CARIBBEAN
PORTS OF CALL

Dominica

Jamaica

Jamaica

Key West

Trinidad

St. Thomas/
U.S. Virgin Islands

Trinidad

Aruba

Aruba

Jamaica

Guatemala

Riviera Maya

Guatemala

Puerto Rico

Praise for Kay Showker's
Caribbean Ports of Call series

"Written by travel expert Kay Showker is a first-of-its-kind guide that shows anyone how to plan a carefree vacation at sea and make the most of the limited time in each port of call."
—*Modern Bride*

"Adds to cruise clients' enjoyment by tipping them off to fun things to do while ashore."
—*Travel Life*

"There are shelffuls of guidebooks on the Caribbean, and there are books that deal with cruising in general (and with ships in particular), but there has been no comprehensive work that effectively combines the two. Kay Showker's admirably fills that void."
—*Oceans*

"Very, very comprehensive, a complete and invaluable book."
—Joel Rapp, WABC Radio, New York

"Check out *Caribbean Ports of Call* to get an inside line not only on the cruise 'personalities' and itineraries, but also where to go, what to do, and what to skip when the ship pulls into shore."
—*Self* magazine

"Her book will become a standard in its field that fills a need people have referred to but no one has taken the time to prepare. For both the first-time cruiser as well as the aficionado, this book is perfect. It is absolutely indispensable to any person taking a cruise and can lend a totally added dimension to the cruise experience."
—Arthur Frommer, "Arthur Frommer's Almanac of Travel," The Travel Channel

"Has much to offer both the most experienced old salt and the first-time passenger . . . Pulls together various aspects of Caribbean cruising that often are covered in separate books . . . More than lives up to its title."
—*Washington Times*

also by Kay Showker
The 100 Best Resorts of the Caribbean

HELP US KEEP THIS GUIDE UP TO DATE

We would love to hear from you concerning your experiences with this guide and how you feel it could be improved and kept up to date. Please send your comments and suggestions to:

editorial@GlobePequot.com

Thanks for your input, and happy travels!

Caribbean
Ports of Call

A GUIDE FOR TODAY'S
CRUISE PASSENGERS

KAY SHOWKER WITH MARY BRENNAN

gpp

travel

Guilford, Connecticut

In memory of Audrey Palmer Hawks, a credit to her homeland of Grenada and a beloved friend who radiated the warmth and charm of the Caribbean and the strength of its women.

All the information in this guidebook is subject to change. We recommend that you call ahead to obtain current information before traveling.

To buy books in quantity for corporate use or incentives, call **(800) 962–0973** or e-mail **premiums@GlobePequot.com.**

Editor: Amy Lyons
Project Editor: Lynn Zelem
Layout: Joanna Beyer
Text Design: Nancy Freeborn
Maps: Multi-Mapping, Ltd. © Morris Book Publishing, LLC

Library of Congress Cataloging-in-Publication Data is available on file.

ISBN 978-0-7627-6035-0

Printed in the United States of America
10 9 8 7 6 5 4 3 2 1

Contents

Part Five
The Eastern Caribbean

Antigua

St. Barthélemy (St. Barts)

St. Kitts and Nevis

Montserrat

Guadeloupe

Dominica

Martinique

Central America and the Panama Canal

Index

List of Maps

MAP LEGEND

Boundary:

National Park / Forest	
International	
Provincial	

Transportation:

Major	
Other	
Trail	

Hydrology:

Rivers/Creeks	
Lake	
Waterfall	

Symbols:

Accommodation	
Archaeological Site / Ruin	
Bank	
Bus Station	
Cemetery	

Symbols (cont):

Church	
Customs / Immigration	
Ferry / Cruise	
Fort	
Golf Course	
Hospital	
Important Building	
Information	
International / Domestic	
Library	
Lighthouse	
Museum	
Observatory	
Point of Interest	
Post Office	
Sanctuary	
School	
Taxi	
View Point	
Volcano	

The Caribbean

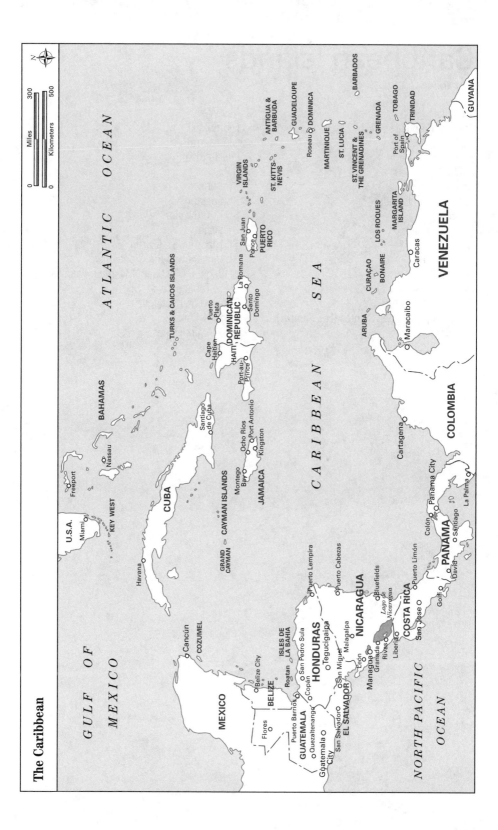

Caribbean Islands

Anguilla
Antigua/Barbuda
Aruba
Bahamas
Barbados
Bonaire
British Virgin Islands
Cancun
Cayman Islands
Cozumel
Curaçao
Dominica
Dominican Republic
Grenada/Carriacou
Guadeloupe/Iles des Saintes (Les Saintes)
Jamaica

Key West
Martinique
Montserrat
Puerto Rico
Saba
St. Barts
St. Eustatius
St. Kitts/Nevis
St. Lucia
St. Maarten/St. Martin
St. Vincent and the Grenadines
     (Bequia, Mustique, Mayreau, Palm, Union,
     Tobago Cays)
Trinidad and Tobago
Turks & Caicos
U.S. Virgin Islands

Caribbean Ports of Call

Anegada, British Virgin Islands
Basse-Terre, Guadeloupe, French West Indies
Basseterre, St. Kitts
Belize City, Belize
Bequia, St. Vincent and the Grenadines
Bimini, the Bahamas
Bluefields, Nicaragua
Bridgetown, Barbados
Calica, Mexico
Cancún, Mexico
Castries, St. Lucia
Caye Caulker, Belize
Charlestown, Nevis
Charlotte Amalie, St. Thomas, U.S. Virgin Islands
Christiansted, St. Croix, U.S. Virgin Islands
Codrington, Barbuda
Costa Maya, Mexico
Cristobal (Colon), Panama
Cruz Bay, St. John, U.S. Virgin Islands
English Harbour, Antigua
Falmouth, Antigua
Fort Bay, Saba
Fort-de-France, Martinique
Frederiksted, St. Croix, U.S. Virgin Islands
Freeport, Grand Bahama, the Bahamas
Grand Cayman, Cayman Islands
Grand Turk, Turks & Caicos Islands
Great Guana Cay, Abaco, the Bahamas
Guanaja, Bay Islands, Honduras
Gustavia, St. Barthélemy (St. Barts), French West Indies
Hillsborough, Carriacou
Iles des Saintes, Guadeloupe, French West Indies
Jost Van Dyke, British Virgin Islands
Key West, United States
Kingston, Jamaica
Kingstown, St. Vincent
Kralendijk, Bonaire
La Ceiba, Honduras
Livingston, Guatemala
Marie Galante, French West Indies
Marigot, St. Martin, French West Indies
Mayreau, St. Vincent and the Grenadines
Montego Bay, Jamaica

Mustique, St. Vincent and the Grenadines
Nassau, New Providence, the Bahamas
Norman Island, British Virgin Islands
Ocho Rios, Jamaica
Oranjestad, Aruba
Oranjestad, St. Eustatius
Palm Island, St. Vincent and the Grenadines
Panama Canal, Panama
Philipsburg, St. Maarten
Pigeon Point/Rodney Bay, St. Lucia
Pigeon Point, Tobago
Placencia, Belize
Playa del Carmen, Mexico
Plymouth, Montserrat
Pointe du Bout, Martinique
Pointe-à-Pitre, Guadeloupe, French West Indies
Ponce, Puerto Rico
Port Antonio, Jamaica
Port Cristobál, Panama
Port of Spain, Trinidad
Porto Progreso (Mérida), Mexico
Portsmouth/Prince Rupert Bay, Dominica
Puerto Barrios, Guatemala
Puerto Cortes, Honduras
Puerto Limón, Costa Rica
Punta Gorda, Belize
Road Town, Tortola, British Virgin Islands
Roatan, Bay Islands, Honduras
Roseau, Dominica
San Blas Islands, Panama
Sandy Ground, Anguilla
San Juan, Puerto Rico
San Miguel, Cozumel, Mexico
San Pedro, Ambergris Caye, Belize
Santo Domingo, Dominican Republic
Santo Tomás de Castella, Guatemala
Scarborough, Tobago
Soufrière, St. Lucia
St. George's, Grenada
St. John's, Antigua
Tortola, British Virgin Islands
Vieques, Puerto Rico
Virgin Gorda, British Virgin Islands
Willemstad, Curaçao

Cruising and the Caribbean

The Winning Combination

Every year, more than 13 million people take cruises, and almost half of them cruise in the waters of the Bahamas and the Caribbean. Superb year-round weather, proximity, prices, and the region's great variety—of cultures, activity, scenery, sports, and attractions—all are reasons that make the combination of cruising and the Caribbean a vacation choice that's hard to beat.

Caribbean Ports of Call: A Guide for Today's Cruise Passengers is intended to fill the gap between two kinds of books: books about cruising and books about the Caribbean.

Typically, books about cruising describe the ships in great detail and are useful in selecting a cruise; however, these books give little or no attention to ports of call. Generally, once you are on board your ship heading to the Bahamas or the Caribbean, their value is marginal.

Guidebooks on the Bahamas and the Caribbean invariably assume that their readers will arrive at a destination by plane and remain several days or longer and have plenty of time to explore the attractions. They are not written for cruise passengers who spend only a few hours in port and need a special kind of guidance.

Indeed, neither the standard cruise guide nor the typical Caribbean guidebook has the kind of information cruise passengers need to help them plan and set priorities for their time in port. That has been the aim of this book from the outset.

Other cruise guides and Caribbean books may appear with "Ports of Call" added to their titles, but a comparison of their content would show that this book is the only one designed specifically to help readers plan their time in each port of call as well as a guide to be taken along in port.

How to Use This Guide

Part One is an introduction to the Caribbean with an overview of its attractions and contrasts of the different regions. It is also a guide for selecting and buying your cruise, with information on ways to save money on your cabin, no matter which ship you select, and tips for getting ready for your trip.

Part Two is a guide to the cruise lines that sail in the Caribbean. It is designed to help you find the line and ship most likely to match your tastes and pocketbook. **Parts Three through Seven** cover the ports of call in two geographic patterns: From the Bahamas south through the Eastern and Southern Caribbean to Aruba; and west from Jamaica to the Mexican Caribbean, Central America, and the Panama Canal. Every effort has been made to be consistent in the presentation of information for each port of call, but some slight variations are inevitable.

All major port chapters open with At a Glance, a generic list of attractions with one ★ star to five ★★★★★ stars. The stars are not used in the sense of a restaurant critique; rather, they are intended as an objective guide to what the island has to offer, that is, which of its attractions are comparatively the best. The purpose is to give you an instant picture of the port to help you judge how best to use your time. Major port chapters include an introduction to the country with a general map, Fast Facts, Budget Planning, and brief descriptions of popular tours, or shore excursions, as cruise lines call them.

The Port Profile has information on embarkation, port location and facilities, and local transportation. The Author's Favorite Attractions' list can be used as a guide to tailor your own priority list. Sections on the capital or main city, historic, and other attractions are followed by those on shopping, sports, dining, entertainment, cultural events, holidays, and festivals.

For those who want to be on their own, each chapter has a walking tour with map, where appropriate, and descriptions of island attractions to see when you rent a car or hire a taxi.

Prices are not uniform in the Caribbean; they tend to be highest in the most popular places. You might sometimes have the feeling that there's a "soak the tourist" attitude, but try to remember that a place like St. Maarten, which has no industry and only minimal agriculture, must import almost all of its food and other supplies, driving up costs to satisfy American tastes.

The Delights of the Caribbean

Take a cruise to the Caribbean, and you will discover a world that is foreign but familiar, close yet far. It is an exotic world of vivid color and gentle trade winds. The Caribbean is often called Paradise, and you will see why as your ship glides gently through aquamarine and sapphire waters to reach places thick with tropical greenery down to their white-sand shorelines.

The seas of the Bahamas and the Caribbean stretch across more than a million square miles from the coast of Florida to the shores of Central and South America. On the east, the islands form an arc that cradles the Caribbean Sea and separates it from the Atlantic Ocean, and on the west, Mexico and Central America form the landmass that separates the Caribbean Sea from the Pacific Ocean. The Caribbean region, often called the Eighth Continent of the World, contains large and small countries, islands, and tiny islets, some no more than the peaks of long-submerged mountains. Others are larger than fifteen states of the United States and have the geographic variety of a continent. The Caribbean region has as many independent nations and island-states as there are countries in Europe, and they draw their heritage from around the globe.

Mapping the Caribbean

The Caribbean roughly has the shape of a rectangle. The sides of the rectangle—north, east, south, and west—represent four regions that are quite different from one another, each with its particular qualities and special appeal.

The northern side—Cuba, Jamaica, Haiti, Dominican Republic, and Puerto Rico—is known as the Greater Antilles. These are the largest, most developed islands, with the largest populations and closest to the United States, with direct air service (except for Cuba). Historically they have had the closest ties with the United States and from

a visitor's standpoint, cater mainly to American tourists. Indeed, for most Americans, they are the Caribbean.

But far more numerous and more "Caribbean" in the tropical sense are the islands of the "other" Caribbean—the string of tiny jewels that starts east of Puerto Rico and arches south to South America. Sometimes called the Bali Hai of the Western Hemisphere, the islands of the Eastern Caribbean are serene, seductive hideaways with grand landscapes of savage beauty. Most are intensely green and very mountainous, often rising almost directly from turquoise seas to jagged, cloud-covered peaks.

Known in history as the Lesser Antilles, they fall into two groups: the Leewards on the north (composed of U.S. and British Virgin Islands that bridge the northern and eastern Caribbean, Anguilla, St. Maarten/St. Martin, St. Barts, Saba, St. Eustatius, St. Kitts/Nevis, Antigua/Barbuda, Montserrat, and Guadeloupe); and the Windwards on the south (Dominica, Martinique, St. Lucia, St. Vincent and the Grenadines, and Grenada). Barbados, technically neither a Leeward nor a Windward island, is 100 miles to the east of St. Vincent. On the south side of the Caribbean rectangle are Trinidad and Tobago, Aruba, Curaçao, and Bonaire, forming what is known as the Southern Caribbean or the Deep Caribbean.

Often called the Undiscovered Caribbean, most of the Eastern Caribbean islands are idyllic hideaways, still natural and unspoiled. It is of course difficult to generalize, since the islands are at various stages of development and sophistication, but with a few exceptions the Eastern Caribbean islands are less developed and hence less commercial than those of the Northern Caribbean. The island chain acts as a barrier between the Atlantic and Caribbean. On the east, or windward side, the rolling Atlantic Ocean pounds against rocky shores often covered with wind-sheared vegetation. On the west, or leeward side, the crystal waters of the calm Caribbean lap gently at the white—or black—sand beaches of reef-trimmed coves. These protected leeward waters have long been among the world's most popular yachting waters. Added to the visual diversity of the land and the coral gardens of the sea, the Eastern Caribbean is a cultural kaleidoscope. It changes from the Spanish heritage in San Juan to the Danish legacy in the U.S. Virgin Islands, to the Dutch in the Dutch Windwards, the French in the French West Indies, and the British in a dozen or so stops from Anguilla to Barbados.

The southernmost islands—Trinidad and Tobago, the Dutch islands of Aruba, Curaçao, and Bonaire—form separate units and are quite different in appearance, culture, and history from the islands of the Eastern Caribbean. Due to their location they are often ports of call on itineraries of longer than one week from Florida and San Juan and on cruises en route to the Panama Canal.

The Bahamas and the Turks & Caicos lie southeast of Florida and north of the Greater Antilles. They are entirely in the Atlantic Ocean, but because their tropical environment is so similar to that of the Caribbean, they are thought of as part of the region. Both have daily air service from the United States.

In addition to Jamaica and the Cayman Islands, the Western Caribbean has come to mean Mexico's Yucatán Peninsula with Cozumel, Cancún, the Riviera Maya, and Costa Maya as well as Belize and Honduras and their islands fronting the longest barrier reef in the Western Hemisphere; plus the Central American countries of Guatemala, Nicaragua, Costa Rica, and Panama, bracketing the Caribbean's western shores.

Caribbean destinations make interesting itineraries because they are distinctive, both topographically and culturally. For example, in the Western Caribbean they range from English-speaking Jamaica, Cayman Islands, and Belize to Spanish-speaking Mexico and Central America. Some places are tropical and lush like Jamaica; others are sandy and arid like Cozumel. Places like Belize and Honduras have towering mountains, rain forests, vast jungles, deserts, and low-lying islets encircled with white sand beach—all within one country.

Nature's Extravagance

Along the 2,000 miles of the Caribbean, whether to the east or the west, nature has been extravagant with its color, variety, and beauty. Between the towering peaks and the sea, rivers and streams cascade over rocks and hillsides and disappear into mangrove swamps and deserts. Fields of flowers, trees with brilliant scarlet and magenta blossoms, and a multitude of birds and butterflies fill the landscape. The air, refreshed by quick tropical showers, is scented with spices and fruit.

And this is only nature's act above the ground. Below the sea is a wonderland of brilliantly colored fish of every size and shape darting endlessly through the crystal waters to hide in caves and grottos, mingle among the swaying purple sea fans, and burrow into boulders of coral and sponge.

Yet what makes the Caribbean region unique is not simply its beauty or geography but rather the combination of this lovely and exotic scenery and the kaleidoscope of rich and diverse cultures. Like the vibrant landscape they reflect, the people and their cultures have evolved from a wide range of traditions, music, dance, art, architecture, and religions from around the world into the greatest of the world's melting pots.

Enter Columbus

Before 1492, when Columbus sighted the New World, the lands of the Caribbean region were populated by Indian tribes, some of whom may have migrated to the region from Asia 20,000 years ago. In more recent history we know that the Ciboneys, who probably came from South America, arrived in the Caribbean region about 3,000 years ago. They were followed by the peaceful Tainos (known as the Arawaks, their more frequently used linguistic name) and the fierce Caribs, who had been in the region for about 600 years when Columbus arrived. It is from the latter group that the Caribbean Sea takes its name.

But in less than a century after Columbus's voyages, the Native population in the islands had almost vanished because of war, disease, and enslavement. Their only survivors are a small group of the descendants of the Carib Indians on the island of Dominica and the Afro-Amerindians, known as Black Caribs in St. Vincent and as Garifunas, after their distinct language, in Belize and Honduras.

Columbus's discoveries brought waves of explorers, conquerors, settlers, merchant sailors, pirates, privateers, traders, and slavers from Europe, the Middle East, Africa, and Asia. For two centuries the West Indies, as the region came to be known, were a pawn in the battle for the New World that raged among the European nations. While they fought, they plundered the region's riches and searched for a route to the East. These were savage times that disgraced even the noblest of aims.

By the dawn of the 18th century, Spain, England, France, Denmark, and Holland had sliced up the region, had planted their flags on various islands, and had begun to colonize their new territories. Gradually the decimated Indian population was replaced with African slaves to work the land that yielded fortunes in sugar, rum, cotton, and tobacco. After slavery was abolished in the British colonies in the 19th century (three decades before its abolition in the United States), the Africans were replaced by indentured laborers from Asia. They were in turn followed by waves of immigrants from the Mediterranean to the Americas in search of a better life.

Once entrenched in the Caribbean, the European governments began to make burdensome demands on their colonies. There were many rebellions. Haiti's revolt was the only one to succeed in a complete break and led to the establishment of the first black republic in the Western Hemisphere two decades after the American Revolution.

Following abolition and the invention of the steam engine and cotton gin, the West Indies lost the base of their economy and soon became neglected outposts of European empires. With the end of the Spanish-American War, Spain gave up its holdings in the New World, and after World War II, Britain, France, and the Netherlands were forced to change their relationships with most of their colonies, granting them independence in most cases.

But the road to independence was a rough one. The troubled 1960s in the United States, with their shock waves of black power demands and rising expectations, washed ashore in the Caribbean. Adding to their burdens, the 1970s, with the oil crisis, inflation, and the worldwide recession, were particularly hard on the islands, which have few resources other than their people and natural beauty. But from the experience a new Caribbean has taken shape.

Caribbean Culture

Down through the centuries, those who came to the Caribbean—conquerors and settlers, sailors and slaves, merchants and workers, and visitors and vacationers—brought with them parts of their cultures: their church steeples, temples, brogues, high tea, High Mass, masks, drums, colors, songs, dances, high-rises, and hamburgers. Out of this mélange has grown a new Caribbean as colorful, rich, and diverse as the landscape in which it flowers.

Although it might be difficult to single out a Caymanian or a Cruzan by sight, there is no mistaking the lilt of a Jamaican's voice when she speaks or a Trinidadian when he sings. Haitian art is instantly recognizable. The beguine began in Martinique, the merengue in the Dominican Republic. Calypso and steel bands were born in Trinidad, reggae in Jamaica, and salsa in Puerto Rico.

Today the region pulsates with creative energy in the arts. The best time to see the evidence is during Carnival, when tradition vies with innovation as part of the show. Trinidad's Carnival is the best known and is held at the traditional pre-Lenten time, but Carnival in the Caribbean, often developed from local events, is held at different times of the year. For example, Crop-Over in Barbados in July stems from the celebration of the harvest, and Antigua's Carnival in Aug started as a welcome to the British monarch during her visit in the 1960s.

Caribbean architecture, like its art, is a composite of world cultures. English churches and Spanish cathedrals stand alongside warm-weather adaptations of Dutch farmhouses and French manors. Victorian gingerbread mansions are pauses in the tango of brightly painted houses in the towns and villages. Minarets and steeples pierce the sky of Trinidad; the oldest synagogue in the Western Hemisphere is a Curaçao landmark.

New Cuisine

Caribbean cuisine, too, is a cornucopia of tastes from the four corners of the world—a unique blend that evolved over the centuries and combines nature's bounty with the richness of the region's culinary heritage. The Spaniards discovered not only the New World but also a continent of exotic foods, fruits, and vegetables Europeans had never seen—avocado, cassava, maize, peppers, papaya, chocolate, and potatoes, to name a few. From the native people, the Spaniards learned how to use the new ingredients and eventually adapted them for their own cooking; many became basic elements in classic Spanish and French cuisine. The Danes, Dutch, Portuguese, English, Africans, Chinese, Indians, Greeks, Turks, Indonesians, and Arabs all made their contributions.

Out of this potpourri evolved a Creole or West Indian cuisine that includes such standards as Cuban and Puerto Rican black bean soup, Jamaican pepper pot, St. Kitts goat water or mutton stew, Grenadian callaloo, and Guadeloupan accra. Now, a new generation of hotel and restaurant chefs have been developing a new and sophisticated Caribbean cuisine that has resulted in such wonderful creations as cold papaya bisque, crab and callaloo soup, breadfruit vichyssoise, callaloo quiche, chicken Creole with mango, and avocado ice cream, to name a few.

The starting point in the making of Caribbean cuisine is the market—a cultural potpourri where Africa meets the Caribbean and mixes with Asia. Mountains of mango, melon, and banana and pyramids of papaya, pineapple, and pomegranate are stacked next to the plantain, okra, dasheen, coconut, cassava, cloves, coffee, and cinnamon— alongside piles of clothes and shoes to be haggled over by the townsfolk and villagers. Visitors, too, frequently join the mélange because there is no better place than a market to take in the Caribbean kaleidoscope.

A Wealth of Activity

Against the Caribbean's rich and varied geographic and cultural landscape, visitors enjoy a cornucopia of sports and recreational facilities, entertainment, sightseeing, and shopping possibilities. For sports the Caribbean has few rivals. Across the region, sailing is suited for any type of boat, from Sailfish to ocean yachts. Yachters often call the stretch south from St. Vincent through the Grenadines the finest sailing water in the world. Snorkeling and scuba diving are excellent throughout the warm and exceptionally clear waters of the region.

Golf on championship layouts created by the most famous names in golf course design is available at many ports of call. Puerto Rico offers more than two dozen championship courses; Jamaica has six of them and even the smallest islands like Nevis and Canouan have world famous layouts. Most cruise lines have golf programs or can arrange for their passengers to play golf at most ports of call.

You can also play tennis, squash, or polo and fish in the ocean or in mountain streams. There is horseback riding, jogging, hiking, biking, surfing, windsurfing, rafting, kayaking, tubing, waterskiing, parasailing, and more. Throughout the region are national parks, bird sanctuaries, mountain trails, and panoramas of magnificent scenery. Visitors can have a close-up look at a rain forest, drive into the crater of a volcano, bike across meadows, hike through deep ravines, and explore some caves along the way. But, if you are less athletically inclined or simply want to enjoy nature and the outdoors, there are mile-long, powdery sand beaches where you can stretch out for the day with no more company than a couple of birds.

Diversity of Destinations

All cruise lines would like you to believe that their ships are the main reason to take a cruise, but they are the first to admit that most passengers select a cruise for its destinations. Together, the ports on a Caribbean cruise provide a kaleidoscope of the region's history and cultures, scenery and sights, language and music. It is a window onto the islands with an ever-changing panorama.

No two Caribbean destinations are alike: Each has a personality, distinctive geographic features, and special charm with which it beguiles its admirers. Some places are tiny idyllic hideaways far from the beaten path with names familiar only to mapmakers and yachters. Others are big in size or seem big because of their strong character and regional influence, while still others are big on action, with gambling, shopping, and sophisticated dining and nightlife. Some locales have enough sports and entertainment to keep you busy every hour of the day; others test your ability to enjoy simple pleasures. The Caribbean is a learning experience, too. The region is rich in historic monuments, old forts, plantation homes, sugar mills, churches, and synagogues that have been beautifully restored and put to contemporary use as art galleries, boutiques, cafes, restaurants, inns, and museums. They help bring the region's history to life. Few Caribbean destinations fit neatly into only one category: Most have features that contrast and overlap. One of the great advantages of a cruise is the chance to visit several places during one vacation and sample some of this variety.

A cruise is the best and sometimes the only way to visit several Caribbean islands in one vacation—that's another of cruising's attractions. But if you don't plan, you might come back thinking the islands are all alike. You can maximize your enjoyment by taking advantage of the unique or unusual features of each port of call and selecting an activity at each location that you cannot do elsewhere. In other words, if you were to spend all your time on a walking tour in Old San Juan, you might want to snorkel or take a diving lesson in St. Maarten, and go hiking in a rain forest in St. Lucia.

Life and Leisure in Paradise

Finally, a word about the people and pace of Paradise. Life in the Caribbean is leisurely. It is easy for Americans to become impatient with the slow pace, but remember, it's precisely the unhurried atmosphere you have come to enjoy. Americans often misinterpret a shyness and conservative nature toward strangers as unfriendliness. But after traveling from one end of the Caribbean to the other for almost three decades, I know from experience that the people of the Caribbean are as friendly as their music and as warm as their sunshine. They have wit, talent, dignity, and grace. They are generous and kind and will go out of their way to be helpful if you meet them with respect and greet them with a genuine smile.

I love the Caribbean. It's like magic. I recognize the elements that create the magic, although I don't quite know what makes it happen. Yet the experience is so delightful that I'm happy to let the mystery remain.

The Delights of Cruising

People take cruises for various reasons. Some people are looking for fun, companionship, excitement, and romance—whether it's the romance of the sea or romance at sea. A cruise offers a change of pace and relaxation, new faces, new places, and a foreign environment. It is a different kind of holiday. Indeed, a cruise is so completely unlike other holiday experiences, it is difficult for those who have never taken one to imagine its pleasures or realize its true built-in value.

Changing Lifestyles

In the past, people saved all their lives to make a single trip. The ultimate dream was a trip around the world by ship. Today the stresses of modern life and the pressures of work and urban living have made it desirable, even necessary, to get away often, if only for a few days. Shorter, less expensive cruises have enabled more people to take them and to take them more often. Speedier modes of transportation combined with greater affluence have made a short break the norm, especially for city dwellers. And nothing could be more ideal for a short, recuperative break than a cruise, offering a complete break from the workaday world.

The Ultimate Convenience

Once you have checked in at the airport in your hometown, you won't have to bother with your luggage again. It will be waiting in your cabin. You will be brought from the airport by motor coach to the ship that awaits you at your port of embarkation without having to tote bags or give out tips.

The ease and comfort with which you can visit places that are hard to reach on your own are part of cruising's great attractions. Almost anyplace in the Caribbean can be reached by plane, but if you tried visiting Key West, Jamaica, and Cozumel or Nassau, St. Thomas, and Martinique in a week, you would spend most of your vacation in airports! Indeed, the more changes of hotels, trains, buses, and planes that a similar itinerary by land requires, the more attractive travel by ship can be. Your ship is not only your transportation, it is also your hotel. It's the ultimate convenience—you pack and unpack only once. In my book, that's a real vacation!

Cruising is the ultimate escape. For a few days you can turn off your worries and live out your fantasies. Without even working at it, you relax. The pure air, the gentle movement of the ship gliding through the water, and the unhurried rhythm of shipboard life are instant antidotes to the noise, pollution, and pressures of daily life.

Onboard Activities

A cruise is what a vacation should be—fun! In fact, there are more ways to have fun on a cruise than there are hours in the day to enjoy them all. People often have the false notion they will become bored on a cruise, but there's little chance of boredom if you take advantage of all that is available.

For active people there are swimming, fitness classes, yoga, deck tennis, table tennis, workout gyms, exercise and dance classes, and even rock climbing. On some ships, onboard sports and fitness programs are combined with organized in-port snorkeling, diving, sailing, windsurfing, tennis, golf, and fishing. Or you can simply head for a beach and participate in these activities on your own.

Those who like to learn are kept busy, too. Ships frequently have instructors and tournaments for bridge, language, arts and crafts, wine tasting, cooking, and computers, to name a few subjects. These enrichment programs, as the cruise lines call them, vary from ship to ship and cruise to cruise. Some ships build a cruise around a special theme such as mystery or photography; others offer annual cruises featuring classical music or jazz festivals at sea. Bingo is alive and well on ships, along with casinos.

Movies—new releases and old favorites—are shown daily in the ship's theater or on closed-circuit television in your cabin. The theater is also used for such special events as concerts by visiting artists, fashion shows, or Broadway-style shows.

Every evening before you go to bed, a schedule of the next day's activities is slipped under your door. You can take in all of them, pick and choose, or ignore the lot of it.

A Movable Feast

Cruising has given new meaning to the term, a movable feast. The feasting starts with morning coffee and tea for the early birds and breakfast in the dining room or on one of the parlor decks. Every day at every meal, the menu has three, four, or more selections for each course and half a dozen courses for each meal. All the new mid-size and large ships have several alternative restaurants; those of Norwegian Caribbean Line have up to ten or more dining venues. If you are worried about gaining weight, menus have low carb and low cal selections. The ships also cater to special dietary requirements and can provide salt-free, diabetic, vegetarian, or kosher meals. The food, wine, music, dances, language, and people—all give a ship its personality and ambience and make a cruise a special kind of holiday.

Nightlife is another attraction on a cruise. Cruise lines go out of their way to provide a variety of entertainment for different age groups and interests. All but the smallest ships have nightclubs and discos, and most have casinos. Most large ships offer full-scale Broadway– and Las Vegas–style shows. Best of all, they're there to enjoy only one or two decks from your cabin.

Cruising with Children

A cruise is one of the best possible vacations for families with children. There is no end to a child's fascination with a ship. It is a totally new experience, with an environment different from anything he or she has known at home. It's also an education. The crew members—many of whom are away from their own children—are wonderful with young passengers. There are always babysitters around, and you are never far from the children when you want to spend time on your own.

Once strictly adult territory, some cruise ships are so well equipped for children, they could be called floating camps. Trained youth counselors plan and supervise shipboard activities geared to specific age groups. On the first day at sea, the counselors meet with parents and their children to review the week's activities and answer questions about facilities. Each morning a printed schedule especially for children is slipped under their door with the program for the day.

Teenagers are likely to shun structured activities, and many prefer to be on their own. But the ship helps them get acquainted with a party. Some ships give the teenagers exclusive use of the disco while the adults are at cocktails or dinner. The newest big ships have special lounges and facilities specifically designed for tweens and teens.

Shows with magicians, puppets, dancers, and singers are big hits with kids and parents alike. Children often get their own tours of the ship and even get to meet the captain. They often learn more about the ship and how it operates than many adults do. They learn about travel etiquette and different foods, experience new kinds of service, and learn how to socialize in new environments.

Family Reunions

Cruises are great not only for families with children but those with grandchildren, too. And they are ideal for family reunions, especially for families scattered around the country who find it hard to gather in one place—and do all that cooking! A cruise gives all members of the family equal time to spend with their favorite aunts, uncles, and cousins. Thanks to a ship's wide range of activities, there's always plenty to do, regardless of age. By sailing together, family members across the country can take advantage of group rates. Your travel agent can piece the parts together for you. All you need to do is agree on the cruise and the date.

Ideal Honeymoon

A cruise is what a honeymoon should be—romantic, relaxing, glamorous, different, and fun. It is a fairy tale come true. And it has the ingredients for a perfect honeymoon: privacy when you want it, attention when you need it; sports, music, dancing, and entertainment to share; sightseeing to enjoy. The atmosphere is a happy one. Honeymooners

need not have a worry in the world. Everything is at their fingertips, including breakfast in bed. There are no big decisions to make, no travel hassles to face.

A cruise offers them total flexibility in making plans. And thanks to the all-inclusive nature of a cruise, a couple can know the cost of the honeymoon in advance and plan accordingly.

A travel agent can also arrange for the honeymooners' extras that most ships offer. These might include champagne on the first night, flowers in the cabin, a wedding cake, an album for honeymoon photos, and a reception by the captain. Almost all ships have tables for two and cabins with double beds, which a travel agent can request when the reservations are made. Princess Cruises' newest ships have a real wedding chapel where you can be married in full ceremony in a lovely setting. Now other cruise lines are following Princess' lead and adding a wedding chapel, too.

Selecting a Cruise: Tips and Advice

With so many cruises going to so many different places, selecting one can be difficult. My suggestion is to start your planning at a travel agency. About 75 percent of all cruises are purchased through travel agents. It will not cost more than buying a cruise directly from a cruise line, and it will save you time and could save you money. A good travel agency stocks the brochures of the leading cruise lines; these show prices and details on the ship's itineraries and facilities. An experienced agent will help you understand the language of a cruise brochure, read a deck plan, and make reservations. The knowledgeable agent can help you make comparisons and guide you in the selection of a ship and an itinerary to match your interests. Your agent can book your dining room table and handle a particular request such as for an anniversary party or a special diet. Agents also know about packages and discounts that can help you save money.

The Internet has a wealth of information on cruises. All cruise lines have their own sites with descriptions of their ships and itineraries—none of them objective, of course, any more than the cruise line brochures are objective. Many travel agencies also have sites, which usually service sales via e-mail. For ship reviews and the latest deals, check out AOL's Cruise Critic or www.cruisemates.com, or subscribe to some of the e-mail newsletters published by cruise lines or large travel agencies that feature weekly cruise specials. In all cases, however, be guided by your interests and needs— and not by price alone. If it's your first cruise, you should seek the expertise of a travel agent.

Cruise Vacation's Built-In Value

Of all the attractions of cruising, none is more important than value. For one price you get accommodations, meals, entertainment, use of all facilities, and a host of recreational activity. Air transportation may or may not be included, depending on the cruise line and the destination (see Cruise-Only Fares). The only items not included are tips, drinks, photographs, shore excursions, personal services such as spa services and hair-dressers, and, in some cases, port tax. There are no hidden costs.

Dollar for dollar, it's hard to beat a cruise for value. To make an accurate assessment of how the cost of a cruise compares with other types of holi-days, be sure to compare similar elements. A holi-day at sea should be compared with a holiday at a luxury resort, because the quality of service, food, and entertainment on most cruises is available only at posh resorts or top-level all-inclusive resorts.

The average brochure price of a one-week Caribbean cruise can range from under $100 to $1,000 per person per day including the ingredients previously described, but with current discounts and advance purchase plans, these prices can be cut in half. Shorter three- and four-day Bahamas cruises range from $75 to $250 per day, and there are plenty of low promotion fares available for them, too. No luxury resorts give you a hotel room, four full meals plus two or three snacks each day, nightly entertainment plus a myriad of activity—all for one price.

Stretching Your Budget

Air/sea combinations are available in two forms: an all-in-one package combining a cruise and air

transportation in one price; or a second type, in which the cruise is priced separately and an air supplement is added on to the cruise price or a credit for air transportation from one's hometown to the ship's nearest departure port is offered. The amount of the supplement or credit varies from one cruise line to another. But, usually, the supplement is slightly more the farther away from the departure port you live. Still, the total cost is normally less to you than if the cruise and air transportation were purchased separately. The details are spelled out in the cruise line's brochure. Ask your travel agent to explain how the package works as it can be confusing.

Cruise-Only Fares

Most cruise line brochures quote "cruise-only" fares rather than air/sea packages. The reasons: Crowded airplanes and crowded skies have often made it difficult for cruise lines to negotiate the low airfares of the past. Even when they can, the airlines—not cruise lines—control the routing, which often has deviations that lead to passenger complaints. Also, many cruise passengers have acquired frequent-flyer miles they want to use for vacation travel.

Selecting a Ship

The ship and the cruise line's reputation are other considerations in making your selection. Not only do ships differ, so do their passengers. You are more likely to enjoy a cruise with people who are seeking a similar type of holiday and with whom you share a community of interests and activities. A good travel agent who specializes in selling cruises is aware of the differences and should be able to steer you to a ship that's right for you. But before you visit an agent or begin to cull the colorful and enticing brochures, here are some tips on the items affecting cost that can help you in making a selection.

Selecting a Cabin

The largest single item in the cost of a cruise is the cabin, also known as a stateroom. The cost of a cabin varies greatly and is determined by its size and location. Generally, the cabins on the top deck are the largest and most expensive; the prices drop and the cabins narrow on each deck down from the top. (Elevators and stairs provide access between decks.) But the most expensive cabins are not necessarily the best. There are other factors to consider.

Almost all cruise ship cabins have private bathrooms, but the size and fittings vary and affect cost. For example, cabins with full bathtubs are more expensive than those with showers only. Greater standardization of cabins is a feature of most new cruise ships.

Outside cabins are more costly than inside ones. There is a common misconception that inside cabins are to be avoided. It dates back to the days before air-conditioning when an outside cabin above the waterline was desirable because the porthole could be opened for ventilation. Today's ships are climate-controlled; an inside cabin is as comfortable as an outside one. What's more, on a Caribbean cruise particularly, you will spend very little time in your cabin; it is mainly a place to sleep and change clothes. An inside cabin often provides genuine savings and is definitely worth investigating for those on a limited budget.

For the most stable ride, the deck at water level or below has less roll (side-to-side motion) and the cabins in the center of the ship have the least pitch (back-and-forth motion). But often, these cabins also cost more than those in the front (fore) or the back (aft) of the ship. Fore (or the bow) has less motion and is therefore preferable to aft (or the stern), where sometimes there is vibration from the ship's engines.

A ship's deck plan shows the exact location of each cabin and is usually accompanied by diagrams of the fittings in the cruise line's brochures. It does not give the dimensions of the cabin, but you can have a reasonable estimate since beds are standard single size—about 3 x 6 feet. Some ships have double beds, but most have twin beds that can be converted to doubles on request.

Singles

A few ships have single cabins; otherwise, a passenger booking a cabin alone pays a rate that is one and a half times the price per person for two sharing a cabin. A few ships offer special single rates on certain cruises or reserve a few cabins for single occupancy at the same rate as the per person rate on a shared basis plus a small supplement. Your travel agent should be able to give you specific information about single rates. Norwegian Cruise Line's new *Norwegian Epic* has "Studio" cabins, priced specifically for single occupancy with no added supplement—a first among the modern cruise ships that have debuted in the last two decades.

Other Cost Factors

As might be expected, rates for the winter season in the Caribbean are higher than in the spring, summer, or fall. Cruises over Christmas, New Year's, and other major holidays are usually the year's most expensive, but often, real bargains are to be found on cruises immediately before or after a holiday season when demand drops and lines are eager to stimulate business.

The length of the cruise bears directly on its cost. Longer cruises provide more elegance and fancier dining and service. The cost also varies depending on the ship's itinerary. For example, it is more economical for a cruise line to operate a set schedule of the same ports throughout the year, such as the ships departing weekly from Florida to the Caribbean, than it is to change itineraries every few weeks.

Family Rates

If you are planning a family cruise, look for cruise lines that actively promote family travel and offer special rates for children or for third and fourth persons in a cabin. It means a bit of crowding but can yield big savings. Family rates vary from one cruise line to another. As a rule, children sharing a cabin with two paying adults get discounts of 50 percent or more of the minimum fare. Qualifying ages vary, too, with a child usually defined as two to twelve, and sometimes up to eighteen years. Some lines have teen fares, while at certain times of the year others have free or special rates for the third or fourth person sharing a cabin with two full-fare adults, regardless of age. Most lines permit infants under two years to travel free of charge. Some cruise lines, particularly MSC Cruises, offer "Kids Free" programs year-round.

Cruise Discounts

In today's highly competitive market, discounts have become a way of life. Cruise lines use them to publicize a new ship or itinerary, to attract families, younger passengers, singles, and a diversity of people. Some low fares are available year-round but may be limited to a certain number of cabins on each sailing; others are seasonal or may apply to specific cruises.

You can take advantage of fare discounts in two ways. If you book early, you can usually benefit from early-bird discounts, often up to 50 percent or more, and of course, you can be sure you have the cruise and cabin you want. On the other hand, if you are in a position to be flexible, you can wait to catch the last-minute "fire sales." These specials are most often available on the Internet only. To take advantage of this situation, you need to have maximum flexibility.

Remember, when you are buying a cruise, you will have already paid for all your accommodations, all meals (three meals a day is only the beginning; most ships have five or more food services daily), all entertainment, and all recreational facilities aboard ship, and in some cases, round-trip airfare to the ship's departure port, baggage handling, and transfers. It is this all-inclusive aspect of a cruise that makes it a good value—a particularly significant advantage for families with children and those who need to know in advance the cost of a vacation.

Shore Excursions

Sightseeing tours, called shore excursions by the cruise lines, are available for an additional cost at every port of call in the Caribbean. A pamphlet on the shore excursions offered by the cruise line is often included in the literature you receive before sailing. If not, ask for one. However, more and more cruise lines now post their shore excursions on their Web sites and enable passengers to book their excursions in advance online. If not, you can buy them on board ship from the purser, cruise director, or tour office. Some people prefer buying them on board, since frequently their interests and plans change once the cruise is under way. Sometimes, but not often enough, there are savings by buying on the Internet.

A word of caution: There used to be very little difference between the cruise ships' prices for tours and those of local tour companies if you were staying in a hotel. However, the situation has changed dramatically. In their need to keep their cruise prices down in the face of intense competition and rampant discounting, many cruise lines now regard shore excursions (as well as other ancillary services such as shipboard shopping, bars, and spa facilities) as profit centers; often selling their tours at exorbitant prices.

Since tours vary from vendor to vendor and cruise ship to cruise ship, it is difficult to generalize. Therefore, when you check prices, it is important that you compare like items and, when necessary, factor in such additional costs as insurance and transportation from the pier to the vendor's office or starting point. The information and prices provided here are intended as guidelines. Even if they change, the increase is not likely to be more than a dollar or two. If you come across shore excursion prices that appear to be out of line, please write to me and enclose a copy of the tour.

Port Talks

All ships offer what is known as a port talk—a brief description of the country or island and port where the ship will dock as well as shopping tips. The quality of these talks varies enormously, not only with the cruise line but also with the ship, and can depend on such wide-ranging considerations as the knowledge and skill of the cruise director and the policy of the cruise line as to the true purpose of the information. Be aware that most cruise lines in the Caribbean have turned these port talks into sales pitches for certain products and stores with which they have exclusive promotional agreements and in which the cruise lines take commissions or are paid directly by the stores. You will receive a map of the port with "recommended" shops. What that really means is that the shop has paid the cruise line for being promoted in port talks and advertising in the ship's magazine that might appear in your cabin. Also, sometimes cruise directors receive commissions from local stores, even though they deny it. Hence, their vested interest could color their presentation and recommendations.

There are three ways to avoid being misled. If a cruise line, a cruise director, a guide, or anyone else recommends one store to the exclusion of all others, that should alert you to shop around before buying. The recommended store may actually be the best place to buy—but it may not. Second, if you are planning to make sizable purchases of jewelry, cameras, china, etc., check prices at home before you leave, and bring a list of prices with you. Be sure, however, you are comparing like products. Finally, check the prices in shipboard shops, which are usually very competitive with those at ports of call.

Happily, because you have this book, you do not need to rely on port talks for information, but if you do attend your ship's port talks and find that they have been more sales pitch than enlightenment, please write and tell me about your experience.

Know Before You Go

Climate: While the sun keeps the islands warm, the trade winds that blow from the northeast and east throughout the year keep the temperatures comfortable and consistent, averaging about 78 to 82 degrees Fahrenheit year-round. The difference between summer and winter temperatures seldom varies more than five to ten degrees. Dec through Mar are normally the driest, coolest months, when temperatures on some islands might drop to 65 degrees Fahrenheit on mountain peaks. July, Aug, and Sept are the hottest, wettest months, when temperatures reach 86 to 90 degrees Fahrenheit and the humidity can be 100 percent. Fortunately, during this period, frequent tropical showers quickly cool the air.

The lay of the land has a direct impact on weather on every island. Some islands, such as Antigua and Barbados which do not have the high mountains and thick foliage characteristic of most Eastern Caribbean islands, tend to be dry, with rainfall averaging only 46 inches annually. Even on the islands with high mountains, such as St. Kitts, the climate can vary, from 148 inches of annual rain on forested mountain peaks to less than 40 inches per year in dry lowlands. Trinidad and Tobago,

Aruba, Bonaire, and Curaçao fall south of the Caribbean hurricane belt. Aruba, Bonaire, and Curaçao are similar in climate, which, typically, is much drier than in other parts of the Eastern Caribbean. On these islands where the terrain is low, the winds are strong and constant, reaching their greatest intensity in June and July.

Clothing: Cotton and lightweight fabrics are recommended year-round. Informal, casual, but conservative dress is appropriate throughout the islands. Bathing suits, tank tops, and revealing attire are not acceptable anywhere except on the beach. West Indians generally are conservative and are offended by tourists wearing such attire in public places. Some casinos require jackets. In the French West Indies, as in France, topless is not only allowed, it's expected. Guadeloupe and St. Martin have topless and nudist beaches, but Martinique does not.

Luggage and Wardrobe: There are no limits on the amount of luggage you can bring on board ship, but most cabins do not have much closet and storage space. More important, since you are likely to be flying to your departure port, you need to be guided by airline regulations regarding baggage. Life on a Caribbean cruise is casual. It is needless to be burdened with a lot of baggage; you will spend your days in sports clothes—slacks, shorts, T-shirts, bathing suits. Men are often asked to wear a jacket at dinner in the main dining room or fancy specialty restaurants.

The first and last nights of your cruise and the nights your ship is in port almost always call for casual dress. At least one night will be the captain's gala party, where tuxedos for men and long dresses for women may be requested but are never mandatory. Another night might be a masquerade party; it's entirely up to you whether to participate.

A gentleman who does not have a tuxedo should bring a basic dark suit and white shirt. Add a selection of slacks and sport shirts, one or two sports jackets, and two pairs of bathing trunks. Women will find nylon and similar synthetics are good to use on a cruise because they are easy to handle, but these fabrics can be hot under the tropical sun. It largely depends on your tolerance for synthetic fabrics in hot weather. Personally, I find cottons and cotton blends to be the most comfortable. You will need two cocktail dresses or dressy pants suits for evening wear. A long dress for the captain's party is appropriate but not compulsory. Add a sweater or wrap for cool evening breezes and the ship's air-conditioning in the dining room and lounges. Take cosmetics and sun lotion, but don't worry if you forget something. It will most likely be available in shipboard or portside shops.

You will need rubber-soled shoes for walking on deck and a comfortable pair of walking shoes for sightseeing. Sunglasses and a hat or sun visor for protection against the strong Caribbean sun are essential. A tote bag comes in handy for carrying odds and ends; include several plastic bags for wet towels and bathing suits upon returning from a visit to a beach. Keep camera equipment in plastic bags as protection against the salt air and water and sand. And don't forget to pack a bathing suit and whatever sporting equipment and clothes you will need. Remember, the Caribbean sun is very strong. Wear a sun hat or visor for protection, and always use sunscreen lotion. For hiking at high altitudes, take a sweater and wear good hiking shoes.

Electricity/Electrical Appliances: Aruba, St. Maarten, and U.S. Virgin Islands have 120 volts AC, 60 cycles; Barbados, Bonaire, Curaçao, and Puerto Rico have 110–120 volts AC, 50 cycles. The French West Indies and all other former British islands (Anguilla, Antigua/Barbuda, British Virgin Islands, Cayman Islands, Dominica, Grenada, Jamaica, Montserrat, St. Kitts/Nevis, St. Lucia, St. Vincent, Trinidad and Tobago) have 220 volts AC, 60 or 50 cycles. Appliances made in the United States need transformers or models with converters built into them. Hotels on most islands, however, have 110 volts AC, 60 cycles or both currents. If in doubt, inquire at the hotel front desk.

Cabins on almost all new ships have hair dryers and outlets for electric razors or are wired for them, but the oldest ships are not. Instead, rooms with special outlets are provided. Normally, ships do not allow you to use electric irons in your cabin because of the potential fire hazard. Electric current is usually 115–120 volts—but not always—and plugs are the two-prong, American-type ones. Check with your cruise line for specific information.

Laundry and Dry Cleaning: All ships have either laundry service for your personal clothing (for which there is an extra charge) or coin-operated laundry rooms. Only a very few have dry-cleaning facilities. In the Caribbean, this is not an important consideration since the clothes required are cotton or cotton blends and should be easy to wash.

Documentation: Among the Caribbean's many advantages is that normally no destination (except Cuba) requires visas of U.S. and Canadian citizens arriving as cruise passengers. If you leave your ship, you will need proof of citizenship with photo (passport in most cases). Most islands also require visitors arriving by air to have a valid onward or return ticket. Since Jan 1, 2009, all U.S. citizens are required to show a passport to enter or leave the United States. Actually, every traveler should have a passport—it's the best identification you can carry. In Guadeloupe, Martinique, St. Barts, St. Martin, if proof of citizenship is a document other than a passport (such as a notarized birth certificate), it must have a raised seal and photo identification.

Vaccination Requirements: There are no inoculation requirements for U.S. and Canadian citizens to visit any island in the Caribbean.

Port Security: No special identity or security measures are required on any island covered in this book. Passengers are allowed to come and go from their ships freely; every cruise ship has its own system for identifying its passengers. Large ships usually issue identity cards like a credit card, whereas small ships may simply use cabin keys or tabs.

Time: The Eastern Caribbean falls into the Atlantic Standard Time zone, which is one hour ahead of Eastern Standard Time. When daylight saving time is in effect in the United States, only a few of the islands change their time. In those months Atlantic Standard Time is the same as Eastern Daylight time. The Western Caribbean is on Eastern Standard time, while the Mexican Caribbean, generally, is on Central Standard time.

Mealtimes: All but the most luxurious Caribbean cruise ships, adventure-type, and most small ships have two sittings for the main meals. Early-sitting breakfast is from 7 to 8 a.m., lunch is from noon to 1 p.m., and dinner is from 6:15 to 7:30 p.m. On the late sitting, breakfast is from 8 to 9 a.m., lunch is from 1:30 to 2:30 p.m., and dinner is from 8:15 to 9:30 p.m. Most mainstream lines (Norwegian Cruise Line, Princess, Carnival) have introduced flexible plans, enabling passengers to eat when and where they chose. If you are an early riser, you will probably be happy with the early sitting. If you are likely to close the disco every night, you might prefer the late one. Of course, you will not be confined to these meals as there are usually a buffet breakfast, lunch on deck, afternoon tea, and late night snacks. Also, more and more ships, particularly the new ones, have alternative restaurants for dinner, as well as turning part of the lido restaurant into a casual evening dining venue. In an effort to provide greater flexibility, many ships have open seating for breakfast and lunch and assigned seats for dinner only.

Requesting a Table: Your travel agent can request your table in advance, if you want a table for two or for your family, as well as your preference for early or late seating. Some cruise lines will confirm your reservation in advance; and more and more, enable you to select your dining choice on line.

Spa Services/Hair Salon: Almost all Caribbean cruise ships have spas and hairdressers for both men and women. Prices are comparable to those at deluxe resorts.

Religious Services: All ships hold interdenominational services; many also have a daily Catholic mass. Services will be conducted by the captain or a clergyman. At ports of call you will be welcome to attend local services. It can be an interesting experience and a highlight of your cruise.

Medical Needs: All cruise ships are required by law to have at least one doctor, nurse, and infirmary or mini-hospital. Doctor visits and medicine are extra—and usually overpriced—costs.

Seasickness: First-time cruise passengers probably worry more about becoming seasick than about any other aspect of cruising. Certainly they worry more than they should, particularly on a Caribbean cruise, where the sea is calm almost

year-round. Ships today have stabilizers, which steady them in all but the roughest seas. But if you are still worried, there are several types of nonprescription medicines such as Dramamine and Bonine that help to guard against motion sickness. Buy some to bring along—you may not need it, but having it with you might be comforting. Also, the ship's doctor can provide you with medication that will be immediately effective, should you need it.

Sea Bands are a reliable product for seasickness prevention. They are a pair of elasticized wristbands, each with a small plastic disk that, based on the principle of acupuncture, applies pressure on the inside wrist. I use Sea Bands and have given them to friends to use and can attest to their effectiveness. They are particularly useful for people who have difficulty taking medication. Sea Bands are found in drug, toiletry, and health-care stores and can be ordered from Travel Accessories, P.O. Box 391162, Solon, OH 44139, (216) 248-8432. They even make sequined covers in a dozen colors to wear over the bands for evening.

There are two important things to remember about seasickness: Don't dwell on your fear. Even the best sailors and frequent cruisers need a day to get their "sea legs." If you should happen to get a queasy feeling, take some medicine immediately. The worst mistake you can make is to play the hero, thinking it will go away. When you deal with the symptoms immediately, relief is fast, and you are seldom likely to be sick. If you wait, the queasy feeling will linger, and you run a much greater risk of being sick.

Caution Against the Caribbean Sun: You should be extra careful about the sun in the tropics. It is much stronger than the sun to which most people are accustomed. Do not stay in the direct sun for long stretches at a time, and use a sunscreen at all times. Nothing can spoil a vacation faster than a sunburn.

Shipboard Shops: There's always a shop for essentials you might have forgotten or that can't wait until the next port of call. Many ships—particularly the new ones—have elaborate shops competitive with stores at ports of call. It's another reason to pack lightly, since you are almost sure to buy gifts and souvenirs during the cruise.

Tipping: Tipping is a matter of a great deal of discussion but much less agreement. How much do you tip in a restaurant or a hotel? Normally, the tip should be about $3.50 per person per day for each of your cabin stewards and dining room waiters. On some ships, particularly those with Greek crews and adventure-type cruises, the custom is to contribute to the ship's common kitty in the belief that those behind the scenes such as kitchen staffs should share in the bounty. On some ships dining room staffs also pool their tips. Tipping guidelines are usually printed in literature your cruise line sends in advance, enabling you to factor the expense into your budget even before booking a cruise. The cruise director, as part of his advice-giving session at the end of the cruise, also explains the ship's policy and offers guidelines.

More recently, when cruise lines have introduced flexible meal plans—Norwegian Cruise Line's FreeStyle, Princess's Personal Choice, and Carnival's Total Choice—they include the tip, particularly for the cabin and dining staffs, to your shipboard bill. The amount—about 10 percent of your bill—is established by the cruise lines, but you can elect to increase or decrease the amount.

Communications: Most new ships have telephones in cabins with international direct dialing capability and fax facilities in their offices. Be warned, however, the service is very expensive—about $9 to $15 per minute. If someone at home or in your office needs to reach you in an emergency, they can telephone your ship directly. Those calling from the continental United States would dial 011 plus 874 (the ocean area code for the Caribbean), followed by the seven-digit telephone number of your ship. Someone calling from Puerto Rico should dial 128 and ask for the long-distance operator. Instructions on making such calls, how to reach the ship, or whom to notify in case of an emergency are usually included in the information sent to you by your cruise line along with your tickets and luggage tags. If not, your travel agent can obtain them. You should have this information before you leave home.

Staying in touch when you are on a cruise is getting easier all the time as more and more ships now have Internet access, as well as WiFi enabling passengers to send and receive e-mail almost around the clock and to use their wireless-enabled computers at sea—for a fee.

Regarding cell phones, there are no restrictions about using them on a cruise ship, but the range can be limited and useful only in or near port. More and more cruise ships are being equipped with the technology to enable cell phone connection virtually anywhere the ships sail. Be aware, however, that you will be billed by your phone company at its long-distance or international rates, which are likely to cost as much as $5 per minute.

PART TWO

Caribbean Cruise Lines and Their Ships

Every effort has been made to ensure the accuracy of the information on the cruise lines and their ships, but do keep in mind that cruise lines change their ships' itineraries often for a variety of reasons. Always check with the cruise line or with a travel agent before making plans.

Azamara Club Cruises

1050 Caribbean Way, Miami, FL 33132; (305) 539-6000; (800) 646-1456; fax: (800) 437-5111; www.azamaracruises.com

Ships (passengers): *Azamara Journey* (710); *Azamara Quest* (710)

Departure ports: Fort Lauderdale, Miami, San Juan, others seasonally

Type of cruises: 7 to 10 or more nights, Eastern/Western Caribbean

Lifestyle tips: Moderately priced, upscale cruises at comfortable pace; emphasis on quality and destinations.

In 2006, when Royal Caribbean International (RCI) acquired Pullmantur, a Spanish tour and cruise operator, it also got two ships (originally Renaissance's *R6* and *R7*). First, they moved the ships to Celebrity Cruises and added some facilities and attractions to make them more consistent with the Celebrity fleet. But soon after, RCI decided to create a new brand, Azamara Cruises in a new category, "deluxe," meant to fill the gap between the premium (such as Celebrity and Holland America) and luxury categories (Seabourn and Silverseas) cruises.

The two ships were renamed *Azamara Journey* and *Azamara Quest*. The name, Azamara, was created from two words—*aza* from the Italian azzurro, meaning blue, and *mar* or mare, meaning sea. Azamara's cruises are designed mainly for experienced travelers who seek an alternative to big cruise ships at affordable prices and are intended specifically to compete with the popular Oceania Cruises. In 2010, "Club" was added to the name to project more of a country club image as part of a concerted effort to appeal to a more upscale traveler.

Azamara ships combine the glamour of traditional cruising with opulent, yet comfortable, decor in a relaxing atmosphere. For example, dress is usually resort-casual and no evenings require formal attire. Azamara offers more long cruises and itineraries with two- to three-night overnights. The ships have specialty restaurants, spas, Internet access, and WiFi.

Blount Small Ship Adventures

(formerly American Canadian Caribbean Line)

461 Water St., Warren, RI 02885; (401) 247-0955; (800) 556-7450; fax: (401) 245-8303; www.accl-smallships.com

Ships (passengers): *Grande Caribe* (100); *Grande Mariner* (96); *Niagara Prince* (90)

Departure ports: Various ports

Types of cruises: 7 to 12 days of Bahamas; Virgin Islands; Belize, Honduras

Lifestyle tips: Family-style dining; mature and experienced passengers; light adventure; no frills; emphasis on natural attraction and local culture. If you are looking for tranquility, informality, and conversation with fellow passengers instead of floor shows and casinos, Blount Small Ship Adventures (BSSA) offers low-key cruises around the Bahamas archipelago and the Western Caribbean during the winter season.

In 1964, the late Luther Blount designed his first small ship for cruising Canada's inland waterways. By 1988 the line had expanded to the extent that it could add Caribbean to its name. In the intervening years, BSSA remained faithful to the concept that small, intimate ships with limited planned entertainment can be successful. The ships' innovative bow ramps and shallow drafts give passengers direct access to beaches, coves, and places that are inaccessible to larger ships.

BSSA's ships are popular with mature, well-traveled passengers who like hearty American fare and the informal atmosphere of family-style dining. It is an atmosphere for instant friendships and complete relaxation. The line's large number of repeaters would seem to indicate that passengers agree with its concept and appreciate the "in-close" facility the ships bring to the cruise experience.

3655 NW Eighty-seventh Ave., Miami, FL 33178-2428; (305) 599-2600; (800) 438-6744; fax: (305) 599-8630; www.carnival.com

Ships (passengers): *Carnival Conquest* (2,974); *Carnival Destiny* (2,642); *Carnival Dream* (3,652); *Carnival Ecstasy* (2,052); *Carnival Elation* (2,052); *Carnival Fantasy* (2,056); *Carnival Fascination* (2,052); *Carnival Freedom* (2,974); *Carnival Glory* (2,974); *Carnival Imagination* (2,052); *Carnival Inspiration* (2,052); *Carnival Legend* (2,124); *Carnival Liberty* (2,974); *Carnival Magic* (3,652); *Carnival Miracle* (2,124); *Carnival Paradise* (2,052); *Carnival Pride* (2,124); *Carnival Sensation* (2,052); *Carnival Spirit* (2,124); *Carnival Splendor* (3,006); *Carnival Triumph* (2,758); *Carnival Valor* (2,974); *Carnival Victory* (2,758)

Departure ports: Miami, Port Canaveral, Tampa, New Orleans, San Juan, Galveston, Charleston, Jacksonville, Mobile, Fort Lauderdale, year-round. New York, Baltimore, Norfolk, summer/fall.

Types of cruises: 3, 4, and 5 days to Bahamas and Key West; 4 to 10 days to Western, Northern, Eastern, and Southern Caribbean, and the Panama Canal

Lifestyle tips: The "Fun Ships"; youthful, casual, action-filled; high value for money

Carnival Cruise Lines is the stuff of legends. In 1972 the late Florida-based cruise executive Ted Arison and an innovative Boston-based travel agency bought the *Empress of Canada,* which they renamed the *Mardi Gras,* to start a cruise line that would stand the stodgy old steamship business on its ear. But alas, the *Mardi Gras* ran aground on her maiden cruise. After staring at losses three years in a row, Arison took full ownership of the company, assuming its $5 million debt, buying its assets—the ship—for $1, and launched the "Fun Ships" concept that is Carnival's hallmark.

The idea was to get away from the class-conscious elitism that had long been associated with luxury liners and to fill the ship with so much action-packed fun that the ship itself would be the cruise experience. The line also aimed at lowering the average age of passengers by removing the for-mality associated with cruising and providing a wide

selection of activity and entertainment to attract active young adults, young couples, honeymooners, and families with children at reasonable prices. In only a few months, Carnival turned a profit, and in the next two years, it added two more ships.

The line's next move was as surprising as it was bold. In 1978, when shipbuilding costs and fuel prices were skyrocketing—threatening the very future of vacations-at-sea—Carnival ordered a new ship, larger and more technologically advanced than any cruise ship in service. It changed the profile of ships and enhanced the "fun" aspects of cruises. But it was Carnival's next move that really set the trend of the 1980s and beyond.

In 1982, less than ten years after its rocky start, Carnival ordered three "superliners," each carrying 1,800 passengers, with design and decor so different, it was zany and with as much glitz and glitter as the neon on Broadway.

In the 1990s Carnival outdid itself with the Fantasy group, eight megaliners even more dazzling than the earlier superliners with flashy decor and high-energy ambience. The ships have full-fledged gyms and spas and so many entertainment and recreation outlets that you need more than one cruise to find them all. Beginning in 2007, the Fantasy class ships were renovated and major new facilities, such as a water park for children and a "serenity" section for adults, were added. By 2010, Carnival had added three new classes of ships—four 110,000-ton megaliners, four 88,500-ton super-liners, and two 130,000-ton ships carrying 3,652 passengers. Carnival's largest ships are called "post-Panamax," meaning that they are too large to transit the Panama Canal—at least until the new third channel opens in 2014. All Carnival ships have Internet cafes and are fitted for WiFi.

Now headed by Arison's son, Micky, Carnival is directed by an energetic and aggressive team that seems determined to entice everybody—single; married; families; children; retirees; disabled; first-time cruisers; repeat cruisers; people from the North, South, East, and West; and from all walks of life—to take a cruise. To that end, the cruises are priced aggressively and offer among the best values in cruising.

Carnival has a 24-hour, toll-free hot line to help passengers who encounter a travel emergency, such as severe weather or an airline delay or strike, en route or returning from their cruise. The U.S. number is (800) 885-4856; outside the United States, call collect (305) 406-4779. Do all these ideas work? You bet they do! Carnival carries more than three million passengers a year. That's up from 80,000 passengers in its first year.

Carnival Cruise Lines is a public company and owns the long-established Holland America Line, Costa Cruises, Cunard, Princess Cruises, and Seabourn Cruise Line. Altogether, Carnival Corporation ships account for more than 49 percent of the U.S. cruise market. These lines operate under their own banners, but the combination makes Carnival one of the world's largest cruise lines and gives it enormous marketing clout across the widest possible spectrum.

Celebrity Cruises

1050 Caribbean Way, Miami, FL 33132; (305) 539-6000; (800) 646-1456; fax: (800) 437-5111; www .celebrity.com

Ships (passengers): *Celebrity Century* (1,750); *Celebrity Constellation* (1,950); *Celebrity Eclipse* (2,850); *Celebrity Equinox* (2,850); *Celebrity Infinity* (1,950); *Celebrity Mercury* (1,750); *Celebrity Millennium* (1,950); *Celebrity Silhouette* (2,850); *Celebrity Solstice* (2,850); *Celebrity Summit* (1,950); *Celebrity Xpedition* (94)

Departure ports: Fort Lauderdale, San Juan, Miami, Cape Liberty

Types of cruises: 5 nights to the Bahamas; 7 to 14 nights to Caribbean; Bermuda.

Lifestyle tip: Deluxe cruises at moderate prices

In 1989 when John Chandris, the nephew of the founder of Chandris Cruises, announced the creation of a new deluxe, midpriced cruise line, he said the goal was "to bring more luxurious cruises to experienced travelers at affordable prices." He was met with a great skepticism; "deluxe" and "midpriced" seemed a contradiction in terms. But three years later, he had made believers out of all his doubters.

Not only did Celebrity Cruises accomplish what it set out to do, it did it better than anyone had imagined and in record-breaking time. A Celebrity cruise is not only deluxe; it also offers true value for the money. It was a completely new product with a new generation of ships designed for the 1990s and beyond and set new standards of service and cuisine in its price category.

Celebrity's ships are tony, not glitzy, and they are spacious and have a similar array of entertainment and recreation as the new megaliners. The once-standard one-lounge-for-all was replaced by small, separate lounges, each with its own decor, ambience, and entertainment, and a variety of bars to give passengers a range of options. They have stunning, stylish decor that brought back some of the glamour of cruising in bygone days, but with a fresh, contemporary look.

From its inception, Celebrity Cruises aimed at creating superior cuisine as one way to distinguish itself. It engaged as its food consultant an award-winning master French chef with two Michelin three-star restaurants in England. Celebrity set a new standard for other cruise lines. The food is high quality, sophisticated but unpretentious. Celebrity's stylish, elegant ships have mostly outside cabins equipped with television, mini-fridge, first-run movies; piano bar; nightclub; duplex show lounge with state-of-the-art sound and lighting systems; disco; casino; and an observation lounge. There are shops, sports and fitness center, swimming pools, Jacuzzis, and Internet cafes. In the suites, butler service is available. In 2008, Celebrity introduced the 118,000-ton *Celebrity Solstice*, a new class of ships and the first of five being introduced at the pace of one per year to 2012. They have already, proven to be so popular that Celebrity is "Solsticizing" all its fleet by adding favorite features of the new class. Celebrity Cruises is owned by Royal Caribbean but operates as a separate company.

Club Méditerranée, S.A.

40 West Fifty-seventh St., New York, NY 10019; (212) 977-2100; (800) CLUB-MED; fax: (212) 315-5392

Ships (passengers): *Club Med II* (392)

Departure port: Martinique

Type of cruises: 7 days to Eastern and Southern Caribbean

Lifestyle tip: Casual and sports oriented Club Med, a name synonymous with all-inclusive vacations and an easy lifestyle, took its popular formula to sea in 1990 with the introduction of the world's largest sailboat and geared it to upscale, sophisticated, and active vacationers. But theirs was no ordinary sailing ship.

Longer than two football fields, *Club Med II* is 610 feet long and is rigged with five 164-foot masts. The $100 million ship was the last word in 21st-century technology, with seven computer-monitored sails. All 191 outside staterooms have a twin porthole and hand-rubbed mahogany cabinetwork. The spacious, 188-square-foot cabins are fitted with twin or king-size beds. All cabins have private bath, closed-circuit television, radio, safe, and minibar.

The ship has two restaurants: One, on the top deck, offers casual dining and has an outdoor veranda for breakfast and luncheon buffets; the other, directly below, is a more formal dining room with waiter service and a la carte menu. Complimentary wine and beer accompany both luncheon and dinner. The ship has a fitness center with a panoramic view from the top deck, pine saunas and licensed massage therapists, tanning salon, two swimming pools, a disco, casino, 24-hour room service, and satellite telecommunications. Other facilities include a boutique, theater, hair salon, and observation deck. The ship carries water-sports equipment and has a special sports platform that unfolds into the sea from which passengers can sail, windsurf, scuba dive, water-ski, and snorkel. During the winter season *Club Med II* is based in Martinique, from where it sails on alternating itineraries to the islands of the Eastern and Southern Caribbean.

Costa Cruise Lines

Venture Corporate Center II, 200 South Park Rd., Suite 200, Hollywood, FL 33021-8541; (954) 266-5600; (954) 266-2100; (800) GO-COSTA; www .costacruise.com

Ships (passengers): *Costa Allegra* (1,000); *Costa Atlantica* (2,114); *Costa Classica* (1,356); *Costa Concordia* (3,300); *Costa Deliziosa* (2,260); *Costa Fascinosa* (3,000); *Costa Favolosa* (3,000); *Costa Fortuna* (2,720); *Costa Luminosa* (2,260); *Costa Magica* (2,720); *Costa Marina* (1,000); *Costa Mediterranea* (2,114); *Costa Pacifica* (2,260); *Costa Romantica* (1,356); *Costa Serena* (3,300); *Costa Victoria* (1,928)

Departure ports: Miami, Ft. Lauderdale, Guadeloupe

Types of cruises: 7 days to Eastern/Western Caribbean

Lifestyle tip: More European atmosphere and service than similar mass-market ships.

"Cruising Italian Style" has long been Costa Cruise Lines' stock in trade, with a fun and friendly atmosphere created by its Italian staff. The emphasis is on Italian food, which means pasta and pizza (there are other kinds of cuisine, too); European-style service, particularly in the dining room; and, not to forget the Italians' ancestry, a toga party, which is usually a hilarious affair, one night of the cruise.

Founded by the Genoa-based Costa family, which has been in the shipping business for more than one hundred years and in the passenger business for almost seventy years, Costa began offering one-week Caribbean cruises from Miami in 1959. Costa launched the 1990s with new ships, introducing interesting new features in its design, combining classic qualities with modern features and boasting unusually large cabins for their price categories. Among the ships' nicest features are canvas-covered outdoor cafes and pizzerias serving pizza throughout the day without additional charge. The ships also have Internet cafes.

Catalina Island is Costa's "private" beach off the southeast coast of the Dominican Republic featured on Eastern Caribbean cruises. The island is near the sprawling resort of Casa de Campo, which has, among its many facilities, three of the best golf courses in the Caribbean, a tennis village, horseback riding, and polo. Costa's ships have fitness centers and spas (services are extra), along with a health and fitness program.

You can combine two consecutive cruises into one fourteen-day cruise, at a price considerably less than that of two separate cruises. Another popular feature: During a Caribbean cruise a couple can renew their wedding vows in a special shipboard ceremony.

Costa is owned by Carnival Cruise Lines but operates as a separate entity.

Crystal Cruises

2049 Century Park East, Suite 1400, Los Angeles, CA 90067; (310) 785-9300; fax: (310) 785-3891; www.crystalcruises.com

Ships (passengers): *Crystal Serenity* (1,080); *Crystal Symphony* (960)

Departure ports: Miami and worldwide

Types of cruises: 10- to 17-day Eastern/Western transcanal

Lifestyle tip: Ultra luxury for sophisticated travelers

The launching of Crystal Cruises in 1989 was one of the most anticipated in the cruising world. The owners spared no expense to ensure that its sleek new ship would live up to its advance billing. Its goal was to create luxury cruises that would return elegance and personalized service to cruising and be designed for an upscale mass market at deluxe prices. The ship exceeded expectations and quickly became the ship by which others in its class—or trying to be in its class—are measured.

The *Crystal Serenity* took luxury to another level, with larger cabins (no inside ones), more cabins with balconies, a larger spa, and more dining options, including a specialty restaurant by famed master chef Nobu Matsuhisa. The ships are magnificent, with exquisite attention to detail. The food is excellent and the service superb, with the staff at every level smiling and gracious and always willing to go the extra mile.

These are spacious ships for experienced travelers with sophisticated lifestyles. The luxury is evident from the moment you step aboard. Staterooms have sitting areas, minibars, spacious closets, and such amenities as hair dryers, plush robes, DVDs, and 24-hour hookup with CNN and ESPN; more than half have verandas. The ships' penthouses have Jacuzzis and butler service. Facilities include spa and fitness centers and full promenade decks for jogging. The indoor/outdoor swimming pools have swim-up bars and lap pools with adjacent whirlpools. The ships have casinos and a choice of dinner restaurants—Japanese or Asian and Italian—at no extra cost. These restaurants are in addition to standard meal service in the main dining room and 24-hour room service.

Crystal's ships offer Computer University@Sea, with hands-on lab sessions. Laptop computers can be rented. Crystal also offers passengers individual e-mail addresses to use onboard.

Cunard

24303 Town Center Dr., Suite 200, Valencia, CA 91355-0908; (661) 753-1035; (800) 7-CUNARD; fax: (661) 259-3103; www.cunard.com

Ships (passengers): *Queen Elizabeth* (2,000); *Queen Mary 2* (2,620); *Queen Victoria* (2,014)

Departure ports: New York, Fort Lauderdale

Types of cruises: 8 to 14 days for Caribbean on seasonal schedules

Lifestyle tips: Deluxe, and no mistaking the British touch; caters mostly to affluent travelers

The 150,000-ton *Queen Mary 2*, the largest cruise ship ever built at the time she was launched, is heir to a family of transatlantic liners reaching back more than a century and a half and the only ship still on regular transatlantic service, from Apr to Dec.

The *Queens* set the standard of elegance at sea in times of peace and served their country with distinction in times of war. *QM2*, which made her maiden voyage in Jan 2004, sets the tone for Cunard for the years to come. She is an ocean liner reminiscent of the great steamships and, in Cunard's words, was meant to "relaunch the golden age of travel for those who missed the first one."

Costing more than $800 million, the *QM2* is one of the world's fastest ships, with speeds up to 30 knots. She offers a "quasi-class system," with cabin category determining assignments in each of three restaurants—one with a grand staircase similar to that seen by moviegoers in *Titanic*. Seventy-five percent of the cabins have balconies. The *QM2* also boasts one of the largest spas afloat, designed by the famous Canyon Ranch, which operates it.

In 1998 Cunard was purchased by Carnival Cruises but operates as a separate company. Even though Cunard is one of the oldest lines afloat, it has been an innovator, responding to today's changing lifestyles and the impact of the electronic revolution on people's lives—including their holidays. Its ships were the first to have a computer learning center, and satellite-delivered world news.

Queen Victoria made her debut in December 2007 with a world cruise; and the new *Queen Elizabeth* launched in October 2010.

Disney Cruise Line

210 Celebration Place, Suite 400, Celebration, FL 34747-4600; (407) 566-3500; (800) 939-CRUISE; fax: (407) 566-6910; www.disneycruise.com

Ships (passengers): *Disney Dream* (2,500); *Disney Fantasy* (2,500); *Disney Magic* (1,760); *Disney Wonder* (1,760)

Departure port: Port Canaveral

Types of cruises: 3-, 4-, 5-, and 7-day Eastern and Western cruises combined with Disney World vacations

Lifestyle tip: Family oriented but designed for all ages

Disney Cruise Line was launched in July 1998, with ships that have classic exteriors reminiscent of the great transatlantic ocean liners of the past, but up-to-the-minute inside with Disney innovation and family entertainment. Disney Cruises' two new megaliners at sea in 2011 and 2012 are full of spectacular innovations.

The line combines a three- or four-day stay at a Walt Disney World resort with a three- or four-day cruise aboard ship, sailing round-trip from Port Canaveral. Most itineraries also include a day at Castaway Cay, Disney's own private island in the Bahamas. In addition to catering to families, the ships' major innovations were three themed restaurants as well as an adults-only alternative restaurant, swimming pool, and nightclub on each ship. Nightly entertainment features Disney-produced shows with Broadway-quality entertainers, cabaret, and a comedy club.

The children's programs are the most extensive in the industry, with the largest children-dedicated space and age-specific activities and a large number of counselors. The ships have a separate pool, lounge, teen club, and game arcade for older kids.

The ships sport spacious suites and cabins, with 73 percent outside and almost half with small verandas.

Holland America Line

300 Elliott Ave. West, Seattle, WA 98119; (206) 281-3535; (800) 426-0327; fax: (206) 301-5327; www.hollandamerica.com

Ships (passengers): *Amsterdam* (1,380); *Eurodam* (2041); *Maasdam* (1,266); *Nieuw Amsterdam* (2,104); *Noordam* (1,848); *Oosterdam* (1,848); *Prinsendam* (794); *Rotterdam* (1,316); *Ryndam* (1,266); *Statendam* (1,266); *Veendam* (1,266); *Volendam* (1,440); *Westerdam* (1,848); *Zaandam* (1,440); *Zuiderdam* (1,848)

Departure ports: Fort Lauderdale, Tampa, New York; Boston, Norfolk seasonally

Types of cruises: 5 to 11 days to Western and Eastern Caribbean; 10 days to Southern Caribbean; 10 to 23 days to Panama Canal

Lifestyle tip: Classic but contemporary

Begun in 1873 as a transatlantic shipping company between Rotterdam and the Americas, Holland America Line stems from one of the oldest steamship companies in the world. Through the years and two world wars, its ships became an important part of maritime history, particularly significant in the westward passage of immigrants to America. The line also owned Westours, the Seattle-based tour company that pioneered tours and cruises to Alaska in the 1950s. Both were purchased by Carnival Cruise Lines.

Holland America now has one of the newest fleets in cruising, having added ten magnificent, brand-new ships in less than ten years. The ships combine the Old World with the New in decor and ambience and boast million-dollar art and antiques collections reflecting Holland's association with trade and exploration in the Americas and Asia.

Their Dutch officers and Indonesian and Filipino crews are another reminder of Holland's historical ties to Asia.

The ships have the space and elegance for long cruises of two weeks or more, for which they were designed. They feature a three-level atrium lobby with unusual sculpture, an elegant two-level dining room, small lounges and bars, disco, casino, spa, a sliding-glass dome for the swimming pool, spacious cabins, and premium amenities. All suites and 120 deluxe cabins have private verandas, whirlpool baths, minibars, and DVDs. There are bathtubs in all outside cabins.

Holland America's Caribbean cruises include a day at the line's 2,400-acre Bahamian island of Little San Salvador, located between Eleuthera and Cat Island, and renamed Half Moon Cay. Developed as a private island, the multimillion-dollar facility, covering 45 acres along a gorgeous white-sand beach, has a plaza built to resemble the ruins of an old Spanish fort, a shopping area, and a food pavilion—all connected by walkways and a tram. There is a children's playground, wedding chapel, and post office that sells Bahamian stamps and has its own postmark. The sports center offers snorkeling and diving on nearby reefs, Sunfish sailing and other water sports, volleyball, and basketball. Parts of the island with nature trails were designated as a bird sanctuary by the Bahamian National Trust.

Signature of Excellence, a program launched in 2004 to update its ships, has added new features such as Internet cafes, expanded spa facilities, alternative dining venues, and larger children's facilities, making the ships more relevant to baby boomers and multigenerational families. During the winter the fleet sails on Caribbean and Panama Canal cruises, some departing from Tampa, a port Holland America helped to develop for cruise ships.

MSC Cruises

6750 North Andrews Ave., #605, Fort Lauderdale, FL 33309; (954) 772-6262; (800) 666-9333; fax: (954) 776-5881; www.msccruises.com

Ships (passengers): *MSC Armonia* (1,556); *MSC Fantasia* (3,300); *MSC Favolosa* (2,550); *MSC Lirica*

(1,590); *MSC Magnifica* (2,550); *MSC Melody* (1,062); *MSC Meraviglia* (2,550); *MSC Musica* (3,000); *MSC Opera* (1,756); *MSC Orchestra* (3,000); *MSC Poesia* (2,550) *MSC Sinfonia* (1,556); *MSC Splendida* (3,300)

Departure port: Fort Lauderdale

Type of cruises: 7, 10, and 11 days to Eastern/Western Caribbean, Panama Canal

Lifestyle tip: Classic but contemporary, Italian style

Privately-owned by the world's second-largest operator of container ships and fast ferries, Mediterranean Shipping Company (MSC) acquired three cruise ships in less than four years and by 2009 had added nine ships with another three ships under construction. Actress Sophia Loren has christened all MSC Cruises ships since the *MSC Lirica* in 2003. (Most of the ships sail primarily in Europe.)

With an Italian staff and ambience, the ships offer classic cruises with good food and service. MSC aims for a mix of 85 percent American and 15 percent international passengers when its Florida-based ships sail the Caribbean. Onboard, MSC made changes to appeal to American tastes, such as prices being in dollars rather than euros, cabin television with CNN and American movies, and breakfast and lunch buffets with choices that American passengers prefer. Among the ships amenities are two swimming pools, a gym and jogging track, two hot tubs and a sauna, a virtual-reality center, and an Internet cafe. The ships also have a disco and a theater with shows nightly, a supervised Mini Club for children, a shopping gallery, and two or more restaurants as well as a grill and pizzeria. All cabins have satellite television, minibar, safe, radio, and 24-hour room service.

Norwegian Cruise Line

7665 Corporate Center Dr., Miami, FL 33126; (305) 436-4000; (800) 327-7030; fax: (305) 436-4120; www.ncl.com

Ships (passengers): *Norwegian Dawn* (2,240); *Norwegian Epic* (4,200); *Norwegian Gem* (2,376); *Norwegian Jade* (2,466); *Norwegian Jewel* (2,376); *Norwegian Pearl* (2,376); *Norwegian Sky* (2,002);

Norwegian Spirit (1,966); *Norwegian Star* (2,240); *Norwegian Sun* (2,002)

Departure ports: Miami, New York, Port Canaveral, Houston year-round; Boston, Charleston, New Orleans seasonally

Types of cruises: 3, 4, and 7 days to the Bahamas; Eastern/Western Caribbean; Bermuda

Lifestyle tip: Mainstream of modern cruising

Norwegian Cruise Line (NCL) was started in 1966 by Knut Kloster, whose family has been in the steamship business in Scandinavia since 1906. Kloster is credited with launching modern cruising when he introduced year-round three- and four-day cruises from Miami to the Bahamas, thus creating the first mass-market packaging of cruises.

By 1971 NCL had added three new ships and pioneered weekly cruises to Jamaica and other Caribbean destinations, and bought a Bahamian island to add a day-on-a-private-island to the line's Bahamas cruises. The idea has since been adopted by most cruise lines sailing the Bahamas and Caribbean.

Yet, in its history loaded with "firsts," nothing was as significant as the entry of the *Norway* (now retired) in 1980. After buying the former *France* for $18 million, NCL spent $100 million to transform her from the great ocean liner to a trendsetting Caribbean cruise ship. Her size enabled NCL to create a completely new environment on board with restaurants, bars, and lounges of great diversity; shopping malls with "sidewalk" cafes; full Broadway shows and Las Vegas revues in its enormous theater; full casino; and sports and entertainment facilities that could keep passengers in motion almost around the clock. These innovations set the pattern for all cruise ships that followed and are common features on all large ships today.

NCL is known for its entertainment—ranging from comedy clubs and cabaret stars to Broadway shows, and has an extensive youth and children's program.

In 2000 NCL was bought by the Asian cruise line, Star Cruises, which stepped up NCL's expansion with seven new megaliners in five years. The new ships reflect NCL's FreeStyle Cruising, one of the line's most significant innovations, provides passengers with the utmost flexibility, enabling

them to dine where, when, and with whom they choose, with up to ten and more restaurants, along with choice of attire and other features. NCL was one of the first cruise lines to provide wireless capability on its newest ships. The new *Norwegian Epic,* launched in July 2010, promises to be one of the most innovative ships of the decade.

Oceania Cruises

8300 Northwest Thirty-third St., Suite 308, Miami, FL 33122; (305) 514-2300; (800) 531-5658; fax: (305) 514-2222; www.oceaniacruises.com

Ships (passengers): *Insignia* (684); *Marina* (1,200); *Nautica* (684); *Regatta* (684)

Departure port: Miami

Type of cruises: 10 to 16 days to the Caribbean, Panama Canal, Central and South America in winter

Lifestyle tip: Casual country-club elegance without pretension

Formed in late 2002 by two well-known cruise industry veterans, Oceania Cruises carved out a niche between the premium and luxury categories similar to the now-defunct Renaissance Cruises, using three of the former line's ships. Appealing to discerning, sophisticated travelers, the cruise line created an outstanding product with its cuisine, service, and destination-oriented itineraries and offers it at moderate prices. The relaxed onboard atmosphere is meant to resemble the casual elegance of a country club, neither stuffy nor pretentious. Formal wear is never required.

The ships—small compared with today's megaships—provide an intimate atmosphere while having the facilities of larger ships. For example, each ship has four restaurants with open seating, enabling passengers to dine when, where, and with whom they choose, and offering a different type of cuisine and ambience. Menus have been crafted by master chef Jacques Pepin, the line's executive culinary director and one of America's best-known chefs. Of the total 340 spacious cabins and suites, 92 percent are outside, and almost 70 percent have verandas. The ships have spas and fitness centers and personal trainers are available. Oceania@Sea, the 24-hour computer center, has Internet access, and there's a library, card room, medical center, self-service launderette, and four elevators. Some itineraries include overnight port stays to allow passengers to immerse themselves in the local flavor of the region. Passengers are registered in the line's Repeaters Club from their first cruise, making them eligible for travel rewards and other benefits.

Oceania is building two 1,200 passengers ships to be launched in 2011 and 2012.

Princess Cruises

24305 Town Center Dr., Santa Clarita, CA 91355; (800) 774-6237; fax: (661) 284-4771; www.princess .com

Ships (passengers): *Caribbean Princess* (3,100); *Coral Princess* (2,000); *Crown Princess* (3,100); *Dawn Princess* (1,950); *Diamond Princess* (2,700); *Emerald Princess* (3,100); *Golden Princess* (2,600); *Grand Princess* (2,600); *Island Princess* (2,000); *Ocean Princess* (670); *Pacific Princess* (700); *Ruby Princess* (3,100); *Sapphire Princess* (2,700); *Sea Princess* (1,950); *Star Princess* (2,600); *Sun Princess* (1,950)

Departure ports: Fort Lauderdale, San Juan, Acapulco, Los Angeles, New York (summer), Barbados (winter)

Types of cruises: 7 to 14 days, combining Western/Eastern/Southern Caribbean, and Panama Canal

Lifestyle tip: Casually stylish and modestly affluent

Princess Cruises, a West Coast pioneer begun in 1965, is credited with helping to create the relaxed and casual atmosphere that typifies life aboard today's cruises. One of its ships, the former *Pacific Princess* (now retired), was the ship used in the popular television series *The Love Boat*. That show probably did more to popularize modern cruising than all other cruise publicity combined. It was certainly a factor in dispelling cruising's elitist image and enabling people who might have never considered a cruise holiday to identify with it.

When the *Royal Princess* (now retired), which was christened by Diana, Princess of Wales, made her debut in 1983, she set new standards in passenger comfort with all outside cabins, and refrigerators, televisions, and bathrooms fitted with

tubs as well as showers in every cabin category. All suites, deluxe cabins, and some of those in lesser categories had private outside balconies—a first for cruising.

In 1995 and for the next decade, Princess launched two new classes of megaships for a total of ten ships which were among the largest cruise ships ever built. Designed by NjalEide, the architect of the elegant *Royal Princess*, they are some of the most beautiful large ships afloat, with exquisite interiors of the finest Italian workmanship. They introduced many new features, including two atrium lobbies and two main show lounges, a true theater at sea, and a restaurant offering 24-hour dining. About 70 percent of the outside cabins have verandas. *Grand Princess* and her sister ships came with even more choices— three show lounges with different shows each night, three dining rooms, three alternative restaurants, and more. All have elaborate spas and Internet cafes. With the new ships, the cruise line introduced a flexible dining program enabling passengers to dine when and with whom they wish as in a restaurant, along with traditional dining in the main dining room.

In recent years Princess has had one of the strongest presences in the Caribbean in the winter season. The line has a private beach, Princess Cays (on south Eleuthera in the Bahamas) with just about every water sport a passenger could want, nature trails with guided walks, games, kiosks for local crafts, and a large dining pavilion where passengers are served lunch.

In 2003 Princess Cruises was purchased by Carnival Corporation, outbidding Royal Caribbean Lines for this prize. Princess caters to a modestly affluent clientele from thirty-five years of age plus, with a median age of fifty-five.

Regent Seven Seas Cruises

600 Corporate Dr., No. 410, Fort Lauderdale, FL 33334; (954) 776-6123; (800) 477-7500; fax: (954) 772-3763; www.rssc.com

Ships (passengers): *Seven Seas Mariner* (729); *Seven Seas Navigator* (490); *Seven Seas Voyager* (708)

Departure ports: Fort Lauderdale seasonally

Types of cruises: 7 to 14 days; transcanal, Eastern Caribbean

Lifestyle tip: Luxury for affluent travelers

The cruise line operates three ultra luxurious ships that sail the world. They are among the most spacious ocean liners afloat. The *Seven Seas Mariner* and *Seven Seas Voyager* were cruising's first all-suite-with-balcony ships. Throughout the fleet, the decor is one of understated elegance. The ships have several lounges and bars, a spa, and a fitness center with a gym, sauna, and jogging track. The dining rooms and alternative restaurants serve as fine cuisine as one finds in top restaurants in New York or Paris.

Only one ship sails in the Caribbean, and only for a limited time in winter. These cruises are usually combined with the Panama Canal or South America. The cruises are expensive and cater to affluent passengers who are accustomed to the best, but the price is more inclusive than their competitors as it includes most shore excursions.

Royal Caribbean International

1050 Caribbean Way, Miami, FL 33132; (305) 539-6000; (800) 659-7225; (800) 722-5329; fax: (305) 373-4394; www.royalcaribbean.com

Ships (passengers): *Adventure of the Seas* (3,114); *Allure of the Seas* (6,200); *Brilliance of the Seas* (2,000); *Enchantment of the Seas* (1,950); *Explorer of the Seas* (3,114); *Freedom of the Seas* (3,600); *Grandeur of the Seas* (1,950); *Independence of the Seas* (3,634); *Jewel of the Seas* (2,100); *Legend of the Seas* (1,808); *Liberty of the Seas* (3,634); *Majesty of the Seas* (2,354); *Mariner of the Seas* (3,114); *Monarch of the Seas* (2,354); *Navigator of the Seas* (3,114); *Oasis of the Seas* (6,200); *Radiance of the Seas* (2,000); *Rhapsody of the Seas* (2,000); *Serenade of the Seas* (2,100); *Splendor of the Seas* (1,800); *Vision of the Seas* (1,950); *Voyager of the Seas* (3,114)

Departure ports: Miami, San Juan, Fort Lauderdale, Port Canaveral, Bayonne, Philadelphia, Baltimore, Boston, Tampa, Galveston, New Orleans

Types of cruises: 3 to 10 days to the Bahamas and Western/Eastern/Southern Caribbean

Lifestyle tip: Active, wholesome ambience

Royal Caribbean Cruise Line (RCI), launched in the early 1970s, was the first line to build a fleet of ships designed specially for year-round Caribbean cruising. The ships were established so quickly that within five years RCI needed more capacity and did so by "stretching" two of the vessels with midsection inserts. In the 1980s and 1990s, RCI added superliners with unique design features including the *Sovereign of the Seas,* the first of the new generation of megaliners and the largest cruise ship afloat at the time. Few ships in history have received so much attention. With *Legend of the Seas,* it introduced the first miniature golf course at sea and a spectacular "solarium"—an indoor/outdoor swimming, sunning, and fitness facility. *Voyager of the Seas* came with cruising's first rock-climbing wall, skating rink, cabins overlooking the atrium, and more.

But the showstopper of all times was the 220,000 ton *Oasis of the Sea,* the largest cruise ship ever built, launched in 2009. Her sister followed in 2010. As Royal Caribbean added ships, it has expanded its itineraries and now homeports ships in Europe and Asia, as well. It would be impossible for even the most active passenger to participate in all the daily activities offered on an RCI ship. Fitness folks have health clubs, complete with ballet bars, computerized exercise equipment, and a high-energy staff to put them through their paces. The sports deck has twin pools and a basketball court. RCI ships have acres of open sundecks and large pools. The line's ShipShape program is often combined with sports in port. Golf Ahoy! enables passengers to play golf at courses throughout the Caribbean.

For those with something less strenuous in mind, there are small, sophisticated lounges for drinks, dancing, and cabaret entertainment. Enrichment programs run the gamut from napkin folding to wine tasting. Two feature films run daily in twin cinemas and the show lounge, a multi-tiered theater with unobstructed views, runs two different Las Vegas–style revues and variety shows. A top-deck lounge cantilevered from the funnel provides fabulous views from twelve or more stories above the sea. These lounges are RCI's signature.

RCI blankets the Caribbean year-round. Coco-Cay, a small island in the Bahamas, is used for the ships' day-at-the-beach. Labadee, RCCL's private resort on the north coast of Haiti, is very popular.

Founded in 1969 as a partnership of three prominent Norwegian shipping companies, RCI went public in Apr 1993. In 1997 RCI purchased Celebrity Cruises, which it operates as a separate company. RCI caters to a moderately upscale market in a friendly and casual atmosphere. All RCI ships have programs for children and teenagers because the line believes that a happy kid on a cruise now will still be a customer in twenty or thirty years.

cleaning mechanisms. The ships have spas and computer learning centers.

Passengers dine on gourmet cuisine served on Royal Doulton china and have open seating. They may also dine from the restaurant menu in their suites. Seabourn's ships have sleek profiles that resemble the most modern of yachts. A water sports platform at the stern has a "cage" that can be lowered into the water for passengers to swim in the open sea without fear. The ships carry sailboards, snorkeling and dive equipment, and two high-speed boats.

In 2009, Seabourn launched the first of three new ships, almost double in size of the original three, and even more luxurious; two more ships debut in 2010 and 2011. The company is owned by Carnival Cruise Lines but operates as a separate entity.

Seabourn Cruise Line

6100 Blue Lagoon Dr., Suite 400, Miami, FL 33126; (305) 463-3000; (800) 929-9391; fax: (305) 463-3010; www.seabourn.com

Ships (passengers): *Seabourn Legend* (214); *Seabourn Odyssey* (450); *Seabourn Pride* (214); *Seabourn Sojourn* (450); *Seabourn Spirit* (214)

Departure ports: Fort Lauderdale, Barbados, others

Types of cruises: 3 to 21 days in Eastern/Southern Caribbean, Panama Canal in winter

Lifestyle tip: The ultimate luxury cruise

When Seabourn was formed in 1987, it set out to create the world's most deluxe cruises on the most elegant, luxurious ships afloat. Despite very high per diem rates, Seabourn quickly won enough fans to add more ships.

The ships and cruises were designed with a certain type of person in mind—one who normally stays in the best rooms at a luxury hotel and books a deluxe suite on a luxury liner. The staterooms are luxuriously appointed in soft, warm colors and have television with CNN, CD and DVD players, stocked bars, refrigerators, walk-in closets, and large marble bathrooms with tub and shower. Each has a roomy sitting area beside a large picture window with electrically manipulated shades and outside

SeaDream Yacht Club

2601 South Bayshore Dr., Penthouse 1B, Coconut Grove, FL 33133-5417; (305) 631-6100; (800) 707-4911; fax: (305) 631-6110; www.seadreamyachtclub.com

Ships (passengers): *SeaDream I/SeaDream II* (110)

Departure ports: San Juan, Barbados, St. Thomas, St. Maarten

Types of cruises: 7-day Caribbean, seasonally

Lifestyle tip: Luxury but casual

SeaDream Yacht Club, a venture of two cruise-industry veterans, began operating in late 2001 with the luxury twin ships *SeaDream I* and *II* (formerly *Sea Goddess I* and *II*). The handsome twins, which the line calls mega-yachts, are meant to provide a totally different experience from today's typical cruise, one that more closely resembles yachting. Like yachts, the ships offer an open, unstructured ambience for passengers to move at their own pace. "No clocks, no crowds, no lines, no stress" could be the company's motto.

The cruises have flexible schedules and itineraries, departing their first port and arriving at their last port as scheduled, but the port calls in between are not run by a strict timetable. Captains have the authority to adjust for local opportunities. Sometimes, SeaDream yachts overnight at popular ports where the action doesn't get started until late evening. While the ship is in port, passengers may visit a small-town pastry shop with the chef, go snorkeling with the captain, or go hiking, biking, or golfing with the officers. What better guides to have.

The ships have alcoves for sunning on trendy double sun beds, a private massage tent on deck, a large-screen golf simulator that also can be used to watch sports events or movies, and a water sports marina at the stern equipped for kayaking, waterskiing, windsurfing, snorkeling, and Sunfish sailing. Tai chi, yoga, and aerobics classes are also offered.

Indoors, passengers have an Asian-style spa and fitness center. The ships have a Main Lounge, piano bar, casino, and library with books, CDs, DVDs, and computer outlets. Laptop computers are available. Passengers are given their own onboard e-mail address.

All cabins are Internet ready and have an entertainment center with a flat-screen television, CD and DVD systems with movies and other selections. SeaDream has no dress code; rather it stresses the casual nature of yachting.

Silversea Cruises

110 East Broward Blvd., Fort Lauderdale, FL 33301; (954) 522-4477; (800) 722-6655; fax: (954) 522-4499; www.silversea.com

Ships (passengers): *HSH Prince Albert II* (132); *Silver Cloud* (306); *Silver Shadow* (388); *Silver Spirit* (540); *Silver Whisper* (388); *Silver Wind* (306)

Departure ports: Fort Lauderdale, Barbados

Type of cruise: Caribbean, seasonally

Lifestyle tip: Ultra luxurious surroundings in a relaxing, friendly—not stuffy—atmosphere

Silversea Cruises was launched in late 1994 with the luxurious all-suite *Silver Cloud,* designed by Oslo-based Petter Yran and Bjorn Storbraaten, the architects of the Seabourn ships. Silversea's large suites, averaging 300 square feet, have a spacious sitting area, walk-in closet, fully stocked bar, hair dryer, TV with DVD, direct-dial telephone, and marble-floored bathroom with tub. Passengers are

welcomed to their staterooms with fresh flowers, a bottle of champagne, a basket of fruit replenished daily, personalized stationery, and plush terry robes for use during their cruise.

There is open seating in the dining room and 24-hour room service. The ships have a tiered show lounge spanning two decks, with a nightclub at the upper level, plus a casino, a spa, and a library.

In 2000 and 2001, the line added two new, slightly larger, and even more spacious ships, but almost identical in style to the earlier ships. In 2009, Silversea added a new slightly larger ship of 36,000 tons. The ships sail on worldwide itineraries throughout the year, but at least one is in the Caribbean for transcanal, Central, and South American itineraries in winter.

Star Clippers, Inc.

7200 Northwest Nineteenth St., Suite 206, Miami, FL 33126; (305) 442-0550; (800) 442-0551; fax: (305) 442-1611; www.starclippers.com

Ships (passengers): *Royal Clipper* (224); *Star Clipper* (180); *Star Flyer* (180)

Departure ports: St. Maarten; Barbados

Type of cruises: 7 to 14 days on alternating itineraries in the Eastern Caribbean

Lifestyle tip: For active travelers looking for the romance of sailing to out-of-the-way places Star Clippers is the brainchild of Swedish shipping entrepreneur Mikael Krafft, whose passions for sailing and building yachts and his love of the clipper ship (which he says is one of America's greatest inventions) led him in 1991 to create a cruise line with ships that are direct descendents of the fast, sleek clipper ships that ruled the seas in the mid-1800s. Built in Belgium, the vessels are 357 feet long with four masts and square-rigged sails in the forward mast—a Barguentine configuration—with a total of seventeen sails (36,000 square feet of sail area). They are manned, not computerized, and capable of attaining speeds of 19.4 knots. At 208 feet tall, they are among the tallest of the tall ships.

Today's clippers retain the romance of sailing under canvas coupled with the excitement of participating in the sailing of an authentic square rigger. They are further enhanced by the out-of-the-way Caribbean destinations that the cruises visit. Passengers quickly get to know the youthful crew, who double in their duties as deckhands, as sports instructors, and in other capacities.

The cruises focus on an active, casual, and even educational experience, so it's more like being on a private yacht. The food is good but not gourmet. Dress is very casual, with shorts and deck shoes the uniform of the day, and only slightly less casual in the evening. Fellow passengers will be kindred souls—you hope—and 50 percent or more might be Europeans, depending on the time of the year. The cruises are also a great environment for families with children ages seven to seventeen.

All cabins have air-conditioning, carpeting, and private bathrooms with showers. Most cabins are outside-facing and fitted with twin beds that can be converted to a bed slightly larger than the standard queen size. The top staterooms on the main deck have marble bathrooms with bathtubs and hair dryers. All passengers dine at one seating, although when the ship is full the room can be very crowded. The dining room converts into a meeting room with screen projectors and video monitors.

Adjoining the aft end of the Piano Bar is the Tropical Bar, protected from the elements by a broad canvas awning, under which is found the bar, a dance floor, and the stage where the captain holds his daily talks, and where much of the entertainment takes place. Also on the main deck is a library that resembles an English club with large brass-framed windows, carved paneling, and a marble fireplace. It doubles as a reception desk and is used for small meetings.

Royal Clipper is more than twice the size of its sister ships but with a capacity for only 224 passengers. The *Royal Clipper* is also more upscale. It has three small swimming pools, one with a glass bottom that allows light into the three-deck atrium below; an observation lounge with wraparound windows on the deck below the bridge; and a dining room accommodating all passengers at a single seating. The ship also has a water-sports platform and an inflatable floating raft for swimmers.

Cabins are larger than those on the sister ships, and some have a third fold-down bed. The

suites have private verandas and bathrooms with whirlpool tubs. The clippers can anchor in bays that large cruise ships cannot reach. Launches take passengers to isolated beaches and scuba and snorkeling spots or to enjoy other water sports. Snorkeling gear, water skis, sailboards, and volleyballs are carried on board. The cruises are priced to fit between budget-conscious cruises and pricey yacht-like ships.

Windstar Cruises

300 Elliot Ave. West, Seattle, WA 98119; (206) 281-3535; (800) 258-7245; fax: (206) 281-0627; www .windstarcruises.com

Ships (passengers): *Wind Spirit* (148); *Wind Star* (148); *Wind Surf* (308)

Departure ports: Barbados, Puerto Caldera, St. Thomas

Types of cruises: 7 days to the Eastern and Southern Caribbean, Costa Rica, Belize, and Panama Canal

Lifestyle tips: Combination of sailing yacht and deluxe cruise ship; for active people.

Imagine a deck one and a half times the length of a football field and half its width. Now, look up to the sky and imagine four masts in a row, each as high as a twenty-story building and each with two enormous triangular sails. If you can picture these dimensions, you will have a mental image of the windcruiser, which was, when she debuted, the most revolutionary vessel since the introduction of the steamship in the last century. The six great sails are controlled by computers instead of deckhands. The computer is designed to monitor the direction and velocity of the wind to keep the ship from heeling no more than six degrees. The sails can be furled in less than two minutes.

The windcruiser marries the romance and tradition of sailing with the comfort and amenities of a cruise ship. The ship has seventy-five identical, outside 182-square-foot staterooms. The well-designed cabins make optimum use of space and are fitted with twin- or queen-size beds, minibar, color television, VCR, satellite phone, and safe.

Cabins, gym, and sauna are on the bottom two of four passenger decks. The third deck has a main lounge and dining salon; both are handsome rooms that have the ambience of a private yacht. The dining room, which has open seating, serves sophisticated gourmet cuisine. The ship has a tiny casino, boutique, and beauty salon. The top deck has a swimming pool, bar, and veranda lounge used for lunch during the day and a disco at night. Through the overhead skylight of the lounge, passengers can have a dramatic view of the majestic sails overhead.

The vessels have a shallow 13½-foot draft that enables it to stop at less-visited ports and secluded beaches and coves. The ships are fitted with a water sports platform that gives passengers direct access to the sea. Sailboats and windsurfing boards are carried on board, as are Zodiacs (inflatable boats) to take passengers snorkeling, scuba diving, waterskiing, and fishing. The gear for these activities is available for use without additional charge. Any passenger lucky enough to hook a fish can have it cooked to order by the ship's chefs.

Windsurf is a larger version of *Windstar*. It has thirty-one deluxe suites and a 10,000-square-foot spa. In addition to the standard amenities, the suites boast his-and-hers bathrooms with shower, complete with teak flooring, plush terry towels and robes, and vanity lighting. The ship has a computer center, an outdoor barbecue station, and a fully equipped conference center.

PART THREE

The Bahamas, Turks & Caicos, and Key West

The Bahamas

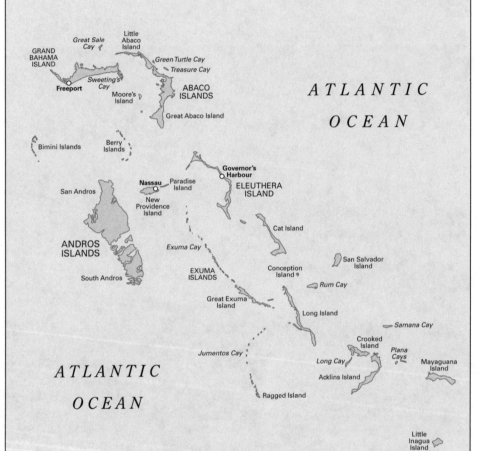

The Bahamas

Miles 0 100

Kilometers 0 200

N

GRAND BAHAMA ISLAND

Great Sale Cay

Little Abaco Island

Green Turtle Cay

Treasure Cay

Sweeting's Cay

Freeport

Moore's Island

ABACO ISLANDS

Great Abaco Island

ATLANTIC OCEAN

Bimini Islands

Berry Islands

Governor's Harbour

Nassau

Paradise Island

ELEUTHERA ISLAND

San Andros

New Providence Island

Cat Island

ANDROS ISLANDS

Exuma Cay

San Salvador Island

EXUMA ISLANDS

Conception Island

South Andros

Rum Cay

Great Exuma Island

Long Island

Samana Cay

Crooked Island

Plana Cays

ATLANTIC OCEAN

Jumentos Cay

Long Cay

Mayaguana Island

Acklins Island

Ragged Island

Little Inagua Island

Great Inagua Island

Distant Neighbors

Whether your destination is Nassau, Freeport, or one of the Family Islands, your first impression of the Bahamas and the image you are likely to carry away with you is of water. Intensely beautiful with shades of aqua, turquoise, cobalt, and peacock blue, these waters have long attracted boating and fishing enthusiasts, and now they are being discovered by snorkelers, scuba divers, and cruise passengers.

The Bahamas is an archipelago of more than 700 low-lying tropical islands and islets dotting 100,000 square miles of sea. They start only 50 miles from the eastern coast of Florida and stretch for 750 miles to the Turks & Caicos and the northern coasts of Haiti and Cuba. They are strategically situated between the Atlantic on the north, south, and east, and the Gulf of Mexico on the west. About half of the archipelago lies north of the Tropic of Cancer.

The Bahamas derives its name from the Spanish *baja mar* shallows—a term that early explorers used in mapping the group. Of the hundreds of islands, islets, and cays that make up the island-nation, only about three dozen are populated. Of these, three ports—Nassau, Paradise Island, and Freeport—get the lion's share of visitors and almost all of the cruise passengers.

The Bahamas is so close to the U.S. mainland that many people hop over for the weekend in their own boats or private planes, and ships board thousands of passengers every week for one-, two-, three-, and four-day cruises between Florida and Bahamian ports.

Yet the Bahamas is foreign. A British colony for more than two centuries and independent since 1973, the Bahamas in many ways is still more British than the queen. This despite the fact that throughout the history of the islands—from the time Columbus made his first landfall on the Bahamian island of San Salvador and Ponce de León came in search of the Fountain of Youth—the Bahamas has been as closely linked to events in the United States as to any in Britain.

Today the British flavor combined with American familiarity, the magnificent waters and endless days of clear skies, the outstanding facilities, the variety of sports and entertainment all have made the Bahamas one of the most frequently visited destinations in the tropics, with more than five million visitors a year—of whom 71 percent arrive by cruise ship.

On any given day in port, you can play tennis and golf or bike and jog in the countryside. The shallow, warm waters provide a carnival of life for snorkelers and scuba divers. Protected bays and shallow waters near shore are ideal for windsurfing, waterskiing, Jet Skiing, and parasailing. You'll find an abundance of fish in the deep waters only a short distance from port and excellent opportunities for deep-sea fishing year-round.

If the sporting life is not your first requirement, a walking tour of Nassau is a stroll through history and a chance to check out the bargains in the shops and straw markets along the way. You can do it on your own or in the company of a Bahamian host

At a Glance

Antiquities . . . . ★
Architecture . . . . ★★★
Art and Artists . . . . ★★
Beaches . . . . ★★★★★
Colonial Buildings . . . . ★★★★
Crafts . . . . ★★
Cuisine . . . . ★★
Dining/Restaurants . . . . ★★★
Entertainment . . . . ★★★★
Forts . . . . ★★
Gambling Casinos . . . . ★★★★★
History . . . . ★★
Monuments . . . . ★★
Museums . . . . ★
Nightlife . . . . ★★★★
Scenery . . . . ★★★
Shopping . . . . ★★
Sightseeing . . . . ★★
Sports . . . . ★★★★★
Transportation . . . . ★★

Fast Facts

Population: 350,000, of which two-thirds live in New Providence (Nassau). Except for Nassau and Freeport, there are no towns with more than 1,500 people.

Government: The Parliament, more than 250 years old, has two houses. The House of Assembly has members elected every five years; the Senate is an advisory group of sixteen appointed members. The Bahamas is a member of the Commonwealth, and the British queen is its monarch, too.

Climate: Strictly speaking, the Bahamas is not part of the Caribbean, but it enjoys a similar idyllic tropical climate. The Gulf Stream bathes the western coast with clear warm waters, and easterly trade winds caress the shores. As a result, temperatures in the northernmost islands seldom drop below 60°F or rise above 90°F.

Clothing: Casual but proper. Bahamians tend to be conservative and are offended by the overly revealing dress of some tourists on the streets. Informal spring/summer sportswear for day and evening will suit most occasions, although elegant attire is not out of place in the evening, depending on your choice of dining place and activities. Generally, men neatly dressed in slacks, sport shirt, and jacket will be comfortable at any nightspot in the islands. For women, a cocktail dress or stylish pantsuit is appropriate.

Currency: The Bahamian dollar (B$) is freely exchanged with the U.S. dollar at par.

Departure Tax: When you leave the Bahamas by air, you pay $15 ($18 departing Grand Bahama) per adult and per child ages six and older. Children ages five and under are not charged.

Electricity: 120 volts AC, 60 cycle. Standard U.S. shavers, hair dryers, and other appliances can be used.

Emergency Numbers: Police: Nassau, 919 or (242) 322-4444. Medical Services: Nassau, Princess Margaret Hospital, (242) 322-2861. Ambulance: Nassau, (242) 322-2221.

Entry Formalities: All U.S. citizens must have a passport.

Language: English—more British than American—with a lilt and influences from the early settlers, African slaves, and Caribbean islanders who came here to work.

Postal Service: A letter to the United States costs 85 cents per half ounce; a postcard, 50 cents. The post office nearest the pier in Nassau is at Parliament and East Hill Streets, 3 blocks south of Rawson Square. In Freeport, the post office nearest the pier is at Adventurer's Way. Hours: 9 a.m. to 5 p.m.

Public Holidays: Jan 1, New Year's Day; Good Friday, Easter Sunday and Monday; Whit Monday (six weeks after Easter); Labor Day (first Fri in June); July 10, Independence Day; Emancipation Day (first Mon in Aug); Oct 12, Discovery Day; Dec 25, Christmas; Dec 26, Boxing Day.

Telephone Area Code: 242. (Dial exactly as you do for a long-distance call within the United States.)

Time: Eastern Standard Time. Daylight saving time is adopted in the summer months as in the United States.

Vaccination Requirement: None.

Airlines: Direct flights from major U.S. gateways by AirTran, American Airlines, American Eagle, Bahamasair, Caribbean Airlines, Continental/Gulfstream, Delta, JetBlue, Spirit Airlines, United, US Airways; from Canada by Air Canada, WestJet.

Information: www.bahamas.com

In the United States:

Bahamas Tourist Offices: (800) 422-4262, (800) BAHAMAS

Miami: 1200 South Pine Island Rd., Suite 750, Plantation, FL 33324; (954) 236-9292; (800) 327-7678; fax: (954) 236-9282. Grand Bahamas Tourist Bureau, Freeport (242) 350-8600; (800) 448-3386; fax: (242) 352-2714. Bahamas Out Islands Promotion Board, (305) 931-6612; (800) 688-4752; fax: (305) 931-6867

New York: 60 East Forty-second St., Suite 1850, New York, NY 10165; (212) 758-2777; (800) 224-3681; fax: (212) 753-6531

In Canada:

Toronto: 6725 Airport Rd., Suite 202, Mississauga, ON, L4V 1V2; (905) 672-9017; (800) 667-3777 (Canada only); fax: (905) 672-2092

In Nassau:

The Ministry of Tourism has information booths at Prince George Dock, (242) 325-9155; Ministry of Tourism Headquarters, Bolam House, George and Marlborough Streets, (242) 302-2000; (800) BAHAMAS (422-4262)

In Grand Bahama Island:

The Tourist Information Centre is located in the Sir Charles Hayward Library, (242) 352-8044, and there are booths at Freeport Harbor, (242) 352-9651, and in the International Bazaar. Hours: 8:30 a.m. to 5 p.m. Mon through Sat.

arranged for through the Tourist Office's People-to-People Program. Evening entertainment in port can range from the music of a scratch band in a rustic tavern by the sea to an extravaganza with Las Vegas sizzle at a cavernous casino.

Columbus and the Aftermath

The diversity of the Bahamas is the result of its variegated past. The islands' recorded history begins on the most significant date in the annals of the New World—Oct 12, 1492—with Christopher Columbus making his first landfall on an island the Native Lucayans called Guanahani and that Columbus christened San Salvador, the Savior.

When the Spaniards who followed Columbus found no gold, they abandoned all interest in the Bahamas, but not before enslaving the entire Lucayan Indian population of 20,000 and shipping them to work the mines in Cuba and Hispaniola. Ponce de León was apparently an exception. He came to the Bahamas in search of the Fountain of Youth before moving on to Florida to continue his quest. Today four places on the island of Bimini claim to have been stops in his epic journey.

In 1648—a century after the Spaniards departed from the islands, English settlers fleeing religious conflict in Bermuda arrived on Sigatoo Island, which they named Eleuthera after a Greek word meaning "freedom." In time, the Bahamas was granted to the lords of the Carolinas, absentee landlords whose lack of interest allowed the infestation of pirates, such as the infamous Edward Teach, known as Blackbeard, and Henry Morgan. The hundreds of harbors were ideal havens for smuggling and piracy; their reefs and shallows ensured—by accident or design—frequent wrecks.

Finally in 1718 the ironfisted British captain Woodes Rogers took command of the Bahamas and established order. Rogers gave the scavengers a clear choice: Give up piracy and be pardoned, or be hanged. Eight who tested Rogers will were hanged in public, thus helping to bring a chapter of the Bahamas's history to a close. Ten years later, the islands were officially made a British colony, with Rogers the first royal governor.

In an effort to destroy British supply lines during the American Revolution, the American navy

captured Nassau and held it for two weeks. Later the Spanish held it for a year when they were forced out by Col. Andrew Deveaux, a Loyalist from the Carolinas and one of 8,000 who had fled to the Bahamas after the American Revolution. Deveaux and the other Loyalists brought with them all their possessions, including slaves, and in the Bahamas they replicated the plantation society they had left behind. The old order lasted until slavery was abolished in 1834.

Twice again events in the United States led to direct Bahamian involvement and a boom: gunrunning during the Civil War and rum running during Prohibition. After that, the American–Bahamian connection became more respectable, but no less flamboyant. During World War II the royal governor of the Bahamas was none other than the Duke of Windsor, who along with his glamorous American-born duchess set the style for what was to become the Bahamas's most important postwar enterprise, tourism.

The New Bahamas

After the war, a weak and weary Britain welcomed foreign investments that would enable its colonies to become self-supporting. At the same time, several wealthy Americans saw the opportunity to create playgrounds in the Bahamas, which could benefit from the islands' proximity to the U.S. mainland. The most significant venture turned a spit of land facing Nassau Harbor into the most complete resort in the tropics.

In the 1950s A&P grocery heir Huntington Hartford bought most of Hog Island, as it was known, from another millionaire and renamed it Paradise. His estate, set in landscaped gardens adorned with classic marble statues and enclosed with stones from a 12th-century French monastery, became the centerpiece of the fashionable Ocean Club.

During the following decade Paradise Island was acquired by Resorts International, which added hotels, a casino, and extensive sporting facilities. It also made Paradise more accessible by building a multimillion-dollar bridge between the island and Nassau, and later by adding an airline. Then, in 1989, famed television star Merv Griffin bought Resorts International and put his stamp on the island. But the greatest transformation of all came after Sun International bought out Griffin and transformed Resort International's holdings into a new resort named Atlantis, creating an entirely new landscape of lakes, parks, and attractions, investing over a billion dollars to make it the largest resort and theme park in the tropics.

About the same time that Hartford was creating Paradise, American financier Wallace Groves was transforming Grand Bahama Island, a little-known stretch of limestone and pine forest only 60 miles from Florida. Freeport, as it is better known, became the showplace of its day with hotels, casinos, a flashy international shopping bazaar, and six championship golf courses.

In the 1970s, with the recession, inflation, oil crisis, and competition from newer resorts in Florida and the Caribbean, Freeport lost a great deal of its luster. But by the mid-1980s a renaissance was under way, with millions of dollars being invested by the government and private developers, particularly in the Lucayan area.

Another transformation took place in the 1980s and 1990s at Cable Beach, a 5-mile stretch west of downtown Nassau with multimillion-dollar hotels and casinos opened. The Royal Bahamian Hotel, the colonial grande dame of Cable Beach, which served as the fashionable resort of royalty and heads of state in its heyday as the Balmoral Beach Club when the Duke of Windsor was governor, was transformed into a Sandals, the Jamaican-based, all-inclusive group, and after extensive renovation into one of the chain's most luxurious resorts.

Down the road Breezes Bahamas, formerly the Ambassador Beach, was the first Bahamas member of Superclubs, also a Jamaican all-inclusive chain. On the west side of Nassau, the landmark British Colonial Hotel was gutted and rebuilt as the British Colonial Hilton International.

But all that seems to be merely a prelude to the current developments at Cable Beach (see the description later in the Attractions West of Nassau section). As your ship steams into Nassau Harbor, look south and you can spot Cable Beach on the ship's starboard side. The stretch of green north of the harbor on the port side of the ship is Paradise Island. Long before it became a famous playground, the island served as a natural breakwater for Nassau Harbor, protecting the only safe entrance to New Providence. In the distance the arched bridges connecting Paradise Island to Nassau are the most visible evidence of the long-standing American–Bahamian connection.

An Introduction to Nassau

www.nassauparadiseisland.com

Old World charm and New World glamour come together in Nassau and its elaborate resorts of Cable Beach and Paradise Island. Nassau is one of the most sophisticated and popular destinations in the tropics.

For most people Nassau is the Bahamas. However, Nassau is not an island but a town—to be sure, the main town—on the island of New Providence, located at the center of the Bahamas archipelago. As the seat of government, the hub of commercial activity, and the crossroads of the nation's air and sea-lanes, Nassau has acquired the bustle and worldliness of an international capital. Yet it is the only place throughout the 700 islands of the Bahamas archipelago, including Freeport, that comes even close to having this character.

For cruise passengers Nassau's combination of the old and the new in an international city surrounded by lovely beaches is perfect. Stretched along the north coast of the island, the town is compact and easy to explore on foot in a leisurely morning or afternoon. The low-lying island, only 21 miles long and 7 miles wide, is easy to see by car, bus, or moped in a few hours. It is also possible to combine some sightseeing with a sport or a shopping expedition and have time at the beach.

Perhaps more than any other place in the Bahamas, Nassau reflects the country's British past visually in the colonial buildings of Old Nassau and in the trappings of tradition that have lasted through three centuries. Cruise passengers encounter the British legacy almost from the moment they step off their ship. Street traffic is directed by "bobbies" whose uniforms—white jacket, blue trousers with a red stripe, and pith helmet—are a tropical version of their London counterparts' garb. Driving is on the LEFT side, as in Britain.

The graceful colonial buildings of Parliament Square are the backdrop for a statue of Queen Victoria, and visitors on hand for the annual opening of Parliament will see the members of the legislature dressed in striped pants and morning coats. Were you to step into the Supreme Court while it is in session, you would find the judges and lawyers dressed in robes and wearing the traditional white wigs.

Nassau's Origins

Nassau, originally known as Sayle's Island, was settled for the first time around 1666 by a group of Bermudians and English, and within five years it had more than 900 settlers. By the time the Bahamas was granted to the Six Lords Proprietors of Carolina by the British Crown in 1670, the population had reached almost 1,000, including slaves. But the settlement developed into a pirate stronghold, which led to Spanish raids in 1684—raids so effective, apparently, that the town was abandoned. Some settlers returned two years later, but growth was slow until 1695, when one of the governors, Nicholas Trott, laid out a town plan for Charlestown, as it was called. To protect the western entrance to the harbor, he built Fort Nassau, which he named in honor of the prince of Orange-Nassau, who later became William III of England.

Except for Trott, however, the Carolina landlords were not interested in the Bahamas and allowed it to become a haven for pirates and privateers. Finally, from 1718 to 1721 under the first royal governor, Woodes Rogers, Nassau was cleaned up, Fort Nassau restored, an assembly established, and a town plan created, which has remained, more or less, the same to the present day. Nassau had a burst of prosperity later in

the century when Loyalist refugees fleeing the American Revolutionary War came here to settle. Both administratively and architecturally, the new arrivals made a major impact on the island and transformed the scrappy little port into a pretty and prosperous town with new streets and wharfs and city ordinances for fire and health.

In 1787 the last royal governor of Virginia, John Murray, better known to history as Lord Dunmore, became the governor of the Bahamas. Arrogant, incompetent, and thoroughly disliked, Dunmore left an indelible mark on the Bahamas with his passion for building. He cost both the Crown and the Bahamians a great deal of money and grief. To fortify the island he built Fort Charlotte on the west, Fort Fincastle and Fort Winton on the east; he added gun emplacements on Hog (Paradise) Island. His home, Dunmore House, served as the governor's residence until Government House was completed. On the eastern end of New Providence, he built the Hermitage as his summer home. The present mansion, reconstructed in the early 1900s, is the residence of the Roman Catholic bishop of Nassau.

Port Profile: Nassau

Embarkation: In Nassau the piers are located on the north side of New Providence Island, less than a ten-minute walk from the heart of town. Ships pull dockside to the modern piers, known as Prince George Wharf, 1 block from Bay Street, the main shopping street of Nassau, accessible by an attractive pedestrian walk from the piers to the square. Taxis and motor coaches are waiting for passengers at the dock when ships arrive.

Passengers are allowed to come and go freely between their ship and town. On returning to your ship, however, you will have to show your passport, your government-issued ID and cabin key, or some other form of identification distributed by your ship. After leaving the pier, en route to Rawson Square, you can pass through the large, brightly colored building marked FESTIVAL PLACE with the Welcome Center of the Bahamas Ministry of Tourism, where you can pick up maps, brochures, and other information. Festival Place also has a post office and about two dozen shops for books, spices, souvenirs, and the like.

Local Transportation: Taxis are readily available and are zoned, but you can also request to be put on the meter. Rates are supposed to be fixed at $3 flag-fall and 40 cents each ⅕ mile for one or two passengers, $2 for each additional passenger. Some zone rates are: downtown to Cable Beach $17; Cable Beach to Paradise Island $20, each additional passenger $3, and $1 bridge toll. For a typical city and country tour, a party of four pays approximately $60 for two hours. Unfortunately, some Nassau taxi drivers pretend their meters do not work in order to overcharge tourists.

If you plan to engage a taxi for sightseeing, negotiate the price in advance. Be aware that there are freelancers who are not legal taxis and who will charge whatever they think they can get. Look for a taxi with a Bahama host sticker on its windshield. The drivers are reliable and the best informed to be tour guides.

In Nassau, city buses or jitneys (US$1 to $2 fare) run frequently throughout the day and early evening from two downtown departure points only 3 blocks from the pier. At Bay and Frederick Streets is the station for buses to the northern and eastern parts of the island; those to Cable Beach and residential areas on the western side of the island leave from Bay Street and Navy Lion Road, next to the British Colonial Hilton. For Paradise Island, you'll need to take a taxi or water taxi. The Paradise Island Bridge Toll is $1 per motorized vehicle. Taxis from Prince George Wharf to Paradise Island charge $8 plus toll for a one-way trip.

Surreys—horse-drawn carriages that can be hired at Rawson Square—are strictly for tourists and cost $10 per person. If there are more than two of you or if you want to keep the surrey for a longer period than the usual half hour, be sure to negotiate the price in advance.

Ferry Services: Ferries (water taxis) for Paradise Island depart from Woodes Rogers Wharf every thirty minutes from early morning until 6 p.m. and cost $3 per person. **Bahamas Fast Ferry** (242-323-2166; www.bahamasferries.com) offers regularly scheduled service to Harbour Island as well as to Spanish Wells, North Eleuthera, and Governor's Harbour. The Harbour Island tour costs $184 adults, $124 children round-trip.

Car Rentals: Car rentals from major U.S. companies are available at major hotels and various locations throughout Nassau. Those with offices nearest the pier are **Avis** (242-377-7121) and **Dollar Rent-A-Car** (242-377-8300) at the British Colonial Hilton. Expect to pay $50 and up for a subcompact with unlimited mileage. If you rent a car with a credit card, you must be twenty-one years or older; without the card, twenty-five or older. Americans may use U.S. driver's licenses for up to three months. Remember: Bahamians drive on the LEFT. The speed limit is generally 30 mph, but not many drivers observe it, least of all the bus drivers.

Mopeds/Bicycles: Rental agencies for motor scooters and bicycles are located by the pier. A valid driver's license and a helmet supplied by the rental agency are compulsory for using a motor scooter, and you must be eighteen or over. Inside Festival Place, there is a counter for renting motorbikes. The price is $30 per hour, $40 for two hours, and $50 for a full day, plus $5 gassing charge, or you can opt to get gas yourself. You must leave a $20 deposit, and insurance is $5. To repeat, driving is on the LEFT.

Budget Planning

Nassau is not a cheap port. Taxis, car rentals, admission fees to privately operated sightseeing and other attractions, deluxe restaurants, and drinks are usually 20 percent higher than comparable facilities in the United States and other Caribbean ports of call. These costs, however, can be avoided or offset. Here are some ways, particularly for visitors on limited budgets.

- Walk. Nassau is a compact town that's easy and pleasurable to cover on foot.
- Use public transportation, which is good and low cost.
- Enjoy the abundant, beautiful, free, easy-to-reach beaches.
- Dine in restaurants serving local specialties. They are reasonably priced and clean.

Drugs, Crime, and Today's Realities

The Bahamas, like other places, is not immune to today's social ills. Although you might be approached to buy drugs, the possession, sale, or purchase of drugs is prohibited. Penalties for breaking the law apply to tourists as much as to Bahamians. They are severe, and the jails unpleasant.

Theft and crime, particularly in Nassau and Freeport, are on the rise. As a tourist, you are an easy target. Rented cars and motor scooters, for example, have special plates that make them easy to identify. However, you can reduce your vulnerability with prudence.

Do not park in secluded or isolated areas, particularly on the south coast of Nassau. Never leave valuables in your car or on the beach, including hotel beaches. Do not walk alone in remote or lightly trafficked areas, and most of all, do not engage someone as a guide who approaches you on the street or beach. All guides and taxi drivers in the Bahamas are licensed; if you have any doubt about a person's credentials, you need only step into the nearest tourist office or police station.

Nassau Shore Excursions

Because Nassau is easy to manage on your own and has a wide selection of activities to enjoy, shore excursions offered by cruise lines tended to be limited, but the selection has greatly improved in the last decade, responding to the demands of cruise passengers. The attractions and sports on these tours are described elsewhere in this chapter.

City and County Tour: Three hours; $60 per person. A drive through Old Nassau and around the island is combined with a visit to the Ardastra Gardens. Some visit Paradise Island, including Versailles Gardens. Suggested for those on their first visit who cannot make the walking tour. You might want to check out www.bahamasforaday.com for its selection and prices.

Excursion Boat Trips: Glass-bottomed boats, catamarans, and other excursion boats depart from the pier area frequently throughout the day on guided tours to nearby reefs, beaches, and Blue Lagoon. Some boats stop for a swim and snorkeling. Some offer sunset and moonlight dinner cruises, too. Prices range upward from $60–$70 for half day.

The *Seaworld Explorer:* $45 adult; $25 child. This semi submarine drops about 5 feet below the surface of the water for you to view the gardens.

Golf: Most cruise lines offer packages, or you can make your own arrangements. Majestic Tours (242-322-2606), one of the major local companies, has golf packages starting at $210. See the Sports in Nassau section later in this chapter.

Dolphin Encounters: At Blue Lagoon, an islet off Nassau, Close Encounters with dolphins are available for $98 per person, and swimming with dolphins for $185 per person (242-363-1003; www.dolphinencounters.com).

Biking Excursions: See the Sports in Nassau section later in this chapter.

Nightclub Tour: $30; $50 with dinner. The tour includes admission to a nightclub with Bahamian and West Indian music and show, drink, tips, and transfers. (See Entertainment later in this chapter for more selections.)

People-to-People

The Bahamas Ministry of Tourism gives you the opportunity to meet Bahamians as you would a friend through its People-to-People program, which brings tourists together with Bahamians who have volunteered to host visitors.

People-to-People volunteers—more than 1,200 on seven islands—come from a cross section of the community. They might belong to the same service club, such as Rotary or Kiwanis, as you do; or practice your profession or trade; or share your hobby. Many have traveled themselves and know what it is like to be on your own in a strange place. They know, too, how much more meaningful a visit can be when it is enriched with a personal experience.

These nice folks are volunteers. Although the program is operated by the Bahamas Ministry of Tourism, the volunteers are neither employed nor subsidized by the government. They offer their time and friendship without compensation and neither ask nor expect anything in return. They are involved because they enjoy meeting people from other

Walking Tour of Old Nassau

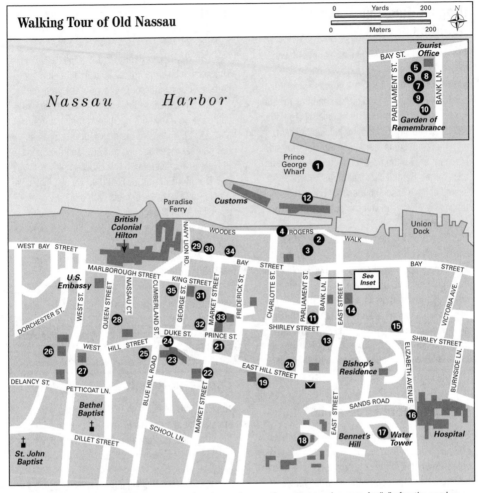

NOTE: Numbers in the walking tour correspond to the numbers on the accompanying map. An "x" after the number means the house or building is not open to the public; "s" means it can be visited by special arrangement.

1. Prince George Wharf
2. Tourist Information Office
3. Rawson Square
4. Woodes Rogers Walk
5. Parliament Square
6. House of Assembly
7. Senate Building
8. Colonial Secretary's Office and Treasury
9. Supreme Court
10. Central Police Station
11. Public Library
12. Welcome Center
13. Curry House and Zion Church
14x. Cascadilla
15. Bahamas Historical Society and Museum
16. Queen's Staircase
17. Fort Fincastle and Water Tower
18. Police Headquarters
19. Ministry of Foreign Affairs
20x. Jacaranda House
21. St. Andrew's Presbyterian Church
22. Gregory's Arch
23s. Government House
24. Christopher Columbus Statue
25. Graycliff House
26. Cathedral of St. Francis Xavier/The Priory (Dunmore House)
27. National Art Gallery/Junkanoo Museum
28. The Deanery
29. Cable Beach/West End Bus Stand
30. Vendue House/Pompey Museum
31. Christ Church Cathedral and Pirates of Nassau Museum
32. Balcony House
33. Central Bank/Trinity Place
34. Straw Market; North and East End Bus Stand
35. Ministry of Tourism

countries and they want visitors to know their country in a natural, noncommercial atmosphere.

The form that the welcome takes depends on your Bahamian hosts. Because they, too, work for a living, they generally entertain in the evenings or on weekends. They might take you sightseeing or to their favorite beach for a picnic or to a Sunday service at their church. Or hosts might invite you to share an afternoon or evening of conversation with light refreshments, join a family gathering, or take a meal at their home. You will be enjoying facets of Bahamian life that most visitors never see.

To participate in the People-to-People program, contact an office of the Bahamas Ministry of Tourism for a request form to be submitted about two to three weeks in advance of your visit. Write to the Ministry of Tourism, P.O. Box N-3701, Nassau, Bahamas; or P.O. Box F-251, Freeport, Bahamas. You can also visit www.bahamas.com or e-mail peopletopeople@bahamas.com. You will be contacted by a Ministry of Tourism People-to-People coordinator about the arrangements made especially for you.

Garden tea parties, sponsored jointly with the Bahamas Ministry of Tourism, are another part of the People-to-People program. In Nassau the parties are held from 4 to 5 p.m. in Jan to June and Oct and Nov on the fourth Fri of the month at historic Government House and hosted by the wife of the governor-general.

In Freeport the Garden of the Groves is the venue. In Exuma, high tea is held every other month from Nov through Mar/Apr; the venue revolves among Grand Isles Villas and Spas, Peace and Plenty Club, and the **Palm Bay Beach Club** (242-366-2430).

Nassau on Your Own

Unless you have already been to Nassau several times, you will probably find a walking tour of Old Nassau or a boat excursion as interesting a way to enjoy your day in port as any alternative. Neither requires transportation from the pier, but visiting the attractions east and west of town and on Paradise Island does. Public buses are available, but they do not take you directly to the sites;

from the main road, you will have a short walk. If you engage a taxi to a specific location, be sure to arrange your return transportation and set the price in advance.

A Walking Tour of Old Nassau

The entire walk, following the sequence as numbered, takes three to four hours depending on your pace. At several points along the way, you can stop for a refreshment or break off entirely and return to your ship or to Bay Street for shopping.

A walking tour of Old Nassau in the heart of town is a stroll through Bahamian history, particularly its British past. The town plan, laid out in grid fashion in 1788, is virtually intact and comprises four long, parallel east-west streets crossed by ten small north-south streets running from the harbor and Bay Street on the north to a hillside (East Hill and West Hill Streets) on the south. Although modern encroachments are everywhere, many streets have retained enough of their 18th- and 19th-century buildings, gardens, and broad steps to give visitors a real sense of Nassau in bygone days.

Prince George Wharf (1): From Prince George Wharf where the cruise ships dock, it is only a few steps to Rawson Square, the **Tourist Information Office (2)** inside Festival Place, and Parliament Square, the heart of downtown. En route you will pass a statue dedicated to the women of the Bahamas, by Randolph Johnston of Abaco.

The docks have a Welcome Plaza, a taxi dispatch station, and shelter for the horse-drawn surreys. Festival Place contains a **Welcome Centre (12)**, as well as information, communication, and banking services; shops selling Bahamian products. **Rawson Square (3):** In 1985, as part of the beautification project for the visit of Queen Elizabeth II and the meeting of the Commonwealth nations, Old Nassau's stately buildings and monuments in the heart of downtown were spruced up, and a garden and mosaic walkways were laid to connect Rawson Square and Parliament Square on the south side of Bay Street. The square is named for Sir William Rawson, governor of the Bahamas from 1864 to 1869, and it has a small statue of Sir Milo Butler, the first governor-general of the Bahamas after independence in 1973. The Churchill Building on the east side of the square was formerly the prime minister's office. On the west side, you can engage a horse-drawn surrey for a tour or stop to have your hair braided for $2 per braid at the open-air pavilion.

Woodes Rogers Walk (4): The waterfront walkway west of Rawson Square, known as Woodes Rogers Walk, was named for the first British governor of the Bahamas. The tiny lanes are lined with shops. The town's famous **Straw Market (34)** is a lively bazaar of Bahamian crafts facing Bay Street, the town's oldest street and main thoroughfare. It is lined with department stores and boutiques selling anything from $2 T-shirts to French perfumes and English china at about 20 percent less than stateside prices. The **Ministry of Tourism (35),** is located in the Commerce Centre at the British Colonial Hilton Hotel, farther west at the end of Bay Street. If you were to continue west on Bay Street beyond the British Colonial Hilton, you would be on West Bay Street, the road leading to Ardastra Gardens and Cable Beach. East on Bay Street about 2 miles is the bridge to Paradise Island. Potters Cay has a native market where Bahamians buy fresh fish and provisions.

Parliament Square (5): The traditional center of Bahamian government activity, Parliament Square is graced by a marble statue of a youthful Queen Victoria seated upon a throne and holding a sword and scepter. Framing the statue is the lovely Georgian architecture of the **House of Assembly (6)** on the west, the **Senate Building (7)** on the south, and the old **Colonial Secretary's Office and Treasury (8)** on the east. The buildings were constructed from 1805 to 1813 and are based on Tryon's Palace of New Bern, the old capital of North Carolina, praised as the most beautiful building of its time. South of these buildings facing the Garden of Remembrance, with a cenotaph commemorating the dead of the two world wars, is the **Supreme Court (9).** The garden with stately royal palms and tropical flowers is one of the prettiest spots in the downtown area. On the east side of the square on Bank Lane is the **Central Police Station (10). Public Library (11):** The octagonal structure, built in about 1798 as a prison, was made into a library and museum in 1879. The structure, contemporary with buildings in Williamsburg,

Virginia, is thought to have been modeled after the Old Powder Magazine there. The first and second floors had prison cells on each of their eight sides; a central open area provided fresh air. These alcoves now hold library stacks. A domed gallery on the third floor was originally unroofed; it once held a bell that was rung to summon members of the House of Assembly to meetings. The upper floor has a collection of books and artifacts on the Bahamas, including old maps dating from 1750 and prints from 1891. Hours: 10 a.m. to 8 p.m. Mon through Thurs, 10 a.m. to 5 p.m. Fri, 10 a.m. to 4 p.m. Sat.; (242) 322-4907.

Magistrate's Court No. 3 on Parliament Street was originally built in 1894 as a chapel for the Salem Union Baptist congregation on a site known as the Livery Stable Grounds. It is still owned by the church. South of the library, the old Royal Victorian Gardens was the site of the once grand Victorian Hotel, the center of social activity when it opened in 1861 during the American Civil War. Among its first guests were those fleeing the war; others were blockade-runners, officers of the Confederacy, spies of the northern states, and "ladies of high quality" who were invited to the nightly parties.

In 1876 the hotel was leased to the brother of former U.S. president Grover Cleveland and later purchased in 1898 by Henry M. Flagler, the American railroad czar who drew up plans for a rail/ferry service to connect the Bahamas to the U.S. mainland. In its heyday the hotel hosted a long list of distinguished guests that included Winston Churchill, Prince Albert, and an array of European royalty and celebrities. The hotel changed hands many times before it closed in 1971 and was later destroyed by fire.

Curry House (13), located on Shirley Street immediately west of Zion Church, is a three-story building that opened in 1890 as a private hotel. Later it became an annex of the Royal Victoria Hotel, and in 1972 it was acquired by the government and is used by the Ministry of Finance.

From here, you have a choice of walking east to Bennet's Hill and the Water Tower or west to Government House. If you plan to cover this entire walking tour on foot, you might do well to take the uphill climb to the Water Tower first. To reach the Water Tower, walk east on Shirley Street and turn south onto Elizabeth Avenue. It leads directly to the Queen's Staircase and hence the Water Tower.

Cascadilla (14x) is one of the Nassau houses thought to have been built by ships' carpenters—the island's only craftsmen for many decades. (Certain Bahamian architectural features later transplanted to Key West by Bahamians derive from this origin.) The oldest part of the house dates from 1840, when it marked the eastern boundary of town. **Bahamas Historical Society and Museum (15):** Founded in 1959, the society is a nonprofit cultural and educational organization dedicated to stimulating interest in Bahamian history and collecting and preserving material related to it. Admission: $1 adult; 50 cents ages five through twelve. Hours: 10 a.m. to 4 p.m. Tues through Fri, 10 a.m. to 1 p.m. Mon, 10 a.m. to noon Sat (242-322-4231; www.bahamashistoricalsociety.com).

Queen's Staircase (16): At the head of Elizabeth Avenue is a passageway of sixty-six steps carved out of limestone, draped with thick tropical foliage, and cooled by a waterfall. Local lore says the steps represent each year of Queen Victoria's reign. Actually, they were carved by slaves a century earlier and form a passageway to Fort Fincastle, thus enabling troops to reach the fort from town without being exposed to fire from enemy ships (242-326-9772).

Fort Fincastle (17): Situated on Bennet's Hill overlooking the town, Paradise Island, and the eastern approaches to New Providence, Fort Fincastle was built in 1793 and takes its name from Lord Dunmore's title as the Viscount Fincastle. The fort was constructed in the shape of a ship's bow and has served as a lighthouse and signal station. Hours: 8 a.m. to 4 p.m. Mon through Fri, 9 a.m. to 6 p.m. Sat and Sun.

Water Tower (17): Next to the fort, the 126-foot Water Tower built in 1928 is the highest point on the island, 216 feet above sea level. The tower was closed for repairs and had not reopened at press time (242-326-9781).

From the tower you can continue your walking tour by returning to East Street via Sands Road or Prison Lane and walking north to East Hill Street. The **Police Headquarters (18)** was built in 1900. The green-and-white building on the north side of the complex is a typical example of Bahamian

wooden architecture and is reminiscent of houses built in Key West by Bahamian transplants.

When the Loyalists came to Nassau after the American Revolution, they brought with them ideas about colonial architecture, particularly of the South. Although it evolved into a decidedly Bahamian version with different types of building materials, the influence is evident. Typical building materials included limestone with pink-washed walls and peaked roofs; wood was used in colonnades, fretwork balconies, and jalousies, or louvered shutters that shielded the verandas from the hot sun and allowed the air to circulate. In the late 19th and early 20th centuries, economic hardship forced many Bahamians to leave the islands. Some became the early settlers of Key West, bringing their building habits with them.

From East Street, turn west onto East Hill Street. You will pass the modern post office building and the former East Hill Club, which houses the **Ministry of Foreign Affairs (19).** The club was built around 1850 by the socially prominent Matthews family, who were lawyers and government officials. The Georgian colonial house was first renovated when it was owned by Lord Beaverbrook.

Jacaranda House (20x), on the corner of East Hill and Parliament Streets, was built about 1840 by Chief Justice Sir George Anderson, of Georgia stone previously used as ship's ballast. During World War II the house was owned by Capt. Vyvian Drury, aide-de-camp to the Duke of Windsor. It was bought in 1949 by the widow of Sir Harry Oakes and later passed to her daughter. The house is furnished with lovely antiques and has exterior features typical of classical Bahamian architecture, such as interlocking corners of large projecting stones used for strength (known as chamfered quoins).

St. Andrew's Presbyterian Church (21): The pretty white church at the corner of Prince and Market Streets was begun in 1810 and expanded many times over the next five decades. It was completely renovated early in the 20th century.

Gregory's Arch (22): Spanning Market Street is a picturesque entrance to Grant's Town, one of the early settlements of former slaves, referred to locally as "Over the Hill" as it is literally over the ridge that divides north Nassau from the south side.

The arch, named for Governor John Gregory, was built in 1852 by J. J. Burnside, the surveyor-general who laid out Grant's Town. Broad stone stairways at the foot of Charlotte and Frederick Streets lead from East Hill Street directly to Bay Street.

Government House (23s): The imposing Government House (at Blue Hill Road and East Hill Street) stands on Mount Fitzwilliam, a hillside overlooking Nassau. It is home of the governor-general, the queen's personal representative to the Commonwealth of the Bahamas. In 1787, Lord Dunmore moved to the house he built on West Street (now a priory) and sold the government house and its land to another Loyalist. The present house was built between 1803 and 1806 and expanded several times. The hurricane of 1929 caused a great deal of damage to the structure, and, subsequently, the interior and front facade were entirely redesigned, the main entrance changed, and the main hall added. In 1940 the house was extensively redecorated, and living quarters in the west wing, known as the Windsor Wing, were added for the personal staff of the Duke of Windsor, who lived here for four years as the royal governor of the Bahamas.

More changes were made in 1964 and again in 1977 for the visit of Queen Elizabeth II. Many members of the royal family, heads of state including President John F. Kennedy, and other celebrities have been guests here. **Christopher Columbus Statue (24):** The entrance to Government House is marked by a 12-foot-tall statue of Christopher Columbus, made in London by an aide to American novelist and historian Washington Irving and placed here in 1830 by Governor Sir James Carmichael Smyth. It commemorates Columbus's arrival in the New World on the Bahamian island of San Salvador. The ceremonial Changing of the Guard with the famous Royal Bahamas Police Force Band takes place on alternate Sat at 10 a.m. sharp (242-322-3622).

From the statue you can walk down George Street in front of the Columbus statue to the Straw Market on Bay Street, or continue your walking tour to see some of Nassau's oldest and loveliest houses.

Graycliff House (25): This Georgian mansion set in a lovely tropical garden dates from about 1726. Now a hotel and restaurant, it was originally built by a notorious pirate, Capt. John H. Graysmith, as his home. The building may have been used as a garrison for the British West Indies Regiment, judging from the thick walls and other structural elements in the cellars, which are now used by the hotel for its wine collection. The house is known to have been a hotel as early as 1844, but it became a private residence again in 1937 when it belonged to a Canadian couple who added a swimming pool and made alterations. In 1966 the estate was bought by Lord Dudley, earl of Staffordshire, as his winter home. The present owners acquired it in 1974.

Farther west on West Hill Street are several beautifully restored private homes and the **Priory (26),** formerly known as Dunmore House. After serving as the governor's residence, the house became the officers' quarters and mess hall for the 22nd West Indies Regiment. It later became a military hospital and in 1893 was purchased by the Roman Catholic Church and made into the Priory; the Cathedral of St. Francis Xavier is adjacent.

National Art Gallery (27): Opened in 2003 and housed in a magnificently restored mansion built in the 1860s, the National Art Gallery of the Bahamas, at the corner of West and West Hill Streets, contains impressive examples of the Bahamas's art development from colonial times to the present. Although the collection is in its early stage of acquisition, it is the only place you can get a comprehensive view and gain an appreciation for the Bahamas's young art movement. Among the established artists in the collection are the late Amos Ferguson, Brent Malone, Maxwell Taylor, the brothers Jackson and Stanley Burnside, Alton Lowe, Edison G. Rolle, Edward Minnis, Dorman Stubbs, Ricardo Knowles, and others. The gallery renovation took three years to complete at the cost of $3.4 million. The museum shop sells the richly illustrated book *Bahamian Art, 1492–1992,* an excellent introduction to the Bahamas's art history, published to commemorate the Columbus Quincentennial. Admission: $5 adult; $3 senior, student; under 12 free. Hours: 10 a.m. to 4 p.m. Tues through Sat (242-328-5800; www.nagb.org.bs).

The annual national festival of the Bahamas, Junkanoo, held Dec 26 and Jan 1, is now an integral part of Bahamian culture, and the creation of its elaborate costumes has played an important role in the development of Bahamian art and artists. At the **Educulture/Junkanoo Museum (27)** (West and Delancy Streets, www.educulturebahamas .com), visitors see some of the costumes and get a comprehensive tour of Junkanoo by a guide who is an active and enthusiastic member of the festival. Admission: $20 adult; $10 child; (242) 328-DRUM.

The Deanery (28): From West Hill Street continue north and turn into Queen Street to the Deanery, at No. 28. Built in 1710, it is thought to be the oldest house in the Bahamas. The building was acquired by the Anglican Church in 1800 and is the rectory of Christ Church Cathedral. The three-story house is built of stone with chamfered quoins; originally it had three tiers of verandas on three sides. A one-story building on the west side was the stone kitchen with an 8-foot fireplace and a domed oven; it has a small room thought to have been used as sleeping quarters for domestic slaves. Across the street is the U.S. embassy.

On the north side of Marlborough Street is the British Colonial Hilton, the pink colonial building that dominates the waterfront. It is on the site of the town's first fortification, Fort Nassau, built in 1670. On its east side is the stand for buses to **Cable Beach (29).**

Vendue House/Pompey Museum (30): At the head of George Street facing Bay Street is the site of the former slave market, originally a colonnade structure without walls dating from about 1769. It was rebuilt in the early 1900s and occupied by the Bahamas Electricity Corporation. In 1992, as part of the Columbus Quincentennial, it was renovated to house a museum—Pompey Museum of Slavery and Emancipation—funded by a grant from Bacardi Corporation. The exhibit on the African experience in the Bahamas was named for Pompey, a slave on one of five estates in Exuma owned by Lord Rolle and a hero in Bahamian history. Admission: $3 adult; $2 senior; $1 child. Hours: 9:30 a.m. to 4 p.m., closed Thurs and Sun; (242) 356-0495.

Christ Church Cathedral (31): Turn east onto Marlborough Street and walk to the corner of King and George Streets to Christ Church Cathedral. In the original layout of the town, this area was a park known as George's Square, the site of the colony's first church.

Pirates of Nassau Museum (31) (King and George Streets). The attraction, two years in the making, is part museum, part Disneyesque entertainment. Housed in three adjoining structures, the 150-year-old Lofthouse, a 200-year-old slave kitchen, and the modern Marlborough Arms building, the museum offers an interactive, educational journey into the early 18th century when pirates such as Blackbeard ruled Bahamian waters. Designed and built in Canada, Switzerland, and Britain, as well as Nassau, the museum has as its centerpiece a 75-foot replica of the pirate ship *Revenge* and a re-created wharf. The scent of tar, the sound of water lapping against the wooden ships, scenes of life at sea, and a pirate marooned on a deserted island are some of the come-to-life details that depict the age of piracy at its zenith. A tour takes about forty-five minutes and is suitable for all ages. Hours: 9 a.m. to 6 p.m. Mon through Sat, 9 a.m. to noon Sun. Admission: $12 adult; $6 ages twelve or under; (242-356-3759; www.pirates-of-nassau.com).

Balcony House (32): Facing the Central Bank on Market Street is the two-story Balcony House, whose construction indicates it may have been built by ships' carpenters around 1790. The house was constructed of American soft cedar and has a second-floor balcony that hangs over the street. An unusual inside staircase is said to have come from a ship. The property, which includes three other houses and slave kitchens, was acquired by Lord Beaverbrook, who sold it in 1947. More recently it was acquired by the Central Bank and renovated as a museum by the Department of Archives to show life of a prosperous family in the 19th century. Hours: 10 a.m. to 5 p.m. weekdays except holidays; (242) 302-2621.

The Central Bank (33) has a collection of the Bahamas's leading artists on display in its lobby. The bank is on Trinity Place, a small street between Market and Frederick Streets. One of the oldest streets in Nassau, Trinity Place is home to the Trinity Church. Both Market and Frederick Streets lead to Bay Street and the local bus stand for buses to the North and East End. You can return to your ship by walking east on Bay Street.

Nassau and Its Environs

New Providence has many good roads, making any section of the island accessible with a few minutes' drive. At least four highways cut the island north–south, making it easy to reach the south coast from Nassau by a direct route.

Attractions West of Nassau

In contrast with the Old World ambience of Old Nassau are the modern resorts of **Cable Beach** that stretch west from town along 5 miles of lovely, white-sand beaches on the north shore. Dubbed the Bahamian Riviera, they include the Sheraton Cable Beach Resort; Breezes Bahamas, next to Nassau's oldest golf course; and Sandals Royal Bahamian. All are undergoing a transformation, creating, the largest destination resort in the Caribbean here. Baha Mar, as it is known, will offer approximately 3,000 guest rooms and the largest casino in the Caribbean. Starwood has committed to operate hotels under its W, St. Regis, Westin, and Sheraton brands. An 18-hole golf course, 20-acre pool and beachfront complex, retail village, restaurants, and entertainment venues are scheduled for completion in 2012. Between Old Nassau and modern Cable Beach, in the shadow of Fort Charlotte, there are several attractions that usually can be visited in one tour.

If you visit any of the following places on your own by taxi, be sure to arrange for your return transportation. In most cases, public buses pass within walking distance.

Ardastra Gardens and Zoo: One mile west of town in the shadow of Fort Charlotte is a nature park with the world's only trained flamingo corps. The pink birds are put through their paces in a twenty-five-minute show three times a day. The pretty birds, which are the national bird of the Bahamas, have a mating display of strutting that lends itself to being trained to parade. The five-acre gardens also offer the chance to see in one place a wide variety of tropical plants as well as endemic birds, four species of iguana (which look like miniature dinosaurs), and other wildlife remaining in the Bahamas.

Visitors are allowed to take photographs, including ones of themselves amid the flapping flamingos. The flamingos come from the southern island of Great Inagua, where 50,000 birds—the world's largest breeding colony—are protected in a nature preserve administered by the Bahamas National Trust. Ardastra also has several beautiful Bahama parrots in a captive breeding program with the trust. This endangered species, one of sixteen Amazon parrot species in the Caribbean, is found only in Inagua and the Abacos in a sanctuary within a large forest reserve. Hours: 9 a.m. to 5 p.m. daily. Admission: $15 adult; $7.50 child. Shows are Mon through Sat, 10:30 a.m., 2:10 p.m., and 4:10 p.m. (242-323-5806; www.ardastra.com).

Nassau Botanical Gardens: Adjacent to Fort Charlotte is an 18-acre spread of tropical plants and flowers, a delightful oasis with a large variety of flora typical of the tropics. The gardens are popular for weddings. They also have a re-created Lucayan village. Admission: $1 adult; 50 cents child. Hours: 9 a.m. to 4:30 p.m. daily; (242) 323-5975.

Fort Charlotte: One mile west of town. Named in honor of the wife of George III, the fort was begun by Lord Dunmore in 1787 and built in three stages. The eastern part is the oldest; the middle portion was named Fort Stanley; and the western section, Fort D'Arcy. Much of it was cut out of solid rock, and the walls were buttressed with cedar to "last to eternity," according to Dunmore. It still has its moat, open battlements, and dungeons, plus a good view of the harbor. The fort was restored extensively in 1992. Admission: $5 adult; $2 child under twelve. Hours: 9 a.m. to 4 p.m. daily. Tours throughout the day; (242) 325-9186.

Arawak Cay: What started a few years ago as a few stalls of fishermen shucking conch—Bahamians' favorite food—for local conch lovers has blossomed into one of Nassau's main attractions. Here, at any of two dozen stalls, you can sample fresh conch prepared in one of several ways—cracked, fritters, jerk, and more. Those in the know agree that the best is conch salad, the Bahamian answer to seviche, the popular South American lime-and-onion-flavored fish appetizer. A fish fry with local bands making music is held here on weekends (242-323-2227).

From Cable Beach, a road hugging the coast continues west around the island to Love Beach, one of the island's loveliest beaches. Farther west is Lyford Cay, a private, 4,000-acre residential

New Providence Island

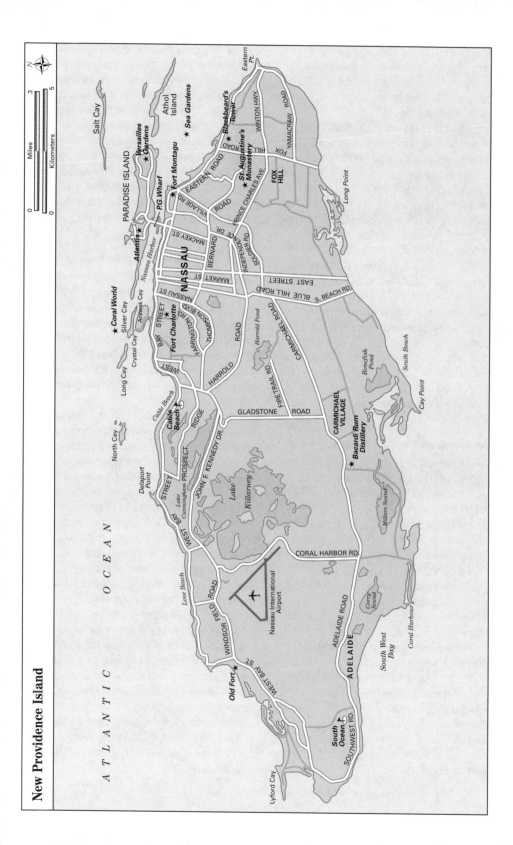

ATLANTIC OCEAN

Salt Cay

PARADISE ISLAND

★ Versailles Gardens

Athol Island

★ Sea Gardens

★ P.G. Wharf

★ Fort Montagu

Eastern Pt.

★ Blackbeard's Tower

EASTERN ROAD

VILLAGE RD.

★ St. Augustine's Monastery

WINTON HWY.

FOX HILL ROAD

YAMACRAW ROAD

PRINCE CHARLES AVE.

FOX HILL

★ Atlantis

MACKEY ST.

Nassau Harbor

NASSAU

BERNARD RD.

INDEPENDENCE DR.

SOLDIER RD.

MARKET ST.

EAST STREET

Long Point

★ Coral World

Silver Cay

Crystal Cay

Arawak Cay

BAY STREET

NASSAU ST.

★ Fort Charlotte

FARRINGTON RD.

THOMPSON BLVD.

BLUE HILL ROAD

S. BEACH RD.

Harrold Pond

CARMICHAEL ROAD

Bonefish Pond

South Beach

Cay Point

North Cay

WEST STREET

Cable Beach

Cable Beach

HARROLD ROAD

FIRE TRAIL RD.

GLADSTONE ROAD

CARMICHAEL VILLAGE

★ Bacardi Rum Distillery

Delaport Point

BAY STREET

RIDGE

PROSPECT

JOHN F. KENNEDY DR.

Lake Cunningham

Lake Killarney

Millars Sound

Love Beach

WEST BAY STREET

WINDSOR FIELD ROAD

Nassau International Airport

CORAL HARBOR RD.

ADELAIDE ROAD

Corry Sound

Coral Harbour

Lyford Cay

★ Old Fort

WEST BAY ST.

SOUTHWEST RD.

ADELAIDE

South West Bay

🛬 South Ocean

N

0   3   Miles

0   5   Kilometers

resort that you can visit only as a guest of a member. Lyford Cay, as much as any development, caused the Bahamas to be called the jet-set capital because of the many famous international personalities who own homes here.

The western end of the island has many elegant Bahamian mansions, frequently painted in the deep pink color associated with the Bahamas or other pastels with white trim, and surrounded by tropical gardens. Among the loveliest are the home of the former prime minister, on Skyline Drive; the residence of the U.S. ambassador to the Bahamas, on Saffron Hill; and on Sandford Drive, the mansion of Canadian millionaire Sir Harry Oakes, one of the island's most famous residents and benefactors, whose murder in 1943 sent shock waves through the island and continues to be a mystery.

Large areas of the south side of the island are uninhabited and covered by miles of pine forests. From Adelaide and Carmichael Roads, you can circle back via Gladstone Road over Prospect Ridge to see one of the island's biggest surprises—Lake Killarney and Lake Cunningham—large bodies of water whose wooded shores are richly populated with birds.

Attractions East of Nassau

Fort Montagu: The first fortification at the northeastern end of the island was built in 1728 to protect the eastern approach to Nassau Harbor. In 1741 it was replaced by the present structure, designed by Peter Henry Bruce, an engineer previously employed by Peter the Great of Russia. The fort was seized by the Americans briefly during the Revolutionary War.

The Retreat, Bahamas National Trust: The trust's headquarters, east of Nassau near Queen's College, is on an 11-acre site where Arthur and Margaret Langlois, beginning in 1925, created one of the world's largest private collections of palm trees—about 175 species from around the world. The property was donated to the trust and officially opened in 1985. The palm trees grow in a thick coppice forest with other native trees and shrubs. The gardens are maintained by volunteers from local garden clubs. Admission: $2. Hours: 9 a.m. to 5 p.m. Mon through Fri (242-393-1317; www.bnt.bs).

St. Augustine's Monastery: Near Fox Hill village. Father Jerome, the architect of several Anglican and Catholic churches in the Bahamas, designed the school and cloister of the monastery.

Wealthy colonialists originally settled in the area east of Nassau; there, dozens of fine mansions stand witness to the enormous wealth the early settlers amassed. Some sections also have small settlements of colorful West Indian–style houses built, after slavery was abolished, by former slaves granted plots of land. Four of the original settlements are Adelaide, Carmichael, Fox Hill, and Gambier.

Attractions on Paradise Island

Facing Nassau's north shore is Paradise Island, connected to Nassau by two ½-mile bridges and a ferry from Prince George Wharf. Initially, the island resort was put on the map by A&P grocery heir Huntington Hartford, whose home became the centerpiece of the fashionable Ocean Club. In 1994 Sun International acquired Resorts International, changing the name to Atlantis and making major changes.

Atlantis Resort and Casino: The complex includes a dozen hotels, several dozen restaurants, a cavernous casino, an enormous dinner theater, an 18-hole championship golf course, a twelve-court tennis complex, horseback riding, a marina, a full range of water sports, and an international airport with flights to several Florida cities. Atlantis's centerpiece is the 63-acre Aquaventure water experience with "master blaster" waterslides, water escalators, and wave surges all accentuated by smoke, fog, and video effects. There is a near-vertical 50-foot drop at the 120-foot tall Power Tower; you'll also find 7-foot ups-and-downs into white-water rapids on a mile-long river loop. The 14-acre Waterscape is said to have the largest outdoor, open-water aquarium in the world, six exhibit lagoons, more than forty waterfalls, five swimming pools, three underground grottos, and an underwater walkway with windows for viewing sharks and artificial coral reefs. Dig and Marine Aquarium Tour (given frequently throughout the day, 9 a.m. to 5 p.m. daily) admission: $29 adult; $14.50 ages four to twelve. Aquaventure: $105 adult; $75 child (242-364-1317).

Versailles Gardens and French Cloister:
Landscaped gardens, adjacent to the Ocean Club on the island's northeast side, are enclosed by the stones and arches of a 12th-century Augustinian monastery, which Huntington Hartford had shipped from France stone by stone and reconstructed here. From the hotel's swimming pool, the gardens rise in seven terraces to the cloisters, which overlook a small garden and the sea. Each terrace is embellished with ancient as well as modern statues of historic figures, such as Empress Josephine of France, Franklin D. Roosevelt, and Dr. Stanley Livingstone.

Shopping

Shopping in Nassau closely rivals St. Thomas, with goods from around the globe. The Tourist Information Center inside Festival Place can provide information. There are shops and services there, too.

At Rawson Square you can turn east or west onto Bay Street, and you will find every type of shop—dress, sportswear, shoes, men's clothing, liquor, perfume, and more. The newest shops and small shopping plazas are east of the square, while the stores on the west are generally the more established ones. The free promotional booklet *Best Buys in the Bahamas* is useful for maps and store descriptions. It usually has coupons for free gifts and discounts, too.

Before the day has ended, you will certainly want to visit the **Straw Market** on Bay Street; it is open daily. One of the best of its kind in the tropics, it's crammed full of handcrafted baskets, hats, handbags, dolls, and other inexpensive gifts to take home. You can watch the items emerge from the skilled fingers of a Bahamian craftswoman and even have them handmade to order with your own design and initials. Don't hesitate to bargain in the market; the women expect it and enjoy the exchange. And it's fun!

In addition to Bay Street, there are shopping arcades in hotels, particularly on Paradise Island at Atlantis, where the Crystal Court, includes such high-fashion boutiques as Ferragamo, Versace, and Gucci, as well as more moderate ones. The Marina Village shopping mall is also part of Atlantis but outside the hotel structures. In stores designed to resemble the houses in a Bahamian village are found art shops, clothing and jewelry boutiques, and a variety of restaurants. Some are included in the information below.

Nassau stores are open 9 a.m. to 5 or 6 p.m. Mon through Sat. Many are also open on Sun; some close on Thurs afternoon. All of the following stores are on Bay Street unless indicated otherwise.

Art and Antiques: Nassau Art Gallery (East Bay Shopping Center) and **Doongalik Art Gallery** (Marina Village; 242-363-1313) have limited selections of contemporary local artists. **The Plait Lady** (Marina Village; 242-363-1416), after an absence of several years, reopened in the shopping mall. The owner, Clare Sands, employs more than 1,000 craftspeople throughout the Bahamas who produce the most authentic, best-made straw products in Nassau. All are handmade from the silver top palm, mostly from Long Island, and the pond top from Eleuthera. The products are expensive. And indeed, it would appear that some of these craftspeople are supplying other vendors, such as the **Bahamas Craft Centre** (Paradise Island Shopping Centre), with similar, if not the same, finely woven baskets of improved style and design for modest prices.

For a humorous view, Jaff Cooper, a political cartoonist for local newspapers, has a kiosk at the Marina Village, where he sells his Bahama Mama cartoon characters, children's coloring books, and other souvenirs.

Balmain Antiques (Bay Street at Charlotte Street, second floor; 242-323-7421; fax: 242-323-7422) has a great collection of old prints and maps.

Bahamian Batiks: Native Bahamian designs on cotton and other fabrics are printed by Androsia (www.androsia.com) on the Bahamian island of Andros and made into sportswear sold in high-quality stores. Selections are available at **Royal Palm Trading Co.** A similar, more expensive product, **Bahama Hand Prints** (Marina Village; 242-94-4111), is made in Nassau. Their silk-screened designs, usually on voile-type fabrics, have a more flowing look. New prints and colors are introduced each season.

Books: The Island Book Shop is something of a department store and sells everything from cameras to cashmeres, swimsuits, and sportswear. The book department on the second floor is the best in town.

Children's Gifts: If you want a fun, unusual, and interesting gift for a small child, bookstores, newsstands, and pharmacies stock a series of coloring books on Bahamian flowers, birds, fish, shells, ships, and Junkanoo. For expensive items, The Linen Shop (242-322-4266) has lovely hand-smocked and embroidered children's clothes.

China and Crystal: For the best selections of English bone china, Waterford, and other fine crystal, Solomon Mines (Bay Street; 242-356-6920) has a large selection, with savings of up to 35 percent on china and crystal, among some the best buys in duty-free goods in the Bahamas. You will be better prepared to recognize a bargain when you come with prices from home. Have the name of the pattern as well as the manufacturer for accurate comparisons. Tiffany and Co. (284 Bay St.) has a boutique inside John Bull, a major department store.

Dive Supplies: Bahamas Divers outfits divers and snorkelers; Pyfrom's carries T-shirts, Sea Island cotton shirts, and souvenirs, as well as masks and flippers for children and adults.

Jewelry: Coin of the Realm (14 Charlotte St.; 242-322-4682) has not only coins but also a large selection of precious and semiprecious stones, gold and silver jewelry, and stamps. Bulgari (Crystal Court, Atlantis) is the first boutique of the famous Italian designer in the Bahamas.

Leather: Leather Masters (Parliament Street; 242-322-7597) and the Brass and Leather Shops (14 Charlotte St.) carry fine Italian bags, briefcases, shoes, and other leather goods. Fendi and Gucci have their own shops in prime locations. Savings are about 20 percent, if that much, over U.S. prices. Ferragamo, Versace, and other famous designers have shops at the Atlantis resort.

Perfumes: The Perfume Shop has several outlets on Bay Street and in the Paradise Island Shopping Centre. Their prices are as competitive as any we have found. Actually, French perfume prices are set by French perfume makers; any dealer who undercuts the price is cut off from the supply.

For local products, **Bahamaspa** (Festival Place; 242-327-2772; bahamaspa@aol.com) has luxury soaps made in small batches by hand with natural ingredients and oils. At Sundrop Creations (Montrose Avenue and Sears Road; 242-325-4469; www.sundropcreations.com) offerings include bath salts made with sea salt from the local waters, hand-poured candles, body butter, and sea bubbles.

Sportswear: There are many low-priced and discount shoe stores and sports- and casualwear shops along East Bay Street. Seventeen Shop (Bay Street; 242-322-2456) has a large selection of mod fashions, in dresses as well as shorts, shirts, and slacks. Venue (Bay Street; 242-326-8079) has both casual and evening wear for women.

Watches: John Bull (Bay Street and Paradise Island; 242-322-4253; www.johnbull.com) is one of the oldest and largest stores in the Bahamas. It carries all the famous makes from novelty watches to Corum and Cartier, as well as a full line of cameras and photo equipment, as well as leather goods and jewelry.

Women's Fashions: Calypso Carousel (Marina Village; 242-363-0380) sells the latest mod fashions with lots of glitter for $300 and up. Cole's of Nassau (Parliament Street, Lyford Cay, Crystal Court; 242-322-8393; www.colesofnassau.com) has the largest selection of sophisticated women's fashions, but many are familiar labels that sell for less in New York. For less expensive clothes, check the shops on Bay Street east of Rawson Square.

Dining and Restaurants

Restaurants and hotel dining rooms range from elegant and sophisticated—as befits a world capital—to simple and unpretentious, as suits an unhurried tropical resort. You can enjoy a barbecue on the beach, a fish fry by the harbor, or a gourmet treat in the romantic ambience of a colonial home.

The variety of international cuisine includes French, English, Italian, American, Chinese, Indian, and Greek, but you really should try some Bahamian specialties. The best known are johnnycakes, a corn bread; conch chowder, spicy and delicious; conch fritters or deep-fried grouper; and pigeon peas with rice, to mention a few. Prices range from $8 for lunch at a typical local restaurant to $100 for dinner at the top gourmet havens.

Always check your bill before you leave a tip. Many restaurants in the Bahamas and the Caribbean have taken up the European custom of adding a 15 percent service charge to the bill. If so, you do not need to leave a tip, unless the service has been exceptional and you want to leave something more.

Bahamian Kitchen (Trinity Place; 242-325-0702), 1 block from the Straw Market. Has Bahamian specialties. Moderate.

Humidor Churrascaria (Graycliff, West Hill Street; 242-322-2796; www.graycliff.com) is a steak house like no other. Start at the salad and pasta bar, where selections can be a meal by themselves; then wait for the waiters to come to your table every few minutes with a skewer of hot roasted beef, lamb, pork, chicken, and more; and finish with a scrumptious dessert. Expensive. The Humidor part of the name comes from the cigar-rolling center adjacent to the restaurant.

Dune (Ocean Club, Paradise Island; 242-363-2501; 800-321-3000). Set in the dunes at the water's edge, the restaurant of renowned chef Jean-Georges Vongerichten, and designed by famed French designer Christian Liaigre, is casual and elegant at the same time. Liaigre blended natural woods and fabrics with a sophisticated palette of color from the ash of weathered wood to the slate of the chairs and the charcoal of hardwood tabletops.

Dune offers signature dishes from Jean-Georges's top-rated New York restaurants—Jean Georges, and others—with Bahamian ingredients, often seasoned with herbs from the restaurant's small garden. Open daily for three meals. Diners may sit inside under a high-pitched, beamed ceiling and enjoy views of the turquoise sea; watch the activity in the display kitchen that runs across the back of the restaurant; or dine under white umbrellas on the outdoor patio by the beach. Reservations are necessary to get past the security gate at the hotel entrance. Jean-Georges's other venture, **Café Martinique** (Marina Village), is an elegant French restaurant.

The Taj Mahal (Parliament Street; 242-356-3004). A restaurant by the operators of Gaylords, the international Indian restaurant chain. The menu includes tandoori, Punjabi, Nepalese, and Mughali dishes. It has carry-out service, too. Moderate.

Nobu (Atlantis, Royal Towers). Fans of the famous Japanese chef Nobu Matsuhisa will want to try this Bahama-based version. Expensive.

Mama Lyddys (Market Street; 242-328-6849) serves seafood and authentic Bahamian cuisine in a lovely setting that was once an old Bahamian home. Inexpensive.

The Poop Deck (East Bay Street; 242-393-8175; www.thepoopdeckrestaurants.com) offers Bahamian and seafood specialties in a rustic atmosphere at lunch or dinner. The restaurant has great conch chowder, fritters, and Key lime pie in a fabulous setting by the water overlooking Paradise Island Bridge. Moderate. There's a more upscale version of The Poop Deck west of town at Sandy Port (242-327-3325).

Traveller's Rest (West Bay Street; 242-327-7633) is something of a drive from town, but it's worth it for the food and delightful country setting under huge shade trees overlooking the aqua sea. Here you can try fried grouper with peas and rice, and plantains, which are similar to fried bananas. Moderate.

There are also lots of places to satisfy your steak cravings—like Outback Steakhouse—or your pizza yearnings, including Domino's and Swank's. You'll also find a Hard Rock Cafe and a Señor Frog's.

Sports in Nassau

The Bahamas has some of the best sports facilities in the tropics, available in or near enough to Nassau or Freeport for cruise passengers to use them with relative ease. When facilities for sports such as tennis or golf are available at a hotel, contact the hotel or the sports operator in advance, particularly during the peak season, when demand is likely to be high. When you want specific information on any sport, phone the Bahamas Tourist Office, (800) 327-7678.

Beaches: So fine are the beaches that picking the best is difficult. For hotel beaches, the nearest to the port is the British Colonial Hilton, but if you go a little farther west, you have all of Cable Beach, dubbed the Bahamian Riviera. Most of Paradise Island is fringed with white sand.

Biking: The island is rather flat, and roads away from the main arteries with heavy traffic are easy for biking. Bikes can be rented for $15 per day and up. Inquire at the Bahama Tourist Office by the pier.

Bahamas Outdoors (242-362-1574; fax: 242-362-2044; www.bahamasoutdoors.com) offers a variety of tours for bikers of average skill on easy trails through woodland and along the seashore, visiting historic Adelaide Village. Easier or more challenging tours are available. Tour includes off-road bicycle, water bottle, helmet, and backpack. Minimum age nine years; maximum weight 200 pounds. Half-day tours, $69, require advance booking; maximum six persons. Birding tours are available in winter and include an ecotour guide.

Boating: Almost any size or type of boat, sail or power, with or without crew, is available. You can explore, swim, and picnic at your own pace. **Nassau Yacht Haven** (East Bay Street; 242-393-8173; www.nassauyachthaven.com) can provide information on yachts and fishing boats.

Half-day sailing/snorkeling ($70) and sunset excursions ($70) are offered by **Flying Cloud** (Paradise Island Ferry Dock; 242-363-4430; www.flyingcloud.info). **Seahorse Sailing Adventures** (Atlantis Marina; 242-363-5510; 800-821-4505; www.seahorsesailingadventures.com) has three catamarans departing at 9 a.m. and 1 p.m.; $60 adult; $30 under twelve. **Barefoot Sailing Cruises** (242-393-0820; www.barefootsailingcruises.com) also offers sail and snorkel excursions, half-day, $75.

For more adventure, **Powerboat Adventures** (East Bay Street; 242-363-1466; www.powerboat adventures.com) has fast boats to Exuma Cays (fifty-five minutes) for a day of drift snorkeling, shark and stingray feedings, nature walks, and more, departing at 9 a.m. and returning about 5:30 p.m.; $199 adult; $140 ages two through twelve, including transfers, lunch, open bar. A similar excursion to the Exumas is available from **Island World Adventures** (242-363-3333; www.islandworld adventures.com) for $200 adult; $150 under twelve.

Canoeing Lake Nancy: (J. F. Kennedy Drive; 242-323-3382). Lake Nancy's clear, shallow waters are home to fish and bird life such as ospreys, coots, egrets, cranes, and endangered white-crowned pigeons. Canoes are available for rent by the hour or day. Refreshments and light snacks are available.

Deep-Sea Fishing: The Bahamas is a magnet for sportfishermen. World records for marlin and other big game are made and broken year after year. Jan to late Apr is the best season for white marlin and amberjack; June through Aug for blue marlin and kingfish. Ocean bonito, blackfin tuna, and Allison tuna are caught from May to Sept. Grouper can be found in reef areas year-round, and you'll find bluefin tuna, sailfish, wahoo, and more. Andros calls itself the bonefishing capital of the world.

Boats depart from Nassau Yacht Harbor on regular half-day fishing trips at 8:30 a.m. and 12:30 p.m. for $60 per person, with six persons per boat. The price includes bait and tackle. Contact **Chubasco Charters,** Capt. Mike Russell (242-324-3474; www.chubascocharters.com). Charter rates, which include tackle, bait, ice, and fuel, are about $450 to $700 for a half day; $900 to $1400 for a full day for boats accommodating up to six people. The **Bahamas Tourist Office** (800-327-7678) has copies of the *Bahamas Fishing Guide,* with pictures and descriptions of the main sportfishing targets and their seasons, plus a wealth of other information. The center can provide you with an up-to-date schedule of the fishing tournaments held during the year.

Golf: A baker's dozen of Bahamian courses, designed by famous architects, are as beautiful to see as they are challenging to play. Most courses are part of resort complexes and have resident pros, pro shops, and clubhouses.

Nassau/Paradise Island has four courses. The closest to the port is the **Cable Beach Golf Course** (7,040 yards, par 72; 242-327-6000; www.bahamasgolf.com). This championship course was the Bahamas's first when it was built in 1926. It has a clubhouse, pro shop, and restaurant. Greens fees are $180 for 18 holes, including cart.

Ocean Club Golf Course (242-363-6680; 6,776 yards, par 72) was redesigned by well-known golfer Tom Weiskopf, and reopened in late 2000. It is open to members and Atlantis and Ocean Club hotel guests only.

In development as part of the Baha Mar megaresort at Cable Beach is an 18-hole Jack Nicklaus Signature course that will be accessible via a specially designed waterway and will feature play for all skill levels. (For Freeport golf clubs, see the section on Grand Bahama Island.)

Horseback Riding: Happy Trails Stables/ Windsor Equestrian Centre (Coral Harbour; 242-362-1820; www.windsorequestriancentre.com), open daily except Sun. A riding tour costs about $150, including round-trip transportation to the stables from town.

Snorkeling/Scuba Diving: The spectacular underwater world of the Bahamas has something for everyone, no matter what your level of expertise. Snorkelers and novice divers can simply swim off a beach to discover fantastic coral gardens only 10 or 20 feet below the surface of the water. More experienced divers can explore drop-offs that start at 40 feet and plunge thousands. They can swim into underwater caverns and tunnels teeming with fish and roam through waters with visibility as great as 200 feet. Masks and flippers are readily available, as are diving equipment and instruction (www.bahamasdiving.com).

Bahamas Divers (East Bay Street; 242-393-6054; 800-398-DIVE; www.bahamasdivers.com) has daily snorkeling excursions for $39. It also offers dive trips (all gear provided) with one-tank dives for $55 and two-tank dives for $89. **Stuart Cove's Aqua Adventures** (South West Bay Road; 242-362-4171; www.stuartcove.com) offers the full range of dive excursions as well as shark diving. Prices start at $48 snorkeling; $89 diving. It also offers "Sub Bahamas," a personal underwater scooter. **Dive Dive Dive Ltd.** (242-362-1143; 800-368-3483; www.divedivedive.com) takes experienced divers to see bull, reef, and silky sharks several days a week, $120.

Tennis/Squash/Racquetball: In the Bahamas, where the weather is ideal to play year-round, tennis is as popular as any water sport. There are no fewer than one hundred courts and excellent facilities with pros and pro shops, instruction, and daily clinics available at hotels and resorts in Nassau, Cable Beach, and Paradise Island. Many courts

are lighted for evening play. Since most hotels do not charge guests for the use of courts, you will need to make special arrangements in advance by contacting the hotel to request court time.

Underwater Adventures: The Seaworld Explorer (Moses Plaza, Bay Street; 242-356-2548; www.seaworldtours.com), a semi submarine, originally developed in Australia for use on the Great Barrier Reef, glides over Nassau Sea Gardens while you sit in air-conditioned comfort 5 feet below the surface of the water. Price: $45 per adult and $25, children.

Hartley's Undersea Walk (Nassau Yacht Haven, East Bay Street; 242-393-8234; www.underseawalk.com). Explore the reefs like early marine biologists did before scuba was invented. Your head stays dry. It's safe for all ages, nonswimmers, and those who wear contact lenses. Two trips daily. Price: $125 per person, adults and children.

Dolphin Encounters (Blue Lagoon Island; 242-363-1003; fax: 242-363-4438; www.dolphinencounters.com) offers two options at Blue Lagoon, an islet off Nassau used by many cruise ships for beach and snorkeling excursions. The Close Encounters program with dolphins costs $98 per person; swimming with dolphins, $185 per person.

Windsurfing: The protection the shallows and reefs give to most parts of the Bahamian coast also makes its many bays excellent places to learn to windsurf. The cost is about $20. The annual Windsurfing Regatta is held in Jan.

Entertainment

Bahamians—and visitors—make something of a ritual of watching the pretty sunsets. So when the air begins to cool and the sun starts its fall, you can grab a Bahama Mama (that's the local rum punch) and head for the beach. You'll probably be joined by kindred spirits, a scratch band, or other local musicians for some impromptu jamming.

After the sun disappears and the stars are out, you can stay on the beach with the calypso beat or change into something a bit dressier for a round of the Bahamas's razzle-dazzle nightlife. The 1,000-seat theater of the **Atlantis Show Room** (Paradise Island) hosts Las Vegas–style shows nightly. At the

Crystal Palace Casino you can choose blackjack, roulette, craps, baccarat, or slot machines to play, and if your luck runs out, you can laugh it off at Atlantis's Joker's Wild Comedy Club.

Hard Rock Cafe (Charlotte Street; 242-325-7625; www.hardrock.com) near the port, offers live music along with the chain's usual menu. Some other noted nightspots are Bambu (Prince George Dock; 242-326-6627; www.bambunassau.com), a music bar and lounge for dancing with a rooftop SkyLounge overlooking the harbor open Thurs, Fri, Sat from 9 p.m. to the wee hours; admission $20. Club Waterloo (East Bay Street; 242-393-9732), popular with the young crowd; admission $20; and Uptown Night Club (Across from British Colonial Hilton, West Bay Street); admission $20. Club Aura (in Atlantis Casino); admission $50 for females, $100 for men; sophisticated dress required. To sample the current sounds of the hot new generation of Bahamian musicians who blend Junkanoo whistles, cowbells, and goatskin drums with hip-hop and funk, check out Charlies (East Bay Street; 242-322-3041), the hot nightspot where Baha Men (of "Who Let the Dogs Out" fame), Visage, Spank Band, and other local bands hang out.

For those who want something on the cultural side, the Dundas Centre for the Performing Arts (Mackey Street; 242-393-3728) offers plays, musicals, ballets, and folkloric shows.

Festivals and Celebrations

Bahamians love to celebrate. From Jan to Dec the calendar is full of sporting events, music festivals, historic commemorations, religious feasts, and national holidays. All are windows on island life not open to visitors at other times of the year. You can watch the fun from the sidelines or join in. Bring your camera.

Junkanoo, a National Festival

Of all the festivals, none compares to Junkanoo, an exuberant Bahamian celebration full of color and creativity, humor, rhythm and music, dance, fun, and festivity. The national extravaganza traces its origins to the West African dance and mask traditions kept alive throughout the West Indies by slaves brought to the New World in the 17th and 18th centuries. After emancipation in the early 19th century, Junkanoo was suppressed by religious zealots, both black and white. It had nearly died out when it was revived in the 1970s as part of the effort to preserve the Bahamas's multifaceted heritage.

Now, once again, Junkanoo is part of the Bahamian tradition reflected in the art, dance, and music. It has been taken into the schools, where the construction of costumes is part of the curriculum, and sent abroad by the musicians and entertainers, where it is receiving international recognition.

Junkanoo is the Bahamian version of Carnival, with parades, costumes, and music, but unlike traditional Carnival, it is held at the end of the year and the start of the new one. The first Junkanoo parade starts at daybreak on Dec 26, Boxing Day, a public holiday stemming from British tradition. Bahamians and visitors who feel the spirit don brilliant costumes and parade through downtown Nassau to the clatter of cowbells, horns, whistles, and the driving beat of African drums. Prizes are awarded to those with the most unusual and elaborate costumes—all made from cardboard and strips of paper laid down in tight layers. Every display must be able to be carried by one person; nothing on wheels is allowed.

Participants and viewers need to be on the street before daylight—it's all over by 8 a.m. (Photographers need fast film, as the light is still low at parade time.) Bleachers are set up in the judging area on Bay Street west of Rawson Square, and the judging takes place from 6 to 7 a.m. Costumes that do not win are often dumped in the street and make fine souvenirs.

The celebration is repeated on New Year's Eve after the private parties at homes and hotels wind down and the streets begin to fill with late-night revelers. It lasts through New Year's Day. But you don't have to wait to the year's end to see Junkanoo. You can sample it at some nightclub and folkloric shows and other celebrations throughout the year.

Other Festivals and Events

Independence Week in early July celebrates the Bahamas independence. It culminates on

Independence Day, July 10, with fireworks at Clifford Park.

Emancipation Day, the first Mon in Aug, is a public holiday that commemorates the abolition of slavery in 1834. It is followed on Tues by Fox Hill Day. In the old days Fox Hill was isolated from Nassau; hence, the residents did not learn about the Emancipation until later. And so, symbolically, they celebrate on the second day.

Oct 12, Discovery Day, is a public holiday with special meaning in the Bahamas. It was on a Bahamian island, which the native Lucayan Indians called Guanahani, that Christopher Columbus landed in 1492. Columbus renamed the island San Salvador.

Another Oct highlight is the formal opening of the Supreme Court, when the chief justice, dressed in the traditional robe and wig, is escorted by the commissioner of police to inspect the Police Honor Guard while the famous Police Band strikes up. An equally colorful event with pomp and pageantry is the formal opening of Parliament, usually in Feb.

The Christmas festivities begin in mid-Dec with an annual candlelight procession staged by the Renaissance Singers. The group performs at the Government House ballroom and the Dundas Centre for the Performing Arts with a repertoire ranging from Renaissance classics to modern spirituals. For information on tickets, contact the **Ministry of Education, Division of Cultural Affairs** (242-322-8119).

Grand Bahama Island

www.grandbahama.bahamas.com

When American financier Wallace Groves began to turn his dream into reality in the 1950s, Grand Bahama Island, 60 miles from Florida, was little more than limestone, pine trees, and brush. From the money he earned lumbering the pine, he began developing the island. Today Freeport, as it came to be known, developed into the second largest town and largest industrial area in the Bahamas and a major international resort and port. In recent years the name Freeport has been consigned to the port/airport area only; the Bahamians prefer their island be called by its proper name, Grand Bahama Island.

Freeport spent the 1960s in the limelight, particularly after Cuba went by the board as an American playground, but by the 1970s it had lost much of its luster. The recession, worldwide economic problems, and competition from new resorts in Florida and elsewhere resulted in a setback for the island.

A renaissance began in 1984 with the multimillion-dollar renovation of hotels and casinos. This was followed the next year by the development of Port Lucaya, a shopping and entertainment complex, along with the Dolphin Experience attraction.

Grand Bahama got another boost when it became a popular cruise stop, especially for short cruises from Florida. These cruises bring more visitors to the island in a month than many islands see in a year. The island has an active People-to-People program similar to that in Nassau, as well as a large variety of restaurants, casinos, golf courses, and an international shopping bazaar.

In Brief

Location: Grand Bahama Island is about 96 miles from end to end. The cruise ship port, situated on the south coast at the mouth of Hawksbill Creek, is about 5 miles from the town of Freeport, where the International Bazaar is located. Another 5 miles east along Sunrise Highway takes you to the Lucaya residential and resort area and the Port Lucaya Marketplace, where major hotels front expansive white-sand beaches on the south shore and offer an array of water sports.

Transportation: Metered taxis are available at the port, downtown Freeport, and at hotels. Rates are zoned from the cruise port to the two resort areas: Cruise port to Freeport and the International Bazaar environs, $20 for two passengers; cruise port to Lucaya area, $27. An option is shared rides at $5 for a minimum of six passengers.

If you plan to engage a taxi for sightseeing, you should negotiate the price in advance. Also, be aware there are freelancers who are not legal taxis and who will charge whatever they think they can get. Look for taxis with a Bahama Host sticker on the windshield. They are reliable, and their drivers are the best informed.

Town buses or jitneys ($1) run during the day from town to Lucayan and ($4) West End. However, as a cruise passenger with limited time, you are better off hiring a taxi or renting a car if you want to visit either end of the island.

Car Rentals: To rent a car with a credit card, you must be twenty-one years or older; without the card, twenty-five or older. Americans may use U.S. driver's licenses for up to three months. Car rentals are available from several locations in town and at major hotels. When you have reserved a car in advance with Hertz or Avis, it will deliver your car free of charge to the port. Expect to pay $50 and up for a subcompact with unlimited mileage. Jeeps are available, too. **Avis,** (242) 352-7666; **Dollar Rent-A-Car,** (242) 352-9325; **Econo Car & Bike Rental,** (242) 351-6700; **Hertz,** (242) 352-9250; and **Thrifty,** (242) 352-9308.

And remember, Bahamians drive on the LEFT. You will need a map and a good sense of direction, because even new maps are not up-to-date. Do not hesitate to ask anyone for directions.

Information: The Tourist Information Centre has booths at Lucaya Cruise Facility (242) 352-9651, the airport (242) 352-2032, and the Port Lucaya Marketplace (242) 373-8988. Booth hours: 8:30 a.m. to 5 p.m. Mon through Sat. In the United States: Bahamas Tourist Office 800-BAHAMAS (800-224-2627).

Emergency Numbers: Medical Services: Rand Memorial Hospital; (242) 352-6735. Police: Freeport; 919. Ambulance: Freeport; (242) 352-2689.

Mopeds/Bicycles: Inquire at the Tourist Information Office for rental locations. A valid driver's license and a helmet supplied by the rental agency are compulsory. Prices are about $30 per day. To repeat, driving is on the LEFT.

Grand Bahama Nature Tours (242-373-2485; 866-440-4542; www.grandbahamanaturetours.com) offers a guided bicycle tour that covers 20 miles in about five hours. It's an easy-paced ride to see Taino Beach, the dolphins at Sanctuary Bay, and the old settlement of Smith Point. A native snack at a seaside restaurant, a dip in the sea, or relaxing in a beach hammock are also included for $79. **Calabash Eco-Adventures** (242-352-1455; www .calabashecoadventures.com) has a guided bike/ nature/snorkel tour to West End; from $89.

Shopping: The **International Bazaar,** housing dozens of boutiques with merchandise set the standard for other tourist destinations when it first opened in the 1960s. Other shopping centers in the Freeport area are Town Centre and Churchill Square.

Next to the International Bazaar, the **Perfume Factory** (www.theperfumefactory.com), which houses **Fragrance of the Bahamas,** is set in a replica of an old Bahamian mansion, where various scents for ladies and gents are made. Guides dressed in period costumes give visitors a tour and explain how the essences, made only from natural plants, are blended into perfumes and other products. There are six standard fragrances; you can also create your own, which will be officially registered in your name. Port Lucaya Marketplace, a waterside shopping, entertainment, and water sports complex in the heart of the Lucayan resort area, has more than forty stores, snack bars, and restaurants in attractive, colonial-style buildings. Count Basie Square, the entertainment center, features steel bands, reggae groups, and other entertainment.

Many of the best-known Nassau stores have outlets in Freeport and Lucaya. Generally, shops are open 9:30 a.m. to 5 p.m. weekdays. Most stay open at night on weekends. Oasis, which sells perfumes, toiletries, and jewelry, is open until 10:30 p.m. The Straw Market and pharmacies are open on Sun.

Beaches and Water Sports: Grand Bahama has some of the finest beaches in the Bahamas. Among the best with hotels and facilities are Xanadu Beach, not far from the port, and Lucayan Beach, 11 miles east of the port. The Lucayan National Park on the south coast is a drive of about thirty minutes from town. Grand Bahama Island also has terrific fishing, sailing, and windsurfing. All beachfront hotels have windsurfing equipment.

The island's facilities for scuba and snorkeling are not only the best in the Bahamas, but among the best in the world. It is home base for UNEXSO, the **Underwater Explorers Society** (Royal Palm Way, Freeport; 242-373-1244; 800-922-3483; www .unexso.com). Its facility, adjacent to Port Lucaya, offers eight levels of instruction and includes a 17-foot-deep diver training pool, outdoor bar and cafe, and pro shop. Introduction to diving begins with a lesson in the pool followed by exploring the shallow reefs with a scuba instructor ($109). One-tank dive, $59; two-tank dive with all gear, $99. Shark dives are available for $99. Wreck and night dives for experienced divers are also available.

The Dolphin Experience: UNEXSO, the firm that operates the Dolphin Experience, has a pod of Atlantic bottlenose dolphins that live in Sanctuary Bay, where they are the star attraction of the visitor programs.

Close Encounters is a two-hour, hands-on learning experience in which guests are briefed on dolphin behavior before touching the friendly creatures as they swim by. You sit on the edge of the enclosure with only your feet in the water. Participants are picked up at Port Lucaya and ferried to Sanctuary Bay. Cost is $75 adult; $50 ages four to twelve; under four free. Other programs include Swim with Dolphins ($169), interaction in the water at the lagoon pen. After hearing the dolphin trainer instructions, you get a brief encounter to know a little about the dolphin you will be swimming with and then you will swim with them for about 25 minutes. During this time a photographer will take your picture with the dolphins. The water depth is 15–20 feet; life jackets as well as fins are provided upon request.

Golf: The course nearest the port is the championship, PGA Ruby Golf Courses. Additional courses are those in the Lucayan area, about 11 miles from the port; normally, cruise ships offering golf packages use these courses.

The Reef Course, laid out by the Robert Trent Jones II Group, is links style, featuring water on thirteen of its 18 holes. Fees at both courses are $130; club rentals, $45 per set. The 9-hole course at **Fortune Hills Golf & Country Club** (242-373-4500) complements this luxurious country club community. Designed by Dick Wilson and Joe Lee, its challenging holes have the most expansive elevated greens in the Bahamas. Greens fees: $50–$64 for 18 holes; $35 for 9 holes, including cart. Club rental: $20. If your cruise lines does not have golf packages, call ahead for reservations. For cruise passengers who are planning to overnight here, some hotels have golf packages.

Horseback Riding: Pinetree Stables (Beachway Drive; 242-373-3600; www.pinetree-stables .com) offers two-hour guided trail rides at 9 a.m. and 11:30 a.m. daily. The trails wind through pine forests and rocky coppices and emerge onto the beach for an ocean splash. A two-hour tour costs $85 per person. The stable is located midway between Freeport and Port Lucaya. **Trikk Pony Adventures** (242-374-4449; www.trikkpony.com) has a morning beach ride daily except Sun and a sunset one on Sat, 10 a.m. and 12:30 p.m. The cost is $95.

Tennis: Tennis, too, is popular and readily available at hotel courts convenient to the port. Rates are reasonable.

Sightseeing

In contrast to its high-living, high-stakes image, Grand Bahama Island has several low-key attractions that tell its history and highlight its tropical variety.

Lucayan National Park: Located 25 miles west of Freeport near the former U.S. Army Missile Tracking Base, Lucayan National Park (242-352-5438; www.bnt.bs/parks_lucayan.php) is about a thirty-minute drive from downtown. The 40-acre park, opened in 1985, is situated on land donated to the National Trust by the Grand Bahama Development Company and is composed of four different ecological zones. The park, designed by Freeport planner Peter Barratt, has a 1,000-foot-wide beach with some of the highest dunes on the island. Gold Rock Creek, which is bounded by extensive mangroves, flows through the park to the sea. Among the flora are coca plums, sea grapes, sea oats, and casuarinas. Another area has Ming trees, wild tamarind, mahogany, and cedar trees.

The park is also the entrance to one of the world's longest charted cave systems, but access to the caves is restricted to scientists and archaeologists who have permission from the National Trust. Lucayan Indian relics have been found inside the caverns.

There are footpaths and raised wooden walkways over the mangroves to the beach and a map on display at the car park. Further information is available from the Rand Nature Center. The area is popular with bird-watchers, but the main reason to visit this area of the island is the lovely, untouched beaches.

Rand Memorial Nature Center: (P.O. Box F-42441, Freeport; 242-352-5438). Located 3 miles from the International Bazaar, the center, which is also the headquarters of the Bahamas National Trust, comprises 100 acres of tropical plants, trees, birds, and butterflies and is home to hundreds of species of plants and approximately ninety-six species of birds. A preserve for the native pine forests that once covered the island, it contains many species endangered by the island's continuing development.

An hour-long walking tour along winding trails provides an opportunity to see and photograph tropical flora, including many species of wild orchids and a great variety of birds. At the end of the trail, surrounded by numerous flowering exotic plants, is a pond that is home to a small group of flamingos. Hours: 9 a.m. to 4 p.m. Mon through Fri. Admission: $5 adult; $3 ages five to twelve. The park is a prime birding location, and naturalists are on hand. A guided tour Mon through Fri at 10 a.m. combines Bahamian history and culture, flora, and bird-watching.

The Heritage Trail: Before 1955 the main transportation artery on Grand Bahama Island was the Old Freetown Road, a dirt path leading from Old Freetown in the east to Eight Mile Rock and other settlements in the west. After the development of Freeport began and a modern highway was built, the old road was abandoned. Eventually, nature did such a good job of reclaiming it that a stretch of the road near Freetown has become a nature walk. Along the easy, 5-mile path, you can see more than thirty species of plants, eighteen types of bird, and seven butterfly species and the remains of the Hermitage, the oldest building intact on Grand Bahama, dating from 1901.

Adventure Tours: Several companies offer adventure and nature-oriented excursions. **Grand**

Bahama Nature Tours (242-373-2485; 866-440-4542; www.grandbahamanaturetours.com): offerings include a Lucayan National Park Kayak & Cave Tour, which involves ninety minutes of moderate paddling in shallow waters; a guided nature walk through the park's diverse ecosystems, including the caves; and a stop at Gold Rock Beach in the National Park for a light picnic lunch and a swim, $79. Biking, bird-watching, and snorkeling are also available. All tours include lunch and refreshments, equipment, and admission to parks and attractions visited. Children's discounts are available on some tours. **Calabash Eco-Adventures** (242-352-1455; www.calabash ecoadventures.com) offers a guided bike, nature, snorkeling, and kayak tours. Prices start at $89.

Boat Excursions: Snorkeling trips, picnic trips, and sunset party cruises are available from **Pat & Diane Fantasia Tours** (242-373-8681; www .snorkelingbahamas.com), $40 adults, $25 children; and **Reef Tours** (242-373-5880; www.bahamasvg .com/reeftours); all depart from Port Lucaya. The latter also claims to have the largest glass-bottomed boat on the island. It departs daily from the Port Lucaya marina at 9:30 and 11:15 a.m. and 1:15 and 3:15 p.m. on reef cruises; $30 adult; $18 child (under five free). **Exotic Adventures** (242-374-2278; www.exoticadventuresbahamas.com) and **H. Forbes Charter & Tours** (242-352-9311; www.forbescharter.com) operate fishing (half day, $95; full day, $139 per person). Also available are snorkeling, sunset, and glass-bottomed boat excursions. Forbes also offers city tours, $40; beach party with lunch, $50; and other excursions.

Dining and Restaurants in Freeport

Like Nassau, Grand Bahama has a great variety of restaurants, including inexpensive ones specializing in Bahamian dishes. **Port Lucaya Marketplace** (www.portlucayamarketplace.com) has more than 30 restaurants, snack bars, and other food outlets, while the International Bazaar and large resorts also provide many choices. **Mamadoo's** (Port Lucaya Marketplace; 242-373-8520) offers patio dining on Bahamian specialties such as cracked conch. **Stoned Crab** (Taino Beach; 242-373-1442; www.bahamasvg.com), which is popular in the Lucayan area, specializes in lobster and steaks.

Sabor's Restaurant (Pelican Bay Hotel, Port Lucaya; 242-373-9550) is on the more expensive side, but well worth it, and touted by locals as the best dining experience on the island. The elegant ambience at water's edge complements superb dishes, created by the Icelandic chef. Open for lunch and dinner daily except Mon.

Every Wed evening a native fish fry dinner is held at Smith's Point, a small beachside settlement. Visitors dine on fresh seafood and can meet local residents. It's not an advertised event, but local taxi drivers know about it.

Nightlife centers on the large hotels and casinos, but if you want to mix and mingle with Bahamians, Port Lucaya Marketplace has nightly entertainment on stage at the square, plus dancing—and it's free. Shenanigan's (242-373-4734), a lively Irish pub, is just behind the square. The Prop Room (on the beach behind the Treasure Bay Casino) offers big-screen sports, big drinks, singing waiters, and karaoke nightly.

A Drive Around Grand Bahama Island

To explore the less commercial side of Grand Bahama, a drive of 21 miles to West End will take you to the oldest settlements and some of the quieter corners of this surprising island.

If you are driving from the port or town, head west on Queens Highway to Eight Mile Rock, the largest Native settlement on the island, aptly named for the 8 miles or so of rocky shore on its south coast. The colorful village of brightly painted wooden houses was settled around 1830. The picturesque St. Stephens Anglican Church, built directly on the sea, dates from 1851.

Queens Highway continues to Seagrape, a tiny hamlet with a reputation for making the best bread in the Bahamas. As you near West End, you pass the saltwater Pelican Lake and Bootle Bay.

West End hugs the westernmost tip of Grand Bahama Island and is less than 60 speedboat miles from the Florida coast. It is the oldest settlement on the island and has had at least two fast but fleeting booms—during the American Civil War as a base for southerners running ammunition and supplies through the Yankee blockade to Confederate forces,

and during Prohibition, when the likes of Al Capone found it a convenient shipping point for liquor from Europe.

After 1933, West End went back to being a sleepy fishing village, attracting such occasional deep-sea fishermen as Ernest Hemingway. But over the last decade, West End has gotten the biggest makeover ever with a multimillion-dollar resort and residential community on 150 acres that is expected to grow to more than 2,000 acres. Called Old Bahama Bay, the privately-owned Ginn Sur Mer hotel-condominium complex has a deepwater marina, which is a port of entry. Pine Island, the residential community, has luxurious homes, each on an acre or more of land, and private docks for yachts up to 125 feet.

The road into West End takes you by tiny wooden stalls beside mounds of conch shells where you can stop to watch one of the local fishermen prepare the day's catch for tomorrow's market. There's an old church built in 1893 as well as the Star Hotel (242-346-6207), the island's first, built in 1946. The rickety wooden building, no longer a hotel, got a new lease on life when it was renovated by the grandchildren of the original builder. At present it houses a bar and a restaurant serving local food.

On your return trip, stop by Sunset Village in Jones Town at Eight Mile Rock. It was originally one of the small shacks along that stretch of coast, but has grown in all directions, and is the weekend hot spot for lobster and great seafood, music, and dancing—but if you linger too long, you are likely to miss your boat.

The Out Islands

The Other Bahamas—the hundreds of islands, islets, and cays that make up the Bahamas archipelago—are known as the Out Islands (meaning out beyond the main center of Nassau). They are the serene hideaways of our dreams, where endless miles of white- and pink-sand beaches are surrounded by gin-clear waters and where life is so laid-back, ten people make a crowd. Only about three dozen islands have permanent settlements.

No cruise lines offer year-round cruises, but several small ships occasionally call at one or two locations, and most ships on three- and four-night Bahama cruises from Florida stop for the day at one of the typical uninhabited islands. These are leased from the Bahamas government for an extended period of time and outfitted with the facilities and amenities to give their passengers a comfortable and fun-filled day at the beach.

The Abacos: At the northern end of the Bahamas archipelago, a group of islands and cays is strung in boomerang fashion for 130 miles, enveloping the Sea of Abaco, whose sheltered waters offer some of the Bahamas's best sailing. Two main islands, Little Abaco and Great Abaco, are joined by a causeway.

Walker's Cay, a well-known fishing resort, lies off the north tip of Little Abaco. Hole in the Wall, at the south end of Great Abaco, was a strategic location throughout the 18th century for guarding the shipping lanes to Nassau.

Marsh Harbour, the capital and main hub of the Abacos, is the third largest town of the Bahamas and one of the main boat-chartering centers of the Caribbean. It has a resident population of about 1,000 and an airport. Its small resorts are operated by Native islanders or American and Canadian transplants.

Of the Loyalists from New York who came in 1783 to join the English settlers living in the Abacos, some stayed at New Plymouth, a Cape Cod village in the tropics, on Green Turtle Cay. For many years it was the largest settlement and capital of the Abacos. In recent times the old fishing village has become something of an artist colony. Two native sons—Alton Roland Lowe, a historian and one of the Bahamas's leading landscape artists, and James Mastin, an outstanding sculptor—led the way.

The **Albert Lowe Museum** (242-367-4094; www.bahamas.com/vendor/albert-lowe-museum), created by Alton Lowe in honor of his father, who was a noted carver of ship models, is devoted to the history of the Abacos and to shipbuilding. Lowe's paintings, most of which depict local island subjects and settings, and Mastin's works are on view, and prints are available for sale.

A few steps from the museum on the same street is the Loyalist Memorial Sculpture Garden, Mastin's contribution to the island. Opened in 1983 for the bicentennial of the island's Loyalist settlements, the bronze statues represent the people who shaped the history of the Bahamas down through the centuries, from the first settlers to the present. Almost as famous as the artists is **Blue Bee Bar** (242-365-4181), whose walls and ceiling are covered with thousands of business cards from around the world. Miss Emily, as Emily Cooper, the former proprietress, was affectionately known, is credited with creating the Goombay Smash, a famous tropical drink served in bars throughout the Bahamas—although this churchgoing lady was a teetotaler. Now the bar and its traditions are carried on by her daughter. Less than an hour's drive west of Marsh Harbour through forested land is Treasure Cay, where the 1973 movie *The Day of the Dolphin* with George C. Scott was filmed. Legend has it that seventeen Spanish treasure galleons sank here in 1595. Some have been found; exploration for the others continues. The self-contained resort, Treasure Cay, on a 3½-mile, half-moon beach, is best known for its golf course.

Andros: A thirty-minute flight west of Nassau will bring you to Andros, the largest island of the Bahamas and one of the least developed. The interior of the island is covered with pine forests interspersed with mangroves; other parts are mudflats or barren. Off the east coast of Andros lies the Barrier Reef, more than 100 miles long, the third largest in the world. Just beyond is the Tongue of the Ocean, a depression that plunges as deep as 6,000 feet at the north end. These natural phenomena attract divers and sportfishers from around the world. Andros also calls itself the bonefishing capital of the world. Among the resorts, **Small Hope Bay Lodge** (242-368-2015, 800-223-6961; www.smallhope.com) at Fresh Creek was the first organized diving resort in the Bahamas.

Berry Islands: The group of about thirty islands with a total land area of only 14 square miles is located between New Providence (Nassau) and Grand Bahama Island (Freeport). Most are uninhabited, and several are popular stops for cruise ships whose passengers spend the day on "their" island, enjoying the beaches and swimming and snorkeling in clear water. Their lovely little harbors, coves, and protected waters make them popular with the yachting crowd.

The Biminis: South of Freeport where the Bahamas Banks meet the Gulf Stream are the Biminis, the Bahamian islands only 50 miles from Florida. Ernest Hemingway was a frequent caller, and Adam Clayton Powell, the flamboyant Harlem minister and member of Congress, made Bimini his second home. Long before either of them, however, Ponce de León stopped here in his search for the Fountain of Youth. No less than four places commemorate his landing.

The group is divided into the North Biminis and South Biminis. They, along with Cat Cay, are among the prime gamefishing centers in the Western Hemisphere. Because of their proximity to the Gulf Stream, Bimini waters teem with sea life. Vestiges of old ships in Bahamian waters number in the hundreds. Among the most famous is the *Sapona,* which lies between South Bimini and Cat Cay. Built by Henry Ford around 1915, the ship served as a private club and is said to have been a rumrunner's storehouse in the 1920s until it was blown ashore by a hurricane in 1929. The main settlement is Alicetown on North Bimini. You can walk or bike around most of the island in an hour or so. Although the island takes on something of a rowdy party atmosphere in the evening (the fishing crowd at one of its favorite bars), during the day it is a sleepy little place, pleasant for picnicking and lazing on the beach.

Cat Island: East of the Exumas lies Cat Island (not to be confused with Cat Cay). It is covered with forested, rolling hills that soar to the great height of 204 feet—the highest natural point in the Bahamas. Once prosperous with sugar plantations of the Loyalists who had fled the American Revolution, Cat Island is largely untouched today and is best known as the childhood home of actor Sidney Poitier. Its four tiny hotels and wide white beaches are made for ardent escapists.

Eleuthera: First-time visitors to the Other Bahamas often select Eleuthera because of its combination of faraway tranquility, the pretty setting of pastel-painted houses surrounded by gentle green hills, and its 300 years of history. It also has comfortable, unpretentious hotels, good dining and sports facilities, and more roads and transportation than the other islands. The island is famous for its pink-sand beaches.

Situated 60 miles east of Nassau, Eleuthera is a 110-mile skinny spine never more than 2 miles wide, except for splays at both ends. It has six official ports of call and three airports, with direct flights from Nassau, Freeport, Fort Lauderdale, and Miami.

Eleuthera has three of the Bahamas's oldest and prettiest settlements: Governor's Harbour, the main town near the center of the island and the hub of commercial activity, more than 300 years old; Dunmore Town on Harbour Island; and Spanish Wells off the northern end, is a popular fishing and yachting center.

Harbour Island, almost touching the northeastern tip of Eleuthera, is one of the most beautiful spots in the Bahamas and the site of Dunmore Town, its original capital and now a tranquil village of neat old houses and flower-filled lanes. A high green ridge dotted with pink and white colonial homes separates the 17th-century village from a 3-mile beach of pink, powdery sand, whose color comes from the coral. The island has about a dozen small hotels.

Princess Cay: The "private island" used by Princess Cruises for most of its Caribbean itineraries is a recreational facility spread along a lovely beach at the southern tip of Eleuthera. Here Princess has developed excellent facilities for a day at the beach for its passengers, offering a wide range of water sports, beach games, guided nature walks, several bars, a boutique, small markets for local Bahamian crafts, and local entertainment. Lunch is served at a large pavilion to all passengers who choose to spend the day at the beach. Continuous tender service is provided by the line between the ship and the beach.

The Exumas: From 35 miles south of Nassau, the Exumas stretch southeast over an area of 130 square miles. The group is particularly popular with the yachting set, for whom the variety of color and subtle shades of the waters around the Exumas have no equal. Snorkelers and divers sing their praises, too. The **Exuma Land and Sea Park**

(242-359-1821) is a preserve accessible only by boat.

George Town, the capital, is a quiet village of 800 people and several small hotels. Across the bay is Stocking Island, whose lovely stretches of white-sand beach are rich with seashells. About a dozen resorts are dotted through the Exuma chain, as are hundreds of beaches and coves. This sea lover's mecca becomes busiest in Apr, when the islands host the annual Out Islands Regatta, the Bahamas's most prestigious sailing race. The luxury Sandals Resort Great Exuma has the Exumas' first championship golf course.

Inagua: The Bahamas's third largest island is one of the least visited. Flamingos outnumber people 50 to 1. The 287-square-mile Inagua Park is the largest flamingo preserve in the Western Hemisphere. Union Creek National Park is a reserve for giant green turtles.

San Salvador: Situated east-southeast of Nassau and directly east of Cat Island, San Salvador is the island "where it all began," so to speak. The island had been neglected until 1992, when it received a great deal of attention during the Quincentennial celebrations as the site of Columbus's first landfall in the New World. The island has four monuments commemorating this event. (The landing site has been disputed as much as the landing!)

The New World Museum is in a renovated building that was originally constructed in the early 19th century and served until 1966 as a courthouse, a jail, and the commissioner's office. The building was restored by the Kiwanis Club of San Salvador with help from other service clubs and private groups. The exhibits are arranged in four groups: Columbus, 1492; the Lucayans, A.D. 600–1492; San Salvador, 1492–1838; and San Salvador in the late 19th and 20th centuries. The Lucayan exhibit has a map that shows the forty-eight known Indian archaeological sites on San Salvador.

Transportation Serving the Out Islands

Airlines: Bahamasair (800-222-4262; www.bahamasair.com) serves all the airport centers of the Out Islands from Nassau.

Ferries: Bahamas Fast Ferry (242-323-2166; www.bahamasferries.com) offers interisland service among Nassau, Harbour Island, and North Eleuthera. The Bahamas Class Catamaran travels at about 40 knots, making the trip between Nassau and Harbour Island in about an hour and forty minutes.

Two scheduled daily round trips operate between Nassau and Harbour Island and North Eleuthera, and twice weekly between Nassau and Governor's Harbour. The air-conditioned ferry accommodates 177 passengers. Round-trip transportation costs $184 per person. A one-day excursion, including a historical/cultural tour of Harbour Island and lunch, visits the island's pink-sand beach.

Turks & Caicos Islands

Turks & Caicos Islands

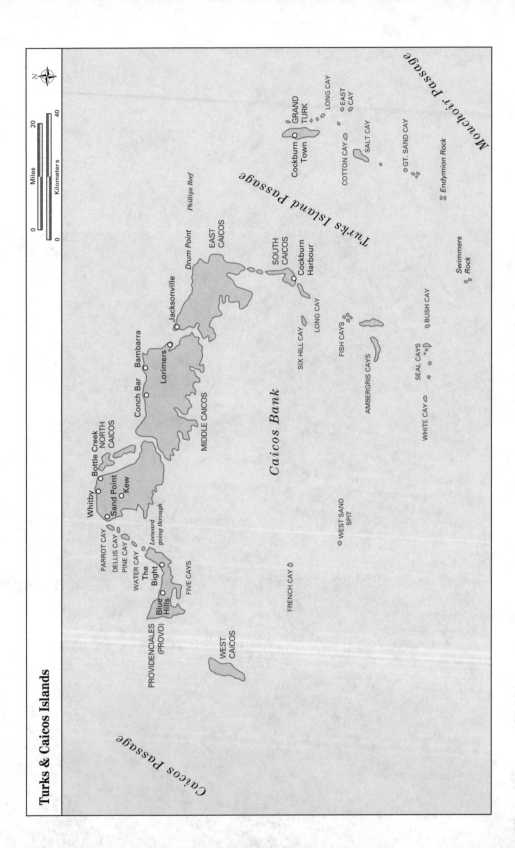

Fast Facts

Population: Grand Turk, 7,000

Location: 575 miles southeast of Miami, Florida

Climate: Average temperature 85–90 degrees, June to Oct; 80–84 degrees, Nov to May. Constant tradewinds help keep climate comfortable. Normally, 350 days of sunshine.

Language: English

Currency: U.S. dollar is the official currency.

Telephone Area Code: 649

Time: EST; Daylight Saving Time, Mar to Nov

Information: www.turksandcaicos tourism.com

In the United States:

Turks & Caicos Islands Tourist Board, HC1 Box B8, Swiftwater, PA 18370; 800-241-0824, fax: 646-375-8830; Mrs. Pamela Ewing, manager; pewing@tcigny.com

In Grand Turk:

Grand Turk Tourist Office, Front Street, Grand Turk, Turks & Caicos Islands, British West Indies; P.O. Box 128; 649-946-2321, fax: 649-946-2733; info@turksandcaicos tourism.com

The Last Frontier

Located at the end of the Bahamas chain directly north of Hispaniola, the Turks & Caicos (pronounced KAY-kos), are often called the Caribbean's Last Frontier. A British Crown Colony made up of eight islands and several dozen cays, the islands stretch across 90 miles in two groups separated by the Turks Island Passage, a deep-water channel of 22 miles surrounded by magnificent seas with some of the most spectacular marine life in the world.

To the west are the Caicos Islands—South, East, Middle, North—which form an arch on the northern side of Caicos Bank. Provo, as Providenciales is known, is the commercial center and the location of most of the resort and commercial development. Provo has a marina for yachts, but it is not a port of call for cruise ships.

To the east is the Turks group with Grand Turk, the capital which has been the seat of government since 1766; a dozen of tiny cays, most protected sanctuaries for nesting birds and marine life; and neighboring Salt Cay, a historic settlement with windmills and salt ponds, declared a Heritage Site under UNESCO's World Heritage program. Grand Turk's most historic claim to fame is the much disputed one as having been the island on which Christopher Columbus made landfall (rather than San Salvador in the Bahamas) on his discovery of the New World in 1492.

Surrounded by virgin reefs, most uncharted, the Turks & Caicos are known as a diver's heaven, while the Turks Island Passage, a thoroughfare for migratory humpback whales and giant manta rays in spring and autumn and home to large fish year-round makes them a sportsman's dream. The islands with a surprising variety of flora, endless miles of untouched white sand beaches, acres of tropical wilderness and wetlands—some protected in national parks and bird sanctuaries—are a nature lover's paradise, too.

Grand Turk

www.grandturkcc.com

Note: In Sept 2008, Grand Turk was hit by Hurricane Ike, a category 5 storm which damaged or destroyed 80 percent of the homes and businesses on the island. Fortunately, most of the island has been restored and new construction can be seen throughout, but there is still work to be done and some places normally on sightseeing excursions had not reopened at press time.

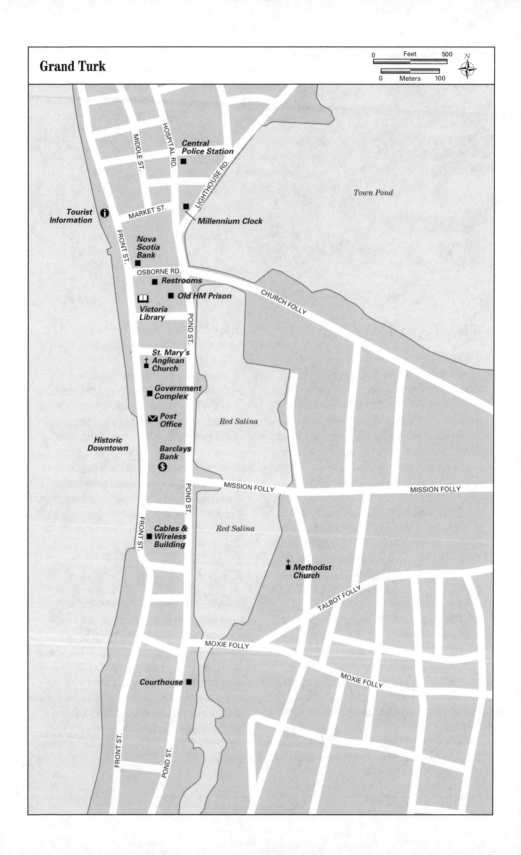

Profile

Grand Turk is a long, skinny island, 7 miles long and 2 miles wide, along the Turks Island Passage. Until 2006, when the $60 million Grand Turk Cruise Center opened, it was little known to travelers, except perhaps scuba divers. Built and financed mostly by Carnival Cruise Lines, the world-class, beach front cruise facility sits on the southwestern leeward coast on 37 acres of which 14 landscaped acres encompass the Cruise Center, approximately 3 miles south of historic Cockburn Town, Grand Turk's main settlement.

Cockburn Town: Founded three centuries ago by Bermudian salt rakers, Cockburn Town (pronounced "Coburn") is a sleepy, quaint Caribbean hamlet at the edge of white sand beaches and easily explored on foot. The interesting walk will take you along Duke and Front streets where 18th- and 19th-century landmarks of Bermudian/British colonial architecture reflect the island's history as a center of the salt industry. Most of these structures were built by the wealthy Bermudian who dominated the salt trade. Most have been converted into the inns, restaurants, a public library, and government offices, amid colorful, Caribbean-style houses, small gift and craft shops, and some laid-back bars.

The **Oddfellows Lodge/Eunice Lodge** (Front and Market Streets) probably dates from about 1796. According to local lore, the proclamation abolishing slavery was read here in 1834. South of Oddfellows on Victoria Street is Her Majesty's Prison, which mostly held runaway slaves. The structure was restored by Carnival Corporation, which added a cafe, gift shop, and medicinal garden. Take note of the old street lamps and don't be surprised to see donkeys and horses, used for transporting salt in olden days, grazing nearby.

Turks & Caicos National Museum: Housed in Guinep House, one of the island's oldest stone buildings, the museum covers the islands' history from the arrival of the Lucaya Indians in 700 A.D. to modern times, including the arrival of John Glenn who splashed down here after his historic Mercury Space mission in 1962. Another exhibit tells the story of the Molasses Reef Wreck with recovered artifacts on display. Dating from around 1513, it is said to be the oldest European shipwreck yet discovered in the Western Hemisphere. The museum also has a natural history gallery with exhibits on the island's geology and ecology as well as manuscripts, prints, and other items relating to the Turks & Caicos Islands history. Admission fee: $5 per person. The museum has a nice gift shop with books, crafts, postcards, posters, and a verandah overlooking the sea. Stamp collectors will also want to visit the Grand Turk Philatelic Bureau in the Franklin Missick Building. (There's a Philatelic Bureau now at the cruise center.)

In the middle of Grand Turk, a salt pond known as the Town Salina has an island at its center which contains the ruins of a hospital station built in the early-mid 1800s. Here ship passengers or residents who showed signs of a contagious disease—cholera, typhoid fever, etc. were consigned. Apparently many did not recover judging from the many graves left behind.

Grand Turk Lighthouse: On the northern tip of the island stands a lighthouse that was brought from Britain in 1852. As the story goes, the lighthouse was erected at the insistence of the U.S. government, which grew tired of islanders waving lanterns near the rocky eastern shores to lure ships to their watery end so they could plunder their cargo. The cast-iron lighthouse structure was recently sandblasted and restored by Carnival and the former residence of the lighthouse keeper made into an outdoor pavilion picnic area. The lighthouse's old lens is on display in the Turks & Caicos National Museum.

The site, now protected by the National Trust, is a popular viewing spot for the whales in Feb and Mar. Two short nature trails, cleared by Carnival, lead east and west from the lighthouse. From the eastern overlook, you can see cliff faces eroded by the strong wind and washed by the turquoise sea. On the west coast is the site of the former U.S. Air Force tracking station, closed in 1984. The lighthouse hill overlooks North Creek, an inland body of water that some historians maintain fits Columbus' description for the island that he first encountered on his voyage in 1492. Today, North Creek is known in yachting circles as the only hurricane shelter between Nassau and Puerto Rico.

At Coralie Gardens, private land at the edge of North Creek, a considerable amount of archeological research has been done by Earthwatch under the aegis of the Turks & Caicos National Museum and Florida Museum of Natural History, Gainesville. Here, a Lucayan canoe paddle, on display in the Turks & Caicos National Museum, was found. The shallow water area here borders a pre-Columbian site, dating about A.D. 700 and said to be the oldest known Indian site in the Bahamian archipelago.

Both the extreme northern and southern ends of the North Creek have extensive wetlands and are significant nursery habitat for the marine life outside the mouth of North Creek, supplying juvenile fish and lobsters in large numbers. Birds, especially wading birds, are many, and the southern end is often visited by flamingos.

The Columbus Landfall Marine National Park: Before cruise passengers discovered Grand Turk, its main attraction was diving and a major part of the island's income came from dive-orientated tourism. Part of what makes Grand Turk grand is that only a few hundred yards from shore the shallow continental shelf plunges 7,000 feet. The coral reefs on the sea wall and the abundant, healthy marine life in these pristine waters have made it one of the top diving destinations in the world. Fortunately, Grand Turk has had the foresight to protect its waters. The Columbus Park covers an area of 1,280 acres of sea from the high water mark to the 330 feet depth from the mouth of North Creek and along the western shores with an extensive barrier reef averaging a quarter-mile from shore and including the beach and seashore bordering Cockburn Town. Certain beach areas are bird and turtle nesting habitat. Since the early 1980s, Grand Turk has had a mooring buoy system in place.

Several other national parks and sanctuaries cover the western and southern shores and offshore islets and their surrounding 400 feet of sea. All are nurseries for fish, conch, and lobster, and nesting sites for migrant birds, especially Sooty and Noddy terns (Gibbs, Pear Cay), Brown boobies (Pinzon Cay), and Frigatebirds (Penniston Cay). Gibbs Cay also has a Lucayan site and a small, colonial era emplacement, thought to be a French-built gun or observation post dating from the late 1700s.

South Creek National Park, a 183-acre tidal salt water estuary, contains the largest stand of Red Mangroves in the Turks Bank; the mangroves and surrounding grass flats are nurseries for lobster, conch, and reef fish. The lagoon is a bonefish and tarpon habitat. On the southeast, undeveloped Long Cay and nearby islets comprise a 198-acre sanctuary for iguana and nesting migrant birds. A permit is required to visit. Further south, Big Sand Cay Sanctuary has a large iguana population and abundant Turks Head cactus (often cited as the source of the Turks & Caicos Islands' name.) It is also a breeding ground of Nurse sharks. A permit is required to visit.

Salt Cay: South of Grand Turk, Salt Cay is the best known and historical most significant of the cays neighboring Grand Turk. A place where time has passed by, it was once the center of the salt industry and the basis of the Turks & Caicos economy for more than 300 years. Declared a World Heritage Site by UNESCO, it is almost like a moment frozen in time with a landscape of windmills that no longer turn and slowly evaporating salt ponds. Balfour Town, the only settlement, has 200 people and is a treasure trove of architecturally significant structures, including the White House, owned by descendants of Bermudan salt rakers and containing the original antique furniture; Brown House, Dean's Dock, St. John's Anglican Church, dwellings, rock walls, canals, and other structures connected with the salt industry. Whale House Bay was the headquarters of a short-lived whaling industry in the late 1800s, when Humpback whales were caught in the Turks Island Passage during their winter migration.

Grand Turk Cruise Center

The Cruise Center has been an almost overnight success and expects to welcome over half-million cruise passengers per year. In addition to its 800-feet-long beach, the facility boasts an array of stores and duty-free shops in its large shopping complex as well as sports facilities, including a large, lagoon-shaped swimming pool, a variety of tours and sporting excursions, car rental services, restaurants, and entertainment, and more are being added frequently.

Designed as a colorful village, the Welcome Center buildings were inspired by the local architecture, even down to chimneys on the main buildings—after all, the temperature is in the high 80s year-round. But apparently, the transplanted Bermudians considered chimneys essential to recreate the look of their former homes. The Welcome Center has restrooms, locker rooms, lounge chairs in the pool and beach areas, and free umbrellas (by the pool only); clam shells for lounge chairs can be rented for US$20. Passengers can swim in the ocean and relax on the beach or by the pool and rent floats and snorkeling equipment from the Beach Rental Hut. For those who want a little pampering, Spa Anani offers beach side massages.

There are also some poolside cabanas for rent for the day through your ship's shore excursion desk for US$99. The cabanas, complete with an outdoor shower and private waiter service, have ceiling fans, but no air conditioning and accommodate up to four people.

The shopping options range from a dozen or so high-end jewelers and well-known tropical apparel merchants such as Piranha Joe's to specialty outlets like Starfish Oils and locally crafted souvenirs, gifts, T-shirt shops, and The Trading Post at Jimmy Buffett's Margaritaville—Buffett's largest bar, restaurant, and retail shop in the Caribbean. Among other food and beverage outlets are Rasta Pasta and Bonefish Charlie's.

Added in 2010, adjacent to Margaritaville and the swimming pool, is a Flowrider, the first, and until now, the only one of its kind in a cruise center. The surfing facility operates by using a pair of high pressure water jets that produce a thin, two-to three-inch layer of water moving over a pre-formed and cushioned surface at high speed. Tickets for this shore excursion can been purchased onboard your cruise ship. You can use a body board (US$24 for half-hour) or if you are an experienced surfer, you can try the more challenging stand-up ride (US$34 for one hour).

Conch World: Created by Cockburn Village & Farm, Ltd. in partnership with Carnival Cruise Lines, Conch World is a new attraction, four years in the making. The million-dollar-plus attraction has several brightly colored, air-conditioned buildings that showcase the Queen conch, which is native to Grand Turk and which plays a vital role in the health of coral reefs as a food source for lobsters, turtles, and other marine animals. A guided tour begins with a video, followed by a review of displays, pictures, and dioramas regarding conch farming. There's a cafe and gift shop. The farm is also developing a commercial conch farm.

Guana Island Bus Loop: A specially-designed Hop On/Hop Off bus, operated by Island Routes, a Jamaica-based tour company, runs in a continuous loop around the island, stopping approximately every 15 minutes. The bus takes about one hour to complete the loop and operates continuously throughout the day. Passengers can hop on and off the bus as often as they like at any of the scheduled stops and spend as much time as they like at each venue. They are given a wristband for identification. The bus fare of US$20 provides admission to several of Grand Turk's main attractions. Tickets must be purchased onboard your ship; some of the money is donated to the island's rebuilding fund.

Shore Excursions

Cruise passengers have more than two dozen excursions to enjoy, provided by seven different tour operators—some local, others such as Jamaica-based Chukka Caribbean and Island Routes operating throughout the Caribbean. They include horseback riding with an ocean swim, a bike and hike combination ending with a short hike to Matterson Beach for a swim, 4x4 vehicle adventures, horse-drawn carriage tours, dune buggy tours, and visits to Grand Turk's outer islands.

Among the water-based options are Sea Trekkin', an underwater walking tour; Semi Sub, a narrated tour of the coral reefs and colorful marine life aboard a semi submersible craft; Snuba, an apparatus that's something between snorkeling and scuba; an excursion to Gibbs Cay to snorkel with stingrays; kayaking on a guided tour through the gentle, shallow waters of South Creek, learning about the plant and animal life along the way. Or, you can do your sightseeing aboard a luxury yacht with a rum punch in hand.

Deep sea and flats fishing can be arranged. In July, Grand Turk hosts the annual Grand Turk Heineken Game Fishing Tournament, a fun-filled event for locals and visitors alike. Serious scuba divers should make arrangements directly with one of the dive operators in Cockburn Town in advance. Blue Water Divers (649-946-2432; www.grandturk scuba.com), located by the beach, just south of the Turks & Caicos National Museum, has been running diving, snorkeling, and cay trips since 1983. Prices per person for a single tank dive US$50; two tanks, US$85; snorkel trip (includes mask/fins) US$40–$45. It also offers a resort course US$150 (includes one dive and gear).

For those who prefer to be on their own, Grand Turk Inn (Front Street, 649-946-2827; www.grandturkinn.com) about 3 miles from the port or a US$6 per person taxi fare offers the Day Pass for the cruise ship passengers for US$40 per person plus 11% government tax. It faces a small white sand beach where use of snorkel, fins, beach mat, noodle float chair, and a beach umbrella is included along with lunch of coleslaw, potato salad, club sandwiches, and a desert, served in its breezeway. It's a very relaxed, casual atmosphere, and owner Katrina Birt from Australia, adds in little history of the islands for their guests.

Key West

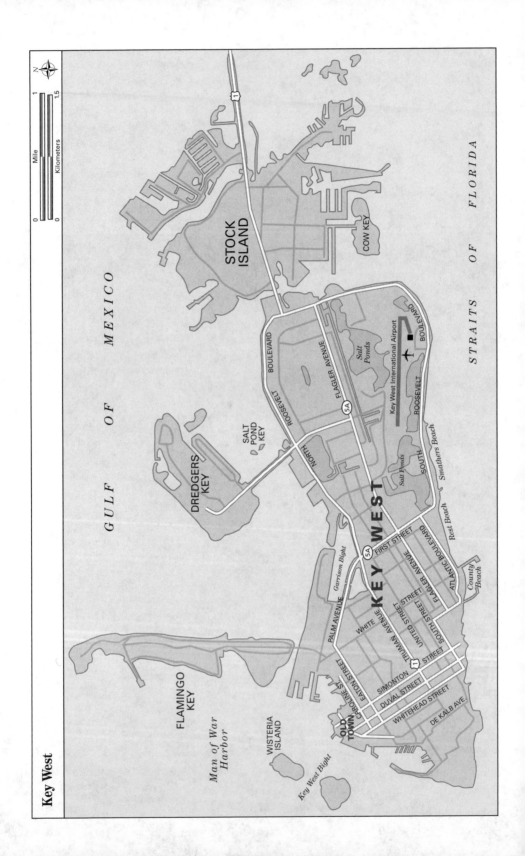

Key West

America's First Caribbean Island

Key West is a state of mind as much as a place. Earthy and stylish at the same time, America's southernmost town is one of the most delightful places in the world—one of a kind and infectious. Decades of writers, artists, and loads of eccentrics have made it that way—none more famous than author Ernest Hemingway, playwright Tennessee Williams, and nature artist John James Audubon. The first gave it his lust for living; the second, his flair for eccentricity; and the third, a cause for preservation. Combined, they set the stage for the theater that is Key West.

In recent years Key West has become one of cruising's most popular ports of call, visited by more than two dozen cruise ships at last count. And why not? It's one of the country's most interesting and charming towns—easy, convenient, and ideal for a day's visit. Cruise ships dock almost at the heart of Old Town, the oldest and most interesting part of Key West and within walking distance of major attractions, shops, and restaurants.

In the 1920s and 1930s, before Key West became a popular vacation destination, it barely qualified as a stopover on the way to Havana. Passengers in New York would board a train called the Havana Special and, on arrival in Key West, transfer from the train to their ship without leaving the pier for the overnight voyage to Cuba.

Key West began its transformation from a small, historic southern town to a major international resort in the 1950s and 1960s, attracting artists, writers, and people from the fashion world. But even with the changes, it kept its traditional resident communities: Cuban Americans (from the time of the Spanish-American War), blacks (who came even earlier as freemen, runaway slaves, and shipwreck survivors), and Conchs, longtime residents whose forebears came as traders, merchant sailors, wreckers, and fishers. (No one can say how many generations of living on the island it takes to be considered a Conch.) In any case, the mix of artists and shrimpers, rednecks and blacks, yuppies and blue collars, gays and straights, writers, hippies, expatriates, and escapists from all over has given Key West an unusual combination of style and luxury and working-class simplicity (at least, until recently). Key Westers think of themselves as far removed from the Upper 48—and they are.

Key West has a long history of rags to riches. It was discovered by early Spanish explorers who, it is said, found piles of human bones on the island and called it Cayo Hueso (Island of Bones). History has not learned to whom these bones belonged, but the assumption is they were an Indian tribe, the Caloosa or Seminoles, who roamed the Keys.

Throughout the 17th and 18th centuries, Key West—indeed, all the Keys—was the lair of pirates who preyed on Spanish galleons laden with gold, silver, and gems from Mexico and South America that had to pass through these waters to return to Spain.

In 1822 the island was sold by a Spaniard to John Simonton, an American businessman, for $2,000, and the American flag was raised in the vicinity of Mallory Square the same year. Over the next fifty years the population quadrupled to almost 3,000 and was made up of New England merchant seamen and white Bahamian traders, most of whom were engaged in the wrecking business—the very profitable enterprise of salvaging goods from ships that hit the reefs fronting the Keys. It was not uncommon for wreckers to cause such mishaps purposely by posting false signal lights for approaching ships during storms.

The construction of a lighthouse in the 1850s put a big dent in their business, and Key West had to wait for its next boom—first from sponging, then cigar making. Both were attributed to the influx of Cubans in the last quarter of the century. Once again the town flourished and was said to have been the richest town per capita in the country. But by the 1930s Key West was down on its luck to such an extent that 80 percent of the town's 12,000 people relied on public assistance.

World War II and the U.S. Navy brought life back to Key West, but it was abandoned again after the war. President Truman visited in 1946 and continued to return frequently. Hemingway had been living there since 1931, and Tennessee Williams came frequently in the 1940s, encouraging his literary friends to join him. By the late 1950s and for the next decade, investment filtered in, but it was not until the 1980s—when Key West

Population: About 50,000 permanent residents; the population doubles or triples with tourists, particularly in winter.

Climate: Balmy weather almost year-round. Temperatures average 75°F in Jan and 82°F in summer. Short tropical rains come often in fall and spring.

Clothing: Tropical-casual. Seldom do men wear ties. A sweater or jacket is needed in the shade in winter and almost any time for air-conditioning.

Currency: US dollar. Traveler's checks and credit cards are widely accepted.

Customs Regulations: Cruise passengers are admitted without formalities (you're still in the United States), but it is wise to carry a passport, or some official identification.

Electricity: 110 volts AC, 60 cycles

Language: English with a twang

Postal Service: The post office is located on Whitehead and Fleming Streets.

Public Holidays: All U.S. holidays, plus a few special local ones.

Telephone Area Code: 305

Airlines: American/American Eagle, Cape Air, Comair/Delta, Gulfstream, and US Airways Express have

frequent flights daily from Miami International.

Information: www.fla-keys.com

Key West Chamber of Commerce, 402 Wall St./Mallory Square, Key West, FL 33040; 305-294-2587; (800) 527-8539. Hours: 8:30 a.m. to 5 p.m. Mon through Fri, 9 a.m. to 5 p.m. Sat and Sun. The office has maps, brochures, and information on self-guided walking tours.

Old Island Restoration Foundation, Hospitality House, Mallory Square, Box 689, Key West, FL 33041; 305-294-9501. Key West Attractions Association, www.keywestattractions.org.

---

became fashionable and restoration of Old Town, which had started in the 1970s, was well under

At a Glance

Antiquities . . . . ★
Art and Artists . . . . ★★★★
Beaches . . . . ★
Crafts . . . . ★★★
Cuisine . . . . ★★★
Dining/Restaurants . . . . ★★★
Entertainment . . . . ★★★
History . . . . ★★★★
Museums . . . . ★★★★
Nature . . . . ★★★★
Nightlife . . . . ★★★★
Scenery . . . . ★★
Shopping . . . . ★★★
Sightseeing . . . . ★★★★
Sports . . . . ★★★★
Transportation . . . . ★★★

way—that real estate prices skyrocketed and the boom was on again.

Key West is small and easy to find your way around in, and it has something for everyone—historic sites enhanced by their colorful past, unusual architecture, and the famous writers and artists who lived and worked here; funky as well as smart shops, restaurants, bars, and entertainment; sports, including snorkeling and diving on the only coral reef offshore the continental United States; and, of course, the famous Key West sunsets, not to mention Key lime pie and margaritas.

Key West is both an island and a city, with a population of fewer than 50,000 residents that is swollen by more than a million tourists annually. Closer to Cuba than to Miami, Key West, with its graceful palms and masses of bougainvillea, its tropical climate, and easy-living ambience, seems as Caribbean as any of the islands bathed by that sea.

Key West will probably remind you of New Orleans in more ways than one. Conch, like the term Creole in New Orleans, refers to people, food, and a style of architecture. As you will quickly learn, the Conchs are proud of their name. In 1882 they even declared Key West the Conch Republic and seceded from the Union—but that's another story.

Local lore says the name conch (pronounced konk) comes from the 17th century, when the Eleuthran Adventurers, a group from Bermuda that had established a colony in the Bahamas, fled to Key West after the British tried to tax them, declaring they would "eat conchs" before paying taxes to the Crown. As enduring as the conch, some might muse, has been the legacy of piracy—reflected not only in real estate prices but also in the town's anything-goes attitude, relishing the unexpected and keeping rules only to break them.

Budget Planning

Key West is as expensive as you want to make it. Fortunately, your feet can get you around town to almost all the main attractions. There are bikes and mopeds for rent and public buses, as well as car rentals. If you are on a tight budget, you should plan your sightseeing because the museums, historic homes, and other attractions charge admission—$5 to $15 for adults and half that amount for children. There are restaurants in every price range, and souvenirs from $5 T-shirts to $5,000 paintings.

Port Profile: Key West

Location/Embarkation: The port in Key West is located in the northwest corner of the island. Downtown, known as Old Town, stretches directly behind the dock to the south and east. Duval Street, the main thoroughfare of Old Key West, runs for about a mile from the dock to Southernmost Point, and in a bit of hyperbole is called the longest street in the world because it runs from the Gulf of Mexico to the Atlantic Ocean. Some cruise ships anchor at piers fronting Old Town, but megaliners dock at a facility on the west side of town, from where passengers are transported to Mallory Square by the Conch Train. It's hard to get lost: The center of town is only about 10 blocks square, laid out in a grid and easy to follow with maps available at the Key West Chamber of Commerce on Wall Street by Mallory Square. Key West has the feel of a tropical port with the added

advantage of good transportation, communications, and technical facilities not always available in the Caribbean.

Local Transportation: Taxis are readily available, but you do not need them unless you have trouble walking. In that case, you might want to use public buses or take one of the town tours offered by the Conch Train or Old Town Trolley (see details under Shore Excursions). All major car rental companies are represented here. Because of the heavy demand during the peak winter season, you would be wise to make reservations from home through a rental company's 800 number before departing on your cruise.

Bikes and Scooters: Bikes and scooters are the best way to get around Key West. The island is only a mile wide, 7 miles long, and entirely flat. Rentals are available from the **Bike Shop** (1110 Truman Ave. at Varela Street; 305-294-1073) as well as **The Moped Hospital** (601 Truman Ave., at Simonton Street; 866-296-1625; www.moped hospital.com) where all bikes are custom-made, specially geared with high handlebars, comfortable seats, and safety yellow baskets, and bikes with baby seats and adult tricycles. All $12. Scooters rent for $35 for the day; those for two persons (carrying capacity of 550 pounds) are $55 per day. **Pirate Scooters** (401 Southard/Whitehead St.; 305-295-0000; 877-PIRATE-6; www.piratescooter rentals.com) offers shorter rentals for cruise ship passengers; call for price. **Paradise Scooters & Bikes** (430 Duval, at Whitehead Street; 305-292-6441; www.paradisescooterrentals.com) offers bikes at $8 for two hours; $10 for four hours from 9 a.m. to 4:30 p.m.; single scooter costs $35 for three

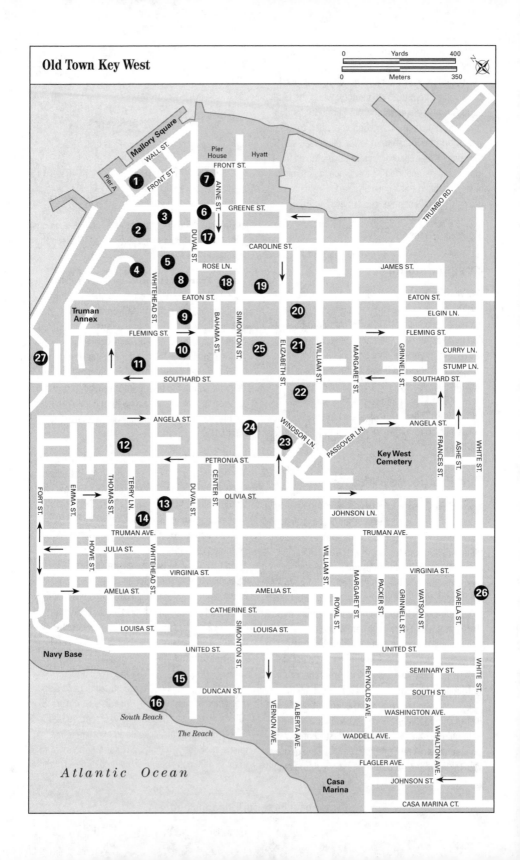

Old Town Key West

0	Yards 400
0	Meters 350

Mallory Square

WALL ST.

Pier A

FRONT ST.

Pier House   Hyatt

FRONT ST.

TRUMBO RD.

ANNE ST.

GREENE ST.

DUVAL ST.

CAROLINE ST.

JAMES ST.

ROSE LN.

WHITEHEAD ST.

EATON ST.

EATON ST.

ELGIN LN.

Truman Annex

BAHAMA ST.

SIMONTON ST.

FLEMING ST.

FLEMING ST.

CURRY LN.

STUMP LN.

ELIZABETH ST.

WILLIAM ST.

MARGARET ST.

GRINNELL ST.

SOUTHARD ST.

SOUTHARD ST.

ANGELA ST.

WINDSOR LN.

PASSOVER LN.

ANGELA ST.

FRANCES ST.

ASHE ST.

WHITE ST.

Key West Cemetery

PETRONIA ST.

CENTER ST.

DUVAL ST.

OLIVIA ST.

FORT ST.

EMMA ST.

THOMAS ST.

TERRY LN.

JOHNSON LN.

TRUMAN AVE.

TRUMAN AVE.

HOWE ST.

JULIA ST.

WHITEHEAD ST.

VIRGINIA ST.

WILLIAM ST.

VIRGINIA ST.

AMELIA ST.

ROYAL ST.

MARGARET ST.

PACKER ST.

GRINNELL ST.

WATSON ST.

AMELIA ST.

VARELA ST.

CATHERINE ST.

SIMONTON ST.

LOUISA ST.

LOUISA ST.

UNITED ST.

UNITED ST.

WHITE ST.

Navy Base

SEMINARY ST.

DUNCAN ST.

REYNOLDS AVE.

SOUTH ST.

South Beach

VERNON AVE.

ALBERTA AVE.

WASHINGTON AVE.

The Reach

WHALTON AVE.

WADDELL AVE.

FLAGLER AVE.

Casa Marina

JOHNSON ST.

Atlantic Ocean

CASA MARINA CT.

1. Mallory Square/Wall and Front Streets
    Key West Aquarium
    Waterfront Playhouse
    Hospitality House/Old Island Restoration
    Foundation
    Chamber of Commerce
    Key West Shipwreck Historeum
    Key West Art Center
    Clinton Square Market/Naval Coal Depot
    Key West Museum of Art and History
    (Custom House)
2. Mel Fisher's Maritime Heritage Museum
3. Audubon House and Tropical Gardens
4. Little White House
    Kelly's Caribbean/PanAm
5. Heritage House
6. Sloppy Joe's
7. Pirate Soul Museum
8. Wrecker's Museum/Oldest House
9. La Concha
10. Fast Buck Freddie's

    Jimmy Buffett's Margaritaville
    San Carlos Opera House
    Ripley's Believe It or Not Odditorium
11. Monroe County Courthouse/Post Office
12. Blue Heaven/Bahama Village
13. Hemingway Home and Museum
14. Key West Lighthouse and Military Museum
15. Key West Butterfly & Nature Conservatory
16. Southernmost Point
    Harris House/Southernmost House
17. Curry Mansion Inn
18. Casa Antigua
19. Donkey Milk House
20. Octagon House
21. Monroe County Public Library
22. Gingerbread House
23. Windsor Compound
24. Burton House
25. Secret Garden
26. Tennessee Williams Theatre
27. Fort Zachary Taylor

hours or less, and two-person model $48. **Barracuda Scooter Rentals** (1800 North Roosevelt Blvd.; 305-296-8007; www.coolkeywest.com) offers bikes for $12, scooters for $45 single, $75 double. Barracuda also has kayaks for half-day ($30) and full-day ($45) rentals, and offers three-hour kayak tours daily at 9:30 a.m. and 2 p.m.

Shore Excursions

Conch Tour Train (Mallory Square/Front Street; 305-294-5161; www.conchtourtrain.com) $29 adult; $14 ages four through twelve; 10 percent discount for Internet tickets; tour ticket usually includes discount coupons. A leisurely hour-and-a-half orientation to Key West with commentary by the driver-guide on dozens of sites en route. The train is made up of three or four open-sided cars pulled by a truck disguised as a caboose. Some driver-guides are better than others. You can take the tour on your own; tours depart from the Conch Train's depot about every thirty minutes. Hours: 9 a.m. to 4:30 p.m., daily year-round.

Old Town Trolley (Mallory Square/Wall Street; 305-296-6688; www.trolleytours.com) $29 adult; $14 ages four through twelve. Trolley cars similar to those in San Francisco (except that they are motorized) have the same owners as the Conch Train and offer a similar tour—but with one important advantage. Passengers may get on and off the trolley at any of the ten stops along the route, making it a more useful vehicle for those who want to explore a particular area of the town. You can easily take the trolley on your own; tours depart about every thirty minutes 9 a.m. to 4:30 p.m.

Conch Train/Trolley, Aquarium/Historeum: 2.5 hours; $35 adult; $23 child. Trolley or train tour is followed by Key West Aquarium for a self-guided tour of about forty-five minutes and the Shipwreck Historeum (described later in this chapter). Aquarium and Historeum, both by Mallory Square, can be visited on your own.

Island City Strolls with Sharon Wells (305-294-0566; www.seekeywest.com) are offered several times per week, each with a different focus, for a four-person minimum. Sharon Wells, a historian, photographer, and expert on Key West, writes and publishes *Walking & Biking Guide to Historic Key West,* a periodical with fourteen illustrated, self-guided tours, $9 on Web site.

Key West Nature Bike Tour (Lloyd Mager, 305-294-1882; www.lloydstropicalbiketour.com).

Mager leads a two-hour bike trip with a lesson in Key West history, architecture, and flora, daily except Mon, departing at 9:45 a.m. from Moped Hospital (601 Truman Ave.); call 305-294-1073 for a recorded message announcing the next tour. Cost: $37 per adult, $26 children, plus bike rental.

Pelican Path (Old Island Restoration Foundation, Hospitality House, Mallory Square; 305-294-9501). A carefully laid out, self-guided route leads past many of Key West's landmarks and famous old houses in Old Town. A folder with a route map and brief descriptions of the houses, prepared by the Foundation, is available from its office. The foundation offers guided house and garden tours during winter for about $10 per person.

Walking Tours: Inquire with Denison Temple, 305-296-1866; fax: 305-296-0922. Temple, a Key West resident, offers walking or biking tours with a focus on Key West history, architecture, or its literary highlights by appointment. Charges: $15 to $20 per hour. Tours usually about one and a half hours. Another walking tour of historic Key West departs daily at 10 a.m. from Key West Shipwreck Historeum where information and tickets are available.

Catamaran Sailing and Snorkeling: Three hours; $49 adult; $24 child. A 65-foot catamaran sails to the continental United States' only living coral reef, about 7 miles southeast of Key West. Snorkeling equipment, flotation devices, and instruction are included. B boat has changing facilities and freshwater showers. Complimentary soft drinks, beer, and wine served. Children age eleven and under cannot participate in the snorkeling.

Coral Reef Glassbottom Boat: Discovery, operated by **Discovery Undersea Tours** (251 Margaret St., Key West; 305-293-0099; 800-262-0099; www.discoveryunderseatours.com), a catamaran with a specially fitted underwater viewing room, is wheelchair accessible. Daily departures: 10:30 a.m. and 1:30 p.m. Cost: $40 adult; $16 child (5 to 11) for a two-hour excursion. Similar excursions available from **Fury Water Adventures** (400 Wall St., 305-292-7260; www.furykeywest.com).

Key West Scuba: Three hours; $66 and up. For certified divers, PADI five-star instructors offer a full range of services for diving on one of two sites: the Sambos, a collection of three shallow reefs 15 to 40 feet deep, 1.5 to 2.5 miles apart and richly populated with reef fish; or an artificial reef formed by the 187-foot Cayman Salvager, sunk in 1985. Equipment is included. (See the Sports section later in this chapter.)

Back Country Kayaking: Two and a half hours; $49. Great experience for beginners or experienced kayakers. After receiving instructions on paddling, you tour a cluster of mangroves with a guide and learn about flora, fauna, and folklore.

Seaplanes of Key West (Key West Airport; 305-294-0709; 800-950-2359; www.seaplanesofkeywest.com). Seaplanes fly to the Dry Tortugas and Fort Jefferson National Park, 70 miles into the Gulf of Mexico, where you can spot marine life, shipwrecks, and Mel Fisher's treasure site and enjoy swimming, snorkeling (free gear), bird-watching, and sightseeing.

Key West on Your Own

Mallory Square and Vicinity

Mallory Square (1), on the island's northwest corner at the foot of Duval Street, a short walk from the pier, was the heart of Key West in the old days, and it's the center of activity for visitors today. The old buildings beside the square once quartered the trades (read: wrecking) that made Key West rich; now they house shops, restaurants, bars, and museums. You will need some imagination to picture the setting in seafaring days, as the square itself has been reduced to a small area by the sea where sunset devotees come to watch the nightly show. The rest is a parking lot.

On the east side of the square in a building dating from 1850 is the **Waterfront Playhouse** (305-294-5015; www.waterfrontplayhouse.org), home of the Key West Players. On the west is **Hospitality House,** the headquarters of the Old Island Restoration Foundation, in a Conch house dating from the late 19th century. And behind it on Wall Street is the **Chamber of Commerce,** in a former warehouse. Wall, Front, Whitehead, Greene, and Duval Streets—with many of Old Town's main attractions—parallel or lead off the square. Most sightseeing excursions start from here.

Key West Aquarium (1): (1 Whitehead St.; 305-296-2051; www.keywestaquarium.com). Exhibits of Atlantic marine life are a hit with kids, especially watching sharks and turtles being fed by hand. Admission: $12 adult; $5 ages four to twelve; slightly less online; free for kids under four. Hours: 9 a.m. to 6 p.m. daily. Frequent guided tours between 11 a.m. and 4:30 p.m.

Key West Shipwreck Historeum (1): (Wall and Front Streets; 305-292-8990; www.shipwreck historeum.com) offers an excellent presentation of the Keys' famous—and infamous—wrecking era with artifacts from the *Isaac Allerton,* said to have carried the richest manifest of any ship of its day when it went down in 1865. Key West's colorful history is brought to life by actors and exhibits that help viewers understand the times that revolved around shipping and the town that built its fortune rescuing shipwrecks survivors and salvaging their cargoes. The building has a 65-foot observation tower, similar to those used in olden days to spot ships and now offering visitors a great view. Admission: $12 adult; $5 ages four through twelve. Hours: 9:40 a.m. to 5 p.m. daily. Presentations every twenty minutes; the last full presentation at 4:40 p.m. If you only have time for one historic museum, this is the one to select.

On the corner at Front Street, the **Key West Art Center** (301 Front St.; 305-294-1241; www.key westartcenter.com) is a nonprofit artist cooperative, housed in a late-19th-century wooden structure that was used in the 1930s under the New Deal for the WPA Arts Project headquarters.

Next to the Aquarium, the **Clinton Square Market** was formerly a naval storehouse dating from 1861 and is now the town's oldest brick building, housing attractive specialty shops.

Key West Museum of Art and History (1): (281 Front St.; 305-295-6616; www.kwahs.com). Next to the market is the massive U.S. Customs House, dating from 1891, said to be the only structure in Florida in Romanesque Revival style. Used for various government agencies over the century, it was put on the National Register of Historic Places in 1973 and renovated by the Key West Art and Historical Society as a museum. Opened in 1999 as the main repository for the island's art and history, this architectural gem houses permanent

collections and stages touring exhibitions. Admission: $10 adult; $9 senior; $5 student; kids under six free. Hours: 9 a.m. to 5 p.m. daily.

Front Street, as the name implies, fronted the harbor in olden days and was the main commercial street, with banks, trading offices, bars, and flophouses for merchant seamen. Apparently one of the most raucous, the **Havana-Madrid,** was a tavern and striptease joint; its namesake today is a seafood specialty restaurant at 410 Wall St.

Mel Fisher's Maritime Heritage Museum (2): (200 Greene St.; 305-294-2633; www.melfisher .org; info@melfisher.org). A visit to this museum, with the discoveries by America's most noted shipwreck sleuth, Key West's own Mel Fisher, can turn anyone into a hopeful treasure hunter. In 1985, after many tries, Fisher found *Nuestra Senora de Atocha,* a 17th-century Spanish galleon that went down in 1622 only 45 miles west of Key West, with an estimated $400 million in gold and silver. On display is a copy of the ship's manifest, heavy gold crosses and chains, emeralds, coins, weapons, and other artifacts recovered from the sunken treasure. Admission: $11 adult; $6 ages six to twelve; free for kids five or younger. Hours: 8:30 a.m. to 5 p.m. The museum is ADA-compliant and air-conditioned.

Key West Cigar Factory (306 Front St., 3 Pirates Alley; www.keywestcigarfactory.com) is the last of a once major industry in Key West, brought here by Cubans in the late 19th century. In a setting of old equipment and furnishings that has not changed in a century, two people demonstrate the old method of hand rolling cigars. There are several other cigar stores in town; most now have their factories in the Dominican Republic.

Audubon House and Tropical Gardens (3): (205 Whitehead at Greene St.; 305-294-2116; 877-281-2473; www.audubonhouse.com). Built in 1830 for Capt. John H. Geiger, a skilled harbor pilot and master wrecker, the house is typical of Key West architecture of the period and is surrounded by lush gardens. When nature artist John James Audubon visited Key West in 1832 to hunt and sketch local birds, tradition has it that he stayed at Geiger's home, although there is apparently no historical record to substantiate the claim.

Nonetheless, more than a century later Key West native son and prominent Miami businessman

Mitchell Wolfson acquired the Key West landmark, restored it, and dedicated it as a public museum. The restoration is credited with sparking a preservation trend in the mid-1970s, led by a pair of Old Town merchants who teamed up to renovate fifteen buildings along the 600 block of Duval Street. Today the downtown restoration is nearly complete, with the renovated buildings and homes housing smart boutiques, art galleries, restaurants, and pubs.

Audubon House, run by the Florida Audubon Society, has been elegantly furnished with antiques of the period. The original furnishings probably came from the salvaged cargo of wrecked ships, as was customary at the time. Some of Audubon's most famous engravings, such as the roseate spoonbill, hang on the walls, and in the garden is the Geiger tree used as a background by Audubon for his engraving of the white-crowned pigeon, which he named the Key West pigeon; it was one of eighteen species new to Audubon. A fine collection of porcelain birds by Dorothy Doughty is also on display. The museum offers a videotape presentation of Audubon's *Birds of Florida*. The entrance is through the museum's store, where you can buy Audubon posters and books. Admission: $11 adult; $6.50 student; $5 ages six to twelve; free for kids five or younger. Hours: 9:30 a.m. to 5 p.m. daily. Tours are self-guided; the last tour is at 4:30 p.m.

Little White House (4): (111 Front St.; 305-294-9911; www.trumanlittlewhitehouse.com). After his first visit in Nov 1946, Harry Truman became enamored of Key West and returned frequently, making the estate his presidential vacation retreat. The house, built by the U.S. Navy in 1890 for a naval commandant, is now a museum with Truman memorabilia. Admission: $15 adult, $13 senior, $5 ages twelve and younger. Hours: 9 a.m. to 4:30 p.m. daily. Guided tour about every fifteen minutes.

The 44-acre Truman Annex extending south along Whitehead Street was part of the former U.S. Naval Base, bought some years ago by private developers who created a luxury residential and resort community, and a Hilton Hotel, with retail shops, restaurants, a deepwater marina, a beach club, and condos. The hotel faces Sunset Island (formerly known as Tank Island), with beach facilities and frequent ferry service.

Florida Keys Eco-Discovery Center (305-292-0311; http://floridakeys.noaa.gov/eco_discovery.html), located on the waterfront at the end of Southard Street at Truman Annex, is one of Key West's newest attractions. Incorporating 6,400 square feet of interactive exhibits, the center showcases the underwater and upland habitats that characterize the Keys, emphasizing North America's only living contiguous barrier coral reef, which parallels the Keys. Through interactive and touch-screen modules, text and audio-video components, visitors can explore the region's mangrove, patch reef, seagrass, Dry Tortugas environments, and more. There's a walk-through version of the Aquarius Undersea Lab, the world's only operational underwater laboratory, located off Key Largo. The center is a cooperative effort of the National Oceanic and Atmospheric Administration's Florida Keys National Marine Sanctuary, the National Park Service, U.S. Fish and Wildlife Service, and South Florida Water Management District. Admission: free. Hours: 9 a.m. to 4 p.m. Tues through Sat.

USS *Mohawk* Coast Guard Cutter Memorial Museum (305-799-1143; www.ussmohawk.org), another new museum on the Truman Waterfront, set in the USS *Mohawk*, believed to be the only remaining Coast Guard submarine chaser in existence. Built in 1934, the 165-foot-long historic ship was assigned North Atlantic escort operations in World War II. Regarded as the memorial ship of the Battle of the Atlantic, the vessel launched fourteen attacks against Nazi submarines and rescued hundreds of people at sea. Visitors can view the original radio room, bridge, galley, officers' staterooms, crew quarters, and weapons, as well as the sonar room where crew members listened for German submarines during the war. Admission: $5 per person ($1 for veterans with identification). Hours: 10 a.m. to 5 p.m. Tues through Sun.

On the corner across from the Little White House gates is **Kelly's Caribbean Bar & Grill** (303 Whitehead St.; 305-293-9405; www.kellyskeywest.com), a garden restaurant in the former building of Aero-Marine Airways, which provided mail service between Key West and Havana in the 1920s. The building once occupied the site where Pier House is today, and it became the headquarters of Pan American World Airways after the airline launched its service to Havana in 1928, ushering in the era of international passenger air travel. Kelly's belongs to actress Kelly McGillis of *Top Gun* and *Witness* fame.

Heritage House Museum and Robert Frost Cottage (5): (410 Caroline St.; 305-296-3573; www .heritagehousemuseum.org). Built about 1834—but it's not clear by whom—the house was owned by George Carey, a liquor merchant who expanded it in 1844 for his bride, adding the front rooms and porch. The house remained in the family for almost a century and was bought in 1934 by Jessie Porter Newton, one of the driving forces behind Key West's preservation efforts. She renovated the house and added a garden and swimming pool in place of the cookhouse and cistern, and another room (called the Chinese porch) decorated with Asian art and antiques. Later, she built a second house for herself at the rear of the property, and turned the old house into a museum brimming with furniture and collectibles from the four corners of the world.

Miss Jessie, as the guides refer to her, was a longtime friend of Robert Frost, who visited Key West frequently in the 1940s, finally taking up semi residence in the small, tin-roofed cottage at the rear of Miss Jessie's house, where he spent fourteen winters. Hours: 10 a.m. to 4 p.m. Mon through Sat. Admission: $6 self-guided tour. Guided tours of Heritage House are available, $9, but the Frost cottage is not included as it is often used for literary meetings and seminars. A Robert Frost poetry reading and seminar is held in Mar. The gardens are often used for weddings.

On the corner of Caroline and Duval stands one of the town's largest houses, built in the last century for Dr. J. Y. Porter, Florida's first public health officer, credited with significant research on yellow fever. The building now houses several art galleries.

Duval Street

Key West's famous Duval Street, named for the first governor of the Florida territory, is the main drag of Old Town, awash with bars, shops, art galleries, and old houses with a slice of history at every address. The street from the north end at

Mallory Square to the south end at the Southern-most House has been invaded by T-shirt and knick-knack shops, but happily there are plenty of other stores with attractive art, objets d'art, restaurants and sidewalk cafes, and clothing boutiques to make it interesting and easy to combine a shopping expedition with a stroll through history.

Sloppy Joe's (6) (201 Duval St.; www.sloppy joes.com) was one of Hemingway's favorite haunts and is still a mecca for Hemingway fans. Owner Joe Russell, a Key West boatman, was immortalized by Hemingway as "Freddie" in *To Have and Have Not*. In 1937, when the rent on Russell's Greene Street location (the original site) was to be raised, Joe moved his bar to Duval Street in the middle of the night. Note the painting on the south wall by the bar; it shows a young Hemingway with a typewriter and Sloppy Joe wearing the crown of grapes and sitting at a table surrounded by friends—a rough bunch known as "The Mob." The painting was done by an artist in the WPA Arts Project.

When Hemingway left Key West to live in Cuba, he stored some of his belongings in a back room here. In 1962, after his death, Mary, Hemingway's last wife, discovered among those belongings the original manuscript of *A Farewell to Arms* and *To Have and Have Not,* and even some uncashed royalty checks.

The bar is full and noisy from morning to night, and no tourist to Key West would think a visit complete without a stop here. The adjoining T-shirt shop probably does as much business as the watering hole.

Pirate Soul Museum (7): (524 Front St.; 305-292-1113; www.piratesoul.com). Those fascinated with pirates can take a 1-block detour from Sloppy Joe's to one of Key West's newest museums. The collection includes authentic pirate artifacts along with interactive technology for a historic adventure through the "Golden Age of Piracy" and learn about the infamous pirates of the period. Admission: $13 adult; $8 child, plus tax. Hours: 9 a.m. to 7 p.m. daily.

Wrecker's Museum/Oldest House (8): (322 Duval St.; 305-294-9502; http://oirf.org). Built about 1829, it claims to be the oldest house in Key West and was the home of Capt. Francis B. Watlington, a merchant seaman and wrecker. Key West's piracy and wrecking days are described in pictures, old documents, and ship models; the furnishings reflect the family life of a sea captain of the time. The kitchen in the back is separate from the house, as was characteristic in those days. The building is now operated by the Old Island Restoration Foundation as a nonprofit museum. Among its original furnishings, is an unusual miniature 1850–style dollhouse fashioned after the "Conch"–style houses of Key West and furnished in colonial and mid-Victorian styles. There is also an interactive map showing the locations of shipwrecks along the Keys. Admission: $5 adult; $1 child. Hours: 10 a.m. to 4 p.m. daily.

La Concha (9): (430 Duval St.; 305-296-2991; 800-745-2191; www.laconchakeywest.com). It's a Crown Plaza unlike any other in the chain. Opened in 1926 at a time when Key West—then a major port and link for tourists en route to Havana—needed a first-class hotel, La Concha quickly became the social center of the town. The seven-story building was—and still is—the tallest building in Key West, with fabulous newer features such as rooms adjoined by baths, hot and cold running water in all rooms, an elevator, telephone booths, a haberdashery, a bakery, and a bank.

Now listed on the National Register of Historic Places, the hotel has seen a great deal of history. Here in 1927, Juan Trippe, founding president of Pan American World Airways, formally announced the start of passenger service between Key West and Havana, launching international air travel. Hemingway, a guest and frequent patron of La Concha's Duval Street bar, included the hotel in his *To Have and Have Not*. And Williams wrote much of *A Streetcar Named Desire* while he was staying here in 1947.

The hotel's fortunes and misfortunes paralleled those of the town, and during the 1930s both fell on hard times. By the time Atlanta architect Richard Rauh was brought in to rescue it, the hotel had been badly vandalized and was boarded up. In 1986, after a multimillion-dollar renovation, the hotel reopened and quickly took its place once again as the belle of Duval.

Fast Buck Freddie's (10) (500 Duval St.; 305-294-2007; www.fastbuckfreddies.com) is Key West's answer to Bloomingdale's. Those who are old enough to remember will immediately recognize the exterior as a former Kress Five & Dime store, built in 1913, but inside, it is a chic emporium. The building is shared with Jimmy Buffett's Margaritaville, the store and restaurant of Key West's most famous citizen (after Hemingway), who got his start here. And he does show up here from time to time.

There's a second store, **Half-Buck Freddie's** (306 William St., 305-294-2007), a discount outlet.

San Carlos Opera House (10): (516 Duval St.). Restored in 1990, the building is the third on the site and has served the Cuban community since 1871, when the first structure was dedicated. It is used as a center for music, plays, and other cultural activities.

Ripley's Believe It or Not Odditorium (10): (108 Duval St.; 305-293-9939; www.ripleyskeywest .com). The fun-house museum, based on the works and collection of Robert Ripley. Admission: $16 adult; $13 ages four through eleven. Hours: 10 a.m. to 11 p.m. daily. Across the street is the renovated Strand Theater, a former movie house with a fanciful facade built in the 1930s as one of the WPA projects to employ local artists and workers; it now houses a Walgreens, a 24-hour pharmacy, 305-292-9833).

If you continue south on Duval Street, the walk from Southard Street to the ocean becomes an art and shopping excursion more than a sightseeing one, as many of the best art galleries and boutiques are in these blocks.

*Alternatively, you could turn west on Southard and continue 1 block to Whitehead, where you will find the post office to your right and the **Monroe County Courthouse (11)** at Jackson Square to your left. The Green Parrot Bar, a watering hole popular with locals, has held down the corner of Whitehead and Southard since 1890. Straight ahead, Southard Street continues to **Fort Zachary Taylor (27)**.*

Blue Heaven (12): (Thomas and Petronia Streets; http://blueheavenkw.homestead.com/ blue_heaven_restaurant_key_west.html). If it's lunchtime, you may want to detour another block south to Key West's most written-about restaurant/

art gallery in the heart of Bahama Village, the town's oldest black neighborhood.

Bahama Village historically was made up mostly of Bahamians and Cubans of African origin and has had various names—La Africana in the 1880s, Jungle Town in the 1950s and 1960s, and now Bahama Village. Indeed, a ceremonial arch with the Bahamian coat of arms mounted over Petronia Street at Duval proclaims it thus. The area is something of a hodgepodge architecturally and culturally, with tiny houses, narrow lanes, churches, funky art galleries, and men sitting under shade trees playing dominoes—a picture you're likely to see in any barrio south of Miami. Although some restoration has been done, enough of the neighborhood's character remains to get the feel of Key West in another era.

Blue Heaven, which dates from 1884, has had quite a past—as a pool hall, ice-cream parlor, dance hall, bordello, and artists' studios. Hemingway used to referee boxing matches in an outdoor arena under the Spanish lime tree, and young black boxers such as "Iron Baby" Roberts and "Battlin' Geech" Kermit Forbes sparred with him on Friday. Apparently cockfights were frequent, too, as there's a "Rooster Graveyard" with tombstones intact in the northeast corner.

At the back of the outdoor restaurant, set under enormous shade trees and showers of bougainvillea, stands a water tower dating from about 1920; it was moved here from Little Torch Key, where it had been used for the men building the Flagler Railroad that once brought mainlanders to Key West on the Havana Special.

Oh, yes, the food. It's as eclectic as the setting, and quite good, and you can't beat the price. Several handsome roosters strut about underfoot, stopping from time to time to crow. But it's the fresh flowers on the tables in this chicken patch that's the pièce de résistance.

Hemingway Home and Museum (13): (907 Whitehead St.; 305-294-1136; www.hemingway home.com). The large house suggesting Spanish colonial design is set back from the street in lush tropical gardens. Built by a Connecticut merchant in 1851, it is now a National Historic Landmark and museum and one of Key West's most unusual structures. Constructed of native rock hewn from the grounds, the house has features unusual for Key West, such as arched windows with shutters and a second-floor wraparound veranda with an iron balustrade that would seem to fit better in New Orleans than Key West.

Hemingway bought the house in 1931 and added a swimming pool, the first in Key West. He lived here for two decades, during which he wrote many of his greatest works, including *For Whom the Bell Tolls, Death in the Afternoon, Snows of Kilimanjaro, To Have and Have Not,* and many short stories. It was his most productive period, when he was idolized and imitated by writers the world over. The house was sold shortly before his death in 1961.

The gardens are beautiful, but the house is disappointing—sparsely furnished, with almost none of the furnishings having belonged to Hemingway except a collection of his childhood books in a glass case on the second floor and some family photographs. There are numerous cats, which tour guides say are descendants of Hemingway's cats, but that's questionable. Admission: $11 adult; $6 ages six through twelve. Hours: 9 a.m. to 5 p.m. daily. Guided tours start about every half hour.

Sloppy Joe's, Hemingway's favorite bar, originally located on Greene Street (see earlier description) is still there but is known as **Captain Tony's Saloon** (428 Greene St.; 305-294-1838). Although Tony Tarracino, the former owner and mayor of Key West, no longer owns the colorful bar, which claims to be the oldest in town, it has changed little since Hemingway's day. The ceiling is covered with thousands of calling cards and almost as many bras, and a motley crew of loyal patrons occupy the bar stools, talking and vaguely listening to the entertainer plucking a guitar.

Key West Lighthouse (14): (938 Whitehead St.; 305-295-6616; www.kwahs.com/lighthouse .htm). Across the street from the Hemingway House, a 110-foot lighthouse, built in 1847, marked the water's edge in those days. It is still the best location for a panoramic view of Key West, with the Atlantic Ocean on the east and the Gulf of Mexico on the west. There are eighty-eight steps to the balcony and another ten steps to the light station.

The **Lighthouse Military Museum,** in a small building on the south side of the compound, has interesting exhibits of old military uniforms, ship models, and other seafaring paraphernalia. Admission: $10 adult; $9 senior; $5 student and child (under age six free). Hours: 9:30 a.m. to 4:15 p.m. daily.

Key West Butterfly & Nature Conservatory (15): (1316 Duval St.; 305-296-2988; 800-839-4647; www.keywestbutterfly.com). Walk through gardens filled with butterflies and colorful birds, flowers, and waterfalls. The facility has a learning center, gift shop, and gallery where original art work is available. Admission: $12 adult; $9 senior; $8.50 ages four through twelve; three and under free. Hours: 9 a.m. to 5 p.m. daily.

Truman Avenue, which you will cross when you continue south, is the southern terminus of US 1.

Southernmost Point (16), a red, black, and yellow marker at the end of Whitehead Street, is a Key West landmark, establishing the spot as the most southerly in the continental United States. It also indicates that Cuba is 90 miles away. In the past a more portable sign—irresistible to souvenir hounds—was here until the townsfolk got fed up with having to replace it. They could hardly have thought up an uglier monument than the present one, yet no one passes here without stopping to take a picture. As you will discover, all the surrounding streets have places claiming to be the "southernmost" hotel, motel, guesthouse, cafe, laundry, church, or whatever. Harris House, the large home occupying most of the block at South and Duval Streets, claims to be the Southernmost House. Built for a judge around 1905, it was a fashionable restaurant frequented by Tennessee Williams and his friends in the 1950s. It is now a private residence.

Caroline Street and Beyond

For literary, theater, and architecture buffs, the streets east of Duval from Caroline to Angela have some of the finest houses in Key West. Most are private residences, but some have been converted to inns and stores, and many are the homes and haunts of famous writers, playwrights, and celebrities who have lived in Key West all or part of the year.

Curry Mansion Inn (17): (511 Caroline St.; 305-294-5349; 800-253-3466; www.currymansion

.com). The elaborate Victorian house was built by Milton Curry, Florida's first millionaire, who made his fortune as a wrecker. The rear of the house is part of the original structure built in 1855; the front part was added in 1899 when Curry married. The mansion was restored by the present owners, beginning in 1974, and includes the kitchen where the first Key lime pie is said to have been baked. The guest wing, added in 1989, houses the bed-and-breakfast inn, with fifteen rooms, each with private bath.

Among the many interesting features to note is the 1853 Chickering grand piano in the music room, which belonged to Henry James and came from his home in Newport. A glass case in the library has Hemingway's favorite big-game gun, a Westley Richards .577, with which he was often photographed. In the dining room, the gold-colored tableware is meant to suggest the original solid gold Tiffany service for twenty-four that Curry had made. Some pieces are on display at the Audubon House. Daily tours: $5. Hours: 10 a.m. to 5 p.m. daily.

Casa Antigua (18) (312 Simonton St. at the corner of Rose Lane) was Hemingway's first Key West pad and the place where he wrote most of *A Farewell to Arms*. Papa and his wife Pauline came to Key West in 1928 by ferry from Cuba after a voyage from France, having heard about the island from writer John Dos Passos, who joined them later. Key West's freewheeling atmosphere in 1929 is described by Dos Passos in his autobiography, *The Best of Times*. Casa Antigua was once an inn; now the large building is a private residence separated by a fabulous tropical garden and swimming pool from the owners' craft store, **Pelican Poop** (314 Simonton St., 305-296-3887; www.pelican poop.com), at the front. The gardens may be visited, but not the house.

Donkey Milk House (19): (613 Eaton St.; 305-296-1866). Built in the 1860s and occupied by the same family for more than 120 years, the house was saved from the Great Fire of 1886 by a U.S. marshal who dynamited the nearby structures along Eaton Street. It is a good example of the architectural style known as Classical Revival in Key West and won an award in 1992 for its restoration.

There's a century-old Cuban rainwater vessel out front, now filled with plants; inside, the floors have Spanish tiles and hand-decorated ceilings dating from 1890. The owners live in the ten-room house filled with fine period furniture and open it to the public as a house museum. There is a small antiques shop on the first floor. Self-guided tours: $5 adult; $4 seniors. Hours: 10 a.m. to 5 p.m. daily.

Octagon House (20) (712 Eaton St.), a wood frame house built at the turn of the 20th century by Richard Peacon, a grocery store owner, has been given its name because of its unusual multisided front. Angelo Donghia, one of the best-known interior decorators of the 1960s, bought the house in 1974 for $45,000 and renovated it. Six years later fashion designer Calvin Klein paid the princely sum of $975,000 for it—the highest amount ever paid for a Conch house up to that time. Now on the National Register of Historic Places, it recently was listed for sale for a reported $3 million plus.

On Peacon Lane, a small street facing the Octagon House, No. 328 is said to be the least altered of any Key West home. The kitchen in the rear is detached from the house, a precaution against fire seen in the design of houses in olden times. In the 1970s Henry Faulkner, an artist and every inch as much an eccentric as his friend Tennessee Williams, lived here with his goat, Alice, whom he often dressed up and took to parties. The house is now owned by the son of Bertolt Brecht.

Monroe County Public Library (21) (700 Fleming St.), in an art-deco-style building, houses a wonderful collection of old photographs, local historical documents, and genealogy records that researchers and other interested parties are welcome to use. The west side of the building opens onto a garden festooned with palms.

Across the street, the twin Victorian houses (701 and 703 Fleming St.) with wraparound verandas were dilapidated when Jerry Herman of Broadway fame (*Auntie Mame, Hello Dolly!, La Cage aux Folles*) bought them in the early 1980s. After a superb two-year restoration, Herman sold the corner house and lived at the other.

Down the street, **Fausto's Food Palace** (522 Fleming St.; www.faustos.com) calls itself a social center and the town's oldest grocery store; and **Key West Island Bookstore** (513 Fleming St.) is the town's best for books about Key West and those by writers associated with the town.

Gingerbread House (22) (615 Elizabeth St. at Baker's Lane) has so much filigree trim it could be called the Wedding Cake House. The name would be appropriate because it was built in the 1880s by Benjamin Baker, a lumber-mill owner and builder, as a wedding present to his daughter. The house, which won a Preservation Award in 1995, was so well built that during a tornado in 1972 the structure was lifted 7 feet off its foundation but not damaged.

Around the corner the small, dark wood house at 709 Baker's Lane was the home of James Herlihy, author of *Midnight Cowboy* and *Blue Denim*, among others, in the late 1960s. He, too, was a good friend of Tennessee Williams. Note the stained-glass window above the front door.

Windsor Compound (23): (713–727 Windsor Lane). At several locations in Key West, groups of adjoining dilapidated houses have been renovated as residences for writers. The Windsor Compound has served as the winter residence for such important writers as 1993 poet laureate Richard Wilbur and Pulitzer Prize winner John Hersey, who wrote *A Bell for Adano* and *Hiroshima*, among others.

Farther along at Margaret and Angela Streets is the Key West Cemetery (www.keywest.com/cemetery.html) where burials are in aboveground tombs, as in New Orleans. The cemetery is famous for some of the inscriptions on the tombstones; the one most often cited reads, I TOLD YOU I WAS SICK. Some of the deceased were buried with their pets. The gates close at sunset.

Burton House (24): (608 Angela St.). Philip Burton, a playwright, author, and Shakespearean scholar, served as headmaster at the Port Talbot School early in his career and became the foster parent of actor Richard Burton. The elder Burton bought the Key West cottage in 1974 and lived there until his death in 1995. Elizabeth Taylor was a frequent visitor.

Secret Garden (25): (1 Free School Lane; 305-294-0015; www.nancyforrester.com). Immediately after 521 Simonton (across the street from the Heron Hotel) is Free School Lane, which leads to the entrance of Nancy Forrester's Secret Garden, the largest private tropical garden in Key West and jungle-thick with enormous trees, flowers, and birds. Hours: 10 a.m. to 5 p.m. daily. Admission:

$10; private tour, $15 for a minimum of four people. Walking tours led by historian Sharon Wells and other guides depart from here daily at 10 a.m. (305-294-8380).

Tennessee Williams House (26): (1431 Duncan St.). The famous playwright visited Key West for a few months in 1941, when he finished *Battle of Angels,* and returned frequently for visits. In 1951 he bought a modest house and had it moved from Bahama Street, a lane just east of Duval, to Duncan Street, about a mile to the east, for greater privacy. The one-story white frame cottage with red shutters was his home for three decades until his death in 1983. During those years he won two Pulitzers—for *A Streetcar Named Desire* and *Cat on a Hot Tin Roof.* Among the other plays he wrote here were *Night of the Iguana* and *The Rose Tattoo,* which was later filmed in Key West, with some of the scenes shot at Williams's house. The swimming pool has a mosaic tile rose tattoo on the pool floor.

Tennessee Williams Theatre (5901 College Rd., 305-296-1520; www.tennesseewilliamstheatre .com), at Florida Keys Community College on Stock Island, was built in Williams's honor. The center stages plays, dance, films, and concerts during the winter season.

Fort Zachary Taylor (27): (305-292-6713). On the southwestern end of the island (about a ten-minute bike ride from Mallory Square) stands a trapezoid-shaped fort, which was begun in 1854 and finished in 1875. During the Civil War it was controlled by Union forces who used it as a base for blockading Confederate ships. Buried under tons of sand and largely forgotten, it was restored in the 1960s, mainly through the efforts of historian Howard England. The fort has a large collection of Civil War artifacts. The grounds of the fort are a park with a large artificial beach and picnic areas, popular with families. Hours: 8 a.m. to sunset daily. Admission: $3. There's also a charge for bikes. Free tour of the fort at 2 p.m.

The Other Key West

Three miles from the pier and Mallory Square at the eastern end of the island along US 1 is another Key West, as different as the 150 years that separate them. A city bus connects the two, but unless you

have a particular fondness for shopping centers, you need not bother.

East Martello: (3501 South Roosevelt Blvd., next to Key West International Airport). The historic brick-and-masonry Civil War fort is a National Historic Site. The East Martello Museum and Art Gallery, located in the tower, holds a large collection of artifacts from the Keys and Key West. Admission: $6 adult; $5 senior; $3 student and child (under six free). Hours: 9:30 a.m. to 4:30 p.m. daily.

Thomas Riggs Wildlife Refuge: (South Roosevelt Boulevard; 305-294-2116). Bird-watchers and nature lovers find this spot a refuge away from the crowds. An observation platform provides views of Key West's historic salt ponds and a chance to see heron, ibis, osprey, and small wading birds. Phone ahead to be sure the reserve's gates are open.

Sports

Beaches: If you really prefer a day in the sun, Smathers Beach (South Roosevelt Boulevard) is a 3-mile stretch favored by sporty types. It's body-to-body during college spring break. Water sports equipment is available for rent. Higgs Beach (Atlantic Boulevard) is popular with gay men. There are shaded picnic tables and a snack stand.

Diving and Snorkeling: The water sports center at the Hyatt Key West arranges diving and snorkeling excursions. **Key West Dive Center** (866-563-1805; www.keywestdivecenter.com) has several departures convenient for cruise for dives at two locations, for $99 with all equipment; $45 for snorkelers. **Dive Key West** (3128 North Roosevelt Blvd.; 305-296-3823; 800-426-0707) has daily excursions for snorkelers to advanced divers; instruction and equipment are available.

If you are not ready for diving but want something more than snorkeling, you might try Snuba, an apparatus attached to a boat that provides oxygen and greater range for swimming over the reef. Contact **Snuba of Key West** (Garrison Bight Marina, Palm Avenue; 305-292-4616; www.snubakeywest .com). There are three departures daily. Cost: $99 adult; $79 ages eight to twelve.

Fishing: Key West offers good deep-sea fishing in the Atlantic and bonefishing in the shallow-water backcountry on the north and west side of the Keys. Dozens of private sportfishing boats offer excursions on an individual or charter basis. Check out **Capt. Bill Wickers' Charter Boat** *Linda D* (City Marina; 305-296-9798; 800-299-9798; www.charterboat lindad.com), half-day charters $600, full-day charters $800; **Lucky Fleet** (Lands End Marina, Margaret Street; 305-294-7988; 800-292-3096; www.lucky-fleet.com); or **The Galleon Marina** (619 Front St.; 305-292-1292; 800-544-3030; www.galleonresort .com), which has a water sports center. Half- and full-day charters are available from **Capt. Dan's Fishing Charters** (Galleon Marina, 305-294-3815; www.captdans.com) for $450 for four hours. **Key West Fishing Club** (Garrison Bight Marina; 305-294-3618; www.keywestfishingclub.com) has guided fishing trips and charters. **The Saltwater Angler** (Hilton Resort & Marina; 305-296-0700; www.salt waterangler.com) offers professional guides for flats and offshore fishing; thirty licensed and insured boat captains. Half-day $400 to $900, depending on the type of fishing. Hours: 9 a.m. to 9 p.m. daily.

Golf: Key West Resort Golf Course (6450 East College Rd.; 305-294-5232; www.keywestgolf.com). The 18-hole course (6,500 yards, par 70) is located on Stock Island, about 3 miles east of the pier. Greens fees: $95 winter; $70 off-season, including cart. Call for tee times and club rental information.

Kayaking/Nature in the Wild: The north/ northwest side of the Keys, known as the back-country, is a region of shallow flats and mangroves that, for the most part, lies along the north side of US 1. Not easily navigable or accessible to major boat traffic, the area is largely untraveled, unspoiled, and rich in plant and animal life. Kayak-ing is ideal for excursions here, and tours are avail-able with guides eager to share their knowledge about the Keys' environment. Wildlife abounds; kayakers frequently spot roseate spoonbills, ospreys, great white herons, and even bald eagles. The flats support small lobsters, young reef fish, turtles, stingrays, and big predators such as sharks and barracudas. Guided kayaking excursions are available. **Outdoor Adventures** (5106 US 1, Stock Island; 305-295-9898; www.kayakthekeys.com) has a two-hour nature tour for $35; single kayak rental $20 half-day, $30 full day. **Sunset Watersports**

(305-296-2554; www.sunsetwatersports.info) offers two-and-a-half-hour boat excursions in the back-country, departing at 9 a.m., noon, and 3 p.m. for $69 per person, two persons per boat. The company also offers kayaking and other water sports.

Dolphin Encounters: Wild About Dolphins, Inc. (P.O. Box 747, Key West, FL 33041; 305-294-5026; 800-593-6574; www.wildaboutdolphins.com) offers two four-hour excursions to the dolphin "playground" daily at 8 a.m. and 1 p.m. aboard the custom-designed vessel *Amazing Grace*, guided by Capt. Sheri Sullenger. Participants observe, swim, or snorkel, and learn about wild dolphins in their natural habitat, as well as birds and other wildlife in the backcountry. Cost: $89 adult, $69 child under ten. Boat departs from Key West Yacht Club of Americas Marina (6000 Peninsular Ave.), a fifteen-minute taxi ride from downtown.

Sailing: Sebago Watersports (328 Simonton St.; 305-292-5687; www.keywestsebago.com) offers catamaran sailing with snorkeling and kayak-ing. Excursions depart at 9 a.m. and 1 p.m. from Key West Heritage, at the end of William Street. Cost: $49. Discounts available online with advance reservations. **Floridays** (601 Front St., 305-744-8335; 888-733-5455; www.floridays.org), a 60-foot luxury sailboat, offers two snorkeling excursions daily, departing from the Hyatt Resort Hotel at 9 a.m. and 1 p.m. in winter, 9:30 a.m. and 2 p.m. in summer for $45; sunset, $35.

Shopping

Art and Antiquities: Key West has a lively art community and almost forty art galleries showing their works; most are on or near Duval Street and feature almost every kind of art. **Key West Art Center** (301 Front St.; 305-294-1241) is a nonprofit artist cooperative housed in a turn-of-the-20th-century structure where members, who must be local property owners, showcase their work.

Guild Hall Gallery (614 Duval St.; 305-296-6076; www.guildhallgallerykw.com) is a coopera-tive of local women artists. **Gingerbread Square** (1207 Duval St.; 305-296-8900; www.gingerbread squaregallery.com) is the oldest private gallery in Key West and represents many of the best artists.

The Key West Art Gallery Association publishes a brochure with a map and brief descriptions of the specialty of each of its twenty-two members. A list of art galleries/antiques shops is found at www .fla-keys.com.

Candy, Coffee, and Wine: Jim Garrahy's Fudge Kitchen (Clinton Square) makes Key lime fudge, which you can watch being made in the afternoon and try a free sample, or buy a slice for about $10 a pound. **Key West Candy Company** (810 Duval St.; 305-292-1496) also has Key lime fudge. **The Key West Winery** (103 Simonton St.; 305-292-1717; www.thekeywestwinery.com) offers free wine tasting daily for its Key lime, mango, and other fruit wines, as well as Key lime and other products.

Clothing, Books, and Gifts: Lilly Pulitzer (600 Front St.; 305-295-0995; www.lillypulitzer.com) is known for tropical resort wear. **Jackie Arevalo** (310 Duval St.; 305-292-3100; www.keywestbeadco .com) has custom-designed jewelry created by this Key West artist. **Besame Mucho** (315 Petronia St.; 305-294-1928; www.besamemucho.net) sells body care products and accessories. **Kermit's Key Lime** (200 Elizabeth St.; 305-296-0806; www .keylimeshop.com) sells Key lime sweets. **Peppers of Key West** (602 Greene St.; 305-295-0333; www .peppersofkeywest.com) has some 600 sauces from around the world. **Design Store** (620 Duval St.; 305-292-7800; www.islandstylegalleries.com) sells Purplebabydaddies designs, funky eclectic gifts, art, sculpture, jewelry, and other treasures from more than seventy-five artists. **Key West Aloe** (Front Street; 800-445-2563) makes a full line of skin and body care products; Baskets, which is part of the store, makes up spice, candle, herb, and many other types of pretty gift baskets. **Arches** (1208 Duval St.; 305-294-3771) specializes in African art and rugs, as well as furniture from Indonesia. **Kindred Spirit** (1204 Simonton St.; 305-296-1515; www.kindredspiritkeywest.com) is a bookstore-cum-tearoom.

Dining and Restaurants

Abbondanza (1208 Simonton St.; 305-292-1199). This moderately priced Italian restaurant, very

popular with Key Westers, serves excellent food (huge portions) at reasonable prices in a very pleasant atmosphere.

Alice's Key West (1114 Duval St.; 305-292-5733) specializes in New American cuisine by famous chef Alice Weingarten. Expensive.

Blue Heaven (729 Thomas St.; 305-296-8666; http://blueheavenkw.homestead.com/ blue_heaven_restaurant_key_west.html) serves Caribbean and vegetarian soul food in an outdoor setting with huge shade trees overhead and roosters underfoot. (See No. 12 earlier description.) Inexpensive.

Camille's Key West (1202 Simonton St.; 305-296-4811; www.camilleskeywest.com). A funky establishment that's been pure Key West for more than 20 years. Eclectic menus, posted on its Web site, change from time to time. Everything is cooked to order with freshest ingredients available. Moderate.

Grand Café Key West (314 Duval St.; 305-292-4740; www.grandcafekeywest.com). Praised for its fresh seafood, steaks, and big martinis to be enjoyed in the courtyard or on wraparound porches while watching the passing Duval Street parade. Panini and sandwiches at lunch. Menus are posted on the Web site. Moderately expensive.

Hogfish Bar and Grill (6810 Front St., 305-293-4041; www.hogfishbar.com). On Stock Island, the next island to Key West, this fun and funky eatery is totally old Key West in flavor. It may not be easy to find; ask locally for directions. The menu is mostly fresh fish; it's famous for its "KILLER" Hogfish sandwich. If you catch a fish, the restaurant will cook it for you.

Jimmy Buffett's Margaritaville (500 Duval St.; 305-292-1435; www.margaritavillekeywest .com). Enjoy "cheeseburgers in paradise" with a front-row seat on Duval for the passing parade. Music in the afternoon and evening. Moderate.

Origami (1075 Duval St.; 305-294-0092). Often voted Best Sushi Bar by annual local award; other Japanese selections. Seating inside in air-conditioning or outside on the garden patio. Dinner only. Moderately expensive.

Pepe's Cafe & Steak House (806 Caroline St.; 305-294-7192; www.pepescafe.net) has served breakfast, lunch, and dinner for ages at surprisingly low prices. In season, Apalachicola Bay oysters are a specialty.

Pisces (1007 Simonton St.; 305-294-7100; www.pisceskeywest.com). Seafood is the specialty. Expensive.

Rooftop Cafe (308 Front St.; 305-294-2042; http://rooftopcafekeywest.com) in a pretty setting on the second floor overlooks Front Street and Mallory Square. The main dining room has sliding glass doors on three sides, left open for tropical breezes or closed for air-conditioned comfort. Its terrace is bordered by flowering plants and shaded by a large mahogany tree. Lunch is more brunch than lunch. Moderate.

Entertainment

After the sun goes down, Key West's nightlife lights up all over town with comedy and combos—rock, pop, reggae, soul, Cuban, country, and more. Key West even has its own brand of music—Conchtown rhythm, a mix of New Orleans jazz and calypso.

Unfortunately, cruise ships must leave their dock by 6 p.m.—that's part of the agreement the lines made with the city. But you don't have to miss out on all the fun, as some places, such as **Rick's** (208 Duval St.; 305-296-4890), gets started with music in the afternoon, and others, such as **Sloppy Joe's** (201 Duval St.; 305-294-5717), never seem to stop. **The Keys Piano Bar** (1114 Duval St., 305-294-8859; www.akeywestpianobar.com) and Off-Key Bar (behind Keys Piano) have music on Wed to Sun, 3 to 11 p.m.

Celebrations

Jan through Apr: Old Islands Days highlight the Keys' history and culture with Key West's House & Garden Tours, Feb to Mar (www.oirf.org), Art Fest, Literary Seminar, and others. A calendar of events is available from the Chamber of Commerce (Mallory Square/Wall Street).

Apr: A ten-day festival in late Apr celebrates the Conch Republic Independence, when in 1982 Key West declared war and "seceded" from the Union.

July: Hemingway Days is a week of activities to celebrate the birthday of Ernest Hemingway on July 21. The seven-day festival, rich in nostalgia for Hemingway buffs, includes Hemingway Look-Alike, short story, and story-telling contests; a writer's workshop and conference; and more.

Oct: Fantasy Fest, a ten-day event in late Oct embracing Halloween, is Key West's answer to New Orleans's Mardi Gras.

Sunsets

Key West abounds with wonders—both natural and created by people—but its famous sunset is something of both. Daily as sunset nears, islanders joined by tourists, young and old, arrive at Mallory Square pier. Hotel desk clerks watch for the exact second the sun is to set and alert guests so they can go barreling down to see it. Soon the place is alive with entertainment: jugglers here, tumblers there, foot-tapping music all around; a unicyclist wriggling free of a straitjacket; a gaily dressed young woman beating out a tune on a washboard. There is applause for not only the entertainers but the entire celebration. The applause grows louder when the Key West sun—that massive fireball symbolizing life—falls below the horizon.

PART FOUR

Gateways to the Eastern and Southern Caribbean

Three of the islands —Puerto Rico, St. Thomas, and St. Maarten—are gateways or home ports, from which some ships depart en route to destinations in the Eastern and Southern Caribbean. These, together with their neighboring islands—the Dominican Republic, St. John, St. Croix, the British Virgin Islands, Saba, St. Eustatius, and Anguilla—form a bridge between the Northern and Eastern Caribbean.

Puerto Rico

San Juan, Ponce

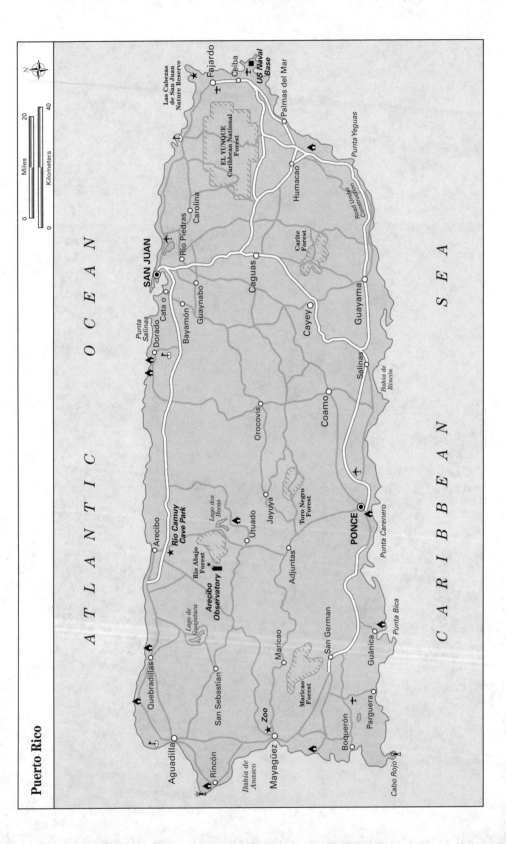

Puerto Rico

The Complete Island

Cruise passengers sailing into San Juan Bay have a breathtaking view of Puerto Rico. From afar the green peaks of the thickly wooded Cordillera Central, rising to 4,398 feet, are outlined against the blue Caribbean sky. By the sea, palms etch miles of white-sand beaches. As the ship approaches the harbor, it passes the colossal fortress of El Morro to dock in Old San Juan, the oldest city now under the American flag. Beyond the ramparts of the fortress, the skyline of new San Juan is juxtaposed against the Old World grace of the colonial city.

Puerto Rico, the easternmost island of the Greater Antilles, has been under the American flag since 1898, but it was under Spanish rule for almost four centuries. From the intermingling of the two cultures comes modern Puerto Rico. It offers visitors the best of both worlds—the familiarity of home in a setting that is distinctly foreign. And it offers a great deal more.

Rectangular in shape, Puerto Rico is only 110 miles long and 35 miles wide, yet it has the range of scenery and geographic features of a country fifty times its size. From the quiet, palm-fringed beaches on the east, the land rises to two rugged mountain ranges that fall off in an ocean of rolling surf on the west. The mountainous spine of the island peaks toward the center at more than 4,390 feet, separating the north coast on the Atlantic Ocean from the south coast facing the Caribbean Sea. The slopes are thick with rain forests; the foothills are covered with breadfruit, mango, and coffee trees and rolling hills planted with sugar and pineapple.

The island has desert, salt flats, mangroves, and three phosphorescent bays that glow in the night. On the west end is the Maricao State Forest, one of the island's ten forest reserves; near the east end is the 28,000-acre Caribbean National Forest, known locally as El Yunque, the only tropical rain forest in the U.S. National Forest Service system.

Puerto Rico has long been a popular port of call. Among the many reasons for its popularity is the variety of activities and attractions it offers.

Sports enthusiasts can enjoy Puerto Rico's miles of beaches for swimming, windsurfing, kite sailing or kiting, sailing, and even surfing. Anglers can try to beat one of the three dozen sportsfishing world records previously set in Puerto Rican waters. Golfers have twenty-three courses to test; tennis buffs can choose from one hundred courts in and near San Juan. A dozen or more places around Puerto Rico and its offshore islands attract snorkelers and divers. There are caves to explore, hikes in the rain forest, and horseback riding and racing. Puerto Rico even has its own special breed of horse, Paso Fino.

In a country whose culture spans more than five hundred years, attractions for history buffs are abundant. Shoppers can be diverted at street markets and boutiques in the Old City, arcades in hotels, or the Texas-size shopping centers of the suburbs. But what will interest them most are the crafts made in Puerto Rico.

Entertainment and nightlife offer so much variety, you could stay in Puerto Rico a month, try a different restaurant and nightclub every night, and still have plenty left for your next visit. There are discos, cabarets, casinos, and the Puerto Rican specialty—lobby bars with salsa and other Latin beats, where you can catch the beat in the afternoon and dance the night away.

The variety of arts and cultural attractions is equally impressive. No week goes by without art exhibits in galleries and museums. The performing arts calendar is filled year-round with concerts, opera, ballet, and theater and highlighted by the annual Casals Festival in late Feb/early Mar.

For those planning a stay before or after their cruise, Puerto Rico offers a large variety of hotels in San Juan and around the island to suit any lifestyle or pocketbook. Remember, too, that it's part of the United States, so you can use your U.S. dollars, credit cards, and driver's license.

A 10 million-square-foot mixed-use urban plan to reshape the San Juan waterfront has been underway since 2007. This project has included an outstanding convention center, hotels, and a mega yacht marina with retail stores, residences, and an aquarium to come. New pier facilities include the Pan American Pier in Isla Grande, managed by Royal Caribbean International and a completely renovated Pier #4, managed by Carnival Cruise Lines. Ponce's Port of the Americas Vieques, and the Port of Mayaguez receive cruise ships occasionally.

Budget Planning

Costs in Puerto Rico are similar to those on the mainland. In San Juan they are comparable to those in a large metropolitan area, such as New York City or Chicago; those in the Puerto Rico countryside, to small-town America. The best way to save money is to walk, which is delightful in Old San Juan, and to use public transportation, which is inexpensive and plentiful. All but the most deluxe restaurants are reasonably priced. Outside of San Juan they are cheap by any standard.

Port Profile: San Juan

Location/Embarkation: One of the biggest attractions of San Juan for cruise passengers is the location of the port. Quite literally, you step off your ship into the oldest, most interesting part of town. All ships pull in dockside unless there is an unusually large number in port. The piers are within walking distance of the city's main sightseeing, shopping, dining, and transportation to other parts of the city.

The ride from the airport to the pier takes twenty-five to forty minutes, depending on traffic. Taxis Turísticos, a program in the San Juan tourist area, is sponsored by the Puerto Rico Tourism Company. Participating taxis are white and have the Taxis Turísticos logo on the door. They follow set fares: Airport to Isla Verde $10; to Condado/Miramar $15; to Old San Juan/piers $19; to Plaza Las Américas $20. From piers to Old San Juan $7; to Condado/Miramar $12; to Isla Verde $19. These rates apply only from Luis Muñoz International Airport or the cruise ship piers in Old San Juan. There is a charge of $1 each for luggage. Between and beyond the tourism areas, taxi rates are metered. If you are arriving as part of an air/sea package, your cruise line arranges the transfer. Tourist police (wearing white hats) are available to help visitors.

Local Transportation: Fleets of taxis are on hand to meet all ships. Taxis operate on meters and are comparable in price to those in stateside cities. You can hire them by the hour or half day, but settle the price in advance. A taxi dispatcher is available at the port to help passengers.

City buses to Condado and all parts of San Juan leave frequently from the bus station near Pier 3. A list of bus routes can be found in Que Pasa. Free motorized trolleys, sponsored by the Old San Juan Merchants Association, operate on two routes: from in front of the bus depot in Cavadonga to Plaza de Armas via San Francisco and Fortaleza Streets; and to Calle del Cristo and Fortaleza via Boulevard del Valle and Calle Norzagaray.

Roads and Rentals: Puerto Rico has an excellent network of roads. You can drive around the entire island on a road that skirts the coast; drive through its mountainous center on the Panoramic Highway, one of the Caribbean's most scenic routes; and detour to rural mountain-town or seaside fishing villages along the way. All major U.S. rental firms are represented in San Juan, but none has offices at the port. The nearest offices are in Condado, ten minutes from the port. There are

At a Glance

Antiquities	★★★★
Architecture	★★★★★
Art and Artists	★★★★
Beaches	★★
Colonial Buildings	★★★★★
Crafts	★★★★
Cuisine	★★★★
Culture	★★★★★
Dining/Restaurants	★★★★
Entertainment	★★★★
Forts	★★★★★
History	★★★★
Monuments	★★★★★
Museums	★★★★
Nightlife	★★★★★
Scenery	★★★★
Shopping	★★★
Sightseeing	★★★
Sports	★★★★★
Transportation	★★★★

Population: 3.9 million

Size: 3,421 square miles

Main Cities: San Juan, Ponce, Mayagüez, Caguas, Arecibo

Government: Following the Spanish-American War, Puerto Rico was formally turned over to the United States in 1898. Puerto Ricans were made U.S. citizens and given the right to vote in local elections in 1917; the island was made a commonwealth in 1952. It is represented in the U.S. Congress by a resident commissioner with a voice but no vote, except in the committees on which he or she may serve.

Currency: U.S. dollar

Customs Regulations: Cruise passengers who disembark in San Juan to return to the United States by plane after visiting other islands and countries must go through U.S. customs here.

Departure Tax: None

Emergency Numbers: General emergency: 911; Medical service: (787) 343-2550; Ambulance: (787) 343-2550; Police: (787) 343-2020; Tourist Zone Police, 24 hours, emergencies, (787) 726-7015 (Old San Juan to Ocean Park); (787) 726-2981 (Isla Verde)

Alcoholics Anonymous: (787) 723-4187; (787) 786-8287

Language: Spanish. English widely spoken.

Postal Service: Same as U.S. mainland

Public Holidays: Jan 1, New Year's Day; Jan 6, Three Kings Day; Jan 11, Patriot de Hostos; Jan 20, Martin Luther King Day; Feb, Presidents' Birthday; Mar 23, Emancipation Day; Good Friday; Apr 16, Patriot de Diego Day; May, Memorial Day; July 4, U.S. Independence Day; July 17, Muñoz Rivera Day; July 25, Constitution Day; July 27, Barbosa Day; Sept 1, Labor Day; Oct 14, Columbus Day; Nov 11, Veteran's Day; Nov 19, Discovery of Puerto Rico (by Columbus); Nov, Thanksgiving; Dec 25, Christmas.

Smoking Ban: Effective Mar 2007, a comprehensive smoking ban prohibits smoking in all food establishments, cultural centers, casinos, bars, shopping centers, public and government buildings, and schools.

Telephone Area Code: 787 and 939. All local calls in the San Juan area must be preceded by 787; those outside are preceded by 1-787 or 939. When dialing from a land line that does not have the same area code as the number you are calling, it is necessary to dial a "1."

Airlines: *From the United States mainland:* Air Tran, American, Continental, Delta, JetBlue, Spirit, United, and US Airways. *Regional:* Air

Sunshine, American Eagle, Cape Air, LIAT. *Local:* Isla Nena Air Service, Vieques Air Link.

Information: www.gotopuertorico.com

In the United States:

Puerto Rico Tourism Company:

New York: 135 West Fiftieth St., 22nd Floor, New York, NY 10013; (212) 586-6262; (800) 223-6530; fax: (212) 586-1212

Los Angeles: 3575 West Cahuenga Blvd., No. 405, Los Angeles, CA 90068; (323) 874-5991; (800) 874-1230; fax: (323) 874-7257

In Canada:

6-295 Queen St. East, Suite 465, Brampton, Ontario LGW456; (416) 368-2680; (800) 667-0394 (Canada only); fax: (416) 368-5350

In San Juan:

La Casita: Puerto Rico Tourism Information Center (PRTC), Comercio Street, Old San Juan; (787) 722-1709; fax: (787) 722-5208. Hours: Mon to Wed 8:30 a.m. to 8 p.m.; Thurs and Fri 8:30 a.m. to 5:30 p.m.; Sat and Sun 9 a.m. to 8 p.m. *Que Pasa* is the free quarterly official tourist guide.

Paseo de la Princesa #2, Old San Juan, San Juan, PR 00901; (787) 721-2400; (800) 866-7827; fax: (787) 722-1093

also many local companies with lower rates. A list appears in *Que Pasa.*

Ferry Service: Ferries leave frequently from San Juan pier to Cataño across the harbor. Cost is 50 cents. On Sunday sightseeing ferries operate cruises around the harbor.

Urban Train/Tren Urbano: The new rail system, primarily above ground, connects Bayamón with eastern Santurce near Sagrado Corazón–University via Guaynabo, Centro Médico, University of Puerto Rico at Río Piedras, and the financial district of Hato Rey. It has thirteen stations and air-conditioned cars. The trains run daily from 5:30 a.m. to 11:30 p.m. and cost $1.50 per ride with one transfer to a local bus; 75 cents for students and seniors. For information, (866) 900-1284; www.ati.gobierno.pr.

Domestic and Regional Air Service:
American Airlines/American Eagle (800-981-4757) flies to Mayagüez, Vieques, and throughout the Eastern Caribbean. **Air Flamenco** (787-724-1818), Isla Nena Air Service (787-863-4447), and **Vieques Air Link** (787-741-8331) serve Vieques and Culebra. Air service to Ponce is very limited.

Shore Excursions

The first tour listed is available on almost all cruise ships, but the second might not be or may vary in length and price. Both sites are described elsewhere in the chapter.

City Tour—Old and New San Juan: 2–4 hours, $25–$40. San Juan is a large, sprawling metropolis; a brief tour can be a useful introduction on a first visit.

El Yunque Rain Forest and Luquillo Beach: 7–8 hours, $40–$60. A drive in El Yunque is combined with a stop at palm-fringed Luquillo Beach, the most popular *balneario,* or public beach.

Rum Distillery and Old San Juan: Half-day, $40. A guided tour of the Barcardi rum distillery followed by a tour of Old San Juan.

These and other tours are available from **Rico Suntours,** (787-722-2080, www.ricosuntours.com); **Castillo Tours & Watersports,** (787-791-6195, www.castillotours.com); **Tour Co-op of Puerto Rico,** (787-762-7475); and United Tour Guides Co-op, (787-723-5578).

San Juan on Your Own

San Juan, the air and cruise hub of the Caribbean, with a population exceeding one million, has the bustle of a large American city, the grace of its Spanish heritage, and the beat of the Caribbean. It also has a wonderful variety of big-city activity and attractions, yet it is only a stone's throw from quiet fishing villages and quaint mountain hamlets.

Beautifully restored Old San Juan is a living city bursting with activity from morning to night and ideal for walking. (For more than 350 years, it was a walled and fortified city.) Then, beginning in the 1900s with growth and expansion to new areas along Condado and Isla Verde beaches, the old part of San Juan became seedy. It might easily have been lost to the bulldozers had it not been for some farsighted Puerto Ricans who banded together to save it, by first getting it made a protected historic zone in 1949. In 1955 the Society for the Development and Conservation of San Juan got a ten-year tax exemption for those restoring Spanish colonial buildings, and the Institute of Puerto Rican Culture designed a twenty-year plan to guide the preservation effort.

The renovations sparked a renaissance that recaptured the town's old charm and ambience. Along streets paved with the blue cobblestones and in lovely old Spanish houses with flower-filled balconies and colonnaded courtyards, you can browse in shops, museums, and art galleries, enjoy lunch or refreshments at restaurants and cafes, and visit some of the oldest monuments in the Western Hemisphere.

An Old San Juan Walkabout

Old San Juan was laid out in typical Spanish colonial fashion as a grid and built on a hill, which slopes from El Morro and San Cristobal fortresses on the north to the port on the south. With the exception of the perimeter roads that follow the contour of the Old City walls, streets run north-south and east-west, making it easy to find your way. **Colonial Adventure** (787-793-2992; 888-774-9919) conducts two- to three-hour-long walking

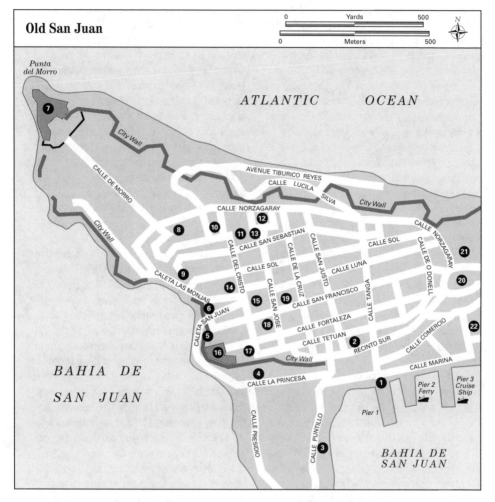

Old San Juan

| 0 | Yards | 500 |
| 0 | Meters | 500 |

N

Punta del Morro

ATLANTIC OCEAN

City Wall

CALLE DE MORRO

City Wall

AVENUE TIBURICO REYES

CALLE LUCILA

SILVA

City Wall

CALLE NORZAGARAY

CALLE NORZAGARAY

CALLE SAN SEBASTIAN

CALLE DEL CRISTO

CALLE SOL

CALLE SOL

CALLE SAN JUSTO

CALLE DE LA CRUZ

CALLE LUNA

CALLE DE O DONELL

CALETA LAS MONJAS

CALETA SAN JUAN

CALLE SAN JOSE

CALLE SAN FRANCISCO

CALLE TANGA

CALLE FORTALEZA

CALLE TETUAN

RECINTO SUR

CALLE COMERCIO

City Wall

CALLE MARINA

CALLE LA PRINCESA

BAHIA DE SAN JUAN

CALLE PRESIDIO

CALLE PUNTILLO

Pier 1

Pier 2 Ferry

Pier 3 Cruise Ship

BAHIA DE SAN JUAN

1. San Juan Pier and Plazoleta del Puerto
2. La Casita
3. Museum of Puerto Rican Culture (The Arsenal)
4. La Princesa Jail and City Walls
5. Gate of San Juan
6. Plaza de la Rogativa
7. El Morro Fortress
8. Ballaja Barracks (Museum of the Americas) and Casa de Beneficencia
9. Casa Blanca
10. Plaza of Five Centuries
11. Church of San José and Dominican Convent
12. San Juan Museum
13. San José Plaza and Casals Museum
14. Hotel El Convento
15. San Juan Cathedral
16. La Fortaleza
17. Pigeon Park and Christ Chapel
18. Department of State and Provincial Deputation Building
19. City Hall
20. Plaza Colón, Tapia Theatre, and Old Casino of Puerto Rico
21. Fort San Cristobal
22. Municipal Bus Station

tours for groups of ten or more. **Legends of Puerto Rico** (787-605-9060; www.legendsofpr.com) is a tourist guide service company specializing in innovative heritage and nature tours, including a nighttime walking tour of Old San Juan, an arts and crafts tour, rain-forest walks, and more. You can book online as well as by phone or fax.

From your ship the twenty-five-minute walk west-northwest along the Old City walls to El Morro is a lovely introduction to Old San Juan and the way visitors in olden times had to approach it. If you want to conserve time and energy, take a taxi to El Morro ($7) and start your walking tour from there. Upon leaving the **piers (1)** turn left (west) to Plaza de Hostos, passing **La Casita (2)**, with a Puerto Rico Tourist Information Office. On certain weekends, Festival La Casita, combining miniconcerts and street theater with an arts fair, takes place here. **The Arsenal (3):** South of Calle La Princesa is the 18th-century building known as the Arsenal, which houses the Institute of Puerto Rican Culture, with changing art exhibits. Here in 1898 the last Spanish general, Ricardo Ortego, turned over Puerto Rico to the United States. Hours: Wed through Sun, 9 a.m. to 4:30 p.m.; (787) 724-5949/0700.

La Princesa (4): At the west end of Calle La Princesa is a former jail, built in 1837. It was restored to house the offices of the Puerto Rico Tourism Company. The beautiful building is also used as a gallery for contemporary Puerto Rican art. Calle La Princesa rounds the corner along the massive City Walls, which rise to 70 feet above the sea and once completely surrounded the city.

Gate of San Juan (5): Walking north along the walls, you come to the small park and the Gate of San Juan, one of the four original gates to the city, built in 1639. On the south is **La Fortaleza (16)**, the residence of the governor of Puerto Rico for almost five hundred years. Originally it was the fort where the early Spaniards stored their gold and silver. Open weekdays, 9 a.m. to 4 p.m.; (787) 721-7000, ext. 2211.

La Rogativa (6): After you pass through the Gate of San Juan, turn left to the Plaza de La Rogativa. The spectacular sculpture of *La Rogativa* is one of the most forceful, inspired works in iron ever conceived. It was done by Lindsay Daen to mark

the city's 450th anniversary in 1971. *La Rogativa,* meaning the Procession, commemorates the saving of San Juan in 1797, after the British had laid siege to it from the sea. As the saga goes, after two weeks city leaders thought their defeat was imminent and asked the bishop to lead a night vigil in honor of St. Catherine, the governor's patron saint. Marchers bearing torches started from San Juan Cathedral at the top of the hill above La Rogativa, proceeded through the streets, and returned to the church for mass. The British commander, seeing the torchlights and hearing the ringing of church bells, thought reinforcements had arrived by land from the east. Rather than face an uncertain battle, he hoisted anchor and quietly slipped away under the cover of night. The next morning the townspeople found their prayers had been answered. A path north of La Rogativa leads directly to El Morro.

El Morro (7): A magnificent fortress begun in 1539, El Morro was part of the Spanish defense system that stretched from Puerto Rico on the Atlantic to the coast of South America. It was built to protect the ships carrying gold and silver from Mexico and South America to Spain.

El Morro is built on a promontory, or morro, in the shape of a head of a longhorn steer. The fortress was built with such strength that it withstood all attempts to take it from the sea for more than 350 years. During the Spanish-American War, the U.S. Navy bombarded El Morro; after the war, when the Spaniards left Puerto Rico, the U.S. Army occupied the site for several years.

El Morro was a living citadel, with seven levels of tunnels, storage rooms, barracks, and artillery emplacements, plus kitchens, a chapel, and foundry. Be sure to go up to the level of the lighthouse for splendid views. The fort has been beautifully restored and is maintained by the U.S. National Park Service; it is listed on the National Register of Historic Sites. El Morro and its companion fort, San Cristobal; San Juan Gate and the City Walls; and La Fortaleza have been designated by UNESCO as landmarks on the World Heritage List. Orientation is available in English and Spanish; there is a museum and bookshop. Hours: daily 9 a.m. to 5 p.m. June to Nov, and until 6 p.m. Dec to May. Entrance: persons age sixteen and older, $3 per fort or $5 for both forts; age fifteen and younger, free. (787) 729-6960/6754; www.nps.gov/saju.

Ballaja Barracks and Casa de Beneficencia (8): As the centerpiece of San Juan's Quincentennial effort, the Ballaja district was transformed by the $60 million restoration of the buildings and grounds that once constituted Fort Brooke (decommissioned in 1967). The district covers the 5 blocks from the Dominican Convent and Church of San José on the east to Casa Blanca, the ancestral home of the Ponce de Leon family, on the west. Now part of the San Juan National Historic Site, Ballaja contains some of Old San Juan's largest, most historically significant buildings.

Most of the buildings date from the 19th century, but Ballaja was the name of the barrio, or district, as early as the 18th century. In 1857, after the construction of the Ballaja Military Barracks (El Cuartel de Ballaja) as the headquarters of the Spanish Army, the barrio became more integrated with its contingent areas, and the Dominican Convent (1523), Conception Hospital (1774), and other nearby buildings were taken over by the military. After the Spanish-American War, the U.S. Army occupied the buildings and added three small structures. All were turned over to the Commonwealth in 1976.

The Barracks, the largest, most imposing of the buildings, is used by the University of Puerto Rico and houses the **Museum of the Americas,** created by Ricardo Alegria, the founding director of the Institute of Puerto Rican Culture. Facing the Barracks, another huge building, dating from 1861, Casa de Beneficencia, is the home of the **Institute of Puerto Rican Culture** (www.icp.gobierno.pr). The facades of the two buildings define a triangle that has a small plaza and park. Here, the street leads directly to El Morro, which is in full view. Museum hours: Tues to Sun 10 a.m. to 4 p.m. (787) 724-5052; www.museolasamericas.org.

Casa Blanca (9): The first structure, a modest wooden house, was built in 1521, but after it was partially destroyed by fire, Ponce de Leon's son-in-law built a stone-and-masonry structure, which also served as a fort against Indian attacks. In 1540, when La Fortaleza was completed, Casa Blanca became the Ponce de Leon family home and so remained until 1779, when it was sold to the Spanish government as a residence for the army

engineer corps. After the Spanish-American War, Casa Blanca was occupied by the U.S. military until 1967. The following year the house was declared a National Historic Monument and is used for exhibits. Hours: Tues to Sun 9 a.m. to noon and 1 to 4 p.m. Entrance: $3 adults; $2 seniors and children. (787) 725-1454.

Plaza of Five Centuries (10): The historic and symbolic centerpiece of the Ballaja restorations is the Plaza of Five Centuries, a three-tiered urban park highlighted by a monumental commemorative sculpture. Beneath the plaza is an underground parking lot.

Church of San José and Dominican Convent (11): The east side of the plaza is bordered by the Church of San José and Dominican Convent. The church is the second-oldest Roman Catholic church in the Americas and one of the purest examples of Gothic architecture in the world. Built in the early 16th century as a chapel of the Dominican monastery on land donated by Ponce de Leon's family, it was used as a family church until the last century. Ponce de Leon was buried here after his remains were brought from Cuba in 1559; his body was moved to San Juan Cathedral in 1908. The Church of San José has undergone lengthy renovation to strip away centuries of coatings on the walls and reveal the beautiful apricot stone and magnificent cross-vaulting of the ceiling.

Next to the Church of San José is the convent, which dates from 1523. It was one of the first buildings to be constructed after Ponce de Leon moved from Caparra, the site of his original settlement, to establish San Juan. The convent was converted into a barracks for the Spanish Army and later became the U.S. Antilles Command headquarters. It now houses the Center for Popular Arts.

San Juan Museum (12): Next to the convent, but facing Calle Norzagaray, is a large structure originally built in 1855 as a marketplace. Restored in 1979, it is used as a cultural center, with an exhibit about San Juan and changing art and cultural events staged in its large courtyard. An audiovisual show on the history of San Juan is available. Open Tues to Sun 9 a.m. to 4 p.m., admission is free. (787) 723-4317.

San José Plaza and Casals Museum (13): On the south side of the church is San José Plaza, with a statue of Ponce de Leon. Made in 1882, the statue is said to have been cast from the melted-down cannons used by the British during their attack on San Juan in 1797. On the east side of the plaza, a town house holds the Casals Museum, devoted to the great Spanish cellist who made his home in Puerto Rico for more than twenty years. Pablo Casals spearheaded the founding of the performing arts festival that bears his name. The island's leading cultural event, the festival is held annually in late Feb. Hours: Tues to Sat 9:30 a.m. to 4:30 p.m.; (787) 723-9185. Small admission fee. Next door is the **Museum of Our African Roots** (787) 724-4294, highlighting Puerto Rico's African heritage. Open Tues to Sat 8:30 a.m. to noon and 1 p.m. to 4:20 p.m. Small admission fee.

The plaza, **Calle San Sebastian,** and adjacent streets are the setting for the *Festival of San Sebastian,* an annual art and music show in mid-Jan. Walk west on Calle San Sebastian to a set of stone steps, Calle del Hospital, leading to Calle Sol and a second set of stairs, **Stairway of the Nuns,** leading directly to Hotel El Convento.

Hotel el Convento (14): Built in 1646 as a convent for the Carmelite nuns, it was first made into a deluxe hotel in the 1970s, but altered several times in the 1980s. After extensive renovation in the 1990s, the hotel reopened under new owner-ship. The first two levels have boutiques and res-taurants; third to fifth floors house the deluxe hotel. The lovely colonial architecture was retained, and furnishings throughout are antiques or authentic reproductions from the 17th and 18th centuries. The project was directed by Jorge Rosello, the archi-tectural genius behind the renovation of La Concha and other leading hotels.

On the west side of the pocket park in front of the hotel is the **Museo del Nino** (Museum of the Child), which features fun and educational hands-on exhibits and a staff of youth counselors to help kids get the most out of their visit. Hours: Tues to Thurs 9 a.m. to 3:30 p.m.; Fri 9 a.m. to 5 p.m.; Sat and Sun 12:30 to 5 p.m. Entrance: $7 children (age one through fifteen), $5 adults. (787) 722-3791; www.museodelninopr.org.

San Juan Cathedral (15): Facing El Convento on Calle del Cristo, San Juan Cathedral enjoys a commanding position at the top of the hill leading

up from San Juan Gate. It was from here that the procession commemorated by La Rogativa set out in 1797 and miraculously saved the city. The pres-ent 19th-century structure stands on the site of the first chapel built soon after the city was founded. Ponce de Leon's tomb is on the north wall. Open daily 8 a.m. to 5 p.m. (787) 722-0861.

La Fortaleza (16): Continuing south on Calle del Cristo, you'll pass some of the best shops and art galleries in the city; turn west on Calle Fortaleza. La Fortaleza, the official residence of the governor of Puerto Rico, is said to be the old-est executive mansion in continuous use in the Western Hemisphere. Hours: daily, 9 a.m. to 4 p.m.; Sun to 2 p.m. Tours in English through the lovely grounds are available weekdays, every hour. Visi-tors must be properly dressed. (787) 721-7000, ext. 2211.

Pigeon Park (17): From Fortaleza, return to Calle del Cristo, and turn right at the corner onto the pretty little street with outdoor cafes leading to Pigeon Park (Las Palomas), where you can get a great view of San Juan Harbor and spot your ship at the pier. **Christ Chapel,** with a silver altar, is said to have been placed here after a horseman racing down the hill from El Morro missed the turn in the road and was thrown over the wall to the sea below to seemingly certain death. Miraculously, he did not die, according to the legend.

Department of State (18): At Calle San José, turn left (north) for a stop at the Department of State, whose interior courtyard is one of the loveli-est examples of colonial architecture in San Juan. Note especially the staircase on the right of the entrance. **City Hall (19):** Across Plaza de Armas is City Hall, dating from 1602 and the site of many important events in Puerto Rico's history, including the abolition of slavery in 1873.

Here on the square, you can pick up the trolley to return to the port or walk east 2 blocks to Calle Tanca, which leads south directly to the pier where you started. One block farther east on Fortaleza is Plaza Colon.

Plaza Colón (20): The plaza is dominated by the statue of Christopher Columbus (whose Span-ish name is Colón) placed here in 1893 to mark the 400th anniversary of Columbus's discovery of Puerto Rico. On its south side is the **Tapia**

Theatre, built early in the 19th century. It has been renovated many times, but claims to be the oldest theater in continuous use in the Western Hemisphere. The theater has a year-round schedule of concerts and drama. Check *Que Pasa,* or call (787) 722-0407.

On the east side of the plaza is the **Old Casino of Puerto Rico,** built in 1915 to be the most elegant social hall in the Americas. Because of the war, however, the building never realized its potential and came to be used for many purposes, deteriorating all the while. It was renovated in 1985, its magnificent drawing rooms restored to their former elegance. Renamed the Manuel Pavia Fernandez Government Reception Center, it is used mainly by the Puerto Rico State Department for special occasions and receptions. Hours: weekdays 8 a.m. to 4 p.m.

Fort San Cristobal (21): Northeast of Plaza Colón is the entrance to Fort San Cristobal, part of the defense structure begun in 1633. The impressive fortress is larger than El Morro, with several levels of ramparts, moats, tunnels, and storerooms, and is considered a masterpiece of strategic military design. It, too, is maintained by the U.S. National Park Service. Hours: daily 9 a.m. to 5 p.m. Orientation is available in English and Spanish. Small entrance fee. (787) 729-6960/6754.

Museum of Puerto Rican Art (Museo de Arte de Puerto Rico) (299 De Diego Ave., Santurce; 787-977-6277; www.mapr.org). The museum is not within walking distance of the port, but it is accessible by taxi and certainly worth a visit.

Located in Santurce, near the Condado hotel district, the world-class museum is housed in two wings. The west wing, the main entrance, is a neoclassical structure built in the 1920s as part of the Municipal Hospital. Now restored, it houses the permanent collection in eighteen exhibition halls and showcases Puerto Rican artists, with paintings, drawings, sculptures, ceramics, printmaking, and photography reflecting the history of Puerto Rican culture through its art.

The east wing is a modern, five-story structure, designed by well-established Puerto Rican architects Otto Reyes and Luis Gutierrez. It has a three-story atrium, an interactive family gallery called ActivArte, a computer learning center, studios and workshops, a 400-seat theater, and a museum shop. There are two large galleries for local and international exhibitions.

The works of fourteen Puerto Rican artists are displayed in the museum's five-acre sculpture garden, complete with a lake, trails, and gazebos where visitors can sit and reflect. The museum is a private, nonprofit corporation whose $55 million development and construction was financed by the Puerto Rican government. Hours: Tues to Sat 10 a.m. to 5 p.m.; Wed to 8 p.m.; Sun 11 a.m. to 6 p.m. Admission: $6 adults, $3 children, students, and seniors. For special tours, contact the Education Department (787-977-6277, ext. 2230).

For those who wish to view contemporary Puerto Rican art, visit the **Museum of Contemporary Art** in its new location (Ponce de León Avenue, corner R. H. Todd, Parada 18; 787-977-4030; www.museocontemporaneopr.org; open Tues to Sat 10 a.m. to 4 p.m., Sun noon to 5 p.m.) in a lovely two-story brick building.

Shopping

Old San Juan with its pretty boutiques and specialty shops is the best area of the city for shopping. In the Condado hotel area, you will find the high fashion boutiques of Ferragamo, Louis Vuitton, Gucci, and Cartier on Ashford Avenue; and in the suburbs Texas-style shopping centers, such as Plaza Las Americas, in Hato Rey. And for those last-minute needs, there's a Walgreens (Plaza de Armas) a short walk from the port. Because cruise passengers frequently visit duty-free ports, such as the U.S. Virgin Islands, they are often understandably confused about Puerto Rico's status. Puerto Rico is not a duty-free port. Imported goods such as gold jewelry and Scottish cashmeres have the same duties levied on them here as in New York or Miami. Advertisements for "duty-free" merchandise mean only that you will not have to pay additional customs duties upon your return home, and, of course, you save state and local taxes. The best buys are for art, crafts, clothing, and rum made in Puerto Rico.

Art and Artists: On a walk in Old San Juan, you will see art galleries where you can discover many fine Puerto Rican and other artists living and working here. Gallery nights are held on the first Tues of the month during Feb to May and Sept to Dec, when twenty or more art galleries and museums remain open from 6 to 9 p.m. and there's a festive atmosphere throughout the Old City. For information: (787) 723-7080.

Galeria Botello in Old San Juan (208 Calle del Cristo; 787-723-9987; www.botello.com) showcases fine international artists and represents the estate of the gallery founder, Angel Botello, one of Puerto Rico's best-known artists with a very distinctive style.

Galeria San Juan (204 Boulevard del Valle; 787-722-1808; www.thegalleryinn.com), set in three restored 17th-century buildings, is the home and studio of American-born artist Jan D'Esopo, known for her Old San Juan street scenes.

Galeria Arte Espinal (304 Calle San Francisco), the gallery of artist Santiago Espinal, has changing exhibits of high quality Puerto Rican, Caribbean, and South American artists.

Amparo Porcelain Inn (53 Calle de Cristo, 787-722-1777), the studio—and home of artist Amparo Cuillar is open only on Wed from 11 a.m. to 5 p.m. or by appointment.

The Butterfly People (257 Calle de la Cruz; 787-723-2432; www.butterflypeople.com) is in a beautifully restored Spanish colonial mansion, where all artwork on display features butterflies in the design.

Cigars: Cigar stores, as well as cigar bars, have proliferated. Near Pier 3, opposite the Sheraton San Juan Hotel in the Covadonga building near the trolley station, is **Cigarros Antillas,** where you can watch a Dominican craftsman roll tobacco into shape and purchase the product. One hand-rolled cigar costs about $2.50; a box of twenty-five cigars, $55.

Clothing: In Old San Juan on Calle del Cristo, you will find **Coach** (787-722-6830), **Dooney & Bourke Factory Store** (787-289-0075), **Polo Ralph Lauren Factory Store** (787-722-2136), and **Guess** (787-977-1550).

T-shirt shops are everywhere. The most attractive have designs adapted from Taino Indian petroglyphs. Hand-painted T-shirt dresses and bathing cover-ups are also popular.

Not to be overlooked are Puerto Rican designers. **Nono Maldonado** (787-721-0456), a former fashion editor of *Esquire,* has a boutique on Ashford Avenue and **David Antonio** has a shop (69 Avenida Condado) in Condado. **Lisa Cappelli** (206 Calle O'Donnell, Old San Juan; 787-724-6575) is a young designer who creates fun, fresh, funky outfits that are sold at several shops around town.

Crafts: An Artisan's Market is held next to La Casita Information Center in Old San Juan on weekends and during the week when cruise ships are in, from noon to 6 p.m. The carving of santos—small wooden figures representing a saint or depicting a religious scene—is considered Puerto Rico's most distinctive craft. The santeros' style and techniques have been passed from father to son for generations.

Musical instruments and masks are two of the oldest crafts. The cuatro is a five-double-string guitar inherited from the Spaniards; the *guiro,* or gourd, comes from a tradition that goes back to the Taino Indians. Mask making is found mainly in Loiza, a town east of San Juan that has maintained its African heritage. Papier-mâché masks, a Spanish tradition, are used in Carnival, particularly in Ponce. Hammocks are another skill that was taught to the early Spaniards by the Taino Indians. Mundillo, handmade bobbin lace, came with the Spaniards and Portuguese.

Aguadilla en San Juan (205 Calle de la Cruz) and **Puerto Rican Art & Crafts** (204 Calle Fortaleza; 787-725-5596; www.puertoricanart-crafts.com) specialize in Puerto Rican crafts. Calle Fortaleza has a tiny lane known simply as **La Calle,** with a variety of attractive shops selling jewelry, leather handbags and belts, and other accessories, masks, and crafts.

Jewelry: Calle Fortaleza has so many jewelry stores, especially for gold, you might think they were giving it away! (A check of stateside prices will convince you they are not.) Some cruise directors and guides direct passengers to certain stores, where they have something to gain. The practice is no different here than in other places around the world, so a good dose of skepticism on your part is healthy. If you plan to buy expensive jewelry, become familiar with prices at home, and do not buy in San Juan or any other Caribbean port without looking around and comparing prices. **Boveda** (209 Calle del Cristo; 787-725-0263) has unusual, one-of-a-kind mod jewelry, accessories, and women's clothing.

Leather: Several shops in Old San Juan import leather goods from Spain and South America. Prices are often much less than those in the United States. The best buys are in the small shops of **La Calle**, a-cul-de-sac near Calle del Cristo and Fortaleza. **Coach** (158 Calle del Cristo; 787-722-6830) has fine leather goods. Most cost about 20 percent less than mainland ones, but some go up to 40 percent.

Dining and Restaurants

Puerto Rico has a cuisine of its own, which you can enjoy at pretty restaurants set in town houses of Old San Juan. Some dishes you might find on menus are black-bean soup; *asopao,* a spicy chicken stew; *pionono,* ripe plantain stuffed with ground beef; *mechada,* stuffed eye of round beef; *pernil,* roast pork; *arroz con gandules,* rice with pigeon peas; and *tostones,* fried plantain. Entries range from moderate (less than $10) to moderately expensive ($10 to $25) to expensive (more than $25).

Old San Juan

Aguaviva (364 Calle Fortaleza; 787-722-0665; www.oofrestaurants.com) offers seafood with Latin pizzazz and even has a ceviche bar. Expensive.

Amadeus (106 Calle San Sebastian; 787-641-7450; www.amadeuspr.com) was one of the first to offer nouvelle Puerto Rican cuisine, sophisticated creations based on local products. Moderately expensive.

Baru (150 Calle San Sebastian; 787-977-7107; www.barupr.com) offers Mediterranean/Caribbean cuisine in one of the most beautiful settings in the Old City, with a spectacular inner courtyard. Especially popular on weekends. Moderately expensive.

Cafe Berlin (407 San Francisco/Plaza Colón; 787-722-5205) is a pastry shop and sidewalk cafe with light fare and vegetarian specialties. Great people-watching spot. Moderate.

Dragonfly (364 Calle Fortaleza; 787-977-3886; www.oofrestaurants.com) is the best of trendy

Asian/Latin fusion cuisine eateries. Expensive.

El Patio de Sam (102 Calle San Sebastian; 787-723-1149) is perfect for a snack or light meal of Puerto Rican and other cuisine during your walking or shopping tour. Moderate.

Il Perugino (105 Calle del Cristo; 787-722-5481; www.ilperugino.com) has a wide selection of veal dishes and fresh fish. Moderately expensive.

La Mallorquina (207 Calle San Justo; 787-722-3261), in operation since 1850, claims to be the oldest restaurant in Puerto Rico. Its menu has the most typical Puerto Rican dishes, along with Spanish and Cuban ones. Moderate.

The Parrot Club (363 Calle Fortaleza; 787-725-7370; www.oofrestaurants.com) offers an eclectic menu of spicy Caribbean cuisine. Moderately expensive. Parrot Club was the first of the culinary enterprises of Emilo and Gigi Figueroa which are among the best and most popular in Old San Juan. In addition to Aguaviva and Dragonfly [described above], there are **Sonne** (364 Calle Fortaleza), a steakhouse with live jazz six nights weekly; **Toro Salao** (367 Calle Tetuan), a tapas bar; Koco at the El San Juan Hotel; and **Sofia** (355 San Francisco), an Italian restaurant offering live jazz Thurs through Sat.

Condado—Isla Verde

BLT Steak at the Ritz-Carlton (Ritz-Carlton, San Juan Hotel, 787-253-1700) was the first Caribbean member of French chef Laurent Tourondel's BLT group. BLT (which stands for Bistro Laurent Tourondel) has a raw bar and seafood entries, but the specialty is steak, particularly Kobe beef and Wagyu Skirt, the American version. There's also a selection of fifteen scrumptious desserts and a kid's menu. Dinner only. Expensive

Budatai (1056 Ashford Ave., 787-725-6919) is a hot, new eatery for Asian fusion, especially Japanese. Expensive.

Chayote (603 Avenida Miramar, Olimpio Court Hotel; 787-722-9385) features fresh local fruits, vegetables, and fish. Moderately expensive.

Marisqueria Atlantica (2475 Loiza St., Ocean Park; 787-726-6654) offers seafood as its specialty. You can select your fish fresh from the display and have it cooked to order. Its sister restaurant (7 Lugo Viñas St.; 787-722-0890) is located at the entrance to Old San Juan. Moderately expensive.

Pikayo (Conrad Condado Plaza Hotel, 999 Ashford Ave., Condado; 787-721-6194; www.pikayo.com). The iconic fine dining restaurant of Puerto Rico's best-known chef Wilo Benet recently moved into elegant new surroundings. Expensive.

Sports

Puerto Rico has some of the best sports facilities in the Caribbean, near enough to the pier for cruise passengers to use them with ease. Contact the hotel or sports operator in advance to make arrangements, particularly during the peak season. And don't overlook spectator sports, especially baseball. In the winter season, from Oct through Feb, all six of the local professional teams have major league players in their lineups. Check newspapers or the **Professional Baseball League of Puerto Rico** (Hato Rey, San Juan; 787-765-6285; www.puertoricobaseballleague.com).

Horse races are held on Mon, Wed, Fri, Sat, Sun, and holidays at **El Commandante** (787-724-6060). Buses leave from Plaza Colón, timed for the starting race, and return according to the racing schedule. Horse shows are often held when a village celebrates a saint's day or festival. The local breed, Paso Fino, is a small, spirited horse noted for its gait. Check *Que Pasa.*

Beaches/Swimming: All beaches are public, including hotel beaches. Those operated by the government or municipality have *balneario* facilities (lockers, showers, and parking) at nominal fees. Hotels on or near Condado Beach are the closest to the port; Isla Verde Beach, where El San Juan Hotel and Ritz-Carlton Hotel are located, is 1 mile from the airport.

Deep-Sea Fishing: San Juan is one of the world's favorite sportsfishing spots. Half- or full-day and split-boat charters with crew and equipment are available; expect to pay about $550 and up for a half day and $900 and up for a full day for up to six people. Contact **Benitez Fishing Charters** (Club Nautico San Juan, Miramar; 787-723-2292; www.mikebenitezsportfishing.com) or **Caribbean Outfitters** (787-396-8346; www.fishinginpuertorico.com).

Golf: The quartet of Robert Trent Jones championship courses at the **Dorado Beach Resort & Club** (787-796-8961; www.doradobeachclubs.com) are not only among the best in the Caribbean, but in the world. Located at Dorado 15 miles west of San Juan, these courses are famous for their layouts and natural settings. East and West greens fees for non-guests: $195 morning, $119 afternoon, $60 after 4 p.m. in the low season; Sugar Cane and Pineapple: $135 morning, $89 afternoon, $45 after 4 p.m. Reserve in advance. **Rico Suntours** (787-722-2080; www.ricosuntours.com) can make arrangements to play the Dorado Beach Club courses as well as other courses in Puerto Rico.

Rio Mar Beach Resort & Spa, a Wyndham Grand Resort (787-888-6000; www.wyndhamriomar.com) east of San Juan (a forty-minute drive from the port), has two 18-hole courses: one designed by Tom and George Fazio and another by Greg Norman, his first in the Caribbean. Both are dotted with lakes and have El Yunque as a backdrop and a palm-fringed beach in the foreground. The St. Regis Bahia Beach Golf Course is the first in Puerto Rico by Robert Trent Jones Jr. Water will be a strong component of this course overlooking the Atlantic Ocean. Reservations, (787) 809-8000. The course is part of a 483-acre residential and vacation enclave in Rio Grande anchored by the St. Regis Resort & Residences, 2 miles east of San Juan.

Hiking: The best trails are in the rain forest of the Caribbean National Forest of El Yunque and range from an easy fifteen-minute walk to arduous eight-hour treks. Information and maps are available from El Portal, the visitor and interpretive center that opened in 1996. Hours: daily 9 a.m. to 5 p.m. Admission: $3 adults, $1.50 seniors; children younger than age fifteen are free. For hiking information call Caribbean National Forest (787-888-1880; www.fs.fed.us/r8/caribbean). See El Yunque section for more information.

A list of companies that offer hiking excursions is available from the Puerto Rico Tourism Company. The following are samples:

- **AdvenTours** (Luquillo; 787-530-8311; www.adventourspr.com). Excursions with environmental and cultural focus, bird and wildlife observation, hiking, biking, kayaking. Reservations required.

- **Aventuras Tierra Adentro** (San Juan; 787-766-0470; www.adventurespr.com). Rappelling, caving, rock climbing, canyoning, body rafting.

- **Copladet Nature & Adventure Travel** (San Juan; 787-765-8595; www.copladet.com). Nature and adventure excursions with environmental education: bird-watching, rappelling, caving, hiking, body rafting, trips to Mona Island.

- **Encantos Ecotours** (San Juan; 787-272-0005; www.ecotourspr.com). Historic, cultural, and nature tours; kayaking, snorkeling, biking, hiking, and sailing lessons and gear rental. Also custom design excursions.

Horseback Riding: East of San Juan near Luquillo Beach, **Hacienda Carabali** (787-889-5820; www.haciendacarabalipuertorico.com) offers group riding along the coast and foothills of El Yunque. Rico Suntours (800-844-2080) offers a half-day guided riding excursion for $85.

Kayaking: Kayaks can be rented by the hour at the Condado Plaza Hotel water-sports center. **Yokahú Kayak Trips** (Fajardo; 787-604-7375) offers eco-adventure kayak tours to the bioluminescent bay and lagoon, with licensed guides and equipment included. Also see companies under Hiking.

Scuba and Snorkeling: Some of Puerto Rico's best snorkeling and diving are found on the east coast around the coral-fringed islands facing Fajardo. Boats operated by water-sports centers at San Juan resort hotels depart daily for these locations. Equipment for certified divers is available for rent. Several catamarans offer full-day picnic sails with snorkeling to Icacos. An outstanding scuba location, dubbed the Puerto Rican Wall and as exciting for divers as the Cayman Wall, is off the south coast at La Parguera.

Caribe Aquatic Adventures (Park Plaza Normandie in Condado; 787-281-8858; www.diveguide.com/p2046.htm) is one of the oldest dive operations on the island and a member of the Puerto Rico Water Sport Federation. It has daily dive trips and arranges kayaking, sailing, windsurfing, and kite sailing. A list of dive operators is available in *Que Pasa*.

Tennis: Courts and full-time pros are available at more than a dozen San Juan hotels. Nearest the port is Caribe Hilton, with three night-lit courts. **San Juan Central Park** (Cerra Street; 787-722-1646) has more than a dozen public courts with night lighting. Hours: open daily.

Entertainment/Cultural Events

San Juan has a full calendar of seasonal concerts by the Puerto Rico Symphony Orchestra, San Juan Opera Company, several ballet and theater groups, Broadway productions, and performances by visiting artists. Most are given at the **Fine Arts Center** (El Centro de Bellas Artes; 787-620-4444; www.cba.gobierno.pr), also known as the Performing Arts Center, a multi-auditorium complex and one of the best-equipped facilities in the Caribbean. Another venue is the **Tapia Theatre,** in Old San Juan.

The year's biggest cultural event is the **Casals Festival of the Performing Arts** in late Feb/early Mar, but there are many art and music festivals throughout the year. *Que Pasa* lists all major cultural and sporting events.

The **LeLoLai Festival** offers weekly shows highlighting Puerto Rico's folklore with song, dance, and crafts. Each show has a different theme to reflect Puerto Rico's long and rich culture and blends the island's Spanish, African, and Taino Indian heritages. The festival, staged at participating hotels, is sponsored by the Puerto Rico Tourism Company and is usually available to cruise passengers as part of a shore excursion.

You also have a choice of small bars with Spanish guitars or jazz in the Old City or nightclubs, discos, cabarets, and casinos in Condado or Isla Verde. Some of the liveliest action is at lobby bars that have combos playing salsa and other Latin and disco beats, and there's even a **Hard Rock Cafe.**

Small-scale **Carli Café Concierto** (206 Tetuan St.; 787-725-4927) in Old San Juan is the place to hear jazz. Some other nightspots:

- **Nuyorican Café** (312 San Francisco St.; 787-977-1276; www.nuyoricancafepr.com) is a cafe theater with live music, theatrical performances, and poetry readings; live salsa Fri and Sat nights, Charanga on Sat after 10:30 p.m. Mick Jagger and other celebrities use it as an after-concert hangout.

- **Parrot Club** (363 Fortaleza St.; 787-725-7370; www.oofrestaurants.com) offers background jazz and live Latin music Tues, Thurs, and Sat.
- **Borinquen Grill & Brewing Company** (800 Av. Isla Verde, San Juan; 787-268-1900; www.borinquenbrewing.com) is the island's first and only microbrewery, offering hard-to-find draft beer.

Casinos: All of San Juan's casinos are in hotels, and some, like the Conrad Condado Plaza and El San Juan, are practically in the lobby.

San Juan's Environs

Catano and Palo Seco: Across the bay from San Juan in Catano is the home of the **Bacardi Rum Distillery**, the largest single producer of rum in the world. There are a gift shop and open-air patio bar with beautiful views across manicured grounds and the bay to Old San Juan. At the plant's visitor center, Casa Bacardi (www.casabacardi.com), you wander through interactive exhibits chronicling the Bacardi family and its rum with the help of individual audio guides. A rum tour is usually offered as a shore excursion by cruise ships.

On your own, the ferry for **Catano** (787-788-0940; www.prpa.gobierno.pr) departs every fifteen minutes on weekdays and every half hour on Sat and Sun from 5:45 a.m. to 9:45 p.m. from a small dock situated between Pier 1 and Pier 2. The ride takes about twenty minutes. On the opposite side of the bay, you can get a publico (shared minibus) to the Bacardi Rum Distillery. Open Mon to Sat, 8:30 a.m. to 5:30 p.m. (the last tour is at 4:15 p.m.), and Sun, 10 a.m. to 5 p.m. (last tour at 3:45 p.m.).

Botanical Gardens: In the San Juan suburb of Rio Piedras, about a thirty-minute drive from the port, are the **Agricultural Experiment Station Botanical Gardens,** which is part of the University of Puerto Rico, and the Institute of Tropical Forestry (787-766-5335; www.tropicalforestry.net), which is part of the U.S. Forest Service. Spanning both sides of a stream and a series of ponds, the gardens cover an area of 270 acres, 45 of which are

developed in a park setting, providing a delightful introduction to the enormous variety of plants, flowers, and trees of Puerto Rico and the Caribbean. At **Casa Rosada** (787-767-1710, open weekdays), the headquarters, an orientation and a leaflet guide in Spanish are available.

East of San Juan

El Yunque: In the Luquillo Mountains, about thirty minutes east of San Juan, is the Caribbean National Forest, more commonly known as El Yunque—the only tropical rain forest in the U.S. Forest Service system. Long a research center on tropical flora and fauna, El Yunque has 240 species of trees, more than 200 types of fern, and 60 species of birds. One of its most important projects has been the effort to save the Puerto Rican parrot, decimated from an estimated million birds at the time of Columbus to only twenty-two in 1975. Now the bird's numbers are slowly being rebuilt.

You can drive through El Yunque on a tarmac road (No. 191) that goes into the heart of the rain forest, passing waterfalls, lookouts, and picnic areas. At the northern boundary of the forest, you'll find the office of the Caribbean National Forest and El Portal, the visitor and interpretive center, open daily (787-888-1810). Maps—essential for hiking—and an orientation are available. Look for *Where Dwarfs Reign: A Tropical Rain Forest in Puerto Rico* by Kathryn Robinson (University of Puerto Rico Press, 1997). Written in readable layman language, it is the most comprehensive book available on El Yunque.

La Mina/Big Tree Trail, a paved path leading to La Mina Falls, takes about an hour, round-trip. It runs along the Mina River and passes through a forest of stately tabonuco trees, one of the four types of forest found in the reserve.

Las Cabezas de San Juan: In the northeastern corner of the island, about a thirty-minute drive from El Yunque, is **Las Cabezas de San Juan Nature Reserve,** a 316-acre peninsula of forest land, mangroves, lagoons, beaches, cliffs, cays, and coral reefs, marked by a 19th-century lighthouse, **El Faro,** which serves as the visitor center. Opened in 1991 by the Conservation Trust of Puerto Rico, there are nature exhibits in the lighthouse and walkways through the mangroves. Guided tours on trolleys introduce visitors to the peninsula's ecology. Reservations (787-860-2560) are required. A spectacular view from the lighthouse extends 40 miles east to the Virgin Islands and west over El Yunque and the Caribbean.

Fajardo: South of the reserve on the coast is Fajardo, home to Puerto Rico's largest marina and an occasional port for small cruise ships. Nearby is El Conquistador Resort and Golden Door Spa (787-863-1000; www.elconresort.com), a large elaborate resort with a championship golf course and excellent tennis and water-sports facilities.

West of San Juan

Rio Camuy Cave Park: The Camuy Caves are the largest on the island, with a surface area of 268 acres. Seven miles of passageways have been explored, including chambers as high as a twenty-five-story building. The Camuy River, the third-largest underground river in the world, passes through the complex system.

At the visitor center a film provides an orientation. At the cave entrance visitors accompanied by bilingual guides board a tram for the tour. The tram winds through a ravine with rain-forest vegetation to the first of sixteen chambers, where passengers begin a forty-five-minute walk. The room is illuminated by natural light that penetrates the entrance. It leads to another huge chamber, tall enough to hold a 17-foot-high stalagmite. The trail winds along a path from which the Camuy River, 150 feet below, comes into view. The park (787-898-3100) is open Wed to Sun and on holidays. Entrance: $10 adults, $7 children, $5 seniors. From Old San Juan it is a one-and-a-half-hour drive west via Arecibo and inland on Route 129. Not far from the park, you can detour to the small mountain town of Lares, which is famous for its ice-cream parlor (Heladería de Lares; Plaza de Recreo, Lecaroz Street; 787-897-3290), where you can sample any of the sometimes bizarre flavors, such as tomato, garlic, cabbage, chickpea, celery, and beer. Not to worry, there are the customary flavors: chocolate, strawberry, and many more.

Arecibo Observatory: Nearby, the Arecibo Observatory (787-878-2612; www.naic.edu) is the largest radar/radio telescope in the world—a 20-acre dish set in a sinkhole equal in size to thirteen football fields—where scientists listen for signs of intelligent life in the universe. Many exciting discoveries have been made here, including the mapping of one of the largest structures in the universe—a cluster of galaxies—and observations from which scientists determined the true rotation of the planet Mercury. Here, too, the first planets outside our solar system were found.

Operated by Cornell University, the observatory has the wonderful Arecibo Observatory Visitor and Educational Facility. It makes the research being undertaken here more accessible to the nonscientific community. The building houses interactive exhibits, a theater, meeting rooms, work space, and a science-related book and gift shop. Hours: Wed to Fri noon to 4 p.m.; weekends and holidays 9 a.m. to 4 p.m. Admission: $5 adults, $3 seniors, students, and children younger than age twelve.

The Panoramic Route: Crossing the center of Puerto Rico is a spine of tall green mountains, Cordillera Central, with peaks that are often concealed by clouds. The Panoramic Route, a 165-mile road made up of forty different routes, winds through the mountains, from Yabucoa on the southeast to Mayagüez on the west coast, providing spectacular panoramas through forests and rural landscapes—light-years away from the bustle and glitter of San Juan. The route divides into three sections, each requiring a day to cover with stops along the way. There are trails, picnic areas, a spring-fed swimming hole, and man-made lakes—reservoirs created in the 1930s to harness the island's water resources.

Ponce

Puerto Rico's second-largest city, Ponce, was founded in 1692 by a great-grandson of Ponce de Leon, for whom it was named. The site is thought to be an ancient one, since a huge Indian burial ground lies a short distance north of town.

Ponce is a treasure of architecture, with streets of colonial houses with balconies and wrought-iron railings reminiscent of Savannah and New Orleans. Other houses are turn-of-the-20th-century Victorian gems, with gingerbread trim reminiscent of Key West; still others built in the 1930s and 1940s are straight off the drawing boards of art deco architects.

On the main square, the Old Firehouse is painted bright red and black, Ponce's colors. It's all the more startling, standing as it does next to the classic Cathedral of Our Lady of Guadaloupe, which dates from 1670. The firehouse has a collection of memorabilia pertaining to the history of the building.

Ponce is especially proud of its **Museo de Arte de Ponce** (2325 Avenue Las Americas; 787-848-0505; www.museoarteponce.org), housed in a building designed by Edward Durrell Stone. The collection, one of the largest in the Caribbean, has more than one thousand paintings and four hundred sculptures representing all periods of Western art from ancient to contemporary. Hours: daily 10 a.m. to 5 p.m. Admission: $5 adults, $2.50 children. The Visitor's Information Center (Cristina and Mayor Streets) is directly across from La Perla Theatre, where plays, concerts, and other events are held throughout the year.

Castillo Serralles, the former mansion of a wealthy local rum-producing family, sits high on a hillside overlooking the city and has been converted into a museum. Open Tues to Sun. (787-259-1774; www.castilloserralles.org). Admission: $4 to $9 adults; $1 to $4 children, students, seniors.

Indian Ceremonial Park: One of the oldest, most important burial grounds ever discovered in the Caribbean is the Tibes Indian Ceremonial Park, 2 miles north of town. Here, seven ceremonial plazas belonging to the Igneri culture, dating from A.D. 600 to 1000, were found. The museum has displays pertaining to the Taino Indians and other pre-Columbian cultures. A film on the first Puerto Ricans is shown every forty-five minutes as an orientation to the site. Guides are available; 787-840-2255. Open Tues to Sun.

Hacienda Buena Vista: In the foothills of the Cordillera Central north of Ponce is an old estate that was once one of the largest working plantations in Puerto Rico, growing coffee and other cash crops. Now a property of the Puerto Rico Conservation Trust, it has been extensively renovated as an interpretive center and museum. A footpath through the pretty woods leads to waterfalls along an aqueduct that once carried water to a huge waterwheel supplying the estate with its power. Multilingual guides lead visitors through the grounds. Reservations are required. (787) 722-5882 (San Juan); (787) 284-7020 (Buena Vista).

The Dominican Republic

Land of Superlatives

The Dominican Republic is the oldest European settlement in the New World, and it has the tallest mountains in the region. It also has some of the longest beaches, the best golf and tennis facilities, the best museums, the best restaurants and the hottest nightclubs, and among the lowest prices in the region. Within its boundaries is a diverse landscape of great green mountains that climb to 10,400 feet, rain forests, rolling hills, plains, lowlands, and a lake, 144 feet below sea level—the only saltwater body in the world with crocodiles. Yet, despite its extensive tourism development of the past two decades, which resulted in more hotel rooms than any other destination in the Caribbean, the Dominican Republic has been the region's best kept secret for cruise passengers. Now that's beginning to change.

Second only to Cuba as the largest country of the Caribbean's island nations, the Dominican Republic covers 19,000 square miles or about two-thirds of Hispaniola, the island it shares with Haiti. It lies between Cuba on the west and Puerto Rico on the east and faces the Atlantic on the north and the Caribbean on the south.

Santo Domingo, the capital of this Spanish-speaking country, is located on the Caribbean coast. A cosmopolitan and sophisticated city with more than two million people, it combines modern comforts and conveniences with Old World history and charm. New port developments aim at making the city a major port of call.

Meanwhile, the east coast, with its miles of palm-fringed beaches, has been the setting for extensive resort development, particularly in the area of **Punta Cana**. Further north on the east coast, the **Bay of Samana**, a major whale

watching location from December to March and the new focus of resort development, has some of the country's most outstanding natural attractions. The island of **Cayo Levantado** at the mouth of the bay is a day-at-the-beach stop for several cruise lines for its lovely beaches. On the southeast coast near the sugar mill town of **La Romana** are the islands of **Catalina** and **Casa de Campo**, a 7,000-acre resort famous for its three golf courses, tennis complex, polo fields, and artists' village. The entire region is also known for deep-sea fishing.

On the island's north coast, **Puerto Plata** is near the site of **La Isabela,** where Christopher Columbus landed on his first voyage in 1492. The 80 miles of white sand beaches east of Puerto Plata was one of the first areas of extensive resort development; it is known as the windsurfing and kitesurfing capital of the Caribbean. At one time Puerto Plata was a frequent port of call, but as the country concentrated on resort development with the employment and tourists it brings, the port was neglected and finally abandoned. There is talk of reviving it, but major investment would be needed to bring it up to today's requirements. For now, there's more interest in Santo Domingo's potential.

When Columbus returned to the island, which he called *La Isla Espanola*, in 1493, he established a settlement at La Isabela, but within a few years the Spaniards moved south, where they founded **Santo Domingo.** It became their capital and for the next century, it was their base of operation to explore and conquer the New World. By 1697, however, the Spaniards were no longer able to hold the entire island and ceded the western part (now Haiti) to France. A century later in 1795, Spain, due to her greater interests in Latin America, gave up the entire island to France. But France's ownership was not to last either.

Demands by French colonists, who sniffed the winds of the French and American revolutions and revolts by slaves in the western portion, gave Napoleon all he could handle and enabled the Dominicans to call in the English for help in recapturing Santo Domingo. Over the next fifty years, the island was under the control of the Dominicans, French, Spanish, and Haitians. Finally, on February 27, 1844, the Dominicans, led by Juan Pablo Duarte and two colleagues in a movement

known as La Trinitaria, declared their independence. But they had great difficulty making it stick. Disorder, dictatorships, and intermittent peace characterized the country's history until World War I, when the United States sent in the Marines. The United States administered the country from 1916 to 1924.

In 1930 after a coup d'etat and a rigged election, Rafael Trujillo began what was to become a thirty-year dictatorship during which he was so exploitive and corrupt that even now his name is used almost generically to describe the most ruthless of rulers. His reign ended with his assassination in 1961, by which time he and his family had amassed a legendary fortune. Two attempts at civilian government were followed by coups and a civil war. In 1965 the United States, worried that another Cuba was in the making, sent in the Marines again. Fortunately, a democratic government was established and has prevailed to the present.

After the Spanish conquistadors had depleted the country of its gold and its native Indian population, they imported African slaves and established a plantation society to exploit the country's rich agricultural potential. To this day, although the country has made great efforts to diversify, its economy is still basically agricultural with sugar as the major crop. The country passed through an extremely difficult period during the early 1990s when the economy was in terrible shape and inflation was running over 100 percent. The tide began to turn in 1992 and the picture brightened so that by 1993, inflation had been reduced to 4 percent. In the years that followed, the economy has grown at a healthy rate, with tourism being the fastest growing segment.

Santo Domingo has been named the Cultural Capital of the Americas for 2010, underscoring its wealth of landmarks, monuments, arts, theater, and culture ranging from cobblestone streets in the Old City, a World Heritage site, to its modern architecture and transportation systems. And not to be forgotten, baseball is not just a sport here but a national passion, and many major league players, such as Sammy Sosa, Alex Rodriguez, Pedro Martinez, David Ortiz, Manny Ramirez, to name a few, hail from the Dominican Republic.

Population: 9,760,000

Main Towns: Santo Domingo, Santiago, Puerto Plata, Punta Cana, La Romana, Sosua, Higuey

Government: Democratic form of government with executive, legislative, and judicial branches. Elections held every four years.

Climate: Pleasant, warm weather year-round along the coast and lowlands averaging 77°F in winter, 82°F in summer, and up to 30 degrees cooler in the high mountain regions.

Clothing: Casual, informal dress is worn throughout the country, but in any elegant restaurant in Santo Domingo, patrons are fashionably dressed.

Currency: Dominican peso fluctuates around 37 pesos to the U.S. dollar. U.S. dollars are readily accepted.

Customs Regulations: Cruise passengers who disembark in the Dominican Republic to return to the United States by plane must have a tourist card (US $10).

Departure Tax: US $20, which is usually included in the airline ticket.

Electricity: 120 volts; 60 cycles.

Entry Formalities: A tourist card ($10), required for U.S. citizens, is a formality handled by a cruise line for its passengers. However, you will need a passport to leave and reenter the United States.

Language: Spanish. On the tourist track, you will find English widely used, but if you do not speak any Spanish, a Spanish language phrase book or small dictionary is handy.

Public Holidays: Jan 1, New Year's Day; Jan 6, Kings Day (Epiphany); Jan 21, Our Lady of Altagracia; Jan 26, Duarte's Birthday; Feb 27, Independence Day (also the start of Carnival); Good Friday; Easter Sunday; May 1, Labor Day; Corpus Christi (60 days after Good Friday); Aug 16, Restoration Day; Sept 24, Our Lady of Las Mercedes; Oct 12, Columbus Day; Nov 6, Constitution Day; Dec 25, Christmas.

Telephone Area Code: 809. Direct dial to and from the United States is available.

Time: One hour ahead of Eastern Standard Time, Nov through Apr; same as Eastern Standard Time, May through Oct.

Airlines: From the United States, American, American Eagle, Continental, Delta, JetBlue, Spirit, US Airways. The airport in Santo Domingo is 16 miles east of the city. Domestic service: Aerodomca (www.aerodomca.com), Air Century (www.aircentury.com), Take Off (www.takeoffweb.com), and VolAir (www.govolair.com).

Information: www.godominicanrepublic.com

In the United States:

Dominican Tourism, 136 East 57th St., #803, New York, NY 10022; (212) 588-1012; (888) 374-6361; newyork@godominicanrepublic.com. Other offices in Miami and Chicago.

In Canada:

26 Wellington St. East, Suite 201, Toronto, M5E-1S2; (514) 499-1918; (800) 563-1611; montreal@godominicanrepublic.com.

In Santo Domingo:

Consejo de Promocion Turistica, Dominican Republic Ministry of Tourism, Mexico Ave.; (809) 221-4660; www.godominicanrepublic.com

American Chamber of Commerce, Hotel Santo Domingo, (809) 381-0777.

U.S. Consulate, Maximo Gomez Ave. and Cesar Nicolas Penson St.; (809) 221-2171.

The cruise ships that stop here do not spend enough time for passengers to take advantage of all the attractions and facilities the country has to offer. But, as is often the case with cruise passengers, if you are looking for places to return for a longer holiday, the Dominican Republic should be high on your list for its value and endless attractions.

Budget Planning

The Dominican Republic is one of the least expensive countries for visitors in the Caribbean. Food and restaurant prices are low compared to most other islands, and Dominican-made jewelry and crafts are bargains. However, by law a 16% sales tax and a 10% service charge are added to restaurant bills. Taxis can be expensive but shared taxis, buses, and the new metro are cheap.

Port Profile: Santo Domingo

Location/Embarkation: One of the biggest attractions of Santo Domingo for cruise passengers is the port's proximity to the city. The Port of Santo Domingo actually encompasses three separate areas. The **Don Diego dock and terminal (2)**, renovated and upgraded in 2006, is located on the west side of the Ozama River directly below the walls of the **Colonial Zone**. Steps from the water-front lead up to the historic city. Don Diego dock handles ships with up to 2,000 passengers.

On the east side of the river almost directly across from the Colonial Zone is the new **San Souci terminal (1)** which is the first phase of a large development that will include extensive residential, commercial, and entertainment facilities. San Souci dock has the capacity to handle ships with up to 4,000 passengers and is equipped for home porting operations. At the mouth of the river at the foot of the Colonial Zone is a marina for yachts that is being expanded. The former Navy base had to be moved to Boca Chica to make way for the new port developments.

On the southeast coast, **La Romana Port** can receive large cruise ships that mostly offer tours to nearby **Casa de Campo**, famous for its golf courses and polo fields, and **Altos de Chavón**, an artists' village; and to **Catalina Island** (or Serena Cay) for a day-at-the-beach excursion. On the northeast coast, **Samaná Peninsula and Bay** is attracting more and more cruise ships for its remarkable natural attractions, including whale watching from January to March, bird life and unusual terrain in the **Los Haitises National Park**, and beautiful beaches and water sports at **Cayo Levantado** in the Bay, and at **Las Terrenas** and **Playa Rincón** on the north shore.

Local Transportation: The city has eight different, very inexpensive bus routes. *Collectivos* (seat-in-taxi), known here as *publicos,* are inexpensive, and those that run along major arteries are easy to use with a little Spanish and a sense of adventure. Taxis are plentiful but do not have meters. They are usually cream colored and have a sign, Taxi Turistico, along with a number assigned them by the Tourism Office painted on their door. The **Santo Domingo Metro** (subway), opened in

early 2009, cuts through the heart of the city, and has fourteen station stops. Work has begun on a second line with twenty stations, and four more lines have been planned.

Roads and Rentals: The Dominican Republic has a large network of roads, often crossing beautiful landscapes, such as the newest route through the Los Haitises National Park hills to the Samaná Peninsula and the north coast. Expect to pay from $60 to $90 per day, depending on the model, for automatic shift and unlimited mileage, including insurance. You can drive here with a valid U.S. or Canadian driver's license. Driving is on the right side of the road. Gas stations close at 8 or 9 p.m. In Santo Domingo: **Budget** (J.F. Kennedy Ave., 809-566-6666; www.budget.com) and **Nelly Rent**

a Car (654 Independence Ave., 809-687-7997; www.nellyrac.com) offer pick up and delivery service; Avis, Dollar, National-Alamo, and EuropCar are also represented. Information is available from the National Association of Rental Cars (www.andri.com.do).

Shore Excursions

If this is your first visit to Santo Domingo, you will probably want to take a city tour, either by motorcoach or private car, since the city is too spread out to cover on foot. However, if you are a history buff and like walking, you can easily cover the Colonial City on foot. For more adventurous passengers, several tour companies in Santo Domingo offer nature-oriented excursions that must be arranged in advance, if your cruise ship does not offer them. Contact **Prieto Tours** (Avenida Francia No. 125, 685-0102, www.prieto-tours.com.do; and **Turinter Tours** (Leopoldo Navarro No. 4, 809-686-4020; www.turinter.com), among others.

From Santo Domingo

City Tour: Old and New, three to four hours. Visit the Colonial City with stops at the **Cathedral, Alcazar,** and **National Pantheon,** followed by the modern city, passing the **National Palace** and the **Cultural Plaza.** A full day might add **Columbus Lighthouse, Three Eye Cave, National Aquarium, Botanical Garden, Museum of the Dominican Man,** and the **Gallery of Modern Art.** Optional lunch at local restaurant.

Beach Tour: Full day. En route to **Boca Chica Beach,** a thirty-minute drive east of Santo Domingo, visit Los Tres Ojos. At the beach, you have a hotel room for changing and access to the pool, chaise lounges, and other facilities.

Night Tour: Three hours, Thurs through Sun, departing at 9 p.m. Most tours include **Guacara Taino,** a nightclub in a cave, as well as visits to a disco, hotel casino, and show.

Jarabacoa, the Dominican Alps: Full day. To the countryside with the highest mountains in the Caribbean, ride horses and hike to a waterfall where you can swim in clear—but cold—water. Lunch at restaurant in Jarabacoa village.

Santo Domingo on Your Own

Santo Domingo is the oldest continuously inhabited city established by the Spaniards in the Americas. Its precise origins are blurred between fairy tale and fact, but in 1496, after Columbus returned to Spain from his second voyage, he sent word to his brother, Bartholomew (whom he had left to govern in La Isabela, Columbus's first settlement), to go south to find a suitable place for a new settlement. History is unclear about Columbus's motives but it was probably to be closer to the mother lode of the island's gold, which Columbus had learned was in the south.

Bartholomew selected a site near the mouth of the Ozama River on the east bank to establish an outpost and named it La Isabela Nueva. Today, the site is marked by the **Chapel of the Rosario.** The chapel is near the enormous **Columbus Lighthouse,** which was completed in 1992 to commemorate the 500th anniversary of Columbus's arrival in the New World.

In 1498, the settlement was moved across the river to the west bank, where the Colonial City now stands, and was renamed Santo Domingo. In an area of one square mile the Spaniards built their first fortress, first hospital, first cathedral, and first university in the New World. Within a decade, the new town had become Spain's colonial capital, where such men as Hernan Cortes, Diego de Velazquez, Ponce de Leon, and Alonso de Ojeda planned the conquest of Mexico and the New World. Today, such history is a lively part of a modern city that extends 15 miles or more in all directions from its 16th-century origin. With a day in port it is possible, if you move quickly, to see both old and new Santo Domingo.

Santo Domingo is much more than history and sightseeing. It's lots of fun and has an atmosphere of warmth and friendliness. In 2009, Santo Domingo was named the Cultural Capital of the Americas for 2010. The city bounces with every sort of entertainment, from romantic piano bars to pulsating discotheques, smart supper clubs to brassy cabarets and casinos. It has restaurants of great variety to suit most anyone's taste, from hamburgers and pizza to

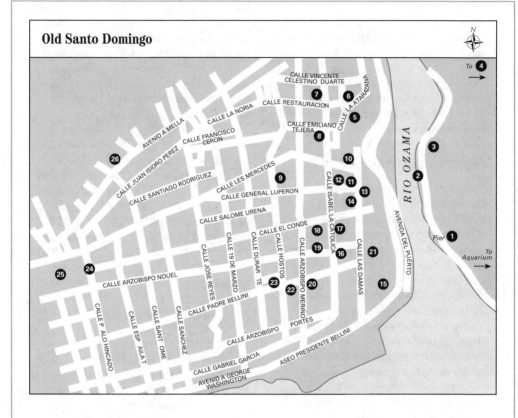

Old Santo Domingo

1. San Souci Cruise Terminal
2. Don Diego Pier
3. Chapel of the Rosary
4. Columbus Lighthouse
5. Alcazar and Plaza de la Hispanidad
6. Las Atarazanas/Museo de las Atarazanas Reales
7. Duarte Museum
8. House of the Cord
9. Hospital of San Nicolas de Bari
10. Museo de las Casas Reales
11. National Pantheon
12. Plaza de Maria de Toledo
13. Hostal de Nicolas de Ovando
14. Casa de Francia (Hernan Cortes House)
15. Tower of Homage
16. Casa de Sacramento (Archbishop of Santo Domingo)
17. Borgella Palace
18. Plaza Colon
19. Cathedral of Santa Maria la Menor
20. Casa de Tostado (Museum of the Dominican Family)
21. House of Bastidas
22. Las Casas Park; Convent of the Dominicans
23. Duarte Park
24. El Conde Gate
25. Independence Park
26. Mercado Modelo

seafood and Dominican specialties. They also have a wide range in price and ambience. The city offers a variety of sports, including tennis, golf, bowling, boating, horseback riding, fishing, and diving. And then there's baseball. Baseball, the national sport of the Dominican Republic, with fans as ardent as those in the United States, has two seasons: the professional winter season, from late October through January, when local teams are joined by some greats from the United States; and the summer season, from April through September. Many games are played at **Quisqueya Stadium;** check local newspapers.

Exploring the Colonial City

If walls could speak, those in the **Colonial Zone** of Santo Domingo would have 500 years of stories to tell. Particularly interesting would be the tales of the city's early years, which would weave a tapestry of the courage and glory, the greed and intrigue, and the triumphs and tragedies that fell on Christopher Columbus, his brother, Bartholomew, his son, Diego, and on all the conquistadors who followed them.

The 16th-century town, defined by remnants of the original walls overlooking the Ozama River, covers less than a square mile and contains seventy-six churches, chapels, old houses, palaces, monuments, forts, gates, parks, plazas, and other points of interest. In 1992 for the Columbus Quincentennial, the entire Old City was beautifully restored and its historic buildings and monuments were renovated with aid from Spain. The cathedral, the oldest in the Americas, was given particular attention. The waterfront was made accessible with a boulevard and a series of steps leading directly from the waterfront into the heart of the Colonial City. The improvements brought renewed life to the ancient district, where restaurants, art galleries, shops, and museums are housed in the lovely historic buildings that line the pretty little streets and overlook the graceful parks. The Colonial Zone, along with some 300 monuments throughout the country, was declared a World Heritage site by UNESCO in 1990.

Depending on where your ship docks—**Don Diego pier (2)** or **San Souci pier (1)**—will

determine the ease to reach the Old City. Once in the Colonial Zone, you can start your walk at the **Alcazar (5)** or **Plaza Colon (18).** Normally, you can cover the main parts on a walking tour of three hours or so, but a visit to all the sites with time to linger in the museums and shops and relax over lunch at one of the restaurants needs a full day. The big central market, the **Mercado Modelo (26),** is within walking distance of the Colonial Zone. Admission to most sites is free unless noted otherwise. Most are open daily Tues to Sun from 9 a.m. to 5 or 6 p.m.

Calle las Damas: The town Columbus knew was a typical, walled Spanish town laid out in the grid with a central plaza anchored by a church. You could start at almost any spot, but if you enjoy historic symmetry, **Calle Las Damas** which runs north-south paralleling the eastern walls and the Ozama River, is the oldest street of the Americas. It was named for the women brought to the New World to form the court for Columbus's son, Diego, the first viceroy, and his wife, Maria de Toledo, the niece of King Ferdinand of Spain who financed Columbus's expeditions. The northern end of the street was made into a huge esplanade in front of the Alcazar.

Alcazar (5): Situated on the edge of the fort overlooking the river, the palace was built in 1514 for Diego Columbus. It is now a museum, and the reception rooms, galleries, and state apartments furnished with antiques or reproductions of the early Spanish period give viewers a good idea about life at the court in the early history of the New World. In Saturday evening shows, players in period costume depict Don Diego, his wife, and their court and reenact those historic times. There is a small admission fee. Call (809) 682-4750 for more information.

Plaza de la Hispanidad, the large courtyard in front of the palace, is frequently used for outdoor concerts. From here, you can look across the Ozama River to the Columbus Lighthouse in the distance and to the **Chapel of the Rosary (3),** the site of Bartholomew's Nueva Isabela, in the foreground. Between the Alcazar and the Ozama River, centuries of debris and modern obstructions were removed in the renovations to reveal the old city walls. Steps on both sides of the Alcazar lead through ancient gates in the walls to the waterfront boulevard.

Las Atarazanas (6): The north and west sides of the plaza in front of the Alcazar are renovated former warehouses of the port and the arsenal of the fort. Today, they house attractive restaurants, boutiques, art galleries, and shops selling native Dominican crafts. Several sidewalk cafes line the west side of the plaza and are especially popular in the late afternoon and evening. They also are the best vantage point for viewing the cross in the sky formed by the floodlights atop the Columbus Lighthouse Monument. On the north side of the plaza, directly in front of the Gate of the Royal Arsenals, is the Museo De Las Atarazanas Reales devoted to the history of navigation in Dominican waters. Among its displays are the gold, silver, jewelry, Ming china, and other articles recovered from sunken galleons: the 17th-century *Concepcion* and the 18th-century *Guadalupe* and *Tolosa,* found in the late 1970s off the north coast and Samana Bay. The museum has miniature models of Columbus's three ships. The oldest artifacts are the cannons from the ship of Nicolas de Ovando, the first governor, dating from 1502.

House of the Cord (*Casa de Cordon*) (8): So named because of the cord decoration on the facade representing the Franciscan order, this is thought to be the oldest stone building in Santo Domingo, and thus, the oldest European structure in the Western Hemisphere. Diego Columbus and his wife lived here while the Alcazar was being built. It is now a bank and open during regular business hours. At the end of Tejera Street are the ruins of the Monastery of San Francisco.

Duarte Museum (7): Located at 308 Isabel La Catolica St.,(809-687-1436), the house where Juan Pablo Duarte, the Father of Dominican Independence, was born on January 26, 1813. After his return from study in Europe Duarte formed a secret society, La Trinitaria, together with Ramon Mella and Juan Sanchez Ramirez. His house became a center of revolutionary activity against the much-hated Haitian occupation that lasted twenty-two years. In 1844 he led the move to proclaim the nation's independence.

Museo de las Casas Reales (10): At the corner of Mercedes and Las Damas is the Museum of the Royal Houses, the first Palace of Justice and, later, the headquarters of the colonial government. Today, the stately buildings house a museum covering Dominican history from the Spanish conquest to independence. There is a small admission fee. Call (809) 682-4202 for information.

National Pantheon (11): On the corner at Luperon Street, a Jesuit seminary of the 18th century was made into a monument to the heroes of the nation. Many prominent Dominicans are entombed there. The building was restored in 1955 by Trujillo for his monumental tomb. The irony is that one chapel preserves the ashes of the martyrs of the 1959 uprising which tried, unsuccessfully, to overthrow him. Call (809) 682-0185 for information. On the south side of the Pantheon is a pedestrian walk, Plaza de Maria de Toledo (12), where there is an outdoor market on Sun. Two blocks west of the Pantheon at Calle Hostos are the ruins of the Hospital of San Nicolas de Bari (9), the first hospital in the New World.

Farther along on Calle las Damas on the corner of Calle de Conde stands Casa de Francia (14), the house where Hernan Cortes lived while he prepared for the expedition that led to the conquest of Mexico. Today it houses the French Embassy. Across the street, Hostal de Nicolas de Ovando (13) was once the home of the city's founder. It is now a hotel.

Calle de Conde, the main east-west street of the Colonial Zone running for ten blocks from Calle Las Damas to El Conde Gate (24) and Independence Square (25), is a pedestrian mall and the district's main shopping street. The easternmost end has a pocket park and the next block passes several popular restaurants with sidewalk cafes and the former Borgella Palace (17) on Calle Isabel La Catholica.

Plaza Colon (18): Columbus Square, the main square of the Colonial Zone, is bordered by Calle Conde on the north and the Cathedral on the south. The plaza is dominated by a noble statue of the admiral in bronze made by the French sculptor Gilbert in 1897 to commemorate the 400th anniversary of Santo Domingo.

Cathedral of Santa Maria la Menor (19): The church, the oldest cathedral in the Western Hemisphere, is still in use. Built in 1523, it became the Metropolitan and Primate Cathedral of the Indies in 1542. In 1586 the English captain Sir Francis Drake camped in the church for about three weeks. Drake, who has something of a noble swashbuckler image in English history, was nothing but a scoundrel here, forcing women to give up their jewelry, churches to denude their altars, and the government to empty its treasures to meet his ransom demands. He pressed his point further by burning and destroying most of the town in a siege from which it never quite recovered.

The facade of the cathedral, built of native apricot-colored coral limestone that has mellowed with age, is an outstanding example of Spanish Renaissance architecture. The cleansing and restoration in the 1990s (the first time in 20th century) made it more beautiful than ever, with the exquisite details of the carved stone more easily seen. The interior is Gothic with lovely high pointed arches. The high altar of carved mahogany covered with silver and a silver carillon are said to have been made by the 16th-century Italian sculptor Benvenuto Cellini.

In addition to the main altar there are fifteen small chapels where Maria de Toledo, several Dominican presidents, an ancestor of Simon Bolivar, the liberator of South America, and other leaders are buried. The marble sarcophagus of Columbus rested in the nave of the Cathedral until 1992 when it was moved to the Columbus Lighthouse Monument across the river. Like everything else about the Admiral, his tomb has long been a matter of dispute; Cuba and Spain claim to be his final resting place, as well.

During the most recent restoration, the tombs of 300 priests, high ranking military and other government officials, and some of Columbus's descendants were found beneath the presbytery. The catacombs were renovated extensively and faced with marble, and then rededicated during the Pope's visit at the time of the Quincentennial commemorations in October 1992. Hours: Daily Mon through Sat, 9 a.m. to 4 p.m.; mass is held at 5 p.m. on Sat, noon and 4:30 p.m. on Sun.

The south side of the church has a small plaza, leading to Calle Isabel La Catholica and a pedestrian lane, next to Casa de Sacramento (16), the house of the Archbishop of Santo Domingo.

House of Bastidas (21): At the south end of Calle Las Damas, Fort Ozama and a group of buildings, known as Casa de Bastidas, served as houses, warehouses, and military barracks at different times. Now they are used to stage exhibitions of local artists and to house the Centro Artesanal, a craft shop of a government-sponsored craft cooperative that sells pottery, leather, dolls, masks, and other items made by local craftsmen.

Tower of Homage (15): Further south overlooking the river is a military structure known as the Tower of Homage (Torre de Homenaje) from which ships entering port were saluted. The tower was significant from its earliest days and was used as a symbol of nobility. As late as the 19th century the queen of Spain conferred upon the governor of Cuba the title of duke of the Tower of Homage of Santo Domingo. From here you can look over the city walls to the Ozama River below and probably see your ship.

Museum of the Dominican Family (20): Around the corner from the fort, Calle Billini leads past the Church of Santa Clara to the corner of Padre Billini and Merino Streets, where a building dating from 1516 is known as Casa de Tostado. It houses the Museum of the Dominican Family and is furnished as it might have been by a prosperous family of the late 19th century. The building is noted for its Gothic double window, an architectural feature said to be unique in the New World. Hours: Daily 9 a.m. to 2:30 p.m. There is a small admission fee. Call (809) 689-5000 for information.

Las Casas Park (22): The next block has a small, tree-shaded park dedicated to Bartolome de Las Casas, the Franciscan friar whose writings are a major source of our knowledge of the Conquest period and particularly of the indigenous people. The sculpture of Las Casas is by Joaquin Vaquero Turcios. Next to the park is the Convento de los Dominicos dating from 1510. It once housed the University of St. Thomas Aquinas, the first university in the New World. It is now part of the Autonomous University of Santo Domingo, located west of the Colonial City. Across the street from the convent is the Duarte Park (23), dominated by a monument and commanding statue of Juan Pablo Duarte, the father of the country.

Independence Park (25): At the western end of Calle Conde, eleven streets of the city converge at the large square. **Independence Park** is as much a point of departure from the Colonial Zone historically as it is architecturally. Independence Day is marked here annually by the reenactment of the 1844 events in which the nation's independence was proclaimed by La Trinitaria, a secret society formed by Juan Pablo Duarte to rid the country of the much-hated twenty-two years of Haitian occupation. The **Altar de la Patria** (Monument to the Founders of the Republic), where the three founders of the modern Dominican Republic are buried, was placed here in 1944 to commemorate the 100th anniversary of independence.

The New City

Modern Santo Domingo, laid out between wide tree-lined boulevards on both sides of the Ozama River, is a sprawling city of more than two million inhabitants that stretches from the sea on the south across more than 15 miles east, west, and north. It's best covered by tour and worth the effort for a window onto this multifaceted city. It is a complete contrast to the Old City.

Public buses and *publicos* (shared taxis running on specific routes) are plentiful and reasonable, but given the limited time cruise ships are in port, the use of public transportation is not practical. If you choose not to take an organized tour or to rent a car, you can arrange a city tour with a taxi driver or through a taxi company. Be sure your driver speaks English unless, of course, you are fluent in Spanish. Information (in Spanish) is available from the **Association of Tourist Guides** (El Conde St. 53, 809-682-0209) from 9 a.m. to 4 p.m.

From the Colonial Zone, George Washington Ave. (known locally as the Malecon and undergoing renovation through a joint public-private initiative) is complete with a miniature copy of the Washington Monument. It runs along the sea past some of the city's leading hotels and University City. It parallels Independence Ave. to Abraham Lincoln Ave., a north-south artery that leads to John F. Kennedy Ave. The names remind Americans that they are unlikely to visit a country where they will find a more genuine welcome. And they will probably never meet a Dominican

who does not have at least one relative in the United States.

Plaza de la Cultura

Another north-south artery, Maximo Gomez Ave. (in part, the route of the metro) leads to the modern **Plaza de la Cultura,** the heart of the capital's cultural life, built on a former estate of the infamous dictator Trujillo. The plaza is a park with a complex of five buildings of contemporary design. Hours: Tues to Sun from 10 a.m. to 5 p.m.

The National Theatre (809-687-3191) is used for plays, classical ballet by the National Ballet Company, folkloric performances by the National Folkloric Group, weekly concerts by the National Symphony Orchestra, and chamber and jazz ensembles and visiting artists.

The Gallery of Modern Art (*Galeria de Arte Moderno*) (809-685-2154) is the repository of the nation's leading contemporary artists along with an international collection.

The Museum of Dominican Man (*Museo de Hombre Dominicano*) (809-687-3622) holds the country's main collection of Taino Indian artifacts and other archaeological exhibits, which constitute the most important collection in the Caribbean on the inhabitants of the Western Hemisphere before Columbus. Other displays cover Dominican history and folklore. There is a small admission fee.

Other buildings hold the **National Library,** a center for West Indies research; **Museum of National History and Geography** (809-686-6668), and **Museum of Natural History** (809-689-0106).

Sala de Arte Prehispanico: The private museum (279 San Martin Ave. at Lope de Vega St.; 809-540-7777) is often overlooked because of its unlikely location on the second floor of the Seven-Up Bottling Company. The collection is outstanding, exquisitely displayed, and should not be missed. (Labels here, as in most museums in the Dominican Republic, are in Spanish, but don't let that deter you.) The exhibits are worth viewing if you have even a passing interest in and knowledge of pre-Columbian art. Call in advance.

Columbus Lighthouse Monument: In a large park near the site of the founding of Santo Domingo on the east bank of the Ozama River stands the colossal monument commemorating the 500th anniversary of Christopher Columbus's discovery of the Americas. It was inaugurated in October 1992 with the transfer of Columbus's mortal remains from the Cathedral in the old city to the $70 million memorial. The Lighthouse, first conceived in 1852 and designed in 1926, was a longtime dream of former Dominican President Joaquin Balaguer, who predicted that it would become "the greatest tourism attraction in the Caribbean."

The gargantuan structure is 693 feet long, 132 feet at the widest point, and rises to 99 feet in seven stories. Designed in the shape of a cross, it reclines at a 45 degree angle on a base with steps resembling those of an Aztec or Mayan pyramid, as if to suggest the overlaying of Christianity on the pagan culture of the New World. Columbus's marble sarcophagus is at the center. On the roof directly above the sarcophagus is a crown made up of linked arms, one for each country of the Americas, and a center light with a rotating beam like the beacon of a lighthouse. The roof has 149 floodlights beamed to the heavens; they project the shape of an enormous cross that is visible for miles in the sky.

After Columbus's death and burial in 1506 in Valladolid, Spain, his remains were taken, as he had requested, to Santo Domingo by his daughter-in-law, Maria de Toledo, on her fifth and last voyage to the New World in 1544 and buried in the cathedral. But in 1795, Columbus's remains or what was thought to be his remains were removed from the cathedral and taken to Havana and later to Seville. However, in 1877 the Dominicans discovered in the cathedral a coffer with an inscription which they believe proves conclusively that its contents are the bones of the great explorer. Scholars have concluded that the remains in Seville are those of Columbus's grandson. The most valuable artifact is an anchor, said to be from the *Santa Maria,* Columbus's flagship, which went aground off the coast of Hispaniola on his first voyage. The anchor was taken to Chicago for the Exhibition in 1892 and remained with the Chicago Historical Society until 1992 when it was returned to the Dominican Republic.

Intended solely as a tomb by its original designer, the Lighthouse has exhibits in the crypt-like interior that were intended to enhance its role as a tourist attraction, but most are disappointing. Also, the U.S. exhibit is so puny that it's embarrassing. The most interesting display deals with the Lighthouse's history, drawings, and models of earlier commemorative projects. There is a small admission fee. No shorts, tank tops, or bare feet allowed.

The National Aquarium: By the sea, about 1 mile east of the Columbus Lighthouse, is one of the Caribbean's best aquariums, with large windows onto a great variety of Caribbean marine life. At the center of the building, a glass tunnel passes directly through an area of the sea. An orientation film (in Spanish) is shown frequently in the center's auditorium; English-speaking guides are available for visitors. There is a small admission fee.

Los Tres Ojos (Three Eyes): A grotto at the edge of town on the airport road is a geological curiosity. At the entrance, steps lead down 50 feet through tropical foliage to an underground world of stalactites and stalagmites and three pools of water—one sweet, one salt, one sulphur. There is a small admission fee.

Paseo de los Indios: On the west side of town, Paseo de los Indios is a linear park that runs for 8 miles through residential sections to the western edge where the industrial district begins. The park is especially popular with Dominicans on weekends as it has playgrounds, a miniature lake representing Lake Enriquillo in the western part of the country, and samples of Dominican trees and flowers. At the entrance to the park stands a statue of an Indian in chains, meant to represent the native Tainos whom Columbus took back with him from Hispaniola to prove to his Spanish backers that he had found the Orient, a belief he carried with him to his grave.

National Botanic Gardens: Located on the northwest side of town at Colombia Ave., the tree-shaded lawns and gardens of the National Botanic Gardens (*Jardin Botanico Nacional*) are popular with residents as places for relaxing and picnicking, but are little-known to tourists. Named for a prominent Dominican botanist Dr. Rafael Moscoso, author and founder of the Botanical Institute of the Autonomous University of Santo Domingo, the gardens have a pretty entrance with colorful bougainvillea and stately palms leading to fountains and pools and a large floral clock. Here and on many streets of the capital, you can see Dominican mahogany, which blooms from Feb to Apr. Its tiny blossoms are the national flower and used in the design on Dominican money. The gardens have a stream with row boats available for rent, a Japanese garden with an arched bridge over a pond, and a small tram that provides transportation through the gardens. An annual flower show is usually held in Apr. There is a small admission fee and another for the tram. Call (809) 565-2860 for information.

National Zoo: Situated on 400 acres on the north side of town at Arroya Salado Ave., the zoo has many native animals as well as elephants and hippos in simulated natural settings without cages. There are ponds with swans, geese, ducks, and flamingos; a serpent and reptile house featuring the native American crocodile; the Hispaniolan hutia, a rodent; an anteater from the Los Haitises region in the northeast; and two native iguana. A large walk-through aviary with exotic and native birds includes the Hispaniolan parrot and the palmchat, the national bird. Known as *cigua palmera* in Spanish, it builds its unusual nest, sometimes 6 feet long and 3 feet wide with many compartments, in the palm trees. A tram provides transportation around the grounds. Hours: Daily 8:30 a.m. to 5:30 p.m. There is a small admission fee and another for the tram. Call (80) 562-2080 for information.

Shopping in Santo Domingo

Shopping for Dominican products can be a highlight of a visit to Santo Domingo if you make your way to the big central market, **Mercado Modelo (26)** on Mella Ave., within walking distance of the Colonial Zone. You'll know you are in the right place when you smell freshly roasted coffee, on sale at the entrance and purchasable by the pound in bags or in vacuum-packed tins for about half the price of coffee in the United States. Dominican coffee is excellent and is a wonderful gift to take home to friends. The Mercado covers a city block and is crowded with stalls stacked with pyramids of fruits and vegetables in the central aisles and grains, groceries, and handicrafts along the sides. Look around and bargain hard.

Arts and Artists: The Dominican Republic has a very active art community and exhibits are held year-round at galleries, museums, and sometimes hotels. The Colonial City has many galleries that feature Dominican artists. Among the best are **Galeria Toledo** (Isabel La Catolica 163/Plaza Maria de Toledo; 809-688-7649), which fills two floors of a restored town house and spills onto a tree-shaded pedestrian lane where gallery owner Bettye Marshall, a native of Tennessee, has a sidewalk cafe serving light meals. The gallery has works by established Dominican and Haitian artists in a wide range of styles and prices, and crafts of artistic merit. **Nader Gallery** (9 La Atarazana St., 809-688-0969) is one of the oldest galleries. Next door, **Sala de Arte Rosemaria** features outstanding art and gaily painted life-size wood sculpture in a school of art and sculpture that has come to be known as Prats Ventos. This name is after one of the Dominican Republic's best known sculptors, Antonio Prats-Ventos, who created a series of figures meant to represent the women of the court in colonial times. The faces of the women are white on one side, black on the other, and have been interpreted to mean the embodiment of the country's European and African heritage—a duality that permeated all of Dominican life. Members of the **School of Dominican Plastic Arts** (58 Calle El Conde) exhibits their work in shows that are changed monthly.

The work of Candido Bido, one of the country's best known artists with an international reputation, is available in oils, prints, and miniatures at his shop, **Candido Bido Gallery** (5 Calle Dr. Baez; 809-687-0115); nearby is another gallery, **Arawak** (104 Pasteur Ave., 809-685-1661).

Circuito de Galerias de Arte (Art Gallery Circuit) sponsored by the Dominican Republic Art Galleries Association (AGA), and Tequia Experiences, a local tour operator that specializes in cultural experiences, links nineteen art galleries in a guided tour on the third Thurs of every month from 7 to 11 p.m. For readers who are visiting La Romana/Casa de Campo, see the information about the art center Altos de Chavon later in the chapter on page 130.

Crafts: Local crafts, such as ceramics, straw bags, baskets and planters, macramé, and hand-carved mahogany salad bowls, are well made and sell for one-third of their U.S. prices. A craft shop next door to the **Museo de Las Atarazanas Reales** has a very good selection of ceramics from artisans around the country; **Casa Verde** (Calle Isabel La Catolica 152), a craft and souvenir shop, features a large selection of Carnival masks, a specialty of Santiago, and other folk art. A variety of local crafts is available at the Mercado Modelo and at the **Centro Artesanal** (Calle Las Damas) and there are many craft and souvenir stores along Calle El Conde, the main shopping street of the Colonial City. La Tienda is the official outlet for crafts made at **Altos de Chavon**. The crafts are based on designs created by the Dominican artists at the Central Design Center, including weaving, pottery, and silk screening.

Jewelry: Two Dominican gemstones (larimar and a special type of amber) are unique to the Caribbean. Amber, a fossilized resin, ranges in color from pale yellow to dark brown and is embedded with particles of plants and insects millions of years old. Larimar, a milky blue stone similar to turquoise found in the Bahoruco Mountains near the Haitian border, was discovered to be suitable as a gemstone in 1974 by Miguel Mendez, a well-known jeweler, and Norman Rilling, a Peace Corps volunteer. The name larimar came from a combination of "Larissa," the name of Mendez's daughter, and "mar," the sea, as suggested by the color of the stone.

Amber and larimar are fashioned into bracelets, necklaces, and earrings by local craftsmen and range from as little as $1 to $100 and more. The Mercado is full of cheaply made jewelry, but if you like the unusual amber or larimar stones and want to buy a good piece of jewelry with Dominican gold or silver, go to a real jeweler such as **Amber Colonial Gift Shop** (Colonial Zone), or top stores at **Plaza Naco** (Tiradentes Avenue) in the city's most elegant residential area of Naco. But before you buy any jewelry, you might want to visit the **Larimar Museum** (Calle Isabel La Católica 55; 809-689-6605, www.larimarmuseum.com). The ground floor store has a selection of good quality larimar and amber and upstairs is an educational museum.

A word of caution: Jewelry, combs, and other gifts made from tortoise shells are Dominican crafts. It is illegal to bring them into the United States since tortoises are on the endangered species list and these items will be confiscated by U.S. customs officials.

Dining and Evening Entertainment

Santo Domingo has a large number and variety of restaurants, patronized by Dominicans as much as, if not more than, by tourists. Dominicans tend to follow their Spanish ancestors when it comes to lunch and dinner hours, seldom having lunch before 1 or 2 p.m. and dinner at 9 or 10 p.m. Music, a significant part of Dominican life, is often provided in restaurants by strolling troubadours, guitarists, or dance bands. Dominican cuisine is Spanish influenced, too, but the nation has a cuisine of its own, which is celebrated with annual festivals and contests.

The sidewalk cafes and tapas bars on the **Plaza de la Hispanidad** in the old city are popular sundown rendezvous points for Santo Domingo's diverse expatriate community of artists and writers. The main casinos are in hotels.

Sports in Santo Domingo and Environs

Beaches: The most accessible beaches are about thirty to forty-five minutes east of Santo Domingo beyond the airport at Boca Chica where the water is calm and shallow. Several hotels have packages which enable day visitors to use their facilities and have a room for changing. Next to the airport is **La Caleta Marine Park** (*Parque Nacional Submarino La Caleta*), an underwater park created in 1987 to protect three miles of the coastline. A wrecked ship was sunk here to create an artificial reef. Although the Dominican Republic is bordered by reefs along much of its coasts, diving is a fairly new sport.

Golf: The Dominican Republic has twenty-three golf courses, including some of the best golf courses in the Caribbean. Those in Santo Domingo and at Casa de Campo are convenient for cruise passengers. **Guavaberry Golf & Country Club** (www.guavaberrygolf.com) is an 18-hole championship course designed by Gary Player. **Las Lagunas Country Club** (www.laslagunas.com.do) was inspired by Pete Dye. **Cayacoa Golf Club** (809-561-7288) is the capital's beauty. Designed by Pete

Dye with a variety of hazards, the course (par 71, 5,869 yards) is challenging and blends in with its tropical setting and breathtaking view.

Casa de Campo (809-523-3333) has three of the most beautiful 18-hole championship courses in the Caribbean. **The Links** (par 71, 6,461 yards) and its companion course, **The Teeth of the Dog,** as well as **Dye Fore,** a Pete Dye layout famous for its challenge and natural beauty with seven holes next to the sea, are considered among the best in the world.

Deep-sea Fishing: The clear waters off the Dominican shores teem with fish. If your cruise ship does not offer deep-sea fishing excursions, one can be arranged through **Mundo Submarino** (809-566-0340). Two boating clubs at Boca Chica are **Andres Boca Chica Club** (809-685-4940) and **Santo Domingo Nautical Club** (809-566-4522). You can also arrange in advance a day of deep-sea fishing through the Jaragua Renaissance Hotel.

Other Sports: Tennis is available at the **Jaragua Renaissance Hotel,** which has four courts, conveniently located near the city center. There is horse racing at the **Perla Antillana Race Track** (Avenue San Martin) several days a week. Cockfighting can be seen at the **Coliseo Gallistico** (Avenue Luperon) in Herrera, a suburb on the northwest side of the city. As noted previously, baseball is a national passion and can be enjoyed year-round. During the professional winter season from late October through January, well-known players from the United States join local teams. Check local newspapers.

Cultural Events

The performing arts are very important in the Dominican Republic. The country has its own national symphony orchestra, chamber orchestra, opera company, ballet company, folkloric company, and national theatre, plus a number of smaller groups. The Plaza of Culture is the center of activity, but there are concerts, ballet, folklore, and other performances in other parts of the city. Check the local newspapers for events during your visit.

Casa de Teatro (110 Arzobispo Merino; 809-689-3430; www.casedeteatro.com) is the gathering place of avant-garde artists, actors, and musicians. It stages art and literature exhibitions, offers painting, drama, and dancing courses, as well as monthly contests for poetry, short stories, and other writings. On weekends, there are plays and concerts. Performers that you might see here and around town, known as Perico Ripiado, are genuine *campesino* (country) scratch bands that play traditional merengue on homemade instruments that are African in origin. Casa de Teatro is opened from 8 a.m. to 6 p.m. on weekdays; check locally for the weekend schedule.

As for other Dominican popular artists, **Wilfrido Vargas y Los Beduinos** is one of the most exciting, syncopated groups around. Grammy-winner **Micheal Camilo,** a composer and pianist of sophisticated jazz, is a recognized force in the jazz world. His composition "Caribe" is samba, merengue, and jazz that melts in your ears. He now lives in New York but performs often in Santo Domingo. **Juan Luis Guerra y 4-40** (Cuatro-Cuarenta) is a group with an international following and blends original music with jazz and Latin rhythms.

Festivals

Villages throughout this country of rich traditions mark their patron saints' days with feasts and festivals. One of the largest festivals is **Independence Day** on February 27, and it marks the start of **Carnival.** It is celebrated with several days of festive parades. The religious procession of **Epiphany** (January 5) and **Holy Week** just before Easter are also colorful occasions in Santo Domingo.

The annual **Merengue Festival** is held in late July in Santo Domingo and offers concerts, ballet, craft and food fairs, folk dancing, parades, and other events. The fiesta takes its name from the merengue, the dance that originated in the Dominican Republic two centuries ago.

Casa de Campo (La Romana)

Casa de Campo, an hour-and-a-half drive east of Santo Domingo near the sugar mill town of La Romana, is the most elaborate resort in the Dominican Republic, set on 7,000 acres of a former ranch near miles of sugar plantations. Developed by the

U.S. conglomerate Gulf & Western in the 1970s, the resort was sold in 1984 to the Florida-based Premier Hotel Corporation. In addition to its magnificent championship golf courses, Casa de Campo has a tennis village with thirteen courts, some lighted for night play, and a full-time pro and professional staff; horseback riding and polo; sailing and deep-sea fishing; more than a dozen swimming pools; a fitness center; a secluded beach; and its own international airport. The hotel interiors were created by Dominican fashion designer Oscar de la Renta. No structure is more than two stories high.

On the north side of the resort is **Altos de Chavon,** an artisans' village, unique in concept and design. It is a 16th-century Mediterranean village built entirely in the 20th century from the imagination of its architect. Here, noted artists, writers, and performers are in residence for several months, during which time they both teach and do their own work. Several times annually the artists-in-residence show their works; year-round the art galleries exhibit the works of well-known and emerging Dominican talent. Altos's affiliation with the Parsons School of Design in New York and a university in Santo Domingo enables it to offer an associate's degree for its two-year university program.

The Regional Museum of Archaeology, a teaching museum, grew from a private collection of a La Romana resident who had gathered the unusual and valuable Indian artifacts from his immediate area. They are beautifully displayed, and the labels, fortunately, are in English.

Altos has a small inn, several restaurants, art galleries, craft and gift shops, and a 5,000-seat amphitheatre inaugurated in 1982 by Frank Sinatra. Performances by international artists such as Sergio Mendes and Julio Iglesias are part of a year-round calendar of events.

The cruise ships call at Casa de Campo and spend the day, which is about enough time for passengers to play a round of golf or some tennis, or to enjoy the hotel's other facilities and explore Altos de Chavon.

Catalina Island/Serena Cay

Off the coast at La Romana the small island of Catalina (renamed by some as Serena Cay) is a stop for a day-at-the-beach by some cruise ships. It is scalloped with pearly white beaches and surrounded by crystal clear waters. Here, passengers enjoy water sports and a buffet, open bar, and entertainment by a merengue dance group on the beach. (You will need your sunscreen and insect repellant.) Or, they take excursions to Casa de Campo or enjoy the resort's golf or tennis facilities. Passengers are tendered to the pier where a motorcoach takes them on a tour of the resort and village. Casa de Campo's Equestrian Center offers riding for all levels. For sports fishing, passengers depart from Catalina on a fully equipped sport fishing vessel that provides captain and mate, tackle, bait, beer and soft drinks, and box lunch.

Samana Peninsula and Bay

In the northeastern corner of the Dominican Republic is a 30-mile-long peninsula extending into the Atlantic and cupping a bay whose waters and shores hold a great deal of interest to nature lovers and water sports enthusiasts. **Samana,** the name of the bay, the peninsula, and the main town, had only one paved road less than a decade ago, but now, with the opening of an international airport and an express highway to Santo Domingo, it's become the fastest resort development area in the country.

The town of Samana, located on the south side of the peninsula overlooking the bay, is the port of call for most cruise ships. The bay has small islands with pretty beaches and good snorkeling, such as **Cayo de Levantado,** where several cruise ships spend their day-at-the-beach. On the northeast corner of Samana peninsula is a two-mile stretch of palm-shaded sands, called **Playa Rincón.** It is often cited as the most beautiful beach in the Dominican Republic. Located forty-five minutes from Samana, at the base of 2,000-foot high mountains, it nestles at the west end of Rincon Bay overlooking crystal clear turquoise waters. At last count, we are told, fourteen resorts are underway or planned for the area.

From Samana town a newly paved road leads to **Limon** on the Rio Limon in the center of the peninsula from where a trail goes to a magnificent waterfall, all but hidden amidst the savage beauty of the thickly forested mountains. The falls drop 165 feet with such force that one can get wet from the spray standing 100 feet away. Some cruise ships offer an excursion to the falls; otherwise, you will need to go with a local guide. Here, too, you can rent horses if you do not want to walk the steep trail of 2 miles. The trail crosses the river twice and hikers get wet to their knees. Once there, you can reward yourself with a swim in the deep pool under the falls.

The north coast of Samana peninsula is accessible by road that leads over the mountains to resort areas of **Las Terrenas and Portillo** with more beautiful beaches. Fifty miles off shore, **Silver Bank** (Santario de Ballenas Jorobadas del Banco de la Plata) is a marine sanctuary of the humpback whale. The underwater lagoon, 100 feet below sea level, attracts herds of up to 3,000 migrating humpback whales from late December to early March. Here, whales give birth and nurture their young, and there are large schools of fish, coral formations, and sea turtles. During this period, whales can be seen at the mouth of Samana Bay which is where cruise ship excursions take passengers. Whale watching and scuba diving trips also depart daily from Samana port.

On the south side of the Samana Bay is **Los Haitises National Park** (*Parque Nacional Los Haitises*), a karst region of land and mangrove estuaries stretching 15 miles west from the mouth of Rio Barracote at the west end of Samana Bay. Ordinarily, the area would be semi-desert due to the nature of the rocky terrain, but due to the heavy rainfall—over 90 inches per year—and frequent cloud cover, the small limestone knolls (some up to 1,000 feet or more in elevation) and the narrow valley bottoms are densely covered with trees.

The many tiny, rocky islands or cays along the coast, once part of the main land, are alive with birds. **Bird Island** (*Isla de los Pajaros*) has a small forest atop the rock where brown pelicans, flocks of snowy egrets, roseate terns, and other water birds roost in the trees and soar overhead. Some cruise ships offer excursions to the Park, departing by boat directly from the ship. Tours are also organized from Samana town by local travel agencies. The trip is best made in the morning when the bay is calm; sometimes winds pick up in the afternoon making the water very choppy. Be sure to have insect repellant as sand flies and mosquitoes are very active here.

The Virgin Islands

U.S. Virgin Islands

**Charlotte Amalie, St. Thomas; Cruz Bay, St. John;
Frederiksted, St. Croix; Christiansted, St. Croix**

U.S. Virgin Islands

The American Paradise

They are our corner of the Caribbean, and, topside or beneath the sea, you will not find a more beautiful place under the American flag. Every turn in the road reveals spectacular scenes of white beaches washed by gentle turquoise water, backed by forest-green hills, and colored by a rainbow of flowers with such marvelous names as Catch-and-Keep and Jump-Up-and-Kiss-Me. Easy breezes carrying the light scent of jasmine cool the air.

The Virgin Islands are divided between the United States and Britain into two groups of about fifty islands and cays each. They are situated in the northeastern Caribbean adjacent to the Anegada Passage, a strategic gateway between the Atlantic Ocean and the Caribbean Sea, 40 miles east of

Puerto Rico, where the Lesser Antilles begin.

The U.S. Virgin Islands constitute a "territory" rather than a state. Only four islands are inhabited: St. Croix, the largest, lies entirely in the Caribbean and is the easternmost point of the United States; St. Thomas, the most populated and developed, is 40 miles north of St. Croix, between the Caribbean and the Atlantic Ocean; and neighboring St. John, the smallest, is 3.5 miles east of St. Thomas. The islands are so close together that they can be visited in a day, yet no three in the Caribbean are more different from one another than our American trio.

Columbus first sighted the Virgin Islands on his second voyage in 1493. He arrived at an island native Carib Indians called Ayay and named it Santa Cruz, or Holy Cross (we call the island by its French name, St. Croix). There Columbus sailed into

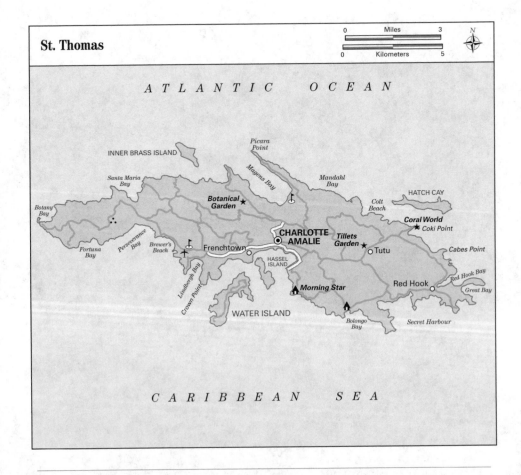

the Salt River estuary on the island's north coast to replenish his ships' supply of fresh water. (Hence, St. Croix's claim: that it is the first land now under the American flag to have been visited by the great explorer.)

But the fierce Caribs did not welcome Columbus as the peaceful Arawaks had done elsewhere. Columbus made a hasty withdrawal and continued north through the archipelago. The admiral, like all those who have followed him, was dazzled by the islands' exquisite beauty. Seeing so many clustered together, he named the group after the ancient legend of St. Ursula and the eleven thousand virgins.

Columbus claimed the islands for Spain, but the Spaniards paid little attention to them for a century or more. Sir Francis Drake, the dashing corsair of English history, was among those who sailed the Virgins' waters—long enough to form the basis of England's claim to them. The islands' jagged coastlines, good harbors, and proximity to major shipping lanes made them natural havens for pirates and privateers. By 1625 the English and Dutch had recognized the islands' strategic location and began colonizing St. Croix.

The Danes took possession of St. Thomas in 1672, adding St. John in 1717 and St. Croix in 1733. Two decades later Denmark declared the islands a crown colony and subsequently made St. Thomas a free port that flourished as the center of contraband for the entire Caribbean, while St. Croix and St. John became rich with sugar plantations.

In 1917 the United States, concerned about protecting the Panama Canal, bought the Virgin Islands for $25 million—or about $300 an acre—a high price at the time. Island residents were made U.S. citizens in 1927; the present structure of territorial government was established by the U.S. Congress in 1954. Although the islands are American—with fast-food shops and supermarkets, direct dial and cable television—they have retained enough of their past to give visitors a sense of being in a foreign yet familiar place.

Budget Planning

Prices for sports and tours in St. Thomas and St. John generally are typical for the Caribbean; St. Croix is slightly lower. The largest expenses for visitors are taxi fares and fancy restaurants. On the other hand there is an ample selection of moderately priced, attractive restaurants serving local dishes; public transportation is plentiful and inexpensive; and beaches are free or have minimal charges.

Port Profile: St. Thomas

St. Thomas is the ideal cruise port. The green mountainous island rises dramatically from the deep turquoise sea to peaks of 1,550 feet that frame an irregular coastline of fingers and coves, idyllic bays, and white-sand beaches. Steeped in history, St. Thomas is as up-to-date as Fifth Avenue; it is small enough to see in a day, yet it has the diversity and facilities to offer cruise passengers a wide choice, with every kind of warm-weather sport a visitor could want. There are inviting restaurants—some in historic settings,

At a Glance

Antiquities	★
Architecture	★
Art and Artists	★★
Beaches	★★★★★
Colonial Buildings	★★★★
Crafts	★
Cuisine	★★
Culture	★
Dining/Restaurants	★★
Entertainment	★★
Forts	★★★★
History	★★★★
Monuments	★
Museums	★★
Nightlife	★
Scenery	★★★★★
Shopping	★★★★
Sightseeing	★★★
Sports	★★★★★
Transportation	★★★★

Fast Facts

Population: St. Croix, 54,000; St. John, 4,300; St. Thomas, 52,000

Size: St. Croix, 27 miles long, 84 square miles; St. John, 9 miles long, 19 square miles; St. Thomas, 13 miles long, 32 square miles.

Main Towns: Christiansted and Frederiksted, St. Croix; Cruz Bay, St. John; Charlotte Amalie, St. Thomas

Government: Executive power is vested in the governor, who appoints the heads of his twelve departments. Residents were granted the right to vote for their governor in 1970. The legislature, which has convened since 1852, is a single body of fifteen senators from the three islands, elected for two-year terms. Residents vote in local elections and, since 1972, have sent a representative to Congress. They pay federal income tax to the local government but cannot vote in national elections, and their congressperson does not vote on the floor of the House of Representatives.

Currency: U.S. dollar

Customs Regulations: Cruise passengers who disembark in the U.S. Virgin Islands and plan to return to the mainland by plane pass through customs here. The U.S. Virgin Islands have a special status, enabling U.S. residents to bring back up to $1,600 worth of goods—twice that of other islands in the Caribbean—free of customs tax. Persons over twenty-one years old are allowed five fifths of liquor, plus a sixth one of a Virgin Islands spirit (such as Cruzan Rum) and five cartons of cigarettes or one hundred cigars. You can also mail home gifts (other than perfume, liquor, or tobacco), each valued up to $100.

Departure Tax: None

Emergency Numbers: Medical: St. Thomas Hospital, (340) 776-8311; Ambulance, Fire, Police: 911; Recompression Chamber: (340) 776-2686; Alcoholics Anonymous: (340) 776-5283

Language: English. But don't be surprised if you have trouble understanding some Virgin Islanders. The local dialect is an English-Creole, which has had a profound influence on their speech. If you have trouble with the dialect, ask the person to speak slowly—and you should do the same.

Public Holidays: Jan 1, New Year's Day; Jan 6, Three Kings Day; third Mon in Jan, Martin Luther King's Birthday; Feb, Presidents' Day; Easter Thursday, Good Friday, Easter Sunday and Monday; Mar 31, Transfer Day (from Denmark to United States); May, Memorial Day; July 3, Emancipation; July 4, Independence; Sept, Labor Day; Oct 14, Columbus Day; Oct 21, Hurricane Thanksgiving; Nov 1, Liberty Day; Nov 11, Veteran's Day; Nov, Thanksgiving Day; Dec 25, 26, Christmas. Banks and stores are closed on some major holidays; stores remain open on local and federal ones.

Telephone Area Code: 340

Airlines: *From the United States mainland:* American, Continental, Delta, Spirit Airlines, US Airways, and United Airlines. *Intraregional:* Air Sunshine, American Eagle, Cape Air (USVI/San Juan), LIAT, Seaborne Seaplane (340-773-6442; www.seaborneairlines.com). Air Center Helicopters (www.aircenterhelicopters.com; Sea Flight (340-714-3000)

Information: www.visitusvi.com; www.stcroixhotelandtourism.com

In the United States:

U.S. Virgin Islands Tourist Information: (800) 372-USVI

Atlanta: (404) 688-0906; fax: (404) 525-1102; atlanta@usvitourism.vi

Chicago: (312) 670-8784; fax: (312) 670-8784; chicago@usvitourism.vi

Los Angeles: (213) 739-0138; fax: (213) 739-2005; losangeles@usvitourism.vi

Miami: (305) 442-7200; fax: (305) 445-9044; miami@usvitourism.vi

New York: 1 Penn Plaza, Ste. 3525, New York, NY 10019-0002; (212) 502-5300; fax: (212) 465-2324; newyork@usvitourism.vi

Washington: (202) 624-3590; fax: (202) 624-3594; washington@usvitourism.vi

In Canada:

Elaine Carnegie, CANLINK, www.canlinktravel.com

In St. Croix: Frederiksted, USVI 00840; (340) 772-0357; fax: (340) 773-5074. Christiansted Government House Office; (340) 773-1404

In St. John: P.O. Box 200, Cruz Bay, USVI 00830; (340) 776-6450

In St. Thomas: P.O. Box 6400, Charlotte Amalie, USVI 00804; (340) 774-8784; fax: (340) 774-4390

others with lovely views—and enough colonial buildings, old homes, forts, and monuments for history buffs easily to fill their day.

Location/Embarkation: Set on a deep horseshoe bay, Charlotte Amalie (pronounced Ah-mahl-ya) is the busiest cruise port in the Caribbean—a role it played for two hundred years during the colonial era as a major trading port on the sea-lanes between the Old and New Worlds.

The heart of town—both historic and commercial—hugs the shore and climbs the mountainsides overlooking the port. The harbor has three docks; the size of your ship usually dictates which one is used. On the east, about 1.5 miles from downtown, is the West Indian Company Dock, where the majority of ships arrive. Six cruise ships can berth in the harbor at one time. **Yacht Haven Grande,** a multi-million dollar megayacht marina complex, is next to the cruise ship piers. It includes a marina that accommodates fifty large yachts, three restaurants, and 80,000 square feet of retail space with high-end shops; and a hotel; other facilities are to be added.

Small ships (fewer than two hundred passengers) often sail directly to the waterfront in town. On the west side is the Austin (Babe) Monsanto Crown Bay facility about 1.5 miles from town, hosts a number of cruise ships. Since more cruise ships call at St. Thomas than at any other port in the Caribbean, it is not surprising to find the port crowded. The system operates more or less on a first-come, first-served basis; the number of ships in port will determine whether your ship draws dockside or tenders.

At the West Indian Company Dock, you can find telephones for local and long-distance calls, an Internet cafe, a U.S. post office, a tourist information center where you can get maps and information, and a large shopping complex with bars and restaurants, Havensight Mall and Port of Sale, where many of the Main Street stores have branches. After its most recent development, Crown Bay Dock, which is now used for the largest cruise ships, is now a very attractive arrival pier with many new facilities and shops. Tourist Helpers, dressed in orange top uniforms, are stationed at both ports.

Local Transportation: The transportation system at the ports is well organized and convenient. You will find taxis, minibuses, and open jitneys (locals call them safaris) for twenty passengers lined up by the dozens for transportation from the port to Emancipation Garden in downtown Charlotte Amalie. Average cost is $6 per passenger one-way, $5 if more than one person is traveling; prices vary depending on location. The garden is located at the head of Main Street, the central shopping street. It is also the ideal place from which to start a walking tour. To return to your ship, jitneys and taxis leave frequently from the square to the docks; you can almost always share a taxi with other returning passengers. Be sure to give yourself ample time to return to your ship, particularly around the noon hour and from 4 to 6 p.m., when local traffic is extremely heavy and moves at a snail's pace. It can take forty-five minutes to drive the 1.5 miles between town and the West Indian Company Dock.

Taxi rates, set by the government, are based on destination rather than mileage; a copy of the rates should be available from the driver. Rates for most locations beyond town are $6 to $18 one-way. Coki Beach is $12–14 for one person and $9 per person for two or more. Taxis are available for island tours. Drivers, who act as guides, are usually informed on the basics, but some are definitely better than others—be prepared to take potluck. Cost is $50 for two persons for a two-hour tour, $15 for each additional passenger. The open-sided "safari" buses, or jitneys, run frequently from the Airport Road to Red Hook; one-way fare is $2.

Buses: Regular bus service connects Charlotte Amalie with Red Hook, at the eastern end of the island, where ferries leave for St. John and Bordeaux at the west end. Buses run about hourly, with the last returning to town about 10 p.m.; cost is $1.

Roads and Rentals: Roads on St. Thomas are generally well marked with route signs, but pay close attention because the roads are very winding and frequently branch onto small roads. In addition, driving is on the LEFT side of the road, and it is very easy to get distracted by the views.

Route 38 traverses the island east-west from Charlotte Amalie to the eastern end, forking northeast to Coki Point and southeast to Red Hook. Route 40, known as Skyline Drive, runs parallel along the north side of the mountains, affording magnificent views, and leads to Mountain Top, the highest accessible point on St. Thomas.

You need a valid U.S. driver's license to rent a car here. Expect to pay about $55 to $70 per day for a compact with unlimited mileage from an international chain and about $50 from independent dealers. Jeep rentals cost about $65, but unless you have had experience with driving on the left and on mountain roads, you may be wiser to rent a car. Some car-rental companies have agreements with local merchants offering discounts on rentals and/or merchandise. Some also have free pickup and delivery service at the port, but during the winter season, when demand is greatest, availability of cars is uneven and pickup service unreliable.

A list of rental firms is available in *St. Thomas This Week,* a free booklet widely distributed in tourist offices and elsewhere. Among them are **Amalie Car Rental** (340-774-0688; www.amaliecar .com); **Avis** (340-774-1468); **Budget** (340-776-5774; 800-626-4516; www.budgetstt.com); **Dependable Car Rental** (340-774-2253; 800-522-3076; www .dependablecar.com); **Discount** (340-776-4858; 877-478-2833; www.discountcar.vi); and **Thrifty** (340-776-1500).

Ferry Service: Ferries between downtown and Marriott Frenchman's Reef Hotel leave every half hour 8 a.m. to 5:30 p.m., daily except Sun; and from the downtown waterfront, 8:30 a.m. to 5:30 p.m. Cost is $6. St. John is connected by hourly service from Red Hook from 6:30 a.m. to midnight; the trip

takes twenty minutes. Another ferry, less frequent but more convenient for cruise passengers, leaves from the downtown waterfront several times daily, beginning at 9 a.m.

Ferries to Tortola, B.V.I.—**Smith's Ferry** (340-775-7292; www.smithsferry.com) and **Native Son** (340-774-8685; nativesonferry@aol.com)—both leave from Charlotte Amalie frequently and take forty-five minutes; some continue to Virgin Gorda. You need a passport to reenter the United States. Schedules are printed in *St. Thomas This Week.*

Interisland Air: Sea Flight has service between St. Thomas and St. Croix' **Seaborne Airlines** (340-773-6442; 888-359-8687; www.seaborneairlines .com) flies seaplanes between St. Thomas and St. Croix almost hourly during the day. It also has service between St. Thomas and Old San Juan, Puerto Rico, as well as from St. Thomas to Virgin Gorda. **American Eagle** connects St. Thomas and St. Croix with Puerto Rico. **Cape Air** (800-352-0714; 866-CAPEAIR; www.flycapeair.com) flies almost hourly between San Juan, St. Thomas, and St. Croix.

Shore Excursions

What to do in St. Thomas largely depends on your personal interest—the choices are plentiful. Be sure to plan some activity: Despite all you have heard about the wonderful shopping here, most people complete their shopping within two hours and then are disappointed if they have not planned something else, too.

St. Thomas Island Tour: 2 to 3 hours, $25–$45. Drive to Bluebeard's Castle for the view; Mafolie Hill and Drake's Seat for scenic panorama of Magens Bay and British Virgin Islands; and return to town. Same drive available by taxis for $50 for two.

St. John Safari: 4 to 4.5 hours, $60–$80. Recommended for those who have visited St. Thomas before or who prefer outdoor activity to shopping. The excursion goes by ferry to Cruz Bay, tours St. John, and visits Trunk Bay for a swim and snorkel. Bring a towel and plastic bag for swimsuits.

Underwater Life: 3 hours, snorkelers, $50 to $60; introductory dive lesson, $110. Some cruise ships send snorkelers and divers in separate groups; others combine them. They are accompanied by an instructor. For sightseeing or hiking and snorkeling combination, see **Captain Nautica, Inc.** (340-715-3379; www.captainnautica.com) in the Sports section.

Horseback Riding and Kayaking: See Sports section later in this chapter.

Golf: See Sports section and **Mahogany Run Golf Course** (340-777-6250; 800-253-7103; www.mahoganyrungolf.com).

Accessible Adventures (340-344-8302; www.accessvi.com) provides tours on St. Thomas for those with restricted mobility. Each of its vehicles has a lifting device, four-point tie-down system, and flip-up seats to accommodate up to three wheelchairs. Tours begin at $64 for adults, $46 for children.

Day Pass: Bolongo Bay Beach Resort (340-775-1800; 800-766-2840; www.bolongobay.com) offers a Day Pass for a full day's use of the resort's facilities—1,000 feet of palm-lined beach; swimming pool with swim-up bar; tennis, basketball, and volleyball courts; a room to shower and change; use of the resort's non-motorized equipment including kayaks, Sunfish, paddleboats, and snorkel equipment. Cost: $60 adult; $30 children age twelve and younger, or $150 for a family of four (two adults/two children).

Walk Through Old St. Thomas: (340-714-1672; www.st-thomas.com). Two hours, $40–45 per person. Contact Historic Preservation, see number below. Ocean Racing (On Deck, Yacht Haven Grande) two hours; $99. One of the newest attractions is a chance to learn and help crew a six-passenger Farr 40 in a race with On Deck's other three boats.

St. Thomas on Your Own

The historic district of Charlotte Amalie is listed in the National Register of Historic Places. Most restorations were done by private owners who gave the old structures new life as stores, business and government offices, hotels, restaurants, and residences—uses not far removed from their original purposes. A walk through these streets

is a chance to learn something about the island's history and shop in lanes made charming by the past. The **St. Thomas Historical Trust** (340-642-4074; www.stthomashistoricaltrust.org) can provide information.

A Charlotte Amalie Walkabout

Historic Charlotte Amalie is a grid of 3 blocks deep from the waterfront on the south to the hillsides on the north, intersected by long east-west streets extending from old Hospital Gade on the east to just below General Gade on the west. A walk takes two to three hours, depending on your pace. Taxis from the cruise ports discharge passengers at or near Emancipation Garden at the head of Main Street.

Emancipation Garden (1): A small park that was originally the town square was named to commemorate the abolition of slavery on July 3, 1848. It has a bandstand and benches where locals and visitors can watch entertainment. Adjacent to the garden is the Vendor's Market, an open-air market where T-shirts and souvenirs are sold. There is a bust of the Danish King Christian IX and a small replica of the Philadelphia Liberty Bell. At the southwest corner is the Native Arts and Craft store which has restrooms, telephones, and information on St. Thomas.

Grand Galleria (2): The building on the north side of the park, built in 1839 as the Commercial Hotel, was the town's leading accommodation for more than a century and known as the Grand Hotel. Originally the Greek Revival structure occupied an entire block overlooking the square. The complex, now a commercial building has had a multimillion-dollar reconstruction in its interiors, which includes more shops with local arts and crafts; a two-floor, centrally air-conditioned atrium; and interior courtyard with an outdoor cafe. An ATM and public toilets are available.

Fort Christian and Museum (3): East of the park, Fort Christian is the oldest building in the Virgin Islands and a National Historic Landmark. The red-brick fortress, built between 1666 and 1680, was named for Denmark's King Christian V and was the center of the community for three centuries, housing the colony's first governors and

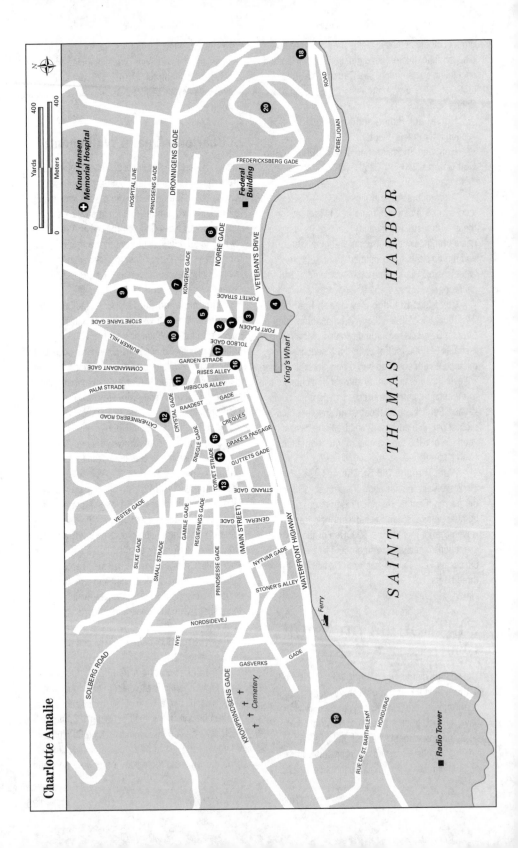

Charlotte Amalie

SAINT THOMAS HARBOR

Knud Hansen Memorial Hospital

Federal Building

King's Wharf

Radio Tower

Cemetery

Ferry

HOSPITAL LINE
PRINDSENS GADE
DRONNIGENS GADE
FREDERICKSBERG GADE
NORRE GADE
KONGENS GADE
STORE TARNE GADE
FORTET STRADE
VETERAN'S DRIVE
FORT PLADEN
TOLBOD GADE
COMMANDANT GADE
BUNKER HILL
GARDEN STRADE
RIISES ALLEY
PALM STRADE
HIBISCUS ALLEY
RAADEST GADE
CATHERINEBERG ROAD
CRYSTAL GADE
CREQUES
DRAKE'S PASSAGE
SNEGLE GADE
TORVET STRADE
GUTTETS GADE
STRAND GADE
VESTER GADE
GAMILE GADE
REGIERINGS GADE
(MAIN STREET)
GENERAL GADE
NYTVAR GADE
WATERFRONT HIGHWAY
SMALL STRADE
SILKE GADE
PRINDSESSE GADE
STONER'S ALLEY
SOLBERG ROAD
NYE
NORDSIDEVEJ
KRONPRINDSENS GADE
GASVERKS GADE
RUE DE ST. BARTHELEMY
HONDURAS
DEBELJOIAN ROAD

Yards 0   400
Meters 0   400

N

later serving as a church, garrison, surgeons' quarters, prison, police station, and courthouse. Hours: weekdays 8:30 a.m. to 4:30 p.m. (340-776-4566). [The building is undergoing major renovation and may not be opened during your visit.]

Legislative Building (4): The Italian Renaissance structure on the waterfront is the home of the Virgin Islands Legislature. Here in 1917, the Danish flag was lowered for the last time, transferring ownership to the United States. Built in 1874 as barracks for the Danish police, it served as a U.S. Marine Corps barracks from 1917 to 1930 and as a public school until 1957. Open weekdays.

Frederick Lutheran Church (5): Built in 1820 to replace an earlier one destroyed by fire, it is the second oldest church on the island. The church was originally established in 1666, the year Erik Nielson Smith took formal possession of St. Thomas in the name of the Danish West India Company. The charter that the royal government granted to the company stockholders included a provision for the Lutheran church, the state church of Denmark. When St. Thomas became a Crown colony in 1754, the church quickly expanded its role, increasing the number of schools it operated and adding a hospital.

The Parsonage (23 Kongen's Gade) behind the church is more than 250 years old and is one of the oldest structures in continuous use on the island. The original walls, partially exposed in several rooms, consist of bricks and stones brought from Denmark as ballast for sailing ships and exchanged for cargoes of sugar, cotton, and rum.

Moravian Memorial Church (6): Farther east on Norre Gade is another 19th-century church. The two-story structure is built of local volcanic rock called blue-bitch stone and beveled sandstone cornerstones. Atop the hip roof is a bell tower with a delicate wooden cupola dating from 1882.

Government House (7): Built from 1865 to 1867 for the Danish Colonial Council, Government House is the office of the governor of the U.S. Virgin Islands. The first two floors are open to the public and have paintings and objets d'art relating to the islands' history and works by the French Impressionist Camille Pissarro, who was born in St. Thomas in 1830. Hours: weekdays 8 a.m. to noon and 1 to 5 p.m. Closed holidays.

The 99 Steps (8): The steep hills made it difficult to build roads; instead, access between the higher and lower parts of town was gained by a series of stone stairs. Two of the best preserved ones, built by the Danes in the mid-18th century, are west of Government House—one immediately west of the mansion and a second, known as the 99 Steps, a short walk beyond.

Fort Skytsborg (9): Both passageways lead to Fort Skytsborg, a five-story conical watchtower known as Blackbeard's Tower, built by the Danes in 1678. Legend has it that the infamous pirate used the tower to scout his prey and hide his treasures. The view from here is reward enough for climbing the 99 Steps.

Hotel 1829 (10): At the foot of the 99 Steps on Kongen's Gade is Hotel 1829, formerly known as Lavalette House after its builder, a French sea captain. The initial L of the original owner can still be seen in the wrought-iron grillwork at the entrance. The two-story stucco town house, begun in 1819, was designed by an Italian architect in a Spanish style. It has had extensive restoration down to the two-hundred-year-old Moroccan tiles in the main dining room. The bar is in the original Danish kitchen. The Caribbean World Amber Museum is a recent addition.

Continue to Garden Street, and turn west onto Crystal Gade.

St. Thomas Dutch Reform Church (11) is the oldest church on St. Thomas. The first church was built in the mid-1670s and had several locations prior to the present one. The Greek Revival building, constructed in 1846, has such classical features that it looks more like a temple than a church. Its two-story facade is surmounted by a large triangular pediment supported by four Doric columns.

Synagogue Hill (12): Farther along, **Beracha Veshalom Vegemilith Hasidim Synagogue,** built in 1833 on the site of two earlier structures, is one of the oldest synagogues in North America. (As early as 1684 Gabriel Milan, a member of a prominent European Jewish family, was appointed governor by the Danish Crown.) The synagogue marked its 200th anniversary in 1996. In 2000, following a year's restoration, the synagogue was designated a National Historic Landmark.

The synagogue is a freestanding, one-story structure of cut stone and brick. Inside, the exposed walls are composed of native stone with a mortar made of sand and molasses. Mahogany pews face the center of the sanctuary; the mechitzah that once separated the men and women can be seen behind the fourth row. The furniture and many of the fixtures and ornaments date from 1833. On the east wall the Holy Ark contains scrolls of the Torah, three of which are more than two hundred years old; one set of *rimonim* (handles of the scrolls) were saved from a fire in 1831; and the old mahogany doors have ivory insets. Above the Ark are the blue-and-gilded Tablets of the Decalogue; the lamp of eternal light hanging in front can be raised and lowered with a counterweight. Overhead in the center of the dome is a Magen David encircled with designs; from it hangs an eighteen-armed candle chandelier with Baccarat crystal hurricane shades.

There are four corner columns with Doric capitals, said to represent the four mothers of Israel: Sarah, Rebecca, Rachel, and Leah. Hours: weekdays 9:30 a.m. to 4:30 p.m. Docent-led thirty-minute

tours begin at 10:30 a.m. weekdays. For information, (340) 774-4312; hebrewcong@islands.vi.

The Weibel Museum (at rear of synagogue; 340-774-4312) covers the three-hundred-year-old history of the Jews of St. Thomas; gift shop sells ritual items and Judaic arts and crafts. Hours: weekdays 10 a.m. to 4 p.m.; weekends 12:30 to 4 p.m.

Market Square (13): Continuing west on Backstreet, Market Square is the site of the notorious slave market, one of the biggest in the West Indies. Today it is covered by an iron market shed built in the early 20th century and used as the town's open-air fruit-and-vegetable market, and it's now called the Sanderilla Thomas Bungalow, after a woman who sold produce there for fifty years. It reopened in July 2007 following a $1 million rebuilding project. Saturday is market day.

One block west on Main Street is the Cathedral of St. Peter and St. Paul, built in 1844. The cathedral offers daily tours for visitors by appointment, and guided by their school's students. For information: 340-774-0201; www.catholicvi.com.

Public Library (14): East of Market Square on Main Street is the Enid M. Baa Public Library, built around 1800 as the Lange residence. The library is named for one of the island's first female university graduates, who served as librarian for many years and was instrumental in creating the von Scholten Memorial Collection with books, prints, and documents on the Virgin Islands and the West Indies.

Pissarro's Birthplace (15): No. 14 Dronningens Gade (Main Street) is the birthplace of Camille Pissarro (1830–1903), a Sephardic Jew who lived here until he went to Paris to study at the age of twelve. Pissarro lived in Paris most of his life, but he is known to have returned to St. Thomas at least once. The building is marked by a small oval sign. On the second floor is the **Pissarro Gallery,** directed by Debra Wombold and featuring local artists. On both sides of Main Street, small lanes have been made into palm-shaded shopping plazas where shops are housed in 18th-century buildings that were houses of the old port; some are recent structures made to look old.

Riise Alley (16): One of the first old structures to be renovated, helping to spark the renaissance of the historic district, was **A. H. Riise Store and**

Alley, belonging to the Paiewonsky family. In olden days each warehouse had its own lift to haul cargo from the ships at the waterfront and load it onto a flatbed car that ran on rails through the alleyway to Main Street. The sample here is the only one remaining. At the end of Riise Alley, the 18th-century building was the **Danish Harbor Office.**

At the end of Main Street by the Emancipation Garden is the **post office (17)**, with murals by illustrator Stephen Dohanos. They were painted in the 1940s as a WPA project, before he gained his reputation as an illustrator for the *Saturday Evening Post.* Next to the post office, the Continental Building is the old Danish Customs House. Next door is the **Territorial Building (18).**

Frenchtown (19): At the west end of town is the old fishing village of Frenchtown, settled by French immigrants fleeing the Swedish invasion of St. Barts in the late 18th century. Some of their descendants continue to speak a Norman dialect. While many of the old structures have given way to new houses and buildings, Frenchtown has retained a community feeling, and fishermen can occasionally be seen bringing in their catches to sell on the dock. This small area has a concentration of some of St. Thomas' best restaurants popular with islanders and a pretty village church, the Church of St. Anne. Frenchtown is known as Cha Cha Town for the pointed straw hat called *cha cha,* once woven by the town's women.

Paradise Point Tramway: Directly behind the West Indian Company Dock is the station (340-774-9809; www.paradisepointtramway.com), where a cable car whisks passengers up a steep mountainside in four minutes to Paradise Point, the summit. There are spectacular views of Charlotte Amalie and St. Thomas. Cost is $21 for adults, $10.50 for children round-trip. The restaurant/bar at the peak is a popular spot for cocktails at sunset. Paradise Point can also be reached by road from the harbor. At the summit, there is a nature trail of 1 mile for hiking. The tramway station has a pretty gazebo where couples can be married and from where there are fantastic views, along with a Bird Show and a Wednesday Caribbean happy hour. Information is available on the Web site.

The **Butterfly Farm** (Havensight Mall; 340-715-3366; www.thebutterflyfarm.com) located near the main cruise ship, has hundreds of butterflies from around the world and offers guided tours. Entrance: US$15.

Driving Tour of St. Thomas

Remember: KEEP TO THE LEFT. East of Charlotte Amalie the waterfront boulevard, called Veterans Drive (Route 30), forks and leads up to **Bluebeard's Castle Hotel (20)**, high on a hill from which you can enjoy a spectacular view of Charlotte Amalie and spot your ship at the West Indian Company Dock directly below. The hotel is set in gardens of tropical plants, and its 17th-century Danish watchtower, for which it is named. Look closely among the hibiscus and you might see an iguana, a reptile that looks like a miniature dinosaur. Unlike other Caribbean islands, where the iguana is elusive and endangered, it is something of a pet on St. Thomas and will often remain still for a photograph.

From Bluebeard's, Routes 35/40 lead to **Drake's Seat,** a small lookout named for the British sea captain Sir Francis Drake, who is said to have used this vantage point to watch for the Spanish treasure galleons on which he preyed. You may not see any treasure ships, but you will be richly rewarded with a magnificent view of Magens Bay and neighboring islands; off to the east is Drake's Passage, a sea channel first explored by Drake in 1580. On Route 40, the **Estate St. Peter Greathouse and Botanical Garden** (St. Peter Mountain Rd.; 340-774-4999 or 340-690-4499; www.greathouse-mountaintop.com) was once part of an 18th-century plantation. It is now a 12-acre landscaped spread 1,000 feet above Magens Bay Beach. The estate's modern West Indian–style house is furnished with works by fifty local artists. Self-guided nature trails are also offered. Hours: daily 9 a.m. to 5 p.m.; $5 adults, $2 children.

Crown Mountain Road (Route 33 west) circles Crown Mountain at 1,550 feet, the highest peak. Solberg Hill Road (Route 40 south) returns to Charlotte Amalie, providing extensive views of the town, harbor, and Hassel Island in the foreground and Water Island beyond.

West of Charlotte Amalie, Veterans Drive passes Frenchtown, the turn off for Crown Bay Dock, and the airport, continuing to the **University** of the Virgin Islands, situated on 175 acres. Not far from the entryway to Botany Bay, the Bordeaux Farmers' Market, sponsored by a growers' co-op, is held the last Sun of every month. In addition to delicious prepared dishes and organic fruits and vegetables, there is live music by steel drummers and reggae musicians.

Shopping

Main Street and side lanes such as Palm Passage have pretty stores and smart boutiques housed in renovated old warehouses from its heyday as a trading post. You will find top-brand watches, jewelry, cameras, electronic equipment, china (340-777-5313; www.havensightmall.com) remain open until 6 p.m. Stores close on Sun unless a cruise ship is in port, when some may open for half a day. The Havensight Mall's Web site has a diagram and a list by location of all its stores and services. Check out also "Port of $ale," a complex of colorfully painted boutiques next to the Havensight Mall. The shops at Yacht Haven Grande are the newest addition to St. Thomas shopping scene and include many well known high-end brands. A diagram and list of its shops are available to its Web site.

Duty-free Shopping: The matter of "duty-free" needs some explanation. All stores in the U.S. Virgin Islands are duty-free. Even so, the goods they sell are not entirely without import taxes. Local merchants pay taxes on the merchandise they import, but the levies are lower in the U.S. Virgin Islands than on the mainland.

A Word of Caution: Merchandise in St. Thomas is not always the bargain that is claimed. The proliferation of discount houses in the United States, particularly for cameras and electronic equipment, has cut into the traditional savings on duty-free merchandise. The only way to know a real bargain is to come prepared with prices from home and to do some comparative shopping before you buy. Cigarettes and liquor have the lowest prices and represent the greatest savings.

Art and Artists: A. H. Riise Gifts and Art Gallery (Main Street; 800-524-2037; www.ahriise.com) has a collection by local as well as Haitian artists. In late Mar, Aug, and Nov, **Tillett's Gardens** (Route 38, Tutu; 340-775-1929; www.tillett gardens.com), where some artists and jewelry designers work and sell their products year-round, holds an arts fair, **Arts Alive,** with more than fifty local artists and artisans. The colorful Mocko Jumbies, clowns, acrobats, and folkloric dancers are part of the entertainment. Admission is free. Tillett's also offers a series of musical concerts in the winter season and there is wireless Internet service in the garden. **Mango Tango** (340-777-3060; www.mangotango-art.com) is one of the best places in St. Thomas to buy quality art by local artists. The gallery has a second location in the Yacht Haven Grande complex; from Nov to May, emerging artists are featured. **Jonna White Gallery** (30 Main St.; 340-774-1201; 877-860-3600) is the gallery of the artist who has a distinctive style, using Caribbean colors on handmade paper.

Gallery St. Thomas (Palm Passage; 340-777-6363; http://gallerystthomas.com) promotes art from or inspired by the Virgin Islands. Owner Claire Ochoa carries a variety of artists and mediums, creating an interesting showcase for local art. **Cloud 9 Studio** (1 Norre Gade; 340-514-2432; www.artbylucinda.com/studioinfo.htm) is owned and operated by well-known local artist Lucinda Schutte O'Connell. Lucinda is artist-in-residence at the Ritz Carlton St. Thomas and offers art classes to locals as well as visitors on Tues at 2 p.m. and Fri at 9:30 a.m.; $65 for two-hour session. **David Hill Gallery** (340-714-4400) is the gallery of a local artist. For antiques, check out the **Carson Company** (Royal Dane Mall; 340-774-6175), where you can find unusual antiques and ethnic artifacts.

Books: Dockside Bookshop (Havensight Mall; 340-777-8786; www.docksidebooks.com) has the largest selection of books and carries stateside newspapers—costing $2 or more. Hours: Mon through Thurs and Sat, 9 a.m. to 5 p.m., Fri to 6 p.m., Sun, 11 a.m. to 3 p.m.

Cameras/Electronics: All leading makes are available, but bring stateside prices for comparison. The largest selections are at **Boolchand's** (31 Main St. and Havensight Mall; 340-774-8027; www.boolchand.com). Prices are comparable to those of discount houses in New York.

China/Crystal: Little Switzerland (Main Street, Havensight, and Yacht Haven Grande; 340-779-2546; www.littleswitzerland.com) carries a wide selection of English china, French crystal, and similar high-quality goods. You can get a catalog by calling (800) 524-2010. **A. H. Riise Gifts** (Main Street) is something of a department store with a collection of boutiques for gifts, jewelry, perfume, china, silver, and crystal, as well as liquor.

Clothing: In the narrow passageways between Main Street and the waterfront, you can find boutiques with designer fashions, while **Fendi, DKNY, Nicole Miller, Tommy Hilfiger,** and **Polo Ralph Lauren** (Palm Passage) have their own stores. **Local Color** (on the waterfront; 340-774-3727) has handpainted T-shirts, dresses, and sportswear; **Fresh Produce** (Riise Mall; 340-774-0807) is similar. Look for the label **Sloop Jones** (www.sloopjones.com), which is based at Hansen Bay, St. John.

Zora's of St. Thomas (5040 Norre Gade; 340-774-2559; www.zoraofstthomas.com) has custommade sandals and leather goods and a wide variety of canvas bags, backpacks, and travel bags. The **Doubloon Company Store** (www.doubloon.com) sells boat merchandise from both of their boats, the *Doubloon* and the *Dancing Dolphin,* including flags and shirts with the Jolly Roger design. **Caribbean Marketplace** (Havensight Mall; 340-776-5400) sells a wide selection of crafts from the region. The new **Yacht Haven Grande** complex (340-774-5030; YHGST@igymarinas.com) houses a variety of famous-label stores, including **Bvlgari, Ferragamo, Gucci, Caché, Coach,** and **Louis Vuitton.**

Crafts: Don't overlook locally made products, especially for gifts and souvenirs. You do not have to count these products in your $1,600 customs allowance. Products you will find include straw hats, mats, and baskets; candles with scents of local herbs and spices; candies and preserved fruits and spices; pottery and ceramics; folkloric dolls; macramé and scrimshaw; and perfume and suntan lotions made from native flowers and herbs.

A. H. Riise (48 AB Norre Gade; 340-766-2303) sells preserves, herbs, and spices as well as imported teas and coffees. The **Native Arts and**

Crafts Cooperative (Tolbod Gade; 340-777-1153) specializes in island-made art and other crafts from ninety different craftspeople. **Caribbean Chocolate** (15 Main St.; 340-774-6675) sells handmade chocolates as well as Virgin Islands rum cake. On site good, but expensive, chocolate candy is made at the **Belgian Chocolate Factory** (Riise Alley; 340-777-5247; www.thebelgianchocolatefactory.com).

Jewelry: Stores such as **Cardow, Cartier,** and **H. Stern** (all on Main Street) have international reputations; **A. H. Riise Gifts** has a large jewelry department and is the exclusive Mikimoto dealer and official Rolex retailer. The **Caribbean Bracelet Company** (www.caribbeanbracelet.com) makes the popular handcrafted bracelet of the same name and sold at Cardow and other jewelers. Many smaller jewelry stores on Main Street and adjacent malls sell gold jewelry. Look around before you buy.

Leather/Luggage: Royal Dane Mall has several shops with high-quality Italian and Spanish handbags. **Cuckoo's Nest** (International Plaza; 340-776-4005) specializes in men's clothing. **Gucci** (340-776-4244) is located in the Yacht Haven complex.

Linens: Table linens are among the best bargains here. Most come from India and China. **Linen House** (340-774-8117) and **Mr. Tablecloth** (6 Main St.; 340-774-4343; www.mrtablecloth-vi.com) have large collections, and you might also check out some of the general stores on Main Street.

Liquor: Prices are very competitive, but **Al Cohen's** near the port claims to have the best prices in St. Thomas. Check *St. Thomas This Week* and other free pamphlets distributed for tourists. The centerfold or back page often has a list of current liquor prices.

Perfumes: Perfume Palace (Main Street) has nothing but perfume. **West Indies Bay Company** (Estates Thomas; 800-422-9786; www.stjohns bayrum.com) makes St. Johns Bay Rum for men, J'Ouvert for women, and other fragrances packaged in bottles with handwoven palm fronds in a traditional design used by Caribbean fishermen for their fish pots. The company offers factory tours.

Dining and Nightlife

The Virgin Islands did not gain their reputation as Paradise in the kitchen. It's not that innkeepers and restaurateurs don't try. They try very hard, perhaps too hard, to create gourmet havens. But for myriad reasons they are unable to maintain a consistently high level. (Herman Wouk's hilarious *Don't Stop the Carnival* was written from his trials and tribulations in trying to operate a hotel in St. Thomas.) Aspiring places can quickly become pretentious disappointments at very high prices instead. With this caveat, the selection here is based less on the great gourmet experience you are unlikely to have than on the aesthetic one you are sure to experience, either thanks to a view, a historic setting, or both. Some of the best establishments are open for dinner only. Expensive means more than $30 per person. If wine is added, the bill can quickly climb to $50 per person and more. Most are open daily, but check locally.

With a View or Historic Setting

Hervé Restaurant and Wine Bar (Government Hill; 340-777-9703; www.herverestaurant.com) one of the island's most popular restaurants, is set in a renovated 18th-century building with a panoramic view of Charlotte Amalie. Herve Paul Chassin is a St. Thomas restaurateur for more than thirty years. You lunch and dine in an informal atmosphere on contemporary American and classic French selections, all touched by a bit of Caribbean. Closed Sun. Expensive. Newly added to Herve's veranda is **Paulette's Patio**, offering Mediterranean fare in a breezy, alfresco setting with a view of the harbor. Look for the burgundy awning.

Light and Local

Beni Iguana (Havensight Mall; 340-777-4711) is a sushi bar and restaurant, now enlarged in its new location. The bar serves domestic and Japanese beer and sake. Open daily. Moderate.

Café Amici (Riise's Alley; 340-776-5670; www.cafeamicivi.com), a sidewalk cafe in the heart of town, is perfect for lunch or a refreshment break during a shopping expedition. The menu offers light fare and usually a specialty of the day. Moderate.

Craig and Sally's (Frenchtown; 340-777-9949; www.craigandsallys.com) is a family-run restaurant/bar with owners Craig at the door and Sally in the kitchen. The bar, open daily 11:30 a.m. to 1 a.m. except Mon, serves wine by the glass. The restaurant offers an eclectic menu that's changed daily. Closed Sat and Sun lunch. Moderately expensive.

Cuzzin (7 Backstreet; 340-777-4711) is a lively restaurant-bar in the heart of Charlotte Amalie featuring West Indian dishes, sandwiches, and pasta. Moderate.

Gladys' Cafe (Royal Dane Mall; 340-774-6604), a charming cafe in town, serves lunch plus dinner on Fri with jazz, 6 to 9 p.m. Lunch offers fresh fish, hamburgers, and local specials. Gladys's hot sauce, attractively packaged for gifts, sells for $6 a bottle. Moderate.

Havana Blue (MorningStar Beach Resort; 340-715-2583; www.havanabluerestaurant.com) offers Pacific Rim and Cuban– and Latin American– inspired dishes. Favorites include grouper encrusted with red chili and avocado, seared Thai tenderloin, and duck lettuce cups. Moderate. Owners also have two newer eateries, **Lotus**, and **Fat Boys**.

Randy's Bar & Bistro (4002 Raphune Hill; 340-775-5001) is a wine and gourmet shop that doubles as an eatery with a creative menu that changes daily. Moderate.

The **Old Stone Farmhouse** (Mahogany Run Golf Course, 340-777-6277; www.oldstonefarmhouse.com), situated in a 200-year-old restored field house, was recently renovated. The menu offers a range of internationally inspired, eclectic cuisine, such as upside-down spinach "martini" and "calypso" seafood hot pot. Expensive.

W!kked (Yacht Haven Grande; 340-777-8WKD; www.wikkedrestaurant.com) a hip, rustic waterfront restaurant offering island fare and favorites like wings and tacos. Open 7 a.m. to midnight. Moderately expensive.

XO Bistro (Red Hook Plaza, behind Duffy's Love Shack and by the Grateful Deli; 340-779-2069), a wine and champagne bar popular with locals is little known to tourists. Open daily with different theme or specialty each evening, some with live music. Some say it's the place to be on Fri nights. Moderate.

Evening Entertainment

Nightlife is small-scale—steel bands, combos, discos—and mostly revolves around hotels and restaurants. Check local newspaper and tourist publications such as *St. Thomas This Week* for what's happening. Green House, Bamboo, Fat Turtle, and Fat Boys are some of the bars, restaurants and clubs with nightly entertainment. A terrace at **Paradise Point** and **Room with a View** (Bluebeard's Castle; 340-774-1600) provide a good perch for cocktails at sunset and offer a fabulous view of Charlotte Amalie.

Duffy's Love Shack (Red Hook Plaza; 340-779-2080; www.duffysloveshack.com). Nightly, a parking lot is transformed into a popular local watering hole. The rustic, thatch-roofed bar serves up exotic concoctions like the Love Shack Volcano and Revenge of Godzilla (in a big green Godzilla you can take home). For lunch and dinner, you can grill your own meat or fish. After 9 p.m. on "Taco Tues," tacos are $1.25; "Chicks Rule" on Wed is ladies' night with free drinks and $2 beer; and Fri is dancing under the stars. Open daily from 11:30 a.m. to 2 a.m. No credit cards.

St. Thomas This Week (340-774-2500; www.stthomasthisweek.com) has a full page of the island's entertainment, from steel band to calypso to guitar and jazz.

Sports

St. Thomas boasts good facilities for almost every warm-weather sport—fishing, golf, tennis, parasailing, waterskiing, windsurfing—and those for sailing and diving are outstanding.

Beaches/Swimming: The coves and bays that sheltered pirates in the old days are among St. Thomas's biggest attractions for tourists today. The most celebrated—and the most crowded—beach is at Magens Bay on the north side of the island. Beaches closest to Charlotte Amalie are Morningstar, Limetree, and Bolongo on the south/southeast, and Lindbergh, close to Crown Bay Marina. Tranquil Honeymoon Beach on Water Island, which is slowly—very slowly—getting a face-lift, is open for visitors and can be reached by a short ferry ride from town. You'll find a list of beaches and facilities in *St. Thomas This Week*.

Biking: Water Island Adventures (340-714-2186; www.waterislandadventures.com) offers a bike tour and swim on Water Island.

Boating: Calm seas and year-round balmy weather make the Virgin Islands a boating mecca. Every type of craft is available for chartered, bare boat, or crewed, and with all provisions. Many charter operators have stateside offices and toll-free numbers for information and reservations. **Yacht Haven Marina** (www.yachthavengrande.com) is the home port for the V.I. **Charter Yacht League** (340-774-3944) and the venue for the league's annual boat show in mid-Nov. On the east end at Red Hook are **American Yacht Harbor** (340-775-6454; www.igy-americanyachtharbor.com) and **Charter Boat Center** (Piccola Marina; 340-775-7990; www.charterboat.vi), among others. Several dozen boats operate day sails that take passengers to pretty beaches for swimming and snorkeling. Some boats hold only six people, whereas party boats can take several dozen. Among them are *Daydream* (www.daydreamervi.com) and *Independence* (www.independence44.us). Cost is about $90 for a full day.

Deep-Sea Fishing: Experts say the Virgin Islands are among the best places in the world for blue marlin, and the records set here support the claim. Other fish—maho, kingfish, sailfish, wahoo, tuna, and skipjack—are plentiful, too. American Yacht Harbor, **St. Thomas Sports Fishing Center** (340-775-7990), and a dozen or more boat operators offer half- and full-day trips; they provide bait, tackle, ice, and beer. Half-day trips cost $500 to $700; $900 to $1,500 for six hours for up to six people. The time of year makes a difference in the prices; the marlin season is mainly July and Aug. The **Virgin Islands Game Fishing Club** (340-775-9144; www.vigfc.com) Web site has information on tournaments and other competitions in the Virgin Islands and nearby islands, social events, and other information. The club was a pioneer in conserving fish resources by banning the use of double hooks in competition. At **Deep Sea Fishing** (340-775-6147; red@sportfishvi.com) a half-day starts at $650. Also see www.stthomassportfishing.com.

Golf: Mahogany Run Golf Course (340-777-6006; www.mahoganyrungolf.com) is St. Thomas's only 18-hole course. The championship layout is one of the Caribbean's most challenging. Located about twenty minutes from Charlotte Amalie, the spectacular course (6,100 yards, par 70) by George and Tom Fazio extends over verdant hills and rocky cliffs overlooking the north coast. It has a pro shop, driving range, and practice green. Greens fees: $165 including cart fee for 18 holes; $115 for 9 holes. After 1:30 p.m., twilight fee, $100; all include shared cart. Call for tee time. Ship golf package may cost $200 or more, but will include transportation from the port.

Hiking: Captain Nautica, Inc. (340-715-3379; www.captainnautica.com) offers hiking, sightseeing, and snorkeling excursions. The snorkel package combines two hours of sightseeing and two hours snorkeling at two locations; $58 per person with snorkel equipment, snacks, and beverages.

Magens Bay Trail: Guided hikes on a nature trail on 75 acres above Magens Baywas created by the Nature Conservancy with environmental experts. The trail runs downhill from 450 feet elevation and passes through forests and dense vegetation to the beach. The sixty- to ninety-minute hike is moderately strenuous.

Virgin Islands Ecotours (340-779-2155; www.viecotours.com), an ecotour operator, has a guided three-hour tour that begins with exploring the mangrove ecosystem by kayak followed by a hike in Cas Cay, a 15-acre wildlife sanctuary, with stops at a natural whirlpool and blowhole, followed by snorkeling in the protected reserve; cost is $79. For honeymooners, the outfitter provides pick-up and drop-off service for a day of secluded fun. Children can celebrate their birthday with a treasure hunt party and swim at Cas Cay.

Kayaking: Virgin Islands Ecotours (340-779-2155; www.viecotours.com) offers two-and-a-half-hour guided kayak tours of the Virgin Islands Marine Sanctuary Mangrove Lagoon, led by marine biologists and naturalists from the University of the Virgin Islands. It uses single- or two-person ocean kayaks that are easy to paddle. Tours start from the Holmberg Marina and cost $69, with a fifteen-minute orientation and slide show to introduce

kayakers to local flora and fauna. Kayaks may also be rented for individual exploration.

Snorkeling and Scuba Diving: The Virgin Islands are rated by dive experts among the best in the world for both novice and experienced divers. Visibility ranges up to 150 feet, water temperatures average 82 degrees Fahrenheit in summer and 78 degrees Fahrenheit in winter, and there's great variety plus excellent facilities. Three dozen of the Virgin Islands' one hundred dive sites lie within a twenty-minute boat ride of St. Thomas. Most dive operators have their own tanks and boats and offer packages ranging from half-day to weeklong certification. A list of operators is available at www.visitusvi.com and V.I. tourist offices. Many cruise ships offer a half-day introduction to scuba diving course.

Coral World Ocean Park (340-775-1555; 888-695-2073; www.coralworldvi.com), an underwater observatory and park at Coki Point, is St. Thomas's most popular attraction. Admission: $19 adults, $10 children age three to twelve years, and $60 for families (two adults and up to four children). Hours: daily 9 a.m. to 4 p.m. Daily talks and feeds.

Coral World's Lorikeet Garden, a 1,600-square-foot walk-through aviary is home to a collection of lorikeet parrots. Visitors can purchase a cup of nectar to feed them by hand. Also not to be missed is Sea Trekkin', where you can walk on the floor of the Caribbean Sea and enjoy its incredible marine life. Participants (eight years of age and older) wear a special helmet and are led by a guide along a trail equipped with a handrail, 12 to 30 feet deep into the crystal-clear water. The helmet provides air and allows communication with the guide while keeping your head dry. The two-and-a-half-hour tours are offered from 9 a.m. to 4 p.m. daily; in summer, usually closed on Fri and Sun. Rates: $77 adults, $68 children, including park admission.

The more adventurous will want to try the **Shark Encounter at Coral World.** There are no cages or barriers, just you and your guide in the Shark Shallows Pool, home to more than a dozen juvenile lemon, blacktip, and nurse sharks. Cost: $51 adults and $42 children, including Coral World admission. Participants must be a minimum of 54 inches tall. Coral World also offers swimming with sea lions.

If you are not quite ready for diving, there's an alternative called **Snuba** (340-693-8063; www .visnuba.com), a cross between scuba diving and snorkeling. It, too, is available at Coral World. Cost: $68, including your Coral World pass. Participants must be at least eight years old.

Homer's Scuba and Snorkel Tours and Berry Charters (Hull Bay; 340-774-7606; www .nightsnorkel.com) offers boat diving, kayak dives, snorkel trips for small groups, and fishing, as well as surfboard, kayak, dive, and snorkel gear rentals. Hull Bay, on the north side of St. Thomas, is the island's best-kept secret with great snorkeling, fishing, and diving on reefs little touched by crowds. Kayak/scuba and snorkel trips use two-person inflatable Diveyaks, in groups of eight with never more than four divers, accompanied by a dive master. Kayak scuba $80; kayak snorkel $59. Morning trips only, departing at 9:30 a.m., returning about 1:30 p.m. The company also has power snorkel or scuba with seascooters. Two-hour excursions (at 10 a.m. and 1 p.m.) costs $50 per person includes free pick up at your ship and guided tour and limited to four persons at a time.

Tennis: About a dozen hotels have tennis courts. Those closest to the West Indian Company Dock and open to nonguests are at **Frenchman's Reef & Morning Star Marriott Beach Resort** (340-776-8500), two courts, $10 per hour. Courts nearest to Crown Bay Dock are two public ones, lighted until 10 p.m.

Windsurfing/Kiteboarding: Morningstar Beach is nearest the West Indian Company Dock, but the eastern end of the island has the best windsurfing. **Sapphire Beach** (340-775-6100) offers instruction on a simulator and instruction in the water. **West Indies Windsurfing** (340-775-6530), on the beach in Red Hook, has the best rentals.

On the southside of Red Hook, Vessup, known locally as **Bluebeard's Beach,** is a popular venue for windsurfing and kiteboarding contests.

Cultural Events and Festivals

The Virgin Islands observe all the U.S. national holidays, plus a few of their own. Leading the list is **Carnival,** which on St. Thomas is held during the last two weeks of Apr. It begins officially with a weeklong calypso competition for the coveted title of the Calypso King; followed by a week of festivities with the crowning of a Carnival Queen and an elaborate all-day parade featuring the Mocko Jumbi Dancers.

Reichhold Center for the Performing Arts (340-693-1559; www.reichholdcenter.com) offers a year-round schedule of concerts, opera, ballet, Broadway musicals, jazz, gospel, and plays at its wonderful outdoor theater.

St. John: A Gift of Nature

www.stjohnisland.com
www.gotostjohn.com
www.stjohnusvi.com

Serene St. John, the least developed of the U.S. Virgin Islands, is truly America the Beautiful. Almost two-thirds of the heavily forested, mountainous island—9,485 acres—is covered by national park on land donated in 1956 by Laurance Rockefeller. The island is edged by lovely coves with pristine, white-sand beaches and some of the most spectacular aquamarine waters in the Caribbean. Beneath these waters is a tropical wonderland, also protected by the park.

Development is restricted; it has occurred mainly in the area of the lilliputian port of Cruz Bay and in the southwest corner. On the north coast is the superdeluxe Caneel Bay, set on an old sugar plantation in the magnificent gardens fronting seven—yes, seven—of the prettiest beaches in the Caribbean. The tennis facilities are great, too.

Several cruise ships call at St. John, but the majority of its visitors come on day trips from St. Thomas; it is one of the most delightful excursions available for cruise passengers, whether as an organized tour, a day sail, or on your own. The day's target for most visitors is a circle route along North Shore Road (Route 20) and Centerline Road (Route 10), the two main roads, with stops for a swim, picnic, and short hikes.

Ferry Service: Ferries depart Red Hook hourly from 6:30 a.m. to midnight for Cruz Bay and return

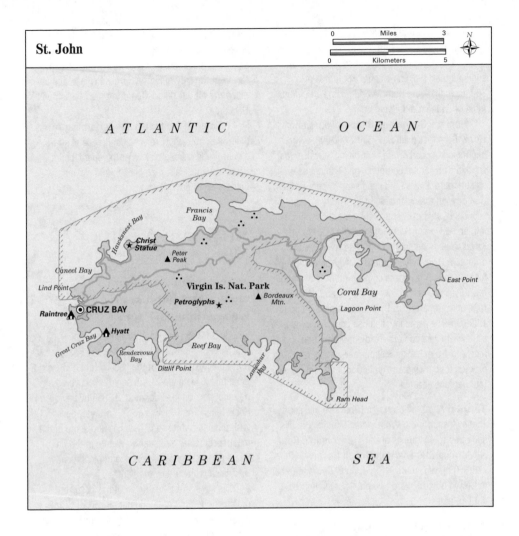

St. John

0   Miles   3

0   Kilometers   5

ATLANTIC   OCEAN

Francis Bay

Hawksnest Bay

Christ Statue

Peter Peak

Caneel Bay

Lind Point

Virgin Is. Nat. Park

Petroglyphs

Bordeaux Mtn.

Coral Bay

East Point

Lagoon Point

Raintree   CRUZ BAY

Great Cruz Bay   Hyatt

Rendezvous Bay

Reef Bay

Dittlif Point

Lameshur Bay

Ram Head

CARIBBEAN   SEA

from 6 a.m. to 11 p.m. One-way fare is $6. Others depart from the Charlotte Amalie waterfront at two-hour intervals from 9 a.m. to 5:30 p.m. Cost is $12 one-way and takes forty-five minutes. There is also ferry service from St. John to Jost Van Dyke and Tortola, B.V.I.

Transportation: Taxis with driver/guides can be hired in Cruz Bay at the pier, or you can rent a car or jeep for about $55 per day. A two-hour island tour costs $50 for one or two persons, $25 per person for three or more. Several St. Thomas tour companies provide service in St. John and combine the two islands into one package. Drivers take and return you to the ferry docks on both islands. After

a tour of St. John, your driver leaves you at a beach to fetch you later. St. John has buses, including a van for wheelchair passengers and senior citizens. The service operates hourly from Cruz Bay and Coral Bay from 5:30 a.m. to 8:30 p.m. Fares are $1 for the bus, $4 to $24 for the van, depending on location. Call 340-776-6346.

St. John Community Foundation (340-693-693-9410; www.sjcf.org) offers tours for mobility restricted visitors, sponsored by the United Way St. Thomas/St. John and Virgin Islands Department of Human Services. They operate weekdays from 8:30 a.m. to 4:30 p.m. The accessible van has space for two wheelchairs. Inquire for rates.

Cruz Bay

Tiny, yacht-filled Cruz Bay hugs a narrow strip of land between the harbor and the mountains. Most of the buildings and houses are West Indian–style in architecture and painted a medley of pastel colors. Until recently the structures were small and blended into the landscape as naturally as the bougainvillea. Regretfully, new construction is drastically altering the character of the town by crowding the space around the harbor and turning the once-natural setting into a tacky T-shirt and fast-food mall. Nonetheless, the town—three streets wide and four streets deep—is worth exploring and easy to do on foot. Facing the pier is a park, and on its north are the Taxi Association and Tourist Information Center.

Park Service Visitor Center: Northwest of the harbor is the Virgin Islands National Park Service Visitor Center (340-776-6201; www.nps .gov/viis), open from 8 a.m. to 4:30 p.m. The center is well organized and offers a variety of activities, including ranger-led tours, hikes, snorkeling trips, cultural and wildlife lectures, and film presentations. A schedule is available in advance from the park service (340-776-6201, ext. 238). Reservations during the winter season are strongly recommended. The park's user fee is $4 per adult. Information is also available from **Friends of the Park** (340-779-4940; www.friendsvinp.org), which holds a variety of interesting workshops and educational excursions during the winter season.

Hikes and Tours: *Trail Guide for Safe Hiking* is a park brochure outlining twenty-one trails with a map and tips on preparations. Most trails are designed in clusters of two or three contiguous paths to be taken in segments as short as ten minutes, or, when strung together, as long as two to four hours. The most popular is **Reef Bay,** a 2.5-mile trail that takes about two hours to cover in a downhill direction. The park ranger-led Reef Bay hike is available at 10 a.m. on Mon, Tues, Thurs, and Fri for $15 per person. Hikers must arrange their own transportation to the trailhead. Taxis ($7 per person) can take hikers there; local buses, too. At the end of the trail, the Park Service ferries hikers back to its dock in Cruz Bay. Reservations required: (340) 776-6201, ext. 238.

Among the historic programs is the Annaberg Cultural Demonstrations (three hours; free), which visits the partially restored ruins of the Annaberg Plantation, where you can learn about tropical food, plants, weaving, baking, charcoal making, and other skills islanders once needed to subsist.

Cruise-ship excursions usually stop at Trunk Bay, a lovely beach on the north shore, about twenty minutes from town and the site of an underwater trail laid out for snorkelers by the Park Service. Unfortunately, the reef is now badly deteriorated from overuse. Snorkelers and divers on their own have many other reefs around St. John to explore. At Honeymoon Beach, one of the palm-studded coves of Caneel Bay, snorkelers can swim with spotted eagle rays.

Thunderhawk Trail Guides (340-774-1112; 340-774-1030), specializing in hiking tours, provides two-hour guided tours of St. John's nature trails from Cruz Bay to Lind Point, Honeymoon Beach, and the Caneel Hill spur trail. Guides provide information on history and culture of the Taino Indians, the island's ancient inhabitants.

The **National Park Service** (340-776-6201) offers a Culture Walk at Cinnamon Bay Tues from 9:30 to 10:30 a.m. and a Waters Edge Walk every Wed from 9:30 a.m. to noon that meets at Leinster Bay trailhead. The snorkeling trip at Trunk Bay operates every Mon from 9:30 to 10:30 a.m.; bird watching at the Francis Bay trailhead goes on every Sun from 7:30 to 9 a.m.; and a full-day, guided Reef Bay hike occurs from 9:30 a.m. to 3 p.m. on Mon and Thurs. Recently, the park completed new Accessible Trails at Francis Bay and is working on one at Cinnamon Bay. These trails enable visitors in wheelchairs, families with young children and other people less surefooted to enjoy the park.

Shopping

St. John's beauty and tranquility have made it something of an artists' community. Several artists have stores in town sandwiched between the T-shirt and junky-merchandise shops.

The **Pink Papaya** (Lemon Tree Mall; 340-693-8535; www.pinkpapaya.com) is the gallery and gift shop of Virgin Islands artist Lisa Etre, whose distinctive style reflects her West Indian environment in a sophisticated way. In addition to original paintings and prints, elements from her drawings are used in designs on tableware, greeting cards, and lovely gifts.

Mongoose Junction (www.mongoosejunction stjohn.com), a ten-minute walk north of the pier, is a shopping plaza designed as an artist's enclave with rustic wooden buildings incorporating the trees in a natural setting. You will probably want to browse, as each shop is different. Among the boutique/studios of local artists and transplanted mainlanders, the Clothing Studio (340-776-6210; www.clothingstudio.com) has handpainted tropical wear and swimwear. Fabric Mill, belonging to interior designer Trisha Maize, carries unusual fabrics and accessories. Bajo El Sol Gallery/ Under the Sun (Reef Building, 2nd Level, 340-593-7070; 866-593-7070; www.bajoelsolgallery .com) is one of St. John's largest galleries, featuring Caribbean-inspired original art, prints, jewelry, and crafts. Sea Leathers & Antique Jewels (340-777-6850) carries an unusual array of goods made from skins such as salmon and eel. Not far from Mongoose Junction, the Amore Center has the Donald Schnell Studio (800-253-7107; www .donaldschnell.com/studio) featuring ceramics of natural materials—coral sand, woods—by an American artist who comes originally from Michigan.

South of the pier, Wharfside Village (www .wharfsidevillage.com) is a multilevel mall of West Indian–style structures awash in cool pastels, with more than forty shops and restaurants. Freebird Creations (340-693-8625; www.freebirdcreations .com), one of the island's longest-established businesses, sells unusual and many one-of-a-kind jewelry crafted by Caribbean artists. Spyglass Restaurant (340-774-8470) (formerly The Balcony at Cruz Bay) offers a Euro-Caribe fusion menu with fresh seafood from local waters.

The Marketplace (Cruz Bay; 340-776-6455; www.stjohnusvi.com) is a shopping center with a variety of stores and services. Built in native stone and mahogany, with verandas and courtyards, the center is anchored by the Starfish Market (340-779-4949) and St. John Hardware (340-693-8780). Other stores include the Artists' Association of St. John Gallery (340-774-2275; www.stjohnarts.org), Surf da Web Cyber Cafe, Baked in the Sun, Chelsea Drug Store (340-776-4888), and Book & Bean (340-779-2665), among others.

The Kareso (Cruz Bay; 340-714-5511) art gallery exhibits local art, including paintings by owner Karen Samuel, whose contemporary style features island landscapes and people. The gallery also has Karen's brother's turn-wood pieces, such as bowls, vases, and other decorative items made from exotic tropical hardwoods. The gallery sells local handmade baskets, painted clothing, photography, watercolors, prints, and furniture. Open daily.

Dining

Asolare (Cruz Bay; 340-779-4747; www.asolare stjohn.com) is an island favorite for Pacific Rim cuisine, which can be enjoyed along with spectacular views. Moderately expensive.

Chilly Billy's Lumberyard Café (Lumberyard Shopping Center, Boulon Center Road; 340-693-8708), a sandwich shop by day, gets transformed in the evening into an intimate French restaurant, seating only twenty-four people, at 6 and 8 p.m. Open Mon to Sat, reservations recommended. Moderately expensive.

Happy Fish (The Marketplace; 340-776-1717) is a new popular sushi and martini bar open for lunch Mon through Fri 10:30 a.m. to 2 p.m. and for dinner daily 5 to 10 p.m. Nightly music entertainment as well as kung fu movies. Moderately expensive.

The Lime Inn (Lemon Tree Mall, Cruz Bay; 340-776-6425) serves lunch and dinner in a tropical setting and features fresh fish, charcoal steaks, and creative specials. Moderate.

St. John Waterfront Bistro (Cruz Bay Beach; 340-777-7755; www.thewaterfrontbistro.com) offers ocean views while you enjoy French cuisine with a Caribbean twist, Open daily from 11 a.m. to 11 p.m.

Sports

Horseback Riding: Carolina Corral (340-693-5778; www.carolinacorral.vi) offers horse and donkey rides by the hour or half-day with guide. Little instruction is given, and trails are steep and narrow. Cost: $75 for ninety-minute ride; $65 for children age twelve and younger. Carriage rides are also available.

Kayaking: The sport of kayaking is very popular in St. John and available from several operators, who for $65 offer guided tours of the beautiful coastal waters with time for swimming, snorkeling, and exploring isolated beaches accessible only by boat. **Low Key Watersports** (340-693-8999; 800-835-7718; www.divelowkey.com) will tailor the trip to your interest.

Arawak Expeditions (P.O. Box 853, Cruz Bay, St. John; 340-693-8312; 800-238-8687; www.arawakexp.com) offers guided kayaking and mountain-biking excursions to remote parts of St. John and nearby islands. No previous experience is necessary. Full-day (six hours) kayaking excursion leaves from Cruz Bay at 10 a.m. to Henley Cay for snorkeling and to Lovango Cay for lunch and more snorkeling. Cost is $110 per person including lunch. Half-day (three hours) excursions depart at 9 a.m. and 2 p.m. for Henley Cay or other snorkeling spot; $50.

Water Sports: Low Key Watersports (Cruz Bay, St. John; 340-693-8999; 800-835-7718; www.divelowkey.com) offers reef and wreck dives departing daily at 8:30 a.m. Cost is $90, including gear, for a two-tank dive. Resort course is $115. The operator offers a customized package for minimum of four people. The day sail is $125 with lunch; sportsfishing charter, $550 for half day; $950 for full day.

Cruz Bay Watersports (Box 252, St. John 00830; 340-776-6234; www.divestjohn.com) has similar programs as well as day sails with snorkeling, drinks, and lunch for $120. For information: www.divestjohn.com. For a new experience, try snuba. It's something like scuba without the serious gear. Snuba of St. John (Trunk Bay; 340-693-8063; www.visnuba.com) has daily guided tours, starting at 9:30 a.m., for $65 plus the $4 National Park entrance fee.

St. Croix: The Sleeping Virgin

www.gotostcroix.com

St. Croix, 40 miles south of St. Thomas, is the largest of the U.S. Virgin Islands and served as the capital for more than two hundred years, but today it is less developed and generally less known to tourists than St. Thomas.

St. Croix has much to offer: scenery, sightseeing, sports, shopping, historic towns, pretty beaches, good restaurants, and some attractions that not even St. Thomas or St. John can boast. It has two 18-hole golf courses, a "rain forest," botanic gardens, wildlife refuges for birds and leatherback turtles, and three parks, including the only underwater park in the U.S. National Park Service.

A low-lying island of gentle landscape and rolling hills, St. Croix is vastly different from its mountainous sisters. From the time Columbus sighted the island in 1493 to the United States' purchase in 1917, it saw seven flags fly over the land. Whereas St. Thomas prospered on trade, St. Croix became a rich sugar producer and developed a plantation society that prevailed long after the abolition of slavery. Today many of the sugar mills and plantation homes have been restored as hotels and restaurants; and the colonial hearts of Christiansted, the main town, and Frederiksted, are on the National Historic Registry.

Frederiksted, on the west coast, has a deep-water harbor used by most cruise lines and is convenient to popular attractions included on most shore excursions. Christiansted, 17 miles east of Frederiksted on the north shore, has a pretty yacht-filled harbor trimmed by a colorful, historic waterfront anchored by a grand fort—all beautifully restored. Although Christiansted is more developed than Frederiksted for shopping, restaurants, and water sports, unless the harbor is dredged, it is limited to receiving small, shallow draft ships—a situation many local people prefer. St. Croix has good roads and transportation, and travel is easy regardless of which port is used. In the shopping plazas in Christiansted and at the King Christian Hotel facing the waterfront, there are car-rental firms

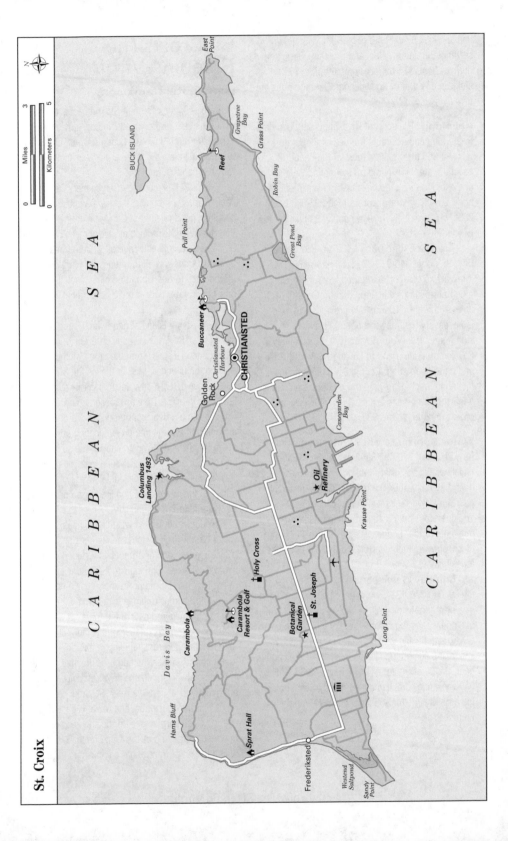

and watersports operators who make excursions to Buck Island and offer diving and other sports.

Most ships offer **St. Croix Island Tour** (3.5 hours, $35; or by taxi, $80) and a **Buck Island Tour** ($60 to $100, depending on the boat and duration of the excursion).

In addition to sailing, beach party, shopping, and diving for certified divers, passengers can snorkel or learn to snorkel or get initiated to diving, take a 12-mile guided bike tour, a walking tour of Frederiksted and the Botanical Gardens, or a nature hike in the western, forest-clad mountains.

For those on their first visit who prefer to travel on their own, we recommend an island tour, preferably by taxi with a driver/guide. It is not worthwhile renting a car unless your ship remains in port for a full day. A shuttle bus is usually available between the Frederiksted pier and Christiansted; a taxi between the two towns is $24. The average charge for a three-hour tour for one to four persons is $100.

Taxi and tour prices are posted at the Visitor's Bureau office by the pier. The **Taxi Federation** (340-277-0202; fax: 340-692-1214) has more than one hundred members, who must take tourism/guide refresher courses every six months. **St. Croix Safari Tours** (340-773-6700; www.gotostcroix.com/safaritours) offers rides in colorful open-air safari buses with a covered top and visits to the island's main heritage sites. Sweeny is probably the best-known guide in the Virgin Islands, with extensive knowledge of St. Croix. **Tan Tan Tours** (340-473-6446; www.stxtantantours.com) and owner Wave Phillip take you off the beaten path by jeep to parts of St. Croix only accessible with four-wheel drive. Half-day, $100 per person.

St. Croix Environmental Association (340-773-1989; www.stxenvironmental.org) offers nature hikes into the rain forest, snorkel trips, bird-watching tours, turtle nesting and hatchling watches, and stargazing. **Crucian Nature & Heritage Tourism** (CHANT) (340-719-5455; www.chantvi.org) has a variety of heritage and nature tours, including historic and eco walking tours; hands on art studio tour and medicinal tours with an herbalist.

AirVentures in Paradise (340-277-1433; www.airventuresinparadise.com) can take you on a 45-minute flight-seeing for $180 for up to three persons.

Frederiksted

A Williamsburg in the Making

Frederiksted was an almost deserted town in the 1970s, but federal legislation granting tax benefits to historic preservation galvanized community action, and many old buildings were renovated. Despite the setback of Hurricane Hugo in 1989, city fathers dream of someday making Frederiksted a Williamsburg of the Caribbean. Recently, the Frederiksted pier area was given a major facelift with a lush park, fountains, and cobbled pedestrian paths stretching a quarter mile along the town's waterfront. The pier was upgraded to accommodate two of the largest cruise ships and two mini-cruise vessels. A shopping area with vendors' booths is within walking distance of the pier. Taxis and tour buses are readily available. Among the innovations is a Webcam on the waterfront, courtesy of www.gotostcroix.com. Residents and visitors can be seen live; cruise ship and other visitors can connect with friends and family around the world via the Internet. It is free to the public and the live image, which refreshes every 15–20 seconds, can also be viewed on the iPhone.

Cruise passengers have a choice of staying close to town to enjoy the beach and stroll through its historic center, taking an island tour, or enjoying a specific sport—diving, horseback riding, golf, or hiking.

The old district of Frederiksted, directly in front of the pier, is laid out in a grid running 7 blocks from Fort Frederik and the Customs House on the north, to the Library and Queen Cross Street on the south, and 5 blocks deep from the waterfront (Strand Street) east to Prince Street. **Fort Frederik**, which dates from 1752, was the site of the emancipation of the slaves in 1848. Other important buildings include **Government House,** built in 1747; **St. Paul's Anglican Church,** 1817; and **St. Patrick's Roman Catholic Church,** 1848. Many historic homes and commercial buildings line the old streets.

Sandy Point National Wildlife Refuge: Just 3 miles south of Frederiksted is a protected area that is one of only two nesting grounds for the leatherback turtle in the United States. From Mar through June the enormous turtles—up to

6 feet long and 1,000 pounds—come ashore to dig holes where each lays as many as eighty eggs. Afterward they cover the eggs with sand for protection and lumber back to the sea, returning to repeat the ritual as many as six times during nesting season. After about two months the hatchlings emerge from the sand pits and dash to the sea under the cover of night. Earthwatch, a U.S.–based, nonprofit research organization, and the **St. Croix Environmental Association** (340-773-1989; www.stxenvironmental.org) maintain a turtle watch in which visitors can participate from Apr through June and in Aug. Reservations must be made in advance. Inquiries should be made to the association. The group also conducts guided environmental tours.

St. Croix Heritage Trail (340-772-0598; www.stcroixlandmarks.com), a self-guided tour of the island's historic and cultural heritage, is entertaining as well as enlightening. Supported by the USVI Department of Tourism, the St. Croix Landmarks Society, and many St. Croix businesses, it was named one of fifty national Millennium Legacy Trails by the White House Millennium Council. The St. Croix Heritage Trail traverses the entire 28-mile length of St. Croix, from Frederiksted on the west end to Point Udall, the easternmost point of the United States, and links the history of the island's diverse inhabitants, and agricultural and historic attractions.

The Heritage Trail traces St. Croix's evolution, which was influenced by a variety of nationalities—European planters and merchants, African slaves, free people of color, Caribbean immigrants, and American settlers—that have lived here during the past 350 years and have profoundly shaped the island's history and culture.

With a trail map, and following the Heritage Trail road signs, travelers can explore the island on a self-guided driving tour, stopping at places of interest. They can also learn about the island's oral traditions, music, and food. Some sites charge an admission fee. Trail brochures with maps are available at the U.S. Virgin Islands Department of Tourism offices and select island locations.

Christiansted
The Picture-Perfect Port

Christiansted is one of the Caribbean's prettiest little towns. In an area of about 5 square blocks, you will find some of the best-preserved and most interesting landmarks in the Virgin Islands. Alongside them are shops, making it easy to combine a walking tour with a shopping excursion.

Scalehouse: Once part of the Customs House where goods were weighed for tax purposes, Scalehouse, now houses an information office connected to the national park. The building is thought to date from 1855. In 1989 the winds and sea surge of Hurricane Hugo were so powerful they lifted the base of the heavy scales out of the ground. Hours: weekdays 8 a.m. to 5 p.m.

Fort Christian: Overlooking the harbor is the best preserved of the five Danish forts in the West Indies. Built in 1749, Fort Christian is now under the supervision of the U.S. National Park Service. You can get a brochure for a self-guided tour, and park rangers who know their history well are on hand to answer questions and provide fascinating tidbits not available in brochures. For one thing, they'll show you the cell where Alexander Hamilton's mother was jailed for her "improprieties." Tut tut! Interpretive exhibits have been installed in some of the rooms to demonstrate life in the fort in the mid-18th century. Hours: weekdays 8 a.m. to 4:45 p.m.; weekends and holidays 9 a.m. to 4:45 p.m. Between the fort and Scalehouse is the old Customs House and Post Office, built in 1751. It is used now as a library.

Government House: One block west on King Street, an imposing 18th-century town house that was built as a private home was later used as the residence and offices of the Danish governor. A handsome outside staircase leads to a beautiful ballroom on the first floor. In 2000 a six-year restoration project was completed, adding air-conditioning, elevators, and other modern conveniences.

Steeple Building: The first church the Danes built after acquiring St. Croix in 1733 stands at the corner of Church and Company Streets. Completed in 1750, it was a Lutheran church until 1831, and afterward served as a school, hospital, and storehouse. It now has a small museum with Amer-Indian and other types of artifacts.

Nearby, the **St. Croix Archaeology Museum** (Company Street; 340-277-4072; http://stcroix archaeology.org) has exhibits of ritualistic, ceremonial, and utilitarian artifacts found on St. Croix that date back to 2000 B.C. and continue up to the Taino culture (A.D. 1200–1492) at the time of Columbus. Entrance: $4.

Buck Island: The Buck Island Reef National Monument (www.nps.gov/buis), 3.5 miles northeast of St. Croix, is a volcanic rock of about 300 acres surrounded by 550 acres of underwater coral gardens of unusual beauty and scientific interest. The reef around Buck Island makes up the only underwater park in the U.S. National Park Service. A Park Service pamphlet explains the reef and pictures some of the fish that swimmers are likely to see; it is usually distributed to participants of snorkeling excursions. Glass-bottom boats, catamarans, and motorboats with snorkeling equipment operate daily from Ann E. Abramson pier in Frederiksted and King's Wharf in Christiansted to Buck Island. (See snorkeling in the Sports section.) The ride to Buck Island takes about thirty minutes. The time spent at the reef is usually an hour, but it can be longer, depending on your interest.

A Drive Around St. Croix

A driving tour by bus or car is usually made in a circular fashion from Frederiksted to Christiansted via Mahogany Road (Route 76), a scenic east-west road through the rain forest, a stretch of lush tropical vegetation very different from the rest of the island. The return uses Centerline Road, the island's main east-west highway, convenient for stops at three of St. Croix's main attractions. In the I-have-to-see-it-to-believe-it department, you can watch the world-famous beer-drinking pigs at the **Mt. Pellier Hut Domino Club** (340-713-9052), a restaurant/bar on Mahogany Road in the forest. The original beer-drinker has passed on to pig heaven, but her siblings and offspring are carrying on the family tradition without missing a can.

St. George Village Botanical Garden: On the north side of Centerline Road, about 5 miles east of Frederiksted, are 16 acres of tropical gardens, landscaped around the ruins of a Danish sugar-plantation workers' village dating from the 18th and 19th centuries. The garden began in 1972 as a cleanup project of the local garden club, but when the debris was cleared away, the members recognized the site as one of historic significance. Archaeologists excavated the area and found beneath the colonial ruins an Arawak settlement dating from A.D. 100 to 900. It is believed to have been the largest of the ninety-six Indian villages that existed on St. Croix at the time of Columbus.

Designed to incorporate the colonial ruins, the garden combines natural growth, landscaped plantings, and open land. The standout is the cactus garden. Among the restored ruins you will see the bake oven, which is operating again, and the blacksmith's shop, where volunteer smiths using original tools produce items sold in the gift shop. An excellent map is available, and walkways are signposted for self-guided tours. The garden is open daily. Admission is $8 adults, $6 seniors, $1 children. The garden (127 Estate, St. George; 340-692-2874; www.sgvbg.org) is privately supported and volunteer managed.

Cruzan Rum Distillery: At the pavilion of the Virgin Islands' leading rum maker, visitors are offered a free tour, rum cocktails, and recipe booklets. Tours run weekdays from 9 to 11:30 a.m. and 1 to 4 p.m. Call 340-692-2280 or visit www .cruzanrum.com.

Whim Greathouse: St. Croix's pride is Whim Greathouse, a restoration project of the St. Croix Landmarks Society (340-772-0598; www.stcroix landmarks.com). The beautifully restored plantation house, built in 1803, is furnished with lovely antiques; and the old kitchens, mill, and other buildings give visitors a good picture of life on a sugar plantation in the 18th and 19th centuries. You will also see the cook house, bathhouse, apothecary, 1856 steam engines, animal mill, windmill, boiling shed, rum still, and sugar factory. It has a museum, gift shop, and furniture showroom. Hours: daily 10 a.m. to 4 p.m. Admission with guided tour: $10 adults, $4 children.

Lawaetz Museum: Another of the St. Croix Landmarks Society's project is **Estate Little La Grange,** where an exhibit of St. Croix life in its sugar production heyday can be seen in the

18th-century estate house. The manor is furnished with antiques and heirlooms of the Lawaetz family, who have lived on the estate since the family arrived in St. Croix from Denmark in 1890. The grounds also have the remains of a windmill, mill, and the only aqueduct on the island. Guided tours: Tues to Sat 10 a.m. to 3 p.m. Tours cost $10 adults, $4 children. For information: 340-722-1539. A 2-mile walking trail is part of the St. Croix Heritage Trail. With the help of interpretive signs, brochures, and an information kiosk, visitors can learn about the cultural significance of the trees and other vegetation along the trail.

Cramer Park and Point Udall: The eastern end of St. Croix with Point Udall is covered by Cramer Park, a dry, low-lying area that is a marked contrast to the western end. The park has a public beach with changing rooms and bathrooms. Point Udall is the easternmost extension of the United States in the Western Hemisphere.

St. Croix East End Marine Park (340-718-3367; www.stxeastendmarinepark.org): In 2003, the Virgin Islands Department of Planning and National Resources created a new marine park to protect a 60-square-mile area along St. Croix's easternmost tip. Legislation made the area an official (and the first) territorial park, encompassing a magnificent barrier reef less than half a mile offshore and home to a great array of fish, sponges, coral heads, and patch reefs. The park covers one of St. Croix's few remaining mangrove systems located at Great Pond, and it includes a turtle preserve that protects a variety of endangered species that nest on its beaches. Leatherbacks and green and hawksbill turtles populate the remote beaches throughout the year. An interpretive tour is available to the public.

Casino: On the southeastern shores of St. Croix at Grapetree Bay, the **Divi Carina Bay Beach Resort** (www.divicarina.com) has St. Croix's and the Virgin Islands' first casino. It also has two restaurants and three snack bars, gift shop, live entertainment, and complimentary high-speed Internet service.

Columbus Landing Site and the Salt River Bay National Park: On the north shore at the mouth of the Salt River, Salt River Bay is an estuary, an important Arawak Indian site, a major dive location, and the site of Columbus's landing. The site was designated a national park in 1992 to commemorate the Columbus Quincentennial. Southeast of the estuary at Triton Bay, the Nature Conservancy has a 12-acre preserve.

Shopping

St. Croix's best shopping is in Christiansted, where 18th- and 19th-century warehouses have been made into attractive, palm-shaded shopping plazas. The streets paralleling King Street—Company Street on the east, Strand Street on the west—also have attractive shops. The historic buildings around Market Square, between Company and Queen Streets, have been renovated and house many smart shops. Shopping in Frederiksted is limited, but a few Christiansted stores have branches there. Crucians, as the people of St. Croix are called, maintain that their prices are better than those in St. Thomas because they do not have to pay St. Thomas's high rents or the high commission demanded by some cruise directors.

Art and Artists: St. Croix has an active art community of local artists and mainlanders who live there part of the year. But since artists and galleries come and go, you should consult *St. Croix This Week* (340-773-9864; www.stcroixthisweek.com) for a current list of artists and galleries. The **Yellow House** (3A Queen Cross St.; 340-719-6656; www.judithkingart.com) is the studio-gallery of artist Judith King, who works in bright, colorful acrylics. The shop also has handmade jewelry and a small collection of works by other local artists. Hours: Mon to Sat 10 a.m. to 5 p.m. **Danica Art Gallery** (54 King St.; 340-719-6000; www.danicaartvi.com) is owned by St. Croix–born artist Danica David and showcases original art, including jewelry, pottery, clocks, tiles, and mahogany sculptures by David and several other local artists. Hours: Mon to Fri 11 a.m. to 5 p.m. **Maria Henle Studio** (55 Company St.; 340-773-0372; www.mariahenlestudio.com) in the historic inn upstairs above Indies Restaurant, has a permanent exhibit of the late owner/artist's paintings and a display of photographs by her famous father, the late Fritz Henle, a leading recorder of Caribbean scenes. Hours: Mon to Sat 10 a.m. to 5 p.m.

Mitchell–Larsen Studio (Company Street; 340-719-1000; www.janmitchellcollection.com) is the home of the delightful artistry in glass by Jan Mitchell. Visitors can watch the work in progress and shop for gifts in the setting of a historic building. Upstairs, in a historic town house, the **Christiansted Gallery** (1 Company St.; 340-773-4443) is a showcase for local art, including original works and prints, along with paintings by artist/gallery owner Marjorie P. Robbins. Hours: Mon to Fri 10 a.m. to 4 p.m.; Sat 11 a.m. to 2 p.m.

Akin Studio (340-713-8419) showcases watercolors by St. Croix resident Jane Akin. The artist's depiction of tropical flora and architectural subjects captures the elegant essence of the Caribbean. By appointment. Local artist **Mark Austin**'s creations include handpainted furniture and buckets, sculpture, original paintings, prints, and more. He works from home.

In Frederiksted, **Island Webe** (210 Strand St., across the pier; 340-772-2555) is the permanent home of the colorful works of Caribbean-born artist Joffre George. The gallery features works in various media by other local artists as well. You may also want to visit the **Caribbean Museum Center** (10 Strand St.; 340-772-2622; www.cmcarts.org). Hours: Thurs to Sat 10 a.m. to 4 p.m.

And don't forget, original works of art are exempt from customs duty and do not count in your $1,600 exemption.

Books/Maps: St. Croix Landmark Museum Store (Fredericksted) and **Undercover Books** (Gallows Bay, 340-719-1567; www.undercoverbooksvi.com) sells books and periodicals.

China/Crystal: Baci (55 Company St.; 340-773-5040) has quality English china, French crystal, Swiss watches, Hummel figurines, and other gift items.

Clothing/Sportswear: Trends (1115 Strand St.) boutique specializing in eclectic mix of clothing, shoes, and accessories with an island flare. PacifiCotton (36C Strand St.) features sportswear of 100 percent cotton for women and children. From The Gecko (1233 Queen Cross St.; 340-778-9433; http://fromthegecko.com) features hand-crafted jewelry, accessories, and exclusive clothing lines

for the whole family, including the handpainted Sloop Jones Collection made on St. John. **Hotheads** (King's Alley Walk; 340-773-7888) sells beach apparel for all shapes and sizes. Full-figured women can find attractive styles in swimwear, sarongs, cover-ups, bags and accessories, and as the name suggests—hats.

Crafts: Many Hands (Pan Am Pavilion; 340-773-1990; http://manyhands.stcroixtravelusvi.com) displays handcrafts by three hundred artisans living in the Virgin Islands. The products range from jewelry and ceramics to sculpture and paintings. The **St. Croix Landmarks Society Museum Store** (52 Estate Whim, Frederiksted; 340-772-0598; www.stcroixlandmarks.com) has a wide selection of West Indian crafts, art prints, teak furniture reproductions, maps, and home furnishings. Open Mon to Sat 10 a.m. to 4 p.m. **St. Croix Leap** (Mahogany Road, Route 76; 340-772-0421; www.usvi.net/usvi/stxsi.html) is a great place to stop if you are touring the eastern end of the island. You can watch crafters make bowls, vases, and other practical home products from native woods. The items can be purchased. Crafts and original art are duty-free upon your return through U.S. Customs.

Tesoro (36C Strand St.; 340-773-1212) carries a wide range of Haitian art and crafts from the Dominican Republic. **Gone Tropical** (5 Company St.; 340-773-4696; www.gonetropical.com) is stuffed floor to ceiling with interesting crafts and art from Indonesia, India, the Philippines, Africa, and other exotic places, which the owner, Margot Meacham, selects herself. The **Royal Ponciana** (1111 Strand St.; 340-773-9892) stocks crafts and locally made soaps, herbs, and spices. Not to be overlooked is the **Whim Plantation Museum** gift shop, which has a very good selection of fine gifts and crafts. **Designworks/Island Living Store** (Apothecary Hall; 340-713-8102) features works by island artists (originals and prints, ceramics, metalwork, and photography), gifts, jewelry, maps, and cards. **Jewelry Sonya Ltd.** (1 Company St.; 340-773-8924; www.sonyaltd.com) specializes in handwrought gold and silver jewelry, as does **Crucian Gold** (Strand Street; http://cruciangold.com). Others to check out are **Tropical Bracelet** (Queen Cross Street; 340-719-0672); **Silver Angel**

(Caravelle Arcade); **Nelthropp and Low** (Pan Am Pavilion; 340-773-0365; www.nelthropp-low.com) and **JCove** (Company Street; 340-713-COVE; www.jcove.com) with original, locally designed jewelry. The **Caribbean Bracelet Company** (Strand Street, Frederiksted; 340-773-9110; www.stcroixbracelet company.com) specializes in silver bracelets with a horseshoe clasp that has come to be known as the "St. Croix" design, though it was not originated here. The bracelets, which make nice gifts to take home, come in all sizes, from those small enough for a child to those for a large adult, and vary in price from $25 and up. An explanation of the design is included with every purchase. **ib Designs** (Christiansted; 340-773-4322; www.islandboydesigns.com) is the studio of artist/metalsmith Whealan Massicott, whose specialty is distinctive, diverse and imaginative handcrafted designs in sterling silver and gold, usually connected to and inspired by nature.

Perfume: Violette Boutique (Caravelle Arcade; 340-773-2148) has as complete a selection as any store in town—and at competitive prices. You can call ahead for a price list: (800) 544-5912.

Dining

In Frederiksted: Blue Moon (Frederiksted Waterfront; 340-772-2222; www.bluemoonstcroix.com) is a pleasant outdoor bistro serving award-winning cuisine with a Cajun Flair. Moderate.

The **Sustainable Farm** (Frederiksted; www.visfi.org), known for its monthly slow-down dinners, prepares lunch if requested well in advance). Owner Ben Jones also has a farm in Georgia.

Polly's at the Pier (Frederiksted; 3 Strand St.) is a new cafe on the waterfront serving coffee, tea, ice cream, and sandwiches. Owners Steve Schawl and Seth Wilcoxon, host Frederiksted's new Harbor Cam. The cafe also has Internet stations and WiFi access.

In Christiansted: Longtime favorites **Kendrick's** (340-773-9199; www.kendricksdining.com) and **Bacchus** (Queen Cross; 340-692-9922), serve dinner only.

The **Avocado Pitt** (on the boardwalk; 340-773-9843), is a casual downtown restaurant offering a diverse menu for breakfast and lunch, takeout and boxed lunches. Open 8 a.m. to 5 p.m. daily. Moderately expensive.

Café Fresco (Penthany Courtyard; 340-719-0126), a favorite lunch spot for locals and visitors, where the food is fresh and creative, offering soups, salads, wraps, and fun specials by chef/owner Jill Dedinsky.

Rum Runners Steaks & Seafood (Hotel Caravelle; 340-773-6585; www.rumrunnersstcroix.com), the waterfront bar and cafe next to the Seaplane landing, is a delightful setting for lunch. In addition to Caribbean specialties, Rum Runners serves hand-rolled sushi and sashimi, and fresh lobster. Moderately expensive.

Salud! Bistro (340-718-7900; www.salud bistro.com) serves Mediterranean-inspired fare by owner Tavia Babbs; winner of *Wine Spectator* Award for its wine list.

Singhs Fast Food (King Street), whose owners were originally from Trinidad—so you can imagine the great food!

Zebos Wine Bar and Restaurant (1111 Strand St., 340-692-2864; www.zeboswinebar.com) is popular, fun and always packed with locals and tourists. **Eat @ Cane** (110c Cane Bay; 340-718-0360; www.eatatcanebay.com) features build your own salads and burgers and a menu for the kids.

Rowdy Joe's North Shore Eatery (Northshore Road; 340-718-0055) offers a menu using fresh ingredients from St. Croix's farms and local fisherman, as well as espresso, wireless Internet, on the open air deck.

Sports

Beach/Boating: Frederiksted has a pretty public beach only a few minutes' walk from the pier and, south of town at Sandy Point, one of the most beautiful stretches of sand in the Caribbean.

Fishing: St. Croix's deep waters teem with wahoo, yellowfin, and marlin. Among the sportsfishing specialists are **Irie Feeling Sportsfishing Charters** (340-244-4232; www.virginislands outfitters.com); **Sea Hunter Fishing Charters** (340-277-1751; www.islandsportfishing.com); and **St. Croix Deep Blue Fishing Charters** (340-626-0060; www.stxdeepbluecharters.com).

Golf and Tennis: Equidistant between Frederiksted and Christiansted, on the north side of the island, is **Carambola Beach Resort and Golf Club** (http://carambolabeach.com), a lovely, 18-hole layout (6,856 yards, par 72) designed by Robert Trent Jones. It has a clubhouse and pro shop. Call in advance for tee-off times (340-778-5638; www.golfvi.com); greens fee 18 holes, $129, including cart and transfers. **The 19th Hole** serves lunch Tues to Fri and brunch on Sunday.

A mile east of Christiansted, **Buccaneer Hotel** (340-714-2100; www.thebuccaneer.com) sprawls over 240 landscaped acres with great views, beaches, spa, and water-sports facilities. It has an 18-hole golf course, and its eight Laykold tennis courts are the largest complex on the island. Greens fee including cart: 18 holes, $100 winter; $60 summer; 9 holes, $70 winter, $45 summer. **Reef Golf Course** (East End, 340-773-8844) is a 9-hole layout.

Hiking and Biking: In the northwest corner of St. Croix, an area known as the **Rain Forest** has winding roads with light traffic and paths in the woods that lead to seasonal streams and waterfalls. The most scenic route, Western Scenic Road, begins (or ends) at Hams Bay on the northwest coast. The coastal road (Route 63) north passes Butler Bay, where a nature preserve of the St. Croix Landmarks Society is popular for bird-watching. Caledonia Valley, on the south side of the ridge, has the island's only year-round stream and is also popular for bird-watching.

Freedom City Cycles (340-277-2433/332-4054; www.freedomcitycycles.com) has one of a kind bike tours of Frederiksted, focusing on the island's history and architectural trends, continuing north on the coastal road to historic sugar estates with descriptions of sugar industry and their significance in Virgin Islands history. At Hams Bluff participants get a description of the area's geology and coastal ecosystems, along with its flora and fauna.

Caribbean Adventure Tours (340-778-1522; www.stcroixkayak.com) offers kayaking and hiking to Salt River National Park, learning about the island's history and ecology along the way; moonlight kayaking, with a guide sharing local folk tales

and ghost stories; sunset kayaks along the north shore; and hikes along Annaly Bay or Jack and Isaac's Bay. Two hours and half, $45 per person.

Ay-Ay Eco Hike and Tours (340-772-4079), owned by Ras Lumumba, a gardener and herbalist who came to St. Croix from Dominica in 1964, offers two- to four-hour ecotours to such locations as Salt River Bay, Annaly Bay, and Caledonia Rain Forest, focusing on the island's environment and history.

The **St. Croix Hiking Association** (340-772-2073, 340-778-9087; www.stcroixhiking.org), a nonprofit organization, is dedicated to educating the local community and visitors about the island's nature, culture, and history, and facilitates preservation by enforcement of legislation and other appropriate means. It organizes hikes on a regular basis, including a 4-mile hiking tour of Castle Nugent, a 300-acre working farm established in the 1730s on the island's south shore. The hike, over moderate to strenuous terrain, covers the area's cultural, historical, agricultural, and ecological significance. The great house is listed in the National Historic Register. Cost: $10.

Horseback Riding: Paul and Jill's Equestrian Stable (340-772-2880; www.paulandjills.com), next to Sprat Hall Estate 2 miles north of Frederiksted, is operated by a member of the family that has owned Sprat Hall, one of the island's most historic inns, for more than two hundred years. The stable offers two-hour scenic trail rides for about $75. Buccaneer Hotel (near Christiansted) has riding over trails on its property. Both facilities require advance reservations. Others are **Equus Riding Tours** (340-513-4873) and **Gecko's Island Adventures** (340-713-8820; www.geckosislandadventures.com).

Kayaking: Caribbean Adventure Tours (340-778-1522; 800-532-3483, www.stcroixkayak.com) offers kayaking excursions of Salt River National Park as well as the north shore. Departures are daily at 9 a.m. and 2 p.m.; tours are approximately two-and-a-half hours. (See the Hiking and Biking section.) **Virgin Kayak Company** (340-778-0071; virginkayak@stcroixlink.com) offers guided north shore tours and rentals.

Kiting: Kite St. Croix (340-643-5824; www.kite stcroix.com) rents equipment and offers lessons to get students airborne. Introductory three-hour course, $225.

Snorkeling and Scuba Diving: St. Croix is almost completely surrounded by coral reefs. In addition to Buck Island, there are forty-seven dive sites near St. Croix. The greatest variety of coral and fish is found along 6 miles of the north shore where the reef is only 500 yards from the coast in water about 35 feet deep. It is most accessible from Christiansted, which is also the location of **Caribbean Sea Adventures** (340-773-2628; www .caribbeanseaadventures.com), which has several daily excursions to Buck Island: A powerboat or glass-bottom boat leaves at 9:30 a.m. and returns at 1:30 p.m., cost is about $50 adult, $35 child.

Cruzan Watersports & Tours (north of Frederiksted Pier; 340-277-8295 and at Protestant Cay across from Christiansted boardwalk, 340-773-7060; www.cruzanwatersports.com) offers kayak rentals as well as two-hour open water rides with snorkeling and beach stop.

On the south of St. Croix, **Anchor Dive Center** (340-778-1522; www.anchordivestcroix.com), in the Salt River National Park, has daily dives to what it calls the "seven wonders of St. Croix." One tank dive, $65; five departures daily.

The Salt River Dropoff at the mouth of the river is a prime diving location made up of two sites: the east and west walls of a submerged canyon, which shelve and plunge more than 1,000 feet. The walls are encrusted with corals, sponges, and forests of black coral and attract large schools of fish. Frederiksted is not without interest, particularly for shipwrecks and the abundance of tiny seahorses around the harbor.

The Virgin Islands

The British Virgin Islands

Tortola, Norman Island, Jost Van Dyke, Virgin Gorda, Anegada

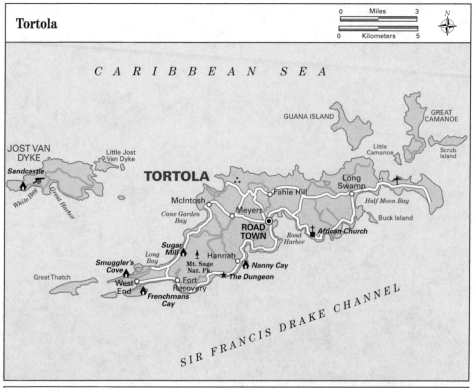

Tortola

0 — Miles — 3
0 — Kilometers — 5

N

C A R I B B E A N   S E A

GUANA ISLAND

GREAT
CAMANOE

Little
Camanoe

Scrub
Island

**JOST VAN
DYKE**

Little Jost
Van Dyke

TORTOLA

Long
Swamp

Half Moon Bay

Sandcastle

McIntosh

Fahie Hill

Buck Island

White Bay

Great Harbor

*Cane Garden
Bay*

Meyers

**ROAD
TOWN**

*Road
Harbor*

African Church

Great Thatch

*Long
Bay*

**Sugar
Mill**

Hannah
Mt. Sage
Nat. Pk.

Nanny Cay

The Dungeon

**Smuggler's
Cove**

West
End

Fort
Recovery

*Frenchmans
Cay*

S I R   F R A N C I S   D R A K E   C H A N N E L

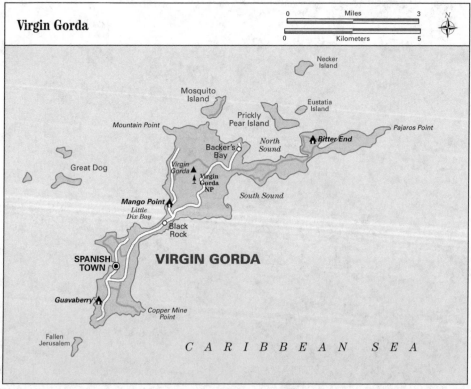

Virgin Gorda

0 — Miles — 3
0 — Kilometers — 5

N

Necker
Island

Mosquito
Island

Eustatia
Island

Prickly
Pear Island

Mountain Point

Pajaros Point

Backer's
Bay

*North
Sound*

Bitter End

Great Dog

*Virgin
Gorda*

Virgin
Gorda
NP

South Sound

Mango Point

*Little
Dix Bay*

Black
Rock

**SPANISH
TOWN**

VIRGIN GORDA

Guavaberry

*Copper Mine
Point*

Fallen
Jerusalem

C A R I B B E A N   S E A

The British Virgin Islands

Yachtsman's Haven

The British Virgin Islands, an archipelago of about fifty green, mountainous islands, cays, and rocks, are spread over 59 square miles of sapphire waters along the Anegada Passage between the Caribbean Sea and the Atlantic Ocean. Mostly volcanic in origin and uninhabited, they have scalloped coastlines and idyllic little coves with white-sand beaches. In olden days their strategic location made them a favorite hiding place of pirates who plundered ships carrying treasures and cargo between the Old and New Worlds. Today the islands of this British Crown Colony are favorite hideaways for yachtsmen drawn by the good anchorage, vacationers drawn by the beaches, and a growing number of cruise ships determined to get away from the crowd.

The largest and most populated islands are Tortola, the capital; Virgin Gorda; and Anegada. Others such as Peter Island and Guana Island have become popular after being developed as private resorts, but for the most part the British Virgin Islands are almost as virgin as the day Christopher Columbus discovered them.

The BVI, as the aficionados call them, say frankly that they do not appeal to everyone. They have no golf courses or casinos, and what little nighttime activity exists is low-key. But what these islands lack in flashy entertainment is more than made up for in facilities for boating, scuba diving, deep-sea fishing, and windsurfing.

The British Virgin Islands are next-door neighbors of the U.S. group, and without a map it's hard to tell the difference. On the other hand, when you ask someone from the BVI if there is a difference between their islands and America's, they will delight in answering, "Yes, the British Virgins are still virgin."

Arriving in the British Virgin Islands

Most visitors arrive in the BVI on a cruise ship, ferry, or private yacht—their own or one they have chartered. Frequent ferry service connects Tortola with St. Thomas and St. John in less than an hour.

Round-trip fare is $40. Less frequent service is available between either St. Thomas or Tortola and Virgin Gorda.

Tortola is the home of the largest yacht charter fleet in the Caribbean, where boats with or without crew can be chartered for a day or a year. Lying in close proximity astride Drake's Passage, the islands create a sheltered waterway that is one of the world's prime sailing locations. From their base in Tortola, boats crisscross the passage to visit Peter and Norman Islands directly across from Road Town, Virgin Gorda to the east/northeast, and Jost Van Dyke on the northwest. These are also the stops made most often by cruise ships. In only the last few years, after the new pier in Road Town was complete, has Tortola become a cruise port of some significance, growing in the availability of services and activities to meet the needs of cruise passengers.

Local Transportation: Tortola's three entry points—Road Town, the main town on the south coast; the Soper's Hole West End ferry landing; and the airport on Beef Island at the east end—are linked by paved roads. Beef Island is connected to Tortola by a bridge. Paved roads wind over the mountains to Brewers Bay, Cane Garden Bay, and other resort areas on the northwest coast. More remote areas are accessible by dirt roads, some requiring four-wheel drive. Taxis are plentiful in Tortola; they use fixed rates, based on distance.

Sightseeing: Taxis and travel agencies offer half-day tours by minivan and open-air safari buses. Major car-rental firms, as well as independent ones, have offices in Tortola and on Virgin Gorda; no service is available on the other islands. Remember: In this British colony, driving is on the LEFT. The following are samples of shore excursions; attractions are described later in this chapter:

Snorkeling Tour: 2.5 hours, $40–$59. View colorful corals and exotic fish on a guided snorkel tour of a nearby island. A similar four-hour excursion ($69) by yacht sails across Sir Francis Drake Channel for snorkeling and swimming at Cooper, Salt, or Peter Islands.

Tortola Sightseeing and Cane Garden Bay Beach: 3.5 hours, $59–$70. In Road Town, visit the Botanical Gardens, then drive to Skyworld, from where you can see Puerto Rico on a clear day, and across mountainous Tortola with many heart-stopping views along the winding route. End at Cane Garden Bay for swimming at this beautiful white-sand beach.

Virgin Gorda Tour: 4 hours, $69–$80. An excursion launch picks you up shipside and cruises along Sir Francis Drake Channel to Spanish Town, Virgin Gorda, where an open-air safari bus takes you on a short drive to the famous Baths for swimming, snorkeling, and sunning.

Dolphin Swim: 2 hours, $159. Participants are transferred by bus to Dolphin Lagoon for a thirty-minute introductory talk followed by a thirty-minute swim session with the dolphins.

X-BOB: 3.5 hours, $109. X-BOB is an underwater bike tethered to the surface on a floating buoy, allowing a maximum depth of less than 7 feet. A safety briefing is followed by thirty minutes of underwater fun. The X-BOBs are led and followed by the diving team throughout the underwater trail.

At a Glance

If you prefer to make your own arrangements, these are some resources and local vendors to contact in advance:

On Tortola

National Parks Trust (61 Main St., Road Town; 284-494-2069; www.bvinationalparkstrust.org) has maps of parks and hiking trail tours.

B.V.I. Taxi Association (284-494-2322), **Quality Taxi Association** (284-494-8397), and **Romney Associates Consultants** (284-494-2872)—all at Wickham's Cay 1, Road Town—offer guided open-air safari bus tours or air-conditioned vans for sightseeing and trips to the beach.

Travel Plan Tours (Waterfront Drive, Tortola and Spanish Town, Virgin Gorda; 284-494-2872; 284-494-4000; www.aroundthebvi.com) provides tours by glass-bottom boat and to X-BOB (see above), island tours by vans and buses, and snorkel and scuba day sails.

Island Helicopters International (Beef Island Airport; 284-495-2538; www.helicoptersbvi.com) offers half-hour flight-seeing, day trips to other islands, and other services.

On Virgin Gorda

Andy's Taxi and Jeep Rental (284-495-5252; fischers@candwbvi.net) and **Mahogany Taxi Service** (284-495-5469; www.mahoganyrentals .puzzlepiece.net)—both at the Valley—have guided island tours by safari buses and vans. The latter's Island Tour, one-and-a-half hours, costs $15 per person.

Virgin Gorda has an open-air jitney bus that shuttles between Spanish Town, the Baths, and some resort areas. With it you can see most of the island on your own in less than three hours.

Tortola and Its Neighbors

In the past, Tortola was a sleepy little place with not a great deal of activity, but with its development as a cruise port and the bustle that accompanies hundreds of cruise passengers roaming the island almost daily, particularly during the winter season, its character is beginning to change. New, modern buildings are replacing the colorful West Indian ones; new cars and buses are crowding the roads; and more and more people, attracted by

Population: 28,882

Size: Anegada, 15 square miles; Tortola, 21.5 square miles; Virgin Gorda, 8.5 square miles

Main Towns: Road Town, Tortola; Spanish Town, Virgin Gorda

Government: Overseas Territory of the United Kingdom

Currency: U.S. dollar

Departure Tax: $20 by air; $5 by boat; $7 by cruise ship

Emergency Numbers: Peebles Hospital: 284-496-8422; Police, Fire, Ambulance: 999

Language: English

Public Holidays: Jan 1, New Year's Day; Mar 4, Commemoration of H. Lavity Stoutt Day; Mar 11, Commonwealth Day; Apr, Good Friday, Easter Monday; May 20, Whit Monday; June, Sovereign's Birthday; July 1, Territory Day; Aug, Festival Mon, Tues, Wed; Oct 21, St. Ursula's Day; Dec 25, Christmas Day; Dec 26, Boxing Day.

Telephone Code: 284

Airlines: *From North America:* via Antigua, Puerto Rico, St. Maarten, St. Thomas connecting to Air Sunshine, American Eagle, Cape Air, LIAT, or Winair. Seaborne Airlines (www.seaborneairlines.com) offers scheduled seaplane service on Fri from San Juan to Virgin Gorda via St. Thomas.

Smoking Policy: A law passed in 2007, by the Legislative Council bans smoking in public places including bars, restaurants, nightclubs, airports, offices, and sports facilities. It also bans smoking within 50 feet of any public space.

Information: www.bvitourism.com; www.bviwelcome.com; www.british virginislands.com

In the United States:

British Virgin Islands Tourist Board:

Atlanta: 1275 Shiloh Rd., Suite 2930, Kennesaw, GA 30144; (770) 874-5951; fax: (770) 874-5953

Los Angeles: 3450 Wilshire Blvd., Suite 1202, Los Angeles, CA 90010; (213) 736-8931; fax: (213) 736-8935; bvila@bvitourism.com

New York: 1 West Thirty-fourth St., #302, New York, NY 10001; (212) 563-3117; (800) 835-8530; fax: (212) 563-2263; info@bvitourism.com

In Tortola:

BVI Tourist Board, Akara Building, 2nd Floor, DeCastro Street, Road Town, Tortola; (284) 494-3134; fax: (284) 494-3866; info@bvitourism .com

---

jobs and business opportunities, are swelling the island's population. Road Town is still the only sizable residential center. It has shops, hotels, restaurants, and bars with local bands. Most are located along the south shore road and on Main Street.

If you want to know more about the BVI, visit the **Virgin Islands Folk Museum,** operated by the Virgin Islands Historical Society.

For shoppers, the first stop is likely to be **Crafts Alive,** the government-funded crafts village of local craftspeople and artists in Road Town. Here, an array of locally made goods are housed in small, colorful wooden buildings meant to resemble an island village of the past. The center is only a short walk from the cruise ship pier and was motivated, in part, by the ready market cruise passengers bring.

At the **B.V.I. Handicrafts Association,** all the crafts are handmade by ten women who make up the group. Among their crafts are the dancing "Mocko Jumbie" dolls of acting president Frances Springette. Colorful batik fabrics of original designs, hats, baskets, and prints are available. Next door, **B.V.I. Social Development Department,** a government-sponsored shop, carries crochet work, rag rugs, and straw hats made by elderly craftspeople of the islands. A specialty to note are handmade Afro-Caribbean dolls with two heads—two dolls each skillfully hidden under the skirt of the other. Turn one over, and you see another doll with a completely different costume.

Creative Crafts and Things displays one-of-a-kind banana leaf dolls, using the contours of scorched banana leaves to fashion the dolls' clothing. The **Bush Tea Doctor,** Ashley Nibbs, brews up hot sauce, guavaberry liquor, and gooseberry syrup from family recipes under the label A. Nibbs Sons & Daughters.

The effort to keep local crafts alive is reflected elsewhere in other ventures: **Bamboushay** (284-494-0393; www.bamboushay.com), a pottery studio and art shop located at the Nanny Cay Hotel and

Marina, features the work of English artisan Val Anderson as well as a large selection of locally made cards, paintings, prints, photographs, and baskets; Pat Faulkner of **Pat's Pottery** on Anegada, known for the whimsical dancing crabs and seascapes that decorate her work, has a shop at Nutmeg Point. Aragorn Dick-Read, a local sculptor, has **Aragorn's Studio** (284-495-1849; www.aragornsstudio.com), a Caribbean arts and crafts shop at Trellis Bay, and gives lessons in pottery, woodcarving, and basketry. The studio's Art Centre provides an outlet for the crafts of the Carib Indians. Aragorn's connection to local agricultural communities has led to the creation of a line of Island Spices as well as a Fruit Depot where local farmers come to sell their organic produce.

Among the island's master weavers, ninety-two-year-old Estelle Dawson, who has been weaving straw hats since she was a child, continues to work in her small house by the sea on the East End. She uses a palm known locally as broom teyer palm (*Cocothrinix alta*) that grows in shallow, rocky ground by the sea. **Sunny Caribbee Spice Shop** (284-494-2178; www.sunnycaribbee.com), one of the best-known Caribbean labels, displays the work of master basket weaver Darwin "Gun" Scatliffe, who uses the local hoop vine in his creations. On Main Street, **Serendipity Bookshop** (284-494-5865; www.bvibooks.com) specializes in Caribbean and children's books, along with best sellers. It has a cafe with an eclectic menu and an Internet cafe upstairs. **The Gallery** (284-494-2096; www.thegallerybvi.com), set in a historical West Indian house, has a large selection of BVI paintings & prints as well as Haitian and other Caribbean ones and offers shipping. **Samarkand Jewellers** (284-494-6415; www.samarkandjewellers.com) offers handcrafted gold and silver jewelry and repair services. **Pusser's** (284-499-4428; www.pussers.com) is something of a department store.

J. R. O'Neal Botanical Gardens: One of Road Town's most prized attractions is the tropical Botanical Gardens, created on a neglected site formerly occupied by the BVI Agricultural Station. The four-acre spread, opened in 1987, is the work of the BVI National Parks Trust and volunteers from the Botanic Society and Garden Club. The garden

is divided into about twenty collections of rare and indigenous tropical plants. Entrance fee: $3.

Mount Sage National Park: In the 1960s Sage Mountain, on Tortola, and Virgin Gorda's Spring Bay and Devil's Bay were donated to the BVI government by Laurance Rockefeller. The gift led to the creation of the BVI National Parks Trust (www.bvinationalparkstrust.org) and the start of a land- and sea-conservation program with eleven of twenty-three proposed areas under management.

The 92-acre **Mount Sage National Park** (www.b-v-i.com/nature/mtsage.htm) is located on the peaks of the tall volcanic mountains that cross the center of Tortola, reaching 1,780 feet, the highest elevation in either the U.S. or the British Virgin Islands. Its vegetation, characteristic of a rain forest, is thought to be similar to that of the island's original growth. A road leads to the park entrance, where you will find panoramic views. Two graveled, signposted trails, each about an hour's hike, wind through the forest past huge elephant ears, hanging vines, lacy ferns, and a variety of trees common to the Caribbean, such as kapok, mahogany, and white cedar. Entrance fee: $3.

Norman Island: Across Drake's Passage from Tortola is uninhabited Norman Island said to be the "Treasure Island" of Robert Louis Stevenson's novel. The island has old ruins, a salt pond with abundant bird life, and footpaths. One path is a thirty-minute hike up Spy Glass Hill with fabulous 360-degree views. In olden days pirates used this vantage point to watch for Spanish treasure ships; hence its name. More recently, Norman Island was purchased by the owners of Guana Island and is slated for development in a fashion similar to Mustique Island in the Grenadines.

Rhone National Marine Park: Southeast of Tortola at Salt Island lies the wreck of the *Rhone*, the most famous—and popular—shipwreck dive in the Virgin Islands, if not the entire Caribbean. The movie *The Deep* was filmed here. The wreck, lying at 20- to 80-foot depths west of Salt Island, has been made into a marine park covering 800 acres. Along with nearby reefs and caves, the park includes Dead Chest Island on the west, where seabirds nest on the tall cliffs.

The 310-foot Royal Mail Steamer *Rhone* sank in 1867 during a terrible hurricane. Anchored in calm seas off Peter Island, the ship was loading passengers and stores for its return trip to England when a storm blew in suddenly. The ship lost its anchor when its cable broke, and, no longer safe at anchor, with her rigging torn by the winds, she steamed at top speed for open water to ride out the storm. But the hurricane struck again from another direction, forcing the *Rhone* onto the rocks at Salt Island. She split apart and sank. Parts of the ship can be seen by snorkelers.

Salt Island has a few residents who still tend the salt ponds, trails that lead up a hill to a wonderful view, and a good beach.

Jost Van Dyke: Off the northwest coast of Tortola and directly north of St. John, Jost Van Dyke's good anchorage and beautiful beaches make it a popular stop for yachts and small cruise ships that sail regularly through the Virgin Islands. Most anchor at yacht-filled Great Harbour, the main settlement surrounded by green hills. Two of the best-known beach bars in these parts are **The Soggy Dollar** (284-495-9888; www.soggydollar .com) at the Sand Castle Hotel and **Foxy's Tamarind Bar and Restaurant** (284-495-9258; www .foxysbar.com). They are favorites of the yachting crowd, where a beach party with calypso music is the order of the day—any day.

Sports

Biking: In recent years, cycling has become a major sport in the BVI. It's a great way to explore the islands. **Last Stop Sports** (Nanny Cay, Tortola; 284-494-1120; www.laststopsports.com), a fully equipped cycle and water-sports shop, recommends that you bring cycling shoes for mountain biking or casual cycling. Helmets (mandatory), locks, and racks are provided at no extra charge.

Boating: Experienced yachtsmen consider the waters of the BVI to be among the finest sailing in the world. Little wonder that it's home to five sailing schools. As noted earlier, Tortola is also the base for the largest yacht charter fleet in the Caribbean. A complete list of charter companies is available on the BVI Tourist Board's Web site and its publication *Welcome,* available from the board's U.S. offices. For day sailing excursions, **Day Sail BVI** (284-494-0740; www.daysailbvi

.com) for trips to Jost Van Dyke for $115 and Virgin Gorda for $125.

In Jan 2009, **The Moorings** (888-952-8420; www.moorings.com), one of the Caribbean's largest yacht charter companies, inaugurated The Moorings Village, a $15 million expansion of its flagship operations base in Road Town. The reception area opens to a landscaped plaza, with views of the Drake Channel. There are new retail shops, cafe for pastries, ice cream, and coffee; spa facilities, a business center with free WiFi, swimming pool, dockside market, the renovated Mariner Inn Hotel, a new full-service marina and Charlie's Bar & Restaurant, named after The Moorings founder, Charlie Cary.

Diving and Snorkeling: Few places in the Caribbean match the BVI for the clarity of the water, the variety and accessibility of marine life and shipwrecks, the quality of the dive operations, and the ease, particularly for beginners, for enjoying snorkeling and diving. **B.V.I. Scuba Organization** (www.bvitourism.com; www.bviscuba .org) has a complete list of dive operations, along with their services and rates. These are a few sample prices: One-tank dive, $65–$95; two tanks, $90–$120; resort course, $125; lesson and excursion, $120; snorkeler/rider, $40. **UBS Dive Center** (Harbour View Marina, East End, Box 852, Road Town, Tortola; 284-494-0024; www.scubabvi.com) is somewhat unusual in that it offers private diving services: your own boat for the day; your schedule, instruction, and tours.

Fishing: Avid anglers the world over come to the BVI to test their skill, particularly in the deep waters off Anegada. Fishing charters range from $700 to $1,000 for half-day excursions and $900 to $1,600 for full-day trips and are offered by **Blue Ocean Adventures** (284-499-2837; fax: 284-495-5820; blueocean@hotmail.com), among others. You must have a permit from the **Fisheries Division** (284-494-3429). For fly fishing, see www.caribbean flyfishing.com, offering a half-day trip for $480.

Hiking: Sage Mountain on Tortola and Gorda Peak on Virgin Gorda are the most popular hikes. Both are part of BVI's National Parks System and have maintained trails. **National Parks Trust**

(Fishlock Road, Road Town; 284-494-2069; www
.bvinationalparkstrust.org; bvinpt@caribsurf.com)
has park maps and hiking trail tours.

Horseback Riding: Shadows Stables (Ridge
Road; 284-494-2262) will take you through the rain
forest on Sage Mountain or down to Cane Garden
Cay.

Kayaking: The BVI's warm, protected waters and
unspoiled nature are ideal for kayaking, especially
for beginners and intermediates, in the mangroves
or the bays; experienced kayakers can venture farther out to Drake Channel. Rental companies offer
advice on where to kayak and what conditions to
expect. They stock a range of kayaks and supply
life vests. Those named here are on Tortola and are
open from 8 a.m. to 5 p.m. daily.

  Boardsailing B.V.I. Shop (Trellis Bay, Beef
Island, Box 537, Long Look; 284-495-2447; fax: 284-
495-1626; www.windsurfing.vi) has surfboards and
single and double kayaks. Hourly rentals; rates on
request. Two-hour lessons available.

  Last Stop Sports (Nanny Cay and The Moorings, Box 3208, Road Town; 284-494-0564; fax:
284-494-0593; www.laststopsports.com) offers sailboards, kayaks, surfboards, laser sailboats, water
skis, and body boards. Rentals from $28 per day.

Windsurfing/Kitesurfing: The northwest
coast of Tortola is one of the prime windsurfing
locations in the Eastern Caribbean. See Boardsailing BVI Shop mentioned above. Island Surf & Sail
(284-494-0123; www.bviwatertoys.com) offers
kitesurfing lessons from $100 per person; windsurf-
ing $40 for half-day rental; and surf boards for $30
per day.

Virgin Gorda

Virgin Gorda is known for the Baths, an extraordinary grotto created by toppled gigantic rocks
that have puzzled geologists for years. They are
completely different from any other rock formation
of the area. Worn smooth by wind and water over
the millennia, the enormous rocks have fallen in
such a way as to create labyrinths and caves that
are fun to explore, although they are not real caves,
of course. Where the sea rushes in and out, the

formations near the shore catch the water, creating pools of crystal-clear water shimmering from
the sunlight that filters between the rocks. They
are delightful for a refreshing splash—hence their
name. The area can be reached by land or sea,
and the reefs fronting the Baths are popular for
snorkeling.

  Virgin Gorda rises from its boulder-strewn
coast and sandy beaches on the south in a northerly
direction to 1,370-foot Gorda Peak near the island's
center. The top of the mountain is protected by
the **Virgin Gorda Peak Park,** which covers 265
acres of forests. The park has a self-guided hiking
trail leading to an observation point; it is actually the end of a paved road leading to Little Dix
Bay—one of the Caribbean's famous resorts and
the sister resort to Caneel Bay on St. John. Equally
as expensive, exclusive, and low-key, the resorts
were begun by Laurance Rockefeller as Rockresorts
and were among the Caribbean's first ecologically
designed hotels, encompassing the natural environment in which they are set and harmonizing their
architecture with it.

  Virgin Gorda's other famous spots are **Bitter
End,** a hotel/restaurant/bar that is probably the
most popular watering hole in the Caribbean for the
yachting crowd; and Necker Island, across the bay
from Bitter End, which belongs to English entrepreneur Sir Richard Branson, who built his sumptuous
nest on its summit. This ten-bedroom perch is available for rent at a mere $32,000 and up per day!

Anegada

Unlike the other BVI, which are green and mountainous, Anegada is a flat, dry coral atoll fringed
by miles of sandy beaches and horseshoe-shaped
reefs. The most northerly of the BVI, it was once a
pirates' lair, where the low-lying reefs caught pur-
suers unaware. An estimated three hundred ships
are thought to have gone down here. Today those
wrecks and the reefs attract divers, and the fish
attracted to the reefs make the island's waters a
prime fishing location.

  In addition to sailing, the BVI's healthy and
abundant reefs are popular for snorkeling and
scuba diving. The BVI waters are also popular for
live-aboard dive boats, which carry passengers in

cruise ship–style comfort. Some are based in Tortola year-round, whereas others visit from time to time. Dive operators, based in Tortola, offer a full range of excursions. Glass-bottom boat tours are available, too.

Tortola Fast Ferry, operated by Smith's Ferry Service: (284-494-4454; www.smithsferry.com), offers twice daily ferries from Road Town to Anegada.

The BVI waters teem with fish, and the islands are adjacent to the 50-mile Puerto Rican Trench. But surprisingly, deep-sea fishing has only recently been developed here. Sportfishing boats are available for charter in Tortola and Virgin Gorda, which are both a forty-five-minute boat ride from the trench.

You can get windsurfing equipment at most resorts. Experienced surfers say the northwest coast of Tortola, where the swells roll in from the Atlantic and break against the north end of Cane Garden Bay, is the Virgin Islands' best surfing location.

There's talk that Anegada, something of the Caribbean's last frontier, is slated for development. Hopefully, should it happen, it will be slow, careful, and controlled.

St. Maarten/St. Martin

and Neighbors

Philipsburg, St. Maarten; Marigot, St. Martin; Fort Bay, Saba; Oranjestad, St. Eustatius; Sandy Ground, Anguilla

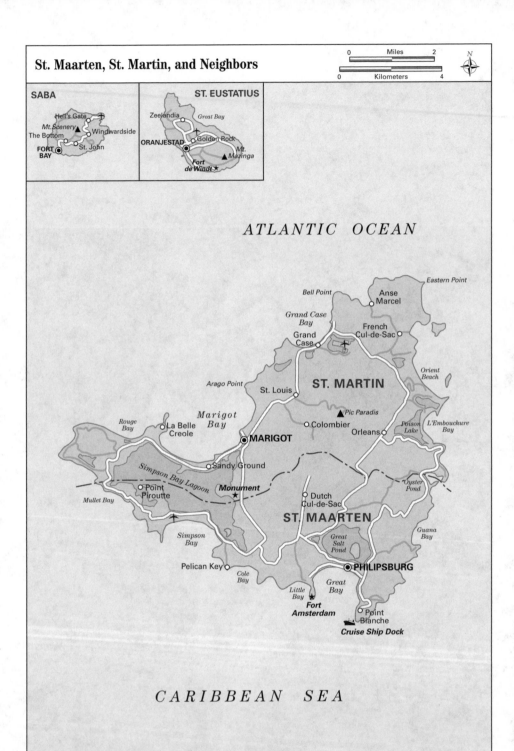

St. Maarten, St. Martin, and Neighbors

Miles
0 · 2

Kilometers
0 · 4

N

SABA

Hell's Gate
Mt. Scenery
The Bottom · Windwardside
St. John
FORT BAY

ST. EUSTATIUS

Zeelandia · Great Bay
ORANJESTAD · Golden Rock
Mt. Mazinga
Fort de Windt

ATLANTIC OCEAN

Eastern Point

Bell Point
Anse Marcel
Grand Case Bay
French Cul-de-Sac
Grand Case
Orient Beach

Arago Point
St. Louis
ST. MARTIN

Rouge Bay
Marigot Bay
Pic Paradis
Poison Lake
L'Embouchure Bay
La Belle Creole
Colombier
Orleans
MARIGOT
Sandy Ground
Oyster Pond
Simpson Bay Lagoon
Point Pirouette
Monument
Dutch Cul-de-Sac
Mullet Bay
ST MAARTEN
Simpson Bay
Great Salt Pond
Guana Bay
Pelican Key
Cole Bay
PHILIPSBURG
Little Bay
Great Bay
Fort Amsterdam
Point Blanche
Cruise Ship Dock

CARIBBEAN SEA

The Dutch Windward Islands

And Their Neighbors

Centered at a cluster of lovely hideaways in the northeastern Caribbean are three of the most distinctive islands in the entire region. They share their seas with a neighbor that is one of the most talked-about gems in the ocean.

Sint Maarten (commonly written as St. Maarten), the capital of the Dutch Windward Islands and the major cruise-ship port of the group, is an island of green mountain peaks that swoop down to scalloped bays and stretches of powdery white-sand beaches and the shimmering, turquoise sea. Situated on an island of only 37 square miles, Sint Maarten shares more than half of the land with French St. Martin. Their split personality—Dutch on one side, French on the other—enables visitors to dine, tour, sail, and play tennis in two languages, under two flags, without ever leaving the island.

Saba (pronounced SAY-ba), another member of the Dutch group, is unique. The 5-square-mile volcanic peak, 28 miles southwest of St. Maarten, rises straight up from the sea. Its history reads like a fairy tale.

St. Eustatius, known as Statia, is the third of the Dutch Windwards and is ten minutes by plane south of Saba. This island of 8 square miles was once the richest free port in the Americas, though today it takes some imagination to picture it.

Anguilla, a British colony 5 miles north of St. Martin, was the best-kept secret in the Caribbean until the addition of some highly publicized superdeluxe resorts brought trendsetters flocking to this spot of tranquility. You can easily discover Anguilla for yourself on a day trip from St. Maarten.

Before Concordia

Before Columbus got to St. Maarten in 1493 and claimed it for Spain, the island was inhabited by the Carib Indians. More than a century later—after the island had bounced among the Dutch, French, and Spanish—a young Dutchman of later New York fame, Peter Stuyvesant, tried to wrestle it from Spain. He lost a limb instead—only to see the Spaniards abandon their claim to the island to the Dutch just four years later, in 1648.

When the Dutch sent their commander from St. Eustatius to take possession, they found the French waiting to do battle. But the Dutch and French soon agreed to stop fighting over the island and split the spoils instead. Legend says the accord has lasted more than three centuries; in fact, the island changed hands another sixteen times. The place where the agreement was reached is known as Mt. Concordia, nonetheless, and the old accord is celebrated as an annual holiday. More important: The two sides have no real border between them. The only way you know you are crossing from one country to the other is by a welcome sign on the side of the road.

Yet the two sides of this island are noticeably different, beginning with the spelling of the names: Sint Maarten and Saint Martin. Signs are in Dutch and French (also in English), and the people speak

At a Glance	
Antiquities	★
Architecture	★
Art and Artists	★★
Beaches	★★★★★
Colonial Buildings	★
Crafts	★
Cuisine	★★★★★
Culture	★
Dining/Restaurants	★★★★★
Entertainment	★★★★★
Forts	★
History	★
Monuments	★
Museums	★★
Nightlife	★★★★★
Scenery	★★★
Shopping	★★★★★
Sightseeing	★★★
Sports	★★★★★
Transportation	★★

St. Maarten

Population: St. Maarten, 41,000; Saba, 1,090; St. Eustatius, 2,089

Size: 16 square miles

Main Town: Philipsburg

Government: The three Dutch Windward Islands, together with Bonaire and Curaçao in the South Caribbean, make up the Netherlands Antilles. The government is a parliamentary democracy, headed by a governor who is appointed by and represents the queen of the Netherlands. The central government is in Curaçao; each island has its own representative body called the Island Council. However, scheduled for Nov 10, 2010, St. Maarten will no longer be part of the Netherlands Antilles and will become an independent country. Bonaire, Saba, and St. Eustatius will become overseas territories of the Netherlands.

Currency: Netherlands Antilles guilder, written NAf. US$1 equals NAf 1.80.

Departure Tax: The departure tax, approximately US$30, is included in the airfare. Boat trips to neighboring islands: $30 adults, $15 children. For islands within the Netherlands Antilles, the departure tax is US$15.

Electricity: St. Maarten and St. Martin have separate systems: the Dutch side uses 110–120 volts AC, 60 cycles.

Emergency Numbers: Medical: Philipsburg Hospital, 599-543-1111; Ambulance: 599-542-2111

Police: St. Maarten, 599-542-2222 and 111.

Language: Dutch is the official language, but English is a common second language.

Public Holidays: Jan 1, New Year's Day; Good Friday; Easter Monday; Apr 30, Coronation Day (Dutch); May 1, Labor Day; Whit Monday; Ascension Thurs; Nov 11, St. Maarten's Day; Dec 25 and 26, Christmas.

Telephone Area Code: St. Maarten and St. Martin have separate telephone systems, and that's where the island's two-country quaintness can lose some of its charm. A call between the two is an international phone call; sometimes it's easier to call New York from Philipsburg than to call Marigot, less than 8 miles away. So much for Concordia! To make matters even more confusing, the telephone numbers on the Dutch side have seven numbers rendered as 344-4444; while those on the French side have six, written as 22-22-22 or 22.22.22, the traditional French way. To call St. Maarten from the United States, dial 011-599-54 plus the five-digit local number. To call from the Dutch to the French side, dial 00-590-590 plus the local number.

Wireless: In Jan 2005 Philipsburg became the first Caribbean town to go wireless, allowing residents and visitors alike to use their enabled computers or other mobile devices anywhere in town. SMITCOMS (St. Maarten International Telecommunications Services) teamed up with Lucent Technologies and BelAir Networks to provide a WiFi network for the St. Maarten capital.

Airlines: *From the United States:* American, Continental, Delta, JetBlue, Spirit, United, US Airways; American Airlines/American Eagle from San Juan to St. Maarten. *Interisland:* from Princess Juliana International Airport (www.pjiae.com) in St. Maarten, Winair (Windward Islands Airways) has daily service to Montserrat, Saba, St. Eustatius, Anguilla, St. Barts; Air Caraibes flies frequently to St. Barts and Guadeloupe. LIAT, Caribbean Airlines (www.caribbean-airlines.com) also has service to neighboring islands.

Information: www.st-maarten .com; www.mrstm.com; www.saint-martin-online.com

In the United States:

St. Maarten Tourist Office, 675 Third Ave., No. 1807, New York, NY 10017; (212) 953-2084; (800) STMAARTEN; fax: (212) 953-2145

In Canada:

St. Maarten Tourist Board, 2810 Matheson Blvd. E, Suite 200, Toronto, Ontario, L4W 4X7; (416) 622-4300; fax: (416) 622-3431

In Port:

St. Maarten Tourist Bureau, Vineyard Office Park, W. G. Buncamper Road 33, Philipsburg; 011-599-542-2337; fax: 011-599-542-2734; info@ st-maarten.com

Dutch or French (also English). Two currencies—guilders and euros—circulate, but everyone takes dollars (even vending machines on the Dutch side take U.S. coins). There are two governments, two flags, and two sets of stamps—which your philatelic friends will love. Most important, each side has a distinctive, unmistakable ambience.

Small as it is, St. Maarten has as many diversions as places ten times its size. The beaches are gorgeous, the water spectacular, and the sports facilities excellent. There's golf, scuba, tennis, windsurfing, fishing, riding, sailing, snorkeling, and biking. St. Maarten has bouncing showplaces and quiet corners, fancy restaurants, discos, and twelve casinos.

Located in the heart of the Caribbean between the Virgin Islands and the French West Indies, St. Maarten is an air- and sea-transportation hub for the northeastern Caribbean. Its central location enables cruise passengers to explore the neighboring islands—Anguilla, Saba, and Statia—by air or boat in a day.

Note to readers: This chapter is oriented to St. Maarten for practical reasons. An estimated 80 percent of all cruise ships arrive in Philipsburg; hence most passengers are likely to want information on the facilities and services convenient to it. Separate entries for French St. Martin have been made when it seemed pertinent and clearer to do so.

Budget Planning

If you choose the beachcomber's St. Maarten, costs are reasonable. You can take advantage of the beaches near the pier, snack at one of the modest places in town, and do your shopping on Front Street, where you will find bargains galore. If you choose the elegant side, however, for haute cuisine and shops with designer clothes, you will find St. Maarten/St. Martin to be expensive. Top French restaurants cost US$200 or more for dinner for two persons; chic shops with fashions by Armani, and other top designers may be 20 percent lower than U.S. prices, but they are still expensive. It pays to look around, and do not be shy about asking the price. You should know that some restaurants have two sets of prices—one for local clientele and one for tourists.

Taxis, unless you share with others, are expensive. If you plan to tour on your own, a car rental is the best deal.

Shore Excursions

Cruise lines usually offer several excursions, but St. Maarten is easy to see and enjoy on your own.

Island Tour: 3 hours, $25–$30 by bus (or by taxi, 2 hours, $45–$50 for two people; each additional person is $10). For first-time visitors reluctant to drive, a bus tour is a quick look at the island.

America's Cup 12 Metre Challenge: 3 hours, $85 per person, when bought directly from the operator and includes a tee shirt. $100 and more, depending on the cruise line. Experience the fun and thrill of racing an authentic America's Cup 12-meter yacht in an actual race. It's the most popular excursion in St. Maarten. You don't need experience, but you do need to be in good physical condition.

Diving or Snorkeling Package: 3 hours, single tank, $65–75; snorkeling, $50–$60. Most cruise ships offer a variety of snorkeling and dive packages; some include an island tour, and others include sailing around the island to the uninhabited islets off the northeast coast.

Port Profile: Philipsburg

As your ship approaches St. Maarten, the green mountains make the island seem much larger than it is; and when you walk down the streets of Philipsburg, its capital, the crowds make it seem larger than it is, too.

Philipsburg, situated on a crest of land facing Great Bay, was founded in 1733 as a free port and named for John Philips, who served as the commander from 1735 to 1746. It is still a free port. Frontstreet and the lanes leading to Backstreet are lined with trendy boutiques and air-conditioned malls selling duty-free goods from around the world. The Dutch side, which saw its first hotel open in 1947, developed sooner than its French counterpart. In addition to the international airport and cruise-ship port, the Dutch side has the majority of hotels, banks, and stores.

Location/Embarkation: St. Maarten's cruise facility at Pointe Blanche (www.portofstmaarten .com) on the eastern tip of Great Bay includes a multi-million dollar shopping and entertainment complex called Harbor Point Village. With the most recent expansion, the port can accommodate the very largest ships The terminal has a tourist information kiosk, post office, deli, ATM machines, Internet access, pay phones, craft and gift shops, car rentals, and conference space for rent. There are covered taxi stands and space for a host of tour buses.

All the shops, the open-air market, restaurants, bars, and entertainment areas adhere to the same theme and color scheme as the terminal building: yellow walls with red and purple roofs, and gray and red cement block walkways. To go to the center of town, cruise passengers have the option of walking on the new sidewalk from the port to Philipsburg (about a mile) or taking a taxi or a water taxi ($4 one-way, $6 round-trip unlimited access) that departs every fifteen minutes from the pier to Bobby's Marine at the east end of the bay; or Capt. Hodge's Wharf in Wathey Square, directly in front of the Frontstreet shopping area where ships dropped passengers in the past; or further west where an addition dock has been added to serve the western end of the bay.

When you walk, you will pass Great Bay Marina and Bobby's Marina, where you can sign up for diving or a picnic sail to a secluded beach or a day sail to a neighboring island. Most boats leave about 9 or 9:30 a.m.

Local Transportation: Taxis do not have meters; rates, which must have government approval, are based on destination for two passengers per trip. A charge of $4 is added for each additional person. There is a 25 percent surcharge

after 10 p.m. and 50 percent between midnight and 6 a.m. Always ask for the fare in advance. Cab drivers usually quote prices in U.S. dollars, but to avoid misunderstandings, be sure to ask which currency is quoted. Your driver will expect a 10 to 15 percent tip.

Approximate fares in U.S. dollars from Philipsburg: west to Little Bay, $7; airport, $12; Maho, $17; La Samanna, $17; east to Oyster Pond and Dawn Beach, $15; north to Marigot, $15; Grande Case, $25; or Orient Beach, $18. Fares are posted at the arrival area at the cruise port. Licensed taxi drivers can be recognized by their orange golf shirts.

For budget-minded travelers, public buses run between Philipsburg and Marigot throughout the day. The fare is $1.50. Other buses run every half hour between Mullet Bay, Simpson Bay, Cole Bay, and Grand Case; every hour to Mullet Bay; and every fifteen to twenty minutes to the French Quarter. Bus stops on the Dutch side are marked "Bushalte"; on the French side, "Arret"; or you can usually stop an approaching bus by waving to it.

Roads and Rentals: St. Maarten's narrow, winding roads are barely adequate for the traffic around town and the airport. Driving is on the RIGHT. Most companies have pickup and delivery service and offer unlimited mileage. You should book in advance, particularly in high season, and don't be surprised if your confirmed reservation is not fulfilled. As we have noted many times in this book, although intentions are good, execution often falls short of them. Expect to pay about $50 for a standard shift and $60 for automatic with air-conditioning.

Among the rental companies are Budget (599-545-4030), which has cars and jeeps; Alamo, Avis, Hertz, National, and Thrifty are also represented.

Motorbikes: Super Bikes St. Martin/Harley-Davidson Rental (599-544-2704, www.h-dstmartin .com) Harleys from $100; **St. Maarten Scooter Rental** (866-826-2205; www.stmaartenscooter rental.com); and **TriSports** (mountain bikes; 599-545-4384; www.trisportsxm.com) bikes rent for $17 half-day. We do not recommend bikes even for experienced, careful drivers, however, because St. Maarten's roads are narrow, hilly, and replete with

St. Martin

Population: 39,000

Size: 21 square miles

Government: St. Martin and its neighboring St. Barts officially broke away from Guadeloupe in 2007, becoming Overseas Collectivities. As French territories, the residents are citizens of France with the same rights and privileges as their countrymen in metropolitan France. St. Martin has a legislative body elected by the people whose representative is a member in the French parliament.

Main Towns: Marigot and Grand Case

Currency: Euro. US$1 equals about €.50 or € 1 equals about US$1.50

Electricity: St. Martin's electricity system is separate from the Dutch side and is 220 volts AC, 50 cycles.

Emergency Numbers: Medical, Marigot Hospital: 590-29-57-57; Gendarmerie (police): 17; Fire, accident, ambulance: 18

Language: French is the official language; English, although widely used, is not spoken by the local French people with the fluency of those with a Dutch language background.

Postal Service: You must use French stamps to mail post cards and letters from St. Martin. The post office (Rue d'Anguille) is open weekdays, 8 a.m. to noon; 1 to 4:30 p.m. and on Sat morning and closed on Wed afternoon.

Public Holidays: Jan 1, New Year's Day; Good Friday; Easter Monday; May 1, Labor Day; Whit Monday; July 14, Bastille Day; Ascension Thurs; Nov 11, St. Martin's Day; Dec 25 and 26, Christmas.

Telephone Area Code: St. Martin and Sint Maarten have separate telephone systems. To call St. Martin from the United States, dial 011-590-590 plus the six digits local number. To call from the French to the Dutch side, dial 00-599-54 plus local number.

Airlines: For service from the United States and intra-island, see Sint Maarten Fast Facts. Esperance Airport, a small domestic airport in St. Martin, is served by Air Caraibes flying to Guadeloupe and Martinique and St. Barth Commuter to St. Barts.

Information: www.st-martin.org; info@st-martin.org

In the United States:

St. Martin Tourist Board, 825 Third Ave., New York, NY 10022; (212) 745-0967

In Canada:

French Government Tourist Board, 1981 Avenue McGill College, #490, Montreal, QC H34 2W9; (514) 288-4264; and One Dundas St. W, #2405, Toronto, ON M5G 1Z3; (416) 593-4717

In Port:

St. Martin Tourist Office, Route de Sandy Ground 97150, Marigot (590) 87-27-21/23; fax: (590) 87-56-43; hours: 8 a.m. to 12:30 p.m.; 2 to 5 p.m.

---

potholes and blind curves. You are likely to have to stop dead for a cow or goat that has strayed onto the road, particularly in the rural northeast side—and animals have the right of way.

Ferry Service: High-speed ferries to St. Barts (forty to sixty minutes): *The Edge*, operated by **Aqua Mania Adventures** (599-544-2640/2631; www.stmartin-activities.com), departs daily (9 a.m.) from Pelican Marina, Simpson Bay; $65 round-trip adult, $35 child. *Voyager* (590-87-10-68; www.voy12.com) departs from Philipsburg daily at 12:30 and 4 p.m., $72 round-trip, $61 one-way. To Saba: *The Edge* departs (9 a.m.) Wed to Sun from Pelican Marina and returns by 5 p.m.; $65 round-trip adults, $35 child. Ferries have a start-and-stop

history here. Always check in advance before making plans.

Marigot: A French Delight

Marigot is less than a twenty-minute drive from Philipsburg, but the differences make it light-years away. Marigot is so unmistakably Gallic you don't need the language, the signs, the food, the wine, or the khaki-clad gendarme to tell you so. The ambience is St. Tropez in the tropics—complete with sidewalk cafes, fishing boats, and a topless beach or two. You will find boutiques with French perfumes and fashionable sportswear, and gourmet shops and grocery stores where you can stock up on French products.

The little French capital is definitely worth a stroll. Despite modern incursions from new hotels, stores, and a marina with a large shopping and restaurant complex, the town retains its old character thanks to many West Indian–style houses, colonial buildings, and the main streets beautified with flowers.

At the harbor filled with fish and ferry boats, there are outdoor markets for fruit and vegetables and souvenirs. The waterfront has recently been expanded by landfill, adding a larger market area and parking space and outdoor cafes. In Marigot a taxi service is located at the port near the ferries. Sample fares from Marigot: to Grand Case Beach Club, $12 to $15; to Philipsburg, $15. A 25 percent surcharge is added after 9 p.m. and 50 percent after midnight.

Ferries: From Marigot Harbor, service to Anguilla leaves approximately every half hour, takes fifteen minutes, and costs $10 one-way plus $2 departure tax. You can buy tickets at a kiosk by the dock. The ferry dock in Anguilla is on the south side of the island. Don't forget to bring your passport or travel identification documents. Also from Marigot to St. Barts, *Voyager* (590-87-10-68; www.voy12.com) departs Mon and Tues and Thurs through Sat twice a day (9:15 a.m. and 6:45 p.m.); $72 round-trip, $61 one-way.

St. Maarten on Your Own

Philipsburg sits on a thin crest of land hemmed in by two bodies of water: Great Bay on the south and Great Salt Pond on the north, and anchored by high hills at both ends of the crest. As a result, the downtown in the past was only 2 blocks deep with two main streets: Frontstreet (Vorstraat, in Dutch) with traffic one-way east; Backstreet (Achterstraat), one-way west. Since 2002, St. Maarten has been working on a long-term redevelopment and beautification plan for Philipsburg with fabulous results. The lovely crescent-shaped, white sand beach of Great Bay has been widened and an attractive boardwalk stretching from end to end of the beach, added. Now the beach is dotted with lounges and

colorful umbrellas which can be rented for the day for a small fee and the boardwalk is lined with shops restaurants, and bars and has become the center of the action for Philipsburg. Wathey Square, the town center, and Frontstreet and Backstreet have been made into pretty pedestrian malls which are often closed to traffic when several cruise ships are in port.

Two new roads—Cannegieter Street and Walter Nisbet Road (better known as Pondfill Road)— were added through landfill of Great Salt Pond in order to relieve the downtown traffic congestion. Yet another road is being created to circle the pond and enable traffic to move more freely between Philipsburg, Simpson Bay, the airport, and Marigot. The pond once provided the island with its major source of income: salt, once an important commodity in world trade.

A stroll around town takes less than an hour unless you get sidetracked with shopping. Frontstreet and the little lanes, or steegjes, that connect it to Backstreet have boutiques, restaurants, air-conditioned shopping malls, and small hotels.

Courthouse: On the north side of Wathey Square, a white clapboard building with green trim is the old Courthouse, built in 1793 and rebuilt in 1825. Originally the house of the colony's commander, in subsequent years it was used as the council chambers, courts, fire hall, and jail. Today the upper floor is still used by the courts, and the building serves as the town hall.

Guavaberry Emporium (599-542-2965; www.guavaberry.com) St. Maarten liquor made from rum and a local fruit, guavaberry, can be purchased from a shop at the east end of Frontstreet housed in a historic building dating from the late 18th century. Once the home of a St. Maarten governor, it is said to occupy the former site of a synagogue. The shop sells many flavors, any of which you can sample before you buy.

Royal Guest House: Across the street is the Pasanggrahan Hotel (599-542-3588; www.pasanhotel.com), once the Royal Guest House, which hosted Queen Wilhelmina of the Netherlands when she was en route to exile in Canada after the Nazi invasion of her country. The modest inn, hidden behind its tropical gardens, was the favorite of those who discovered St. Maarten before the boom. The front porch and restaurant are directly on Great Bay Beach.

Museum of St. Maarten: At the east end of Frontstreet is the Museum of St. Maarten (599-542-4917; www.stmaarten.com), created in 1989 by the St. Maarten Historic Foundation. Located on the second floor of a small shopping complex, the modest museum has displays from excavations on the island and artifacts donated by residents. Next door is the gallery-museum of Mosera, one of St. Maarten's leading artists. Hours: Mon to Fri from 10 a.m. to 4 p.m., Sat to 2 p.m. Admission is $1.

Sint Maarten Nature Foundation: Established in 1997 to preserve St. Maarten's environment, the foundation (599-542-0267; www.naturefoundationsxm.org) is creating two nature parks accessible to the public with funding from the World Wildlife Fund–Holland.

The **Sint Maarten Marine Park** (Great Bay Marina, #3 P.O. Box 863, Philipsburg; 599-542-0267) focuses on the eastern and southeastern areas of Dutch St. Maarten, protecting coastal waters and some adjacent coastline from Oyster Pond to Cupecoy Beach, including four small islands that serve as breeding grounds for birds and fish. The first step was to install moorings along the reefs so that dive operators and other vessels no longer had to anchor directly to the reefs. Now there are more than twenty-eight moorings and a large area designated for local fishermen, as well as areas for diving sites and other water sports.

The foundation's second effort is being aided by a group in Holland and the local government to purchase and restore Emilio Wilson Estate, the home of Commander John Philips, the island's first governor under British rule, and the adjacent Mary's Fancy Estate, two historical estates in the Cul-de-Sac area. Phase One, which entailed developing the Emilio Wilson Historical and Cultural Park, called Doctor's Yard, opened in 2002 with the first structure, a wood and guinea–grass thatched slave watch house.

Located on L. B. Scott Road in Dutch Cul-de-Sac, the interesting property was originally a sugar plantation where slaves worked and lived. The estate changed owners many times until 1954, when it was sold to Emilio Wilson, the son of a former slave. Wilson died in 2001, leaving an

arrangement that enabled the foundation to establish the park. The park has a restaurant and visitor facilities. Hours: daily 10 a.m. to 5 p.m. Donations are welcomed.

The foundation has also been involved in a mangrove planting program at Little Bay and Fresh Bay Ponds, organized a Sea Turtle Club with volunteers to help identify and safeguard nesting sites, and started an environmental awareness program in the local schools. St. Maarten Park (599-543-2030).

Fort Amsterdam: Philipsburg does not have any "must see" historic sites, but a pavement at the foot of Frontstreet goes over the hill to Little Bay to the ruins of Fort Amsterdam, on the finger of land separating Great Bay and Little Bay. The fort dates from the 17th century.

A Drive Around the Island

The best way to see and enjoy St. Maarten is to rent a car and drive around the island on your own. When you find a pretty beach or a scenic view, stop for a swim, a photo, or a picnic. One road circles the island, and secondary ones go inland or to secluded beaches. You can leave Philipsburg by the Ring Road, which runs west along Great Salt Pond and over Cole Bay Hill.

Cole Bay Hill Cemetery: The Scottish adventurer John Philips is buried on the hill overlooking the town he founded. The hill separates Philipsburg from the west end of the island, where its best-known resorts are located. From an observation platform at the summit, you can see neighboring Saba, St. Eustatius, St. Kitts, and Nevis. The valley below overlooking Cay Bay was where Peter Stuyvesant unsuccessfully battled the Spaniards in 1644.

Simpson Bay Lagoon: After several winding miles the road intersects with Welfare Road, where you can turn north to Marigot or continue west along Simpson Bay Lagoon, the island's main setting for water sports. The road parallels the airport on the south; at the end of the runway is Maho Bay, the smart "suburb" of St. Maarten with attractive shops, good restaurants, and entertainment.

The main road west continues to Cupecoy and the French side, where secondary roads lead to La Samanna, a very expensive luxury resort on Long Beach, one of the island's most magnificent stretches of sand. The western end is hilly and provides good views of the island and coastline. West of Cupecoy is the dividing line between the two parts of the island.

Marigot: The little French capital, even with its modern incursions, is definitely worth a stroll. For the most part the town has retained its character, with many Creole or West Indian–style houses and colonial buildings. Most now house chic little boutiques, perfume shops, restaurants, or the occasional sidewalk cafe, where the croissants are as tasty as in Paris.

At the harbor, filled with fishing and ferry boats, there is a daily outdoor arts and crafts market on the landfill-widened seafront promenade and a major fresh fruit, vegetable, and seafood market under its own roof on Wed and Sat from 7 a.m. to 1 p.m. The **Marina Fort Louis** offers dock space, a landscaped area, and extended parking, and the West Indies Mall has very high-end shops (don't look for bargains here) and one of the town's best dinner restaurants, **Le Gaiac** (590-51-97-66). Bordering the harbor square on three sides are restaurants and sidewalk cafes. Those on the south side are tiny stalls, popular with townsfolk and tourists at lunchtime.

Branching out from here are the three main shopping streets—rue de la République, rue Kennedy, and rue General Charles de Gaulle—lined with shops in balconied buildings, some trimmed with gingerbread and wrought iron, reminiscent of New Orleans.

The town's most delightful spot is the yacht-filled Marina Royale, which you pass on your way into town. It is lined with seafood restaurants and sidewalk cafes—the best people-watching spots in town—where you really do feel you are in St. Tropez. Marigot has several supermarkets, where you can buy French cheese, wine, and other picnic supplies.

Louis Fort: Built in 1776 on a strategic hilltop above Marigot Harbor, the fort is St. Martin's largest colonial fortification and at one time had fifteen cannons. Under the guidance of the St. Martin Historic and Cultural Foundation, the fort has been made more accessible and is being restored. Steps

from the car park of the Sous-Prefectus lead up the hill; from here there are grand views south, across the islands to Simpson Lagoon and the leeward coast, and north, across the sea to Anguilla. The best time for a visit is early morning or late afternoon.

St. Martin Museum: At Sandy Ground on the south side of Marigot is the St. Martin Museum, also called "On the Trail of the Arawaks." Three permanent exhibits are on view. The first displays artifacts from the archaeological excavations in St. Martin over the past decade, some dating from 1800 B.C.; a second display covers early explorers and colonization; and the third presents the island from 1900 to the 1960s. The exhibits are labeled in French and English. There are also changing exhibits of works by local artists. Hours: Mon to Fri, 9 a.m. to 1 p.m. and 3 to 6 p.m., Sat to 1 p.m. Entrance: $5. Historic tours of St. Martin can be reserved through the museum: phone/fax: 590-29-22-84; museestmartin@powerantilles.com; tours depart at 9 a.m. and return at 11 a.m. Cost is US$30.

Paradise Peak: After Marigot en route to Grand Case, country roads on the east lead to the village of Colombier and Paradise Peak, the island's highest mountaintop. There is a short trail at the top, from which there are panoramic views. Look for the sign for **Loterie Farm** (Pic Paradise; 590-87-86-16; www.loteriefarm.net; visit@loteriefarm.com.), a former sugar plantation whose long-hidden structures were uncovered when Hurricane Luis swept away the vegetation in 1995. This private nature reserve's 150 acres of untouched farmland, tropical forest, and hills provide excellent hiking trails as well as a unique setting for musical events and theme evenings around its rustic Hidden Forest Café. An informative one-and-a-half-hour guided ecotour begins at 10 a.m. some mornings for $25. A canopy tour, which the Californian owner of the farm calls "fly the trees," has three levels: a higher and more challenging tour for adults and a lower, easier one for children at least 4 feet tall.

Grand Case: Five miles north of Marigot is Grand Case, a small town with an international reputation as a gourmet haven that now counts more than thirty dining establishments, including half a dozen that rank among the island's best. In the middle of all the haute cuisine are the lolos (seaside barbecue shacks) serving fresh West Indian fare, from Creole dishes to lobster, with lots of local atmosphere and down-to-earth prices. At the north end of town a dirt road west leads to Grand Case Beach Club, an American-operated beachfront hotel.

On Tues in Jan to May, Grand Case is enlivened by a big Arts and Crafts market with costumed participants, performances of traditional dances, exhibits of sixty or more local arts and crafts people, and food offerings by several dozen local restaurants. The village is also the departure location for Seaworld Explorer excursions, $39 adults, $25 children.

French Cul-de-Sac: From Grand Case the road cuts east across the north tip of the island, the most mountainous part, to French Cul-de-Sac and the eastern side of the island fronting the Atlantic Ocean. A very hilly road continues north to Anse Marcel, one of St. Martin's prettiest beaches.

Orient Beach: From the main east-coast route, secondary roads lead to Orient Beach. The long stretch of beautiful white sand is now densely populated with restaurants and beach clubs. The beach and swimming are free, but you will have to pay if you want to use one of the beach lounges and any other amenities or sports equipment. (There is a nudist beach at its eastern end.) Several of the water-sports operators here offer boat trips to the nearby islands that face the beach.

Continuing south, you will pass through the most rural part of the island. A side road takes you into the interior to Orleans.

The Butterfly Farm: On Le Galion Beach Road (about a thirty-minute drive from Philipsburg) is La Ferme des Papillons (590-87-31-21; www.thebutterflyfarm.com; info@thebutterflyfarm.com). In 1,000 square meters of tropical gardens fenced with wire mesh like an aviary, you can see hundreds of rare exotic butterflies flitting about freely. The gardens have a montage of blossoms to provide nectar for the butterflies and special plants to feed the caterpillars.

A guide leads visitors through the exhibit area, identifying species, pointing out courtship and mating displays, and relating interesting facts and stories about these beautiful creatures. Visitors also see the stages of the butterflies' life cycle, from laying their eggs to caterpillars hatching, growing, and forming their chrysalis. Visitors may wander through the gardens to take photos and video film or sit in the shaded areas to absorb the tranquil atmosphere, watch the butterflies, and listen to the soothing pan music heard quietly in the background. Guests are warmly welcomed by English owners William and Karin Slayter, general manager John Coward, and a staff that is always on hand to answer questions. Hours: 9 a.m. to 3 p.m. Admission US$14 adults, US$7 children, which includes a complimentary pass for the duration of one's vacation. Visitors from cruise ships receive a $2 discount in lieu of the pass. A shop sells unusual butterfly gifts.

The Old House: (590-87-32-67) Just beyond the entrance to Le Galion Beach is a rambling, traditional-style house with a green roof. A prominent family, the Beauperthuys, have occupied this hilltop structure for six generations. The present owner, Pierre, recently converted his ancestral home into a rum museum, where he displays many of his family's treasures and personally recounts their fascinating history. The rum-related poster collection and rums from around the world are as amusing as they are unusual. Hours: 10 a.m. to 4 p.m. daily except Mon. Admission: $10.

Oyster Pond/Dawn Beach: Immediately after crossing the Dutch/French border, the road takes a sharp turn to the east, and after another mile it forks east to the Dawn Beach and Oyster Pond resort areas. The return to Philipsburg can be made via Naked Boy Hill Road, a winding road south along Great Salt Pond.

This drive can easily be taken in the reverse direction. If it is an afternoon drive, time your return to the western side for late afternoon to watch a St. Martin sunset. Don't miss it!

Shopping

On this half-Dutch, half-French island with its duty-free goods and smart boutiques, shopping is as much an attraction as are its restaurants and sports. You can buy delftware and Gouda cheese as easily as Limoges and Brie, not to mention Japanese cameras, Italian leather, Chinese linens,

Colombian emeralds, and a host of other quality products from around the world. Savings range from 20 to 40 percent off U.S. prices, but, as we always emphasize, the best way to know if you are getting a good buy is to come with prices from home. St. Maarten shopkeepers are very competitive; it pays to shop around. Yet even the most ardent shoppers will probably find they can check out the best in either Philipsburg or Marigot in an hour or two.

Attractive shopping complexes with quality stores are also in the resort areas west of Philipsburg. The Maho Bay shops are centered around Maho Beach Hotel, and the attractive Cinnamon Grove Plaza is designed around an outdoor courtyard with boutiques in low-rise buildings of colorful West Indian–style architecture.

Stores named below are on Philipsburg's Frontstreet unless otherwise indicated. Some close for lunch from noon to 1 p.m. When cruise ships are in port on Sun and holidays, some shops—not the best—open briefly.

Art and Artists: St. Maarten/St. Martin have become a mecca for artists, many of whom have their own galleries or open their studios to visitors. The **Art Lovers Association** is the Association of St. Martin Artists (www.artlovers-sxm .com; contact@artlovers-sxm.com); its Web site has an extensive list of artists and galleries with addresses.

Greenwith Galleries (599-542-3842) specializes in fine art of the Caribbean and represents thirty-six artists living in St. Maarten and nearby islands. **Simpson Bay Art Gallery** (Airport Road; 599-544-4360), situated in a lovely stone-and-wood "dollhouse," features the fanciful and sometimes whimsical works of Mounette Radot, a French artist who has lived on St. Maarten for many years. She also shows the work of local artists. Open daily, including Sun.

Art Lovers Association, the Association of St. Maarten Artists (7 Speetjens Arcade, Frontstreet; phone/fax: 599-542-0554). Among the artists shown here is the talented Mosera Henry (www.speetjens .com/mosera), who is originally from St. Lucia. Other artists are shown and poetry readings and plays are held from time to time. Opening hours are fluid; inquire locally. Among other St. Maarten artists are Ria Zonneveld, who creates unusual

clay busts with a touch of whimsy; Ruby Bute, Joe Dominique, and Cyrnic Griffith are some of the best-known painters of local scenes.

The French side is particularly active, with several dozen galleries. Most are located in Marigot or Grand Case; many show French or other Europeans and Americans living in St. Martin for part or all of the year. Many restaurants show local artists throughout the year. *Ti Gourmet,* a local guide to dining and restaurants, has a list of galleries and artists who show at their homes, along with their phone numbers. **Roland Richardson Gallery** (6 rue de la République, 590-87-84-08; 590-87-32-24; www.rolandrichardson.com) is the gallery of Roland Richardson, the island's best-known artist, situated in a handsome, renovated 19th-century Creole house next door to the house where he was born.

On the main road at Orient is **The Potters,** where you can watch master potters and their apprentices at work and buy their products.

Books/Maps: In addition to crafts, **Shipwreck Shop** carries books, magazines, maps, and postcards reproduced from paintings, prints by island artists, and stamps.

Cameras/Electronics: Boolchand's (www .boolchand.com) has three downtown stores where you will find the leading names in Japanese cameras and electronic equipment. Bring prices from home for comparison. The shops also carry linens, jewelry, and Bally and Adidas shoes.

China/Crystal: Little Switzerland, a familiar name throughout the Caribbean, carries only the highest-quality English china, French crystal, Swiss watches, Hummel figurines, and other gift items. You can request a catalog in advance by calling (800) 524-2010. **Dutch Delft Blue Gallery** is a specialty shop for delftware.

Clothing: There are dozens of shops along the main streets, most with beach and casual wear. **Liz Claiborne, Ralph Lauren, Hugo Boss,** and **Tommy Hilfiger** are the most familiar name-labels with their own stores here. The **Sint Rose Shopping Mall** in the heart of town has a variety of shops facing Frontstreet and restaurants, bars, an art gallery, and other attractions on the other side along the boardwalk. Old Town is a similar Mall between Front and Back Streets. **Endless Summer** (27 Frontstreet; 599-542-1510) has an impressive selection of international beachwear, particularly bathing suits in all shapes and sizes.

Crafts: Impressions (Promenade Arcade) specializes in authentic native arts and crafts from the Caribbean, folklore, occult artifacts, and herbs and spices. The best craftwork comes from Moro of Haiti, whose artisans make carved and painted wood pieces that are original and distinctive. Another unusual craft, bread and fruit baskets made from fired coconut shells, comes from Nevis. **Sea-breeze** (Promenade Arcade) carries handpainted T-shirts by Ruby Bute as well as her postcards. The **Shipwreck Shops** (at the port and a dozen more branches around the island) carry quality Caribbean crafts and souvenirs.

Food Specialties: The Antilles Spice Clipper (599-542-5358; www.lordandhunter.com; info@shipwreckshops.com) line of sauces and Caribbean condiments carried at **Lord & Hunter** and a dozen other stores, including Shipwreck, are perfect small carry-home gifts. The stores also carry island clothing, souvenir items, and gifts.

Jewelry: Little Switzerland has a full line of quality brands. If emeralds are your passion, **Colombian Emeralds** has the largest collection, and the staff is quick to remind you that unmounted emeralds can be brought into the United States free of customs duty. The merchandise also carries a guarantee honored by the company's Miami office. The best selection of high-end watches is found at **Oro de Sol** (Cartier, Chopard, Ebel, and Harry Winston), along with exclusive jewelry, and Goldfinger's, which is also the island's Rolex agent. **Pearl Gems** has the Caribbean's largest selection of cultured and freshwater pearls; Artistic Jewelers is the Mikimoto specialist.

Leather/Luggage: Several stores, such as MCM (Simpson Bay; 599-545-5470) and **Fifth Avenue** (599-542-3401) carry high-quality Italian-leather handbags and accessories. If you want the best knock-offs of famous international brands head to **Everest Enterprises** (Frontstreet, 599-542-9734).

Linens: Mr. Tablecloth (599-542-2193) and Linens Galore (599-543-0099) specialize in hand-embroidered linens and quality gifts.

Liquor: Philipsburg Liquor Store and Rum Jumbie Liquor (Point Blanche; 599-542-3587; www.rumjumbie.com) adjacent to the cruise-ship dock is hard to miss. It's St. Maarten's best, with a full line of liquors and wine. And don't overlook the **Guavaberry Tasting Shop** (www.guavaberry.com; described earlier in the Philipsburg walking tour). Their attractively bottled liqueurs made from a local fruit, guavaberry, make unusual, inexpensive gifts to take home. Don't miss **Ma Doudou's** flavored rums and spices in their unique handpainted bottles found in the better souvenir shops and markets on both sides of the island.

Perfumes: Lipstick and Penha have large stocks of cosmetics and French perfumes. The latter store also carries sportswear and fashion jewelry.

Marigot

Shops along rue de la République, rue Kennedy, rue General Charles de Gaulle, and around the Marina Royale feature French and Italian designer clothes at designer prices, including such prestigious names as Armani, Chloe, Jean-Paul Gaultier, Hermes, Max Mara, and Versace. The craft market has expanded into more spacious waterfront stalls, and shopping is as good as in Philipsburg. The better shops have branches on both sides.

The area around and beyond the Ferry Dock has been upgraded with the addition of the Marina Fort Louis, with space for mega-yachts, and Le West Indies Mall, a glossy trilevel structure providing luxury shopping, wining, and dining in air-conditioned comfort with twenty-two boutiques (Lancel, Newman, Lacoste, among others), a piano bar, and two restaurants, including a rooftop gourmet gathering place, **Le Gaiac,** with 180-degree views and a chef from Michel Guerard. Store hours are Mon to Sat from 9 a.m. to 1 p.m. and 3 to 7 p.m. Some stores open when ships are in port on Sun and holidays.

Dining and Restaurants

The number and variety of good restaurants on this small island are astonishing. The best gourmet selections, which have won the island international recognition, are on the French side, particularly in the tiny village of Grand Case. But be prepared for the bill. Many are as expensive as top French restaurants in New York. The restaurants listed below in Philipsburg are located on Frontstreet unless otherwise indicated. Moderate means less than $20 per person, expensive means $35 or more, and very expensive means $50 or more per person. Expensive gourmet restaurants close one day during the week, usually Sun or Mon, but it is best to check in advance, as opening hours and days vary.

St. Maarten

Cheri's Cafe (Maho Shopping Center; 599-545-3361), a lively open-air cafe and bar, with music and dancing every evening, serves food from 11 a.m. to midnight; the varied menu has salads, fresh fish, steaks, and hamburgers. Moderate.

Kangaroo Court (Frontstreet; 599-542-4278), a popular cafe/deli in a historic building across from the courthouse, serves big salads, hearty sandwiches on home-baked bread, fresh-squeezed lemonade, and scrumptious cakes and pastries in a lovely hidden garden. Moderate.

Oualichi (Boardwalk; 599-542-4316) offers air-conditioned inside seating or outdoor seating on the terrace for pizza, pasta, lobster, and a variety of other selections. Huge portions. Moderate.

Saratoga (Simpson Bay; 599-545-2421; www .sxmsaratoga.com) was created by a Culinary Institute of America graduate who creates contemporary American cuisine with a Pacific Rim touch. It has a delightful terrace setting overlooking the bay. Expensive.

Sheer (44 Frontstreet; 599-542 9635), one of the town's newest, elegant restaurants serves European and Asian fusion cuisine with a Caribbean flair.

Taloula Mango's (Boardwalk; 599-542-1645), an early newcomer to the boardwalk, serves burgers, ribs, and seafood. Jazz on Sun. Moderate.

Temptation (Atlantis Casino Courtyard; 599-545-2254; www.nouveaucaribbean.com) is the restaurant of the well-known local chef Dino Jagtiani, who is St. Maarten's first native-born graduate of the Culinary Institute of America. His French–Caribbean fusion garners rave reviews.

In the same location, he also has **Rare** (599-545-5714; www.daretoberare.com), an American-style steakhouse. Expensive.

Turtle Pier Bar (Simpson Bay Lagoon; 599-545-2562), in a delightful setting on the lagoon, has its own boat dock and sundeck, where you can enjoy light fare or nightly entertainment. Moderate.

St. Martin

Marigot and Beyond: Bar de la Mer (on the waterfront; 590-87-81-79; bardelamer@power antilles.com), a casual, friendly cafe and bar serving salads, pizza, and steak, is a great people-watching and rendezvous place. They lend backgammon sets, too! Moderate.

Mini Club (590-87-50-69) is an old-time rustic favorite, especially on Wed and Sat evenings for the large buffet ($35). Moderate.

Tropicana (Marina Royale; 590-87-79-07) has terrace tables overlooking Marigot's popular marina, which are much in demand at both lunch and dinner and require a reservation. The small brasserie-style menu is creative, the daily specials are always excellent, the ambience is convivial, and the prices just can't be beat for the consistently high quality. Moderate.

Grand Case and Environs: L'Alabama (590-87-81-66) is a local favorite for French cuisine. (This is despite its unlikely name; one owner, Karin, is from Austria and the other, Pascal, is from France.) Fish and steak dishes with wonderful sauces and great desserts are served for very reasonable prices. Closed Mon.

L'Auberge Gourmande (Grand Case; 590-87-73-37; www.laubergegourmande.com) offers the best value of the town's leading dozen restaurants. Moderately expensive. The owner's other restaurant, **Le Tastevin** (across the street; 590-87-55-45) has a contemporary French menu. Expensive.

Captain Oliver's Restaurant & Marina (Oyster Pond; 590-87-30-00; www.captainolivers.com) has a delightful waterfront setting where you—and its loyal local patrons—can enjoy French and continental cuisine. Moderate.

Rainbow (176 Boulevard de Grand Case; 590-87-55-80). Many St. Martin cognoscenti consider this airy beachfront restaurant the best on the island for contemporary French cuisine. It's expensive but worth the price. Open for dinner daily except Sun.

Sunset Cafe (Grand Case Beach Club; 590-87-37-37; www.gcbc.com), extending out over the water, is a great relaxing and informal location to enjoy excellent seafood. Moderate.

Sports

In most cases you should contact the hotel or sports operator in advance to make arrangements, particularly during the peak season, when demand is likely to be high.

Beaches/Swimming: St. Maarten is famous for its beaches—more than three dozen lovely white-sand stretches and coves where you might easily spend the day. Some are busy with people, facilities, and concessioners; others are quiet and secluded. Some of the beaches on French St. Martin are nude or topless, but none are on St. Maarten. If you take a taxi to one of the more secluded beaches, arrange with the taxi driver a specific time to return, and agree in advance on the price of the round-trip fare. The Web site www.sint-maarten.net has photographs and descriptions, beach by beach, of those on both the Dutch and French coasts.

The beaches are listed here by their proximity to Philipsburg. A taxi to west-side beaches costs about $10 to $15; those to the east side about $15; and north to Orient Bay, $20.

Great Bay, a mile-long strand directly in town on Great Bay, has calm and generally clean water, and now, with the new boardwalk and renovations and the cruise port having been moved to Pointe Blanche, the beach is once again an attractive and convenient place to enjoy a beach day.

Little Bay, west of town within walking distance of town, is a smaller beach with lovely water; there are several hotels on the beach with water sports. Simpson Bay and Maho Bay, by the airport, have hotels with concessioners handling water-sports activities. Farther west, Cupecoy Beach—with sandstone cliffs as a backdrop—is quiet and less accessible. There are no facilities other than a beach bar on the cliffs, where you can rent snorkel gear. The far end of the beach is used for bathing in the buff.

Long Beach, at the far western end of the south shore, is one of the Caribbean's most beautiful beaches, and rounding the point are Plum Bay and Rouge Beach, two secluded beaches more easily reached by boat. Rouge Beach has a beach bar. Both are topless beaches.

On the east side of St. Maarten, Oyster Pond and Dawn Beach constitute a long, wide stretch along Guana Bay where the Atlantic washes the shore. The south end is popular for surfing. Orient Beach, on the northeast, is another very long beach that has been built up with condos and beach bars in recent years. The southeastern end of the beach is a nudist beach.

Boating: St. Maarten offers excursions on two types of boats: large catamarans, holding up to twenty-five or more passengers, which go to Anguilla, Prickly Pear, and Tintamarre, or small sailboats for six to ten passengers, which sail to a secluded beach for a swim, snorkel, and picnic or sunset cruise. Boats leave from Bobby's Marina (599-542-4096; www.bobbysmarina.com) or Pelican Marina (599-544-2640) about 9 or 9:30 a.m. and return about 5 or 5:30 p.m. Prices are $70 to $80 per person plus $5 departure tax.

The America's Cup Regatta (599-542-0045, www.12metre.com) is St. Maarten's most popular excursion for cruise passengers. Participants do actually sail in a race as crew on a boat that has been an America's Cup contender. The price for the excursion can range from $99 and up, depending on your cruise ship. The price is $85 if you buy the excursion directly from the America's Cup operator, but departures are not guaranteed. Booking through your ship's excursion desk gives you a guarantee to sail, so you are better advised to buy your ship's excursion and to book it at your earliest opportunity, because it sells out quickly. There are four sails a day, every day of the year except Christmas.

Deep-Sea Fishing: Charters with tackle, bait, sandwiches, and drinks cost approximately $600 for half-day, $900 for full-day, and are available from Bobby's Marina and Blue Water Sport Fishing (Simpson Bay; 599-545-3230); on the French side, Samaco Sportfishing (590-61-81-61). The season for dolphin, mahi-mahi, and kingfish is Dec to Apr; tuna, year-round. Some cruise ships offer fishing trips for about US$225 per person.

Golf: Mullet Bay Golf Course (599-545-2801) is the island's only golf course. It's open daily but only minimally maintained.

Hiking/Biking: There are 25 miles of hiking trails, and *Nature,* an impressive local magazine published annually, has brief descriptions of them, including length and level of difficulty. Paradise Peak, on the French side, is the highest point on the island and can be reached partway by vehicle, but eventually must be approached by foot. Contact the **Association Action Nature** (590-87-97-87) or the **Dutch Hiking Club** (599-542-4917). **TriSports** (599-545-4384; www.trisportsxm.com) offers hiking, mountain bikes, and kayaking. On the French side try **Authentic French Tours** (Rue de Hollande, Marigot, 590-87-05-11). Other sources are **Loterie Farms-Colombier** (590-87-86-16; see description earlier in this chapter; **Oliver Borensztejn** (0690-62-79-07, oliviersxm@yahoo.fr); **St. Maarten National Heritage Foundation** (599-542-4917); and **St. Maarten Road Runners Club** (599-556-7815). A three-hour mountain biking excursion costs about $75 per person.

Horseback Riding: Bayside Riding Club (Le Galion Beach; 590-87-36-64; www.baysideriding club.com) takes small groups with a guide on rides. Reservations must be made in advance. At the north end in French St. Martin, **OK Corral** (Coralita Beach; 590-87-40-72) offers similar excursions. On the Dutch side is **Lucky Stable** (Cay Bay; 599-544-5255; cell 599-555-7246; http://luckystables.shore adventures.net/2007/05/luck_stables.html), which offers one-hour ($45) and two-hour ($65) trail rides, along with a dip in the ocean.

Kayaking: TriSports (Simpson Bay; 599-545-4384; 599-545-4385; www.trisportsxm.com) rents kayaks for exploring the lagoon. It also has mountain bikes for rent for exploring the island. On the French side there's **Wind Adventures** (590-29-41-57), **Tropical Wave** (590-87-37-25) and **Kayak Tour** (Cul-de-Sac, 599-557-0112; sxmkayaktour@ wanadoo.fr) which rent kayaks.

Kiteboarding: The new craze sweeping the water-sports world is popular in St. Martin. Orient Bay and Le Galion Beach are considered to be good places to start. The island's kitesurfing school, located between Kakao and Kontiki on Orient Beach, is operated by **Club Nathalie Simon** (590-29-41-57). Classes are limited to two persons and are taken off from nearby Green Cay. **Kite Surfing** (Orient Bay; 590-29-41-59) and **Wind Adventures** (Orient Bay Resort, 590-29-41-57; www.wind-adventures.com) offers a three-hour lesson of kiting basics for about € 100.

Snorkeling/Scuba: St. Maarten is a good place to learn to snorkel, because there are reefs near shore in shallow water so clear that visibility to 150 feet is normal. It is also a good place to try your first scuba dive. A one-day resort course is available from **Ocean Explorers Dive Center** (Simpson Bay; 599-544-5252; www.stmaartendiving .com), $70. On the Dutch side are **Aqua Mania Adventures** (Pelican Bay Marina; 599-544-2640; www.stmaarten-activities.com), **Dive Safaris** (Bobby's Marina; 599-542-9001; www.divestmaarten .com), and **Scuba Fun** (Divi Little Bay; 599-542-2333; www.scubafun.com); on the French side, **The Scuba Shop** (Oyster Pond; 590-87-48-01; www .thescubashop.net).

Experienced divers will enjoy St. Maarten's wrecks, as well as a variety of reefs characterized by a descending series of gentle hills and valleys and a rich display of colorful fish. Near the entrance to Great Bay Harbor lies the British man-of-war the HMS *Prostellyte,* sunk in 1801.

Off the northeast coast, **Ilet Pinel** offers shallow diving; **Green Key** is a barrier reef rich in sea life; **Flat Island,** also known as Tintamarre, has sheltered coves and a sunken tugboat. The area comprising Flat Island, Ilet Pinel, Green Key, and **Petite Clef** is protected in the Underwater Nature Reserve. The water-sports operator at Orient Beach has snorkeling trips to Green Key island, two hours, for $30.

Windsurfing: The best windsurfing is at Le Galion Beach, where **Tropical Wave** (590-87-37-25) rents boards for $25 to $30 per hour and has a lesson package, too. Orient Beach is another popular location. **Wind Adventures** (Orient Bay Resort,

590-29-41-57; www.wind-adventures.com) offers a private one-hour lesson.

Entertainment

St. Maarten's very lively nightlife offers music varying from piano bars to discos and calypso bands at large resorts and restaurants specializing in Caribbean cuisine. Small as it is, the Dutch side has thirteen casinos. Most are in or connected with a hotel and open at noon. Those closest to the Philipsburg pier are on Frontstreet: **Beach Plaza** (Walter Nesbitt Road; www.beachplazaxm .com); **Rouge et Noir** at Seaview Hotel and the Coliseum Casino, with a gallery of slot machines and a shopping arcade; and **Jump Up** (Emmaplein; www.jumpupcasino.com), with its Carnival theme. The Maho area is the center of the action, although that's beginning to change somewhat with the new attractions on the new boardwalk in town.

On the French side, Marina Royale and the waterfront by Marigot's market draw the crowds. Clubs start at midnight and go until dawn. Some names to note are **Tantra** and **The Sopranos,** a piano bar, at the Sonesta Maho Beach Resort & Casino, **Bamboo Bernies** (www.bamboobernies .net) at Caravanserai Resort, Club 1-Eleven, a hot new night club, and the **Havana Too** in Marigot.

Festivals: The year's major festival is Carnival, beginning mid-Apr and ending with Coronation Day, Apr 30, a public holiday.

Saba: The Storybook Isle

Saba (pronounced SAY-ba), located 28 miles southwest of St. Maarten, is the most curious island in the Caribbean. It is a cone-shaped volcanic peak rising straight up from the sea to 3,000 feet. It has no flat land and no beaches.

When Dutch engineers surveyed the island's steep mountainous terrain in the 1930s, they concluded that construction of a road would be impossible. Undeterred, a local resident, Lambertus Hassell, decided to prove them wrong even though he had no technical training. He sent away for and

studied an engineering correspondence course, organized the island's citizens, and in 1943 completed the first ¾-mile of road up the mountain face to the capital, The Bottom.

Twenty years later, in 1963, the last stretch was finished. The road drops 1,312 feet in twenty hairpin turns ending at the island's airport, which was cut out of the mountainside, too. It looks something like the deck of an aircraft carrier at sea. Landing here in one of Winair's STOL aircraft is an experience you will never forget.

But then, everything about Saba is unusual and unforgettable. The population of about 1,090 is made up mostly of the descendants of Scottish, Irish, and Dutch settlers. And what a hardy bunch they must have been! Before the airport and road were built, people and goods were hoisted up the side of rock cliffs. The alternative was to climb the steep mountain paths to reach the island's several villages.

Hell's Gate and Windwardside: Today the hand-laid road that zigzags up the mountain from the airport leads first to Hell's Gate and continues to Windwardside, a lilliputian village of gingerbread houses with white picket fences. Were it not for the tropical gardens surrounding them, you could imagine yourself on the set of *Hansel and Gretel* rather than on a Caribbean island. One of the homes, a sea captain's house built in the mid-19th century, is the **Saba Museum,** which has a display of pre-Columbian artifacts found on Saba. It is open Mon to Fri from 10 a.m. to noon and 1 to 3:30 p.m. There is a small donation for admission.

Mount Scenery: From Windwardside a series of 1,064 steps rise through the misty rain forest rich in flora and fauna to the summit of 2,855-foot Mount Scenery—well named for the magnificent panoramas of the Caribbean and neighboring islands that are there to reward hikers. Most trekkers take a picnic lunch and make a day of the climb to enjoy the views and lush vegetation along the way. If you have less time and energy, you can hike to one of several other locations on trails that have been developed by the **Saba Conservation Foundation** (Fort Bay, Saba, N.A.; 599-416-3295; www.sabapark.org).

My Kitchen (Windwardside; 599-416-2539; caru@unspoiledqueen.com) is located near the

Mount Scenery trailhead; you can pick up lunch to carry on your hike. **Scout's Place** (Windwardside; 599-416-2205) restaurant and bar offers a variety of dishes, such as Saba lobster, spit-roasted chicken, and the catch-of-the-day at reasonable prices.

Rainforest Restaurant (599-416-3888; www.ecolodge-saba.com), the restaurant of the Ecolodge, changes its menu daily depending on what can be gotten fresh from its garden and the sea. Moderate.

The Bottom: From Windwardside the road descends to The Bottom, another doll-like village of white clapboard houses with red gabled roofs and neat little gardens. The former **Government Guesthouse,** one of the town's most historic buildings, is Antique Inn.

Saba Artisans' Foundation: At the **Saba Artisans' Foundation** (599-416-3260) you can find needlework, silk-screened fabrics, beachwear, and other island specialties. Open 8 a.m. to noon. and 2:30 to 5 p.m.

Saba Marine Park: Saba's steep volcanic cliffs drop beneath the sea as vertical walls encrusted with a fantastic variety of reefs and other marine life. To protect this treasure, the Saba Marine Park was developed with the help of the Netherlands Antilles National Park Foundation, the World Wildlife Fund of the Netherlands, and others. The park comprises the entire shoreline and seabed from the high-water mark to a depth of 200 feet and two offshore seamounts. It has twenty-six self-guided underwater trails and areas designated for recreation. The park was developed under the guidance of Tom van't Hof, who also directed the marine parks in Bonaire and Curaçao and has written a guidebook to the park. The main dive areas are on the west coast. **Ladder Bay** to **Torrens Point** is an all-purpose recreational zone and includes Saba's only "beach," a stretch of pebble shore with shallow water.

Saba Deep Dive Center (599-416-3347; fax: 599-416-3397; 888-DIVE-SABA; www.sabadeep.com), **Saba Divers** (Scout's Place; 599-416-2740; www.sabadivers.com), and **Sea Saba** (599-416-2246; 800-883-SABA; www.seasaba.com) are the island's fully equipped dive operators with their own dive boats. Each offers several dive trips daily and arranges fishing excursions. The Saba Bank,

3 miles southwest of Saba, is a 32-mile region of shallow water where fishing is terrific. Sea Saba's Web site publishes a newsletter with information on the dive operators' PADI/National Geographic program, a link to its "Sea & Learn" program, and updates and calendar of events of interest to divers and environmentalists.

Sightseeing: Taxis with driver/guides are available at the airport for tours of the island, or, for those who arrive by boat, at Fort Bay, the port on the southwest corner of the island. Guided nature tours of Mount Scenery and other locations can be arranged through the Saba Tourist Office in Windwardside.

Ferry Service: From St. Maarten, *The Edge,* a high-speed ferry, departs Wed to Sun at 9 a.m. from Pelican Marina and returns by 5 p.m.; $65 round-trip adults, $35 children. *Dawn II* (www.sabactransport.com) leaves from Dock Maarten Tues, Thurs, and Sat, $80 round-trip adult, $35 child age two through twelve, same day return.

Telephone Area Code: To phone Saba from the United States, dial 011-599-41 plus the local number.

Information: www.sabatourism.com

From the United States: Saba and St. Eustatius Tourist Information Office, P.O. Box 527, Windwardside, Saba, N.A.; iluvsaba@unspoiledqueen.com

In Saba: Saba Tourist Office, Windwardside, Saba, N.A.; 599-416-2231, 599-416-2322; fax: 599-416-2350; iluvsaba@unspoiledqueen.com; holmglen@hotmail.com

St. Eustatius: A Cruel Twist of Fate

Statia, as St. Eustatius is known, is ten minutes by plane south of Saba. You may need all the imagination you can summon to believe it today, but this island of only 8 square miles was once the richest free port in the Americas, with a population of 8,000 (it has 2,089 today), where everything from cotton to contraband from around the world was traded. In the first two hundred years after Columbus discovered it, the island changed hands twenty-two times!

Fort Oranje: During the American Revolution the neutral position of Holland, which had claimed the island in 1640, was suspect to the British because St. Eustatius was used as a transit point for arms and goods destined for the rebels. On Nov 16, 1776, after the island's garrison saluted the *Andrew Doria* flying the American flag—the first foreign port to do so after the United States declared its independence—the gesture so enraged the British that they sacked the town and destroyed the harbor. The late Barbara Tuchman's book *The First Salute,* published in 1988, is based on this incident.

In one of history's saddest cases of overkill, the British navy left the Dutch flag up long enough to lure 150 merchant ships into the harbor, then confiscated their cargo, burned the town to the ground, and, as the coup de grâce, destroyed the harbor's breakwater. The grand houses and warehouses tumbled into the sea. The island never recovered.

More recent research debunks this version of the events, which has become the embellished truth of local lore. Under President Franklin D. Roosevelt, the United States expressed its belated thanks, and the fort and other buildings dating from the 18th century were restored with U.S. help. Although we can wonder why, Statia-America Day, celebrated on Nov 16, is one of the island's main events.

Oranjestad: The little town of Oranjestad is divided into two parts. Upper Town, a pretty little community of palm-shaded, cobblestoned streets lined with West Indian gingerbread-trimmed houses and flowering gardens, grew up around the old fort atop a 150-foot cliff overlooking the sea. Lower Town, the site of the famous old harbor, is the docking area today, and to the north is the island's main beach. Only a few feet beneath the sea rests centuries-old debris that has led researchers to call Statia "an archaeologist's nightmare and a scuba diver's dream." The two parts of town are connected by the cobblestoned pedestrian walk and a paved road.

St. Eustatius Historical Foundation Museum (Simon Doncker House, Oranjestad,

599-318-2693, www.steustatiushistory.org, secar@ hotmail.com) A colonial house near the fort contains the town's museum, which displays artifacts from Indian settlements dating from A.D. 300, as well as 17th- and 18th-century artifacts found in the underwater ruins of warehouses, wharfs, and shipwrecks. You can get a brochure with a map for a self-guided tour of the fort and surrounding historic buildings. These include the old Government House, a Dutch Reform church, a synagogue that was probably the second or third created in the Western Hemisphere, and other ruins from the 18th century.

The Quill: The crater of an extinct volcano that dominates the south end of the island, the Quill can be seen distinctively in the island's silhouette. A series of eight signposted trails has been developed, enabling you to hike up to and around the crater's rim, down into the cone, and around the outside of the cone at about midgirth. The hikes were designed as a series of contiguous trails that can take from one hour up to a full day.

The most popular trail leads from town up the western slope of the crater to the rim in about an hour. It meets another trail, which is a steep path down to the floor of the crater, passing through steamy thick foliage where trees, protected from winds and hurricanes, grow tall. Their trunks and branches are entwined with enormous elephant ears, other vines, and sometimes tiny orchids. The crater's interior is planted with bananas, but over the years it has been cultivated with coffee, cacao, and cinnamon trees, which now grow wild.

Stenapa (St. Eustatius Marine and National Parks Foundation), a nongovernmental organization for conservation and protection of the natural and cultural heritage of St. Eustatius, manages the national parks. In 1997 the island council adopted the Protection of Flora and Fauna ordinance, which gave particular areas of the island protective status, including the higher parts of the Quill and certain plant and animal species For information: STENAPA, Gallowsbay, P.O. Box 59, St. Eustatius, N.A.; 599-318-2814; fax: 599-318-2913; www.statia park.org.

St. Eustatius Marine Park (www.statiapark .org/parks/marine), opened in 1998, is being developed east of St. Eustatius. Scuba divers have a heyday exploring the ruins of the houses and warehouses in the old harbor that have lain undisturbed for two hundred years. Farther out the sea bottom is littered with hundreds of shipwrecks, some dating back three hundred years. Atop this jumble corals grow, attracting a great variety of fish and marine life. That combination of coral reefs, marine life, and historic shipwrecks, all untouched by commercial development, is what makes Statia extraordinary and so exciting to divers. Most diving is in 20 to 80 feet of crystal-clear water, which makes it accessible to snorkelers, too.

Sixteen sites have been charted to date—a descriptive map is available on the park's Web site. The most popular, dubbed the Supermarket, is located about half mile off the coast from Lower Town at a 60-foot depth. It has two shipwrecks less than 50 yards apart, with patches of beautiful coral and colorful sponges growing over them. There are also rare fish here; the flying gurnards are the most intriguing. About 12 inches long, these fish are black with white spots and iridescent blue pectoral wings, and they move through the water like hovering birds. The park maintains twelve yacht moorings in the bay (yellow buoys) and charges a yacht fee, $10 per night or $30 per week. Snorkelers wishing to use the moorings must buy a dive tag: $3 for a single dive or $15 for an annual pass. Fees go toward maintenance, cleaning, and rope replacement of the moorings.

In 2002 the St. Eustatius government acquired the 300-foot *Charles L. Brown,* a vessel used for cable-laying by AT&T, to be an artificial reef. The vessel crossed many oceans to arrive in Statia. The Web site also provides links to the St. Eustatius Office of Tourism and to Statia's three local dive operators: **Dive Statia** (Lower Town; 599-318-2435; 866-614-3491; United States; 405-843-7846; www.divestatia.com), the island's first water-sports operator, with its own boats making two or three dives daily; **Golden Rock Dive Center** (P.O. Box 93; Lower Town, St. Eustatius; 800-311-6658; 599-318-2964; www.goldenrockdive.com), which offers one-tank dives for $45, two-tank for $75, and snorkeling for $25; and **Scubaqua** (Blue Bead Restaurant; 599-318-2160; www.scubaqua.com), operated by a professional Swiss group.

Interisland Air Service: St. Eustatius is a ten-minute flight south of Saba or seventeen minutes from St. Maarten. Winair has five flights daily; round-trip airfare is about $100. The airport is located mid-island, about 1.5 miles from town. There you can arrange a tour by taxi or rent a car. Donkeys can be hired for climbing up to the crater.

Telephone Area Code: To phone St. Eustatius from the United States, dial 011-599 plus the local number.

Information: www.statiatourism.com

In St. Eustatius: St. Eustatius Tourist Bureau, Fort Oranjestraat 3, Oranjestad, St. Eustatius, N.A.; 599-318-2433 or 599-318-2213.

Anguilla: Tranquility Wrapped in Blue

Anguilla is a British colony that has the distinction of rebelling to remain a colony. Until its super deluxe resorts were spread across the pages of slick travel and fashion magazines in the 1980s, Anguilla was the best-kept secret in the Caribbean. The small coral island 5 miles north of St. Martin is especially noted for its three dozen gleaming white-sand beaches—which you can have practically to yourself—and the clear, blue-green waters surrounding it.

Known to its original Arawak Indian inhabitants as *Malliouhana,* the island takes its name from the French word for eel, *anguille,* or the Spanish, *anguilla*—they were both here—because of its shape. In the past, when it had only a few tiny hotels and guesthouses, the tranquil island appealed to true beachcombers who cared little for social conveniences. Yachtsmen, too, have long been attracted to the spectacular waters around Anguilla, as have snorkelers and scuba divers from neighboring islands. Two large reefs with huge coral formations growing to the surface of the sea lie off the island's shores.

Even with all the attention, the island's unspoiled quality remains. But then, the Anguillans are as appealing as their island. Until the tourism boom began, most were fishermen supplying the restaurants in St. Martin. The 16-mile-long island got its first golf course in 2006, but it still has no casinos, and there may still be as many goats and sheep as people.

Several of the super deluxe hotels attracted much of the attention. **Cap Juluca,** a sybaritic fantasy in Moorish design, graces one of the most magnificent powdery white-sand beaches in the Caribbean. **Malliouhana,** on the island's northwest coast overlooking two spectacular beaches, is Mediterranean in design with graceful interiors by Larry Peabody, known for his stylish decor in other Caribbean resorts. If you want to do any more than look—perhaps have a meal—you will need to make arrangements in advance and be prepared to spend US$100 for lunch.

For such a small island, Anguilla has an extraordinary number of good restaurants; there were eighty at last count.

Hibernia (Island Harbour; 264-264-497-4290; www.hiberniarestaurant.com) is one of the best restaurants in Anguilla. The French owner is a serious chef who smokes his own fish and knows how to combine Asian flavors with fine French cuisine—all to be enjoyed on a terrace overlooking the Caribbean.

Oliver's Seafood Grill (Long Bay, 264-497-8780; www.olivers.ai), set on a double deck by the beach, serves seafood and a refined version of West Indian specialties.

Overlook (South Hill, 264-497-4488), set on a hillside overlooking Sandy Ground, offers fresh fish and Caribbean selections.

PADI dive centers—**Shoal Bay Scuba** (264-497-4371; www.shoalbayscuba.com), directly on Shoal Bay East, and **Anguillan Divers** (264-497-4750; www.anguilliandiver.com), at Meads Bay in the west. Both offer instruction and dive packages.

In 1990 the Anguillan government took its first major step at marine-resource management. Six wrecks resting by Anguilla's shores were towed to sea and sunk to create artificial reefs that have become nurseries for fish and new sites for divers. Their removal also eliminated a potential boating and marine hazard in Road Bay, the island's main harbor.

Concerned about the phenomenal growth in the 1980s, Anguilla created a National Trust with a permanent staff to oversee the preservation of the island's cultural and national heritage and direct already-active volunteer organizations. These include the Archaeological and Historical Society, which organized in 1979 the first scientific survey of the island, which unearthed thirty-three sites of antiquity; the Horticultural Society, which organizes periodic cleanup and beautification drives; the Marine Heritage Society, the driving force behind the creation of marine parks; and various cultural groups working to preserve Anguilla's folklore, music, and other traditions.

Telephone Area Code: 264

Information: www.anguilla-vacation.com

In the United States: Anguilla Tourist Information Office, (877) 4-ANGUILLA; 246 Central Ave., White Plains, NY 10606; (914) 287-2400; fax: (914) 287-2404; mwturnstyle@aol.com

In Anguilla: Anguilla Tourist Board, Coronation Avenue, The Valley, Anguilla, B.W.I.; (264) 497-2759; (800) 553-4939; fax: (264) 497-2710; atbtour@ anguillanet.com

Anguilla Life, a quarterly published by veteran Caribbean writer Claire Devener, is a valuable source of information. Contact P.O. Box 1622, Anguilla, B.W.I.; (264) 497-3080; www.anguilla-beaches.com; anguillalife@anguillanet.com

PART FIVE

The Eastern Caribbean

Antigua
St. John's, Falmouth, English Harbour, Antigua; Codrington, Barbuda

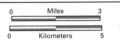

Antigua

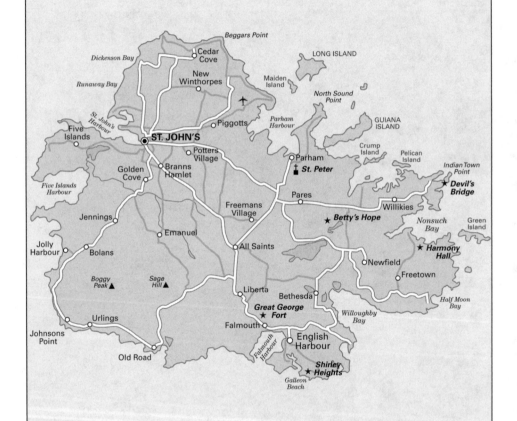

ATLANTIC   OCEAN

Beggars Point

LONG ISLAND

Dickenson Bay

Cedar
Cove

New
Winthorpes

*Maiden
Island*

*North Sound
Point*

GUIANA
ISLAND

Runaway Bay

Piggotts

*Parham
Harbour*

*St. John's
Harbour*

Five
Islands

ST. JOHN'S

Potters
Village

Parham

✝ **St. Peter**

*Crump
Island*

*Pelican
Island*

*Indian Town
Point*

★ **Devil's
Bridge**

Golden
Cove

Branns
Hamlet

Pares

Willikies

*Five Islands
Harbour*

Freemans
Village

★ **Betty's Hope**

*Nonsuch
Bay*

*Green
Island*

Jennings

Emanuel

All Saints

★ **Harmony
Hall**

Jolly
Harbour

Bolans

Newfield

Freetown

*Boggy
Peak* ▲

*Sage
Hill* ▲

Liberta

Bethesda

*Willoughby
Bay*

*Half Moon
Bay*

Urlings

**Great George
★ Fort**

Falmouth

English
Harbour

Johnsons
Point

*Falmouth
Harbour*

Old Road

**Shirley
★ Heights**

*Galleon
Beach*

CARIBBEAN   SEA

A Beach for Every Day of the Year

Relaxed and quietly sophisticated, Antigua is a mecca for those who love the sea. Shaped roughly like a maple leaf, the protruding fingers provide Antigua's coastline with sheltered bays, natural harbors, and extra miles of beautiful beaches—one for every day of the year, the Antiguans say. The coral reefs that fringe the island are a magnet for snorkelers and scuba divers. Together these assets have made Antigua one of the most popular beach and water-sports centers in the Caribbean. As a bonus, low humidity coupled with year-round trade winds create a wonderful climate for tennis, golf, horseback riding, and a variety of other sports—and, of course, for sightseeing.

Antigua (pronounced an-TEE-ga) is the largest of the Leeward Islands. Barbuda, its sister island 30 miles to the north, is largely undeveloped; the third member, Redonda, 36 miles to the southwest, is uninhabited. Located at the heart of the Caribbean, east of Puerto Rico and the Virgin Islands between the French and Dutch West Indies, Antigua is a transportation hub of the region.

Settled by the British in 1632, Antigua was Britain's most strategic Caribbean colony for two centuries due to her protected harbors and position on the trade routes, with the winds blowing almost year-round from the east. The island's historic character is most evident at English Harbour, where the buildings of the old wharf, known as Nelson's Dockyard, have been restored. The British legacy is also seen in the island's passion for cricket, afternoon tea, and driving on the left side of the road.

Of the eighty or more archaeological sites found here, the oldest dates back more than four thousand years to the Ciboney, a Stone Age people about whom little is known. The most extensive excavations have been those of the Arawak Indians, who arrived in Yarumaqui, as they called Antigua, about A.D. 500. They remained about five centuries and moved north, probably to flee pursuing Carib Indians, a warlike people after whom the Caribbean is named.

Wadadli, the Carib name for the island, was sighted by Columbus in 1493. He did not come ashore, but he did name the island Santa Maria de la Antigua, after the virgin saint of the Cathedral of Seville in Spain. Attempts by the Spaniards, and later the French, to settle the island were unsuccessful. Then in 1632 English settlers from St. Kitts, led by Edward Warner, the son of Thomas Warner, who founded the first settlement on St. Kitts, came ashore near Old Road on the south coast, where they established a colony. Except for a brief French occupation in 1666, Antigua remained British for the next three hundred years.

The first settlers cleared the land and planted tobacco, a crop they learned from the Arawaks. But in time tobacco was replaced by sugar, and slaves were imported from Africa to work the cane fields. The island was divided into estates, and a plantation society developed that lasted well into the 20th century. Much of this history is reflected today in village, family, and location names.

In 1784 Horatio Nelson, who later became one of Britain's most celebrated admirals, took command of the Leeward Islands Squadron in which the future king, William IV, served as captain of the HMS *Pegasus*. Antigua became the New World headquarters for the Royal Navy, and English Harbour, as it is known today, was strongly fortified.

After the abolition of slavery in 1834, the sugar-based economies of the Caribbean declined, and the introduction of the steamship changed the course of trade between the Old and New Worlds. For the next century Antigua, like so much of the Caribbean, was largely ignored by its colonial masters. During World War II, the island became a U.S. military base, and the impact was immediate. It brought jobs, new roads, piers, an airport, and technicians, who helped to train Antiguans in skills that served the local population well after the war.

In 1958 Britain granted Antigua and its other colonies semiautonomous status in the West Indies Federation. In 1967 Antigua, with Barbuda and Redonda, became an Associated State within the Commonwealth, governing its own internal affairs. Finally in 1981 full independence was achieved. After two decades on its own, Antigua was transformed from an agricultural economy to a service one, with tourism the major source of jobs and revenue.

Budget Planning

Taxi fares are high, and unless you have others with whom to share them, sightseeing by taxi is expensive. Car rental is more reasonable and recommended. Aside from taxis, prices in Antigua are moderate, and restaurants serving local or West Indian cuisine are inexpensive.

Port Profile: St. John's

Location/Embarkation: St. John's, the capital, is located on the island's northwest Caribbean coast at the head of a deepwater harbor. A pier at the foot of town enables passengers to walk off their ships directly into Heritage Quay, a shopping, food, and entertainment complex. Antigua Deepwater Harbour, another pier on the north side of the harbor about a mile from town, is used for large ships and when there are more ships than the town pier can accommodate. Yachts and some small cruise ships often arrive at English Harbour, one of the prettiest yacht basins in the Caribbean, or at neighboring Falmouth Harbour, both on the southeastern coast.

Local Transportation: The distance from the pier at Deepwater Harbour to St. John's is short enough to walk, but most visitors prefer to take a taxi because the only place to walk is in the road. Taxis are plentiful and cost US$11 and can be shared by up to four people for the ride into town. From St. John's to the airport costs about US$15; to Nelson's Dockyard costs about US$31 one-way. A bus route called "Coolidge" runs from St. John's to the airport area. A taxi with the driver acting as guide can be hired for touring. Rates are set by the government and tend to be expensive, costing US$25 per hour for up to four persons, negotiable for more, or about US$100 and up for an island tour. Be sure to set the price in advance and to confirm whether the price quoted is in U.S. or EC dollars. Local buses are not useful for cruise passengers.

Roads and Rentals: If you have an adventurous spirit, the ideal way to tour the island is by self-drive car. Antigua has an extensive network of roads, but driving can be a bit difficult due to narrow, winding roads that are not well marked. Also, traffic in this former British colony moves on the LEFT. A good map is essential, but even with it, roads can be confusing: Expect to get lost several times. Happily, the Antiguans are friendly and helpful, although not very precise in giving directions; you might need to ask for directions several times. Basically, the road system fans out from St. John's on major arteries that loop around each area of the island—north, southeast, southwest—making it easy to leave from the capital by one route and return by another.

Rental cars and jeeps are reasonably priced, costing from about US$55 to $65 per day for a small car with unlimited mileage plus a set insurance rate of US$10 daily. During the winter season demand is often greater than supply and cars can be difficult to obtain; reservations are recommended. Avis, Budget, Dollar, Hertz, National, Thrifty are represented in addition to some local companies. You'll need a local driver's license, which the car-rental agency will obtain for you upon presentation of a valid U.S. or Canadian one; the fee is US$20. Before starting out be sure to have a full tank of gasoline; there are few gas stations on some roads outside of St. John's.

Shore Excursions

With advance arrangements, local travel companies can tailor a tour to your specifications by using a private car with a driver/guide. But whether on an organized tour in a minibus or by car, local guides are not well trained and cannot be depended upon for much commentary. The shore excursions most often available on cruise ships follow; prices are per person and may vary from ship to ship. Details on the sites are described later in this chapter.

Historic Antigua: 3 hours, US$54. Drive across the heart of the island to English Harbour, Clarence House, and Shirley Heights.

Antigua by Sea: 6 hours, US$94. A coastline sail on a luxury catamaran with stop at Green Island for lunch and snorkeling.

Antigua Canopy Tour: 3.5 hours, US$99. Nine ziplines, two suspension bridges, and optional parachute jump offer a bird's-eye view of the rain forest (268-562-6366; www.antiguarainforest.com).

Population: 80,000

Size: Antigua, 108 square miles; Barbuda, 62 square miles

Main Town: St. John's

Government: Antigua has a parliamentary government headed by a prime minister and is a member of the British Commonwealth. The queen is represented by a governor general.

Currency: Eastern Caribbean (EC) dollar. US$1 equals EC$2.70. Major credit cards and U.S. dollars are widely accepted. Since both currencies are rendered in "dollars," be sure to determine which currency is being discussed whenever you negotiate the price of a service or commodity.

Departure Tax: US$28

Emergency Numbers: Medical: Holberton Hospital, Hospital Road, St. John's; 24-hour service, 268-462-0251; Ambulance: 268-462-0251; Police: 268-462-0125

Language: English has been the language of Antigua for three centuries and adds to the ease of getting around.

Public Holidays: Jan 1, New Year's Day; Good Friday and Easter Monday; Labor Day, first Mon in May; Whit Mon; Queen's Official Birthday, second Sat in June; Carnival, first Mon and Tues in Aug; Nov 1, Independence Day; Dec 25, Christmas; Dec 26, Boxing Day. Although not a public holiday, Sailing Week in mid-late Apr is one of the biggest events of the year and commands the attention of most people.

Telephone Area Code: 268

Airlines: *From North America:* American Airlines, Continental Airlines, Delta Airlines, and US Airways; American Eagle flies from San Juan. Antigua's airport is headquarters for LIAT (Leeward Islands Air Transport; www.liat.com), offering frequent service to the neighboring islands of the Eastern Caribbean as does Caribbean Airlines (www.caribbeanairlines.com) and Winair. Carib Aviation (268-481-2403) operates charters as well as scheduled flights to Barbuda, a trip of ten minutes, and neighboring islands.

Information: www.antigua-barbuda.org; www.searchantigua.com; www.antiguanice.com

In the United States:

Antigua and Barbuda Department of Tourism, 305 East Forty-seventh St., Suite 6A, New York, NY 10017; (212) 541-4117; fax: (212) 541-4789; info@antigua-barbuda.org

25 Southeast Second Ave., No. 300; Miami, FL 33131; (305) 381-6762; fax: (305) 381-7908

In Canada:

Antigua and Barbuda Department of Tourism, 60 St. Clair Ave. East, Toronto, ON M4T 1N5; (416) 961-3085; fax: (416) 961-7218; info@antigua-barbuda-ca.com

In Antigua:

Antigua Tourist Board, Ministry of Tourism, Queen Elizabeth Highway, Box 363, St. John's, Antigua, W.I.; (268) 462-0029, (268) 462-0480; fax: (268) 462-2483. There's also an information office at the Heritage Quay by the port in St. John's. Antigua Historical and Archaeological Society, Museum of Antigua and Barbuda, P.O. Box 103, Market Street, St. John's, Antigua; (268) 463-1060. National Parks Authority, Box 1283, St. John's, Antigua; (268) 481-5028; www.nationalparksantigua.com.

Flight-seeing: Caribbean Helicopters (268-460-5900; www.caribbeanhelicopters.com), operates out of Jolly Harbour, offers half-island tour from about US$85 per person, US$150 for a full-island tour; and a Montserrat Volcano Tour for US$220. Arrange in advance.

Cuisine Tour: Up to 4 hours; about $100 per person. Nichole's Table offers informal cooking classes in Caribbean cuisine for up to 12 people, held in West Indian–style house near Cedar Valley Golf Course, about 10 minutes from St. John's. Takeaway menus and recipes provided (Carib-World Travel, 268-480-2999; reservations@nicolestable.com).

Nature Tours: Valley Ventures (268-723-5858; www.venturesantigua.com) in Christian Valley in the south west offers guided hikes, including to Mount Obama for US$45 per person and horseback ride at the beach for US$50 per person, among others.

Swim with Stingrays: 3 hours, US$69. Short boat ride to calm shallow waters of Stingray City, where you can pet, feed, and learn about Southern Stingrays in their natural environment and snorkel on a coral reef (268-562-7297; stingray@candw.ag).

Barbuda Day Excursion: Adventure Antigua operates day excursion to Barbuda via powerboat that takes about one-and-a-half hours (268-726-6355; www.adventureantigua.com).

Routes Caribbean Adventure Tours (877-768-8370; www.islandroutes.com) has a range of tours for cruise passengers including transfers from the cruise ship terminal.

Kayak/Hiking/Golf/Snorkel Eco-adventure (see Sports later in this chapter).

Antigua on Your Own

Antigua's capital was a sleepy West Indian town that was transformed into a new town by the tourist boom over the past two decades.

A St. John's Walkabout

One of the island's oldest ports, settled in the early 17th century, St. John's was once a scruffy town of hard-drinking sailors and traders and an unsavory reputation to match. It was laid out formally in 1702 and given city status in 1842. Through the centuries the town suffered destruction by fires, hurricanes, and earthquakes, yet enough of its historic buildings and West Indian architecture remain to give it character. The most historic and interesting area is a grid of 6 blocks in the heart of town, best seen on foot in an easy hour's walk.

Redcliffe Quay (1): On the waterfront on the west side of town is a group of former warehouses and other buildings that have been restored and made into attractive boutiques, restaurants, and offices. To the west is pretty **Heritage Quay (2),** a shopping, food, and entertainment center of two stories built around an open-air plaza. Although modern in design, its architecture incorporates colonial and West Indian

elements that blend into the old town. The **Tourist Information Office and the post office (3)** (Thames Street) are a block to the north.

Museum of Antigua and Barbuda (4): The oldest structure in use in St. John's now houses the Museum of Antigua and Barbuda (Market and Long Streets; 268-462-1469; www.antiguamuseums.org). An 18th-century courthouse built from white stone quarried from an island off the northeast coast, the building has been repaired and rebuilt many times over the centuries. It housed the island's parliament until 1974, when the building was damaged by an earthquake. The renovations were undertaken by the Antigua Historical and Archaeological Society with the aid of Canada, UNESCO, and private donors to create the museum. There is no admission fee, but a US$2 donation is suggested. Hours: Mon to Thurs 8.30 a.m. to 4 p.m.; Fri 8.30 a.m. to 3 p.m.; Sat 10 a.m. to 2 p.m.

The collection includes Arawak and pre-Columbian artifacts found in Antigua; other displays interpret Antigua's history from the colonial period to independence. Hours: Mon to Thurs 8 a.m. to 4 p.m.; Fri 8:30 a.m. to 3 p.m.; Sat 10 a.m. to 2 p.m.; 268-462-1469; museum@candw.ag. The Historical and Archaeological Society, which operates the museum, sponsors tours and invites membership.

St. John's Cathedral (5): On the highest rise of town stands the Cathedral of St. John the Divine (Newgate Street and Church Lane), dating from 1847. It is on the site of earlier churches. The first church, dedicated in 1683, was a wooden structure built by the island's largest plantation owner, Sir Christopher Codrington. The iron railings at the entrance date from 1789. The figures of John the Baptist and John the Evangelist at the south gate, originally destined for Dominica, were the spoils of war for an English man-of-war, taken from a French ship in the early 19th century. The church has two towers, topped with silver cupolas; the interior is faced with pitch pine, a type of pine that yields pitch and is intended to strengthen the structure to withstand hurricanes and earthquakes.

Behind the church is **Government House (6),** dating from the 17th century. Originally two houses, one of which was the residence of the minister for the parish of St. John's, it was bought as a residence by Lord Lavington of Carlisle Estate in 1801.

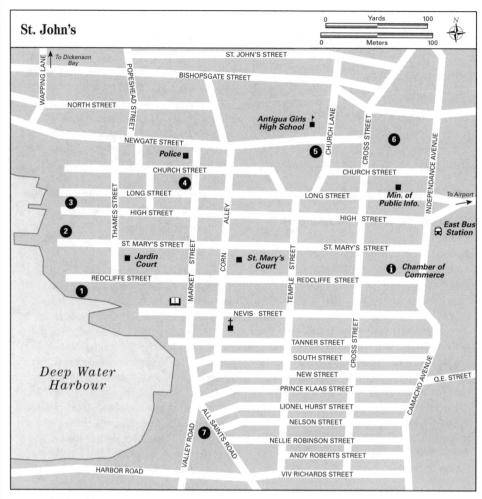

St. John's

1. Redcliffe Quay
2. Heritage Quay and town pier
3. Tourist Information Office and Post Office
4. Museum of Antigua and Barbuda
5. St. John's Cathedral
6. Government House
7. Public Market

Today it is the official residence of the governor general of Antigua and generally is not open to the public.

Public Market (7): By the waterfront on the south end of Market Street is the Public Market, a particularly lively, colorful scene on Fri and Sat mornings and a good place for an introduction to Antigua's local produce and some of the exotic fruits and vegetables of the Caribbean. Next door is the Industrial School for the Blind, where a limited selection of handcrafts is on sale.

St. John's Point, the tip of a 2-mile scenic headland on the north side of the harbor, has the remains of **Fort James,** built in the early 18th century, with ten of its original thirty-six cannons. Its counterpart, **Fort Barrington,** crowns a promontory known as Goat Hill, on the south side of the harbor. The forts, part of the extensive British military installations, attest to the island's strategic importance in colonial times.

Sea View Farm Village: One of Antigua's oldest traditions is pottery making, dating back to the early 18th century, when slaves fashioned cooking vessels from local clay. Today folk pottery is fashioned in several locations, but the center is Sea View Farm Village, west of St. John's. The pottery can be purchased at outlets in the village as well as in shops around the island. Be aware, however, that this pottery can break easily in cold climates.

A Drive Around Antigua

South to Falmouth and English Harbour

Southwest of St. John's along the Caribbean coast are some of Antigua's prettiest beaches. The most immediate road west from St. John's leads to the Royal Antiguan, the island's largest hotel. Secondary roads take you to the Five Islands area, a part of the island with beautiful beaches and reefs and offshore islets popular for boating and water sports.

The main road from St. John's to the southwest coast runs inland through Jennings, the turnoff to 595-foot **Green Castle Hill,** the remnant of a volcano with rock formations whose origin is unknown. A trail climbs to the top. Immediately before Johnson's Point on the southwest tip are **Jolly Beach,** with a large resort, and **Dark Wood Beach,** an exquisite stretch of white sand on the quiet Caribbean, popular with cruise ships for their crews on R&R.

Boggy Peak/Mount Obama: Upon the election of Barak Obama as president of the United States, Antigua changed the name of Boggy Peak to Mount Obama, the highest point on the island (marked by a communications tower). A road inland leads to the top of the hill. The area is famous for the Antigua black pineapple, an unusually sweet, delicious variety cultivated here. Offshore is the 2.5-mile-long Cades Reef, part of which is a marine park.

Old Road: The hamlet of Old Road, at Carlisle Bay, marks the site of the first English settlement in 1632. Curtain Bluff Hotel, perched on a small bluff overlooking two lovely beaches, is one of Antigua's most attractive resorts, embraced in magnificent flowering gardens. Directly on Carlisle Bay is another of the island's luxury resorts named after the bay.

Fig Tree Drive: At Old Road the main route turns inland onto Fig Tree Drive (fig is the Antiguan name for the banana plant) and winds through the hills between Old Road and the village of John Hughes. The 3-mile, sometimes bumpy stretch, overhung with tropical vegetation, is called "The Rain Forest" locally, because the area is more lush than the dry landscape typical of most of Antigua. It's now the location of the zipline attraction.

Antigua's hilly south coast between Old Road and Falmouth is popular for hiking on footpaths leading to hilltops and cliffsides for panoramic views and to beautiful, secluded beaches, otherwise accessible only by boat.

Liberta and Monks Hill: At the tiny village of Swetes en route to Falmouth, the main road bends southeast to Liberta, one of the first settlements founded by freed slaves after the emancipation in 1834. The church of **St. Barnabas,** the parish church, dates from the 19th century. East of Liberta a road leads to Monks Hill and remnants of **Fort George,** built by the British in the 17th century primarily as a place of refuge for women and children in times of attack. The road—used for walking or driving—is marked with a sign to the village of **Table Hill Gordon,** a steep hike of about an hour to Monks Hill. The rough road, best negotiated by jeep, rewards you with fabulous views.

Falmouth: The port of Falmouth, set on a pretty bay, was once Antigua's capital and now is an occasional port of call for small ship. It is surrounded by former sugar plantations whose old mills dot the landscape here as they do throughout Antigua. The restored **St. George's Church,** dating from the 17th century, is one of the island's oldest churches. The Antigua Yacht Club is located here.

English Harbour: A small inlet on the southeast coast barely visible from the sea is one of the best natural harbors in the Caribbean, deep enough for oceangoing ships. Thanks to its deep water, hidden opening, and protective hills sheltering it from hurricanes and providing strategic positions for defense, the harbor served as the main base of the British Admiralty in the West Indies. Throughout the 18th and 19th centuries, it was a base of operations for such famous British admirals as Nelson and Rodney and played a major role in helping to establish British naval superiority over the French.

The naval base, constructed between 1725 and 1746, occupied a narrow promontory that juts into the bay and separates English Harbour from Falmouth Harbour. A series of fortifications were added at the harbor and on the ridge surrounding it. The hills on the east are known as **Shirley Heights,** named for the governor of the Leewards who built the hilltop installations. After the Battle of Waterloo and peace in 1815, English Harbour's strategic importance began to decline. It was formally closed as a royal dockyard in 1889 and fell into decay until 1931, when an effort was launched to preserve the site.

Nelson's Dockyard: English Harbour (www .antiguamuseums.org/nelsonsdockyard.htm), today one of the busiest yacht basins in the region, is still appreciated by sailors. Reconstruction of the old dockyard, now called Nelson's Dockyard after the British admiral, began in 1951 and was officially reopened in 1961, but another decade was needed to complete the task. The beautifully restored historic buildings house charming shops, museums, inns, restaurants, and a marina. The **Admiral's House,** Nelson's former residence, contains a museum of colonial history. (Hours: 8 a.m. to 5 p.m. year-round, Sun and holidays included.) Admiral's Inn is a hotel with a terrace restaurant overlooking the harbor. The old **Copper and Lumber Store** is also a hotel furnished in colonial style. An entrance fee of US$5 includes a guided tour of the dockyard, which is now part of the national park.

Clarence House: The 18th-century residence of Prince William Henry, Duke of Clarence and later King William IV, who was based here as commander of the HMS *Pegasus* in 1787, stands on a hill overlooking English Harbour. The Georgian manor, furnished with antiques loaned by the British National Trust, is now the country house of the governor of Antigua and can be visited. A guide is on duty.

Dow's Hill Interpretation Centre: Operated by the national park, the center is a must stop for those interested in the island's history, culture, and natural attractions. "Reflections in the Sun,"

a multimedia presentation, traces the history of Antigua and Barbuda from prehistoric times to the present. The center is on a hilltop above Nelson's Dockyard en route to Shirley Heights.

Shirley Heights: The military installations on the hillside east of the harbor have been restored and contain a small museum and a restaurant, **The Lookout** (268-728-0636). The main attraction, though, is the magnificent view overlooking English and Falmouth Harbours, the hills, and south coast of Antigua. On a clear day you can see as far away as Redonda and Montserrat, 32 miles to the southwest. The Heights is a popular place to watch a fabulous Antiguan sunset. Jammin' at the Heights is a Sunday tradition, when half the island is on hand to dance, hang out, and watch the sunset.

The **Lookout Trail,** a nature walk created by the National Parks Authority (268-460-1379; www .nationalparksantigua.com), leaves from Galleon Beach Hotel on the east side of English Harbour. A descriptive pamphlet for a self-guided hike, available from the Parks Authority, explains the traditional uses of the trees and plants you'll see along the way. The hike is not difficult and takes about forty minutes to go up and fifteen minutes to descend. Wear sneakers or similar shoes.

A secondary road winds over the heights to **Dow's Hill,** a site used by NASA for a tracking station during the Apollo program. The former NASA building now houses the **Antigua University of Health and Sciences.** Here a footpath leads to Bat's Cave, a small cavern with hundreds of bats.

The fastest return to St. John's from English Harbour is across the center of the island via All Saints, a pretty little village where pottery making is a traditional craft.

North of St. John's

Antigua's main resort center is north of the capital, along the Caribbean coast. The stretch of sand closest to St. John's, known as Runaway Beach, is often used by cruise ships for their "day-at-the-beach" excursions. At the south end, you will find **Miller's by the Sea** (268-462-9414), a beachside restaurant, water-sports, and entertainment center. In recent years, it has become the most popular location for cruise-ship beach excursions, but you can easily go on your own. There's live music at lunch and in the evenings with a different band each day and a beach barbecue on Thurs. Dickinson Bay and Hodges Bay, farther north, have the largest concentration of hotels. Water sports are available from vendors at resorts along the beach. You'll find good snorkeling here.

Parham: Directly east of St. John's on the northeast coast, the little settlement of Parham was the first capital of Antigua. **St. Peter's Church,** built in 1840 to replace an earlier church destroyed by fire, was designed by Thomas Weekes, a famous architect of the time, who was brought from Britain for the purpose. About a mile northeast of Parham is **Crabbs Slipway and Marina,** a boating center and a port of entry for yachts. The area is popular for biking tours.

Great Bird Island National Park (www .antiguamuseums.org/natural.htm): An uninhabited islet offshore, with a pretty little beach, the park is popular for day-sailing excursions. The limestone cliffs of Great Bird Island are home to the red-billed tropic bird that can be seen gliding on the wind currents blowing in from the Atlantic. Bird Island and nearby cays have good snorkeling. There is a trail up to a great view of the Atlantic Ocean from the 100-foot-high cliffs. Some cruise lines offer a sailing excursion for about US$79, including lunch. Local tour companies in St. John's can arrange the trip as a private excursion. Contact **Kiskidee Travel & Tours,** Briggins Road (268-462-4801; fax: 268-462-4802); or **Nicholson's Travel Agency** (268-463-7391); or **Tropical Adventures** (268-480-1122; www.tropicalad.com).

East to the Atlantic Coast

From St. John's, two roads lead east to the Atlantic coast. The more northerly one passes through the villages of Pares and Willikies to Indian Town Creek, a national park on the northeast corner of Antigua. En route feeder roads and tracks extend to the north coast, an area sheltered by cays and reefs that provide calm waters for sailing, snorkeling, and fishing.

Betty's Hope (www.antiguamuseums.org): Near Pares a signposted road turns inland to the ruins of the first large sugar plantation in Antigua, Betty's Hope, founded in the 1650s and granted to Sir Christopher Codrington, a prosperous planter

from Barbados, in 1668. Codrington is credited with introducing large-scale sugar cultivation and innovative processing methods in Antigua. The success of Betty's Hope, named for Sir Christopher's daughter, is said to have led other planters to turn from tobacco and indigo to sugarcane as their main crop.

Codrington and his son served as governor-general of the Leeward Islands, developing the plantation as the seat of government. The estate remained in the Codrington family until 1944. The ruins include two windmill towers and arches of the boiling house, among other structures.

In 1990 a $10 million restoration project was launched to restore Betty's Hope for use as a cultural center and historic attraction. The fundraising activities are spearheaded jointly by the government, business and civic leaders, Partners of the Americas (Rochester, New York—Antigua's sister city), and Antigua Historical Society. There is an interpretive center in the old stables. Hours: Tues to Sat 10 a.m. to 4 p.m. Entrance: US$5. Call 268-462-1469.

Indian Town National Park: The main road beyond Willikies ends at Grand Pineapple Beach, an all-inclusive resort on Long Bay. Tracks branch out across the northeastern peninsula to pretty coves. In a deep cove known as Indian Town Point is Devil's Bridge, a natural bridge that has been carved out of the rocks by the relentless waves of the Atlantic. Alongside it, "blowing holes" send jets of water high into the air. The south side of the peninsula overlooks Nonsuch Bay, one of the prettiest bays on the Atlantic coast, protected by coral reefs. Offshore Green Island is a nature preserve. The reef between Green Island and tiny, uninhabited York Island is a popular area for day-trippers.

The southerly of the two roads from St. John's to the east coast skirts Potworks Reservoir for almost 2 miles. The largest of Antigua's numerous man-made catchments and one of the largest bodies of freshwater in the Eastern Caribbean, it has a pretty wooded setting, popular for bird-watching.

Shopping

The best shopping is found in the heart of St. John's along St. Mary's, High, Redcliffe, and Market Streets, the oldest thoroughfares, where many shops are housed in colorful historic buildings of West Indian architecture. Here you will find a variety of locally made clothing, straw products, pottery, paintings, batiks, and jewelry with local semiprecious stones. Locally made rum and liquor prices are some of the lowest in the Caribbean. The downtown area is relatively small, and shops are within easy walking distance of one another. Stores are open daily (except Sun) 9 a.m. to 5 p.m. Many take an hour's noontime lunch break.

Heritage Quay (www.stjohnsdevelopment .com), a shopping and entertainment complex located directly at the pier, was built with cruise-ship passengers in mind. The center has more than forty stores with high-quality merchandise such as English bone china, French crystal and perfumes, Italian leather, and Swiss watches at duty-free prices.

Art and Artists: Until its recent sale, **Harmony Hall** (Brown's Bay; 268-460-4120; www .harmonyhallantigua.com) was a branch of the well-known art gallery in Jamaica. It stocks work by quality Antiguan, and other Caribbean artists and holds exhibitions frequently. The gallery is part of a six-room inn and outdoor restaurant with a delightful setting on an old sugar plantation. It's almost an hour's drive from St. John's, but worth a stop, if you plan to spend a day rambling about the island. Normally, the gallery closes for the summer months. Among other galleries are **Art Loft** (Lower St. Mary's Street; 268-721-2343), featuring Antiguan artists; **Elvie's Pottery** (Seaview Farm; 268-463-1888), which exhibits authentic Antiguan terra-cotta–colored clay pottery; **Fine Art Framing** (Redcliffe Quay; 268-562-1019), which carries an interesting range of original art and photography by local and regional artists; and **Rhythm of Blue Gallery** (English Harbour; 268-562-2230; arawak art@yahoo.com) with pottery by Nancy Nicholson, scrimshaw by Michael Strzalkowski, as well as paintings, photographs, and sculpture by other leading local artists. Open Nov to Apr.

Books/Maps: The **Map Shop** (High Street; 268-462-3993; cesmap@candw.ag) stocks maps of Antigua and the Caribbean and reproductions of antique maps, as well as postcards and stationery. It also sells British Admiralty charts. BB, the **Best of Books Bookshop** (St. Mary's Street; 268-562-3198; bestofbooks@yahoo.com) carries a wide range of books as well as newspapers.

Clothing: **Benetton** (Heritage Quay; 268-462-3273; www.benetton.com), the well-known Italian clothing and accessories chain, has sportswear in bright coordinated colors. **Sun Seekers** (Heritage Quay; 268-462-3618; www.sunseekers.com) stocks a large selection of swimwear. **Island Woman Boutique** (7 Redcliffe Quay; 268-462-4220) carries locally designed leisure wear for men and women, jazzy swimwear from Jamaica and Brazil, fun design T-shirts, and stuffed batik animals for children. **Noreen Phillips Couturiere** (Redcliffe Quay; 268-462-3127; www.noreenphillipscouturiere.com) designs a full line from elegant casual wear to sophisticated evening wear, which the shop claims can be made in two hours. The **Galley Boutique** (English Harbour; 268-460-1525), the shop of designer Janie Easton, stocks casual clothes and sportswear by the owner and others. Particularly attractive are the fashions by John Warden, a designer from St. Kitts. **A Thousand Flowers** (Redcliffe Quay; 268-462-4264) carries great cottons, accessories, and footwear, ideal for island travel.

Crafts and Souvenirs: The **Pottery Shop** (Redcliffe Quay; 268-462-5503; www.sarahfuller pottery.com) carries mugs, vases, plates, and other pottery made in Antigua. If you are traveling around the island, check out **Cedars Pottery** (Buckley Rd.; 268-460-5293), where a team of potters makes brightly decorated tableware and sculptures. **Jacaranda** (Upper Redcliffe Quay; 268-462-1888) stocks island spices, herbs, teas, and cosmetics, along with prints by Bajan artist Jill Walker. **Shipwreck Shop** (Heritage Quay, 2nd Floor; 268-562-4625) specializes in gifts indigenous to Antigua and the Caribbean, local art, books, and magazines.

Jewelry: The **Goldsmitty** (Redcliffe Quay; 268-462-4601; www.goldsmitty.com) makes fine, handcrafted gold jewelry of original design, often using local stones. **Colombian Emeralds** (Heritage Quay), a major gem dealer, has stores throughout the Caribbean. **Abbott's Jewellery & Perfumery** (Heritage Quay; 268-462-3107) is an authorized dealer for Rolex, Gucci, and other famous brands.

Leather and Luggage: Millennium (Heritage Quay; 268-462-3076) sells top name-brand leatherwear as well as jewelry. **Land** (Heritage Quay; 268-462-0746) carries bags, shoes, and accessories.

Linens: The Linen Shop (Heritage Quay; 268-462-3611) specializes in imported hand-embroidered tablecloths, table mats, sheets, towels, and bedspreads at low prices.

Perfumes: Lipstick (Heritage Quay; 268-562-1130) offers an excellent selection of French perfumes as well as cosmetics and skin care products. There is a similar store in St. Martin, **Q-rios** (Heritage Quay, 268-562-6370).

Smokes: Quin and Farara & Co. (Heritage Quay, www.quinfarara.com) has a large selection of Cuban cigars, kept in a walk-in humidor.

Dining and Restaurants

Antigua is an island of many different lifestyles, reflected in its variety of restaurants—from rustic taverns by the beach, English pubs, and unpretentious establishments for West Indian food to elegant dining rooms where jacket and tie are required. Seafood is a specialty, with fresh local lobster and conch at the top of the list. Exotic Caribbean vegetables include christophene (a type of squash), dasheen (a leafy plant similar to spinach), plantains, and breadfruit. The Antigua black pineapple is one of the sweetest, best-tasting kinds anywhere; mangoes, papayas, and coconuts are abundant. Rum turns up in many recipes and drinks. Normally restaurants open daily for lunch and dinner, unless noted otherwise. This being the laid-back Caribbean, however, it is always wise to check in advance.

St. John's and Environs

The Beach Restaurant (Dickenson Bay; 268-480-6940; www.bigbanana-antigua.com) offers great international cuisine by the beach. Antigua's hot spot on Fri evenings. Moderate. Same group operates Big Banana (Airport) and **Pizzas in Paradise** (Redcliffe Quay; 268-480-6985; www.bigbanana-antigua.com) which has live music on Thurs at lunchtime. Open Mon to Sat 8:30 a.m. to midnight. Moderate.

Coconut Grove (Siboney Beach Club, Dickinson Bay; 268-462-1538; www.coconutgroveantigua.net). Pretty, romantic beachfront setting, specializing in seafood. Live music during the winter season. Reservations advised. Moderate.

Hemingways (St. Mary's Street; 268-462-2763). Second-floor bar and restaurant is situated in one of the oldest houses of West Indian gingerbread, with an attractive veranda overlooking the town center. Great variety of tropical drinks are featured, along with salads, seafood, and sandwiches. Moderate.

Home Restaurant (Gambles Terrace, Luther George Place; 268-461-7651; www.thehomerestaurant.com), made famous by CNN, which featured owner-chef Carl Thomas for his seafood and local dishes. Dinner only.

Cocos (Valley Church; 268-460-2626; www.cocoshotel.com), on a hillside on the south coast with a stunning view of the Caribbean, has a great wine list and a menu of fresh-caught fish and spicy local dishes that make this a popular spot for locals as well as guests. Moderately expensive.

English Harbour

Admiral's Inn (Nelson's Dockyard; 268-463-1027; www.admiralsantigua.com). Built in 1788 as offices for the naval engineers, the inn's tree-shaded dining terrace overlooking the harbor provides one of Antigua's most pleasant settings for seafood and light lunches. Moderate.

OJ's (Crabbe Hill Beach; 268-460-0184). A beachside bar and restaurant is the perfect place to kick back island-style. OJ is famous for his grilled red snapper, and if you have to wait it's only because they're catching it. Open for lunch and dinner with live entertainment on Sun. Moderate.

Nightlife

Nightlife revolves around hotels, small bars, and discos. Almost any evening there will be a barbecue, with steel band music, at one of the hotels. The casinos are **King's Casino** (Heritage Quay; www.kingscasino.com); **Grand Bay Casino**, adjacent to Sandals Grand Antigua; **Paradise Casino** (Runaway Bay). The **Coast Night Club, Bar and Restaurant** (Heritage Quay; 268-562-6278; www

.coast.ag) is the hot late-night party spot and in addition to live music and local DJs, the club offers free WiFi access in both the bar and restaurant. **Rush Entertainment Centre** (Dickerson Bay) has options: piano lounge, sports bar, casino, and upscale restaurant.

Sports

Antigua has some of the best sports facilities in the Caribbean for swimming, sailing, and tennis. In most cases you should contact the sports operator or hotel in advance to make arrangements, particularly during the peak season, when demand is likely to be high.

Beaches/Swimming: Many people would say the best reason to visit Antigua is its beaches— frequently ranked by Caribbean aficionados as the best in the region—and there are plenty of them. Antigua's maple leaf shape gives it extra miles of shore, with beaches in little coves hidden between rocky fingers and long, powdery white sands that often stretch for a mile. Some beaches can be reached only by hiking or from a boat; others have bars, restaurants, music, and facilities for water sports.

The beaches closest to the port are at **Runaway** and **Dickinson Bays** on the north, **Deep Bay** and **Hawksbill** on the south (where one of Hawksbill's four beaches is clothing optional). All are on the Caribbean, or leeward, side, where the sea is calm and gentle. The beaches on the Atlantic, or windward, coast often have wave action and surf, but many coves are protected by reefs and have calm water.

Biking: Bike Plus (St. John's; 268-462-2453) has bicycles for US$17.50 per day. **Paradise Rentals & Charters** (Jolly Harbour; 268-460-7125; www .paradiseboats.com) rents mountain bikes and kid's bikes for US$15 per day. Also rents scooters. **Cheke's Scooter & Car Rental** (268-562-4646; cell: 268-773-3508; chekescooter@hotmail.com) has scooters for US$35–$40 per day. Drivers must be at least eighteen years old and have a valid driving license and temporary Antiguan driving license (cost: US$20).

Boating: Trade winds blowing 90 percent of the year from the east, the spectacular water surrounding the island, the variety of anchorages and sheltered coves with pretty beaches and reefs, plus splendid facilities all have made Antigua one of the major boating centers of the Caribbean. There are daily cruises around Antigua and picnic sails to nearby islands. The large boats have steel-band music and make quite a party of it. **Excellence** (268-480-1225; www.tropicalad.com) is among the most popular and likely to be sold as an excursion by your cruise ship. Others offering day sailing or power catamaran trips are **Wadadli Cats** (268-462-4792; www.wadadlicats.com); **Jabberwocky Yacht Charters** (268-764-0595; www.adventure caribbean.com) offers a 50-foot yacht with crew for two to ten, from US$110 per person with skipper, chef, gourmet lunch and wine, and snorkeling. **Capt. Nash Sailing Cruises** (268-560-0014; nash@ caribbean-marketing.net) caters to small groups.

English Harbour is the main marina and headquarters for **Nicholson Yacht Charters** (www .nicholsonyachts.com), one of the Caribbean's oldest, most respected operations, with an international reputation. Its founders spearheaded the renovation of Nelson's Dockyard. Regattas are held year-round, but for true salts Antigua is the place to be in mid/late Apr when the island hosts **Sailing Week,** the Caribbean's most prestigious annual yachting event, attracting sailing greats and would-be greats from around the world. Since its inception in the 1960s, Sailing Week has become to sailing what Wimbledon is to tennis.

Fishing: Overdraft (268-464-4954; www.antigua fishing.com) has a fully equipped 40-foot sportfishing boat available for four-hour ($495) to eight-hour ($790) charters. Rates include boat, captain, mate, bait and tackle, and soft and alcoholic beverages for up to six persons. **Antigua & Barbuda Sport Fishing Club** (268-460-7400; cell: 268-726-4700; www.antiguabarbudasportfishing.com) holds an Annual Sport Fishing Tournament. Also see www .fishantigua.com.

Golf: The Cedar Valley Golf Club (268-462-0161; www.cedarvalleygolf.ag), located 3 miles from St. John's, has an 18-hole course (6,077 yards, par 70). Greens fees are US$48 for 18 holes; golf cart, US$42; rental clubs, US$30. There is a pro shop and snack bar. **Jolly Harbour Golf Course** (268-462-7771; golf@jollyharbourantigua.com) is an 18-hole course designed by golf course architect Karl Litton of Florida. The course (6,001 yards, par 71) is open to visitors on a daily fee basis. Greens fees are US$57.50 for 18 holes; golf cart, US$40.25; rental clubs, US$28.75.

Hiking: The Historical and Archaeological Society organizes monthly hikes. Inquire at the Antiquities Museum in St. John's. Antigua has a web of dirt roads and tracks that wander from main roads to beaches, where you can swim, or into woodlands and along ponds for bird-watching. The only marked trails are those leading to the heights above English Harbour and a 7-mile marked trail system in the area of **Wallings Reservoir** (268-462-1007). There are short hikes in the hills of the south coast between Old Road and Falmouth that take 30 minutes or an hour to reach lovely beaches accessible only by hiking or by boat. Rendezvous Bay, one of the island's most spectacular beaches, can be reached from Falmouth by four-wheel-drive vehicles or a hike of about forty-five minutes.

Horseback Riding: Spring Hill Riding Club (Falmouth; 268-773-3139; www.springhillridingclub .com) is home to the Antigua & Barbuda Horse Society. The stable offers a two-hour trail ride to Rendezvous Bay, which can be reached only by boat, jeep, or on foot. Another very steep trail leads to Monks Hill, from which there are magnificent views.

Kayaking: Look for turtles and other surprises of nature in bays and coves near Willikies and Seatons. **Tropical Adventures Antigua** (268-480-1225; www.tropicalad.com) offers kayaking, sailing, and jeep safari tours. **Antigua Paddles Kayak Eco Trips** (268-463-1944; www.antiguapaddles .com) include kayaking, swimming, snorkeling, and nature walks on an uninhabited island. From the fisherman's cottage clubhouse at Seatons Village, participants go by motorboat through Mercer's Creek to a long raft where kayaks are moored. After a safety briefing, guides lead the group to tiny islands and fish spawning areas and explain mangrove ecosystems. After kayaking and

refreshments, motorboats whisk the group across to North Sound National Park to Bird Island and snorkeling over coral reefs. The company is a member of the Antigua Environmental Eco Awareness Group.

Snorkeling/Scuba Diving: Antigua is surrounded by coral reefs in crystal-clear, shallow water, ideal for snorkelers. Almost all beaches and offshore islands have reefs within swimming distance or a short boat ride from shore. With a few exceptions diving is in shallow water at sites of less than a 60-foot depth, where colorful reef fish are abundant. North of St. John's above Dickinson Bay is **Paradise Reef,** a popular area for snorkeling. Fronting the palm-fringed beaches on the east coast are miles of reefs that break Atlantic waves and provide calm waters for snorkelers.

South of the capital along the west coast at **Hawksbill Rock,** there is a cave in 15 feet of water. **Sunken Rock,** which drops to a depth of 122 feet, is a deep dive for experienced divers. Along the drop-off divers see sting rays, barracudas, and occasional dolphins.

Cades Reef, a 2.5-mile-long reef about a mile off Cades Bay on the south coast, is typical of the reefs around Antigua. It is dominated by staghorn and elkhorn coral in the shallow areas and rich with colorful reef fish, such as parrotfish and blue tang. Visibility ranges from 80 to 150 feet. The reef is one of Antigua's main dive sites; part of it has been designated a marine park. The most popular of the six wrecks close to Antigua is the *Andes,* a three-masted, fully rigged merchant vessel that sank in 1905. It is located south of St. John's harbor by Deep Bay in only 20 feet of water.

Among the half-dozen dive shops belonging to the **Antigua Dive Operators Association** (www .divetravel.netfirms.com), are **Deep Bay Divers** (268-463-8000), with several locations; **Jolly Dive** (Jolly Beach Resort; 268-462-8305; www.jollydive .com); and **Indigo Divers** (Jolly Harbour; 268-729-3483; www.indigo-divers.com).

Stingray City Antigua: In the lee of a barrier reef on the eastern (Atlantic) side of Antigua, is an area dubbed **Stingray City Antigua** (268-562-7297; www.stingraycityantigua.com; stingray@ candw.ag). Here Southern Stingray have lived for centuries. Excursions depart from the fishing village of Seatons by powerboat to the barrier reef, where guides who are former fishermen take you swimming in the clear water with the rays. You will discover they are like big puppies. Departure times: 9 and 11 a.m., 1 p.m. $50. Snorkeling gear is provided, but ground transportation to Seatons may not be.

Tennis and Squash: Antigua's low humidity makes it suitable for tennis, a sport very popular here. More than a dozen hotels have courts. **Curtain Bluff** often hosts Tennis Week in May, when tournaments feature top-seeded players. **Temo Sports** (English Harbour; 268-463-6376) is a tennis and squash complex. It has locker rooms and showers, snack bar, and pro shop. Courts must be reserved.

Windsurfing/Kitesurfing: The same trade winds that made Antigua a haven for ships of yesteryear and attract yachts today have made it a windsurfing mecca, too. Most beachside hotels have boards for rent. The quiet seas and gentle breezes along the Caribbean shores are ideal for beginners. Strong winds varying from 12 to 25 knots and seas with 2- to 3-foot chops on the Atlantic side attract experienced enthusiasts. Antigua has several internationally known windsurfing schools. Windsurfing Antigua Week, the annual international competition, is usually held in Jan.

Windsurf Antigua (Jabberwock Beach; 268-461-WIND; www.windsurfantigua.net) offers instructions and rentals.

One of Antigua's fastest growing sports was a natural development for an island long known for excellent windsurfing. KiteSurfAntigua (Jabberwock Beach; 268-720-5483; www.kitesurfantigua.com) is affiliated with the International Kiteboarding Organisation (IKO), and adheres to industrywide teaching standards. Lessons, conducted by certified instructors, are an absolute requirement for this extreme sport. All courses from beginners to advanced are taught in two-hour sessions, at 9 a.m. and 1 p.m. daily. Two weeks advance booking is recommended. Open full-time Dec to Aug; closed Sept to Nov (open weather permitting and upon request). Antigua Adventures (268-726-6355; www.antiguaadventures.com) offers quad biking,

fishing, kitesurfing, and an Xtreme visit to Stingray City Antigua.

Festivals and Celebrations

Antigua Sailing Week in late Apr or early May is the most important annual yachting event in the Caribbean. Carnival in Antigua began two decades ago as festivities to celebrate the visit of Queen Elizabeth II. The Antiguans had so much fun doing it, they repeated the celebration the following year, and the next, until it grew into an annual event. Since independence in 1981, Carnival has become an eleven-day arts festival highlighting the island's culture and heritage with parades and other competitions. It is held in late July and early Aug before Emancipation Week, which begins the first Mon in Aug.

Barbuda

Barbuda, Antigua's sister island, is a nature lover's paradise. Scalloped with miles of pink-sand beaches and fringed by reefs, the coral island is a sparsely settled wilderness interspersed with lagoons, marshes, and mangroves, which are home to the largest frigate-bird sanctuary in the Eastern Caribbean. Located 30 miles north of Antigua, the largely undeveloped island is only 143 feet above sea level at its highest point. Codrington, where most of the island's 1,500 people live, is the only village.

Codrington Lagoon: A large estuary along the west coast is the mating ground for thousands of magnificent frigate birds. During the mating season, from late Aug to Dec, the sight is fantastic. Every bush appears to have a dozen or more females on it, and a few feet overhead dozens of males with wingspans up to 8 feet glide through the air in display, ballooning their red throat pouches to get the attention of the flapping females.

Boats are available in Codrington for the short trip to the middle of the lagoon, where you can watch and photograph the birds within a few feet of the bushes. In addition to the frigate bird, Barbuda is said to have 170 bird species. Other wildlife includes white-tailed deer and boar.

South of Codrington in the area of Palmetto Point are the island's most beautiful pink-sand beaches. Offshore, Palaster Reef is a marine reserve established in 1972 to protect the reef, its pristine waters, and historic shipwrecks. **George Jeffries Tours** (Barbuda; 268-460-0143) excursions, including the frigate bird sanctuary, for US$50 for the boat up to four people or US$12 per person over four people, plus US$2 per person dock tax. If you cannot contact him, **Paradise Tours Barbuda** (268-772-0661) operates the same tour for US$25 per person, for a maximum of eight persons to a boat (by law). The company is run by Linton Thomas, the executive chairman of Barbuda's Tourist Board.

Barbuda Ferry: *The Barbuda Express* (268-560-7989; www.antiguaferries.com), an 85-foot power catamaran, departs St. John's daily for Barbuda at 8:30 a.m. and returns by 5 p.m. for US$50 round-trip. The ferry also offers a day tour from St. John's to Barbuda on Wed, Thurs, and Sun, 8:15 a.m. to 4 p.m., for $120. The boat makes the Atlantic crossing to Barbuda in about an hour.

St. Barthélemy (St. Barts)

Gustavia

St. Barts

ATLANTIC   OCEAN

ÎLE CHEVREAU

Anse de
Colombier

Anse Paschal

Anse des
Flamands

Pointe
Étages

Île de
la Petite
Jean

○ Colombier

Les Grenadiers ○

La Tortue

Pointe Lorient

Anse de Marigot

Anse de Grand Cul-de-Sac

Anse de Petit Cul-de-Sac

Anse de
Cayes

Anse de
Lorient

Marigot
○

Grand
Cul-de-Sac
○

○ Corossol

Anse à
Corossol

Baise de
Jean

Lorient
○

Vitet ○

Anse de Public

✈

Les Islettes

□ St. Jean

Morne
du Vitet ▲

Les Saintes ○

● GUSTAVIA

○ Lurin

Morne de
Grand Fond ▲

Anse de
Toiny

Grande
Saline

Anse de
Grand Fond

Grande Pointe

Anse du
Gouverneur

Anse de
Grand Saline

CARIBBEAN   SEA

The Darling of the Jet Set

A seductive paradise of scenic beauty at first sight, serendipitous upon acquaintance, St. Barthélemy—or St. Barts, as it is better known—is a stylish hideaway, 15 miles southeast of St. Maarten. The smallest of the French West Indies, St. Barts is a tiny Eden of green mountains and miniature valleys overlooking two dozen gorgeous white-sand beaches and turquoise water.

Discovered five decades ago by the Rockefellers and Rothschilds, it is something of a St. Tropez-in-the-Tropics, attracting jet-setters and a host of show-biz celebrities and all those who follow in their wake. But the lot of them are mere Johnny-come-latelies. The island was probably inhabited first by the Arawaks. Christopher Columbus came upon the island in 1493 and named it for his brother's patron saint, Bartolomeo. The first French colonists arrived in 1648 from St. Kitts and were followed by the Knights of Malta. After raids by the fierce Carib Indians, the island was abandoned until 1673, when it was again settled by Frenchmen from Normandy and Brittany.

In 1784 the French sold St. Barts to Sweden in exchange for trading rights elsewhere. The Swedes renamed the harbor Gustavia in honor of their king, declared it a free port, and profited handsomely from the enterprise. France repurchased the island in 1878, retaining its free port status to this day.

In addition to being the only Caribbean island the Swedes ever possessed, St. Barts has other features that make it different. Too dry and rocky to be coveted for agriculture, the little island attracted only small farmers who had to scratch for a living. It was never converted to a sugar economy as was most other Caribbean islands, slaves were never imported, and the plantation society typical of the colonial Caribbean never developed here.

Rather, St. Barts is a minuscule remnant of ancient France, with neat little villages surrounded by meadows marked with centuries-old stone fences, and fair-skinned farmers and blue-eyed fishermen who speak a dialect of their 17th-century Norman ancestors that even Frenchmen cannot understand. Against this background of a conservative, closely knit society with Old World traditions,

St. Barts became a modern playground of worldly French sophistication for the rich and famous from both sides of the Atlantic.

Budget Planning

St. Barts offers the best that money can buy—and you will need plenty of it. It is one of the most expensive islands in the Caribbean, particularly so for its restaurants, which are comparable to top New York ones and often cost US$100 or more per person for lunch or dinner. On the other hand, day-sailing excursions and car rentals are reasonable. French products are slightly less than in the United States but, generally, more than on the neighboring St. Martin.

Port Profile: Gustavia

Embarkation/Location: The pretty, yacht-filled harbor of Gustavia is located on the south side of the island. Small cruise ships usually steam directly into the harbor but do not dock; instead, they tender passengers the short ride to the wharf. Larger ships remain outside the harbor and tender passengers to the dock. Bordering the harbor on three sides are fashionable boutiques and outdoor cafes with an unmistakable French ambience.

Local Transportation: There is no public bus system, but since the island is so small—only 25 miles of road—you can walk to many locations. There is a taxi station on rue de la République and another at the airport. You can also call for a taxi (0590-27-66-31). Taxi fare for up to three persons per car from Gustavia to St. Jean Beach is about €5 for rides up to five minutes long and €4 each additional three minutes. After 8 p.m. and on Sun and holidays, fares have a 50 percent surcharge.

Roads and Rentals: The best way to tour St. Barts is by car, which can be rented for about €55–65 per day in winter and €45–55 in the summer with unlimited mileage. Gas is extra. Advance reservations are necessary, especially during the winter season, but be aware that some agencies require a two- or three-day minimum rental. The island has two gas stations; neither is open on Sun. Not all car-rental companies take major credit

Population: 7,000

Size: Approximately 10 square miles

Main Town: Gustavia

Government: St. Barts and neighboring St. Martin officially broke away from Guadeloupe on July 15, 2007, becoming Overseas Collectivities. Considered French territories, the residents have full French citizenship like those on the mainland. St. Barts is run by a territorial council with a president and executive council.

Currency: Euro. US$1 fluctuates at about 1 euro equals about US$1.32. U.S. dollars are widely accepted, and prices are often quoted in dollars. Check locally as the dollar fluctuates constantly against the euro.

Departure Tax: About €5.

Emergency Numbers: Medical: Gustavia Hospital, 0590-27-60-00 or 0590-27-60-35; Police: 0590-27-66-66

Firearms: Yachts are permitted to have firearms aboard, but they must be declared. Otherwise visitors are not allowed to bring them into St. Barts.

Language: French is the official language; the local dialect stems from old Norman speech and is hard to understand, even for Frenchmen.

Public Holidays: Jan 1, New Year's Day; May 1, Labor Day; May, Ascension Thurs; May, Pentecost Mon; July 14, Bastille Day; Aug 15, Assumption Day and St. Barts/Pitea Day, which commemorates the twinning in 1977 of St. Barts and Pitea, Sweden; Nov 1, All Saints Day; Nov 2, All Souls Day; Nov 11, Armistice Day; Dec 25, Christmas.

Telephone Area Code: 590. To call St. Barts from the United States station-to-station, dial 011-0590 plus the St. Barts number; person-to-person, dial 01-0590 plus the St. Barts number. To call St. Barts from other French West Indies islands, dial direct. To call Dutch St. Maarten from St. Barts, dial 00-599-54 plus the St. Maarten number. To call the United States from St. Barts, dial 00-1, followed by the code for the state. To call within the island or Guadeloupe, dial 0590, plus the phone number. For Martinique dial 0596 plus the phone number. There are no coin-operated phones; major credit cards can be used, and telephone cards (Télécartes) are available for purchase.

Airlines: *From the United States to St. Barts:* there are no direct flights. Travelers fly to St. Maarten, San Juan, and other gateways to connect with Winair (599-545-4237; fax: 599-542-2002; www.fly-winair.com), Air Caraibes (0590-27-61-90), St. Barth Commuter (0590-27-54-54; www.st-barths.com/stbarth-commuter). The flight from St. Maarten takes ten minutes. St. Barts's small airport and short landing strip cannot handle anything larger than twenty-seat STOL aircraft. It is not equipped for night landing.

Information: www.st-barths.com

In the United States:

New York: French West Indies Tourist Board, 825 Third Ave., 29th Floor, New York, NY 10022; (212) 745-0950

In Canada:

French Government Tourist Board:

Montreal: 1981 Avenue, McGill College #490, Montreal, QC H3A 2W9; (514) 288-2026; (800) 361-9099; fax: (514) 845-4868

In Port:

Office du Tourisme, Quai General de Gaulle, Gustavia, (0590) 27-87-27; fax: (0590) 27-74-47. Mailing: St. Barts Tourist Office, B.P. 113, Gustavia, 97098 Cedex, St. Barthélemy, F.W.I. Hours: weekdays 8 a.m. to 6 p.m., and 9 a.m. to noon on Sat.

---

cards. The most popular vehicles are open-sided Mini-Mokes, Gurgles, and Volkswagen Beetles—all well suited for the narrow, winding roads and hilly terrain—but drivers of these vehicles need to know how to operate a stick shift. Driving is on the RIGHT side of the road. The speed limit is 28 mph, which suits the roads and terrain—but not the French drivers from the mainland who race around St. Barts as if they were practicing for the Grand Prix.

Motorbikes, mopeds, scooters, and 18-speed mountain bikes are available from **Rent Some Fun** (0590-27-54-83). You'll need to show a motorbike or driver's license, and French law requires drivers to wear helmets. Rentals cost about €35 a day in high season and include helmet and insurance.

Most car-rental firms are located at the airport. There are independent dealers and major names. **Avis/St. Barth Car** (0590-27-71-43; www

.avis-stbarth.com); **Budget/Jean-Marc Greaux** (0590-27.66-30; budgetstbarth@wanadoo.fr); **Hertz/Henri's Car Rental** (0590-27-71-14; hertz .stbarth@wanadoo.fr); and **TropicAll Car Rental** (0590-27-64.76; tropicallrent@saint-barths.com).

Ferry Services: *Voyager* (0590-87-10-68; www.voyager-st-barths.com) departs twice daily from St. Martin for a seventy-five-minute trip; *The Edge* (599-544-2640), a high-speed ferry, leaves once daily, Tues to Sat from Pelican Marina, St. Maarten, and takes forty-five minutes to Gustavia. Fares range from €50–55 one-way; €62–75 round-trip. You can also charter a high-speed boat to pick you up in St. Maarten. Contact **Marine Service** (0590-27-70-34) or **Master Ski Pilou** (www.master ski-pilou.com), who offers a 24/7 St. Maarten water taxi service.

Great Bay Express, a brand new ferry operation belong to the owner of Bobby's Marina in St. Maarten, offers scheduled service between St. Maarten and St. Barts with the 130-passenger *Shantiwa*, a Louisiana-built aluminium 65' monohull flying the Anguilla flag. She has two outside decks (one covered) and one air-conditioned salon. One-way €55 adult, €40 child.

Shore Excursions

Island tours are operated by minibus or by taxi, with the driver acting as guide.

Snorkeling Adventure: 2 hours, US$76. A catamaran cruise to Colombier Bay for snorkeling, including equipment and refreshments.

Semi Submersible: 1 hour, US$99. View marine life while traveling in the *Sea Discoverer,* and pass over the wrecks of the 50-foot freighter *Marginan* and the multimillion-dollar, 110-foot yacht *Non-Stop.*

Trekking in St. Barts: 2 hours, US$94. Ride to Petite Anse in Flamands, where guided hike begins to Anse de Grand Colombies, also known as Rock-efeller Beach, with time for a swim.

St. Barts ATV Adventure: 2 hours, US$169. Explore both the windward and leeward sides of the island following expert guides.

Office du Tourisme can provide a list of independent driver/guides and sailboat operators that provide excursions.

St. Barts on Your Own

The delightful little town of Gustavia with its lilliputian port has a pretty setting: yachts bobbing in the harbor and red-roofed houses climbing the surrounding green hills. Only 3 blocks deep, the town has no must-see historic sites and can be explored easily on foot in an hour, stopping now and then to check out the boutiques and to enjoy refreshments at one of the sidewalk cafes that lend a French air to the setting. A few street signs in Swedish are reminders that the Swedes were here, too.

A Gustavia Walkabout

Old fortifications are located on both sides of the harbor. On the south a five-minute walk passes Fort Karl en route to Petite Anse de Galet, also known as Shell Beach, where there is good shelling. On the north Fort Gustave offers a nice view of the harbor.

The **Town Hall (Mairie de St. Barth)** and some restaurants are housed in old buildings dating from the 18th century. **St. Barth Municipal Museum (Musee Municipal de St. Barthélemy),** on the south side of the harbor, depicts the island's history through photographs, documents, costumes, and antiques. It is open daily.

A steep road by the landmark clock tower on the east side leads over the hill, where a rough road continues to Anse du Gouverneur, a cove with one of the island's most beautiful, secluded beaches bracketed by jagged cliffs. You can see Saba, St. Eustatius, and St. Kitts in the distance.

A Drive Around the Island

The quickest way to get into the St. Barts mode is to rent a Mini-Moke (a canopied jeep) and wander about following your whim. Stop at a beach for a swim or in a village to sip an aperitif, ramble down a country lane, or turn up a road to a hillside for a view. St. Barts can be easily toured by car in half a day. The narrow roads—yesterday's donkey tracks—twist and turn through tiny villages and along rocky shores to secluded, picture-book beaches.

West of Gustavia

On the north side of town, the road forks northeast to the airport and northwest to Corossol, the most traditional of the island's tiny fishing villages, where the old Norman dialect can be heard. Some of Corossol's elderly women still wear long blue-and-white-checkered dresses and the caleche, a stiff-brimmed bonnet derived from 17th-century Breton style. It is sometimes called quichenotte, meaning "kiss me not." The women are very shy and disappear at the first sign of strangers who might try to take their pictures. If you put away your camera and take an interest in the straw hats they want to sell you, you will find the reception quite different. The straw—the finest, most supple in the Caribbean—is handwoven from the fan-shaped fronds of latania palms. Also in Corossol is the Inter Oceans Museum (0590-27-87-27; 0590-27-62-97), a private collection of shells, open daily 10 a.m. to 4 p.m. Admission: about €4.

Farther along, the road winds its way to Anse des Flamands on the north coast, where you will see another of the island's beautiful coves with a wide, half-mile stretch of white sand fringed by latania palms and framed by weather-worn rocks washed by intensely turquoise seas. It is home to several small resorts, including Hotel St. Barth Isle de France, with a popular restaurant. Anse de Colombier on the northwest end is a pretty cove accessible only by foot or boat.

The North Coast and East End

From Gustavia a hilly, twisting road heads northeast, passing the airport and skirting St. Jean Bay on its way to the eastern end. The bay, rimmed by white-sand beaches and bathed by calm, reef-protected turquoise waters, is divided about midpoint by a small promontory topped by tiny Eden Rock (www.edenrockhotel.com), the island's first

hotel, which was renovated and expanded by its new owners in 1997 and quickly reestablished its premier position as the best place to enjoy fabulous views and absorb something of the St. Barts legend, in the place where it began. The bay is the hub of St. Barts's resort and water-sports activity.

Lorient, at the eastern end of St. Jean Bay, is the site of the first French settlement in 1648. Its palm-fringed beach is used by local families, and its long rolling waves make it popular with surfers and Windsurfers. Jutting out to sea between Lorient Bay and Marigot Bay on the east are the jagged cliffs of Milou and Mangin, where Atlantic waves crash against rock. Pointe Milou, almost barren a decade ago, is now a fashionable residential area of elegant homes and resorts.

Rising behind Lorient are the island's highest peaks: 898-foot Morne de Grand Fond on the west and 938-foot Morne du Vitet on the east. One road passes between the mountains to the south coast, another loops around Morne du Vitet via Grand Cul-de-Sac and the south coast, and a third winds up Morne du Vitet. All pass centuries-old rural landscapes of farmhouses, grazing cattle, and patchwork fields outlined by stone fences.

Grand Cul-de-Sac, a large bay on the northeast, is another resort and water-sports center, where shallow, reef-protected waters are ideal for novice Windsurfers and snorkelers. Another road passes over the mountain to Anse de Toiny, with wild landscape that reminds people of the Normandy coast.

Shopping

St. Barts is a duty-free port. Perfumes and famous-brand crystal, silver, china, jewelry, liquor, and tobacco are sold for about 20 percent less than U.S. prices. But as we have said earlier, St. Barts is not a place for bargains. As in most of France, stores close for lunch.

Art and Artists: Pompi (Petit Cul de Sac; 0590-27-75-67) is the local boy who made good. Pompi is an intuitive artist who has his atelier, gallery, and restaurant under one roof. A list of artists and art galleries is found in *Ti Gourmet Saint-Barth*, a local publication issued annually.

Other products on sale include exquisite straw work, woven from latania palm, by the older women in the fishing village of Corossol; lovely jewelry by Annelisa Gee, who also sells it at her boutique **Made in St. Barth** (0590-27-56-57), in St. Jean; and paintings by artists living in St. Barts.

Books and Maps: For books in French and English, try **Librairie de Oasis** (Lorient).

China/Crystal: Several shops around the island carry French china, crystal, and silver; convenient to the port is **Carat** (Quai de la République), which has Baccarat, Lalique, Christofle, and other high-quality brands.

Clothing and Accessories: Boutiques of **Hermés, Louis Vuitton, Ralph Lauren,** and other famous designers are found in Gustavia, St. Jean, and the **La Savane Commercial Center** opposite the airport. A variety of somewhat less expensive stores housed in colorful cottages make up **Villa Creole,** a small shopping mall on St. Jean beach. **Lolita Jaca** (Gustavia; 0590-27-59-98) is best known for straw, leather, or beaded handbags and unusual, sophisticated jewelry; silk and cotton clothing; Lolita's perfume, which comes in a fabric pouch filled with pearls perfumed with the same fragrance, can be used as a sachet. For some specialty shops, **Black Swan** (Gustavia and Villa Creole; 0590-27-65-16) has active sportswear; **C. Demours** (0590-251-14-60) and **Maryvonne & Gerard** (0590-252-37-68), both on rue de la République in Gustavia, have original, one-of-a-kind jewelry designed and crafted in St. Barts.

Crafts and Souvenirs: The women of Corossol and Colombier are famous for their handwoven baskets, broad-brimmed hats for men and women, and handbags, made of delicate, supple straw with designs that resemble old lace. Other locally crafted products include sandals and shell jewelry.

Groceries: If you want to take home some French products, **Match** (St. Jean; 0590-27-68-16) is a useful stop. **Foodland** (Gustavia port; 0590-27-68-37), a grocer-caterer, is patronized by locals and boat people. AMC Grocery is another.

Liqueurs and Wine: Fine French vintages stored in temperature-controlled rooms are found at **La Cave du Port Franc** (Gustavia). The store also sells contemporary paintings and antique objets

d'art. **Cellier du Gouverneur** (Gustavia; 0590-27-99-93) is the place for wines, rums, and passionfruit punch.

Perfumes and Cosmetics: Well-known French labels are available in boutiques, but more unusual are the locally made perfumes, lotions, and suntan oils of natural products. One line, La Ligne de St. Barth (0590-27-82-63; www.lignestbarth .com), is produced and sold by Brigit and Hervé Brin, whose ancestors settled on St. Barts hundreds of years ago. Their boutique and laboratory in Lorient are well worth a visit. Another local face and body product with all natural ingredients is made by **Belou's P d'Helene Muntal**. It includes three body oils named after St. Barts's beaches and a mosquito repellent that nourishes skin as it repels the insects. It is available at Mandarine (www .shopmandarine.com) in Gustavia.

Dining and Restaurants

St. Barts is the gastronomic capital of the Caribbean, where dining is one of the main attractions. Renowned chefs from France frequently visit the island, and some teach classes here during the winter season. Young chefs trained in France's best restaurants come to work in St. Barts, bringing with them a high standard and creativity. By combining local ingredients, Gallic traditions, and modern trends, they have created a new French Caribbean cuisine.

Restaurants are small, and each has something special, either in food, setting, or atmosphere. About half of the ninety or so restaurants are open only for dinner or only during the winter season. Most close on Sun. For three courses without wine, expect to pay per person about US$25 to $30 for a modest meal, $40 to $50 for a moderate one, and $60 and up for an expensive one. Some restaurants do not accept credit cards; inquire in advance.

Gustavia and Environs

La Route des Boucaniers (on the port; 0590-27-73-00; fax: 0590-27-73-05; boucaniers@wanadoo .fr). Lively brasserie overlooking the harbor. Moderately expensive.

Le Bete a Z'ailes (Gustavia port; 0590-29-74-09; bazbar@wanadoo.fr). Sit inside or outside to enjoy the harbor setting, with sailboats bobbing in the water at the shore of the little town, and feast on fresh fish, sushi, sashimi, and pasta salad. Jazz some evenings. Moderately expensive.

L'Esprit Salines (on road to Saline beach; 0590-52-46-10; lesprit3@wanadoo.fr) is in a pretty garden cottage where brothers Guillaume and Christophe prepare refined French fusion cuisine, beautifully presented, in a friendly ambience. Fresh fish specialties are available daily. Moderately expensive.

Maya's (Public Beach; 0590-27-75-73; mayas restaurant@wanadoo.fr). Just around the bend from Gustavia, overlooking the sea, it's the favorite of St. Bart cognoscenti and good for celebrity watching as well as dining. Maya is from Guadeloupe, which is famous for its chefs; her husband is from Nantucket. Menu changes daily and is always fresh. Dinner only; sunset drinks from 4 p.m.; closed Sun. Informal, expensive.

Wall House Restaurant (Quai du Wall House; 0590-27-71-83; fax: 0590-27-69-43). Located in a quiet corner of the harbor, owners Franck and Denis prepare light menus for lunch and more elegant gourmet specialties for dinner to be enjoyed overlooking the water. Moderate.

West of Gustavia

François Plantation (Colombier; 0590-29-80-22; info@francois-plantation.com). Now under new owners, the hillside villa hotel houses one of St. Barts's brightest dining stars. A long arbor covered with blooming vines leads to a plant-filled bar and elegant, terraced dining room with a wine cellar that is partly under a decorative waterfall. The cuisine is French and Mediterranean, and the ambience sophisticated. Dinner only; expensive. Closed Apr 15–Nov 1.

La Case de L'Isle (Hotel Isle de France; 0590-27-61-81; isledefr@saint-barths.com). This intimate beachside eatery of the hotel on Anse des Flamands is one of the island's best. Managed by American Evelyn Weber, the chef de cuisine is Bruce Domain. Moderately expensive.

St. Jean and Beyond

Eden Rock (0590-29-79-99; www.edenrockhotel .com). This completely renovated landmark—St. Barts's first hotel—is worth a visit for the beautiful view, to have a drink at the harbor bar, and to dine in the original bar perched over St. Jean Bay. The Sand Bar, especially popular at lunch, serves grilled fish (and other selections) in a manner reminiscent of the French Riviera and is moderately expensive. The elegant On The Rocks is on the terrace of the original building. Expensive.

Hostellerie des Trois Forces (Vitet; 0590-27-61-25; 3forces@st-barths.com). Grilled shrimp, lobster in basil sauce, fish with fennel, and other dishes are turned out from a wood-burning fireplace and served in the cozy atmosphere of a rustic country inn. The proprietor is an amateur astrologer and yoga practitioner; hotel rooms are named for the signs of the zodiac. Moderate to expensive.

Le Gaiac (Hotel le Toiny; 0590-27-88-88; le toiny@saint-barths.com). If you happen to be on the far eastern side of St. Barts at lunchtime or on a Sunday, you can't do better than the lovely outdoor restaurant setting of this hotel perched high above the sea. Many rate it as the best restaurant on St. Barts. Very expensive.

Nightlife

Leisurely dining is the main evening pastime. St. Barts has no movie houses or casinos. Young locals and visitors gather at such popular hangouts in Gustavia as **Bar de l'Oubli** (0590-27-70-06), where the open porch is a great people-watching spot reminiscent of Saint-Tropez. Its neighbor, **Le Select** (0590-27-86-87), is a long-standing local hangout for snacks, drinks, and people watching. The garden restaurant, **Cheeseburger in Paradise,** is next door; it's named for Jimmy Buffett, an island habitué. *St. Barth Magazine,* a lively French/English publication, is the best source of information on current nighttime attractions.

Sports

St. Barts has good facilities for water sports. You should always contact the hotel or sports operator in advance to make arrangements, particularly during the peak season. There are about a dozen tennis courts but no golf course.

Beaches/Swimming: St. Barts is scalloped with more than two dozen pearly beaches bathed by calm turquoise waters—and few are ever crowded, even in peak season. Signs prohibiting nudism are all around the island, but the teensiest monokini is the fashion. All beaches are public and free.

Anse du Gouverneur, near the port, and Anse de Grande Saline, also on the south coast, are the most secluded beaches; St. Jean on the north coast and Grand Cul-de-Sac on the northeast are the most developed ones, with hotels, restaurants, and water sports.

The Nikki Beach (0590-27-64-64; www.nikki beach.com) has brought a little South Beach and St. Tropez to St. Barts. The beach club, the place to see and be seen, is located on St. Jean beach next to Eden Rock, which certainly doesn't hurt it for attracting a cool crowd. Light lunch and dinner menus include sushi. Moderately expensive.

Boating: St. Barts's popularity for yachting is due in part to its location midway between Antigua and Virgin Gorda, two major sailing centers. Gustavia's harbor, which runs 13 to 16 feet in depth, has mooring and docking facilities. Loulou's Marine (Gustavia; 0590-27-62-74) is known throughout Caribbean yachting circles as one of the best-stocked marine supply stores in the Leeward Islands. The staff speaks English, and its bulletin board is something of a message center.

Sunfish sailing is especially pleasant in St. Barts, because most of the bays have gentle waters. Boats can be rented at St. Jean, Grand Cul-de-Sac, Public, and Colombier beaches.

Ocean Must (0590-27-62-25) and La Marine Service (0590-27-70-34; marine.service.st.barth@wanadoo.fr) have half-day sails and other excursions to nearby beaches and islets. Bare-boat rentals, with gas and ice, cost about €170 for a half day to €400 for a full day at Marine Service. Full-day sailing excursions to Colombier or Ile Fourchue, a desolate island of wild moonscape terrain off the northwest coast, depart Gustavia at about 9 a.m. and return about 5 p.m. The cost is about €110 per person (minimum of four) and includes swimming, snorkeling, cocktails, open bar, and picnic lunch. The island is interesting to explore but hot; bring a generous supply of water, sun protection, and sturdy shoes for hiking.

Deep-Sea Fishing: Fishing charters can be arranged through Ocean Must (0590-27-62-25) and Marine Service (0590-27-70-34). The latter charges about €700 for a half day to €1,200 for a full day, including fishing gear, open bar, and sandwiches for four persons. Popular catches are tuna, bonito, dorado, marlin, and barracuda. Check with local fishermen before eating your catch; not all fish in these waters are edible. Patrick Laplace (0590-27-61-76) is a professional deep-sea fishing guide.

Golf: Golfers, don't get your hopes up, but St. Barts has a small driving range, Golf Driving Range (Cul de Sac; 0590-37-46-45), open in the afternoons.

Hiking: St. Barts's pretty landscapes and country roads with light traffic make walking and hiking popular pastimes. Almost any location is within easy reach, although the hilly terrain and hot sun make distances deceiving.

Horseback Riding: Ranch des Flamands at Anse des Flamands. Contact Laure Nicolas (0590-27-13-87). A two-hour-long excursion that departs at 9 a.m. and 3 p.m. costs €55. Another is St. Barth Equitation (Flamands, 0690-62-99-30).

Snorkeling/Scuba: Diving St. Barts is almost completely surrounded by shallow water reefs, better suited for snorkeling than diving, and often within swimming distance of shore. St. Jean Bay has the most accessible reefs. Equipment can be rented from La Marine Service (0590-27-70-34).

The best dive locations are on the west coast at about 50- to 60-foot depths within easy reach of Gustavia. Immediately outside the harbor is Gros Ilet, a rock poking about 75 feet above the sea, where you can see grouper, snapper, moray eel, lobster, and large schools of reef fish.

Dive operators run boat trips daily. La Marine Service (0590-27-70-34; fax: 0590-27-70-36; www .st-barths.com/marine.service) offers PADI and French certification. Dive trips cost about €75 to €99 per person, gear included. St. Barth Plongee (Gustavia, 0590-41-96-66; birdy.dive@wanadoo.fr) and Plongee Caraibes (Quai de la République; 0590-27-55-94; www.plongee-caraibes.com) also offer PADI certification. The staffs, certified as instructors by their French federation, are familiar with American methods and standards, and the shops maintain American as well as French tanks and regulators. One dive €60; two dives €110, Snorkel, two hours €40; Discover Scuba €80. **Ouanalao Dive St Barth** (Grand Cul de Sac Beach, 0690-63-74-34; www.ouanalao-dive.com, ouanalao-dive@gmail.com) is PADI certified and has three daily diving excursions, at 9 and 11 a.m. and 2.30 p.m., for all skill levels. Also offers snorkeling excursions and private outings upon requests. Gift shop has snorkels, fins, masks, and kayaks for rent.

Surfing: Lorient, east of St. Jean Bay, is the most popular surfing area. You can rent boards at watersports centers and get advice about water conditions at the same time.

Windsurfing/Kiteboarding: Shallow waters and gentle winds make conditions at St. Jean and Grand Cul-de-Sac ideal for learning to windsurf. Rentals are available at beachside water-sports centers. **Carib Water Play** (St. Jean; 0690-61-18-81) and **Wind Wave Power** (St. Barth's Beach Hotel; 0590-27-82-57) offer rentals and lessons.

Rentals average about €30 an hour. Both also offer kayaking. Lorient is the most popular site for experienced sailboarders. Kiteboarding, or Kitesurf, has come to St. Barts, as it has to all the Caribbean. Contact **Kitesurf** (Grand Cul de Sac, 0690-69-26-90; enguerrand7@voila.fr).

Festivals and Celebrations

St. Barts celebrates **Mardi Gras** in the French tradition and has some festivals and events special to the island.

The **St. Barts Music Festival** (www.stbartsmusicfestival.org), under the direction of Frances DeBroff, president of the Pittsburgh Symphony Association, is an annual affair in mid- to late-Jan/early Feb featuring chamber music, dance, and other arts. Artists from the United States and Europe perform in the church of Lorient and at the wharf in Gustavia.

The **Festival of St. Barthélemy,** Aug 24, is the colorful feast day of the island's patron saint. Similarly, the Feast of St. Louis, Aug 25, is celebrated in the village of Corossol.

St. Kitts and Nevis

Basseterre, St. Kitts; Charlestown, Nevis

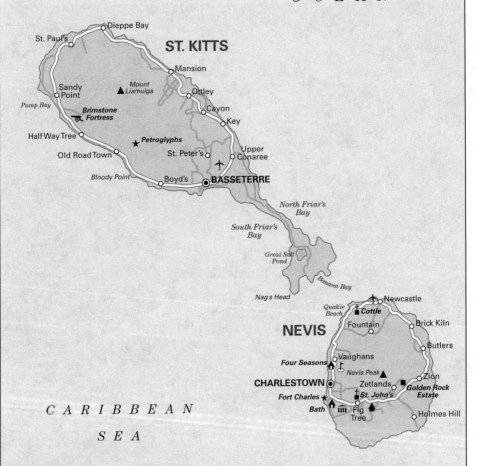

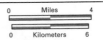

Miles

0   4

Kilometers

0   6

N

ATLANTIC

OCEAN

Dieppe Bay

St. Paul's

ST. KITTS

Mansion

Sandy
Point

*Mount
Liamuiga*

Ottley

Pump Bay

*Brimstone
Fortress*

Cayon

Key

Half Way Tree

★ *Petroglyphs*

Old Road Town

St. Peter's

Upper
Conaree

Bloody Point

Boyd's

●**BASSETERRE**

*North Friar's
Bay*

*South Friar's
Bay*

*Great Salt
Pond*

Banana Bay

Nags Head

Newcastle

*Quakie
Beach*

Cottle

NEVIS

Fountain

Brick Kiln

Butlers

Four Seasons

Vaughans

Nevis Peak ▲

Zion

CHARLESTOWN ◉

Zetlands

*Golden Rock
Estate*

Fort Charles ★

St. John's

Bath

Fig
Tree

Holmes Hill

CARIBBEAN

SEA

The Secret Caribbean

Graceful islands of gentle beauty, St. Kitts and Nevis (pronounced NEE-vis) enchant visitors with their lovely landscapes and unspoiled qualities. Christopher Columbus, who came upon the islands in 1493, selected St. Kitts from all his discoveries to name for his patron saint, St. Christopher. Located in the Leeward Islands west of Antigua, St. Kitts and Nevis call themselves "The Secret Caribbean," being discovered only now by tourists and cruise ships. The irony is that these islands were the first the English settled, and St. Kitts—as St. Christopher came to be known—had the title of the "mother colony" throughout its colonial history.

Here the British gained great wealth from the land that produced the highest-yielding sugar crop in the world. Little wonder that the native Carib Indians called the island Liamuiga (lee-a-MOO-ee-ga), meaning "fertile land." To protect their valuable possession, the British built their most massive fortress in the Eastern Caribbean. From their base in St. Kitts, the British settled Nevis, Antigua, and Montserrat.

Shaped like a paddle, St. Kitts rises from a grassy coastal skirt through intensively cultivated green hills to a central spine of mountains covered with rain forests. Mount Liamuiga, a dormant volcano whose peak, at almost 4,000 feet, is usually hidden under a cap of white clouds, dominates the north. Different in climate and terrain from the main body of St. Kitts, the Southeastern Peninsula, a hilly tongue of land forming the "handle of the paddle," is covered with dry woodlands and salt ponds and scalloped with the island's best beaches.

After a century as a Spanish possession, the first English settlers arrived in St. Kitts in 1623 to stake a claim for Britain. They established a colony near the place known today as Old Road Town. The following year the French arrived and claimed the northern and southern parts of the island. Like the British, they used it as a base for further colonization, laying claim to Guadeloupe, Martinique, St. Martin, and St. Barts—the islands that make up the French West Indies today.

For more than a century Britain and France fought over St. Kitts for possession of this rich prize, but they first had to battle the Carib. It was not until 1783, under the Treaty of Versailles, that the British finally got St. Kitts and Nevis for themselves. The islands remained British colonies until 1983, when full independence was established.

Budget Planning

St. Kitts and Nevis are among the least expensive islands in the Caribbean. If you can share the cost, a taxi is the best way to tour in the short time usually available to cruise passengers. Restaurants (with local cuisine) are moderately priced. As for shopping, the island compares favorably in price with St. Thomas for duty-free goods, but you are likely to find the locally made products of more interest.

Port Profile

Location/Embarkation: Cruise ships arrive in St. Kitts at Basseterre, the capital, on the southwest side of the island. Most ships use Port Zante, the new facility in town where land reclamation extended Basseterre's waterfront from the shore behind Pelican Mall about 800 feet into the bay. Covering the 26 acres, Port Zante has an arrival center with a kiosk of the St. Kitts Tourist Office and shopping mall, and other businesses in a park setting.

In Nevis cruise ships and ferries from St. Kitts arrive in Charlestown, the main town. Its waterfront has been renovated, too. The pier for cruise ships to dock or tender has been rehabilitated, and the historic Cotton Ginnery houses small arts-and-crafts shops, a small museum, and other facilities. Land reclamation has provided parking areas and passenger gazebos in a parklike setting.

Local Transportation: On St. Kitts, private buses operate between villages, but generally they are not used by cruise-ship passengers due to the short time their ships are in port. Taxis, operating on set rates, are available for touring on both islands. Drivers are a loquacious lot and likely to sprinkle their commentary with local lore. Sample rates: one-way from Basseterre to Frigate Bay, US$30 round-trip or US$5 per person for five or more passengers; Deep Water Port, EC$22 (US$8); to South East Peninsula, US$40 round trip;

Fast Facts

Population: St. Kitts, 31,880; Nevis, 9,423

Size: St. Kitts, 68 square miles; Nevis, 36 square miles

Main Towns: Basseterre, St. Kitts; Charlestown, Nevis

Government: St. Kitts and Nevis, officially known as the Federation of St. Christopher and Nevis, belong to the British Commonwealth. They are governed by a parliamentary government headed by a prime minister. Each island has a legislature and assembly. The queen is represented by a governor-general.

Currency: East Caribbean (EC) dollar. EC$2.70 equals US$1. U.S. dollars are widely accepted.

Departure Tax: US$22, including an environmental tax.

Emergency Numbers: Medical: Joseph N. France General Hospital, Basseterre, (869) 465-2551; Alexandra Hospital, Nevis, (869) 469-5473; Police: 911; Fire: 333; Nevis Fire Services, (869) 469-3444.

Language: English

Public Holidays: Jan 1, New Year's Day; Good Friday; Easter Monday; Labor Day, first Mon in May; Whit Mon; Queen's Birthday, second Sat in June; Aug Mon, first Mon in Aug; Sept 19, Independence Day; Dec 25, Christmas; Dec 26, Boxing Day; late Dec, Carnival Day at the end of the two-week festivities that begin a week before Christmas.

Telephone Area Code: 869. From the United States and Canada, dial 869-465 for St. Kitts and 869-469 for Nevis, followed by the four-digit local number. International telex service is operated by Skantel; international collect calls can be made from their office in Basseterre.

Airlines: *From the United States:* American Airlines/American Eagle, Continental, Delta, and US Airways. *From Canada:* Air Canada. *Interisland:* Winair. Other international carriers connect with regional ones via St. Maarten, San Juan, and Antigua. Nevis is served by American Eagle from San Juan, LIAT from Antigua, and Winair from St. Maarten.

Information: www.stkittstourism .kn; http://stkitts-guide.info; www .nevisisland.com

In the United States:

St. Kitts Tourism Authority, 414 East Seventy-fifth St., Suite 5, New York, NY 10021; (212) 535-1234; (800) 582-6208; newyork@stkittstourism .kn

In Canada:

St. Kitts Tourism Authority, 133 Richmond St. West, Suite 311, Toronto, ON M5H 2L3; (416) 368-6707; fax: (416) 368-3934; canada@ stkittstourism.kn

In Port:

St. Kitts: St. Kitts–Nevis Department of Tourism, Pelican Mall, P.O. Box 132, Basseterre, St. Kitts, W.I.; (869) 465-4040; fax: (869) 465-8794; ceo@ stkittstourism.kn

Nevis: Nevis Tourist Authority, Main Street, Charlestown, Nevis, W.I.; (869) 469-7550; (866) 556-3847; fax: (869) 469-7551; info@nevisisland .com

---

Sandy Point, US$16; to Rodney Manor, US$26; Brimstone Hill, US$50 for two hours for one to four people; Ottley's Plantation Inn, US$25 or US$5 per person for five or more. For a taxi from one point to another within Basseterre, US$6. Waiting time charged for every fifteen minutes, EC$5 (US$2). Taxi rates are published in Tourism Department pamphlets.

Roads and Rentals: A good road circumnavigates the main body of St. Kitts, hugging the coast all the way; and a wonderful scenic road, opened in 1989, crosses the Southeast Peninsula to the tip, a stretch of about 7 miles. The coastal road makes it easy to drive—or bike—around the island and

provides access to the mountainous interior, where you'll find splendid hiking. There are no cross-island roads through the central mountains, but there are footpaths. Maps are available from the Tourism Department.

Nevis has about 20 miles of narrow, winding roads that encircle the island, but not always along the coast; some cut across the foothills of Mount Nevis. The south side of the island is honeycombed with country lanes and footpaths, ideal for rambling. Local people use the roads for walking as much as for driving, since traffic is light.

To drive, you must obtain a local driver's license by presenting your valid U.S. or Canadian license and paying a fee of US$25 at the Traffic

Department (Central Police Station, Cayon Street, Basseterre, or the police station in Charlestown). Normally the transaction takes only a few minutes. Driving in this former British colony is on the LEFT.

Car-rental rates are comparable to U.S. ones. Some agencies require that drivers be at least twenty-five years of age. Most offer pickup and delivery service. Some agencies have Mini-Mokes or jeeps, mopeds or motorbikes, as well as popular Japanese and European cars.

In St. Kitts: **Avis** (South Independence Square St.; 869-465-6507; www.avis.com); **Delisle Walwyn Auto Rentals** (Liverpool Row, 869-465-8449; www.delislewalwyn.com); and **Thrifty/T.D.C.** (Central Street; 869-465-2991; www.thrifty.com). These two as well as **Island Moped & Auto** (Sprott Street) have mopeds and bicycles. **Island Scooter Rentals** (Cayon Street, 869-465-8545, fax: 869-465-7833); **Islandwide Scooter Rentals** (Caunt Street, Newtown; 869-466-7841, fax: 869-466-8487).

In Nevis: **Hertz** (Nelson's Spring; 869-469-7467); **Thrifty/T.D.C.** (Main Street; 869-469-5430); **Meadville Bike Rental** (Craddock Road; 869-469-5235) and **Mountain Bike Rentals** (Oualie Beach; 869-469-9692) have bicycles and scooters.

Ferry Service: Four ferry companies—M & M **Transportation** (Carib Breeze/Carib Surf; 869-466-6734), **Wesk Agency** (Sea Hustler/Mark Twain; 869-469-0403), **St. Kitts & Nevis Fast Ferries** (Geronimo Express; 869-662-8930) and **F & F Transportation** (Carib Queen) run frequent service Mon through Sat and limited Sun services between Basseterre and Charlestown. It takes forty-five minutes. Fares from EC$20 (US$8) round-trip. Schedules are available from the Tourist Office on both islands. For information, call (869) 466-INFO.

Shore Excursions

Scenic Railway Tour: 3.5 hours, US$99–109 adults, US$54 children. The old sugar railroad tracks are used by a train built especially for the popular tour. See description later in this chapter.

Island/Brimstone Hill Tour: 3 hours, US$65. The island tour takes in the scenic west coast with a stop at Caribelle Batik and Brimstone Hill. You could take a similar route on your own, with a stop

at Rawlins Plantation Inn on the north coast for lunch or a swim.

Mount Liamuiga Rain Forest: 5–6 hours, US$95. Local companies offer a guided hike to the crater rim of Mount Liamuiga; must arrange in advance. Half-day rainforest hikes can also be arranged.

Snorkel Adventure: 3 hours, US$79 adult, $49 child. Snorkel safari along southeast peninsula stops at White House Bay to explore a sunken Spanish galleon, and other sites.

Sky Safari/St. Kitts Zipline Tours—St. Kitts' newest attraction is set on the Windfield Estate, a sugar plantation with aqueduct and other ruins. The five zip lines vary in length and speed and offer great views of the rainforest. Full tour, two-and-a-half hours, including all ziplines, US$99 with transfers; half-tour, US$50 plus $10 for transfer. The Fly and Walk tour combine zipline with an easy hike on a plantation trail.

St. Kitts on Your Own

The capital of St. Kitts is unmistakably British, despite its French name. Hard by the sea along a wide bay, Basseterre, which means "lowland" in French, is one of the best remaining examples of a traditional West Indian town in the Eastern Caribbean. Despite fires, hurricanes, and earthquakes, many examples of Georgian and Victorian architecture have survived and give the town its historic character.

A Basseterre Walkabout

The historic town center, laid out in a modified grid, is easy to cover on foot and to combine with a shopping tour. **The Circus (1):** One block inland

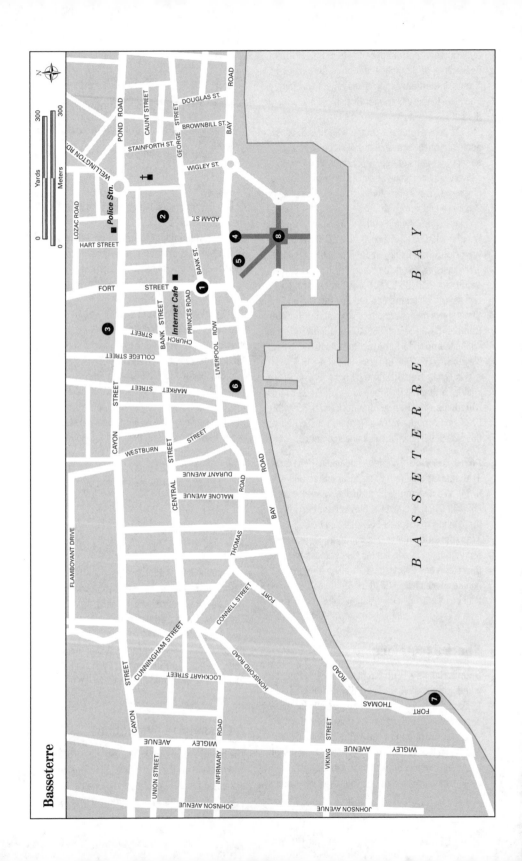

Basseterre

BASSETERRE BAY

from the waterfront, the palm-shaded Circus is a small replica of Piccadilly Circus in London, with a Georgian clock tower and a memorial to Thomas Berkeley, a former president of the Leeward Islands Legislative Council. The roundabout is in the heart of the business district at the intersection of Fort and Bank Streets and Liverpool Row—all with shops, car rentals, tour companies, and restaurants.

Independence Square (2): East of the Circus at the end of Bank Street is Independence Square, a public park with flowering gardens and a central fountain. The square was the site of the slave market in the 18th century and is surrounded by some of the town's best-preserved colonial buildings, many with balconies and gingerbread trim. Its side streets have shops, the island's best art gallery, and restaurants. On the east side stands the **Church of the Immaculate Conception.**

St. George's Anglican Church (3): Originally built as Notre Dame by the French in 1670, the church was destroyed by fire in 1706 by the British, who rebuilt it four years later and renamed it for the patron saint of England. Over the next century it suffered from fires and natural disasters and was rebuilt several times (the last time was in 1869).

At the foot of the Circus on the waterfront is a landmark building known as the **Treasury (5)**, dating from 1894; the post office is located here. The St. Kitts Philatelic Bureau is west of the Treasury on Bay Road. St. Kitts and Nevis each issues its own stamps, which make them prized by stamp collectors—and a nice source of revenue for the government. Next door the **Pelican Mall** is a small shopping center with quality shops that opens on to Port Zante. The **St. Kitts Tourism Authority (4)** is on the second floor.

Farther west along the bay, the **Market (6)**, liveliest on market day (Sat), is a good place to learn about local fruits and vegetables. At the west end of the bay, **Fisherman's Wharf** and **Pelican**

Cove Marina (7) are the main dive and watersports centers. From the gardens of the Ocean Terrace Inn on the hillside above the wharf, you can have a splendid view of Basseterre and see your ship docked at **Port Zante (8)**.

A Drive Around St. Kitts

The road north from Basseterre along the leeward coast hugs the shoreline and borders the tracks of the sugar train fringing the sugarcane fields; Mount Liamuiga towers in the background on the north. Most of the coast is rockbound except for an occasional small cove with a tiny beach or stretch of golden sand, particularly between Old Road Town and Half Way Tree.

Bloody Point: Stonefort Ravine, north of Boyd's, was the scene of a terrible massacre in 1626. The British and French joined forces to wipe out almost an entire population of 2,000 Caribs, after receiving word of an attack planned by the Carib Indians against the new colonists who had settled farther up the coast. The site is known today as Bloody Point, because it is said that the ravine ran with blood for three days.

Old Road Town: On the shores of Old Road Bay in 1623, Sir Thomas Warner, his family, and fourteen followers landed to establish the first British settlement in the West Indies. It served as the capital of St. Kitts until 1727. The tomb of Warner, who died in 1648, lies in a churchyard nearby at Middle Island.

Romney Manor: Inland from Old Road Town en route to Romney Manor and Wingfield Estate, former plantations in the foothills of the central mountains, there are small boulders with Carib petroglyphs. The land of Wingfield Estate once belonged to a Carib tribe whose chief, Tegreman, befriended Warner and permitted him to make a settlement on St. Kitts—much to the chief's later regret.

Romney Manor, a 17th-century plantation house partially rebuilt after a fire in 1996, is the home of **Caribelle Batik** (869-465-6253; www .caribellebatikstkitts.com), surrounded by lovely gardens and shaded by an enormous saman, or rain tree, as it is known locally, said to be more than 350 years old. At Caribelle Batik you can watch artisans—mostly girls from the surrounding villages—at work, re-creating drawings taken from the Carib petroglyphs, scenes of Caribbean life, and West Indian motifs. Caribelle Batik uses the ancient Javanese method of making batik; its sole concession to the twenty-first century is the use of colorfast dyes rather than traditional vegetable dyes, which fade. Next to Caribelle Batik is the new Zipline launching site and Wingfield Estate building ruins recently uncovered in on-going archeological excavations.

Brimstone Hill National Park: Begun in 1690 by the French, and completed by the British over a century, Brimstone Hill (www.brimstonehillfortress .org) has been dubbed the Gibraltar of the West Indies. Perched on an 800-foot spur of Mount Liamuiga overlooking the west coast, the fortress covers 38 acres. It's one of the most massive fortifications built during the colonial era. Made into a park in 1965, the fort has been beautifully restored with British assistance; it has three redoubts, officer's quarters, hospital, ordnance stores, kitchen, and drainage system. A museum was added in 1982.

The view from the ramparts brings into focus St. Kitts's strategic location to the colonial powers. Beyond the green cultivated fields on the north lie the islands of Saba, St. Eustatius, and St. Barts. On the south beyond the sugarcane fields that cover the hills forming the backbone of St. Kitts are the peaks of Nevis and Montserrat. Admission: US$8 adult, US$4 child.

Mount Liamuiga: The brooding volcano known in colonial times as Mount Misery rises behind Brimstone's gray stone walls. From its rainforested peaks, the mountain slopes down through a quilt of green cultivated hills to a sapphire sea. The rim of the crater, at 2,625 feet, is not the actual peak, which is located east of the crater, but it is the area that can be climbed. The trail is a gradual ascent along deep ravines under a dense canopy of trees more than 50 feet high and dangling with curtains of vines, ferns, and philodendron. There are magnificent views down the coast and across St. Kitts to the surrounding islands. At the rim you have the unusual opportunity to walk down (crawl is more accurate) into the crater of a dormant volcano, but it is an arduous trek requiring stamina and agility.

Hikers usually approach the volcano from the north, at Belmont Estates, where a dirt road leads to the trailhead at about 1,500 feet elevation. The hike to the crater rim takes about two-and-a-half hours on the ascent and about one-and-a-half on the descent. There are no facilities whatsoever on the trail. If you want to go down into the crater, it is essential to have a local guide, because it is easy to become disoriented and lost.

Black Rocks: On the northern tip of St. Kitts at Dieppe Bay, the coast is fringed by coral stone and black-sand beaches.

Beaumont Park: Part of the multimillion-dollar development in the Deippe Bay area, Beaumont Park is a racetrack for horse and greyhound racing, opened in Dec 2009. The facility has six stables, each with twenty stalls, and over four hundred greyhound kennels. Currently, seventy horses are being housed and worked out by jockeys from various countries including Barbados, Guyana, and Ireland. Future plans call for a butterfly farm and bird aviary, petting zoo, retail village, and residential lots.

At Belle Vue, on the windward coast, huge boulders of molten lava from prehistoric volcanic eruptions rest at the edge of the sea, where the pounding surf has shaped and weathered them into spectacular, wild scenery. You can return to Basseterre along the east coast via Conaree and the international airport. You will pass Ottley's, a plantation acquired in 1989 by an American family and converted into a hotel using the 1832 greathouse as the centerpiece. **Ottley's Plantation Inn** (869-465-7234; 800-772-3039; www.ottleys.com).

Scenic Railway Tour (869-465-7263; www .stkittsscenicrailway.com). When the St. Kitts Scenic Railway National Tour began service in 2002, it made history on two counts. It's the first luxury train tour in the Caribbean, and the train itself travels over the essence of St. Kitts's history—sugar.

From the early 1700s, sugar plantations were located near the coast and in the foothills of the mountains rising in the center of the island. The scenic train uses the same rail lines built in 1912 to deliver the cane from the plantations to the sugar mill in Basseterre.

The tour, which encircles about two-thirds of the island, departs from the Needsmust Station in Basseterre and heads north, counterclockwise across the coastline, passing small villages and providing passengers with great views. The conductor narrates the tour, describing the scenery: old sugar estates with abandoned windmills and chimneys; slave quarters that housed Africans imported to work the plantations; Brimstone Hill Fortress; Old Road Town, where Thomas Jefferson's great-grandfather is buried; and other historic sites. Because of the deep canyons, or ghuts, that run from St. Kitts's mountainous center to the coast, the train travels over twenty-three bridges. The trip takes less than three hours and when offered as a cruise ship excursion, passengers return via the coast by motor coach.

The scenic railway has ten twenty-eight-passenger double-decker railway coaches, built especially for the tour. Every passenger has two seats—one on the first level in the air-conditioned cabin with 6-foot-wide vaulted windows and another on the open-air observation deck. The coaches are equipped with water coolers, restrooms, and a sound system. Car attendants are on board to assist passengers. The railway tour schedule varies according to demand. Price: US$89 adults, US$44.50 children, including beverages and musical entertainment. Tickets can be purchased at the Needsmust train station or the St. Kitts Scenic Railway office in Basseterre.

Frigate Bay and the Southeastern Peninsula

On the south side of Basseterre, a narrow strip of land stretches southeasterly in a series of knolls, ponds, and coves with St. Kitts's prettiest white-sand beaches. In the late 1970s the first phase of a long-range resort development of the peninsula began with the first mile or so in an area known as **Frigate Bay**. The remaining 7-mile strip was accessible only on foot or by boat until the completion of the first road through the area in 1989. The road affords lovely views throughout the drive and ends at the peninsula's most beautiful beaches. Frigate Bay where the large St. Kitts Marriott Resort and the Royal St. Kitts Golf Course are located has seen intensive development, mostly with villas and condominiums. On the opposite coast from Frigate Bay on South Friar's Bay Beach, construction has begun on the four-acre Marine World St. Kitts which will have a stingray lagoon, dolphin encounters, an educational program on marine life, nature trail, an aviary with tropical birds, and a beach bar/grill. The $16 million park will also offer water sports.

Further to the southeast at the tip of the peninsula, **Christophe Harbour** fronting Turtle Beach, Major Bay, and Banana Bay is one of the largest projects, scheduled to launch in 2012. Led by Kiawah Development Partners, the 2,500-acre luxury resort development will include a mega-yacht marina, Tom Fazio championship golf course, two five-star hotels, restaurants, shops, boutiques, and oceanfront and hillside homesites. Christophe Harbour already operates the Beach House restaurant at **Turtle Beach,** which fronts the island's best snorkeling reefs. With some developments approved for St. Kitts' Economic Citizenship Program, persons who make a minimum investment of US$350,000 in an approved project or a minimum contribution of US$200,000 into the Sugar Industry Diversification Foundation, will be entitled to apply for citizenship.

Shopping

The development of tourism and the island's growing economy is reflected in the increasing number of shops in Basseterre, particularly those offering island crafts and duty-free gifts. Generally, store hours are from 8 a.m. to noon and 1 to 4 p.m. daily except Sun. Most shops of interest to visitors are found in a compact area, from the Port Zante pier to the Circus and Independence Square.

Art and Antiques: Spencer-Cameron Art Gallery (10 North Independence Sq.; 869-465-1617; www.spencercameron.com). Housed in a restored colonial building dating from the 1860s, the art gallery and workshop of artist Rosey Cameron-Smith has works by artists from St. Kitts/Nevis and around the Caribbean. **Kate Design** (Mount

Pleasant House, St. Pauls; 869-465-7740; www
.katedesign.com). Set in a restored West Indian
house on a hillside below Rawlins Plantation, the
gallery belongs to English-born Kate Spencer who
uses St. Kitts and the Caribbean as her subjects.
The gallery also has lithographs, place mats, table
mats, and more. **Carla Astaphan** (Bay Road West;
869-465-5947), one of St. Kitts' best-known potters,
uses selected blends of local and specially imported
clays and glazes to create unique ceramics and
masks. Her studio-home is also a gallery for other
local artists whose paintings and photographs are
shown along with her own works. More information
on artists is available at www.stkittstourism.kn.

Books and Music: Mini Wall's (Princes
Street) and **Harpers** (Fort Street, above the Circus)
have local guidebooks, stationery and greeting
cards, cookbooks, magazines, and Caribbean music.

China/Crystal: Ashbury's (Liverpool Row;
www.ashburys.com) and **Ram's Duty Free** (Port
Zante and Frigate Bay; 869-466-RAMS; www
.ramstrading.com) carry fine china, crystal, famous
name watches, and jewelry.

Clothing and Accessories: Brown Sugar
(Bay Road; 869-466-4664; www.mybrownsugar
.com) is the store, gallery, and label of Judith Rawlins. Her fashion designs are simple yet stunning,
ranging from comfortable day-wear to sophisticated
looks for evening. **Island Hopper** (the Circus; 869-
465-1640) carries a variety of tropical wear and
souvenirs. **Glass Island** (Independence Square ;
869-466-9067) sells jewelry as well as colorful,
handblown vases, bowls, and plates.

Crafts: Caribelle Batik (Liverpool Row; 869-465-
6253; www.caribellebatikstkitts.com) is the in-town
outlet for the batik maker at Romney Manor. The
shop features colorful, handmade, and original wall
hangings and sportswear in fine sea-island cotton. **The Crafthouse** (Shoreline Plaza, Bay Road;
869-465-7754; www.stkittscrafthouse.com) is a
government-sponsored center for local craftspeople
to work and improve their skills as well as to display their wares. In addition to crafts and souvenirs,
they sell perfume, gold jewelry, and fashion accessories. **The Linen Shop** (Port Zante Mall; 869-465-
9766) offers handcrafted linen items.

Jewelry: At Port Zante jewelry stores line both
sides of the walkway leading from the ships to
downtown. All are very commercial and it's hard to
distinguish one from the other.

Perfume: Ashbury (Liverpool Row) sells perfumes as well as watches and jewelry, china, crystal, and leather goods at duty-free prices that claim
to beat those in St. Maarten.

Dining and Restaurants

St. Kitts has a delicious local cuisine that reflects
the Caribbean melting pot as well as any place in
the region. Carib, African, European, Asian, and
Middle Eastern influences are found in the taste
and variety of dishes, which use exotic vegetables
such as breadfruit and christophene (a type of
squash), eggplant and okra, herbs, and fresh seafood. Peter Mallalieu, a fifth-generation Kittian and
food specialist, says such dishes as pepperpot, a
meat stew, was learned from the Caribs; *konki,*
a cassava, yam, and coconut bread steamed in
banana leaves, came with the African slaves;
paelau, a rice-and-peas dish served for celebrations, mingles Spanish and East Indian traditions;
and *kibbe* and rolled grape leaves arrived with the
Lebanese traders at the turn of the 19th century.

Restaurants are open daily except Sun, unless
otherwise noted. Not all take credit cards; inquire
in advance. Inexpensive, not including wine,
means less than US$15–$20 per person; moderate,
US$20–25; expensive, more than US$25.

The Ballahoo Restaurant (the Circus; 869-
465-4197). A good place to relax after shopping, it
is popular with locals and tourists for seafood and
local fare and for its location, which offers seating
on a second-floor balcony overlooking the town.
Moderate.

Bobsy's Bar & Grill (869-466-6133; lahkwf@
caribsurf.com) features fresh lobster as well as
local and international dishes in a Caribbean atmosphere. Open for lunch and dinner daily. Karaoke,
dancing, and entertainment. Moderately expensive.

Mr. X's Shiggidy Shack Bar & Grill (Frigate
Bay, 869-663-3983; www.mrxshiggidyshack.com)
serves grilled fish, lobster, and chicken in traditional Kittian style. Open bar, live music. Its water
taxi is available to transport passengers from the

Port Zante Cruise Terminal for US$10 round-trip. Inexpensive.

The Pizza Place (Central Street; 869-465-2546). In addition to pizza, you can get rôti, chicken, and fried conch to enjoy in its courtyard or to take out. Inexpensive.

Rawlins Plantation (869-465-6221; www.rawlinsplantation.com). The dining room of this small plantation inn is famous for its luncheon buffets of West Indian cuisine. The inn has a magnificent setting at the foot of Mount Liamuiga. Moderately expensive.

Royal Palm (Ottley's Plantation Inn; 869-465-7234; www.ottleys.com). Innovative cuisine by chef Pamela Yahn, who creates Caribbean-inspired dishes with Asian flavors, can be enjoyed in a spectacular al fresco setting. Expensive.

The Spice Mill (Cockleshell Beach). The new restaurant at the water's edge offers an eclectic menu of West Indian-influenced dishes for lunch daily and for dinner six nights a week. Its upscale, casually decor includes local and regional elements, such as hand-woven crayfish baskets; a canoe replicating the original Carib Indian design has been transformed into a bar.

StoneWalls Tropical Bar and Eating Place (Princes Street; 869-465-5248;) enjoys an international reputation as a bar, thanks to *Newsweek* magazine, but you can also dine in a tropical garden setting with selections as varied as jerk chicken and sushi. Moderate. Next door is Stonewalls Tropical Boutique offering a range of clothing and accessories and featuring the Island-to-Island brand of John Warden, an established designer based in St. Kitts.

Nightlife

St. Kitts is very low-key. Nighttime entertainment takes the form of live dance music by a small combo at the main hotels, bars, or discos. There is a casino at Frigate Bay.

Sports

Beaches/Swimming: Beaches are open to the public, but access may be private along some stretches. St. Kitts's best beaches are on the southeastern peninsula. The northern Atlantic coast has stretches of black sand, which are more of a natural curiosity than good bathing beaches. On the east coast south of Black Rock, there are strong currents and undertow. Conaree Beach, on the east coast, has surf.

Biking: St. Kitts, with a good road on the lowland skirt of the mountains, reasonably light traffic, and friendly people, is well suited for biking. Inquire in advance through the Tourist Board about the availability of equipment. **Fun Bikes** (Cayon Street; 869-662-2088) has quad bike tours, call ahead for reservations.

Boating/Kayaking: Several boats offer day trips, but boating as a sport is not well developed in St. Kitts. **Blue Water Safaris** (869-466-4933, fax: 869-466-6740; www.bluewatersafaris.com) and **Leeward Island Charters** (869-465-7474; fax: 869-465-7070) offer a day excursion to secluded Friar's Bay for a swim, snorkeling, and fine view of Nevis. **Tropical Tours** (Cayon Street; 869-465-4039; fax: 869-465-6400; www.tropicalstkitts-nevis.com) has boat charters, sightseeing, and dive excursions. A half-day trip is US$55; full day, $85. These companies arrange deep-sea fishing charters, too. Although the waters around St. Kitts are rich in fish, sportfishing is not developed. Local fishermen catch mackerel, barracuda, kingfish, snapper, grouper, and marlin, among others. A three-hour kayak excursion costs US$45.

Golf: The Royal St. Kitts Golf Club (869-466-2700; www.royalstkittsgolfclub.com), located at Frigate Bay adjacent to the St. Kitts Marriott Resort, features two holes on the Caribbean Sea and three on the Atlantic Ocean with water hazards on 10 holes and 80 bunkers. The course plays as an 18-hole, par 71 course at 6,900 yards from the back tees. Greens fees: $180 from Nov to May; $140 June to Oct.

Hiking: Hiking on St. Kitts ranges from easy rambling on country lanes to arduous trekking on volcanic peaks. With a map you can easily find your way in the lowlands and foothills. In the rain-forested mountains, however, you should have a local guide, as vegetation often obscures trails. Guided hikes are available from **Greg's Safaris** (869-465-4121;

www.gregsafaris.com) and range for US$65; hiking the volcano, $95.

Horseback Riding: Plantation roads through lush sugarcane and banana fields in the shadow of brooding volcanic peaks are ideal for horseback riding. **Trinity Stables** (Frigate Bay; 869-465-9603; 869-662-3098; fax: 869-465-9464; www.trinityinn apartments.com/stables.asp) offers half-day excursions in the rain forest departing daily at 9 a.m. Cost $55, call in advance to reserve. **Royal Stables** (West Farm; 869-465-2222; fax: 869-465-4444) has similar two-and-a-half- to three-hour excursions departing at 8:45 a.m. and 1:30 p.m. Cost: US$60 adult.

Snorkeling/Scuba Diving: Under the sea St. Kitts remains largely unexplored. It has extensive reefs and a diversity of sites offering walls, canyons, and caves and drift diving in some locations. But the biggest attraction is wrecks. Of 350 unexplored wrecks known to be in St. Kitts waters, only a dozen or so have been identified. Historic records show that approximately one hundred ships were lost in Basseterre harbor in one hurricane alone. The reef in front of Banana Bay is in about 15 feet of water and is one of the island's best snorkeling locations. It has star coral, elkhorn and brain corals, and a large variety of colorful reef fish.

A long barrier reef, known as the Grid Iron, stretches for more than 6 miles from Conaree on the east coast of St. Kitts to Newcastle Bay on Nevis at depths varying from 6 to 50 feet. It helps protect the Narrows, the shallow seabed connecting St. Kitts and Nevis. Here, a large circular reef spread over an area of about a half mile ranges from 18 feet to 50 feet. On the south side of the reef, an area known as Monkey Shoals is thick with black coral at 35 feet. It also has a few nurse sharks, rays, and lobsters.

Facilities for diving and other water sports can be found at **Dive St. Kitts** (Bird Rock Beach Hotel; 869-465-1189; www.divestkitts.com). Daily 9 a.m. departures for nearby reefs and shipwrecks return at 12:30 p.m. **Kenneth's Dive Center** (Bay Road, Newtown; 869-465-2670; www.kennethdivecenter .com) offers a range of dive excursion, from US$80 for one-tank.

Zipline: **Sky Safari Zipline** (www.stkittstourism .kn/enjoystkitts/thrills.asp) opened in 2009, is set on the grounds of the old Wingfield Estate, where estate ruins include original structures, equipment, chimney, aqueduct, and other interesting historical elements that guests can view and tour. Sky Safari St. Kitts offers excursions on 5 zip lines over the rainforest on ziplines that vary in length and speed.

Nevis

Separated from St. Kitts by a 2-mile channel and linked by ferry, Nevis appears to be a perfect, dark-green cone rising with graceful symmetry from the sea. Mount Nevis, at more than 3,000 feet, is usually crowned with white clouds, as though the mountain were covered with snow. Apparently the illusion was enough to inspire Columbus to name it Las Nieves, after a range of snowcapped mountains in Spain.

After its discovery by Columbus in 1493, little happened to Nevis until 1627, when it was granted to the Earl of Carlisle. The following year Thomas Warner sent one hundred settlers from St. Kitts to establish a settlement at Jamestown. After it was destroyed by a tidal wave in 1680, the capital was moved 2 miles south to Charlestown, where it is today. Although the colony started with tobacco as its first export, by the 18th century sugar had become the main crop, bringing with it large plantations and great wealth.

The rich plantation society soon made Nevis the social hub of the Caribbean, with an international reputation as the "Queen of the Caribbees." The Bath House Hotel, built in 1778 immediately south of Charlestown amid elaborate gardens, was said to be the finest building in the Caribbean: It had a casino, where planters and traders won and lost fortunes and made big deals, and a tiny brothel for the officers of visiting ships. It became the most fashionable spa in the region, attracting English and other European aristocrats, who came to its mineral springs to cure their rheumatism, gout, and similar ailments. But even before the Europeans, the Carib must have appreciated the waters, too, because their name for Nevis was Oualie (pronounced WAL-lee), meaning "land of beautiful water."

The springs still flow, and tourists still come to Nevis, but not for the old spa, a historic ruin that awaits renovation, but for the former plantation houses that are now some of the finest small resorts in the Caribbean. Nevis is ideal for travelers who like to wander about, curious to learn what lies down an unnamed lane or over the next hill, stopping to chat with folks they meet along the way. It's what the West Indians call "limin'," or doing nothing in particular.

Charlestown

Located on the west side of the island, **Charlestown** is a West Indian colonial village so perfectly caught in time it could be a movie set. Only 2 blocks deep and about 4 blocks long, its streets are lined with a medley of pretty old buildings, many with gingerbread trim, and only a few modern intrusions. You step off your ship onto a pier with facilities built specifically to attract more cruise ships. The **Cotton Ginnery,** a small complex of shops designed in traditional architecture, was the historic site where farmers came to sell their products and cotton was ginned, baled, and made ready for shipping. Check out **Nevis Craft House** (869-469-5505) for locally made handicrafts and souvenirs.

On the south side of the pier is the Market, best on Sat morning, market day, when folks from all around the island come to town to buy and sell. A few steps away are the Tourist Board Office, which has maps and books on Nevis for sale, and the **Nevis Philatelic Bureau,** one of the busiest places in town.

The street directly in front of the pier leads to Main Street, with the **Nevis Handicraft Cooperative** (869-469-1746) on the south, and the post office and landmark Treasury building, dating from the 18th century, on the north. A turn south on Main Street leads past shops to the courthouse and public library, a handsome stone building dating from the late 19th century. In front is a memorial to the fallen sons of Nevis in World Wars I and II. Farther along, at the corner of Government Road, an old Jewish cemetery has tombstones dating from the 17th century and the ruins of what may be the oldest synagogue in the Eastern Caribbean.

You can visit Nevis's small galleries and see artists and craftspeople at work; inquire at **Cafe des Arts** (Main Street; phone/fax: 869-469-7098), a gallery/cafe in Charlestown, where you can browse the artwork of Kittian and other Caribbean artists.

North on Main Street you pass some attractive shops, particularly the **Island Hopper** (869-469-0873), known for its batik clothing; and **Island Fever Boutique** (869-469-0887), with a good selection of beachwear, and island fashions. On the west side of Main Street is the **Museum of Nevis History** (www.nevis-nhcs.org), the home of Alexander Hamilton, the first U.S. secretary of the treasury, who was born here in 1755. Hours: Mon to Fri, 9 a.m. to 4 p.m., Sat to noon; cost US$5 adults, $2 children.

Horatio Nelson Museum (Belle Vue, next to Government House east of town; 869-469-0408) contains memorabilia of the famous admiral. Entrance: US$5 adults, $2 children. **Knick Knacks Boutique** (869-469-5784; knickknacks@sisterisles .kn), located at Henville's Plaza on Samuel Hunkins Drive, sells some of the most delightful, fun crafts by local artists to be found in the Caribbean. Best of all are cloth and carnival dolls by artist/owner Jeannie Rigby.

Pinney's Beach: North of Charlestown, the road to Newcastle, where the airport is located, skirts the coast along 4-mile-long Pinney's Beach, an idyllic, palm-fringed stretch of golden sand where the Four Seasons Nevis Resort is located. (The hotel has been closed since 2008, due to hurricane damages but is scheduled to reopen in Dec 2010.) At Cades Point a steep road leads to a hilltop high above Tamarind Bay, from which there are breathtaking views of St. Kitts and the Caribbean. It is the best place on the island to watch a spectacular Caribbean sunset. Nevis's coast is sprinkled with springs and seasonal lagoons that fill after heavy rains, often catching fish when the waters spill over to the sea. At Nelson's Spring, a freshwater pond on the north end of Pinney's Beach, cattle egrets flock in the late afternoon to roost. This area had not been developed until 1991, when the **Four Seasons Nevis Resort** opened Nevis's first international deluxe resort. Located 3 miles north of Charlestown, its most outstanding feature is its golf course Another mile north is **Oualie Beach Resort**

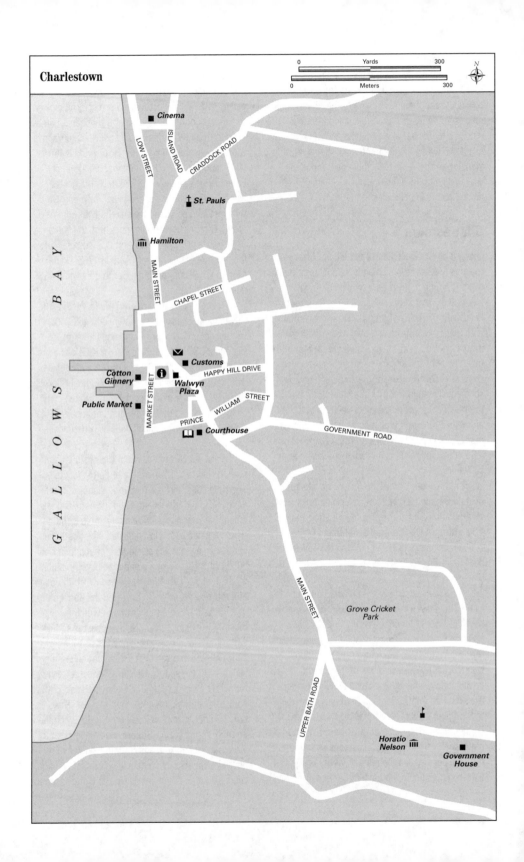

(www.oualiebeach.com), an attractive beachfront resort with cottages in West Indian style, which has one of the island's main dive and water-sports centers.

Newcastle: On the north coast Nisbet Plantation, once the estate of Frances Nisbet, the wife of the famous British admiral Lord Nelson, is now an antiques-filled plantation inn, Nisbet Beach Resort (www.nisbetplantation.com), with a magnificent lawn that flows to the beach between double rows of stately palms and flowering gardens. With a little imagination you can easily envision the opulent life here in Nevis's heyday.

Nearby at Newcastle Pottery, you can watch pottery made from Nevis's rich red-clay soil being shaped and fired in traditional ways. The pottery is available for sale.

Bath Stream: On the south side of Charlestown are the ruins of the famous Bath spa and stream whose waters supply the spa. There is a small bathhouse still in use by local people. Plans to rebuild the spa have been discussed often but languish for lack of funds.

Fig Tree Village: The main road turns inland to Fig Tree Village and St. John's Church, where the book of records is open to the page that recorded the marriage of Lord Nelson and Frances Nisbet in 1787. Admiral Nelson, who was headquartered at the British naval base in Antigua, was first attracted to Nevis for its fresh water to supply his ships. Then he discovered Frances Nisbet, a widow of a wealthy plantation owner. The best man at their wedding—the Duke of Clarence—later became King William IV of England. The marriage took place at the Montpelier great house, which belonged to Frances Nisbet's uncle at the time. It is now restored as an inn (www.montpeliernevis .com), set in beautiful gardens.

Gingerland: Beyond Morning Star, the area known locally as Gingerland has Hermitage Plantation, Croney's Old Manor Estate, and Golden Rock Estate—former plantations whose great houses or sugar mills have been converted into inns. All are situated at about 1,000 feet elevation, on the southern slopes of Mount Nevis.

Rainforest Trail: A trail through the rain forest on the side of Mount Nevis leaves from Stonyhill, above Golden Rock Estate, and winds north through groves of cacao, breadfruit, and nutmeg trees and overlooks the Atlantic coast. Vervet monkeys can be seen frequently on the walk. Golden Rock Estate has a map for a self-guided walk.

Mount Nevis: Dominating the landscape in every direction is cloud-covered Mount Nevis. Dormant since its last eruption in 1692, it continues to emit hot sulfurous gases. The crater is a half-mile wide and almost 800 feet deep. A very difficult trail of about 2 miles leads to the crater rim—for experienced hikers only. New, less strenuous trails have been developed at a lower level on the mountainside. (See Hiking section.)

Botanical Gardens of Nevis (Mount Pelier Estate; 869-469-3509; www.botanicalgardennevis .com) is an eight-acre spread of tropical gardens, divided into sections: cactus, bamboo, lily pools, fruit, and more. A rain-forest conservatory, Mayan temple, and waterfalls are part of the attraction. There is a gift shop and a teahouse/bar. Hours: Mon to Fri, 10 a.m. to 3 p.m. Admission: US$10 adults, $7 children age six to twelve, younger than age six free.

Saddle Hill Battery: Built by the British with slave labor in the 18th century, at about 1,700 feet, the fort is the only fortification on Nevis that is not on the coast. The site has been converted by the Nevis Historical and Conservation Society (www .nevis1.com/nevis-museum-history) into a tourist attraction with a trail and interpretive markers. Along the way, hikers enjoy the panoramic view of St. Kitts, Statia, Montserrat, Redondo, and Antigua. Saddle Hill has an observation center with a telescope at about 1,200 feet above sea level. The telescope was given to Nevis by Greenpeace to watch migrating whales.

Plantation Carriage Rides: Hermitage Plantation Inn (869-469-3477; nevherm@caribsurf.com) has authentic, classic Creole adaptations of Victorian-style carriages, crafted of West Indian mahogany, and offers 2- to 3-mile trips that wind through historic Gingerland or scenic back roads where you can see everyday West Indian country life.

Sports

Beaches/Swimming: All beaches are open to the public, and the 4-mile stretch of reef-protected

Pinney's Beach is the standout. **Oualie Beach,** north of Pinney's Beach, is another fine, more open strand of golden sand with surf and is popular for windsurfing and kayaking.

Deep-Sea Fishing: Mount Nevis Beach Club (869-469-9373; 800-756-3847; www.mountnevis hotel.com) and **Oualie Beach Resort** (869-469-9735; fax: 869-469-9176; www.oualiebeach.com) arrange sportfishing trips. *Deep Venture* (869-469-5110), with professional fisherman Matt Lloyd, offers half- and full-day charters. On *Venture II* (869-469-9837) champion fisherman Claude Nisbett gives half- and full-day trips on a 28-foot sportfishing boat with a bar on board.

Golf: The 18-hole championship layout by Robert Trent Jones is part of the **Four Seasons Nevis Resort** (800-332-3442; www.fourseasons.com/nevis). Greens fee for 18 holes: US$195. Considered one of the best—and certainly one of the most beautiful—courses in the Caribbean, it overlooks Pinney's Beach and the Caribbean, with lofty Mount Nevis as a backdrop.

Hiking and Biking: Nevis's web of country lanes and footpaths provides a delightful variety of hiking for ramblers. With a map it is easy to find your way. **Rainforest Trail** on the slopes of Mount Nevis can be covered without a guide. The **Nevis Historical and Conservation Society** (869-469-5786), with help from the U.S. Peace Corps, developed six easy to strenuous trails on Mount Nevis accessible from various locations and has a brochure describing them. **Upper Round Road,** a 9-mile road constructed in the 1600s, is being developed for hiking, horseback riding, and off-road mountain biking. It was part of an extensive road system built to provide access to the sugarcane fields and communities that once surrounded Mount Nevis. The road connects Golden Rock Plantation Inn on the east side of Nevis with the Nisbet Plantation Beach Club on the northern tip. It passes through local villages with quaint West Indian houses, a seasonal rain forest, orchards, and vegetable gardens. Hikers are likely to see monkeys frolicking and mongoose scampering by. Organized

by the Nevis Historical and Conservation Society, with a grant from RARE, Center for Tropical Conservation, the project has received an ecotourism award from *Islands* magazine.

Golden Rock Nature Trail, behind the Golden Rock Plantation Inn (869-469-3346; info@golden-rock.com; www.golden-rock.com), is an easily accessible trail that runs along a ridgeline and meanders down a gentle sloping ravine bed with huge rain-forest plants, fruit trees, and flowers. Here a troop of African green, or vervet, monkeys make their home and are seen often peering from behind the trees. Trail maps are available at the inn.

Expert guides can make your trip more meaningful with their knowledge of the flora, fauna, and history. It's also safer than hiking on your own. Michael Herbert, **Heb's Nature Tours,** (869-469-3512; hebnature@hotmail.com) is known as the "bush doctor" for his knowledge of local bush remedies, which he shares on his rain-forest hikes. Earla Liburd (869-469-2758; www.nevisnaturetours .com; info@nevisnaturetours.com), a local teacher with **Sunrise Tours,** leads moderately challenging hikes to little-known areas and three waterfalls.

Snorkeling/Scuba: Diving Nevis's underwater world is even less explored than that of St. Kitts. The island is completely surrounded by reefs, some within swimming distance of shore. The best snorkeling locations are off **Pinney's Beach.** The Grid Iron, the barrier reef that stretches across the Narrows between Nevis and St. Kitts, starts at Newcastle Bay on the north coast of Nevis. **Scuba Safaris** (Oualie Beach; 869-469-9518; www .scubanevis.com) has PADI and NAUI instructors and offers diving trips for US$65 for one-tank and US$95 for two-tank excursions. It also has glass-bottom boat cruises and kayaks.

Windsurfing: The best location is the northwest coast from Cades Bay to Newcastle. Equipment can be rented from the **Oualie Beach Resort** (869-469-5329; fax: 869-469-9176). You can also rent mountain bikes and kayaks here, as well as arrange for guided excursions.

Montserrat

Plymouth

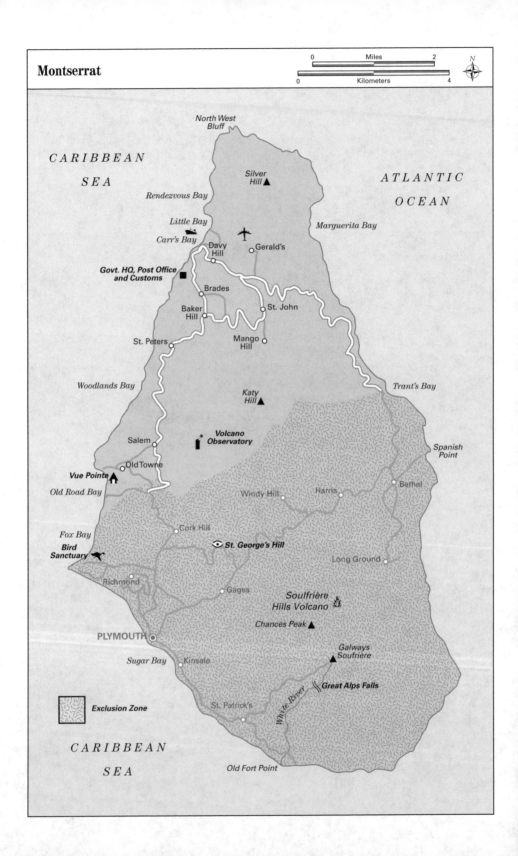

A Quiet Corner of the Caribbean

Note to readers: For a decade beginning in July 1995, volcanic eruptions in the southern half of the island plagued Montserrat, and the area south of the Belham Valley has been declared off-limits to both visitors and residents. The residents and businesses that were in this area, including those in the capital of Plymouth, had to leave and move north. Most resettled north of Plymouth in the area of Salem, where life continues as normally as can be expected.

The good news is that the volcano seems to have calmed down, and people, who have shown remarkable resilience, hope the worst is behind them. A new airport was completed in spring 2005 when Princess Anne came to Montserrat to dedicate it, and air service by Winair was launched. The Montserrat Tourist Board has a promotional campaign to attract visitors. Indeed, for naturalists, environmentalists, and adventurous travelers, now is probably the most interesting time of all to visit Montserrat. In 2007, Montserrat's new $2 million Cultural Centre (664-491-4242; montserratcultural centre@candw.ms) opened, a big step in the long-term strategy to develop Little Bay, on the west coast, as the country's new urban area.

Known as the Emerald Isle of the West, Montserrat has the distinction of being the only place in the Caribbean settled by the Irish. The title also comes from the island's physical resemblance to Ireland, as velvet green as ever a place could be. The early settlers also left their mark in the names of people and places, evident throughout the island. And to honor them all, a shamrock was mounted on the governor's mansion, visitors' passports are stamped with a shamrock, and St. Patrick's Day is a public holiday.

This quiet corner of the Leeward Islands, 27 miles southwest of Antigua, promotes itself as "The Caribbean as It Used to Be," in praise of its uncommercialized ambience and natural environment. Mostly of volcanic origin, pear-shaped Montserrat rises quickly from a narrow belt of lowlands and foothills to mountains formerly covered with tropical rain forests dominated by 3,002-foot Chance's Peak, the highest point.

Montserrat was sighted by Christopher Columbus in 1493, and, according to tradition, he gave the island its name because its serrated peaks reminded him of the mountain range surrounding Santa Marie de Monserrate, a monastery near Barcelona. The Spaniards apparently had no interest in the island, and the hills and forests were left to the Carib Indians until the middle of the 17th century, when the first European settlers arrived.

The Irish came to Montserrat in 1632, fleeing religious persecution on nearby St. Kitts. The French and British subsequently fought over the island until 1783, when Montserrat was ceded to Britain in the Treaty of Versailles. It remains a British crown colony.

Sugar and a plantation society based on the labor of African slaves dominated the island throughout the 18th century. Limes and, later, cotton were introduced after emancipation in the early 19th century. Today bananas are the main crop, with some production of limes and cotton, but farming has been severely disrupted by the volcanic eruptions.

Port Profile

www.visitmontserrat.com

Location/Embarkation: The former cruise-ship port of entry and capital, Plymouth, was destroyed by the volcanic eruptions of 1995. A new port on the northwest coast at Little Bay is being developed for small cruise ships and private vessels and where a commercial port is operating. For information, Montserrat Port Authority, Little Bay (664-491-2791; fax: 664-491-8063).

Local Transportation: A list of taxi and van operators and car-rental agencies is available from the Montserrat Tourist Board. If you hire a taxi, settle the cost in advance and be sure to determine whether the agreed amount is U.S. or EC dollars. If you rent a car, you'll need a temporary driver's license, which can be obtained for US$19 (EC$50) from police headquarters in Salem (664-491-2555), open 24 hours a day, Mon to Fri.

Roads and Rentals: Montserrat has a network of paved roads that wind north around hillsides

Population: 4,700

Size: 11 miles long and 7 miles wide; 39 square miles

Main Town: Brades

Government: Montserrat is a British crown colony, whose governor is appointed by the queen.

Currency: Eastern Caribbean (EC) dollar. US$1 equals EC$2.70. U.S. dollars are used widely, but credit cards are not.

Departure Tax: US$21

Emergency Numbers: Medical: Hospital, (664) 491-2552; Operator Assistance: 411; Emergencies: (664) 491-2802; Police: 999; Fire: 911

Language: English

Public Holidays: Jan 1, New Year's Day; Mar 17, St. Patrick's Day; Good Friday; May, Labour Day; Whit Mon; June 9, Queen's Birthday; Aug Mon (first Mon); Dec 25, Christmas Day; Dec 26, Boxing Day; Dec 31, Festival Day.

Telephone Area Code: 664. When calling from the United States, dial 491 plus the local four-digit number.

Airlines: Blackburne Airport on the east coast was destroyed by volcanic eruption. However, a new airport located at Geralds (between Sweeneys and St. John's) was inaugurated in spring 2005 from where Winair (www.fly-winair.com) operates scheduled flights between Montserrat, Antigua, and St. Maarten on nineteen-seater Twin Otter aircraft. Reservations can be made online. Fly Montserrat operates nine-seat Islander on scheduled and on-demand flights. Montserrat can also be reached by ferry from Antigua: 300-passenger *Opale Express* (Carib World Travel, Lower Redcliffe Street, St. John's, Antigua; 268-460-6101, fax: 268-480-2995); and by an occasional cruise ship. Ondeck (Antigua) offers four weekly sailing trips (see Sailing later in this chapter).

Information: www.visitmontserrat.com

In the United States:

Montserrat Tourist Board, Cheryl Andrews Marketing, 331 Almeria Ave., Coral Gables, Fl 33134

In Port:

Montserrat Tourist Board, & Farara Plaza, Buildings B&C, P.O. Box 7, Brades, Montserrat; (664) 491-2230, fax: (664) 491-7430; info@montserrattourism.ms

Montserrat National Trust, Salem Main Road, Salem, Montserrat; (664) 491-3086; www.montserratnationaltrust.ms

and skirt the island's coast and beaches. Driving is on the LEFT. If you're unfamiliar with the narrow mountain roads and left-handed driving, you might prefer to hire a taxi. This way you are free to enjoy the beautiful scenery and listen to the driver, who is likely to be an animated storyteller as well as a guide.

Shore Excursions

Sightseeing excursions are available by taxi, for four persons, or by small minibuses for up to eight people, or you might prefer to enjoy a sport—sportfishing, kayaking, diving, or hiking—because sights such as the **Great Alps Waterfalls** and **Galways Soufrière** are covered by volcano ash in the region where travel is prohibited.

Montserrat on Your Own

Montserrat Museum (P.O. Box 393, Salem Main Road, Olveston, 664-491-3086, fax: 664-491-3046) Housed in the mill of a former sugar plantation, the museum covers Montserrat's history from pre-Columbian times to the present. There are natural-history exhibits as well. The museum, operated by the Montserrat National Trust with a volunteer staff, is also responsible for the renovation of historic sites around the island; excavation of pre-Columbian sites; conservation programs that have established the Woodlands Beach Picnic Area and the former Fox's Bay Bird Sanctuary; and flora and fauna research that brings scientists and other experts to the island. **Oriole,** a shop located in the museum, carries T-shirts, local crafts, postcards and volcano photos, local books, and videotapes.

Visitors can obtain a map of Montserrat here. Hours: Mon to Fri 8:30 a.m. to 4 p.m., Sat 9 a.m. to 1 p.m.

Fox's Bay Bird Sanctuary: On the coast 3 miles northwest of Plymouth was once is a 15-acre protected wildlife area established by the trust in 1979. The sanctuary was a mangrove and bog with a central pond that is the nesting area for coots, gallinules, and other waterfowl. There are several species of heron, of which the most numerous is the cattle egret. The sanctuary was encircled by a nature trail that ends at the beach. (Check locally to learn if the area is off-limits.) The endemic black-and-yellow Montserrat oriole, the national bird, dwells in mountainous areas. Among the island's thirty breeding species are three species of hummingbirds. All these species have since migrated to the northern end of the island.

Castle Peak: Up the hill from Salem is the volcano's scientific observatory. Travelers interested in volcanoes are welcome to visit and speak to the experts who man the center 24 hours a day. Castle Peak is also the name of the island's newest volcano, which seems to be teasing the islanders with its capricious behavior from time to time. Indeed, volcano watching has become a full-time pastime for both visitors and residents.

Garibaldi Hill: Located behind Fox's Bay on the west coast, Garibaldi Hill is the best location to look across to deserted Plymouth and to view Soufrière Hills Volcano, whose growing summit now makes it the island's highest point. **Richmond Hill,** also behind Fox's Bay is another place to see the sharp contrast between the barren flanks of the mountains to the south and the lush rain-forested hills in the north. Only a few vertical struts jutting from rocks and other debris are all that can be seen of the Belham Valley Bridge, but the effect is dramatic and gives a clue as to how deep beneath the surface lies the bridge, now concealed by the mud flows from the volcano. From **Jack Boy Hill,** near the east coast, you get a panoramic view of the coastline and the abandoned airport.

Volcano Observatory: The Montserrat Volcano Observatory (664-491-5647; www.mvo.ms), established in 1996 following volcanic eruptions in the Soufrière Hills, is located 3 miles northwest of the still active peak, providing visitors with a safe,

front-row seat to the continuing spectacle. The facility has sophisticated visual and seismic equipment to monitor volcanic activity, and has played an important role in attracting scientists and scholars as well as visitors. Tours of the observatory by the staff are available Mon to Sat at 3:30 p.m. Fee: EC$10 (US$4) for those age twelve and older; there is a small gift shop.

Southern Montserrat

Montserrat's most popular attractions in the southern third of the island are no longer accessible, and travel in the region is prohibited for visitors and even for residents without special permission. Nonetheless, we have retained the information for those interested in reading about the area and in the hope that someday people will be able to visit some of the places again.

Plymouth: Called a modern day Pompeii, buried in ash and volcanic debris of house size

At a Glance	
Antiquities	★
Architecture	★
Art and Artists	★
Beaches	★
Colonial Buildings	★
Crafts	★
Cuisine	★★
Culture	★
Dining/Restaurants	★
Entertainment	★
Forts	★
History	★
Monuments	★
Museums	★★
Nightlife	★
Scenery	★★★★★
Shopping	★
Sightseeing	★★
Sports	★★
Transportation	★

boulders, the once thriving business and commercial center now resembles a lunar landscape where deep canyons have been gouged.

Galways Estate: Three miles south of Plymouth were the ruins of a sugar plantation dating from the mid-17th century and operated more than 250 years. Selected in 1990 by the Smithsonian Institute as a preservation project for the Columbus Quincentennial, excavations were undertaken for almost a decade by the Montserrat National Trust, aided by specialists from the University of Tennessee and Boston University, as well as Earthwatch and Partners for Liveable Places, among others.

Before excavation began in 1981, the foliage, allowed to run wild after the plantation was abandoned, had become so dense that structures could no longer be recognized. The ruins include a sugar mill and boiling house, windmill tower, great house, and other structures, many of beautifully cut stone.

Galways Soufrière: The southern third of Montserrat is dominated by the Soufrière Hills, several of whose peaks were covered with rain forest before the volcanic eruptions. Galways Soufrière, an active boiling volcanic fissure at 1,700 feet, known as the Devil's Playground, was a treacherous field of unstable rocks with a witch's brew of boiling mud, hissing steam, and the strong smell of sulfurous vapors. It has been the main area of volcanic eruption since 1995. In Aug 2005, dome growth began with renewed activity but in Feb 2010, the dome partially collapsed, in part due to heavy rains. The volcano is continuously monitored.

Dining and Restaurants

Montserrat's native cuisine is West Indian with British and French influences. The most popular dish is mountain chicken, or frog legs, as we know them. Known locally by its Creole name, *crapaud,* the large frog is hunted at night after rainy spells. Also hunted for its meat is the agouti, a rabbit-size, tailless rodent that was once abundant in the Lesser Antilles and is now extinct on most islands. Goat Water, another popular dish, is an adaptation of Irish stew substituting goat meat for beef and seasoned with rum and cloves.

Two restaurants to try are **Tina's Restaurant** (Brades; 664-491-3538) housed in a pretty, green

and white wooden building, offers a varied menu of local dishes including pumpkin soup, shrimp, and the popular lobster burgers; and **Olveston House,** the restaurant of the guesthouse set in one of Montserrat's most historic homes and run by Carol Osborne, owner of Vue Point Hotel, the island's leading hotel before volcanic eruptions forced its closure.

Ask a resident and you'll find Alla (known to one and all for her famous rôtis). Seek out, too, **John Watts Ice Cream,** which specializes in tropical flavors such as mango, coconut, and passion fruit.

Sports

Beaches/Swimming: The island's best and most accessible beaches stretch north along the Caribbean coast. Most are secluded strands of black or gray sand bracketed by rock cliffs with calm, clear water for swimming and snorkeling. None have been developed commercially: They are **Woodlands Beach,** where the National Trust has a picnic site; **Carrs Bay,** and **Little Bay,** where the sand is a butterscotch color.

The only white-sand stretch, **Rendezvous Beach,** is surrounded by steep cliffs and is usually reached by boat from Little Bay, directly to the south. Alternatively, you can hike on an inland path from Little Bay to Rendezvous in about forty minutes, or make a steep thirty-minute climb over the bluff separating the two bays.

Hiking: The Montserrat National Trust, together with the Forestry Department and Montserrat Tourist Board, has cleared several trails: **Runaway Ghaut Trail** has a variety of bird species as well as the dwarf gecko; a trail from Duck Pond to Duberry Estate offers superb views of Plymouth, the island's sputtering volcano, and surrounding environs; the **Forgathy to Cassava Ghaut Trail** has a profusion of flowers and offers a possible glimpse of the rare Montserrat oriole, the shy bridled quail dove, and the rarely seen galliwasp (part lizard, part snake).

Blackwood Allen Trail, about one-and-a-half hours to traverse, takes hikers from Baker Hill near the west coast to Mango Hill in the center of the island. Visitors can see a broad spectrum of island flora, a lovely spring filled with crayfish, and, maybe, agoutis. From a viewing platform, hikers can see Lookout Village and out to sea to neighboring Antigua. Interpretive signs on all trails are planned. Guides are available through the Montserrat National Trust and hikes for up to two hours can be organized on request for US$25, one person; US$20 per two to three persons; and US$15 per four to five persons. After that, is US$10 per hour per person.

Sailing: Ondeck (268-562-6696; www.ondeck oceanracing.com/antigua/montserrat-adventure .htm) based in Antigua, offers sailing trips to Montserrat on a 65-footer Farr Ocean Racing Yacht, departing Falmouth at 8 a.m. on Mon, Wed, Fri, and Sat for Little Bay. The trip takes up to four hours. The return departs Montserrat at 1 p.m. on the same days and takes up to five hours. Cost: US$189 round-trip. Passengers can remain overnight or longer in Montserrat.

Scuba Diving/Snorkeling: If any possible good has come from Montserrat's volcanic activity, it's that her sea life is healthier than ever. Apparently, the environment of coral, fish, sponges, and other creatures has been enriched, and as a result, the island's dive spots are teeming with more life than ever. The dive-able area stretches for some 13 coastal miles from Old Road Bluff on the west to the northeast corner and along the eastern shore to the border of the Maritime Exclusion Zone.

Green Monkey Dive (Green Monkey Inn, Little Bay; 664-491-2960; www.divemontserrat .com), operated by master dive trainer Troy Deppermann, a 20-plus years veteran, offers all levels of dive experiences. With wife Melody, the shop can arrange top-side eco-tours and nature hikes. Green Monkey also offers round-island boat tours, jet boat rentals, and a shuttle service to Rendezvous beach for snorkeling or picnicking.

Scuba Montserrat (Little Bay; 664-496-807; www.divedestinationmontserrat.com), Montserrat's newest dive shop, is run by Andrew Myers and Emmy Aston who have worked in the Bahamas, South Africa, and other locations. They offer lessons as well as dive and snorkel excursions, and boat tours with local guides who experienced the volcanic eruptions first hand.

Festivals and Celebrations

The **Christmas Festival** is Montserrat's version of Carnival and begins officially on Dec 20. But actually it starts in Nov with preview activities, when masqueraders begin rehearsing their quadrilles and polkas. There are calypso contests and performances by bands, groups, and schools. Once an adult art rooted in African folklore, masquerading is now done by children, who perform on holidays and for arriving cruise ships. Competitions, concerts, pageants, and parties keep revelers on the go during the festival until New Year's Day.

Guadeloupe

Pointe-à-Pitre, Guadeloupe; Basse-Terre, Guadeloupe; Iles des Saintes; Marie-Galante

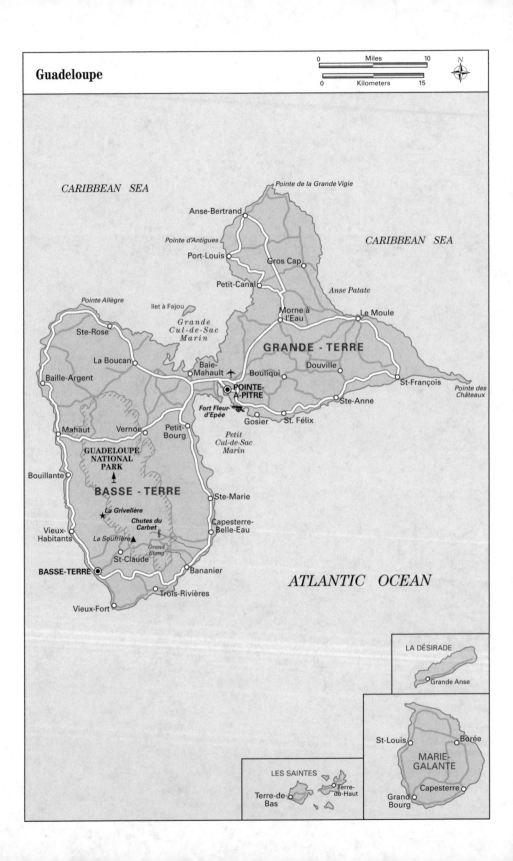

Guadeloupe

Miles 0 10
Kilometers 0 15

N

CARIBBEAN SEA

CARIBBEAN SEA

Pointe de la Grande Vigie

Anse-Bertrand

Pointe d'Antigues

Port-Louis

Gros Cap

Petit-Canal

Anse Patate

Pointe Allègre

Ilet à Fajou

Grande Cul-de-Sac Marin

Morne à l'Eau

Le Moule

Ste-Rose

La Boucan

GRANDE - TERRE

Baille-Argent

Baie-Mahault

Bouliqui

Douville

St-François

Pointe des Châteaux

Mahaut

Vernou

Petit-Bourg

POINTE-À-PITRE

Ste-Anne

Fort Fleur-d'Epée

Gosier

St. Félix

Petit Cul-de-Sac Marin

GUADELOUPE NATIONAL PARK

Bouillante

BASSE - TERRE

Ste-Marie

La Grivelière

Chutes du Carbet

Capesterre-Belle-Eau

Vieux-Habitants

La Soufrière

Grand Etang

St-Claude

Bananier

BASSE-TERRE

Trois-Rivières

ATLANTIC OCEAN

Vieux-Fort

LA DÉSIRADE

Grande Anse

St-Louis

Borée

MARIE-GALANTE

Capesterre

LES SAINTES

Terre-de-Haut

Grand Bourg

Terre-de-Bas

The Caribbean in Miniature

Guadeloupe is actually two islands shaped like butterfly wings. The two parts—Basse-Terre and Grande-Terre—are separated by a narrow channel and connected by a short bridge. No two islands in the Caribbean are more different.

Guadeloupe is also a small archipelago composed of Marie-Galante, Les Saintes, and La Désirade. Together they make up a Caribbean in miniature with the full range of natural features and beauty for which the region is known, along with good facilities to enjoy them.

Grande-Terre, the eastern wing of Guadeloupe, is a flat, dry limestone island, densely populated and developed. It has Guadeloupe's largest town, Pointe-à-Pitre, the business and commercial capital and main cruise port. The south coast is the main resort area, with long strands of white-sand beaches along its quiet Caribbean shores, where many cruise passengers often elect to spend their day.

In contrast, Basse-Terre, the western wing, is a volcanic island dominated by a spine of steep, forest-green mountains climbing to 5,000 feet and mostly covered by the 74,100-acre National Park. From their lofty peaks, where up to 400 inches of rain falls annually, spectacular waterfalls rush over rocky cliffs, crash through canyons, and career through the mountains, forming the rivers and streams that irrigate an emerald skirt of sugarcane and banana fields along Basse-Terre's east coast. Basse-Terre is the name both of the island and of its main town, which is also the capital of Guadeloupe, on the southwest coast. Offshore are the Iles des Saintes, or Les Saintes, also of volcanic origin.

When Christopher Columbus came upon the islands in 1493, he sailed north from Dominica to the island he named Marie-Galante for his flagship, which had brought him there. He arrived in Guadeloupe at the place known today as Sainte-Marie de la Capesterre, on the east coast of Basse-Terre, and claimed the island for Spain. Several attempts by the Spaniards to settle Guadeloupe were repulsed by the fierce Caribs, and a permanent European settlement was not established until after France took possession of the island in the early 17th century. Under the patronage of Cardinal Richelieu, French entrepreneurs formed La Compagnie des Iles d'Amérique to develop Guadeloupe.

In 1635 it sent two noblemen, Charles Liénard de l'Olive and Jean Duplessis d'Ossonville, and a group from Normandy and Touraine to make a settlement.

For the next five years they fought the Caribs and drove them away to neighboring islands. The French cleared the land, introduced sugar and other crops, and imported slaves from Africa to work the land. In 1674 Guadeloupe was officially annexed by France, but for the next century it continued to be the scene of intense rivalry between France and Britain.

During the French Revolution Guadeloupe was occupied by Britain, but it was reconquered in 1794 by Victor Hugues, who abolished slavery. When Napoleon came to power, however, he reinstituted slavery. Through the efforts of Victor Schoelcher, a national hero today, slavery was abolished permanently in 1848. In the following years indentured workers from India were imported to work the cane fields.

In 1946 Guadeloupe was officially designated a French département with the same status as a département of metropolitan France, in the way that the Hawaiian Islands are a state of the United States. In 1974 Guadeloupe and its satellite islands, were given the further status of région. Martinique is a separate région. The people of the French West Indies are culturally French and citizens of France in all respects.

Budget Planning

Guadeloupe is an expensive island, particularly for taxis and restaurants. An average meal for one person in an ordinary restaurant can cost US$25, and in one of the better establishments, it will be US$40 and up. All service charges—taxes and tips—are included in the prices. You do not need to add more tip unless you want to. If you speak French and have the time to use local buses, you can travel economically. Otherwise you should plan to take one of the shore excursions offered by your cruise line, or if you can share with others, hire a taxi or rent a car for touring.

Population: 435,000

Size: 583 square miles

Main Towns: Basse-Terre, Pointe-à-Pitre

Government: Guadeloupe is a région of France with a prefect appointed by the French Minister of the Interior.

Currency: € euro. US$1 fluctuates around €0.73. One euro equals about US$1.36. U.S. and Canadian currency are widely accepted. Banks are open Mon to Fri from 8 a.m. to noon and 2 to 4 p.m.

Departure Tax: None

Emergency Numbers: Medical: Centre Hospitalier de Pointe-à-Pitre, (0590) 89-10-10. Tourist Office can assist in locating English-speaking doctors. Ambulance/SOS service: 24 hours a day, (0590) 87-65-43, (0590) 91-39-39; Police: Pointe-à-Pitre, 17; (0590) 82-00-89; Basse-Terre, (0590) 81-11-55.

Firearms: Yachts are permitted to have firearms on board, but they must be declared.

Language: French and Creole. English is spoken in hotels by the manager and front-desk staff, but personnel in stores, restaurants, and other tourist facilities are likely to speak French only. Non-French speakers should carry a French phrase book and a pocket dictionary when they strike out on their own.

Public Holidays: Jan 1, New Year's Day; Easter Monday; May 1, Labor Day; Ascension Thurs; Pentecost Mon; May 27, Slavery Abolition Day; July 14, Bastille Day; July 21, Schoelcher Day; Aug 15, Assumption Day; Nov 1, All Saints Day; Nov 11, Armistice Day; Dec 25, Christmas.

Telephone: To phone station-to-station from the United States, dial 011-590-0590 plus the six-digit local number; for person-to-person, dial 01-590-0590 plus the six-digit local number. Guadeloupe telephone/fax numbers have a total of ten numbers. To phone from Guadeloupe, Télécartes (sold at post offices and outlets marked TÉLÉCARTE VENTE ICI) are used in special booths marked Télécom throughout the island. Visa and MasterCard may also be used.

Airlines: From United States, American Airlines/American Eagle via San Juan. Other carriers make connections through St. Maarten. LIAT (0590-21-42-93) provides scheduled service between Guadeloupe and major islands in the Eastern Caribbean. Air Caraibes (0590-82-47-00), serves the French West Indies islands daily and flies to Puerto Rico, St. Maarten, and Santo Domingo. Caraibes Air Tourisme flies to Les Saintes daily.

Information: www.antilles-info-tourisme.com; www.lesilesdeguadeloupe.com

In the United States:

New York: French Government Tourist Board, 825 Third Ave., New York, NY 10022; (212) 838-7855; fax: (212) 838-7855

In Canada:

Montreal: 1981 Avenue McGill College, No. 490, Montreal, QC H3A 2W9; (514) 288-2026; (800) 361-9099; fax: (514) 844-8901

In Port:

Guadeloupe Islands Tourist Board (Les Iles de Guadeloupe Comite du Tourisme), 5 Square de la Banque, 97166 Cedex Pointe-à-Pitre, Guadeloupe, FWI; (0590) 82-09-30; www.lesilesdeguadeloupe.com; info@lesilesdeguadeloupe.com. Maps, magazines, and brochures are available.

National Park of Guadeloupe, Habitation Beausoleil, Monteran, F97120 Saint-Claude, Guadeloupe; (0590) 80-8600; fax: (0590) 80-0546; www.guadeloupe-parcnational.com

Port Profile

Location/Embarkation: Pointe-à-Pitre, Basse-Terre, and the offshore islands of Les Saintes are cruise ports; Marie-Galante is an occasional one. Pointe-à-Pitre can accommodate large liners. Most cruise ships use Pointe-à-Pitre, where they dock west of the downtown shopping district and the Tourist Office. In the last few years, Pointe à Pitre suffered with the development of Destrelland, the very large commercial center of Baie Mahault, located west of Pointe à Pitre, and Millenis, a complex near the airport, where many of the downtown shops have moved their business and now, where people do their shopping. In an effort to revitalize the city's economy, a law was passed several years ago to make Pointe à Pitre a tax-free area and now Rue Rue Brissac and Rue Delgres, have become nice shopping streets.

Local Transportation: Inexpensive easy-to-use public buses linking the main towns of Guadeloupe operate from 5:30 a.m. to 7:30 p.m. In Pointe-à-Pitre buses for Gosier and the south coast depart from Dares Station, near the dock and Tourist Office; those to the north and central regions depart from Moreno Station. Buses connecting Grande-Terre with Basse-Terre leave from the Bergevin Station on the north side of town. Buses stop at signs marked ARRÊT-BUS, or you can wave to the driver to stop. Few drivers—very few—speak English.

Due to their short time in port, cruise passengers usually prefer to use taxis, but they are expensive. They are plentiful at the port upon the arrival of cruise ships. Most drivers are looking for cruise passengers they can take on island tours, so expect a certain amount of hustling. (Do not count on them to speak English.) Half-day tours about €75; full-day €125.

The taxi stand closest to the St. John Perse Center is Place de la Victoire near the Tourist Office. From Pointe-à-Pitre to the airport is about US$30–$35, and to Gosier hotels US$35–$40. A 40 percent surcharge is added from 9 p.m. to 7 a.m. and all day Sun and holidays. For radio cabs, call (0590) 90-70-70; (0590) 20-74-74; and (0590) 83-89-98.

Roads and Rentals: Guadeloupe has a network of excellent roads covering 1,225 miles. You can make a complete loop around Basse-Terre or Grande-Terre and explore their interiors, except for certain parts of Basse-Terre. But due to the nature of the terrain, distances can be deceiving and often take double the amount of time you are likely to plan. Car rentals rates are comparable to those in the United States and Europe. A valid driver's license is needed. Driving is on the RIGHT, and traffic regulations and road signs are like those in Europe. Drivers here tend to speed.

Car-rental companies in Pointe-à-Pitre are open weekdays from 8 a.m. to noon and 2:30 to 5 p.m.; Sat to noon or 1 p.m. Among the major car-rental companies are **Rent-a-Car** (0590-21-13-62; 0590-22-74-14); at the Pole Caraibe International Airport and major hotels, the major companies are **Budget** (0590-21-13-49) and **Europcar** (0590-21-13-52; www.europcar-gpe.com). There are also independent companies, you can get a list from the Tourist Office. Or try the online rental service: http://guadeloupe.rentalcargroup.com.

Bicycles and motorbikes can be rented from **Dingo** (Place de la Victoire, 2 blocks from the port; 0590-83-81-19). Vespas cost about US$20 to $30 per day with unlimited mileage.

Ferry Services: From Pointe-à-Pitre to Les Saintes, **Express des Iles** (0590-83-12-45; www.express-des-iles.com), **TMA Archipel** (0590-83-19-89), and **Brudey Freres** (0590-90-04-48) operate daily. To Marie-Galante, ferries leave most days at 8 a.m. from Pointe-à-Pitre. (Both locations have daily air service from Pointe-à-Pitre.)

From Trois-Rivières on Basse-Terre (one-and-a-half hours' drive from Pointe-à-Pitre), ferries leave twice daily at 8 a.m. and 4 p.m. for Les Saintes; the trip takes about thirty minutes. They also depart from the town of Basse-Terre to Les Saintes.

Shore Excursions

If you enjoy spectacular scenery, hiking in a rain forest, and picnicking in the woods, Basse-Terre will be your first choice. If beaching and biking are preferences, you will have the best of both in Grande-Terre. A Tourist Office booklet entitled *Guadeloupe Excursions* maps out six itineraries for self-drive tours. Similar tours can be made by taxi, and some are available as motor coach tours. **Tropical Tours** (0590-83-12-35; www.tropical-tour.com) offers similar tours and a range of sporting excursions. From my experience, guides in Guadeloupe score the best in the Caribbean for knowledge about their island. Tours begin in Pointe-à-Pitre; prices and duration will vary, depending on the cruise line and tour company. Places mentioned here are described later in the chapter.

Basse-Terre to the Carbet Falls/Grand Etang: 4 hours. After skirting the east coast of Basse-Terre to St-Sauveur, you turn inland to Carbet Falls. Longer versions include Grand Etang, an inland lake, or the town of Basse-Terre.

Basse-Terre to the Soufrière Volcano: 8 hours. Same as above tour but instead of Carbet Falls, it continues to Basse-Terre and winds up the mountains to the volcano.

National Park/Southern Basse-Terre: 8 hours. The route crosses the National Park from east to west, where there are trails and picnic sites. On the west coast it turns south to Vieux-Habitants, along the magnificent scenery of Grande Rivière to La Grivelière, a coffee plantation. Return via Basse-Terre, Archaeological Park, and east coast.

Grand Tour of Grande-Terre: 4–5 hours. From resort town of Gosier, drive follows the south coast to Pointe-des-Châteaux; east coast to Le Moule; and around to the west coast at Petit-Canal and Morne-à-l'Eau.

Discover the Mangroves: Clarisma Tour (3 Chemins Gros Cap 97131, Petit-Canal; 0590-22-51-15; fax: 0590-20-11-86) has a two-hour boat excursion in the bird-rich mangroves between Grand-Terre and Basse-Terre. Cost: €20; excursions are in French. Jungle Safari Adventure (0590-56-17-03; junglesafariadventure@wanadoo.fr). Explore off the beaten track in daylong four-wheel-drive tours.

Le Attelages du Comté (Ste. Rose; 0590-56-61-12; www.lesattelagesducomte.fr) offers horse-driven wagon rides. Per person €30 for one hour; €45 for half-day.

Guadeloupe on Your Own

Pointe-à-Pitre is the main city of Guadeloupe. As early as the mid-18th century, its value as a well-protected, deep-water harbor was recognized by the English and the French, who took turns at building the city and fortifying the nearby hills. It thrived despite fires, earthquakes, and hurricanes. Today the city has a slightly tatty look, with an architectural diversity of wooden houses with wrought-iron balconies in the small narrow streets of the old town juxtaposed against modern commercial and government buildings.

A Pointe-à-Pitre Walkabout

Pointe-à-Pitre can be explored easily on foot. The St. John Perse Center (1), a hotel and shopping complex at the port, was designed with cruise passengers in mind. The center is accessible to local citizens as well. A short walk will put you in the heart of Pointe-à-Pitre at Place de la Victoire (2), a garden square shaded by royal palms and sandbox trees. They were planted in 1794 by Victor Hugues on the day after his victory against the British. The square is bordered by colonial-style houses that lend an Old World atmosphere to the town. Many have been renovated to house boutiques and sidewalk cafes. The Tourist Office (3) is on the southwest corner of the square. One of the town's several markets, a lively vegetable-and-fish market, is on the south by the harbor front. Walking west along rue Peynier, you will cross the main shopping streets of rue Nozières, rue Frébault, and rue Schoelcher, where boutiques stock perfume, china, and other French goods. At the corner of Peynier and Frébault is the Central Market (4), a large town plaza where vendors sell tropical flowers, fruits and vegetables, spices, and crafts. West of the market, in a pink ornate colonial building on rue Peynier, is the Schoelcher Museum (5). It is dedicated to the leading French abolitionist of his time, who led the fight to end slavery in the French West Indies. Nearby on rue René-Boisneuf, a plaque at No. 54 marks the birthplace of Nobel Prize–winning poet St. John Perse and the Saint-John Perse Museum, which opened for his centennial in 1987.

A Drive Around the Island

To Basse-Terre: From Pointe-à-Pitre, you cross Pont de la Gabare, the bridge over the Rivière Salée, the channel separating the two parts of Guadeloupe. After 2 miles you'll come to the Destrellan traffic circle, where you can turn south on highway N 1 to Basse-Terre town and the Soufrière Volcano; or turn north on N 2 to Le Lamentin, Ste-Rose, and the beaches and fishing villages of northern Basse-Terre. A third option is to go to the N 1/D 23 intersection at Versailles and turn west on Route de la Traversée, the east-west highway that crosses the heart of the National Park.

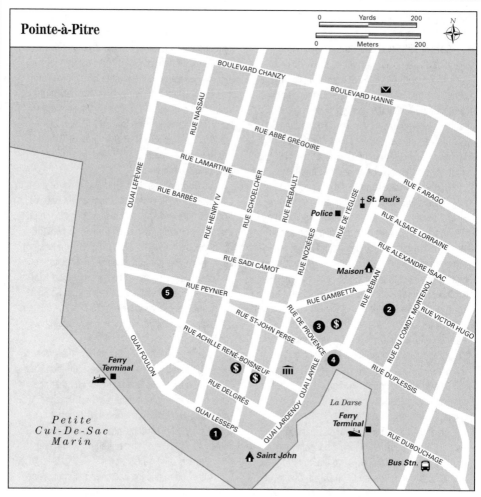

Pointe-à-Pitre

BOULEVARD CHANZY
BOULEVARD HANNE
RUE NASSAU
RUE ABBÉ GRÉGOIRE
RUE LAMARTINE
QUAI LEFÈVRE
RUE BARBÈS
RUE SCHOELCHER
RUE FRÉBAULT
RUE F. ARAGO
St. Paul's
RUE DE L'ÉGLISE
Police ■
RUE HENRY IV
RUE ALSACE LORRAINE
RUE NOZIÈRES
RUE ALEXANDRE ISAAC
RUE SADI CÁMOT
Maison
RUE BÉBIAN
5 RUE PEYNIER
RUE GAMBETTA
2
RUE DU COMDT. MORTENOL
RUE VICTOR HUGO
RUE ST-JOHN PERSE
RUE DE PROVENCE
3 **$**
RUE ACHILLE RENÉ-BOISNEUF
QUAI FOULON
$
Ferry
Terminal ■
$
RUE DELGRÈS
QUAI LARDENOY
QUAI LAYRLE
4
RUE DUPLESSIS
QUAI LESSEPS
La Darse
Petite
Cul-De-Sac
Marin
Ferry
Terminal ■
RUE DUBOUCHAGE
1
Saint John
Bus Stn.

1. St. John Perse Center
2. Place de la Victoire
3. Tourist Office
4. Central Market
5. Schoelcher Museum

Southern Basse-Terre

Basse-Terre's southeastern coast, from Petit-Bourg to Capesterre-Belle-Eau and Bananier, stretches in green fields of banana plantations from the sea, bordered by small villages and pretty beaches, to the brooding peaks of the Soufrière Mountains. The coast south of Petit-Bourg is popular for swimming and scuba diving; offshore, tiny Ilet Fortune is a nudist beach. Farther along, Ste-Marie has a monument commemorating Columbus's landing in 1493. At Changy a Hindu temple is one of several reminders of the multiracial makeup of the French West Indies.

Capesterre-Belle-Eau has a cassava-processing plant where you can watch cassava flour and bread being made. Cassava was a staple of the Amerindians, who taught early European explorers to use it, and it continues to be a basic food of the West Indies. En route from Capesterre to St-Sauveur, the road passes through Allée Dumanoir, one of the most photographed settings of Guadeloupe, where the route is lined with stately century-old royal palms.

Carbet Falls (Chutes du Carbet): A detour inland at St-Sauveur takes you to the imposing Carbet Falls and the Grand Etang, an inland lake whose tranquil waters mirror the lush landscape surrounding it. From the eastern slopes of the Soufrière Volcano, waters cascade more than 800 feet in three stages, forming the tallest falls in the Caribbean and creating the Grand Carbet River that empties into the sea at Capesterre-Belle-Eau.

Grand Etang (Grand Pond): Situated at 1,312 feet altitude, Grand Etang is the largest of several ponds in the area, covering 50 acres in a hot, humid atmosphere and creating a greenhouse that nurtures giant philodendron and ferns, orchids, anthurium, bromeliads, and other rain-forest vegetation not normally found at lower altitudes.

Archaeological Park (Parc Archéologique des Roches Gravées): Near Trois-Rivières on the road to the ferry for Les Saintes, there is an outdoor museum with petroglyphs of the Carib Indians, the pre-Columbian inhabitants of Guadeloupe. The drawings date from about A.D. 300 and depict animal and human figures. A footpath is bordered with cassava, cacao, calabash, pimiento, and other plants the Indians cultivated.

All along the drive of southern Basse-Terre, the dark green Soufrière Mountains loom high on the western landscape. To go directly to the Soufrière Volcano, turn north on D9 via Choisy, a hamlet surrounded by vast banana plantations, to St-Claude and La Savane à Mulets, a plateau and parking area where the hike to the volcano's summit begins.

Basse-Terre: The capital of Guadeloupe, which sits at the foot of the Soufrière Mountains, is one of the best-kept secrets in the Caribbean. A delightful town almost untouched by tourism, it was founded in the early 17th century and occupied several times by the British during the two centuries of rivalry between France and Britain over the Caribbean. To the south on a promontory was Fort St-Charles; the Gallion River, which originates on the slopes of La Soufrière, runs under the fort's ramparts on its way to the sea. The fort was surrounded by the Carmel quarter, the traditional

military and government section. Today it has the Palais d'Orléans with the Prefecture, the Palace of Justice, and the General Council building—all handsome examples of colonial architecture.

To the north was St-François parish, the commercial district with the streets laid out in a grid. It is still the commercial section, and behind the Town Hall on avenue Général de Gaulle are the main downtown streets. Rue du Docteur Cabre leads to the **Cathedral of Our Lady of Guadeloupe,** with a facade that's been classified as a historical monument.

St-Claude: The drive from Basse-Terre town to La Savane à Mulets, at 3,747 feet at the base of La Soufrière, takes thirty minutes and passes through the pretty hillside town of St-Claude. A wealthy residential community, its West Indian houses are set in flowering gardens against rainforest greenery and cascading streams. A visitor center, **La Maison du Volcan,** has displays relating to La Soufrière and the other volcanic regions of the Eastern Caribbean, as well as on volcanology throughout the world.

Soufrière Volcano: The forest green, deeply creviced mountains that dominate southern Basse-Terre are part of the National Park and take their name from the highest peak, La Soufrière, the brimstone-belching volcano at 4,813 feet. It is surrounded by other volcanic peaks more than 4,000 feet—all with waterfalls, hot springs, rain and cloud forests, and trails.

Although rumblings had been recorded since the 15th century, La Soufrière had been dormant for centuries when it began to erupt in 1975. Warnings had come as early as 1956, when tremors sent up rocks and ash and caused new fractures. La Soufrière continues to boil and bubble, but it is quiet enough to be climbed. You can go by car as far as the base of the cone at La Savane à Mulets, from which four marked trails—Red, Yellow, Green, and Blue—lead to the summit. When combined the trails take three-and-a-half hours to cover. One trail (Red) leads from the La Savane parking lot directly to the top in a series of switchbacks that gain 1,000 feet in forty-five heart-pounding minutes. Composed of solidified lava, the crown has a deep split through the center, where continuing volcanic action can be seen. You should wear sturdy shoes and protection against the rain and wind, and be extremely cautious walking around fumaroles at the summit. Some parts of the trails are very difficult; mist and clouds often make it difficult to see your way. If you do not have the time or stamina to go to the summit, you can choose from several easy walks in the La Savane area.

Matouba: Two miles northwest of St-Claude, the town of Matouba, at 2,234 feet in altitude, was settled by the East Indians brought to the French West Indies as laborers in the mid-19th century after the abolition of slavery. The hot springs of Matouba are well known for their therapeutic properties.

Vieux-Fort: At the southern tip of Basse-Terre, where the Atlantic Ocean meets the Caribbean Sea, is an old town that takes its name from the fort that once guarded the strategic point. Today the town is known for a delicate embroidery art made by the women of the village.

National Park of Guadeloupe (Parc National de Guadeloupe): The spine of forested mountains that run almost the length of Basse-Terre constitute the 74,100-acre National Park. You'll find exhibits throughout on particular aspects—volcano, forest, coffee, sugarcane, archaeology, and wildlife—of the park, but explanations are in French only. The exhibits are intended as learning centers as well as outdoor museums. The centers are accessible on paved roads and are usually the starting point for one of the park's 200 miles of signposted trails.

Route de la Traversée: The highway through the center of the park starts from the banana and sugarcane fields on the east coast at Versailles and climbs to 600 feet at Vernou, a fashionable residential district of pretty villas with tropical gardens overlooking the serpentine Lézarde River Valley. After Vernou the highway winds through the park to a pass, **Col des Deux Mamelles,** where it crosses the ridge to the west coast. The scenic drive provides access to more than a half-dozen walks and hikes from a ten-minute stroll to a 10-mile trek.

Ecrivisses Falls (The Falls of the Crayfish): About a mile from the park entrance on the south side of the Route de la Traversée, a path along the Corossol River leads in a ten-minute walk to the **Cascade aux Ecrevisses.** The pretty waterfall is the most accessible one in the park and is usually included on motor coach tours of eastern Basse-Terre. It is also popular for swimming and picnicking. (Do not leave valuables unattended. Young boys, finding tourists easy prey here, sometimes sneak out from the woods to grab a handbag or camera and disappear into the foliage.)

The Forest House and Bras David Tropical Park: About halfway on the Route de la Traversée is the Forest House (La Maison de la Forêt; Hours: 9 a.m. to 4:30 p.m.) in the Bras David Tropical Park, which takes its name from a nearby river. It has picnic grounds, trails, and a nature center with outdoor displays and three short trails.

Les Mamelles: When the Route de la Traversée crosses over the main ridge, it passes several peaks where there are roads or footpaths for hiking. On the south are the Deux Mamelles: Petit-Bourg, 2,349 feet; and Pigeon, 2,526 feet. The latter has a path of forty-five minutes with a lookout at 1,969 feet that takes in a grandstand view of the mountains and the coasts. From the pass of the Deux Mamelles, the Route de la Traversée winds down to the coast under a 2-mile umbrella of flamboyant trees that are magnificent when they are in bloom, from May to Oct.

At Mahaut on the west coast, you can turn north to Pointe-Noire and Deshaies or south on the scenic road known as the Golden Corniche, which winds along pretty little coves between cliffs and gorges to Basse-Terre town.

Pigeon Island/Cousteau Underwater Nature Park: At Malendure Beach you can take a five-minute boat ride to Pigeon Island or a glass-bottom boat excursion to the Underwater Park of Pigeon Island, also known as the Cousteau Underwater Reserve, Guadeloupe's main diving location.

Maison du Café: Inland from Vieux-Habitants, a scenic drive winds along the Grande Rivière through the wooded mountains with magnificent views of the park, Soufrière Volcano, and the coast. It ends at the Maison du Cafe, one of the interpretive centers of the park, and La Grivelière, a small coffee plantation that has been in the same family for more than a century. A tour is available. Vieux-Habitants, one of the island's oldest villages, has the oldest parish church in Guadeloupe (1650), which was recently restored.

Northern Basse-Terre

You can approach northern Basse-Terre from either the east or west coast. On the east coast the drive skirts miles of banana and sugar plantations and mangroves; on the west coast the wooded highlands of the park fall almost directly to the sea. The fishing villages of the north coast are popular for their Creole and seafood restaurants. **Domaine de Séverin** (0590-28-91-86; fax: 0590-28-36-66; domaine.de.severin@wanadoo.fr) in Ste-Rose and Grosse-Montagne in Lamentin are long-established rum makers where guided tours are offered.

From Mahaut at the western end of Route de la Traversée, the road north passes Pointe-Noire, a town known for its wood craftsmen. Here the **House of Wood** (0590-98-16-90; www.guadeloupe-parcnational.com) is a display center and forestry museum. Another attraction in the vicinity is the 18th-century coffee plantation, located on a hillside above Pointe-Noire, with a restaurant, **Caféière Beauséjour,** and boutique of local products (0590-98-10-09; fax: 0590-98-12-49; www.cafeiere beausejour.com). Farther north Deshaies has a marina and **Le Jardin Botanique de Deshaies** (Botanical Garden of Deshaies; 0590-28-43-02; fax: 0590-28-51-37; www.jardinbotanique.com), with walkways, birds, and waterfalls. Entrance fee: US$15–$20. Hours: 9 a.m. to 4:30 p.m.

Around Grande-Terre

Grande-Terre, Guadeloupe's eastern wing, is flat in comparison to Basse-Terre and is as popular for biking as Basse-Terre is for hiking. From Pointe-à-Pitre the highway east passes Bas du Fort, with its large yacht-filled marina and the **Guadeloupe Aquarium** (Place Creole; 0590-90-92-38; www.guadeloupeaquarium.com; aquarium-guadeloupe@wanadoo.fr). Here you can see exhibits of Caribbean marine life and walk through the glass tunnel of a 21,000-gallon tank with sharks. There is a boutique and restaurant. Admission: €8.50 adults, €5 children age five to twelve. Hours: 9 a.m. to 7 p.m. daily.

After passing the campus of the university, the road continues along the south coast to Guadeloupe's main resort centers—Gosier, Ste-Anne, and St-François—which are set on attractive beaches or on hillsides overlooking the sea; they offer the full range of water sports. Petit-Havre, between Gosier and Ste-Anne, and Raisins-Clairs Beach at St-François are public beaches. St-François, a fishing village, is known for its seafood restaurants.

Pointe des Châteaux: The easternmost point of Grande-Terre at Pointe des Châteaux, which is marked by a large white cross, has a dramatic setting with big Atlantic waves rolling in from the north and smashing against the cliffs of the rocky headlands.

Le Moule: Once the capital of Guadeloupe, Le Moule was the site of fierce fighting between the early French settlers and the Caribs. Today it is the main town on the Atlantic coast with a horseshoe beach and a picturesque church that is a historic monument. The neighboring village, La Rosette, has the **Edgar Clerc Archaeological Museum** (Musee d'Archéologie Precolombienne Edgar Clerc), where Amerindian artifacts gathered from the islands of the Eastern Caribbean are displayed. Hours: daily except Tues 10:30 a.m. to 6:30 p.m.; (0590) 23-57-57. Admission is free.

The region around Le Moule is covered with cane fields and dotted with sugar mills, some with their original machinery, as well as the ruins of old plantation houses. There are several rum distilleries in the area. The contrast between the pastoral landscape of Grande-Terre and the brooding peaks of Basse-Terre is particularly noticeable here.

At **Rhum Damoiseau,** the old windmill, complete with its arms and together with the mill works, was restored in 1996 and can be visited (Distillerie Bellevue, 97160 Le Moule, Guadeloupe, FWI; 0590-23-55-55; fax: 0590-23-48-50; http://damoiseau.fr/fr; rhum@damoiseau.com). Hours: Mon to Sat 7:30 a.m. to 2 p.m.

Les Grands Fonds: Across central Grande-Terre, between Pointe-à-Pitre and Abymes on the west and Le Moule on the east, is the roller-coaster terrain of *mornes* and *fonds*, the hills and valleys that characterize this region, known locally as *montagnes russes*. Les Grands Fonds is inhabited by the descendants of the Blancs Matignon, a small group of white settlers who retreated here after the abolition of slavery in 1848. They formed a unique ethnic and social group, but today they are distinguishable from the rest of the population only by race.

Morne-à-l'Eau: South of Abymes in the town of Morne-à-l'Eau is one of the island's best-known landmarks, an amphitheater-shaped cemetery in checkerboard black and white. It is a place of pilgrimage on All Saints Day, Nov 1, when people from all over the island—as well as visitors—come to light candles for their deceased loved ones.

Petit-Canal: The **Monument to Liberty** in the small village of Petit-Canal is one of the most poignant sites in the Caribbean. It stands on a hillside at the head of fifty-three steps—one for each plantation that once flourished in Guadeloupe. During slavery, plantation owners punished their rebellious slaves by putting them in barrels with spikes driven into the sides and rolling them down these steps. North of the fishing villages of Port-Louis, the inviting beaches are all but deserted on weekdays.

Exploring the Offshore Islands

Iles des Saintes (Les Saintes): Off the south coast of Basse-Terre is an archipelago of eight tiny volcanic islands with quiet bays and rocky coves etched with white-sand beaches. These idyllic hideaways, where time seems to have stood still, are popular with day-trippers from Guadeloupe and small cruise ships.

Only Terre-de-Bas and Terre-de-Haut, the largest of the group, are inhabited, and only the latter has tourist facilities. Most inhabitants are descended from the settlers from Brittany, who were often the pioneers of the French West Indies. Many are fishermen who still wear the salako, a broad-brim, flat straw hat covered with white cloth, which they inherited from their seagoing ancestors.

Mountainous Terre-de-Haut, usually called Les Saintes, has one village, Bourg des Saintes, and one road, a flower-filled lane that runs from one end of the 3-mile-long island to the other. From the harbor situated on the north side of the island, the walk in either direction is delightful. On a hilltop overlooking the village is **Fort Napoleon,** built in the 17th century to defend Pointe-à-Pitre harbor. The fort has a botanic garden and, surprisingly, contains a museum of modern art. South of town, 1,020-foot Le Chameau is the island's highest hill, where a track zigzags up to an old watchtower and a panoramic view of Terre-de-Haut and its neighbors, Basse-Terre and La Soufrière.

West from the harbor the road leads up a hill along a row of small, colorful houses with gingerbread trim and flowering gardens to delightful beaches with small hotels, good restaurants, and water-sports facilities. On the east end of the island, pretty St-Pierre Bay has a white-sand beach; there is an entrance fee. On the south side of the island where the small airport is located, the beach is usually too windy and rough for swimming.

The island has taxis; daily ferry service from Trois-Rivières and Basse-Terre takes thirty minutes, from Pointe-à-Pitre about an hour. There is also air service from Pointe-à-Pitre.

Marie-Galante: Located 27 miles south of Grande-Terre, Marie-Galante is an occasional cruise port of call. Similar in appearance to Grande-Terre, the slightly pear-shaped island has green rolling hills and long, reef-protected white-sand beaches along the west and south coast. The east side is mostly rockbound. Historic Marie-Galante is called the island of a hundred windmills. Some of the old mills that dot the landscape still produce cotton and sugar, the island's mainstay. Château Murat, an old plantation manor house, is now a museum.

The three main towns—St-Louis on the west, Grand-Bourg on the southwest, and Capesterre on the southeast—are connected by good roads. Each town has narrow streets with tiny stores and pastel houses. The good roads, low terrain, and light traffic make biking a delightful mode of travel for the island.

One of the main roads crosses the southern third of the island from St-Louis and the beaches of the west coast over rolling hills to the eastern part of the island. About midway the road branches to **Trou à Diable,** a grotto of stalactites. From St-Louis and Anse-Canot on the northwest coast, there are scenic routes along **La Grande Barre,** a high green ridge dividing the northern half of the island into two plateaus. Anse-Canot and Vieux-Fort have beautiful beaches with reefs.

Marie-Galante is the most populous of the offshore islands and has restaurants and small hotels. Daily flights from Pointe-à-Pitre take fifteen minutes; ferries take one-and-a-half hours.

Shopping

Perfumes, china, crystal, leather goods, cosmetics, clothing and accessories, fine wines, and liqueurs are some of the French products' famous labels that will attract your immediate attention, but don't overlook local products. You will find rum, coffee, spices, handcrafted pottery, straw, gold jewelry, madras dolls, shell figurines, and much more. French perfumes are about 20 percent lower in price here than in the United States. When you pay in U.S. travelers' checks, 20 percent is sometimes deducted on certain luxury items in specialized shops.

The main downtown shopping streets run about 6 blocks deep from the port between rues Frébault, Nozières, and Schoelcher. All are picturesque with colorful old, balconied houses between the chic boutiques with fashions from Paris and the trendsetting Côte d'Azur. Don't expect much English to be spoken. Shops in town are open on weekdays from 8:30 or 9 a.m. to 12:30 or 1 p.m. and from 2:30 or 3 to 5:30 or 6 p.m.; on Sat to 1 p.m.

Destreland (www.destreland.com), ideally situated on a spit of land between Grande-Terre and Basse-Terre, with Creole-style architecture, is the largest commercial center in Guadeloupe with more than one hundred boutiques, services, and restaurants. It is open daily except Sun.

Even more fun than chic boutiques is a visit to the open-air markets. The main market is found at **Place du Marché,** north of rue Peynier. Here in the mélange of colors, sounds, and aroma, Creole-speaking market women in madras dress sell exotic flowers and fruits, vegetables, and fresh spices, and they know how to drive a hard bargain.

Books and Maps: Espace St. John Perse (3 rue Boisneuf) and **Librairie Générale** (46 rue Schoelcher) are main outlets for books in French. For books on Guadeloupe and the French West Indies in English, try the gift shops in hotels.

Cheese and Groceries: Cora Supermarket on the east side of Pointe-à-Pitre is a large supermarket where you can find pâtés, cheese, canned delicacies, liquor, wine, and kitchen gadgets, as well as inexpensive beachwear and boutiques for jewelry, shoes, and more.

Clothing and Shoes: As noted earlier the **Destreland Shopping Center,** on the west side of Pointe-à-Pitre, is the island's largest shopping center with more than one hundred shops, including designer labels and well-known fashion brands, jewelry, shoes, accessories, and fancy leather goods, plus banks, a drugstore, food, liquor, wine, cheese, and sports wear, **Roger Albert** (perfume, accessories), and restaurants, including Subway, McDonald's, and a pizzeria. A fashionable boutique in town is **Paul et Virginie** (rue Schoelcher). Stylish sandals and inexpensive shoes are found at **Bata** and **100,000 Chaussures** (both on rue Frébault).

Crafts and Souvenirs: Handicrafts such as dolls dressed in madras, known as *doudou* dolls; madras table linens; aprons; cards with colorful collages; straw hats and bags; baskets of spices; shells; and wooden carvings can be found at various shopping centers. **Galerie de l'Artisanat** (Destreland Center; 0590-25-45-15; fax: 0590-25-02-04; espace .art@wanadoo.fr) has the Craft Gallery, a boutique with crafts by local artisans. **Grain d'Or** (47 rue Frebault) sells costume jewelry and unusual gifts. **Eurogold** (Rue Frabault) is another jewelry store.

Music: Zouk is the French West Indies' answer to calypso or *soca*. Kassav is the best-known group of the zouk artists. Two locations of **Debs** (27 and 116 rue Frébault) sell their recordings. Selections are greater here, but prices are higher than in New York.

Perfume: Phoenicia (rue Frébault) has a wide selection of perfumes and cosmetics, as well as ties, scarves, and small accessories.

Dining and Restaurants

Although other French islands are famous for their gourmet restaurants, Guadeloupe has traditionally been the culinary capital of the French West Indies—and it is the only island in the Caribbean with an annual feast honoring the patron saint of cooking. The island's distinctive Creole cuisine reflects its multifaceted heritage: the French interest in careful preparation of fine cuisine, the ingredients inherited from the Arawaks, and the spices and traditions introduced by Africans, Indians, and Asians. Fresh seafood is an important element, as are conch and stuffed land crabs. To start your meal the traditional way, try a ti-punch, a small but potent mixture of rum, lime juice, and sugarcane syrup that is meant to stimulate the appetite.

Cruise-ship passengers normally do not have the luxury of spending two or three hours over a meal as the French traditionally do, but if trying new and exotic cuisine is high on your list of priorities, you might want to spend part of your day enjoying a Creole meal. It is easy to combine sightseeing with lunch in an out-of-the-way place, since some of the best restaurants are rustic establishments on the south coast of Grande-Terre, the north coast of Basse-Terre, and in small villages along the way. Prices are on the high side. An inexpensive three-course meal for one person, without wine, costs about US$30; moderate, US$30–$45; and expensive, US$45 and higher. Inquire in advance about the use of credit cards and serving hours.

Pointe-à-Pitre/Gosier Area

Auberge de la Vieille Tour (Montauban, Gosier; 0590-84-23-23) in a long established hotel has one of the best restaurants in Guadeloupe and special-izes in French cuisine and seafood with a Creole flair. Moderately expensive.

Côte Jardin (La Marina; 0590-90-91-28) heads the list for Guadeloupe's movers, shakers, and gourmets for its excellent cuisine and service in a lovely indoor garden setting. Expensive, but worth it for those who appreciate fine dining.

Quatre Épices (25 Général-de-Gaulle Blvd.; 0590-84-76-01), situated in a 200-year-old Creole house, serves high quality French Creole cuisine.

Villa Fleur d'Epée (rue du Fort Fleur d'Epée, 97190 Gosier; 0590-90-86-59; fleurdepee@wanadoo.fr). Fine French cuisine with a Creole touch. Nice garden. Expensive.

St-François Area

Iguana Café (route de la Pointe des Chateaux, St-François; 0590-85-03-09). Fine, innovative cuisine served in a renovated Creole house. Moderately expensive.

Northern Basse-Terre

Chez Clara (Ste-Rose; 0590-28-91-86). Charm-ing rustic restaurant facing small fish port of Ste-Rose, specializing in Creole cuisine. Moderately expensive.

Domaine de Séverin (Cadet Ste-Rose; 0590-28-34-54). Colonial house nestled in a magnificent tropical garden. French and Creole cuisine with fish and ouassous (crayfish) specialties. Moderately expensive.

Le Karacoli (Deshaies; 0590-28-53-40). Open-air terrace in the shadow of coconut trees, facing Grand-Anse. Excellent authentic Creole cuisine. Moderately expensive.

Southern Grand Terre

La Paillotte de Pêcheur (Trois-Rivières; 0590-92-94-98) is a family-run "fisherman's hut" that spe-cializes in seafood, particularly fresh lobster. Open daily for lunch and dinner except Sun. Moderate.

La Rocher de Malendure (Bouillante, Basse-Terre; 0590-98-70-84). Enjoy views of Pigeon Island and the sea from a rustic terrace setting amid tropical gardens while you lunch on fresh seafood. Moderately expensive.

Le Caprice des Iles (Baillif; 0590-81-74-97). Dining room and covered terrace overlooking the sea, offering fish and chicken specialties. Moder-ately expensive.

Ti Cafe (St-Claude; 0590-80-06-05; fax: 0590-80-31-63). Situated in an 18th-century estate house of a coffee plantation, the cafe specializes in Creole cuisine made from fresh local products and fresh fish. Moderately expensive.

Nightlife

In addition to hotel discos and nightclubs, there are nightspots for zouk, the pop music craze. Guade-loupe has two casinos: one in Gosier and the other in St-François. The legal age is twenty-one, and proof of identity (passport or driver's license with photo) is required. Jacket and tie are not required, but dress is fashionable.

Sports

Beaches/Swimming: Guadeloupe has a great variety of beaches, from long stretches of white sand and sheltered coves to black-sand beaches and surf-washed Atlantic shores. Public beaches are free, though some may charge for parking.

Unlike hotel beaches, they have no facilities. Generally, hotels welcome nonguests but charge for the use of facilities. There are several officially designated nudist beaches, the most popular being Pointe Tarare near Pointe des Châteaux. Topless is common at hotel beaches, but less so on village beaches.

Biking: Cycling is a national sport whose popularity gets an annual boost from the Tour de la Guadeloupe, a ten-day international race in Aug that is as hotly contested as the Tour de France on the mainland. For visitors biking is best in Grande-Terre. **Cyclo-Tours** (0590-84-11-34) and **Dingo** (0590-83-81-19) in Pointe-à-Pitre have bikes for rent.

Boating: Strong winds and currents make yachting a challenging sport in Guadeloupe. Boats of all sizes are available for charter with crew or bareboat. Safe anchorages and pretty beaches make Les Saintes popular destinations for day excursions. Full-day picnic sails are organized by local travel companies. **Port de Plaisance Marina** (Bas-du-Fort; 0590-90-84-85), the largest of three marinas, is located ten minutes from Pointe-à-Pitre and is considered in yachting circles to be one of the best in the Western Hemisphere for its facilities. The **Capitainerie** (Harbormaster, 0590-82-54-85) is open weekdays 8 a.m. to 1 p.m. and 3 to 5 p.m., and Sat to 11:30 p.m.

Canyoning/Rappeling: Canopée (Plage de Malendure, Bouillante; 0590-26-95-59; www .canopeeguadeloupe.com); **Mangofil** (St. Claude; 0590-81-10-43; mangofil1@wanadoo.fr). Sequence of fifty crossings from tree to tree on Tyrolean traverses and rope bridges. **Vert Intense** (www .vertintense.com) is a specialist.

Deep-Sea Fishing: Sportfishing boats are based at **Port de Plaisance Marina** (Bas-du-Fort; 0590-82-74-94), the **Fishing Club Antilles** (Bouillante; 0590-90-70-10), and **Guadeloupe Marlin Club** (0590-98-70-10).

Golf: Golf International (St-François, 0590-88-41-87; fax: 0590-88-42-20) on the southeastern end of Grande-Terre is within walking distance of several hotels. The 18-hole course, designed by Robert Trent Jones, has a clubhouse with pro shop, lockers, and restaurant and an English-speaking pro.

Hiking: Basse-Terre's National Park, with its spectacular scenery and good trails, offers some of the best hiking in the Caribbean. The 200 miles of signposted trails range from easy walks through tropical rain forests to arduous treks through wild mountain terrain. Many short hikes lead to pretty picnic spots, waterfalls, and mountain pools. The Tourist Office in Pointe-à-Pitre has brochures on the park. Guided hikes can be arranged through the **Bureau des Guides de Moyenne Montague,** (Maison Forestière, Matouba; 0590-81-24-83).

Jacky Action Sport (Baie Malhaut, 14 res Louverture, La Jaille; 0590-26-02-34; jacky.noc@ wanadoo.fr) offers mountain guides, hiking, canopy tours, equestrian sports. **Vert Intense** (Basse-Terre, Marine Rivière Sens; 0590-99-34-73; www .vertintense.com) arranges hiking La Soufrière and rivers in the heart of the national park; mountain biking; canyoning.

Horseback Riding: Among the stables are **Domaine de Belle plaine** (Ste. Rose; 0590-58-01-09; www.cheval-guadeloupe.com) offers rides on forest trails, by rivers, waterfalls and surrounding farmlands. **Le Haras de Saint-François** (St. François; 0590-58-99-92; leharasdesaintfrancois@ wanadoo.fr) has horseback outings; and **La Bellencroupe** (St. Louis; 0590-97-18-69; la.bellen croupe@wanadoo.fr) offers horseback rides and trekking.

Kayaking/Canoeing: The lagoons and mangroves of Grand Cul-de-Sac Marin on the northwest of Basse-Terre are ideal for kayaking. Guided excursions are available from **Nature Passion Ecotourisme** (Ste-Rose; 0590-28-98-73; fax: 0590-68-47-55; nature-passion-ecotourisme@wanadoo.fr) and **Guadeloupe-Adventure** (0590-35-45-78) which also offers canyoning and hiking. **Tam Tam Pagaie** (Ste-Rose; phone/fax: 0590-28-13-85; tamtam-pagaie@wanadoo.fr). Offers kayak trips.

Snorkeling/Scuba Diving: The snorkeling locations nearest to the port in Pointe-à-Pitre are the reefs fronting Gosier and the offshore island, Ilet du Gosier. Equipment is available from water-sports operators based at beachside hotels in Grande-Terre.

The most popular dive area is Pigeon Island off the west coast of Basse-Terre. It is actually two tiny volcanic islands with abundant marine life. Each dive location is different in character. The west side has a wall that begins at the surface, drops to 25 feet, slopes to 40 feet, and drops again. Here soft corals, large brain coral, seafans, and sponges and colorful fish are abundant, making it interesting for undersea photographers and popular with snorkelers. The north side has a reef beginning in shallow water suitable for novice divers; it drops off to small canyons and walls, interesting for experienced divers. On the northeast side, a wall begins at the surface and drops to 40 feet. It is rich in sponges, pillar corals, and a great variety of fish. Ilet à Fajou, off the north coast of Basse-Terre, is another location visited on day trips from Grande-Terre.

Individual dives range from about US$50 to $75, depending on distance to dive sites. Dive operators in Grande-Terre usually take groups to Pigeon Island. On Malendure Beach, facing Pigeon Island, there are four dive operators: **Les Heures Saines** (0590-98-86-63); **Plaisir Plongee Karukera** (0590-98-82-43); **UCPA** (Bouillante, 0590-98-89-00; ucpa .bouillante@wanadoo.fr) which also offers hiking excursions and windsurfing; and **Archipel Plongee Guadeloupe** (0590-98-93-93; www.archipel-plongee.fr), with departures at 10:15 a.m. and 12:45 p.m. Cost: Snorkeling, €20; novice dive from €50; two dives €90. Nondivers can take the *Nautiles,* a glass-bottom boat at Plage de Malendure which departs several times daily. The eighty-minute ride passes over the Cousteau Marine Reserve, a protected area just off the coast at Malendure. American visitors should be aware that the French, who pioneered the sport of diving, use a system for dive tables and apparatus that is different from the American one. As a safety matter, divers (including certified ones) are checked on the use of the equipment before they are permitted to don tanks. Courses for certification by CMAS (Confédération

Mondiale des Activités Subaquatique), the French national scuba association, are rigorous.

Windsurfing/Kitesurfing: Guadeloupe was a pioneer of windsurfing in the 1970s, and it is a frequent venue for international meets. Lessons and rental equipment are available from most beachfront hotels. **Loisirs Nautiques** (Callinago; 0590-84-25-25) and **Nauticase** (Salako Hotel) rent boards for about US$15 to $20 per hour. Beginner's lessons cost about US$25. **Ecole de Voile** (0590-88-12-32). Kitesurfing is the new attraction. Contact **Sports & Adventure** (Gosier; 0590-38-00-25; www .sport-adventure.com; sportdav@wanadoo.fr).

Festivals and Celebrations

Fête des Cuisinières (Festival of the Women Cooks), one of the Caribbean's most colorful festivals, takes place on the second weekend in Aug. It is the feast day of St. Laurent, the patron saint of cooking. But this is no ordinary feast. For days the women cooks of the island prepare their specialties and make their costumes for a special parade. The celebration begins with a High Mass at the Cathedral in Pointe-à-Pitre to bless the food, which is placed at the altar. Afterward the women promenade through the streets in their Creole finery, carrying their elaborately decorated plates of island specialties and gaily decorated baskets of fruits and vegetables trimmed with miniature kitchen utensils. The parade ends at a local school for a ceremony attended by the mayor and other dignitaries, followed by a feast and dancing. Visitors are invited to participate.

Other celebrations include **Carnival,** held in the traditional pre-Lenten period. For the last five days of Carnival, all business stops, and by Shrove Tues, or Mardi Gras, festivities reach a frenzy with parades of floats, costumed red devils, and dancing in the streets of Pointe-à-Pitre. In the French West Indies Carnival continues through Ash Wed, when participants dress in black and white, King Carnival is burned on a funeral pyre, and a night parade with torches is held to bury Vaval.

Dominica
Roseau, Portsmouth/Prince Rupert Bay

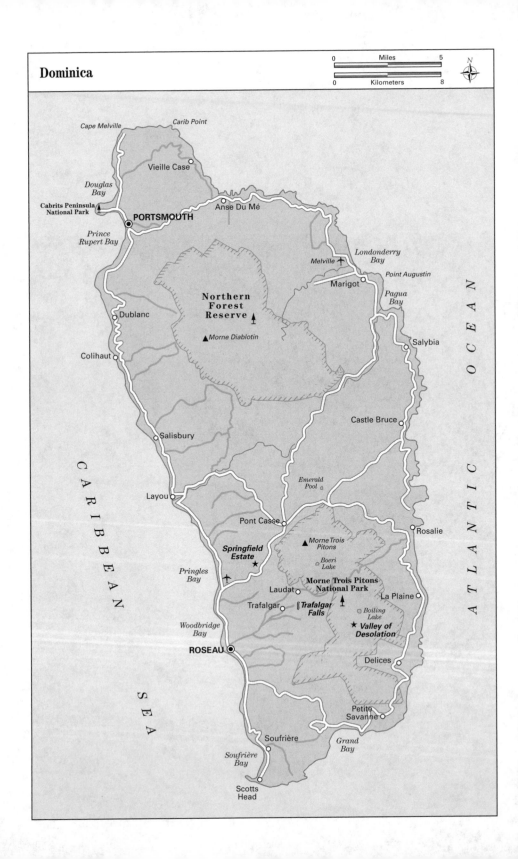

Dominica

Miles 0 5
Kilometers 0 8

N

Cape Melville
Carib Point
Vieille Case
Douglas Bay
Cabrits Peninsula National Park
PORTSMOUTH
Anse Du Mé
Prince Rupert Bay

Londonderry Bay
Melville ✈
Point Augustin
Marigot
Pagua Bay

Northern Forest Reserve
▲ *Morne Diablotin*

Dublanc

Colihaut

Salybia

Salisbury

Castle Bruce

Emerald Pool

Layou

Pont Casse

Rosalie

▲ *Morne Trois Pitons*

Springfield Estate ★

Boeri Lake

Pringles Bay
✈

Morne Trois Pitons National Park

Laudat

La Plaine

Trafalgar

‖ *Trafalgar Falls*

Boiling Lake

Woodbridge Bay

★ **Valley of Desolation**

ROSEAU ◉

Delices

Petite Savanne

Soufrière

Grand Bay

Soufrière Bay

Scotts Head

C A R I B B E A N   S E A

A T L A N T I C   O C E A N

The Gift of Nature

Covered from end to end with towering volcanic mountains and spectacular tropical scenery, Dominica is the gift of nature. Mists rise from the green valleys and fall softly over the blue-green peaks densely carpeted with rain forests and exotic plants that host more than 135 species of birds. Natural wonders hide in the mountain vastness, and rivers and streams cascade over cliffs and rush down steep mountains.

Located in the heart of the Eastern Caribbean between Guadeloupe and Martinique, Dominica—not to be confused with the Dominican Republic—bridges the Leeward and the Windward Islands. The most mountainous of the Lesser Antilles, the land rises steeply from the shore to peaks that reach almost 5,000 feet. The native Carib Indians called their island by the descriptive name of *Wai'tukubuli,* meaning "tall is her body." Moisture-laden trade winds from the east hang over the mountains, where they condense and release 250 inches of rain per year.

Dominica does not fit the usual image of a Caribbean island. Tourism's role is secondary in the economy. The island has no large resorts or shopping centers and does not want them. There are only a few beaches, and except for a stretch on the north coast, they consist mostly of black, volcanic sand—a matter of little importance, since the exquisite beauty of Dominica's interior more than compensates for the absence of beach-scalloped shores.

Columbus came upon Dominica on a Sunday in 1493 and named it for the day. The French and British fought over the island but in 1686 agreed in a treaty to recognize Dominica as a neutral territory to be left to the Caribs forever. But neither honored the agreement, and in practice Dominica became a sort of no-man's land of endless battles, with the French and British encroaching increasingly on Carib lands.

In 1805 Britain took possession of Dominica, and after almost two centuries of more turbulence, the island became independent in 1978. The French influence on the culture lingers to this day almost as much as that of the British. It is particularly apparent in the Creole speech, the cuisine, and the names of people and places.

Budget Planning

In some ways Dominica is one of the least expensive islands in the Eastern Caribbean, but it is also one of the least developed for tourism. Restaurants serving locals are cheap; some catering to tourists are outrageously expensive. Outside of the capital and Portsmouth, tourist facilities are extremely limited or nonexistent. If the shore excursions offered by your cruise ship do not suit your interests, it is best to arrange a tour or hike with one of the local travel companies rather than go on your own.

Port Profile

Location/Embarkation: Dominica has three ports. Roseau, the capital on the southwest coast, has a passenger port in the heart of town. (The exit gate is directly in front of the museum.) A second, deepwater harbor and commercial port is at

At a Glance

Antiquities	★
Architecture	★
Art and Artists	★
Beaches	★
Colonial Buildings	★★
Crafts	★★★★
Cuisine	★★★
Culture	★★★
Dining/Restaurants	★★
Entertainment	★
Forts	★★
History	★★★
Monuments	★
Museums	★★★
Nightlife	★
Scenery	★★★★★
Shopping	★★
Sightseeing	★★★
Sports	★★★★★
Transportation	★

Fast Facts

Population: 75,000

Size: 29 miles long and 16 miles wide; 290.8 square miles

Main Towns: Roseau, Portsmouth

Government: Dominica is a democratic republic headed by a president. The constitution provides for seven ministers, including a prime minister who is the leader of the party with a majority in the House of Assembly. The cabinet, comprising the prime minister, ministers of government, and attorney general, is the chief policy-making body.

Currency: Eastern Caribbean (EC) dollar. US$1 equals EC$2.70. Credit cards are accepted at major hotels but are not widely used.

Departure Tax: US$20

Emergency Numbers: Medical: Harlsbro Medical Centre, Hillsborough Street; contact local operator, or dial 999; Police: 999

Language: English is the official language, but Creole, a French-based patois, is spoken widely.

Public Holidays: Jan 1, New Year's Day; Carnival, Shrove Mon and Tues; Good Friday; Easter Monday; May 1, Labor Day; May/June, Whit Mon; first Mon in Aug; Nov 3 and 4, National Day Celebrations; Dec 25, Christmas; Dec 26, Boxing Day.

Telephone Area Code: 767. Direct telephone and fax services to all parts of the world are operated by Cable and Wireless Ltd.

Airlines: There is no direct service from the U.S. mainland to Dominica. Rather, you must fly to San Juan, Antigua, or another of the Caribbean's main gateways, and transfer to American Eagle, Dominica Air Taxi, LIAT, or other local airlines that fly to Dominica.

Dominica has two airports: Canefield, 3 miles north of Roseau, accommodates aircraft up to a nineteen-seater twin otter; and

Melville Hall on the northeast coast, 29 miles from Roseau and 20 miles from Portsmouth, takes larger aircraft. LIAT operates daily flights to both airports.

Information: www.dominica.dm; www.visit-dominica.com

In the United States:

In lieu of an office, the Discover Dominica Authority (DDA) has a toll-free number (866) 522-4057 for callers from the United States and Canada to assist with tourism-related inquires. The number is answered by tourism representatives from the DDA, Mon to Fri between 9 a.m. and 5 p.m.; dominicany@ dominica.dm.

In Port:

Discover Dominica Authority, Valley Road, Roseau, Commonwealth of Dominica, W.I.; (767) 448-2045; fax: (767) 488-5840; tourism@discover dominica.com

Forestry Division, (767) 448-2401

Woodbridge Bay, about 1 mile north of town, which is sometimes used by cruise ships. The third port is Portsmouth, the second-largest town, and is located 25 miles north of Roseau on Prince Rupert Bay, a wide bay adjacent to the historic Cabrits Peninsula National Park. Dominica built the port here to develop Portsmouth and the Cabrits as a tourist attraction. The dock and modern terminal, designed in West Indian architecture typical of the 18th century, enable passengers to disembark directly into the national park.

Local Transportation: Dominica's public transport is provided by private taxis and minivans in Roseau and between towns and villages.

Roads and Rentals: Dominica has more than 300 miles of good roads built in the mid-1980s with the help of the United States. They connect Roseau

with the main towns and villages, making many of the island's most scenic parts—heretofore almost inaccessible—easy to reach. No highway completely encircles the island, but it is possible to loop around the northern end. Three highways connect Roseau on the west coast with the main east-coast villages of Rosalie, Castle Bruce, and Marigot.

And now for the bad news. The secondary roads and tracks feeding from the paved roads range from passable to terrible, and none are well marked. You must have a good map to find your way, but even detailed maps do not show all the important places. To see the most beautiful parts of Dominica, you need to leave your car and hike into the interior to the forests, lakes, waterfalls, and mountain heights.

Cars are available for rent; you need a visitor's driving permit, which can be obtained upon presentation of a valid driver's license to the Police Traffic

Department (High Street, Roseau) and select car-rental agencies, and payment of EC$30 (US$12). You must be between the ages of 25 and 65. Rental rates start at about US$50 per day; a deposit, payable by credit card, is sometimes required. Driving in this former British colony is on the LEFT. And, be aware, driving here is hazardous. Some car-rental firms in Roseau are **Island Car Rental** (767-448-0737; fax: 767-448-0737; www.islandcar.dm), **Garraway Rent-a-Car** (17 Old St., Roseau; 767-448-2891; fax: 767-448-0541; www.avirtualdominica.com/garraway carrental/index.html), and **Valley Rent-a-Car** (767-448-3233; www.valleyrentacar.com).

Ferry Service: L'Express des Iles (767-448-2181; www.express-des-iles.com) provides high-speed catamaran services between Dominica and Guadeloupe on the north and Martinique on the south. Since ferries have a start-and-stop history in the Caribbean, you should check with the ferry company before making plans.

Shore Excursions

Dominica has good, reasonably priced tour compa-nies, and their tours are recommended for first-time visitors. You can waste a great deal of time trying to find your way in Dominica's mountainous terrain, where distances are very deceiving, routes often taking two or three times the normal amount of time to cover. Descriptions of sites mentioned here are provided elsewhere in the chapter. All rates are per person.

City/Trafalgar Waterfalls: 4 hours, US$40–$58. Drive to Morne Bruce for a spectacular view of Roseau and harbor, visit the Botanical Gardens, and continue to Trafalgar Falls and a short walk in the rain forest.

Trafalgar/Emerald Falls/Carib Reserve: Full-day, US$50–$69. Trafalgar Falls, Emerald Falls Trail, and a drive to Carib Indian Reservation. Return via Layou River Valley. Some versions might include a hike to Freshwater Lake.

Whale Watching: 3.5 hours, $68 (see Sports section).

Rain Forest Aerial Tram: 4 hours, $95–$119 (see description later in this chapter).

Cooking Caribbean Adventure Tour: 3.5 hrs, $85, including transfers. For an interesting

Author's Favorite Attractions

★ Trafalgar Falls and Papillote Nature Center

★ Indian River boat ride

★ Hiking in the rain forest

and fun experience, Daria Eugene teaches you to prepare traditional Creole dishes along with some Dominican culture and heritage at her home, high on a hillside above Roseau. Information: **Jungle Trekking Adventures** (767-367-4264).

Hiking Safaris: 6 hours, US$44–50; US$200 for four people. To hike in the rain forest, you must have a guide. They can be obtained through the Dominica Tourist Office or from tour companies (see Sports/Hiking).

Dominica on Your Own

Dominica's capital is situated on a flat river delta at the mouth of the Roseau River on the site of a former Indian village. It takes its name from a wild reed, roseau, that once grew here in abundance. The French, the first Europeans to settle here, built a fort around which their colony developed. When the British took control of the island, they expanded the French fort and renamed it Fort Young, for the first British governor.

A Roseau Walkabout

A typical West Indian port, Roseau sprawls along the waterfront and climbs Morne Bruce and the other steep hills that frame it. The town has retained much of its old character, despite the devastation caused by Hurricane David in 1979. The oldest part is laid out in a modified grid of about 10 blocks and can be covered easily in an hour or so.

Museum and Market: At the waterfront in front of the **cruise dock (1)** is the **Museum of Dominica (2)** (767-448-8923), with a small,

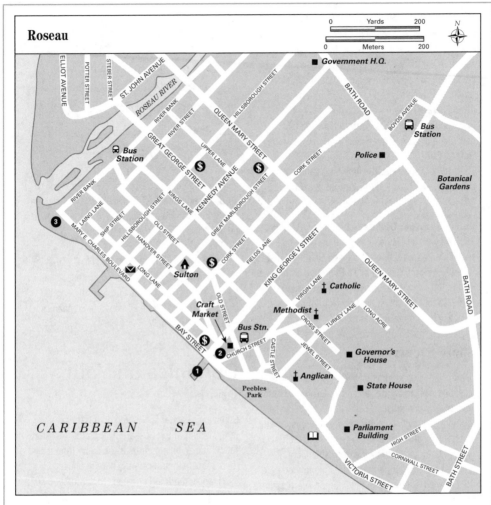

Roseau

CARIBBEAN SEA

1. Dock
2. Museum of Dominica
3. Market

beautifully displayed collection that traces the island's history from pre-Columbian times to the present. Admission: $3. Next door is the tourist information office, and directly behind it is an outdoor market of Dominican crafts on the spot that was once the island's slave market.

The **fruit-and-vegetable market (3)** at the north end of Bay Street is a wonderful place to visit, particularly on Sat mornings, when it is jammed with people from the countryside selling exotic fruits and flowers in a kaleidoscope of colors.

Fort Young: South of the museum on Victoria Street is Fort Young, constructed in 1770 to replace the original fort built by the French. It served as the main defense of the town and the harbor; some of its cannons can be seen at the entrance. In more recent times the building was used as the police headquarters and later was made into a hotel.

Government House: Across from the Fort Young Hotel is Government House, built in the 1840s to replace an earlier building on the same site. It was altered and improved over the years as the official residence of the queen's representative. After independence it became the residence of the president of Dominica.

Also opposite the Fort Young Hotel is the 19th-century St. George's Anglican Church and the public library, one of several built in the Caribbean by the Andrew Carnegie Foundation in 1905.

The Cathedral: East of Old Market Square on Virgin Lane, the Roman Catholic Cathedral of Our Lady of Fair Haven was built in 1854 to replace an earlier church and cemetery on the site. The side walls have old stained-glass windows; behind the main altar are modern ones. One of the old windows in the west wall depicts Columbus's discovery of the New World.

The town center has a number of wooden houses with second-story balconies and gingerbread trim. One of the oldest was once the home of novelist Jean Rhys.

Dominica Botanical Gardens: (www.da-academy.org/dagardens.html) Originally laid out in 1890 on 110 acres at the foot of the wooded cliffs of Morne Bruce, the Dominica Botanical Gardens have been reduced to 40 acres. Despite urban growth, they are still the largest area of open space in town. Near the entrance to the gardens, which were devastated by Hurricane David in 1979, is a poignant reminder of David's visit: a yellow school bus crushed by a toppled African baobab tree. The wreck now supports new life. The gardens retain about 150 of the original 500 species of trees and shrubs; a replanting program has been in progress for many years. Among the significant trees is Carib Wood, whose red blossom is Dominica's national flower; it blooms from Mar to May. Others to note are the pretty orchid trees near the entrance and two unusual bottle palms, whose name comes from the shape of the trunk, which is similar to the shape of the original Coca-Cola bottle. The gardens' most curious tree is the no-name tree, so called because specialists have not been able to identify it. Spectacular views of Roseau and the coast can be seen from Morne Bruce, an elegant residential hillside above the gardens.

A Drive Around the Island

Roads east and north of Roseau lead to the edge of the national park, from which hiking trails ascend the mountains through rain forests to the lakes and waterfalls. Information on trail conditions and brochures prepared by the Park Service are available from the Dominican Tourist Board. Some of the following nature sites have been developed with access roads, forest trails, interpretive centers, restroom facilities, picnic shelters, and ancillary services: Soufrière Sulfur Springs, east of Soufrière; Fresh Water Lake; Middleham Falls and nature trails; and Emerald Pool—all located within the Morne Trois Pitons National Park. Similar improvements have been made at Trafalgar Falls.

Dominica National Park (www.natureisland.com) Established in 1975 on 7,000 acres in the central and southern highlands, Dominica National Park has magnificent scenery and a great variety of plant and animal life. Known also as the **Morne Trois Pitons National Park** after the highest of four peaks in the park, it has hiking trails ranging from a comfortable thirty-minute walk to Emerald Pool to a tortuous four-hour trek to Boiling Lake. On the north side of Roseau, a road inland winds through the lush Roseau River Valley to the tiny village of Laudat on Mount Micotrin (site of the Aerial Tram) and the "gateway" to the main attractions in the park's central region. In 1998 the park was declared a World Heritage Site by UNESCO. It covers five major peaks as well as Boiling Lake, Freshwater and Boeri Lakes, and associated waterfalls and a thermal area.

Trafalgar Falls: One of the most beautiful, accessible sites in the park is also the one closest to Roseau. Spectacular Trafalgar Falls are actually three separate cascades, which tumble down the steep sides of Mount Micotrin into pools several hundred feet below. The falls are quite far apart. The trail is an easy fifteen-minute walk and provides a good introduction to tropical rain forests. Entrance fee: US$5.

At the base of the cliff and the entrance to the trail at a 1,000-foot elevation is the **Papillote Inn** (www.papillote.dm), a wilderness retreat and nature sanctuary with a rain-forest garden. Begun in 1969 by former New Yorker Anne G. J. Baptiste, the proprietor of the inn, the garden follows the natural contour of the mountainside, although some terraces were added. More than fifty species of nesting birds can be seen from the inn's terrace or nearby. The rustic inn organizes guided nature walks and trail hikes.

Freshwater and Boeri Lakes: Laudat is also the start of hikes to Freshwater Lake at 2,779 feet and Boeri Lake at 2,800 feet. The two bodies of water were once a single lake in the crater of an ancient volcano until Morne Micotrin, a young cone, formed in the crater and separated the water. Freshwater Lake, the largest of Dominica's five lakes and the source of its hydroelectric power, is surrounded by dense forests. Hummingbirds are seen often. The walk from the Laudat trailhead to Freshwater Lake takes about forty minutes. The views across the park are wonderful.

North of Freshwater Lake, a steep, narrow trail of about one hour's hiking winds up the mountain along the ridge separating the two lakes to Boeri Lake. It passes through different types of forests with giant tree ferns and many types of plants, and along small streams and hot and cold springs. Throughout the hike there are sweeping views across the island to the Atlantic coast. Boeri Lake has a magnificent setting between Morne Micotrin on the south and Morne Trois Pitons on the north, where it is difficult to believe you are in the Caribbean. The lake and its wooded surroundings look more like Vermont than the tropics.

Rainforest Aerial Tram: Located near Laudat village, about a thirty-minute drive from Roseau over terrible roads, the tram starts in the wooded area at the end of a road and returns to the same location. On the ride up, the tram, a modified ski lift, travels up a steep slope on the side of Mount Micotrin and over a spectacular ravine where passengers see waterfalls, and then it passes through the lower canopy of the forest. Passengers, accompanied by a naturalist guide, discover plants and life-forms that are usually hidden from view in the forest treetops. Halfway through the tour, passengers get off the tram for a ten-minute walk across a suspension bridge spanning the Breakfast River Gorge and through the forest understory. Price: US$95–119 adult. For cruise-ship passengers who

have booked a shore excursion or a tour through a local tour company, transportation to the tram is included. If you go on your own, you will need to arrange your own transportation. At the site there are restroom facilities, a nature walkway, a juice bar, and a gift shop. The tram owners/operators are **Rainforest Aerial Tram** (2250 Southwest Third Ave., Suite 301, Miami, FL 33129; 767-448-8775; 866-759-8726; www.rainforestaerialtrams.com), which also operates aerial trams in Costa Rica. The Web site has a useful video and commentary.

Titou Gorge—Valley of Desolation—Boiling Lake: South of Laudat, the Titou Gorge, a narrow, deep, water-filled defile, is the start of the trail to the Valley of Desolation and Boiling Lake, the world's second-largest solfatara lake. Boiling Lake is 6 miles east of Roseau as the crow flies, but to reach it on the ground takes four hours over a 6-mile roller-coaster trail. Some of the most difficult hiking in the Caribbean, this is an undertaking for experienced hikers and then only with a guide. As an alternative, you can go as far as Titou Gorge or go halfway on the trail to the edge of the Valley of Desolation, a hike of three hours round-trip. First studied by British scientists in the 1870s, Boiling Lake resembles a huge cauldron of bubbling gray-khaki water smothered in mist. It is thought to be a flooded fumarole, or hole in a volcanic region, that releases hot gases and boiling vapors from the molten lava below.

Soufrière: On the south end of Dominica, 5 miles from Roseau, is the fishing village of Soufrière. It is situated on a wide scenic bay that ends at Scotts Head, a promontory that offers great views of the Martinique Channel where the Atlantic and Caribbean collide. Martinique is in view on the south. Scotts Head has some of the island's main dive sites. According to local legend, the cliffs above Soufrière Bay were used by Carib men to punish unfaithful wives—they threw them into the sea. Soufrière takes its name from the Sulfur Springs that can be found less than a mile east of the village. From Soufrière, the road west takes a wide swing around the bay along a narrow stretch of road to Scotts Head village, where you can see fishermen mending their nets and repairing their boats. On Fri nights the area is transformed into a street fair attracting Dominicans from the capital and all over the area coming for a raucous good time.

At Pointe Michel, a village between Roseau and Soufrière settled by survivors of the catastrophic 1902 eruption of Mount Pélé in Martinique, farmers grew the grass used to make Dominica's distinctive rugs. Traditionally, the tough grass, khuskhus, was put on the road for cars to run over in order to make it more pliable to weave.

Soufrière/Scotts Head Marine Reserve: (www.dominicamarinereserves.com) Dominica's first marine reserve on the southwest coast protects the area's important marine resource and manages its use by traditional as well as recreational users. The Reserve is under the Local Area Management Authority (LAMA), made up of community groups, private sector operators, the Fisheries Department, and the Dominica Watersports Association and is responsible for training wardens for beach and shore patrol. All users pay US$2 per dive to help support the Reserve. The reserve starts at the impressive "Champagne," a dive site named for its champagne-like bubbles, as the northern limit and runs through Scotts Head/ Soufrière Bay, along the south shore of the Scotts Head peninsula to "Lost Horizons," another dive site, as the southern limit. There are four user zones: diving, fishing, general recreation, and research. Among other popular dive sites in the reserve are the pinnacles at Soufrière and Scotts Head, Dangleben's Reef, and L'Abym (also called "the Wall"). For information: National Development Corporation, Valley Road, Roseau; (767) 448-2045; fax: (767) 448-5840.

Middleham Trails: North of Roseau the road to Pont Casse, a junction in the center of the island, winds east along hairpin curves through the steep mountains. It passes Springfield Estate, an old plantation at 1,200 feet, and now a rustic, eco-tourist inn, and skirts the Middleham Estate on the northwest edge of the national park. Here a 950-acre tract was donated to the park in 1975 by John D. Archbold, the American owner of Springfield Plantations. It has some of Dominica's finest rain forests with trails. One trail begins in Providence near the village of Laudat; the other, at the village of Cochrane. Both lead, in about a one- to two-hour hike, to the waterfalls, where you can rejuvenate in the freshwater pool at the base of the falls. Entrance: US$5.

Emerald Pool Nature Trail: At the north end of the national park near the Pont Casse junction, a sign on the road to Castle Bruce marks the turnoff for Emerald Pool Nature Trail, the national park's most accessible trail. An easy thirty-minute walk on a good half-mile footpath, it passes through lush forest to a beautiful cascade that drops 20 feet into a grotto of black rock with emerald walls of ferns, orchids, and dense foliage. (The pool is large enough for a swim. Bring a towel. There are new facilities at the entrance, including an information center, bar, and toilets.) Entrance: US$5.

The trail has lookouts over the magnificent Belle Fille Valley, an area of banana groves backed by jungle-thick mountains, and a stretch of the wild east coast at Castle Bruce. A short paved section of the trail is part of the old road—an ancient Indian trail—to Castle Bruce used by the Caribs before the main road was built in the 1960s.

The Imperial Road: The 20-mile stretch known as the Imperial Road, between Pont Casse and Marigot on the northeast coast, crosses the heart of the Central Forest Reserve, one of two reserves in northern Dominica. The other, the enormous Northern Forest Reserve, is dominated by the island's highest peak, Morne Diablotin, at 4,748 feet. The northern reserve is the last refuge of the rare imperial parrot, known locally as the sisserou, and its smaller relative, the red-necked parrot, or jacquot. In 2000, 842 acres of Morne Diablotin were set aside as a national park. You can climb to the summit of the morne on a trail classified as moderate to difficult.

The Central Forest Reserve protects a small gommier forest with gigantic trees up to 120 feet in height. The gommier is a beautiful hardwood used to make furniture, but for centuries it has been used by the Amerindians to make oceangoing canoes. The top branches of the gommier are the principal nesting places for Dominica's endangered parrots. Before strong conservation measures were put in place, commercial logging was destroying the forests at an alarming rate. The trend has been stopped, but poaching of trees and birds does continue.

From the gommier forest the road drops into lime and banana plantations laced with ferns along the Pagua River. At Pagua Bay a wide crest of golden sand bracketed by rocky cliffs is washed by the crashing waves of the Atlantic, where wind-sheared vegetation clings hard to the cliffs. The bay is the north boundary of the Carib Indian Reservation.

Carib Indian Reservation: (www.centrelink.org) Dominica is the only place in the Caribbean where the Carib, after whom the Caribbean is named, have survived. In 1903 approximately 3,750 acres, including eight hamlets in the northeastern part of Dominica from Castle Bruce to Pagua Bay, were set aside as a reserve for the Caribs. The land is held in common by the 3,202 descendants of the Caribs who inhabited the island at the time of Columbus. To be eligible, claimants must have at least one parent of Carib origin and must reside on the reservation. About 10 percent of the descendants are considered predominantly of Carib stock, but there are probably no pure-blooded Caribs today. Those who survived the wars or were not hunted down by the earlier settlers eventually intermingled with other people who came to the island. Today the Caribs you meet usually have rather distinct Asian features and straight black hair and bear some resemblance to the Amerindians of South America. Until recently some lived in traditional thatched huts, but those dwellings have been replaced by modern houses.

Visitors are often misled by descriptions in brochures and some guidebooks and go to the Carib reserve expecting to see a Stone Age people living as they did when Columbus arrived five hundred years ago. The Carib villages, as well as most of the people themselves, are indistinguishable from others on the island. A few Carib traditions that link them with their past have survived. The Carib straw craft is instantly recognizable by its design and fabric and is different from any other straw woven in the Caribbean.

Another legacy—but one that is getting harder to find—is the oceangoing canoe that the Indians make from the trunk of the gommier tree. On the beach at Castle Bruce, you can sometimes see boatmen making dugout canoes in the same method used by the Indians since before Columbus. A modified version is still made and used as fishing boats in other Eastern Caribbean islands.

Kalinago Barana Autê (Carib Cultural Village by the Sea; Old Coast Road, Crayfish River; 767-445-7979; www.kalinagobaranaaute.com). Opened in Feb 2006, the facility provides a unique opportunity to learn and appreciate the heritage of the Carib people. It has an arts and crafts gallery where Kalingo artisans use the Larouma plant to weave functional items like bottles, mats, and baskets, create crafts from calabash, make pottery, and build canoes. They harvest plants and herbs for medicine. A cassava mill is used to grind this dietary staple, which is converted into bread and farine. Beautiful Kalingo structures include the "karbet" that serves as the center for daily performances of traditional dance, drama, and song. Hours: daily, 10 a.m. to 5 p.m.; Oct 15 to Apr 15, closed Mon; Apr 16 to Oct 14, closed Wed and Thurs. Admission: US$5 adult, $3 child.

Portsmouth: The small, sleepy village of about 2,000 people overlooks Portsmouth Bay, known in history as Prince Rupert Bay. This wide natural harbor has a freshwater source, Indian River, on the south end. Behind the town rises Morne Diablotin, Dominica's highest peak. The natural harbor, a freshwater supply, and a defensive headland—the Cabrits Peninsula on the north side of the bay—were reasons enough for the area to be strategically important to the British and French and heavily fortified during their colonial wars. Indeed, one of the most decisive naval battles of the colonial wars was fought here in 1782. The British victory helped Britain establish its sea supremacy over the French and, hence, the trade routes and wealth of the West Indies.

Portsmouth has a few modest beachfront hotels and restaurants on the beach, which is currently being upgraded and beautified. Windsurfing and snorkeling are the main water sports to enjoy here.

Cabrits Historical and Marine Park: The silhouette of the 260-acre Cabrits Peninsula can be recognized by its two steep hills, remnants of ancient volcanoes. The peninsula, a freshwater swamp that joins it to the mainland, and an 800-acre marine reserve in adjoining Douglas Bay make up the Cabrits Historical and Marine Park, which is part of the Dominica National Park. *Cabrit* is said to come from the word meaning "goat" in several

European languages. Early exploration ships had the habit of leaving goats here to graze so that they would have fresh meat to eat on future visits.

From 1770 to 1815, on a promontory of the peninsula, the British built Fort Shirley, one of their most impressive military installations in the Caribbean. Since 1982 the extensive ruins have been under restoration following the original plans, which were found preserved in England. In addition to the battlements, there is a museum in the former powder magazines and trails—one leading to the ghostly remnants of the commander's house, now choked by enormous roots of ficus and sandbox trees.

When restoration began, the growth all but obscured the ruins. Before the area became a national park, the Forestry Division had planted trees on an experimental basis; even earlier, orchards of tropical fruit trees were cultivated here, so that now the park has an interesting variety of Caribbean flora. The adjoining swamp hosts a variety of plants and birds; and on the park's beaches, two species of sea turtles nest here from Apr to Sept. The marine park of Douglas Bay is a popular snorkeling area.

In the terminal reception hall, passengers are introduced to the attractions with audiovisual displays. Entrance fee: US$5.

The Indian River: South of Portsmouth at the mouth of the Indian River, a rowboat with a nature guide can be rented for a trip upriver. The tranquil estuary is so thick with tropical vegetation, it forms a tunnel over the river so dense only slim rays of light filter through the foliage, dancing on the leaves and water, creating a hauntingly beautiful setting. About thirty minutes up the river, your boatman stops at a clearing, where he leads his group on a hike, identifying the birds and flora along the way. Fee: half-day US$40–$60.

Gingerette Nature Sanctuary: This sanctuary (767-440-3412; rastours@cwdom.dm) is the first phase of a 35-acre ecological preserve along the Layou River. Intended as a model agrotourism project, the sanctuary is a showcase for native vegetation such as cocoa trees, breadnuts, avocados, sugarcane, and bananas. There is a waterfall and a mineral-water spring; river bathing, bird-watching, nature walks, and guided tours are available.

Shopping

Dominica is not a place for fancy duty-free shopping for designer fashions or the latest electronics, but some handcrafts are distinctive, particularly the woven straw products of the Carib Indians. An outdoor market next to the museum (facing the cruise-ship pier) has crafts and souvenirs; however, they are not always the best available. Before buying, if you are interested in quality crafts, visit some of the specialty stores in Roseau, such as **Shanice's Craft Centre** (Hanover Street; 767-225-1429; sharonjoyn@hotmail.com); **Dominica Pottery** (Bayfront Street at Kennedy Ave.); and **Balisier** (135 Great George St.). Other good buys include soaps made locally from fresh coconut oil, leather crafts, cigars, and cassette recordings of traditional "jingping" folk music. **Luxury Emporium** (Bay Front, 767-448-5247) carries Cuban cigars, rum and other spirits, and **Land** (land@archip.com) leather products. Among other duty-free shops for luxury goods, **Asbury's** and **Colombian Emeralds** are located in the Fort Young Hotel, within walking distance of the cruise-ship dock.

Dining and Restaurants

Dominica has a Creole cuisine incorporating a great array of locally grown vegetables, fruits, and herbs that reflects its African and French heritage more than its British one. The most popular specialty is mountain chicken, or frog legs, known locally by its Creole name, *crapaud;* crayfish, or river shrimp, and stuffed land crabs are others. Among the common vegetables are bananas, plantains, and dasheen, a root vegetable with green heart-shaped leaves, which can be seen growing throughout the country. The root is used like potatoes, and the young spinach-like leaves are used to make callaloo, a thick soup.

Evergreen Hotel Terrace Restaurant (Castle Comfort; 767-448-3288; evergreen@cwdom.cm). In a delightful terrace setting overlooking the Caribbean, you can enjoy well-prepared local specialties at reasonable prices as well as a magnificent view. Moderate.

La Robe Creole (3 Victoria St., Roseau; 767-448-2896). Known particularly for callaloo and crab soup and mountain chicken but it's almost too overpriced to recommend. Expensive.

The Orchard (King George V and Great George Streets, Roseau; 767-448-3051). The menu has Creole favorites like black pudding, rôti, crabbacks, conch, and lobster. No credit cards. Moderate.

The Sutton Place Grill (25 Old St.; 767-449-8700). Set in one-hundred-year-old stone walls, the restaurant is part of the family-run Sutton Place Hotel and offers traditional West Indian cooking with international inspiration. (Be sure to see one of the hotel's guest rooms—they may just be the prettiest hotel rooms in the Caribbean.) Moderately expensive.

Pearl's Cuisine (50 King George V St.; 767-448-8707). Set in a restored Creole house, this eatery is popular with local folks for outstanding Dominican/Caribbean cuisine by chef Pearl.

Cocorico Café (Bay Front; 767-449-8686). The casual waterfront cafe offers indoor/outdoor seating for light selections fresh from the market.

Sports

Beaches/Swimming: Except for the golden strands of the northeast, most of Dominica's beaches are steel-gray volcanic sand. But the best swimming in Dominica is not always at seaside beaches. Lakes, rivers, and waterfalls of the interior provide some of the most pleasant spots. On the west coast at Layou, a ten-minute walk along the lush banks takes you to a spring-fed pool popular for swimming.

Biking: Mountain biking is available from **Nature Island Dive** (767-449-8181; www.natureislanddive.com) and other tour operators, but you'll need to be in top physical condition with lots of stamina to negotiate the island's steep mountains and rugged trails.

Fishing: Sportfishing is a relatively new tourist attraction, although fishing has been a livelihood for people as long as they have lived in Dominica. Fishing charters are arranged by **Rainbow Sportsfishing** (Castaway Beach Hotel; 767-448-8650; fax: 767-448-8834; rollei@cwdom.dm). The operator also offers whale-watching excursions for US$40 per person, minimum of four.

Hiking: The best and sometimes the only way to see Dominica's attractions is hiking. The easiest short walks are the Emerald Pool Nature Trail, Trafalgar Falls near Roseau, and Cabrits National Park. Longer, more strenuous hikes go to Freshwater Lake, Boeri Lake, and Middleham Falls. For hiking in the rain forest, you must have a guide; fast-growing vegetation often obscures trails, and it is easy to get disoriented and lost. *Hike Dominica,* a booklet published by the government (www.discover dominica.com), describe a dozen or so main sites and trails, indicating their length, level of ease or difficulty, and directions to reach them. Site passes (US$5 per site) are required of all non-resident users and can be purchased at the site entrance. The fees are used toward site maintenance.

Most local companies specialize in safari-type excursions with nature guides who convey passengers in minivans or jeeps to points in the mountains from where hikes begin. In Roseau, **Ken's Hinterland Adventure Tours** (767-448-1660; www.khattstours.com) is among the dozen or more local companies offering hiking, diving, kayaking and other watersports, and bird and whale watching. The operator has an extensive Web site with detailed descriptions and prices. Others include **Dominica Tours** (Anchorage Hotel, 767-448-2638; fax: 767-448-5680); and WRAVE, **Wacky Rollers Adventure Vacations and Expeditions** (767-440-4FUN; www.wackyrollers.com) which uses a fleet of former military vehicles, colorfully painted by Dominica's leading artist, Earl Etienne. WRAVE also has a river tubing tour, three hours, $64.

Horseback Riding: Highride Nature Adventures (New Florida Estate, P.O. Box 467, Roseau; 767-448-6296; highriders@cwdom.dm) is one of the last remaining estates in Dominica to maintain a family tradition of horsemanship. For more than fifty years, horses have been an integral part of estate operations, both for pleasure riding and farming activities.

Kayaking/River Tubing: Nature Island Dive (767-449-8181; fax: 767-449-8182; www.natureislanddive.com) and other dive and watersports operators also provide kayaking excursions, and some combine kayaking and snorkeling. Costs range from US$25 per person per hour; $55 half-day double kayak. Also available through **Wacky Rollers** (767-449-8276; fax: 767-513-7638; www.wackyrollers.com), which offers river to ocean kayaking and river tubing; and **Cobra Tours** (Portsmouth; 767-445-3333), which offers kayaking and snorkeling, including lessons and rentals, as well as windsurfing, surfing, and bodyboarding.

Snorkeling/Scuba Diving: Dominica was only recently discovered as a dive location. It has reefs on the north and west coasts. Hodges Beach, a white-sand beach on the northeast coast, faces three small offshore islands with banks of brain corals and an abundance of tropical fish. On the northwest shore the best snorkeling is found in Douglas Bay, where there is a large reef about 180 feet from shore in 20 to 50 feet of water.

On the south side of Roseau and about 300 feet north of the Anchorage Hotel, a reef approximately 180 feet from shore starts at about a 45-foot depth. Wall diving at Pointe Guignard, less than a mile north of Soufrière, holds the greatest interest for divers due to the variety of attractions: caves, lobsters, black and brown coral, sponges, and diverse marine life. Anchorage Dive Centre is based at the hotel.

On the south end of the island, Scotts Head has a variety of diving locations from the Caribbean around to the Atlantic side of the promontory. These are mainly drop-offs and reef dives with characteristics similar to those of Pointe Guignard. The beach on the north side of Scotts Head is rocky, but it is popular for snorkeling, as the coral is within swimming distance. The area is small and features mostly finger corals, but it has a large variety of small, colorful reef fish.

Dive Dominica (767-448-2188; www.divedominica.com) is a qualified dive operation offering a full range of services, including PADI instruction and a ten-passenger dive boat. Deep-sea fishing can also be arranged. Single-tank dive, US$55; two tanks, US$90. Participants must show a certification card.

Whale Watching: Twenty-one species of whales and four dolphin species have been identified in waters off Dominica. Although whale watching is available year-round, the best months are from Oct to Apr, when sperm whales cavort only 3 to 8 miles offshore. Whale-watching excursions are well organized and readily available from **Castle Comfort Diving Lodge/Dive Dominica** (P.O. Box 2253, Roseau; 767-448-2188; 888-414-7626; fax: 767-448-6088; www.divedominica.com), **Anchorage Hotel and Dive Center** (767-448-2638; www.anchoragehotel.dm), and other local tour companies that offer daily excursions. Cost for a three-and-a-half hour excursion is about US$68 per person.

Festivals and Celebrations

Creole Day, which coincides with Dominica's Independence Day, is the year's main celebration. Schoolchildren, teachers, and other adults don the traditional, colorful madras costume for a day filled with parades, competitions, and other festive activities. The **World Creole Music Festival** takes place the last weekend in Oct. The annual event brings together Creole bands from the English-, French-, and Spanish-speaking islands, as well as West Africa.

Martinique
Fort-de-France

Martinique

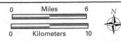

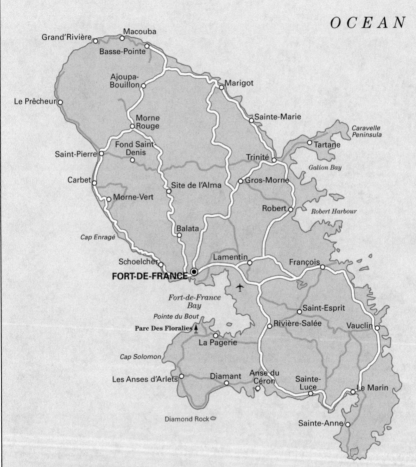

ATLANTIC

OCEAN

Grand'Rivière
Macouba
Basse-Pointe
Ajoupa-Bouillon
Marigot
Le Prêcheur
Sainte-Marie
Morne Rouge
Caravelle Peninsula
Fond Saint-Denis
Tartane
Saint-Pierre
Trinité
Galion Bay
Carbet
Site de l'Alma
Gros-Morne
Morne-Vert
Robert
Robert Harbour
Cap Enragé
Balata
Schoelcher
Lamentin
François
FORT-DE-FRANCE
Fort-de-France Bay
Saint-Esprit
Pointe du Bout
Rivière-Salée
Vauclin
Parc Des Floralies
La Pagerie
Cap Solomon
Les Anses d'Arlets
Diamant
Anse du Céron
Sainte-Luce
Le Marin
Diamond Rock
Sainte-Anne

CARIBBEAN

SEA

The Isle of Flowers

Beautiful and beguiling, Martinique is a paradox of razorback ridges and undulating meadows, steep peaks and soft hills, and possesses the diversity of a continent rather than a small Caribbean island. Its three distinct regions of greatly varied terrain leave visitors with the impression that it is a much larger island.

Volcanic mountains, their peaks hiding under a hood of clouds, dominate the northern end of the island, where windswept cliffs hang high above the sea and the land climbs steeply along deeply creviced mountain slopes to the cone of Mount Pelée, an active volcano more than 4,500 feet high. From these rain-forested slopes, the land drops to skirts of fertile green fields of banana and pineapple plantations. The central region rises in spiked peaks and ridges carved by rivers and streams that fall quickly to meadows with grazing cattle and sugar-cane fields. Even greater in contrast is the dry, flat south end with parched lowland and saline flats bordered by white-sand beaches.

Some authorities say that when Columbus first sighted the island in 1493, he named it for a saint, as was his usual custom. Others claim that the name derives from a Carib word, *madinina*, meaning "isle of flowers"—a theory that's easy to believe, since masses of flowers color the landscape in every direction.

Columbus is believed to have come ashore at Carbet, on the Caribbean coast, on his fourth voyage, in 1502. The first settlers did not arrive until 1635, however, under Pierre Belain d'Esnambuc, a French nobleman from Dieppe. For the next quarter of a century, many other settlers arrived, and battles with the native Carib Indians were frequent. So too were skirmishes with the British and Dutch for control of the island. Then in 1763 Louis XV, in the Treaty of Paris, gave up Canada—which he reportedly called "a few snowy acres"—rather than his territory in the West Indies. The decision was later to be as pivotal for the young United States as it was for France, which used Fort-de-France as a supply base to aid the Americans during the American Revolution.

By the early 19th century, the voices of emancipation had grown strong. Through efforts led by Victor Schoelcher, an Alsatian deputy and one of the leading French abolitionists of the time, slavery in the French West Indies was abolished in 1848. Soon after, indentured workers from Asia were imported to work the sugar plantations. Some of this ethnic diversity—French, African, Asian—remains, but for the most part it has blended into an exotic combination, creating Martinique's character today—which is as distinctive as its landscape.

Budget Planning

Taxis and leading restaurants are expensive. Collective taxis and the ferry to Pointe du Bout are cheap. Sports facilities are comparable to prices in other popular Caribbean locations. The most economical way to tour the island is on an organized motor coach tour or on your own, by rented car, if you can

At a Glance

Antiquities	★
Architecture	★★
Art and Artists	★★★
Beaches	★★★
Colonial Buildings	★★
Crafts	★★
Cuisine	★★★★
Culture	★★★
Dining/Restaurants	★★★★
Entertainment	★
Forts	★
History	★★
Monuments	★★
Museums	★★★★
Nightlife	★
Scenery	★★★★★
Shopping	★★★
Sightseeing	★★★★
Sports	★★★
Transportation	★★

share the expense with others. Don't overlook the many walking excursions to be taken in Fort-de-France and the endless hiking opportunities around the island.

Port Profile

Location/Embarkation: The main passenger port, Pointe Simon, is on the north side of the Bay within walking distance of town. Sometimes the largest ships anchor in the bay and tender passengers to the pier. Small ships sometimes dock at Pointe du Bout, the main resort area on the south side of the bay.

At Pointe Simon the terminal building has an information desk to help arrange island tours, public phones that accept credit and phone cards, and restrooms.

A team of young English-speaking Martiniquais members of the Welcome Brigade (Brigade d'Accueil) circulate in town to provide visitors with information and assistance. They are easily recognizable by their uniforms: white polo shirts, blue vests, and jeans, Bermuda shorts or skirts. Members report regularly to fixed posts—near Pointe Simon dock and south edge of La Savane—and are on duty from 8 a.m. to noon (Tues 12:30 to 4:30 p.m.); schedules are also adjusted to coincide with cruise-ship arrivals.

Local Transportation: Taxis are plentiful but tend to be expensive. There are taxi stands at the port, in town, and at major hotels. Sample fares from the port terminal: to Fort-de-France, about €13; to Pointe du Bout, about €44. Between 8 p.m. and 6 a.m., there is a surcharge of 40 percent. **Cooperative Martinique Taxis** (0596-63-63-62). Collective taxis, eight-seat limousines with the sign TC, are less costly and are used widely by tourists, particularly those who speak some French. The collectives depart frequently from the main terminal, on the waterfront at Pointe Simon, to outlying areas, discharging passengers en route. Public buses serve all parts of the island.

Roads and Rentals: Martinique has some of the best roads in the Caribbean, although those over the mountainous interior are very winding. Essentially the network fans out from

Fort-de-France and intersects with cross-island highways. The Tourist Office has seven "Circuits Touristiques" for self-drive tours, which depart from Fort-de-France and vary in driving time from a half to a full day. They use one road on the outbound and a different one for the return, covering the north of the island in three circuits, the central in one, and the south in three. Each is named—North Caribbean, North Atlantic, and so on—with a color-coded map to match the route's road signs. You need a valid driver's license to rent a car. There are many car-rental companies, and most have French-made cars such as Peugeot, Citröen, and Renault. Those in Fort-de-France are **Avis** (596-42-11-00; www.avis.fr); and **Budget** (30 rue Ernest Deproge; 596-70-22-75; www.budget-antilles.com). They are open weekdays 8 a.m. to noon and 2:30 to 5 or 5:30 p.m.; Sat to noon.

Bicycles and motorbikes can be rented from **Discount** (Pointe du Bout; 596-66-54-37) and **Funny** (80 rue Ernest Deproge, Fort-de-France; 596-63-33-05). The **Regional Natural Park of Martinique** in cooperation with local bicycle organizations has designed off-the-beaten-track biking itineraries. For information, call (596) 70-54-88.

Ferry Service: Fort-de-France is linked to Pointe du Bout, the main resort center, by frequent ferries that run daily from early morning until after midnight. Between Fort-de-France and Pointe du Bout costs €7 round-trip, adults, €4 children age two to eleven. In Fort-de-France all ferries (known locally as vedettes) depart the Quai d'Esnambuc, the pier at the foot of the town center.

Shore Excursions

Any of the seven self-drive circuits designed by the Tourist Office could be made by taxi, and local tour companies offer some by motor coach. Taxis charge $50 per hour for up to four passengers. The most popular are likely to be sold as shore excursions on your ship. A list of tour companies is available on the Martinique Tourist Office Web site. Places mentioned here are described later in the chapter.

To Saint-Pierre along the West Coast: 2.5 hours, US$125. The classic island tour runs north

Population: 392,000

Size: 50 miles long and 22 miles wide; 425 square miles

Main Town: Fort-de-France

Government: In 1946 Martinique was made a French département with representation in the French Parliament. More recently it was made a région. Martinique, along with Guadeloupe, St. Barts, and St. Martin, make up the French West Indies. Its people are French citizens sharing the same culture and privileges as those in mainland France. The electorate sends four deputies and two senators to the French Parliament. It is governed by two elective bodies: the Conseil Général, with thirty-six representatives, and the Conseil Régional, with forty-one members.

Currency: € euro; US$1 fluctuates around €0.75, or I € equals US$1.32. U.S. and Canadian traveler's checks and credit cards are readily accepted.

Departure Tax: None

Electricity: 220 volts AC, 50 cycles. U.S. and Canada appliances require French plug converters and transformers.

Emergency Numbers: Medical: 15; La Meynard (Quartier La Meynard; 596-55-20-00) on the east side of Fort-de-France is one of the main hospitals. The Tourist Office can assist in locating English-speaking doctors. Police: 17 or 590-63-00-00; Fire: 18

Language: French and Creole. English is spoken in most tourist facilities, but a French phrase book and pocket dictionary are useful.

Public Holidays: Jan 1, New Year's Day; Easter Monday; May 1, Labor Day; Ascension Thurs; Pentecost Mon; May 22, Slavery Abolition Day; July 14, Bastille Day; Aug 15, Assumption Day; Nov 1, All Saints Day; Nov 11, Armistice Day; Dec 25, Christmas Day.

Telephone Area Code: 596. To phone station-to-station from the United States, dial 011-596-596 plus the local number. In Martinique, Télécartes, sold at post offices and outlets indicating *télécartes en vente ici*, are used in special booths marked TÉLÉCOM and make local and international calling easier and less expensive. Visa and MasterCard can also be used.

Airlines: Air France via Miami; Air Canada from Montreal; LIAT, Air Caraibes to neighboring islands. American Airlines/American Eagle service from New York via San Juan to Fort-de-France.

By Sea: L'Express des Iles (596-42-04-05; fax: 596-63-34-47; www.express-des-iles.com; info-reservations@express-des-iles) and **Brudey Frères** (596-90-04-48; fax: 596-70-53-75; www.brudey-freres.fr) provide high-speed catamaran services between Guadeloupe and Martinique. Since ferries have a start-and-stop history in the Caribbean, you should check with the ferry company before making plans.

Information: www.martinique.org

In the United States:

(800) 391-4909

New York: Martinique Promotion Bureau/CMT USA, 825 Third Ave., 29th Floor, New York, NY 10022; (212) 838-6887; (800) 371-4909; fax: 838-7855; www.martinique.org; info@martinique.org

In Canada:

Office du Tourisme de la Martinique au Canada

Montreal: 4000 Rue St. Ambroise, Suite 265, Montreal, QC H4C2C7; (514) 288-2026; (800) 361-9099 (Canada only); fax: (514) 845-4868

In Port:

Office Départemental du Tourisme (Martinique Tourist Office), Immeuble Beaupré, Pointe de Jaham, 97233 Schoelcher, Martinique, F.W.I.; (596) 61-61-77; fax: (596) 61-22-72; www.martiniquetourisme.com; info.cmf@martiniquetourism.com. Hours: weekdays 7:30 a.m. to 12:30 p.m. and 2:30 to 5:30 p.m. (Fri to 5 p.m.); Sat 8 a.m. to noon. The office has maps, literature, and an English-speaking staff (www.martiniquetourisme.com).

---

18 miles along the Caribbean coast through picturesque fishing villages to Saint-Pierre, and return via the volcanic observatory to the Route de la Trace or **Leyritz Plantation, St. James Rum Distillery,** and **Balata Gardens.** The tour is made in the reverse direction.

To Trois-Ilets and La Pagerie: 3 hours, US$150. South of the capital, a westbound circuit follows the expressway on a wide swing around Fort-de-France Bay to Rivière-Salée, where a detour west leads to Trois-Ilets, Pointe du Bout, and Caribbean coast beaches.

Martinique on Your Own

The pretty capital of Martinique stretches from the Bay of Fort-de-France to the foothills of the Pitons du Carbet, rising more than 3,500 feet in the background. A natural port and commercial center, Fort-de-France did not become the capital until 1902, after the old capital, Saint-Pierre, was buried under volcanic ash from Mount Pelée.

A Fort-de-France Walkabout

Fort-de-France is a delightful place to explore on foot. Its narrow streets, reminiscent of the French Quarter in New Orleans, are lined with pastel-colored houses and lacy wrought-iron balconies housing boutiques with fashions from Paris. The main business and shopping district is a 6-block area bounded by rue de la Liberté and rue de la République, from rue Victor Hugo to rue Perrinon—all to the west of La Savane.

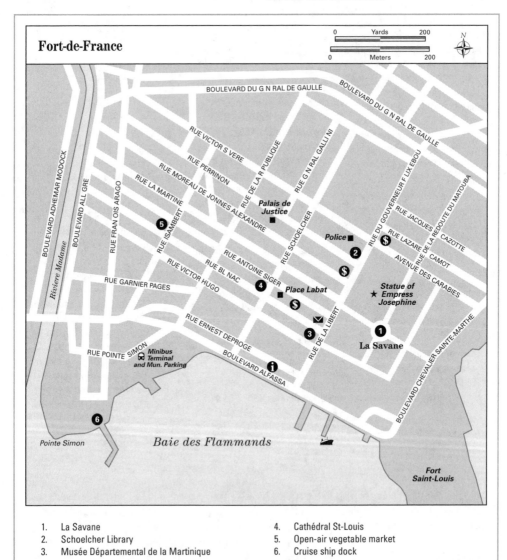

Fort-de-France

1. La Savane
2. Schoelcher Library
3. Musée Départemental de la Martinique
4. Cathédral St-Louis
5. Open-air vegetable market
6. Cruise ship dock

La Savane (1): A large public square by the bay is the heart of the city, with spacious lawns shaded by royal palms, flamboyant, and other flowering trees. The houses, hotels, and cafes around the square are in buildings dating from the 19th century that help give the city its colonial character. The square, a good people-watching spot, serves both as a playground and promenade often used for parades and other events on special occasions and public holidays.

The park has a statue of Marie Josephe Rose Tascher de la Pagerie, better known in history as Napoleon's Josephine. The white Carrara-marble statue by Vital Dubray shows her in the flowing high-waisted dress of the First Empire and looking across the bay to Trois-Ilets, where she was born (looking, that is, before someone made off with her head). A relief on the base depicts Josephine's coronation. At the southeast end of the park, the 17th-century Fort Saint-Louis, surrounded by water on three sides, commands the harbor. Closed to visitors.

The southwest corner also has a lively open-air market where you can find madras-costumed dolls, ceramics, shell figures, and wicker and straw products, as well as inexpensive costume jewelry and Haitian paintings. **Centre des Métiers d'Art,** west of the park beyond the Tourist Office, also has a small selection of local crafts, particularly bright patchwork tapestries, a Martinique specialty.

Schoelcher Library (2): On the northwest corner of La Savane is the city's architectural showpiece, the Schoelcher Library (rue de la Liberté; 596-70-26-27; biblio-schoelcher-dep@cg972.fr). A Romanesque-Byzantine gem built for the Paris Exposition of 1889, it was dismantled and shipped piece by piece to Fort-de-France, where it was reconstructed on the site of the old Hotel du Petit Gouvernement, where the Empress Josephine once resided. Named for the French abolitionist Victor Schoelcher, who donated his library of nine thousand volumes to Martinique in 1883, the building has an elaborate fanciful facade. Hours: weekdays 8:30 a.m. to noon and 2:30 to 6 p.m.; Sat to noon.

Musée Départemental de la Martinique (3): Situated in a beautifully restored colonial house on the west side of **La Savane,** the Archaeological Museum (9 rue de la Liberté; 596-71-57-05) has artifacts from pre-Columbian Amerindian cultures and representations of the island's everyday life and folklore in literature, art, music, clothing, and crafts. Two companion galleries are the **Musée de l'Esclavage** (Route de Didier), on the history of slavery, and **Archival Services of Martinique** (Tartenson; rue St-John Perse; 596-63-88-46), with a collection of maps and engravings from the 16th and 17th centuries.

Cathedral St-Louis (4): Also west of La Savane, rue Blenac leads to the Cathédral St-Louis, on the site of previous churches destroyed by war or natural catastrophes. The present church, built in 1978 following the design of the earlier 19th-century church, is earthquake-proof. Its fine stained-glass windows were restored.

Another block west at the rues Isambert and Blenac is the **open-air vegetable market (5),** particularly lively on Sat mornings. It is the best place to see the exotic vegetables and herbs that inspire island cooks to the taste treats of Creole cuisine.

Walking Tours: Azimut Tourisme Urbain (13 rue du Taillis, Clairiere; Fort-de-France; 596-70-07-00; fax: 596-63-05-46) has four walking excursions of Fort-de-France accompanied by multilingual guides. (Azimut also has a kiosk in the craft market at La Savane.) *Traces* is a two-and-a-half-hour historic/architectural tour; *Verso* reveals the unknown heart of the city; *Ship-Shop* is a shopping/sightseeing excursion designed for cruise-ship passengers; and *Bet Afe* (Creole words for "firefly") is Fort-de-France-by-night with dinner and entertainment.

A Drive Around Martinique

North to Mount Pelée along the West Coast

The coastal road passes the large suburb of Schoelcher—once merely a small fishing village named for the French abolitionist—to Case-Pilote, one of the oldest settlements on the island, named after a Carib chief who befriended the French. Carbet, the probable site of Columbus's landing in 1502, has an 18th-century church.

Gauguin Art Center and Museum (596-78-22-66). Nearby at Anse Turin, a village where Paul Gauguin lived for four months in 1887, is a small memorial to the noted French painter.

The contemporary structure is in a rustic setting designed to encompass the natural surroundings that inspired Gauguin and contains reproductions of the dozen pictures he painted on the island, including *Two Women of Martinique* and *The Bay of St-Pierre*. There are books about the painter, biographical information, and some of his letters. Hours: daily 10 a.m. to 5 p.m. Admission: about €4 adult.

Habitation Anse Latouche, at Carbet's Botanical Garden, is situated among the ruins of the earliest 17th-century settlements of Martinique. Admission: about €5.50 adults, €2.50 children; younger than age seven admitted free.

Farther north at Fond Capot you can enjoy panoramic views of the Caribbean, Mount Pelée, and the Pitons du Carbet. All along the serpentine coast, roads climb inland to pretty mountain villages and trails on the Pitons du Carbet. The landscape and cool climate has earned it the name of Little Switzerland.

Saint-Pierre: The once-fashionable capital, Saint-Pierre was totally devastated by the eruption of Mount Pelée on May 8, 1902, when a cloud of burning gas with temperatures higher than 3,600 degrees Fahrenheit, ash, and stones rained down onto it. In minutes the entire population of 30,000 perished, except for one survivor, a prisoner named Cyparis, who was protected by the walls of his underground cell. The town never recovered. Today St-Pierre is only a village.

Saint-Pierre Museum (Musée Volcano-logique; 596-78-15-16). Created by American volcanologist Franck A. Perret, the contents of this museum are a poignant memorial to the fatal eruption. A number of clocks on display— all stopped at the same time—mark the historic moment. Photographs and documents of the old town and exhibits of molten glass and twisted metal reveal its ferocity. Among the bizarre relics are petrified spaghetti, teapots fused with lava, and twisted musical instruments, melted by the heat. Hours: Mon to Fri 9 a.m. to noon and 3 to 5 p.m. Small admission fee.

The Cyparis Express (596-55-50-92), known as the Little Train of Saint-Pierre, offers tours of the historic town. On weekdays the tour lasts one hour. Price is €8 adult, €2 children. Resting on the seafloor in Saint-Pierre Bay are twelve ships that were destroyed in the harbor at the time of Mount Pelée's eruption. Because the bones of survivors were found, the site is a memorial grave kept intact. Jacques Cousteau headed the team that researched the site and made a film of it.

Le Prêcheur: North of Saint-Pierre the coastal road skirts the spectacular scenery of Mount Pelée's western flank. Le Prêcheur, one of the oldest villages on the island, is a base for climbing the mountain. Beyond Le Prêcheur a secondary road twists along the coast to Anse Céron, a beautiful beach with heavy surf and a tiny offshore island, La Perle, a dive site.

Habitation Céron (Anse Céron, Le Prêcheur; 596-52-94-53; habitation.ceron@wanadoo.fr). The manor house of a 17th-century sugar plantation in a beautiful park setting by a stream has impressive remains of its ancient mill. Surrounded by fields where coffee, cocoa, tapioca, and bananas once flourished, the principal crop today is avocados. Céron, historically, is connected to Françoise d'Aubigue, the celebrated Madame de Maintenon, who secretly wed France's King Louis XIV. Individuals are welcome, and day trips for small groups can be organized by bus or boat from Fort-de-France. The outing includes a Creole luncheon, a swim, and a guided tour of the estate by the English-speaking owner, Madame Laurence des Grottes. The estate also offers horseback riding.

From Saint-Pierre two routes cross the island. One passes the **Observatoire du Morne des Cadets,** the observatory that monitors Mount Pelée's activity, and the village of Fond St-Denis, where the slopes on both sides of the road are covered with gardens. Fond St-Denis is a frequent winner of an annual, islandwide contest for the village with the most beautiful flowers. After Fond St-Denis, the cross-island highway joins the Route de la Trace.

North of Fort-de-France over the Pitons

Behind Fort-de-France are the Pitons du Carbet, traversed by the most scenic route on the island, Route de la Trace, known simply as the Trace, a central highland road that winds through the rain forests of the Regional Natural Park of Martinique (PNRM) to the foot of Mount Pelée. As the narrow road leaves Fort-de-France and snakes up the mountains, you can enjoy sweeping views of the city and the bay. In the distance on the north is **Sacre-Coeur de Balata,** a miniature of Montmartre in Paris, set, incongruously, in the tropical landscape of the Pitons.

Balata Botanical Gardens (596-64-48-73; www.jardindebalata.com). On a hillside at 1,475 feet, overlooking the capital, is a private botanical park created by its owner, an artist and landscape designer. It is centered by a restored Creole house furnished with antiques and has more than a thousand varieties of tropical plants. At the entrance are hedges of brilliant magenta bougainvillea, a flower that grows profusely in Martinique in many colors and named for Louis de Bougainville, who imported it from Brazil in 1768. Walkways through the gardens have lookouts that take advantage of the fabulous views of Fort-de-France and Cap Solomon; one path leads to a lily pond framed by a dramatic view of the Pitons. Along the way, look closely, and you probably will see hummingbirds flitting about the hibiscus. Hours: daily 9 a.m. to 6 p.m. Admission: about €6.50 adult; €2.50 children age seven to eleven; signs and literature are in French.

Absalon Mineral Springs: On the west side of the Trace, the Absalon Mineral Springs are the starting place of trails through the central mountains. In the immediate vicinity of the springs is a loop trail of about three hours' hiking.

A mile north of the springs, the Trace reaches its highest altitude at 2,133 feet. A tunnel on the north side of the Pitons, Deux Choux, marks a junction of the Trace with D1, a major east-west artery. The road west runs through a deep gorge known as the Porte d'Enfer, or Gate of Hell, to Fond St-Denis and Saint-Pierre, on the coast.

Trace des Jésuites: East of the Trace and the cross-island highway is the Jesuits' Trail (Trace des Jésuites), one of the most popular rain-forest hikes in Martinique. The signposted trail, maintained by the Forestry and Parks departments, starts less than a mile north of Deux Choux and passes through beautiful forest under a canopy of giant hardwoods, such as mahogany and gommier, typical of the Eastern Caribbean. The gommier, also known as white gum, has a tall, straight trunk whose sap the early Jesuit missionaries used in making incense—hence the trail's name. The Amerindians used the trunks of the gommier for their dugout canoes. Today a boat called gommiers, or gomye, used by local fishermen, derives from the tradition. It is about an hour's walk to the Lorrain River, which is a pleasant spot for a picnic. Scheduled hikes led by park guides are available.

Mount Pelée: Towering over the northern part of Martinique from almost any location is cloud-capped Mount Pelée, the island's highest peak, at 4,584 feet. The outward signs of volcanic activity have subsided, but the volcano is still boiling and belching. The hike to the summit takes a strenuous five hours round-trip.

At Morne-Rouge you can turn west to Saint-Pierre and return to Fort-de-France via the Caribbean coast. Or turn east to continue to Grand'Rivière on the north coast.

Ajoupa-Bouillon: The route east snakes through a beautiful part of the highlands under a canopy of tall tree ferns, bamboos, and palms to Ajoupa-Bouillon. It is a delightful mountain hamlet, dating from the 17th century, where flowering hedges and colorful gardens border the highway. A narrow dirt road and trail marked Gorge de la Falaise leads to a trail to a narrow river canyon with a beautiful waterfall. Guide, about €7.

Les Ombrages: On the east side of Ajoupa-Bouillon is one of the island's most beautiful attractions, Les Ombrages—tropical gardens and rain-forest trail in a magnificent natural setting. Heliconia and other colorful flowers natural to the rain forest have been added along a signposted footpath, which follows the natural contours of the land, winding beside a brook under a canopy of enormous trees and stands of bamboo that reach more than 60 feet in height. The privately maintained park provides a map for the forty-five-minute self-guided hike. There is an admission fee of about €5 for adults, €2.50 for children five to eleven years (596-53-31-90; fax: 596-53-32-04).

Basse-Pointe: From Ajoupa-Bouillon the highway winds through green hillsides of banana, sugarcane, and pineapple plantations to Basse-Pointe, the main town on the northern Atlantic coast. Basse-Pointe (which means "low point") is situated at the base of windswept cliffs that plunge into the sea. They are covered with heavy foliage sheared by the alizés, or northeast winds, that blow off the Atlantic. Basse-Pointe has a high concentration of East Indians brought to Martinique to work the cane fields after slavery was abolished. There is a Hindu temple in the area.

Musée de Poupées Végétales (Plantation Leyritz; 596-78-53-92). Created by artist Will Fenton, the small museum has a display of fifty or so elegantly dressed miniature dolls of celebrated women, such as Madame de Pompadour and Josephine Baker. The dolls are made from six hundred different natural fibers and plants. Hours: daily 8 a.m. to 5 p.m. Fee: about €5; children younger than age twelve admitted free with visit to the Leyritz gardens and plantation house, which dates from the 18th century.

Farther north, Macouba has one of the oldest churches of the island, and from there the road weaves north through banana, coffee, and tobacco fields to Grand'Rivière, crossing some of the most spectacular scenery on the island. Big volcano rocks that have tumbled down the mountains from Mount Pelée rest at the edge of black-sand beaches, where huge white-capped waves crash against the vertical-sided cliffs carpeted with wind-sheared foliage.

Grand'Rivière: On the isolated north coast is an old fishing village where time has stood still. Grand'Rivière is set against the deep green, wind-sheared cliffs of Mount Pelée under palms and giant breadfruit trees. Village fishermen returning with the day's catch must perform a feat of great skill by riding the swells and, with split-second timing, pulling their boat onto the beach to avoid being slammed against the rocks by the crashing waves. From Grand'Rivière a trail through the forests of Mount Pelée's northern flank rounds the coast.

East of Fort-de-France to the Atlantic Coast

Fort-de-France is separated on the south and east by a wide savanna, grazed by cattle and oxen and edged by a landscape of tumbling hills. The region is watered by the Blanche River and other streams that flow from the Pitons into the Lézarde River, Martinique's longest river, which empties into Fort-de-France Bay at Lamentin. Robert, a fishing village

on the Atlantic, is connected to Fort-de-France by an expressway. Le François is one of the prettiest spots on the east coast, with offshore islets and shallow, calm water; boat excursions are available. Two islets have plantation houses converted into inns.

Caravelle Peninsula and Nature Reserve: Jutting into the Atlantic directly east of Fort-de-France at La Trinité is Presqu'ile de la Caravelle, a peninsula with a nature reserve on the eastern half. A road of about 5 miles crosses the peninsula to the ruins of Château Dubuc, a 17th-century plantation house, where there are trails to the easternmost point of the peninsula, marked by a 19th-century lighthouse. The chateau museum (596-58-09-00) is open weekdays 8:30 a.m. to 12:30 p.m. and 2:30 to 5:30 p.m. There is a small admission fee.

La Trinité, once one of the island's most prosperous towns, sits in the elbow of the Caravelle Peninsula on a sheltered bay with beaches for safe swimming, overlooking the rockbound north coast. Between Sainte-Marie and Marigot at Pointe Ténos, there is a wooded park with a picnic area and marked trails overlooking a beautiful bay with wild windswept scenery.

St. James Distillery Rum Museum (596-69-30-02; rhums.st.james@wanadoo.fr). The museum at Sainte-Marie is set on a sugar plantation in an old Creole plantation house. It has displays of engravings, artifacts, and machinery on the history of sugar and rum production from 1765 to the present; visitors can sample St. James products. Hours: weekdays 9 a.m. to 5:30 p.m.; weekends 9 a.m. to 1 p.m. The Plantation Train provides a ride through the sugarcane and banana fields surrounding the distillery. There is a small admission fee. Another of the oldest distilleries and museum, Habitation Clement (596-54-62-70; www.habitation-clement .fr/fr/accueil.html), is located in Le Francois.

Banana Museum (Sainte Marie, Habitation Limbe, 596-69-45-52; www.lemuseedelabanane .com). The first of its kind in the Caribbean, the museum is located on an authentic 17th-century banana plantation. Its exhibits cover the history, cultivation, and medicinal properties of the banana and its importance to the island's economy. Banana beverages and pastries are available. Admission:

€7.50 adult, €4 children ages five to twelve. Hours: daily 9 a.m. to 5 p.m. Call (596) 69-45-52.

Farther north, **Fonds Saint-Jacques** is one of the best-preserved estates on Martinique. Built by Dominican Fathers in 1658, it was the home from 1693 to 1705 of Père Labat, the French Dominican priest who was an explorer, architect, engineer, historian—and even warrior against the British. The chapel, windmill, and workshops remain, and there is a museum. Hours: daily 9 a.m. to noon. Admission is free; guided tours are available.

South of Fort-de-France along the Caribbean

The Caribbean coast south of the capital bulges with a peninsula that stretches west to Cap Solomon and is scalloped by pretty coves and white-sand beaches. Although there are good roads to the area, the quickest and most direct way to get there from Fort-de-France is the twenty-minute ferry ride across the bay to Pointe du Bout, a small finger of land with luxury hotels and a marina. Small cruise ships dock here occasionally, and boats sail from here daily on excursions down the coast for swimming and snorkeling. Some of Martinique's main attractions are only a few miles from Pointe du Bout.

Les Trois-Ilets: On the bay, halfway between Pointe du Bout and Rivière-Salée, is the historic town of Les Trois-Ilets, one of the prettiest villages in Martinique. In its heyday the town prospered from the nine refineries that served the nearby sugar plantations. Much of that history has been preserved in nearby attractions.

Maison de la Canne (Pointe de la Vatable; 596-68-32-04). Opened in 1987, the House of Sugar is a modern museum in the ruins of an old distillery, with exceptionally good exhibits on sugar and rum in a park setting, labeled in French and English for a self-guided tour. Hours: daily except Mon 9 a.m. to 5 p.m. There is a small admission fee.

Pottery Center (Centre Artisasnal de la Poterie; 596-68-03-44) East of Les Trois-Ilets a pottery-making center, established in the 18th century, was restored in 1987 to serve as an artisan's center. Using the rich terra-cotta–colored clay of the area, potters make a mixture of three types of clay, which they fashion on hand-thrown wheels into objects such as carafes, bowls, ashtrays, and copies of pre-Columbian artifacts. Hours: weekdays 9 a.m. to 3 p.m.

La Pagerie: South of Les Trois-Ilets is La Pagerie, the former sugar plantation where Empress Josephine was born. The remaining stone structures of the estate house now contain the **Musée de La Pagerie** (596-68-38-34; fax: 596-68-33-96), set in landscaped gardens. The museum has a collection of furniture (including the bed that Josephine slept in until her departure for France at age sixteen), portraits of her and of Napoleon, invitations to great balls in Paris, medals, bills attesting to her extravagance as the empress, and letters—notably a passionate one from the lovelorn Napoleon. Hours: daily except Mon from 9 a.m. to 5:30 p.m. There is a small admission fee.

The Caribbean coast from Pointe du Bout south to Sainte-Anne has a series of pretty coves and beaches. Anse (or cove) Mitan is one of the island's main restaurant, bar, and water-sports centers.

The road winds south over hilly terrain to Les Anses d'Arlets, a large bay with mile-long, palm-shaded white-sand beaches cupped by Cap Solomon, the westernmost point of Martinique's Caribbean coast. Popular weekend yacht havens today, these idyllic coves inspired Paul Gauguin, who lived here in 1887. Grande Anse, a fishing village, has colorful gommiers, fishing boats made in the traditional manner of the Amerindian dugouts.

Diamond Rock: Two miles off the south coast, at Diamond Bay, is a steep-sided volcanic rock jutting from the sea to 590 feet. The multisided rock has the shape of a cut gem, hence its name, Diamond Rock. It is the only known rock in history to be declared a warship. In the early 19th century, during the endless battles between Britain and France, the British landed two hundred sailors with cannons and arms on the rock, declaring it the HMS *Diamond Rock.* For eighteen months, they were able to hold the French at bay, bombarding any French vessel that came within range. When the French learned—through an "indiscretion"—that the British defenders had grown weary of their isolation, they devised an ingenious scheme to regain the rock. They loaded a boat with rum and caused it to run aground on the rock. As expected, the British garrison quickly consumed the rum, and the French took the rock without difficulty.

Two miles of tree-shaded beach stretch along the bay overlooking Diamond Rock, and at the eastern end is Le Diamant, one of the island's oldest villages. You can rent a boat to go to the rock, but the crossing is often rough. Diamond Bay is one of Martinique's main windsurfing locations. From Le Diamant you can return on the expressway to Fort-de-France, or continue south to Sainte-Luce, a fishing village and popular resort. The route south of Sainte-Luce to Sainte-Anne passes Le Marin, a picturesque old village with a large, yacht-filled marina.

Do not miss the **Slave Memorial** (Memorial de l'Anse Caffard) at Le Diamant, fifteen larger-than-life statues (each more than 8 feet tall) looking out to sea. They were erected in 1998 to commemorate the 150th anniversary of the abolition of slavery. The group immortalizes an incident in the 19th century when a ship carrying slaves sank off Martinique. Eighty-six of the captives were saved, mostly women and children, but their fate is unknown. Although the slave trade was outlawed in 1815 by the Congress of Vienna, it was still legal to own slaves in Martinique until 1848.

Sainte-Anne: An idyllic colonial village with a tree-shaded square anchored by an 18th-century stone church, the popular resort of Sainte-Anne has good seafood restaurants and water-sports facilities, as well as a pretty beach. At the south tip of the island, **Grande Anse des Salines** is a mile-long crescent of powdery white sand shaded by coconut palms that bow to the sea. The beach is trimmed with almond and white pear trees and huge sea grape with bent, knotted trunks. A similar tree, the manchineel, is marked with bands of red paint as a warning: Its small green apples are poisonous. Do not sit under the tree, particularly while it is raining, because the water washes sap from the leaves and bark that can cause a rash and severe blisters. The Caribs used its sap to coat their arrowheads.

Shopping

French perfume, crystal, jewelry, sandals, leather goods, designer scarves, and liqueurs, as well as locally made dolls, patchwork tapestries, and other crafts and rums, are among the good buys. At the time of purchase, when you pay with traveler's checks or certain credit cards, shops selling duty-free items to tourists deduct the 20 percent tax on perfumes and other luxury items that local residents must pay. Downtown stores are open weekdays from 8:30 a.m. to 6 p.m.; Sat to noon. **La Galleria** (596-50-66-63; www.galleria.mq), one of the largest shopping centers in the Caribbean, is a five-minute drive from the airport and about twenty minutes from the port, depending on the traffic. Many of the best stores that were formally in the downtown area have moved to La Galleria. Another popular shopping area, particularly for tourists, is the **Village Creole** (www.villagecreole.com) at Pointe du Bout next to the casino. It has mostly small, specialty shops—some funky, most expensive.

Art and Artists: Galerie Artibijoux (89 rue Victor Hugo) specializes in Haitian painting and some local artists. It stocks a few French and English art books and has a small costume-jewelry section. The Gold Dolphin (7 boulevard Chevalier, Sainte-Marthe) is a gallery with an exposition salon. Paintings by native-born Martiniquais and other artists who live on the island are shown year-round in some hotels.

Caribbean Art Center (Savane Park) has colorful patchwork tapestries that are considered original works of art; the best carry such artists' names as Réné Corail and Balisier. Prices range from €135 and up. **Boutique Tam Tam** (60 rue Victor Hugo) has tasteful, inexpensive crafts from Haiti, South America, and Bali. **Artisanat and Poterie des Trois-Ilets** (Les Trois-Ilets; 596-68-18-01) is the shop of the Pottery Factory, where you can watch artisans at work.

China and Crystal: Cadet Daniel (72 rue Antoine Siger) stocks Christofle silver, Limoges china, and crystal from Baccarat, Lalique, and others. **Roger Albert** (rue Victor Hugo) is another long-established emporium for crystal.

Clothing: In fashion-conscious Martinique a new crop of boutiques blossoms each season. Some that carry stylish pret-à-porter (ready-to-wear): **La Chamade** (38 rue Victor Hugo) and **Georgia** (56 rue

Victor Hugo). For the hottest new look in sportswear from Paris and Côte d'Azur, try **Parenthése** (6 rue Schoelcher). **Samourai** (rue Antoine Siger) and **New Borsalino** (27 rue Blenac) are exclusive men's shops. The latter has handsome Italian-made linen sports shirts in a variety of fashion colors for US$75 to $100.

Mounia (rue Perrinon) carries top French designers including Claude Montana, Dorothée Bis, and Yves St. Laurent. It is owned by Mounia, a beautiful Martiniquaise who was one of the top models for St. Laurent.

Shows presenting collections by young Martinique designers are held in Fort-de-France hotels in spring and fall. Among the prominent names are Yves Gérard, Daniel Rodap, and Gilbert Basson, whose ready-to-wear label is Gigi, and Paul-Herve Elizabeth, who returned from Paris and opened his elegant **Le Showroom** in a Fort de France suburb.

The streets alongside the cathedral and open-air vegetable market are lined with shoe stores. Most carry reasonably priced shoes of mediocre quality for men and women, but a terrific buy are stylish, inexpensive summer sandals, averaging €13 to €25. Try **Sergio Valenti** (corner of rues Isambert and Blenac) and **Vankris** (46 rue Lamartine).

Jewelry: Gerbe d'Or and L'Or et L'Argent sell pretty island-made 18-karat gold baubles, including the beaded collier chou, or "darling's necklace," the traditional ornament for the Creole costume. You can find great costume jewelry for low prices at **Cleopatre** (72 rue Victor Hugo) and in some of the stalls at the craft market (La Savane). **Cadet Daniel** carries the work of Emile Mothie, a top designer of both classic and modern Creole jewelry.

Leather and Luggage: Roger Albert (rue Victor Hugo) has moved its leather goods department to the Galleria Shopping Center, but the best, most attractive selections can be found at **La Calèche** (41 rue Victor Hugo).

Liqueur and Wine: Martinique rum is some of the Caribbean's best and least expensive. **La Case à Rhum** (rue de la Liberté) has a good selection. The dozen or so members of Le Comité de Défense du Rhum welcome visitors at their distilleries from Jan to July to see the processing and sample their products.

Music: Records and tapes from folk music to zouk, the French West Indies answer to calypso, are found at **Georges Debs, Hit Parade,** and other downtown shops, but prices are often higher than at record/video shops in New York.

Perfumes: Martinique boasts that it has the lowest prices for French perfume in the Caribbean, but prices are now so standardized by French suppliers, I have found little difference. The best savings are to be found on quantities of an ounce or more. The exchange rate fluctuates, however, so check prices in advance at home to know how much of a bargain you can get. **Roger Albert** (rue Victor Hugo) has the largest selection but the least helpful staff.

Spices and Groceries: Gourmet chefs can have a field day here buying spices in the open-air markets and pâté or canned quail at local supermarkets. **Galeries Lafayette,** a department store, sells shredders, graters, and other culinary collectibles. French wines and champagnes are sold in grocery stores. One of the best products is fruit preserved in rum, attractively packaged in glass jars and sold at the **St. James Distillery in Sainte-Marie** (596-69-30-02). In the village of Bezaudin, near Sainte-Marie, **Ella,** a "boutique gourmande," specializes in exotic homegrown spices, preserves, and syrups. Another homemade delicacy, rillettes landaises au foie gras, is prepared at **Habitation Durocher,** a duck farm near Lamentin. At Christmas its specialty is a terrine de foie gras made with Armagnac and packaged in attractive crockery made by Pottery Center of Les Trois-Ilets.

Dining and Restaurants

Martinique has excellent restaurants, most offering traditional French and Creole cuisine. Fresh seafood is always on the menu, prepared in Creole style or in a more sophisticated French manner. Classic French dishes are often served with exotic tropical fruits and vegetables, such as guava, soursop, cassava, christophene, and breadfruit. Specialties vary according to the morning's catch. Typical are *soudons* (small clams), *z'habitants or cribiches* (freshwater crayfish), *lambi* (conch), *oursin* (sea urchin), and *langouste* (clawless Caribbean lobster). Prices for a three-course meal for one person, without wine, can be inexpensive (less than US$30) to moderate (US$30–$45) to expensive (US$45 and up). Most restaurants include tax and service charges in the menu prices. Restaurants close one day each week, but there is no uniformity about it. Check in advance, and also inquire about the use of credit cards.

Fort-de-France

La Cave à Vin (118 rue Victor Hugo; 596-70-33-02). Fine French cuisine along with excellent wines. Lunch and dinner daily except Sun. Expensive.

Chez Carole (Grand Marché, Fort de France) provides Creole cuisine and fresh seafood dishes daily for lunch at the main fruit and vegetable market in the heart of town.

Le Mareyeur (183 Blvd de la Point des Nègres; 596-61-74-70). Lobster and other seafood specialties. Moderate.

South of Fort-de-France

La Langouste (by the ferry jetty, Plage de l'Anse Mitan; 596-66-04-99). Dine on seafood and Creole specialties on the veranda by the water. Moderately expensive.

La Villa Creole (Anse Mitan; 596-66-05-53; www.la-villa-creole.fr) As the name implies, the restaurant features traditional Creole cuisine on the terrace of a creole house set in a tropical garden. Live music nightly by owner Bruyère-Dawson. Moderately expensive.

Manoir de Beauregard (Sainte-Anne; 596-76-73-40). The old manor house/hotel has been restored and its restaurant is well-known for its good food. Open daily for lunch and dinner. Moderately expensive.

North of Fort-de-France

Auberge de la Montagne Pelée (596-52-32-09). Dine on good French cuisine under the volcano, with a magnificent view of the Atlantic coast. Moderately expensive.

Chez Tante Arlette (3, Rue Lucy de Fossarieu, Grand Rivière; 596-55-75-75; fax: 596-55-74-77) has been serving traditional Creole cuisine daily at noon for three generations. Moderate. **Le Colibri Parfume** (Morne-des-Esses; 596-69-91-95). Clotilde Palladino's small home is the setting of a family

restaurant. English is limited, but the Creole food is so good and the atmosphere so pleasant you won't notice. Take one of the seven back terrace tables, relax, and enjoy the view and a ti punch while your meal is prepared to order. Phone ahead. Moderate.

East of Fort-de-France

Le Plein Soleil (Le Francois (596-38-07-77; pleinsoleil1@wanadoo.fr). Set on the Plein Soleil Hotel terrace, its restaurant offers French/Creole fusion cuisine in a garden setting. Chef Natanael Ducteil was trained by renowned French chef Alain Ducasse and the pricey menu reflects it.

Nightlife

Fort-de-France has more than a half-dozen little nightspots with zouk or jazz, in addition to the nightclubs and discos in the larger hotels. There are also several piano bars.

Les Grands Ballets de la Martinique, the island's leading folkloric troupe, performs at different hotels each night and often comes on board cruise ships to perform. Dancers in traditional costume perform a spirited mazurka brought to the islands from the ballrooms of Europe; the exotic beguine, born in the French West Indies; and an erotic calenda, danced to the beat of an African drum.

The **Casino Bateliere Plaza,** north of Fort-de-France near the Bateliere Hotel, is housed in a handsome building with a gaming room at one end and slot machines at the other. The casino at **Trois-Ilets** (Pointe du Bout near the Village Creole) is open nightly. Photo identification is required. Dress code is casual. The legal gambling age is eighteen.

Sports

Beaches/Swimming: The beaches south of Fort-de-France are white sand, while those of the north are mostly gray and black sand. The best beaches are found on the south Caribbean coast with the mile-long crest at Grand Anse des Salines, the standout. Swimming on the Atlantic coast is generally not recommended except at coves protected by coral reef, such as Cap Ferré. Public beaches do not have changing cabins or showers, and hotels normally charge nonguests for use of facilities. You won't find any nudist beaches here, but large hotels generally permit topless bathing.

Biking: V T Tilt (Anse Mitan, Les Trois-Ilets; 596-66-01-01; cell: 596-60-69-64; www.vttilt.com) has a fleet of specialized bicycles and a nine-seat vehicle that can accommodate nine bicycles. The company organizes trips that highlight Martinique's diverse landscape, explore places not visited by most tourists, and offer contact with the Martiniquais. Tours with guide cost about €45 per person.

Boating: Martinique's irregular coastline and many coves have long made it a favorite of yachtsmen. Yachts, bareboat or with crew, can be chartered for the day or longer. Day-sailing excursions on large catamarans and schooners leave from Pointe du Bout and other marinas for Saint-Pierre in the north and Diamond Rock in the south, stopping for snorkeling and picnic; cost is about €90–115 with lobster lunch.

Fort-de-France Bay is a popular departure point for yacht charters sailing to the Grenadines. Yacht-club members (showing membership cards) may use the facilities of the Yacht Club de la Martinique (Sainte-Marthe; 596-63-26-76; ycmq@orange.fr). *A Cruising Guide to Martinique* is a French/English publication designed for experienced yachtsmen. The Martinique Tourist Office can provide information on boat rental and charter companies in Fort-de-France, including trips on Martinique fishing yawls.

Canyoning: An unusual experience—canyoning in the rain forest—awaits with Aventures Tropical (14 Chemin bois Thibault; 596-64-58-49; aventures-tropicales@wanadoo.fr). The company also offers kayaking and hiking.

Deep-Sea Fishing: Deep-sea fishing must be arranged a day or two in advance. The most popular catches in Martinique waters are tuna, barracuda, dolphin, kingfish, and bonito. A full-day charter for up to six persons costs approximately €600 to €900. Caribtours (596-50-93-52) and Martin Caraibes Fishing (596-45-30-36; marlincaraibesfishing@wanadoo.fr) arrange sportfishing trips. For an unusual adventure, contact the Association Coup

de Senne (phone/fax: 596-55-03-88) if you would like to fish in typical island manner with local fishermen.

Golf: Golf de l'Impératrice Josephine (Les Trois-Ilets; 596-68-32-81; fax: 596-68-38-97; www.martiniquegolf.com), a five-minute drive from the Pointe du Bout ferry, is an 18-hole course (par 71) designed by Robert Trent Jones. Set on 150 landscaped acres of the rolling terrain overlooking the sea, it has a clubhouse, pro shop, and restaurant. Greens fees are about €60, cart about €40, and club rentals about €20. It also has three tennis courts with night lights. Cruise ships often have golf packages for this course.

Hiking: Thirty-one marked trails, most designed as self-guided hikes, laid out by the Regional Natural Park of Martinique (PNRM), National Forestry Office (ONF), and Le Club des Randonneurs (Hiking Club), are detailed (in French) in a guide, with maps, available from the Tourist Office. For information on trail conditions, call PNRM (596-64-42-59; pnrm@wanadoo.fr). Sunday hikes with PNRM guides are organized year-round on a published agenda. They are mainly intended to acquaint local people with the natural environment, but visitors are welcome (commentary is in French). Guided hikes are also organized by Aventures Tropicales (596-75-24-24; aventures-tropicales@wanadoo.fr); Maison du Tourisme Vert (9 boulevard General de Gaulle, Fort-de-France; 596-73-19-30); and Rediscover Martinique (www.cg972.fr).

Horseback Riding: Ranch Jack (near Les Anses d'Arlets; 596-68-37-69; www.martinique-equitation.fr), Black Horse Ranch (Les Trois-Ilets near La Pagerie; 596-68-37-80; fax: 596-68-40-87), and Centre Equestre du Diamant (Le Diamant; 596-76-29-41) offer riding excursions along scenic beach routes and through tropical hillsides. A one-hour ride costs about €25 per person; a half-day ride with guide, about €50 per person.

Kayaking: There are several locations, but Belle Fontaine, about 10 miles north of Fort-de-France, is one of the best. Equipment is available there from Aventures Tropicales (596-64-58-49; www.aventurastropicales.com; aventures-tropicales@wanadoo.fr), Fun Kayak (37, Lot Votable, Trois

Ilets; 596-48-22-45), and **Madinina Tours** (596-70-65-25) in Fort-de-France; also **Caraibes Coast Kayak** (Sainte-Anne; phone/fax: 596-76-76-02) and **Kayaks du Robert** (Robert; 596-65-33-89, fax. 596-65-70-68).

Snorkeling/Scuba Diving: Martinique is surrounded by reefs, but take the advice of local experts before snorkeling or diving on your own—many places have rough seas and tricky waters. There is a great variety of sea life, with walls, caves, and reefs with colorful sponges and corals. In the south Pointe du Bout, Anse Mitan, the small bays around Les Anses d'Arlets, and Sainte-Anne offer super snorkeling, most directly from the beach. Area hotels have glass-bottom boats and equipment for rent. Les Anses d'Arlets is for novice divers, Diamond Rock for advanced ones.

North of Fort-de-France, Cap Enragé, near Case Pointe, is popular for walls and caves where there are large schools of soldierfish, triggerfish, and lobster. La Perle Island, north of Le Prêcheur, a site for experienced divers, has moray eels, lobsters, groupers, and other fish. Dive operators are located in the main tourist centers and serve the hotels of a particular area. The Pointe du Bout operators have American and French licensed instructors and provide instruction for beginners. A list of operators is available from the Martinique Tourist Office.

Tennis: Hotels with tennis facilities nearest the port are the Bakoua with two courts, on the south, and La Batelière, with six courts, north of the capital. **Tennis Club of Fort de France** (596-64-72-24) has three courts.

Windsurfing/Kitesurfing: Beachfront hotels have windsurfing equipment, and many offer lessons. Beginners start in the calm coves of the Caribbean southwest coast; advanced ones find Diamond Bay challenging. Boards rent for about €18 per hour; a half-hour private lesson costs about €14–20. Martinique is a frequent venue for international windsurfing competition. **Alize Fun** (Sainte Anne; 596-74-71-58; www.alizefun.com) has kite-surfing instructions and rentals. **Fun Caraibes** (Cap Est, Le Francois; 596-54-88-34; www.funcaraibes .com) has a school and shop for kilesurfing.

Festivals and Celebrations

Carnival is a five-day celebration when all business comes to a halt and the streets are filled with parades and revelers costumed as "red devils." Carnival continues to Ash Wednesday, when more devils, costumed in black and white, jam the streets for King Carnival's funeral procession and burial at La Savane.

In July the annual **Festival de Fort-de-France** is a monthlong celebration of the arts that attracts major names in theater, art, music, and dance from the Caribbean and around the world. The festival is organized by SERMAC (Service Municipal d'Action Culturelle, Place José-Marti; 596-71-66-25).

In the first week in Dec of alternating years, the **International Jazz Festival** (odd years) and **International Guitar Festival** (even years) attract international artists. The festivals are sponsored by the **Centre Martiniquais d'Animation Culturelle** (596-70-79-29).

The **Atrium Cultural Center** (596-60-78-78), the premier facility in Martinique, offers a yearlong schedule of the performing arts and features international artists. Generally, performances are in the evening.

St. Lucia

Castries, Soufrière, Pigeon Point/Rodney Bay

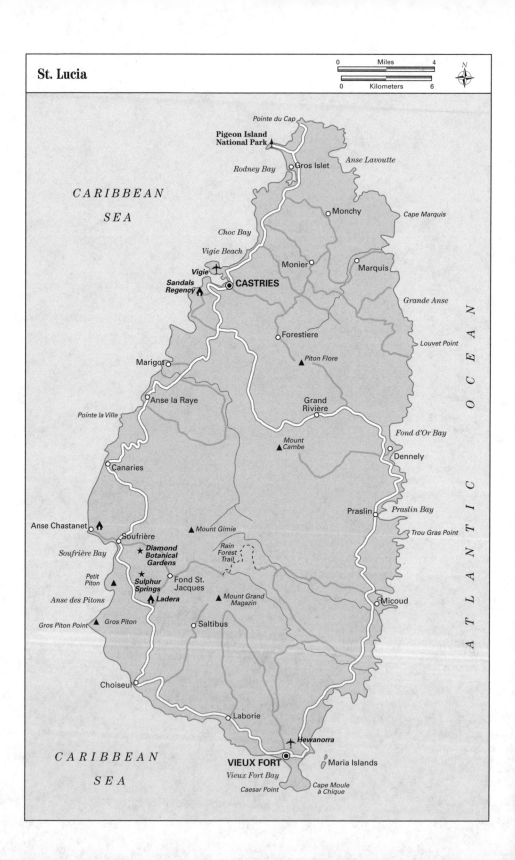

St. Lucia

Miles
0   4
Kilometers
0   6

N

Pointe du Cap

Pigeon Island National Park

Rodney Bay   Gros Islet

Anse Lavoutte

CARIBBEAN

SEA

Monchy

Cape Marquis

Choc Bay

Vigie Beach

Vigie

Monier

Marquis

CASTRIES

Sandals Regency

Grande Anse

Forestiere

Louvet Point

▲ *Piton Flore*

Marigot

Anse la Raye

Grand Rivière

Pointe la Ville

Fond d'Or Bay

Mount
▲ *Cambe*

Dennely

Canaries

Praslin   *Praslin Bay*

Anse Chastanet

▲ *Mount Gimie*

Trou Gras Point

Soufrière

Rain Forest Trail

Soufrière Bay

★ **Diamond Botanical Gardens**

Petit Piton

★ **Sulphur Springs**

Fond St. Jacques

▲ ▲ **Ladera**

Anse des Pitons

Mount Grand
▲ *Magazin*

Micoud

Gros Piton Point   ▲ *Gros Piton*

Saltibus

Choiseul

Laborie

✈ *Hewanorra*

CARIBBEAN

VIEUX FORT

Maria Islands

SEA

Vieux Fort Bay

Cape Moule à Chique

Caesar Point

A T L A N T I C   O C E A N

The Bali Hai of the Caribbean

An island of surprises with scenic wonders on a grand scale, St. Lucia is a nature lover's dream, where every turn in the road—and there are many—reveals spectacular landscapes of lushly covered mountains and valleys colored with tropical fruits and flowers. Among its most celebrated natural attractions are a drive-in volcano and the ultimate postcard image of the tropics: the magnificent Pitons, sugarloaf twins that rise dramatically at the water's edge.

St. Lucia, mostly volcanic in origin, is the second largest of the Windward Islands. From the north, where the hills are up to about 1,640 feet, the terrain rises to a central mountain range with peaks more than 3,000 feet and quickly drops south to rolling hills and a coastal plain. In some places on the coast, cliffs rise almost directly from the sea, hiding tiny coves bathed by quiet Caribbean waters; in others rocky fingers bracket long stretches of white-sand beaches where Atlantic rollers wash the shores.

St. Lucia was inhabited by the Arawaks about A.D. 200 and the Caribs about A.D. 800. It has traditionally commemorated Dec 13, 1502, as the date of Columbus's discovery of the island on his fourth voyage. Some historians say Columbus was never there, however, and that it was Juan de la Cosa, Columbus's navigator, who actually made the discovery in 1499.

The first European colonists to arrive here were sixty-seven English settlers who were blown off course on their way to Guyana in 1605. They landed near Vieux Fort, on the south coast. Within a few weeks the Caribs had massacred most of them but allowed the nineteen survivors to leave the island in a canoe. Thirty years later the English tried again but failed. Then in 1650 two Frenchmen purchased St. Lucia, along with Martinique and Grenada, for the grand sum of £1,660 from the French West India Company, which had come to possess them. The following year French settlers arrived, and for the next 150 years the English and French fought over St. Lucia. By 1815, when the British finally won, St. Lucia had changed hands fourteen times.

Their constant presence in St. Lucia gave birth to a fascinating blend of English and French traditions, which, in turn, were overlaid by the African ones that came with the slaves who were imported to work the sugar plantations. Today the language, feasts, festivals, and cuisine of this richly textured society reflect the curious cultural mix.

After slavery was abolished in 1838, sugar production declined. Britain reorganized its colonies of St. Lucia, Barbados, Grenada, St. Vincent, and Tobago into one administrative unit, called the Windward Islands Government. During World War II the United States established a military base on the island and built an airport at Vieux Fort, which is now the international jetport. St. Lucia got its independence in 1979. Although sugar has long since been replaced by bananas as the main crop, St. Lucia remains an agricultural country. Over the last two decades tourism has gained steadily.

At a Glance

Antiquities	★
Architecture	★★
Art and Artists	★★
Beaches	★★★
Colonial Buildings	★★
Crafts	★★★★
Cuisine	★★★★
Culture	★★
Dining/Restaurants	★★★
Entertainment	★
Forts	★★★
History	★★★
Monuments	★
Museums	★
Nightlife	★★
Scenery	★★★★★
Shopping	★★★
Sightseeing	★★★★★
Sports	★★★★★
Transportation	★

Population: 150,000

Size: 27 miles long and 2 to 14 miles wide; 238 square miles

Main Towns: Castries, Vieux Fort

Government: St. Lucia, a member of the British Commonwealth, has a parliamentary government with two chambers: the seventeen-member House of Assembly, whose members are elected for a five-year term, and a Senate, whose members are nominated. The prime minister is the leader of the major political party in the Assembly. The head of state is the governor-general, appointed by the queen on the advice of the prime minister.

Currency: Eastern Caribbean (EC) dollar. US$1 equals about EC$2.70. U.S. and Canadian dollars, traveler's checks, and most major credit cards are accepted by stores, restaurants, and hotels.

Departure Tax: EC$68 (US$26)

Emergency Numbers: Medical: Victoria Hospital in Castries has 24-hour emergency service. Dial the operator from any island location to be connected with the nearest medical facility or police. Ambulance: 911; Police: (758) 452-2854.

Language: English is the official language, but Creole, a French-based patois, is the common language; many people also speak French.

Public Holidays: Jan 1–2, New Year's holiday; Feb 22, Independence Day; Carnival; Good Friday; Easter Monday; May 1, Labour Day; late May/early June, Whit Mon; May 25, Corpus Christi; Aug 7, Emancipation Day; Oct 2, Thanksgiving; Dec 13, National Day; Dec 25, Christmas; Dec 26, Boxing Day.

Telephone Area Code: 758. From the United States, dial 758 plus 45, plus the five-digit local number. International direct-dial telephone, fax, and telex services are available at the cruise-ship terminal.

Airlines: St. Lucia has two international airports: George Charles (Vigie) Airport at Castries served by American Eagle from San Juan, Air Caraibes, and LIAT; and Hewanorra International at Vieux Fort for wide-bodied aircraft and served by Air Canada, American Airlines, Caribbean Airlines, Delta, Jet Blue, US Airways, and West Jet from North America. By Sea: Express des Iles (www.lexpressdesiles.net) offers high-speed ferry service to Martinique in one hour and twenty minutes. It also has service to Dominica and Guadeloupe. Information: www.stlucia.org.

In the United States:

St. Lucia Tourist Board, 800 Second Ave., New York, NY 10017; (212) 867-2950; (800) 456-3984; fax: (212) 297-2795; stluciatourism@aol.com; slutour@candw.lc

In Canada:

St. Lucia Tourist Board, 65 Overlea Blvd., Suite 250; Toronto, ON M4H 1P1; (416) 362-4242; fax: (416) 362-7832; sltbcanada@aol.com

In Port:

St. Lucia Tourist Board, Pointe Séraphine, P.O. Box 221, Castries, St. Lucia, W.I.; (758) 452-4094; slu tour@candw.lc

St. Lucia National Trust, P.O. Box 525, Castries, St. Lucia, W.I.; (758) 452-5005; fax: (758) 453-2791; tours: (758) 453-7656; www.slunatrust.org; natrust@candw.lc

St. Lucia gained attention when one of its native sons, poet and playwright Derek Walcott, won the Nobel Prize in literature in 1992 (he was the second Nobel Prize winner from St. Lucia, Sir Arthur Lewis having won for economics in 1979). More recently, St. Lucia was the film location for the Disney production *Pirates of the Caribbean*.

Budget Planning

In recent years St. Lucia has become an expensive island for tourists. Taxi and tour prices, particularly, seem to be out of line when compared to some other islands of the Eastern Caribbean. Shopping and restaurants (except those in deluxe hotels) are moderate. Restaurants may add a service charge or tax of about 10 percent to the bill.

Port Profile

Location/Embarkation: The busy port of Castries, the capital, is located on the northwest coast overlooking a deep natural harbor with a narrow neck and sheltered by an amphitheater of green hills. In colonial days this anchorage was of immense strategic value. Today's cruise ships sail into the pretty harbor to an attractive facility, Pointe Séraphine (758-452-2036). It has berths for two cruise ships and a jetty for tenders, a shopping plaza with duty-free shops, and an outdoor cafe. The Tourist Board's information desk (758-452-7577; Soufrière, 758-454-7419) can arrange sports activities. Numerous tour and car-rental agencies, as well as taxi and minibus operators, also have desks where passengers can make arrangements. There is shuttle-bus service to town. Pointe Séraphine is close to Vigie Airport.

Some of the largest ships dock on the south side of the harbor at the commercial port. While this location is not as attractive as Pointe Séraphine, it has the merit of being directly at the foot of town, within walking distance of shops and Derek Walcott Square.

Cruise ships also stop at Soufrière, a small picturesque port at the foot of the Pitons on the southwest coast and at Rodney Bay, the main tourist center of the northern part of St. Lucia. The stop also enables passengers to visit Pigeon Island on the north side of Rodney Bay. Some ships stop in both ports.

Local Transportation: Public transportation is operated privately rather than by the government. A popular (though not comfortable) mode of travel are jitneys (wooden-seat buses) that connect Castries with other towns and villages. They leave from the Castries Market on Jeremie Street in the town center.

Taxis are plentiful, but expensive. Rates are not fixed, but they are fairly standard. (Always agree on the fare with the driver before departure.) The one-way fare from Pointe Séraphine to Castries is US$10; from Castries south to Caribelle Batik, US$16; Hewanorra Airport, US$75 for up to four persons; and north to Rodney Bay Marina, US$20.

Roads and Rentals: No roads encircle the island completely, but you can make a loop around the southern half, which has the main attractions. An alternative is a forty-five-minute motorboat trip, available daily from Castries to Soufrière, which provides wonderful views from the sea. South of Soufrière there is a west-coast road to Vieux Fort that takes about forty-five minutes.

You might enjoy your sightseeing more if you do not have to concentrate on those narrow, winding roads, particularly since driving in this former British colony is on the LEFT. Local travel companies offer well-organized tours for small groups to the main attractions. Or, if you have others with whom to share costs, you could hire a taxi to tour. Be sure to set duration, in addition to the price, in advance. The cost is about US$200 per day for up to four people.

If you prefer to do your own driving, you will need a temporary driver's license, which can be arranged by your rental company. The cost is EC$54 (US$20). Car-rental companies in Castries include **Avis** (758-452-2700; www.avisstlucia.com) and **Budget** (758-452-9887; www.budget-stlucia.com), which has Suzukis for about US$50 to $60 and jeeps for about US$80 per day with unlimited mileage and free pickup. Rental cars cost US$55 and up per day plus insurance ranging from US$15 to $22 per day.

Shore Excursions

St. Lucia divides conveniently for touring into a southern circuit and a west/north-coast tour. The following tours may be offered as shore excursions by your cruise ship, but their length and cost will vary, depending on the port—Castries, Soufrière, or Rodney Bay—from which your tour commences. Often Caribbean cruise ships northbound from the Panama Canal or Barbados stop at Soufrière long enough to tender passengers to shore to pick up their tour and return overland. Meanwhile their ships sail on to Castries, where they dock, and the passengers on tours rejoin their ships there. The reverse procedure may be followed on southbound cruises. All attractions named here are described later in this chapter.

Soufrière and Drive-in Volcano: 3 hours, US$80 to $130 round-trip for up to four persons in taxi. From Castries the tour drops south along the west coast to Soufrière, with views of the Pitons, visits the drive-in volcano, Diamond Falls, and returns to Castries via the east coast.

Day sail to Soufrière: Full-day, US$100. Sail down the west coast from Castries to Soufrière on a yacht or party boat, such as the Brig *Unicorn*, a miniature clipper ship (seen in the film *Pirates of the Caribbean*), with a stop for swimming and snorkeling.

Rain Forest Walk: 5 hours, US$90 via west coast from Castries (shorter and less expensive when originating from Soufrière). See later in this chapter for descriptions.

Canopy Tour: See Sports later in this chapter

Flight-seeing: St. Lucia Helicopters (758-453-6950; www.stluciahelicopters.com). From $85 per person for 10 minutes to $145 for 30 minutes.

Special Excursions: In the past few years, many new, interesting excursions have become available, some by jeep or horseback, that enable visitors to hike on new trails and visit working plantations and out-of-the-way villages. **Sunlink Tours** (758-452-8232; www.sunlinktours.com) offers a large number of excursions, all described in an attractive four-color brochure and on its Web site. Sunlink is a division of **St. Lucia Representative Services** (758-456-9100; www.sunlinktours .com). **St. Lucia Tours** (www.stlucia.com) has an extensive list of tours with descriptions, including some that are specifically designed for cruise-ship passengers. Also, **St. Lucia Naturalist's Society** (c/o St. Lucia National Trust; 758-452-5005; tours: 758-453-7656; www.slunatrust.org; natrust@candw .lc) conducts regular field trips.

Rhythm of Rum: US$45 adult, $25 child. Available to the **Roseau Sugar Factory** (758-451-4258; fax: 758-451-4221) in the Roseau Valley set amid a vast banana plantation, about twenty minutes from Castries, near Marigot Bay. The tour with a short video on the rum industry, takes visitors through the history of rum and the distillery. You climb to a viewing platform to see the distilling columns, fermentation tanks, and a pot still, as the distillation process is explained. You can sample rums and liqueurs and make a purchase.

St. Lucia on Your Own

Castries dates from the mid-18th century, but it is now a fairly new town, rebuilt in 1948 after a fire destroyed many of its historic homes and churches, including 80 percent of its old wooden houses.

A Castries Walkabout

Derek Walcott Square: The square in the center of the city, formerly known as Columbus Square, was renamed in honor of St. Lucia's native son Derek Walcott, who won the 1992 Nobel Prize in literature. It is shaded by an enormous saman, or rain tree, said to have been planted by Governor Sir Dudley Hill in 1833. (Some sources claim the tree is more than three hundred years old.) The square, which was the Place d'Armes under the French, has a cenotaph, or monument, to the fallen of two world wars. On Nov 11, Remembrance Day, wreaths are laid in an official ceremony. The square has the bust of Derek Walcott, as well as the bust of Sir Arthur Lewis, the first Nobel Prize winner from St. Lucia, who won for economics in 1979.

Cathedral of the Immaculate Conception: On the east side of the square is the one of the largest churches in the West Indies, built in 1897 and consecrated in 1931. It became a cathedral in 1957, when the Castries diocese was established. Facing the square on the south side, Brazil Street has several 19th-century buildings, the best known being a white-and-green Victorian building with gingerbread trim. It is one of the few colonial houses to have survived the 1948 fire. The building is said to have been a setting in Sinclair Lewis's *Arrowsmith*, which takes place on a fictitious Caribbean island, "St. Huberts," that was, in reality, St. Lucia. Farther east at Brazil and Chisel Streets is the **Anglican Holy Trinity Church,** dating from the early 19th century. West of the square on Bourbon Street is the **Central Library,** built in 1925 by the Andrew Carnegie Foundation.

Castries Market: One of the most interesting places in town is Castries Market (Jeremie Street), with a bright red facade and a clock over the entrance. Built in 1894 by engineers from Liverpool, the structure has had only minor repairs over the years and is virtually unchanged architecturally.

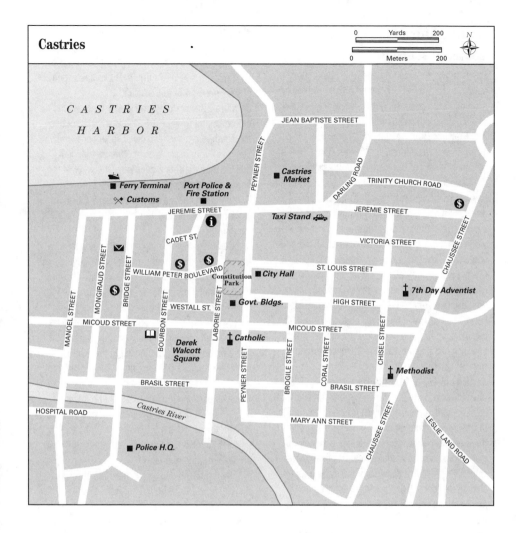

Castries

CASTRIES HARBOR

JEAN BAPTISTE STREET

PEYNIER STREET

DARLING ROAD

TRINITY CHURCH ROAD

Ferry Terminal

Customs

Port Police & Fire Station

Castries Market

JEREMIE STREET

JEREMIE STREET

CHAUSSEE STREET

Taxi Stand

CADET ST.

VICTORIA STREET

MONGIRAUD STREET

BRIDGE STREET

WILLIAM PETER BOULEVARD

Constitution Park

ST. LOUIS STREET

City Hall

7th Day Adventist

MANOEL STREET

WESTALL ST.

BOURBON STREET

LABORIE STREET

Govt. Bldgs.

HIGH STREET

MICOUD STREET

MICOUD STREET

CHISEL STREET

Derek Walcott Square

Catholic

PEYNIER STREET

BROGILE STREET

CORAL STREET

Methodist

BRASIL STREET

BRASIL STREET

HOSPITAL ROAD

Castries River

MARY ANN STREET

CHAUSSEE STREET

LESLIE LAND ROAD

Police H.Q.

The clean, well-organized market is a feast for the eyes as well as the table, with its colorfully dressed vendors selling an array of exotic fruits, vegetables, and spices. Saturday is market day, when farmers bring their produce to sell, crowding into the market and spilling over into adjoining streets. There are also vendors selling kitchen and other useful items, such as brooms made of palm fronds, clay pots, and straw craft, often made by the person selling them.

Government House: On the south side of town is an ornate Victorian mansion perched on the side of Morne Fortune (which means "hill of good fortune" and is often referred to locally simply as the Morne). It is the official residence of the governor-general. You will consider it your good fortune, too, if you are there to see a St. Lucia sunset.

Fort Charlotte: Due to its strategic importance, the hills surrounding Castries harbor were rung with batteries and forts built by the French and British. The best preserved is Fort Charlotte, which crowns the summit of Morne Fortune at 853 feet. Fort Charlotte was begun by the French in 1764 as part of a plan to build Citadelle du Morne Fortune, but was completed by the British in 1794. Many of the original fortifications are still in place. The view from Morne Fortune takes in Castries and stretches from Pigeon Island on the north to the Pitons on the south.

A Drive Around the Island

South to Soufrière

South of Morne Fortune the road winds around hairpin turns, up and over steep hills to the lower reaches of the beautiful Cul-de-Sac Valley, intensively green with vast banana plantations.

Marigot Bay: At Marigot a corkscrew road drops down precipitously to Marigot Bay, a teardrop lagoon with one of the most beautiful settings in the Caribbean. At sunset the scene is exquisite. The bay, almost completely hidden by steep, heavily wooded hills, is a natural harbor that used to make a dandy hideout for pirate ships and warships in the olden days. In the past, the bay's tropical splendor was used frequently as a movie location. Today it is a popular anchorage for yachts and base of the Moorings, one of the leading yachting companies in the Caribbean (its home base is Clearwater, Florida; 888-952-8420; www.moorings.com). Recently, the bay has seen a great deal of development, much of which has taken away from its once gorgeous tropical setting.

Discovery at Marigot Bay (758-458-5300; www.discoverystlucia.com), a large resort and villa development is operated by GLA Hotels. In addition to fifty-seven suites and sixty-seven luxury rooms, there are several restaurants, a spa, a sixty-berth marina, and a marina village with shops and water sports. The resort, we are sorry to say, is an intrusion on this once idyllic setting. It's called "progress" and it's enough to make you weep. Across from the resort on the north side of the bay is **The Rainforest Hideaway** (758-286-0511), a rustic, moderately priced restaurant at the water's edge serving very good Caribbean and Pacific Rim fusion cuisine.

After the Marigot turnoff, the main road crosses the Roseau River Valley and passes the fishing villages of Anse la Raye and Canaries, skirting deserted beaches framed by high rocky cliffs, some accessible only by boat. A small side road leads to the old fishing village of Anse la Raye, where you can tour **La Sikwi Sugar Museum** (758-452-6323; www.lasikwi.com), a cultural theater, a restored 40-foot water wheel, and botanical gardens by advance arrangements. There is a small admission fee. The serpentine route makes its way along the magnificently lush Duval Ravine and over the hills to the ridge overlooking Soufrière—one of the most fabulous views in the Caribbean. There, on the south side of Soufrière, the majestic peaks of the Pitons jut out of the sea.

The Pitons: Petit Piton (2,438 feet), the northern peak, and Gros or Grand Piton (2,619 feet), on the south, are ancient volcanic spikes or extrusions. They rise from either side of a steep, wooded hillside that shelters a deep bay. The view of the Pitons is magnificent from several hilltops above Soufrière. One of the best, particularly for photographs, is at Ladera, a hotel perched high on a cliff south of Soufrière.

Of all the views, nothing beats the approach from the sea, an experience offered by several cruise ships and available on day sails from Castries. To sail into Soufrière Bay, watching the Pitons grow in their dimensions as the ship nears, and to anchor directly in front of them where their peaks tower a half-mile overhead is to enjoy one of the most extraordinary experiences in the world of travel—on par with seeing the pyramids of Egypt and the Taj Mahal. Here the sight is all the more fabulous because it is a natural phenomenon. If your arrival is timed for the late afternoon before sunset, the scene is more magical still as the peaks, bathed in the light of the setting sun, have an almost ethereal quality.

By the beach and on the hillsides between the Pitons is **Jalousie**, a resort that took its name from a former plantation on the site. The hotel was controversial from the day the first stone was laid because it has marred one of the Caribbean's most magnificent natural sites. For hiking the Pitons, see the Sports section later in this chapter.

Soufrière: The quaint little port of Soufrière has a spectacular setting at the foot of the Pitons with the mountains of the St. Lucia Rain Forest rising behind it. The town is the oldest settlement on St. Lucia and was an important center of trade and commerce under the French. At its prime in the late 18th century, there were as many as one hundred sugar and coffee plantations in the vicinity. During the French Revolution, which took as bloody a turn here as it did in France, members of the aristocracy were put to the guillotine erected in Soufrière's town square. Even after almost two centuries of British rule, the French legacy is still very apparent in the names of people and places, their speech, and to some extent, the architecture of the old town.

Although a great deal of the town's historic houses have been lost to fires and hurricanes over the centuries, there are enough Victorian and French colonial buildings around the main square to give the town character. Restoration of the historic center has been under way since 1989 and will take many years to complete.

Soufrière and southern St. Lucia are known for their wood craftsmen. The furnishings of the Tourist Bureau's visitor center at the pier were created entirely by local craftsmen using cedar, mahogany, teak, and other local woods. In addition to its fabulous setting, Soufrière is surrounded by scenic wonders and is the gateway to some of St. Lucia's most interesting natural attractions.

Drive-In Volcano: Southeast of Soufrière is the remnant of a volcanic crater, which St. Lucians have dubbed "the world's only drive-in volcano." Actually, a road does lead into an area of barren, grayish earth and gravel, with pools of boiling mud. At regular intervals clouds of steam, accompanied by hissing sounds, shoot 50 feet in the air, as sulfuric gases are released from the earth's inner core. Where water flows the rocks have been streaked with yellow, orange, green, purple, and brown, indicating the presence of sulfur, iron, copper, magnesium, and zinc washed from them by the water. A slight, but not offensive, sulfur odor can be detected. There is a small entrance fee, and a park guide must accompany visitors.

Diamond Falls and Mineral Baths (758-459-7565; www.diamondstlucia.com; soufestate@candw.lc). After fresh rain water collects in the boiling crater, where it is saturated with minerals and heated to about 180 degrees Fahrenheit, it runs down the mountainside, dropping about 1,800 feet in six waterfalls. You can actually follow the course of the water on mountain trails, but an easier way to see at least one of the falls—lowest and prettiest of the six—is to visit the Diamond Falls and Mineral Baths, less than a mile east of Soufrière. From the entrance to the privately owned Diamond Waterfalls, a narrow bricked path bordered by hedges of tropical plants and shaded by stately palms and gigantic tree ferns leads to the bathhouse and the falls. The beautiful cascade roars out of dense tropical foliage down a mineral-streaked gorge into a stream that flows through the gardens to underground pipes and a series of pools, each a different temperature.

The baths were built originally in 1784 for the soldiers of Louis XVI. The French governor of St. Lucia had had the water analyzed and found its curative properties to be similar to that of Aix-les-Bains in France. The baths were almost totally destroyed during the French Revolution, and in 1836 the British governor tried to restore them, but without success. Only in recent times, after restoration by their present owner, have the baths functioned again; a part of the original 18th-century baths is still in use. The water reputedly has curative powers for arthritis and rheumatism, but even if you do not take the baths, you will find the peaceful gardens a cool, refreshing respite for sun-weary travelers. Hours: daily 10 a.m. to 5 p.m., Sun to 3 p.m. Gardens entry fee US$5; baths $4 public, $6 private. There is not charge for a guide.

Anse Chastanet (758-459-7000; www.ansechastanet.com). On the north side of Soufrière is one of the most enchanting resorts in the Caribbean, with a setting so idyllic you will forgive, if not forget, the terrible road leading there. The road has the merit, however, of having a splendid view of Soufrière and the Pitons. Anse Chastanet is built along a precipitous hillside overlooking a lovely beach. Sunsets here must be seen to be believed. Some of the hotel's furnishings have been made by local wood craftsmen. Take particular notice of the columns of the dining terrace; they are made of local wood and beautifully carved with wildlife scenes by a local self-taught woodcarver, Lawrence Deligny. Anse Chastanet's beach fronts some of the best reefs in St. Lucia only 20 feet from shore. The hotel's dive facilities are open to nonguests (see Sports section later in the chapter).

St. Lucia Rain Forest: The Central Forest Reserve, part of the 54,252 acres of forest and woodlands that cover St. Lucia, is a nature reserve of the central highlands, commonly called the St. Lucia Rain Forest. The Rain Forest Walk, a 7-mile trail, crosses the island through the reserve, between the villages of Mahaut on the east and Fond St. Jacques on the west. From the high ridge there are panoramic views of the central mountains, the Pitons, and Morne Gimie, the highest peak on the island (3,117 feet). Don't be surprised to see farmers emerge from the valleys and mountainsides carrying sacks of produce. The forest, with up to 150 inches of rain per year, has a great variety of ferns, bromeliads, wild orchids, anthuriums, and other rain-forest vegetation. Overhead the canopy is often so dense that little sunlight gets through. On the approach to the trail, the air is perfumed by pretty white flowers called wild orchids that grow profusely by the roadside. Bird life is abundant and includes three species of hummingbirds and the highly endangered St. Lucia green parrot, the national bird. Since 1979 St. Lucia has had a tough conservation program to save the parrot, bringing it back from the edge of extinction.

The Rain Forest Trail can be approached from either the east or west coasts, and many people hike straight from coast to coast. The hike is not difficult and takes three-and-a-half hours, but there are no facilities on or approaching the trail. Permission from the Forestry Department is needed. Forestry Department hikes with naturalists provide the most practical way to go. Now, too, most tour companies in St. Lucia that offer adventure type excursion have the Rain Forest Trail hike among their program. Usually, you will need to contact them in advance of your arrival. The Tourist Office in Soufrière or Anse Chastanet Hotel organizes hikes with one of the best naturalists in St. Lucia.

The drive from Soufrière to Fond St. Jacques takes about thirty minutes, but the road to the top of the ridge and the trailhead is rutted and must be taken by jeep or on foot. The ridge road runs for about 2 miles to the signposted entrance of the reserve and the start of the trail. From here the hike to the eastern exit takes about three-and-a-half hours. If your time is limited, an alternative would be to hike for only an hour or two and return to waiting transportation at the western entrance. Wear comfortable walking shoes; trails are often muddy, and showers are frequent.

Morne Coubaril (758-459-7340; fax: 758-459-5759; coubaril@candw.lc). The 200-acre Morne Coubaril Estate, just outside Soufrière, is a working coconut and cocoa plantation and cultural center

with costumed guides. It can be visited on foot or horseback. After many years of neglect the property, said to be the oldest estate in St. Lucia, has been restored and is meant to give a glimpse of daily life on a plantation in olden days. In addition to the restored manor house, there is a stable, **Trekkers,** offering rides through the plantation and the surrounding countryside and to the Sulfur Springs. The estate also offers a two-hour hiking excursion to a waterfall with explanations of plants and herbs.

To the South Coast

Choiseul: The forty-five-minute drive to the southern end of the island passes through the fishing village of Choiseul, known as the arts-and-crafts center of St. Lucia, where many villagers work in their homes as wood carvers, potters, and straw weavers. Their products can be purchased at the **Choiseul Arts and Craft Centre** (758-459-3226), a teaching center, and Victoria Arts and Crafts, a roadside stand.

On the north side of town by the roadside, you will pass a rock with a clearly visible Amerindian petroglyph often pictured in St. Lucia brochures. After the fishing village of Laborie, the landscape is flat and dry, unlike most of the island.

Moule-à-Chique Peninsula: Vieux Fort is the main town of the south and the location of Hewanorra International Airport. Hewanorra, meaning "land of the iguana," was the original Arawak name for St. Lucia. Regrettably, very few iguana remain. On the tip of the island, a narrow finger of land, Moule-à-Chique Peninsula, ends in an 800-foot-high promontory overlooking the sea, where the Atlantic Ocean and the Caribbean Sea collide. The view takes in the dramatic seascape, with St. Vincent in the distance on the south and the Maria Islands on the east.

Maria Islands Nature Reserve: At the end of the airport runway by Sables Bay is the Maria Islands Nature Centre and a half-mile offshore the two small islands of the Maria Islands Nature Reserve. Created in 1982 and operated by the National Trust, the reserve is home to a variety of wildlife including the Maria Islands ground lizard and the kouwes, a small, harmless, nocturnal snake said to be the rarest snake in the world. The Maria

Islands are also a bird refuge, and the waters around the islands are rich in marine life. A visit to the islands must be arranged with the National Trust, but you do not need permission to snorkel, which is best on the southwest side of Maria Major, the larger of the two islands.

The East Coast

The scenery along the east coast is lovely. In some parts there are dramatic rock formations created by pounding Atlantic waves, and other parts have deep bays with quiet waters. Savannes Bay, north of Vieux Fort, is a protected area, with the island's most extensive mangroves. Along this road, if you are lucky, you might see men making dugout canoes from the gommier tree in the same manner used by the Arawak and Carib Indians five hundred years ago.

Continuing en route to Dennery, the largest town on the east coast, the road passes through some of the island's most beautiful, lush scenery, with huge banana groves swooping down from rain-forested mountain peaks to the edge of the sea, where the Atlantic breaks against rocky fingers and barrier islets near the coast.

Mamiku Gardens (758-455-3729; fax: 758-452-9023). The 22-acre botanic gardens at Micoud (on the east coast, about a forty-five-minute drive from Castries) have been carved out of the woodlands surrounding the ruins of an 18th-century estate house that originally belonged to Baron de Micoud, a French governor of St. Lucia. Later, it served as a British military post and was destroyed during a battle between the British and the brigands, as slave freedom fighters were known.

The gardens, created by owner-designer Veronica Shingleton-Smith, whose family has owned the estate since 1906, have four distinct selections: **Mystic Garden,** approached by a pretty archway of hybrid gingers, has orchids and a variety of flowers and trees, as well as a small restaurant and souvenir shop in one of the plantation's old buildings. Another path meanders through stands of bay trees, a typical species throughout the estate, to the **Secret Garden,** reminiscent of an English summer garden with a great variety of sage, oleander, and flowering plants. Benches made by local craftsmen from local wood are placed in shady areas throughout the gardens for visitors to sit and enjoy the tranquil surroundings.

The **Woodland's Path** leads to **Grandpa's House,** an old wooden house, formerly used by the estate owners, with a typical Creole garden of fruit trees and herbs and spices used traditionally as natural remedies, as well as in cooking. **Bougainvillea Walk** connects with another path that zigzags up the mountainside to the high point of the estate. Benches along the way are conveniently placed to enable visitors to enjoy panoramic views of the Atlantic coast and Praslin Island. At the summit there is a small wooded picnic area and the ruins of an 18th-century plantation house. Banana Walk has signs that explain banana cultivation.

Veronica's Garden and the Casse (a small stream), the fourth area, can be visited on the downhill return. The garden follows a watercourse with anthurium along the banks. A fifteen-year-old galba tree, one of the rare indigenous varieties on St. Lucia, can be seen here; Mamiku has an estimated five hundred varieties of plants. Accommodation for the handicapped has been made.

Praslin Bay: Once a quiet fishing village, Praslin is now the site of a major billion-dollar resort and residential development, Le Paradis St. Lucia (www.leparadisstlucia.com), covering 554 acres along 2.5 miles of coastline and reefs facing Fregate Island; however the project has been delayed. Offshore at Praslin Bay, Fregate Island is a nature preserve for the Magnificent Fregatebird that nests here. Through the St. Lucia National Trust, you can arrange to hike the milelong nature trail circling the national park. In addition to Fregates, the island is home to some rare species of birds and boa constrictors. On a hillside above Praslin Bay is **Fox Grove Inn,** which some call the best-kept secret in St. Lucia for its restaurant where patrons enjoy a magnificent view of the coast and Frigate Islands. (See Dining section later in this chapter.) Further north, Dennery at the foot of the rain forest–covered mountains is the starting point for the **Treetop Canopy Adventure,** one of St. Lucia's rainforest canopy tours. (See Sports section later in this chapter.)

Beyond Dennery, the east-coast road meets the cross-island highway with the Barre de L'isle on its south. About halfway along the road to Castries is the trailhead to the Barre de L'isle Rain Forest Trail that runs along the edge of the rain forest and climbs to the top of Morne la Combe, which towers 1,446 feet on the Barre de L'isle ridge. Those who have the stamina for the difficult, three-hour hike are rewarded with fabulous panoramic views west to the Roseau and Mabouya valleys; shorter hikes have their rewards, too. For information: (758) 450-2231.

North to Pigeon Island

St. Lucia's main resorts and some of its best beaches lie along a stretch of coast between Castries and Rodney Bay. Some of the hotels are all-inclusive resorts whose sports and other facilities are available only to their guests; others accommodate day visitors. Inquire at the Tourist Information Desk at Pointe Séraphine.

Union Nature Trail: A few miles inland from Sandals Halcyon Beach Hotel on Choc Beach, a nature center at Union has a forty-five-minute trail for a self-guided walk, an herb garden featuring bush remedies used in St. Lucia, and a small zoo of local wildlife, developed in 1987 by the **Forestry Department** (www.slumaffe.org) to acquaint children with their natural heritage and provide a convenient place to introduce these attractions to cruise passengers and other visitors. The trail is an easy graveled path through a dry forest where hikers are likely to see hummingbirds, warblers, and finches. There is a small admission fee.

Gros Islet: Normally a quiet fishing village on the northwest coast, Gros Islet comes to life on Fri nights. A street fair and outdoor disco has become the island's biggest weekly event, with visitors joining residents in a "jump up," the street dancing of Carnival, which has come to mean a big party.

Rodney Bay: As part of a development plan for northern St. Lucia, a causeway was built in 1971 to connect Pigeon Island to the mainland by closing the north end of Rodney Bay and creating a long sandy beach. Over the years, the land area has been expanded and the south end of the bay, with its yacht basin, has become a major resort area and nightlife center with bars, restaurants, shops, and hotels at the edge of hip Rodney Bay Village, which bills itself as St. Lucia's answer to South Beach.

The Body Holiday at LeSport, an all-inclusive spa-resort and the first of its kind in the Caribbean,

is only a short drive from Rodney Bay. It has several day passes: Lunch with a swim in the pool or at the beach from 12:30 to 3 p.m. costs US$31; half-day package from 10 a.m. to 6 p.m. includes lunch, drinks, activities, and afternoon tea for US$60; and full-day from 10 a.m. to midnight includes lunch and dinner, all beverages, sports, and exercise facilities (except scuba and waterskiing) for US$118 per person. Spa treatments are separate.

Pigeon Island National Park: Pigeon Island (www.slunatrust.org) has a long and colorful history going back to the Arawaks. It was used as a hideaway by pirates who preyed on merchant ships in the 16th century and was a strategic British fort in the 18th century. It has been a quarantine station, whaling station, U.S. naval station, and even a hideaway of an English actress. After the causeway was constructed, the island was made into a park. It has trails leading to a promontory, now known as Pigeon Point, with the ruins of Fort Rodney and grandstand views of Rodney Bay and the north coast. The Pigeon Island Museum and Interpretive Centre is housed in the former British officer's mess, which was completely remodeled to the original 1808 plans. The history is brought to life in exhibits and an audiovisual reenactment of Rodney's famous victory over the French. The park is open daily from 9:30 a.m. to 4:30 p.m. There is a small admission fee. Cruise ships that stop at Rodney Bay often arrange a barbecue on the beach with water sports, a visit of the park, or tours of the northern part of St. Lucia.

Roads inland from Choc Bay or Rodney Bay lead to mountainous interior of the north and to Chassin in Babonneau where the Rainforest Aerial Tram and zipline are located. (See Sports later in this section.)

Shopping

Pointe Séraphine has an attractive shopping complex set around a Spanish-style courtyard with dozens of shops selling duty-free goods. Selections are small, but prices are among the best in the Caribbean. You will find fine china, crystal, perfume, liquor, cigarettes, jewelry, and leather goods, as well as locally made fashions and crafts. Although Pointe Séraphine is primarily for cruise-ship passengers, it is open to other visitors and to St. Lucia residents.

Cruise passengers must show their cabin key, landing card, or passport to claim duty-free privileges; island residents pay duty on their purchases. Liquor and cigarettes are delivered to the ship. Store hours are Mon to Fri 8:30 a.m. to 12:30 p.m. and 1:30 to 4:30 p.m. and Sat to 1 p.m., but the hours are usually extended when cruise ships are in port.

On the south side of the harbor, **La Place Carenage Shopping Plaza** is an attractive shopping complex in West Indian design, located at the foot of town and directly in front of the piers. It has many of the same shops as Pointe Séraphine, along with some unique attractions as well. The walk-in **Desmond Skeete Animation Centre,** said to be the only one of its kind in this area of the Caribbean, reproduces the island's colorful history through animation technology. The **Promenade of Artisans** is a showcase of local artisans, where visitors can browse and buy local art and crafts and watch some of the local artists at work on a range of pieces from self-portraits to pottery. The **Arcade of Indigenous Products** reflects St. Lucia's heritage, with cottage industry items such as jams, jellies, sauces, candy, and more, some to be sampled before buying.

The island has other shopping centers: **Sunset Shopping Plaza** and **Rodney Bay Marina Shopping Complex.** Beach and street vendors who are licensed by the government and permitted to operate in certain areas usually sell coral and freshwater pearl jewelry. They can sometimes be overzealous, but normally they are good natured and will move on after a smile and a "no, thank you." Artists, often Rastafarians, sell their woodcarvings on the street or beach, too. And don't overlook the **Castries Market**—it's fun, even if you buy nothing.

Art and Artists: Eudovic Art Studio (Goodlands, Castries; 758-452-2747; www.eudovicart .com; info@eudovicart.com). Joseph Eudovic is the dean of St. Lucia's wood sculptors and possibly the best of his style in the Caribbean. His works stand on an international level, with many being museum pieces. He carves from the trunks and limbs of local trees—gliricidia, red cedar, eucalyptus, and mahogany—allowing the natural wood to inspire the shape. Each piece is lyric with tension and energy that seem to be struggling to break out, but, at the same time, lines that flow with a calm and

grace only a master craftsman can achieve. Prices range from US$300 to $3,000 and up.

Eudovic is also a teacher, and other artists and students work at his studio. Visitors are welcome to view works in progress. The small shop also has beautiful trays, masks, and other gifts made from local woods and coconut. Eudovic's wife makes madras-costumed dolls that are whisk brooms and brushes. The fifteen-minute drive south of Castries is well worthwhile it for serious art lovers.

Another well-known artist, Llewellyn Xavier, whose work is in the permanent collection of New York City's Museum of Modern Art, has his studio at Silver Point, **Cap Estate** (Gros Islet; phone/fax: 758-450-9155). Call for an appointment. Xavier and his wife operate **Art and Antiques** (Point Seraphine; 758-451-4150), an art gallery selling fine art and antique maps and prints, silver, jewelry and collectibles. The gallery also holds auctions from time to time. In 2007, a 208-page retrospective of Xavier's work was published by Macmillan Caribbean as part of the latter's series on Caribbean artists. The book, *Llewellyn Xavier: His Life and Work,* covers the artist's forty-year creative journey.

In Castries, **Artsibit Gallery** (Brazil and Mongiraud Streets; 758-452-7865) carries local and Caribbean art, as well as posters and prints. The St. Lucia's Artists Association, organized in 1987 to help local artists and create a permanent national collection, exhibits its members' work here. Among the other galleries are **Modern Art Gallery** (Bois d'Orange Highway; 758-452-9079) and, at Rodney Bay; **Caribbean Art Gallery** (758-452-8071), and **Zaka** (758-457-1504; www.zaka-art.com), which specializes in colorfully painted masks.

Books and Maps: Sunshine Bookshop (Brazil Street; 758-458-0633; sunbooks@candw.lc) has the largest stock in town. **Noah's Arkad**e (Pointe Séraphine) and gift shops at hotels usually carry tourist books on St. Lucia.

China and Crystal: Harry Edwards Jewelers (Pointe Séraphine and La Place Carenage; 758-451-6799) has duty-free china and crystal.

Clothing and Accessories: Several companies design and manufacture clothing in their factories in St. Lucia. **Pickwick & Co.** has the best of Britain in cashmere, china, and other goods. **Timbuktoo** (La Place Carenage) has a large selection of casual tropical wear.

Crafts and Souvenirs: Batiks, hand-printed fabrics, and silkscreen designs are among the island's nicest products and are available as shirts, skirts, dresses, and a large variety of gifts. The oldest and most distinctive producer is **Bagshaws** (La Toc Road, La Place Carenage, and Pointe Séraphine; www.bagshawsstlucia.com), which has been in business more than three decades and still uses the colorful designs created by the late founder. The enterprise is now operated by daughter-in-law Alice Bagshaw, a dynamic American who has lived on the island most of her adult life. Bagshaws makes sportswear, leisure wear, and gift items with two dozen distinctive silkscreen designs on a variety of fabrics, including sea island cotton. The fabrics are designed, printed, and sold only in St. Lucia. Prices are reasonable. The retail shop is next to the art studio, where you can watch artisans at work.

Caribelle Batik (Old Victorian Road) has its workshop in a more-than-one-hundred-year-old house on the Morne, where you can watch artists at work making batik using antique Asian hot-wax methods on cotton. Their batik wall hangings, pareos (beach wraps), shirts, skirts, sundresses, evening wear, and more are sold at **Sea Island Cotton** (Rodney Bay), and other quality shops. **Arts and Crafts Cooperative of St. Lucia** (La Place Carenage) has a wide selection of gifts and souvenirs made in St. Lucia by different artisans.

The **Noah's Arkade** stores (Pointe Séraphine, Castries, and Rodney Bay) carry a large variety of crafts: wooden bowls, trays, and carvings; straw mats, baskets, and hats; ornamental shells and shell jewelry; and hammocks, as well as postcards and books on St. Lucia. **Handicraft St. Lucie** (Sunset Shopping Plaza) is an art gallery with souvenir items of red clay pottery, straw, and wood carvings.

Herbs and Spices: Caribelle Batik (Pointe Plaza) stocks Sunny Caribbee Herbs and Spices. **Erma of St. Lucia** (Rodney Bay Marina) has local products, perfumes and spices from Grenada, and unusual crafts that owner Erma Compton uncovers in her travels throughout the Caribbean and South America.

Jewelry: Colombian Emeralds (Pointe Séraphine and La Place Carenage) with stores throughout the Caribbean, has fully guaranteed sapphires, rubies, diamonds, and emeralds. **Y. de Lima** (William Peter Boulevard) is one of the top stores for fine jewelry, also selling cameras and film. **Touch of Class** (Pointe Séraphine) has jewelry and electronics.

Liquor and Wines: Rums made in St. Lucia are **Denros Bounty, Admiral Rodney,** and **Five Blondes.** The latter is particularly popular with visitors as souvenirs for its label, which pictures . . . yes, five blondes. (Presumably the name originally referred to blond or light rum.) Stores at Pointe Séraphine are well stocked and competitively priced; some are even lower than in St. Thomas.

Perfumes and Cosmetics: Images (Pointe Séraphine and La Place Carenage) has the best selection of perfume and cosmetics. Perfumes are made locally by **Caribbean Perfumes** (Vigie Cove; 758-453-7249; www.caribbeanperfumes.com) and come in several floral scents.

Dining and Restaurants

Dining choices in St. Lucia range from elegant restaurants in the hills overlooking Castries to rustic seafood ones in villages by the sea. All have the personal stamp of their owners and reflect the island's diverse makeup. European and American fare is readily available, but it is the island's Creole cuisine that deserves your attention. Be sure to sample such dishes as callaloo soup, stuffed breadfruit, banana bread, fried plantain, pumpkin soup, flying fish, and stuffed crab backs. Prices are not high, except in deluxe restaurants. Generally, lunch per person in an inexpensive restaurant will be less than US$15; moderate, US$15 to $25; and expensive, more than US$25. Most restaurants are open daily; some close on Sun, others close on Mon or Tues. Check in advance.

Castries and Environs

Buzz Seafood and Grill (Rodney Bay; 758-458-0450; www.buzzstlucia.com). From the outset, Buzz got lots of buzz because its owner is Pat Bowden, a former owner of San Antonio, the island's trendsetter for many years. Together with Chef Marie, they have created an eclectic, modern, and internationally inspired menu tested from several of their other ventures. But unless your ship remains in port for an evening or calls on Sunday during the winter season in time for brunch, you cannot learn what all the buzz is about because Buzz is only open for dinner. Expensive.

The Coal Pot (Vigie Marina; 758-452-5566; www.coalpotrestaurant.com) is a long-established open-air restaurant at the water's edge. Owners Xavier, the chef, and Michelle Elliot, who is an artist and acts as hostess, specialize in New World cuisine, a fusion of fresh Caribbean ingredients with French cooking. Moderately expensive.

The Green Parrot (Morne Fortune; 758-452-3399; www.greenparrothotel.com). A local favorite with a grand view of Castries offers West Indian dishes, along with steaks, watched over by Chef Harry, a St. Lucian who trained at London's prestigious Claridges Hotel. There is also a pool and darts room with an English pub atmosphere. Expensive.

The Edge Restaurant Bar and Sushi (Harmony Suites Hotel, Rodney Bay; 758-450-EDGE; www.edge-restaurant.com) is popular for award-winning Swedish chef Bobo Bergstrom's unusual Eurobbean fusion cuisine. The gourmet fare is served in a stunning, torch-lit waterfront setting. Open daily from 8 a.m. to 11 p.m. Reservations are recommended; closed Sept. Moderately expensive.

Ti Bananne Caribbean Bistro & Bar (Coco Palm Resort, Rodney Bay; 758-456-2800; www.coco-resorts.com) Chef Richardson Skinner combines Trinidadian and French cuisine amid colorful murals in a relaxed and distinctly St. Lucian ambience. Moderate.

Jacques Waterfront Dining (Vigie Cove; 758-458-1900; www.froggiejacques.com). Open-air waterside dining on seafood and local specialties in a pleasant, casual setting. Moderately expensive.

The New Lime (Rodney Bay; 758-452-0761). Popular at lunch for rôti and light fare, it is a favorite for "limin'" at happy hour and in the evening for the Rodney Bay crowd. Moderate.

Oceana Seafood Restaurant (Castries; 758-456-0300; fax: 758-453-2102). Great food; a local favorite. Inexpensive.

Spinnakers Beach Bar and Carvery (Rodney Bay; 758-452-8491; fax: 758-458-0301). On the beach and very popular, the food is always fresh. Great atmosphere, particularly at lunchtime. Moderate.

Tao (LeSport; 758-450-8551; www.bodyholiday .com). The gourmet restaurant of the spa-resort is one of the best in the Caribbean for its innovative Pacific Rim cuisine. Tao is a nonsmoking restaurant and the dress code is resort elegant. Expensive.

Soufrière to the East Coast

Trou au Diable Restaurant (Anse Chastanet Resort; 758-459-7000; ansechastanet@candw.lc). Situated directly on the beach just north of Soufrière, the open-air restaurant is popular with swimmers, divers, and snorkelers who enjoy the reefs only 20 yards offshore. The menu has a choice of salads, sandwiches, seafood, and other dishes. Best reached by water taxi from Soufrière. Moderate.

Dasheene Restaurant & Bar (Ladera Resort; 758-459-7323; 866-290-0978; www.ladera.com). Set on a mountainside 1,000 feet above sea level with a spectacular view of the Pitons, the restaurant is casual, yet sophisticated, and serving light cuisine that combines Caribbean Creole fare with modern American cooking. Open seven days a week. Moderately expensive.

Whispering Palms (Fox Grove Inn, Mon Repos; 758-455-3271; foxgroveinn@candw.lc) on a hillside above Praslin Bay on the east coast is probably the best-kept secret in St. Lucia for its fine restaurant with a wonderful view. The friendly owner/chef Franz Louis-Fernand, who has had thirty-five years experience at restaurants in Europe and is aided by wife Esther, serves fish and lobster bought fresh from local fishermen and vegetables, fruits and herbs from local farms. Moderate.

Nightlife

St. Lucia is low-key, with nightlife revolving around hotels and a few restaurants with light entertainment. There are romantic cocktail and moonlight cruises, and everyone on the island heads for Gros Islet on Fri night.

Rodney Bay has become the center of night action with bars and restaurants, offering live musical entertainment on different nights of the week. Check *Tropical Traveler*, a free tourist newspaper that lists nighttime entertainment daily for the week. The **Derek Walcott Theatre** (at the Great House) offers music, dance, and drama productions in a small, open-air theater located in the ruins of the old Cap Estate House. An annual performance by the Trinidad Theatre Workshop and Sun brunch productions are among the theater's highlights.

Sports

Beaches/Swimming: St. Lucia claims to have more than 120 beaches, many accessible only by boat. The beaches closest to Castries are north of the port and easy to reach by bus or taxi. The prettiest ones are in the secluded coves south of the capital, reached by motorboat in about thirty minutes.

Biking: Bike St. Lucia (758-451-2453; www .junglereefadventures.com; junglereef@candw.lc), developed by Anse Chastanet resort, is St. Lucia's only biking-in-the-forest facility, located adjacent to the resort on Anse Mamin, site of one of St. Lucia's oldest plantations. The prepared trails, designed to accommodate both first-time and experienced riders, weave through the plantation grounds, deep into the tropical jungle. There is also a skills-training area where instructors provide an introductory class or refresher course. The trails also offer a window into history as participants pedal by the 18th-century French-colonial ruins of a sugar mill, an old church, a freshwater reservoir, and more. The area has fruit trees such as mango, coconut, banana, guava, cocoa, and citrus, as well as wild orchids, birds, and an old-fashioned river swimming hole. The Jungle Biking Adventure costs US$95 per person and includes equipment rentals, water bottle, and introductory lesson; round-trip transfers by water taxi and lunch served at the plantation. Another company is **Cycle St. Lucia** (Rodney Bay; 758-458-0908; www.cyclestlucia.com).

Boating: Sailing is one of St. Lucia's most popular sports, where yachtsmen can enjoy safe harbors on the island's deeply indented coastline. Marigot Bay is the base for **The Moorings St. Lucia** (758-451-4357; www.moorings.com), a major Caribbean boat charterer. It offers day-sailing from Marigot Bay and has a dive shop and water-sports center. **Rodney Bay Marina** (www.igy-rodneybay.com) at Gros Islet has **Sunsail Stevens Yachts** (758-452-8648), one of the oldest yachting specialists in the Eastern Caribbean, and **Destination Saint Lucia Yachting** (758-452-8531; www.dsl-yachting.com). Both offer day sails and longer charters.

Castries is the base for large party boats that sail on picnic and snorkeling excursions, such as the Brig *Unicorn* (758-456-9100), US$100, which departs about 8:30 a.m. and returns at 4:30 p.m. Soufrière is the most popular destination; Anse Jambette is also popular.

Endless Summer Cruises (Castries; 758-450-8651; fax: 758-452-0659; www.stluciaboattours .com) offers full-day catamaran cruises from Rodney Bay to Soufrière with tours, buffet lunch on board, and stops for swimming and snorkeling at secluded beaches as well as at Marigot Bay, about US$90.

Canopy Tours: St. Lucia has two canopy tour locations. Both are offered by **Sunlink Tours** (758-456-9100; www.sunlinktours.com); Island Routes (www.islandroutes.com); and other tour companies offering adventure type excursions.

Treetop Canopy Adventure, located on the east coast inland from Dennery at the foot of the rainforest–covered Central Mountains, is the operated by Palm Services Ltd. (758-458-0908; www .adventuretoursstlucia.com), a St. Lucia company specializing in adventure tours. The ride, along a system of integrated cables, rigging, and platforms has eleven zip lines ranging from 83 feet to 800 feet between platforms, for a total span of 5100 feet, and reaching heights up to 150 feet above the forest floor. The four-hour tour is graded as low to moderate activity level and has minimum height and maximum weight restrictions. Cost: $100. The operator offers a variety of others excursions. For example, one combines the zipline with a cycling excursion, about US$150.

Rainforest Sky Ride, operated by Rain Forest Aerial Tram St. Lucia (758-458-5151; www.rainforest adventure.com), is located in the north at Babonneau in the highland community of Chassin at approximately 2,000 feet above sea level. It offers an aerial tram excursion providing a spectacular ride over the rain forest, as well as a ten-stage zipline adventure, US$92. Recently, the operator added a more adventuresome excursion that it bills as the "Adrena Line Zip Line." After an orientation and safety briefing, the adventure starts with a short hike through the rainforest that becomes an adrenaline rush as participants scramble across floating stairs suspended above the ground past the eagle's claw (so named for the grip of the root system that has consumed volcanic boulders) that delivers them to the first of fourteen platforms. There, guides hitch riders up to a series of cables to zip from platform to platform and ending in a heart-dropping slide off a platform down to terra firma.

Rain Forest Aerial Trams St. Lucia (U.S./Canada 866-759-8726; www.rainforestrams.com) belongs to the company that originated zipline excursions in Costa Rica and operates them in Dominica and Jamaica.

Deep-Sea Fishing: Fully equipped sportfishing boats are available for half-day and full-day charters. Contact **Captain Mike's Sport Fishing & Pleasure Cruises** (Vigie Marina; 758-452-7044; www.captmikes.com), **Mako Water Sports** (Rodney Bay Marina; 758-452-0412; makosportfishing@yahoo.com), or **Hackshaw's Boat Charters & Sport Fishing** (Castries; 758-453-0553; www.hackshaws.com). The main seasons are Dec to June for open-sea species, such as wahoo, sailfish, tuna, and kingfish, and July to Dec, when the catch is best closer to shore. Fishing is an old tradition and a way of life for many St. Lucians. Normally, a half-day charter costs $450 to $550; full day $800 to $950.

Dolphin and Whale Watching: St. Lucian waters are home to resident and migrating dolphins and whales. The claim is made that twenty-five varieties have been spotted in St. Lucia waters. Most frequent are sperm, pilot, and humpback whales and on rare occasion the orca (killer whale). On occasion, large pods of dolphin, up to 150 at a time are sighted. **Hackshaw's Boat Charters** (758-453-0553 or 758-452-3909; www.hackshaws.com; hackshawc@candw.lc), operates four boats—three for sportfishing and a custom-designed whale-watching boat. Hackshaw's is a member of the St. Lucia Whale Watching Association and follows the international whale-watching rules for the safety of the mammals. *Whale Watch*

Safari departs from Vigie Marina in Castries; some excursions include lunch and swimming. **Sunlink Tours** (758-456-9100; www.sunlinktours.com) arranges excursions upon request; US$70 adult, $45 child.

Golf: The **St. Lucia Golf & Country Club** (Cap Estates; 758-450-8523; www.stluciagolf.com), about 1 mile from Rodney Bay, is an 18-hole layout. Greens fees are US$95–$120 for 9 holes, US$105–$145 for 18 holes depending on the season, US$20 to $50 for golf club rentals. The course is fully irrigated with an automatic system. The Cap Grill is open daily for breakfast and lunch and Thurs to Sat for dinner. The 9-hole golf course at **Sandals Regency Golf Resort & Spa at La Toc** (758-452-3081), about 5 miles from the port, is reserved for its guests but available to others by prior arrangement.

Hiking: The central mountains, particularly the short trail of the Barre de l'Isle, St. Lucia Rain Forest Trail, and Union Nature Trail, are the most popular for hiking. (See previous sections in this chapter for details.) These hikes do not require a great deal of experience or endurance. Wear comfortable shoes, and keep cameras in waterproof covers. Experienced hikers are allowed to hike the Gros Piton, a strenuous 2,619 feet up, but they should have permission of the **Forestry Department** (758-468-5649; deptforest@slumaffe.org) and a knowledgeable guide, which can be arranged by contacting the **Pitons Tour Guide Association** (758-459-9748); maximum three hikers per guide. **St. Lucia National Trust** (758-452-5005; www.slunatrust.org) and **Heritage Tourism Programme** (758-451-6058) also arrange hiking excursions.

Horseback Riding: St. Lucia can be explored by horseback on trips organized by **Trim's National Riding Academy** (758-452-8273; www.trimsnationalridingacademy.com) at Cap Estate. The stable offers picnic rides along the Atlantic coast and trail rides overlooking the Caribbean and horse-and-carriage tours of Pigeon Point. US$80 per person. **International Pony Club** (Gros Islet; 758-452-8139) offers a beach picnic to Cas en Bas with time for swimming. In the Soufrière area, **Trekkers** (Morne Coubaril Estate; 758-459-7340) has similar excursions.

Kayaking: A fairly new sport in St. Lucia, kayaking excursions are available from **Jungle Reef Adventures** (Soufrière; 758-459-7755; www.jungle reefadventures.com). The company also offers mountain biking and scuba diving excursions.

Snorkeling/Scuba Diving: St. Lucia has lovely, unspoiled reefs with abundant fish along 24 miles of its Caribbean coast, with many sites yet to be explored. Some of its best reefs with spectacular coral and marine life are found at Anse Cochon and in the few miles between Anse Chastanet Beach and the Pitons. Here, dive sites are found in calm and protected waters near the shore; some in only 20 feet of water are close enough to reach directly from the beach. Indeed, the proximity to shore of shallow-water reefs makes St. Lucia a good place to learn to snorkel and dive.

The Pitons drop as deep into the water as they rise above the ground, and their walls offer an exciting and unusual experience for divers, who see huge sponges, underwater caves, and a great variety of fish.

Scuba St. Lucia (Anse Chastanet; 758-459-7755; www.scubastlucia.com) is the island's leading dive shop and offers beach and boat dives four times daily. It has resort courses for beginners, certification courses, night dives, underwater photography, and others. Facilities include changing rooms, freshwater showers, beach bar/restaurant, and boutiques. **The Moorings St. Lucia** (Marigot Bay) and **Windjammer Landing,** north of Castries, have dive operations as well.

Soufrière Marine Management was founded in 1995 to protect and properly manage 7 miles of St. Lucia's most spectacular underwater coastline in the Soufrière area. Rather than simply impose measures to safeguard the marine environment, the SMMA project over a period of three years consulted every community member—fishermen, taxi drivers, dive operators, community groups, restaurateurs, and church organizations—before legislation was implemented. As a result, the coastline was carefully zoned to fill the needs of all users, establishing fishing priority areas, marine reserves, mooring areas, recreational sites, and multiuse zones. Since the SMMA was established, the reefs have started to regenerate, and fish stocks in certain areas have tripled. The SMMA has been recognized for its work with several awards and is seen as the blueprint for marine management to be set up around Anse la Raye and Canaries, and ultimately to create an umbrella organization to manage the entire St. Lucian coastline.

Windsurfing/Kiteboarding: Sables Bay facing the Maria Islands is the most popular location for windsurfing, but the entire south coast, bordering both the Atlantic and the Caribbean, is ideal. Strong Atlantic winds and choppy waves are a challenge to experts, whereas the Caribbean's gentle breezes are suitable for learning or improving your skills. Most beachside hotels offer rental equipment and instruction.

The sport of kiteboarding or kitesurfing has come recently to St. Lucia, along with the rest of the Caribbean. For information, contact **Club Mistral St. Lucia** (758-454-3418; www.stluciakite boarding.com; www.slucia.com/windsurf) or **Reef Kite & Surf** (Anse de Sables Beach, Vieux Fort, 758-454-3418; kitesurf@slucia.com).

Festivals and Celebrations

St. Lucia's festivities are a blend of its French, British, and African heritage—to the extent that it is hard to tell where one ends and another begins. Two festivals unique to the island are the **Feast of St. Rose de Lima,** Aug 30, and **Feast of St. Marguerite Mary Alocoque of France,** Oct 17. Both were founded by St. Lucian singing societies, La Rosa and La Marguerite, and are held on the feast days of the patron saints for which they are named. Each festival is preceded by months of nightly singing practices called séances, which take place in festive settings. A king and queen, who serve as leaders for the events, are selected for each festival. Strict protocol is observed, with participants and visitors bowing to the chosen leaders upon entering the practice hall. A church service is followed by a costumed procession of members clad as kings and queens, princes and princesses, policemen and soldiers—singing and dancing in the streets. The parades are topped off with sumptuous banquets and dancing, with the king and queen leading the grand waltz at midnight.

St. Vincent and the Grenadines

Kingstown, Bequia, Mustique, Mayreau, Tobago Cays, Palm Island, Union Island

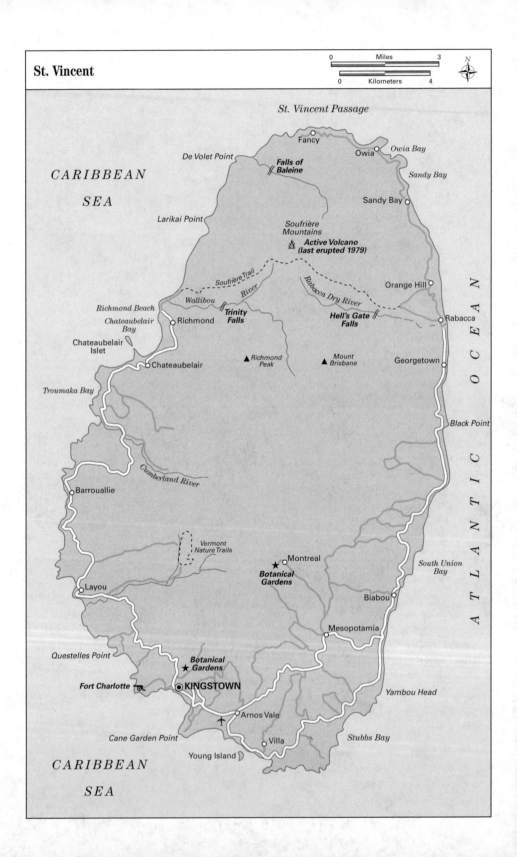

St. Vincent

Rugged Terrain and Gentle Beauty

Majestic emerald mountains rising almost directly from a sapphire sea anchor a chain of three dozen exquisite gems that make up the country of St. Vincent and the Grenadines. Situated in the Windward Islands between St. Lucia and Grenada, they are the idyllic Caribbean hideaways for nature lovers, boating enthusiasts, and true beachcombers.

St. Vincent, the capital and largest of the group, is surprisingly different in composition and appearance from the Grenadines. It is covered almost end to end with intensely green, deeply creviced mountains that peak at 4,500 feet in an active volcano that displayed its awesome power as recently as 1979. Roads twist through the steep mountains, providing spectacular views of the interior, thick with tropical forests and cultivated with banana and arrowroot. On the Caribbean coast sheer cliffs drop to the sea, and white- or black-sand beaches hide in the crevices of an irregular coastline. On the windward side the Atlantic crashes against the rockbound shores.

The Grenadines, by contrast, are low-lying islets trimmed with palm-fringed, pristine beaches facing coral gardens. They stretch south from St. Vincent to Grenada over 65 miles of sparkling seas that yachtsmen often call the most beautiful sailing waters in the world. Now cruise ships are discovering them, too. Out of thirty-two islands and cays, six are ports of call.

Discovered by Columbus on his third voyage in 1498, St. Vincent was probably inhabited first by the Ciboneys and later by the Arawak and Carib Indians. Pre-Columbian artifacts have been found throughout the islands, and Amerindian petroglyphs can be seen on rock faces in many places. The island was still occupied by Caribs in 1672 when it was claimed by Britain.

In 1675 a slave ship sank in the channel between St. Vincent and Bequia. Survivors reached both islands and, in time, were assimilated with the Caribs. Their offspring came to be called the "Black Caribs," a name sometimes still used to refer to the villagers on St. Vincent's northeast coast, where their descendants concentrated.

Britain and France fought over St. Vincent for a century, but the Caribs put up such fierce resistance that neither country was able to colonize it. In 1748 the European combatants declared St. Vincent a neutral island. Under the Treaty of Paris, however, St. Vincent was ceded to England in 1763 and, together with Grenada, the Grenadines, and Dominica, formed the Windward Islands Federation. The Grenadines were divided administratively; Grenada got Petit Martinique and Carriaçou, at the south end of the chain, and St. Vincent was made responsible for all the islands north of Petit Martinique.

Except for a brief period of French occupation from 1779 to 1783, St. Vincent remained in British hands. With French support the Caribs made a final attempt in 1795 to regain their territory, but the rebellion was squashed. Hundreds of Caribs were shipped off to Balliceaux, an islet east of Bequia, and then deported to the island of Roatan,

At a Glance

Antiquities	★
Architecture	★
Art and Artists	★
Beaches	★★★★★
Colonial Buildings	★
Crafts	★
Cuisine	★★
Culture	★★
Dining/Restaurants	★★
Entertainment	★
Forts	★★★
History	★★★
Monuments	★
Museums	★
Nightlife	★
Scenery	★★★★★
Shopping	★
Sightseeing	★★★★★
Sports	★★★★
Transportation	★

Fast Facts

Population: 109,022

Size: St. Vincent, 18 miles long and 11 miles wide, 133 square miles; Bequia, 7 square miles; Mustique, 4 square miles

Main Towns: Kingstown, St. Vincent; Port Elizabeth, Bequia; and Clifton, Union Island

Government: St. Vincent and the Grenadines, a member of the British Commonwealth, has a parliamentary government headed by a prime minister. The parliament is made up of a House of Assembly, elected every five years. The governor-general is appointed by the queen on the advice of the prime minister.

Currency: East Caribbean (EC) dollar. US$1 equals about EC$2.70.

Departure Tax: EC$40 (US$15)

Emergency Numbers: Medical: Milton Cato Memorial Hospital, Kingstown; (784) 456-1185; Police and Coast Guard: 999; 911

Language: English

Public Holidays: Jan 1, New Year's Day; Mar 14, National Heroes Day; Good Friday; Easter Monday; May 1, Labor Day; May 31, Whit Mon; July 5, Caricom Day, Carnival Mon; July 6, Mardi Gras; Aug 1, Emancipation Day; Oct 27, Independence Day; Dec 25, Christmas Day; Dec 26, Boxing Day.

Telephone Area Code: 784

Airlines: There are no direct flights from the United States to St. Vincent. American Airlines, Air Canada, Caribbean Airlines, Delta, Jet Blue, and US Airways connect in San Juan, Barbados, St. Lucia, and Antigua with American Eagle (to Canouan only), LIAT, SVG Air (784-457-5124; www.svgair.com), and Mustique Airways (784-458-4380; www.mustique.com). St. Vincent has an information desk in the arrivals hall at Barbados airport, open daily from 1 to 8 p.m. to assist passengers traveling to/from St. Vincent and the Grenadines.

Information: www.stvincent.com; www.bequiatourism.com

In the United States:

St. Vincent and the Grenadines Tourist Information Office, 801 Second Ave., New York, NY 10017; (212) 687-4981; (800) 729-1726; fax: (212) 949-5946; svgtony@aol.com

In Canada:

St. Vincent and the Grenadines Tourist Information Office, 333 Wilson Ave., Suite 601, Toronto, ON M3H IT2; (416) 457-1502; fax: (416) 633-3123; svgtourismtoronto@rogers.com

In Port:

Kingstown: St. Vincent and the Grenadines Tourism Authority, P.O. Box 834, 2nd Floor, NIS Building, Upper Bay Street, Kingstown, St. Vincent and the Grenadines; (784) 456-6222; fax: (784) 485-6020; tourism@vincysurf.com. Hours: weekdays 8 a.m. to 4:15 p.m.

Bequia: Bequia Tourism Association, Port Elizabeth; (784) 458-3286; fax: (784) 458-3964; bequiatourism@caribsurf.com. Hours: Mon to Fri from 8:30 a.m. to 6 p.m., Sat from 8:30 a.m. to 2 p.m., and Sun from 8:30 a.m. to noon.

Union Island: Union Island Tourist Bureau; (784) 458-8350. Hours: daily, including weekends, 8 a.m. to noon and 1 to 4 p.m.

which was part of British Honduras at the time. St. Vincent and the Grenadines became independent in 1979.

Today, St. Vincent and the Grenadines hit the big time with their starring role in Disney's *Pirates of the Caribbean: The Curse of the Black Pearl*. St. Vincent became the base of operations for the cast and crew, and Walillabou was transformed into the bustling Port Royal. The set is still standing and is a popular tour stop.

Budget Planning

St. Vincent is one of the least expensive destinations in the Caribbean, but the limited tourist development limits your options as well. On the other hand, its unspoiled quality is part of the attraction. Plan to enjoy St. Vincent and the Grenadines for their unrivaled natural beauty, and leave your shopping for other ports. Some of the Grenadines—Bequia and Union—are also inexpensive, but those that have been developed as deluxe, private-island resorts, such as Petit St. Vincent and Young Island, are expensive. The islands frequented by cruise ships—Bequia and Mayreau—are visited for their beaches and water sports; activities are generally prearranged by the cruise line.

Port Profile

Location/Embarkation: The port is on the southwestern corner of St. Vincent at Kingstown Bay. It is a vital commercial artery for this pre-dominantly agricultural country as well as being its cruise and ferry port. A new pier exclusively for cruise ships was part of a major reclamation project to improve the appearance, access, and facilities of the port area. A walkway from the pier leads directly into the city center, 2 blocks from the Department of Tourism and main shopping street. The Cruise Ship Pier and Terminal offers a number of shops and a Tourism Information Bureau.

Local Transportation: Minibuses to all parts of St. Vincent depart from Market Square, or you can wave at a passing bus to stop for you. Sample fares from Kingstown to the main locations: Arnos Vale, EC$1; Mesopotamia, EC$3; Georgetown, EC$6. Cruise-ship passengers seldom use buses except for short distances near Kingstown.

Taxi rates are fixed by the government. The hourly rate is EC$50 (US$19). Taxis can be hired for sightseeing. Some examples of one-way fares from Kingstown to popular destinations: airport, EC$25; Young Island dock, EC$30; Blue Lagoon, EC$35; Mesopotamia EC$60. Lists of bus and taxi fares are available from the Department of Tourism.

Roads and Rentals: On St. Vincent the main road system is confined to the southern, most populated, third of the island between Kingstown and Richmond on the west and Sandy Bay on the east. Most are narrow roads that wind through the mountains and along irregular coastlines. No road circumnavigates the island, and only roads on the south coast cross the island between the east and west coasts. There are very few roads in the central area, and almost none in the northern third. The east-coast road north of Georgetown is best covered by four-wheel drive.

Cars and jeeps are available for rent in Kingstown for US$45 and up per day, but you might

enjoy your sightseeing more if you do not have to negotiate the winding roads. Taxis can be hired by the hour or for the day; be sure to agree on the route and price in advance. Guides for hiking can be obtained through the Forestry Division or the Government Tourist Office; you should consult them about trail conditions. Local tour companies organize hikes to Soufrière, as well.

Rental companies include **Ben's Auto Rental** (Arnos Vale; 784-456-2907; www.bensautorentals .com), which has all-terrain Suzukis and pickup service available; **Greg's Rental Services** (784-457-9814; www.gregsrental.com); **Avis** (784-456-4389); and some independent dealers. A local driving license is required and can be obtained for EC$100 upon presentation of your U.S. or Canadian driver's license at the Licensing Authority, Halifax Street, or at the police station on Bay Street. For bike and scooter rentals, check out **Sailor's Cycle Centre** (784-457-1712) and **Trotman's Depot** (784-482-9498). Driving in this former British colony is on the LEFT.

Ferry Service: Between Kingstown and Bequia ferries leave at two- and three-hour intervals from 6 a.m. to 7 p.m. Cost is EC$20 one-way. Schedules are subject to seasonal changes. For schedule information contact **Bequia Express** (784-457-3539) or **Admiral** (784-458-3348). Ferries to Canouan, Mayreau, and Union operate several days a week. You will find schedules in the Tourist Department's information booklet.

Shore Excursions

Shore excursions vary from a three-hour island tour with a visit to the Botanical Gardens, to a drive to Mesopotamia for about US$50–$60; to hikes on nature trails in the Buccament Valley or to Trinity

Falls for about US$70–$80, to dive and/or snorkeling trips or trips to Bequia and other Grenadine islands, US$85–$135 to a boat excursion to the Falls of Baleine—a magnificent waterfall accessible only by boat—passing spectacular scenery, with stops for swimming and snorkeling. This trip is offered as a day excursion by tour and water-sports companies in Kingstown. Another option is to hike to the summit of the Soufrière Volcano, for about US$70–$80. The excursion from Kingstown takes six hours; **Fantasea Tours** (784-457-4477; www.fantaseatours.com) excursion departs Kingstown at 9 a.m. and returns at 4:30 p.m. A six-hour tour to the Darvue Waterfall stops in Wallilabou where fans of *Pirates of the Caribbean* will see the film set for the movie's town of Port Royal firsthand. A three-hour motor cruise provides an opportunity to view some of the seven species of whales and eleven species of dolphins that frequent the waters off St. Vincent for US$50.

For travelers arriving by yacht or coming to St. Vincent to begin a sailing excursion through the Grenadines, these tours can be arranged through your chartering company.

Some tour companies: **Vincy Aviation Services Ltd.** (Arnos Vale; 784-456-5600; www.vincy aviation.com) specializes in island tours and charter flights, among other services. Yacht cruises to the Grenadines (with or without crew) are available through **Barefoot Yacht Charters** (784-456-9526; www.barefootyachts.com; barebum@vincysurf.com).

Fantasea Tours (784-457-4477; www.fanta seatours.com) and **Hazeco Tours** (Box 325, St. Vincent; 784-457-8634; fax: 784-457-8105; www .hazecotours.com) offer ecotours to volcano and other nature sites; boat tour to the Falls of Baleine and whale watching and bird-watching excursions. **Sailor's Wilderness Tours** (Middle Street; 784-457-1712; fax: 784-456-2821; www.sailortours .com, sailortours@hotmail.com) has a variety of tour packages, including Mesopotamia Valley, Falls of Baleine; Rain Forest and Parrot Reserve; biking/ picnicking volcano tour; catamaran sailing tours; Bike 'n Cruise the Grenadines. **Sea Breeze Nature Tours** (784-458-4969; www.seabreezenaturetours .com), hiking and horseback riding as does the **Richmond Vale Nature and Hiking Center** (784-492-4058; www.richmondvalehiking.com) at the northwest corner of the island.

St. Vincent on Your Own

Kingstown is the only sizable town on St. Vincent. Founded in the early 18th century, the historic town stretches around Kingstown Bay and climbs the surrounding hills. It is laid out in a grid of three streets deep and about 10 blocks long. The historic sites, along with browsing in a few shops, can be covered on foot in an hour or so.

A Kingstown Walkabout

In the Cruise Ship Terminal, after you have browsed the shops selling local and imported items, you can walk out onto Upper Bay Street, turn left, and walk along to old, renovated warehouses that now house the Cobblestone Inn, **Basil's Bar and Restaurant,** and a number of small shops.

One block west of this complex is the Kingstown Market, a large building that is open every day except Sun. At the north end of the market, on Halifax Street, is the **Courthouse and Parliament** building, a large colonial structure and small square at the town's center.

West of the parliament Halifax Street becomes Grenville Street, which has two landmark churches. **St. George's Anglican Cathedral,** at the corner of North River Road, is the oldest church in St. Vincent (1820) and is noted for its stained-glass windows. But more curious is St. Mary's Catholic Church, an extraordinary mixture of Romanesque, Gothic, Renaissance, and baroque styles with pointed arches, round arches, turrets, and square and wedding towers. It was created from pictures of famous European cathedrals by a bishop-architect in 1823, enlarged in 1877 and 1891, and restored in the early 1940s. The interior is as ornate as the exterior. North of the church is **Victoria Park,** a parade ground.

Botanical Gardens: About a mile north of town are the oldest botanic gardens in the Western Hemisphere, established in 1765 on 20 hillside acres north of town. The gardens were begun mainly to grow herbs and spices, which in those days were the source of most drugs; the first curators were medical men as well as horticulturists.

After being allowed to deteriorate in the mid-19th century, the gardens were reactivated by 1890 as part of a larger agricultural and botanical scheme. Today they are beautifully maintained, though not well signposted, and have enormous variety; they rank among the most outstanding in the Caribbean. They have nine varieties of ixora, a flowering bush whose small clustered blossom is the national flower. Along with huge mahogany and teak, you might see African tulip, yellow poui, flamboyant, or others in bloom, depending on the month. In Oct, for example, the nutmeg are laden with fruit, and the cannonball tree, an ugly wiry tree, shows its magnificent, delicate coral blossom.

The gardens' prized species is a sucker from the breadfruit tree planted in 1793 from the original plant brought to the Caribbean from Tahiti by Captain Bligh of *Mutiny on the Bounty* fame. When he arrived in Kingstown in 1793 on the HMS *Providence* on his second voyage, he off-loaded 530 breadfruit plants, of which 50 were planted in the gardens. The gardens' specimen is said to be a third-generation sucker of an original plant. As a clone of the original root, it can be referred to as an "original." The entrance to the gardens opens onto a manicured grass path bordered by hibiscus hedges and shaded by enormous Honduras mahogany trees. The famous breadfruit tree is nearby. Guides are available.

On the east side of the gardens is an aviary for the St. Vincent parrot, the national bird and one of the most endangered parrot species. Their number has decreased from thousands to an estimated five hundred birds today. Their habitat is being destroyed by clearing of the forest for agriculture, logging, hunting, and by the lucrative international pet market for exotic birds. The bird has magnificent coloring, with a distinctive white head and a brownish mauve body and green, deep lavender, and gold on the tail, neck, and wings.

A major effort to preserve the parrot is under way by the Forestry Division with the aid of Peace Corps volunteers, World Wildlife Fund, and RARE, the Philadelphia-based tropical-bird conservation group. A reserve has been established on about 600 acres of rain forests in the Upper Buccament Valley. The program has involved the entire population—from schoolchildren, dressed as parrots, dancing to a calypso tune written especially for "Vincy," the parrot's nickname, to businessmen who use the parrot in their promotions.

Fort Charlotte: From its 650-foot-high perch about 2 miles west of town, Fort Charlotte commands a magnificent view across Kingstown Bay to some of the Grenadines. Built around 1791 during the reign of King George III and named for his queen, the fort was completed about 1812 and was occupied by British troops until 1873. The gun emplacements, which are intact, point inland. This and the moat location, between the promontory and the main island, indicates that the builders may have been more concerned about attacks from the land—from the Caribs or the French—than from the sea. Today an area of the fort is used as a women's prison.

Fort Duvernette: Built about 1800 to protect the entrance to Kingstown, the fort sits atop a volcanic spike, 195 feet above the sea, next to Young Island (www.youngisland.com) at the entrance to Young Cut, a narrow channel on the south coast where water sports are centered.

A Drive Around the Island

The South Coast to the Mesopotamia Valley

From the capital, Queen Elizabeth Drive, one of the main arteries, runs east over Sion and Dorsetshire Hills, providing fabulous views over Kingstown and Fort Charlotte. At Arnos Vale, by the airport, the road splits. One branch skirts the coast along Calliaqua Bay, where most of the hotels and popular beaches are located; and the other climbs the mountains. The east end of Calliaqua Bay, known as the Careenage or Blue Lagoon, is the center for sailing charters.

Mesopotamia Valley: The southern third of St. Vincent has two high mountain ridges bridged at two 3,000-foot peaks—Grand Bonhomme and Petit Bonhomme. They form the heads of two large, intensively cultivated valleys: the Mesopotamia Valley on the east and the Buccament Valley on the west. The high slopes of the Mesopotamia Valley are thick with tree ferns and bamboo and planted with nutmeg, cacao, and coconut. The panoramic views are spectacular. The lower reaches of the valley are the country's breadbasket, planted with West Indian staples that include breadfruit, banana, plantain, and root crops such as eddo and dasheen—all plants with huge leaves that enhance the valley's lush appearance. High on the windward slopes of Grand Bonhomme at Richland Park are the Montreal Gardens, a botanical garden and nursery.

Yambou Gorge: You can return from the gardens via the Yambou Gorge, where the streams that drain through the Mesopotamia Valley tumble over volcanic rocks on their way to the sea. On the coast large Atlantic rollers break against the rocks and the black-sand beaches at Argyle. Views along the way across the ridges and through the valley to the sea are magnificent.

The West Coast to the Buccament Valley

West of Kingstown the Leeward Highway snakes along the west coast and after about 5 miles crosses the Buccament Valley. The former Pembroke Estate was once a prosperous 1,000-acre sugar plantation whose aqueduct supplied water to power the mill. A road inland along the Buccament River leads to the head of the valley and a rainforest trail on the slopes of Grand Bonhomme.

Nature Trail: A loop trail of one-and-a-half miles, developed by the Forestry Department with the aid of Peace Corps volunteers in 1988, rises from about 1,000 feet to almost 2,500 feet and passes under towering teak, mahogany, silk cotton, gommier, and other hardwoods that form a dense canopy overhead. The forest floor is carpeted with enormous ferns; tree trunks and their limbs are festooned with epiphytes (leafy air plants) and entangled in a curtain of vines. The buttress roots of the oldest trees are among the largest seen in any Caribbean rain forest. The trail has a lookout for viewing parrots.

Beyond Buccament the Leeward Highway snakes north along steep ridges that drop into the sea, passing fishing villages on the way to Chateaubelair and Richmond Beach, where the road ends. This region of jagged peaks, high bluffs, and deep ravines is the less-accessible part of the island.

Falls of Baleine: St. Vincent's prettiest waterfalls are almost at the water's edge on the northwest coast, about 7 miles north of Richmond

Beach and 18 miles from Kingstown as the crow flies. At the head of a steep-sided gorge on the northern face of the Soufrière Volcano, the falls cascade more than 70 feet in one stage through thick tropical foliage into a rockbound pool ideal for swimming.

Access to the falls from Kingstown is by boat. The forty-five-minute trip is as fascinating as the falls are enjoyable and provide a view of St. Vincent's spectacular scenery from the sea. The falls are located about 500 yards from a small pebble beach. The boat anchors by a pier that provides easy access to the beach. A walkway, including a bridge with handrail, also helps in providing easy access to the falls. Trips to the falls are offered daily by most tour companies.

Exploring the East Coast

Soufrière Volcano: The northern third of St. Vincent is dominated by the Soufrière Mountains, which have one of the most active volcanoes in the Eastern Caribbean. Five eruptions between 1718 and 1979 are documented, but archaeological evidence indicates the volcano probably erupted as early as A.D. 160. During an 1812 eruption—one of the worst, killing two thousand people—ash fell as far away as Barbados, 90 miles to the east. In 1902, the same year as the devastating eruption of Mount Pelée in Martinique, an eruption of Soufrière created the present width of the crater: 1 mile in diameter. In 1971 another eruption caused an island of lava to form in the center of the crater lake.

The most recent, in Apr 1979, sent ash and stone thousands of feet into the air and rivers of molten lava down the mountainsides. More than twenty thousand people were evacuated, but, miraculously, no one was killed.

Once again the volcano is safe to climb and may be approached from either the eastern or western side on a trail running along the southern ridge of the crater. The eastern trail is used most frequently and can be followed by experienced hikers on their own. It starts 1 mile north of Georgetown at Rabacca, where the peak first comes in view. A guide and jeep can be provided by a local safari outfitter.

From Kingstown to the start of the eastern trail is 26 miles and takes one-and-a-half to two hours to drive. It is followed by a 2.5-mile drive on a very rutted plantation road north of the Rabacca Dry River, passing through the extensive banana and coconut groves of Rabacca Farms—formerly the 3,000-acre Orange Hill Estate, once the largest coconut plantation in the Caribbean—to the base of the crater at about a 700-foot altitude. From there a 3-mile trail ascends gradually through a rain forest to the crater rim. Along the way are wonderful vistas, sometimes looking back to the coast. The hike to the rim takes about three hours. You should check with the Forestry or Tourism Offices about trail conditions. Bring water and a picnic lunch, and start early to avoid the heat of the sun (but temperatures at the summit are chilly). There are no facilities of any kind once you leave the coast.

Rabacca Dry River: A remarkable phenomenon of the St. Vincent volcanic eruptions are the "dry rivers": riverbeds that were filled and choked with scoriae, or lava cinder, and gravel after the eruptions of 1812 and 1902. Water flowing into the river seeps through the scoriae and disappears, becoming a subterranean river as it nears the coast. At the mouth of the river, the surface is bone-dry.

The best examples of dry rivers are at Wallilabou, on the west coast, and on the east coast at the Rabacca Dry River, which enters the sea at Rabacca, north of Georgetown. Where the main highway crosses the riverbed, the dry river is more than a half-mile wide and covered with several feet of loose ash; no water is visible on the surface. But toward the mountain, where the terrain begins to rise, water can be seen. Depending on the time of the year, it might be a small stream or a raging torrent after a sudden downpour.

Sandy Bay and Fancy: On the north coast at the base of La Soufrière are the villages of Sandy Bay, Owia, and Fancy. Traditionally, Sandy Bay had the largest concentration of the descendants of the "Black Caribs," who came from the union of African slaves and indigenous Amerindians. After Sandy Bay the coastal road is paved to Owia Salt Pond.

Shopping

The town center of Kingstown is small, and the shopping of interest to cruise passengers is modest, involving only a few stores on Bay and Halifax Streets. Stores are open weekdays from 8 a.m. to 4 p.m. and Sat to noon.

The best selection of crafts, as well as books on St. Vincent, can be found at the **Cruise Ship Shopping Complex.** The courtyard at the Kingstown Market is another place to find everything from jewelry to wood carvings.

The **St. Vincent Crafts Centre** on the east side of town is a marketing outlet and craft shop for locally made jewelry, dolls, baskets, and other crafts made from straw, clay, coconut, wood, and bamboo; quality is not consistent.

Fibreworks (Penniston; 784-456-7118; fibre works@caribsurf.com), in the Buccament Valley, was founded in 1997 by artist Vonnie Roudette, who uses local materials to create unique handcrafted items.

Dining and Restaurants

Kingstown has only a few restaurants outside of hotels. Prices are moderate. Check locally about days and hours for serving lunch and dinner.

Basil's Bar and Restaurant (Cobblestone Inn; 784-457-2713; www.basilsbar.com). The famous watering hole on Mustique has a twin. Situated in a pretty, historic building within walking distance of the pier in Kingstown, the pub offers classic cuisine and seafood. Basil's also has **At Basil's** (784-456-2602), an antiques and furniture store.

The Bounty Restaurant and Art Gallery (Kingstown; 784-456-1776) serves Creole dishes using fresh local produce and catch-of-the day.

The French Verandah Restaurant (Mariners Hotel, Villa Bay, 784-457-4000). Quality international cuisine to be enjoyed in a lovely open-air setting by the sea. Moderately expensive.

Paradise Beach Hotel (784-457-4795; www .paradisesvg.com). The hotel's restaurant offers local and international selections and has a "Grillin' with the Captain" every Fri.

Young Island Resort (784-458-4826; www .youngisland.com), St. Vincent's only luxury resort, has long enjoyed a reputation for fine cuisine, enhanced by the private-island resort's romantic setting with dining under thatched gazebos smothered in tropical gardens at the water's edge. Reservations required. Expensive.

Sports

Beaches/Swimming: The white-sand beaches on the south and black-sand ones on the west are the safest for swimming. The windward, or east, coast is generally too rough and the shoreline too rocky for swimming. All beaches are public. On the south coast a two-minute dock-to-dock boat ride across the cut takes you to Young Island, a private-island resort. Except for a few thatched-roof pavilions by the beach, most of the villas are hidden under curtains of tropical foliage. The resort does not provide changing facilities for day visitors, but you can swim at the beach and lunch in the restaurant.

Boating: A sailing trip through beautiful waters of the Grenadines usually starts from St. Vincent. Yachts for up to eight people can be chartered, with or without crew, from **Sunsail Lagoon Marina & Hotel** (Blue Lagoon; 784-458-4308; www.lagoon marina.com; sunsailsvg@vincysurf.com), **Barefoot Yacht Charters** (Blue Lagoon; 784-456-9526; www .barefootyachts.com; barebum@caribsurf.com), and **TMM Bareboat Vacations** (Blue Lagoon; 784-456-9608; www.sailtmm.com; tmmsvg@ sailtmm.com). Also see **St. Vincent Yacht Club** (784-457-2827).

Deep-Sea Fishing: Sportfishing is not a developed sport, although the seas around St. Vincent and the Grenadines have abundant fish. Watersports operators can arrange deep-sea fishing upon request, and in the Grenadines you can often go out to sea with a local fisherman. **Crystal Blue Sportsfishing** (Indian Bay, Box 175, Kingstown; 784-457-4532; www.wefishin.com; wefishin@ yahoo.com).

Hiking and Biking: St. Vincent has some of the most spectacular scenery in the Caribbean, and it's best seen by hiking. There are easy trails in lush, mountainous settings and arduous ones over rugged terrain. For local people the lack of roads in many places makes walking and hiking a necessity. Guides for hiking are available through the Forestry Division and the Department of Tourism. Local travel companies organize hiking to Soufrière. Contact **Fantasea Tours** (784-457-4477; www.fanta seatours.com) or **Hazeco Tours** (784-457-8634; fax: 784-457-8105; www.hazecotours.com) for hiking trips and sightseeing tours. **Sailor's Wilderness Tours** or **Sailor's Cycle Centre** (784-457-1712; fax: 784-456-2821; sailorscyclecentre@yahoo .com) organizes bike tours to remote areas.

Snorkeling/Scuba Diving: The best snorkeling in St. Vincent is found along Young Island Cut and the west coast, but even better snorkeling is in the Grenadines, where shallow-water reefs surround almost every island, and huge schools of fish travel through the archipelago. Diving in St. Vincent has been recognized in only the past decade or so, and experts have been excited by what they have found. Reef life normally found at 80 feet in other locations grows here at depths of 25 feet, and there is an extraordinary amount and variety of tropical reef fish. **Dive St. Vincent** (784-457-4928; www.divestvincent.com; bill2@divestvincent.com) is located on St. Vincent's south coast; **Bequia Dive Adventures** (784-458-3826; www.bequiadive adventure.com; adventures@caribsurf.com), and **Dive Bequia** (784-458-3504; fax: 784-458-3886; www.dive-bequia.com, bobsax@caribsurf.com) are in Bequia. Generally, prices for dive excursions and use of equipment are lower than in other Caribbean locations.

Tennis and Squash: Grand View Hotel (784-458-4811; fax: 784-457-4174; www.grandviewhotel .com; grandview@caribsurf.com) on the south coast has a sports center with tennis and squash courts, gym, and an outside pool. Nonguests may use the facilities upon payment of a fee. Tennis facilities are also located at the National Sports Centre in Villa; contact the **National Sports Council** (784-458-4201). For squash, contact the **National Squash Center** (784-485-6411).

Windsurfing: Equipment is available for rent from hotels on the south coast. In the Grenadines, all beachside resorts have windsurfing equipment.

Festivals and Celebrations

St. Vincent's Carnival, or **Vincy Mas,** as the Vincentians call it, is a ten-day festival held from the last Sun in June to the first Tues in July. It is one of the biggest celebrations in the Eastern Caribbean, and people from neighboring islands participate.

The last two weeks in Dec have Christmas celebrations. Starting on the 16th people parade and dance through Kingstown every day (except Sun) for the following nine mornings. Other festivals are National Heritage Month (Mar), Emancipation Month Celebrations (Aug), and Independence Month Celebrations (Oct).

The Grenadines

The three dozen enchanted islands and cays that make up the Grenadines are like stepping-stones across the 65 miles between St. Vincent and Grenada. These idyllic islands-in-the-sun, where the news comes with the mail boat, so to speak, are about as far off the beaten track as you can get in the Caribbean.

Scalloped with porcelain-white beaches protected by coral reefs, the Grenadines float on a deep turquoise sea. Long admired by yachtsmen, in recent years they have drawn the attention of cruise ships. Nine islands have settlements; the others are sanctuaries for birds and hideaways for those who love the sea.

Bequia

Information: Bequia Tourism Association (784-458-3286; fax: 458-3964; www.bequiatourism.com).

Lying 9 miles south of St. Vincent across the Bequia Channel, Bequia (pronounced BECK-wee) is the largest of the Grenadines and a cruise-ship port of call. An island of rolling green hills, Bequia has only a few roads, but walking on unpaved roads and footpaths is easy. The island has many pretty beaches with reefs that are often within swimming distance from shore.

Bequia is known throughout the Eastern Caribbean for its skilled seamen, boat builders, and fishermen—descendants of New England whalers, European traders, pirates, and shipwrecked slaves. A haven for yachtsmen from around the world for its excellent anchorage at Admiralty Bay, Bequia has become a mecca for artists, writers, and assorted city dwellers who have opted for the laid-back island life. Unlike some of the Grenadines, Bequia has not been developed for tourists. Most hotels and guesthouses—some in former plantation houses with flowering gardens—are small and unpretentious.

Port Elizabeth, the main town and port where ships dock, can easily be covered on foot. The tourist information office at the pier has free maps and literature. A short walk north of the harbor takes you to the workshops of the island's best carvers of model boats, a craft for which Bequia is famous.

If you walk south from the pier along the main street, you will find the Bequia Bookshop, Noah's Ark, and other small stores. By the bay, **Frangipani Hotel** (www.frangipanibequia.com) belongs to a former prime minister of St. Vincent and the Grenadines, who hails from Bequia. The hotel is one of the oldest on the island, and its bar is something of an institution for residents and visiting salts. Next door the Gingerbread is a tiny hotel with a delightful restaurant open to the breezes, an ice-cream parlor, and Dive Bequia, one of several local dive shops. Some of Bequia's best snorkeling is found at Friendship Bay on the south coast where a half-mile beach is protected by reef; Spring Bay on the east coast is another. The breakers at Hope Bay are popular for bodysurfing. Every spring the Bequia Easter Regatta attracts sailors and spectators from distant lands who join local fishing boats in four days of competition and celebration. Bequia's fishing vessels are wooden craft still made by hand. There are also competitions for model "gum boats" made by young Bequia craftsmen and gaily rigged miniatures made from coconut husks by children. The festival includes sports competitions, music, food, and exhibition of island products. For day-sailing excursions, contact **Michael Tours** (Paget Farm; 784-458-3782; www.bequia.net/michael_tours; michaeltoursbequia@yahoo.com).

Frequent daily ferry service connects Port Elizabeth and Kingstown in about one hour. Bequia has an airstrip.

Mustique

Developed in the early 1970s by British and international investors, Mustique was put on the map by the British royal family, Mick Jagger, Raquel Welch, and a host of international celebrities who vacation here. The former home of the late Princess Margaret, a six-acre perch overlooking Galizeau

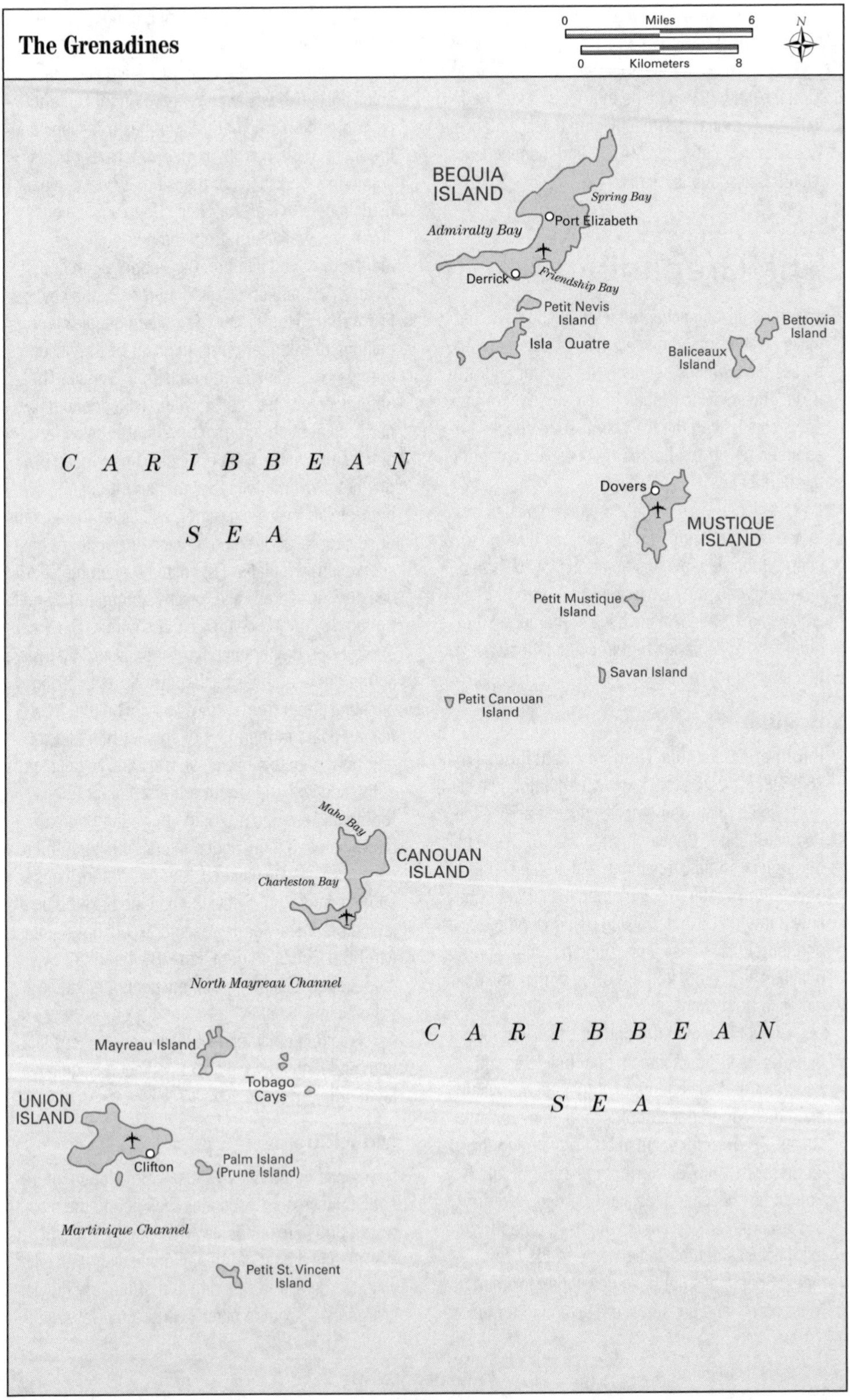

The Grenadines

Miles 0 — 6
Kilometers 0 — 8
N

BEQUIA ISLAND
Spring Bay
Admiralty Bay
○ Port Elizabeth
Derrick ○
Friendship Bay
Petit Nevis Island
Isla Quatre
Bettowia Island
Baliceaux Island

CARIBBEAN

SEA

Dovers ○
MUSTIQUE ISLAND

Petit Mustique Island

Savan Island

Petit Canouan Island

Maho Bay
CANOUAN ISLAND
Charleston Bay

North Mayreau Channel

Mayreau Island

CARIBBEAN

Tobago Cays

SEA

UNION ISLAND
Clifton ○
Palm Island (Prune Island)

Martinique Channel

Petit St. Vincent Island

Bay on the south coast, is available for rent. **Basil's Bar and Restaurant,** the parent of Basil's Restaurant in St. Vincent, is the best celebrity-watching spot on the island. It also has water-sports equipment for rent. Mustique welcomes visiting yachts but not cruise ships.

Mustique has a more manicured appearance than its sister islands. From the north end covered with gentle hills, the land rises to a steep range in the center and south. Sandy Bay on the north coast has a milelong crest of white sand with spectacular water whose colors run the full spectrum of blue and green. Off the western point of the bay lies the wreck of the *Antilles.* Other good beaches are found at Pastor Bay on the east and Landing Cove on the west. There is good snorkeling, particularly at Britannia and Lagoon bays.

In colonial times the island had seven sugar plantations, one of whose estate houses is now the Cotton House, the only deluxe hotel in Mustique. There are frequent flights from St. Vincent, which take ten minutes. Mustique Airways flies daily from Barbados.

Canouan

Located between Mustique and Mayreau, the island is a popular stop for yachts, with a marina for one hundred boats. **Raffles Resort at Canouan Island** (784-458-8000; fax: 784-458-8885; www .rafflescanouan.com; canouan@raffles.com) is the largest hotel in St. Vincent and the Grenadines; another is the **Tamarind Beach Hotel** (784-458-8044; fax: 784-458-8851; www.tamarindbeachhotel .com). Both have facilities for water sports. The Trump International Golf Club at Raffles Resort, designed by Jim Fazio, has been called the "St. Andrews of the Caribbean." There is one main road and a renovated and upgraded airport.

One of the driest islands of the group, Canouan is encircled by beautiful beaches. Charleston Bay on the west is the main port. The mushroom-shaped harbor has a milelong beach. From the bay a half-milelong footpath over the hill leads to more beautiful beaches and to some of the best snorkeling in an area called the Pool, where the colors of the water are fabulous.

Moorings Yacht Charters (Raffles Resort; 784-458-8044, www.moorings.com), one of the

major sailing and bare-boat chartering companies in the Caribbean, has a base at the Raffles Resort.

Mayreau

Until Salt Whistle Bay Resort opened in 1987, Mayreau had no facilities. The resort is situated on a palm-fringed crescent of beach; at the north end, a short trail crosses over to the east side and a long stretch of beach. The island's tiny village is on a hill from which there is a lovely view over Tobago Cays and Horseshoe Reef, an area with extraordinary multihued aquamarine waters for which the Grenadines are famous. Mayreau is popular as a cruise-ship stop for its beautiful beaches and reefs. The wreck of a British gunboat, about 300 yards off Grand Col Point on the west coast, is a favorite of divers.

Tobago Cays

East of Mayreau about halfway between Canouan and Union is one of the most beautiful spots in the Caribbean and a highlight of cruising the Grenadines. Tobago Cays are four uninhabited palm-fringed islets etched by pristine white-sand beaches and incredibly clear aquamarine waters. The setting is so serene it seems unreal. From a beach on any islet, you can walk or swim to clusters of reef to view the spectacular marine life. The water flowing between the islands has strong currents, which bring huge schools of fish. On the east the cays are encircled by Horseshoe Reef, the northern half of which has spectacular reefs; parts are shallow enough to wade.

In 1989 at the tenth anniversary of its independence, St. Vincent and the Grenadines' prime minister declared the 1990s as the Decade of the Environment, placing conservation at the top of the priority list. One of its first projects was the Tobago Cays National Park—and not a minute too soon. The islets were declared a marine reserve more than a decade ago, but lack of attention and careless use by fishermen and boaters, coupled with the lack of strong government regulation, put tremendous stress on the coral gardens.

Palm Island

A private resort on a 110-acre island, Palm Island was known as Prune Island until the late Texan

John Caldwell came along. Known as the Johnny Appleseed of the Caribbean, Caldwell obtained a ninety-nine-year lease (for which he paid US$1 per year) from the St. Vincent government and built a resort, where he replaced the scrub and swamp—not to mention mosquitoes—with two thousand palm trees and hundreds of other flowering trees and plants. He also planted another three thousand palm trees on neighboring islands. The resort was purchased in 1999 by Rob Barrett, who owns Galley Bay and other hotels in Antigua and who made extensive renovations and improvements. **Palm** (www.eliteislandresorts.com) is popular with yachtsmen and is an occasional stop for small cruise ships. It is surrounded by pretty beaches protected by reefs that are only a wade or a short swim away.

Petit St. Vincent

Another deluxe, private-island resort, Petit St. Vincent often appears on the Caribbean's "ten best" list. Half of the 113-acre property was left in a natural state, and the other half was turned into a manicured park setting. The island is scalloped with pretty spectacular beaches, and on its north side are two sandbars with gorgeous white sand—Punaise and Mopion—floating in fantastically beautiful water and reefs. In fact, the islands are the western extreme of a 3-mile reef that runs along the north and east sides of Petit St. Vincent to Petit Martinique, one of Grenada's Grenadines.

The shallow water offers some of the best snorkeling in the area. Petit St. Vincent welcomes visiting yachts but not cruise ships.

Union Island

Located about halfway between St. Vincent and Grenada, Union Island is 1.5 miles from Palm Island and 4 miles from Tobago Cays. The second-most populated of the Grenadines, Union's 2,500 inhabitants live mostly in Clifton, which is the government and commercial center as well as port. It has a bank, police station, doctor and clinic, and several buildings dating from the early 1800s. A footpath leads to Fort Hills, where there is a gun emplacement with old cannons and a panoramic view.

The T-shaped island has a spine of jagged, slab-faced mountains running north-south along the T-bar with Mount Tabor, at 999 feet, the highest peak in the Grenadines. A road connects Clifton, on the east coast, and Ashton, a fishing village on the south coast. Bloody Bay on the northwest coast and Chatham Bay on the west coast are popular anchorages.

Union has small hotels and an airstrip served by scheduled flights from St. Vincent, Grenada, St. Lucia, and Martinique. Union celebrates Easter with boat races, calypso competitions, and cultural shows. In May the Big Drum Festival is a cultural event to mark the end of the dry season and culminates with the Big Drum Dance, a celebration also seen on Carriacou.

Grenada

St. George's, Grenada; Hillsborough, Carriacou

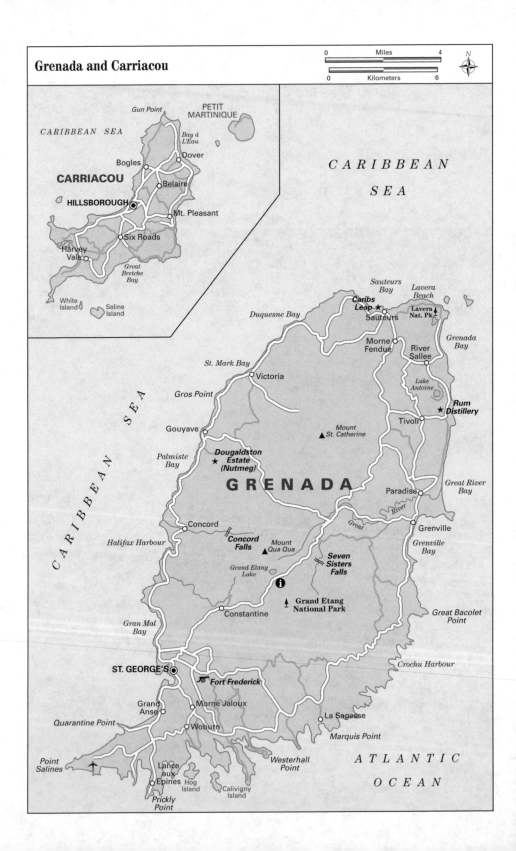

Grenada and Carriacou

Miles
0 — 4

Kilometers
0 — 6

N

CARIBBEAN SEA

PETIT MARTINIQUE

Gun Point

Bay á L'Eau

Dover

Bogles

CARRIACOU

Belaire

HILLSBOROUGH

Mt. Pleasant

Six Roads

Harvey Vale

Great Bretche Bay

White Island

Saline Island

C A R I B B E A N

S E A

Duquesne Bay

Sauteurs Bay

Lavera Beach

Caribs Leap ★

Lavera Nat. Pk.

Sauteurs

Morne Fendue

River Sallee

Grenada Bay

St. Mark Bay

Victoria

Gros Point

Lake Antoine

Rum Distillery ★

Gouyave

Tivoli

Palmiste Bay

Mount St. Catherine ▲

Dougaldston Estate (Nutmeg) ★

G R E N A D A

Paradise

Great River Bay

River

C   A   R   I   B   B   E   A   N

Concord

Concord Falls

Mount Qua Qua ▲

Great

Grenville

Halifax Harbour

Seven Sisters Falls

Grenville Bay

Grand Etang Lake

ℹ

S   E   A

Grand Etang National Park

Constantine

Great Bacolet Point

Gran Mal Bay

Crochu Harbour

ST. GEORGE'S ◉

⚔ **Fort Frederick**

Grand Anse

Morne Jaloux

Quarantine Point

Woburn

La Sagesse

Marquis Point

Point Salines

Lance aux Epines

Hog Island

Calivigny Island

Westerhall Point

A T L A N T I C

Prickly Point

O C E A N

The Spice Island

Mountainous and lush, Grenada is a tapestry of tropical splendor that leaves you breathless with its beauty. Here, where the air is filled with the scent of cinnamon and nutmeg, thick vines climb the telephone poles and trail along overhead wires; the banana trees by the side of the road grow as tall as the palm trees that shade the beaches. Waterfalls cascade through the forested mountains decorated with 450 species of flowering plants and 150 species of birds. Nutmeg, ginger, vanilla, and almost every herb and fruit of the tropics fill the landscape.

The Spice Island, as Grenada is known, is the southernmost island of the Windwards, located 100 miles north of Venezuela. Off the north coast are its dependencies of Carriacou and Petit Martinique—two islands of the Grenadines chain that stretches north to St. Vincent. The trade winds that cool the island—only 12 degrees north of the equator—bring more than 160 inches of rain annually to the interior, creating lush forests and rivers that rush down the mountains to the sea.

From its forested, volcanic peaks, Grenada drops to a varied coastline of steep cliffs with hidden coves of black sand, wide bays with long stretches of white sand, deep harbors sheltering sailing craft, and lagoons and estuaries that host wildlife. Beneath the sea volcanic action continues nearby. Kick 'em Jenny, a volcano, lies submerged only 500 feet under the water off Grenada's north coast.

Sighted by Columbus on his third voyage in 1498, Grenada was probably occupied first by the Ciboneys and later the Arawaks, who were driven north by the fierce Carib Indians around A.D. 1000. English traders attempted to establish a colony on Grenada's west coast in 1609, but they failed due to Carib resistance. In 1650 the French had better luck and established a settlement on the southeast coast at the present site of La Sagesse, which paved the way for it to become a French possession two decades later.

Because of its strategic location, Grenada was coveted by the British, too. Consequently, the island changed hands several times between the French and the British until 1783, when it was ceded to Britain under the Treaty of Versailles. The British expanded sugar production, stepped up the importation of slaves, and established a plantation system. In 1795 Julien Fedon, a mulatto planter of French origin inspired by the ideas of the French Revolution, led a bloody but unsuccessful rebellion against the British. After slavery was abolished in 1834, attempts to continue sugar cultivation by importing indentured laborers from Asia failed. In 1877 Grenada became a British crown colony, and in 1974 it gained full independence.

A few years later in 1979, a bloodless coup led by Maurice Bishop and six of his followers, known as the New Jewel Movement, threw out the government of Sir Eric Gairy, a controversial character with a secret police known as the "Mongoose Gang." Bishop and his group might have been a welcome relief had they not changed the island's name to the People's Revolutionary Government of Grenada and begun waltzing with Cuba. The Cubans wasted no time in sending experts to train

At a Glance

Antiquities . . . . ★
Architecture . . . . ★★
Art and Artists . . . . ★★
Beaches . . . . ★★★★★
Colonial Buildings . . . . ★★★
Crafts . . . . ★
Cuisine . . . . ★★★★
Culture . . . . ★★
Dining/Restaurants . . . . ★★★
Entertainment . . . . ★
Forts . . . . ★★★
History . . . . ★★★
Monuments . . . . ★
Museums . . . . ★
Nightlife . . . . ★
Scenery . . . . ★★★★★
Shopping . . . . ★★
Sightseeing . . . . ★★★
Sports . . . . ★★★★
Transportation . . . . ★

Fast Facts

Population: 102,000

Size: Grenada, including Carriacou and Petit Martinique, covers 133 square miles. Grenada itself is 12 miles wide and 21 miles long.

Main Towns: St. George's and Grenville, Grenada; Hillsborough, Carriacou.

Government: Grenada has a parliamentary form of government and is a member of the British Commonwealth. Parliament consists of two chambers: a Senate of thirteen appointed members and a House of Representatives of fifteen elected members. The cabinet, headed by the prime minister, is responsible to parliament. The queen is represented by a governor-general.

Currency: Eastern Caribbean (EC) dollar. US$1 equals EC$2.70. U.S. dollars and traveler's checks are widely accepted.

Departure Tax: Included in the cost of a plane ticket

Emergency Numbers: Medical: General Hospital, St. George's; (473) 440-2050; Ambulance: St. George's area, (473) 473-434; Police: 911

Electricity: 220 volts AC, 50 cycles

Language: English

Public Holidays: Jan 1, New Year's Day; Good Friday; Easter Monday; May 1, Labor Day; May, Whit Mon; June, Corpus Christi; First Mon and Tues in Aug, Emancipation Holidays; Oct 25, Thanksgiving Day; Dec 25, Christmas Day; Dec 26, Boxing Day.

Telephone Area Code: 473

Airlines: *From the United States:* American/American Eagle, Delta. *From Canada:* Air Canada. *Regional:* LIAT from various Caribbean islands. SVGAir serve Carriacou from Grenada; the latter connects to Union Island. Grenada's Maurice Bishop International Airport has services for private aircraft including a VIP lounge with dedicated customs and immigration personnel.

Information: www.grenada grenadines.com

In the United States:

Grenada Board of Tourism: P.O. Box 1668, Lake Worth, FL 33460; (561) 588-8176; (800) 927-9554 for travel information; fax: (561) 588-7267; cnoel@grenadagrenadines.com

In Canada:

Grenada Board of Tourism, 439 University Ave., Suite 920, Toronto, ON M5G 1Y8; (416) 595-1339; fax: (416) 595-8278; tourism@grenada consulate.com

In Port:

Grenada Board of Tourism, Burns Point, P.O. Box 293; St. George's, Grenada, W.I.; (473) 440-2001/2279; fax: (473) 440-6637; www.grenada grenadines.com; gbt@spiceisle.com

In Carriacou:

Grenada Board of Tourism, Main Street, Hillsborough; (473) 443-7948; fax: (473) 443-6127; carrgbt@spice isle.com

---

Grenada's security forces and help with its most pressing need: the construction of a new airport. The airport became a bone of contention for the United States, which saw Cuba's involvement as a camouflage to turn Grenada into a military base, enabling Cuba to control the two ends of the Caribbean.

Thus in 1983, when an internal struggle for power resulted in the assassination of Bishop and an attempt by a pro-Cuban faction to seize power, the United States saw an opportunity, and, with the endorsement of the Eastern Caribbean states, it intervened militarily to stop the coup and restore order. The following year a parliamentary government was returned to power. The irony is that the United States completed the construction of the airport, which it had claimed Grenada did not need, and President Ronald Reagan landed there sixteen months after its opening, pointing with pride to its completion.

Despite its turbulent history, Grenada is an easy-living sort of place, with hotels set in flowering gardens alongside beautiful beaches, old fishing villages, and gentle folk whose diverse heritage matches the colorful tapestry of their tropical landscape. British traditions run as deep as African and Asian ones, but the French legacy, too, has endured: in the names of the people and places, the patois that is more French than English, and the cuisine, which is some of the best in the Caribbean.

Budget Planning

Grenada is not an expensive island, with the notable exception of taxis, but since many cruise ships do not stay a full day in port, a taxi with the driver/guide might be your best way to tour—particularly if you have others with whom to share the cost. If you plan to do nothing more than go to the beach, public buses run frequently from town to Grand Anse Beach.

Port Profile

Location/Embarkation: St. George's, the capital and port, has one of the most picturesque settings in the Caribbean. The harbor has two sections: one is the docking area for large cruise ships; the other is a well-sheltered inner harbor used as a yacht basin. The $24 million Melville Streetcruise ship port, opened in Dec 2004, can accommodate at least two mega cruise ships. The facility has a welcome center and parking areas for taxis and tour operators. The US$11 million Esplanade Mall, added a year later, has shops selling local crafts, fragrances, electronics, jewelry, gifts, and liquor at duty-free prices. At the Welcome Center you can get information and make phone calls using a major credit card. Simply dial 111 from pay phones.

Local Transportation: Grenada does not have a fully developed public transportation system. Instead, private minibuses provide in-town and intra-island services at low rates. They leave frequently from the Melville Street Bus Terminal in St. George's.

Taxis are available at the port and in town, rates are set by the government in cooperation with the taxi union. Sample taxi fares from the pier for up to four persons: to town center, US$10; Grand Anse/Morne Rouge, US$15; golf course, US$15; Maurice Bishop International Airport, US$20. Taxi hire per hour: US$25.

Roads and Rentals: One road circumnavigates the island, and another crosses it from coast to coast over the central highlands. By combining the routes it is easy to make a loop around the northern or southern half of the island. The time most cruise ships remain in port is usually insufficient, however,

to cover both circuits in one day. The best roads are those between St. George's and the south coast, and the cross-island highway. Major arteries deteriorate farther north along both the west and east coasts. Secondary roads and dirt tracks reach most villages throughout the island. If you have a good map (on sale at the Grenada National Museum), you can rent a car, but if you are not accustomed to left-side-of-the-road driving, you are probably better advised to hire a taxi, with the driver acting as guide. Often roads are narrow, winding, and in poor condition, and Grenadians drive fast, making for a daunting experience.

Car rentals cost about US$60 per day. In winter you should reserve in advance. You need to be twenty-one years of age and have a valid driver's license to obtain a local permit from the traffic department, which the car rental agency will handle for you. Cost is EC$30 or US$12. Driving in this former British colony is on the LEFT. Rental agencies in St. George's include **Avis/Spice Island Rentals** (473-440-3936; avisgrenada@spiceisle .com); **Azar Auto Rentals** (473-414-2911; www .azarsrentals.com); **Dollar** (airport; 473-444-4786; reservations@dollargrenada.com); and **McIntyre Bros.** (473-444-3944; www.caribbeanhorizons .com), among others. Bikes can be rented for about US$15 from **Trailblazers Mountain Bike Tours & Rentals** and jeeps from **Adventure Jeep Tours,** (both at 473-444-5337; www.adventuregrenada .com). Both companies also operate biking and jeep tours.

Ferry Service: The *Osprey Express* (473-440-8126; www.ospreylines.com; osprey@spiceisle .com), a high-speed catamaran, takes passengers twice daily (only once on Sat) from St. George's to Hillsborough, Carriacou, and to Petit Martinique in about one-and-a-half hours. EC$80 or US$30 one-way; EC$160 or US$60 round-trip.

Shore Excursions

The places mentioned are described later in this chapter. Prices are for up to four persons unless otherwise indicated.

Grand Etang and the Central Highlands: 2–3 hours, US$100 for four persons. After climbing the lush hillsides with grand views of the harbor, the route crosses the central spine of mountains with the Grand Etang National Park to the East Coast. From the visitor center there are self-guided, signposted trails in the rain forest.

The West Coast: 4–6 hours, US$150. A west coast drive reveals Grenada's fabulous scenery. Stops are usually made at a nutmeg plantation and a processing plant in Gouyave. Return inland for forty-five-minute hike to the Concord Falls. The longer, 6 hours, version from Gouyave continues to Sauteurs and historic Caribs Leap, stopping for lunch at Morne Fendue, and returning to Grenville via the east coast and the cross-island highway.

The Southern Route: 4–5 hours, US$100. City tour continues to Westerhall Point, a deluxe residential area with a dramatic seascape, and to Grand Anse Beach. Or, continue southeast to La Sagesse, a nature reserve and estuary, for a swim or a walk in the woods.

Kayaking/River Tubing/Whale watching: See Sports section later in this chapter.

Some companies offering light adventure and nature tours:

Adventure Jeep Tours (473-444-5337; www.grenadajeeptours.com), in addition to river tubing, specializes in nature tours by jeep to rain forests for hiking; repast on local cuisine at a restaurant deep in the interior; to beach for a swim and snorkel. **Henry Safari Tours** (473-445-5313; www.henrysafari.com); and **Telfor Bedeau** (473-442-6200) were among the first to specialize in hiking and nature tours two decades ago.

Caribbean Horizons Tours & Services (True Blue Bay Resort; 473-444-1555; www.caribbeanhorizons.com). Day tours to major attractions; rain-forest hikes to waterfalls or mountain peaks.

Deep-sea fishing, day sails. Twenty-four-hour answering service.

Sunsation Tours (Marquis Complex, Grand Anse; 473-444-1594; www.grenadasunsation.com) offers similar excursions and jeep rentals.

Published prices for a taxi with a driver/guide for up to four persons from the cruise port: **Annandale Falls,** 2 hour, US$50; **Morne Jaloux/Woburn/Grand Anse Beach,** 3 hours, US$60; **Fort Frederick/Bay Gardens,** 3 hours, US$75; **Grand Etang/St. Margaret Falls,** 4 hours, US$100; **Grand Etang/Grenville/La Sagesse,** 3–4 hours, US$100; **Dougaldston/Gouyave/Spice Factory,** 3 hours including tours, US$75; **Concord Falls,** US$60. A complete list of car-rental and tour companies is available at www.grenadagrenadines.com.

Grenada on Your Own

The capital of Grenada is set on a deep bay with a tango of yellow, blue, and pink houses topped with red-tile roofs, clinging to the slopes of the green hills that frame the harbor. One of the Caribbean's most beautiful natural harbors and an important trading center since its founding by the French in the early 18th century, St. George's is a popular port of call for cruise ships and yachts sailing the Grenadines.

A St. George's Walkabout

Like its history, St. George's character is part French and part English, yet distinctively West Indian. It is divided into two parts separated by a promontory crowned by Fort George. The lower town hugs the inner harbor, known as the Carenage, and the new town is "over the hill" along the seaside Esplanade. The two are connected by a tunnel under the hill, used by motor vehicles, and by a road and narrow sidewalk over the hill, used by cars and pedestrians. Both parts are best seen on foot, which takes about two hours, but it could take longer if you stop frequently to admire the views or browse in shops and historic sites along the way.

The Carenage (1): A perfect horseshoe in shape, the Carenage is one of the best anchorages in the West Indies and always busy with boats of all sizes and description. It is also a lively center, where schooners loaded with Grenada's bountiful harvest of fruits and vegetables sail for markets in Barbados and Trinidad. On the south side of the Carenage, a second harbor known as the **Lagoon (2)** is the yacht basin, marina, commercial port, and the new Port Louis development. The Lagoon is actually the submerged crater of an ancient volcano. On its east are the **Botanical Gardens,** begun in 1887; buildings on the grounds house government offices.

To the **north (3),** Lagoon Road/Wharf Road skirt the Carenage past the post office, the **Department of Tourism Bureau (4),** the public library, and small shops on the waterfront. Near the Department of Tourism, overlooking the water, is a shaded pedestrian plaza with seats and pretty flowers around a statue, *Christ of the Deeps.* It was given to Grenada by Costa Cruise Line in appreciation of the island's help to the passengers and crew of the *Bianca C,* which caught fire in the harbor in 1961. Climbing the hill above the Carenage are old churches that combine West Indian and European architectural elements and government buildings dating from the early 1800s. **York House** holds the supreme court; the neighboring **Registry Building** was built about 1780; and **Government House,** remodeled in 1802, is a fine example of early Georgian architecture. **St. George's Anglican Church (5),** rebuilt in the 20th century, has wall plaques from the 18th and 19th centuries; **St. Andrew's Presbyterian Church** dates from 1830 and **St. George's Methodist Church** from 1820. These old buildings were considerably damaged during the severe hurricane, Ivan, in 2004; there are plans to restore them as funds become available.

Grenada National Museum (6): On the hill up from the Carenage in an 18th-century building, once part of a French army barracks and prison, that now is the National Museum. Here artifacts from archaeological excavation around the island and exhibits trace Grenada's history from the Ciboneys to colonial times. The museum sells books, pamphlets, and maps of Grenada. Hours: weekdays 9 a.m. to 4:30 p.m., Sat 10:30 a.m. to 2 p.m., closed Sun. Admission: US$2.

Market Square (7): A walk from the Carenage up Young Street over the hill or a drive through

Sendall Tunnel (8) takes you to the other side of St. George's, with Market Square at the center of town. The market is one of the liveliest, most colorful in the Caribbean, particularly on Sat morning. Vendors, each with their tiny plot and brightly colored umbrella, sell brooms, baskets, and an array of exotic tropical fruits, vegetables, and spices. West of the square the **Esplanade (9)** and Melville Street, the coastal road along the outer harbor, is the new cruise terminal where your cruise ship will dock.

At strategic hilltops around the harbor, the French and the British built a series of fortifications to defend the island. Today they stand as testimony to the rivalry that raged between the two powers throughout most of Grenada's colonial history, as well as offering grandstand views.

Fort George (10): The harbor entrance is guarded by an imposing fort built in 1706 by the French as Fort Royal and later seized by the British, who renamed it for their monarch. Built on a promontory with walls more than 4 feet thick, the fort was a master feat of engineering in its day. It has two levels with barracks, ammunition storage rooms, dungeons, and a maze of underground passages. The fort served as police headquarters for many years, and in 1983, it witnessed the coup in which Prime Minister Bishop and many of his supporters were killed.

Fort Frederick: Built in 1779 soon after the French recaptured the island from the British, Fort Frederick is located on the summit of Richmond Hill, between Fort Matthew to the north and Fort Adolphus to the south, occupying the most strategic position of all the fortresses and commanding extensive views. Its thick stone walls, barracks, watchtowers, and underground tunnels are similar to those of Fort George. In the 1983 coup attempt, the fort was the headquarters of the People's Revolutionary Army, the faction that tried to seize power from Bishop. The carcass of a Soviet armored truck, left to rust where it was abandoned, seems a fitting reminder of the grim events.

Bay Gardens: East of Fort Frederick in the hillside suburb of St. Paul's on the site of an old sugar mill is a private three-acre spread with an estimated 3,000 different species of flora found in Grenada and the Caribbean. Footpaths covered

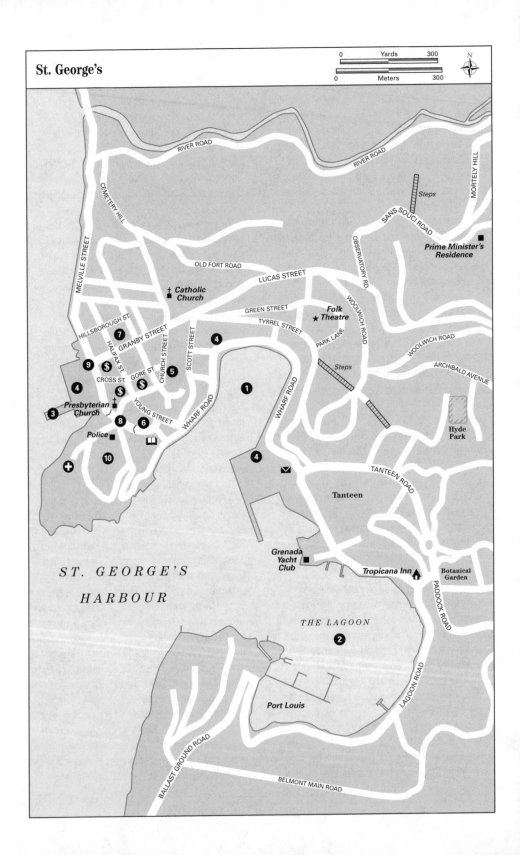

St. George's

0   Yards   300

0   Meters   300

N

RIVER ROAD

RIVER ROAD

MORTELY HILL

Steps

SANS SOUCI ROAD

OBSERVATORY RD.

Prime Minister's
Residence

CEMETERY HILL

OLD FORT ROAD

LUCAS STREET

MELVILLE STREET

† Catholic
Church

GREEN STREET

Folk
Theatre

WOOLWICH ROAD

HILLSBOROUGH ST.

GRANBY STREET

TYRREL STREET

PARK LANE

WOOLWICH ROAD

ARCHIBALD AVENUE

7

HALIFAX ST.

CHURCH STREET

SCOTT STREET

Steps

9 **$**

CROSS ST.

GORE ST.

5

4

1

Steps

Hyde
Park

4

$

WHARF ROAD

WHARF ROAD

3

Presbyterian
Church

YOUNG STREET

8 **6**

4

TANTEEN ROAD

Police

Tanteen

10

ST. GEORGE'S

HARBOUR

Grenada
Yacht
Club

Tropicana Inn

Botanical
Garden

THE LAGOON

PADDOCK ROAD

2

LAGOON ROAD

Port Louis

BALLAST GROUND ROAD

BELMONT MAIN ROAD

with nutmeg shells wind through exotic vegetation. In addition to spice and fruit trees—all labeled—Bay Gardens has sections for flowers and various kinds of orchids. The entrance fee includes a walk through the gardens with a guide.

The Tower: A private home east of Bay Gardens on St. Paul's Road is the estate house of a working fruit-and-spice plantation, set in gardens of exotic plants. The Tower, built in 1916, is one of the island's few remaining old houses constructed of volcanic rock. It is open to the public by appointment. The owner's private collection of Carib artifacts and antiques is on display.

A Drive Around the Island

Along the West Coast

Underwater Sculpture Park: North of St. George's the road hugs the coast, passing through small fishing villages and magnificent scenery of lush, thickly carpeted mountainsides that drop almost straight into the sea and coves, their black-sand beaches almost hidden from view. Offshore at Molinere Bay is the fabulous *Underwater Sculpture Park* by British artist, Jason Taylor. Located 2 miles north of St. George's, the park has sixty-five sunken figures, positioned in a circle on the sandy bottom, in depths between 6 and 24 feet.

Concord Valley: Inland from Halifax Harbour a road along the Black Bay River leads to the head of the Concord Valley, where a triple-stage waterfall in a setting of dense tropical foliage cascades down the central mountains. Above Concord village the road stops directly in front of the falls' lower stage, where concrete steps lead down to a swimming area.

The second stage has a much more beautiful setting, which is accessible, thanks to a footpath laid by U.S. Peace Corps volunteers. Large rocks

and a few small bridges were placed at strategic points, making it less difficult to cross the river against rushing water. Even so, the hike is not easy unless you are nimble and dressed appropriately in shorts or bathing suit, and sneakers (the rocks are slippery). Your effort will be richly rewarded: The cascade spills through jungle-thick vegetation into a pool where you can have a delightful swim surrounded by magnificent scenery.

VIV's Design Studio/Veronica's Visions (473-437-8154; www.grenadaspicecloth.com), located on the road to the Concord Falls, uses nutmeg and other spices as inspiration for the designs of the fabrics it uses in making garments for women and men, tote bags, and other products under the label, SpiceWear.

Gouyave: Grenada is the world's second-largest producer of nutmeg; the main production center is the area around Gouyave on the west coast north of St. George's. Inland about a half mile immediately before Gouyave is Dougladston Estates, one of the island's oldest and largest nutmeg plantations. Its staff members explain the cultivation of nutmeg and other spices to visitors. In Gouyave you can have a free walk-through tour of a growers' cooperative that is the country's major nutmeg-processing station. You will see workers clean, grade, and prepare nutmeg for shipping.

Gouyave, the main fishing town on the west coast, was one of the sites of a British attempt to establish a colony in 1609, when they were forced to leave after encountering fierce Carib resistance. Today the town has a reputation for rowdiness.

The North Coast

Caribs Leap: North of Gouyave the road passes through Victoria, a quiet town at the foot of 2,757-foot Mount St. Catherine, Grenada's highest peak, and continues to the town of Sauteurs (which in

French means "leapers"). There is a promontory alongside St. Patrick's Roman Catholic Church and Cemetery, a historic landmark. The steep-faced north side of the promontory, known as Caribs Leap or Leapers Hill, drops more than 100 feet into the sea. The last of the Carib, the inhabitants of the island at the time of Columbus, leaped to their death here rather than surrender to the French, who were intent on exterminating them. Nearby is the new **Glebe Street Museum & Exhibition Centre** which has a collection of artifacts, sculptures, paintings, art, and antique furniture. It has a museum shop and tea shop. Hours: Mon-Fri, 10 a.m. to 5 p.m.

Helvellyn House (Sauteurs, 473-442-9252; www.travelgrenadagrenadines.com) Located on a hilltop at the northern tip of Grenada, Helvellyn House surrounded by tropical gardens, commands a great view across the sea to Carriacou. The stone structure was built by the current owner's grandfather, who also made the furniture. A lunch of West Indian specialties is served daily and there are three rooms available for rent. Nearby is the **Helvellyn Pottery and Learning Centre,** which makes vases, bowls, plates, and other pottery, designed and fired onsite.

Morne Fendue: On the south side of Sauteurs, the estate house of a former plantation, Morne Fendue, was built at the turn of the 20th century in the traditional method: with hand-cut local stones and mortar made with lime and molasses. The late owner, Betty Mascoll—the island's best-known hostess of kings, queens, and presidents—opened her house for a Grenadian lunch. You can still enjoy lunch provided you call in advance (473-442-9330) and dine on local dishes, usually fresh vegetables from the garden.

Belmont Estate (473-442-9524; www.belmontestate.net) The 400-acre estate, dating from the 18th century, has been in continuous operation and still produces nutmeg and cocoa. There is a museum and a forty-five-minute tour of the working plantation. Visitors also enjoy demonstrations of traditional cultural activities, such as stick fighting, drumming, and local dances. The estate serves a three-course lunch of local dishes for US$21 for adults; It is open Sun to Fri; reservations are required. **Sunsation Tours** (www

.grenadasunsation.com) among other tour companies, visit the estate on their island tours.

Grenada Chocolate Company (Hermitage, St. Patrick's; 473-442-0050; http://grenadachocolate.com). Part of Belmont Estate amid the cocoa groves is the chocolate company, founded in 1999 to produce high-quality, organic dark chocolate from local cocoa. The company has its own organic 100-acre cocoa farm, and its little factory can perform all the steps in the production of chocolate, from the planting and growing of cocoa trees to the fermenting of fresh cocoa beans to the processing of fine dark chocolate. Its cocoa is grown without use of chemicals, and solar energy is used to power its machines. The company had to create its own processing methods, designing its own machines based on early 1900s designs and refurbishing antique ones. Its goal is to revolutionize the cocoa-chocolate system that typically keeps production separate from chocolate-making and thus, takes advantage of cocoa farmers, by enabling farmers to be part of the entire process. The company's products are sold online in the United States. A colorfully wrapped 3-ounce chocolate bar costs about US$5.

Levera National Park: East of Sauteurs is a long white-sand beach popular with Grenadians on weekends, but usually deserted during the week. The scenic coast is part of the Levera National Park and nesting grounds for sea turtles, protected from May to Sept. South of the park the coastline changes to gray sand and weathered rock cliffs.

Lake Antoine and River Antoine Distillery: South of Levera Park, the 18th-century River Antoine Rum Distillery is a historic landmark on a sugar plantation where cane for rum making is processed in the same way it was two hundred years ago when the plant was built. The distillery has an electrical pump and new boiling machinery, but water from the river is still used to turn the old waterwheel to power the plant. It is the last operational waterwheel in Grenada. Lake Antoine, a crater lake, can be reached on a footpath from the distillery or nearby road.

The Central Highlands

Annandale Falls: On the highway from St. George's to the Grand Etang Forest Reserve, on the mountain spine down the center of the island, a short detour can be made to Annandale Falls, the most accessible waterfall in Grenada. Located only a few yards from the road in an area of lush tropical vegetation, the small hillside with steps leading to the falls is planted with an herb and spice garden. A welcome center at the entrance to the falls sells local spices and crafts. There is a small entrance fee.

Grand Etang Forest Reserve: The ridge of mountains that bisect the interior of Grenada are covered by the Grand Etang Forest Reserve, part of a new national parks system established by the government of Grenada with the help of U.S. development agencies, including the Peace Corps and the Organization of American States. The highway that zigzags up the forested mountains crosses the reserve almost at its center at a 1,910-foot altitude and within a few hundred yards of Grand Etang, an extinct volcano that gave the reserve its name; its crater is filled with a lake. (Grand Etang means "large pond" in French.) North of the crater is Mount Qua Qua Peak, one of Grenada's three highest peaks. Grand Etang Lake is only about 500 yards from the visitor center, where there are displays and information on the self-guided nature trails. The trails range from fifteen minutes to three hours and lead to the lake and surrounding rain forests, which have some of the island's most exotic vegetation and wildlife.

Seven Sisters Trail: Southwest of Grand Etang Lake, a trail leads to an area with waterfalls that drop in several stages into a large pool delightful for swimming. The trail takes three hours roundtrip for experienced hikers and crosses a cultivated area to reach the virgin forest. Parts of the trail, along steep ridges, are difficult, particularly during the rainy season when the ground is very muddy. An experienced nature guide is essential.

The South Coast

From St. George's, along the Lagoon Road, the highway leads to Grand Anse Beach, one of the most beautiful beaches in the Caribbean, and the southern part of the island. At the southernmost point, Fort Jeudy, the Atlantic crashes against high cliffs, and the scenery is magnificent.

Port Louis Grenada (Lagoon Road, 473-439-0000; www.portlouisgrenada.com). A comprehensive resort, spa, marina, and residential development, representing an investment of about US$555 million, includes a world-class marina with 350 slips and yachting facilities for yachts up to 100 meters, lots for individual homes, 200 residential units varying in size from 900-square-foot apartments to turnkey 3,000-square-foot houses; a 120-room luxury hotel; a mid-priced hotel; reclamation and renovation of the seafront; water sports, beach extension, diving, and employment and training of up to 800 staff. The development has been spearheaded by Peter de Savary, a well-known British developer of luxury properties, who has also developed Mount Cinnamon, a resort on Grand Anse.

The entire south and southeast coasts from Point Salines on the west, where the international airport is located, to Great Bacolet Bay on the east, is made up of hilly peninsulas, bluffs, islets, and deep bays. Some fingers have hotels and marinas, and others are elegant residential areas with pretty views. The deep bays and islets have recently become popular locations for kayaking. At the water's edge of Lance aux Epines peninsula is **Prickly Bay Waterside,** one of Grenada's newest marina and residential resorts.

La Sagesse Nature Center (473-444-6458) In the southeast corner, La Sagesse is the site of the first European settlement on Grenada. A nature center here, developed as part of the national parks system, includes palm-fringed beaches and coral reefs, mangrove, a salt pond, woodlands, and an estuary with a large variety of birds. A small guesthouse with a delightful bar and outdoor restaurant has equipment for water sports. Its **La Sagesse Arts & Craft Market** showcases the work of Grenada's finest artists and artisans.

You can return to St. George's via Marquis, Grenada's capital under the French. The road passes cacao and banana plantations and fields of wild pine whose fiber is widely used in making baskets and other straw handicrafts. In this area of the east coast, the island's French heritage is particularly evident in the names of people and places.

Shopping

The shopping area of St. George's is compact and easy to cover on foot in an hour or so. Some of the shops are on the waterfront by the Carenage, and others are in the "upper" town, where Young Street becomes Halifax and leads to Market Square. Most stores are open weekdays from 8 or 9 a.m. to noon and 1 to 4 or 4:30 p.m.; Sat 8 a.m. to noon. Not all close for lunch. Over the past several years, shopping malls have blossomed in the Grand Anse area, but the most convenient is the new Esplanade Mall at the cruise-ship terminal, which offers a variety of duty-free and other stores as well as an Internet cafe. A 15% value added tax will be added in some cases.

Art and Artists: Yellow Poui Art Gallery (9 Young St.; 473-440-3001; yellowpoui@spiceisle .com) features local artists including Grenada's best-known primitive artist, internationally known, the late Canute Caliste, and such well-known Caribbean artists as Boscoe Holder from Trinidad. Also find prints, rare antique maps and engravings, watercolors, and photographs; look for brightly decorated masks on calabash by local artist Ottley Dennis. Closed Mon except by appointment. **Art & Soul** (Spiceland Mall; 473-439-450); **Arts of the Caribbean** (Esplanade Mall; 473-435-6820); and **Fidel Productions** (Port Louis; 473-435-8866) are other shops with selections of local artists. In addition to Canute Caliste, look for works by Susan Mains, Roger Brathwaite, and Richard Buchanan.

Books and Maps: Sea Change Book & Gift Shop (Carenage; 473-440-3402) stocks American and British paperbacks and best-sellers and books on Grenada and the Caribbean.

China and Crystal: The Gift Shop (Carenage and Grand Anse Shopping Complex) has famous-name crystal and china, such as Wedgwood and Royal Copenhagen. **Caribbean Duty Free** (Esplanade Mall; 473-440-5356) carries a large selection of china and crystal, fine jewelry, and other duty-free items.

Clothing and Accessories: Art Fabrik (9 Young St.; 473-440-0568; www.artfabrikgrenada .com) is a batik shop with a selection of hand painted batik art, clothing, and accessories made in its studios. **Imagine** (Grand Anse Shopping Center; 473-444-4028) carries Caribbean handcrafts as well as island batiks and casual wear. **Gatsby** (Spice

Island Beach Resort; 473-444-4258) has separate, duty-free boutiques of designer resort wear for men and women.

Crafts and Souvenirs: Arawak Islands, Ltd. (Frequente Industrial Park; 473-444-3577; www .arawak-islands.com) has attractively packaged island products that make great gifts to take home. Sold in outlets around the island, the best of the collection are handmade, hand painted ladies' sachets and kits of island specialties packaged in a fabric pouch. **Figleaf** (Carenage) carries gifts, local handcrafts, resort wear, and Cuban cigars. Closed weekends.

Tikal (Young Street; 473-440-2310; fisher@ spiceisle.com), the leading store for handcrafts made in Grenada and other Caribbean islands, has batiks, hand painted T-shirts, and jewelry.

White Cane Industries (Carenage; 473-440-0112), formerly the Blind Workshop, is managed by the Grenada National Council for the Disabled. It is an outlet for handwork by local blind and disabled artisans and their products include straw bags, hats, baskets, jewelry, and mats, often made from recycled material. The artisans excel in high quality re-caning of chairs and other furniture, hence, the company's name.

Grand Anse Craft and Spice Market (north end of Grand Anse Beach; 473-444-3780), managed by the Grenada Tourist Board, was created in response to complaints about persistent vendors roaming the beach. Here, you can find a wide range of local art and crafts, from carvings to homemade sweets and hair braiding. There's a refreshment bar, phones, toilets, and tourist information desk. Hours: daily 8 a.m. to 7 p.m.

Jewelry: Lisa's Island Jewellery/The Jewellery Store (Spiceland Mall, Morne Rouge Road, and Grenville Street; 473-439-4404) specializes in handmade gold and silver jewelry in West Indian designs as well as international brands. **Colombian Emeralds** (Melville Street Cruise Terminal; 473-440-1746), with stores throughout the Caribbean, has a large selection of jewels and jewelry. **Spice Island Jewellery Mfg. Co.** (Grenville Street, St. George's; 473-440-3155) features handcrafted gold and silver jewelry.

Liquor and Wines: Renwick-Thompson & Co. (Carenage; 473-440-2625) claims to be "the best little liquor store in town." **Tourist Gift Shop** (St. George's Pier) stocks duty-free liquor and gifts.

Perfumes and Cosmetics: Arawak Islands (Belmont Road) is a store and workshop that produces perfumes, lotions, potpourri, and teas made from native flowers, spices, and herbs. The staff will explain the manufacturing process and let you sample scents such as frangipani, jasmine, and other unusual fragrances. Shampoo, body lotion, and suntan lotion also are available. Products can be purchased at gift stores in town.

Dining and Restaurants

Fresh fish, fresh vegetables and fruit, soups, desserts made from exotic herbs and spices, and tangy cool drinks punched with island rum are some of the taste treats of Grenadian cuisine, one of the most original in the Caribbean. In addition to traditional West Indian dishes, the French, Chinese, Indian, and Middle Eastern influences have added a distinctive variety and nurtured an interest in food not usually found in former British colonies.

Restaurants are small and operated by their owners, who take personal pride in every dish. Many close on Sun. Major credit cards are accepted unless noted otherwise. For lunch inexpensive means less than US$10; moderate, US$10–$20; expensive, more than US$20. A 10 percent service charge and a 15 percent value added tax are added to the bill. As mentioned earlier in the chapter, several estate homes in the northern part of Grenada serve lunch, usually offering an array of delicious Grenadian dishes. You will want to make it part of your sightseeing, but normally, you will need to make reservations in advance.

Aquarium Beach Club and Restaurant (Magazine Beach, 473-444-1410; www.aquarium-grenada.com). The fashionable beachside restaurant with its great location in tropical gardens by the sea is one of the island's favorites for lunch or dinner. Fresh fish, local and international specialties. Wed night is lobster night; Sun brunch's beach-side barbecue is the place to be. Moderately expensive.

The Beach House Restaurant and Bar (Point Salines/Ball's Beach; 473-444-4455). International cuisine with a Grenadian flavor, seafood, and steaks in a relaxed setting by a pretty beach. Closed Sun. Moderate.

Coconut's Beach (Grand Anse Beach; 473-444-4644). Delightful sand-in-your-feet setting for Creole specialties or refreshing tropical drinks. No credit cards. Moderate.

La Belle Creole (Blue Horizons Hotel; 473-444-4316; www.grenadabluehorizons.com). Set in pretty tropical gardens, the hotel belongs to a family known throughout the Eastern Caribbean for its inventive, Creole cuisine. Moderate.

The Nutmeg (Carenage; 473-440-2539). A longtime favorite of townsfolk and tourists for its convenient location, this restaurant features a harbor view, sandwiches, and snacks. Moderate.

Rhodes Restaurant (Calabash Hotel, Lance aux Epines; 473-444-4334; www.calabashhotel.com). One of Grenada's best restaurants serves continental cuisine with a Caribbean touch. Dinner only. Moderate to expensive.

Savvy Restaurant (Mount Cinnamon at Grand Anse; 473-439-0000; www.mountcinnamongrenada.com). Located at Mount Cinnamon resort overlooking Grand Anse Beach, Savvy serves Mediterranean fusion cuisine laced with Grenadian spices in a casual-chic atmosphere in a beautiful setting with a spectacular view stretching to St. George's. Expensive.

Tropicana (Lagoon Road; 473-440-1586). West Indian and Chinese cuisine and the best Indian rôtis (meat or chicken roll flavored with curry) in town. Moderate.

The Victory Bar & Grill II (Port Louis Marina, Lagoon Road) is an unusual bar with casual barbecue grill and the new marina. Open Tues to Sun from 11 a.m. until 11 p.m.

Water's Edge (Bel Air Plantation Resort; 473-443-2822; watersedge@belairplantation.com) features Caribbean cuisine with a contemporary flair. Be sure to try the calalou soup. Moderately expensive.

Nightlife

In low-key Grenada nightlife means watching a magnificent sunset while sipping on an exotic sundowner, a leisurely dinner, and maybe a stop at a disco. Larger hotels have a West Indian buffet and live music on different nights of the week. The **Marryshow Folk Theatre** (Tyrrel Street; 473-440-2385) has concerts, plays, and special events from time to time.

The **Rhum Runner** (473-440-4386; runner@spiceisle.com), a large catamaran, sails on Fri and Sat evenings, departing the Carenage at 7:30 p.m. and returning at midnight. There's music for dancing and free-flowing rum punch. Price is US$12; a dinner cruise on Wed evening from 6 to 9 p.m. for US$40 is also offered. Some cruise ships offer *The Rhum Runner* as a three-hour excursion along the coast to a beach for a swim and rum drinks, US$27.

Sports

Beaches/Swimming: Grand Anse Beach is a 2-mile band of beautiful white sand framed by palm trees bowing to a calm Caribbean Sea. It is not only the prettiest beach in Grenada, but one of the loveliest in the Caribbean and the island's resort and water-sports center. The south shore has quiet coves with white-sand beaches hidden between the fingers of its deeply indented coast. The west-coast beaches north of St. George's have steel gray, volcanic sand. Carriacou and its offshore islands are rung by fabulous white-sand beaches that seldom see a footprint.

Boating: Grenada is the southern gateway to the Grenadines and has long been known in yachting circles for its sheltered bays, which provide some of the best anchorages in the Caribbean. The **Grenada Yacht Club** (Lagoon Road, 473-440-6826; gyc@caribsurf.com), located just outside of St. George, offers docking and re-fueling facilities and can accommodate boats up to 75 feet long. The south coast offers short excursions for snorkeling and beach picnics and complete charter facilities. Contact **Prickly Bay Waterside** (L'Anse aux Epines; 473-439-5659; www.pricklybay.com). For day cruises, contact **First Impressions** (473-440-3678; www.catamarancharters.com, starwindsailing@

spiceisle.com); or **Rhum Runner** (473-440-2198; renthom@spiceisle.com). Its party cruises are offered frequently as cruise-ship excursions.

Deep-Sea Fishing: Fish are plentiful in Grenadian waters, but sportfishing is not well developed here. The catch includes barracuda, kingfish, red snapper, and grouper offshore; ocean species are sailfish, black-fin tuna, and blue marlin, among others. **Sanvics** (Grenada Grand Beach Resort; 473-444-4371; www.sanvics.com/grenada.htm) arranges half-day charters for about US$350 and US$500 for six hours, or contact **Evans Fishing Charters** (473-444-4422; fax: 473-444-4718; bevans@caribsurf.com).

Golf: Grenada Golf and Country Club (Woodlands; 473-444-4128; www.grenadagolfclub.com) has a 9-hole course, which is one of the best natural courses in the Caribbean. Visitors may use the facilities. Greens fees US$23 for 9 holes; club rental and, caddie available for small fee. Club hours: Mon to Sat 8 a.m. to sunset; Sun to 1:30 p.m.

Hiking: With its magnificent scenery and accessible self-guided nature trails in the Grand Etang National Park, hiking is one of Grenada's top attractions for nature lovers. To arrange more difficult hikes requiring a guide, contact **Telfour Hiking Tours** (473-442-6200) whose owner, Telfour Bedeau, is the most experienced hiking guide in Grenada; **Phinton Ferrier** (473-444-9241), or Denis Henry of **Henry's Tours** (473-443-5313; www.henrysafari.com). The latter's rates are posted on his Web site and range from US$130 for one person to US$55 per person for four or more persons for a hike to Concord or Seven Sisters falls. **Caribbean Horizons Tours** (473-444-1555; www.caribbeanhorizons.com) is among others that arrange hiking. (See Shore Excursions earlier in this chapter for details.)

Over the last few years, Grenada has developed a new, groundbreaking National Forest Policy involving people from all over the country. One result has been a decision to ban all logging in forest reserves and national parks and establish management priorities such as water production, biodiversity, wildlife conservation, and recreation.

Regarding the last, the National Parks and Tourism sector is developing a network of nutmeg-shell-covered nature trails, such as the Morne Gazo Trail in St. David's Parish, the southeastern district of the island. The trailhead can be reached by bus or car; there is a cafe/shop and restrooms near the car park. The 1-mile trail has steps and handrails where necessary, but you need to be fairly fit to climb the 200 steps to the summit. There, a platform provides views across most of southern Grenada. Entrance: EC$5; information sheet in English is available; open 9 a.m. to 4 p.m. Mon through Sat, 10 a.m. to 3 p.m. Sun. Other trails are Annandale, starting from the falls; and Cross, near where the St. George–Grenville highway crosses Grand Etang, among others.

Kayaking: The sport is a natural one with the island multi-indented coastline offering so many shelter bays and off-shore islets. Spice Kayaking & Eco Tours (P.O. Box 1518; Allamanda Beach Resort, Grand Anse; 473-439-4942; cell: 473-407-1147; spicekayaking@spiceisle.com) offer a variety of tours. The half day begins from Clarke's Court Bay to explore Hog Island and untouched bays and coves of Grenada's southeast with a stop for a swim or snorkel in crystal-clear waters. Pedal boats are also available. A full-day six-hour adventure takes in Calivigny Island and snorkeling and continues to a secluded beach at Fort Jeudy where a Grenadian lunch awaits. All excursions are accompanied by guides.

River Tubing: Balthazar River, fed from sources deep in the interior, flows through tropical rain forest and the historic Balthazar Estate. A forty-five-minute drive from St. George's through the Grand Etang Reserve takes you to the launch site, where participants get a briefing and are provided with a life vest and tube. Guides accompany you down the river, as you gently spin in the currents. At the end, there's an opportunity to swim. It's wet, wild, and wonderful. Age requirement: eight years and older; maximum weight: 250 lbs. Departures: 9 a.m., 11:30 a.m., and 2 p.m. from launch site. Bring a towel; wear swimsuit, sunblock, and water shoes. Reservations required. Adventure Jeep Tours (P.O. Box 857, St. George's; 473-444-5337; www.grenadajeeptours.com).

Snorkeling/Scuba Diving: The best reefs are off Carriacou and its surrounding islands, but in the immediate vicinity of Grenada, you can find reefs along the west coast, some within swimming distance of shore. The south end of Grand Anse Beach is well suited for snorkeling. It has some of the largest sea fans in the Caribbean and a great variety of small fish. The north side of Grand Anse Beach at Martin's Bay is a popular dive site and has patch reefs in 30 to 50 feet of water.

About 3 miles from Grand Anse Beach lies Costa Cruise Lines' former ship, *Bianca C,* which caught fire and sank in 1961. The wreck, one of the largest in the Caribbean, is in water more than 100 feet deep and attracts huge turtles, rays, and a variety of other fish. It has been a very popular wreck for experienced divers. Unfortunately, hurricanes have left the wreck broken up and strewn over a larger area, and the lack of protection has enabled souvenir collectors to strip the ship bare of its furnishings.

Molinière Reef, about 3 miles north of St. George's, is the most frequented area for diving. The reef begins at a 30-foot depth and slopes to 60 feet before dropping to 120 feet. Recently, it has become even more popular with the addition of the wonderful Underwater Sculpture Park by British artist Jason Taylor. The site, only a short boat ride from the cruise port, is easily accessible to snorkelers as well as divers.

Aquanauts Grenada (Grand Anse Beach and True Blue Bay Resort; 473-444-1126; www.aquanautsgrenada.com) and Dive Grenada (Grand Anse Beach; 473-444-1092; 444-5875; www.divegrenada.com) have daily excursions and certified diving courses at all levels. Of Aquanauts Grenada's two locations: The nearest to the cruise port is located on the beach of Spice Island Beach Resort. It is a full-service operation with two dive boats and modern dive equipment. It offers daily two-tank dives in the morning, US$70, and single dive in the afternoon, US$40, and trips to Isle de Ronde, a volcanic island 4 miles north of Grenada and one of the Caribbean's last virgin dive sites, US$75.

Tennis: Public courts are located at the Tanteen Public Court and Grand Anse Public Court. The Richmond Hill Tennis Club allows visitors to use its facilities for a small fee.

Whale and Dolphin Watching: An estimated fifteen species of whales can be seen in Grenada waters. The best viewing times run from Dec to Apr. **First Impressions** (phone/fax: 473-444-3678; www.catamaranchartering.com) is one of many watersports company offering excursions.

Festivals and Celebrations

Grenada's three biggest events are Carriacou Maroon and String Band Music Festival, Rainbow Festival, and Carnival. The Carriacou Maroon Festival which began in 2001, has evolved into the **Carriacou Maroon & Regional String Band Music Festival** (www.carriacoumaroon.com) being held for the first time in 2010. The **Rainbow Festival** in Grenville draws the entire parish of St. Andrew, in which the town is located, to paint the town with brilliant colors; music, food, and crafts fill the streets. In mid-Aug the festivities move into high gear with **Carnival.** The celebrations culminate in the final "jump-up," with the picturesque harbor of St. George's filled with color, music, and dance, and visitors joining the Grenadians in celebration.

The **Carriacou Regatta,** begun in 1965, and usually held the first weekend of Aug, is one of the Grenadines' main sailing events. All types of boats participate—work boats, sloops, five-masted schooners, canoes, and even miniature sailboats propelled by hand. Banana boats exchange their cargo for people, and sailors from throughout the Grenadines converge on the island and camp on its nearby islets to be part of the three days of festivities. The biggest celebration is the Big Drum Dance, a ritual of the islanders' African heritage that has been reborn into the national culture of the Eastern Caribbean.

Carriacou

Twenty-three miles northeast of Grenada is one of its two Grenadine Islands. Carriacou, a port of call for several small cruise ships, is a 13-square-mile island with an interesting history and a diverse cultural and natural heritage. It is scalloped with white-sand beaches and surrounded by tiny islets and cays with even more beautiful, pristine beaches—all set in turquoise waters with fabulous reefs. A national parks system is being developed to bring the main areas under protection.

About two-thirds of Carriacou is of volcanic origin. The remainder is limestone and contains fossils that have made Carriacou particularly interesting to scientists.

Hillsborough: The port and main town is a village where time seems to have stood still. About 4 blocks long and 3 deep, it is worth a quick walkabout, particularly to visit the museum, where there is a collection of Amerindian and other artifacts. It is situated in the island's oldest house, which was recently restored. Sandy Island, facing the harbor, is a popular snorkeling location with a shallow-water reef only a few feet from shore. You can rent a boat at the pier for the five-minute ride to the island, but you'll need to bring your own snorkeling gear or rent it from **Carriacou Silver Diving.**

Most parts of the island have adequate roads; you can make a tour in a leisurely hour's drive. From a hilltop on the north end of the island, known as the Hospital Scenic Overlook, you can get a grandstand view and a quick orientation of the island. High North Peak, the highest point in Carriacou, at 955 feet, is being made into a national park; it is the least-altered area of the island. The forested northwest slope of the peak drops down to L'Anse La Roche, a beautiful reef-protected cove and beach. Here, too, are the stone ruins of an 18th-century plantation that once covered about 266 acres of forest and grazing lands.

The northeast coast at Petit Carenage Bay has extensive mangroves that attract a large variety of birds. South of the swamp at Watering Bay is the village of Windward, founded by Scottish seamen and known throughout the Eastern Caribbean for its skilled boat builders. You can often see them by the waterfront making their fishing and sailing boats, which they construct by hand without a blueprint in a traditional manner handed down from generation to generation.

Off the south coast are tiny Saline Island and White Island, surrounded on three sides by sandy white beaches and protected by the best coral reefs in Grenada's waters. Saline is interesting to scientists for its geological formations and to bird-watchers for its shore birds. Red-billed tropic birds, which grow tails up to 20 inches long, breed here from Apr to May.

Carriacou Silver Diving (Main Street, Hillsborough; phone/fax: 473-443-7882; www.scubamax .com), the first dive school on Carriacou, opened in 1993. It offers PADI and CMAS-certified international diving instruction and certification and a variety of dive packages. The thirty sites in the vicinity of Carriacou offer diverse diving grounds, from flat coral reefs to steep, sloped reefs. **Arawak Divers** (Tyrrel Bay; 473-443-6906; fax: 473-443-8312; www.arawak.de; arawakdivers@caribsurf .com) is another PADI dive operation and offers daily excursions.

Carriacou has small, attractive hotels with dining facilities. Seafood is the specialty—with dining on the water's edge at **Scraper's** (Tyrrel Bay; 473-443-1403).

Carriacou, eighteen minutes from Grenada on Airlines of Carriacou or Region Air Services, is an easy day trip. The taxis are available from Carriacou Airport to Hillsborough. The **Osprey Express** (473-440-8126; www.ospreylines.com) catamaran operates between Grenada and Carriacou twice daily.

Petit Martinique: Located 2.5 miles off the east coast of Carriacou is its sister island of Petit Martinique. The largest and only one of Carriacou's offshore islands that is inhabited, it covers 486 acres and is dominated by a 745-foot volcanic cone. The 900 residents are mainly fishermen and boat builders. The island is also served by the Osprey Express, which makes the trip in one-and-a-half hours and costs US$30 one-way, US$60 round-trip.

Barbados

Bridgetown

Barbados

Miles
0 ——— 4

Kilometers
0 ——— 6

N

A T L A N T I C

O C E A N

Archer's Bay

North Point

Flatfield

ST. LUCY

Harrisons

Nesfield

St. Nicholas Abbey ■   ▲ *Cherry Tree Hill*

Diamond Corner

Morgan Lewis Beach

Six Men's Bay

Farley Hill Nat. Pk. ▲   ★ **Wildlife Reserve**

Speightstown

ST. ANDREW

Belleplaine

ST. PETER

Turners Hall Woods ▲

Chalky Mount

Weston

Mount Hillaby ▲

ST. JOSEPH

Bathsheba

Orange Hill

Flower Forest ▲

▲ **Andromeda Gardens**

ST. JAMES

Welchman Hall Gully ★

Sherbourne

St. Johns †

Folkstone Marine Park

Welchman Hall

★ *Harrison's Cave*

Villa Nova ■

ST. JOHN

Holetown

▲ *Sandy Lane*

ST. THOMAS

Market Hill

★ *Ashfold Bird Sanctuary*

Ragged Point

Paynes Bay

Bailey Hill

Francia House ■   ○ Gun Hill

Cottage Vale

ⓘ

Tyrol Cot ■

ST. GEORGE

Sunbury House ■

ST. PHILIP

Sam Lord's Castle ★

Turnpike

Six Cross Roads

ST. MICHAEL

Mapp Hill

CHRIST CHURCH

Crane Beach

BRIDGETOWN ◉

■ *Government House*

Carlisle Bay

Charnocks ○

Needham's Point

IIII *Barbados*

Hastings

† *Grantley Adams*

St. Lawrence

Oistins

Long Bay

Oistins Bay

South Point

C A R I B B E A N   *S E A*

Masterpiece Theatre in the Tropics

Barbados is an elegant sort of place in a quiet way. Whether it comes from the three hundred uninterrupted years of British rule, the pride and natural gentility of the Bajans—as its people are called— or from the blue-stocking vacationers who return annually like homing birds to their roost, this Caribbean island is tony. Something like *Masterpiece Theatre* in the tropics.

A limestone and coral island of soft, rolling green hills, Barbados is the easternmost land in the Caribbean, located 100 miles east of the Lesser Antilles. Surrounded by coral reefs that are often within swimming distance from shore, Barbados is fringed with white-sand beaches and calm Caribbean waters on the west and pounded by white-topped Atlantic rollers on the east.

The island's first inhabitants, the Barrancoids, were an Indian tribe from South America who came in the first century A.D. and remained six hundred years. There appears to have been a two-hundred-year gap before the arrival of the peaceful Arawaks, another South American tribe that remained until they were forced north or conquered in about A.D. 1200 by the more warlike Caribs. Early in the 16th century, the Caribs met their fate at the hands of the Spaniards who took them as slaves to work in Hispaniola.

Thus when the Portuguese arrived in 1536, they found the island deserted but decided not to settle. A century later, due to a navigational miscalculation by the skipper, Henry Powell, the first English ship arrived in Barbados in 1625, on the west coast at the site Powell called Jamestown for the English monarch. Two years later he returned with eighty settlers to establish the first British colony at the site, known today as Holetown. The settlers raised crops such as yams, cassava, and tobacco, which they had learned from the Indians. But it was sugar, introduced in 1637, that brought Barbados the riches and gave birth to a plantation society that ran the island for almost three hundred years. Unlike most other Caribbean islands, which seesawed between rivaling European powers, Barbados remained British. This continuity helped to make it one of the most stable countries in the Caribbean.

Barbados lays claim to being the third-oldest democracy in the Commonwealth, having established its first parliament in 1639. But, of course, it was hardly a democracy for everyone. As the island developed, the planters imported white indentured servants to fill the need for increased labor. But their treatment of these workers was so inhumane it led to riots in 1634 and 1649, and new arrivals fell to a trickle. To relieve the labor shortage, African slaves were introduced, but from the first slave uprising in 1675 until the abolition of slavery in 1833, rebellion was continuous. In the following century, the majority black population matured politically and economically, and a middle class developed.

Although Barbados has been independent of British rule since 1966, in some ways it seems more British than the queen. In Bridgetown, the capital, bewigged judges preside over the country's law courts, and hotels stop for afternoon tea. Even

At a Glance

Antiquities	★★
Architecture	★★★★
Art and Artists	★★★
Beaches	★★★
Colonial Buildings	★★★★
Crafts	★★
Cuisine	★★★
Culture	★★★
Dining/Restaurants	★★★★
Entertainment	★★
Forts	★★
History	★★★★
Monuments	★★
Museums	★★★★★
Nightlife	★★
Scenery	★★★
Shopping	★★
Sightseeing	★★★★
Sports	★★★★
Transportation	★★★

Fast Facts

Population: 288,000

Size: 166 square miles

Main Town: Bridgetown

Government: Barbados, a member of the British Commonwealth, has two houses of parliament: the House of Assembly, the lower house, with twenty-eight members elected from each of Barbados's eleven parishes and the City of Bridgetown for five-year terms; the Senate, or upper house, with twenty-one appointed members. The governor-general is appointed by the queen.

Currency: Barbados (BD) dollar. US$1 equals BD$2. U.S. dollars, traveler's checks, and major credit cards are widely accepted.

Emergency Numbers: Medical, Queen Elizabeth Hospital: (246) 436-6450; Ambulance: 511 or (246) 426-0016; Police: 211 or (246) 430-7100; Fire: 311

Entry Requirements: All visitors must have a valid passport.

Departure Tax: Included in airline ticket cost.

Language: English

Public Holidays: Jan 1, New Year's Day; Jan 21 (or nearest Mon), Errol Barrow Day; Good Friday; Easter Monday; May 1, Labour Day; May 15, Whit Mon; Oct 2, United Nations Day; first Mon in Aug, Kadooment Day; Nov 30, Independence Day; Dec 25, Christmas Day; Dec 26, Boxing Day.

Telephone Area Code: 246

Airlines: Barbados is one of the major transportation hubs of the Eastern Caribbean. *From the United States:* direct service is provided by: American Airlines, Caribbean Airlines, Delta, JetBlue, and US Airways. *From Canada:* Air Canada flies directly to Barbados. *Interisland:* American Eagle, Air Caraibe, Caribbean Airlines, LIAT, Mustique Airways, and SVG Air.

Information: www.barbados.org; www.visitbarbados.org

In the United States:

Barbados Tourism Authority

New York: 800 Second Ave., New York, NY 10017; (212) 986-6516; (800) 221-9831; fax: (212) 573-9850; btany@barbados.org

Coral Gables: 150 Alhambra Circle, No. 1000, Coral Gables, FL 33134; (305) 442-7471; fax: (305) 567-2844; btamiami@barbados.org

Los Angeles: 3440 Wilshire Blvd., No. 1215, Los Angeles, CA 90010; (213) 380-2198; (800) 221-9831; fax: (213) 384-2763; btala@barbados.org

In Canada:

105 Adelaide St. West #1010, Toronto, ON M5H 1P9; (416) 214-9880; (800) 268-9122; canada@barbados.org

In Port:

Harbour Road, P.O. Box 242, Bridgetown; (246) 427-2623; (800) 744-6244; www.barbados.org; btainfo@barbados.org

Barbados National Trust, Wildey House, St. Michael, Barbados; (246) 426-2421; http://trust.funbarbados.com; natrust@sunbeach.net. The trust is a private organization concerned with the country's cultural, historic, and natural heritage and responsible for many of its major tourist attractions.

The Inns and Outs of Barbados (www.insandoutsofbarbados.com), an annual publication, contains a wealth of information useful to visitors. There's also information on www.funbarbados.com and on www.totallybarbados.com. Barbados is on Facebook at www.tinyurl.com/barbadosbeat; and Twitter, www.twitter.com/barbadostourism.

---

the rolling countryside bears a striking resemblance to England.

Budget Planning

Barbados has a reputation for being an expensive island, but this may be unfair without some qualification. Certainly, if you travel by private taxi and dine at top restaurants and posh resorts, you will find prices on par with those in New York. But to enjoy Barbados you do not have to go the expensive route. It has good public transportation; taxis for touring, when shared with others, are not unreasonable; and Barbados has many areas where it is easy and pleasant to walk or hike. There are moderately priced restaurants, particularly for Bajan food.

Port Profile

Location/Embarkation: Bridgetown, the capital, is situated on the southwest corner of Carlisle Bay. Known as Deep Water Harbour, the port is about 1 mile west of the city center. Cruise ships dock next to the commercial port, which is part of an industrial park; however, it has a separate section of piers with a terminal for cruise passengers. The terminal has a Tourist Information Desk and duty-free shops. Outside the terminal taxis authorized to be in the port area await passengers, most hoping to take you on a tour rather than merely transport you into town.

Local Transportation: Barbados has good public transportation serving all corners of the island. Buses operated by the state-owned Transport Board are blue with yellow trim; smaller, privately operated minibuses are yellow with blue trim. To ride the bus you need the exact fare, BD$1.50; you can buy tokens at the bus depot in town. You need have no hesitation about using buses here, but be forewarned: Some bus drivers appear to be in training for the Indy 500. If they are not already deaf from the blast of their bus radios, they—or you—soon will be. Buses operate frequently, from 5 a.m. to midnight, but they are crowded from 3 to 7 p.m.

You can easily identify taxis by the taxi sign on the roof and the letter Z on their license plates. They are not metered, but rates are regulated by law. As always, agree on the price with the driver in advance. Expect to pay about US$100 for a four-hour tour; up to five persons may share the car. Drivers are supposed to be trained to act as guides, but you have to settle for potluck. (The taxi union here is very strong, and some of their members would do well to retire.) The taxi fare from the port to Bridgetown is BD$12. Some one-way fares from Bridgetown: St. Lawrence Gap, BD$36; airport, BD$50; Harrison's Cave, BD$60; Holetown, BD$50; Speightstown, BD$60; and east to Bathsheba, BD$76.

Roads and Rentals: Barbados has more than 800 miles of paved roads. The main arteries are fairly easy to follow, but the maze of small roads and country lanes bordered by tall khuskhus grass

and sugarcane tend to look alike to newcomers and can sometimes make even the most accessible place hard to find. The road network starts from Bridgetown, in the southwest, and fans out across the island like sun rays. The main arteries are numbered 1 to 7 and branch often to connect with other highways, creating a web across the island. A modern 12-mile highway between the airport and west coast skirts the congested Bridgetown/south coast area.

It is easy to take one road on the outbound and return by another route. For example, if you leave the port by Route 1, bordering the west coast where many top resorts are located, and return by Route 2, which is slightly inland from the west coast, you will pass near many of the main attractions.

Good maps are available, but adequate road signs are not. Fortunately, Bajans are friendly and helpful. Their directions, however, are not always clear, because they use the name of the parish—rather than a town or specific locations—as a frame of reference. Bridgetown traffic is heavy; give yourself plenty of time to return to your ship.

Cars, Mini-Mokes, and vans are available for rent. You can use your valid U.S. or Canadian driver's license, but you must register with the police and pay a fee of BD$10. Your car-rental firm will handle all the formalities for you. *NOTE:* Travelers age 70 and older must present a medical form signed by a doctor verifying their fitness to drive. Rental firms adhere closely to this regulation. Those affected should request the medical form in advance from a car rental company in Barbados and have it completed by their doctor prior to their departure from home.

Daily rates for cars start at about US$50 for standard shift and US$75 for automatic. Rental companies often offer discounts to customers booking online. Some companies will not rent cars for less than two days; it is wise to check in advance. Among those that offer one-day rentals are **Courtesy Car Rentals** (246-431-4160; www.courtesyrentacar.com), which has free pickup and delivery; **Voyager Rent-A-Car** (246-243-0427; www.voyager-rent-a-car.com); **Direct Car Rentals** (246-420-6372; www.barbadoscars.com), which has Mini-Mokes and jeeps, also free pickup and delivery; and **Bajan Car Rentals** (246-429-4327; www.bcrbarbados.com).

Shore Excursions

Because of its large number of sightseeing attractions and the extensive road network, there are many routes to be taken for an island tour, and each local tour company has its version. Those described here are typical, but the excursions offered on your ship are likely to differ slightly. The sites mentioned are described elsewhere in the chapter.

Harrison's Cave/St. Nicholas Abbey/Farley Hill National Park: 4.5 hours, US$70–$90, depending on itinerary. Shorter versions available for about US$40–$50.

Gun Hill/Flower Forest/Sunbury Plantation: 3.5 hours, US$45. **Atlantis Submarine** (866-546-7820; www.atlantissubmarines.com/barbados), US$106 adults, US$64 children; Above and Below Barbados Tour, US$140 adults, US$89 children, combines an island tour or snorkeling adventure with an underwater tour on *Atlantis III.*

Golf/Hiking/Biking Tours. See Sports section.

Rum Factory Tours: Three of Barbados's historic rum factories offer tours, each with a slightly different spin on the tale, which you can take your own. *Mount Gay*, within walking distance of the port, is the oldest factory; *Malibu*, about a mile from the port, is the only working distillery on a beach; and *Heritage Park* in near the east coast, is a modern plant in a historic park. (See descriptions later in this chapter.) For something a bit more spicy, **Island Safari** (246-432-5337; www.islandsafari.bb) has a Rum Shop Safari on Sat from 10 a.m. to 3 p.m.

Plantation House Tours: Several of Barbados's many old manor houses are included on island tours, and the one visited usually depends on the route. Those such as Sunbury and Tyrol Cot can be visited on your own. From Jan to mid-Apr, the National Trust offers special home and garden tours on Wed afternoon. Check local newspapers or the National Trust for information.

Island Tours: Among the independent tour companies that offer regular island tours, **Adventureland** (246-429-3687; fax: 246-426-3687; www.adventurelandbarbados.com) has an off-road, full-day excursion to less-traveled Barbados for US$80 adult, US$45 children. **Island Safari Barbados** (246-432-5337; www.islandsafari.bb) organizes off-beat, caravan-style safari excursions in Land Rovers, among others. **Boyce's Tours** (246-425-5366; www.toursbarbados.com) has heritage, cultural, and nature tours, with departures almost daily, from US$45 to US$62.50 per person. Theirs are among the most moderately-priced tours available. **Bajan Helicopters** (Bridgetown Heliport; 246-431-0069; www.barbadosbarbados.com) has two flight-seeing tours of Barbados: 20 minute tour costs US$140 per adult, US$80 per child; 30 minutes, US$180 per adult, US$110 per child. Tours depart around 10 a.m. to 11 a.m. Mon to Fri.

Barbados on Your Own

Bridgetown, where approximately one-third of the population lives, has retained enough of its historic character to make a walk interesting. When you come into Bridgetown at **Deep Water Harbour (1)**, you drive (or walk) along Princess Alice Highway, a road built on reclaimed land and paralleling Broad Street, a thoroughfare to the north. You pass **Pelican Village (2)**, a center for local arts and crafts; and to the north, the 18th-century St. Mary's Church. The main road ends by the **Careenage (3)**, the picturesque old harbor where the town began in 1628.

A Bridgetown Walkabout

Careenage: Still the heart of town, the Careenage lies at the mouth of Constitution River and

Bridgetown

0   Yards   300

0   Meters   300

N

1.   Deep Water Harbour
2.   Pelican Village
3.   Careenage
4.   National Heroes Square
5.   Barbados Parliament

6.   Old Town Hall
7.   Synagogue
8.   St. Michael's Cathedral
9.   Queen's Park

is spanned by the two small bridges from which Bridgetown takes its name. On the north bank, **National Heroes Square (4)** has a statue of Admiral Nelson by Sir Richard Westmacott, dating from 1815 and predating by twenty-seven years the more famous Nelson Monument in London.

North of National Heroes Square is a group of neo-Gothic buildings, which house the **Barbados Parliament (5)** (www.barbadosparliament.com), originally constructed in 1635. The structures were rebuilt to replace buildings destroyed by fire in 1860. The west wing, dating from 1872, houses the Senate; and the east wing, built in 1874, is the House of Assembly. Note the stained-glass windows with portraits of British monarchs and the speaker's chair, which was a gift from the Indian government when Barbados got its independence.

From the square, Broad Street runs west toward the port, crossing Prince William Henry Street, named for the young naval captain around whom one of the island's favorite tales was spun. It involves a character named Rachel Pringle, an innkeeper and madam who ran the best little brothel in Barbados, where the prince and his rowdy sailor friends spent a raucous evening. Miss Rachel, history tells us, had no hesitation about sending the prince—who later ascended to the English throne as William IV—a bill for damages. He paid it.

North of Broad Street is Victoria Street, a narrow street with small shops, and Swan Street, a picturesque lane with old balconied buildings, stores selling clothing and jewelry, and pushcarts piled with tropical fruits. Farther north the 18th-century **Old Town Hall (6),** at James and Coleridge Streets, houses the police headquarters. It neighbors the supreme court and the public library, built in 1905 with a grant from the Andrew Carnegie Foundation.

In a triangle east of the library on Magazine Lane (the name comes from a powder storehouse, or magazine, once here) you will see the Montefiore Fountain, donated by a member of the Jewish community in 1864. Across from it stands the restored **Nidhe Israel Synagogue (7),** the second oldest in North America. Originally built in 1656 by Jews from Brazil, the synagogue was rebuilt in the 19th century, but the building had long ceased serving as a temple and was in ruins when it was rescued from demolition in the early 1980s. It was restored through the efforts of the local Jewish community, the National Trust, and Jewish groups in the United States, Canada, and the United Kingdom.

Today the building's exterior appears much as it did in the 1830s and has a balustraded roofline, lancet-shaped windows, and thick walls rounded at the corners. Inside, all the additions made in the 20th century—when it was used alternately as a racing club, warehouse, law library, and business office—were removed, and the walls were stripped to the original coral stone and roof timbers.

To re-create the 1833 temple appearance, the original benches were copied in native mahogany,

and eight chandeliers were copied from the originals (now in the Winterthur Museum in Delaware). The cemetery, with 400 old graves, was cleaned and tombstones were repaired. The Nidhe Israel Synagogue Museum, adjacent to the synagogue, exhibits artifacts discovered in the cemetery. They are exhibited on a bed of sand, connecting with the religious observance of the sand covered floor in a 17th-century synagogue. Hours: Mon to Sat, 9 a.m. to 4 p.m. Admission: US$12.50 adult, $6 children. For information, Synagogue Restoration, Box 256, Bridgetown; (246) 436-8043.

East of National Heroes Square, St. Michael's Row leads to **St. Michael's Cathedral (8),** built originally in 1665 and rebuilt in 1789 after being destroyed by a hurricane. It was elevated to a cathedral on the arrival of the first bishop of Barbados in 1825. On the south is Queen's College, a prominent girls' school, opened in 1880. At the end of the street is a public park, **Queen's Park (9),** that was once the residence of the commander of the British troops of the West Indies.

From the Careenage, Bay Street (which becomes Route 7) runs south past the Harbour Police Station and St. Patrick's Cathedral, the island's first Roman Catholic church, built in 1849. The road passes the Carlisle Bay Centre, a recreational and water-sports center.

At the corner of Bay Street and Chelsea Road stands a house, once identified as the place where George Washington stayed with his brother in 1751 as a lad of nineteen. Recently, however, this historic error was corrected and Bush Hill House in the Garrison, now called **George Washington House** (246-228-5461; www.georgewashingtonbarbados .org), was identified as the home where Washington stayed. Barbados was the only foreign land the first president of the United States ever visited. Hours: weekdays, 9:30 a.m. to 4:30 p.m. Admission: US$10 adult, $5 children age five to ten, younger than age five admitted free.

At the south end of Carlisle Bay, Needham's Point is a popular resort area with hotels, pretty beaches, and sports and recreational facilities. On the tip are the ruins of Fort Charles and St. Anne's Fort, which were part of a defense system begun in 1694. Behind the forts is the **Garrison Savannah,** a parade ground that is now the racetrack. It is surrounded by more than seventy historic buildings, one of which—a former colonial prison—houses the Barbados Museum.

Barbados Museum (246-427-0201; customerservice@barbmuse.org.bb) For history buffs, a visit to the museum is a Barbados highlight where they can enjoy a magnificently displayed, comprehensive collection on the history, culture, and natural history of Barbados and the Caribbean. Among the outstanding exhibits are those tracing the routes of the pre-Columbian people into the Caribbean, along with displays of their artifacts. The "Charles A. Robertson African Gallery: Connections and Continuities" introduces the viewer to the geography, history, and heritage of Africa and its legacy in the creation of Caribbean society. The museum has a fine library of old maps and documents on the West Indies and a good bookshop. Hours: Mon to Sat 9 a.m. to 5 p.m., Sun 2 to 6 p.m. Admission: BD$15 adults, BD$7.50 children.

Bordering the residential district of Belleville (too far to walk) on the east is **Government House,** set in lovely gardens. It has been the residence of the governor since 1702. Nearby **Ronald Tree House** (No. 2, Tenth Avenue), formerly the headquarters of the Barbados National Trust, is a restored Victorian town house named for the trust's founder, Ronald Tree, who also built the original luxury hotel Sandy Lane.

Barbados National Trust (246-426-2421; fax: 246-429-9055; http://trust.funbarbados.com), is now housed in Wildey House, a beautifully restored Georgian greathouse set in five acres in St Michael parish. The house and its contents, including the elegant furniture and family memorabilia, bequeathed to the Trust by Edna Leacock. Hours: 8 a.m. to 4 p.m. Many of the historic homes and sites in Barbados maintained by the Trust rank among the island's main attractions. On Wed from mid-Jan to early Apr, the trust sponsors Open Houses, a house and garden tour. The houses, often furnished with antiques and rare collections, have beautiful interiors. Fee: US$ 10.

Tyrol Cot Heritage Village (St. Michael; 246-424-2074; www.barbados.org/tyrolcot.htm). High on the list of Barbados's heritage attractions is the house that belonged to both Sir Grantley Adams, the first premier of Barbados, honored as the "father of democracy," and his son Tom Adams, who followed in his father's footsteps and was the country's second prime minister. Built in 1854, and restored by the National Trust, the manor is a good example of mid-19th-century architecture. In the gardens is **Heritage Village,** an outdoor "living" museum housed in chattel houses, the folk architecture of old Barbados. Each cottage displays the work of a traditional craftsman or artist, who usually can be seen at work. Traditional Bajan food and snacks are served in a "rum shop." Hours: weekdays, 8 a.m. to 4 p.m. Admission: BD$16 adults, $10 children.

A Drive Around the Island

Barbados has so many historic homes, gardens, old churches, parks, nature reserves, and scenic sites that you could strike out in almost any direction and find plenty to fill a day. We have divided the excursions into segments to be taken separately as leisurely drives of two to three hours; they can also be combined, depending on your time.

North to Speightstown
(Parishes: St. Michael, St. James, St. Peter)

From Bridgetown, Route 1, skirting the palm-fringed beaches of the Caribbean known as the Platinum Coast, has many of Barbados's most fashionable resorts and fabulous villas.

Mount Gay: North of the cruise ship pier, within walking distance, is **Mount Gay Visitor Center** (Spring Garden Highway; 246-425-8757; www.mountgay.com), Barbados's oldest rum factory, begun in 1703. On the tour you get a taste of the island's history, culture, rum making, and rum. There is a gift shop and a garden cafe. Hours: Mon to Fri, 9:30 a.m. to 3:30 p.m.; tours every half hour. Admission: BD$14. There is also a Bajan buffet luncheon tour on Tues and Thurs, BD$100 with transportation, BD$68 without transportation. Call in advance to reserve tours.

Farther along, **Malibu Visitors Centre** (Brighton, Black Rock; 246-425-9393; www.malibu-rum.com), by West Indies Rum Distillery and the home of Malibu, is Barbados's only working distillery on the beach and offers distillery tours. Hours: Mon to Fri, 9 a.m. to 4 p.m. The last morning tour is at 10:30 a.m.; last afternoon tour at 3:45 p.m. After a tour you can spend the day on the beautiful beach where chairs, umbrellas, changing rooms, showers, and a small restaurant and bar (where you receive a complimentary drink) are available. Special day pass and lunch tours, including transportation, are also available.

Sandy Lane: Once the dowager queen of the group, **Sandy Lane Hotel and Golf Club** (www .sandylane.com) is set in 380 acres of a former sugar plantation just south of Holetown. Designed by the well-known Caribbean architect Robertson "Happy" Ward, Sandy Lane was built in 1961 by Sir Ronald Tree, M.P., whose famous aristocratic friends helped him establish the resort's reputation as the most exclusive in the Caribbean. The resort was torn down totally and rebuilt from the ground up. It reopened in 2001 as a brand-new hotel, resembling the old one somewhat, but with quite a difference. The rooms are larger and more luxurious, with push-button electronics that even Batman could envy. There's one to open the draperies, another to adjust the lights or the volume on the television or the DVD, and still another to tell the butler on the outside that you are inside your room. The resort, which has a huge spa with eye-popping prices, redesigned and expanded its golf course to 45 holes, including two 18-hole championship courses by famed architect Tom Fazio.

Holetown: The site of the island's first settlement, Jamestown, is marked by a memorial and the St. James Parish Church, first built about 1660 and thought to be the oldest on the island. The south porch has an old bell on a pillar, bearing an inscription to King William, 1696—making it older than the Liberty Bell in Philadelphia, which was cast in London in 1750. At the entrance to Holetown is **Chattel House Shopping Village,** which has craft and other shops in colorful cottages patterned after typical local houses. A map of other Chattel House Shopping Village locations around the island can be found at www.barbados.org/maps. With so many of Barbados's best hotels along the west coast, this area is also a center for many of the island's best restaurants and more sophisticated nightlife.

Folkestone Park/Barbados Marine Reserve (www.nccbarbados.gov.bb) North of Holetown,

the Folkestone Park is a picnic and swimming spot popular with Bajans and part of the complex that includes the Barbados Marine Reserve, a small marine museum, and the Belair Research Laboratory. Offshore, the marine park is divided into zones according to use for water sports or scientific research.

If you are short on time, you can turn east at Holetown onto Route 1A, for Harrison's Cave, Welchman Hall Gully, and Flower Forest.

Glitter Bay: Immediately upon entering the front gate, which opens onto 12 beachfront acres of landscaped gardens, you get the impression that someone important lived here. Glitter Bay, formerly the seaside retreat of Sir Edward Cunard of British steamship fame, was the gathering place of a glittering array of lords and ladies when Cunard's passengers came to winter in the tropics. Stately royal palms lead the way to flower-trimmed walkways, a mile-long beach, and a split-level swimming pool with a waterfall and footbridge. The equally stylish Royal Pavilion is next door.

Cobblers Cove: Farther north, Cobblers Cove (www.cobblerscove.com) is a small, romantic resort set snugly in three acres of tropical gardens overlooking a quiet crescent of pearly sand, with just enough history to lend it charm. Cobblers Cove made its American television debut in 1982 when its former neighbor, actress Claudette Colbert, whose house shared the same beach, had old chum Ronald Reagan as a guest. The resort's centerpiece is a pale pink villa built as a summer home by a Bajan sugar baron early in 20th century.

Speightstown: Once an important sugar port, Barbados's second-largest town was founded between 1630 and 1635 by a firm called Speight of Bristol (England). So close were the links in trade that the town was known as Little Bristol until the turn of the century. The Manse, the oldest building in the town, dates from the 17th century.

Arlington House and Museum (246-422-4064) on Queen Street was restored to house has an interactive museum on all three floors: "Speightstown Memories" on the ground floor; "Plantation Memories" on the second floor; "Wharf Memories" on the third floor celebrating Speightstown's former glory as a leading port and hub connecting three continents. Hours: Mon to Sat, 10 a.m. to 5 p.m. Admission: BD$12.50.

East to Farley Hill
(Parishes: St. Peter, St. Andrew)

At Speightstown, Route 1 leaves the coast and turns east to Farley Hill.

Farley Hill National Park: Approached by an avenue of royal palms and casuarina trees, the park is named after a mansion built in 1861 for the visit of Prince Alfred, Duke of Edinburgh. Later it housed George V and other members of the British royal family. After a fire in 1965, the house was taken over by the government, but not rebuilt. The grounds were made into a park of 30 wooded acres and gardens with picnic tables and a children's playground. The views south and east of the Scotland District and the Atlantic coast are spectacular. Several times a year Farley Hill is transformed into a stage for musical and theatrical events, such as the Barbados Jazz Festival in Jan (www.barbadosjazzfestival.com). Hours: daily from 7 a.m. to 6 p.m.

Barbados Wildlife Reserve: Opposite the park entrance a track leads through a sugarcane field to the Barbados Wildlife Reserve (246-422-8826; www.barbados.org/reserve.htm; info@ barbadosmonkey.org), primarily a sanctuary for the green, or vervet, monkey, created in 1985 by primatologist Jean Baulou of the Barbados Primate Research Centre. Monkeys, brought to Barbados from West Africa, were considered agricultural pests as early as 1680. In recent years they had become so numerous and destructive that the government turned to the Primate Research Centre to organize a humane trapping and wildlife management program.

The monkeys, although called green, are brownish gray with yellow and olive green flecks. Naturally shy and difficult to observe in the wild, the monkeys are uncaged here and can be seen in a mahogany grove along with agoutis, caimans, deer, opossums, raccoons, tortoises, and wallabies. The three-acre reserve has tree-shaded paths, a stream with otters, swans, and ducks, and a walk-in aviary of tropical birds. Hours: daily 10 a.m. to 5 p.m. Admission: BD$23 adults, BD$11.50 children three to twelve years old. Information: 246-422-8826.

St. Nicholas Abbey: East of the park en route to Cherry Tree Hill is St. Nicholas Abbey (www .stnicholasabbey.com), a plantation house built in 1650 and owned a decade later by Sir John Yeamans, the third governor of South Carolina. Still the estate house of a working sugar plantation, the well-preserved structure with curved gables and four chimneys is a fine example of Jacobean architecture. The mansion was recently renovated by the new owner, architect Larry Warren. Hours: weekdays, 10 a.m. to 3:30 p.m.; admission: BD$30 adults; BD$20 children.

To the east, the 850-foot Cherry Tree Hill commands a fabulous view of the Atlantic coast and Scotland District, a large bowl-shaped area that differs geologically from the rest of the island. It is in St. Andrew parish, named for the patron saint of Scotland.

Morgan Lewis Mill: About a mile south of Cherry Tree Hill stands the 17th-century Morgan Lewis Mill (www.barbados.org/morgan.htm), the only windmill of the three hundred that once operated in Barbados that still has its wheelhouse and arms intact. It was built in Dutch style by Dutch Jews from Brazil who settled in Barbados and pioneered sugar cultivation. The mill was restored by the National Trust. Admission: BD$10 adults, BD$5 children.

South of Morgan Lewis you can continue along the east coast to Bathsheba or join Route 2 to return to Bridgetown through the heart of the island. Mount Hillaby, Barbados's highest point, is in view, and inland, Turners Hall Woods is a 46-acre reserve of natural forest popular with hikers and naturalists.

The Central Highlands
(Parishes: St. Michael, St. Thomas)

Three of Barbados's most popular attractions— Harrison's Cave, Flower Forest, and Welchman Hall Gully—are located within a mile of one another about a thirty-minute drive from the port on Route 2. A stop at Earthworks Pottery could be made en route.

Harrison's Cave (www.harrisonscave.com) Among Barbados's many limestone caverns, the most accessible and impressive is Harrison's Cave. First explored in 1781, the cave was developed in the 1970s as an attraction by the government with the aid of Danish speleologists. A battery-powered tram with a driver and guide takes visitors down into the lighted chambers. The spectacular Great Hall, which rises more than 150 feet, has a waterfall set among beautiful stalagmites and stalactites glittering under artificial lights. Near the bottom the tram rounds a curve where you see the falls again, plunging into a blue-green pool below. Renovations in 2007, were followed by major redevelopment. Harrison's Cave reopened in Feb 2010, with a new visitor center, restaurant, interpretive center, glass-fronted elevators, and more. Tours operate daily every hour from 8:45 a.m. to 3:45 p.m. Admission: US$30, children US$15.

Welchman Hall Gully: Across the road from the cave is the south entrance to Welchman Hall Gully, a split in the coral limestone where a nature reserve has been created. The gully, humid and protected from high winds, was converted into a tropical-fruit-and-spice garden in the mid-19th century but was later abandoned. In 1962 the site was acquired and developed as an attraction by the National Trust. A half-milelong path starts at the south entrance and meanders through the reserve, thick with vegetation that appears to be growing out of the rocks. It ends at the parking lot on the north side, having passed six different sections with trees and plants common to the Caribbean, including huge samples of the bearded fig. Open daily; admission is BD$14. Harrison's Cave and Welchman Hall Gully (246-438-6671, www.welchmanhallgullybarbados.com) can be reached by public bus.

Flower Forest: North of Harrison's Cave is a tropical garden developed on 50 acres by a private group of Bajans and foreigners as a "legacy of beauty, peace and quiet . . . to leave our children." Situated on Richmond Plantation, an old sugar estate at 850 feet in altitude, the gardens have a great variety of tropical fruit trees and herbs. Footpaths along the contours of the steep hillside lead past bougainvillea and other tropical flowers. The walk is a bit strenuous, but there are benches and lookouts where you can stop to enjoy views. There is a bar at the entrance serving exotic fruit drinks and also a gift shop. Hours: daily, 9 a.m. to 5 p.m. Admission: BD$20 adults, BD$10 children five to

thirteen years old (246-433-8152; www.barbados.org/sightseeing/flowerforest).

The Central Highlands II (Parishes: St. George, St. John)

Another excursion from Bridgetown through the central part of the island winds east, past tiny chattel houses and fields of swaying sugarcane, to the windswept Atlantic coast at Bathsheba on Routes 4 and 3B.

The parish Church of St. George, dating from the 17th century, was rebuilt after being devastated by a hurricane in 1780. It has an altarpiece painting by the 18th-century American painter Benjamin West.

Gun Hill: About midway a secondary road leads uphill to Gun Hill at about a 700-foot elevation. Once an important British military camp, it was part of a chain of signal stations. On a hillside stands a huge British lion, 10 feet high and 16 feet long, hewn from a limestone outcrop in 1868. This emblem of Imperial Britain looks a bit incongruous now. Gun Hill, a National Trust property, is open daily. Admission: BD$10 adults, BD$5 children (246-429-1358).

Heritage Park: The historic site of the Four-square Sugar Factory in St. Philip has been made into a tourist attraction by the owners in conjunction with the National Trust. Historic buildings (246-420-9954; www.windmillworld.com) are alongside the modern distillery of ESAF White Rum. Hours: Mon to Fri, 9 a.m. to 5 p.m. Admission: free, tours are self-guided.

Orchid World: On Highway 3B between Gun Hill and St. John's Church. One of Barbados's newest attractions set in lovely, rolling countryside, Orchid World (246-433-0306; ffl@sunbeach.net) is a treasure for orchid lovers, with dozens of exotic species from around the world. Hours: daily, 9 a.m. to 5 p.m. Admission: BD$20 adults, children half-price.

On the southwest, Drax Hall, built in 1650, is one of the oldest, finest plantation houses in Barbados and still owned by the Drax family. It is one of the private homes open to the public on the National Trust's homes and garden tours.

The East Coast
(Parishes: St. Philip, St. John, St. Joseph)

The lighthouse at Ragged Point marks the easternmost reach of Barbados; beyond, the next stop is the coast of Africa. North of the point the coast stretches for 16 miles along the Atlantic to Bathsheba and Pico Tenerife. The scenic area is popular for hiking and beachcombing.

Codrington College: Founded in the 17th century by Christopher Codrington, a wealthy planter who became governor of the Leeward Islands, Codrington College (www.codrington.org) is the oldest British school in the West Indies and one of the earliest institutions of higher education in the Western Hemisphere. Now a theological school, the entrance is marked by a fabulous avenue of stately royal palms—one of Barbados's most frequently pictured settings.

St. John's Church: On a hillside above Codrington College, St. John's Church was built in 1836 to replace an earlier one destroyed by a hurricane. The churchyard contains tombstones from 1678; one is the grave of Ferdinando Palaeologus, said to be a descendant of Byzantine emperor Constantine. The hillside offers wonderful views of the Atlantic coast.

Bathsheba: Overlooking beautiful Tent Bay and framed by the 1,000-foot-high limestone walls of Hackleton's Cliff, Bathsheba is a fishing village and holiday resort. Often described as Cornwall-in-miniature, it has room-size boulders resting at the water's edge, where large white-topped Atlantic waves break against the shore. Flying fish can be seen here. The Atlantis Hotel (www.atlantishotel barbados.com) overlooking a dramatic seascape and long famous for its Sunday brunch of Bajan cuisine, has recently emerged from major redevelopment as a stylish ten-room boutique hotel.

Andromeda Gardens (246-433-9384; www .andromedagardens.com) On a cliffside above Bathsheba, the Andromeda Gardens, a mature tropical spread acquired by the National Trust in 1989, have a particular interest to botanists and horticulturists. The late owner's hobby was to transplant species here from different climatic conditions around the world to test their ability to grow in the Caribbean's tropical environment. Laid out along the hillside by a meandering stream, the gardens are known for their orchids. Hours: daily, 9 a.m. to 5 p.m. Admission: BD$17.50 adults, BD$9 children.

To the South and Southeast
Parishes: Christ Church, St. Philip)

South of Bridgetown, Route 7 leads 16 miles to Ragged Point. A detour through St. Lawrence Gap or at Maxwell Road takes you through lanes that Bajans call "the Strip." But it's much tonier than the name might suggest, with small resorts and something of a Cape Cod ambience.

Oistins: From the fishing village of Oistins, one of the most historic towns on the island, a road leads to South Point, the southernmost tip of Barbados, where there is a lighthouse. The southeastern end of the island has rocky fingers and pretty bays protected by reefs lying just off the coast. The village is especially known for its Fri night fish fries when all Barbados—or so it seems—shows up for the party.

Concorde Experience Museum (www .barbadosconcorde.com): The G-BOAE, the final Concorde to fly supersonically over the Atlantic, is opened for public tours at Grantely Adams Airport. The experience includes a virtual flight school, a departure lounge, an observation deck, a multimedia presentation, and a tour of the aircraft. The project was done in partnership with GAIA Inc., the Barbados Museum and Historical Society, and British Airways. Hours: daily, 9 a.m. to 6 p.m. Admission: US$20 adults, $12.50 child.

Sam Lord's Castle: The elegant Georgian mansion was built on the foundation of an old plantation house in the early 1800s by Samuel Hall Lord, who reputedly made his fortune as a wrecker—a pirate who lured ships onto the rocks to plunder them. Now a National Trust property, the mansion boasts a fine collection of art and antiques. Sunbury Plantation House (246-423-6270; www.barbadosgreathouse.com): An early-18th-century plantation house that was extensively renovated after a fire in 1995, Sunbury House is furnished with antiques and artifacts meant to reflect life on a sugar estate in the colonial era. Hours: daily, 9:30 a.m. to 4:30 p.m. Admission: BD$18 adults, half-price for children under twelve years. Its bar and restaurant has an a la carte menu plus a weekday buffet of Bajan food for BD$40 per person.

Shopping

Broad Street in Bridgetown is the main shopping center of the island, complete with department stores, shopping malls, and a host of boutiques. The two largest department stores—Cave Shepherd & Co. and Harrison's, with branches at the port—stock duty-free imports such as perfumes and English bone china. Stores are open weekdays from 8 a.m. to 4 p.m. and Sat to 1 p.m. Colorful Swan Street is a place for bargains. Chic boutiques are found on Bay Street. Shopping villages have mushroomed around the island, making it easy to combine a sightseeing and shopping excursion.

Antiques: Greenwich House Antiques (Greenwich, St. James; 246-432-1169), in an old plantation house, is crammed full of wonderful old china, furniture, books, and prints.

Art and Artists: Barbados is in the midst of an art explosion, judging from the number of galleries that have opened in recent years. In addition to those named here, there are another dozen or so around the island. For a list and descriptions of galleries, see http://artshappeningsbarbados .blogspot.com. For those with a serious interest, *Art in Barbados, What Kind of Mirror Image?* by Alissandra Cummins, Barbados Museum and Historical Society director; Alison Thompson, an art history teacher; and Nick Whittle, an artist and art teacher, is a book published by the society.

The Barbados Arts Council Gallery (Pelican Village; 246-426-4385; www.barbadosartscouncil .com) has group and one-person shows year-round in its open-air gallery. It features everything from batik and photography to sculpture and ceramics. A schedule of shows is posted on its Web site. Queen's Park Gallery (Queens Park; 246-427-2345), operated by the National Cultural Foundation, stages monthlong exhibitions throughout the year. The spacious gallery is open daily Mon through Sat 10 a.m. to 6 p.m.

The Gallery of Caribbean Art (Queen Street, Speightstown; 246-419-0858; www.artgallery caribbean.com) specializes in art from around the

Caribbean as well as some of Barbados's leading artists. Hours: Mon to Fri 9:30 a.m. to 4:30 p.m., Sat to 2 p.m. Kirby Gallery (The Courtyard, Hastings, Christ Church; 246-430-3032; www.kirbyartgallery .com), directed by artist Vanita Comissiong, features art by Bajan artists.

Books and Maps: The best is the Cloister Bookstore (Hincks Street; 246-426-2662). Others are Brydens (Victoria Street), Cave Shepherd & Co. (Broad Street), and Barbados Museum Bookshop.

China and Crystal: Cave Shepherd & Co. (Broad Street and branches at deluxe hotels; www .shopatcaveshepherd.com) stocks china and crystal such as Wedgwood, Royal Doulton, and Waterford, to name a few. Little Switzerland (Broad Street) is another.

Cigars: The Caribbean Cigar Co., at the western end of Pelican Village, walking distance from the port, produces four sizes of cigars with tobacco from Cuba, Ecuador, and Cameroon under the brand Royal Barbados. At the workshop you can watch women at work while a guide explains the process done partly by hand, partly by machine.

Clothing and Accessories: In addition to department stores, you can find boutiques for beach and leisure wear throughout the island. The most interesting are those of Bajan designers. Gatsby, with nine boutiques at Bridgetown Harbour and in west coast hotels, has international designer-label fashions. Upbeat (Broad Street and other locations) carries beachwear, including swimwear by local designers, such as Ripples (www .ripples-swimwear.com). The Monkey Pot (Pelican Village) sells hand-painted dresses and ties. Dingolay (Bridgetown, Holetown, Christ Church; 246-432-8709) stocks tropical chic fashion made in Barbados.

Crafts and Souvenirs: The recent explosion of crafts has resulted in a bewildering variety of decorative and functional products by sophisticated artists, who set the standards and style, and by local craftspeople, who use their intuitive skills and ingenuity to transform clay, beads, seeds, rope, coral, wood, and grass into pottery, sculpture, jewelry, fabrics, and household items. The Barbados Investment and Development Corporation (BIDC), a government agency that provides training, is credited with helping to improve the quality and sophistication of local crafts. BIDC markets the products as Pridecraft. Craft fairs are held throughout the year. The main fairs are Holetown Festival, Feb; Oistins Festival, Easter; Crop Over, Aug; and Barbados Museum Annual Craft Fair, Dec.

Pelican Village (Princess Alice Highway) is a cluster of small shops with curios and crafts. Nearby Temple Yard is the craft center of the Rastafarians, who specialize in leather and paintings with strong African identification. Visit http://cruise barbados.com for a list of the stores in Pelican Village.

Earthworks Pottery (Edgehill, St. Thomas; 246-425-0223; www.earthworks-pottery.com) is the workshop of Goldie Spieler, whose imaginative collection ranges from decorative chattel houses to functional microwave and kitchenware. Hours: weekdays 9 a.m. to 5 p.m., Sat 9 a.m. to 1 p.m. Next door, **On the Wall Art Gallery** (2 Edgehill Heights, St. Thomas; 246-425-0223) specializes in Bajan artists.

Articrafts (Broad Street; 246-427-5767) showcases the work of Roslyn Watson, an artist, designer, and handweaving specialist noted for pretty yet durable basketry and tapestry. Hours: Mon to Thurs 8:30 a.m. to 5 p.m., Fri until 6 p.m., Sat to 4 p.m. Quality work by other artists is also on display. **Best of Barbados** (outlets at hotels and tourist attractions; www.best-of-barbados.com) is both a group of shops and a marketing label for the distinctive work of Jill Walker, which is widely distributed throughout the Caribbean. She is best known for her watercolors of island folk scenes, which are reproduced in a wide range of gifts and small household items.

The Chattel Village (Holetown) Borrowing from the colorful style of local architecture known as chattel houses, developers have created attractive, colorful shopping villages with each small house devoted to a specialty shop—Barbados's answer to shopping malls, although the island has them, too. Convenient to the port and hotels is the west coast village with a variety of shops and an outdoor cafe.

Wild Feathers (Bayshore entrance near Sam Lord's Castle; 246-423-7758) is the small home studio where Geoffrey and Joanie Skeete carve and re-create indigenous and migratory birds of Barbados. You usually can watch them at work. On display is their collection of more than thirty birds, including some made by their son and daughter-in-law. Larger carvings are made to order, but miniatures are available for sale. Joanie also paints watercolors of Caribbean birdlife. Call for an appointment.

Medford Craft World (Whitehall, Main Road, 246-425-1919; www.medfordcraftworld.com) is the workshop of Reggie Medford, a self-taught woodcarver with an eye for business who has developed an unusual method of carving native mahogany with an electric blade normally used for sanding. His mass-produced products—clocks, dolphins, bowls—range from US$20 to $150, depending on the size and design. His abstract sculptures, which follow the natural contours of the raw wood, are his most interesting work; they start at US$200.

Jewelry: You'll find fine jewelry at **Cave Shepherd** and **Harrison's,** among others. Craft stores and trendy boutiques carry handcrafted jewelry of local materials and semiprecious stones.

Liquor and Wines: Bajan rum, some of the best in the Caribbean, has been made here since the early 17th century. Barbados claims to be the first island in the West Indies from which rum was exported. The best known is **Mount Gay,** whose factory (246-425-8757) offers one of the most comprehensive tours of a rum factory. Other rum factory tours are described earlier in this chapter. A popular brand of aged rum is Cockspur Old Gold.

Perfumes and Cosmetics: Harrison's (Broad Street, hotel outlets, and at the port) stocks most of the well-known French perfumes and at prices competitive with St. Thomas and other Caribbean islands.

Dining and Restaurants

Neither the gourmet capital of the Caribbean nor its Creole center, Barbados nevertheless can hold its own for the range and variety of restaurants, and it's getting better with each passing year. More restaurants are offering West Indian dishes. Local seafood, especially Barbados's famous flying fish, a small fish that can be seen often skipping over the waves on the Atlantic coast, is the star, as are fresh fruits and vegetables. Other Bajan specialties are pumpkin fritters, curried chicken, pepper pot (a savory stew derived from the Arawak Indians), cou cou (a cornmeal and okra dish), and pickled breadfruit, to name a few. Mauby, a traditional Bajan drink made from tree bark, has a pungent, bittersweet taste meant to stimulate the appetite.

Prices at the best restaurants are high. Inexpensive means less than BD$40; moderate, BD$40–$60; and expensive, BD$60 and up. Reservations are advised. Major credit cards are usually accepted, but inquire in advance. Dress is casual but conservative. Some hotels require a jacket for men at dinner. Some of the best restaurants serve only dinner. Those listed here serve lunch unless stated otherwise, but check locally for times, as these vary.

Bridgetown/Christ Church Area/St. Lawrence Gap

Chefette (246-435-6000; www.chefette.com). Barbados's largest fast-food chain with thirteen restaurants, many with playgrounds, offers steaks, chicken, burgers, pizza, salad bar, ice cream. Moderate.

Josef's (St. Lawrence Gap; 246-420-7638; www.josefsinbarbados.com). Set in a renovated house with an airy touch, the cozy ambience conveys the feeling of dining at a friend's home. A garden has tables at the water's edge. Lunch weekdays; closed Sun. Expensive.

Pisces (St. Lawrence Gap; 246-435-6564; www.piscesbarbados.com). Elegant restaurant of chef Larry Rogers and wife, Michelle, (formerly La Terra at the Royal Westmoreland Clubhouse). Imaginative West Indian–inspired menu features an extensive variety of seafood to be enjoyed in relaxed, sophisticated seaside ambience.

Olives Bar & Bistro (Holetown; 246-432-2112), situated in an old Bajan house and serving earthy Mediterranean and Caribbean favorites. Dinner only. Expensive.

The Waterfront Cafe (Careenage; 246-427-0093; www.waterfrontcafe.com.bb). You can enjoy seafood specialties here along with the picturesque setting of the Careenage. Moderate.

West Coast

The Cliff (Derricks, St. James; 246-432-1922; www.thecliffbarbados.com). In a lovely seaside location and cleverly terraced to guarantee an ocean view for every table, this is the best restaurant in Barbados for sophisticated fare by the creative chef and manager team of Paul "Scally" Owens and "Mannie" Ward. Expensive.

Daphne's (Paynes Bay, St. James; 246-432-2731; www.daphnesbarbados.com), a sister to the famous London eatery, offers contemporary Italian cuisine at the water's edge at the heart of the island's Caribbean coast. Cocktail hour (5 to 7 p.m.) offers drinks at half price. Extensive wine list. Expensive.

Fish Pot (Little Good Harbour Hotel, St. Peter; 246-439-3000; www.littlegoodharbourbarbados.com), at the water's edge in the fishing village of Shermans, north of Speightstown, is an informal, relaxing, yet smart alternative to Holetown's more snooty establishments. Menu and daily specials are mostly seafood, plus local vegetables and fruit. Reservations suggested. Moderately expensive.

Fusion (South Beach Hotel; 246-436-1538), a newcomer serving Asian fusion with a popular outside bar and lounge. Moderate.

Sassafras (Sugar Hill Resort, St. James; 246-422-6684; www.sassafras246.com). An original and creative menu combines Caribbean and Asian flavors. The wine list is good and prices reasonable. Moderate.

The Tides (Holetown, St. James; 246-432-8356; www.tidesbarbados.com). Chef Guy Beasley and his wife, Tammie, have teamed up with manager Trevor Parris to create one of the area's most delightful restaurants. Fresh local fish is a specialty presented in an innovative, contemporary fashion, with European, Asian, or Caribbean influences. Meat and vegetarian dishes are also on the menu, and there's an extensive wine list. Diners can choose a romantic setting on the seafront terrace with orchids on the table, a more casual bistro style in the courtyard, or a blackboard menu of light fare in the busy bar. The Tides is something of an art gallery, with paintings decorating the walls. Expensive.

Nightlife

Bajan Roots & Rhythms is staged Wed and Fri from 6:30 to 10:15 p.m. at the **Plantation Garden Theatre** (St. Lawrence Road; 246-428-5048; www .plantationtheatre.com). Cost is US$97.50 adults, $75 teens age thirteen to eighteen, $45 children age three to twelve and includes transportation, dinner, and drinks. Or, show only: US$57.50 adults, $40 teens, $30 children. Two clubs, both by the beach on Bay Street, are **Harbour Lights** (246-436-7225; www.harbourlightsbarbados.com) and the **Boatyard** (246-436-2622; www.theboatyard.com). At the former, you are likely to see more tourists and ex-pats; the latter is more popular with locals than tourists. Both have live music on some nights, free drinks on others, and dancing on the beach and under the stars. **The Waterfront Cafe** (Careenage; 246-427-0093; www.waterfrontcafe.com.bb) has jazz on Fri and Sat. **De Kitchen,** next to the Boatyard, is the place to mix with Bajan yuppies on Fri night.

If you want to sample the island's late-night action, head for Baxters Road, a sort of ongoing food fair for Bajan snacks with more rum shops per block than any place on the island or maybe the Caribbean. It's busiest after midnight. The **Pink Star** is a late-night favorite. As noted earlier, the Oisins Fish Fry on weekends is one of the most popular places to be in Barbados.

On the cultural scene, **Frank Collymore Hall** (246-436-9083; www.fch.org.bb), a modern concert and conference hall in Bridgetown, has a wide range of programs, from poetry reading and jazz to ballet and symphony concerts. Theater has a long history in Barbados, and long-established groups stage plays by West Indian and international playwrights at island theaters regularly. Consult local newspaper or the tourism authority.

Sports

Beaches/Swimming: All beaches are public, but access is often restricted by the presence of

hotels that crowd the beaches on the west and south coasts. Hotels do not have facilities for day visitors, but you can still use the beach. Much of the north and east coasts is rockbound, with stretches of beaches washed by strong Atlantic waves and too rough for swimming, except in certain places such as Bath, which is protected by a barrier reef. A government-operated picnic site here has showers and toilet facilities. Crane Beach, on the southeast, is one of the prettiest beaches, but it's often rough with Atlantic waves.

Weiser's on the Bay, on Brandon's Beach about a mile from port, is a beautiful stretch of white sand with calm waters. You'll find beach chairs, lockers, and umbrellas, each US$5, with half credited back for bar drinks. Equipment per hour: snorkeling, US$10; kayaks, US$10; Sunfish, US$20; surf, windsurfing boards, US$10. Flag service on beach 9 a.m. to midnight daily. Just up the road is **Malibu Beach Club and Visitor Centre** (Brighton, Black Rock, St. Michael; 246-425-9393; www .malibu-rum.com). In addition to tours of the distillery where Malibu and Cockspur Rum are made, the complex fronts a fine beach and gift shop. Daily tours about every half an hour, US$15 for adults; US$8 children under twelve. Lunch tour, US$42.50 for adults, half-price for children, includes transfers, distillery tour, lunch and four drinks, and use of all facilities such as lounge chairs, beach umbrellas, showers, and changing rooms.

Biking: Highland Adventure Centre (Cane Field, St. Thomas; 246-431-8928; fax: 246-438-8070; neilhighland@hotmail.com) offers a one-and-a-half-hour, 7-mile mountain bike ride from Highland (15 percent uphill), traveling at a leisurely pace on secondary roads through the heart of Barbados, in heavily wooded areas and small remote villages, seeing a side of Barbados that few tourists experience.

Boating: At water-sports centers on the beach, Hobie-cats can be rented for about BD$30 per half hour. Day sails along the west coast with food, drinks, snorkeling, and swimming are available from several companies. The custom-built *Harbor Master* departs on Wed from 11 a.m. to 3 p.m. Cost: US$75. *Tiami Catamaran Lunch Cruise* departs daily at 10 a.m. and returns at 3 p.m.;

cost: US$85. Contact **Tall Ship Cruises** (246-430-0900; http://tallshipscruises.com). **Cool Runnings** (246-436-0911; www.coolrunningsbarbados.com) offers a daily *Snorkel Lunch Cruise* from 9:30 a.m. to 2:30 p.m. from the Careenage for US$85. Boats often change their schedules seasonally; check locally. The **Barbados Yacht Club** (246-427-1125; www.barbadosyachtclub.com) is located east of Bridgetown on the south coast.

Deep-Sea Fishing: Sportfishing is good here, with bottom fishing over reefs, trolling along the coast, and deep-sea fishing for big game. Blue marlin is caught year-round but is more plentiful during the winter months. Other fish include wahoo, tuna, kingfish, bonito, mackerel, yellowtail, and amberjack. Anglers who cast from rocks or shallow water can catch small barracuda, jacks, snook, and tarpon. Half- and full-day charters are available from **Blue Jay Charters** (246-422-2326), **Cannon Charters** (246-424-6107), and **Blue Marlin** (246-435-6669; http://bluemarlinbarbados .com). Most half-day trips run from 8 a.m. to noon and 1 to 5 p.m. and cost US$500–$600 for half-day or $175 per person for four hours, sharing; full-day trips cost $950.

Golf: Barbados's golf course most convenient to the port is the spread at **Sandy Lane Hotel** (St. James; 246-444-2500; golf@sandylane.com); only the 9-hole course is available to nonguests. Farther north **Royal Westmoreland** golf course (www .royalwestmoreland.com/golf) is a private club reserved for the owners of the million-dollar homes in this pricey real estate development, and their friends, and guests at hotels with whom the club has agreements.

The **Barbados Golf Club** (Durants, Christ Church; 246-428-8463; www.barbadosgolfclub .com), the island's first public championship golf course, was redesigned so completely, that it's really a new golf course. Designed by Ron Kirby, the 18-hole, par 72 course is located on the south side of the island and has a clubhouse, bar, and restaurant. Reservations can be made online. The newest links are the **Apes Hill Club** (www.apeshillclub.com), a new resort/residence development.

Hiking: Barbados has many places to hike that combine beautiful scenery and interesting history. On Sunday you can join an early-morning walk organized by the Barbados National Trust. Led by young Bajans, the hikes are designed to highlight the island's history and natural beauty. They are organized into three groups—fast, medium, and slow—start at 6 a.m. and 3:30 p.m. and last about three hours. Wear comfortable walking shoes or sneakers and a wide-brim hat for protection against the sun. Schedules are available from the **National Trust** (246-426-2421; www.hikingbarbados.com) and published in local newspapers. The hikes are free but donations can be made to the Barbados National Trust to help with their efforts to preserve the island's natural environment.

Horseback Riding: Several stables offer beach, trail, and cross-country riding: **Brighton Stables** (246-425-9381), **Ye Old Congo Road Stables** (St. Philip; 246-423-6180); and **Caribbean International Riding Centre** (246-422-7433) which offers a one-and-a-half-hour mountain and beach tour for $70 or $90.

Just Breezing Watersports (Holetown; 246-262-7960; www.justbreezingwatersports.com) offers a five-hour tour for a minimum of four and maximum of six people that begins with a horse-back ride on the Atlantic side, a stop for lunch at the stables, and then, riders are transported to the Caribbean side where they continue with a ride on the beach. The tour then takes to the water on a glass-bottom boat for snorkeling with green sea turtles and over a shipwreck teeming with fish. Cost: US$166.67 per person. **Boyce's Tours** (246-425-5366; www.toursbarbados.com) pairs a horseback ride on the moors of Waterford and a visit to the Arbib Nature and Heritage Trail with a visit to the Mallalieu Motor Collection that includes a Bentley, a Triumph, and Austins. Cost: US$40 per person.

Polo: Introduced in Barbados at the turn of the 20th century by the British Army, polo is played at the **Barbados Polo Club** (St. James; 246-432-1802; www.barbadospoloclub.com) on Wed, Sat, and Sun from Dec to Apr/May. There is a small admission fee. Polo ponies are bred on Barbados.

Snorkeling/Scuba Diving: Barbados is surrounded by coral reefs—an inner one suitable for snorkeling and learning to scuba dive and a barrier reef less than a mile from shore, which has the main dive sites. The best area for snorkeling is the quiet, clear waters of the Caribbean on the west, where reefs in 20 to 30 feet of water are within swimming distance of shore. Equipment is available for rent from the dive shops and water-sport operators. The main dive locations on the west coast are reached by boat. The formation of the reefs is one of peaks and valleys, with the first dropoff ranging from about 50 to 100 feet. North of Holetown, the Barbados Marine Reserve has an artificial reef and marine park with a marked underwater trail for snorkelers and a segment of the 7-mile outer reef for divers.

An artificial reef lies about a half-mile offshore at Prospect and was created by sinking the Greek freighter *Stavronikita,* which had been destroyed by fire in 1976. Most of the ship rests from a 40- to 90-foot depth, but the top of the main mast, marked by a buoy, is only 15 feet below the surface. Other nearby shipwrecks are two in Carlisle Bay, south of Bridgetown. The bay, too, is interesting for divers, because the bottom is littered with bottles of different shapes and sizes dating from colonial times, when the Customs House was located here and ships anchored in the bay.

Among the leading dive operators are **Coral Isle Divers** (Careenage, Bridgetown; 246-434-8377; www.coralisle.net), **Dive Barbados** (Mount Standfast, St. James; 246-422-3133; www.dive barbados.net), **Eco Dive Barbados** (246-243-5816; www.ecodivebarbados.com) and **Dive Shop Ltd.** (246-426-9947; www.divebds.com). Most have trips daily, departing at 9:30 or 10:30 a.m., 12:30 p.m., and 2:30 p.m. Cost: US$65–$85 for one tank, US$110–$150 for two tanks. Barbados is one of the few places in the Eastern Caribbean with a recompression chamber.

If you are not a scuba diver, there are several alternatives. Snuba is something between snorkeling and scuba diving, with special apparatus, offered by **Snuba** (246-436-2088; www .oceanadventures.bb). *Atlantis III,* a recreational submarine, takes passengers to depths of 150 feet on the barrier reef. It operates daily with morning and afternoon departure times from the Careenage, where **Atlantis Submarine** (246-436-8929; http:// atlantisadventures.com) is based, and takes about two-and-a-half hours, with forty-five minutes spent on the reef. Cost: US$101.50 adults, US$52 children. **Heatwave** (246-228-8142) offers a five hour snorkeling and lunch excursions for US$ 75 adults, $38 children.

Surfing/Windsurfing/Kiteboarding: The Atlantic coast in the vicinity of Bathsheba has been the venue for several surfing championships. **Barbados Surf Trips** (246-262-1099; www.surf barbados.com) and **Zed's Surfing Adventure** (Inch Marlow; 246-428-SURF; www.barbadossurfholidays .com), rent boards of all types. Daily rates: US$25– $50. Lessons start at US$50 per person for two hours. Zed Layson, a fifth-generation Bajan and a pioneer of the sport, has been a competitive surfer for more than twenty-four years and is ranked in the top twenty amateurs in the world.

A combination of assets has made Barbados one of the prime windsurfing locations in the world, with conditions particularly well suited for competition. The World Windsurfing Championships have been held here. The main location is the south coast, where there is a reef almost 5 miles long. It protects the inner waters near the shore and provides a calm sea for beginners. Outside the reef, strong Atlantic waves break against and over the reef, providing a real challenge for competitors. Particularly exciting for advanced Windsurfers is the sport of wave jumping. In addition, on the south coast the trade winds blow from the east for nine months of the year and enable Windsurfers to reach for long distances. Barbados is a popular training base for competitors. For lessons and board rentals contact **Silver Sands Resort** (246-428-6001; www.silversandsbarbados.com).

The same assets that made Barbados so popular for surfing and windsurfing are also the features that have made it a center for the fast-growing sport of kitesurfing or kiteboarding. Wind conditions and ocean temperature are said to be best for someone wanting to learn the sport. **Redeye Kiteboarding** (Inch Marlow; 246-262-KITE; www .kitesurfbarbados.com) rents equipment and boards from $35–$65 per day. Kitesurf lessons cost US$80 per person for two hours; private lessons, US$75 per hour.

Tennis and Squash: Tennis is available at two dozen hotels and at other sites operated by the government. Of the six squash facilities, the one with air-conditioned courts nearest the port is **Barbados Squash Club** (The Marine, Christ Church; 246-427-7913).

Festivals and Celebrations

Crop Over, mid-July to early Aug, is an annual arts festival that is similar to Carnival in fanfare, but different in origin. Based on a 17th-century plantation tradition of celebrating the annual sugarcane harvest, the event was revived in the late 1970s as a local festival. It was so popular it evolved into the island's major annual event. In the old tradition the festival began on the last day of harvesting the cane, when the workers decorated themselves and drove to the mill singing that the "crop was over." The next day plantation owners feted the workers with Crop Over parties. Today's version re-creates some of these events with fun and frolic, beginning with the Ceremonial Delivery of Sugarcane and a Decorated Cart Parade. There are concerts, plays, regattas, fancy dress balls, contests, and parades, but the most important event is the Calypso Contest.

PART SIX

The Southern Caribbean

Trinidad and Tobago

**Port of Spain, Trinidad; Scarborough, Tobago;
Pigeon Point, Tobago**

Trinidad

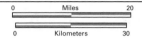

CARIBBEAN   SEA

Galera
Point

Blanchisseuse

Toco

Medine Point

Salibea

Monos Island

Chaguaramas

Northern   Range

*Chacachacar
Island*

**Asa Wright
Nature Center** ★

San
Juan

Tunapuna

**Aripo
Caves** ★

Valencia

Gaspar Island

PORT OF SPAIN

Arima

*Matura
Bay*

Caroni River

**Caroni Bird
Sanctuary**

Sangre
Grande

Cunupia

*Caroni
Dam*

Manzanilla Point

Chaguanas

Talparo

Lower
Manzanilla

GULF OF

Barracones Bay

*Nariva
Swamp*

*Cocos
Bay*

PARIA

Couva

Biche

*Navet
Dam*

Navet River

Point Lisas

*Guatuaro
Point*

Pointe-à-Pierre

Princes
Town

Rio Claro

Mayaro

San Fernando

*Mayaro
Bay*

Point Galba

La Brea

River

Pitch Lake

Ortoire

Guapo Bay

Galeota Point

Irois Bay

Rushville

Granville

San
Francique

Moruga

*Isolate
Bay*

Erin Point

*Icacos
Point*

OCEAN

ATLANTIC

COLUMBUS   CHANNEL

The Odd Couple

A dual-island nation with some of the most spectacular scenery, wildlife, and unusual attractions in
the Caribbean, Trinidad and Tobago are as different
in lifestyle and tempo as any two islands in the
region.

Trinidad, the birthplace of calypso and steel
drums, is the ultimate Caribbean kaleidoscope,
with more than four dozen nationalities and ethnic
groups making up this richly textured society. Hindu
temples stand beside mosques, cathedrals, and
Anglican steeples, and rôti and rijsttafel count as
local cuisine as much as pepperpot, fish cakes, and
shish kebab. A veteran of oil boom and bust, Trinidad is the center of the country's commerce and
trade, where visitors are usually more interested in
business than beaches. But once a year all business
stops and Trinidad explodes in C-A-R-N-I-V-A-L.

Twenty-two miles to the northeast lies tiny
Tobago, a quiet and tranquil island so extravagantly beautiful it makes even the worst Caribbean cynic smile. Tobago is the ultimate tropical
paradise, scalloped with palm-fringed alabaster
beaches bathed by aquamarine waters and framed
by lush green mountains that host hundreds of
exotic birds.

Even the origin of the two islands differs. Trinidad, only 7 miles off the coast of Venezuela near
the delta of the Orinoco River, was originally part of
the South American mainland, although scientists
are not sure exactly how or when the separa-
tion occurred. Tobago, however, was not part of
South America; it was volcanic in origin and more
closely associated with the islands of the Eastern
Caribbean.

Trinidad is only 10 degrees north of the equator. It has three parallel mountain ranges, separated by wide plains that run east-west across the
island. The mountainous Northern Range, covering
the northern third of the island, is considered to be
an extension of the Andes of Venezuela. It has the
country's highest peaks, reaching more than 3,000
feet, which separate the Caribbean coast on the
north from the rest of the country. The south side of
the Northern Range gives way to the wide Caroni
Plain, where nine rivers flow from the mountains
into the Oropouche River, which runs east to the
Atlantic; and the Caroni River, which meanders
west through marshland to the Gulf of Paria.

Due to its proximity to and association with
South America, Trinidad has flora and fauna found
nowhere else in the Caribbean. In contrast to its
bustling capital of Port of Spain, Trinidad's forest-
clad countryside is home to 700 orchids, 600 varieties of butterflies, and more than 425 species of
birds. It also has such strange natural phenomena
as mud volcanoes and the world's largest asphalt
lake.

Trinidad was first settled by the Arawaks from
Venezuela and Guyana more than two thousand
years ago. They called the island Iere, meaning
"land of the hummingbirds," and remained for many
centuries before moving north to the Eastern Caribbean. The Arawaks were followed by the Caribs,
also from South America, but apparently the Caribs
did not stay long and moved north, too.

At a Glance

Antiquities	★
Architecture	★★★
Art and Artists	★★★★
Beaches	★★★★
Colonial Buildings	★★★
Crafts	★★
Cuisine	★★★
Culture	★★★★★
Dining/Restaurants	★★★
Entertainment	★★★★★
Forts	★★
History	★★★
Monuments	★★
Museums	★★
Nightlife	★★★★
Scenery	★★★★★
Shopping	★★
Sightseeing	★★★
Sports	★★★★
Transportation	★★

Fast Facts

Population: 1.3 million

Size: Trinidad, 50 miles long, 37 miles wide; 1,900 square miles. Tobago, 27 miles long, 7.5 miles wide; approximately 200 square miles.

Main Towns: Port of Spain and San Fernando, Trinidad; Scarborough and Plymouth, Tobago

Government: Trinidad and Tobago is a parliamentary democracy based on the British Westminster system. The president, elected by parliament, is chief of state and appoints the prime minister.

Currency: Trinidad and Tobago (TT) dollar. US$1 equals about TT$6.33. Since both currencies are rendered as dollars, be sure you understand which currency is being quoted. U.S. and Canadian money can be exchanged at banks, where you receive an official receipt. It entitles you to reconvert your unused TT dollars back to your original currency on departure. Without this receipt you will not be able to reconvert TT dollars legally. Major U.S. credit cards and traveler's checks are accepted in most hotels, stores catering to tourists, restaurants, and car-rental firms, but at small operations and out-of-the-way places, be prepared to pay in the local currency.

Departure Tax: Included in one's plane ticket

Entry Requirements: Passports are required for U.S. and Canadian citizens.

Emergency Numbers: Medical: Port of Spain General Hospital, (868) 623-2951; Fire: 990; Ambulance: 811; 990

Tobago: Scarborough Regional Hospital, (868) 639-2551; Police: 999

Language: English is the national language, but in this polyglot nation Chinese, Arabic, Urdu, Hindi, and other exotic languages are spoken, too.

Public Holidays: Jan 1, New Year's Day; Good Friday; Easter Monday; May or June, Whit Mon; June, Corpus Christi; June 19, Labor Day; first Mon in Aug, Emancipation/Discovery Day; Aug 31, Independence Day; Sept 24, Republic Day; Dec 25, Christmas Day; Dec 26, Boxing Day. Eid-il-Fitr, a Muslim feast, changes from year to year, as does Divali, a Hindu festival. Carnival is not a national holiday, but Carnival Week, and particularly the final two days, might as well be, since little business is transacted.

Telephone Area Code: 868

Airlines: *From the United States:* American Airlines and Caribbean Airlines from Miami. New York, and the latter from several Caribbean locations; Continental from Newark and Houston; and LIAT from various Caribbean islands to Piarco International Airport, 20 miles southeast of Port of Spain. *From Canada:* Caribbean Airlines from Toronto; and it operates shuttles between Trinidad and Tobago throughout the day, beginning at 6:30 a.m.

Information: www.gotrinidadand tobago.com; www.visittobago.gov.tt; www.tntisland.com; its directories are better than the phone book.

In the United States:

Marketing Challenges International Inc., 915 Broadway, Ste. 600, New York, NY 10010; (212) 529-8484; (800) 816-7541; fax: (212) 460-8287; t&t@mcintl.com

In Port of Spain:

Trinidad and Tobado Tourism Development Company Ltd. (TDC), Level 1, Maritime Centre, 29 Tenth Ave., Barataria, Trinidad; (868) 675-7034; fax: (868) 638-7962; www.tdc.co.tt

Tobago Department of Tourism and Transportation, House of Assembly #12, Sangster Hill, Scarborough; (868) 660-7517; fax: (868) 635-1337; contact@visittobago.gov.tt

Columbus came upon Trinidad on his third voyage and went ashore at Moruga, on the south coast (some authorities say it was farther east at Erin). He named the island La Trinidad for the three peaks of the southeast mountains, which symbolized to him the Holy Trinity and are known today as the Trinity Hills. Trinidad seemed to have been a low priority for the rivaling European powers, thus enabling the Spaniards to hold it until 1797, when they were dislodged by the British.

In contrast, Tobago was so highly prized for its rich agricultural potential and its strategic location that it changed hands more than a dozen times between Spain, England, France, and other European powers battling for control of the New World. Finally, in 1889, Tobago asked to become a part of Trinidad. The two islands received their independence from Britain in 1962 and became a republic in 1976.

Budget Planning

For many years, the government of Trinidad and Tobago has had a love-hate relationship with tourists and an on-again, off-again desire to attract them. Until the oil bust in the mid-1980s, Trinidad had little need for tourism and indeed, its first prime minister, who ruled the country for thirty years, was openly hostile to it. This attitude manifests itself, I think, in the costs for visitors. You can get the impression that for Trinidadians, costs are reasonable, but if you are a tourist, costs are high. This assessment may be unfair, and, rather, may simply reflect the absence of a well-developed tourist industry with competitive services. Another factor of cost is the 15 percent VAT (value-added tax), which is added to the price of most services.

Generally, food and public transportation are cheap. Taxis are expensive, and tours are overpriced. If you know how to bargain or if a local person negotiates the price for you, the price of a taxi for the day can be reduced by as much as 30 to 50 percent.

Port Profile: Port of Spain

Location/Embarkation: Port of Spain, the capital and main port, is situated on the west coast of Trinidad, overlooking the Gulf of Paria. Its cruise-ship terminal is part of a complex covering four acres located at the foot of Port of Spain. The complex has a reception area, exchange bureau, post office, communications center from which AT&T calls can be made collect, and a shopping mall with duty-free shops. The Trinidad and Tobago Tourist Development Authority offices are on the second floor. Outside the terminal building are a craft market, a rustic outdoor pub, and the Breakfast Shed, one of the town's best inexpensive restaurants for local food.

Local Transportation: Taxis are available at the port to take you sightseeing or to other parts of the city. Fares are posted on a board by the terminal door and in Port Authority literature. In the heart of Port of Spain (walking distance from the port), walking is the most practical way to get around, as traffic moves at a snail's pace. Private taxis are expensive, but there are inexpensive collective taxis

and minibuses (Port of Spain, yellow stripe; Tobago, blue stripe) called maxi-taxis. They follow specific routes, stopping to pick up and discharge passengers along the way. Fares are standard; occasionally drivers will take a passenger a short distance off the regular course for an extra fare. Maxi-taxis can be hailed by a hand signal. Port of Spain also has inexpensive bus service on main routes and between major towns.

Taxi rates increase by 50 percent after 9 p.m. All taxis have an H as the first letter on their license plates. Sample rates from the port in Trinidad: to the Trinidad Hilton, TT$60; airport, TT$170; Asa Wright Nature Center, TT$500. Taxi for the day costs about US$25 per hour. In Tobago from Pigeon Point: to Plymouth, TT$70; Scarborough, TT$60; Buccoo Point, TT$60; Arnos Vale Hotel, TT$80; Speyside, TT$265.

Roads and Rentals: Trinidad has a fairly wide network of roads, including some super highways, reaching most areas of the country within one to two hours from the capital. Roads in and around towns are generally well signposted, but they have very heavy traffic. Small towns have secondary roads, but remote mountain and rural regions are reached by track or walking.

Two north-south roads connect Port of Spain with the northwest Caribbean coast. Directly north, Saddle Road winds up the mountains to the North Coast Road and continues to Las Cuevas and Blanchisseuse. East of the capital the only road across the Northern Range is a steep corkscrew route between Arima on the south and Blanchisseuse on the north coast.

East from Port of Spain, two parallel highways run along the south side of the Northern Range.

Eastern Main Road, the older of the two, passes through densely populated suburbs to towns at the base of mountains, from which secondary roads climb the southern face of the mountains. Just before Valencia, Eastern Main Road branches north to Toco, on the northeast tip, where it rounds the corner to the Caribbean coast. The other branch of the Eastern Main Road turns southeast via Sangre Grande, the largest town of the eastern region, to Manzanilla, on the Atlantic coast. The Beetham Churchill-Roosevelt Highway, the alternate express-way east from Port of Spain, terminates at Fort Reed (Wallerfield), a former U.S. Army base. It crosses several north-south roads, the main one being Uriah Butler (Princess Margaret) Highway, an expressway between Port of Spain and San Fernando, Trinidad's second-largest city and the heart of the oil industry.

Car rentals are available. Rates start at about US$50 for a well-used car, plus 15 percent VAT. Some firms require deposits. Check out your car carefully, and make notes of all the dents and other signs of wear to avoid being charged for them when you return. U.S. and Canadian visitors with a valid driver's license may drive here for up to three months. At all times, drivers must have with them their driver's license and any travel document that certifies their date of arrival in Trinidad and Tobago. Driving in this former British colony is on the LEFT.

The Tourist Board has a list of car-rental companies and rates. In Port of Spain these include Autocenter (6 Ariappita Ave.; 868-628-4400; fax: 868-622-2959; autocenter@wow.net), Bacchus Taxi and Car Rentals (868-622-5588), Thrifty (868-669-0602; 800-367-2277), Econo-Car Rentals (868-622-8072; fax: 868-622-8074; econocar@trinidad.net), and Singh's Auto Rentals (868-623-0150; fax: 627-8476; www.singhs.com; singhsautorentals@singhs.com).

In Tobago, Autocenter (868-639-4400; autocenter@wow.net) and Baird's Car Rentals (Scarborough, 868-639-2528) also rent motorbikes and bicycles, as does Modern Bikes (868-868-639-3275). Econo-Car Rentals (Local Road, Crown Point, opposite airport; 868-660-8728; econo_car@hotmail.com) and Sheppy's Car Rentals (868-639-1543; www.tobagocarrental.com) also have motorcycles, jeeps, and minivans; Sherman's Auto Rentals (868-639-2292; www.shermansrental.com), Singh's Auto Rentals (Grafton Beach Resort; 868-639-0624; www.singhs.com), Thrifty (Crown Point airport; 868-639-8507), and Tobago United Auto Rentals (868-639-9973; www.tobagoautorentals.com) have jeeps and small buses, as well as cars.

Shore Excursions

For Trinidad

Local tour companies offer excursions as varied as a visit to a wildlife sanctuary or a working plantation to a day at the beach, golf, or fishing. Tours are expensive unless you are part of a group, and even some group tours are expensive. Prices vary considerably from one vendor to another; and are subject to a 15 percent VAT.

If you have a keen interest in natural attractions, an excursion led by an experienced nature guide will be more rewarding than traveling on your own. Trinidad has good nature guides who cater to bird-watchers and naturalists. One of the most outstanding is Jogie Ramial (Milepost 3¾, Blanchisseuse Road, Arima, Trinidad); write to him in advance to make arrangements. Sites mentioned here are described elsewhere in this chapter.

Caroni Bird Sanctuary: 3 hours, US$64 per person. The 450-acre sanctuary for the scarlet ibis is visited at sunset. See description later in this chapter.

Port of Spain/Maracas/Saddle Drive: 3.5 hours, US$59 per person. City tour followed by a drive over the Northern Range to north coast. Or less city sightseeing and more time at the beach.

Asa Wright Nature Centre: 5 hours, US$84 per person. (See section later in chapter.) A list of tour companies is available from the Tourist Office and from Trinidad & Tobago Incoming Tour Operators Association (868-633-4733; www.ttitoa.com). In Port of Spain these include Travel Centre, Ltd. (868-622-0112; fax: 868-622-0894; www.the-travel-centre.com), which features nature tours, bird-watching, and sightseeing, and Trinidad and Tobago Sightseeing Tours (868-628-1051; fax: 868-622-9205; www.trintours.com), with nature tours, sightseeing, and sailing excursions. Caribbean Discovery Tours (868-624-7281; fax:

868-624-8596; www.caribbeandiscoverytours.com) offers ecological, cultural, and historical tours. Also check out **Sensational Tours** (#47 Reservoir Rd., Santa Cruz; 868-676-2937; sensationaltours@gmail .com).

For Tobago

Buccoo Coral Reef: 1.5 hours, US$25 with transfers. Glass-bottom boat trip over the reef or longer with snorkeling. US$15 for boat excursion directly from Pigeon Point.

Island Tour: 2.5 hours, US$50 per person for two; or five hours, US$120 per person for two; US$30 for three or more.

Island Tour with Hiking: 4–5 hours, US$55 per person. Nature-guide specialists combine an island tour with stops at places for birding and Main Ridge Nature Trail for hiking. Tobago nature specialists are listed in the Hiking/Birding section later in the chapter.

Other tour companies: **Yes-Tourism Ltd.** (Bamboo Walk Hotel, Hampden/Lowlands; 868-631-0286; www.yes-tourism.com) offers island tours in both Tobago and Trinidad. **Fresh Tours Tobago** (Scarborough; 868-748-1220) a small tour company specializing in tailor-made tours for two or more persons to off-the-track nature and beach locations. **Frankie Tours and Rentals** (Mt. Irvine, Tobago; 868-631-0369; www.frankietours.com) arranges personalized, flexible itineraries and has a wide selection of prearranged activities—taxi service, auto rentals, airport shuttle, and tours to Trinidad.

Trinidad on Your Own

If Trinidad and Tobago are the odd couple, Trinidad is a study in contradiction, beginning with the name of its capital. Facing south on the Gulf of Paria with the foothills of the Northern Range rising behind it, Port of Spain is turned inward to its city squares, savanna, and interior streets where the city pulsates. Hot, crowded, and congested, Port of Spain is a defiant city that almost dares you to like it. It is a vibrant, lived-in city with strong, competing images reflecting the multiracial, multifaceted society that makes up the twin-island nation. And, almost in spite of itself, it even has a plan. The

quickest way to get a sense of Port of Spain is to walk through its heart, where the architecture, music, museums, and restaurants mirror Trinidad's cultural mosaic.

A Port of Spain Walkabout

For 250 years under the Spanish, Port of Spain was little more than a tiny village amid swamps and mangroves. The actual Spanish capital, San José de Oruna, was 12 miles inland at St. Joseph, today a suburb. The early 1780s were a turning point, when French and other settlers who had been given land grants in Trinidad arrived and an agricultural and social transformation of the country began. To market their products and supply their needs, the port was improved and expanded. Then, in 1784, José Maria Chacon, the last of the Spanish governors, made Port of Spain the official capital. Merchants built town houses, sugar barons added mansions, and the new prosperity attracted a great variety of people who further contributed to the town's growth. The British arrived in 1797 and added the streets that they named for their kings, queens, and admirals, and which are the heart of the city today.

A fire in 1808 destroyed much of the earlier town, but in 1813 a young and able British governor, Ralph Woodford, set about rebuilding it—a task he apparently relished—his layout remains basically the same.

Now teeming with people, Port of Spain has grown far beyond its 19th-century heart into a complex of communities, each with a distinct identity. On the west are the old middle-class suburbs such as Newtown and Woodbrook. St. James, with streets named Bombay and Bengal, has a large Indian community whose ancestors came as indentured laborers after slavery was abolished. On the north are the newer affluent suburbs of St. Clair, Maraval, St. Ann's, and Cascade climbing the hills; and on the east in the foothills are Belmont and Laventille, Afro-Trinidadian communities where the steel band was born and the air is filled with the pulsating rhythms of calypso.

As your ship sails into **port (1),** the twin towers of the Financial Complex, pictured on Trinidad and Tobago currency and housing the Central Bank and

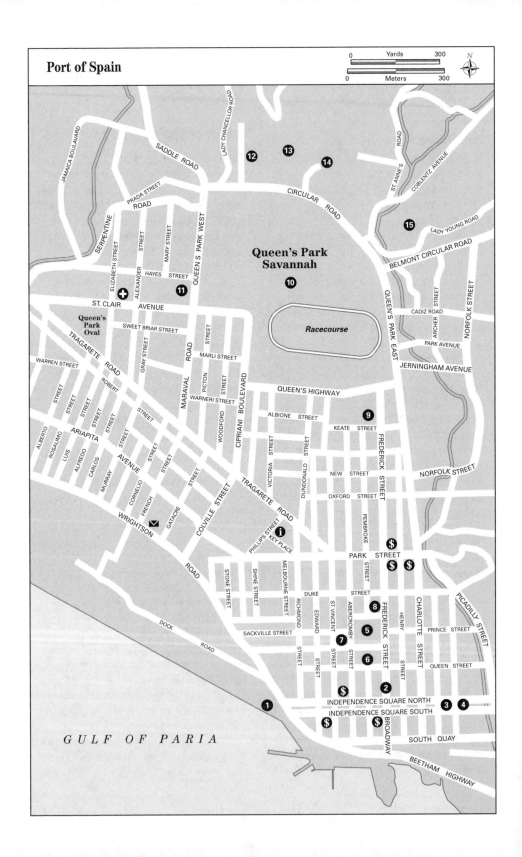

Port of Spain

0 — Yards — 300
0 — Meters — 300

N

JAMAICA BOULEVARD

LADY CHANCELLOR ROAD

SADDLE ROAD

12 **13** **14**

ST. ANNE'S ROAD

COBLENTZ AVENUE

CIRCULAR ROAD

15 LADY YOUNG ROAD

PRADA STREET

ROAD

SERPENTINE

BELMONT CIRCULAR ROAD

ELIZABETH STREET

STREET

MARY STREET

QUEEN'S PARK WEST

Queen's Park Savannah

10

ALEXANDER HAYES STREET

11

NORFOLK STREET

ARCHER STREET

ST. CLAIR AVENUE

CADIZ ROAD

Queen's Park Oval

SWEET BRIAR STREET

QUEEN'S PARK EAST

PARK AVENUE

Racecourse

JERNINGHAM AVENUE

TRAGARETE ROAD

GRAY STREET

MARAVAL ROAD

STREET

MARLI STREET

WARREN STREET

QUEEN'S HIGHWAY

PICTON STREET

WARNERI STREET

WOODFORD STREET

CIPRIANI BOULEVARD

ALBIONE STREET

9

KEATE STREET

FREDERICK STREET

NORFOLK STREET

STREET STREET STREET STREET

ALBERTO

ROSALIMO

LUIS

ALFREDO

CARLOS

MURRAY

ROBERT

STREET

STREET

ARIAPITA AVENUE

CORNELIO

FRENCH

GATACRE

COLVILLE STREET

TRAGARETE ROAD

VICTORIA STREET

DUNDONALD STREET

NEW STREET

OXFORD STREET

PEMBROKE STREET

WRIGHTSON

ROAD

PHILLIPS STREET

KEY PLACE **i**

$

PARK STREET

$** **$

DOCK

ROAD

STONE STREET

SHINE STREET

MELBOURNE STREET

RICHMOND STREET

STREET

DUKE STREET

EDWARD STREET

ST. VINCENT STREET

ABERCROMBY STREET

8 FREDERICK STREET

HENRY STREET

CHARLOTTE STREET

PICADILLY STREET

PRINCE STREET

SACKVILLE STREET

5

7

6

QUEEN STREET

$

2

INDEPENDENCE SQUARE NORTH

3 **4**

1

INDEPENDENCE SQUARE SOUTH

$** **$

BROADWAY

SOUTH QUAY

GULF OF PARIA

BEETHAM HIGHWAY

Ministry of Finance, and the Crowne Plaza, stand out in the foreground against the city, which is still mostly low rise. Some of the old buildings, which have been restored, lend the city grace; those that have fallen into disrepair give it a tawdry touch; and here and there, a new high-rise lifts your eyes up from the shacks and rum shops that often greet your view at eye level.

The center of Port of Spain, from the harbor on the south to the Queen's Park Savannah on the north, is laid out in a modified grid of 10 blocks. From the port you cross Wrightson Road, the highway that separates the city from the port at the foot of Independence Square. Once lined with bars and brothels and dubbed the Gaza Strip during World War II when Trinidad was home to an American army and navy base, Wrightson Road was built on part of the 400 acres of landfill when the bay was dredged in 1935 to create a deep-water harbor.

Independence Square (2), a tree-lined plaza by the sea when it was laid out in 1816, is not a square but two parallel east-west streets. It has the atmosphere and noise of a Middle Eastern bazaar and the confusion of an African market, with honking taxis and cars jostling people and pushcarts while calypso blares from sidewalk stands and storefronts. *(Although I have walked along these streets alone without fear or incident, many Trinis, as Trinidadians call themselves, do not consider the area safe, particularly from petty theft, and warn visitors to be careful with their purses and wallets.)*

In the center of Independence Square at the base of Frederick Street is a statue of Arthur Andrew Cipriani, a pioneer of the independence movement and a former mayor of the city. The east end of Independence Square is anchored by the **Roman Catholic Cathedral (3),** one of the two cathedrals added by Woodford. It is built of blue stone from the Laventille hills in the shape of a cross. Behind the cathedral is **Columbus Square (4),** with a statue of a young Christopher Columbus—an area that is badly in need of renovation.

Frederick Street is the most direct connection between Independence Square and **Queen's Park Savannah.** Traditionally, it has been the main shopping street, but in recent years, as modern shopping centers have been built in the suburbs and the downtown streets have become congested with traffic, better-quality stores have moved away.

Woodford Square (5): The main square, laid out by Woodford, is one of the town's prettiest areas, with enormous flowering trees shading its lawn and walkways. Down through history the square has been a favorite location for political rallies. On the south side is the **Cathedral of the Holy Trinity (6),** the Anglican cathedral built by Woodford to replace one destroyed by the fire of 1808. On the west is the **Red House (7),** the home of Parliament and other government departments. The sprawling neo-Renaissance structure got its name in 1897 when it was painted red for the diamond jubilee of Queen Victoria. Originally built in 1844, the enormous building was burned down in 1903 during demonstrations that started over hikes in water rates and ended in protests against the colonial government. Defiantly, the British rebuilt it. Again in the summer of 1990, the Red House was at the center of conflict when militants took the prime minister and parliament members hostage, and the building was badly damaged. The north side of the square, once lined with town houses, has **Town or City Hall (8),** built in 1961 to replace an earlier structure destroyed by fire; the public library; and the modern Hall of Justice.

National Museum and Art Gallery (9): (117 Frederick St.; 868-623-5941; museum@tstt.net.tt) Founded in 1872 and housed in the Royal Victoria Institute (Keate and Frederick Streets), the Gallery has an art collection ranging from primitive to abstract to folklore, as well as prints by Cazabon, a Trinidadian landscape artist whose paintings have provided a valuable historical record of Trinidad from about 1850 to his death in 1888. Periodic exhibitions of modern Trinidadian art are held here. The museum has a natural history section and exhibitions on the country's oil industry, transportation, and its history from the Arawaks to the colonial period. Hours: Tues to Sat 10 a.m. to 6 p.m., Sun from 2 to 6 p.m., closed on public holidays.

Queen's Park Savannah (10): Once an area of 200 acres, the Savannah now covers 80 acres of open land with enormous shade and flowering trees. Stretching between the city and the hills, it is both the city's lungs and playground. In the northwest corner a depression known as the Hollows, with enormous shade trees along walkways with flower beds, lily ponds, and rock gardens, is a popular picnic spot. In recent years the park has become a huge traffic circle, with cars circling it in a clockwise direction—not entirely a new role, as the route was a toll road in colonial times. Annually it is the center of Carnival activity.

A group of historic houses of imposing architecture frame the western perimeter of the park. Built at the turn of the 20th century and known as the Magnificent Seven, each of the ornate structures has distinguishing characteristics. From Frederick Street, walking west along Queen's Park West, you pass **Knowsley**, which houses the Foreign Ministry. After the road bends north, you pass the American Embassy, and then the stately **Queen's Royal College (11)**, a boys' school; **Hayes Court**, the residence of the Anglican bishop of Trinidad; and **Roomor**, built in French baroque style, with soaring towers, pinnacles, dormers, and cupolas. Mille Fleurs is a typical town house, with lacy iron fretwork; it is followed by the **Archbishop's House**, the home of the Roman Catholic archbishop of Trinidad and Tobago.

Whitehall, in Moorish style, was built in 1904 as a private residence and served until recently as the office of the prime minister. The last in line is

Stollmeyer's Castle, also known as **Killarney**, also built in 1904. It is a copy of a German Rhine castle. Although not one of the Seven, **Boissiere House** (26 Queen's Park West), an eccentric structure known as the Gingerbread House, is the photographer's favorite. On the north side of the park is the home of the president of the republic.

Emperor Valley Zoo (12): (868-622-3530; http://emperorvalleyzoo.110mb.com) Begun in 1952, the zoo has animals from around the world, but emphasizes tropical fauna. Among the natives are the tree porcupine, ocelot, and two species of monkeys, weeping capuchin and red howler. There are agouti; lappe (or paca), an enormous rodent hunted in South America for its meat; and deer. The large number of reptiles includes iguana; spectacled caiman, a small crocodile called an alligator locally; and some samples of Trinidad's forty-seven types of snake. The most colorful birds are the toucan and macaw, but, in fact, the grounds of the zoo, gardens, and park are like an aviary. The zoo gets its name from the once abundant emperor butterfly, one of Trinidad's six hundred varieties.

Royal Botanical Gardens (13): (868-622-1221 x2160-5) Laid out in 1820, the 70-acre Botanical Gardens has manicured lawns with pretty walkways along an avenue of palms and hedges of hibiscus and bougainvillea shaded by large tamarind and saman. Among the flowering trees is the wild poinsettia known as chaconia, named for the Spanish governor who made Port of Spain the capital. The tree's brilliant red blossom is the national flower. Hours: daily 6 a.m. to 6 p.m.

President's House (14): Built in 1857 in Italian Renaissance style, the home of the president of the republic has Victorian cast-iron columns and railings. Its flowering gardens adjoin the Royal Botanical Gardens and zoo.

Overlooking the park from the east is the **Trinidad Hilton (15)**, known as the upside-down hotel because of the manner in which it was built into the hillside. You enter the lobby at the upper level, where there is a magnificent view, and from there descend to the restaurants and guest rooms.

To the west of the capital, Fort George, built in 1804, has been restored as a historic monument. It crowns a promontory at 1,100 feet with a fabulous view. Next to the harbor Fort San Andres, built in

1785, is said to be the place Don Cosmo Damien de Churruca, a Spanish naval officer and astronomer to the king, fixed the first meridian of longitude in the New World in 1792.

On the east edge of town is the most obvious architectural reflection of Trinidad's multifaceted society. The **Jinnah Memorial Mosque,** built in 1947 in South Asian–Islamic style, is named for the founder of Pakistan.

A Drive Around Trinidad

Port of Spain makes a good base from which to see the countryside—as different from Port of Spain as Trinidad is from Tobago. Three of Trinidad's national parks—Chaguaramas on the west, Maracas on the north, and Caroni on the south—are less than 10 miles from the capital. Each park is completely different in nature from the others.

Chaguaramas Peninsula: The northwestern reach of Trinidad, and its offshore islands, are part of the Chaguaramas National Park, whose highest peak is 1,768-foot Mount Catherine. About a mile off the south shore is Gaspar Grand, a local beach resort connected by daily boat service. The island has caves with stalactites and stalagmites that can be viewed along lighted walkways. There are picnic facilities near the cave entrance. Other islands are popular for sailing and water sports.

Maracas: On the north side of Port of Spain, Saddle Road winds up the mountains through the suburbs and descends along forested mountains to Maracas Bay on the Caribbean coast. Long strands of golden sands framed by the lush mountains of the Northern Range stretch from Maracas Bay to Las Cuevas Bay—all part of the Maracas National Park and the most popular beaches in the Port of Spain vicinity.

Caroni Bird Sanctuary National Park: After meandering through the Caroni plains and mangroves, the Caroni River empties into the Gulf of Paria 7 miles south of Port of Spain. Within the mangroves, which cover 40 square miles, is the 450-acre Caroni Bird Sanctuary, the home of the scarlet ibis, Trinidad's national bird. Daily at sunset the brilliant scarlet birds stage one of nature's most spectacular shows. As the sun begins to drop, a few of the bright red adults and their smoky pink

juveniles appear in the sky. Then they arrive by the dozens, and finally by the hundreds, loudly flapping their 3-foot span of wings as they swoop down to perch on mangrove trees to roost for the night. They are joined by large numbers of snowy egrets and herons, and, by dusk the birds cover the green trees in such numbers that the sanctuary looks like a lake of Christmas trees.

Naturalist Frank Graham Jr., writing in *Audubon, the Magazine of the National Audubon Society* (May 1987), says, "The arrival of the scarlet ibises at their roosting place in the mangroves is the most spectacular exhibition in the avian world. . . ." The ibis gets its fire engine red plumage from the carotene in the crabs, shrimp, and snails on which it feeds. Boat trips are available from near the signposted entrance to the park, west of the Uriah Butler Highway. The boats wind through lagoons and mangrove swamps to the sanctuary. Along the way a guide describes the vegetation and wildlife of the swamp, which includes more than 150 species of birds, 80 kinds of fish, and a variety of reptiles and other animals. Tours also leave daily from Port of Spain. Birders and those with a keen interest in nature should arrange to visit with a naturalist guide, however; otherwise you will get a standard tour—little more than a boat ride to the sanctuary at sunset.

Pointe-â-Pierre Wild Fowl Trust: Less than an hour's drive south from Port of Spain is an unlikely combination of conservation and industry, which has resulted in one of the most beautiful spots in Trinidad. Within the compound of the TRINTOC (Trinidad and Tobago Petroleum Company) refineries and petrochemical complex are two lakes surrounded by 15 acres of coastal wilderness turned into a bird refuge for endangered species and migrants. Established in 1966 with the help of Texaco (former owner of TRINTOC), the trust is a private, nonprofit effort to protect Trinidad's endangered species and help to rejuvenate their numbers to return them to the wild. It also serves as an environmental educational center, particularly for children.

On nature walks in a beautiful park setting, you can watch a great variety of waterfowl and forest species at close range. If you wish to make a day of it, bring a picnic lunch. The sanctuary is operated by volunteers, and visits must be arranged in advance (868-658-4200 ext. 2512; www.pointeapierrewild fowltrust.org; wildfowl.trust@petrotrin.com).

Devil's Woodyard: At Princes Town, east of San Fernando, a mud volcano known as the Devil's Woodyard is regarded as a holy site by some Hindus. Mud volcanoes are formations in the earth's surface created by methyl gases sweeping through the subsurface mud. As the mud dries, it builds up platforms that form cones sometimes as high as 20 feet. Twenty mud volcanoes have now been registered in southern Trinidad and are thought to be associated with oil production.

Pitch Lake: Trinidad's largest oil fields lie south of San Fernando. To the west, near the coast at La Brea, is Pitch Lake, the largest deposit of asphalt in the world, discovered in 1595 by Sir Walter Raleigh, who used the pitch to caulk his ships. Often described as resembling a gigantic parking lot, the lake covers approximately 89 acres.

The Northern Range

Mount St. Benedict: The ridges and river valleys on the southern side of the Northern Range resemble the folds of an accordion. Almost any part of the mountains has great hiking and birding, but the areas most frequented are those near picnic, camping, or lodging sites. A popular one near the capital is Mount Tabor, where the Mount St. Benedict Guest House caters to bird-watchers and naturalists. A road there leads past the Abbey of St. Benedict to the peak of Mount Tabor at 1,800 feet. Lookouts along the way provide fabulous views of Port of Spain and the Caroni Plains. The trees around the guesthouse and the abbey, particularly in the early morning and late afternoon, are alive with so many birds you can see three dozen or more species on a two-hour walk. For guided tours, contact **Pax Nature Tours** (Mount St. Benedict, Tunapana; 868-662-4084; fax: 868-645-4234; www.paxguesthouse.com).

Over the next ridge in the Caura Valley, the Forestry Division has a recreation center with picnic facilities, and over the next ridge, a road along the Arouca River leads to Lopinot, the valley's first coffee and cocoa plantation restored as a tourist attraction.

At Arima, a 10-mile road crosses from the south side of the Northern Range to Blanchisseuse

on the Caribbean coast. The spectacularly scenic route climbs from sea level to about 2,000 feet in 387 turns, passing through forests laced with gigantic bamboos and carpeted with ferns. Logging tracks and old plantation roads branch from the main road and make good trails on which to explore the rain forest. Arima has about three hundred descendants of the Arawaks, the Amerindians who inhabited Trinidad when the Spaniards arrived. They have a social organization that is trying to keep their heritage alive. The most easily recognized tradition is their distinctive straw craft, similar in design and fabric to that of the Caribs in Dominica and Guyana.

Asa Wright Nature Centre: Deep in a rain forest on the slopes of the Northern Range overlooking the Arima Valley is the Asa Wright Nature Centre (868-667-4655; fax: 868-667-4540; 800-426-7810; www.asawright.org; dayvisit@asawright .org), a private institution unique in the Caribbean. Established in 1967 on the Spring Hill Estate, it is a former coffee, citrus, and cocoa plantation at 1,200 feet, located 7.5 miles north of Arima. The center includes a bird sanctuary and wildlife reserve with an inn (in the former estate house) and hiking trails that day visitors may use upon payment of a small fee. Guided hikes are available at 10:30 a.m. and 1:30 p.m. Hours: 9 a.m. to 5 p.m.

The **William Beebe Tropical Research Station** (www.wbtrs.org), begun by Dr. William Beebe of the New York Zoological Society in 1950, is part of the Nature Centre.

The inn's veranda, surrounded by dense tropical vegetation, is like an aviary, except that the birds come and go freely from the surrounding rain forest. The most celebrated species here is a nesting colony of oilbirds, which make their home in a cave located on the property. The oilbirds are found only here and in the northern parts of South America.

The center's five trails, ranging from half-hour strolls to three-hour hikes, are designed to maximize viewing of particular species. The fee for day visitors: US$10 adults, $6 children. Lunch is served from noon to 1 p.m. for TT$140, Sun TT$200. Reservations necessary. Located, about one-and-a-half hours' drive from Port of Spain, excursions to the center are available from travel companies in the capital. After crossing the ridge, the Arima-Blanchisseuse Road descends through a pass into the valley with magnificent views of the Northern Range and the Caribbean. In recent years, the once-secluded Blanchisseuse area has become a popular weekend getaway, with holiday homes and guest-houses. The coast is scalloped with small bays and beaches set dramatically at the foot of rain-forest-clad mountains. Small beachside bars offer lunch and shark-and-bake, a specialty of the north coast. Marianne Bay, where the road ends, is the largest and most popular beach, with a freshwater lagoon at its eastern end.

In Blanchisseuse, **Surf's Country Inn** (868-669-2475), a daytime facility designed as a replica of a 17th-century ranch cottage, has a bar, restaurant, and tea terrace overlooking the Caribbean Sea. You will find nature trails and boats available for a cruise along the north coast. Las Cuevas is about 5 miles to the west. The northeast region is wild; even local naturalists do not go hiking without guides.

Matura Beach: Matura, on the Atlantic coast, is the nesting beach of the leatherback turtle. The species is protected, and local environmentalists maintain a turtle watch during the nesting season, from Mar to Sept, when hunting is prohibited. Black with pink and white spots on its neck and flippers, the leatherback is the largest of the sea turtles and grows up to 7 feet in length and more than 1,000 pounds in weight.

Brigand Hill: The best location in eastern Trinidad to enjoy magnificent views and see lots of birds is Brigand Hill, a little-known hilltop near the town of Plum. Once a cocoa plantation overtaken by rain forest, it is now a reserve with a forestry station and lighthouse. The diverse concentration of colorful fruit and flowering trees and forest vegetation attracts an enormous variety of birds. From the summit you have a sweeping view of the east coast from Manzanilla Point on the north to Point Radix on the south, one of the longest stretches of golden sands in the Caribbean.

On the coast the Tourist Board maintains bathing and picnicking facilities. An undertow makes parts of the coast dangerous; ask locally before going into the water to swim, and always stay close to shore. This narrow strip of land, shaded for

17 miles by an estimated one million coconut palm trees, separates the waves of the Atlantic from the great expanse of the Nariva plains and swamp. There is no organized boat trip here such as those at Caroni Swamp, but there is a great variety of birds, easily spotted by the road and along the rice paddies that are characteristic of the area.

Shopping

Local crafts, good art, and an array of fashions by local designers are the attractions of shopping in Trinidad. Among the best crafts are wood carvings, hand-beaten copper, dolls, straw products, steel drums, paintings, fabrics, and jewelry. Don't overlook the locally made rum and world-famous Angostura bitters, which can be purchased at the Angostura shop in the port.

Port of Spain's main downtown shopping area is Frederick Street and nearby streets. The stores more likely to be of interest to visitors, however, are in the port terminal and at the Trinidad Hilton (Lady Young Road) and the Hotel Normandie (10 Nook Ave., St. Ann's), which have quality shops. Shopping malls, popular with Trinis, are found on Frederick and Edward Streets in town and Long Circular Road and Western Main Road in the suburbs and elsewhere.

Art and Artists: Art Creators (Aldegonda Park, Apartment 402, 7 St. Ann's Rd., St. Ann's, Port of Spain; phone/fax: 868-624-4369) is one of the town's most serious galleries, with year-round exhibits of aspiring artists and established Trinidadian ones such as Boscoe Holders. Other galleries include **Aquarela Galleries** (Suite 4, 1A Dere St., Port of Spain; 868-625-5982; fax: 868-624-5217; gml@wow.net); **101 Art Gallery** (101 Tragarete Rd., Woodbrook, Port of Spain; 868-628-4081; www.101artgallery.com). The Falls at **West Mall** has art exhibits and craft markets throughout the year. The **Art Society of Trinidad and Tobago** (868-623-5461; www.artsocietytt.org) has information about exhibitions and has sample photos of artists work.

Books and Maps: RIK Services/Trinidad Book World (87 Queen St.) and **Ishmael M. Khan & Sons** (20 Henry St.) are leading bookshops.

Popular travel guides on Trinidad and Tobago are available in shops at the Trinidad Hilton and **Paria Publishing Co.**, which has a branch at the port terminal.

Clothing and Accessories: The most attractive fashions by local designers are found at the boutiques that make up the **Village Hall,** the shopping gallery of the Hotel Normandie. These include batiks at the 3rd Door. Cool, breezy linen casuals are the trademark of one of Trinidad's best-known designers at **Meiling** (made to order at Satchel's House, 6 Carlos Street; 868-627-6975; www.meilinginc.com). Meiling's fashions are sold at the **Kapok Hotel** (868-628-6205). **Radical** (The Falls at West Mall, Western Main Road; 868-632-5800), with several locations around Port of Spain, is something of the Gap of the Caribbean and carries men's and women's clothing.

Crafts and Souvenirs: Athea Bastien (The Batique; 43 Sydenham Ave., St. Ann's; 868-624-3274) is Trinidad's best-known batik artist. Others are **Bambu Ltd.** (The Falls at West Mall, 16–18 Cotton Hill, St. Clair; 868-628-4003; fax: 637-6324) and **Pamela Marshall** (Poui Design) (Ellerslie Plaza, Boissiere Village, Maraval; 868-622-5597; pouides@tstt.net.tt). The **Trinidad and Tobago Blind Welfare Association** (118 Duke St.; 868-624-4675) has gifts, accessories, and household products of rattan, grass, and banana leaves made by the blind. **Art Potters Ltd.** (port terminal) specializes in pottery. **Craft Mart** (Long Circular Mall and port) stocks crafts and souvenirs.

Jewelry: Baksh Bros (66 Prince St.) has fine silver work. **Kanhai Ragubir** (13 Eastern Main Rd., Curepe) is a jeweler in the port terminal.

Music: Calypso and steel-band CDs and DVDs can be found at **Rhyner's Record Shop** (www.rhyners.com), which has branches at Piarco International Airport.

Dining and Restaurants

Perhaps nothing reflects the multinational heritage of this dual-island nation better than its cuisine, which includes ingredients and dishes from its Spanish, French, Dutch, African, Indian, Chinese, Syrian, Portuguese, and English ancestry. Add to this melting pot an abundance of exotic fruits, herbs, and vegetables—and an imaginative people whose urge to create is as lively in the kitchen as it is in the costumes of Carnival. Moderate means less than US$20. Check locally for days restaurants are open.

Aura (51 Cipriani Blvd; 868-627-AURA; www.auratt.com). The newcomer was an almost instant favorite, especially for seafood for which chef Paul Mowser is well known. Moderately expensive.

Chaud (2 Queen's Park West, 868-623-0375; www.chaudkm.com). One of the city's newest restaurants offers Caribbean fusion, fine dining by one of the country's best known chefs, Khalid Mohammed, celebrated for his innovative, eclectic cuisine. Very expensive.

Melange (Ariapita Avenue, Woodbrook; 868-628-8687), noted for nouvelle Creole cuisine, is set in a colonial house painted blue. Expensive.

Solimar (6 Nook Ave., St. Ann; phone/fax: 868-624-6267) features local specialties and international cuisine in an open-air garden. Moderate.

Tamnak Thai (13 Queen's Park East; 868-625-0647), a restaurant in a renovated mansion facing the Savannah and decorated with Thai artifacts, is the setting for delicious Thai and fusion cuisine. Rooftop bar. Expensive.

Tiki Village (Kapok Hotel, 16 Cotton Hill; 868-622-5765; www.kapokhotel.com). An excellent Chinese restaurant atop a hotel that has been in the Chan family since 1928. Moderate.

Veni Mange (67A Ariapita Ave., Woodbrook; phone/fax: 868-624-4597; www.venimange.com). Cordon Bleu–trained Allyson Hennessy and her exuberant sister, Rosemary Hezekiah, prepare some of the best food in town from this small Victorian house. Not to be missed are specialties such as callaloo soup; stewed beef with eggplant fritters; Trinidad hot-pot; and oildown, a classic West Indian dish of breadfruit, pigs' tails, salted beef, and coconut. Lunch, weekdays 11:30 a.m. to 3 p.m. Dinner, Wed and Fri from 7 p.m. On Fri people linger in an informal late-afternoon party atmosphere. No credit cards. Moderate.

Nightlife

Evenings in Port of Spain start when people else-where are ready for bed. Clubs pulsate with calypso and soca, and major hotels have everything from piano bars to limbo and steel bands. Check local publications to learn what's happening.

Queen's Hall (St. Ann's Road, off the northeast corner of Queen's Park Savannah; 868-624-1284; www.queenshalltt.com) is a venue for popular shows, concerts, and other cultural events. Movie Towne (www.movietowne.com), a short distance from the port, is a new multiplex with a casino, movie theater, restaurants, and clothing and other shops.

Trinidad Theatre Workshop (3 Hart St.; 868-624-4681) produces plays that are staged in Trinidad and other Caribbean islands.

Mas Camp Pub (Ariapita Avenue and French Street; 868-627-4042) has calypso, pan, and danc-ing on weekends and live calypso talent night on Wed. When the Mighty Sparrow—one of the world's best-known calypsonians—is in town, his Hideaway in Petit Valley is a great place to get into calypso.

Sports

Beaches/Swimming: The most popular beaches near the capital are on the Caribbean coast from Maracas Bay to Las Cuevas, where there are snack bars and changing facilities. Gas-par, Monos, and other islands off the northwest peninsula are popular for day trips. On the east coast, Salibia is the main resort, and south of Man-zanilla a palm-fringed beach stretches for 17 miles, but bathers must be careful about undertow. Don't overlook rivers and pools by waterfalls in the moun-tains, where there are picnic facilities.

Boating: Powerboat racing is a popular sport, with the major race, a 90-mile run between Trini-dad and Tobago, in Aug. Sailing is big but only as a private sport. The Trinidad and Tobado Yatching Association (P.O. Box 2852, TT Post, Chaguara-mas; 868-634-4938; www.ysatt.org; www.ttsailing .org) holds races almost weekly and welcomes members of other yacht clubs with prior arrange-ments. Several tour companies offer cruises from Port of Spain to islands off the northwest penin-sula, usually stopping at Gaspar Grande or one of the islands for a buffet lunch and swim. Contact Travel Trinidad and Tobago (868-625-2201).

Deep-Sea Fishing: The Bocas Islands off Trinidad are the prime location for deep-sea fishing. Among the companies that arrange sportfishing trips are Classic Tours (868-680-7993; www.classic toursltd.com) and Island Yacht Charters (868-637-7389; fax: 868-628-0437; pdella@trinidad.net). For information, contact Trinidad and Tobado Game Fishing Association (59 Pinewood Dr., Diego Mar-tin; 868-632-6608; www.ttgfa.com).

Golf: Millennium Lakes Golf & Country Club (Trincity; 868-640-8337; www.millenniumlakes.com) is Trinidad's newest 18 hole championship course (6,500 yards, par 71). Located near the airport, its clubhouse has a pro shop, restaurant, sports bar, and locker rooms. Greens fees: TT$400 per person including shared cart; club rentals, TT$150. The 18-hole Moka Golf Course (6,705 yards), contact Trinidad and Tobado Golf Association (868-629-7127; www.trinidadandtobagogolfassociation.com; ttga@live.com).

Hiking: Trinidad's Northern Range is honey-combed with trails. Monthly field trips are arranged by the Trinidad and Tobago Field Naturalists' Club (c/o The Secretary, P.O. Box 642, Port of Spain; 868-624-8017; www.ttfnc.org; admin@ttfnc .org). Visitors can be accommodated with prior arrangements. Its members are also the best source of information on trails. Recently, some tour compa-nies offering hiking, birding, and nature excursions have blossomed. Among them are Caribbean Dis-covery Tours (see Shore Excursions earlier in this chapter), Paria Springs (www.pariasprings.com), and David Rooks Nature Tours (868-631-1630; www.rookstobago.com). Another useful source on guided nature tours and hiking is the Forestry Division (Long Circular Road, Port of Spain; 868-622-3217). For Chaguaramas, Chaguaramas Development Authority Guided Tours (868-634-4364; www.chagdev.com).

Kayaking: The Kayak Center (Williams Bay; 868-633-7871; kayak@wow.net) and Kayak Adventures (7 St. Vincent, Port of Spain;

868-625-5472) offer rentals and a variety of excursions.

Surfing: The north and northeast coasts are the main areas for surfing, a popular sport here. At Maracas Bay wave heights up to 10 feet are best for bodysurfing. The northwestern end of Las Cuevas, known as "the Bowl," has strong wave action for experienced surfers. Damiens Bay, at Blanchisseuse, has the most consistent surf, with waves from 4 to 13 feet. For information, contact **Surfing Association of Trinidad and Tobado** (92 Edward St.; 868-625-6463; www.surfingtt.blogspot.com; onamission420@yahoo.com).

Windsurfing: The main areas for windsurfing are Chaguaramas Bay, on the west side of the capital, and the north coast. Contact the **Windsurfing Association of Trinidad and Tobago** (32 Dundonald St., Port of Spain; 868-659-2457).

Tobago on Your Own

www.visittobago.gov.tt;
www.tobagotoday.com

Cloaked almost from end to end in deep green foliage brightened by flowering trees and colorful tropical flowers, tiny Tobago is an enchanted island scalloped with some of the Caribbean's most idyllic beaches and encircled by incredibly beautiful aqua waters. This quiet, tranquil Eden of tropical splendor rises almost directly from the sea to about 2,000 feet in the Main Ridge, a mountain spine down the center of the island. From the steep slopes covered with magnificent rain forests, hundreds of tiny streams carve their way through the mountains and cascade over rocky cliffs to the sea. The foothills are covered with cocoa and banana plantations and orchards.

Tobago has long been ambiguous toward tourists—most of whom come from Trinidad. An array of stop-and-go development projects by the government in Trinidad has left this out-of-the-way Nirvana with an assortment of rustic inns, funky guesthouses, and overpriced tourist-class hotels. In 1990 the island welcomed its first deluxe hotel, Grafton Beach Resort, in two decades. Yet, in this day of overdevelopment in Paradise, Trinidad's benign neglect may have been a blessing in disguise.

A cruise-ship dock is in Scarborough, the island's main town; some ships dock off the western tip and tender passengers to Pigeon Point, a spit of land with a picture-perfect, palm-fringed, white-sand beach overlooking the Caribbean, within walking distance of many hotels. It has bathing facilities for day visitors (for a fee).

Occasionally, cruise ships dock off the village of Charlottesville in the northeastern end of Tobago and tender passengers to the jetty located in the center of the village.

Tobago has a limited network of roads, which wind along the coast and twist through the mountains. The newest roads are excellent, the old ones are terrible, and others have simply been abandoned. One road crosses the Main Ridge between the leeward and windward coasts, but no road completely circles the island.

You can rent a car or hire a taxi for the day. In planning an excursion, be aware that distances are deceiving, due to the nature of the terrain and the roads. For example, the 25-mile drive from Pigeon Point along the windward coast to Speyside can take more than one-and-a-half hours.

A Driving Tour of Tobago

Scarborough, about 8 miles northeast of Pigeon Point, is a quiet West Indian village with a small botanic garden and a Handicraft Center (Bacolet Street). Fort King George, a well-restored fortification built by the British in 1777, overlooks the town and provides a fabulous view of the Atlantic, or windward, coast. The **Tobago Museum,** housed in the Barrack Guard House, has Amerindian artifacts, military relics, and documents from the colonial period. The former officer's mess houses a craft shop and the military hospital has the National Fine Arts Centre which displays Tobago art and sculpture. Hours: Mon to Fri, 9 a.m. to 5 p.m. Admission: TT$5. Its other historic buildings are St. Andrew's Church, constructed in 1819, and the Courthouse, which dates from 1825.

Directly north of Pigeon Point on the Caribbean, or leeward, coast and across the island from Scarborough is Plymouth, Tobago's second town. It, too,

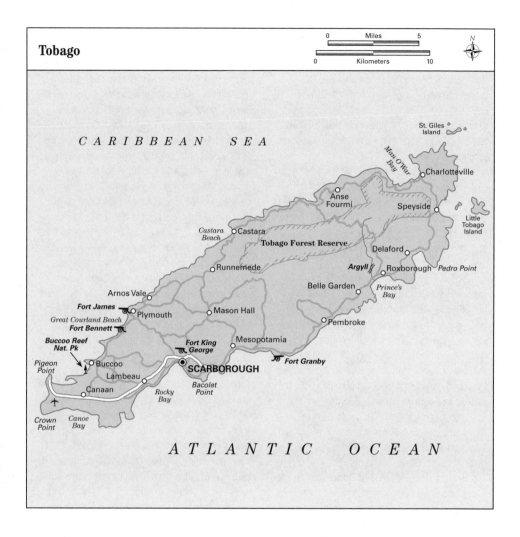

Miles

Kilometers

CARIBBEAN SEA

St. Giles
Island

Man O'War
Bay

Charlotteville

Anse
Fourmi

Speyside

Little
Tobago
Island

Castara
Beach

Castara

Tobago Forest Reserve

Delaford

Runnemede

Argyll

Roxborough

Pedro Point

Belle Garden

*Prince's
Bay*

Arnos Vale

Fort James

Plymouth

Mason Hall

Great Courland Beach

Fort Bennett

Pembroke

**Buccoo Reef
Nat. Pk**

**Fort King
George**

Mesopotamia

*Pigeon
Point*

Buccoo

Fort Granby

Lambeau

SCARBOROUGH

Canaan

*Bacolet
Point*

*Rocky
Bay*

*Crown
Point*

*Canoe
Bay*

ATLANTIC   OCEAN

has a historic fort, Fort James, built in 1768. One of the island's prettiest strands is just south of the town: Great Courland Bay, better known as Turtle Beach for the turtles who come to nest here in Apr and May.

Buccoo Reef National Park/Buccoo Reef Trust: In the quiet waters between Pigeon Point and Buccoo Bay is the Buccoo Reef National Park, a sea-and-land reserve with shallow-water reefs in the form of a wide horseshoe that shelters the inner reef and a lagoon at the center, where the water is less than 30 feet deep. An area of exceptionally clear water on the east is known as Nylon Pool. The gardens have a great variety of coral—staghorn,

starlet, brain, sea fans, and others—that attracts an enormous array of fish.

At low tide the water in parts of the reef is only about 3 feet deep, a feature that has made it popular with snorkelers and nonswimmers who, unfortunately, walk around the reef in sneakers. Although there have been laws on the books for almost three decades to protect the reef, the government has never seriously enforced them, and the reef is in great danger of being destroyed by misuse. The Crusoe Reef Society, a marine research and conservation group in Trinidad, has tried hard to pressure the government for greater conservation measures but has had only limited results. The **Buccoo Reef Trust** (Cowie's Building, Auchenskeoch Road, Carnbee, Tobago, 868-635-2000, fax: 868-639-7333; www.buccooreef.org), established in 2004, was awarded the Environmental Management Authority's Green Leaf Award in 2007 for its contribution to environmental conservation and protection in Trinidad and Tobago. Perhaps that's a reflection that some progress is being made.

Bon Accord, another lagoon on the south side of the park, is edged by mangroves which host a great number of birds, including the rufous-vented chachalaca, Tobago's national bird. A trail east of Pigeon Point borders the mangroves. Glass-bottom boat and snorkeling trips to Buccoo Reef leave daily from Pigeon Point.

East of Plymouth is **Adventure Farm and Nature Reserve** (Arnes Vale Road, 868-639-2839; fax: 868-639-4157; www.adventure-ecovillas.com), a 12-acre estate and organic farm with birds, butterflies, iguanas, mango and citrus orchards, and nature trails. The reserve, which claims to have the largest number of hummingbirds on the island, has a bird observation area. Admission: US$5, per person, half-price for children. Guided tours are available for groups only on request. Mon to Sat 7 a.m. to 5 p.m., Sun by arrangement. Visitors can also purchase homemade drinks from fresh organic fruits in season on the estate.

Grafton Caledonian Bird Sanctuary: Grafton Estate was a working plantation until it was hit by a hurricane in 1963. The damage was so extensive that the owner, Eleanor Alefounder, decided not to restore it. Another consequence of the hurricane was that the island's birds were desperately short of food. Recognizing this, Alefounder started a feeding program and turned part of her estate into a wildlife sanctuary. After her death in 1983, the estate was placed in trust to preserve the reserve and maintain the feeding program. Birds are fed by the caretaker, James Sampson, daily at 8 a.m. and 4 p.m., when visitors can see the beautiful mot-mot, cocrico, blue-gray tanagers, bananaquit, doves, and more. On request, Sampson, who is a mine of information on the birdlife of Tobago and the estate, takes visitors on property trails to spot more wildlife. Located north of Plymouth, the entrance is marked by the sanctuary sign across from the Grand Courlan Hotel. There is no charge, but contributions are welcome.

Kimme Museum (868-639-0257; www.luisekimme.com; hoppingstick@tstt.net.tt) Located near Bethel village overlooking the Mt. Irvine Golf Course, the museum houses a collection of one hundred incredible, unique works of German sculptor Luise Kimme, who has lived in Tobago since 1979. Her unique, colorful, larger-than-life size sculptures—some 14 feet high—of Caribbean dancers, folklore and religious characters, dancing couples, Nijinsky ballet dancers, and mythological figures, are carved out of oak, lime, cypress, and cedar wood; some are created in bronze. The fascinating sculptures capture the essence of the Tobago people and their culture. The museum, locally called "The Castle" for its fancy, bazaar architecture, is very much worth a visit. The studio and workshop are only open on Sun, from 10 a.m. to 2 p.m.; visits at other times can be arranged. Entrance: TT$20 (US$3.50) per person.

The Leeward Coast

Tobago's entire Caribbean coast is made up of one beautiful beach after another—some with resorts, others untouched. North of Plymouth, Arnos Vale, a tiny cove with a hillside hotel, is one of the most romantic spots in the Caribbean. Once part of a sugar plantation, the hotel's oldest building is completely encased in tropical foliage like a tree house, with a choir of birds to serenade it. Sunsets here are incredible. The idyllic cove has a fine coral reef suitable for snorkelers and novice divers. North of Arnos Vale an abandoned road of about 2 miles is now a hiking trail to Golden Lane and Culloden Bay.

Arnos Vale: West of Arnos Vale on the road between Scarborough and Golden Lane, the ruins of the Arnos Vale plantation (with a waterwheel and other machinery bearing 1857 markings) are the centerpiece of a lovely culture park and museum created by the owners of the Arnos Vale Hotel. There is a guided nature trail through the surrounding woods to a waterfall. Hours: daily 8:30 a.m. to 10:30 p.m.; (868) 660-0815. Admission: TT$10. The open-air **Arnos Vale Waterwheel Restaurant** (Franklyn Road, 868-660-0815; www.arnosvalehotel.com; reservations@arnosvalehotel.com) has an eclectic menu of local specialties and light fare.

Tobago has begun to develop specialized eco-resorts that you can visit. **Footprints Eco-Resort** (868-660-0118; 800-814-1396; www.footprintseco-resort.com), at the end of a long, steep road from Golden Lane to Culloden Bay, opened in 1997 on a magnificent 61 acres surrounded by hills and over-looking the sea. The inn uses solar panels, local timber, and recycled piping; produces much of its food; and offers great birding and snorkeling. The resort has two nature trails Where non-resident guests may wander on their own.

Inland, at the end of a rough road from the village of Runnemede is **Cuffie River Nature Retreat** (Scarborough, Tobago; phone/fax: 868-660-0505; www.cuffieriver.com) on a 21-acre site perched above the gently flowing Cuffie River, a tributary of the Courland River. The center, on the edge of the Forest Reserve amidst lush bamboo groves, wild heliconia, and cocoa trees, has locally made furnishings and fixtures and is an ideal center for birding and hiking. It serves local dishes based on fresh produce. The retreat offers walks through their nature trails for a TT$50 fee, and lunch is available to nonresident guests for TT$80.

North of Golden Lane along the Caribbean coast, the road snakes through forested mountains along steep cliffs that fall almost directly to the sea. From **Mount Dillon,** a windswept promontory rising 800 feet above the sea, you can have a spectacular view of the leeward coast with Pigeon Point in the southwest and Trinidad on the horizon. Behind the white-sand beaches rise the green slopes of the Main Ridge.

Castara, a tiny village with a popular swimming beach, has bathing facilities. There are a few local restaurants and rustic inns. Farther north, Englishman's Bay, Parlatuvier Bay, and Bloody Bay—lovely enclaves of white-sand beaches shaded by giant ferns, bamboo, and palms—can be reached by short trails from the main road. Other trails inland lead to pretty waterfalls.

Main Ridge Rain Forest Trail: North of the island's midgirth a good road crosses the Main Ridge between Parlatuvier Bay, on the leeward coast, and Roxborough, on the windward side. At the crest of the ridge is the entrance to the Main Ridge Rain Forest Trail, the most accessible and best-maintained trail in the Tobago Forest

Reserve, the oldest forest preserve in the Western Hemisphere (established in 1765). The entrance is marked by Bloody Bay Lookout Site, where the Forestry Department has a small cabin with a map of the trail. The lookout sits high above Bloody Bay and offers magnificent views.

From here a looped footpath of three hours winds down the steep slopes through the rain forest along a stream that empties into Bloody Bay. After the trail crosses the stream, it levels out and returns on an easy walking path to the eastern entrance on the main highway, about 2 miles west of the lookout.

The Windward Coast

Between Scarborough and Speyside, a fishing village near the north end of the island, the Windward Road hugs the serpentine coast, overhung with trees laden with mango, lime, and papaya as it weaves through fishing villages and bayside hamlets. Almost any road into the mountains leads to waterfalls, wooded slopes, and beautiful vistas. Roxborough, the largest town on this stretch, is the access point to the 175 foot **Argyle Waterfalls,** the island's highest falls, which drops in stages and at the bottom forms a pool where you can swim. The walk to the falls from the car park area takes about twenty minutes. Admission: TT$30 including guide. Further along at the 110-foot Kings Bay Waterfall, the Tourist Board has trails and facilities, but unfortunately very little water falls except during the rainy season.

Speyside: Set against the thick forests of the Main Ridge, the little fishing town of Speyside overlooks Goat Island, one of the most unusual dive sites in the Caribbean, which the Tobago government bought to make it into a nature reserve. A mile offshore is **Little Tobago,** a 280-acre bird sanctuary, also known as Bird of Paradise Island. There in 1909 an Englishman introduced four dozen birds of paradise, hoping to establish a safe haven for the species, which was being decimated by poachers supplying feathers to the European fashion market. The birds lived until 1963, when a hurricane devastated the island. Seven birds survived, but none have been sighted since 1983. The island has many other birds and wildlife and has been a sanctuary since 1934. Nature trails lead to the eastern side of the island, where the beautiful tropic bird nests in the cliffs. Often birds on their nest can be observed and photographed at very close range.

A boat from Speyside to Little Tobago takes about twenty minutes and is often a rough crossing over white-capped seas. Be prepared for wet landings, as there are no docks, and take water because there is no supply on Little Tobago. Arrangements are best made through a local guide or the Blue Waters Inn in Speyside.

Charlotteville: At the north end of Tobago on the leeward coast is Charlotteville, a fishing village on Man o' War Bay. Directly behind the wide horseshoe bay rises heavily forested 1,890-foot Pigeon Peak, the tallest mountain. Due to its isolation, Charlotteville has kept the island's folkways more than any location on Tobago. The Man o' War Bay Cottages on the north side of the bay is a small naturalists' retreat on a 1,000-acre cocoa plantation, open to visitors to wander at will. The road from Charlotteville to L'Anse Fourmi farther south on the leeward coast gives access to a part of Tobago that is truly untouched and making possible a longer route to circle the island. Cruise ships occasionally call here.

Dining and Restaurants

The following restaurants are moderately priced, ranging from about US$10 to $30.

Blue Crab (Main and Robinson Streets, Scarborough; 868-639-2737; http://tobagobluecrab .com). In a hillside house near the harbor, you will find home cooking offered for lunch. Flying fish, curried or rolled around sweet peppers and eggplant, is a specialty, along with homemade ice cream and locally made fruit wines.

Ciao Cafe' Italian Gelato & Bar (Burnett Street, Scarborough, 868-639-3001; www.latartaruga tobago.com) makes two dozen flavors of Italian gelato onsite and serves espresso, cappuccino, and pastries as well as being a wine bar and offering light snacks. Open Mon to Sat 9 a.m. to 10 p.m. and Sun and holidays 5 to 10 p.m.

Jemma's Seaview Kitchen (south of Speyside; 868-660-4066). The day's catch is cooked to order at this rustic beach tavern, where it's enjoyed on a little "tree-house" veranda by the sea. Only a one-room shack a few years ago, Jemma's has grown into the best-known restaurant on the island and something of an institution. If Jemma's is crowded and there's a wait, we are told by some locals that at two nearby restaurants, **Bird Watchers** (868-639-5438), and **Redman Simple,** the food is as good and prices better.

Grafton Beach Resort (Black Rock; 868-639-0191; www.graftonbeachresorttobago.com). One of Tobago's main hotels has a delightful terrace restaurant open to the breezes. Its buffet and a la carte menu have local specialties and international dishes, and they are all good.

Miss Esmee's stand at Store Bay Beach has great tamarind and sesame balls, coconut muffins, and rôti (Indian burritos stuffed with meat or chicken and flavored with curry). Miss Esmee is no longer with us but her daughter runs the stand. If you are heading in a different direction, ask your driver to stop at his favorite rôti maker. It's sure to be fresh, hot, and mighty good.

Sports

Beaches/Swimming: Almost any place on the island has powder-fine beaches, many that seldom see a footprint. Pigeon Point and Store Bay are the most convenient for ships anchoring off Pigeon Point. Parlatuvier and Bloody Bays, on the Caribbean coast, where bathers arrive by boat or hike in from the main road, are tranquil and secluded.

Biking: Mountain bikes are available for rent from **Paria Springs** (Maraval; 868-628-1525; www .pariasprings.com). Rates: Bike rentals, US$10 per day; 3 hour tour, US$50 per person, 4 hour, US$65 and include bikes, helmet, and an experienced guide. **Mountain Biking Tobago** (Bon Accord, 868-639-9709, cell: 868-681-5695; www.mountainbiking tobago.com) and **Tobago Mountain Bike/Slow Leak Tours** (868-332-5872; www.tobagomountain bike.com) offer fun and challenging mountain bike tours around Tobago. The latter's Web site has tour descriptions, including level of difficulty, prices, and tour guide profiles.

Boating: Island Girl (868-639-7245, www.sail tobago.com) offers day-sail tours on the *Island Girl* catamaran. Tours depart from Mt. Irvine Bay and sail up the Caribbean coast to secluded Cotton Bay. Refreshments and lunch are included. **Tobago Carnival Regatta** (www.sailweek.com) (formerly Angostura Tobago Sail Week), racing in the waters off Tobago in Feb is the biggest sailing event of the year and attracts yachties from around the world.

Birdwatching: See Hiking section.

Deep-Sea Fishing: The north shore of Tobago and the waters around nearby St. Giles Island are the main locations for game fishing. Arrangements must be made in advance through a local travel company. Fishing charters are available from **Dream Catcher** (868-868-680-7457, Bon Accord, Tobago; tobagodreamcatcher@hotmail.com). **Dillon's Fishing Charter** (Crown Point, 868-678-3195) offers year-round sportfishing on a fully-fitted 38-foot Bertram Sportfisherman with Captain Stanley, who counts thirty years experience in these waters, for full day/nine hours, US$700 including food, drinks, all tackle and bait. It also does fishing/cruising combos with four hours of fishing followed by a stop at a secluded beach for swimming while the fish is prepared for you for lunch. Dillon's also has a restaurant where seafood is the specialty. **Frankie Tours and Rentals** (Mt. Irvine Beach, Tobago; 868-631-0369; www.frankietours.com) offers several daily excursions: Deep Sea Fishing, all equipment provided, four persons maximum, US$350 half day, US$550 full day; Shark Fishing, four persons, five hours, US$400; Fly Fishing, two persons maximum, five hours, US$200.

Golf: The 18-hole championship **Mount Irvine Golf Course** (6,800 yards, par 72) at the Mount Irvine Hotel (868-639-8737; www.mtirvine.com, mtirvine@tstt.net.tt) is about 5 miles from Pigeon Point. One of the Caribbean's most scenic golf courses, it is situated on 125 landscaped acres of gentle rolling hills overlooking the sea. The clubhouse, which is the headquarters of the Tobago Golf Club, is on a promontory with superb views. It has changing rooms, pro shop, and restaurant. Greens fees are US$30 for 9 holes; US$48 for 18 holes; cart, US$20 and $36; caddy, US$7 and $18. **Tobago Plantations Golf and Country Club** (7,000 yards, par 72), is the island's only

PGA-designed course. Created by architects Bob Hunt and Narcus Blackburn of PGA Management Ltd, its Golf Academy is staffed by PGA-qualified pros and offers all levels of instruction; there's a pro shop, with rentals. Greens fees: 18 holes US$95; 9 holes US$65 (868-639-8000; www.tobago plantations.com).

Hiking/Birding and Nature Tours: Tobago offers endless opportunities for hiking. The most accessible is the Main Ridge Rain Forest Trail, a loop off the main highway between Bloody Bay and Roxborough. You can take it as a short walk of an hour from its eastern entrance or try a three-hour hike from the western one. **Environment Tobago** (868-290-3797; www.sos-tobago.org), a local environment organization, arranges free hikes to interesting locations monthly on Sun mornings. The hikes are meant to be fun and an opportunity to meet new people and join Environment Tobago. Contact for information and the current month's hike. Other nature tour specialists on Tobago are **Newton George** (868-660-5463, cell: 868-754-7881; www.newtongeorge.com); **Wayne Gray** (868-780-7020; www.waynesworld-tours.com), who specializes in bird watching and Tobago's natural history; **Jeb McEachnie**, (868-660-6228, cell: 868-757-4281; www.angelfire.com/nt2/naturestouch2), who offers bird watching, turtle watching, and nature tours and has more than fifteen years of experience; and **David Rooks Nature Tours** (Scarborough; 868-631-1630; cell: 868-352-1222; www.rookstobago.com), headed by Rooks, Tobago's best-known ornithologist and nature tour guide. His Web site has bird lists, tour descriptions, and prices.

Nature Lovers of Tobago (868-639-4559; cell 868-767-9298; www.tobagobirding.com) is headed by Darren Henry, a dendrologist (one who studies trees) and birding tour guide. His Web site has bird lists and photos, plus information on his tours, which range from two hours to full day, and prices. Henry, a trained forester and certified tour guide with a vast knowledge of Tobago's flora and fauna, is a group leader for the Audubon Society's annual Christmas bird count in Tobago.

Peter Cox Tobago Nature Tours (Milford Road, Canaan; 868-385-3909, cell: 868-751-5822;

www.tobagonaturetours.com) provides a wide variety of individualized (no buses except by request) nature and sightseeing tours to the main attractions on Tobago and to Little Tobago, including leatherback turtle–watching tours during the nesting season (Mar to Aug). Tour descriptions and prices can be found on the company's Web site. The birdwatching section of the Web site (www.simply tobago.com) has the most complete information on birding in Tobago, as well as Trinidad, I have found. It also includes an extensive daily diary and bird list written by a contributor.

Kayaking: Tobago Sea Kayak Experience (Charlotteville; 868-660-6186, www.seakayak tobago.com) has kayaking excursions that leave from either Man o' War Bay in Charlotteville or from Conrado Hotel on the road to Pigeon Point. The excursions range from an instructional program and some kayaking for US$40, to a half day for novices to a full day geared to experienced paddlers and including kayaking and hiking into the rain forest and lunch for US$60.

Snorkeling/Scuba Diving: Tobago is almost completely surrounded by shallow-water reefs, most within swimming distance from shore and easily accessible to snorkelers and novice divers. Marine life is rich in color and the water exceptionally clear. Tobago was one of the earliest locations to be discovered by pioneer divers five decades ago, but the advanced skill needed for diving the best sites has left it as something of a last frontier. It offers great diversity, but the most interesting feature for advanced divers is drift diving.

The main area for snorkelers and novice divers is Buccoo Reef and the reefs along the Caribbean coast. Grouper Ground, on the western tip of the island opposite Pigeon Point, has gentle drift diving for experienced divers. Here basket sponges are the size of bathtubs. The clarity of the waters makes it a delight for underwater photographers.

The northeast coast around Goat Island offers some of the finest diving in the West Indies. Due to the strong surf and surge, the reefs have been dubbed "Flying Reefs" and are only for advanced divers with experience in drift diving. Tobago has dive operators at Pigeon Point, Crown Reef, Turtle Beach, and Speyside. A recompression chamber

is in operation at Roxborough. The **Association of Tobago Dive Operators** (868-660-5445; fax: 868-639-4416) sets standards for membership and operations. Among the members are **Undersea Tobago** (Coco Reef Resort, Crown Point; 868-631-2626), **Aquamarine Dive** (Blue Waters Inn, Speyside; 868-660-5445), **Tobago Dive Experience Manta Lodge** (Speyside and Arnos Vale Hotel; 868-660-4888; fax: 868-660-5030; www.tobago diveexperience.com).

Windsurfing/Kitesurfing: Pigeon Point beach, protected by Buccoo Reef, is an ideal tropical lagoon for windsurfing and kitesurfing. The main season is mid-Dec to June with winds averaging 12 to 20 knots from east to northeast. Kitesurfing is fairly new to Tobago. The lagoon is good for beginners, but more adventurous conditions for experienced kitesurfers are found on windward side of the island at Rockley Bay. **Radical Sports Ltd.** (868-631-5150, cell 868-688-2628; www.radical sportstobago.com), at the northern end of Pigeon Point Heritage Park, has kitesurfing and windsurfing equipment for rent. Board and rig rental, TT$250 for one hour or TT $350 for three hours. It also offers kitesurfing lessons, kayaking, and other water sports.

Festivals and Celebrations
Carnival in Trinidad

Trinidadians say they have two seasons: Carnival and the rest of the year. **Carnival in Trinidad** is the biggest, most colorful and creative of all Caribbean Carnivals and the one after which the others are patterned. Carnival is not simply another event, but a celebration of life—a folk festival, sports competition, art exhibit, and dance and music concert rolled into one, involving every age at every level of society. It's street theater where, after months of work, all the island's talent and energy are released in a few delirious days of mirth and madness. It's CAAR-NA-VAAL!

Although Carnival culminates in the last two days before Ash Wed and the start of Lent in the Catholic tradition, Carnival in Trinidad actually begins the day after the new year is born. The tradition began in 1783, when French settlers and others who were given land grants in Trinidad arrived in large numbers, and a festive season from Christmas to Ash Wed was initiated. Masked bands of people, often accompanied by musicians, paraded through the streets, stopping to visit friends at homes where elaborate balls were given. But this was sport for the privileged. "Free persons of color," as free blacks and mixed races were known, were not forbidden to mask, but they did not participate in the affairs of high society. Black slaves were prohibited by law from joining the festivities.

The most radical change came with the emancipation of the slaves in 1833, when the celebrations became the people's festival and the scene shifted from fancy dress balls for a few to the masses in the street. With it also came a confluence of national traditions that, over the century, became as mixed as a pot of callaloo, often totally reversing their original meanings. The music of the old bamboo bands was replaced by rudimentary pan bands whose metallic tones were beat out on dustpans, paint cans, and any other metal objects on which innately talented musicians could improvise rhythm and tone.

During World War II Carnival was suspended, but in the backyards of Trinidad the pan technique continued to develop (leading to the term panyard), and the number of instruments and their complexity grew. Not everyone embraced them; many people branded the players as hooligans and tried to prohibit them from playing in the streets.

In 1948 the commercial 55-gallon oil drum appeared in Trinidad for the first time. Soon the discarded drums were being used by pan players who found that tempered steel enabled them to extend their musical range. Rapidly the drums replaced all other pans in use, and a steel band association was formed. The first pan recital, with selections ranging from calypso to the classics, received such acclaim that the respectability of steel band music was assured. Unfortunately, the steel band, which has been an essential element of Carnival, has recently become an endangered species during Carnival parade. Gigantic boom boxes mounted on flatbed trucks now accompany the paraders. The canned music is so loud that steel pans wouldn't stand a chance to be heard, even if they tried. It's having a serious impact on Carnival, too; many

revelers often seem as mechanical and uninspired as the canned music.

Today Mas Bands, as the masqueraders are known, are divided into three sizes—small, medium, and large—with the largest having four thousand people. Large groups are broken down into three dozen or more sections, each costumed differently to portray an element in an overall theme created by the band leader, who must excel as an artist, showman, director, and producer with the genius to choreograph theater on a grand scale. The winner of the Mas Band competition is crowned King of Carnival. What greater honor is there? The best are household names throughout the Caribbean.

Calypso is the very essence of Carnival. Always witty, rich in innuendo and satire, calypso contains a variety of verses followed by a set refrain. The lyrics often satirize island politics, society, and other local matters, so you are likely to miss the biting humor of the calypsonian, but this will not lessen your enjoyment. The music is infectious.

From Dec through the end of Carnival, top calypsonians and two or three dozen hopefuls perform their newest songs nightly at calypso tents. (Years ago the artists performed in outdoor tents and makeshift structures; today's calypsonians hold their shows in theaters with stages, but the term tent remains.) Each calypsonian has his or her own style and fans. The top ones are as well known in the Caribbean as Michael Jackson.

Although the Road Mar, or Carnival Parade, is the greatest spectacle, the competitions for calypsonians, steel bands, and costumed bands are the heart of Carnival activity for Trinis. About three weeks before Carnival, the Steelband Panorama preliminaries are held over two days and bring together as many as one hundred steel orchestras from around the country, each with as many as fifty or one hundred players. The finals are held on the Sat before Carnival, when a dozen or so orchestras compete for the championship.

Kiddies' Carnival, also held on the Sat morning, is when children dressed in full regalia "play mas."

Dimanche Gras: On the Sun before the two last days of Carnival, the finals of three major competitions take place: Calypso Monarch, the best calypsonian of the year; and the King and Queen of Carnival, chosen for the most beautiful, creative, and magnificently costumed male and female masqueraders. The Dimanche Gras show is staged at the Queen's Park Savannah.

Carnival Monday: Dawn, or J'ouvert (French for "the day begins"), is the official start of Carnival Monday and symbolizes the opening of the doors to let King Carnival in. At the end of the Dimanche Gras show, people join the crowds at *fêtes*—public parties that anyone can attend by buying a ticket. (Dozens of *fêtes* are advertised in daily newspapers, many being held at hotels.) On Carnival Monday the *fêtes* end at 4 a.m., when the dawn breaks and people spill into the streets to jump to the music of the steel bands. Everyone—young and old, visitors and Trinis—joins "Joovay" and lets the music move them along.

Carnival Tuesday: Early in the morning bands of brilliantly costumed masqueraders line up for the spectacular parade through the streets of Port of Spain to the Savannah, dancing to the music. Carnival ends at midnight with the "Las Lap," an expression for the wind down of the festivities— the last chance to jump in the streets before King Carnival disappears for another year.

Other Festivals in Trinidad

Steelband Music Festival in Sept/Oct is almost as important as Carnival.

Festival of Hosay, a Muslim observance, is held in Muharram (first month of the Islamic calendar) and commemorates the martyrdom of Hassan and Hussein, the sons of Ali, at the battle of Kerbala in early Islam.

Phagwa or **Holi,** the Hindu Festival of Color, celebrated in Trinidad and Tobago since 1845, takes place on the full moon of Phagun (Feb to Mar), the most beautiful time of the year in North India at the dawn of spring.

Tobago Heritage Festival, held for two weeks beginning in mid-July, is a celebration of Tobago's history and culture, keeping alive the island's traditions.

Bonaire

Miles 0 — 5

Kilometers 0 — 10

N

ATLANTIC

OCEAN

Playa Funchi

Chikitu Beach

▲ Brandaris

Washington Slagbaai National Park

Goto Meer

Boca Onima

Playa Frans

Rincón

Boca Olivia

Flamingo Sanctuary

Karpata

Seru Largu

Boca Chikitu

Lagoon

Hato

Noord di Salina

KLEIN BONAIRE

Antriol

Nikiboko

CARIBBEAN

Tera Kora

KRALENDIJK

SEA

Hoop

Bachelor's Beach

Punt Vierkant

Lac Bay

Sorobon

Pink Beach

Solar Salt Works

Flamingo Sanctuary

Pekel Meer

Lacre Punt

Nature's Child

Bonaire is an unspoiled island with small-town charm. Although it has seen considerable development in the past decade, the island is devoid of slick commercialism. It has only low-rise hotels along white-sand beaches fronting crystal-clear Caribbean waters within a five- to ten-minute ride from town, the port, and the airport.

Shaped like a boomerang, the island is blessed with a bounty of natural beauty preserved in three nature parks—one for flora and wildlife, another for flamingos, and a third for its coastal waters and marine life. Bonaire has been a mecca for scuba divers from around the world since they discovered its fabulous underwater life three decades ago. But even for those who do not dive or have no higher aspirations than snorkeling, there is more than enough to see here to make a visit worthwhile.

The second-largest island of the Netherlands Antilles, Bonaire is located 86 miles east of Aruba and 38 miles east of Curaçao, its sister Dutch island; Venezuela is 50 miles to the south. The island's landscape is almost as diverse as its seascape and has three distinct areas: The north end, mostly covered by the national park, is hilly and greener than the rest of the island and has freshwater and saltwater lakes.

The central region is semiarid, somewhat flatter, and has a landscape similar to the American Southwest. The south end is the flattest part and is covered with salt pans, sand dunes, and mangroves. Less than a mile off Bonaire's south coast is Klein (meaning little) Bonaire, a flat, uninhabited island of about 3 square miles, which acts like a barrier reef protecting the main island's leeward waters.

In contrast to the calm south coast, Bonaire's north side is battered by strong waves that break against black volcanic and coral rocks, as well as unusual coastal formations with grottoes and caves with Indian petroglyphs. Throughout the island the landscape is dominated by enormous candle and other cacti and the ever-present divi-divi tree, whose asymmetrical shape is sculpted by the strong winds that help keep Bonaire cool.

Bonaire, one of the Caribbean's youngest tourist destinations, was discovered five centuries ago in 1499 by Amerigo Vespucci, the Italian navigator for whom the Americas were named. The tranquil island was inhabited by Arawak Indians at the time, and Vespucci named it Bo-nah, from the Arawak word meaning "low land." For the next century the Spaniards attempted to colonize it but failed. Instead they took the Arawak population to Hispaniola as slaves. In the years that followed, the island was colonized by the Dutch, fought over by the French and British, and leased to a New York merchant.

From 1639, and for the next 160 years, the island was managed by the Dutch West India Company, which developed salt production, and the Dutch imported African slaves to work the salt pans. In 1816 the Dutch government took over Bonaire, after an interlude of British control, and it has remained Dutch to the present.

At a Glance

Antiquities	★
Architecture	★★
Art and Artists	★
Beaches	★★★★
Colonial Buildings	★★★
Crafts	★
Cuisine	★★
Culture	★
Dining/Restaurants	★★
Entertainment	★
Forts	★
History	★
Monuments	★
Museums	★
Nightlife	★
Scenery	★★★★
Shopping	★★
Sightseeing	★★★
Sports	★★★★★
Transportation	★

Fast Facts

Population: 12,000

Size: 24 miles long, 3 to 7 miles wide; 112 square miles

Main Town: Kralendijk

Government: Bonaire is part of the Dutch Caribbean, an autonomous region of the Kingdom of the Netherlands. As of Oct 2010, Bonaire's status, along with other members of the former Netherlands Antilles, changes. Bonaire along with Saba and St. Eustatius become overseas municipalities of the Netherlands, giving them a more direct relationship to the Netherlands government.

Entry Requirements: U.S. and Canadian citizens must have a valid passport and a return or ongoing ticket.

Currency: Netherland Antilles florin (NAf) or guilder. US$1 equals NAf1.79. U.S. dollars are readily accepted.

Departure Tax: US$35 on international flights; US$5.75 (NAf10) to Curaçao and other islands.

Electricity: 127 volts AC, 50 cycles

Emergency Numbers: Medical: San Francisco Hospital, (599) 717-8900; Emergency: 191; Police: 114

Language: Dutch is the official language, but Papiamento is the island language. English and Spanish are widely spoken.

Public Holidays: Jan 1, New Year's Day; Feb, Carnival, Carnival Mon; Good Friday; Easter Monday; Apr 30, Coronation Day; May 1, Labor Day; Ascension Day; June 24, St. John's Day; June 29, St. Peter's Day; Sept 6, Bonaire Day; Oct, Sailing Regatta; Dec 25, Christmas Day; Dec 26, Boxing Day.

Telephone Area Code: For international direct dialing from the United States, dial 011-599-7 plus the six-digit local number.

Airlines: *From the United States:* Flamingo International Airport is served by Continental with two non-stops from Newark and from Houston; and American Eagle from Puerto Rico daily. American Airlines serves Bonaire via Curaçao, connecting with Dutch Antilles Express (599-717-0808; www.flydae.com), Divi Divi Air (599-9-839-1515; www.flydivi.com), Insel Air (599-9-733-1521; www.fly-inselair.com), or Tiara Air (599-297-588-4272; www.tiara-air.com) via Aruba.

Information: www.tourismbonaire.com

In the United States and Canada:

Adams Unlimited Public Relations & Marketing, 80 Broad St., 32nd Floor, New York, NY 10004; (212) 956-5912; 800-BONAIRE; fax: (212) 956-5913; usa@tourismbonaire.com

In Port:

Tourism Corporation Bonaire, Kaya Grandi #2, Kralendijk, Bonaire, N.A.; (599) 717-8322; fax: (599) 717-8408; info@tourismbonaire.com.com

---

Never let it be said that small islands can't have big ambitions. Bonaire is aiming to become the first Caribbean island to be powered 100% by sustainable energy. Beginning in 2007, the island government launched a multi-faceted $75 million project to reduce its dependence on fossil fuel by developing an energy system comprised of a wind farm, biodiesel plant utilizing fuel derived from algae, and backup battery. In the first phase, twelve wind turbines were installed on the north coast of the island, where wind conditions are most ideal, and by May 2010 were producing 50% of the island's energy. The next step brought the diesel plant on line, which will gradually be converted into a biodiesel plant running on fuel derived from algae. Stay tuned.

Budget Planning

Bonaire is relatively inexpensive as Caribbean destinations go. Diving, deep-sea fishing, windsurfing, and most water sports are about the least expensive in the region. Tours are reasonably priced. Certain elements, such as good restaurants, however, can be expensive.

Port Profile

www.tourismbonaire.com
www.infobonaire.com

Location/Embarkation: The pier is located on the south side of town, only a short walk from the town center and a few steps from the **Divi Flamingo Beach Resort and Casino.**

Local Transportation: There is no public bus system, but there are taxis and rental cars. To see the most interesting sights, you need a car or a tour, which can be arranged through a local tour company or the Tourist Office. Sample taxi rates: Kralendijk to Harbor Village or to Captain Don's Habitat, US$9; to Lac Bay, US$20. Add 50% from midnight to 6 a.m. and 20% surcharge for each person over age four. Island tour: US$25 per hour each for two people.

Roads and Rentals: Bonaire has a limited number of surfaced roads; the rest are dirt roads and tracks. A car or, in some places, a jeep or four-wheel-drive vehicle is necessary for exploring the island and can be arranged upon arrival. A valid driver's license is required. The minimum age is generally twenty-one, but it can be twenty-six for certain car models. Driving is on the RIGHT. The tourist office and local tour companies distribute a free booklet, *Bonaire Holiday,* which has a road map.

From Kralendijk a surfaced road of 9 miles runs along the west coast, where most of the island's resorts are located, to the national park boundary. Here it forks with the left road, which continues along the west shore to Nukove, a snorkeling area; the right fork runs east along Goto Meer, a lake, to Rincon, where a road leads northeast to the national park entrance.

South of Kralendijk a surfaced road makes a loop around the southern tip of the island along the Pekelmeer Lagoon and returns north along the east coast.

Daily rates for cars, jeeps, and minivans range from US$40 to $65 with air-conditioning. Rental companies in Kralendijk include **Avis** (599-717-5795; www.avisbonaire.com) and **Budget** (599-717-4700, fax: 599-717-3325; www.bonaire-budgetcar.com), among others. **Cycle Bonaire** (599-717-2229; www.bonairediveandadventure .com; info@bonairediveandadventure.com) rents bikes for $20 per day. Half-day excursions cost $55–$65 depending on course and include refreshments, escort vehicle, and nature interpretation. **Bonaire Wellness Connexions** (599-717-4241; www.bonairewellness.com: info@bonairewellness .com) also rents bikes; call for guided tour prices. **Outdoor Bonaire** (599-791-6272; www.outdoor

bonaire.com; hans@outdoorbonaire.com) offers tours from $40 per person.

Shore Excursions

Bonaire Tours (Box 115, Kralendijk; 599-717-8778; fax: 599-717-4890; www.bonairetours.com, info@ bonairetours.com), the island's main tour company, especially for cruise-ship passengers, and Bonaire Dive & Adventure have similar programs. Transportation is by minivan or jeep, depending on the number of people. Prices are per person for adults plus tax; reduced children's prices are available. All locations are described further in this chapter.

Flamingo View Tour: 2 hours, US$23. Drive along the north coast and through the hills inland to Rincon. Highlights are the Thousand Steps, Goto Meer to observe flamingos, the north coast to see Indian petroglyphs, and to Seroe Largo for a fabulous view.

Southern Island Tour: 2 hours, US$23. The low-lying south is a marked contrast to the hilly north. Highlights are 150-year-old salt pans with sparkling white hills; flamingo sanctuary; stone slave huts; and Lac Bay, a lagoon and wildlife area.

Biking Excursions: half day, US$55–$65. **Bonaire Dive & Adventure** (599-717-2229; www .bonairediveandadventure.com) offers guided biking excursions along the coast to Rincon, Goto Lake and Washington Slagbaai Park. The dive shop at **Sand Dollar Condominium Resort** (www.dive sanddollar.com), offers bike tours, too.

Kayaking, Snorkeling, Diving, Fishing Excursions: See Sports section later in this chapter.

Bonaire on Your Own

Hard by the sea on the west coast at about mid-island is the capital, Kralendijk, which means "coral dyke" in Dutch. It is a pretty little town of pastel buildings of Dutch colonial architecture, reflecting the island's commitment to preserve its cultural heritage as much as the parks preserve its natural one.

A Kralendijk Walkabout

Kralendijk (pronounced KRAH-len-dike) can be covered on foot in less than an hour. It comprises two parallel north-south streets, Kaya Hellmund/Kaya Craane (along the waterfront) and Kaya Grandi (the shopping street), and two east-west streets, Kaya Gerharts and Kaya Brion. A principal artery, Simon Bolivarstraat, begins at Kaya Grandi and cuts diagonally across Gerharts and Brion Streets.

Kralendijk's historic and shopping areas are the same, making it easy to combine a walking and shopping excursion. Many of the shops, bars, and restaurants are housed in colorful old structures that give the town its special character. Some of the most historic buildings are located around Willheminaplein (Queen Wilhelmina Park), by the sea on the east side of town. The park has pretty shade trees and benches and three historical monuments: One commemorating Dutchman Van Welbeek's landing on Bonaire in 1634 is in the center of the park; another honoring Bonairean soldiers killed during World War II is by the sea; and the third remembers Eleanor Roosevelt's visit to Bonaire in 1944, when American troops were stationed here.

Directly behind the park on its east side is an 18th-century church; in front by the pier is the customs office; and on the south, Government House. South of Government House is the old fort, which is to be renovated for the Instituto Folklore Bonaire (Folklore Museum), a collection of musical instruments, old utensils, and pre-Columbian and other artifacts.

A Drive Around the Island

To the North

As you drive from town toward the island's north coast, the terrain changes from flat and desertlike with short, pale-colored bushes and hundreds of cactus plants to green rolling hills. The road winds along the west coast hugging the coastline of jagged, black coral rock. About 4 miles north of the capital at Barcadera (across from the Radio Antilles tower), there are seaside steps, known as the **Thousand Steps,** a popular dive site.

Another mile north are rock formations whose appearance is so grotesque they have been dubbed the **Devil's Mouth.** After another mile the road becomes one-way in a northbound direction. At Karpata the first of two roads goes inland to Bonaire's oldest village, Rincon. After another mile the road reaches the gate of Bonaire Petroleum's oil terminal, where the road forks. A left turn continues north to Nukove and Playa Frans, where you will find beaches for swimming, hidden caves, and some of the island's most popular picnicking and snorkeling locations; the right fork takes you along a lake on the southern border of the park to Dos Pos and south again to Rincon. There is no access to the park from the southwest.

Goto Meer: Lying outside the southwest border of the park is a beautiful lake, Goto Meer, once open to the sea and still fed by underground springs. The drive along the lake shore is the prettiest in Bonaire and should be a priority. The vegetation is typical of the park with candle cactus, acacia, mesquite, and other trees usually found in dry lowland tropical forests; it becomes leafy green during the rainy season. The southern end of the lagoon attracts large numbers of flamingos, particularly in Nov and Dec. Early in the morning you are also likely to see parrots and parakeets in the trees around the lake. The island's highest point, 784-foot Brandaris Hill, is in view on the northeast.

Washington/Slagbaai National Park: The northern end of Bonaire is covered by the 13,500-acre Washington/Slagbaai National Park, a wildlife sanctuary and the first of its kind in the Netherlands Antilles when it was established in 1969. Situated on the hilliest, greenest part of the island on a former plantation producing divi-divi trees, aloe, charcoal, and goats, the park showcases the island's flora and fauna and includes Brandaris Hill, which can be seen from most locations in the park.

In 1967 the heir of the Washington estate sold the land to the government on the condition that it would never be developed commercially. The land was designated for a national park, and the Netherlands Antilles National Parks Foundation was made the custodian. Three years later, in 1972, the family of the Slagbaai plantation sold the land to the Parks Foundation, and the two areas were reunited into the Washington/Slagbaai National Park.

The park has a wide variety of birds and landscape that ranges from dry lowland forest and salt licks to freshwater lakes, secluded white-sand beaches, unusual rock formations, and dramatic seascapes along rocky coasts. Candle cactus, which grows as tall as trees; prickly pear cactus; mesquite, a favorite perch of the Bonaire parrot; acacia; and divi-divi trees are abundant.

Bonaire, a flyover for migratory birds between North and South America, has as many as 150 species—some unique to the island. Among the most interesting are the beautiful black, yellow, and white trupial and the colorful parakeets and parrots. The endemic, yellow-winged Bonaire parrot, also called the lora, is protected. The park can be seen by car or on foot.

There are two sign-posted routes over mostly dirt roads: a short one of 15 miles marked by green arrows and a longer one of 22 miles marked by yellow arrows. The routes can also be used for hiking, and there are additional footpaths to places not accessible by motor vehicles.

At the entrance, located on the southeastern side of the park, you can get a free pamphlet with map or purchase more complete guidebooks that detail the routes and the flora and fauna to be seen along the way. Hours: daily 8 a.m. to 5 p.m. Entrance: US$10 adults, US$5 children; cash only. Must enter before 2:45 p.m. Other resources: www.washingtonparkbonaire.org.

Both park roads begin at the entrance gate. The yellow one, the Lagadishi Walking Trail, goes first to Salina Mathijs, a salt pond populated by flamingos during the rainy season (Oct to Jan). After another mile a side road to the right leads to Playa Chiquito, a rockbound cove with a beautiful beach, where the surf is too strong and the water too rough for safe swimming. A short walk north along the rocky coral coast at Boca Chiquito, huge waves crash against the shore with such force they send clouds of spray shooting 30 feet and more into the air.

The yellow route continues to the north end of the park at Boca Cocolishi (meaning "shell" in Papiamento), a small secluded cove divided into two parts—a deep, rough seaward side and a calm, shallow basin with a black-sand beach—separated by a coral ridge. Inland along Salina Bartol, another salt pond, lies Poos di Mangel, a watering hole for a great variety of birds. Boca Bartol, on the coast, is made up of coral rubble and flat, eroded rock. This bay has abundant elkhorn coral and sea fans and many colorful reef fish.

On the green route, the Kasikunda Climbing Trail, about three-quarters of the way from the east to the west coast, the road passes the trailhead for the 1.5-mile hike to the top of Brandaris Hill. Farther on, a side road leads to Put Bronswinkel, a watering hole for parakeets and other birds and one of the park's best birding locations.

Playa Funchi, on the west coast, is the former harbor of the Washington Plantation. Here you can see dozens of multicolored geckos and iguana, particularly bright green baby ones. If you are quiet on the approach, the iguana often remain statue-still and can be photographed.

At Playa Funchi the green route turns south to Boca Slagbaai, a large bay with a white-sand beach popular for swimming, snorkeling, and diving. Used as a harbor for exporting salt and meat in the 1800s, the former storage buildings and customs office have been restored. The buildings sit on a strip of land that once dammed and separated the sea from Salina Slagbaai, the saline lake behind the bay. The lake has flamingos, particularly from about Jan to July.

Bonaire Tours and Vacations (599-717-8778; fax: 599-717-4890; www.bonairetours.com) offers a guided excursion to Washington/Slagbaai National Park for US$65–$85, which includes transportation and stops for swimming and snorkeling. Discover Bonaire (599-717-2229; www.bonaire diveandadventure.com) also has park tours with a naturalist guide.

Across the Central Region and North Coast

The low-lying terrain and scattered hills of the central region stretch from Kralendijk to the north coast through green farm fields with old Dutch colonial farmhouses. The coast is as desolate as the moon, with large fields of coral terraces and deeply eroded rocks, some with petroglyphs. A good road from Kralendijk to Rincon and the entrance to the national park runs through the cunucu (or kunuku), as the countryside is known in Papiamento.

Immediately north of Kralendijk at Noord di Salina, a side road of about 1 mile leads up **Seroe Largo,** a hill of about 500 feet in altitude. There you will be rewarded with a fabulous view of Bonaire stretching from the national park on the north along the resorts of the west coast and Kralendijk to the salt mounds on the south. Another 4 miles north on the main road brings you to a small sign marking the turnoff onto a dirt road for **Onima,** where there are Arawak petroglyphs on rock faces near the road. On the main road, about 2 miles north of the Onima turnoff, you reach Rincon, the first settlement on the island, dating from the 16th century. Set in a pretty green valley, the town is anchored by a brightly colored village church and surrounded by old red tile–roofed houses of typical Dutch architecture. From Rincon to the national park entrance is less than 3 miles.

To the South

In contrast to the hilly north, the southern part of the island is flat, dry, and covered with white mountains of salt that shimmer in the bright sun. The salt pans, which are more than 150 years old, have been reactivated after many years of disuse. It takes seven months for the evaporation process to be completed to make salt. The salt is shipped to the eastern United States, throughout the Caribbean, and as far away as New Zealand for chemical, industrial, water softening, and ice-control applications. On the coast south of the loading pier is **Witte Pan,** or Pink Beach, one of the longest stretches of beach on Bonaire. It parallels the south side of the Pekelmeer Lagoon, the large canal that channels sea water to the salt pans.

Flamingo Sanctuary: Between the salt pans and the **Pekelmeer Lagoon** is a 135-acre flamingo sanctuary, a nesting ground for about five thousand birds. You can tour the perimeter of the pans, but access to the sanctuary is prohibited because of the flamingos' extreme sensitivity. Viewers usually leave their vehicles by the road and walk quietly along the edge of the lagoon, where they can get close enough to see the birds with binoculars and photograph them with telephoto lens.

On the south side of the saltworks, you can see tiny stone huts by the side of the road. Built around 1850—about a decade before slavery was abolished here—the huts were used to house slaves when they worked the salt pans. On the southern tip of the island stands the **Willemstoren Lighthouse,** the oldest lighthouse in Bonaire, built in 1837.

Lac Bay: Here the road turns north for about 4 miles to a lake with extensive mangroves and is the most popular place in Bonaire for kayaking. Here, too, is **KonTiki Beach Club** (www.kontikibonaire .com), a small restaurant serving fish and snacks, open daily from 8 a.m. to 10 p.m. On the south side of the bay at Sorobon is a small naturalist hotel on a pretty beach; its clothes-optional beach may be used by non-guests upon payment of a fee.

Bonaire Marine Park: The growth of Bonaire as a diver's mecca and the development of tourism in the 1970s led to the creation of the park in 1979, as part of a long-term program to protect the island's extraordinary coral reefs and marine life. Bonaire Marine Park (www.bmp.org) incorporates the entire coastline of Bonaire and neighboring Klein Bonaire and is defined as the "seabottom and the overlying waters from the highwater tidemark down to 200 feet." It has more than eighty marked dive sites, often within wading distance from shore. All marine life is completely protected; fishing, spearfishing, and collecting of fish, shells, or corals—dead or alive—are prohibited. All boats must use permanent moorings and cannot anchor except in emergencies. The park monitors the impact of coastal development, resource exploitation, visitor use, and manages services and facilities for visitors, including park brochures, lectures, slide presentations, films, and permanent dive-site moorings.

Bonaire's reefs contain some of the most beautiful coral formations in the Caribbean. They are famous for their variety—the park's guidebook describes eighty-four species—and include an abundance of sponges, particularly purple tube sponges, elkhorn and sheet coral, and four kinds of brain coral. More than 200 species of fish have been identified. *Guide to the Bonaire Marine Park,* available in local dive shops and gift stores, was written by the marine biologists who developed the Bonaire Marine Park, Tom van't Hof and Dee Scarr.

Divers and snorkelers derive the greatest pleasure from the park, but nondivers can see a great deal on glass-bottom boat excursions, because visibility in Bonaire's waters is excellent and major coral formations are close to shore. The park fee, valid for one year, is US$25 for scuba divers; US$10 for snorkelers, Windsurfers, kayakers, sport fishermen, and kiteboarders. Passes are also available at $10 for one day of Scuba diving. The fee goes to maintaining the marine park.

Klein Bonaire: Less than a mile west of Kralendijk is the small, dry, and rocky islet of Klein Bonaire. Covered with desert vegetation, it has several white-sand beaches, which are popular destinations for day-trippers. Its spectacular reefs are part of the marine park and range from shallow-water gardens thick with elkhorn coral to coral slopes with great varieties of sponges, gorgonians, and large star and brain corals.

After being in private hands for 131 years, Klein Bonaire officially became part of Bonaire in 1999, when it was turned over to the Klein Bonaire Preservation Foundation and the Bonaire government. The island was purchased for US$4.6 million from the Development Company of Klein Bonaire, which originally had intended to turn the island into a resort community. The purchase deed specifies that the island is to remain undeveloped and natural forever. It is known to be a nesting place for sea turtles and birds. Water taxis are available from Kralendijk for US$18 round-trip, and private boats usually offer excursions daily.

Shopping

Kralendijk has an assortment of small shops selling jewelry, crystal, leather, perfume, and sportswear at prices competitive with Curaçao and Aruba, but Bonaire is a place for casual, not serious, shoppers. Most shops on Kaya Grandi are housed in brightly painted colonial buildings. Harborside is a small mall in a renovated building with a Dutch colonial facade. Hotels also have small gift shops, and

these are likely to be your best place to find books on Bonaire, particularly its marine life.

Store hours generally are Mon to Sat from 8 a.m. to noon and 2 to 6 p.m., although some stores remain open through the lunch hours. When cruise ships are in port on Sun or holidays, tourist shops usually open for a few hours. U.S. dollars, credit cards, and traveler's checks are accepted; stores often quote prices in dollars.

Art and Artists: At the JanArt Gallery (Kaya Gloria #7; 599-717-5246; www.janartbonaire.com) Janice Huckaby's paintings and sculptures capture the underwater scenes and landscapes of Bonaire. **Richter Art Gallery** (Kaya Statius van Eps 17; 599-717-4112; www.richterart.com) features the works of Linda and Jacke Richter including "Nature Portraits" oil paintings and "digital painting." Driftwood sculptures and furniture, handcrafted jewelry and dolls are for sale at **Art Studio Yellowhouse** (Kaya Gob N. Debrot #29; 599-717-4040).

China/Crystal/Jewelry: Littman's Jewelers (Harborside; 599-717-8160; www.bonairelittman stores.com) is the agent for several well-known brands of European crystal and also carries delft china; it is best known for fine jewelry and quality dive watches. **Atlantis Duty Free** (Kaya Grandi 32B; 599-717-7730; www.atlantisbonaire.com) specializes in hand-crafted, sealife jewelry designs set with precious stones and pearls.

Cameras/Photo Supplies: Paradise Photo (599-717-8741) has cameras and photographic equipment, develops film, and takes passport pictures. **Fish-Eye Photo** (599-717-2001; www .fisheyephoto.com) rents underwater imaging equipment.

Clothing and Accessories: Benetton (19 Kaya Grandi; 599-717-5107) claims its prices are 30 percent less than those in the United States. **Bahia** (Harborside) has pretty sportswear. **Botica Bonaire** (599-717-8905) is like a general store and has a local clientele for clothing, as well as perfume, toiletries, and pharmaceuticals.

Crafts and Souvenirs: Littman's Gifts boutique stocks hand-painted T-shirts, Dutch china, island souvenirs, and casual jewelry. A small deli section has Dutch chocolates, cheeses, and other specialties. **Bonaire Gift Shop** (Kaya Grandi 13; 599-717-2201) has souvenirs, handicrafts, toys, film, wine, liquor, accessories, custom jewelry, and clothing.

Dive and Sporting Goods: Some stores in town have masks and fins, but you will find the best stocks of quality dive equipment in the dive shops at hotels. **DiveFriends @ Dive Retail Outlet** (Kaya Grandi #6; 599-717-3911; www.dive-friends-bonaire.com) sells water-sports equipment, T-shirts, postcards, and souvenirs.

Perfumes and Cosmetics: D'Orsy's (Harborside), a member of a chain found in Aruba and throughout the Netherlands Antilles, has a good selection of French perfumes.

Dining and Restaurants

Bonaire has a surprising selection of restaurants offering fresh seafood and continental specialties, but some of the best are open for dinner only. Those listed here are generally open daily, but may close Sun or Mon and serve lunch and dinner. Check locally. These restaurants and more can be found at www.bonairediningguide.com, which is updated annually. Entries range from inexpensive (less than US$9) and moderate (US$10 to $20) to expensive (more than US$20).

Bistro de Paris (Kaya Gobernor 46; 599-717-7070; www.bistrodeparis.com), a French-owned and -operated restaurant situated in a small white house with a terrace, serves French cuisine. Moderate.

Cactus Blue Bar & Restaurant (J. A. Abraham Blvd. 12, 599-717-4564; www.cactusblue bonaire.com), a colorful downtown eatery, offers contemporary Caribbean cuisine and some familiar American fare to be enjoyed in air-conditioned comfort or outdoors on the terrace. Some specialties are Cajun tuna sashimi, fresh lobster, lime and ginger shrimp, Argentinean filet mignon, and kabritu stoba—Bonairean goat stew. Expensive.

Papaya Moon Cantina (48 Kaya Grandi; 599-717-5025; www.papayamooncantina.com), Bonaire's first and only Tex-Mex restaurant. Serves lunch and dinner in an indoor/outdoor setting. Moderate.

KonTiki Beach Club (64 Kaminda Sorobon; 599-717-5369; www.kontikibonaire.com) features sandwiches, salads, and snacks in the laid-back atmosphere of an outdoor cactus garden. Exhibits art by local artists for sale. Jazz occasionally. Moderate.

Vespucci's Restaurant (Harbour Village Marina; 599-717-2596) offers seafood and Mediterranean-style fare. Moderately expensive.

Zeezicht Bar and Restaurant (10 Curaçao straat, near the pier; 599-717-8434). Established in 1929, its specialties are fresh fish and nasi goring, an Indonesian dish. Happy hour at 4:15 p.m. features live musical entertainment. Moderate.

Nightlife

Bonaire's nightlife is low-key, in keeping with the ambience of the island. **Karel's Beach Bar** (www.karelsbeachbar.com) on the water and **City Café** (www.citybonaire.com) in Kralendijk are popular nightspots. Both are open air and usually have live music on weekends. Bonaire has a casino at **Divi Flamingo Beach Resort and Casino;** minimum age is eighteen.

Sports

Beaches/Swimming: On Bonaire you have the choice of powdery white, pretty pink, or black sand beaches. Most are small reef-protected coves with exceptionally clear water. The best swimming is on the leeward, or western, side where the waters are calm. Swimming on the windward side is generally not recommended due to the strong waves and currents. Pink Beach on the southwest coast takes its name from the pinkish tint of the sand, enhanced by the light of the late-afternoon sun. Popular with Bonaireans on the weekends, it is delightfully empty during the week.

Sorobon Beach Resort is a clothes-optional resort with a private beach on Lac Bay. Nonguests are welcome to use the resort's facilities for a small fee.

Biking: Bonaire has more than 100 miles of trails ranging from goat paths to unpaved roads. Local bike shops offer bike rentals and guided tours. Bonaire's Web site, www.infobonaire.com, has a cycling map and descriptions of six routes. **Cycle Bonaire** (Kaya Gerharts 11d; 599-717-7558; fax: 599-717-7690; www.bonairediveandadventure.com) offers mountain-bike rentals, mapped routes, and guided biking excursions with stops for snorkeling and a seaside picnic, and has permission for mountain-biking tours in Washington/Slagbaai National Park (US$55–$65). Similar tours and rentals are available from **Outdoor Bonaire** (599-785-6272; www.outdoorbonaire.com); and Buddy Dive Resort.

Bird-watching: Bonaire boasts over 190 species including the protected Lora (Amazon parrot). The island has no endemic bird species, but does have subspecies or ones restricted to the Aruba, Bonaire, and Curaçao area. Bonaire's most famous bird is the pink flamingo, which can be seen in the Washington Slagbaai National Park in the north and a reserve in the salt pans on the south. For bird-watching tours contact **Bonaire Dive & Adventure** (599-717-2229). Jerry Ligon, a resident naturalist, leads field trips to the park and bird sanctuaries.

Boating: Sailing yachts offer half-day and full-day excursions; most serve beverages and snacks. The **Woodwind** (599-786-7055; www.woodwindbonaire .com) has trips to Klein Bonaire for swimming and snorkeling, at US$40 per person, half day; US$45 full day with lunch. Other day sails are offered by **Samur Sailing** (599-717-5592; www.samursailing .com), **ABC Cruiseline NV** (599-786-7615; www .bowalie.com); **AquaSpace** (599-701-2782; www .aquaspace-bonaire.com); and **Pirate Cruise of Bonaire** (599-790-8330; www.remarkable.com/bonaire/pirates.html).

Deep-Sea Fishing: Half- and full-day charters with all provisions are available through water-sports operators. Bonaire's offshore fishing grounds beyond the marine park are abundant with mackerel, tuna, wahoo, barracuda, and swordfish, to name a few. **Big Game Sport Fishing** (599-717-6500; www.sportfishingbonaire.com); **Multifish Charters** (599-717-3648; www.multifish.com); and **Piscatur Charters** (Captain Chris Morkos; 599-717-8774; fax: 599-717-2877; www.bonairefishing .com/piscatur) offer deep-sea fishing trips. Piscatur's charters include gear, bait, beer, soda, and

sandwiches: half day, four persons, US$400; and full day, US$550. They also arrange reef fishing, as well as bonefishing and tarpon fishing in the shallows.

Hiking: The best hiking is on the trails and footpaths of the national park. (See section on the Washington/Slagbaai National Park.) Cyclists and hikers must enter no later than noon. The companies listed under Biking above can also arrange hiking guides. **Bonaire Tours and Vacations** (www.bonairetours.com) has a Kunuku Trip with walk-on trails in the Rooi Lamoenchi plantation; 3 hours, US$20.

Horseback Riding: The **Riding Academy Club at Kunuku Warahama** (599-560-7949; www .horsebackridingbonaire.com), is something of an American dude ranch in the Caribbean and is located in the southern wilderness of the island, offering trail rides for groups of two to five.

Kayaking: Kayaks can be rented from most dive shops. Bonaire's calm waters are ideal for kayaking. Kayaks are available to explore Lac Bay, a lagoon with mangroves, which are a nursery for fish life; to view the coast; or to visit Klein Bonaire. **Bonaire Tours and Vacations** (599-717-8778; fax: 599-717-4890; www.bonairetours.com) has a guided kayaking excursion to Lac Bay for US$45, including transportation and equipment. **Discover Bonaire/Bonaire Dive & Adventure** (599-717-2229; www .bonairediveandadventure.com) has kayak rentals and mangrove excursions. Others offering guided kayak trips include **Outdoor Bonaire** (599-785-6272; www.outdoorbonaire.com) and **Mangrove Information Center Bonaire** (599-780-5353; www .mangrovecenter.com), a research and excursion center, established in 2002 by Gerard van Erp. It has an aquarium for basic research and a research partnership with the Rotterdam Zoo in the Netherlands, which built an educational mangrove forest. Lac Bay mangroves excursions: 8:30 a.m. two-hour guided kayak tour, including mangrove snorkeling, $42.50; 9:30 a.m. one-hour solar boat tour, $25; 11 a.m. one-hour guided kayak tour, $25. Call for reservations.

Snorkeling/Scuba Diving: Bonaire is one of the world's leading scuba-diving locations, with more than eighty beautiful dive spots along its magnificent reefs. Rave reviews come from experienced divers because of the great variety and quality of marine life; beginners like it because of the ease and accessibility of the reefs. In many places, you can wade from the shore to the reefs to enjoy unlimited viewing and diving from the beach any time of the day or night. The island is also one of the Caribbean's best-equipped dive centers; all hotels cater to divers and have excellent dive shops on their premises. They offer lessons at every level of training, as well as in underwater photography. Divers can hire an underwater camera person to videotape their diving experiences.

Snorkel Tour: Bonaire is also the first Caribbean island to have a full-fledged snorkeling program. It teaches participants about the reefs and provides trained guides to take them on reef tours. Tours are available at seventeen locations, and each provides a different experience. They are offered one to three times a day, depending on demand; cost is US$50, including rental equipment, map, video presentation, and guide. Tours can be booked through any dive shop in Bonaire.

The best reefs are within the protected lee of the island, where most of the diving and other recreational activity takes place. Here the reefs have a narrow, sloping terrace extending seaward to a dropoff at 33 feet. This is followed by a slope varying from 30 feet to a vertical wall, extending to a depth of 100 to 200 feet. Among the places for walk-in snorkeling and scuba are the Thousand Steps, on the north coast at Barcadera, and farther north at Nukove, where you can picnic and watch birds.

Among the dive operators closest to the port are **Divi Dive Bonaire** (Divi Flamingo Beach Resort; 599-717-8285; 800-367-3484; fax: 599-717-8238; www.diviflamingo.com) and **Captain Don's Habitat Dive Center** (599-717-8290; 800-327-6709; www.habitatbonaire.com). A list of the island's dive operators and their services is available from the Bonaire Tourist Office and at www.infobonaire.com.

Windsurfing: The constant trade winds that keep the island cool make Bonaire an ideal location for windsurfing. All beachfront resorts have windsurfing equipment. **Bonaire Windsurf Place** (Sorobon; 599-717-2288; www.bonairewindsurfplace.com) has rentals and offers lessons. **Jibe City** (Lac Bay, 599-717-5233; www.jibecity.com) rents boards for US$20 an hour or US$60 per day. It also has kayaks.

Festivals and Celebrations

Carnival is celebrated in the traditional pre-Lenten period, and there is the **Bonaire Dive Into Summer** from June to Sept, but the biggest event of the year is the **Bonaire Sailing Regatta** (www.bonaireregatta.org) in mid-Oct. Started as a wager among friends three decades ago, it has evolved into an official event. Fishermen and yachtsmen from all over the Caribbean compete in different categories.

Curaçao
Willemstad

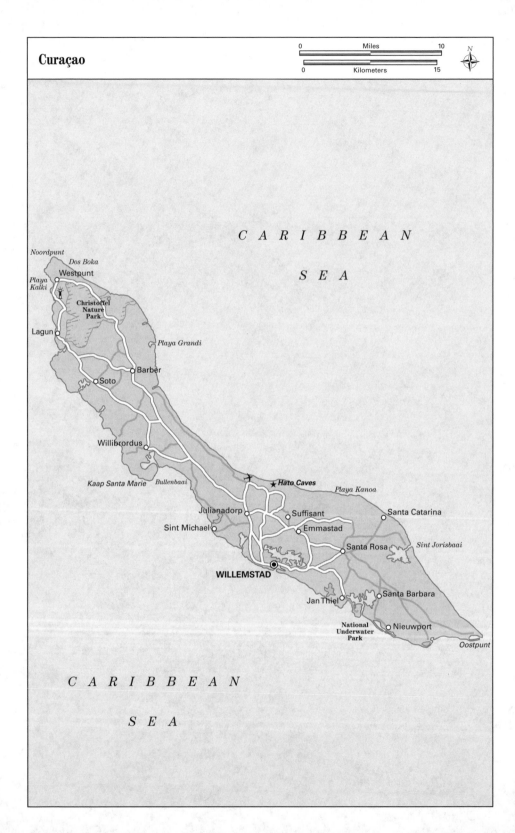

Curaçao

Miles
0   10

Kilometers
0   15

N

CARIBBEAN

SEA

Noordpunt

Dos Boka

Westpunt

Playa Kalki

Christoffel Nature Park

Lagun

Playa Grandi

Barber

Soto

Willibrordus

Kaap Santa Marie   *Bullenbaai*

★ **Hato Caves**

Playa Kanoa

Julianadorp

Suffisant

Santa Catarina

Sint Michael

Emmastad

Santa Rosa

Sint Jorisbaai

WILLEMSTAD

Jan Thiel

Santa Barbara

National Underwater Park

Nieuwport

Oostpunt

CARIBBEAN

SEA

A Dutch Masterpiece in the Tropics

Known throughout its history as a center for international commerce with one of the world's busiest ports, Curaçao, the cosmopolitan heart of the Dutch Caribbean, has stepped into the role of a sun-drenched Caribbean resort rather recently. But over the past several years, in concert with private interests, the government has made up for lost time by renovating, upgrading, and expanding its many attractions. It has added sporting facilities, shopping plazas, new cruise facilities, and a harborside park, as well as restored and beautified an extensive area around the port.

Lying 39 miles off the coast of Venezuela between Aruba and Bonaire, Curaçao is a surprising combination of worldliness and sophistication, resulting from its long trading tradition and polyglot culture, juxtaposed with a rugged landscape reminiscent of the American Southwest, with dry, cactus-covered reddish soil, undulating rocky hills, chalky mountains, and windswept shores. The land is greener toward the north and along the coast, where narrow waterways lead to large lagoons with fingers and islands used for commerce and sport. These waterways are Curaçao's most distinctive features and one of several elements that make it seem like a mini-Holland with palm trees. Surrounded by beautiful reefs that divers are now discovering, Curaçao's rocky north coast is pounded by waves, while on the south a placid turquoise sea laps at small sandy coves. Uninhabited Klein Curaçao lies to the southeast.

Cruise-ship passengers have the best vantage point for an introduction to this unusual island when they sail into Willemstad, the capital. There they are greeted by a colorful harborside of brightly painted and gabled Dutch colonial buildings dating from the 18th century. So distinctive is the setting that it has become Curaçao's signature and led others to call it a "Dutch masterpiece in the tropics."

The island's early inhabitants were the Caiquetios, an Arawak tribe that migrated north to the Caribbean from South America. Discovered in 1499 by the Spanish navigator Alonso de Ojeda, a lieutenant of Christopher Columbus, the Spanish made their first settlement here in 1527. But a century later the Dutch captured the island and founded their own settlement in 1634. It was made a colony of the Dutch West India Company, starting Curaçao's long trading tradition.

Over the next two centuries, the French and British, eager to have Curaçao for its natural harbors and strategic location, battled the Dutch for possession and dislodged them several times for a year or two. In 1642 a young Peter Stuyvesant was made governor, three years before being named director-general of the Dutch colony of New Amsterdam, which today we call New York.

Under the Dutch Curaçao was divided into plantations, some of which prospered on salt mining rather than agriculture. Slave trading was another important source of revenue. But after slavery was abolished here in 1863, Curaçao became a sleepy little island until 1914, when oil was discovered in nearby Venezuela.

Royal Dutch Shell Company, taking advantage of Curaçao's fine harbors, built one of the world's largest oil refineries here. It attracted trade, banks, and other commercial enterprises and created a prosperity that continued throughout the century. Curaçao's trading history had already made it an ethnic melting pot and the oil prosperity that brought workers from many nations enhanced the blend. Today Curaçao claims to be made up of more than fifty nationalities.

Budget Planning

Prices in Curaçao for restaurants and tourist services compare favorably with the rest of the Caribbean. Tourist attractions and facilities are rather spread out; hence touring by taxi tends to be expensive unless you can share costs. Car rentals are moderately priced and public buses inexpensive. You need have no hesitation about using buses since most people speak English and are helpful and friendly. If you like to walk and discover on your own, you'll find Curaçao one of the most delightful ports in the Caribbean.

Population: 130,000

Size: 38 miles long and 2 to 7 miles wide; 180 square miles

Main Town: Willemstad

Government: Curaçao is the largest, most populous of the Dutch Caribbean islands. In Oct 2010, Curaçao's status, along with other members of the former Netherlands Antilles changes to give it a direct relationship to the Netherlands government, similar to that of Aruba. The government is a parliamentary democracy with three councils: legislative, executive, and advisory; whose members are elected for four years.

Entry Requirements: Visitors must have a valid passport.

Currency: Netherlands Antilles guilder (NAf) divided into 100 florin or cents. US$1 equals NAf1.77. U.S. dollars are widely accepted, and prices are often quoted in dollars.

Departure Tax: US$32 on international flights; US$8 for interisland ones.

Electricity: 127/120 volts AC, 50 cycles

Emergency Numbers: Medical: St. Elisabeth Hospital, (599) 9-462-4900; Ambulance: 912; Police and Fire Brigade: 911; Curaçao Dialysis Center: (599) 9-7777; www.curacao-dialysis.com.

Language: Dutch is the official language; English and Spanish are widely spoken. Papiamento is the local language and blends Dutch, Portuguese, English, French, Indian, and African words.

Public Holidays: Jan 1, New Year's Day; Carnival Mon; Good Friday; Easter Monday; Apr 30, Queen's Birthday; May 1, Labor Day; Ascension Day; July 2, Flag Day; Dec 25 to 26, Christmas.

Telephone Area Code: From the United States, dial the prefix 011-599-9 followed by the local number. Cell-phone rentals: VIP Cell Phone Rental, (599) 9-462-6262.

Time Zone: Atlantic Standard Time (one hour later than EST)

Airlines: *From the United States:* American Airlines, Continental Airlines, Delta Airlines, and American Eagle. *Interisland:* Aserca Airlines, Avior Airlines, Divi Divi Air, Dutch Antilles Express (DAE), LIAT, Tiara Air and Insel Air (www.fly-inselair .com) serves interisland routes between Curaçao, Aruba, Bonaire, and St. Maarten.

Information: www.curacao-tourism .com; www.curacao.com; www .curacao-travelguide.com; www .gaycuracao.com; www.tourism-curacao.com; www.curacaomonu ments.org

In the United States:

Curaçao Tourist Office, One Gateway Center, Ste. 2600, Newark, NJ 07102; (973) 353-6200; (800) 3-CURACAO; northamerica@curacao .com

In Port:

Curaçao Department of Tourism, Main Office, Pietermaai 19, Curaçao, N.A.; (599) 9-434-8200; fax: (599) 461-2305; info@curacao.com CARMAB Curaçao, Caribbean Research & Management of Biodiversity, Piscaderabaai z/n, P.O. Box 2090, Willemstad; (599) 462-4242; www.carmabi.org; info@carmabi.org

Port Profile

**www.curacao.com;
www.tourism-curacao.com;
www.curacao-travelguide.com**

Location/Embarkation: Your ship's arrival in Curaçao will be one of the most interesting experiences of your cruise—don't miss it! Willemstad is built around Santa Anna Bay, a large deepwater lagoon, which is entered from the sea through a long, narrow finger whose waterfront is lined on both sides with colorful Dutch colonial buildings. The channel, which is 4,200 feet long and only 270 feet wide, opens onto the Schottegat, the inner harbor, spanning 150 acres—the seventh-largest harbor in the world.

On the east side of the picturesque channel is the Punda, with Fort Amsterdam, the oldest part of town. The west side, where your ship docks, is known as Otrobanda (meaning "the other side"). The two sides are connected by the Queen Emma Pontoon Bridge, a renovated century-old floating bridge that is a pedestrian walkway, near the dock. Another bridge, the Queen Juliana—whose slender, arched profile is in full view from the time your ship enters the harbor—is used for motor traffic. It spans Santa Anna Bay and connects the two sides of town to the roads that circumnavigate the bay. The bridge, stands at a height of 185 feet; your ship is likely to pass directly under the bridge en route to its dock, and if the ship has a tall stack, watching the tricky maneuver can be a heart-stopping moment. Ships too tall to pass under the Queen Juliana Bridge dock at the mega-pier, on the west, before entering the harbor.

The megapier, completed in 1999, was built specifically to accommodate the new megaliners. Passengers step off in the Rif area, next to the 17th-century Rif Fort, which overlooks the harbor entrance. Here, too, is the main bus stop for the Otrobanda area and a short walk via a landscaped walkway to the Queen Emma Pontoon Bridge, more commonly known as the floating bridge, and downtown.

Riffort Village has boutiques, a new Renaissance Hotel, several good restaurants—and an art gallery. There is always some sort of live music, usually a local band in the courtyard. The passenger terminals at both docks have local and international telephones, WiFi, and a tourist information desk and are in walking distance to downtown shopping areas and attractions. In the immediate vicinity of the port are car rentals, taxis, and "Ask Me" personnel provided by the Curaçao Port Authority.

Local Transportation: Taxis are available at the port and taxi stands at hotels. Fares are set by the government but should be agreed upon with the driver in advance. They are for up to four passengers; for a fifth passenger 25 percent is added; there is an additional 25 percent surcharge after 11 p.m. Curaçao taxis can be identified by the sign on their roof and the letters TX after the license number Sample fares from the port: to airport, about US$20; from Punda to Breezes Beach, about US$24. Sightseeing by taxi costs US$30 an hour for one to four passengers, for a one-hour minimum. To phone for a taxi, call (599) 869-0747; to lodge a complaint, call (599) 461-6577.

NOTE: When you leave your ship (in Otrobanda) to go no farther than the downtown shopping area (Punda), it is better to walk across the floating pontoon bridge or take the free ferry; otherwise, a taxi must circle the long distance around the bay.

Public buses operate on regular schedules in Willemstad and to populated areas of the island.

The central departure points are Waaigat (next to the post office) in Punda and Riffort in Otrobanda, a three-minute walk from the docks. Between the two bridges in Otrabanda are the renovated buildings of Porto Paseo, housing hotels, a casino, art gallery, museum, bars, restaurants, parks, and a large crafts center.

Roads and Rentals: In its urban areas Curaçao has a good road network that fans out from Willemstad and the port on the south for a radius of about 6 miles; there are also major east-west arteries crossing the island. But beyond these principal routes, rural roads are sometimes dirt ones, which can become muddy after a heavy rain; inquire locally. East and south of Willemstad, good roads run as far as Spaanse Water (or Spanish Water), a large lagoon on the south coast. On the west a major artery from Willemstad crosses the center of the island to the Christoffel Nature Park and Westpunt (West Point). En route it branches to the west coast in three places: Santa Marta Bay, San Juan, and Santa Cruz, where it continues via the coast to Westpunt. Road maps are available.

Bikes, scooters, Segways, and motorcycles are available for rent, but if this is your first trip to Curaçao, none are a good mode of travel, unless with a tour guide. For bike rentals, **Curaçao Actief** (599-433-8858; www.curacao-actief.com and **Christoffel Park Rental Bike** (Christoffel Park; 599-566-6303); for motorcycles, **Holland Car Rental** (Willem de Zwijgerlaan 15, Willemstad; 599-736-6544; www.hollandcuracao.com); for scooters, **Scooby's Rental Scooters** (Breezes Hotel, Kontiki Resort; 599-523-8618; www.scooters curacao.com; scoobytours@yahoo.com). Car rentals are essential for touring on your own. You need a valid driver's license. Traffic moves on the RIGHT; road signs are in kilometers. Expect to pay about US$50 and up for a small car. Among the rental firms are **Avis** (599-461-1255; www.aviscuracao.com), **Budget** (599-868-3466; www.curacao-budgetcar.com) and **Hertz** (599-888-0088; www.hertzcaribbean.com), which have jeeps. Another dozen local companies, listed on www.curacao.com, may have better rates. Road Assistance: (599) 9-9-24-7.

Ferry Service: A free ferry crosses the harbor between Otrobanda and Punda regularly throughout the day; when the floating pontoon bridge is closed for traffic, pedestrians use the ferry.

Shore Excursions

Cruise ships have tours to the island's best-known attractions, such as the Curaçao Seaquarium and Curaçao Liqueur Distillery, but Curaçao is not a cookie-cutter, beach-lined Caribbean island. It is different, and its differences are what make it interesting, particularly to those with curiosity, a fondness for history, and a sense of adventure. Several local companies offer tours for small groups that will give you a much better picture of this unusual island than do standard tours. They also tailor tours to off-the-beaten-track places.

Walking Tours: The best walking tours of Willemstad are offered by Old City Tours (Julianaplein 26; 599-461-3554), whose architect/owner, Anko van der Woude, is the island's leading expert on historic architecture and sometimes leads the tour himself. The company has several programs of two to three hours, but with advance arrangements, a program can be fitted to your interest. Some other walking tours with an architect or art historian, by appointment, Curaçao Actief (599-433-8858; 599-461-0690; www.curacao-actief.com). Angelina's Walking Tour is a culinary one (see Angelina's Kitchen in Restaurant section later in this chapter).

Banda Ariba (East Side) or Banda Abao (West): 3.5 hours, US$35–45. The half-day tour to the east usually visits Landhuis Chobolobo, which houses the Curaçao Liqueur Distillery, and Landhuis Rooi Catootje Museum, a beautifully restored landhouse, or Hato Caves.

Trolley Train: 1.5 hours, US$20. Guided city tour starting from Fort Amsterdam in a caboose-pulled open-sided trolley. Excellent guides. Operated by Miami-based Atlantis Adventures (Hilton Hotel, 599-461-0011; www.atlantisadventures .com). Cost: US$30–$35 as a ship's shore excursion.

Combination Tours: Half day, US$40–$50 per person. Some island sightseeing, such as the Seaquarium, is combined with swimming or the Botanical Garden and Zoo, a drive west through the countryside, or a visit to a cunucu or kunuku house or Landhuis Jan Kok. Contact Taber Tours (599-737-6637; fax: 599-737-9539; www.tabertours

.com) or Tourism Curaçao (599-462-6262; www .tourism-curacao.com).

Seaworld Explorer: 2 hours, US$39. The semi submarine departs from a dock at the Hilton Curaçao Hotel and Casino. Tours are conducted in several languages; check locally for the English ones (599-461-0011).

Ostrich Farm and Herb Garden: 3 hours, US$54. A visit to the Caribbean's only ostrich farm (branch in Aruba), located in the northeast corner of the island, can be combined with the Caribbean Herb Garden. You will not save money doing it on your own, unless you rent a car, as the drive to the farm takes more than thirty minutes one-way (www .ostrichfarm.net).

Adventure Excursions: For biking, hiking, and other such trips, see the Sports section later in this chapter. Among the companies offering them are Wild Curaçao (6 Scherpenheuvel; 599-561-0027; www.curacaowildtours.com) and Curaçao Actief (www.curacao-actief.com), which offer hikes to the summit of Mount Christoffel as well as historic hikes. Dutch Dream Adventures (599-864-7377) has jeep safaris, canoeing, mountain biking, and hiking excursions.

The Beach Express: US$59 adults, US$30 children. The western end of the island has beaches in secluded coves with crystal-clear water for swimming and snorkeling, but without a car, the trip here can be pricey. An alternative is the Beach Express, a colorful, hand painted open-air bus. En route it makes a short stop at the Christoffel Park and Boka Tabla Cave, then to two of the remote tropical beaches of Banda'bou to swim, snorkel, or relax. Prices include all entrance fees, guide, soft drinks, lunch on the beach, and snorkel gear. For reservations, Yellow Adventures Curaçao's (599-462-6262; www.yellowadventures.com). For more sightseeing options, go to www.tourism-curacao .com.

Curaçao on Your Own

Willemstad is an architectural gem and was given the recognition it deserves when it was named as a World Heritage Site by UNESCO in 1997. The heart of Willemstad, with its colorful historic buildings, straddles Santa Anna Bay. Punda, the east side, has a five-square-block historic zone, including Fort Amsterdam and the main shopping streets—all easily covered on foot. Otrobanda, the west side, is more residential and has clusters of old buildings, newly renovated as hotels, shopping and restaurant complexes, and museums. Both historic districts with their narrow lanes—some closed to traffic—are best explored on foot. (For guided walking tours, see previous Shore Excursions section.)

A Willemstad Walkabout

Curaçao has put an extraordinary effort into the restoration and renovation of the city center, preserving the historic architecture and adding many new facilities. "YOU ARE HERE" signs with maps of the downtown shopping area are posted at the cruise terminal and other key locations.

Queen Emma Pontoon Bridge (2): Only a short walk from the **dock (1),** the bridge connects the Otrobanda and Punda. The bridge swings open regularly to allow ships to pass. The first pontoon bridge was built in 1888 by L. B. Smith, an American entrepreneur from Maine whose ships brought the first ice (packed in sawdust) to Curaçao; he was also involved in building Curaçao's first power and water plant. A series of postage stamps commemorates his achievements.

Handelskade: When you cross the floating pontoon bridge to the east bank, you arrive on Handelskade, the harborfront street lined with brightly painted 18th-century buildings complete with gables and red-tiled roofs. They were once offices of trading companies and warehouses, and were it not for their vivid colors under the bright Caribbean sun, you might imagine yourself in Amsterdam. The red tiles of the roofs came from Europe as ballast in ships. For their return voyages the ships were filled with salt, a major commodity in world trade in colonial days that was used in curing fish and preserving foodstuffs.

Directly in front is the **Penha building (3),** the town's oldest (corner of Handelskade and Breedestraat). Molded on the top is the date 1708, the year of its construction. As you walk along the narrow streets, you will see many old buildings similarly marked. The Penha building was once a social club

with a gallery from which members could watch the passing harbor traffic; today it houses one of the town's leading department stores.

Breedestraat, historically, has been a major thoroughfare of Punda and Otrobanda and can be used as a focal point for your walk. (Incidentally, straat is Dutch for street; we have rendered street names as they appear locally to be easier to follow, if not always to pronounce.) On the south is Fort Amsterdam; on the north the shopping streets and several important historic buildings. Look down Breedestraat and you will see typical Dutch colonial–style galleries with their unusual short, round columns.

Fort Amsterdam (4): Originally constructed in 1634 to protect the harbor entrance, Fort Amsterdam was the largest and most important of the eight forts protecting Curaçao from 1648 to 1861, when the capital was a walled city. Now restored, the fort serves as the seat of government. Within its mustard-colored walls are the governor's residence, several government offices, and the 18th-century Dutch Reformed Church. The governor's mansion is a classic colonial structure whose entrance opens onto a courtyard with buildings that house the offices of the central government. Some buildings have retained their old elements, such as heavy oak beams, wide-pegged floorboards, and handblown glass windows.

Fort Church (5): Across the courtyard, the church dating from 1766 occupies the site where a church has stood since the Protestants first came to Curaçao in 1635. Owned by the United Protestant Community of Curaçao since 1824, the first church was probably a wooden shed that served the military garrison at the fort. According to old town maps, by 1707 it had been replaced by a stone building. The church was rebuilt and expanded many times and now houses a small museum (599-461-1139; info@fortchurch.com). Hours: Mon to Fri, 9:30 a.m. to 1 p.m. Admission: $6 adults, $3 children, under twelve years, free.

Waterford Arches (7): On the south side of the fort, by the sea, the turreted and vaulted ramparts were added in 1826 and 1830 to strengthen the fortifications and house provisions. In 1988 the vaults adjacent to the Van der Valk Plaza Hotel were restored and converted into the Waterfort Arches, a plaza with shops, restaurants, and a seaside

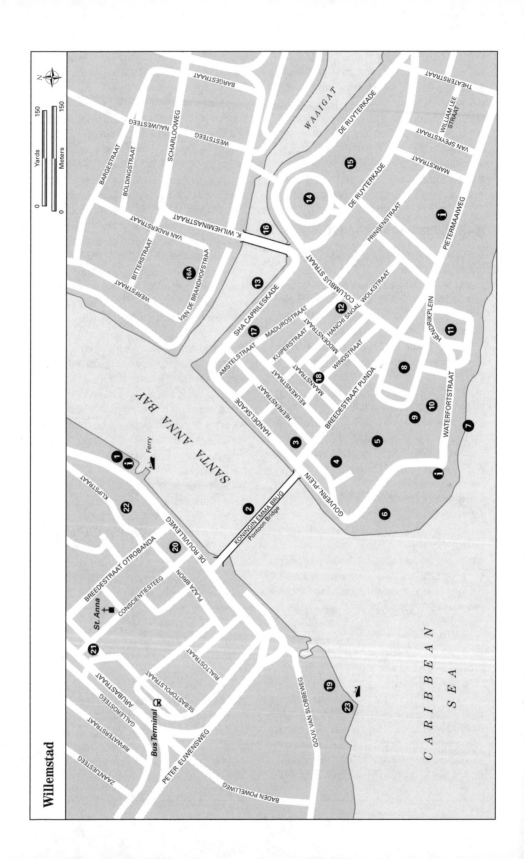

1.	Dock	13.	Floating Market
2.	Queen Emma Pontoon Bridge	14.	Central Market
3.	Penha Building	15.	Post Office
4.	Fort Amsterdam	16.	Wilhelmina Bridge
5.	Fort Church	16a.	Maritime Museum
6.	Plaza Piar	17.	Plaza Jojo Correa
7.	Waterford Arches	18.	Gomezplein
8.	Wilhelmina Park	19.	Riffort
9.	Police Office	20.	Koral Agostini
10.	Courthouse, Council, Bank of Boston	21.	Sebastopol House
11.	Temple Theatre	22.	Museum Kura Hulanda
12.	Mikve Israel-Emanuel Synagogue and Museum	23.	Mega-pier/Renaissance Hotel

promenade where you can stroll along the ramparts. If you were on hand to watch your ship sail into port, you can see why the hotel, built directly on the foundations of fortress walls, is one of the few in the world with marine collision insurance.

Attached to the sea wall below the hotel are links of a heavy iron chain used in olden days for protection against invaders. The chain was placed across the mouth of the harbor, attaching it at the **Riffort (19)**, the counterpart fortification on the west side. Built in 1828, the restored Riffort is home to shops and restaurants which enjoy great harbor views.

Wilhelmina Park (8): East of Fort Amsterdam beyond the **police office (9)** is a small park with a statue of Queen Wilhelmina. On its south are several imposing **buildings (10)**. The first, with an impressive balustrade, houses the Council, or parliament, and Courthouse; another, in Georgian style, was built as a Masonic Temple in 1869.

If you were to continue east for a mile or two, beyond the Avila Beach Hotel—too far to walk— you would come to the Octagon House, a museum dedicated to Simón Bolívar. On two occasions Curaçao gave asylum to Bolívar during his struggle to free South America of Spanish rule. The house was visited by Bolívar when his sisters lived there. Open by appointment. (599-9-461-4377).

Crossing to the north side of Wilhelmina Park, you reach Columbusstraat, which marked the outer city walls until 1861.

Mikve Israel-Emanuel Synagogue and Museum (12): At the corner of Hanchi Snoa is the oldest synagogue in continuous use in the Western Hemisphere. Built in 1732, some of its artistic treasures are even older than the synagogue itself, dating from the founding of the congregation in 1651 by twelve families from Amsterdam. The courtyard museum has artifacts, memorabilia, and replicas of the oldest, most elaborate gravestones in Beth Haim Cemetery, dating from 1659 and said to be the oldest Jewish cemetery in the Western Hemisphere. It is located on the north side of the bay. The architecture of the synagogue, with its curved gables and short columns, is interesting inside and out. As an example, the half columns on the facade do not support the building—they are hollow and function as drains for rainwater. The interior is rich with brassware and woodwork. The symbolism of the white sand on the floor has several interpretations: the wandering of the Jews in the desert, the muffling of the sounds of secret services during the Spanish Inquisition, or God's promise to Abraham that his descendants would be "countless as the sand." Hours: weekdays 9 a.m. to 4:30 p.m.; US$10 entrance fee. Visitors are welcome to attend Sabbath services when tie and jacket are required for men. (599-461-1633; www.snoa.com.)

Floating Market (13): Continuing on Columbusstraat to Madurostraat (another demarcation of the old city walls), you can turn left (west) to see some outstanding examples of rococo gables. The first lane on your right (north) leads to a canal with a picturesque floating market. Each week schooners from Venezuela come here to sell their fruits and vegetables in this open-air market shaded by the sails of the boats. There are also fishermen selling snapper, grouper, conch, and other fish from local waters. Up the street to the east, the large, round building is the **Central Market (14),** a modern town market—but with as much bustle as any Caribbean marketplace. It has a bar and native market-style buffet restaurant serving local food.

Behind the Central Market is the **post office (15),** which has a philatelic window. In front of the market, the **Wilhelmina Bridge (16)** connects Punda with Scharloo, formerly a wealthy residential quarter of early Jewish merchants. The architecture of this area ranges from 18th-century Dutch colonial to Victorian gingerbread. Over the past decade most of these mansions have been restored as private homes or offices; the drive along here is one of the main attractions of a city tour.

Maritime Museum (16A): (Van der Brandhofstraat 7, Scharloo; 599-465-2327; www.curacaomaritime.com), opened in 1999 to commemorate Curaçao's 500th anniversary, celebrates the island's seafaring heritage. The museum has guides and a guided tour by boat. Hours: daily except Mon, 9 a.m. to 4 p.m. Admission: US$6 adults, US$3 children; with harbor tour, US$15 and US$7; request a tour in English.

If you walk west to **Plaza Jojo Correa (17),** you will probably see your ship docked across the bay. At the plaza turn south onto Heerenstraat, one of the main shopping streets, which has several buildings with elaborate gables. At the end of the street is the Penha building, where you began. If you want to take a break, **Gomezplein (18)** is a pretty pedestrian mall with sidewalk cafes, or to Handelskade along the waterfront, also with sidewalk cafes, including the Iguana Café.

Otrobanda

A walk around Otrobanda, except for the immediate vicinity of the port and Breedestraat, is better with a guide through its narrow winding lanes lined with colorful old buildings and private houses, to point out the historic and architectural features that have made them landmarks. If you are truly interested in history, arrange to visit with Old City Tours, whose architect-owner has been one of the driving forces behind the area's preservation.

Museum Kura Hulanda (22): The museum (Klipstraat 9, Otrobanda; 599-434-7765; www.kurahulanda.com) is part of one of the most ambitious restoration projects in the Caribbean. It has included the private restoration of sixty-five historic buildings, mostly former private homes, in an 8-block complex, which has become the Hotel Kura Hulanda and conference center, as well as the museum. Opened in 1999, as one of many projects commemorating Curaçao's 500th anniversary, Museum Kura Hulanda is dedicated to the island's African heritage. A cultural center and cultural studies center with an auditorium, it is situated only a few blocks from the cruise-ship dock on the site of a former slave yard and prison overlooking the harbor. Guides are available. Admission: US$9 adults, US$6 children. Hours: Tues to Sat 10 a.m. to 5 p.m. South of the port terminal on the waterfront is a group of restored buildings known as **Koral Agostini (20),** which date from 1737. It has small shops, a sidewalk cafe, and the Gouverneur, a popular balcony restaurant and bar with live Latin and Caribbean music on weekends.

At Breedestraat, Otrobanda's main shopping street, turn west for 2 blocks to St. Anna Church. One block south is Conscientiesteeg, the oldest lane of the quarter; and directly south of it on Sebastopolstraat, the **Sebastopol House (21)** is a good example of an 18th-century style that combined elements of a colonial town house with those of a plantation house.

West on Conscientiesteeg past **La Moda de Paris,** once the leading clothing shop in town, to the end of the street, a turn south for 1 block takes you to one of the most attractive areas, with a block of renovated town houses called "the Four Alley." Farther south at Zaantjessteeg and Gravenstraat, there is a group of fine houses with their original entrances and pretty gardens facing Pater Eeuwensweg. The houses once overlooked a lagoon that had bridges leading to the Rif area, a sort of lovers' lane in olden days.

You can return to the port via the Riffort area (and to the mega-pier and new Renaissance Hotel) or via Breedestraat for a stop at the **Netto Bar** (599-462-5188; www.nettobar.com), a famous neighborhood rendezvous, where you can buy Cuban cigars (but smoke them before you go back through U.S. Customs, because agents are likely to confiscate them).

Curaçao Museum (Van Leeuwenhoekstraat; Otrobanda; 599-462-3873; www.curacaomuseum .an). A mile or more from Riffort is the Curaçao Museum, housed in a building dating from 1853. Originally it was used as a military hospital—and not a former plantation house, or landhuis, as is sometimes said, although the style is similar. The museum covers the island's history from pre-Columbian times to the Dutch colonial period. Permanent exhibits include a replica of a typical kitchen of the colonial era, antique furniture, old industrial tools, and household utensils. You will find old maps of Curaçao and the Caribbean, a natural-history section, and a garden with island plants and trees. In addition to a permanent collection of contemporary art, the museum organizes exhibitions of works by local artists. Hours: Mon to Fri 9 a.m. to 4 p.m.; Sun 10 a.m. to 4 p.m. Entrance is $5 for adults, $2.50 for children. Monthly on the first Sun, a concert is given in the gardens from 4:30 to 6:30 p.m.

On the south side of Otrobanda by the sea is the Curaçao Marriott Hotel, designed in Curaçao's classic architecture, set in tropical gardens, with three restaurants, a casino, pool with swim-up bar, health club with four tennis courts, and water sports. Farther west at Blaubaai (Blue Bay) is **Blue Bay Curaçao Golf and Beach Resort** (Landhuis Blaauw; 599-868-1755; www.bluebaygolf.com), an oceanfront resort and residential community with a deluxe hotel, conference center and an 18-hole championship course designed by Rocky Roquemore. (See Sports section.)

A Drive Around the Island

Willemstad Environs

You can circle Santa Anna Bay from Piscadera Bay on the west by taking the highway around the bay to the east, or cross over on Queen Juliana Bridge. East of the bridge on the right (south) on a hill is **Roosevelt House,** the U.S. Consul General's residence, a gift from Curaçao to the United States for its assistance in World War II.

Landhuis Chobolobo: On the eastern edge of Willemstad in a 17th-century *landhuis* is the **Curaçao Liqueur Distillery** (599-9-461-3526; www .curacaoliqueur.com), where the orange-flavored liqueur Curaçao is made. The distillery celebrated its 100th anniversary in 1996. The early Spaniards planted Valencia oranges in Curaçao, and after adapting to the aridity and red-clay soil, the trees bore a fruit too bitter to eat—but an oil extracted from its skin proved to be suitable for making liqueur. The colorful liqueur makes a distinctive gifts to take home. Tours are available weekdays 8 a.m. to noon and 1 to 5 p.m.

Landhuis Rooi Catootje: Since 1853 another plantation house, on a hillside beyond the Curaçao Liqueur Distillery, has been in the Maduro family, one of Curaçao's oldest families. After the owner died in 1974, his heirs created the Mongui Maduro Foundation and converted the home into a library to house his unusual collection of books, documents, and photos relating to Curaçao's history, particularly its Jewish community. Hours: weekdays 9 a.m. to noon (599-737-5119; www.madurolibrary.org). If you detour in a northerly direction along Schottegatweg, you pass Peter Stuyvesant High School, with a statue of Peter Stuyvesant in a schoolyard—a reminder of Curaçao's early New York connection.

Landhuis Brievengat: About 9 miles on the northeast, you will see an early-18th-century plantation house that was a 12,000-acre cattle ranch until the mid-19th century. It was saved from demolition by the Preservation of Monuments Foundation.

West of Willemstad

Too often cruise passengers confine their visit to Willemstad and miss some of Curaçao's best attractions: rugged windswept terrain, pretty inland lagoons, adobe houses, and patchwork fields with fences of neatly crisscrossed candle cactus where sheep and goats graze, plus two of the best nature parks in the Caribbean. These are all the more fascinating for their obvious contrast to Curaçao's cosmopolitan capital.

The road crosses the tranquil countryside, or *cunucu* or *kunuku,* an Arawak word originally used to mean a piece of land given by a landowner to a slave to grow crops for his personal needs. The dry landscape is covered with kadushi cactus that grows as tall as trees and the ever-present divi-divi tree, whose wind-sculpted branches grow in one direction at a right angle from the trunk. Dotting the countryside are former plantation houses, or *landhuizen,* some dating from 1650. Most were surrounded by walls and fortified against marauding pirates and rebelling slaves. About sixty houses remain; several are maintained as museums, offices, and private homes.

Landhuis Daniel: Just beyond the Santa Maria turnoff at Daniel is one of the island's oldest plantation houses, dating from 1634. Landhuis Daniel was never a farmhouse, but a rest stop for travelers and their horses traversing the island. The house has been restored and once again is a rustic rest stop, with ten modest rooms, a restaurant, a pool, a herb garden, and facilities for diving nearby (599-864-8400; www.landhuisdaniel.com).

Landhuis Jan Kock: At Daniel the road forks west to Sint Willibrordus, a village, and the 17th-century Landhuis Jan Kock (599-869-4965), where once salt from nearby ponds was produced for the herring industry in Holland. The manor house is now an art gallery and the salt pans are home to Curaçao's only permanent flamingo colony.

Hato Caves: Set on a bluff on the north coast near the airport, the ancient caves have been renovated, lighted, and made more accessible. The caverns have stalagmites, stalactites, and bats. Beautiful orange-and-black orioles, known here as troupial, flit about in nearby trees, and iguanas scamper in the undergrowth near the snack bar and souvenir shop at the caves' entrance (F. D. Rooseveltweg; 599-868-0379; caves@cura.net). Hours: daily 10 a.m. to 5 p.m.; guided tours on the hour until 4 p.m. Admission: US$6.50 adults, US$5 children younger than age thirteen.

Christoffel Nature Park: On the hilly north end of the island is a 3,500-acre nature park whose most prominent feature is Curaçao's highest peak: 1,238-foot Mount Christoffel. The park begins north of Mount Hyronimus, a tabletop mountain, and comprises three contingent plantations—Savonet, Zorgvlied, and Zevenbergen—acquired by the government and managed by Carmabi. The **Savonet Museum** near the park entrance is housed in Landhuis Savonet, the former estate house which

is being restored. Park hours: Mon to Sat 7:30 a.m. to 4 p.m., no admittance after 2:30 p.m., Sun 6 a.m. to 3 p.m., no admittance after 1:30 p.m. Admission: US$10 adults, $4.50 children, including park entrance. The park is a forty-minute drive from Willemstad (599-864-0363; www.savonetmuseum.org, www.christoffelpark.org).

The park has more than 500 varieties of plants and trees, an estimated 150 resident and migrant bird species, iguana, feral donkeys, and the Curaçao deer. You can see unusual rock formations, caves with bats, and Indian petroglyphs. The vegetation is dry with abundant mesquite, century plants, divi-divi, and gigantic cacti.

Twenty miles of road, divided into four color-coded signposted routes, wind through the park. Three are driving routes of about an hour, each highlighting different points of interest. The fourth route is a footpath to the top of Mount Christoffel. A nature guide for hiking, birding, and deer watching can be arranged through the park or the tourist office. Guided nature walks are offered by the park, US$15; check for days and times as they vary by season; reservations should be made in advance.

The park also arranges jeep tours for $20 to $30 per person, including entrance fee; mountain bike tours, for $20; and deer watching year-round. **The White Tail Deer Trails** are a good introduction to the park's vegetation and to the most common trees and plants of Curaçao. They start at the visitor center and wind through the eastern part to the north coast. You might see one of the two hummingbird species—ruby topaz and blue-tailed emerald—that breed here. Near the center of the area is a watchtower from which hikers can spot Curaçao deer that come to a nearby watering trough.

Zorgvlied Trail is a ninety-minute circuit through the central and north areas; it returns along the eastern flank of Mount Christoffel, crossing the footpath to the summit. Two abundant trees and plants are the calabash, whose large fruit has a hard shell used throughout the Caribbean since the time of the Arawaks as a bowl and cooking utensil; and the enormous kadushi, a type of candle cactus, used to make cactus soup.

The Christoffel Mountain Trail winds over the undulating hills of the southwest to the top of Mount Christoffel, offering grand vistas extending the length of the island and, on a clear day, as far east as Bonaire and south to Venezuela. The hike from the visitor center is a three-hour round-trip, but by driving to the base of the mountain, you can cut off an hour.

Westpunt: An old fishing town, Westpunt (or West Point) on the rocky cliffs at the north end of the island sits above a quiet, turquoise sea. Below is a small beach of coarse sand, surrounded by walls of rock. The area has undergone extensive development in recent years with private homes and weekend cottages. The most significant addition is the **Lodge Kura Hulanda & Beach Club,** a deluxe eco-lodge created by the same group that operates the Kura Hulanda Hotel in Willemstad. From Westpunt you can return south through the undulating hills of the west coast.

Landhuis Knip (Kenepa): This restored plantation house is a good example of the island's 17th-century-style. It was one of Curaçao's most prosperous plantations and the site of the island's largest slave rebellion in 1795. It has a small museum and portrait gallery, and occasionally hosts folklore shows with displays of local handicrafts. Hours: Sun to Fri 9 a.m. to 5 p.m. Small admission fee with guided tour (599-864-0244). The landhuis is located in Bandabou, the local name for western Curaçao, near Playa Grandi and Klein Knip, two of the island's best beaches. By the sea is the dive resort **Habitat Curaçao** which enjoys an international reputation. On the south side of Santa Cruz, Santa Marta Bay is a large serpentine lagoon with beaches and rocky shores surrounded by green hillsides. The cultivation of the orange tree, from which the liqueur Curaçao is made, is a specialty of the area.

East of Willemstad

Curaçao Underwater Park: The biggest boost to the development of Curaçao as a dive center has been the creation of the 1,500-acre Curaçao Underwater Park, stretching for more than 12 miles from the Breezes Resort, just west of Jan Thiel Lagoon, to the eastern tip of the island. Developed by STINAPA, the Netherlands Antilles National Parks Foundation, with a grant from the World Wildlife Fund of the Netherlands, it protects some of Curaçao's finest reefs, which can be enjoyed

by snorkelers as well as divers. Jan Thiel Beach provides access to the park, where visibility is up to 150 feet. An excellent guidebook by the marine biologist Jeff Symbesma has an explanatory profile of the reef. There are sixteen permanent mooring buoys for boats. The first mooring in front of the Breezes Resort has diverse and colorful formations typical of Curaçao's reef structure. It starts in shallow water, suitable for snorkelers. The upper slope has mountain star, leaf, flower, and yellow pencil coral, as well as a variety of sponges. On the lower slope are brain, sheet, and star corals.

Seaquarium: On the west end of the marine park is the Curaçao Seaquarium, a private facility with more than four hundred species of marine life native to Curaçao waters. The Seaquarium uses no chemicals, pumps, or filters in the tanks, helping to promote the natural reproduction of sea life. Hours: daily 10 a.m. to 10 p.m. Admission: US$18 adults, $9.50 child younger than age twelve. (Bapor Kibra, 599-461-6666; www.curacao-sea-aquarium.com).

Animal Encounters is your chance to face down a shark or pet a stingray. Next to the Seaquarium divers can enter a 15-foot-deep open-water enclosure, which is a natural tidal pool, to play with the ray, angelfish, grouper, and other fish. At one end of the enclosure, divers are separated by a mesh fence from large sea turtles; on the other side, they can watch reef, lemon, and nurse sharks through a thick Plexiglas wall while they pass food to the sharks through small openings. Admission is US$99, which includes a full dive tank, wet suit, weights, a bucket of fish, and an hour of basic instruction on the use of dive gear from a professional diver who will accompany you. Photographs or a video of you can be taken for an additional charge. It's probably as close to a shark as most people ever want to be, but it's still thrilling. About half of those who participate are donning dive gear for the first time. (I recommend, however, that you have at least taken a scuba diving resort course.) Hours: 8:30 a.m. to 5:30 p.m.

Dolphin Academy Seaquarium offers a variety of programs to interact with dolphins, starting with a free daily educational presentation. Participants are given instructions and accompanied in the water by a trainer. Children younger than age eight must be accompanied by a paying adult. Prices are per person. *Dolphin Encounter:* Interaction with dolphins in shallow water; minimum age 3 years, US$79. *Dolphin Swim:* For experienced swimmers at least 4'3" (1.30 meters) tall, who swim with the dolphins, US$159. Other programs are snorkeling with dolphin, $169; and diving with them, US$214 to $234 depending on certification. Hours: daily 8:30 a.m. to 4:30 p.m. Entrance: US$18 adults, US$9.50 children younger than age twelve. Reservations: (599) 461-8900; www.dolphin-academy.com.

Spanish Water: Near the eastern end of the island, Spaanse Water, one of the island's largest and most beautiful lagoons, is a sheltered natural harbor with many hilly green fingers and coves, islands and beaches, and a long, very narrow opening to the sea. It is the island's boating and fishing center, with marinas and other water-sports facilities. The Curaçao Yacht Club is based here, and many Willemstad residents have weekend houses here. The new **Hyatt Regency Curaçao** (800-55-HYATT; www.curacao.hyatt.com), the first luxury resort in the area and centerpiece of Santa Barbara Plantation, a 1,500-acre luxury resort community, opened in Apr 2010.

East of Spanish Water you can see a chalky table mountain, 637-foot Tafelberg, from almost any height on the island. At one time as much as 100,000 tons of phosphate were mined here yearly; mining continues on a small scale. Beyond to the east is an arid, desolate area of rocky, rugged terrain.

Curaçao Den Paradera: Also known as Dinah Veeris's Botanical Garden (Seru Grandi 105 A, Weg Naar Fuik, 599-767-5608; dinahveeris@ yahoo.com), the owner is on a one-woman crusade to preserve the traditional medicinal flora of Curaçao. Here she grows more than 300 species of wild plants to help save them as well as the knowledge of how to use them—information that was being lost due to urbanization and industrialization that has changed much of the wild landscape of Curaçao. The name "Den Paradera" comes from the Paraguiri Indians who once had a large garden on the island. Veeris, known locally as a healer, blends herbs for medicinal purposes to sell and has published books that are often used by local botanists. Admission with guided tour $6 adult; children $4.

Curaçao Ostrich Farm: Across the island from the Seaquarium on the north coast at St. Joris Bay is a farm, unique to Curaçao and the Caribbean; it's one of the biggest ostrich ranching operations outside Africa. Here you can see the majestic creatures, which are the world's fastest animals on two legs, and learn about all aspects of ostrich ranching in an Africa-like environment. Hours: 9 a.m. to 5 p.m. Reservations: (599) 9-560-1276. Guided tour every hour. Closed Mon. Admission: US$10 adults, US$7 children age two to twelve years (599-747-2777; www.ostrichfarm.net). The farm has a gift shop with African crafts and a restaurant, Zambezi International, serving ostrich meat specialties and South African wines. It is housed in a large thatched-roof hut similar to dwellings that might be seen in Africa. Hours: noon to 10 p.m. daily except Tues (noon to 5 p.m.). Closed on Mon. Moderately expensive.

Aloe Vera Plantation (Weg Naar Groot Sint Joris z/n; 599-9-767-5577; www.aloecuracao.com). Located near the Ostrich Farm on the same dirt road beyond the farm, it is open 9 a.m. to 4 p.m. Mon through Sat. Lotions, gels, sun cream, and other products are available for purchase.

Shopping

Willemstad's cosmopolitan ambience is reflected in its shops filled with goods from around the world, including an abundance of European items: from fine jewelry to designer fashions, perfumes, and electronics. Cruise passengers are often most interested in Dutch goods, such as chocolate, rounds of Edam and Gouda cheese, delftware, and even wooden clogs. Breedestraat and Heerenstraat are the main streets of Punda, where quality stores are housed in colorful 18th-century colonial buildings.

Curaçao is not a duty-free port, but in 1988 the government removed tariffs on most luxury items, so prices represent a savings of 20 to 30 percent off those in the United States. A knowledge of stateside prices is the best way to recognize a good bargain. *Curaçao Events*, a free tourist pamphlet, is a convenient reference guide. Punda stores are open Mon to Sat from 8 a.m. to noon and 2:30 to 6 p.m. Some remain open during lunch, particularly when cruise ships are in port. They also open for cruise passengers on Sun and holidays, except Christmas and Good Friday.

Art and Artists: Curaçao has an active artist community, and in the last few years an amazing number of galleries have opened to showcase the work of local artists. Most galleries are open Mon to Sat from 9 or 10 a.m. to 6 p.m. and on Sun by appointment. Call to confirm hours. In Punda, **Maravia Gallery** (Handelskade #1; 599-461-9866 www.maraviagallery.com) features sculpture, photography, and art jewelry inspired by Curaçao and the diversity of nature and global cultures. The fine gallery represents internationally recognized Curaçao artist Jolanta Pawlak. Near the cruise docks are **Carib Fine Art** (Hotel Kura Hulanda, 599-465-5759; www.caribfineart.com) carries paintings, sculptures, ceramics, glassware, and gift items created by local and Caribbean artists plus a collection of unusual 19th-century engraved sea charts of the New World; and **Gallery Mon Art** (Riffort, 599-462-2977; www.monartgallerycuracao.com), has the paintings, ceramics, and mixed media by a variety of artists. It also sells calendars, diaries, and books.

Slightly farther away is **D'art Gallery** (Bitterstraat 11/Werfstraat 6, 599-462-8680; www.d-artgallery.com) carries contemporary works by local and international artists, including some South American ones. **Gallery Alma Blou** (Frater Radulphusweg 4; 599-462-8896; www.galleryalmablou.com), located in the renovated Landhuis Habaai on the outskirts of Ortobanda, sells local and Curaçao artists living abroad, as well as a nice selection of Curaçao crafts.

Nena Sanchez Gallery (Punda at Gomezplien and Landhuis Jan Kok, 599-738-2377; www.nenasanchez.com), whose Web site shows why this self-taught women is one of Curaçao's most popular artists with a colorful, distinctive style; and **Yubi Kirindongo** (Ser'i Kandela Kaya A 390; 599-869-3268; www.kirindongo.com), one of Curaçao's top artists with international standing, who works with materials and metals that when put together give a rough texture and special energy to his work. Studio and gallery tours, by appointment only. **Landhuis Bloemhof** (Santa Rosaweg 6, 599-737-5775; www.bloemhof.an), the former home and studio of May Henriquez, has been restored and serves

as gallery space for rotating exhibitions, a library dedicated to the arts and artists, and a venue for art related workshops and classes. Admission: US$ 2 per person.

Cameras and Electronics: Boolchand's (Breedestraat 50) and Palais Hindu (Heerenstraat) have large selections of photographic equipment and electronic gadgetry. Come with prices from home to compare.

Clothing and Accessories: The most easily recognized store in Curaçao is the yellow-and-white rococo front of **Penha & Sons** (www.jlpenha.com), a department store in the town's oldest building. It has a wide variety of goods such as perfumes, sunglasses, and designer clothes. **Bamali Boutique** (Breedestraat Punda 2; www.bamali-fashion.com) carries unusual, stylish tropical fashions, costume jewelry, and luxury leather goods. **Wulfsen & Wulfsen** (Gomezplein) specializes in famous European brands exclusively for men. **Emilia** (Gomezplein), a trendy boutique specializes in chic Caribbean style apparel and beach wear for women. Among the familiar brands, Tommy Hilfiger, Calvin Klein, Guess, Converse, and La Costa have boutiques in Punda; Little Holland features Ralph Lauren, and Basic Image has great linen clothing for women.

Crafts and Souvenirs: Obra di Man (Bargestraat in Scharloo) is both a shop and workshop for handmade folkloric dolls, wall hangings, ceramics, and other local crafts, with an outlet on Gomezplein. **Curaçao Creations** (Schrijnwerkerstraat off Breedestraat, in Otrobanda; 599-462-4516) has handicrafts fashioned by Curaçaoans, including pottery, leather goods, glasswork, jewelry, woven baskets, and art. The **New Market** in Punda (near the Wilhelmina Bridge) is another place to find local crafts. Market closes at 2 p.m.

Dutch Antilles Ceramics (Tera Cora, Kaya Diabaas 120, Band Abou; 599-864-9105) makes by hand a large selection of original items that are sold in most souvenir shops. Check the bottom of an item for the trademark. The workshop can be visited weekdays. **Keramos** (Rio Canario, Kaya Col. Kay Winkel 2; 599-737-4676), a twenty-five-year-old pottery store run by local artists, sells handmade ceramic souvenirs, plates, mugs and dishes with local motifs, and miniature landhouses and kunuku cottages.

Gourmet Food Products: Rounds of Gouda or Edam can be purchased in gourmet shops at about a 30 percent savings over U.S. prices. And don't forget Curaçao liqueur. **Zuikertuintje** (meaning "the sugar garden") is a market in a 17th-century landhuis on the east side of town, just beyond the Curaçao Liqueur factory. It has selections of Dutch cheese and chocolates and a large assortment of European gourmet products—plus a cafe where you can sample some of the products. On Handelskade, next to the **Iguana Café** (www .iguanacafe.org) is Iguana Too, an ice-cream shop for the very creamy Curaçao-produced Lover's ice cream, and logo T-shirts, hats, and beach bags. It also serves awesome desserts from a European-trained pastry chef.

Jewelry: Among the best-known names are **Gandelman Jewelers** (Breedestraat 35), which creates its own designs and also sells Piaget and Movado watches and Gucci accessories; and Little Switzerland, a division of Tiffany. For unique fine jewelry **Maravia Gallery** (Handelskade 1; www .maraviagallery.com) features the handmade artisan jewelry of Curaçao artist Jolatna Pawlak—all made in Curaçao. The trendy **Beads & Pieces** (Gomez-plein 3-B and Zuikertuin Mall; 599-465-4781) carries handmade jewelry, handbags and accessories, from modern to classic, for all occasion and budget.

Linens: **Mr. Tablecloth** (Handelskade) has the best selection of linens. Long established stores are **New Amsterdam** (Breedestraat) and **Little Holland** (Breedestraat).

Perfumes and Cosmetics: **Yellow House** (Breedestraat), the leading perfume shop, is as pretty as it is complete in its stock of French and other perfumes and cosmetics.

Dining and Restaurants

Curaçao's long trading history and diverse population made up of Dutch, Portuguese Jews, Africans, Chinese, Indians, Indonesians, and a host of Europeans is reflected in its food and wide selection of restaurants. They range from pizza parlors and

Dutch taverns to French bistros and elegant continental restaurants. Some offer harbor views; others are set in historic forts and charming old plantation houses. Entries range from moderate (less than US$10) and moderately expensive (US$10 to $25) to expensive (more than US$26).

For *criollo*, or local fare, try *empana*, a pastry inherited from the Spaniards; *sopito*, a fish-and-coconut soup served with *funchi*, a cornbread taken from the Africans; *keshi yena*, a cheese shell filled with meat, learned from the Dutch; and *rijsttafel*, a multi-dish treat the Dutch learned in Indonesia.

Angelica's Kitchen (Hoogstraat 49; 599-562-3699; www.angelicas-kitchen.com) is a Curaçao culinary option that enables guests to play chef (with a minimum of ten participants). Beginning at 6 p.m., you'll dress as chefs and read over the recipes that will serve as dinner mostly based on French or Italian cuisine with local influences and Caribbean fare. Dinner is ready by 8:30 p.m., and the evening ends at 10:30 p.m. Owner Angelique Schoop, a Curaçao native, studied in Amsterdam, the Peter Kemp Cooking School in New York, and La Varenne near Paris. Her kitchen is set in her century-old, restored landmark childhood home. Moderately expensive. Angelica also offers two culinary walking tours by request for minimum of four participants. One tour includes lunch of local food at the Old Market; on the other, participants make their lunch at Angelica's Kitchen. Tours start at 9:30 a.m. and visit parts of Otrobanda and Punda, including the historic synagogue and the Floating Market, where participants buy ingredients for their hands-on lunch. Tour ends about 2 p.m. Per person: US$45 with lunch at Old Market; $70 with hands-on lunch. Reservations necessary.

Beach Restaurant (Baoase Luxury Resort, Winterswijkstraat 2; 599-461-1799; U.S. & Canada: 888-409-3506; www.baoase.com) south of Willemstad in a beautiful, new resort by the owners of the Van Der Valk Hotel in town, has a lovely setting directly on the water.

Sculpture Garden Restaurant (Langestraat 8, Willemstad; 599-434-7700; www.kurahulanda .com), in the garden of the Hotel Kurá Hulanda serves contemporary gourmet cuisine indoors and alfresco. Specialties include fresh fish, lobster, and beef dishes. Good wine cellar. Moderately expensive.

Bistro Le Clochard (Riffort, Otrobanda; 599-462-5666; www.bistroleclochard.com). In this restaurant, set in an old fortification and former prison by the harbor, you can sit almost close enough to touch the passing ships. The menu is French and continental with fresh seafood, veal, cheese fondue, and sinful desserts. Expensive.

Fishalicious (Loostraat 1, 599-461-8844) located near Avila Beach Hotel, the restaurant gets high marks for fresh constantly, changing menu of seafood specialties and oyster bar, along with a good selection of wines. Dinner only.

Fort Nassau (599-461-3086; www.fortnassau .com). Known for its view, it offers a pretty hilltop setting overlooking Willemstad, as well as an ideal perch for an aperitif on its terrace bar. Moderately expensive.

Golden Star Bar (Socratesstraat 2; 599-465-4795). The informal bar/restaurant is not much to look at, but it's everyone's favorite for criollo cuisine. You can try a zesty *carco stoba* (conch stew), *bestia chiki* (goat-meat stew), *bakijou* (salted cod), *locrio* (a chicken-mixed rice), *concomber stoba* (stewed meat and cucumber), fish, and *funchi*. Moderate.

Iguana Café (Handelskade 13, 599-465-1956; www.iguanacafe.org) casual waterside dining on international and island specialties, grilled food; live music some evenings.

Le Gourmet (Gomezplein 5; 599-461-6862) in a lovely renovated 17th-century Dutch colonial building with outside terrace dining, serves top class European and Caribbean cuisine with good wine selections. Expensive.

Landhuis Dokterstuin (Dokterstuin in northwest Curaçao; 599-864-2701). If you find yourself on the main road to West Punt or Christoffel Park at lunchtime, this restaurant is worth your stop for authentic Curaçao or criollo cuisine. Here, in an outdoor picnic setting of a 17th-century plantation house (also known as Klein Ascension), you can feast on Creole chicken for only US$6; cactus or okra soup or stewed papaya for US$8; and goat meat, conch, or snapper for US$10. Closed Mon. Inexpensive.

Moon (Pietermaai 152, 599-461-7713; www .mooncuracao.com) the restaurant of Moon Beach Club and Lounge is Curaçao's cool, stylish, ultra modern answer to Nikki Beach complete with large infinity pool, cabanas, daybed lounges, and contemporary cuisine.

Nightlife

Curaçao comes to life at night along waterfront on the Handelskade in Punda at such places as the Iguana Café and across St. Anna Bay on the Rouvilleweg. There's also plenty to do in the resort hotels, casinos, and restaurants that have music for listening or dancing, and at discos. A dozen hotels have casinos; the closest to the port is **Kura Hulanda and the Renaissance Hotel** by the mega pier. There are popular bars for happy hour, piano bars for a quiet rendezvous, and seaside cafes where you can watch the parade of people and ships.

Wet & Wild Beach Club (Seaquarium Beach, Bapor Kibra; 599-561-2477) is a popular local hangout where the dance floor meets the sand along with loud beats and cold drinks. In same area, Mambo Beach restaurant is affordable, fun, and popular with young hip set.

Blues Cafe (Avila Beach Hotel; 599-461-4377) on the east side of town offers jazz by leading local musicians; good menu, too.

Sports

Most of the island's hotels and water-sports centers are located along the south coast immediately east and west of Willemstad. They welcome day visitors.

Beaches/Swimming: Several beaches on the leeward coast within a mile or so of Willemstad have been developed. They have changing facilities and water sports; there is an admission fee. There are pretty bays and coves with beaches, which swimmers are likely to have to themselves, except perhaps on weekends. You will find free public beaches at Westpunt, Knip, Klein Knip, and Daaibooi. Private beaches, charging a fee per car, are Blauw Bay and Jan Thiel, which have changing facilities. On the southeast, Santa Barbara, at the entrance to Spanish Water, is a popular beach with Curaçaoans. The windward coast generally is too turbulent for safe swimming.

Biking: Mountain bikes are available for rent at **Christoffel Park** (599-864-0363; info@christoffel park.org), which is the best place for biking excursions. Several companies offer bike rentals as well as biking excursions: the **Bike Shop** (Sta. Rosaweg 23; 599-560-3882; fax: 599-738-0027; bikeshop@ curacao-travelguide.com), **Dutch Dream** (Landhuis Papaya; 599-864-7377), and **Wanna Bike** (599-527-3720; www.wannabike.com. **Curaçao Actief** (Perseusweg 5t; 599-433-8858; www.curacao-actief .com) organizes mountain biking excursions as well as kayaking, sailing, windsurfing, diving, snorkeling, and eco-safari tours.

Boating: A cruise along the coast to Klein Curaçao off Curaçao's eastern end, to enjoy its sandy beaches and snorkeling, is a favorite sailing excursion offered by water-sports operators. A full-day sail on the *Insulinde,* a 120-foot traditionally rigged sailing vessel, is US$50 (599-560-1340; www.insulinde.com). **Mermaid Boat Trips** (599-560-1530; www.mermaidboattrips.com) sails three times weekly with up to sixty people to Klein Curaçao for the day. The **Katamaran** *Jonalisa* (599-767-9998; www.bountyadventures.com) sails four times weekly. Check with operator for days and time as they vary considerably. For private sailing, contact **Curaçao Yacht Club** (Brakkeput Ariba; 599-767-4627; www.curacaoyachtclub .com).

Deep-Sea Fishing: Half-day charters for about US$400 and full-day ones for about US$600 leave from major hotels and the marinas at Spanish Water almost daily, offering great deep-sea fishing for four to six persons, with tackle and bait provided. Arrangement can be made through water-sports operators. Anglers go for marlin, tuna, wahoo, sailfish, and other large fish. Only hook and line fishing is permitted in the Curaçao Underwater Park. **Let's Fish** (Brakkeput Abou K92; 599-747-4489; www.letsfish.net) offers half-day outings (six people maximum) for US$400; full day, US$575. It also runs day trips to Klein Curaçao (up to eleven people). **Miss Ann Boat Trips** (Jan Sofat 232-A; 599-767-1579; www.missannboattrips.com) has fishing trips for wahoo, tuna, marlin, sailfish, dorado, and barracuda. Six people, half day: US$50, full day, US$800. The Curaçao Yacht Club (see

Boating) organizes an annual Blue Marlin Tournament in early Mar.

Golf and Squash: Blue Bay Curaçao Golf and Beach Resort (Blaubaai, or Blue Bay; 599-868-1755; www.bluebaygolf.com) was the island's first 18-hole championship course, designed by Rocky Roquemore. Located on the south coast west of Willemstad, the 6,815 yard, par 72 course is laid out over the natural undulating terrain between the hills, rocks, and beach, and enjoys views of the sea from many locations. The clubhouse has a pro shop and restaurant. Greens fees: winter US$105 per person or US$85 after noon; off-season, US$90 or $70 after noon. Rental clubs $45; shoes $12.50. The new beachfront **Hyatt Regency Curaçao** (800-55-HYATT; www.curacao.hyatt.com) has the island's first Pete Dye-designed 18-hole championship resort golf course, pro-shop and clubhouse with one of the resort's three eateries, Shor, a seafood restaurant.

The **Curaçao Golf and Squash Club** (Wilhelminalaan, Emmastad; 599-737-3590; www .curacaogolf.com) welcomes visitors. The strong winds and sand greens of the 10-hole course are the challenge. Clubs and pullcarts are available for rent. Greens fee: US$15. There is a clubhouse with bar, open daily in the morning. The club also has two squash courts open daily from 8 a.m. to 6 p.m. There are special hours for visitors.

Hiking: The best hiking is in the Christoffel Nature Park, where marked routes highlight special features and show the variety of Curaçao's natural features and attractions. Many parts of the north coast have only dirt tracks, where hikers can enjoy the wild desolate scenery of strong waves breaking against rock shores. In addition to the guides at Christoffel Park, **Curaçao Actief** (599-462-8858; www.curacao-actief.com) has jeep safaris and organizes hiking excursions as well as kayaking, sailing, windsurfing, diving, snorkeling, and eco-safari tours. **Wild Curaçao** (599-561-0027; www .curacaowildtours.com) offers hiking excursions.

Horseback Riding: Rancho Alegre (Landhuis Groot St. Michiels; 599-868-1181) offers riding in the countryside Tues to Fri, US$50. So too, does **Ashari's Ranch** (599-869-0315). Arrangements should be made in advance. Riding tours of Christoffel Park are offered by **Rancho Alfin** (599-864-0535) and the park by appointment through **Landhuis Savonet** (599-864-0363).

Kayaking/Canoeing: Curaçao's fingered coastline with many bays is ideal for kayaking. Among the companies that offer excursions are **Miss Ann Boat Trips** (599-767-1579) and **Adrenaline Tours** (599-767-6241; www.adrenaline tourscuracao.com). **Dutch Dream** (599-461-9393) offers canoe trips on Thurs from 8 a.m. to 5 p.m., about US$46. **Curaçao Actief** (see Hiking above) offers kayaking excursions.

Snorkeling/Scuba Diving: Long overshadowed by its sister island of Bonaire for diving, Curaçao is finally getting the attention it deserves. The island is surrounded by fringing reef, much of which is virgin territory. The structure comprises gently sloping terraces, shallow walls, and sheer dropoffs. The marine park protects some of Curaçao's finest reefs and can be enjoyed by snorkelers as well as divers. (See the Curaçao Underwater Park section earlier in this chapter.) In addition, Curaçao has more than three dozen coves and beaches with reefs within swimming distance from shore at places that can be reached by car. One of the most convenient is Blauw Bay, 5 miles from Willemstad, just west of Piscadera Bay. Most operators are located at hotels and can make arrangements for fishing, waterskiing, day sailing, and glass-bottom boat excursions, as well as diving and snorkeling.

Among the major dive shops are **Atlantis Diving** (599-465-8288; www.atlantisdiving.com), **Caribbean Sea Sports** (Marriott Beach Resort; 599-462-2620; www.caribseasports.com), **Habitat Divers Curaçao** (Rif Santa Marie; 599-864-8304; www.habitatcuracaoresort.com), **Ocean Encounters** has branches at several hotels and is headquartered in the Seaquarium (Bapor Kibra z/n; 599-461-8131; www.oceanencounters.com). All offer excursions for beginners to experienced divers as well as resort courses. Rates range from US$45–$55 for a single dive and $70–$80 for two dives, including tanks, weights, and belt.

Windsurfing/Kiteboarding: The strong trade winds that cool the island and shape the divi-divi trees have also made windsurfing and kiteboarding two of Curaçao's most popular sports, with international recognition and an Olympic windsurf champion. The most popular windsurfing area is on the southeast coast between Princess and Jan Thiel beaches, which is also the venue for the annual championships. The protected waters of Spanish Water are best for novices. **Top Watersports Curaçao** (by the Seaquarium; Box 3102; 599-461-6666; fax: 599-461-3671) specializes in windsurfing. It rents boards and other water-sports equipment and offers lessons. **Windsurfing Curaçao** (Caracas Bay Island, 599-738-0883; www.windsurfing curacao.com) has boards for rent at Spanish Water, and other locations: one hour US$14, half-day $35, full-day $50; lessons $46 for one hour. **Curaçao Kiteboarding** (599-511-1094; www.curacaokite boarding.com; curacaokiteboarding@gmail.com) provides lessons from beginner to independent kiteboarder.

Kiteboarding, an extreme sport, can be dangerous. Lessons, given at your own risk, start at 9 a.m. at St. Joris Bay. Students must be fifteen years of age or older, be able to swim, and not be afraid of water. They need to have watershoes, T-shirt/rash guard, sunscreen, and insurance. First lesson covers equipment, safety, the wind window, kite setup, kite control, and more. Two hour lesson for one: US$130, for two people: $200. Pickup service: $15. Equipment is available for rent.

Festivals and Celebrations

Curaçao gets the year off to a good start with Carnival and closes it with a big **Christmas**—after all, jolly old St. Nick was Dutch. In between there is a full calendar of sports and cultural events. Curaçao hosts a big fishing tournament in spring, the Tumba Festival in Jan, Heineken Regatta Curaçao in Nov, and the **Curaçao North Sea Jazz Festival** in Aug. For the most complete list of events, tours, attractions, and day- and nighttime activities taking place during your visit, check out the free weekly publication *K-Pasa Curaçao* (www.k-pasa.com).

Aruba
Oranjestad

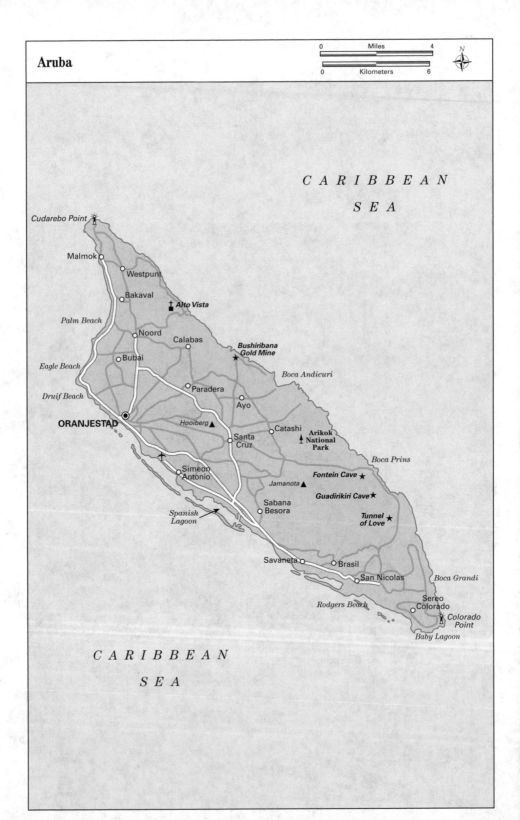

Aruba

0 Miles 4

0 Kilometers 6

N

CARIBBEAN SEA

Cudarebo Point

Malmok

Westpunt

Bakaval

† **Alto Vista**

Palm Beach

Noord

Calabas

Bushiribana Gold Mine ★

Boca Andicuri

Eagle Beach

Bubai

Druif Beach

Paradera

Ayo

ORANJESTAD

Hooiberg ▲

Catashi

Santa Cruz

Arikok National Park

Boca Prins

Simeon Antonio

Fontein Cave ★

Jamanota ▲

Guadirikiri Cave ★

Spanish Lagoon

Sabana Besora

Tunnel of Love ★

Savaneta

Brasil

San Nicolas

Boca Grandi

Sereo Colorado

Rodgers Beach

Colorado Point

Baby Lagoon

CARIBBEAN SEA

Island of Surprises

By any measure Aruba is an unusual island. It combines city polish, frontier ruggedness, and a people who are as warm and gracious as they are ingenious. Dutch orderly and clean, this modern miracle was little more than sand and brush five decades ago. Now the island is one of the most popular, sophisticated destinations in the Caribbean, with tourist facilities catering to visitors from three continents. And it never stops. New hotels, restaurants, shops, and other attractions continue to pop up, adding to Aruba's already impressive range and variety.

In contrast to the glitter and glamour of its resorts, Aruba's arid, rocky terrain is similar to the American Southwest. The land is flat, except for the 541-foot Hooiberg—a conical-shaped hill rising in the center of the island—and small, undulating hills on the north side. Yet for a small, low-lying island, Aruba has surprisingly diverse landscape and natural attractions.

Located only 15 miles off the coast of Venezuela, Aruba is ringed by coral reefs. Its leeward coast, where tourist development has been concentrated, has miles of calm, palm-fringed white-sand beaches, which are among the most beautiful in the Caribbean. In contrast, strong winds and big waves crash against the northeast coast, where the landscape is as desolate as the surface of the moon. Along the rockbound shores are coves with white-sand or black-pebble beaches, caves with prehistoric drawings, and sand dunes. The countryside is dotted with tiny, colorful Dutch colonial villages and farms against a landscape of gigantic rock formations sculpted by the strong winds, and shrub and cactus fields that overnight can turn from a lifeless brown to flowering green after a good rain.

Inhabited by the Arawak Indians of the Caiquetio tribe as early as 500 B.C., more is known about their civilization since the first excavation took place in 1882 by Mr. Van Koolwijk. The island was claimed for Spain in 1499 by Alonso de Ojeda and became a Dutch possession in 1636. Except for a short period of British control in the 19th century, it has remained Dutch. No Europeans settled on Aruba until 1754, but it was another forty years before colonization began.

Aruba was largely ignored until 1824, when gold was discovered. Its production lasted almost a century and was followed by an oil prosperity that began in 1924, when the Lago Oil and Transport Co. built an oil refinery here. Eight years later the company became a subsidiary of Exxon and prospered until 1985, when Exxon closed its refinery due to the drop in world demand. It was a move that might have devastated most islands, but not Aruba. Almost without skipping a beat, the Arubans quickly got their affairs in order—including leaving the Netherlands Antilles in 1986 to become a separate entity under the Dutch crown—and redirected their energies into developing other sectors of their economy.

Arubans say their population is made up of forty-three nationalities. One look at the astonishing range of physical and facial characteristics of the people will convince you the claim is not

At a Glance	
Antiquities	★
Architecture	★
Art and Artists	★
Beaches	★★★★★
Colonial Buildings	★★
Crafts	★
Cuisine	★★★
Culture	★
Dining/Restaurants	★★★★
Entertainment	★★★
Forts	★
History	★
Monuments	★
Museums	★
Nightlife	★★★★
Scenery	★★★
Shopping	★★
Sightseeing	★★★
Sports	★★★★
Transportation	★★★

Population: 97,931

Size: 20 miles in length and 6 miles in width; 70 square miles

Main Town: Oranjestad

Government: Aruba was a member of the Netherlands Antilles until 1986, when it became a separate entity within the Kingdom of the Netherlands with political autonomy, which allows Aruba to conduct its affairs without ratification by the central government as required of the other five Dutch Islands. The Netherlands government is responsible for defense and foreign affairs. Aruba has a governor appointed by the queen for a six-year term of office. The parliament is made up of twenty-one members elected for four-year terms. The Council of Ministers forms the executive power, headed by a prime minister.

Currency: Aruba's currency is the florin (Afl), divided into 100 cents. US$1 equals Afl1.77. Dollars and traveler's checks are widely accepted.

Departure Tax: Afl64.31 (US$36.75). U.S. passengers returning home from Aruba pass through U.S. immigration in Aruba before their departure. Others on international flights, $33.50.

Emergency Numbers: Medical: Dr. Horacio Oduber Hospital, Smith Boulevard; (297) 587-4300; Police: (297) 582-4000; 911; Fire Alarm Center: 115; 911

Language: Dutch is the official language, but Papiamento is the local language, used increasingly in the schools. It evolved from Spanish, Dutch, and Portuguese and is sprinkled with African, English, and French words. Most Arubans have an amazing aptitude for languages and often speak Dutch, English, and Spanish.

Public Holidays: Jan 1, New Year's Day; Carnival Mon; Flag Day; Good Friday; Easter Monday; Apr 30, Coronation Day; May 1, Labor Day; Ascension Day; Dec 25, Christmas; and Dec 26, Boxing Day.

Telephone Area Code: 297. In Feb 2003 Aruba expanded the telephone numbers from six to seven by adding a 5 in front of the former six-digit number. For example, if the old number was 881-111, the new number is 588-1111. To call a cell phone, add a 9 in front of the old number. For example, 981-111 becomes 998-1111. To call Aruba from the United States, dial 011-297 plus the seven-digit local number, which now should always start with 5.

Airlines: *From the United States:* There are daily flights from Atlanta, Boston, Charlotte, New York, Newark, and Miami. Regularly scheduled carriers servicing Aruba include American Airlines, Air Tran, Continental, Delta, JetBlue, Spirit, United Airlines, and US Airways. *From Canada:* Air Canada. *Interisland:* American Airlines/American Eagle, and Tiara Air.

Information: www.aruba.com

In the United States:

Aruba Tourism Authority:

New Jersey: 100 Plaza Dr., First Floor, Secaucus, NJ 07094; (201) 558-1110; (800) TO-ARUBA; fax: (201) 558-47688757; ata.newjersey@aruba.com

Chicago: 1144 E. State St., Suite A Box 300, Geneva, IL, 60134; (630) 262-5580; fax: (847) 262-5581; ata.chicago@aruba.com

Miami: 2334 Ponce De Leon Blvd., Suite 200, Coral Gables, FL 33134; (305) 445-9619; fax; (305) 445-9619; ata.florida@aruba.com

Houston: 10655 Six Pines Dr., Suite 145, The Woodlands, TX 77380-3416; (281) 362-1616; fax: (281) 362-1644; ata.houston@aruba.com

Atlanta: PMB 355, 1750 Powder Springs Rd., Suite 190, Marietta, GA 30064-4861; (404) 89-ARUBA; fax: (404) 873-2193; ata.atlanta@aruba.com

In Canada:

5875 Highway No. 7, Suite 201, Woodbridge, ON L4L 1T9; (905) 264-3434; fax: (905) 264-3437; ata.canada@aruba.com

In Port:

Aruba Tourism Authority, 172 Lloyd G. Smith Blvd., Eagle, Aruba; (297) 582-3777; fax: (297) 583-4702; ata.aruba@aruba.com

far-fetched. But the most pronounced feature the Arubans have retained is the legendary Arawak traits of a gentle, smiling nature. For most visitors this is Aruba's biggest attraction.

Budget Planning

Aruba can be expensive if you travel by taxi and dine at the top restaurants. Bus transportation is reliable and cheap; however, car rentals are reasonable and the best mode of travel; sightseeing tours are moderately priced and well executed; and there is a wide range of restaurants. If you want to tour off-the-beaten-track, you will probably need a guide on rural roads, because there are very few signs and no gasoline stations. There are also savings to be had if you pick up a copy of *Aruba Nights* or *Aruba Experience,* tourist booklets that are chock full of discount coupons.

Port Profile

Location/Embarkation: Ships pull dockside at the port, which is located on the west side of Oranjestad, the capital, less than a quarter mile from the town center and within walking distance of the main shopping area. There are three air-conditioned cruise terminals and facilities include long distance telephone access with worldwide direct-dial capability, an activities desk for immediate bookings and booths selling handicrafts and souvenirs.

Passengers with prearranged rental cars or tours are met inside the terminal lounge. The cruise terminal has three information kiosks with cruise greeters from the Cruise Tourism Authority (CTA) (www.arubabycruise.com) positioned there to offer services to passengers.

Local Transportation: Taxis are at the port to meet ships and can be requested by phone from a dispatch office (297-582-2116). Taxis are expensive, unless you share the cost with others. They do not have meters, but rates are fixed and should be agreed upon in advance. The one-way fare from the port to a Palm Beach hotel is US$12; from Palm Beach hotels to the airport, US$20–$25; and from the port or town to the airport, US$13. All taxi drivers participate in the government's Tourism Awareness Program and receive a Guide Certificate. Local buses are inexpensive and can be recommended. Drivers speak English and are very helpful. The buses run at about fifteen-minute intervals along Smith Boulevard, the main seaside thoroughfare paralleling the port. The main bus terminal is directly across from the cruise dock exit on Smith Boulevard. Buses heading east from the port take you

to the downtown area and beyond. Buses going west take you to the resorts along Eagle and Palm Beaches. Bus stops are marked *bushalte.* One-way fare is US$2.25 and can be paid in U.S. currency. **Arubus** (297-588-2300; www.arubus .com) and the Tourist Bureau have information on buses and schedules.

Roads and Rentals: Aruba has a network of paved and rural roads that make it possible to drive to any part of the island. *Aruba Holiday,* a free tourist guide with a road map, is available from the Aruba Tourism Authority, hotels, and shops. Most roads radiate from Oranjestad, from which the main arteries run west to the resort center of Palm Beach, east to the airport, and southeast to San Nicolas. No road completely encircles the island, but by using a series of connecting roads, you can make a loop from Palm Beach around the northwest end and return via Noord.

Toward the south beyond the airport, the highway continues to Spanish Lagoon, Savaneta, and San Nicolas. You can loop through San Nicolas to the southeast coast and return via Santa Cruz, a crossroad town almost in the center of the island, with roads branching north; west along the Hooiberg, Casibari, and to Palm Beach; and south through Frenchman's Pass (Franse Pas) to Barcadera.

Car rentals are abundant and the best mode of transportation around the island. Cars range from US$40 and up per day. An open-air jeep, the most popular choice, costs about US$60 to $70 per day. A valid foreign driver's license is needed to rent and drive a car. The minimum driving age for rental cars is twenty-one to twenty-five and the maximum age is sixty-five to seventy-five, depending on the rental company. Major U.S. car rental companies have licensees in Aruba, and there are reliable local companies. Driving is on the RIGHT side of the road.

George's ATVs, Scooters & Cycles (297-993-2202) rents jeeps, scooters, and motorcycles and has pickup service. Bikes cost about US$15; scooters, US$20. Open 9 a.m. to 5 p.m. **Pablito's Bike Rental** (297-587-8655) is open 9 a.m. to 6 p.m.

Heli-tours Aruba (297-965-5906; www.aruba helitours.com) offers island tours, using a new R44 helicopter for a minimum of two passengers.

Shore Excursions

An island tour can be taken several ways: a standard motor coach or jeep excursion, on horseback, or by ATV, helicopter, or hiking with a nature guide or other specialist, visiting the less accessible parts of the island and focusing on its more unusual aspects. More information is available on sightseeing and sports later in the chapter. Prices are per person.

Cunucu Safari: 4–5 hours, US$50–70 with lunch. An excursion with more emphasis on the natural environment accompanied by a naturalist guide takes you to the interior. You travel by a jeep-type buggy, breakfast at an Aruban cunucu home, tour the "outback" sites, and end with lunch in town.

Learn to Windsurf: 1 hour, lesson package US$60. Aruba is one of the Caribbean's major windsurfing locations. Lessons are available at beachside hotels and Windsurf Village.

Atlantis **Submarine,** *Seaworld Explorer:* See Sports later in this chapter.

Golf at Tierra del Sol: 5 hours, US$160 in season. The interesting Robert Trent Jones II course is on the northwestern end of Aruba. (See Sports section for details.)

Scuba Diving: 3 hours, US$70. Dive operators offer learn-to-dive courses as well as dive excursions for certified divers: one-tank dive, US$50–$60; two-tank dive, US$65–$75. Snorkeling excursion, US$44.

Sea Trek: Exclusively on De Palm Island. Walk among the fish and marine life on the ocean floor. A large helmet keeps your face out of the water, and you breathe through a tube attached to a floating tank. Half-day US$89, including transfers.

Kayak Adventure: 3 hours, US$99, as ship-to-shore excursion. Kayaking from Spanish Lagoon and mangroves on the south coast to Bacadera Channel to a beach for swimming and snorkeling. Participants must be ten years or older to participate.

Heli-tours Aruba (297-731-9999; www .arubahelitours.com), located behind the Seaport Casino in Oranjestad, offers several tours. The northwestern half of Aruba for fifteen minutes, $85 per person; or combined with the island interior, thirty minutes, $114 per person, for minimum of two passengers.

Aruba on Your Own

The capital of Aruba, Oranjestad, is a neat, clean town of Dutch colonial and modern architecture. It is easy to cover in an hour's stroll or to combine with a shopping excursion. From the port you can walk along Smith Boulevard to the Renaissance Village Complex, a mall with moderate-priced boutiques and outdoor cafes overlooking the harbor. Farther along is Wilhelmina Park, a small tropical garden named for the Dutch queen.

An Oranjestad Walkabout

From Schuttestraat, turn right on Oranjestraat for 1 block to reach **Fort Zoutman,** the oldest-standing structure on Aruba. It was built in 1796 to protect Aruba's harbor; the Willem III Tower was added in 1868 to serve as a lighthouse. The fort houses the **Aruba Historical Museum** (297-588-5199), which focuses on the last one hundred years of Aruba's history. Hours: 8:30 a.m. to 4:30 p.m. Entrance: US$3.

The Bonbini Festival, a folkloric fair, takes place in the courtyard of the fort every Tues evening from 6:30 to 8:30 p.m. year-round. Admission varies from US$3 to $10 depending on what is offered. It features a folkloric show, native food, and crafts by local artisans. The fair proceeds go to local charities whose members man the stalls. (Bonbini in Papiamento means "welcome.")

As an alternative route from Smith Boulevard, just before the small bridge over the Renaissance

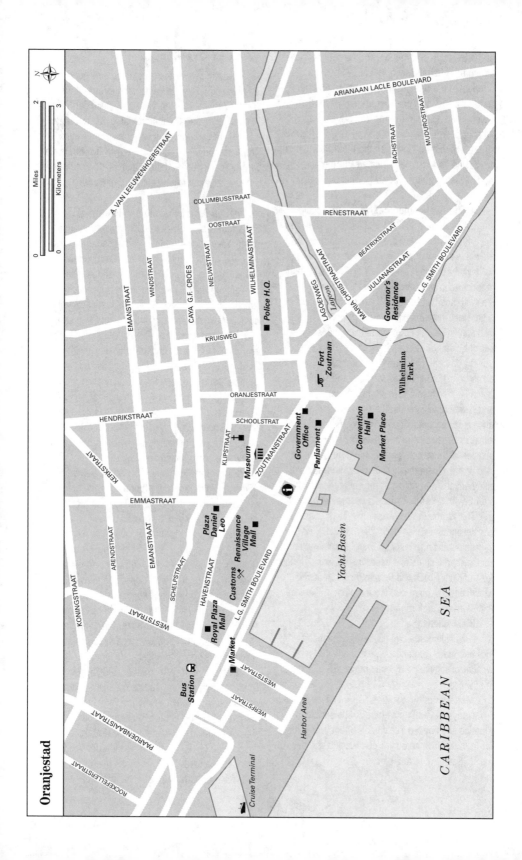

Oranjestad

Aruba Beach Resort lagoon, you can detour through the Renaissance Village, a shopping complex of the Renaissance Aruba, to the town center. Guests board a boat, directly from the lower lobby, to go to the resort's private beach. An escalator in the atrium takes you from the street level by the lagoon to the main floor, where the casino and disco are located. On the north side of the hotel are sidewalk cafes overlooking the town square.

Aruba Archaeological Museum (Schelpstraat 42; 297-582-8979). The museum preserves the artifacts of Aruba from pre-colonial times to the present. Aruba is placing increased emphasis on its cultural and historic heritage for the benefit of its citizens as well as visitors. Hours: weekdays 8 a.m. to noon and 1 to 4:30 p.m. Entrance is free. A booklet, *The Indians of Aruba,* published by the museum, is helpful in understanding the island's ancient history.

On Wilhelminastraat, the Protestant Church dates from 1846 and was rebuilt in the 1950s in Dutch-Aruban architecture. It faces a small square, which was redesigned in the late 1980s as the town plaza and pedestrian mall, surrounded on all sides by shopping complexes behind colorful facades of Dutch colonial architecture. The north side of the square is Nassaustraat, the traditional commercial street. West of the square is Havenstraat, with several of Aruba's best restaurants.

The Numismatic Museum (Weststraat just beyond the cruise dock; 297-582-8831; www.museumaruba.org) displays more than thirty thousand different coins and paper money, some dating from ancient Greek and Roman times. Hours: weekdays 9 a.m. to 4 p.m; Sat 8 a.m. to noon. Entrance fee $5 adults, children free.

Ricki Shells (Salina Serca 35A; 297-586-2119; www.museumaruba.org) displays excavation findings and many rare and unusual shells that make wonderful souvenirs. By appointment only, phone in advance.

Museum of Antiquities (Tanki Leendert 158-G) displays unusual items from Aruba and South America and housed in a complex built with materials from the 17th century. Hour: weekdays 9 a.m. to 5 p.m., Sat 10 a.m. to 2 p.m.

West of Oranjestad

At Druif Bay, where the coastline bends north, a talcum powder–fine white sand stretches for almost 7 miles. It is the most developed part of Aruba, containing the majority of its luxury hotels, casinos, restaurants, and water-sports facilities. The first mile or so, known as **Eagle Beach,** has a jogging track at the western end, and on its north side are wetlands known as **Bubali Pond,** a small bird sanctuary.

Aruba Aloe Museum and Factory (115 Pitastraat, Hato; 297-588-3222; www.arubaaloe .com). Long a local tradition that aloe brings good luck and can cure many ailments, the plant is often found hanging from home ceilings and planted by the front door. In the past the plant brought prosperity to Aruba and is still cultivated commercially for use in lotions, suntan creams, hair-care products, and fragrances. Tours: Mon to Fri, 8 a.m. to 4 p.m., Sat, 9 a.m. to noon. The shop sells aloe products nicely packaged for gifts. They can also be purchased in supermarkets and gift and souvenir shops. Aloe Vera grows wild throughout Aruba and a few of the outdoor ovens where the juice of the leaves is boiled and hardened are still in use. You can treat a cut or sunburn simply by breaking off a leaf and rubbing the sap on your skin.

Palm Beach: The next stretch of 5 miles is gorgeous Palm Beach. Each of its seaside hotels is surrounded by flowering gardens that provide privacy and relieve an otherwise-barren landscape with color. Each hotel has its own swimming pool, beach bar, and water sports. The prettiest of the group is the deluxe **Hyatt Aruba,** designed in Spanish architecture with tropical gardens and terraced pools and lagoons interconnected by waterfalls overlooking a beautiful palm-graced beach. **Red Sail Sports** (297-586-1603 or in the United States 800-255-6425; www.redsailaruba.com) here also handles sports arrangements for day visitors.

Butterfly Farm Aruba (297-586-3656; www .thebutterflyfarm.com). Located near the south end of Palm Beach, Aruba's Butterfly Farm is home to thirty-two species of butterflies from around the world, including eleven native species, accounting for the 600 to 700 large and small butterflies visitors can see here. The farm raises them from egg to caterpillar to butterfly. Visitors are given a guided tour and explanation of the process; afterward, they are free to walk through the different, mesh-enclosed gardens, each intended to attract and sustain various species. Admission: US$15 adults, $8 children four to sixteen years, children three and under are free. Hours: daily 9 a.m. to 4:30 p.m.; last tour at 4 p.m.

California Point: The scenic northern end of Aruba is marked by the California Lighthouse, a historic landmark. It takes its name from the ship *Californian*, wrecked in 1891 and lying in 15 to 30 feet of water off the northwest tip.

Fisherman's Huts: En route to the point after Palm Beach is a stretch of beach that is the island's prime windsurfing area and home of **Windsurf Village.** At the foot of the lighthouse is **Tierra del Sol,** Aruba's golf course (see Sports section).

The main road from California Point returns southeast along a stretch of dry, desolate terrain characterized by towering rocks and scattered hills. The highest is Alto Vista, 236 feet, from which there are lovely views. Here, too, is the chapel of Alto Vista, consecrated in 1750. In the village of Noord, St. Anna Church, with a 17th-century Dutch hand-carved altar, is one of the island's oldest churches and a fine example of Dutch colonial architecture.

A Drive Around the Island

Aruba's surprising diversity can be revealed only on a tour of the island—a total change from the beaches and glittering casinos of the south coast. After leaving the placid turquoise waters and white sands on the leeward shores, the road north passes an area of gigantic rock formations and the ever-present Aruban landmark, the divi-divi tree, whose curious shape is sculpted by strong prevailing winds.

Hooiberg: East from Oranjestad toward the airport is the conical-shaped 541-foot Hooiberg, known as "the Haystack," in view on the eastern horizon. Located almost in the center of the island, the curious volcanic formation is visible from most any location. It is covered with dry woodlands of kibrahacha, or yellow poui, a common tree of the Caribbean that usually blossoms after a rain. A flight of several hundred steps leads to the summit,

where you can see the coast of Venezuela in the distance on a clear day. Among the birds populating the hill is the spectacular orange-and-black trupial (or troupial).

On the south side of the Hooiberg, the Canashito area has caves with Arawak petroglyphs —one of several places where they are found. The area between the Hooiberg and Casibari, on the north, is littered with huge boulders that have been carved and weathered into bizarre shapes by the strong winds that blow across the island.

Ayo: Directly east of Hooiberg, an area strewn with enormous rocks has been dubbed "the Stonehenge of Aruba." Footpaths make it easy to walk through the area and examine the formations at close range. If you are very quiet, you will probably see a variety of birds, particularly colorful parakeets that populate these parts.

Donkey Sanctuary (297-584-1063; www .arubandonkey.org) In Santa Lucia, near the Ayo Rock formations, the Save Our Donkeys Foundation has rescued some ninety animals in a few short years. Visitors are welcome to spend time with the donkeys, feed them, and participate in the adopt-a-donkey program. The guides enjoy explaining the history of the donkeys in Aruba while escorting you around. Hours: weekdays 9 a.m. to 12:30 p.m. and weekends 10 a.m. to 3 p.m.

The Atlantic Coast: Across the island from Oranjestad on the northeast coast between Boca Mahos and Andicuri Bay, the land drops sharply into a turbulent sea where waves crash endlessly against the rocky shores. At a natural bridge— once a prime tourist attraction until it collapsed in Sept 2005—the force of the water was so great it gave rise to the popular notion that the bridge was carved out of the coral by the sea. Scientists say, however, that the bridge and other similar formations along the coast were formed when weak spots in the coral terraces, which make up the north coast, were dissolved and washed away by abrasive action of fresh rainwater. They explain that the sea could have polished, enlarged, and even smashed the bridge by its force, but only fresh water could have dissolved the rock on the land side. Another bridge, known as Boca Druif, or Dragon Mouth, can be seen behind the sand dunes of Boca Prins on the windward coast.

The road between Santa Cruz and Boca Prins runs through the Miralamar Pass between Aruba's highest hills and the countryside of rolling hills, farms, and colorful cunucu houses. Originally, cunucu in the Arawak language meant a plot of land for agriculture; now it is widely used to mean rural areas. Arubans also use the Spanish word *campo* for countryside.

Aruba Ostrich Farm (297-585-9630; www .arubaostrichfarm.com) Located by Bushiribana Goldmine ruins on the road to the former Natural Bridge, the Aruba Ostrich Farm is a sister to the bigger farm on Curaçao. Guided tours by truck are offered daily 9 a.m. to 4 p.m. Cost is US$12 adults, US$6 children. There is no charge to visit the restaurant, bar, or gift shop, which is stocked with interesting African carvings and clothing.

Arikok National Park: Mount Arikok, 577 feet, is the island's second-highest peak and the center of the Arikok National Park (297-585-1234; www.arubanationalpark.com), which lies between Boca Prins, San Fuego, and Boca Keto. It was created by FANAPA, Aruba Foundation for Nature and Parks, the principal group working to preserve Aruba's natural heritage. At the foot of the hill is a restored country house with a small garden that has samples of trees and bushes found on Aruba. Facilities include a Visitor Center, souvenir shop and modernized roads and paths.

Mount Yamanota: The south side of the San Fuego/Boca Prins Road is known as Yamanota (or Jamanota), an area that has been earmarked as a national park and includes the island's highest hill, 617-foot Mount Yamanota. You can take a paved road to the summit, where you will find grand views of the island. The Yamanota area is the home of the Aruban parakeet, a bright green-and-yellow bird that is almost as large as a parrot.

Guadirikiri and Fontein Caves: The most accessible of Aruba's many caves are two on the east coast: the Fontein Cave, with fine Arawak petroglyphs, and the large Guadirikiri Cave, with two high ceiling chambers, one with an opening at the top that allows in some light. A third chamber, entered by a small low opening, is home to a large number of bats. Be forewarned: The room is hot and humid.

South of Oranjestad

Spanish Lagoon: The road south from the airport returns to the coast at Barcadera, where there is a long island waterway, Spanish Lagoon, with mangroves and a bird refuge at its northeastern end. About 600 yards from shore in front of Barcadera Harbor is a reef that starts at the surface and drops to about an 80-foot depth. It is part of a 2-mile reef along the south coast and is popular for snorkeling and diving. The *Atlantis* submarine is based here, and there are also two beach developments: The north one belongs to the Renaissance Hotel; the south one is De Palm Island, a privately developed recreation and sports center. The area is also a favorite for sportfishing. Savaneta, on the south side of Spanish Lagoon, was the first European settlement and the former capital of Aruba.

Frenchmans Pass: A road inland around the north end of Spanish Lagoon goes through Frenchmans Pass (Franse Pas), a tree-lined drive and site of a historic battle between French and Spanish buccaneers in 1700. Tracks from the main road go to the ruins of the Balashi gold mill, a relic of Aruba's gold rush, built in 1898.

San Nicolas (Sint Nicolaas): Aruba's second-largest settlement grew up around the oil refinery, owned by Standard Oil of New Jersey until it closed in 1985. Now, the town will have a new lease on life when an ambitious urban renewal project—to make it a cultural and tourism center—is completed. **Charlie's Bar** (297-584-5086), in the heart of the town, is an island mainstay not to be missed. Charlie came to Aruba several decades ago to work in the oil refinery, but after a time decided a bar was more fun. So too is the bar's decor—everyone who visits is supposed to leave something, and they have!

South of the oil installation, there are two secluded beaches, popularly known as Rodgers Beach and Baby Lagoon, where you can snorkel from shore. Both beaches lie at the foot of Seroe Colorado, a residential community originally built for Exxon Oil executives. Enroute to Baby Beach, you might treat your kids to a stop at the **Aruba Model Trains Museum** (Koolbaaibergstraat 12, Lago Heights, San Nicolas; 297-584-7321), Hours: Tues to Sat 10 a.m. to 5 p.m., Sun by appointment. No entry fee.

The southeastern end of the island, marked by the Colorado Lighthouse, overlooks some of Aruba's main dive locations. Boca Grandi, a wide bay, is a popular picnic spot. The area is popular for windsurfing and sportfishing. North of San Nicolas is an arid, windswept region with little vegetation, even during the rainy season, where the divi-divi tree is abundant. Its asymmetrical shape is caused by the *passaat,* the Papiamento name for the strong winds that blow mainly from the east. Although all wind-sheared trees with this shape are commonly called *divi-divi,* several species grow in this manner. Divi-divi means "ear" in the Arawak language and is derived from the watapana tree, which has thick, curled pods resembling a human ear.

Shopping

Aruba is not officially a duty-free port, but in 1989 duties on luxury items were lowered from 40 to 7.5 percent, turning it into a shopping mecca. Of greatest interest to most visitors are the Dutch products, such as delft blue pottery and Dutch pewter; Gouda, Edam, and a variety of other Dutch cheeses and chocolates; and Indonesian crafts.

Traditionally, Nassaustraat (Caya Croes) has been the shoppers' street, but a downtown renewal project, begun in 1988, changed the face of the town center. Several complexes set behind pastel-colored facades of traditional Dutch Caribbean architecture, complete with gables, added many stores.

The town square is anchored on the west by the Holland Aruba Mall, a shop-and-restaurant complex and on the south, the **Renaissance Mall** (www.shoprenaissancearuba.com), the shopping and restaurant complex of the **Renaissance Aruba Resort and Casino** (297-583-6000). By the waterfront on the east is the Renaissance Marketplace; to the west, directly in front of the port, is the Royal Plaza Mall, with its fancy "Taj Mahal" architecture. The beautiful **Paseo Herencia** (www.paseoherencia.com) is located directly in front of the Holiday Inn and Aruba's newest shopping mall, **Palm Beach Plaza** (www.palmbeachplaza.com) even has a bowling alley and rock-climbing wall. Together these malls have several hundred stores—all within walking distance or a short ride from the docks.

Malls are open Mon to Sat, 9:30 a.m. to 6 p.m. Downtown store hours are Mon to Sat from 8 a.m. to 6 p.m.; although some are closed for lunch between noon and 2 p.m. When cruise ships are in port on Sun and holidays, some shops open.

Art and Artists: Creative Hands (5 Socotorolaan; 297-583-5665) carries ceramic cunucu houses and divi-divi trees, and other folklore objects. **Gasparito** (297-586-7044; www.gasparito.com) near Palm Beach, and **Que Pasa?** (Wilhelminastraat 18; 297-583-4888; www.quepasaaruba.com) are both restaurants and art galleries with local and Caribbean art. **Mopa Mopa** (Renaissance Marketplace) sells unusual gifts that appear to be hand painted but are not. The specialized craft is made from the buds of the mopa mopa tree, which are boiled to form a resin. Vegetable colors are added to the resin, which the artist then stretches by hand. The material is cut into small pieces and layered to form intricate designs on wood.

Access Art Gallery (Caya Betico Croes 16-18, Oranjestad; 297-588-7837) displays local and international artists, with a focus on design as functional art. There are also lectures by exhibiting artists; dance, musical, and theatrical presentations. **Art Studio Insight** (Paradera Park 215; 297-568-9168) emphasizes visual and theater arts. **Eterno Gallery** (Emanstraat 92,Oranjestad; 297-583-9484) carries local and international artwork. **Osaira Muyale Contemporary Art Studio** (Stadionweg 3,Oranjestad; 297-582-1350; osairamuyale@yahoo.com) is the studio of contemporary conceptual artist Osaira Muyale. Rotating exhibits can also be seen at the Cas di Cultura, National Library of Aruba, Numismatic Museum Aruba, and the Aruba Investment Bank in Oranjestad.

In San Nicolas, the **San Nicolas Foundation for the Arts** (SiNFA) (Van Zeppenveldtstraat 10; 297-584-2969) covers the visual arts, theater, music, literature, photography, and dance.

China and Crystal: Aruba Trading Company (Caya G. F. Betico Croes 12; www.arubatrading.com) is a large department store, established in 1930, with a section for china and crystal. **Little**

Switzerland (Royal Plaza, L.G. Smith Blvd.94; 297-583-4057; www.littleswitzerland.com) is one of the Caribbean's mainstays for fine china and crystal.

Clothing and Accessories: There are many boutiques of women's fashions in the various shopping malls, but if you are looking for high fashion, **Agatha at Les Accessoires** (lower level, Renaissance Aruba Resort; 297-583-7965; www.agatha.com) is run by transplanted New York fashion designer Agatha Brown, known for her unique styles. **Benetton** (La Strada) is here, too, but a check of prices did not reflect a savings over U.S. stores. There's also **Louis Vuitton, Cartier,** and **Figaro.** For funky upscale fashions, **Gimmick** (Renaissance Village Mall; 297-583-9244; fax: 587-4195; gimmick@setanet.aw) is operated by a mother and daughter team who import top European lines, from sexy to business attire. **Azul** (Caya G. F. Betico Croes 10; 297-583-0131) is a two-story boutique for men's and women's clothing by **Nautica, Lacoste, Ralph Lauren, Kenneth Cole,** and others. The new **Paseo Herencia** has Diesel, Lacoste, and many other popular brands.

Food Specialties: Supermarkets, such as **Pueblo** and **Ling & Sons,** are good places to buy Dutch cheese, chocolates, and other edibles, as well as liquor.

Jewelry: The best-known jewelers are **Gandelman** (www.boolchand.com), a long-established quality store that has a large selection of fine gold jewelry and watches and a customer-service office in the United States. **Colombian Emeralds,** Cartier, and David Yurman are located in the Renaissance Mall and certain hotels.

Leather: Gucci (Renaissance Mall) has its own store facing the town square, where the savings are about 20 percent over U.S. locations. There are many stores in Oranjestad selling Louis Vuitton–type handbags and luggage at prices considerably lower than in the United States. You would need to be familiar with the manufacturer's goods to know if those here are the genuine item or merely good replicas. But if you don't care, they are very good buys. **Ferragamo** (Emmastraat 1, Plaza Daniel Leo) and **Hugo Boss** (Caya Betico Croes 15) have women and men fashions.

Perfume and Cosmetics: Every shopping complex in town and at resort hotels has perfume shops. **Aruba Trading Company** (Caya G. F. Betico Croes 12) has a well-stocked perfume-and-cosmetics section. The **Aruba Aloe Museum and Factory** (297-588-3222; www.arubaaloe.com) makes a variety of perfumed lotions, sun, skin-, and hair-care products from the gel found in aloe plants grown at the site. Products are sold in the gift shop, along with aloe candles in unusual shapes. Aruba Aloe also has shops downtown and at the airport.

Dining and Restaurants

Oranjestad has a surprising range and variety of restaurants—Chinese, American, Italian, French, Indonesian, and more—reflecting the multifaceted nature of the country. In recent years, too, Aruban specialties have come out of home kitchens onto restaurant menus at places specializing in local cuisine. Some of the best restaurants—**Gasparito** (www.gasparito.com), **Papiamento** (Washington 61; 297-586-4544), **Que Pasa?** (Whilhelminastraat 18; 297-583-4888; www.quepasaaruba.com) —are open for dinner only; some may open for lunch during the winter season. Most restaurants close Sun or Mon like **Chez Matilda.** Inquire in advance. Through a Dine-Around program, monitored by the **Aruba Gastronomic Association** (AGA), visitors can try more than twenty fine restaurants at special rates with purchase of a coupon booklet priced from US$117. Contact AGA (297-586-1266; www.arubadining.com).

Aqua Grill (J. E. Irausquin Boulevard 374, Palm Beach, 297-586-5900; www.aqua-grill.com) serves a wide range of fresh seafood in a setting of contemporary decor that combines New England fish house traditions with Caribbean ones. Moderately expensive.

Cuba's Cookin' (Wilhelminastraat 27; 297-588-0627; www.cubascookin.com) Conveniently located in town, it has a great reputation for authentic Cuban cuisine. Expensive but portions are enough for two meals.

Driftwood Restaurant (Klipstraat 12, 297-583-2515; www.driftwoodaruba.com) Popular for seafood, caught daily by the owner, with an Aruban flavor. Expensive.

Dutch Pancake House (Renaissance Marketplace; 297-583-7180) serves handmade bakes from an old family recipe of the Dutch owners; seventy-five varieties in this seaside setting. Open 10 a.m. to 10 p.m. Moderate.

Flying Fishbone (Savaneta 344; 297-584-2506; www.flyingfishbone.com), a charming beach restaurant specializing in fresh seafood, is set in Aruba's oldest fishing village. You can dine by soft candlelight with your feet in the sand and starlight overhead. Reservations required. Expensive.

Laguna Fish Market (Radisson Aruba Resort and Casino, Irausquin Boulevard 81; 297-526-6612; www.lagunaaruba.com) likes to say that the only thing fresher than the fish is its setting along freshwater lagoons and tropical foliage. Moderate.

Le Petit Cafe (Royal Plaza Mall; 297-583-8471; lepetitecafe1@visitaruba.com) is a lively cafe on the town square where your chicken or meat is cooked on a hot-stone platter in front of you. Moderate to expensive.

For some budget-easy alternatives, try the Grill House (31 Zoutmanstraat; 297-583-1611), which has Aruban-style fish and Dutch steak in a cozy setting; and Mambo Jambo (Royal Plaza Mall; 297-583-3632), which offers light lunch and is open for cocktails during the day and becomes a nightclub in the evening. There's also a Carlos 'n Charlie's of the famous Mexican chain (297-582-0355), Hooters, and pizza parlors galore.

Nightlife

Aruba has a very lively nightlife. Each major hotel has a nightclub with international entertainment or disco with a distinct ambience. If you would like some help in sampling the nightlife, De Palm Tours (297-582-4400) offers a "Bar Hopper" tour. Or, barhop in the gaily painted Kukoo Kunuku Party Bus (297-586-2010; www.kukookunuku.com) or the Banana Bus (297-993-0757; www.banana busaruba.com) with a big yellow banana on its roof. The Banana Bus also runs an island tour with a swim and snorkeling at Baby Beach, Tues to Sat from 9 a.m. to 1:30 p.m. for US$37.50 per person.

The island's ten casinos are found mostly in hotels. The Alhambra (www.casinoalhambra.com), a large independent gaming house, is part of an entertainment-and-shopping complex near Eagle Beach. The complex also has a theater, shops, restaurants (including Dunkin Donuts and Subway), and a big-screen sports bar.

The Lounge (overlooking the casino in Renaissance Aruba Beach Resort; 297-583-6000) is a sophisticated late-nightspot for drinks, light fare, and people-watching until 6 a.m.!

If you would prefer something on the more cultural side, the 220-seat theater Cas di Cultura (Culture Center, Vondellaan 2; 297-582-1010) stages concerts, ballet, folkloric shows, and art exhibits. Check with the Aruba Tourism Authority to learn what's happening during your visit.

Sports

All hotels here have a swimming pool and water sports, and they can arrange scuba, fishing, and windsurfing. De Palm Island, south of Oranjestad, is a water-sports center of De Palm Tours (297-582-4400; in United States, 800-766-6016; www.depalm.com).

Beaches/Swimming: The most beautiful waters for swimming are along the soft sands of Palm Beach, but you can find other white-sand beaches with calm waters along the leeward coast. At Baby Beach on the southern coast, the water is only 4 to 5 feet deep. Its calm waters are especially suited for children.

Biking and Motorcycling: Because most of Aruba is flat, biking can be an easy way to get around, and the trade winds help keep you cool. Bike & Locker Rental (L. G. Smith Boulevard 234, Oranjestad; 297-587-8655) and Pablito's Bike Rental (L. G. Smith Boulevard 234; 297-587-8655) rent bikes for $15 a day. Or, if you have a motorcycle license you can go big time with a Harley Davidson from Big Twin Aruba (L. G. Smith Boulevard 124-A; 297-582-8660, www.harleydavidson-aruba.com; hours: Mon to Sat, 9 a.m. to 6 p.m.) for $130 for a half day; $163 full day, including insurance and helmets, and a $2,500 deposit. The shop also sells Harley clothing and accessories. Donata Car and Cycle (L. G. Smith Boulevard 136-D; 297-583-4343) rents mopeds and motorcycles; George's Cycle Center (L. G. Smith Boulevard 124;

297-593-2202; www.georgecycles.com) has scooters and all-terrain vehicles; and **Semver Cycle Rental** (Noord 22, Noord; 297-586-6851; www.semver.aw) has scooters and motorcycles.

Boating: Water-sports operators offer sail and snorkel cruises on catamarans and other sailboats and glass-bottom ones for viewing the coral.

Deep-Sea Fishing: Sportfishing is a big sport in Aruba. Less than a mile or so from shore, the sea is rich with kingfish, tuna, bonito, wahoo, blue and white marlin, and more. About a dozen boat operators offer half- and full-day, fully equipped charters, some for a maximum of four persons; others for up to six persons. The price ranges from US$240 to $350 for half-day and $450 to $700 full day. You can obtain a list from the Tourist Office.

Golf: Tierra del Sol (866-978-5158; www.tierradelsol.com), Aruba's first 18-hole championship golf course (6,811 yards, par 71) was designed by the Robert Trent Jones II Group and can accommodate golfers of all ages and abilities. There is a driving range, putting green, and practice chipping area complete with a bunker. Reservations: (297-586-0978). Greens fees with cart range from US$92 to $159, depending on time of day and season of the year. Club rentals, US$45.

The Links at Divi Aruba (adjacent to Divi Village Golf and Beach Resort; 297-583-2300; www.divigolf.com) is a 9-hole course that plays as 18 holes. There is a golf school, pro shop, and restaurant. Play is open to the public, but guests at Divi's four hotels get preferred tee times. Non-hotel guests, US$75 to $85 for 9 holes; $29 to $39 for replay; club rentals, $25 per round.

Hiking: Aruba's only marked hiking trails are in Arikok National Park (Piedra Plat 42, 297-585-1234; www.arubanationalpark.org), but there are many tracks branching from main arteries to almost any place of interest. Guided tours for beginners to experienced hikers are $25 per group. For an interesting early-morning climb—and a more accessible one—try the Hooiberg (known locally as the Haystack), the mound rising conspicuously in the center of the island about 6 miles east of Oranjestad. The climb to the top via several hundred carved steps affords great exercise, and you're rewarded with a spectacular view of the island. Information on hiking, jeep, horseback, and bicycle tours through the park are available by contacting the **National Park** offices in advance (297-585-1234, info@aruba nationalpark.org).

Horseback Riding: Rancho Daimari (Palm Beach; 297-586-6284; www.visitaruba.com/ranchodaimari/#rancho) offers a two-hour guided tour including a swim for $64 per person. Others include **Rancho del Campo** (22 East Sombre; 297-585-0290) and **Rancho Notorious** (Boroncana 8–E; 297-586-0508; www.ranchonotorious.com), which offer trail rides daily except Sun. The mounts, imported from South America, are the famous paso fino horses noted for their smooth gait. Trips can be arranged for all levels of skill. Rancho Notorious also offers guided bike tours.

Kayaking: Aruba Kayak Adventures (Ponton 90, Oranjestad; 297-582-5520; www.arubawavedancer.com/arubakayak) offers excursions Mon through Sat starting at 8:30 a.m. and 2:30 p.m. Contact them in advance to make arrangements. A kayaking and snorkeling excursion costs $99 per person.

Landsailing: The sport of gliding over sand and land using a kart with a sail propelled by wind is called landsailing. The small, light kart is mounted on three wheels with the front wheel attached to a system that enables riders to steer the kart with their legs and control the kart with the sail, using techniques similar to sailing. **Aruba Active Vacations** (Salina Cerca 25-K, 297-586-0989; www.aruba-active-vacations.com) offers landsailing as well as other active sports such as windsurfing, kite surfing, and mountain bike rentals and tours.

Rock Climbing: Near Grapefield, a small town at the southeastern end of the island, is a series of 50-foot-high limestone cliffs, known as the Fontein Cliffs. In 1996 some local and Dutch climbers mapped the cliff faces and put in place the material necessary for climbing. Now, the cliffs have become a popular climbing site for locals and visitors. Due to Aruba's intense sun and heat, climbers are advised to plan their climb before 10 a.m. or after 3 p.m.

Snorkeling/Scuba Diving: Aruba is surrounded by coral reefs, and there are interesting shipwrecks. The reefs in the calm leeward waters range from shallow-water corals within swimming distance of shore—suitable for snorkelers and novice divers—to deepwater reefs and walls that drop 100 feet and more. Snorkeling and diving can be arranged directly with dive operators, most of whom are located at the hotels on Eagle and Palm Beaches. A beginner's dive lesson costs about US$70. **Pelican Adventures** (P.O. Box 1194, Oranjestad, Aruba; 297-587-2302; www.pelican-aruba .com), one of the island's oldest dive operators, offers a full range of packages: beginners lesson $95; one-tank dive, US$54; two-tank dive, US$80; night dive, US$62. The dive center is located on Palm Beach next to the Holiday Inn.

There are another dozen dive operators, all PADI certified and with their own boats. A list is available from the Tourism Authority. If you don't dive, you don't have to miss the fun. SNUBA (De Palm Tours; 582-4400; www.depalm.com) is an apparatus that enables you to see more than a snorkel, but it does not require the skills to scuba dive. Cost: US$134.

Arashi Beach, north of Palm Beach, is ideal for snorkeling and shallow-water dives directly from the beach. The reef of elkhorn coral lies on a sandy bottom in 20 to 40 feet of water. There are two shipwrecks that can be viewed by snorkelers as well as divers. The *Pedernales,* an oil tanker from World War II, lies in 20 to 40 feet of water near the Holiday Inn; the *Antilla,* a German cargo ship scuttled by the Germans at the start of the Second World War, lies at 60 feet in two parts.

At Barcadera, a 2-mile reef runs along the south coast and has abundant gorgonians and elkhorn and staghorn corals, which attract a great variety of fish common to the Caribbean. Farther south Baby Lagoon offers the greatest visibility for snorkeling.

If you are in Aruba the first week in July, you can participate in the **Aruba Reef Care Project** (297-582-3777), an annual reef cleanup program.

Atlantis **Submarine** (297-588-6881; www .atlantisadventures.com) departs from the Atlantis downtown office (opposite Aruba Renaissance) where you board a boat that transfers you to the submarine off the southeast coast. The guided excursion takes you over the Barcadera reefs and two sunken wrecks. Price: US$89 adult, $79 teen (twelve to sixteen years old), $49 child.

Seaworld Explorer, a semi submarine with viewing windows onto the underwater sea life, 5 feet below the surface, provides viewing of the Arashi reef and the *Antilla* wreck. The guided excursion departs from the Pelican Pier (Holiday Inn) where you board a transfer boat. Tours daily: 11:30 a.m. and 1:30 p.m. US$37 adult, $22 child (two to twelve years old). Contact Atlantis or **De Palm Tours** (297-582-4400).

Windsurfing/Kiteboarding: The same strong winds that shape the divi-divi tree and keep the island cool have made Aruba one of the leading windsurfing locations in the Caribbean. Most of the year the winds blow at 15 knots and, at times, up to 25 knots. Windsurfers from around the world meet here annually in June for the **Aruba Hi-Winds Pro-Am World Cup,** where the winds get up to 25 knots or more. The most popular windsurfing areas are north of Palm Beach at Fisherman's Huts, the beach fronting **Windsurf Village** (www.arubahouse.com). All beachside hotels have windsurfing equipment. If you want to learn or polish your skills, the **Sailboard Vacations Flight School** (www.sailboardvacations .com) at the Windsurf Village is best. Lessons from a skilled full-time instructor cost US$60 per hour or US$150 for five hours and are given in the warm shallow waters of Fisherman's Huts, where winds are consistent.

Kiteboarding has literally taken off in Aruba, motivated by the same strong winds that made windsurfing so popular. If you know what you're doing, the best spot to "fly" is Arashi Beach near California Lighthouse. At Boca Grande on the south shore, you can watch local experts show off their radical moves. Those eager to learn can take lessons and rent equipment at **Vela Windsurf Resorts/Dare2FlyAruba** (Fisherman's Huts Windsurf Center; 101 L. G. Smith Blvd., Palm Beach, 297-586-9000; 800-223-5443, www.dare2flyaruba .com). Prices range from beginner group lessons for one-hour instruction and one-hour equipment rental afterwards for $55 to two-and-a-half hours of private instruction with equipment for $150. Or, try **Aruba Boardsailing Productions** (486 L. G. Smith Blvd., 297-586-3940 or 297-993-1111, www.aruba-active-vacations.com), where kiteboarding rentals are available after a two-hour lesson for US$60.

Festivals and Celebrations

Carnival, celebrated during the pre-Lenten period, has long been the main celebration in Aruba, and it has all the costumes, color, calypso, parades, and floats of any Caribbean Carnival. Aruba usually has a major music festival in the summer season. For the most complete listing of events, tours, attractions, and day- and nighttime activities taking place during your visit, check out the free weekly publication *Que Pasa.*

PART SEVEN

The Western Caribbean

Jamaica

Jamaica

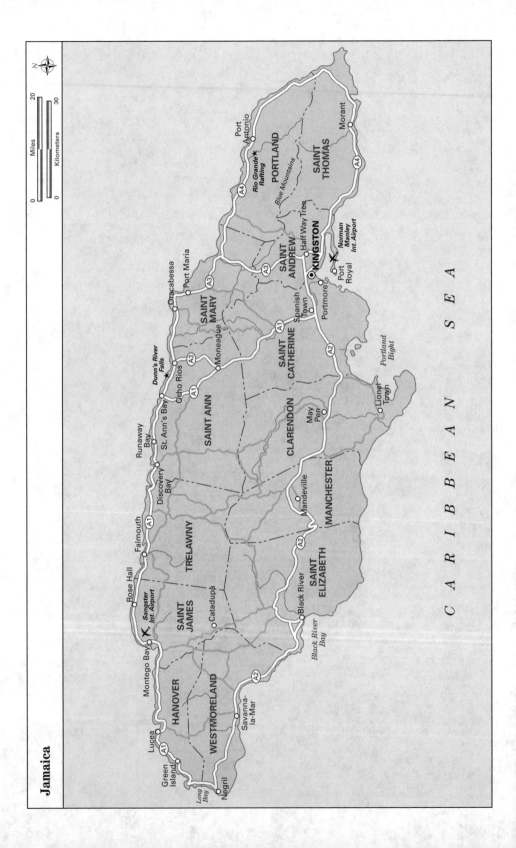

N

Miles
0   20

Kilometers
0   30

Green
Island
Lucea
HANOVER
Rose Hall
Montego Bay
Sangster
Int. Airport
SAINT
JAMES
Catadupa
Falmouth
TRELAWNY
Discovery
Bay
Runaway
Bay
St. Ann's Bay
Ocho Rios
Dunn's River
Falls
SAINT ANN
Moneague
SAINT
MARY
Oracabessa
Port Maria
Rio Grande
Rafting
Port
Antonio
PORTLAND
Blue Mountains
SAINT
THOMAS
Morant
SAINT
ANDREW
Half Way Tree
KINGSTON
Port
Royal
Norman
Manley
Int. Airport
Spanish
Town
Portmore
SAINT
CATHERINE
Lionel
Town
Portland
Bight
CLARENDON
May
Pen
Mandeville
MANCHESTER
SAINT
ELIZABETH
Black River
Black River
Bay
A2
A1
A3
A4
Negril
Long
Bay
Savanna-
la-Mar
WESTMORELAND

C A R I B B E A N   S E A

The Quintessence of the Tropics

How easy it is to fall in love with Jamaica! Awesome blue-green mountains frame its white-sand beaches and turquoise waters and cool the air of the tropical sun. Voluptuous hillsides decorated with brilliant flowers, forests alive with vivid birds, trees laden with exotic fruits, rushing waters, laughing children, gentle people whose voices lilt as though they were singing—these are the charms with which this Caribbean beauty seduces its admirers.

Jamaica, situated 90 miles south of Cuba and an hour and a half flying time from Miami, is the third largest island in the Caribbean and covers 4,411 square miles. Those who think of it simply as another Caribbean island are often surprised by their sense of being in a big country.

The impression comes in part from the thickly forested mountains, which rise to 7,402 feet at their peak and cut the north coast from the south. A further sense of space comes from the land's diversity and richness. More than 126 rivers flow down the mountainsides, and the tropical landscape nurtures 3,000 species of plants, including 600 unique to the island, and hundreds of birds. Indeed, Jamaica's name is derived from the ancient Arawak *Xaymaca,* meaning "land of wood and water."

A third, but more elusive, reason for Jamaica's aura of size is its distinctive culture, built layer upon layer from the Spaniards, who first plundered and victimized the original Arawak inhabitants, to the English, who colonized and exploited it, to the Africans and Asians, who worked the plantations or fled to freedom behind the mountains of the interior. Levantine traders, Christian missionaries, Rastafarian cultists, movie stars, polo players, novelists, Black Power advocates, Third World activists, and pop music superstars are all threads in its richly textured tapestry.

Jamaica's capital, Kingston, is situated on the south coast on one of the best natural harbors in the Caribbean. It is the commercial, cultural, and administrative center of the country, but not the tourist one. The tourist's Jamaica stretches more than 100 miles along the north coast from Negril on the west to Port Antonio on the east. It is dotted with resorts of all styles, where it's easy to be lazy under a bright Caribbean sun or active with kayaking, river tubing, tennis, golf, horseback riding, scuba diving, and a dozen other sports. More adventurous tourists climb the majestic Blue Mountains, camp along less traveled shores, and explore the river valleys and tiny villages of the interior. Near the coast, mountain streams rush headlong to the sea or converge in waterfalls under umbrellas of thick foliage and brilliant flowers—settings that are the quintessence of the tropics as visitors imagine them.

The Jamaican Discovery

Jamaica's history is as vivid as its landscape. It was first sighted by Christopher Columbus on his second voyage in 1494, whereupon its beauty led him to describe it as "the fairest isle that eyes have

At a Glance

Antiquities	★★
Architecture	★★★★
Art and Artists	★★★★
Beaches	★★★★★
Colonial Buildings	★★★
Crafts	★★
Cuisine	★★★
Culture	★★★★★
Dining/Restaurants	★★
Entertainment	★★
Forts	★★
History	★★★★
Monuments	★★
Museums	★★★★
Nature	★★★★★
Nightlife	★★
Scenery	★★★★★
Shopping/Duty-Free	★★
Sightseeing	★★★★★
Sports	★★★★★
Transportation	★★

Population: Three million; 800,000 people live in Kingston and its surrounding metropolitan area

Main Cities: Kingston, Montego Bay, Ocho Rios, Port Antonio, Mandeville, Negril

Climate: Jamaica has no winter. Year-round, the temperature along the coast hovers around 80°F but can go as low as 70 to 75°F between Dec and Mar, and up to 90°F from July through Sept. The rainy seasons are May through June and Sept through Oct, with short tropical downpours. Cool breezes from the sea keep the days pleasant, and mountain regions can be chilly in winter months.

Clothing: Lightweight tropical clothing is best year-round, but beachwear, especially scanty bathing suits (on either sex!), is not acceptable anyplace but at beach and beachside hotels. You should wear a shirt or cover-up while strolling in town. Jamaicans find a too-casual appearance offensive. In winter be sure to pack a light sweater or jacket as evenings, even on the coast, can be chilly.

Currency: Jamaican Dollar (JDS or JD$). The current exchange rate fluctuates around JD$81 to US$1. US currency is widely accepted, and major credit cards can be used in most hotels, shops, and restaurants.

Customs Regulations/Departure Tax: Cruise passengers who disembark in Jamaica and return to the United States by plane must pay a JD$1,000 or about US$17 departure tax plus a new US$10 fee for tourism improvements. Normally, the fee is included in your plane ticket. U.S. Customs will confiscate any fruits, vegetables, or plants from Jamaica. The only exception is flowers sold in departure lounges at the airports that have been specially packaged by the Ministry of Agriculture.

Electricity: 110 to 120 volts AC, 50 cycles

Emergency Numbers: *Montego Bay,* Medical Services: Dial 110 or Cornwall Regional Hospital, (876) 952-5100. Police Department: 119. Ambulance: 110. *Ocho Rios,* Medical Services: Tourist Board Courtesy Unit, (876) 974-2570. Police 119; Ambulance: 110.

Entry Formalities: No visas for U.S. and Canadian citizens; however, a U.S. passport is required for U.S. citizens as proof of citizenship to leave and to return to the United States. A valid driver's license is necessary for car rental identification.

Language: English is the official language and spoken with a melodic lilt that is sometimes difficult to understand. Jamaicans also have a patois, incomprehensible to foreigners, and their colorful speech is peppered with a plethora of words and idiomatic expressions dating from English settler days.

Postal Service: Every port has a conveniently located post office where you can buy colorful Jamaican stamps as souvenirs or mail postcards and letters.

Public Holidays: Jan 1, New Year's Day; Ash Wed; Good Friday; Easter Monday; May 23, Labor Day; first Mon in Aug, Independence Day; third Mon in Oct, National Heroes Day; Dec 25, Christmas; Dec 26, Boxing Day.

Telephone Area Code: 876. Each main town—Montego Bay, Ocho Rios, Kingston, et cetera—has one or more different prefixes (92, 93, 94, etc.) + five digits.

Time Zone: Same as U.S. Eastern Standard Time, but Jamaica does not switch to daylight saving time and is therefore one hour behind Eastern time from Apr through Oct.

Vaccination Requirement: None

Airlines: *From the United States to Montego Bay and Kingston:* Air Tram, American, Caribbean Airlines, Continental, Delta, Jet Blue, Spirit Airlines, United Airlines, and US Airways. *From Canada:* Air Canada, Westjet.

Intraisland: Jamaica Air Shuttle (876-906-9026; www.jamaicaairshuttle.com) scheduled service Montego Bay, Negril, Kingston, Port Antonio, Boscobel. Skylan Airways (876-932-7134; www.skylanairways.com) scheduled service Kingston/Montego Bay; TimAir Limited (876-952-2516; www.timair.com) charter.

Airports: Sangster International Airport (876-952-3124); Norman Manley International Airport, (888-AIRPORT); www.mbjairport.com

Information: www.visitjamaica.com

In the United States:

Jamaica Tourist Board: 5201 Lagoon Dr., Suite 670, Miami, FL 33126; (305) 665-0557; (800) 233-4582; fax: (305) 666-7239; info@visitjamaica-usa.com

In Canada:

Toronto: 303 Eglinton Ave. East, Suite 200, Toronto, ON M4P 1L3; (416) 482-7850; (800) 465-2624; fax: (416) 482-1730; jtb@visitjamaica-ca.com

In Port:

Kingston (main office): 64 Knutsford Blvd., Kingston; (876) 929-9200; fax: (876) 929-9375; info@visitjamaica.com

Montego Bay: Airport Road (876) 952-4425; fax: (876) 952-3587; Sangster Airport, (876) 952-2462

seen" and to name it Santa Gloria. Unfortunately, the island was to become the scene of his most inglorious days.

On Columbus's fourth and final voyage, two of his ships were so badly damaged off the coast of Santa Gloria that he had to beach them at a protected cove that today is identified as St. Ann's Bay. Here Columbus spent a year awaiting rescue by other Spanish expeditioners in nearby Hispaniola. After his return to Spain, Columbus, having fought a long battle with the Spanish Crown to retain the land and titles promised him, was granted Jamaica as part of his family domain. To this day Columbus's heirs carry the title of El Marquis de Jamaica.

After Columbus's death in 1506, his son Diego became the governor of the Indies; from Santo Domingo he sent Juan de Esquivel, a former lieutenant of his father's, to Jamaica to establish a colony. Under him the town of Sevilla Nueva, or New Seville, was laid out in 1509, and other settlements founded. In 1523 they established Villa de la Vega on the south coast, and twelve years later, moved their capital there, renaming it St. Jago de la Vega; later, the English called it simply Spanish Town.

Arrival of the British

By 1655, when the British seized control of the island, the Spaniards had already annihilated the native Arawaks—estimated to have numbered between 60,000 and 100,000—through enslavement or disease and had replaced them with African slaves. The Spaniards fled to nearby Cuba, but their slaves took to the mountains and continued fighting; they became known as the Maroons, from the Spanish *cimarron*, wild. The British were unable to defeat them and finally made an agreement enabling the Maroons to stay in the mountains with a certain autonomy in exchange for peace.

Unfortunately, British rule was no better than Spanish. Rather, the island became the base for the most famous and infamous pirates of the century, who operated with the blessings of the Crown to such an extent that Henry Morgan, one of the most notorious, was actually knighted and made a lieutenant governor of Jamaica. Port Royal, on a spit of land west of Kingston airport, became such a scandalous pirate's port that it earned the title of "the wickedest city in Christendom."

From a pirates' lair, Jamaica became an 18th-century center of the Caribbean slave trade where, it is said, as many as a million Africans were sold to the owners of sugar plantations throughout the region. The British also turned it into a sugar colony of enormous wealth.

The Road to Nationhood

By the 19th century Jamaica had become Britain's most important Caribbean colony, economically. Great plantations of sugar, tobacco, and indigo, and later bananas, created enormous wealth for their owners—often absentee landlords living splendidly in England. There were uprisings by slaves and rebellions by freedmen—the separate mulatto class that had resulted from the unions between white men and black women.

In 1834 slavery was finally abolished, but that was only the first battle. For the next century every attempt by the freed slaves to improve their lot and to have a voice in government was dealt with harshly by the British governors in charge. A naive effort led by a Baptist deacon and small farmer Paul Bogle in 1865 at Morant Bay met such vicious reprisals that the governor was recalled. Soon after, Jamaica was made a Crown Colony.

By the 1930s, after the Depression had taken its toll in Europe and the Americas, Jamaica's struggle for freedom and independence entered its last phase, bringing to the limelight two men whose influence is still felt today. Alexander Bustamante was a leader of the trade union movement, founder of the Jamaica Labour Party, and the first prime minister. Norman Manley, a prominent lawyer, was the founder of the People's National Party and father of the nationalist movement; he also served as premier. In 1944 Britain accepted a new constitution based on universal suffrage and in 1962 granted the country independence.

For almost a decade Jamaica enjoyed a honeymoon as the darling of the Caribbean for winter vacationers. Investment money poured in, and resorts mushroomed along the north coast. Bauxite, which is used to make aluminum, was found in commercial quantities, and its mining brought new wealth.

But in the 1970s the wave of unrest that had swept across the United States in the 1960s washed ashore in the Caribbean. Norman Manley's son Michael, who proved to be as charismatic as his father, sought to chart a new course, and Jamaica became the focal point of radical change. By then, too, the oil crisis and worldwide inflation were taking their toll. Before long Jamaica, in its search for identity and direction, had alienated most of its allies, frightened away potential investors, and mismanaged its wealth to the point of destitution.

By October 1980 Jamaicans concluded that their country's youthful excesses had gone far enough, and they voted in the government of Edward Seaga. Almost overnight the atmosphere changed; confidence was reestablished, and the American-born and Harvard-educated Seaga—with some help from his friends—got Jamaica back on track. In 1989 Manley was returned to power and, having by his own admission learned from past mistakes, steered the country on a more moderate, prudent course. Now his successors are continuing the task of building a new Jamaica.

Lasting Achievements

Although Jamaica's road to nationhood has hardly been filled with sunshine, the country radiates creativity and artistic fervor and can point to a long list of accomplishments by its multifaceted society. In addition to the quarter million slaves who were retained in Jamaica to work the sugar plantations, the colony was a trading center that attracted large numbers of Europeans and traders from the Mediterranean. After slavery was abolished, a new wave of Asians arrived as indentured workers. Thus over the centuries Jamaicans became a thorough mixture of races, nationalities, and cultures from which has grown one of the Caribbean's most dynamic societies, influential throughout the West Indies in music, dance, and art.

For starters, Jamaicans have enriched the English language and made it sing with a soft lilt. And they have made music. Reggae, one of the most influential rhythms on the pop scene today, was born in Jamaica. It, too, is a mixture of folk, soul, and rock. The annual reggae music festival attracts musicians and fans by the thousands from around the world. In the arts, Jamaica has its own national dance company, national theater, national pantomime troupe, national choral group, national art gallery, and national crafts institute.

You cannot see Jamaica in a day or even in a month, but if you take full advantage of your time in this extraordinary port of call, you will come away with some idea of why it enchanted even the most blasé of men like Noel Coward, beguiled suitors as different as Errol Flynn and Johnny Cash, and looms so large on the Caribbean landscape that only excessive images seem to capture the whole of it.

Budget Planning and Other Practical Tips

Jamaica is no longer the bargain it once was. Some things are still inexpensive; some are expensive; the pattern for what's cheap and what's expensive is uneven. As a rule, anything imported—wine, cars—is expensive because of steep import duties, but locally made products—rum, beer, crafts—are cheap.

Taxis are expensive, but when shared with friends or other passengers, they are the best and most economical way to see the island. When you hire a taxi, you usually get a first-rate tour guide and raconteur who will enrich your visit with stories and pithy insights, especially if you enter into the spirit of the occasion with conversation that shows your interest in Jamaica.

Members of JUTA (Jamaica Union of Travellers Association) are trained drivers licensed by the government to transport visitors, and their rates are set by the government. When negotiating with a driver, be sure to agree on the price before you get into the vehicle. Don't be shy. Ask how much your intended time or tour will cost, and add a 10 percent tip at the end (if you have been pleased with the service).

Do not buy cheap crafts on impulse; look around first, as there are considerable differences in quality and variety. And don't be afraid to bargain with craftspeople; they expect it. As a strategy for bargaining, you will be amazed how fast the price drops when you start to walk away. And don't be intimidated by the large numbers of "higglers," as the women street vendors are known, that greet you. If you have no interest in buying, say a polite "No thank you, not today," and keep walking.

Eat in local restaurants featuring Jamaican cuisine, which is unusual, delicious, and reasonably priced. In contrast, meals and drinks at large resorts can be three times the cost of local restaurants. If the goal of exploring on your own is to have a closer look and touch of Jamaica than you can get from a tour bus, you might find these tourist dos and don'ts helpful:

- The Jamaicans are Jamaicans and very proud. Please don't refer to them as "the natives." Nor are they happy to have strangers shove cameras in their faces. If you want to take candid shots, be discreet. If you want a portrait, ask with a smile. It's easy to chat and make friends with Jamaicans. Some will ask to be paid for taking their picture, especially if they are dressed in costume.

- As important as a 10 percent tip may be, a "good morning," a "thank you," and a smile are valued even more. Older Jamaicans, particularly, are almost courtly in their manner, and they very much appreciate your courtesy. Jamaicans have a delightful sense of humor. You can often get rid of a Jamaican peddler with humor faster than with anger.

- Don't leave valuables unattended on the beach, and on crowded streets watch your handbag and wallet as you would in any U.S. city. Despite what you may have heard about ganja, the Jamaican marijuana, drugs are illegal in Jamaica. Foreigners are not immune from arrest and imprisonment if caught with drugs.

Crafts and Duty-Free Shopping

Jamaica has never been considered a mecca for serious shoppers, but there are some unusual buys, especially in certain crafts and food products. Items to buy fall into two categories: those produced on the island and duty-free imports, which can run up to 30 percent lower than U.S. prices.

Art and Artists: The most outstanding and desirable Jamaican products are original paintings

---

Author's Favorite Attractions

- ★ Canopy Tour
- ★ Golf, horseback riding, or tennis
- ★ Day trips: Rose Hall Great House or YS Falls
- ★ Meet-the-People
- ★ Supermarket shopping for Jamaican products

---

and sculpture by contemporary artists who do not mass-produce their work. The best have achieved international recognition and are a source of national pride to Jamaicans. Among the most respected names are the late Edna Manley, mother of former prime minister Michael Manley, noted for her sculpture; 1940s artists John Dunkley and Henry Daley; and the late Kapo, the best known of the intuitive artists.

To learn about current exhibitions during your visit, contact the Jamaica Tourist Board offices (see Fast Facts section). The art galleries on the north coast selling original Jamaican art and sculpture include, in Montego Bay, **Gallery of West Indian Art** (11 Fairfield Rd., Catherine Hall; 876-952-4547; www.galleryofwestindianart.com) and in Ocho Rios, **Harmony Hall** (Highway A-3, 4 miles east of Ocho Rios; 876-974-2870; www.harmonyhall.com) is dedicated to discovering and promoting promising young Jamaican artists. The largest number of galleries is in Kingston.

Crafts: Shopping for Jamaican crafts and products can be fun if you are not deterred by insistent hawkers. A great deal of the straw work is similar to that found in many Caribbean markets. Other products, particularly spices, woodcraft, and dolls, are more distinctive. Prices are lower at markets and from street vendors than in shops, especially when you bargain, but the quality is generally better in hotel gift shops and specialty stores. The Montego Bay and Ocho Rios Craft Markets have almost identical merchandise, making in quantity and cheap prices what they lack in quality. For something different, locally made body oils by **Starfish** (876-901-7113; www.starfishoils.com) are available at its shop in the Island Village in Ocho Rios and in specialty shops and hotel gift shops.

The best wood products are fashioned from mahogany and mahoe, the national tree, a variegated hardwood with a blue tint. These are most attractive when they are combined with a variety of woods into such products as trays and jewelry boxes. In Montego Bay, the best workmanship can be found in products on sale in shops at Rose Hall Shopping Centre; in Ocho Rios, at **Harmony Hall** and **Coyaba Garden Gift Shop** (www.coyaba gardens.com).

The most unusual woodcrafts to blossom are whimsical, brightly painted animals carved from wood. They started with the late Liz DeLisser, an artist/owner of the Gallery of West Indian Art in Montego Bay, who has been credited with discovering the brilliant, self-taught woodcarver Obed Palmer and a dozen other carvers in the Trelawney parish village of Bunkers Hill. The craftsmen turn out an array of whimsical-looking animals, from lions to doctor birds and parrots, and paint them in the colorful and unlikely colors of Carnival—a pink-whiskered lion with red or green dots, a blue alligator with orange and pink scales, and so on. The figures represent a new form of Jamaican intuitive art and are carved from Jamaican cedar, which resists cracking and termites but is easy to carve. The gallery, now operated by DeLisser's daughter, helped Palmer finance the workshop next to his home, and DeLisser added her colorful artistry, helping to make the animals enormously popular. Now they are produced for shops throughout Jamaica and in other Caribbean islands, and they have even been featured at Bloomingdale's in New York.

Groceries: A variety of Jamaican food products make excellent gifts to take home. In supermarkets and hotel gift shops, you can find PickaPeppa, a delicious spicy sauce similar to a barbecue sauce; Hellfire, another savory sauce; local spices such as pimento (allspice), curry powder, ginger, and jerk seasoning; chutney and spicy fruits, and jams and preserves. Some labels to look for are **Busha Browne** and **Walkerswood**. Jamaican coffees are among the world's finest; pure Blue Mountain coffee, however, is also the most expensive. Blends and other brands, including High Mountain, are less costly. They are priced most reasonably at grocery stores, but not at shopping centers or airport boutiques. In Montego Bay, **Wesgate Supermarket** is open daily, and another supermarket, **Bodue,** on the outskirts of town, near the port, is part of a shopping center that also has a good pharmacy, Fortana.

Liquor and Liqueurs: Among the best local products are Jamaica's fine rums and liqueurs. Appleton and Myers rums are US$16 per bottle, as is Tia Maria, the country's famous coffee liqueur. Lesser-known flavors are Rumona, Sangster's Ortanique, Blue Mountain Coffee liqueur, and a wide range of fruit-based rums.

Perfumes and Toiletries: Parfums **Jamaica** (11 West Kings House Rd., Kingston 10; www.parfums-jamaica.com) makes a variety of fragrances for men and women that are sold in hotel shops and specialty stores. They are nicely packaged, inexpensive, and make attractive gifts. So, too, are the soaps and herbal oils by Starfish and Blue Mountain Aromatics. Both are available in gift shops and specialty stores.

Duty-Free Shopping

Procedures for duty-free shopping in Jamaica permit you to take all purchases with you except liquor and tobacco products, which must be delivered in-bond to your ship. In case you are asked, you must be able to prove you are a visitor.

Duty-free stores offer the standard brands of perfumes, gold jewelry, china, and similar products available in other duty-free ports. Shops with the best and most attractive selections are found at large hotels and resorts, such as **The Shoppes at Rose Hall** (876-953-9718; www.rosehallresort .com), a new development that showcases thirty or so luxury outlets.

Cuisine and Dining

Of all the islands you might visit during a Caribbean cruise, Jamaica is the one waiting for those with an inquisitive palate. The country's unusual and exotic national dishes are found no place else in the region. For a morning refreshment, pick an odd-looking fruit from a street vendor balancing her supply in a colorful basket on her head. (She will also be a wonderful portrait in your camera lens—especially when you please her by making a purchase.) Jamaica is a cornucopia of tropical fruits and vegetables: Ortanique (orange-tangerine hybrid), mango, soursop, star apple, and otaheite apple are a few of the delicious ones awaiting you.

The traditional breakfast dish is saltfish and ackee. Ackee is an unusual fruit that looks like a red pepper growing on a tree, but when ripe bursts open to reveal large black seeds covered with yellow lobes. The lobes are boiled and blended with onion, pepper, bacon, and salted cod. This mixture is often served with boiled green banana, johnny-cakes (fried flour dumplings), and bammies (cassava cakes). The flavor and texture of ackee suggest scrambled eggs and blend well with the fish.

For lunch and dinner Jamaican soups are rich and bold enough to make a meal alone. The tastiest are pumpkin soup (hot or cold); red bean soup; and pepperpot, a hearty blend of callaloo (spinach-like greens), crab, pork, coconut milk, root vegetables such as yam, and seasonings. Callaloo, yams, yucca, or cassava are among the most common ingredients.

Among the most popular dishes are escovitched fish, snapper or small reef fish fried whole in a spicy sauce of onions, hot peppers, green peppers, and tomatoes; rundown, which is mackerel or salted cod boiled in coconut milk and eaten with a mush of onions and peppers; and stamp and go, crisp codfish fritters eaten with a meal or as finger food.

Jerk pork or jerk chicken is to Jamaica what barbecue is to Texas—only different. The meat is cooked slowly for hours over an open fire of the pimiento (allspice) tree wood, permeating the meat with the particular flavor. Jerking, as this method of preparation is known, was a specialty of the Port Antonio area, and thirty years ago there was only one jerk place on the entire north coast. Now they are everywhere—a testimony to this dish's great popularity with visitors and Jamaicans alike. In fact, Jerk is so popular it has even inspired the Tourist Board to create a *Jerk Trail*, a culinary adventure, for visitors to follow through Jamaica.

Seafood is plentiful, including local peppery shrimp from the Black River area, lobster, land crabs, and a variety of fish. But of all the selections, smoked marlin is fabulous—more delicate and delicious than smoked salmon. Like jerk pork and chicken, it is cooked slowly over a pimiento wood fire, giving it an unusual flavor. This specialty frequently appears on restaurant menus; you can sometimes buy it packaged in deli shops and supermarkets.

For beverages, Jamaica's Red Stripe beer is the perfect complement to local cuisine. There's Dragon Stout, too, and a variety of liqueurs. Ting, a grapefruit juice soda, is wonderfully refreshing.

Sports and Entertainment

Jamaica has some of the best sports facilities in the Caribbean. If you have the time, you could hike through forests in the Blue Mountains, raft down the Rio Grande in Port Antonio, troll for blue marlin and other gamefish a few miles offshore, ride the treetops on a Canopy tour or a bobsled, practice the equestrian arts at Chukka Cove at St. Ann's Bay, or kayak between Old Fort Bay and Dunn's River Falls.

If you plan to make your own arrangements for your desired sport, here's a word of advice: Call or e-mail ahead or ask your travel agent to make reservations in order to guarantee space, especially during the peak season, Dec through Apr for golf, diving, and deep-sea fishing charters.

Nightlife, Cultural Events, and Festivals

There is plenty of after-dark entertainment, from beach parties to concerts and special events featuring authentic Jamaican folkloric dancing, music, and local food. Most nightspots do not open until 9 p.m. or really get going until midnight. To learn what's happening, check the tourist tabloids, distributed free at hotels and restaurants. Several popular Jamaican evening events highlighting the indigenous culture are held in each of the major resort centers. Check locally. Island Village, an entertainment and shopping center next to the port in Ocho Rios, offers a variety of entertainment daily.

In May 2010, the Jamaican legislature approved a law to allow gambling but before any casinos can open, a commission must write the rules to govern their operation.

In the true sense of festival, Jamaica's vibrant culture, lively spirit, and love of music are most visible and infectious during Carnival in Apr, Independence Week celebrations in Aug, and Junkanoo at Christmas, a sort of Carnival celebrated with lots of music, parties, and street parades highlighted by colorfully costumed participants, masked dancers, and musicians, held between Christmas and New Year. Annually in summer, the famous Reggae Sumfest (www.reggaesumfest.com), featuring top local and foreign reggae artists, is held in the Montego Bay–Ocho Rios area. The five-day event is attended by thousands of music lovers from Jamaica and around the world.

Introduction to Montego Bay

Whether they arrive by cruise ship or by air, many visitors' first glimpse of Jamaica is Montego Bay, the country's second largest town and center of tourist development for five decades. Immediately behind the town and coast rise green-clad mountains with whitewashed houses and flowering gardens in the kind of setting that has earned Jamaica its lush, tropical image.

Even though MoBay, as it is known, looks new, the town was first developed two centuries ago as a port—one of several on the north coast—from which sugar was shipped to Europe and other markets. Freeport, where your ship docks, and the entire waterfront area from the pier to Doctor's Cave Beach are the result of government and private urban development on land reclaimed from the sea. In addition to giving Montego Bay a new harbor, it restored and expanded the beach areas to as much as ten times their size four decades earlier.

The town of Montego Bay divides conveniently into two parts: the town center or western portion, which is the first part you reach coming into Montego Bay from the port, and the tourist district or eastern side. The town center is the business district, which includes banks, professional offices,

stores, and some historic landmarks as well as industrious street sales ladies, called higglers, who peddle their produce and products in the marketplace. Here, too, pushcart vendors sell snacks, cold drinks, and ice cream to the loudspeaker blare of reggae and calypso from streetside record shops. The scene might not be for everyone, but it certainly is Jamaican.

The eastern section of town (approximately a mile from the Montego Bay Craft Market at Market and Harbour Streets) comprises the original tourist area of older hotels, congenial meeting and eating spots, and a wide assortment of shops. If you want nothing more than a golden day on Doctor's Cave Beach and a chance to sample Jamaica's water sports, you won't have to travel any farther than this area of town. Most hotels and restaurants and dozens of shops and craft vendors are located along the main coastal arteries of Gloucester and Kent Avenues; a few are perched on the hillside overlooking the town. Hip Strip, as Gloucester Avenue is known, is where the action is in the evenings.

The touring area of Montego Bay and its nearby attractions covers a 40-mile coastal stretch between Falmouth, 23 miles to the east, and Tryall Golf and Beach Club, 15 miles west of the town. How far to travel and how much to see will largely depend on which attractions—grand plantation houses, lavish gardens, the beach, or sports—have the strongest appeal to you. East of Montego Bay along a coastal road leading to Ocho Rios, there is a series of luxury beach resorts and two of the most splendid plantation houses or "great houses" in Jamaica, both dating from the 18th century. West from the pier for 10 to 12 miles, you come to the fashionable resorts of Round Hill and Tryall Golf and Beach Club, whose centerpiece is an 18th-century plantation house. Farther west, the road leads to Negril, famous for its 7-mile stretch of beach and laid-back lifestyle.

Port Profile: Montego Bay

Embarkation: The cruise ship dock is 3 miles west of downtown in the Freeport area of Montego Bay Harbor, a deepwater pier with eight berths for cruise ships and cargo ships. A fleet of JUTA

(Jamaica Union of Travellers Association) cabs, mini buses, and other ground transportation is on hand to take passengers the short ride to town or on tour. A Jamaica Tourist Board information booth is in the terminal to assist visitors. There are phones, fax, postal service, Internet access, and shops. On the west side of the terminal building is the Montego Freeport in-bond shopping area, which has duty-free stores—that's why it's called "Freeport." Unfortunately, the shops have poor-quality merchandise. We have complained frequently to Jamaican tourism officials about the shops, and we keep being told that there is a master plan to renovate and upgrade the whole area. In the meantime, my advice: Don't hang around the port. Take a tour or go to the beach. The shopping is better elsewhere.

Local Transportation: Taxis: JUTA (Jamaica Union of Travellers Association), the government-licensed, government-approved fleet, is reliable and has something of a monopoly at the docks. Remember, you can share the cost of a taxi with up to three people. From the pier to MoBay city center costs US$5 per person; to Doctor's Cave Beach, US$5 per person; east to Half Moon Club, US$30; west to Tryall Golf and Beach Club, US$40 for one to four persons. A sign in the terminal building lists all prices of taxis and tours to major destinations. From the piers, there is a Hop On/Hop Off service to Doctor's Cave which for $15 you can use all day.

Car Rentals: Bargain Rent-A-Car (800-348-5398), **Budget** (876-952-3838; www.budget jamaica.com), **Elite Car Rental/Hertz** (876-952-4250; hertzja@cwjamaica.com), and **Island Car Rental** (876-929-5875; 866-978-5335; www.islandcarrentals.com) offer reasonable rates by Jamaican standards and have pickup service at the port if you call. As an example of prices, Island Car Rental in Montego Bay charges for a subcompact, standard shift, US$70; automatic, US$75; air-conditioned, US$80. Rates include unlimited mileage and insurance, which is compulsory. If you do not have a major credit card, you must leave a large deposit.

Exploring Jamaica just got easier with the creation of the Caribbean's first GPS Navigation map data known as JAMNAV, developed by the University of the West Indies' Mona GeoInformatics Institute. Currently available from **Avis** (876-952-0762; www.avis.com) at Kingston and Montego Bay airports, JAMNAV offers turn by turn, voice assisted navigation across Jamaica, covering 9,300 miles of roads and 15,000 points of interest including gas stations, hotels, restaurants, shopping places, and attractions.

Major rental companies are located at Sangster International Airport, east of town (about 5 miles from the pier). If you want to rent from one of them, it is better to go directly to its airport office. Although the companies have pickup service at the pier when you reserve in advance, there could be a long wait, as rental companies are inclined to deal with their airport traffic first. Remember, driving is on the LEFT. It is imperative that you be an experienced driver. Jamaican drivers go slightly mad behind the wheel of a car and think the entire road is theirs—blind curves and all!

Montego Bay Shore Excursions

We have selected the most interesting, unique-to-Jamaica tours or those designed for a special interest. These excursions can be taken on your own by hiring a taxi or renting a car or by taking a tour. Descriptions of places and attractions are given elsewhere in the chapter. The prices are based on JUTA's published fees and may vary by a few dollars from one company to another.

Great House Tour: 4 hours; US$25 per hour for one to four persons by car. This half-day trip combines a tour of Montego Bay, a drive east of town and a visit to Rose Hall Great House.

Martha Brae River Rafting: 4 hours; US$55 per person. See description later in this chapter.

Negril Beach Tour: 8 hours; a one-and-a-half-hour motor coach drive west of Montego Bay along the coast to Negril, famous for its 7-mile beach.

Golf, Biking, Canopy Excursions, Scuba Diving: See the Sports section later in the chapter.

Horseback Riding and Swim: 3 hours; US$73 to $80 per person. A mountain-to-sea adventure, riding through old sugar estates to the sea for a ride in the water. See Sports section for details.

Montego Bay on Your Own

A Walk Around Montego Bay

Montego Bay is not a walker's joy in the way Nassau and Old San Juan are, as there is little of its historic past left to see. Yet the old town is not without interest, particularly for people-watchers. Start with a brief taxi tour of Montego Bay to decide which part of town, if any, to explore on foot. Montego Bay is a maze of streets, particularly in the area of Fort and Gloucester Streets, and can be confusing. Fort Street turns into Queen's Drive and curves up a hill to inland hotels and restaurants overlooking the bay. It's not a walk but a hike, and it's hard going under the warm Jamaican sun. We don't suggest it.

Fort Montego: At the roundabout on Harbour Drive (1 block south of Howard Cook Highway) at the base of Miranda Hill are the ruins of Fort Montego, built in 1752, which still has three of its original seventeen cannons pointed seaward. To the south, all roads merge into St. James Street (sometimes shown on maps as Barnett Street), the main road through downtown that leads to Sam Sharpe Square, the town square.

Sam Sharpe Square: The square, a miniature version of the Parade in Kingston, is named for Jamaican hero Sam Sharpe, who was hanged by the British for leading a slave revolt in 1831. It has become traditional in recent years for candidates for national political office to launch their campaigns here. The square is centered on a white-painted, bronze fountain dating from the early 1900s. On the south side, a tableau of five bronze statues by Jamaican sculptor Kay Sullivan depicts Sharpe, Bible in hand, preaching to his followers. At the southeast corner, a very small 18th-century building called "the Cage" was once a prison for runaway slaves.

The Town House: Church Street, which crosses St. James Street on the west of the square, has two fine old buildings. The Town House is a Georgian structure built as a private residence in 1765 by David Morgan, a wealthy merchant. It has been a church manse, a Masonic Lodge, a warehouse, and a lawyer's office, and served as Montego Bay's first synagogue.

St. James Parish Church: Across from the Town House is the beautifully restored St. James Parish Church, established in 1782, which contains ornate monuments erected by wealthy sugar barons. Several nearby streets have nice old balconied houses, which may be interesting to photograph.

Georgian Court: Another block south, at 2 Orange St., are two restored 18th-century town houses connected by a courtyard. One block east at Union Street you can turn south to the City Center, a group of duty-free shops with a limited but well-priced selection of standard goods and souvenir shops with low-quality merchandise, and record stores that carry reggae and other West Indian recordings.

Montego Bay Crafts Market: You should return to the foot of Market Street and the Crafts Market. You can easily spend an hour or so poking around the dozens of crafts stalls and haggling with vendors, but you will quickly discover that most of the stalls sell the same merchandise, and unfortunately very little is of high quality. The stall keepers will vie insistently for your attention, but do not feel under any pressure to buy.

Walter Fletcher Beach: East of the market, Walter Fletcher Beach, a large public park, has good water sports facilities, tennis courts, and clean, protected waters. Entrance fee: US$5 adult; $3 child. **AquaSol Theme Park** (876-979-9447) is the concessionaire that operates the water sports and other facilities here.

A Drive Around Montego Bay

A taxi tour of Montego Bay and its environs is about US$100 for a half day for up to four people. *Agree on the price before you depart.*

Richmond Hill: To get your bearings, Richmond Hill offers a splendid panoramic view of Montego Bay. You will come back down from that lofty perch along Union Street through the downtown marketplace area. Before turning onto Gloucester Avenue to continue to the eastern beach and hotel strip, you pass the sprawling Montego Bay Crafts Market.

Doctor's Cave Beach: One mile east on Gloucester Avenue, a main thoroughfare, brings you to Doctor's Cave Beach, the heart of the tourist

Montego Bay to Ocho Rios

CARIBBEAN SEA

JAMAICA

Holiday Inn Sunspree
Sandals Royal Caribbean
Half Moon
Half Moon
Rose Hall
Montego Bay
Falmouth
Martha Brae
Site of Columbus Landing 1494
Discovery Bay
Site of Seville Nueva 1509 (First Island Capital)
St. Ann's Bay
Dunn's River Falls
Ocho Rios
Fern Gully
Lydford
Moneague

area. It's the prettiest beach in the MoBay area and has a bar and snack counter, water sports, changing facilities, Internet cafe, and entertainment. There is a small entrance fee. A short distance beyond is Cornwall Beach, another nice beach with facilities and water sports.

A Drive East of Montego Bay

Golf, Great Houses, and Rafting

If you rent a car rather than hire a taxi and guide, you should familiarize yourself with a good map first. Maps are available from the Jamaica Tourist Board's information offices. Be especially careful

when driving through busy town streets. The pedestrian is always right. And remember, driving is on the LEFT.

Heading east on Gloucester Avenue, you must turn right onto Sunset Street, which will lead you to a series of roundabouts and Sangster International Airport. The road that passes the airport is the main coastal road, A-1. Two miles beyond the airport, the highway passes several resorts in the Rose Hall area and a cluster of duty-free shops and other stores selling low-quality goods.

Half Moon Beach: After another mile or so, you reach the Half Moon Club, one of the leading hotels in the Caribbean. It is set on 400 acres of landscaped gardens fronting a mile-long beach—the prettiest and longest in the area—and has an 18-hole championship golf course and one of the largest tennis complexes in Jamaica. The Seagrape Terrace is popular for lunch, and there's a delightful bar by the beach. Its Sugar Mill restaurant overlooks its golf course. Most of the hotel's sports and restaurant facilities are available to day visitors with prior arrangements. Reservations are essential in winter.

Rose Hall Great House (876-953-2323; fax: 876-953-2160; greathouse@rosehall.com). About halfway between Half Moon Beach and Hilton Rose Hall Resort & Country Club is Jamaica's most famous plantation house, Rose Hall Great House, a restored mansion with a majestic setting on a hillside overlooking the sea. Built around 1770 by John Palmer when he was the queen's representative for the Parish of St. James, the mansion was acquired in the 1960s by American millionaire John Rollins, a former lieutenant governor of Delaware, in the purchase of a huge tract of land for development. The plantation house was partially damaged in the 1831 slave uprising and unoccupied for more than a century; it was a ruin when Rollins acquired it. He spent several million dollars to restore it as a museum and furnish it with art and antiques to re-create the grandeur of an 18th-century plantation house.

Named for Palmer's first wife, Rose, the mansion is even better known for the legends that surround his fourth wife and last mistress of the house, Annie, although there is little foundation for them in fact. Known as the White Witch of Rose Hall, Annie Palmer, whose ghost was said to haunt the estate after her murder by an unknown hand in 1833, was a beautiful English woman tutored in the black arts by a Haitian priestess. According to the legend, she poisoned one husband, strangled another, murdered a third, and handed out similar fates to a gaggle of lovers (often picked from among her slaves) before meeting her end—and she was only twenty-nine years old! Admission: US$25 adult; $10 child under twelve with a tour by colonial-costumed guides, who embellish the stories of the haunted house with some imagination of their own. Hours: 9 a.m. to 6 p.m. daily; the last tour is at 5:15 p.m.

Nearby, the 427-room **Ritz-Carlton Rose Hall Resort & Country Club** has an 18-hole championship golf course designed by Robert von Hegge—the White Witch—a full-service spa and fitness center, and six restaurants and lounges, among other facilities.

Cinnamon Hill: Another side road past Rose Hall and the walled burial plot of the Moulton Barrett family leads to Cinnamon Hill Great House, the home of relatives of English poet Elizabeth Barrett Browning. The Barrett family was one of the largest plantation owners in Jamaica. The house has been restored and belonged to the late American country-and-western star Johnny Cash, who visited Jamaica frequently. It is not open to the public, but golfers who play the Hilton Rose Hall golf course pass the mansion on the 14th hole.

Greenwood Great House (876-953-1077; www.greenwoodgreathouse.com). Continuing east on Highway A-1, 4 miles past the Hilton Rose Hall and White Witch Riding Stables, a turnoff on the right leads to another Barrett mansion, occupied continuously since it was built in the late 1700s by Sir Richard Barrett, a cousin of the English poet. In the 1980s it was restored and furnished with antiques by its present. The most interesting aspect of the house is the collection of antique musical instruments. From the second-floor balcony there is a spectacular view of the north coast as far as Discovery Bay, 35 miles away. There is a bar in the former kitchen and a gift shop, and outside in the garden, a collection of old carriages. Admission: US$14 adult; $7 child, includes a tour. Hours: 9 a.m. to 6 p.m. daily.

Although these are the most famous historic houses, the north coast of Jamaica has a wealth of lovely old homes and historic buildings. In her book *Jamaican Houses: A Vanishing Legacy,* artist Anghelen Arrington Phillips includes fine sketches of forty such structures.

Falmouth: Built as the capital of Trelawny Parish at the height of the area's sugar-growing prosperity, Falmouth, 23 miles east of MoBay, has a significant group of historic structures dating from the late 18th century. Today, the town is part of the National Trust and preserves Jamaica's Georgian heritage. The most significant buildings are on Market Street west of Water Square. Construction of a new cruise terminal is underway which will not only bring a new cruise port to Jamaica but ultimately, will transform the historic town. As part of a $224 million agreement between the Jamaican government and Royal Caribbean International to modernize the cruise ship pier on Jamaica's north coast, Jamaica is investing $122 million to dredge the harbor and construct the new piers. The remaining $102 million covers infrastructure in and around the cruise pier, renovation of historic buildings, and the addition of an artisans market, retail shops, restaurants, and development of a trolley route and a walking tour with signage. Cruise passengers will have approximately 85 different shore excursions fanning out east and west from Falmouth from which to select. Originally to have been completed in 2009, the target date is now set for Mar 2011. When completed, the port will be able to accommodate two ships the size of RCI's 220,000-ton/6,200 passenger *Oasis of the Seas*—12,000 passengers—simultaneously.

Also in Trelawny is one of Jamaica's newest attractions, the **Outameni Experience** (876-954-4035; genmanger@outameni.com) an interactive journey through 500 years of Jamaican history and culture. Eleven years in the making, the attraction is the concept of Jamaican film producer, Lennie Little-White. It is shown about every half hour, beginning at 10 a.m. and lasts from 75 to 90 minutes.

Martha Brae River (876-954-5168; www.jamaicarafting.com), Falmouth's water source, is the venue for a river-rafting excursion. Signs on the highway point to the turnoff to the Rafter's Village, 4 miles upriver, where the raft trip begins and where there is a restaurant, bar, swimming pool, and boutique. You board a 15-foot bamboo raft, skillfully maneuvered by a Jamaican helmsman, for a relaxing hour's meander downstream through lush riverside vegetation. The raft trip operates from 9 a.m. to 4 p.m. and takes one and a half hours. You are driven back to the village at the end of the trip. Cost: US$55 for two people. Mountain Rafting at Lethe is a similar excursion.

A Drive West of Montego Bay

Natural and Man-Made Splendors

Rocklands Bird Sanctuary (876-952-2009) From the pier, the drive west on Highway A-1 takes less than two hours to Negril. A detour at Reading goes to the Rocklands Bird Sanctuary and Feeding Station, home to large numbers of hummingbirds and many other bird species. The hummingbird species known locally as the "doctor bird" is Jamaica's national bird. The sanctuary is open from 2 to 5 p.m. Call in advance to be sure it's open. At feeding time—3:30 p.m.—you can have the tiny birds eating out of your hand.

At Reading, too, the road to Anchovy leads to Montpelier Plantation, where **Chukka Caribbean Adventures** (888-424-8552; www.chukkacaribbean.com) offers canopy or zipline excursions, similar to those in Costa Rica and built by the same company that created the concept there. The excursions use a harness system of pulleys mounted in the trees that enables participants (supervised by experienced guides) to fly up to 1,000 feet between platforms high in the trees. Cost: US$80 per person. Try it! It's really fun.

Round Hill: After crossing the parish boundary into Hanover at the Great River, you will see the entrance to Round Hill Hotel marked by gateposts. Set on a small peninsula of 98 acres in beautifully terraced gardens overlooking a private beach, the resort is one of the most exclusive, beautiful, and expensive in Jamaica. It was developed in 1953 by Jamaican entrepreneur and later director of tourism John Pringle with a group of investors who included Noel Coward and Oscar Hammerstein. It still attracts a galaxy of stars and celebrities. Hugging the cove in stair-step fashion are the villas, most with private pools and gardens festooned with brilliant flowers.

Tryall Golf and Beach Club: Four miles farther west is the magnificent 2,200-acre sprawl of Tryall Golf and Beach Club. The main house, an 18th-century estate house, and perched on a hillside are forty-three palatial private villas whose wealthy owners come to winter here. The rolling terrain of its 18-hole championship golf course, with an aqueduct and 19th-century waterwheel, serves as a backdrop for the villas, while flowering gardens, the Montego Bay coast, and the sea provide picture-window views.

Kenilworth: Beyond Sandy Bay to the west is the Kenilworth Estate, the finest sugar estate ruins in Jamaica. The factory buildings, impressive stone structures with Palladian windows and arched doorways, lie a mile south of the main road.

Lucea: Another 25 miles west is Lucea, once the main port and center of life for this corner of Jamaica during the heyday of the sugar plantations. Today it is an agricultural center for banana cultivation and molasses production. The town has several historic buildings, including the early-19th-century **Courthouse.** In the restoration the cupola was redesigned and enlarged to fit the clock, whose face measures almost 5 feet. As the story goes, the clock was shipped to Jamaica by mistake and had been intended for the island of St. Lucia, 1,000 miles away!

Negril: Hotels and tourist facilities have been added to Negril in large numbers since it was discovered by the flower children of the 1960s when it was a small village. However, its natural beauty has been saved somewhat because no building can be constructed higher than the tallest tree. Negril is particularly popular for its 7-mile beach and laid back lifestyle. You'll find tennis, horseback riding, diving, and an 18-hole golf course. The nearby region is full of lore and legend dating from the 16th and 17th centuries, when this coast was a pirates' haven. From Montego Bay, Negril is an easy day's excursion for cruise passengers.

Other Sightseeing Options

The following tours depart daily from Montego Bay and cost about US$50 to $60. Most are likely to be incorporated in shore excursions. Alternatively, you can hire a taxi and tour on your own.

Bellefield Great House and Gardens (876-952-2382; www.bellefieldgreathouse.com). In the hills behind Montego Bay is the 3,000-acre Barnett Estate, with an 18th-century great house, the former home of the Kerr-Jarrett family which has owned the estate for more than eleven generations. The 300-year-old estate is still a working plantation producing sugarcane, bananas, mangoes, papayas, and coconuts. The great house, now a museum, was renovated to reflect plantation life in colonial times. It has a dining room, master bedroom, nursery, study, boudoir, and parlor furnished with family heirlooms and mannequins depicting the Kerr family. The "Living History Great House" tour includes the great house and gardens, buffet lunch, and live music by a traditional mento band. Unlike the usual tour, the guides here are dressed in the uniforms or costumes and play the roles of the workers at the great house and on the plantation in colonial times. Cost: US$78 adults, $68 child.

Appleton Estate Tour (876-963-9215; www.appletonrumtour.com). The excursion travels south of Montego Bay, 40 miles deep into the mountains to the Cockpit Country, which was once the region of the Maroons, the runaway slaves and freedmen who fought the British to a truce that allowed them self-government. At the Appleton Rum factory, a guided tour concludes in the tasting room where many different products can be sampled by those over twenty-one years old. The shore excursion is about US$59 adult; $37 ages twelve and under . If you travel to St. Elizabeth on your own, the factory tour is $15. Hours: 9 a.m. to 3:30 p.m. Mon through Sat.

Seaford Town: In 1835, 532 Germans from Hanover and Weserbergland arrived in Jamaica as indentured laborers. Of the group, 251 were to form the township of Seaford, a 500-acre plot given by Lord Seaford from his 10,000-acre estate. After emancipating the slaves, the British colonial government made a policy of bringing European peasants to the island, ostensibly to create thriving communities that would act as both models and employers for the former slaves. But in fact, the new immigrants were to populate the countryside with whites and help keep the peace. The scheme was never a success, and the people who suffered most were the immigrants who had been lured to the tropics by promises of land and a new life in Paradise.

In Seaford Town disease, malnutrition, and migration to the United States reduced the population to one hundred within three years. Originally the settlers were to be given title to the land after five years; it took fifteen. Nonetheless, in the next 150 years the survivors scraped out a small living as farmers and became completely integrated into the mountain life of Jamaica.

In 1978 a minister, Father Francis, completed the **Seaford Town Historical Mini-Museum,** which tells the story of the immigrants. In the same year, St. Boniface Industrial Training Centre was opened with the help of the German and Jamaican governments and German Catholic church. The center is a trade school for more than one hundred boys and girls from throughout Jamaica. Mission Medical Project, opened in 1981, provides a doctor and nurse for the area.

YS Falls (876-634-2454; www.ysfalls.com). Located in the hills behind Montego Bay, about halfway to Black River on the south coast, the beautiful waterfall cascades 120 feet in several stages into the YS River and is the centerpiece of a nature park situated on a 2,000-acre estate. There are food and picnic facilities and river swimming. Chukka Caribbean Adventures (www.chukka caribbean.com) operates a three-stage canopy tour over the falls, US$30 adult, $21 child. Hours: Daily except Mon and holidays.

Meet-the-People: The Jamaica Tourist Board has a Meet-the-People program through which visitors have the opportunity to spend time with a Jamaican host or hostess with whom they may share a common interest. It gives visitors a close look at the lifestyles and culture of the country. To ensure that someone with your particular interest is available, contact the Jamaica Tourist Board nearest you in advance of your cruise or sign up online at www.visitjamaica.com/meetthepeople.

Restaurants

Marguerites, Margaritaville, and The Blue Beat (Gloucester Avenue; 876-952-4777; www.margarita villecaribbean.com). Long MoBay's most popular restaurants, Marguerites has indoor/outdoor terrace dining overlooking the sea and fabulous cuisine for dinner only. It's a bit pricey for Jamaica, but worth it. Margaritaville is open day and night and has several levels: One houses a casual, moderately priced sports bar serving sandwiches and snacks and a boutique; another features an open-air disco with live entertainment; and on the top level you'll find a wild-ride slide that winds three stories down to the sea. The Blue Beat, a third member, is a martini bar and jazz club next door to the restaurant. The multimillion-dollar Blue Beat, with state-of-the-art lighting and sound equipment, features live jazz nightly, hosting established musicians as well as new talent.

The Groovy Grouper Beach Bar & Grill (Gloucester Avenue; 876-954-8287) serves good local cuisine with an emphasis on seafood on decks by the beach. Moderate.

Guangzhou (39 Gloucester Ave.; 876-952-6200) is a Chinese restaurant with a typical large selection of good Cantonese cuisine. Inexpensive.

Juici Patties (36 St. James St.; 876-979-3733; www.juicipatties.com). This islandwide chain is known for inexpensive Jamaican turnovers—the Jamaican version of meat or cheese patties.

The Pelican (Gloucester Avenue; 876-952-3171), the longtime favorite for Jamaican specialties, is comfortable, and convenient. Moderately expensive.

Scotchie's (east of the airport, near Holiday Inn) is an open-air barbecue pit serving some of Jamaica's best jerk meats and fish. Jerk, cooked slowly on a wood fire all morning, is ready by 1 p.m. and can be eaten here or carried out. Inexpensive.

Sports

Beaches/Swimming: The most popular beach in town is Doctor's Cave Beach (876-952-2566; www.doctorscavebathingclub.com), 3 miles east of the cruise ship dock. It has water sports concessions, shops, an Internet cafe, and a snack bar. There are changing areas and showers. A small entrance fee is required.

AquaSol Theme Park (876-979-9447), at Walter Fletcher Park, is the closest-to-port good beach with clean, protected waters and water sports. Pirate's Paradise Water Park at the Sunset Beach Resort & Spa has two 40-foot-high shooting waterslides, a 40-foot-high Pirate's Plank Bridge, Blackbeard's Lazy River, and Buccaneer Beach. Admission: US$60 for those over age eleven.

Kool Runnings Water Park (876-957-5400; www.koolrunnings.com), a five-acre park in Negril has ten waterslides, an interactive children's play area, and a lazy river ride as well as three restaurants a juice bar, and a sports bar. Admission: US$28 adult; $17 senior (sixty-five-plus); $19 child (under 48 inches); under two are free. Hours: 11 a.m. to 6 p.m. Tues through Sun; closed in Sept.

The Sugar Mill Falls Water Park (876-953-2650, www.rosehallresort.com) features waterfalls, a 280-foot thrill slide, lagoons, a lazy river, and three terraced pools, jungle garden with a rope-and-wood suspension bridge, and faux rock formations. The park provides entertainment, including "dive-in" movies, live music, activities, and games as well as poolside food service at two swim-up bars. Admission: US$55 adult; US$35 child.

Boating: For day sails, snorkeling cruises, and boat charters, contact **Pier One** (Howard Cook Highway, opposite Craft Market; 876-952-2452; www.pieronejamaica.com). *The Calico* (876-940-4465), a pirate ship, offers daily cruises at 10 a.m. with stops for snorkeling in the Marine Park. Cost: US$60.

Fishing: A half-day deep-sea fishing charter, with bait and tackle provided, for blue marlin, tuna, dolphin, and wahoo costs US$450 to $550; full day $900 to $1,100. Contact **No Problem Charter** (876-381-3229; fax: 971-5601). Contact **Salty Angler Fishing Charters** (876-863-1599). **Island Routes** (www.islandroutes.com) also offers deep sea fishing.

Golf: For beauty, variety, and challenge, it would be hard for anyplace in the Caribbean to surpass golfing in Jamaica. There are courses within reach of major tourist centers, but for serious golfers Montego Bay, with five championship courses, is the undisputed headquarters. Call for starting times. All locations have clubhouses, restaurant-bars, and pro shops with clubs for rent. East of MoBay, in the Rose Hall area, the 18-hole championship layout by Robert Trent Jones at **Half Moon Club** (7,143 yards, par 72; 876-953-3105; www .halfmoon.com) is characterized by lush, green rolling hills overlooking the sea. It has putting greens, a practice range, a pro shop, and a clubhouse restaurant. Greens fees: US$70 for 9 holes; $130 for 18 holes in summer and US$90 and $150 in the winter for nonguests; cart fees are $25 and $35.

Cinnamon Hill Golf Course (6,930 yards, par 71; 876-953-2650; 800-822-4200; www.rosehall .com), part of the Hilton Rose Hall, is the most unusual course, rebuilt by well-known golf architect Robert von Hagge. The front nine stretch over gentle hills by the sea, but the back nine climb up and around steep hills and are as interesting as they are difficult. The 15th hole has a waterfall

as its backdrop; the 9th and 16th holes are laid out around the ruins of an 18th-century aqueduct; and the 14th plays alongside Cinnamon Hill Great House, the home of the late singer Johnny Cash. Greens fees: US$125 for 18 holes. Club rental $35.

The Ritz-Carlton Rose Hall White Witch Golf Course (6,859 yards, par 71; 800-241-3333; www.ritzcarlton.com) an 18-hole championship layout, named for the famed storybook *The White Witch of Rosehall* by Herbert G. de Lesser. Designed by Robert von Hagge and Associates, the course stretches across more than 200 acres of lush rolling countryside, with 16 holes embracing views of the Caribbean Sea. The clubhouse has a popular open-air restaurant with a veranda that takes in a fabulous view of the greens, the ocean, and the mountains. Greens fees: US$185 winter for 18 holes, $130 summer for nonguests.

About 12 miles west of the pier, the 18-hole championship course of **Tryall Golf and Beach Club** (6,680 yards, par 72; 876-956-5660; www .tryallclub.com) is considered by some to be the island's best in terms of layout, play, and scenery. Greens fees: US$125 winter; $80 summer; cart for two $30; caddie $15 for 9 holes, $30 for 18 holes plus tip. The course is often closed to non-guests in winter; inquire in advance.

Horseback Riding: Available by reservation at the **Half Moon Equestrian Centre** (Half Moon Club; 876-953-2286; www.horsebackridingjamaica .com) The Beach Ride starts with a ride through the Half Moon property and includes a deep swim on horseback. It is scheduled at 7 a.m. and 4 p.m. and costs $60. There's also a tour at 9 a.m. on the Mount Zion Trail through the countryside and Rose Hall Estate, about one-and-a-half hours from the stable. The cost is US$40; riders must be over twelve years old. **Chukka Caribbean Adventures** (876-953-5619; www.chukkacaribbean.com) offers Horseback Ride 'N Swim, a three-hour tour of the countryside with panoramic coastline views, ending with a swim in the sea on horseback. Cost is US$73. Riders must be over six years old and under 250 pounds.

Montego Bay Marine Park: A 15.3-square-kilometer shoreline preserve on the east side of Montego Bay is Jamaica's first Marine National

Park. The preserve is home to mangroves, seagrass beds, and coral reefs and boasts some of the greatest coral diversity in the western Atlantic. The marine sanctuary, together with the Blue Mountain National Park, is part of a project financed in part by aid from the United States. Those who do not dive can enjoy the marine park from the comfort of a semi submersible, usually available as a cruise ship shore excursion. Tours on the semi sub *Coral Viewer* (876-322-8650) were being planned to leave from Pier One for excursions over the reefs. Inquire locally for schedule. **Island Routes** (www.island routes.com) offer snorkeling in the park from aboard the *Red Locks* with a stop at Margaritaville, US$72.

Snorkeling/Scuba: The shallow reefs and drop-offs of Jamaica's north coast offer good diving over unusual underwater sites whose highlights are tunnels, crevasses, mini walls, and what Jacques Cousteau once called "some of the most dramatic sponge life in the Caribbean." *Warning: Do not dive or snorkel with "freelance" guides soliciting business along the beach. Use only established operators, where you must show your certification card.* **Resort Divers** (Royal Decameron Montego Beach, 876-953-9699; www.resortdivers.com) is a PADI operator with shops in several locations on the north shore. An introductory course is US$90; one-tank dive $55; two tank $90, including equipment. Snorkeling, about $40 per trip with equipment.

Tennis: Walter Fletcher Beach has public courts; otherwise, the courts available to cruise passengers are at hotels. Hotel guests are given preference over visitors, who must pay a fee. You need to make arrangements in advance, particularly in high season. **Half Moon Club** (876-953-2211; www .halfmoon.com) has one of the finest facilities in the Caribbean, with thirteen courts, a fully equipped pro shop, and a resident pro. Contact in advance for court time; prices vary by season for non-guests. The hotel also has four squash courts; rental equipment is available.

Windsurfing: You will find the sport at all beachfront resorts on the north coast including **Captain's Watersports** (Half Moon Club, 876-953-2211) Cost: $30 per hour. Hours: 8 a.m. to 4:30 p.m. daily.

Introduction to Ocho Rios

By design and a great deal of help from nature, Ochi, as Ocho Rios is called locally, is a town created for Jamaican tourists as much as foreign ones. Situated on one of the widest, prettiest beaches on the north coast, Ocho Rios, a former fishing village, is said to take its name, meaning "eight rivers" in Spanish, from an English corruption of the town's Spanish name, Las Chorreras, "the waterfalls." There are waterfalls in town near the pier, and Dunn's River Falls, a dramatic cascade of 600 feet, is only a few miles away.

Ocho Rios is centrally located on the north coast within easy reach of three completely different faces of Jamaica, which is one reason for its popularity as a cruise port. In a radius of 20 miles, the beach-trimmed shore is punctuated by tiny fishing villages between major resorts, while the interior behind the coast is dotted with tourist-free small towns and hillside hamlets where Jamaicans earn a simple living from the land.

Separating the tourist coast of the north and the Jamaican's Jamaica of the south are the awesome Blue Mountains, where the famous coffee grows and where the wild forests are home to hundreds of exotic birds and butterflies, tropical plants, and flowers—many unique to Jamaica. The main highway over the towering mountains leads to Kingston, the capital and heart of the country's business, government, and cultural life.

Ocho Rios's location at the center of many varied attractions enables it to offer so many choices that you may have difficulty deciding among them. For water sports enthusiasts, boating, fishing, waterskiing, windsurfing, scuba diving, and snorkeling are all available at the public beach next to the pier from concessioners licensed by the Jamaica Tourist Board. For shoppers, there are crafts markets, boutiques with locally made clothing and other products, duty-free shops, and supermarkets for Jamaican spices, coffee, and other local goods.

For serious explorers, Ocho Rios's attractions stretch from Port Maria on the east to Discovery Bay on the west. Hidden in the hills behind the coast are exquisite gardens, bird sanctuaries, and working plantations of citrus, bananas, mangoes, and other tropical fruits. The lush landscape and its natural beauty are the features that appeal most to visitors and easily convince them that Ocho Rios deserves its title as the Garden of Jamaica.

Port Profile: Ocho Rios

Embarkation: The cruise ship dock and Reynolds Pier (both used by cruise ships) are located on the western side of the town's public beach, anchored at the east end by the Sunset Jamaica Grande Resort and on the west by Island Village, an entertainment and shopping complex, at the cruise passenger exit. A Jamaica Tourist Board representative is on the pier to assist visitors. There is a bank on the pier, but you really do not need to exchange money. U.S. dollars are accepted everywhere.

Upon exiting the dock area, you will find fleets of taxis and tour buses awaiting cruise passengers. Those who are not on an organized tour will be bombarded by taxi drivers who want to be their guide for a tour. Prices are supposed to be set by the taxi association, but do not hesitate to bargain. If you don't want a taxi or tour, just smile, say "No, thank you," and keep walking. In addition to the facilities of Island Village shops, and restaurants, are in the Ocean Village Shopping Center on Main Street, a ½-mile walk east of the pier and the Ocho Rios Crafts Market. Regrettably, this area of Ocho Rios could benefit from a coat of paint and is sorely in need of a beautification. While there are several shopping complexes, such as the Taj Mahal, there's really very little in town, beyond the beach and its sports facilities, of interest to visitors. Since the Ocho Rios area has so many wonderful attractions, my recommendation is to take one of the ship's shore excursions, hire a taxi to tour, or rent a car to explore beyond the port on your own.

Local Transportation: Taxis: JUTA (Jamaica Union of Travellers Association) is the government-licensed/approved fleet, which sets and publishes rates that most companies follow. Remember, in Jamaica you hire the taxi and can share the costs with up to three other people. A taxi from the pier or Main Street to one of the nearby posh hotels, such as Jamaica Inn, is about US$10 to $12 one way. There are no public buses from the piers.

Jamaica has an intracity bus service between Ocho Rios and Montego Bay, but it is seldom used by tourists. Given the limited time most ships are in port, you are better advised to hire a taxi, especially if you have others with whom to share the cost.

Car Rentals: There are two problems with renting a car in Jamaica. First, Jamaicans pay extremely high import duties on cars and parts—thus car rentals can be expensive. Depending on the model, Island Car Rental rates for automatic with air-conditioning and unlimited mileage range from US$50 to $109 winter; US$44 to $99 summer, plus US$12 per day compulsory insurance. In high season there often aren't enough cars to meet the demands of hotel guests; day visitors may find no cars available. Car rental firms in Ocho Rios have pickup service at the port if you have made reservations in advance, but do not be surprised if your car is not on hand for your arrival. If not, go directly to the rental office, as you could waste a great deal of time waiting for your car to show up. Two area firms are **Island Car Rental** (876-929-5875; 866-978-5335; www.islandcarrentals.com) and **Budget** (15 Milford Rd., 876-974-1288; www.budgetjamaica.com).

Ocho Rios Shore Excursions

The following tours are usually offered by cruise ships and local travel agencies such as **Tourwise** (Ocho Rios, 876-974-2323; www.tourwise.org). They can also be arranged with a taxi driver-guide. Descriptions of the attractions are given later in the section. Tour length and prices vary from one tour company to another. Sample prices are per person.

Ocho Rios Highlights Tour: 3 to 4 hours; US$55–$65. Tour combines the area's main mountain and garden attractions: Fern Gully; Shaw Park Gardens or Coyaba River Gardens; and Dunn's River Falls, where you can climb a waterfall and enjoy lunch and Jamaica's lush flora. Because it's the most popular tour in Jamaica, you will do your visiting in a crowd. Bathing suit and sneakers are a must.

Prospect Adventure Tours: 3 to 4 hours; (other plantations are toured as well). Journey by jitney US$32 (or horseback) through citrus groves and forests on a guided tour of a 1,000-acre working estate or take a camel ride US$58. (See description later in this chapter.) When combined with Dunn's River Falls, cost is about $82.

Art, Literary Gems, and Nature: 3 to 4 hours. Several lesser-known attractions east of town make an interesting tour for those on their own. **Harmony Hall** (www.harmonyhall.com), an art gallery in a pretty colonial manor house near Ocho Rios, and Noel Coward's modest hilltop retreat Firefly are among those included. Nearby is the **James Bond Beach Club** (876-975-3663), a beach and entertainment facility with water sports and restaurant; entrance fee: US$5, opened Tues to Sun.

Dolphin Cove: See description later in this section.

Biking, Kayaking, Scuba Diving: (See Sports later in this section.)

Tubing: Floating down the White River in a rubber tube is one of Jamaica's most popular excursions. US$60 adult; $48 ages six and older. (See White River Valley and Sports later in this section.)

Dogsledding: Two tours, US$85. Chukka Farm (888-424-8552; www.jamaicadogsled.com), home to the Jamaica Dogsled Team, offers one-on-one interaction with the team dogs and either a demonstration or a 2½-mile ride. All the dogs are rescues from local animal shelters and have been professionally trained. A fully rigged ride with fourteen dogs costs $180.

Mystic Mountain: See West of Ocho Rios and Sports section later in the chapter

Ocho Rios on Your Own

Be prepared! Cruise ship arrivals turn this town into a beehive of excitement. Like many Caribbean ports, Ocho Rios has a street-fair atmosphere when cruise ships are in port. Everyone in Ocho Rios—or so it seems—will be on hand along the main road to welcome you and try to persuade you not to leave town without taking their tour or buying their necklace, doll, hat, or the hundred other souvenirs they want to sell you.

Taxi drivers, mini bus tour operators, higglers, and crafts peddlers all jockey for the best positions to get your attention. Just smile and keep walking.

If you can enter into the spirit of the affair, you can have fun, try your hand at bargaining, take some great pictures, and come away with attractive souvenirs at cheap prices. Some visitors find this exuberant salesmanship intimidating and others say it's simply irritating, but if you deal with such encounters as sport, you will quickly get the knack of enjoying Ocho Rios.

A note of warning: Ocho Rios has worked hard in the past several years to clean up its act. The great majority of entrepreneurs are warm, friendly, and trusting people, but as in ports anywhere in the world, there are hustlers among them not to be trusted and definitely *not to be hired as guides. Do not go off by yourself in a rented car or on foot with anyone wanting to "show you a special place." They are hustlers posing as guides and could leave you stranded and cashless or worse.* Licensed guides and taxis are just that—licensed. Authorized driver-guides wait near the pier, dressed in uniforms with the company logo clearly visible on their shirts. Anywhere else, you should ask to see their credentials. The Tourist Board maintains a "Courtesy Corps" of men and women specially trained to help tourists; they have the powers of arrest, if that should be necessary. You can recognize them by their uniforms: black trousers, green shirts, and yellow lanyards—the colors of Jamaica's flag. If you have any doubt about a guide or if you feel you are being harassed, don't hesitate to ask one of the uniformed Courtesy Corps or a police officer for assistance.

Meet-the-People: See information in Montego Bay section.

A Walk Around Ocho Rios

Downtown Ocho Rios, except as a place for browsing through shops and crafts stalls or sampling local restaurants, does not merit a walkabout. Your time can be better spent enjoying the beach and water sports or on excursions to interesting attractions in outlying areas.

Island Village: Designed to resemble a small Jamaican village, the complex is something of a theme park, entertainment and sports center, and shopping mall in one. Located next to the cruise ship pier and built primarily for cruise ship passengers, Island Village (www.islandvillageja .com) is the brainchild of Chris Blackwell, who is credited with Bob Marley's success. Island Village is intended to showcase the best of Jamaica. Entrance is free, but some attractions have charges.

Reggae-Xplosion, museum devoted to reggae with interactive displays of its history and best-known artists, and a branch of the National Gallery of Jamaica, with works by Jamaica's finest artists on display. Closed for renovation. At the center of the complex is the Village Stage and Village Green, an outdoor concert venue with a capacity for 3,000 people where a variety of free, local, and international musical performances, as well as other cultural events, can be enjoyed daily. Other attractions include a casino, video games arcade with pool tables, and Internet cafe (US$4 for thirty minutes). From here, walkways lead to colorful cottages housing stores, restaurants, bars, and attractions. There are duty-free stores for jewelry, perfume, cigars, and liquor, and specialty shops, such as Bookland, Cool Gear, and Island Trading Hemp Hut; Starfish Oils for Jamaican incense, candles, and toiletries; and others for Jamaican art, crafts, spices, and jams.

The ice-cream parlor specializes in tropical flavors. There's a photo shop, a Massage Hut with such treatments as "Soul Satisfaction" and "Hot Thighs" costing from US$20 for twenty minutes to $60 for an hour, and a salon for hair braiding and fancy nails.

Jimmy Buffett's Margaritaville (876-675-8813; 888-VILLAGE), serving drinks and snacks, is Action Central all day long. Behind the restaurant is a small, white-sand beach with water sports. Basic entry is US$3, but for $15 or $20 you have use of equipment for snorkeling, kayaking, pedal biking, and more.

Probably the best thing about Island Village is that it improved the port area with an orderly complex and thus improved, however slight, cruise passengers' first impression of Jamaica by reducing the rush of vendors that many passengers find so distasteful.

On Main Street, if you turn east (with the traffic), a ten-minute walk will bring you to the Ocean Village Shopping Center and Crafts Market, and the public beach. Across the road is the Taj Mahal shopping complex and some restaurants and bars. Ten minutes more brings you to the Sunset Jamaica Grande Resort, where there are shops, restaurants, and sports facilities. If you turn west at Island Village, Dunn's River Falls and Dolphin Cove are about one mile. However, traffic being what it is, walking here is hazardous at best.

West of Ocho Rios

Fern Gully: Highway A-3 (a road perpendicular to A-1, the main coastal highway) is the main artery south of town. It winds through an old riverbed bordered by hundreds of species of fern. The lacy branches of the giant ferns and lush vegetation form a natural canopy over the highway, cooling and refreshing the air. The gully is also the first 3 miles of the road to Kingston, the capital of Jamaica.

Shaw Park Gardens (876-974-2723; www .shawparkgardens.com). Watch for the turnoff to Shaw Park Botanical Gardens and Bird Sanctuary, where you will need at least an hour to tour the pretty grounds and enjoy the spectacular view of Ocho Rios. The variety of indigenous flowers, trees, shrubs, and rushing streams and waterfalls makes this a popular photo stop as well. Guided tours every day between 8 a.m. and 4 p.m. Admission: US$10. Refreshments are available.

Coyaba Garden and Mahoe Falls (876-974-6235; www.coyabagardens.com). A garden 1 mile from Ocho Rios, at 420 feet, is named for the Arawak word meaning "paradise." The museum displays pre-Columbian artifacts and exhibits covering the island's history. There are walkways for strolling through the gardens to enjoy natural waterfalls, a gift shop featuring local products, and an art gallery. Admission: US$10 adult; $5 child, which includes tour and welcome drink. Hours: 8 a.m. to 5 p.m. daily.

Dunn's River Falls (876-974-2857; www.dunnsriverfallsja.com). The magnificent waterfall gushes over lush, wooded limestone cliffs along the inland ridge and cascades 600 feet down a series of natural stone steps to the sea. Surefooted tourists climb the rocks—in bathing suits—fighting the rushing water like salmon beating upstream. You can climb with or without an official guide. We strongly recommend a guide. The rocks are very slick, and the water torrents powerful enough to knock you off balance. Daily tours to the falls are available from all of Jamaica's main towns, including Kingston. Hence, the falls are frequently crowded with visitors from not only cruise ships but hotels as well. The later in the day you go, the less crowded the area is likely to be. Admission: US$15 adult; $12 child. Hours: 8:30 a.m. to 5 p.m. daily. The prettiest part of the falls, known as Laughing Waters, is private property where some scenes from the James Bond movies *Dr. No* and *Live and Let Die* were shot.

Dolphin Cove (876-974-5335; www.dolphincovejamaica.com). Located across the road from Dunn's River Falls, Dolphin Cove is set on a lush bank by the sea and offers three programs. Swim with Dolphins, US$195, provides a close, one-to-one encounter as you swim and frolic with a group of dolphins, including the chance for a foot push or dorsal pull. Swim Encounter, US$129, allows you to swim in the deep for thirty minutes with one dolphin. Touch, US$67, offers landlubbers and children a chance to learn about dolphins and touch and enjoy their company. Program times: 9:30 a.m., 11:30 a.m., 1:30 p.m., and 3:30 p.m. Reservations are required, and you must be able to swim. Because the number of participants in the swim programs is limited, you should book ahead. The entrance fee (US$45 adult; $30 child under sixteen for those not participating in a dolphin program) includes a nature walk through the tropical landscape, where you see birds, tropical fish, reptiles, flowers, and dolphins at play. Kayaks and mini boats are available. The facility also has a stingray encounter similar to the dolphin one.

Mystic Mountain: On a mountain side behind Ocho Rios, Rainforest Adventures at Mystic Mountain (876-974-3990; www.rainforestbobsledjamaica.com) is one of Jamaica's newest attractions and a fun way to spend a (pricey) morning or afternoon. Just beyond Dolphin Cove is the entrance and ticket window (US$47) to ride the chair lift—one of fifty in a continuous loop—over the tree tops to the top of the mountain at 750 feet, passing fourteen maintenance towers. At the 11th tower, your picture is taken (for US$12 you can purchase in the pavilion at the top). The ride takes about 15 minutes. At the top, the main building, designed as a replica of an early 1900s Jamaican railway station, has a gift shop and interesting displays of Jamaican history and its heroes and another on its many Olympic athletes. Here, too, is a swimming pool and waterslide; the station for the Bobsled (US$20) that runs on a 3,280-foot track that makes a gravity-drive loop through the forest; and the Zipline (US$65) which has five lines ranging from 99 feet to 560 feet between platforms. The second floor of the main building has a restaurant and steps up to the Lookout from where there are grand views across the forested mountains and down to Ocho Rios and the sea.

Discovery Bay: West of Dunn's River Falls are three small villages that had big moments in Jamaica's history. Until excavations at St. Ann's Bay (1 mile west of the falls) in the 1980s raised doubts, Discovery Bay (15 miles west) was traditionally marked as the site where Christopher Columbus first sighted Jamaica in 1494. The event is commemorated in a seaside monument and memorial park, built by Kaiser Aluminum, the principal company that once mined Jamaica's bauxite. The park has a sugar-refining display—a reminder of Jamaica's plantation economy for most of its colonial history.

On Columbus's fourth voyage in 1503, two of his ships were damaged beyond repair and were beached on Jamaica's north shore. Columbus spent a year on the island awaiting rescue—thus giving Jamaica the unique status as the only place in the New World where the great explorer lived.

New Seville: After Columbus's death in 1506, his son Diego came to the New World as governor of the Indies and from Santo Domingo sent Juan de Esquivel, a former lieutenant of Columbus's, to Jamaica to establish a colony. Under him the town of Sevilla la Nueva, or New Seville, was laid out in 1509. It served as the capital of the Jamaica colony until 1534, when it was abandoned for the new capital of St. Jago de la Vega (present-day Spanish Town) on the south coast. Excavations near the village of St. Ann's Bay uncovered the remains of a settlement and church dating from the 15th and 16th centuries; from artifacts found in the excavations scholars were able to identify it as New Seville.

Seville Great House: About a mile from the site on a hillside is Seville Great House (876-972-2191; www.jnht.com), a 19th-century plantation house; nearby, an Arawak site has also been excavated. It is but one of more than 200 Arawak sites identified in Jamaica. History has recorded that Diego Columbus was the first in a long list of European explorers who succeeded in annihilating the Arawaks within fifty years of Columbus's arrival. Admission: US$5 adult; $2 child. Hours: 9 a.m. to 4 p.m. daily.

Cranbrook Flower Forest (876-995-3097, www.cranbrookff.com). Just west of St. Ann's Bay is 120 acres set by a gentle flowing river with tropical vegetation and gardens. Here guests enjoy nature walks, birding, swimming, volleyball, croquet, and horseback riding. There is a museum of local history and a gift shop in an old sugar mill. Admission and garden tour: US$10 adult; $5 child. Hours: 9 a.m. to 5 p.m. daily. Here, too, **Chukka Caribbean Adventures** (876-972-2506; www.chukkacaribbean .com) operate one of their five Ziplines in Jamaica. The canopy excursion can be combined with snorkeling for US$117 adult; $82 child.

East of Ocho Rios

East from town, Main Street becomes Highway A-3 and passes some of the area's best resorts in ravishingly beautiful settings. If your ship is in port on a Sunday and you are more in the mood for elegance than exploration, you should treat yourself to the luncheon buffet—complete with white-gloved waiters—on the terrace of the **Royal Plantation Resort** (876-974-5601; www.royal plantation.com) overlooking the tropical gardens and beach. But then, Jamaica has many settings equally as beautiful. You need several return visits to see them all.

Prospect Plantation (876-994-1058; www .prospectplantationtours.com). Near the White River, a clearly marked road leads inland 1 mile to a working plantation and wooded estate covering 1,000 acres. Here you will see a great variety of tropical trees, shrubs, and flora typical of Jamaica and the Caribbean, and—unlike so many other locations—species here are labeled. The guides, too, are knowledgeable and make tours interesting and enjoyable, stopping along the way for scenic views of the coast, a lookout over the heavily forested ravine through which the White River flows, and a lane of trees planted by such famous visitors as Winston Churchill, Noel Coward, and Charlie Chaplin. The tour in a jitney leaves the center at 10:30 a.m., 2 p.m., and 3:30 p.m. Cost: US$32 adult; $15 child twelve and under. There is also a camel ride (US$58), hiking, and horseback riding as well as a bar and shop for locally made products. The excursions are operated by **Dolphin Cove Tours** (876-974-5335; www.dolphincovetours.com).

Harmony Hall (876-974-2870; www.harmony hall.com). Beyond White River (4 miles east of Ocho Rios), Harmony Hall is a handsomely restored 19th-century great house of a small pimiento (allspice) plantation, which houses a fine-art gallery and **Toscanini** (876-975-4785), the area's leading restaurant. The gallery (open 10 a.m. to 6 p.m. daily, closed in Sept) specializes in top Jamaican art and sculpture, quality crafts, antiques, and old prints. All works on display are for sale. The 1886 Victorian structure has its original stonework; its new gingerbread trim and balustrade were designed by a batik artist and produced on the property by local artisans.

The gallery has a representative collection of contemporary artists, including Jamaican primitives or intuitives, as they are called, and other young artists whom the gallery owner, Annabella Proudlock, herself an artist, encourages through frequent expositions. There are also prints by the late Australian artist Colin Garland, who lived in Jamaica for more than thirty years and taught in the Ocho Rios area. Garland's paintings were so deeply influenced by his Jamaican environment that he was looked upon as a local artist and included among the Jamaican artists in the National Collection. The gallery has a collection of prints and gifts mounted with miniature copies of prints by the late English artist Jonathan Routh from his popular book *Jamaican Holiday: The Secret Life of Queen Victoria*.

Farther east, Rio Nuevo is the spot where the British finalized their claim to Jamaica by routing the last of the Spanish forces from a stockade at the river's mouth. A small monument marks the battle site.

White River Valley (876-917-3373; www .wrvja.com). An adventure park 7 miles east of town at the hamlet of Cascade is set in the valley on 300 woodland acres and straddles the cool river waters that run for a mile through the property. Here, in this picture of serenity, you can spend the day enjoying river tubing, mountain biking, horseback riding, hiking, and picnicking.

At the entrance is a manicured "village green" surrounded by stands of bamboo, lime and guava trees, and tropical flora beside some colorful cottages of local style. They house the park offices, a juice bar, a coffee bar, a souvenir shop, changing rooms and toilet facilities, horse stables, and a restaurant with an outdoor veranda where you can dine on Jamaican specialties.

The most popular sport—river tubing—begins at the old Spanish Bridge, said to have been built by the Spaniards more than 400 years ago. Here guides instruct you on maneuvering the tubes and lead you throughout the excursion, never losing sight of their charges. The watery ride of about forty-five minutes ends downriver at an embankment with small thatched huts where you can picnic and where transportation awaits to take you back to the village square. Along the way you can enjoy the tropical scenery lining the riverbanks—if you dare take your eyes off the swift-moving river. The entrance fee, which is waived with the purchase of an excursion, is US$10. Sports range from hiking with a guide for US$65 to river tubing, kayaking, biking, or horseback riding for US$69 (www .chukkacaribbean.com).

Goldeneye: At the next town, Oracabessa, a small lane leads to the beach and to **Goldeneye Estate** (876-975-3354; www.islandoutpost.com), the haunt of Ian Fleming, the author of thirteen James Bond novels. Fleming spent winters here from 1946 until his death in 1964, often keeping company with

his friend Noel Coward, whose home is farther east. The estate is now privately owned by Jamaica's most successful music promoter, Christopher Blackwell, who is credited with helping to launch reggae superstar Bob Marley and others. The luxury villa now anchors a 70-acre, expensive boutique hotel and villa complex and next door, the James Bond Club, a beach and entertainment facility with water sports and a restaurant. Entrance: US$5.

Firefly (876-424-5359; www.islandoutpost .com). Farther east, a small sign directs you to turn south off Highway A-3 and up a winding hillside road, past modest homes and through lush vegetation to a lane lined with towering hardwood trees. At the end on a hillside overlooking Port Maria is Firefly, the cottage and refuge of playwright Noel Coward. The modest bachelor pad was donated to the country by his estate after his death in 1973. First renovated by the Jamaica National Trust and opened as a museum in 1985, it was leased in 1993 by Christopher Blackwell, who made extensive renovations, reopening it as a museum evoking its glamorous heyday of the 1950s, when the songwriter and wit entertained his friends—all the most famous stars and celebrities of his day.

Coward is buried, as he had requested, in the far northwest corner of the garden beneath a simple marble slab, protected by a white wrought-iron gazebo. The site was his favorite evening roost to watch the sunset and sip his brandy and ginger. The view from here is one of the finest panoramas in the tropics. The 17th-century pirate Henry Morgan, apparently found the site an ideal lookout for preying on Spanish galleons. That's before he became governor of Jamaica and was knighted! Firefly is used for weddings and special events to augment the museum's income, but this is Blackwell's ode to Jamaica—a labor of love and some nostalgia: Blackwell's uncle had sold the land for Firefly to Coward, and his mother was a longtime friend of the playwright. Admission: US$10 adult, US$5 child. Hours: 9 a.m. to 5 p.m., closed Fri and Sun.

Restaurants

Almond Tree (Hibiscus Lodge, 83 Main St.; 876-974-2813) has good local and continental selections, particularly seafood and soups, in a delightful setting of several terraces that spill down the cliffside overlooking the sea. Smoked marlin is fabulous. Lunch noon to 2:30 p.m.; dinner 6 to 9:30 p.m. Moderate.

Coconuts on the Bay (876-795-0064; www .coconutsrestaurantbarjamaica.com), an Ocho Rios standby, is located by the cruise ship pier. It serves soups, salads, sandwiches, wraps, and a variety of seafood, steaks, and Jamaican specialties. Inexpensive.

Ocho Rios Jerk Centre (Town Center; 876-974-2549) is an open-air restaurant and bar, popular for jerk. Inexpensive.

Passage to India (Sony's Plaza, 2nd Floor, 50 Main St.; 876-795-3182) serves good, authentic Indian cuisine. Moderate.

The Ruins (Da Costa Drive; 876-974-8888; www.ruinsjamaica.com), serves Asian and Jamaican dishes at lunch and Mediterranean and Jamaican cuisine at dinner, in a romantic outdoor setting amid tropical gardens and a waterfall. Moderate.

Scotchies (Highway A-1, St. Ann's Bay; 876-794-9457). The outdoor garden restaurant, across from Draux Hall polo grounds, specializes in jerk pork, chicken, and fish, as well as other popular Jamaican dishes, cooked on grills as close to the original method as to be found. It's about 5 miles from the cruise port, but worth the trip. Inexpensive.

Spring Garden Cafe (Ocho Rios Bypass Road; 876-795-3149). Specializes in seafood, and vegetarian dishes. Situated on a quiet knoll about a mile from the noisy crowd of town, it has inside and outside seating and ample parking space. Moderate.

Toscanini (Harmony Hall; 876-975-4785) is the top restaurant in Ocho Rios, offering seafood as well as excellent Italian food made from fresh ingredients in an attractive setting. Open for lunch and dinner; closed Mon and Sept. Reservations recommended. Moderately expensive.

White River Ranch Bar Restaurant (876-974-6932), a very local eatery on the edge of Ocho Rios in an open shed, serves home-cooked local specialties such as steamed fish, chicken and chips, and fried rice. Inexpensive.

Miss T's Kitchen (second lane east of the Clock Tower in town), a favorite of local folks for Jamaican dishes and recommended, if you can find it. Ask locally for directions.

Sports

Beaches: Within sight of the cruise ship dock upon arrival in Ocho Rios is the public beach, one grand strand of white sand curving from Turtle Beach Towers to the Sunset Jamaica Grande. It is complete with water sports facilities, refreshment stands, and hordes of independent vendors eager to sell you anything from wood carvings to hair braiding.

Reggae Beach, a ½-mile stretch in a quiet cove with a pretty natural setting is 3½ miles east of town. Independent visitors are welcome for an admission fee of US$5, including one drink. The snack bar serves Jamaican dishes; lifeguards, first aid, changing rooms, and showers are available.

Mahogany Beach, a small beach in a cove with a small stream surrounded by low cliffs, is less than a mile east of town, a twenty-minute walk. A lifeguard is on duty, and security is provided day and night. The clear water, less than 6 feet deep, is ideal for novice swimmers. Water sports are available, as are showers and bathrooms, chairs and umbrellas, grill and bar.

Biking: Mountain biking and combinations of biking and river swimming are popular enough to be offered as cruise ship excursions, about US$60 per person. If you want to do it on your own, **Blue Mountain Bicycle Tours** (15–16 Santa Maria Plaza, 121 Main St., Ocho Rios; 876-974-7075; www.bmtoursja.com) offers guided downhill rides on mountain bikes Tues through Sat for US$93 adult; $65 ages twelve and under, including transfers, brunch, lunch, and equipment.

Boating: Heave Ho (180 Main St.; 876-974-5367; www.heavehocharters.com) has large catamarans for charter for ten or more people to go sailing and snorkeling, with drinks and barbecue lunch.

Canopy Excursions (877-424-8552; 888-424-8552; www.chukkacaribbean.com). A facility at Cranbrook Flower Forest in the hills near Ocho Rios enables you to swing high above the treetops in a harness pulled on horizontal traverse cables. US$89 adult; $62 child. (For more options, see Mystic Mountain and White River Valley described earlier in this section.)

Deep-Sea Fishing: Available from Resort Divers (876-881-5760; www.resortdivers.com) with fleet of 42' Bertrams. Book at least one month in advance in winter; two weeks in summer. US$550 half day. Island Routes **Deep Sea Sportfishing Adventure** (www.islandroutes.com) offers fishing excursions aboard 31' Bertram *Sabrina* or 46' Hatteras *Cheryl Ann* with experienced captains and crew fish for blue marlin, yellow tail, and more, US$140 per person.

Golf: In Ocho Rios, **Sandals Golf & Country Club,** 6,600 yards, par 70 (876-974-0119; www.sandals.com), which belongs to the all-inclusive Sandals chain, is an 18-hole course a few miles east of town. Greens fees: US$99; carts $40; caddie $17; club rental $60 with two sleeves of balls. At Runaway Bay, the course belonging to **Breezes Runaway Bay Golf Club** (876-973-7319; 800-467-8737; www.breezes.com/resorts/runaway-bay) charges US$80 for 18 holes, $50 for 9 holes; cart $35 and $23; club rental $20; caddie $16 and $11. Phone in advance for tee times, especially Dec to Apr.

Horseback Riding: Chukka Cove Farm Equestrian Center (877-4-CHUKKA; www.chukkacaribbean.com) is a full-scale operation with facilities for serious and recreational riders. The center offers tours through historic sugar plantations with a bareback swim ($75 adult, $53 child). The farm also stages shows and polo tournaments throughout the year. **Tourwise** (876-974 2323; www.tourwise.org) has Cool Riding, a combination of a horseback beach ride at Drax Hall and a climb of Dunn's River Falls, US$75. **Hooves Limited** (876-972-0905; fax: 876-972-9204; www.hoovesjamaica.com) offers guided horseback tours through the countryside. Its Rain Forest River Ride is for experienced riders. It starts at 1,800 feet, stops for a swim under a waterfall, continues along the river, and makes a second stop for another swim, US$100. Open daily 9 a.m. to 5 p.m.

Kayaking/River Tubing: Chukka Caribbean Adventures (876-953-5619; 877-4-CHUKKA; www.chukkacaribbean.com) offers kayak excursions, US$64 adult; $45 ages twelve and under, includes refreshments; and river tubing at White River Valley, US$63; as well as a combination Zipline and River Tubing, $103 adult, $72 child. Kayak excursions are west of Ocho Rios between Old Fort Bay and Dunn's River Falls.

Polo: Regular polo matches are played at **Chukka Cove** (St. Ann's Bay) and at **Drax Hall Polo Field** (5 miles west of Ocho Rios). Chukka Cove offers lessons at various times of the year, but to play in a match a visitor would need to phone (876-972-2506) or write ahead (P.O. Box 160, Ocho Rios) and include credentials information.

Scuba Diving: Good shallow reefs, tunnels, archways, and drop-offs close to shore make scuba diving interesting in Ocho Rios. Resort courses are available for beginners; boat dive trips require that participants have certification cards. Generally, trips depart at 9 a.m. for four hours and 2 p.m. for two hours, US$50 one tank; $85 two tanks. **Resort Divers** (www.resortdivers.com) is a PADI operator headquartered in Runaway Bay. An introductory course is US$95; one-tank dive US$45; two-tank $85, including tanks and weights. Other water sports operators are found at the Sunset Jamaica Grande Hotel.

Tennis: Courts within walking distance of the pier are at the **Sunset Jamaica Grande,** which has four courts. Non-guest fees are US$8 per hour. Use of courts is subject to availability, and since it is a large hotel, the likelihood of finding a free court is not in your favor.

Windsurfing: On the beach at Sunset Jamaica Grande, windsurfing costs about US$30 per hour and waterskiing US$30 per half hour.

Port Antonio

In the extravagantly beautiful tropical setting of this old port, it is easy to believe that if there is an Eden on this earth, you have found it. You will not be the first to have made this discovery, and you will be in very good company. Yet, despite the steady flock of admirers—all eager to help—Port Antonio always seems to be on the verge of a new day that never comes.

Port Antonio is the place where Jamaica's tourism began. In 1871 a Yankee skipper, Lorenzo Dow Baker, sailed out of Port Antonio with a cargo of bananas—introduced by the Spaniards three centuries earlier. When he sold them in Boston, he made such a killing, he returned to Jamaica, bought land, planted bananas, and began shipping the fruit to markets in the United States and Europe. From that enterprise grew the United Fruit Company, whose name was synonymous with bananas—not to mention banana republics—for most of the 20th century. But Baker did not deal in bananas only. The ships that took the bananas north brought tourists south. They stayed at Baker's inn, the Titchfield Hotel, described in an 1898 guidebook as a "novel hotel admirably adapted to a hot climate."

Mitchell's Folly: The next Yank to fall under Port Antonio's spell was quite eccentric. Alfred Mitchell, a wealthy mining engineer, built a sixty-room palace for his child bride, a Tiffany heiress. As the story goes, the palatial mansion was painted white, white flowers filled the gardens, white birds flitted about the grounds, white horses filled the stables, and white monkeys played on an islet at the shore. But his wife refused to live in the fabled retreat, and it became—you guessed it—a white elephant. In building the mansion, salt water had been used to mix the mortar, and as the salt ate away at the stone, the mansion crumbled. It became known as Mitchell's Folly, although Mitchell lived here until he died in 1912. Today, it is a melancholy ruin that looks like the ideal set for a Greek tragedy.

Flynn Estate: Over the years many others who came to Port Antonio were intoxicated by its beauty, but none as much as matinee idol Errol Flynn. Some say Jamaica was his only lasting love affair. Flynn happened onto Port Antonio in the late 1940s while cruising the Caribbean on his yacht, the *Zacca*. A sudden storm forced him to change course and head for the nearest shelter. When he saw the twin-harbored port, he apparently was so taken with it that he bought Navy Island, an islet at the entrance to the harbor; the Titchfield Hotel; and 2,000 acres of a coconut plantation and cattle ranch. He then set out to create his Eden. But the famous actor died before he could realize the dream. His widow, Patrice Wymore, still lives on the estate, which is a working plantation.

Rafting on the Rio Grande (876-993-5778). Errol Flynn left another legacy that will never die.

Rafting on the Rio Grande had been a Port Antonio pastime since 1911, when Simon Grant, a United Fruit Company representative, got the idea after watching bananas being towed by raft downstream to the docks for loading onto ships. But it was Flynn who popularized the pastime by launching the first rafters' race. Today the excursion is one of Port Antonio's leading tourist attractions. The trip starts about 8 miles upstream at Berrydale, where passengers board a 30-foot-long bamboo raft that seats two. With the Blue Mountains towering in the background, a skilled helmsman guides the raft at a leisurely pace for two to three hours down the Rio Grande while you enjoy the river's tropical setting. You can also stop for a swim.

Along the way you see cattle grazing, children playing, mothers laundering, birds darting about, and banana groves and wild orchids growing in profusion. The serenity makes it easy for anyone to fall in love with Jamaica all over again. Cost is US$45 per person for two and a half hours.

Blue Lagoon: Six miles east of Port Antonio is the Blue Lagoon, which many Jamaica devotees call the most beautiful spot in Jamaica. Well, maybe. Local folks claim the Blue Lagoon is bottomless; others say it's been measured to be 185 feet deep. It is fed by freshwater springs, one of which has the power to increase virility, according to local lore. Blue Lagoon has a restaurant and water sports. The small admission charge is deducted from the meal check when you dine at the restaurant. At San San Bay next to Blue Lagoon is Princess Island, a honeymoon gift of Prince Sadruddin Khan to Nina von Thyssen. And down the road another millionaire built Dragon Bay, a resort, now owned by the Sandals group.

The Castle: Perhaps the most curious story of all is about the Castle, situated on a rocky promontory next to the Trident Hotel. In 1979 a German baroness, Elizabeth Siglindy Stephan von Stephanie, began building an enormous structure complete with turrets that might have a duplicate on the Rhine. Then, as abruptly as construction had begun, it stopped, and the baroness vanished. The then-owner of the former Trident Hotel completed the structure as a private mansion for use in conjunction with the hotel. Ah, but the story does not end. In 1988 the baroness returned and built the

Jamaica Palace, a hotel directly across the bay from the Castle. Less imposing, perhaps, but no less grand, the hotel is furnished with antiques, crystal chandeliers, and splendid Oriental carpets. Among its many bizarre features are round beds with navy-blue satin bedspreads and a swimming pool in the shape of Jamaica—with a full view of the Castle.

Touring Port Antonio

Port Facilities: If you arrive in Port Antonio by sea, you will sail into the **Errol Flynn Marina at Port Antonio** (876-715-6044; www.errolflynn marina.com), a mega-yacht facility in the protected West Harbour. The full-service marina, which can take boats up to 350 feet, is an official port of entry with 24-hour customs and immigration services and security. The harbor also has a cruise ship terminal, information center, gift shop, restaurant, bar, swimming pool, and a pretty white-sand beach.

The town of Port Antonio is very small and can be seen in a few minutes' walk, but the most interesting sights are out of town, too far away for walking. The easiest way to see the area is on a tour that begins with a harbor cruise, followed by a ride to Athenry and a grand view of Port Antonio; a stop at San San Beach for a swim; and last, a visit to Somerset Falls. A guided tour can be arranged through **Joanna's Port Antonio Tour** (876-831-8434; www.portantoniotours.netfirms.com) and can include any of the Port Antonio attractions previously described.

Valley Hikes: Eco-adventures around Port Antonio and the Blue Mountains can be arranged in advance of your cruise through **Unique Destinations** (401-647-4730 or 213-431-1571; 876-993-3881) or **Hotel Mocking Bird Hill** in Port Antonio (876-993-7267; www.hotelmockingbirdhill.com). **Valley Hikes** (876-993-3085; valleyhikes@cw jamaica.com) is a cooperative effort of Port Antonio hotels to promote and protect the diverse environment in the Rio Grande Valley, the Blue and John Crow Mountains National Park. The excursions are led by trained guides from the region who know the vegetation and wildlife as well as herbal medicines used here for generations. The hikes trek through lush valley and mountains on maintained trails that parallel rivers and lead to old banana plantations, little-known streams, and hidden waterfalls. They range from easy, light adventures to moderately challenging and strenuous ones. For history buffs there are tours into the Land-of-Look-Behind and Maroon Country, a meeting with the Colonel (chief of the Maroons, descendants of escaped slaves), and tiny mountain villages.

Kingston

Jamaica's capital, a city of more than 800,000 people, is the hemisphere's largest English-speaking city south of Miami. It is the commercial, political, administrative, and cultural center of Jamaica but largely ignored by tourists. The much-maligned capital is neither the dangerous den nor the ugly duckling that publicity has made it. Indeed, the city enjoys a rather spectacular setting by the sea on the world's seventh-largest natural harbor, with the lofty Blue Mountains in the background.

The capital is the headquarters of Jamaica's theater, music, dance, and art, but the opportunity to enjoy the best talent is a matter of timing. The National Pantomime Theatre performs Jan through Mar; the Jamaica Folk Singers, Mar through Apr; the University Dance Society, May; and the National Dance Theatre, July through Aug. Many also have mini sessions during the Christmas and New Year period.

Plays written by Jamaicans are presented year-round at the Ward Theatre, one of the oldest theaters in the Western Hemisphere; at the University of the West Indies' Creative Arts Centre; and at other playhouses in Kingston. The Cultural Training Center near the Pegasus Hotel in New Kingston has a year-round schedule of cultural activities.

National Gallery of Art (12 Ocean Blvd.; 876-922-1561; http://nationalgalleryofjamaica .wordpress.com). The gallery's collection represents Jamaica's most important native artists from the 19th century to the present as well as foreign artists who have worked here. One room is devoted to the works of the late Kapo, Jamaica's leading primitive artist, known particularly for his sculpture. One of the museum's most outstanding collections is of works by Edna Manley, the wife of the first prime minister and the mother of Michael Manley. Her sculpture *Negro Awakened* is considered one of the most significant works in the body of Caribbean art. Small admission fee. Hours: 10 a.m. to 4 p.m. Tues through Sat.

Institute of Jamaica (12–16 East St.; 876-922-0620; www.instituteofjamaica.org.jm). Founded in 1879 and similar in scope to the Smithsonian Institution, the Institute of Jamaica is an umbrella organization with wide-ranging responsibilities for the Jamaica National Trust Commission, which has identified hundreds of old buildings, churches, houses, and other structures for preservation and oversees archaeological excavations. The institute's West Indian Reference Library chronicles Jamaican and Caribbean political, social, and economic developments and maintains the world's largest collection of books, articles, and prints on the West Indies. It also maintains the Natural History Museum, which collects and studies the flora and fauna of Jamaica, including hundreds of species unique to the Caribbean.

Devon House (26 Hope Rd., Kingston 10; 876-929-6602; www.devonhousejamaica.com). The beautifully restored 19th-century mansion of Jamaica's first black millionaire is a museum and a showplace for Jamaican crafts. Admission: adult US$5, child $3. The coach house of the Devon estate was converted into an attractive restaurant, the **Grog Shoppe** (876-960-9730), serving light lunches and Jamaican dishes; other buildings house shops for Jamaican products, a bakery, a smoke shop, an ice-cream parlor, and displays of musical instruments. Devon House's restaurant, **Norma's on the Terrace** (26 Hope Rd.; 876-929-6602), is managed by Norma Shirley, Jamaica's best-known restaurateur. Moderately expensive.

Bob Marley Museum (56 Hope Rd.; 876-927-9152; www.bobmarley-foundation.com), the former home of the famous reggae superstar, houses a collection of Marley memorabilia, photos, and news clips reflecting his life and career, including the studio where he recorded many of his hits. A twenty-minute video of his best-known concerts is shown. Admission: US$20 adults, $10 child. Hours: 9:30 a.m. to 5 p.m. Mon through Sat.

Port Royal: Jamaica's past is as well represented as its creative present at two important sites within easy reach of the capital. Port Royal, on a spit of land west of Kingston airport, was Jamaica's infamous pirates' port in the 17th century. It was destroyed in 1692 when an earthquake caused 90 percent of the town and its legendary treasures to sink into the sea. The first organized excavations were conducted by the National Geographic Society, the Smithsonian, and the Institute of Jamaica in 1959 and again in 1968 by the National Trust. After several years' restoration work, Port Royal has been made into a park and museum.

Spanish Town: 12 miles west of Kingston. Founded in 1523 by Diego Columbus as Villa de la Vega and renamed St. Jago de la Vega when it became the capital in 1534, the town was destroyed by the English after they seized Jamaica in 1655. They built their own town on the same site but continued to call it Spanish Town. Today the cathedral on the site of the previous Spanish one is the oldest Anglican church in the New World. Tombstones on the church floor date from the 17th century. The Spanish Town Historic Foundation has undertaken an effort to entice private individuals and investors to restore historic homes and buildings to preserve the town's historic character and make it a "living" museum.

Blue Mountain National Park: The main highway between Ocho Rios and Kingston is a scenic drive of 54 miles over the mountains. A narrow, winding, and even more scenic road passes through the heart of the Blue Mountains to Newcastle. The 193,000-acre Blue Mountains and John Crow Mountains National Park protect these rugged mountains that contain some of the most diverse tropical rain forests in the world. Its peaks and valleys are home to seven distinct forest communities and to the endemic swallowtail butterfly, the world's second largest butterfly. Old logging roads and trails provide nature lovers with some of the most beautiful and interesting hiking in the Caribbean. A night hike during full moon to Blue Mountain Peak, arriving at over 7,500 feet in time for the sunrise, is one of the great outdoor experiences of all times.

The Cayman Islands

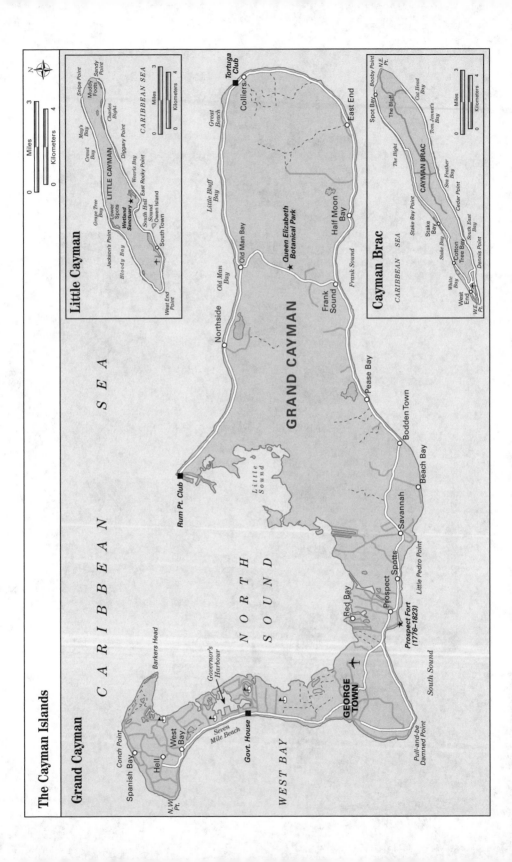

The Cayman Islands

Grand Cayman

Little Cayman

Cayman Brac

The Diver's Mount Everest

The history of the British Crown Colony of the Cayman Islands might be called the tale of the turtles and the pirates. The Cayman Islands were discovered by Columbus in 1503 on his fourth voyage when a chance wind blew the great explorer's ship off course and thrust it onto "two very small islands full of tortoises," which led Columbus to dub them Las Tortugas. On later maps the islands were shown as Caimanas, a Carib Indian name for the marine crocodile. Sir Francis Drake also called them Caymanas when he arrived to claim them for Britain in 1586. That's when the pirates came, too.

At the close of the 16th century and for the next hundred years, the Cayman Islands became a favorite hiding place for Blackbeard, Henry Morgan, Neal Walker, and other pirates (including the infamous women Anne Bonny and Mary Read), buccaneers, privateers, and the whole corps of sea captains and adventurers who preyed on Spanish galleons laden with treasures from Mexico and the Spanish Main. (When one of these entrepreneurs was a dashing corsair like Drake and had the blessing of the Crown, he went down in history as a swashbuckler or privateer, but if he had a reputation like Edward Teach, better known as Blackbeard, history more accurately called him a pirate—the most notorious scoundrel of his day.)

Whether because of the pirates or the turtles, little effort was made to colonize the islands, and as late as the early 19th century fewer than 1,500 people lived here. In 1863, as part of the territory under the British governor of Jamaica, the Cayman Islands became a Crown Colony. But it did not become a separate entity until a century later, when Jamaica got its independence in 1962.

Situated 480 miles south of Miami and about 200 miles from Cuba and Jamaica, the Caymans are made up of three islands: the 22-mile Grand Cayman, with the capital and major port of call, George Town; Cayman Brac, 12 square miles of untamed tropics 86 miles to the northeast of the capital; and Little Cayman, the smallest of the trio, 5 miles from the western end of Cayman Brac.

Today's residents have taken both the turtles and the pirates to heart. A turtle dressed as a pirate has become the emblem of the islands' airline, Cayman Airways. Sea turtles, which are on the endangered species list, are bred at the world's first sea turtle farm at the rate of 20,000 a year. Local menus feature turtle steak and turtle soup. The pirates turn up once a year to reclaim their lair during Pirates Week, the Caymans' Carnival, usually held in late Oct or Nov.

Cynics might also note that the turtle-paced islands are still an ideal place to stash away a treasure or two. As a tax-free haven and offshore banking center, they are favored especially by the fast-track world of international finance. Thanks to their commerce, the Cayman Islands have the best communications, the lowest unemployment, and one of the highest standards of living in the Caribbean.

Yet of all the Caymans' assets, the most appealing and enduring is the gift of nature—magnificent beaches and spectacular coral gardens and marine life, often less than 100 yards from shore and in water so clear that visibility of 200 feet is not unusual. As a further incentive to divers, there are 350 shipwrecks recorded in these waters—apparently, not all of the pirates made it in and out

At a Glance

Antiquities	★
Art and Artists	★★
Beaches	★★★★★
Colonial Buildings	★★
Cuisine	★
Dining/Restaurants	★★
Entertainment	★
History/Culture	★
Museums	★
Nature	★★★★★
Scenery	★★
Shopping	★
Sightseeing	★★
Sports	★★★★★
Transportation	★★

Fast Facts

Population: The Cayman Islands were settled by deserters from Oliver Cromwell's army, shipwrecked sailors, pirates, and freed slaves. To this day the racial and ethnic mix of the original settlers is reflected in the 50,000 people who inhabit the three islands, 90 percent of whom live on Grand Cayman. Intermarriage has made the Cayman Islands one of the best well-integrated societies in the Western Hemisphere.

Main Town: George Town

Government: The Cayman Islands were a dependency of Jamaica until 1961. The following year, Jamaica became independent, but the Caymans chose to remain a British Overseas Territory, self-governing in all internal affairs but administered by a governor appointed by Great Britain.

Climate: Temperatures average 75°F in Jan and 86°F in summer, and more sunny days than elsewhere in the area. Short tropical rains often come by surprise, particularly in the fall and spring, but they rarely last more than a few minutes.

Clothing: Tropic-casual is right here. Lightweight suits are appropriate for those transacting business. A sweater may be needed on cloudy days in the winter.

Currency: The Cayman Island dollar, called the "CI" locally, is tied to the U.S. dollar at a set rate of CI$1.25 to US$1. One hundred U.S. dollars equals 80 CI dollars. Visitor do not need to exchange dollars:

U.S. currency, travelers checks, and credit cards are widely accepted.

Customs Regulations: Since Jan 2009, U.S. government regulations require all U.S. citizens to have a passport to leave and to enter the United States by air or sea.

Departure Tax: US$25 which is normally included in your air ticket.

Electricity: 110 volts, 60 cycles, as in the United States

Language: English, but with a lilt all its own, a delightful mixture of West Indian and Scottish brogue.

Postal Service: In George Town, post offices are located on Cardinal Avenue 2 blocks from the pier and West Shore Plaza on West Bay Road (Seven Mile Beach). Hours: 8:30 a.m. to 5 p.m. Mon through Fri; Sat to 12:30 p.m.

Public Holidays: Jan 1, New Year's Day; annual Agricultural Fair; Ash Wed; Good Friday; Easter Monday; May, Discovery Day; mid-June, Queen's Birthday; July, Constitution Day; Nov, Remembrance Day; Dec 25, Christmas Day; Dec 26, Boxing Day.

Telephone Area Code: 345. When calling from the United States, add "94" in front of the five-digit local number: 1-345-94 + local number. Special direct phones to call the United States are available at the dock and other selected locations where cruise passengers disembark.

Vaccination Requirement: None.

Airlines: Cayman Airways (800-4-CAYMAN, www.caymanairways.com), daily from Miami, and others from Chicago O'Hare, Washington Dulles, Tampa, and New York JFK. Others are Air Canada, American Airlines, Continental, Delta, and US Airways. Island Air provides service from Grand Cayman to Little Cayman and Cayman Brac.

Information: www.caymanislands.ky; www.divecayman.ky

In the United States:

(877) 4-CAYMAN

Cayman Island Tourist Offices:

Chicago: 30 North La Salle St., Suite 1650, Chicago, IL 60602; (312) 263-1750; fax: (312) 263-1753

Houston: 2 Memorial City Plaza, 820 Gessner, Suite 1335, TX 77024; (713) 461-1317; fax: (713) 461-7409

Miami: Trenton Building, 8300 Northwest Fifty-third St., Suite 103, FL 33166; (305) 599-9033; fax: (305) 599-3766

New York: Empire State Building, 350 Fifth Ave., Suite 1801, New York, NY 10118; (212) 889-9009

In Canada:

1200 Bay St., Suite 1101, Toronto, ON M5R 2A5; (416) 485-1550; (800) 263-5805; fax: (416) 485-0835

In Grand Cayman:

Regatta Business Park, Leeward Two, West Bay Road, P.O. Box 67, George Town, Cayman Islands, KY1-1102, British West Indies; (345) 949-0623; fax: (345) 949-4053

Cayman Islands National Trust, Family Park, 558 South Church St., Grand Cayman; (345) 749-1121; fax: (345) 749-1135; www.nationaltrust.org.ky

of the tricky waters of their hideaway. Then, too, not all the wrecks were accidents. Some ships, it is said, were lured onto the reefs by islanders who plundered the wrecks as a means of livelihood.

In addition to their banks and beaches, the Cayman Islands offer many other attractions, including three golf courses, one of which features the "short" ball developed by golfing great Jack Nicklaus.

Budget Planning

The lack of taxes in the Cayman Islands would, at first, seem to be a blessing. As we all know, however, there is no free lunch, either, and the government supports itself with a steep customs duty on everything brought into the islands that run from 15 to 27 percent, including on shipping charges. These prices are passed on to the consumer, making just about everything you buy expensive, with the exception of a limited number of local products and duty-free items. You should always review the prices of anything you buy to avoid unwelcome surprises.

Fortunately, your feet can get you around George Town easily enough. If you are taking a taxi any distance, consider sharing with some fellow passengers. If you are watching your budget, mini buses operate frequently along West Bay Road to all the beaches and can be picked up at bus stop signs en route. The fare is CI$1.50 to CI$2 each way, depending on destination, and can be paid in US currency.

Port Profile: Grand Cayman

Location/Embarkation: George Town, the Caymans' capital and port of call, is located on the west side of Grand Cayman. It is perhaps not what you would expect of a Caribbean port. Downtown George Town, which stretches east directly behind the harbor, looks more like a metropolitan banking and financial center than the capital of a Caribbean island. That's not surprising when you learn that more than 500 banks from more than sixty countries, over 9,000 entities registered or licensed as mutual funds, and approximately 40,000 other companies are doing business here. The Cayman

Islands is now the fifth largest financial center in the world. Little wonder it is called the Switzerland of the Caribbean.

Cruise ships cannot dock in George Town; rather they anchor just outside the harbor and tender passengers to a dock at the center of town. The Port Authority is exploring building the first-ever cruise berthing facilities, two piers to berth four ships, with construction anticipated to begin in 2011. You can hardly get lost as the center of town is only 3 blocks wide and 3 blocks deep, clean and neat, filled primarily with shoppers and businesspeople.

Occasionally when the sea is rough, cruise ships anchor on the south end of the island at Spotts Landing, about 6 miles from George Town. There is a welcome/information center here, and taxis are on hand to take passengers to the town center or on tour.

Facilities: While George Town may not have the "feel" of a typical tropical port, this center of international finance demands and gets about the most efficient transportation, communications, and technical facilities available in the Caribbean. As soon as you get off your tender, there is a special phone available for making calls to the United States, and you can charge the call to a credit card number. Public phones, which almost always work in George Town for local calls, are available, but you will need Caymanian coins or local phone cards to use them. Tourist information booths are located at cruise ship terminals.

Walk straight ahead across North Church Street down Cardinal Avenue and you will find most of the shopping. (U.S. dollars are acceptable everywhere.) If you don't plan to leave George Town by taxi or tour, everything you need in port is within a few hundred yards of the town dock. Your ability to come and go between ship and shore is restricted only by the tender schedule.

Internet Access: As with most Caribbean ports, Internet access facilities have mushroomed. Ask at the tourist information booths at the cruise terminal for facilities nearest the port. Three blocks up on Shedden Road (directly in front of the cruise ship docks) is the **Coffee & Bites Internet Cafe** (Bodmer Building; 345-945-4892). On Seven Mile

Beach **Cafe del Sol** (Marquee Cinema Shopping Centre, 2 miles north of George Town; 345-946-2233); and **PD's Pub** (Galleria Plaza, West Bay Road, 3 miles north of George Town; 345-949-7144) have Internet facilities.

Local Transportation: Taxis are available at the dock whenever there is a ship in port. There are taxi stands in town and near the public beach at Seven Mile Beach on West Bay Road. The drivers speak English, although their lilting accent and their tendency to speak softly take some getting used to. There are no meters, and the rates tend to be high by U.S. standards. Be sure to confirm the rate before you get in the taxi, and be sure, also, that you and your driver understand whether the amount is Cayman Islands dollars or U.S. dollars. As a sample, the fare from the dock to a hotel on Seven Mile Beach costs between US$15 to $18 for one to three people and $5 for each additional passenger, or US$2 to $4 for a seat in a taxi van.

A word of caution: Traffic congestion on Grand Cayman can be terrible, especially along West Bay Road and in town on busy cruise ship days, when it moves at a turtle's pace during the lunch hour (noon to 1:30 p.m.) and around 3 p.m. when passengers are heading back to their ships. Be sure to allow yourself at least double the normal driving time during these peak hours. Also, a mandatory seat belt law requires both drivers and passengers in all vehicles to wear seat belts. Driving is on the LEFT.

Buses: Grand Cayman has an official public transportation system of small buses (sixteen-passenger is average), which run every half hour or hour (depending on the route) Sun through Thurs from 6 a.m. until 11 p.m., Fri and Sat until midnight from downtown George Town to outer districts. The buses are privately owned but government-licensed and operate on routes with fixed fares ranging from CI$1.50 to $2 one way along main routes. All licensed buses have blue-and-white license plates and color-coded stickers that identify the route they follow. The central depot is behind the public library on Edward Street, about 2 blocks from the cruise ship piers. Even so, when your time is limited to tour the island it's better to hire a taxi or rent a car.

Car Rental and Mopeds: Driving is on the LEFT. Several car rental companies on Grand Cayman offer excellent service. For a car, expect to pay about CI$49 a day and up, with unlimited mileage (without insurance); for gas, about CI$4.30 per imperial gallon. You will also need a valid driver's license from home and a visitor's driving permit, which costs US$7.80 and is obtained at the time you sign out the car. You would be wise to make reservations from home before departing on your cruise. Most car rental companies have toll-free 800 numbers. **Andy's Rent a Car** (Seven Mile Beach; 345-949-8111; www.andys.ky), **Avis Cico** (near airport; 345-949-2468; 800-331-1084; www.aviscayman.com), **Budget** (345-949-5605; 800-527-0700; www.budgetcayman.com), **Coconut Car Rentals** (Shedden Road; 345-949-7703; 800-941-4562; www.coconutcarrentals.com), and **Hertz** (Industrial Park; 345-949-2280; 800-654-3131; www.hertzcaribbean.com). Car rental companies will deliver cars anywhere on the island, including the town dock. A moped costs about US$37 a day including helmet and permit, with an additional charge of $5 for insurance and driver's permit,

Ferries: Regular ferry service to Rum Point was suspended after Hurricane Ivan in 2005; rather, you will need to go by car or the shuttle-van service for US$25 per person round trip.

Shore Excursions

If you prefer an easy walk with a little shopping, you can stroll about the center of George Town in only a few blocks. The national museum's gift shop, only a few feet from the dock, has an excellent brochure for a self-guided walk of historic George Town. On the other hand, to see Grand Cayman and get the feel of the Caymans, you will need to get out of town to see the island and its fabulous beaches, get out on the sea to enjoy its lovely waters, or get under the sea to enjoy nature's spectacular show. Whichever you choose, you will need transportation. You can easily negotiate with a taxi driver for a tour of Grand Cayman along West Bay Road to the Turtle Farm or a spin around the island to East End. However, unless you are sharing the cost with friends, that could be expensive. Expect to pay US$75 or more for a half-day excursion.

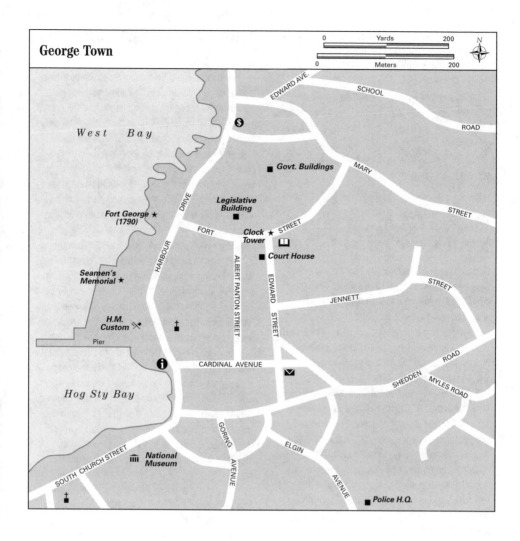

George Town

West Bay

Fort George ★
(1790)

Seamen's
Memorial ★

H.M.
Custom

Pier

Hog Sty Bay

EDWARD AVE.

SCHOOL

ROAD

■ Govt. Buildings

MARY

DRIVE

*Legislative
Building* ■

FORT

Clock ★
Tower

STREET

STREET

■ Court House

HARBOUR

ALBERT PANTON STREET

EDWARD STREET

JENNETT

STREET

†

CARDINAL AVENUE

✉

SHEDDEN

ROAD

MYLES ROAD

ⓘ

GORING AVENUE

ELGIN

AVENUE

🏛 *National
Museum*

SOUTH CHURCH STREET

†

■ Police H.Q.

There are several tours available that will give you a good look at Grand Cayman's shoreside attractions. Among the agencies providing sightseeing are **Reality Tours** (345-947-7200), **Majestic Tours** (345-949-7773; www.majestic-tours.com), and **Tropicana Tours** (345-949-0944; www.tropicana-tours.com).

Often there's a great discrepancy between prices available from local tour companies and sports operators and those being offered by some cruise ships. Prices are U.S. dollars unless specified otherwise.

George Town/West Bay: 3 hours; $45. The tour briefly visits downtown George Town and continues along Seven Mile Beach to West Bay, with stops at Turtle Farm, Tortuga Rum Cake Factory, and Hell to send postcards. You can be dropped off at the beach or returned to town for shopping. A longer version adds lunch at the beach and time for a swim.

Atlantis **Submarine:** (See Unusual Dive Opportunities for Non-divers later in this chapter.)

Stingray City: 3 hours; $40 ($65 adult as a cruise ship shore excursion). For the thrill of a lifetime, you can swim and snorkel with a dozen or so stingrays. (See Scuba Diving/Snorkeling later in this chapter.) There are also glass-bottomed boat trips for $35 and one-tank dives for certified divers at $70. **Stingray City Charters** (345-949-9200) or **Bayside Watersports** (345-949-3200; fax: 345-949-3700) welcome advance reservations from cruise passengers.

Seaworld Explorer Semi Submersible: 1 hour; $34 adult; $19 ages twelve and thirteen. (See Unusual Dive Opportunities for Non-divers later in this chapter.)

Golf, Scuba Diving, Snorkeling: (See Sports section for information.)

Grand Cayman on Your Own

George Town's nickname, the Switzerland of the Caribbean, refers not only to its major position as a financial center for offshore banking and insurance, but also to a certain Swiss-like efficiency, cleanliness, and businesslike attitude. Although the best of Grand Cayman is out of town, a walk in the immediate area of the dock is very worthwhile.

Cayman Islands National Museum (345-949-8368; www.museum.ky). This museum is situated in the Old Courts Building, which dates from the 1830s. The courthouse/jail has served as a public library, bank, church, and local social center. A good example of Cayman-type architecture, the building won an American Express Preservation Award. Although it is an important tourist attraction, the air-conditioned museum was created mainly to give the local population a place to preserve its natural and cultural history.

Exhibits, some with dioramas, highlight the islands' important events. The ground floor is devoted to exhibits on the Caymans' natural history and marine life; the second floor has historical and cultural displays. Admission: CI$5 adult; $3 child. Hours: 9 a.m. to 5 p.m. Mon through Fri; 9 a.m. to 1 p.m. Sat. The section holding the gift shop was once a post office. There is a snack bar with local food.

The Butterfly Farm (345-946-3411; www.the butterflyfarm.com). Located on Lawrence Avenue, east of West Bay Road, the attraction offers guided tours of its tropical garden, resplendent with butterflies from around the world. Admission: US$12 adult; $7 child twelve and under. Hours: 8:30 a.m. to 4 p.m. daily.

Driving Tour of Grand Cayman

Driving is on the LEFT.

Although Grand Cayman is only 22 miles long and about 8 miles wide, you will need to leave yourself plenty of time if you plan to tour the entire island. Unlike many Caribbean ports of call where a road goes around the island, Grand Cayman does not have a loop road encircling it. Rather, the island is shaped something like a boomerang; roads go either to the west side or the east side of the island. You will need to backtrack from any extended drive in either direction to return to town and your ship.

From your starting point at George Town, with a good map in hand (available at the Tourist Office and in bookstores), you have two choices. First, you can follow North Church Street to West Bay Road, the island's main north–south artery along Seven Mile Beach. This plan takes you into the West Bay section, a peninsula that borders the North Sound and contains the vast majority of the island's hotels and condo developments, the Turtle Farm, most restaurants, the island's best beaches, water sports and fishing centers, tennis courts, and golf courses. All the roads in West Bay feed back to West Bay Road, which leads directly into George Town and the harbor. Permitting a reasonable amount of sightseeing time, you can tour West Bay in two hours.

As a second option, you can head south on South Church Street, which leads out of town into rural Grand Cayman to Bodden Town and East End. Eventually, the drive will take you to Rum Point, on the northwestern tip. This tour requires three to four hours or longer if you stop along the way to enjoy the sights, picnic, and swim.

To take in both the west-side and east-side drives, you need a minimum of six hours going at a fast clip. Remember, with each tour you will have to double back to George Town, so plan to turn back when you have used up half of your allotted time.

Also, stick to the main coast road. It adds a few more miles to your trip, but the route is far more scenic, easier to follow, and will bring you directly back to the harbor without any turnoffs. There are shortcuts through the middle of town to or from the harbor, but do not use them if you are unfamiliar with George Town. Traffic is heavy, and you could get lost quickly on the twisting roads, particularly when you are concentrating on staying left while at the same time trying to follow a map. Finally, be aware of roundabouts on many main roads; they can be confusing. You must yield to traffic entering from the right. Familiarize yourself with the traffic flow and proceed carefully.

To the West End

For the western drive, head north from the harbor toward West Bay and along the famed Seven Mile Beach. For the next few miles, you will be traveling straight north with the beach on the left (west), past the hotels and luxury condominiums that line both sides of the road.

Golf Club and Government House: Some points of interest to note are the Britannia Golf Club (which features the Jack Nicklaus short-ball course and lies across the road from the former Hyatt Hotel); the public beach; and Government House, the residence of the governor, also near the public beach. The Links at Safe Haven, an 18-hole championship, par-72 golf course, is located farther north. Farther along at West Bay, a newly developed residential and commercial development area, **Camana Bay,** (www.camanabay.com) has restaurants, shops, cinema, a six-screen cinema, apartments, town houses, a town center for pedestrians only, and water sports. Its latest attraction is an Observation Tower, open to the public free of charge, offers 360-degree views across Seven Mile Beach, George Town and the marine parks of the North Sound. Events held here vary from outdoor concerts to farmers' markets.

Boatswain's Beach/Turtle Farm: After several miles you will come to a fork in the road; the road on the left takes you directly to the **Boatswain's Beach/Turtle Farm** (825 Northwest Point Rd.; 345-949-3894; www.boatswainsbeach.ky). Here at the world's first sea turtle farm, which is also a research station, you will be able to observe turtles in their breeding ponds at various stages of development; you can even pick up one from the water for a photograph. Some grow as long as 4 feet and weigh up to 600 pounds. The farm breeds turtles—at the rate of about 20,000 per year—to

help restock the waters of countries around the world as well as for commercial purposes.

In 2006 the Turtle Farm underwent a major $45 million expansion and was re-located directly across the road from its former location in the new 23 acre marine theme park called Boatwain's Beach. The park has a large saltwater lagoon where visitors can swim with marine life; a predator reef; a turtle hatchery, a nature trail; a free-flight Caribbean Bird Aviary; a Caymanian Heritage Street with artisans and craftspeople; a restaurant serving contemporary Caymanian cuisine; and state-of-the-art research and educational facilities focusing on the conservation of sea turtles. Cost: Wet package (includes all features), $45 adult; $25 ages two through twelve; dry package, $30 adult; $20 child.

We must warn you that tortoiseshell and other turtle products are not allowed into the United States, because these animals are still on the endangered species list.

Hell: You can take a detour to Hell (345-949-6999; www.tab.ky). By following the right fork, the road will take you away from the tourist areas and into the residential sections of West Bay. Follow the signs to Hell, which was given its name because of the area's dramatic and ominous coral and limestone formations known as ironshore, a dominant feature of part of the Cayman shore. In 1986 Hell got a face-lift that added a boardwalk with better access for viewing the rocks, as well as crafts shops, plants, and a new post office. HELL postmarks on your postcards—and, of course, HELL T-shirts—are the main industries here.

North Sound/Stingray City: Across the mouth of North Sound is a barrier reef, and just inside is one of the Caribbean's most unusual sites, dubbed Stingray City. In only 4 to 15 feet of water, divers and snorkelers can touch, feed, and photograph a dozen or more friendly southern Atlantic stingrays. These creatures look prehistoric and frightening, but they are actually very gentle, with skin as soft as velvet.

To the East End

For the second option to the south and eastern parts of the island, South Church Street will take you along the manicured residential areas of the South Sound, around the town, and along South Sound Road, which borders the sea on one side and edges mangroves and ponds on the other—all popular locations for bird-watching. The Caymans, because of their location on the migratory routes of North, Central, and South America, are visited by a large number of bird species in fall and spring. There are, in addition, endemic species. The road turns inland for a short distance before reaching the village of Savannah.

Pedro St. James Historic Site (345-947-3329; www.pedrostjames.ky). In 1991 the Cayman Islands government bought the historic Pedro Castle to restore as a national landmark and develop as a tourist attraction under the supervision of the National Historic Sites Committee. After seven years and $7.5 million, the task was completed.

Built in 1780 by William Eden as a private residence called St. James, the ruins were the oldest standing structure in the Cayman Islands and were constructed from coral rocks common in that area. Here on Dec 5, 1831, the country's first elected legislature was established.

Along with its historical significance, the 7.65-acre site has one of the most scenic and tranquil locations on Grand Cayman's rugged south coast. It lies on Pedro Bluff, a limestone ridge that rises 20 feet from the sea and supports a variety of native flowering plants and shrubs, including the silver thatch palm, a plant that has had an important role in the islands' crafts and heritage. Comprehensive research on the site's history, restoration of the structure, and landscaping were part of the committee's work that went into making the site a national park.

The complex includes a three-story house in 19th-century style and other buildings and a $1.5 million visitor center with a multimedia theater featuring a twenty-four-minute video on Pedro St. James and Cayman history. Other facilities include a resource center, gift shop, wedding gazebo, and cafe.

The Pedro St. James Great House, designated as the Cayman Islands' first national historic landmark, is a historically accurate restoration with every detail reflecting authentic building techniques of early-19th-century Caribbean great houses—from rough-hewn timber beams and wooden pegs to a gabled framework. Other period features include mahogany floors and staircases, wide-beam wooden ceilings, stone walls, outside wooden louvered shutters, and mahogany doors.

The first floor houses the jail, storerooms, kitchen, and pantry. The second level is a dining room, courtroom, and veranda, and the upper level is the living quarters. Furnishings combine original antiques and reproductions. A bake oven and outdoor kitchen are re-creations of the original estate.

An early-20th-century Cayman-style cottage and a traditional hundred-year-old Cayman wattle-and-daub home were added to enhance the site's educational value.

Pedro St. James, with its lovely seaside setting, is a popular venue for weddings and social events. The grounds have been landscaped as a tropical park with native trees and plants, as well as traditional gardens representative of a small early-19th-century West Indian plantation. Interpretative displays and signs allow self-guided tours; guides also are available. Admission: US$10 adult; free for ages twelve and younger. Hours: 9 a.m. to 5 p.m. daily; presentations are on the hour, the first at 10 a.m., the last at 4 p.m.

Bodden Town: After Savannah the main road turns back out again to the small village of Bodden Town, once the capital of Grand Cayman. Here you will get a glimpse of a different Caymanian lifestyle—one that depends on the sea and land for survival. There are caves here that legend says were once pirate hideouts.

After another 6 miles, you will see the **Lighthouse Restaurant** (www.lighthouse.ky) on the right. Use this as a checkpoint to find Frank Sound Road just beyond to the left. If your time is limited, you can use this cross-island highway to drive from the south coast to the north side of the island and trim about an hour off your trip. The cross-island highway passes the entrance to the botanic park.

Queen Elizabeth II Botanic Park (345-947-9462; www.botanic-park.ky). Since 1991 the Cayman Islands National Trust has been developing this nature park to preserve the islands' natural environment and wildlife, provide a place for local people to enjoy their natural heritage, and create an attraction for ecotourists. The park, situated on a 60-acre tract of woodland, was donated to the government by a private owner. As much as 80 percent of the parkland is being preserved as native woodlands with signposted walkways and interpretive displays; a nature walk borders the heart of the area. The park was officially opened in 1993 by Queen Elizabeth II, for whom it is named.

Some areas have been developed as display gardens to showcase vegetation native to the Cayman Islands. An estimated 40 percent of the plants endemic to the Caymans are found in this area, and more species of native flora are being added. The largest garden and main tourist attraction is the Heritage Garden, a historically oriented display of the plants raised by the local population over the years and their uses.

The area is a habitat for the Caymans' two subspecies of Cuban parrots and Grand Cayman's endemic blue iguana, an endangered species estimated to number fewer than fifty in the wild. The park has a captive breeding program for the iguana. There is a wedding gazebo set in pretty landscaped gardens—popular with islanders and visitors alike—a visitor center, and gift shop. Admission: US$10 adult; free for ages twelve and younger.

Mastic Trail: A 200-year-old pedestrian path that once linked the north and south coasts of Grand Cayman is now a hiking trail that links Caymanians with their past and introduces visitors to the island's rich natural history. The 2-mile trail, developed by the **Cayman Islands National Trust** (www.nationaltrust.org.ky), passes through primary dry evergreen forest, now rare throughout the Caribbean, and is amazing for its variety. You can have something of a look at the land as it might have been when Columbus first came upon the Cayman Islands. Named for the massive mastic tree, the trail passes karst pinnacles, mangrove swamps, and ancient woodlands and has a variety of birds. The original path was cut into the woodlands in the north by settlers in search of timber to build ships and export hardwoods such as mahogany and West Indian cedar. About the same time, farmers on the south coast cut a path north, clearing land to grow fruit trees and graze cattle. This part of the trail runs past mango and tamarind trees, as well as through buttonwood swamps. It also includes a short, old causeway across a mangrove swamp,

which demonstrates the great effort required by the settlers to harvest the timber.

By reservations only, the National Trust offers guided nature walks of three hours in small groups (maximum 10) with a trained guide who meets you at the northern trailhead, normally starting at 8:30 a.m. on Wed. Soft drinks and transport back to the southern trailhead at the end of the walk are provided. Price: US$30 per person. Since cruise ships usually do not arrive in time for the scheduled departure, you will need to arrange in advance for your round-trip transportation and rendezvous with the guide. Phone (345) 949-1121 Mon through Fri between 10 a.m. and 3 p.m. The Mastic Trail walk is not suitable for children ages six and younger, the elderly, or persons with physical handicaps or conditions that might require emergency medical assistance.

East End: If you continue straight ahead along the coast instead of turning onto Frank Sound Road, you will soon come to East End, which is the name for both the area and one of the most historically authentic Caymanian villages, where you can have a look at Grand Cayman's past. The shipwreck lying at the fringe of the reef is the remains of the *Ridgefield*, a U.S. cargo vessel that went aground in 1961 during the Bay of Pigs operation—a reminder that the Caymans are located only 200 miles south of Cuba.

As you round the eastern end of the island, you pass Morritt's Tortuga Club and the Reef Resort, two sprawling time-share hotels. They are just beyond where the road bends west onto the Queen's Highway. Several rare species of bird are found only here.

Old Man Bay: Continuing west along Queen's Highway about 5 miles, you will come to Old Man Bay and the northern terminus of Frank Sound Road, the north–south artery connecting the shores of the eastern peninsula. Your fastest way back to George Town, if you are short on time, is to turn left (south) and go back to South Sound Road, which will take you into George Town.

Rum Point: If you continue straight ahead to Rum Point, overlooking North Sound, you come to one of the island's nicest stretches of sand, second only to Seven Mile Beach; in winter it's the site of the island's most spectacular sunsets. Stingray City is just off the coast, although you can't get there from here. At Rum Point there is a snack bar with tree-shaded picnic tables where lunch is served. **Red Sail Sports,** the water sports operator, has a complete facility on the beach and is open daily. To return to George Town from here, you must retrace your route to Frank Sound Road and turn right (south). At South Sound Road, turn right (west) again. Along the way you will come to two forks in the road en route to town. If you hug the coast, always taking the left road at these forks, you will minimize the risk of getting lost on your way back into town.

Shopping

Grand Cayman is not known as a major shopping island. Heavy import duties make most items rather expensive, but duty-free shopping on a limited number of items, such as liquor, jewelry, and luxury products, offers good buys. Cayman Sea Salt is a popular gift. The quality of native art and handicrafts is good, but the supply is limited. The prosperity of the Caymans is reflected in a general appetite for imported high-tech consumer goods. Not surprisingly, Caymanian youth gravitate toward high-paying, skilled jobs and unfortunately show little interest in learning the traditional crafts and artistic skills of the islands. The best of Cayman's artisans are not being replaced, and native art and handicrafts have suffered as a result.

A word of caution: Those highly polished turtle shells and other turtle products for sale in Grand Cayman cannot be imported into the United States. Such products, even when produced on a commercial farm, are prohibited because the sea turtle is on the endangered species list. U.S. Customs will confiscate these items upon your return, and you may be subject to a fine.

Antiques: Artifacts (Harbour Drive; 345-949-2442; www.artifacts.com.ky) has prints, maps, coins, silver, and other interesting pieces mainly from England. The most popular antiques are authentic gold and silver coins set into jewelry by local artisans.

Art and Artists: Several shops, all within walking distance of the harbor in George Town,

are worth visiting. **Pure Art Gallery** (South Church Street; 345-949-9133; www.pureart.ky) is an art lover's dream. If you had to select only one place on the island to shop, this would be the best choice. Even if you do not plan to buy, you will enjoy a visit to see the array. The gallery is set in a charming old Cayman cottage where every nook and cranny is filled with art and usual crafts, herbs, and spices. Most of the items are locally made or come from other Caribbean islands, and all reflect high quality and creativity. Look for the popular birdhouses by Charlie Ebanks.

Kennedy Fine Art Gallery (West Shore Center, 508 West Bay Rd.; 345-949-8077; kgallery@ candw.ky) stocks local and foreign artists who spend time in the Caymans.

Heritage Craft Ltd. (corner of Harbour Drive and Goring Avenue; 345-945-6041). Traditional Caymanian baskets and other woven items are a particularly good buy. Made from thatched palm fibers of a strong species that grows in the Caymans, these baskets are tough and durable. **Cayman Islands National Gallery** (Harbour Place, South Church Street, 345-945-8111; www.nationalgallery.org.ky) is a small gallery focused on contemporary local and international art and has changing exhibits.

Island Glassblowing (189 North Church St.; 345-946-1483; www.islandglassblowing.com). At Cayman's only glassblowing studio, you can watch daily demonstrations while experienced glassblowers shape, blow, and form pieces from hot molten glass. Stingrays, turtles, dolphins, fish, plates, vases, and bowls are some of the items available. **The Craft Market** (waterfront corner of South Church Street and Boilers Road), a short walk from the cruise ship dock in George Town. Vendors in an outdoor plaza offer locally made items of leather, thatch, wood, and shell, as well as Cayman Sea Salt and samples of traditional Caymanian food. **Cayman Sea Salt** (345-943-7258; www.cayman seasalt.com) can also be found at island gift and grocery stores.

China/Crystal: Fine duty-free shops are within an easy walk of the harbor. English crystal and china are specialties. The prices are good, and the selection is wide. **Kirk Freeport Center** (Albert Panton Street, Bayshore Mall; 345-949-7477; www .kirkfreeport.net) and **Waterford/Wedgwood**

Gallery (Cardinal Avenue; 345-949-7477) have the best selections. **Duty Free Stores** (at the harborside Anchorage Center) have excellent selections of perfumes and designer items such as watches.

Clothing: Generally most clothing items are imported from the United States, and the selection is limited. Resortwear is plentiful—but at resort prices. One of the most attractive shops is **Shellections** (Waterfront Centre, Church Street; 345-945-1023), which is a vision in pastels and flowers with hand-painted resortwear for the whole family. There are dresses, summer garden-party hats, painted shirts and dresses, jewelry, and jewelry boxes. Along Edward Street, **Tropical L'Attitude** (Butterfield Place, Edward Street; 345-945-1233; fax: 345-945-1237) and **Aqua World Duty-Free Mall** (Merrendale Drive; 345-946-9219) have batik and colorful island fashions. Tropical L'Attitude is one of the twenty-two shops filling the four-story shopping mall on the harborfront next to the Hard Rock Cafe. It's painted yellow, blue, and red—you can't miss it.

Jewelry: You will see black coral jewelry advertised, but the Cayman Islands prohibited its harvest in 1986, when they passed marine conservation laws. The coral you see is mostly from Asia. Those who care about the environment will have trouble understanding the logic in the Caymans' protecting their own coral but allowing that from other countries to be sold in local stores. If you buy it, you only encourage the practice.

Some of the most attractive ancient coin jewelry is found at **24K-Mon Jewelers** (Buckingham Square, Seven Mile Beach; 345-949-1499); a certificate of authenticity accompanies all purchases. The store also has delightful gold jewelry with sea themes, including stingrays, scuba divers, dolphins, and more.

Many of the waterfront buildings along Harbour Drive have been renovated, giving the downtown an attractive face-lift, splashed with bright Caribbean colors. On Cardinal Avenue, directly in front of the docks, you will find **Cartier Boutique** (345-949-7477), along with the **Kirk Freeport Center** (Bayshore Mall; 345-949-7477; www.kirkfreeport.net) and **Caymania Duty Free** (345-949-7972), one of the oldest establishments.

Liquor: With nearly US$28 per gallon duty on alcohol coming into the Cayman Islands, liquor is no bargain for local residents. However, cruise passengers can buy duty-free liquor in-bond at Tortuga Rum Company outlets (seventeen retail outlets, including four in town and at the Turtle Farm and its modern, spacious headquarters and bakery, which are stops on tours). Be sure to order a few hours in advance. Liquor is delivered in-bond to your ship. You can't take it with you. There are no locally made rums or other spirits. Tortuga rum cake is by far the best buy in Grand Cayman, available at **Tortuga Rum** (South Church Street; 345-949-6322; www.tortugarums.com) and all the company's other outlets. The large bakery handles the volume of vacuum-packed cakes—5,000 a day—using a century-old recipe. Free samples are available. Tortuga Rum has eight flavors of rum cake and a growing line of products from coffee to gourmet sauces. The delicious rum-soaked pound cake is so popular, the company even has offices in Miami (877-486-7884) to handle orders.

Dining and Restaurants

In the last few years, the range and quality of restaurants on Grand Cayman has widened considerably. The bad news about dining in Grand Cayman is that it tends to be expensive. Again, the need to import most ingredients, high labor costs, and a steep duty on imported items keep the prices high. Expect to pay US$50 or more per person with wine in an expensive restaurant.

Native Caymanian cooking emphasizes seafood. Fish served in Grand Cayman's top restaurants is usually ocean-fresh and well prepared. Turtle steak is a national delicacy, which, if properly prepared, can be good. Turtle has a taste best described as a cross between chicken and veal. However, the supply of turtle meat is limited, and it can be hard to find in local restaurants.

Abanks Watersports and Paradise Bar and Grill (just south of George Town on the sea; 345-945-1444). Known locally as Paradise Restaurant, it's a casual bar and cafe with great burgers, daily specials, and some island dishes. You can rent snorkeling equipment here for US$35 for mask, snorkel, and fins and enjoy Devil's Grotto, then dry off, have lunch in your bathing suit, and go back to splash some more. Hours: daily 7 a.m. to 10 p.m.; the water sports shop is open based on cruise ship arrivals. Moderate.

Cracked Conch by the Sea (West Bay, next to the Turtle Farm; 345-945-5217; www .crackedconch.com.ky). This well-known restaurant specializes in local dishes and seafood. A spacious outdoor terrace and bar 15 feet above the ironshore coast and sea offers panoramic views and spectacular sunsets. Expensive.

Grand Old House (South Church Street; 345-949-9333; www.grandoldhouse.com) was the first of Grand Cayman's elegant restaurants. It is located in a turn-of-the-20th-century plantation house and serves seafood and continental cuisine with a distinct West Indian touch. Expensive.

My Bar (Sunset House, South Church Street; 345-949-7111; www.sunsethouse.com). The thatched-roof restaurant of this thirty-plus-year institution overlooking the sea is popular with local folks, from English bankers to taxi drivers, for its chummy atmosphere. Fish-and-chips, snacks, sandwiches, and daily drink specials. Inexpensive lunch. Don't miss **Cathy Church's Underwater Photo Center** (345-949-7415; 607-330-3504; www .cathychurch.com) on the premises, where you will see a gallery of underwater photography by one of the world's top photographers.

Ritz-Carlton Grand Cayman (Seven-Mile Beach/West Bay; 345-815-6851; www.ritzcarlton .com) has seven restaurants and bars offering tradition and novelty: Blue by Eric Ripert (of New York's Le Bernardin) is an open-air eatery for seafood, grill selections, and homemade pastas; Bar Jack provides light fare poolside; Taikun offers sake martinis and forty wines by the glass, in addition to sushi, sashimi, and Japanese green teas; Silver Palm serves a traditional English tea and fifty-six wines by the glass. 7 Prime Cuts & Sunsets, the haute cuisine venue, is only open for dinner. All are expensive.

The Wharf (Seven Mile Beach; 345-949-2231; www.wharf.ky), with its pretty setting of white-washed gazebos stepping down to the water's edge, is one of the island's most popular restaurants. The menu offers an interesting variety of creative fish and meat dishes. Moderately expensive.

Sports

Beach/Swimming: There is but one beach on Grand Cayman worthy of your time. **Seven Mile Beach** runs north of George Town for—yes, 7 miles. It is one of the best anywhere in the Caribbean. A ten-minute taxi ride from the harbor, the crest of white powdery sand edged by tall Australian pines slopes gently into a waveless turquoise sea. For active water sports, head for any of the water sports centers on Seven Mile Beach, where every imaginable type of equipment is available for rent. On the other hand, if you prefer a quiet spot of sand with little to do but swim and sun, have the driver take you farther down the road to the public beach. When you are ready to return to George Town and your ship, walk to the Westin Hotel nearby, where you can pick up a taxi.

Another choice spot is the **Reef Grill/Royal Palms** (345-945-6360; www.reefgrill.com), located on one of the last undeveloped parts of Seven Mile Beach and an ideal place to enjoy the beach. You'll find volleyball, lounge chairs, a full beach bar, and a casual grill/restaurant. There may be a small admission fee.

Boating: You have a choice of several small sailing craft from Sunfish to Hobie Cat Waves which rent for about US$50, and kayaks $25 to $30; there's also a 60-foot catamaran with crew available for charter. **Stingray City Trips** (345-949-9200; www.stingraycitytrips.com) offers daily guided snorkeling excursions to Stingray City and a variety of water sports, and welcome advance reservations from cruise passengers. Stingray City Charters tours depart at 10 a.m., and 2:30 p.m., Mon through Fri, 9 a.m. and 1 p.m., Sat and Sun. Cost: US$40 adult $27.50 ages four through eleven; free to those three and under.

Deep-Sea Fishing: You cannot find a more perfect spot than the Cayman Islands for deep-sea fishing. It's a passion here, and just about every type of boat is available. The waters are noted for marlin, yellowfin tuna, wahoo, mahimahi, and barracuda. All equipment is available for rental, from smaller boats to fully equipped charters for deep-sea fishing. The latter range from US$600 for up to four people for a half day, $1,000 full day; or

$1,000 for up to eight people for a half day, $1,800 full day, depending on the boat. A list of charter boat operators is available in the Tourism Department's booklet *Cayman Islands Travel Planner*. Among them are **Bayside Watersports** (345-949-3200; www.baysidewatersports.com) and **Black Princess Charters** (345-949-0400; www.fishgrand cayman.com).

Golf: Grand Cayman has three golf courses. The first of its kind, **Britannia Golf Club** (www.britannia -golf.com), was designed by Jack Nicklaus as a regulation 9-hole course overlapped by a special short-ball 18-hole course, now known as Cayman Golf. The course is located about a ten-minute taxi ride from the harbor. All equipment is available. The 18-hole Cayman course costs US$150 for non-hotel-guests from Nov 1 to Apr 30; $100, May 1 to Oct 31. The regulation 9-hole course costs US$100. Club rentals $20 for 9 holes, $40 for eighteen. Reservations are necessary and can be made by calling (345) 745-4653. The Blue Tip, 9-hole course at the **Ritz-Carlton** (345-815-6500; www.ritzcarlton.com) designed by Greg Norman, is open to hotel guest and residence owners only.

North Sound Club (345-947-4653; www .northsoundclub.com) is an 18-hole championship course in the West End. The course (6,605 yards, par 71) was designed by Roy Case to suggest the old Scottish coastal courses. Rates are US$105 for 9 holes and US$175 for 18 holes, carts included. Rental clubs for 9 holes, US$30, 18 holes, $50.

Horseback Riding: **Pampered Ponies** (345-945-2262; www.ponies.ky) offers guided trail rides and beach rides, including sunset rides for all levels, on trained horses imported from the United States; US$80 for a ninety-minute beach ride. Cruise passengers must call in advance for reservations and transfers will be arranged. Other options are **Horseback in Paradise with Nicki** (Barkers Beach, 345-945-5839; www.caymanhorseriding .com) and **The Equestrian Centre** (345-949-7360), a riding school that specializes in English riding lessons for ages seven and older.

Scuba Diving/Snorkeling: The Cayman Islands, which have been called the Mount Everest of Diving, are considered by many scuba divers to have the best waters in the Caribbean for diving and snorkeling. If you are a certified diver and have a current PADI, NAUI, or YMCA C-Card, you should certainly put diving the Cayman Islands at the top of your priority list. Although there are dives to be made from shore and even shipwrecks right at George Town Harbor, the particularly interesting features of Cayman diving are gigantic corals, canyons, and walls in areas that you must take a boat to reach. In some places there are freestanding coral heads of 30 feet or more in height and many caves to explore. The Cayman Islands' coast and waters are protected by a marine park and have more than 280 permanent mooring positions off the three islands.

One of the most popular snorkeling and dive sites is just south of George Town harbor near Eden Rocks. It is a complex system of underwater tunnels connecting coral heads in 40 feet of water and rising to within 5 feet of the surface. Fish life, too, is abundant, with schools of yellowtail snapper, blue tangs, and an occasional moray eel and stingray. North of George Town are fine shallow reefs and good drop-offs; at East End and along the south shore to South West Point, the highlight is shallow elkhorn coral reefs that crown labyrinths of limestone caves and grottos housing grouper and giant blue parrotfish.

Because Grand Cayman's North Sound is, in effect, a marine estuary, fish life is abundant. The 20 miles or so of North Wall, off Rum Point, offer great wall diving, with craggy fissures and cuts predominating in certain areas. Circular chimneys that drop 30 to 50 feet and then open out into the ocean are commonplace. However, do not have your heart set on going to one particular place. Dive operators choose the dive sites bases on the weather and currents and on the level of experience of the participants.

Most cruise ships calling at Grand Cayman offer dive packages, but they are often more than double the price than if you make arrangements directly with local operators. In general, a snorkeling trip costs $30 to $35; Scuba beginning resort course, $150; one-tank dive, $60 to $75; two-tank dive, $95 to $120. Call or write from home for a reservation before leaving on your cruise, particularly during the winter season. When you arrive you will have to get yourself to the dive operator by taxi. Timing is very important—most dive trips depart at 9 a.m.

Eden Rock Diving Center (south side of George Town, within sight of the port; 345-949-7243; www.edenrockdive.com), is a PADI training facility and underwater photo center and one of Grand Cayman's top shore-diving facilities. Its proximity to the dock makes it ideal for snorkelers and certified divers (must show C-Card), who can rent diving equipment and tanks and underwater cameras right there and do a shallow dive on spectacular Devil's Grotto and Eden Rock, Cayman's most famous shore dives. You can also reserve a two-tank boat dive for US$100 per person by booking online in advance at edenrock@candw.ky. The boat leaves at 9 a.m. and returns by 1:30 p.m.

The Cayman Islands' Department of Tourism's publications and www.divecayman.ky have maps and a list of the Caymans' three dozen or more dive operators, with their addresses, phone numbers, services, equipment, prices, and other pertinent information.

Among the long established are **Don Foster's Dive Grand Cayman** (345-949-5679; www.don fosters.com) where a one-tank dive costs $60, a two-tank dive $95, and Stingray snorkeling, $35. **Divetech** (345-946-5658; www.divetech.com), the dive shop at Lighthouse Point, offers easy access to a sponge-encrusted mini wall beginning at 30 feet, only 50 yards offshore. Hours: daily, 8 a.m. to 8 p.m.

Stingray City—as the site has been dubbed—is just inside the barrier reef that protects North Sound and is one of the most unusual sites in the Caribbean. Here, in water never more than 15 feet deep, divers and snorkelers can see, touch, and photograph two dozen or more friendly stingrays inhabiting the area. This unusual fish has eyes on top of its body, a wing span of up to 5 feet, and looks like a ship from outer space as it glides gracefully through the water. When purchased directly from a local operator, the going rate for a snorkeling excursion to Stingray City ranges from US$40 half-day to $70 full-day and $65 for a dive. **Stingray City Trips** (345-949-9200) and **Bayside Watersports** (Seven Mile Beach; 345-949-3200) welcome requests for advance arrangements from cruise passengers. Stingray City trips go either to

the original deep site used by divers and snorkelers or to the Sand Bar, which is shallower.

Windsurfing/Kayaking: The calm waters along Seven Mile Beach are a good place to learn to windsurf; most resorts have equipment. For greater challenge, the northeast coast is one of the main windsurfing locations. **Tortuga Divers** (345-947-2097; www.tortugadivers.com) has rentals (US$45 per hour) and an introductory lesson ($65). It also has kayaks for rent. **Cayman Kayaks** (345-926-4467; www.caymankayaks.com) is an adventure tour company offering a range of guided kayak tours in the Rum Point and Cayman Kai area.

Unusual Dive Opportunities for Nondivers

For those who are not divers, Grand Cayman offers several opportunities to see the underwater world. For a close look at Grand Cayman's famous reefs, *The Atlantis,* a submarine designed specifically for recreational undersea travel, dives to a depth of 150 feet. The 50-foot-long ship holds forty-six people and a two-member crew; it boasts one extra-large window in front and eight large viewports along the sides, from which passengers can see nature's display. The ship makes day and night dives along the famous Cayman Wall, where divers normally swim at 40 to 90 feet. Passengers go by motor launch, which leaves about every hour from 9 a.m. throughout the day from George Town Harbor, for a ten-minute ride to the *Atlantis* boarding point. The dive itself is about one hour along the wall to a depth of 90 to 150 feet and is accompanied by a guide who gives a running commentary on the various fish and coral. **Atlantis Expeditions** (345-949-7700; 800-887-8573; www.atlantisadventures.com), US$89 adult; $49 child twelve or younger and over 36 inches tall; $69 ages thirteen to seventeen; three years old and younger are not admitted. You should buy this as a ship's shore excursion, as the price is the same when bought directly. *Seaworld Explorer,* a semi submersible operated by Atlantis, and *Nautilus* (345-945-1355; www.nautilus.ky), a similar semi submersible are less expensive alternatives. The semi submersible has large glass windows at 5 feet below the surface of the water to see the reefs, fish, and shipwrecks near the cruise ship pier. **Nautilus Undersea Tours**

(345-945-1355) submersible a viewing area with wall-to-wall windows.

Entertainment/Nightlife

Cruise ships seldom remain in port in the evening, but if yours does you will find clubs with live entertainment, a comedy club, discos, and even a karaoke bar. The island's famous band, the **Barefoot Man** (www.barefootman.com), plays everything from calypso to pop at the Reef Resort (East End) Tues and Thurs from 7 p.m. to 10 p.m. You can also catch comedy nights at **Legendz Bar** (345-943-3287) in Cayman Falls Plaza. The **Harquail Theatre** (West Bay Road; 345-949-5477; www.artscayman.org) is used for a variety of cultural events and stage performances.

Festivals and Celebrations

High on the list of unique entertainment in Grand Cayman is the annual **Pirates Week Festival** (345-949-5859; www.piratesweekfestival.com) Nov. In celebration of its history as a pirate lair, the whole island is transformed into a pirate encampment complete with a mock invasion of George Town, parades, pageants, parties, and the crowning of a pirate queen. If you happen to land here during Pirates Week, be ready to be swept up into the fun and frolic. The **Batabano Festival** (345-916-1740; www.caymancarnival.com) in May is the more traditional Carnival. **Cayfest** (345-949-5477; www.arts cayman.org), the Caymans' celebration of the arts, runs for several weeks in Apr.

The Mexican
Caribbean

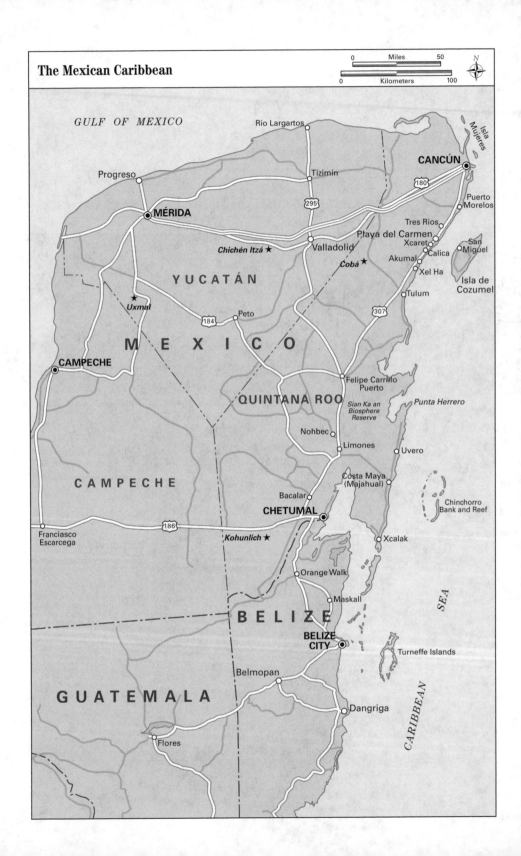

The Mexican Caribbean

Miles 0   50
Kilometers 0   100

N

GULF OF MEXICO

Rio Largartos

Progreso

Tizimin

CANCÚN

180

Puerto Morelos

MÉRIDA

Tres Rios

Playa del Carmen

Xcaret

San Miguel

Chichén Itzá ★

Valladolid

Akumal

Calica

Cobá ★

Xel Ha

Isla de Cozumel

Isla Mujeres

Y U C A T Á N

Tulum

★ Uxmal

Peto

184

M E X I C O

307

CAMPECHE

Felipe Carrillo Puerto

QUINTANA ROO

Sian Ka an Biosphere Reserve

Punta Herrero

Nohbec

Limones

Uvero

C A M P E C H E

Costa Maya (Majahual)

Chinchorro Bank and Reef

Bacalar

CHETUMAL

186

Franciasco Escarcega

Kohunlich ★

Xcalak

Orange Walk

Maskall

B E L I Z E

S E A

BELIZE CITY

Turneffe Islands

Belmopan

G U A T E M A L A

Dangriga

C A R I B B E A N

Flores

Where the Past Meets the Present

The Mexican Caribbean is one of the oldest, most historic regions of Mexico and one of its newest, most popular vacation resorts. It is best known by the names of the two most developed islands, Cancún and Cozumel, famous for their lovely beaches and magnificent water rich in coral gardens and marine life.

Both islands are located on the tip of the Yucatán Peninsula at the easternmost extreme of Mexico, where the Caribbean Sea meets the waters of the Gulf of Mexico. Cancún is connected to the mainland by roads and bridges and seems more like an extension of the mainland than an island. Cozumel is located about 10 miles off the coast, directly east of the port of Playa del Carmen, about 40 miles south of Cancún.

Cancún bills itself as the first resort of the computer age. The site was nothing more than a sandbar in 1973 when it was selected by computer analysis as the best place to start Mexico's long-range development of its coast. Today it is an international playground with glamorous resorts and restaurants, golf, tennis, and a full complement of water sports.

Cozumel, too, has come into its own as a resort since the 1980s, with an array of hotels, restaurants, and sporting activity, but the island was put on the tourist map even earlier by scuba divers. It has been a prime location for diving for more than fifty years. Yet for all their up-to-the-minute fun and facilities, both resorts are part of a land whose history stretches back more than 1,000 years before the arrival of Columbus.

Before Columbus and Cortés

Long before the discovery of America by Columbus and the conquest of Mexico by Cortés, there were civilizations throughout the Americas—the Inca, the Aztec, the Maya—that reached great heights of culture and achievement. One of them, the Maya, dominated the region of the Yucatán from about the first to the 12th century A.D. Today the remnants of their civilization are among Mexico's most important antiquities. At its height the Mayan domain comprised an area extending roughly 550 miles north to south and 350 miles east to west. This included the present states of Yucatán, Campeche, and Quintana Roo in Mexico, as well as Belize, Guatemala, and Honduras. By the time the Spaniards conquered Mexico in the early 16th century, the Mayan culture had already declined, and many of the towns had been abandoned. Why this happened is one of the many mysteries about the Mayas confronting archaeologists.

Indeed, Mayas are almost synonymous with mystery. They stepped into history seemingly from nowhere, spawned a civilization that lasted 1,500 years, and disappeared almost as suddenly as they came. Archaeological evidence shows that the Mayas established cities with as many as 50,000 inhabitants, constructed stone pyramids seventeen stories high and palaces of a hundred rooms or more, chiseled massive sculpture, and painted detailed murals and friezes that can still be seen on their magnificent temples and pyramids throughout the Yucatán.

The Mayas had a complex written language, charted the revolution of the sun and the planets in their observatories, calculated great mathematical

At a Glance	
Antiquities	★★★★★
Archaeology	★★★★★
Art and Artists	★★
Beaches	★★★★★
Crafts	★★★★★
Cuisine	★★★
Dining/Restaurants	★★★
Entertainment	★★★
History	★★★★★
Museums	★★
Nightlife	★★★★
Scenery	★★
Shopping	★★★★
Sightseeing	★★★★
Sports	★★★★★
Transportation	★★

Main Towns: Cancún, 702,873; Playa del Carmen/Calica, 200,000; Chetumal/Costa Maya, 200,000; San Miguel (Cozumel), 72,000

Climate: Consistently warm, around 80°F year-round, and dry

Clothing: Casual and comfortable summer sportswear for day and only a little less casual for evening.

Currency: The unit of currency is the Mexican peso, written with a $ dollar sign or as MXP, meaning "Mexican peso," or N$ to distinguish it from the old peso (fazed out after 1993). US$1 equals about N$12 pesos. Banks are open 9 a.m. to 1:30 p.m. Mon through Fri.

Customs Regulations: If you disembark in Mexico to return to the United States by plane, there is a departure tax of US$17 at 12 pesos to US$1; cash only.

Electricity: 110 volts AC, 60 cycles

Entry Formalities: Normally visitors need tourist cards to enter Mexico. These formalities are handled by the cruise lines. However, you should have your passport with you for identification, and you will need a driver's license and a major credit card to rent a car.

Language: Spanish. English is spoken at hotels and most, but not all, shops.

Postal Service: The post office in Cozumel is located at the corner of Calle 7 Sur and Avenida Rafael Melgar (known as the Malecon).

Telephone Area Code: Mexico, 52; Cancún, 998; Cozumel, 987. From the United States dial 011-52+998 and the local, seven-digit number for Cancún, or 987 and the local, five-digit number for Cozumel. Cancún has expanded its phone numbers, generally with the addition of an 8 as a prefix to the local number, but not all printed matter reflects the change. If you have trouble connecting, try adding an 8 in front of the local number.

Time: Cancún, Playa del Carmen, and Cozumel lie in the Central Standard time zone.

Vaccination Requirements: None

Airlines: *From the United States:* Aeromexico, Alaska Airlines, American, Air Trans, Continental, Delta, Frontier, JetBlue, Mexicana, Spirit, Sun Country, United, US Airways, and Viva Aerobus. *From Canada:* AirCanada and Mexicana. *Between Cozumel/Cancún/Mérida:* Click Mexicana; AeroCosta. *Between Cancún and Chetumal:* Click Mexicana.

Information: www.visitmexico.com; (800) 44-MEXICO. For information on Cancún, (888) 401-3880; www.cancun.info. For updates on the Riviera Maya (Playa Del Carmen, Tulum, Akumal, Puerto Morelos), (877) 7GOMAYA (746-6292) or www.rivieramaya.com.

In the United States:

Mexican Government Tourism Offices:

New York: 400 Madison Ave., Suite 11C, New York, NY 10017; (212) 308-2110; (800) 446-3942; fax: 308-9060; newyork@visitmexico.com

Chicago: 300 North Michigan Ave., Fourth Floor, Chicago, IL 60601; (312) 228-0517, ext. 14; fax: (312) 606-9012

Houston: 4507 San Jacinto, Suite 308, Houston, TX 77004; (713) 772-2581; fax: (713) 772-6058; houston@visitmexico.com

Los Angeles: 1880 Century Park East, Suite 511, Los Angeles, CA 90067; (310) 282-9112, ext. 23; fax: (310) 282-9116; losangeles@visitmexico.com

Miami: 5975 Sunset Dr., Suite 305, South Miami, FL 33143; (786) 621-2909; (786) 621-2907; miami@visitmexico.com

In Canada:

Mexican Government Tourism Offices:

Montreal: 1 Place Ville Marie No. 1931, Montreal, QC H3B 2C3; (514) 871-1052; fax: (514) 871-3825

Toronto: 2 Bloor St. West, Suite 1502, Toronto, ON M4W 3E2; (416) 925-2753; fax: (416) 925-6061

Vancouver: 999 West Hastings St., No. 1610; Vancouver, BC V6C 2W2; (604) 669-2845; fax: (604) 669-3498

---

sums, developed a calendar more accurate than the one we use today, practiced brain surgery, composed music, and wrote books (destroyed by zealous Spanish priests). And what makes the Mayas all the more remarkable is that they gained these achievements without benefit of the wheel, the plow, or other aids usually associated with an advanced civilization.

Archaeologists estimate that less than 10 percent of the Mayan cities have been found. The best known of the archaeology sites today are Chichén Itzá, about 70 miles from Mérida, the capital of the Yucatán near the northwest coast; Uxmal, 35 miles south of Mérida; and Tulum and Cobá, about 35 miles from Playa del Carmen on the east coast.

The combination of superb sports and modern facilities, Mexican crafts, cuisine, and proximity to some of the most important archaeological sites in the Western Hemisphere has made the Mexican Caribbean resorts popular as ports of call.

Budget Planning

Mexico is one of today's best travel bargains, but you may not see the benefit as a cruise passenger because the Mexican Caribbean is a tourist resort area where prices tend to be higher than in the interior of the country. If you are on a budget, stay away from fancy bars and restaurants, particularly in resort hotels. You will do best eating at places that specialize in Mexican fare, drinking local Mexican drinks, and dealing directly with tour companies and dive operators. You do have the alternative of good public transportation, particularly if you speak Spanish.

Shore Excursions

Generalizations about shore excursions for Cozumel, Playa del Carmen/Calica, and Costa Maya are difficult because there is little consistency in cruise ship arrivals and departures, in the ports they use, or in prices. Some ships arrive early in the morning and leave in the afternoon about sunset; others arrive in Cozumel, where they remain through all or most of the next day while passengers make their excursions to the mainland by fast ferry or plane. A few call at Cozumel only or Playa del Carmen or Calica only, while even fewer make stops at both Playa del Carmen or Calica and Cozumel.

Adding to the confusion in terms of planning your day in port is the listing in some brochures of Cozumel and Cancún or Playa del Carmen and Calica as though they were one port. Playa del Carmen is on the mainland, about 10 miles directly west of Cozumel island and 40 miles south of Cancún. Calica is 5 miles south of Playa del Carmen. More often than not when a ship's itinerary is shown as

Cozumel/Playa del Carmen, the ship stops in Cozumel only. To reach the mainland, you must go and return via a thirty-minute ferry ride from Cozumel to Playa del Carmen for the excursion to Tulum. Or, on your own, you can take a fifteen-minute plane ride from the Cozumel airport to Cancún or a thirty-minute plane ride to Chichén Itzá. The "fast" or "express" ferries between Cozumel and Playa del Carmen, depart about every one to two hours during the day from the main pier in town and take thirty-five or so minutes.

When itineraries read Playa del Carmen/ Cozumel, that usually means the ship anchors at Playa del Carmen long enough for passengers to disembark for their excursions, and then the ship continues to Cozumel. Passengers return to their waiting ships in Cozumel by ferry.

Some cruise ships offer a Chichén Itzá excursion; otherwise you must make your own arrangements, and knowing which port or ports your ship visits is essential to your planning. Ask your travel agent to obtain the information you need in advance of your cruise. Another caution when making independent arrangements: Some excursions do not operate daily, except perhaps in high season (from mid-Dec to mid-Apr).

As for prices, to take only one example, the three-hour Tulum/Xel-Ha excursion from Playa del Carmen varies from US$80 to $105; to as low as $45 for seven hours from Cancún—for the same tour. On the Web site of **Cozumel Tours** (www .cozumel-tours.com), a local company, a chart comparing the price cruise ships charge to the tours it offers, makes the point. These are some examples (first is cruise ship prices; second is Cozumel Tour's price): *Dolphin Encounter* $139/$72; *Dolphin Swim Adventure* $189/$83; *Horseback & Beach Hideaway* $99/$50; *Mexican Cuisine Cook & Tasting* $89/$45.

The good news is that in the past several years, cruise lines have significantly added interesting and innovative excursions in Mexican Caribbean ports, ranging from hiking, rock climbing, kayaking to fly fishing to Mayan cooking classes, to name a few. The following tours are described elsewhere in this chapter. You should be guided by your personal interest in making a selection. When shore excursions run longer than four hours, a box lunch will be provided by your ship. Prices are per person in U.S. dollars and are intended merely as guidelines and are subject to change.

Note to photographers: At all archaeological sites, a charge of US$8 or $10 is levied by the Mexican government for video cameras.

Cozumel

Chichén Itzá Air Tour: 5 to 6 hours; $230 and up. Arrangements can be made through local tour companies. Some ships offer an eleven-hour overland Chichén Itzá tour from Cozumel for $79 to $98, but this requires a round-trip ferry ride to Playa del Carmen, where the bus departs and returns. For those who can afford it, the difference for the air tour is worth the price. **Iguanas Tours** (984-127-3123) has daily departures, US$60.

Robinson Crusoe Boat Excursion: Full day; $50 with drinks; $75 with lunch. The boat sails along the leeward coast to a secluded cove for swimming, snorkeling over the reefs, and a seafood lunch. Some are party cruises on boats for 200 people, which is not recommended unless you want this kind of atmosphere, for $65–$70.

Cozumel Diving: $50 to $76 for a one-tank dive; $60 to $80, two-tank dive. The best dive sites are an hour from Cozumel; boats depart between 8 and 9 a.m. (See the Sports section for details.) Some ships offer a two-hour dive course for beginners at $95 to $130.

Snuba: 2 hours, $69. If you are ready to venture beyond snorkeling but not sure about scuba diving, Snuba might be the answer. It's a combination of snorkeling and scuba diving—well, almost. Instead of donning scuba diving equipment, you are tethered to a boat wearing an apparatus that provides a mask and oxygen. After a divemaster's orientation in shallow water, where you try out your skills, you go to deeper water (15 to 18 feet) to spend twenty-five minutes viewing some of Cozumel's famous underwater world. Note: Participants must be at least twelve years old and meet certain medical requirements.

Jeep Safari: 4 hours; $99 per person (four persons per jeep). Many cruise lines offer a wilderness/beach excursion by self-drive jeep that is to be avoided. You travel caravan-style on a very rough dirt and sand path through the jungle to a beautiful beach on the east side of the island that's too rough for swimming. Buffet lunch is served. The excursion is a big rip-off; you can rent a similar jeep for $50 for the full day, tour the entire island on your own at your own pace, have a safe swim at a west coast beach and a great lunch in town, or picnic by the beach for less than $20 per person. The total for four persons would be about $130, instead of the cruise line's $300 to $400 intake.

Cozumel by Horseback: 3.5 hours; $80 to $89. After a briefing by an English-speaking guide, you are assigned a horse suited to your riding ability and experience. Normally, the minimum age is ten and older, maximum weight 275 pounds.

Atlantis **Submarine:** (984-872-5671; 800-715-0804; www.atlantisadventures.com) 1.5 hours; $99 adult; $59 child . The forty-eight-passenger, air-conditioned submarine is a chance for non-divers to see what all the excitement is about since Cozumel is one of the top dive destinations in the world.

Dolphin Royal Swim: 1 hour; $149. Swim with dolphins at Chankanaab National Marine Park. See the Chankanaab Park section later in this chapter, or www.dolphindiscovery.com.

Playa Mia Beach Day: $19 adult; $14 ages three through twelve. Spend the day at a beach club 10 miles south of town where you'll find a bar, pool, lounge chairs, floats, kayaks, and other non-motorized water toys. Deep sea fishing. (See Sports later in this chapter.)

Cooking Class & Beach: Half-day, $50. For a really fun morning or afternoon at Playa Mia, you can take a class learning to prepare some Yucatan specialties with teacher/chef Luis, who is wonderful at keeping the 20 or so participants in the class engaged and entertained. You eat your cooking and are given recipes to take home; afterwards you can spend time on the beach. Cozumel Tours offers a similar program at Mr. Sancho's Beach Club, where you can also take a tequila seminar or a full body massage.

Playa del Carmen or Calica

On the dock as you leave your ship, you may see a list of taxi and tour prices mounted on a large board at the entrance to Playa del Carmen.

Tulum and Xel-Ha Lagoon: 3 hours, $78; (5 to 6 hours, $102–$130, returning by ferry to Cozumel to rejoin your ship). The tour of Tulum and a swim and refreshments at the lagoon. Instead of Xel-Ha, some tours stop at Xcaret, a nature reserve and recreational park a few miles south of Playa del Carmen. The cost will be considerably higher in this case.

Canopy Adventure: 5 hours, $90. Located near Puerto Moreles, the facility has twenty-four platforms and twelve Ziplines. Some packages include a swim in a cenote.

Snorkeling Excursion: 3 hours; $49. Snorkeling at Akumal Bay and Yalku, a spring-fed saltwater lagoon.

Chichén Itzá Tour: 9 hours; $60 to $115. An all-day trip by air-conditioned motor coach to the Yucatán's most important antiquity site. You can easily go on your own by taxi for about $200 for up to four persons.

Sian Ka'an: Full day; $90 to $105 from Playa del Carmen, including bus transportation, and lunch, to the largest nature preserve in Mexico. Some excursions include a hike to Muyil, a Maya antiquity site. (See the description later in this chapter.)

Xcaret: $69; children half-price, entrance fee; sports are extra. The privately owned, 180-acre nature, sports and entertainment theme park is 5 miles south of Playa del Carmen and about a mile before Calica Brightly colored Xcaret buses depart regularly from Playa del Carmen, and Calica. (See the Xcaret section later in the chapter.)

Jeep Safari: 5 hours; $83. Venture by jeep with a driver-guide through the wilderness south of Playa del Carmen to Aktun Chen and to Xpu-Ha for swim and Mayan style lunch, prepared on an open grill. (See Aktun Chen descriptions later in chapter.)

Cancún City and Shopping Tour: 3 to 4 hours; $35–$50. Tour of Cancún City and the Hotel Zone, with stops at the town market or shopping plazas. Some cruise ships provide a shuttle from port to Cancún.

Golf: (See the Sports section later in this chapter.)

Cancún/Puerto Morelos

Almost no cruise ships dock in Cancun per se due to the shallow waters, reefs, and lack of proper docking facilities for large ships. However, some cruise ships are now docking in Puerto Morelos, about 20 miles south of Cancun. **Chichén Itzá Tour:** Full-day; standard tour $77 adult, $46 child. The all-day excursion by air-conditioned motor coach to the archaeological site is available from **Cancún Vista** (998-887-3414; 800-860-5917; www.cancunvista .com/tours.htm), which also offers a wide range of tours in the Cancún/Riviera Maya area.

Isla Mujeres Day Excursion: Full day; $59 adult; $39.50 child. The Dolphin Experience sold in Cancún is actually at Isla de Mujeres. To swim with dolphins: $99.

Golf: (See the Cancun Sports section for details.)

Horseback Riding: 4 hours; $56 plus $15 transportation fee. (See Rancho Viejo Loma Bonita description later in Cancún section.)

Cozumel

Port Profile: Cozumel

www.islacozumel.com.mx; www.cozumelparks.com

Embarkation: Some cruise ships dock at the pier in front of San Miguel, the island's only town. Others dock at the SSA Pier (formerly known as International Pier), about 2 miles south of San Miguel, or Puerta Maya farther south. Passengers are allowed to go to and come from their ships freely provided they show the identity card issued to them by their cruise ship. There are ample taxis between the piers and town. Cozumel is an easy place to be on your own. You can walk the entire length of the Malecon, the main street fronting the

Miles
0   3

Kilometers
0   4

N

CARIBBEAN

SEA

Molas Point

Molas

Cozumel Canal

Passion Island

Bonita Beach

Municipal Pier

★ Cozumel Country Club

★ San Gervasio

SSA Pier

San Miguel

Puerta Maya Pier

Laguna Chankanaab

★ **Chankanaab Nat. Pk.**

Chankanaab

San Francisco Beach

Chen Rio

Cape Moreno

Cedral

National Marine Park

Buena Vista

★

Chen Rio Beach

CARIBBEAN

San Jose

Colombia de Sentos

SEA

Laguna Colombia

Celarian

Observation Tower ★

Palancar Reef

Celarain Point

Punta Sur Ecological Park

---

sea, in thirty minutes—but you will probably need two hours, as you are likely to stop in shops along the way. Shopping is the town's main attraction. For those interested in diving, the main dive operators are located at the south end of town on the Malecon. Don't bother to change your dollars to pesos; every place in Cozumel accepts U.S. dollars.

Local Transportation: Taxis provide local transportation and can be found easily on the Malecon. From SSA Pier at the south end of town to the town center is suppose to be US$6 for the car for up to four passengers but drivers charge each person US$6. Always ask the price in advance, and if you think it is too high, do not hesitate to bargain.

This is particularly true when you hire a taxi for a few hours to tour around the island. The price could range from US$40 to $80 for four hours, depending on your ability to bargain and the driver's eagerness for your business. Be sure to set the price with the driver before you get in the car. To phone for a taxi: (987) 872-0236.

Car Rental: Avis, Budget, Hertz, and several local car rental agencies are located on the Malecon or its side streets. Cars and jeeps range from US$45 to $65 for day rate, 8 a.m. to 8 p.m. Insurance can add another US$25. You will not need a car unless you want to tour the island on your own.

Motorscooters and Bicycles: Motorscooters or mopeds rent for about US$25 to $35 per day at several locations on the Malecon and Avenida 5 Sur, one street east of the waterfront, and on several side streets in between. They are the most popular means of transportation as the island is very flat and distances are not great. **Rentadora Cozumel** (Hotel Flores, 10A, Avenida Sur No. 172, Cozumel; 987-872-1120; 987-872-1429) and **Aguila** (Avenida Rafael E. Melgar No. 685, between Calle 3 and 5 Sur; 987-875-0729; fax: 987-872-3285) rent mopeds for $25; bikes, $10; and Volkswagen cars, $45. They are open from 8 a.m. to 8 p.m. Be aware that when several cruise ships are in port at one time, bikes, scooters, and cars are likely to be in short supply. You can try reserving ahead, but there's no guarantee it will work.

Ferry Service: (987-872-1588). Regular ferries and the Water Jet Mexico depart almost every hour from 5 a.m. to 10 p.m. from the dock in San Miguel for Playa del Carmen. Cost: N$110 (US$10.50) adult, N$60 (US$5.50) child.

Air Transportation: The airport is located 1 mile north of San Miguel. Flights to Cancún Airport (12 miles south of Cancún) leave about every two hours during the day. There are also flights directly to Chichén Itzá and Mérida. Inquire from Aero-Mexico (987-287-1860) or Mexicana (987-872-0157; 800-502-2000), which have offices in San Miguel on the Malecon.

Cozumel Past and Present

The island of Cozumel was the first place in Mexico discovered by Hernando Cortés, the Spanish conqueror, who used it as a staging area for his first expedition to the mainland in 1518.

The island, 30 miles long and 10 miles wide, was also the first of the Yucatán's islands to be discovered by scuba divers who came—as early as the 1950s—to enjoy the world's second longest underwater reef (only Australia's Great Barrier Reef is longer). In the intervening years the divers were joined by deep-sea fishermen, boating enthusiasts, and beachcombers trying to keep one pace ahead of the crowd. But by the 1980s, with an international airport, a host of new hotels, and up to a dozen cruise ships making regular calls, the crowds had come, too.

In antiquity, according to local legend, Cozumel was something of a Garden of Eden from which the gods departed to populate the mainland. Even up to the time of the Spaniards, it was considered a sacred place. Remnants of temples and artifacts used in religious rites have been found throughout the island.

In the days of the Spanish Main, the coves and inlets of Cozumel became favorite hideouts for pirates, including the infamous Henry Morgan and Jean Lafitte, who preyed on Spanish treasure ships as they passed en route from Spain's gold- and silver-rich colonies in South America to the mother country. It seems, however, that many pirates' ships never made it home; there are dozens of old wrecks in these waters. Today they are part of the rich treasures for divers. In the waters surrounding Cozumel, more than two dozen reefs have been named and charted for diving. The south shore of the island alone has a dozen dive sites. The best known is Palancar Reef, which lies about a mile off the south shore and stretches for a distance of 3 miles. Here visibility ranges from 150 to 200 feet. The reef is considered by experts to be one of the most spectacular in the Caribbean for its coral formation.

In the early 1970s—and none too soon—the government introduced strict laws to halt the destruction and exploitation of the reefs. The protected waters lie from the SSA Pier south for 20 miles to Punta Celerain on the south coast. In 1996 the Mexican government created a national marine park, including the beaches, from Paradise Reef (next to the SSA Pier) to Chiqueros Point on the southeast coast. Bird-watchers and naturalists have almost as much to enjoy on land as divers do in the sea. Only about a third of Cozumel is inhabited; the rest of the island has a wild, natural landscape barely touched by development. Cozumel's plants and trees are unusual, even for the Caribbean, and scampering about the undergrowth are lots of weird little creatures, including a 3-foot-long iguana that looks like a miniature dinosaur.

The island is easy to explore by car or jeep; there is a coastal road around about two-thirds of it. At the excellent museum in town, you can learn about the island's natural environment and diversity. A visit is highly recommended, as it will help you plan your sightseeing. San Miguel, the island's port and only town, was a sleepy little village with a World War II airstrip when tourism began in the 1970s. Over the years it grew and prospered, but it didn't really take shape until the 1980s with its growth as a cruise port.

San Miguel is laid out in a grid with streets, or calles, running east–west for more than 30 blocks, with those *norte,* north, having even numbers and those *sur,* south of the plaza, having odd numbers. They are crossed by north–south streets called *avenidas* (avenues). These are numbered in increments of five and carry the suffix *norte* or *sur*—Avenida 5 Sur, Avenida 10 Sur, Avenida 15 Sur, and so on—indicating that the avenue is north or south of Avenida Benito Juarez and the plaza.

The main plaza, closed to traffic, is designed as a pedestrian mall with shops and handicrafts markets. The wide, flower-bedecked street along the waterfront, Avenida Rafael Melgar, better known as the Malecon, is the main drag of the town and has the most fashionable stores. Here you will find the museum, dive shops, jewelry shops, clothing boutiques, pretty open-air restaurants overlooking the sea, lively bars with mariachi music, and more souvenir and T-shirt shops than you would ever want to see.

Since the stores on the Malecon pay a premium for their location, their prices are sometimes higher than the stores on streets farther inland from the waterfront. As Cozumel's tourism has boomed, many shops have opened on side streets and on those deeper into the town. It pays to shop around. You can also find plenty of Internet cafes. The **Calling Station** (Melgar and Calle 3 Sur) has the best prices of any port in the Caribbean—US$1 for thirty minutes and US$2 for sixty minutes. The store also offers telephone, fax, and postal services.

Museum of Cozumel: Museo de la Isla de Cozumel (Rafael Melgar Avenue, between avenues 4 and 6 norte; 872-1545), which opened in 1987, is the best place to start your acquaintance with Cozumel. Comprehensive exhibits utilize relief maps and dioramas to describe the natural environment, including its history of land and sea formations and wildlife; others depict the history of the Mayas

and the arrival of the Spaniards. In the center of the building is a table map that lights up when you press the name of a particular location so you can easily and quickly find places you might want to visit. The museum is situated in a lovely old colonial-style house. On the first floor is a book and gift shop; on the second, a veranda restaurant overlooking the Caribbean Sea. Here, too, you can buy a ticket to three of the main historic sites. Admission: $3; children under eight years old free. Hours: daily 9 a.m. to 5 p.m.

San Gervasio: For those not visiting Mayan antiquities on the mainland, San Gervasio is an interesting site, easily reached from the Cross Island Road, with ruins dating from A.D. 300 to 1500. Usually there is an English-speaking guide at the site. Hours: 8 a.m. to 4 p.m. Admission: $7; children under eleven free.

Discover Mexico (½ mile south of the SSA Pier; www.discovermexico.org) is a cultural theme park where visitors can learn about Mexico and experience the country's amazing history and culture. Admission: $14 adult; $9 child. Hours: 8 a.m. to 6 p.m. Mon through Sat.

Chankanaab National Marine Park (987-872-0914; www.cozumelparks.com): On the coast 5 miles south of San Miguel, the park was built around a natural lagoon that is home to more than sixty species of fish. A nature trail through the botanical gardens showcases more than 400 species of native trees and plants and another 350 from twenty-two tropical countries, and a museum displays shells and information about marine life. A small archaeological park with reproductions of statues, stelae (inscribed stone slabs), and other artifacts represents the different periods and civilizations in Mexico's ancient history. The marine park has a beachside restaurant, La Laguna, and a beach with palapa umbrellas for refuge from the strong sun. The reefs in front of the beach are popular for snorkeling; equipment is available for rent from dive shops in the vicinity. There are restrooms, dressing rooms, and a gift shop. Admission: US$19 adult; $10 ages three through eleven. Hours: 9 a.m. to 5 p.m.

Dolphin Royal Swim (998-193-3360; www.dolphindiscovery.com): Swims with dolphins in Chankanaab National Marine Park are offered daily at 11 a.m., noon, and 1, 2, and 3:30 p.m. The price, which includes a thirty-minute educational program and a thirty-minute swim, is US$149 per person. Participants must be eight years or older. Swimmers start by watching an educational video and for the first twenty minutes in the water, they work with the dolphins and trainers to perform specific exercises. The final ten minutes, they are free to swim with the dolphins under the trainers' supervision. Dolphin Encounters, $88 adult, $74.50 child, does not have a swim.

Punta Sur Ecological Park (www.cozumel parks.com): Three years and US$1.5 million in the making by the Parks and Museum Foundation of Cozumel, the 247-acre park on the southern end of the island is in an area known as the Colombia Lagoon and encompasses mangroves, white-sand beaches, and reef formations. Its goal is to promote conservation of the island's flora and fauna. The information center has a twenty-minute video on the park's ecosystems, birds and wildlife, and marine life. Here, too, visitors can rent electric bikes (US$5 per hour) to explore Punta Sur on their own. An Ecobus circles the park continuously for transportation from site to site.

The reserve has a 30-foot-high observation tower and a dedicated snorkeling and beach recreation area. Snorkeling equipment can be rented for US$5. Between May and Sept snorkelers might see sea turtles that arrive here to nest. At Punta Sur's South Point Camp, a sea turtle research and protection center, visitors learn about turtles and their nesting season. The observation tower offers great views of the lagoon and mangroves and is an ideal perch for bird-watching, which is best between Nov and Mar. Cozumel's bird population includes several species of herons, ibises, and flamingos, among others. The park's other amenities include a recreation area, kayaks, volleyball nets, palapa umbrellas for shade, a restaurant, snack bar, museum, and a souvenir shop. Admission: US$10 per person; ages seven and younger free. Hours: daily 8 a.m. to 6 p.m.

Shopping

For many passengers Cozumel's top attraction has been shopping. Mexico has wonderful crafts.

Unfortunately, crafts are no longer the inexpensive bargains they were in the past—but they are still fun gifts to take home. The best buys are colorful papier-mâché decorations, dolls, birds, and animals; Christmas tree decorations; brightly colored straw place mats; hammocks; leather handbags and sandals; cotton dresses, skirts, and blouses for women and shirts for men; silver plates, pitchers, and dishes; silver jewelry (fine-quality work is not cheap, however); copper plates and cooking utensils; clay and ceramic dishes; toys; handwoven tapestries; colorful paintings on bark; and more.

Larger stores tend to carry some of all these crafts. Quality and workmanship vary a great deal, so look around before you buy and don't hesitate to bargain. Cozumel is a free port, but we have not found the usual duty-free items such as perfume to be particularly good buys. You'll probably do as well aboard your ship. Many stores are open from 9 a.m. to 9 p.m. Using cash rather than credit cards can sometimes get you up to a 20 percent discount.

Punta Langosta, a two-story, open-air shopping mall a few blocks south of San Miguel's main square, is connected directly to the pier by an elevated walkway with stores with such familiar names as Versace and Colombian Emeralds. It may be tempting to linger here, but more interesting shops crammed full of Mexican products await you farther up the street.

At Puerto Maya, 2 miles south of town, you walk directly into an attractive shopping plaza designed to resemble a Mayan village. It has many of the same shops found in town on the Malecon. Puerto Maya was built by Carnival Cruise Lines; all its ships dock here.

Art and Artists: Regrettably, hurricanes in 2004 and 2007 drove away many of the artists and art shops we have visited in the past. One remaining is **Studio One** (25 Avenida 25 Sur, No. 981 between Calle 13 and 15, Cozumel, Quintana Roo 77600; 987-872-2659; www.studioonecozumel.com; jennifer@studioonecozumel.com). It is the gallery of artist Gordon Gilcrest and his wife, Jennifer, both American transplants who have lived in Cozumel many years. Gilcrest's forte is sketches inspired by Maya and other pre-Columbian antiquity sites and motifs, but with an artist's eye and talent that make them more than reproductions.

Clothing: On the Malecon, the **Pirana** (Rafael Melgar, near Calle 2) has cotton sportswear with prices a little high for Cozumel; nearby is **Ron Jon Surf Shop** (Melgar at Calle 4 Norte) for beachwear. **Miro** (on the Malecon south of the Plaza and at the International Plaza) features distinctive sportswear with stylized toucans in bright primary colors. There are so many souvenir and T-shirt shops, it's hard to distinguish any; they stock similar merchandise. Look before you buy. The streets behind the Malecon and east of the Plaza such as **Unicornio** (Avenida 5A Sur, No. 2) are better places to look for typical, inexpensive Mexican cotton dresses with appliqué, and caftans.

Crafts: **Viva Mexico** (on the Malecon; 987-872-5466) has a large selection of Mexican crafts and clothing and offers performances by colorfully costumed folkloric dancers five times a day. All the docks feature arrays of Mexican crafts, toys, resort clothes, and accessories. Take a look to see what's available, but wait until you get to town to buy.

Los Cinco Soles (Avenida Rafael Melgar 27, north end of the Malecon, 987-872-0132; www .loscincosoles.com) is Cozumel's best crafts store, with a vast selection of quality products generally a cut above the others. The well-established shop belongs to Sharon Welch de Morales, an American transplant, and her husband, Francisco. Our advice is to walk as far as this store before you buy anything. You will have passed many similar shops and gotten an idea of prices. Los Cinco Soles, set in a series of colonial-style houses, features a large collection of silver jewelry and some clothing by Mexican designers.

Los Cinco Soles also stocks handsome and unusual pottery that has leather, wooden beads, or cotton cord incorporated into the design. Made in Mexico City, and known as Rainbow Clay, this collection of pottery uses ancient techniques but molded into modern shapes for vases, bowls, and plates. The clay is gathered, cleaned, and then given its form and decorated using only natural adornments. Thus, the potters say, every piece of pottery takes its soul from Mother Earth. At the rear of the store is a courtyard cafe, **Pancho's Backyard,** one of the best restaurants in town for margaritas and Mexican fare.

Gifts and Jewelry: For top-quality modern jewelry inspired by traditional Mexican art, take a look at the work of **Tanya Moss** (Punta Langosta Mall and on the Malecon at Calle 2 Norte), an American who learned her craft while attending college in Mexico City. Her jewelry uses Mexican gold, sterling silver, and turquoise, along with semi-precious stones, and is very expensive. Over the past decade, the number of jewelry shops, such as those of Diamond International, has mushroomed. Most are on the Malecon, and all will be after your business with claims of bargains and other incentives. As we have cautioned throughout this guide, don't be taken in by the sales pitch. Any expensive purchase should come with appropriate guarantees.

Household Accessories: The pottery from Pueblo, Jalisco, Guadalajara, and the other main centers throughout Mexico can be found in crafts stores. Also look for papier-mâché fruits and vegetables; these inexpensive, fun souvenirs can make attractive table centerpieces. **Manuel Azueta** (Avenida 5 and Calle 4 Norte) has hammocks made to order. One of the sections in **Los Cinco Soles** (Avenida Rafael Melgar 27, north end of the Malecon) complex, **Mi Casa,** sells furniture and other household items and has a branch store on the Malecon at Calle 3 Sur.

Leather: If you are in the market for fancy boots or other leather items, Roger's Boots (Avenida Melgar) is known for belts, handbags, wallets, and other leather goods decorated with elaborate tooling. Its boots come in alligator, armadillo, ostrich, frog, and, of course, cowhide. The store also has jackets, hats, and accessories. Prices are moderately expensive, but don't hesitate to bargain.

Liquor/Cigars/Candy/Food: Mexico produces some excellent spirits. Kahlúa is a delicious Mexican liqueur made from coffee. Tequila is the distillation of the agave plant and the basic ingredient of the margarita, Mexico's potent answer to a daiquiri. These and other spirits are available at liquor stores on the plaza and the first and second streets east of the waterfront. The **Havana Club Cigars** store (Avenida Melgar at Calle 10 Norte) is located in the Forum Shops mall at the north end of the Malecon; so, too, is **The Belgian Chocolate**

Factory. Bottled vanilla is a popular purchase with visitors, but remember, all liquids must be packed in your checked luggage when you go through security to board your plane home from your cruise.

Dining and Restaurants

Carlos 'n Charlie's (Melgar at Punta Langosta Mall, 987-869-1646; www.carlosandcharlies.com) is a branch of the famous chain in Mexico City. (The equally famous Señor Frog's is next door.) Carlos 'n Charlie's seems to be a must-do on every cruise passenger's list. Music never stops. Some find it great, wild fun with customers, having drunk enough margaritas, dancing on the tables; for others it's a boisterous bore.

Guidos (2 blocks north of the ferry pier, between Calle 6 and Calle 8; 987-872-0546; www.guidoscozumel.com), set in an outdoor garden profuse with bougainvillea, serves seafood and oven-fired pizzas, its specialty. Hours: 11 a.m. to 11 p.m. Mon through Sat. Moderate.

La Cocay (Calle 8 between Ave. 10 and Ave. 15; 987-872-5533) is popular with local residents and especially divers, for good food at good prices and in a great atmosphere inside in air-conditioning or outdoors. Lunch starts at 1 p.m.

La Lobsteria (Avenida 5 Sur and Calle 7), one long block in from Melgar Street behind Punta Langosta Mall, is situated in an old Mayan house. It offers fresh lobster and shrimp and fresh fish—simply but well prepared to be enjoyed in easygoing atmosphere. Lobster tails tagged with prices are kept on ice; you choose one and it's cooked for you. Hours: 4 to 11 p.m. Mon through Sat. No credit cards. Expensive.

Costa Bravaone, one block in from the Malecon fronting on Calle 7 Sur, has the best, less expensive, lobster and seafood and the biggest, best margaritas we've found in Cozumel.

Las Palmeras (on the Malecon, across from the ferry dock; 987-872-0532) may never win a Michelin star, but it's a classic of a Mexican restaurant catering to tourists, with lively music, generous drinks, and lots of food. Moderately expensive.

And on the Malecon there's also a Hard Rock Cafe that's open until 1 a.m.; Jimmy Buffett's Margaritaville, where you'll want a pair of earplugs to withstand the noise; Pizza Hut and on its second floor, Chi (Chinese-Asian fusion cuisine); and Fat Tuesday on the main square.

Nightlife

Most ships leave Cozumel by 6 p.m. Cozumel's nightlife centers on hotels and a few of the discos in town. As in towns all over Mexico, restaurants frequently have musical entertainment—guitars, mariachis, or the like. Some ships bring local folk dancers and mariachis aboard ship to perform.

If your ship remains in port for the evening, one of its shore excursions will probably be a nightclub show with flamenco dancers and mariachis at one of the hotels. If not, check the Fiesta Americana Sol Caribe Hotel (near the SSA Pier), which usually has the best show in town.

The Mexican Folkloric Ballet performs at Sol Cabanas del Caribe Hotel and other hotels on different nights; inquire locally.

For the disco scene, make your way to Neptuno's on the Malecon at the south end of town or Viva Mexico, for Latin music or Babalu for jazz—all a short walk from the piers in town. There's even karaoke, at Laser Karaoke, about a mile south of town. Some beach clubs also have nighttime entertainment.

Sports

Beaches/Swimming: Cozumel's water is so spectacular, you may want to do nothing more than spend a day on the beach. The nearest one is Sol Caribe Beach, next to the SSA Pier. Better beaches, about 5 miles from the pier, are San Francisco Beach and Palancar Beach on the south shore. Passion Island, offshore, north of San Miguel, is a popular destination for boat day trips. By law, all Cozumel beaches are open to the public. Even so, some are more desirable and accessible than others. The beaches on the west side of the island are safe for swimming; those on the east side, however, no matter how beautiful, are too dangerous for anything more than your toes. For convenience, it's probably best to use one with a "beach club" where there are showers and changing rooms and a restaurant or bar.

Playa Uvas (Carretera Sur, km 8.5; 987-876-1104; www.playauvas.com) about 5 miles south of town, is Cozumel's answer to Nikki Beach (of South Beach fame) with similar white daybeds around the pool and by the beach. There are showers, lockers, a dive shop, kayak rentals, and free snorkel gear. Entrance: US$15 adult, $10 child, includes snorkel gear and two drinks. In the evening it becomes a nightclub and serves dinner to midnight. Mr. Sancho's Beach Club (Carretera Sur, km 15; 987-876-1629, www.mrsanchos.com), about 9 miles south of town, is the polar opposite—crowded with partygoers, beach lovers, screaming kids, and locals on Sun. It has showers, lockers, and a thirty-person hot tub, and its restaurant offers a tequila seminar at lunchtime—no joke!

Deep-Sea Fishing: Cozumel is one of the prime gamefishing areas of the Caribbean, particularly noted for sailfish, blue marlin, white marlin, tuna, dolphin, wahoo, shark, and barracuda, as well as bonefish in quiet lagoons and hidden bays. Boat charters can be arranged through Dive Cozumel (Avenida Rosado Salas, No. 85, and Fifth Avenue, P.O. Box 165, Cozumel; 987-872-4567; 866-319-2649; www.divecozumel.net) or local boat operators and range from US$400 for a half day to $500 or more for a full day, depending on the time of the year and the type of fish. Cozumel has a special fishing resort, Sol Pez Maya (P.O. Box 9, Cozumel; 987-872-0072; fax: 987-872-1599), or contact Club Abrigo Nautico de Cozumel (987-872-1024), Cozumel's fishing headquarters at Puerto de Abrigo, north of town near the airport.

Golf: Cozumel Country Club (Carretera Costera Norte, km 6.5 Interior Casa Club, Cozumel, Quintana Roo 77600; 987-872-9570; fax: 987-872-9590; www.cozumelcountryclub.com.mx) is a Jack Nicklaus–designed 18-hole championship layout (6,847 yards, par 72). It's located on the island's north end about a fifteen-minute drive from the pier, the facility is managed by Clubs Corporation of America. The course incorporates the natural landscape in its design, with fairways built around native trees, mangroves, and wetlands to preserve ecologically sensitive areas. The greens consist of hybrid Bermuda turf. Greens fees: US$169 per person for 18 holes including shared cart. An online package

for greens fees, clubs, balls is $179; $139 without clubs. Tee times are available in advance. There is a practice range, and the clubhouse has a fully stocked pro shop and a snack bar.

Horseback Riding: Rancho Buenvista (987-872-1537; www.buenavistaranch.com) offers half-day riding tours Mon through Sat, including transportation and accompanied by bilingual guides. Cozumel Tours (866-728-1438; 800-822-4577; www.cozumel-tours.com) offer Punta Sur Beach Ride combining riding and beach time, daily from 10:30 a.m. to 2 p.m. $49 adult; and El Cedral Jungle Ride, 2.5 hours; $31.50.

Snorkeling and Scuba: When you've come to one of the world's prime scuba diving locations, you will certainly want to include a dive here if you are a certified diver. The island is surrounded by two dozen or more reefs; those off the south/southwest shore offer the best diving and are protected by the national marine park. Cozumel has both reefs close to shore and drop-offs farther out at sea. Several locations within walking distance of the SSA Pier offer diving from the beach. Paraiso Reef North is about 200 yards off Sol Caribe Beach in depths of 30 to 50 feet, with visibility up to 100 feet. La Ceiba Reef and Plane Wreck, in front of La Ceiba Hotel, next to the pier, has an underwater trail designed by marine ecologist George Lewbel. The trail was created by Pancho Morales, former owner of La Ceiba Hotel and current proprietor of Los Cinco Soles. It starts at the plane, sunk for the filming of a movie, and continues along the reef for 120 yards with signs explaining various types of corals and sponges. The location is popular for cruise ship dive excursions.

Continuing south, the next group of reefs is in the Chankanaab Lagoon area. Close to shore are huge coral heads, and along the shoreline are caves that go back under the shore. These can be reached from the beach; the area can be enjoyed by snorkelers as well. Between Punta Tormentos and Punta Tunich, just before San Francisco Beach, is Tormentos Reef, popular with photographers for its coral heads, sea fans, and abundant fish. Yocab Reef, at a depth of about 30 feet, is a good location for beginning divers. San Francisco Reef, situated about ½ mile directly in front of San Francisco Bay, is popular for its abundant fish.

Palancar Reef, the best known, lies about a mile off the south shore and stretches for 3 miles with visibility up to 200 feet. The variety of formations is the attraction. Here the wall is sloping, rather than a sharp drop-off, and starts about 50 feet down. It is a maze of canyons, tunnels, and caves. The south end has enormous coral pinnacles spiraling up to 60 feet or more. You will find a dozen dive operators on the main street of the town. You should contact them in advance and plan to get to them early; most morning dive trips leave by 9 or 9:30 a.m. You must show a certification card before going out on a boat or renting tanks. Each offers regularly scheduled half- and full-day dive packages, and prices are very competitive. A typical day consists of two dives on different reefs and lunch on a beach for US$70–$80. The exact location of the dives is determined by the divemaster on each boat, depending on weather conditions, currents, and the like.

Among Cozumel operators are **Caribbean Divers** (Calle 3 Sur; 987-872-1080; www.caribbean diverscozumel.com); **Dive Cozumel** (Avenida Rosado Salas, No. 85, and Fifth Avenue, 800-780-5733; 866-319-2649; www.divecozumel.net); and **Aqua Safari** (Avenida Rafael Melgar 1 Sur; 987-872-0101; http://aquasafari.com). **Servicios de Seguridad Sub-Aquatica** (Calle 5 Sur-21b; 987-872-2387; VHF 16 and 21) is a professionally operated recompression center. It is open from 8 a.m. to 8 p.m. and can be reached at other times by radio.

Tennis: Presidente Hotel, an Intercontinental hotel about 1 mile south of the International Pier, has three courts, and there are courts at the Fiesta Americana Sol Caribe. Contact the hotels in advance to request permission to play.

Windsurfing/Kiteboarding: Windsurfing is available at beachside hotels for about US$30. Like most places in the Caribbean, the sport of kiteboarding has come to Cozumel. In fact, Mexico's own Olympic champion, **Raul de Lille** (987-103-6711; www.kitecozumel.com), introduced the sport to Cozumel and became its first certified instructor. He offers instruction, but he's not cheap—US$125 per hour for minimum of three hours for private one-on-one instruction, or $500 per day. If you have

a pal to take lessons with you, it's $300 each. Also check out **Cozumel Kiteboarding** (www.cozumel kiteboarding.com) or contact **Adrian Angulo Romero** (Puro Mar Surf-Kite Co & Bikini Shop, Fifth Avenue at Third Street; 987-876-1558; adrian@ cozumelkiteboarding.com).

Riviera Maya

www.rivieramaya.com

The 100-mile stretch of Caribbean coast south of Cancún Airport to the border of the Sian Ka'an Biosphere Reserve, south of Tulum, is now officially known as the Riviera Maya. It boasts more than five dozen megaresorts and a host of smaller ones, most built only since the mid-1990s.

Playa del Carmen/Calica

Situated 10 miles directly west of Cozumel and equidistant between Cancún on the north and Tulum, a major Mayan temple complex, on the south, Playa del Carmen is the main port of the coast and the gateway to the Yucatán Peninsula for cruise ships. Its growth from a minuscule fishing village to a major town was the result of Riviera Maya's development.

Those who want to be on their own will find ample services in Playa del Carmen for tours, car rental, and taxis. If you have arrived from Cozumel or plan to return to your ship there, you should time your return via ferry either before or after the rush of cruise passengers returning from shore excursions.

When passengers arrive in Playa del Carmen, they find a lively town directly on the beach. On the south side of the pier is Señor Frog's, a member of the Mexican restaurant chain, several beachside hotels, and the Playacar Spa & Golf Club, one of nine golf courses in the Riviera Maya.

On the north side of town is the public beach, with small hotels and beach clubs. From the pier, a short lane lined with tourist shops, leads directly into the main part of town beginning at Fifth Avenue, a north–south pedestrian street lined with shops, restaurants, small hotels, travel companies, dive shops, car rental agencies, and other tourist services. It is intersected about midpoint by Avenida Juarez, the town's main thoroughfare.

Directly in front of the pier next to the kiosk where tickets for the Cozumel ferry are sold, you are likely to find Ricardo waiting to rent you a Hondo Elite scooter (US$28, including gas, insurance, and helmet). Ten steps away will be others offering popular excursions at reasonable prices. There's also a large convenience store selling Kahlúa, the famous Mexican coffee liqueur, and bottles of vanilla, another popular souvenir; and a drugstore next to the office for Xcaret, the popular nature theme park (bus departures hourly, Mon through Fri), and **Budget** (US$45 for small cars to $99 for jeeps, including insurance and taxes). Fishing trips can be arranged through **Pesca Maya Lodge** (888-894-5642; www.pescamaya.com). Prices start at US$430 for two adults for 8 hours, plus 118 pesos for mandatory fishing license; transfers are not included.

Even with Playa del Carmen's growth, it has more Mexican character than Cancún. The action is on the beach during the day—you can even have a massage there—and at the restaurants, bars, and sidewalk cafes of Fifth Avenue in the evening. (Calica information appears later in this chapter.)

Restaurants

Ajua Maya (Calle 4, off Fifth Avenue; 984-873-2523; 818-581-4075; www.ajuamaya.com), pronounced *ahh—who—ahh ma-ya—* is a tequila bar, grill house, and Latin club in one, as serious about food as it is about fun. Nightly, there's live Latin music and dancing waiters. The menu ranges from lobster, USDA Angus steaks, and New York cheesecake, to Mayan and Mexican cuisine, including 19th-century French-influenced mestizo cuisine. **La Casa del Agua** (Fifth Avenue and Second Street, upstairs; 984-803-0232; www.lacasadelagua.com), decorated with wood and Mexican artifacts, with a fountain as part of the decor, the restaurant offers diverse entrees, such as Yucatán seviche, in a romantic atmosphere and great service. Moderately expensive.

La Cueva del Chango (Calle 38, between Av. 5 and the beach; 984-116-3179), a restaurant-bar, is laid-back and cool and a favorite of local residents. Built with wood and natural stone in a jungle garden setting, it's complete with waterfalls, fishponds, monkeys, and birds flying about. Lunch and dinner menus have a wide selection of Mexican dishes and Mexican wines. Moderate.

La Parrilla (Fifth Avenue and North Eighth Street; 984-988-48193) serves steaks and Mexican specialties. Moderately expensive. **Yaxche** (Fifth Avenue and Twenty-second Street; 984-873-2502; www.mayacuisine.com) serves the most authentic Mayan cuisine in Playa del Carmen, if not the Yucatán, at reasonable prices. Be sure to have Mayan coffee—it's quite a show being made.

North of Playa del Carmen/Cancún

The region north of Playa del Carmen offers a great deal of interesting sightseeing. Along with outstanding Mayan archaeological sites, there are caves, underground rivers, cenotes (sacred sinkholes), nature parks, and opportunities for kayaking, biking, trekking, and bird-watching, as well as two golf courses. If you rent a car, there are several important sites of antiquity within a short drive from the pier. Be sure to have a full tank of gas before starting out: Gas stations on the byways are few and far between. Taxis are readily available at reasonable prices.

The main highway (No. 307) between Playa del Carmen and Cancún is an excellent four-lane parkway that runs as straight as an arrow about a mile or so inland from the sea until just south of Cancún. The stretch from Playa del Carmen has been developed with so many small hotels, big resorts, and attractions that it's hard to keep track. To reach most of them, you need to turn off the main road and head toward the sea. (Mileages indicated are measured from Playa del Carmen.)

Mayakoba (3 miles): Directly north of Playa del Carmen is a large hotel and villa resort complex. Among its top hotels are the Fairmont Mayakoba and the Rosewood Mayakoba and the El Camaleon Golf Course, designed by Greg Norman, as its centerpieces. The golf course is open to non-hotel-guests. Greens fees for 18 holes: $170, May through Oct; and $267, Nov through Apr. After 1:30 p.m., $102 and $141, respectively. For tee times: 984-206-3088. El Camaleon is home to the Jim McLean Golf School and the PGA Tour in Mexico.

Its clubhouse has a full-service golf shop with carts, clubs, and shoes for rent; in open-air casual restaurant and an Argentinean steak house.

Playa Xcalacoco (7 miles) is home to The Tides Riviera Maya (984-877-3000), a member of the Kor Hotels group and one of the most luxurious resorts on the coast. Punta Bete (11 miles) is about a 3-mile drive from the highway through typical Yucatán dry brush jungle and banana trees to a rustic, palm-fringed 3 miles of white-sand beach, popular for swimming and snorkeling. La Posada del Capitán Lafitte (998-873-0214) is a modest, attractive beachside resort with a pool, showers, and a restaurant overlooking miles of beautiful, reef-protected white sand. Snorkeling on the reef is available.

Playa Maroma (14 miles). The turnoff at kilometer 51 leads to Maroma Beach Hotel and Spa (998-872-8200; www.maromahotel.com), a small, upscale resort that has received a great deal of publicity for the celebrities it attracts. Small groups of four or six people are welcome to have lunch and swim. It's ideal for those who want to get away from the crowds. Call in advance.

Playa Paraiso (18 miles) has a huge resort complex that includes five Iberostar hotels: including the newest, Iberostar Grand Hotel Paraiso (984-877-2847; www.iberostar.com) and its 18-hole Peter Dye–designed golf course (golfparaiso@iberostar.com.mx), which is open to the public. Greens fee: $190. It has a full-service pro shop and a restaurant.

Puerto Morelos (22 miles) is the oldest port in Mexico. The quiet fishing village, with inexpensive beachfront restaurants where you can enjoy the day's catch, had been bypassed by developers until now. The port is being developed, and a few cruise ships call here. The area between Morelos and Cancún has also undergone intense resort development in the last three years.

Selvatica (998-847-4581; 866-552-8825 www.selvatica.com.mx), a Yucatan adventure company based in Puerto Morelos, offers a Canopy Tour through the jungle that consists of twenty-four platforms and twelve zip lines, mountain biking, and swimming in a cenote, $90 adult; $50 child. Another package combines the Canopy ride with horseback. Selvatica tours depart from Puerto

Morelos, Playa del Carman, and Playacar. Puerto Morelos also has a polo club with a stable of 30 horses. Players and visitors are welcome. Inquire in advance.

Rancho Loma Bonita (km 49, near Puerto Morelos; 998-887-5423), a forty-five-minute bus ride across the Yucatán countryside, takes you to the ranch which offers horseback riding along the beach or jungle trekking. The tour, offered daily, has guide escorts for a leisurely ride along a trail to the Caribbean Sea, where you can ride bareback into the ocean waves. The ride is followed by a Mexican lunch at the ranch. Cost: US$69 adult; $55 ages six through twelve. At the turnoff for Puerto Morelos on the main highway is the 150-acre Dr. Alfredo Barrera Marin Botanical Garden (998-835-0440), which features flora of the Yucatán region. It has a small archaeological site and nature trails through thick, dry forest. The park is maintained by the Quintana Roo State Research Center. There's a small admission fee There's also a gasoline station here.

Crococún and Palancar Aquarium (24 miles): The crocodile farm has several species of crocodiles as well as spider monkeys, Mexican raccoons, and other species native to the Yucatán. There is a small admission fee; a guide is available for an extra tip. Next door, Palancar Aquarium, named for the reef that lies off the coast, has exhibits on all aspects of the region's marine environment.

Beyond Puerto Morelos, 15 miles from Cancún, is the luxury, all-suite Paraiso de la Bonita Resort (www.zoetryresorts.com) nestled in 14 acres of landscaped gardens and mangroves. The architecture is meant to capture the essence of Mayan culture with open courtyards, fountains, and reflecting pools.

Cancún
www.cancun.info

Cancún came out of a computer. Well, almost.

In the late 1960s, when the Mexican government set out to develop the country's coastal regions for tourism, researchers fed a pile of data about climate, water, land, history, and the like into their computers to find the ideal area in which to begin. All the positive signs pointed to a 14-mile

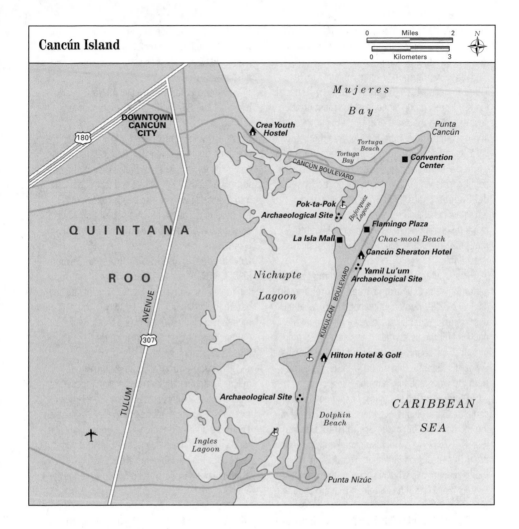

Cancún Island

Miles | 0 | 2
Kilometers | 0 | 3

N

Mujeres Bay

DOWNTOWN CANCÚN CITY

180

Crea Youth Hostel

Punta Cancún

Tortuga Beach

Tortuga Bay

CANCÚN BOULEVARD

Convention Center

Pok-ta-Pok Archaeological Site

Bojorquez Lagoon

Flamingo Plaza

La Isla Mall

Chac-mool Beach

Cancún Sheraton Hotel

QUINTANA

Yamil Lu'um Archaeological Site

ROO

Nichupte

Lagoon

KUKULCAN BOULEVARD

AVENUE

307

Hilton Hotel & Golf

Archaeological Site

CARIBBEAN

SEA

Dolphin Beach

TULUM

Ingles Lagoon

Punta Nizúc

sliver of land off the northeastern Yucatán coast on the Caribbean Sea, known as Cancún.

Most people's response was "Can-who?" And understandably. Cancún was little more than a sandbar, and the eastern zone of the Yucatán was an uninhabited jungle. There were no roads, no water, no electricity, and only about 120 people living there.

Today Cancún has almost 200 hotels in all categories, with such well-known names as Hyatt and Ritz-Carlton. There are approximately 500 restaurants, large shopping centers, native markets, four 18-hole golf courses, a convention center, a wide range of sports and entertainment facilities, and a town of more than 700,000 people.

The island of Cancún has the shape of the number 7 and is connected at both ends to the mainland by bridges. The long side of the island faces the Caribbean on the east and the Nichupté Lagoon on the west. A hotel/resort zone was created on Cancún island and the commercial district was placed on the mainland. Most resorts are located along the beach on the road heading north to Punta Cancún. The hotel area's strict zoning prohibits garish signs and buildings over nine stories. There is frequent bus transportation between the island and town, and the international airport is 12 miles away.

The Beaches: What Cancún lacks in verdant tropical splendor is more than made up for in its beaches and water. (Cancun's beaches were badly damaged from hurricanes in 2004 and 2007. Through 2010, the government has spent millions to restore them and will probably not know how successful the effort has been until after the next hurricane season.) What makes these beaches so spectacular is both the color and the quality of the sand and water. The powder-fine, blinding white sand looks as though it would scorch your feet, but it is actually cool to the touch. That the sand, which is coral and limestone in origin, is very porous accounts for this unusual characteristic and was one of the determining factors in the computer's selection of Cancún. The intense, deep blue-green color of the water is marvel enough, but when you step into it, you will discover it has an unusual silken quality.

That's the good news. The bad news is that some parts of the coast have a strong undertow. Warning signs are posted, but many tourists do not take them seriously. *Never go far from shore, and never swim where someone on shore cannot see you.* The water of the lagoon and the north shore of Cancún island are considered the safest places. Hotels have swimming pools.

Hotel Zone: Hotels—many of which are fabulous architectural creations—line the beach for 14 miles, from Club Med and the huge Hilton Resort and Golf Club on the south to El Presidente Inter-Continental on the north. Most of the hotels tend to be self-contained resorts with their own sports and entertainment, which is helpful for cruise passengers with limited time because they can select one and stay. But if you want to check out the scene at another hotel, it takes more effort than a simple stroll down the beach. A paved pedestrian walkway, the ciclopista, winds through the northern part of the Hotel Zone and is a pleasant walk.

Sports and Attractions: In addition to the water sports facilities at hotels, the Hotel Zone has many water sports centers where you can find equipment for snorkeling, scuba diving, and fishing.

Cancún Golf Club at Pok-ta-Pok (998-883-1230; www.cancungolfclub.com) designed by Robert Trent Jones, is on a series of islands in the lagoon, connected by road to the Cancún Hotel Zone. Hours: 6 a.m. to 6 p.m. Greens fees:

US$145 to $175, depending on the season, for 18 holes with cart; US$45 for clubs. The Club has a restaurant, pro shop, showers, swimming pool, and tennis courts. Another 18-hole championship golf course is part of the complex at the **Hilton Cancún Golf and Spa Resort** (998-881-8000; www.hilton cancun.com). Greens fees for 18 holes, US$199 for non-guests. Some ships have golf packages with this course; otherwise you must make your own arrangements.

When you come into Cancún from Playa del Carmen, as most cruise passengers do, you arrive at the south end of the island where **Club Med** (984-881-8200) is located. The resort has a day pass for $55 per person, which includes lunch, a guided tour (at 10 a.m. or 6 p.m.), and use of the beach, tennis courts, pool, and water sports. The day pass can be booked directly with the hotel.

Farther north, **Dolphin Beach** is a beautiful stretch of open beach. Hard as it may be to imagine, all of Cancún looked like this only four decades ago. On the lagoon side of the road is a Mayan archaeological site, **Ruins del Rey,** uncovered in the late 1980s.

Convention Center: At the north end of the island at Punta Cancún is the Convention Center (www.cancuncenter.com), within walking distance of many hotels and several of the largest shopping plazas. The center has been the venue for many major events. Its showpiece is a tower that rivals Paris's Eiffel Tower in height. The center is also the home of the Museum of Anthropology and History of Cancún.

Shopping: Among the largest shopping malls are **Plaza Caracol** (www.caracolplaza.com), La Fiesta at Punta Cancún, La Isla, and **Plaza Kukulcán** (www.kukulcanplaza.com), about midpoint in the Hotel Zone. Luxury Avenue is a boutique mall in Kukulcan Plaza, which brings together some of the most famous international brands, including Vuitton, Cartier, Ferragamo, Fendi, and more. Incidentally, all of Quintana Roo—the easternmost province of Mexico, in which Cancún and Cozumel are located—is a duty-free zone. Generally, business hours are 10 a.m. to 1 p.m. and 4 to 8 p.m. Not all stores close for the siesta, nor do downtown markets.

Cancún City: From Punta Cancún to Cancún City, the commercial center on the mainland, is 6 miles. Cancún City is a completely new town that is gradually acquiring character. There are wide, tree-lined streets and parks, and an outdoor market with typical Mexican crafts of cheaper quality and price than those found in the large shopping plazas.

Restaurants: Cancún has as many as 500 restaurants, and new ones are opening daily. Some restaurants convenient to the Hotel Zone are Captain's Cove (across from Royal Mayan Hotel; 998-885-0016; www.captainscoverestaurant.com) and Lorenzillo's Live Lobster House (Hotel Zone, km 10.5; 998-883-1254; www.lorenzillos.com.mx), with romantic settings overlooking the lagoon. Both serve seafood and are moderately expensive.

Carlos 'n Charlie's (Forum by the Sea, Boulevard Kukulcan, km 8.5; 998-883-4468; www.carlosandcharlies.com) is a moderately priced member of a famous Mexico City chain specializing in seafood.

Glazz (La Isla Shopping Village, Boulevard Kukulcan, km 12.5; 998-883-1881). A posh restaurant and bar with incredible decor that has been called "South Beach Miami meets Indonesian chic." Moderately expensive.

Labna (Margaritas Street 29, downtown Cancún, 998-892-3056; www.labna.com). Yucatecan specialties. Moderate.

Locanda Paolo (Avenue Bonampak 145 at corner of Jurel Street, downtown Cancún; 998-887-2627; www.locandapaolo.com) is an owner-chef-operated restaurant that gets high marks from Cancún residents for its Italian cuisine. Moderate.

Salute! Cancún (Boulevard Kukulcan, km 11.5; 998-881-5556; www.salute.com.mx), with a wide terrace for great views of the Nichupté Lagoon, offers Mediterranean cuisine, seafood, sushi, steaks, pasta, and daily specials, along with an extensive wine list that includes Mexican wines. Branch in Playa del Carmen. Expensive.

For specialties of the Yucatán, Los Almendros (across from the bullfight ring; 998-884-0807; www.losalmendros.com.mx) is open from noon to 11 p.m.

If you hunger for a Big Mac, McDonald's has eight locations and there's a Jimmy Buffett's Margaritaville. For pizza, there seems to be a pizzeria on every corner; and for a juicy steak, there's an Outback Steakhouse.

Entertainment: Cancún is famous for its nightlife, but unfortunately, most cruise ships leave by sunset, and Cancún's nightlife doesn't even begin to flicker until after 10 p.m. If you are here in the evening, however, you can learn what is happening from one of the free local publications, such as *Cancún Tips.*

Bullfights are staged at the stadium, Plaza de Toros Cancún (Avenida Banampak, Lote 1; 998-884-5629), on Wed at 3:30 p.m. The cost is US$45 adult; child under twelve is admitted free.

Transportation: Taxis are available at all Cancún hotels, and there is frequent bus service between the Cancún resorts and Cancún City. There are car rental offices at major hotels, in the plaza of the Convention Center, and in Cancún City. Budget (Alquiladora Montejo S.A., Avenida Tulum 214; 998-884-6955) has American, European, and Japanese cars that cost from US$60 to $80 per day, depending on the model. If you plan to spend the day exploring on your own, you should either rent a car or moped or hire a taxi with a driver—distances are too great for walking. Bus stops, marked *parada*, are conveniently located throughout the Hotel Zone and in the downtown area; the fare is 6.5 pesos. "Turicun" buses are air-conditioned and more plush.

Useful Numbers: Tourism Office: (998) 881-9000. Police, (998) 884-1107. American Hospital, (998) 884-6133. Red Cross: (998) 884-1616.

Isla Mujeres

Four miles off the north coast of Cancún is Isla Mujeres, the Island of Women, so named by the Spaniards because of the large number of erotic terra-cotta female idols they found when they landed there in 1517. A Mayan temple, believed to have been dedicated to the goddess of childbirth and weaving, suggests it was a sanctuary.

Today the 5-mile-long island, where life is even more carefree and casual than on Cancún, is noted for its scuba diving and snorkeling and good seafood restaurants. During the summer (June 15 through Sept 1, and strictly regulated) whale sharks in their natural habitat can been sighted (www.islawhalesharks.com); the cost is $125. Dolphin Discovery (www.dolphindiscovery.com), located in the heart of the island, offers the 45-minute

Encounter for $89 adult; $79 child. Like Cancún, Isla Mujeres has been transformed and now has a population of 15,000.

The island's newest attraction is an underwater museum, located in the National Park on its west coast. The first 100 sculptures are in place and another 300 sculptures will be added by the end of the year. The project, intended to help conserve natural reefs, is being supervised by prominent creator of the underwater sculptures, Jason de Caires Taylor (www.underwatersculpture.com).

Day trips to Isla Mujeres depart daily from the marina next to El Presidente InterContinental at 10 or 10:30 a.m. and return at 4 or 4:30 p.m; and from the Playa Linda dock at 9:30 a.m. The price (about US$65) includes snorkeling on El Garrafon Reef and a seafood lunch. Fast water taxis make the trip to Isla Mujeres from Puerto Juarez or Punta Sam in about twenty minutes. Cost is US$8 for the boat. Ferries leave frequently throughout the day.

Contoy Island

Approximately 15 miles north of Cancún is Contoy Island, a national bird sanctuary and nature preserve scalloped with pretty beaches. Only 2 miles long and less than ½ mile wide, Contoy is home to many species of birds, including frigate birds, pelicans, cormorants, flamingos, and herons. Until recently the island had been closed to the public because of careless use; it has now reopened, but under more controlled conditions. The boat trip to Contoy (about US$80 round trip), with a stop for snorkeling en route and time on the island is about a five hour excursion. Normally, day excursions depart almost daily.

South of Playa del Carmen

An excellent road, Highway 307, runs directly south from Playa del Carmen and Calica to the Belize border, about 150 miles away. Along the way are many places that you may find more rewarding to visit than Cancún. The choice depends upon your personal interests. In addition to organized tours, car rentals and taxis that can be arranged in port, there are public buses from Playa del Carmen to Tulum town. From there you need to walk a few hundred yards to the temple complex. If you rent a car or hire a taxi, you can combine snorkeling at Xel-Ha or Akumal with sightseeing at Tulum.

Highway 307 runs slightly inland, and because the land is so flat you cannot see the sea from the road. Instead you drive through low, thick brush, which is, frankly, boring from a scenic point of view. (The mileage is indicated from Playa del Carmen.)

Playacar: Next to Playa del Carmen is one of the most extensive resort developments on the Riviera Maya. It is made up of a dozen all-inclusive resorts, running south one after the other along the beach, along with private homes and condominiums, and **Playacar Palace Wyndham Grand Resort** (Paseo Xaman Ha s/n Mza. 26 Fracc; (998-873-4960; 800-635-1836; www.palaceresorts.com; www.golfplayadelcarmen.com), an 18-hole championship golf course, open to the public. Designed by Robert von Hagge, the course (7,202 yards, par 72) has gently sloping hillsides, rock formations, roller-coaster greens, indigenous flora, and wide fairways. It offers a driving range, practice area, putting green and green-side bunker areas, pro shop with Callaway and Titleist equipment and restaurant, the 19th Hole. Greens fees: US$190 with shared cart; $130 after 2 p.m. Club rentals: $35 steel, $50 graphite. The entrance to the golf club is on the main highway, about a mile south of Playa del Carmen. Round-trip transportation to the course US$20. Some ships have golf packages with this club or with several other golf courses on the north side of Playa del Carmen; otherwise, you will need to make arrangements on your own.

Xcaret (pronounced ish-ca-ret; 984-871-5200; www.xcaret.com): A privately owned, 200-acre nature, archaeological, and recreational theme park is 5 miles south of Playa del Carmen and next door to the port of Calica. The site was once an important Mayan commercial port and a ceremonial center where Mayas from all over the peninsula came to purify themselves in the sacred waters of the cenotes (large, natural sinkholes in the limestone that pockmark the Yucatán). The Maya believed the rain god lived in the cenotes and provided the water for their crops.

Xcaret, the Mayan word for "paradise," has nature trails, an aviary, botanical gardens, a museum, recently excavated Mayan ruins, a beach, butterfly attraction, folkloric entertainment, and underwater tunnels and two huge cenotes where you can snorkel in water so clear, you hardly need a mask. The park offers horseback riding, but the most popular and unusual experience is a float down an underground river. There are restaurants, lockers, and thatched umbrellas and chairs for refuge from the bright sun. Xcaret is ideal for families, offering something for everyone. The entrance fee is a steep US$69 adult, $34.50 ages five through twelve, but worth it if you plan to spend the day. Horseback riding and snorkel equipment cost extra. Hours: 8:30 a.m. to 10 p.m. Xcaret's Web site provides details of packages, discounts, and other information.

Xplor (www.xplor.travel): In 2010, the Xcaret group opened a 22 million dollars adventure park next to Xcaret featuring swimming and rafting in underground caverns, zipping along a 2,300 feet zip line and driving in amphibious vehicles through a jungle where crocodiles and jaguars are kept at a safe distance.

Calica (5 miles): South of Playa del Carmen and adjacent to Xcaret is another gateway to the Yucatán, developed primarily as an industrial/commercial port by private investors; cruise ship docking facilities were added later. Calica's protected mooring facilities are its main advantage, enabling cruise ships to dock and remain in port for the entire day—the principal reason cruise lines use it. Its proximity to Xcaret is another advantage. In fact, cruise itineraries that list Xcaret as a port of call most likely dock at Calica. The port facilities include a small restaurant and bar, crafts shop, restrooms, telephone for international calling, and taxi stand, but Calica is not a place to linger. Taxis are plentiful; prices to all the major sites of interest are posted at the dispatcher's kiosk.

Paamul: A short road about 12 miles south of the Xcaret turnoff leads to Paamul Bay with a rocky beach that is popular for beachcombing, bird watching and diving as the reef is only a short distance from shore. Some giant sea turtles come ashore in summer to lay their eggs. Paamul bills itself as the "best kept secret in the Mexican Caribbean" which is probably true, except for RV travelers who have discovered its 200 vehicle trailer park. The small **Hotel Paamul** (www.paamulcabanas.com)

has a beachfront restaurant and **Scuba Mexico** (www.scubamex.com) at the entrance possibly has the less expensive dives in Mexico. One tank dive with equipment is US$39. It also offers cenote dives with 1 instructor for every 4 divers. Excursions depart daily at 9 a.m. and 2 p.m.; reservation required one day in advance. The north side of the bay is a protected area and will not be developed.

Puerto Aventuras (16 miles) (www.puerto aventuras.com): A 766-acre development has a large marina and yacht club, beach club, tennis club, PADI dive center, gym, two hotels and ten condominium buildings, residential homes, nine restaurants, five snack bars, six bars, golf course, shopping complex, disco, bird sanctuary, dolphin aquarium, the CEDAM Nautical Museum, and an archaeological site. It has been designed to retain 65 percent of the area as green space in a natural, park-like setting. If you want to spend the day here and play golf, you should make the arrangements in advance, but you may have to listen to a real estate sales pitch somewhere along the way. Dolphin Discovery (www.dolphindiscovery.com) has a facility here, too.

Kantenah Beach: Farther along, at Kantenah Beach, you can find facilities that make it a good stop for beach lovers—a palapa or thatched-roof restaurant, hammocks rocking in the breeze, volleyball nets, showers, and restrooms.

Bay of Akumal: Sheltered by one of the longest coral reefs in the Western Hemisphere, the Bay of Akumal, 4 miles south of Puerto Aventuras, has seen tremendous development since the early 1990s: fifty hotels, large and small; dive shops; seven restaurants; grocery stores; and more. The beaches are beautiful, and the snorkeling, diving, fishing, and windsurfing are among Mexico's best. You can also explore the surrounding countryside by bike or horseback.

Akumal has seven entrances off the main highway, each leading to a different group of resorts. **Hotel Club Akumal Caribe** (www.hotel akumalcaribe.com), one of the oldest resorts on the bay, welcomes day visitors. You can enjoy the beach, and snorkel gear is available for rent. (Snorkeling packages sold on cruise ships often use this location.) **Akumal Dive Shop** (984-875-9032; www.akumaldiveshop.com) offers a deep dive every morning at 9 a.m., and 40- to 60-foot dives at 11 a.m. and 2 p.m. Single-tank dives are $50; a two-dive package is $70. Freshwater cavern tours are $90 per person. Divers must be open-water-certified.

Xcacel: In another 5 miles or so is a major turtle nesting site.

Aktun-Chen: A road west of the coast between Akumal and Xcacel leads to the 988-acre **Aktunchen Natural Park** (www.aktunchen.com) with trails where visitors might spot local wildlife, such as deer and monkeys, and three caves with an underground river. The main cave, which is more than 600 yards long, has paths and is illuminated. Visitors see stalactites and stalagmites formed more than five million years ago and an underground lake known to ancient Mayans but rediscovered only recently. Hours: 9 a.m. to 4 p.m. daily. Park guided cave tours, US$25 adult; $13 ages three through ten; canopy rides with 10 lines and two suspension bridges; $36; cenote swim $20. Each activity takes about 1 hour 30 minutes. Some cruise ship excursions that visit Aktun-Chen continue on to the beautiful beach at Xpu-Ha for a swim.

Xel-Ha (32 miles): Farther south is Xel-Ha (998-898-1900; www.xel-ha.com), an ecological park set amid tropical forest with an incredible natural aquarium and a network of inlets, lagoons, cenotes, and underground rivers. Here the water is so clear, you don't need a mask to see the fish. It is also a popular swimming and snorkeling spot. Cruise ship shore excursions to Tulum often stop here for passengers to have a swim; some include a picnic lunch. There are trails for hiking or you can explore the park by floating down the waterways in oversize inner tubes. About a mile away, there are Mayan ruins, with murals of birds and jaguars, and a cenote, which attracts wildlife. Visitors have reported seeing jaguars. Admission: daily, basic fee US$39 adult; $15 ages five through eleven, plus tax; under five free. All-inclusive day package (beverage, towels, lockers, snorkel gear, food) $59 adult; $42 child. The park has a **Dolphin Encounters** (998-206-3304; www.delphinusworld .com) facility which has Swim with Dolphins for US$80, and other programs. Reservations can be made online. **Hidden Worlds Cenotes Park** (984-115-4514; www.hiddenworlds.com) offers a variety of excursions here and elsewhere in Riviera Maya, as does **Alltournative** (www.alltournative.com), another adventure style tour company.

Tulum
www.tulum.com

The walled city of Tulum, about 36 miles (less than an hour's drive) from Playa del Carmen, sits dramatically on a cliff overlooking the Caribbean. It is the only known walled city built by the Mayas on the coast. Tulum and other towns of the Yucatán were once connected by an elaborate road system, which is still visible in some sections.

In 1518 a Spanish expedition exploring the Yucatán coast prior to Cortés's conquest of Mexico sighted Tulum. One of its members later wrote, "We saw in the distance a town so large the city of Seville could not be better or larger."

Tulum was one of many coastal towns and temple sites that continued for some time after the Spanish conquest, but for how long we do not know. By the mid-19th century, when Tulum was "rediscovered," most of the former Mayan sites were buried under the growth of the Yucatán jungle—and still are.

When compared with Chichén Itzá or Uxmal, the ruins of Tulum are not grand, but they are interesting. The site dates from about A.D. 700 to 1000, the post-Classic period after the Mayan civilization had reached its peak, and shows the influence of the Toltecs, who conquered the Yucatán in the 10th century. Originally named Zama, "the dawn," because it faced east to the sea, It was protected by the reefs from invasion by way of the sea. The other three sides had walls more than 6 feet thick and varying in height from 4 to 19 feet. There were five entrances; today's entrance is on the west.

The site is dominated by El Castillo, the Castle, the name the Spaniards always gave to the central grand structure of a temple complex. The view of the sea from the top of the castle is lovely. After passing through the entrance and walking directly east, you will see a group of buildings—the Temple of the Frescos on the south and the Great Palace on the north. Directly in front is the Castle, approached by a long series of steps. The first level was the dance platform for religious observances. The Temple of the Frescos is the best preserved and most interesting structure at the site because it still has remnants of the murals that once covered the walls of all the buildings in the complex.

On the east side of the Castle is the Temple of the Descending God, so called because, in the band of decoration over the doorway, the figure of the god is pointed toward the ground. The symbol appears in the Castle ornamentation and elsewhere and is said to represent the bee god of the Mayans. The cultivation of bees was important to the ancient Mexicans, because honey served as their sweetener; they had no sugar.

On the west side of the Castle is the Temple of the Initial Series, which takes its name from the method by which Mayan dates were calculated.

The once-remote ruins of Tulum are now reached by a four-lane highway, and shops line the way near the entrance. From the parking lot, a tram provides transportation to the site for those who do not care to walk the ¼-mile distance. Entrance fee is US$3.50; $3 for video camera use. Guides are available. Booklets are available for purchase at the site as well. Hours: daily 8 a.m. to 5 p.m.

Over the past decade, the town of Tulum has grown from a tiny village to a large one with hotels, restaurants, and shops. The one which has gotten the most publicity and is suggested for a stop is jungle-chic La Zebra (994-115-4627; www .lazebratulum.com), Tulum's hip beach cantina and tequila bar, run by California beach transplant Heather Froeming, manager, and Mexico City native Lina Avila and her sisters—all experienced in the serious tequila and home cooking they serve.

Sian Ka'an
www.siankaan.org;
www.visitsiankaan.com

A vast region covering 2,026 square miles (or 1.3 million acres) of a peninsula and coastal waters, stretching 100 miles south of Tulum down the Caribbean coast, Sian Ka'an was declared a Biosphere Reserve in 1986 and added to UNESCO's World Heritage List. The largest nature preserve in Mexico, it is made up of one-third tropical forest, one-third wetland and mangroves, and one-third coastal and marine environments. It's inhabited by jaguar, margay, cougar, puma, lynx, ocelot, monkey, manatee, tapir, and white-tailed deer, as well as

340 species of birds. It's also rich in flora, with more than 1,200 plant species. Part of the reserve is the barrier reef fronting the Yucatán, which forms part of the world's second longest reef, stretching south to Honduras. Scattered throughout the reef are cays, or islets, that provide nesting grounds for thousands of water birds, including such rare species as the jabiru stork and roseate spoonbill, and four species of endangered sea turtles.

The reserve consists of three parts where environmental conservation and sustainable development are working together: a Buffer Zone, where fishing, tourism activity, and agriculture are permitted under certain guidelines; a Gathering Zone, reserved strictly for local people to hunt, fish, gather food, and build; and a Core Zone, accounting for 80 percent of the area, where only scientific research is allowed. The region is dotted with archaeological sites, some of which are 20,000 years old.

Friends of Sian Ka'an Association (Plaza America, Cobá No. 5, Third Floor, No. 48-50, Cancún; 998-884-9583; fax: 998-887-3080), is a private, nonprofit conservation organization promoting national and international support for the reserve and managing certain projects under the authority of SEDUE (Secretary of Urban Development and Ecology). The association offers an all-day tour escorted by a naturalist guide, with bird-watching and snorkeling in a cenote. During the winter peak season, you need to make reservations at least one month in advance. With advance arrangements, the association's tour bus can pick up cruise passengers at the ferry dock in Playa del Carmen. The tour includes a three-hour boat ride through the coastal lagoons and lunch at Anna y José, a rustic seaside inn.

Excursions are also provided by local tour companies that specialize in adventure travel, such as Eco-Colors (www.ecotravelmexico.com) which has tours on Tues and Thurs for US$146 per person (less 15% online) and offers kayaking, hiking, and snorkeling, $129, as well as private tours. Visit Sian Ka'an (Caapechen Visitor Center, Sian Ka'an Biosphere Reserve, Tulum, Quintana Roo, Mexico; 984-118-2555; 984-111-3812; e-mail@visitsiankaan .com) arranges nature cruises in the mangroves, reef snorkel, and fly fishing and others, from US$ 90 adults, $70 children ages four to twelve.

West of Playa del Carmen

Cobá

The archaeological site of Cobá is 25 miles inland from Tulum. More extensive than Chichén Itzá, Cobá covers 10 square miles with an estimated 6,500 structures. The area is dominated by a building known as the Church, which stands ten stories high. Two miles away is Nohoch Mul, the largest pyramid found in the Yucatán, rising 120 steps to the top at an incline that is almost perpendicular.

Little of the huge site has been excavated, and scholars do not yet know its origin, except to establish that it is older than Tulum, and suggesting it may belong to a civilization even earlier than the Maya, since pre-Classical remnants have been found.

Getting to Inland Archaeological Sites

To visit Chichén Itzá, you should take the shore excursion by air or motor coach offered by your cruise line. If not, and your cruise ship remains in port long enough to make the trip, ask your travel agent to book your arrangements in advance— there probably won't be enough time upon your arrival in port to do so. Excursions leave early in order to maximize time at the site.

There are several alternatives. First, some ships remain in Cozumel overnight or until late in the day, enabling passengers to make the full-day excursion to Chichén Itzá. (See the Shore Excursions section earlier in this chapter.) Second, when a cruise ship visits both Cozumel and Playa del Carmen, it may be possible to leave the ship in one port and rejoin it in another on the same day.

Highway 180 leads to Chichén Itzá and Mérida from either Cancún or Playa del Carmen; the drive takes about two and a half hours. The drive from Chichén Itzá to Mérida is 70 miles or one and a half hours; from Mérida to Uxmal is 35 miles (about an hour). Flights from Cozumel to Cancún take twenty minutes and operate about every two hours throughout the day. There are also flights from Cozumel and Cancún to Chichén Itzá and Mérida. Excursions from Cozumel by air fly directly to Chichén Itzá. Occasionally, cruise ships call at Progreso, the port for Mérida.

Chichén Itzá

The most important site of antiquity in the Yucatán, Chichén Itzá (pronounced che-cha-neat-za) was recently named one of the "New Seven Wonders of the World" by a mail and online vote of a hundred million people from around the world. The site is 125 miles west of Cancún and Playa del Carmen on Highway 180, the road to Mérida. The city was originally founded in A.D. 432 but abandoned in 608. It was settled again in 960 and prospered until about 1200.

Today the site covers an area of about 6 square miles. One part has the great pyramids and temples of the Maya; another was built by their successors, the Toltec, who invaded the Yucatán in the 10th century. The Toltec, a fierce tribe from Tula in central Mexico, brought with them their belief in Kukulcan, the man-god represented as the plumed serpent, and introduced the practice of human sacrifice to the Maya.

El Castillo: The first major excavations were undertaken by Carnegie Tech over a period of twenty years. The site is dominated by El Castillo, a giant pyramid eighteen stories high. An interior tunnel leads into a tiny throne room where you see a red jaguar shaped into a bench and set with jade eyes and turquoise mosaics. It is thought to be a throne. Jade is not native to the Yucatán, so its use here is one more question in the Mayan puzzle.

The Castle is a calendar in three dimensions. On each of the four sides, ninety-one steps lead to the top; these, along with the upper platform, correspond to the 365 days of the year. On each side of the stairways there are nine terraces representing the two seasons; combined, they correspond to the eighteen months of the Mayan year. The steps are about 6 inches wide and rise at least a foot each. The climb is steep, but worthwhile. From the top the Yucatán jungle stretches as far as the eye can see.

At the equinoxes in Mar and Sept, the light and shadow on the steps cast a zigzag pattern from the temple on top of the pyramid to the sculptured snake's head at the bottom of the stairs: The pattern looks like the undulating body of a serpent. For the Maya, the sight represented the return of Kukulcan and heralded the change of season.

The building is so perfectly constructed acoustically that you can clap your hands at its base and hear the echo ripple up each step, and then project itself to listeners standing hundreds of yards away across the giant open courtyard the Castle once dominated.

Temple of the Warriors: The Temple of the Warriors has intricate carving and 1,000 columns.

Ball Court: The 650-foot-long Ball Court is another acoustic wonder: A person standing at one end talking in a normal voice can be heard at the far end. The court was the setting for a ritual game known as pok-a-pok, said to resemble basketball or soccer and played with a hard rubber ball about the size of a baseball. The rules dictated that when the ball was put through a high stone hoop at the side of the court, the game was over. Only the knee, foot, or elbow (but not the hands) could be used. The games sometimes lasted three or four days, and then the defeated captain was conducted to an adjoining ceremonial platform where he forfeited his head to the victors' swords.

New research has led scholars to believe the opponents in this game were prisoners—perhaps of a rival city-state or tribe who may have been Mayan themselves—forced to participate as a final humiliation. The bloodletting at the end of the match was, apparently, a basic element of Mayan life associated with major events such as birth and death. Human sacrifices had mystical meanings we cannot quite fathom, intended to connect the natural and supernatural worlds. (Such scholarly explanations, of course, do not make the knowledge of such brutality any less revolting, but before we condemn the Mayas, it is good to remember that Roman gladiators were little better.)

Another puzzle: No one has discovered what the Maya did with their dead. Human bones have been discovered in only a few of the ruins, a fact that alludes to human sacrifice, introduced into Mayan rites by the Toltec.

Ceremonial Well: A raised ceremonial road leads to the giant ceremonial well, measuring 350 feet long, 150 feet wide, and 60 feet deep, with sinister-looking greenish black water. A sinkhole in limestone known as a cenote, it was once the focal point of the Maya' religious rites where, annually, thousands of people gathered to pray to Chaac, the rain god, who was believed to live in the well and provide water for the crops.

During the ceremony a young maiden clad in precious jewels was fed to the god. These young virgins were trained by the priests to accept their own sacrifice as the high point of the group's religious life. Weighted down with gold and silver ornaments, they quickly drowned, becoming brides of the rain god and ensuring good crops in the coming season. Knowledge of the events has been pieced together from carvings on the sides of the temples and the thousands of silver, gold, jade, and bone relics recovered from the well.

Chac Mool: At Chichén Itzá and elsewhere you will frequently see statues of the ceremonial Chac Mool, a partially reclining stone figure that seems almost whimsical—until you learn that his belly was used to receive the heart of the sacrifice during the temple rites.

There is an entrance fee to the antiquity site. Temple rubbings are available at local shops, as are books, literature, postcards, Mexican crafts, and souvenirs.

Between Chichén Itzá and Uxmal, there are several lesser-known Mayan sites, such as **Izamal**, noted for its yellow facades and its light-and-sound show. However, unless you have visited both Chichén Itzá and Uxmal in the past, you will not have time in a day's visit to take in these sites, too.

Uxmal

The structures of Uxmal are considered the finest pre-Columbian relics in Mexico. Located 35 miles south of Mérida (about an hour's drive), Uxmal (pronounced *oosh-mal*) is pure Maya without the Toltec overlay. It is built of yellowish stone rather than the gray material that gives Chichén Itzá such a sober, forbidding appearance. The site dates from about A.D. 600 and was inhabited for about 800 years. As many as 250,000 people lived in a 4½-square-mile area around the government and religious center, which was filled with magnificent buildings.

Palace of the Governors: The massive, ornately decorated Palace of the Governors, constructed with more than 20,000 cut stones, covers five acres. It is built on an elevated terrace that measures 600 feet by 500 feet. The 320-foot facade has lovely filigree of detailed bas-relief, all the more remarkable when you remember that the Mayas did not have metal tools with which to work.

Pyramid of the Magician: Another imposing structure is the Pyramid of the Magician, also known as the House of the Dwarf, with 118 steep steps leading to the top. According to legend, the pyramid was built on the site of the house of a sorceress who grieved because she had no children. Finally she hatched an egg, and from it came a small child who grew up to be a dwarf. When he was fully grown, she urged him to challenge the Mayan ruler, who in turn condemned him to death unless he could build a house higher than any other in one night. And he did.

Nunnery: The Nunnery, named by the Spaniards, was not a nunnery but part of a quadrangle of four temples that surrounded a courtyard. It is noteworthy for its bas-relief carvings and arches. During the sound-and-light show, presented nightly in Spanish and in English, audiences sit in this area to watch the show.

Authorities on Mayan civilization have reported finding the key to deciphering the glyphs on some Mayan temples. If true, it may mean we can at last begin to unlock the mysteries of the Maya.

Costa Maya

www.puertocostamaya.com

Costa Maya, a new port on Western Caribbean itineraries, is much more than a place to dock ships. It is a broad concept and a major development intended to open up southern Quintana Roo, a part of Mexico mostly unknown to tourists. (Quintana Roo, Mexico's newest state and the same state in which Cancún and Cozumel are located, is one of three states that make up the Yucatán Peninsula.)

Located in the southeastern corner of the peninsula, almost to the Belize border, Costa Maya is the name of both a port complex and an 80-mile finger of land with Caribbean-washed white-sand beaches, jungle-thick scrub, and mangroves running from Punta Herrero—a fishing village on the shores of Espiritu Santo Bay on the south side of the Sian Ka'an Biosphere Reserve—to Xcalak at the southern tip, and only a forty-five-minute ferry ride from Ambergris Caye in the barrier reef off Belize.

Chances are you will not find Costa Maya on a map, but you may find Majahual (or Mahahual) midway along the coast. A small fishing village of about 2,000 people, Majahual is half-mile from the port and the nucleus of the Costa Maya development. Roads, added only in December 2000, run north and south of the port, edging the mangroves and leading to small hotels and hamlets. There is also a small airport, currently served only by charter airlines. Electricity came in 2001; and new infrastructure is some of the US$100 million investment being made here by Fonatur, the quasi-governmental agency that developed Cancún. In Majahual, about a mile of the Malecon, or boardwalk along the waterfront leading to the port, has been completed.

The port and the coast are only part of the story about Costa Maya. The region behind the coast is equally compelling and full of delightful surprises, starting with Chetumal, the pretty capital of the state of Quintana Roo, and its attractions, as well as the prodigious Mayan antiquities—as many as 800 sites—in the surrounding area. Add to this a 30-mile-long lagoon with boating, kayaking, and fishing; seven cenotes for swimming and diving; a tropical jungle alive with birds and wildlife; and one of the most unusual hotels in Mexico, and you can understand why Costa Maya is being called the next Cancún—but with a difference: the promise of low-impact, ecologically sensitive development.

Port Profile: Costa Maya

The first phase of the port of Costa Maya, representing an investment of N$21 million and built by PTM (Promociones Turisticas Mahahual), began operation in Feb 2001. The second phase anticipates the creation of New Majahual, a community for 20,000 people, and excavation and restoration of dozens of Mayan sites and inland attractions in the years to come. Costa Maya is unusual in many ways. First, the builders went to the major cruise lines and asked, "What do you want or need at the port?"—and they listened! Arriving cruise passengers are not likely to be aware of this, but Royal Caribbean, Princess, and Carnival, among others, advised PTM almost every step of the way. The port's design incorporates aspects of Mexico's history—Mayan, Spanish, and modern—in its

Costa Maya

architecture and facilities, beginning with the terminal entrance, which replicates the facade of a Mayan temple with a high pointed arch. Passengers who do not want to walk can ride the short distance from their ship to the terminal entrance in Disney-style trams pulled by a caboose.

Beyond, they enter a large plaza framed on the seaside with three huge palapas whose high, pointed thatched roofs are an expression of indigenous houses seen in villages throughout the Yucatán. The first two palapas are devoted to crafts; the third houses a restaurant serving Mayan dishes and lobster. On the far side of the plaza are two large swimming pools with a swim-up bar. And beyond

the pool you'll find an amphitheater, where performances of Mexican folklore are staged at intervals throughout the day, and another restaurant overlooking the sea.

Around the colonnaded perimeter of the plaza are modern shops, mostly branches of jewelry, clothing, ceramics, and silver stores based in Cancún and Cozumel. At the center of the complex is a bell tower, a typical Spanish feature of every town and village in Mexico. The bell tower marks the exit where passengers find taxis and other services, and sightseeing buses waiting to take them on tours. In spring 2010, a Hard Rock Café opened and a Mayan Museum was added.

On the north side of the port is a beach club owned and operated by the port. It has a restaurant, bar, and full amenities; access to the club is sold as a shore excursion on cruise ships. At Uvero, about 15 miles north of the port, a former naval marina, was converted into a beach club for cruise passengers. It has a restaurant, bar, palapas, hammocks kayaking, and non-motorized water sports. There are freshwater showers, restrooms, and changing rooms. Before the new development began, **Xcalak,** a settlement at the south end of the coast, was merely a spot for divers to pass on their way to Chinchorro Bank, the atoll 18 miles offshore. Now Xcalak is developing, too, with rustic beachfront bungalows and small hotels, and facilities for boating, bird-watching, diving, and sportfishing. Xcalak has a landing strip as well as ferry service to Chetumal.

Banco Chinchorro: The largest atoll in Mexico and part of the second longest barrier reef in the world, Chinchorro, offers superb snorkeling and diving. Larger than the island of Cozumel, the atoll covers about 500 square miles, most of it taken up by a lagoon of crystal-clear water that is 3 to 25 feet deep and drops to 600 feet and more outside the atoll. Chinchorro also has three mangrove areas: Cayo Norte, Cayo Sur, and Cayo Centro, the main one for tourists and local fishermen.

On the reefs, divers and snorkelers can see a great variety of coral—elkhorn, staghorn, brain, star, and soft corals—and sponges of all sizes. Angel, parrot, damsel, and tang are some of the colorful tropical fish that inhabit the atoll, while turtles feed on seagrass beds, and barracuda, snapper, bass, and grouper visit constantly.

Chinchorro has another attraction: sunken ships. Spanish galleons, 19th-century merchant ships, and modern cargo boats—all foundered on the reefs. **Dream Time Diving** (www.dreamtime diving.com) is a local dive operator; however, an excursion would need to be scheduled well in advance as a permit is need. The trip from Majahual to Chinchorro takes about one hour and half.

Costa Maya Excursions

The cruise lines and Costa Maya have added many excursions that provide the opportunity to learn more about the region's rich history, visit more of the Mayan sites that are described later in this chapter, and participate in a wider range of sports. Be sure to review the online listings of shore excursions offered by your cruise line in advance of your trip. Excursions to antiquity sites involve walking and climbing on jungle trails. Bring sunscreen, hat, sunglasses, insect repellent, and wear comfortable walking shoes.

Hiking at Pueblo Chiclero: 3 hours; US$82. After an hour's drive, you hike to a chiclero camp where you can see the chewing gum (Chiclets) production process. En route the guide will tell you about this little-known culture and its traditions.

Beach Snorkel Adventure: 3.5 hours; US$44 to $56 per person, including transportation, equipment, and guide. A forty-five-minute ride to a site where snorkelers have easy entrance into water. Scuba packages are also available.

Bike and Kayak Adventure: 2-3 hours; US$48 to $59 per person. Biking south along a dirt road, you pass long stretches of beach, a mangrove lagoon, and a tiny fishing village. After a swim, you paddle along a nearby reef in a two-person kayak. The return to pier takes a different route.

Kayak Creek: Kayaking in mangroves and water lilies in the emerald lagoon of Uchben Kah Park is a new excursion. There's also a walking and biking tour through the park over the old road the Mayans used to trade with neighboring Belize.

Beach Horseback Riding: 3 hours; $92. Saddle up for an adventure along the Caribbean coast; spend time at the beach. Minimum age: twelve years; maximum weight 250 pounds.

Chacchoben Mayan Ruins: 4 hours; US$72 to $79 per person. (See the description later in this section.)

Kohunlich Mayan Ruins: 7 hours; US$82 to $149 per person. (See the description later in this chapter.) A two-hour drive from the port, the immense site, west of Chetumal, are among the most extensive ruins in the region and encompass a broad range of architectural styles. They are known especially for the enormous masks sculpted on the temples. Another version combines Kohunlich with a visit to the ruins at Dzibanche.

Bacalar Highlights & Seven Color Lagoon: 5 hours; $95 to $115 adult; $88 to $104 child. (See description later in the chapter.)

Biomaya Bacalar: A new zip lining excursion over the trees at eye level with parrots, monkeys, and other wildlife. Afterwards, you can cool off in the Seven Color Lagoon.

Fishing Excursion: 5-6 hours; $219. In this fisherman's paradise, try your hand at fly fishing with a professional guide.

Harley Davidson and ATV Tours: New excursions on Harleys ride along the coast and some inland roads, and an all terrain vehicle version takes to off-road trails.

Exploring the Interior

The interior region offers attractions as interesting and beautiful as the seashore. Cruise lines shore excursions offer a variety of basic tours that include two, three, or perhaps more of the following highlights. (The road west from Majahual meets Highway 307, the main road between Tulum and Chetumal, at the village of Limones. Directly west is the Mayan site of Chacchoben; a turn south leads to Bacalar and Chetumal, 87 miles.)

Chacchoben: In a wooded area a few miles inland from the main road is an important Mayan site that is only now being excavated for the first time. Here the jungle has won: Trees and thick vegetation cover most of the site. Nonetheless, as many as two dozen mounds and pyramids can be distinguished. Of them, nine buildings have been identified and are being studied, and two are being restored.

Three layers of building can be distinguished, indicating a continuation of a dynasty—that is, the son of the ruler built atop his father's structures, and the grandson did likewise. What makes the site particularly fascinating is its state of preservation. In studying and restoring the site, archaeologists are retaining the huge trees growing out of the ancient structures, removing vegetation only in places where they must for research or to stabilize the structures.

A short distance from Chacchoben is the Mayan village of Nohbec, on a small lagoon. Some cruise lines offer a visit to the village for culture/adventure-type excursions. Also, the nearby hamlet of Pedro A Santos has one of several Mennonite communities in this area.

Bacalar and Bacalar Lagoon: The main Tulum–Chetumal highway south skirts the 30-mile-long Bacalar Lagoon to the resort town of Bacalar. Known as the "lagoon of seven colors" for its stunning shades of blue and turquoise, Bacalar Lagoon flows into the Rio Hondo (on the Belize border) and into Chetumal Bay via a network of shallow channels. The banks of the mile-wide lagoon are dotted with vacation villas of Chetumal's prosperous families and waterside cafes serving excellent local seafood and regional cuisine. Boating, fishing, waterskiing, kayaking, and windsurfing can be arranged at the Yacht Club (Club de Yates), a restaurant and boat dock.

Bacalar, 23 miles north of Chetumal, was the most important Mayan community in the region at the time of the Spanish conquest and put up great resistance to it. After the conquistador Gaspar Pacheco won a victory of sorts, he founded Villa de Salaminca de Bacalar in 1545. But the settlement was never a success due to the Mayas' hostility and refusal to work. Nonetheless, with access to the sea via Chetumal Bay, the Spaniards were able to develop Bacalar as a port for goods bound for Europe. Among the most important products was palo de tinte or dyewood, a source of dye prized by Europeans for royal garments.

Fort of San Felipe: The city's wealth made it a target of pirates; it was attacked so often that in 1729, the governor ordered the construction of a fort. Now restored and housing a small museum, the fort is an excellent example of 18th-century military architecture. The layout is a square plaza surrounded by thick stone walls, a deep moat planted with sharp stakes instead of water for defense, and four rhomboid-shaped ramparts mounted with cannons.

Cenote Azul: Directly south of Bacalar is the Cenote Azul, one of seven cenotes in the area and said to be the deepest sinkhole in the Yucatán. Surrounded by lush vegetation, Cenote Azul is filled with cold, clear water almost 200 feet deep. Swimming and diving are allowed.

Chetumal

A Maya center in antiquity covering the area from Bacalar to the Rio Hondo, the natural border between Mexico and Belize, *Chetumal* means "the place where the red cedar is plentiful." Despite their conquest of Mexico, the Spaniards were never able to subjugate the fiercely independent people of this region and, after several attempts, abandoned the area, leaving the Maya to their own devices.

The present town, set on the Bay of Chetumal, was founded in 1898 and is the capital of Quintana Roo province. Today, as in its past, it serves as a gateway to Belize and Central America. A typical Mexican town with a central plaza and market, Chetumal is the real Mexico and the antithesis of Cancún. Its tree-shaded streets are lined with modest, single-story buildings and homes. It has a modern airport, hotels, restaurants, car rental offices, travel agencies, and a ferry linking it to Xcalak across the bay on the Costa Maya. The town market is strictly a local one. For incurable shoppers, Chetumal is famous for its many shoe stores full of inexpensive footwear.

Surprisingly, Chetumal is a more developed and sophisticated town than you would expect in this seemingly isolated corner of Mexico. A pretty town with parks and gardens, it has a graceful parkway skirting the bay, a large botanical garden, three museums, two universities, and an interesting ethnic population of East Indians, Lebanese, Chinese, Western Europeans, and other foreigners who began arriving here in the early 1900s.

Museum of Mayan Culture: Located in the center of town next to the market, the **Museo de la Cultura** (983-832-6838) is by far the most important attraction here. This small museum is exquisitely conceived and executed, and—through the use of sophisticated multimedia—it provides an invaluable introduction to the ancient Maya and their world. The exhibits include miniature displays of important Mayan temples from Chichén Itzá to Tikal to Copan. All exhibits are labeled in Spanish and English. Hours: 9 a.m. to 7 p.m. Tues. Admission: adult $3; child $1. The exhibits are divided into eight sections, each dealing with a different aspect of Mayan culture:

- *The Maya* reflects the people themselves, from their physical appearance and language to their natural environment and history.

- *Between the Mountain and the Sea* portrays the Mayas' relationship with the environment, the technology they developed, and other cultural advances.

- *The Place of Thrones and High Places* displays Mayan architecture and cities, models of civic and ceremonial buildings, and information on urban planning.

- *The Men of Corn* depicts the Mayan economy, daily life, and activities such as hunting, fishing, gathering, farming, and trading.

- *Cosmovision of the Mayan People* focuses on the ties between people and the spiritual world, the myth of creation, and funerary customs.

- *The Wisdom of the Ancients* showcases the Mayas' knowledge of the stars, time, and numerical and writing systems.

- *The Foreigners* shows the Maya cultural contacts and links they forged with peoples such as the Teotihuacan and Toltec, among others.

- *The End of the World* highlights the arrival of the Spanish conquistadores and their deeds and the prophesies predicting the fall of the Mayan civilization.

Chetumal's other museums are the **City Museum** and the **Museo de Constituyentes,** which features a scale model of Payo Obispo, the town's original name, as it appeared in the 1930s when the streets were lined with colorful wooden houses built in the Caribbean style.

Touring the city, you will pass the **Palacio del Gobierno,** or state administration building; the **Congreso del Estado,** or state congress hall; and a monument, **Homenaje al Mestizaje,** depicting a white man, his Indian wife, and their offspring. The statue honors the mestizo race, said to have begun at the dawn of the Spanish era with the union of a Mayan woman and Gonzalo Guerrero, a shipwrecked Spaniard who fathered the first persons of mixed Indian and Spanish blood and who took up the Maya' cause against the conquistadores.

Chetumal Bay is a huge, shallow bay with beaches; it's surrounded by mangroves, marshes, and forest. It offers boating and swimming and a host of moderate waterfront seafood restaurants, such as Christy's in Calderitas, a popular beach

5 miles north of Chetumal. An isolated section in the northeast corner of the bay is a manatee sanctuary.

Mayan Sites in the Chetumal Region

Today, as in ancient times, Chetumal is surrounded by agricultural land and dense forest. Hidden in the jungle fastness are an estimated 800 Mayan sites, according to infrared surveys. Only about two dozen have had serious study and are being restored. Instead of clearing the land that results in the manicured look of Chichén Itzá, the encroaching jungle is being retained, giving scientists a clearer picture of the site's history and providing visitors with remarkable views. All Mexican archaeological sites are protected areas and therefore are havens for wildlife, especially birds.

Oxtankah: (north of Chetumal on the road to Calderitas; turn left at km 11.5 and follow the signs). *Oxtankah* means "three neighborhoods" in the Mayan language, and it has also been translated as the "place of the ramon." The ramon, or breadnut tree, bears a nut gathered by the ancient Maya and ground into flour. The site was first settled by the Maya during the Early Classic period, A.D. 200 to 600. Remnants from the period have survived at the Plaza of the Bees and Plaza of the Columns, the two areas open to visitors.

The buildings, like others in southern Quintana Roo, show the influence of the Peten (Tikal) region of Guatemala, with which the inhabitants traded. Sometime after A.D. 600, Oxtankah was abandoned. Eight hundred or so years later, the Maya returned and used the stones from ancient structures to build a modest settlement. Some of these have survived also.

By 1531 the Spaniards had arrived and christened the settlement Villa Real de Chetumal. But the Mayas' hostility forced them to leave within two years. The Spaniards built a church, of which the archway that supported the roof over the altar and remnants of the baptistery remain. The presence of Mayan and European buildings in one locale makes Oxtankah unusual. There is a small admission fee.

Kohunlich: (40 miles southwest of Chetumal via the Escarcega–Campeche Highway 186; exit south at km 60 to the hamlet of Francisco Villa and follow signs for last 5 miles). One of southern Quintana Roo's most important archaeological sites, Kohunlich was a ceremonial center and home of a powerful dynasty with links to cities in Campeche and Tikal in Guatemala. Despite external influence, experts say, they developed their own distinctive art and architecture. Kohunlich and its surrounding sites were probably inhabited throughout the Classic period, A.D. 250 to 900, and abandoned after 1200.

Kohunlich is named for a nearby logging camp called Cohoon Ridge—a reference to the cohune, a gigantic palm tree abundant here and growing on the ridge (*licht*). The site was discovered in 1912 by explorer Raymond Merwin and excavated in the 1960s by Victor Segovia, who found three periods of construction.

Erected on a slope, the Temple of the Masks is the most important temple on the site and gets its name from the monumental, 6-foot-high stucco masks that line the staircase and reflect the complexity of ancient Mayan society. Experts believe these outstanding works of art represent ancient rulers who portrayed themselves as the sun god, Kinich Ahau, in order to legitimize their rule. The masks are framed with anthropomorphic figures associated with the jaguar, god of the underworld. Thus the symbolism of the masks places the rulers at the center of the universe.

The ceremonial heart of the city during the Late Classic period was dominated by the Palace of the Stelae and the buildings around it, aligned east–west on the central axis and probably used for civic events and administrative functions. The Acropolis, on the northwest, is positioned so that during the spring equinox the moon shines through an opening in the building.

There are many other structures. The majestic North Palace was the residence of a great ruler, built on top of an older building. Another group known as the Complex of the 27 Stairs housed the nobility. It is accessed via stairs that lead to a courtyard with various rooms and terraces. Several tombs have been found in the area. Admission: 30 pesos.

The Explorean Kohunlich

A few miles from the antiquity site might be the biggest surprise in southern Quintana Roo. To call it a rustic jungle lodge, as do the owners, Fiesta Americana, is a little misleading. True, it's a hotel, it's in the jungle, and from a distance the thatched roofs of the cottages piercing the forest canopy appear rustic, but make no mistake, Explorean Kohunlich is luxury in every way.

The lobby, fronted by a reflecting pool, sits under a tall palapa and opens onto a view stretching across the treetops of the surrounding jungle for as far as the eye can see. The reception area steps down to a lounge, fitted with stylish casual sofas and chairs and accessories in natural woods and textures. To one side is the open-air dining room; to the other, a long, narrow swimming pool with lounge chairs and umbrellas perched at the jungle's edge, a health club and spa, and a small meeting room. In the garden at the foot of the pool are two small, igloo-shaped structures where a steam bath treatment is given using local herbs based on a Mayan ritual to drive away bad spirits.

Narrow paths wind down through the forest along stone walls to the cottages, each with two suites. Each of the forty-two rooms has a large bedroom, marbled bath, and a terrace furnished like a living room with views overlooking the jungle canopy—an ideal perch for early-morning bird-watching—and a hammock, just waiting for an occupant.

The decor, uncluttered and understated throughout, uses earth-tone fabrics and local wood, stone, and marble with sophisticated renderings of Mexican motifs. There is an exquisite attention to detail. Explorean Kohunlich (5-201-8350; fax: 52-5-201-8450; www.theexplorean.com.mx) Some cruise ship itineraries stop at the resort.

Dzibanche: (Highway 186 via the turnoff to Morocoy; Dzibanche is 2 miles beyond). Dzibanche, deep in the forest north of Kohunlich, was a powerful city that flourished from A.D. 300 to 1200 and traded with Mayan centers in Campeche and Guatemala. The site was discovered in 1927 by Thomas Gann, who named it *Dzibanche*, meaning "carved in wood," after carvings that deal with the settlement's important dates found on lintels of zapote wood in Temple VI, or the Temple of the Lintels.

The Maya used timber in their art and architecture, but few wooden artifacts have survived due to the region's tropical climate.

Temple I, an Early Classic pyramid and Dzibanche's finest structure, was adorned with giant masks on each side of the staircase. The pyramid is also known as the Temple of the Owl after a fine vessel with a sculpted lid in the shape of an owl, found in the tomb. Here, too, the tomb of an ancient ruler surrounded by offerings of jade, alabaster, obsidian, shell, and ceramic was uncovered. Elements in the design of the buildings on the north and south are said to symbolize the nine levels of the underworld, leading experts to think that they were associated with burials.

Temple II, or the Temple of the Cormorants, the oldest part of the town, has been excavated and restored. The complex owes its name to the polychrome burial vessel decorated with cormorants discovered during excavation. Gann Plaza is a courtyard surrounded by seven buildings, including Structure XII, known as the Temple of the Captives due to the carving of captive warriors on the steps.

Natural Attractions

Southern Quintana Roo has large protected areas of wetlands, where bird life is abundant with more than 300 species, and jungle that is home to the endangered jaguar, howler monkey, tapir, peccary, and other animals. Farmers in villages such as **Tres Garantias,** on the edge of the forest reserve west of Chetumal, live off the land and harvest hardwoods from the forest. A few have converted portions of their land into ecotourism projects designed to protect the land and generate income.

Cenote del Crocodilo Dorado (Sinkhole of the Golden Crocodile). Located by the Hondo River near La Union, the cenote is inhabited by a golden crocodile, according to a local legend, that occasionally makes an appearance. The area is popular for bird-watching and hiking on jungle trails. Excursions can be arranged through agencies in Chetumal.

Rio Hondo: Known to the Mayas as Nohoch Ucum, or great river, the jungle river is the natural border between Mexico and Belize; both countries have equal rights to it. The 63-mile-long river is entirely navigable and was used extensively for trade in ancient times. Particularly lucrative in colonial times was harvesting dyewood, from which a dye prized in Europe was extracted. Rio Hondo has mangrove islets, and its banks are alive with deer, tapir, agouti, and a variety of birds. Cruising the river, you will see herons, ospreys, iguanas, monkeys, and perhaps manatees.

Central America and
the Panama Canal

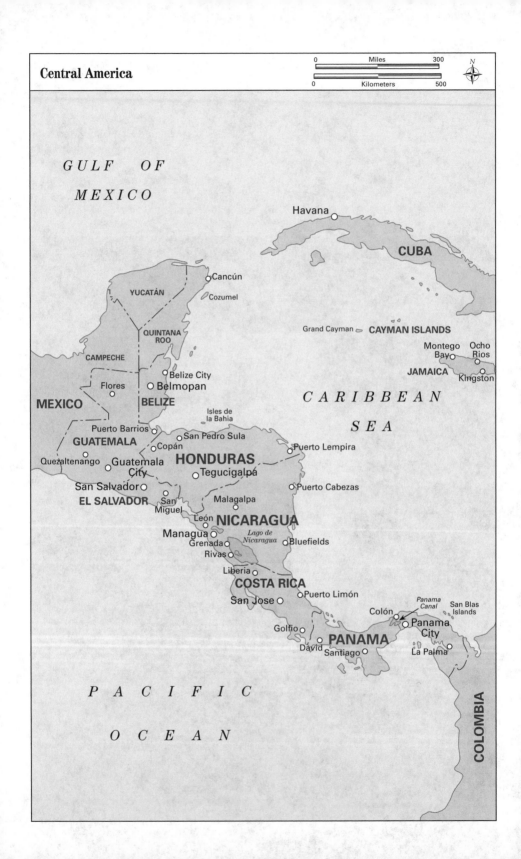

Central America

Miles 0 — 300
Kilometers 0 — 500

N

GULF   OF

MEXICO

Havana

CUBA

Cancún

Cozumel

YUCATÁN

QUINTANA
ROO

CAMPECHE

Grand Cayman **CAYMAN ISLANDS**

Montego
Bay
Ocho
Rios

JAMAICA Kingston

Belize City
Flores Belmopan

MEXICO **BELIZE**

Isles de
la Bahia

CARIBBEAN

Puerto Barrios

SEA

GUATEMALA San Pedro Sula
Copán Puerto Lempira

Quezaltenango Guatemala **HONDURAS**
City
Tegucigalpá

San Salvador Puerto Cabezas

EL SALVADOR San
Miguel Malagalpa

León **NICARAGUA**

Managua *Lago de*
Nicaragua
Grenada Bluefields

Rivas

Liberia

COSTA RICA
Puerto Limón

San Jose *Panama*
Canal San Blas
Islands

Colón
Panama
City
Golfio
David Santiago **PANAMA** La Palma

PACIFIC

COLOMBIA

OCEAN

Central America

The land that forms a bridge between North and South America is a complex of seven nations—Belize, Guatemala, Honduras, El Salvador, Nicaragua, Costa Rica, and Panama—dissimilar as often as they are alike. Although the landmass stretches across some 2,000 miles from Mexico to Colombia, separating the Caribbean Sea from the Pacific Ocean, the area is actually quite small: The seven countries together are not as large as Texas.

To most of us from the United States, the countries of Central America seem exotic and distant, but they are, in fact, among our closest neighbors. All except El Salvador have coastlines washed by the Caribbean Sea. Yet with the exception of Panama and the Panama Canal, the cruise world has largely ignored these countries as places to visit.

Topography, tradition, and turmoil can probably share equal blame. A look at the map reveals a spine of high mountains running almost unbroken from Mexico to Panama and reaching more than 12,500 feet at its highest peaks. From their clouded and rain-forested slopes, the terrain, carved by many rivers, drops to a skirt of lowlands bordering the Caribbean Sea. The Spaniards who arrived on these shores in Columbus's wake found a hot, humid, hostile climate. Little wonder that after they conquered the highlands, with their springlike weather, the Spaniards stayed and built their capitals there. The majority of people who came later did likewise. Hence, the Caribbean coast was never widely populated and was largely ignored, except perhaps by banana growers such as the United Fruit Company, which built some of the towns and ports of the lowlands that exist today.

As for tradition, the countries of Central America, except for Belize and to some extent Honduras, are not usually associated with the Caribbean; their history and culture have been more closely related with the Latin world than with the West Indian one. But then Cuba, the Dominican Republic, and Puerto Rico are tied to the Spanish-speaking world, yet they are the very soul of the Caribbean. And, too, Mexico had very little relationship to the Caribbean in modern times until the creation of Cancún and the development of Cozumel. Now these destinations are promoted as the "Mexican Caribbean" and have become standard ports of call on Western Caribbean itineraries.

More relevant, perhaps, was the political turmoil that dominated the headlines of the 1980s, particularly regarding El Salvador, Guatemala, and Nicaragua, and kept tourists away from much of the region. Coincidentally, the decade paralleled the burgeoning of Caribbean cruising when there was, as yet, little demand or necessity for cruise lines to break out of their traditional itineraries, which sailed east from Florida to the Bahamas and the Eastern Caribbean.

Now that has changed. As Caribbean cruising began to mature in the 1990s, and even today, as the number of ships continues to increase, cruise lines are being driven by competition to develop new itineraries. At the same time, the reservoir of repeat passengers, eager to visit new destinations, is growing steadily. No area of the Caribbean would seem better suited to satisfy these needs than Central America.

Most Central American countries are still held back from any rush of cruise ships by the lack of adequate docking facilities, a developed tourism plant, and other infrastructure requirements. However, a start was made by some small cruise lines with small ships offering adventure-type cruises, usually focusing in depth on one or two destinations. Now major cruise lines with larger ships have added some of these countries to their Western Caribbean and Panama Canal itineraries with regular weekly calls, and more can be expected to do so in the future. Currently cruise ships visit Belize, Guatemala, Honduras, Nicaragua, Costa Rica (although more frequently stop at attractions on its Pacific coast than the Caribbean one), and Panama.

No doubt interest in the area is growing as these nations, young in tourism, develop in the twenty-first century. Meanwhile, anyone who selects a cruise that touches on the region will not be disappointed.

History buffs will find colonial cities, Indian villages, and some of the most important sites of antiquity in the Western Hemisphere; shoppers will be thrilled with the colorful markets filled with excellent and unusual crafts; and outdoor enthusiasts have many new worlds to discover, from palm-fringed coasts with porcelain beaches to mighty mountains with rain forests, volcanoes, and wildlife preserves that are the last refuge for some of the exotic animals and birds once abundant in the Western Hemisphere.

Fronting the Caribbean coast from Mexico to Honduras lies the longest barrier reef in the Western Hemisphere, second in the world only to the Great Barrier Reef of Australia. These pristine waters, particularly off the coasts of Belize and Honduras, offer outstanding snorkeling and diving and some of the best fishing in the world. Several cays, or tiny islets, are nesting places for significant numbers of birds, while mainland marshes and river deltas provide habitat for the manatee and other endangered wildlife.

Belize

www.travelbelize.org; www .belizetourism.org

Long before conservation and environmental protection became fashionable causes, this small country earmarked more than a third of its territory for preservation. Within these borders lie spectacular Mayan ruins, forests, mountains, rivers, waterfalls, and a great variety of wildlife that includes 500 species of birds, 250 types of orchids, howler monkeys, pumas, ocelots, and the 100,000-acre Cockscomb Basin Wildlife Reserve, the world's only jaguar sanctuary.

Belize also has one of the longest chains of caves in the Western Hemisphere and the world's seventh highest waterfall. Its coast faces the world's second longest barrier reef, dotted with hundreds of islets encircled by white-sand beaches and fantastically clear waters rich in coral gardens and teeming with fish.

Formerly known as British Honduras, Belize is bordered by Mexico on the north and by Guatemala on the west and south. About the size of Massachusetts, it is one of Central America's most stable countries, with an English- and Spanish-speaking multicultural population of 250,000. Belmopan, a small interior town, is the capital, but Belize City, on the coast, is the center of commerce, transportation, and activity, as well as a port of call for cruise lines.

Passenger arrival greatly improved when the US$10 million Cruise Tourism Village, opened in 2002. The main arrival hall has tour operator and other tourist services, a water taxi terminal to take visitors to outer islands for diving and snorkeling, and shops with local crafts and duty-free goods. There is a restaurant and bar, a tender terminal, and other hospitality facilities. Car rental services are also available. A list of rental agencies can be found on the Belize Web site www.travelbelize.org.

Shore Excursions

As Belize has improved its infrastructure over the past decade, local tour operators and cruise lines, working in tandem, have become more sophisticated and creative in the types and variety of excursions they offer. Those listed here are a sampling of the more adventurous excursions that are offered by most lines and are sometimes difficult to do on your own. Basic offerings, such as city tours and nearby sites, are noted in the descriptions on the following pages.

Yet keep in mind that while Belize has come a long way, it is still a rough diamond. Roads are often very bumpy and the climate, hot and humid. Most of these tours are not suitable for those with physical limitations. You will need insect repellent, sunscreen, hat, and bottled water; wear comfortable lightweight clothing that covers arms and legs.

Biking in Belize: 6 hours; US$55. An hour's drive takes you to the rain forest, where you get a brief orientation before guides lead a four-hour bike adventure on some of Belize's best trails. You might see such indigenous wildlife as iguanas, possums, anteaters, foxes, forest rabbits, a variety of birds, and natural ponds with crocodiles.

Goff's Caye Snorkeling: 4 hours; US$55. A snorkel boat leaves directly from your ship for a forty-minute ride to the remote atoll, 12 miles east of Belize. Goff's Caye, about the size of a football field, is a coral island in Belize's barrier reef.

Horseback Adventure and Nature Walk: 7 hours; US$90. A one-hour bus ride takes you to a ranch and lodge near Belmopan, the capital. A short river crossing on an old ferry system takes you to the beginning of your horseback ride through some of Belize's most beautiful rain forest trails, with diverse vegetation, birds and wildlife.

Belize

Population: 294,000, comprising Creoles (African-European), Garinagus (African-Amerindian), mestizos (Spanish-Indian), Mayas, Europeans, and Americans.

Government: A democratically elected parliamentary government and a member of the British Commonwealth.

Climate: Hot and tropical year-round; the dry season, from Oct to May, is the most comfortable time.

Clothing: Comfortable, casual light clothing for the coastal areas; hiking clothes and shoes for jungle excursions.

Currency: Belize dollar or BZ. US$1 equals BZ$1.96. In 2006 Belize replaced the value-added tax (VAT) with a general sales tax of 10 percent on goods and services, except hotel accommodations, for which the tax remains 7 percent.

Departure Tax: US$39.25, and must be paid in US currency only

Electricity: 110 volts AC

Entry Formalities: No visa required for U.S. or Canadian citizens, but you must have a valid U.S. passport.

Language: English

Time: Central Standard Time

Telephone Area Code: 501

Vaccination Requirement: None

Airlines: American, Continental, Delta, TACA, US Airways. *Local Airlines:* Tropic Air, (800) 422-3435 (from the United States) or (501) 226-2012; Maya Island Airway, (800) 521-1247 (from the United States) or (501) 226-2435.

Information: www.travelbelize.org; www.belizetourism.org

Belize Tourist Board, P.O. Box 325, 64 Regent St., Belize City, Belize; (501) 227-2420; (800) 624-0686; fax: (501) 227-2423

Shark/Ray Alley Snorkel: 7 hours; US$79. Four miles south of Ambergris Caye, the Hol Chan Marine Reserve and shark/ray alley area are among the most popular snorkeling/dive sites along the barrier reef. For years local fishermen cleaned their catch in this area; now it is a popular site for southern stingrays and nurse sharks. A speedboat leaves directly from your ship for the one-and-a-quarter-hour ride to where you swim and snorkel from the boat among stingrays and nurse sharks in shallow 8 to 10 feet of water.

Belize City: Belize's main city is something of a hodgepodge, with elevated tin-roofed wooden buildings beside British colonial ones, such as the Court House, rebuilt in the 1920s after a fire destroyed the original, and modern ones overlaid with a West Indian atmosphere. Its Cathedral of St. John, built in 1812, is the oldest Anglican church in Central America and today houses a museum. Among the other historic sites spanning two centuries, you will see the 19th-century hand-cranked swing bridge over Haulover Creek, apparently named because cattle were once roped together by their horns and hauled over the river. Nowadays it is opened at 6 a.m. and 5:30 p.m. to let ships pass. The **Museum of Belize**, Belize City's first museum, opened in 2002. It is dedicated to the country's history and culture with exhibits pertaining to Belize's past and present. Otherwise the town is short on sightseeing attractions, but it makes a good base for reaching some of Belize's most interesting sites.

Belize Zoo (www.belizezoo.org): Topping the list of attractions is the unusual, if not funky, Belize Zoo, 30 miles west of town. Here, amid hand-printed, funny, and hokey but charming signs, you can see more than one hundred species of native animals, including jaguars, tapir, howler monkeys, toucans, and more. The zoo was created originally by happenstance. Sharon Madola came to Belize in 1982 to care for a group of native animals that were being used in a nature film, but the project ran out of money before it could finish. The fate of the animals was a big concern. Since Belize did not have a zoo, Sharon asked, why not start one? And she did. Through the schools particularly, she raised interest and awareness, enabling her to get government and private help, and in a decade of hard work she turned the zoo from a noble idea into a Belize institution everyone loves.

Altun Ha: About 30 miles north of Belize City are the country's most accessible Mayan ruins, where thirteen temples and residential structures

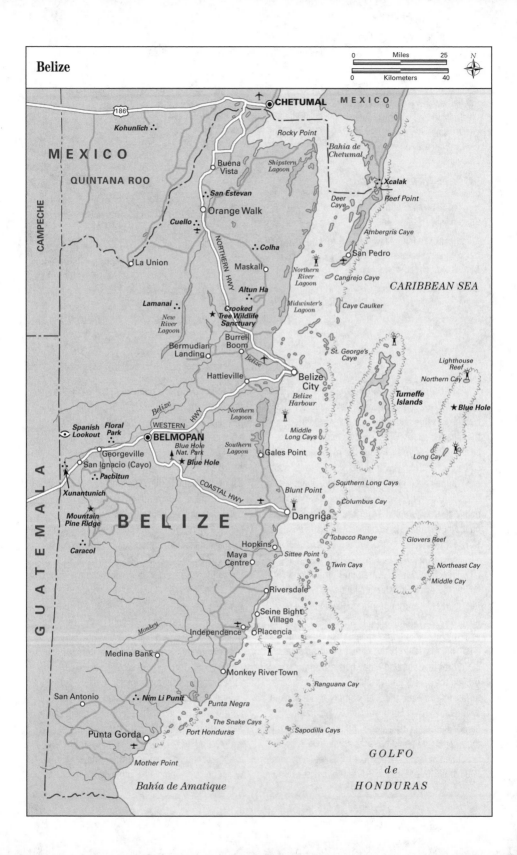

Belize

0   Miles   25

0   Kilometers   40

N

CHETUMAL   M E X I C O

186

M E X I C O

QUINTANA ROO

Kohunlich

CAMPECHE

Rocky Point

Bahía de Chetumal

Buena Vista

Shipstern Lagoon

San Estevan

Orange Walk

Cuello

La Union

Colha

Maskall

Xcalak

Reef Point

Deer Caye

Ambergris Caye

San Pedro

Northern River Lagoon

Cangrejo Caye

CARIBBEAN SEA

Lamanai

Altun Ha

Crooked Tree Wildlife Sanctuary

Midwinter's Lagoon

Caye Caulker

New River Lagoon

Burrell Boom

Bermudian Landing

Belize

St. George's Caye

Lighthouse Reef

Northern Cay

Hattieville

Belize City

Turneffe Islands

Belize

WESTERN

Northern Lagoon

Belize Harbour

Blue Hole

Spanish Lookout

Floral Park

BELMOPAN

Middle Long Cays

Long Cay

Georgeville

Blue Hole Nat. Park

San Ignacio (Cayo)

Blue Hole

Southern Lagoon

Gales Point

Pacbitun

Xunantunich

Blunt Point

Southern Long Cays

Columbus Cay

Mountain Pine Ridge

B E L I Z E

COASTAL HWY

Dangriga

Caracol

G U A T E M A L A

Hopkins

Tobacco Range

Glovers Reef

Maya Centre

Sittee Point

Twin Cays

Northeast Cay

Riversdale

Middle Cay

Seine Bight Village

Independence

Placencia

Medina Bank

Monkey River Town

Ranguana Cay

San Antonio

Nim Li Punit

Punta Negra

The Snake Cays

Punta Gorda

Port Honduras

Sapodilla Cays

Mother Point

GOLFO de HONDURAS

Bahía de Amatique

have been uncovered. Here a jade head—the largest carved jade object ever found in the Mayan region—was uncovered during excavations by David Pendergast of the Royal Ontario Museum from 1964 to 1971. It represents the sun god Kinich Ahau, a national symbol of Belize that can be seen on the nation's currency. Altun Ha was a major ceremonial center in the Classic period from A.D. 250 to 900 and a trading center linking the Caribbean coast with Mayan centers in the interior. A full-day tour departs from Belize City by boat and cruises up the scenic Belize River. En route you might see troops of black howler monkeys and crocodiles basking in the sun on the riverbanks. The site has a gift shop and restrooms.

Bermudian Landing Baboon Sanctuary: The 18-square-mile reserve, an hour's drive north of Belize City, was established in 1985 to protect the black howler monkey through an unusual voluntary grassroots conservation program dependent upon the cooperation of landowners and villagers in farming communities bordering the monkey's habitat on the Belize River.

The black howler monkey, known in Belize as the baboon, is an endangered species whose range is now limited to Belize, southern Mexico, and isolated areas of Guatemala. When the Bermudian Landing community learned of the need to preserve the howlers' dwindling habitat and the benefits they could derive from conservation, its members responded by signing pledges to abide by certain guidelines. These include protecting forests along riverbanks, leaving food trees when clearing land, and maintaining corridors of forest around farmed areas. In turn, the landowners have benefited by reducing erosion, preventing silting of the river, and allowing for more rapid replacement of forests. The community derives some revenue from visitors as well.

In addition to seeing the monkeys, hikers on the reserve's forest trails can see iguanas, coati, anteaters, and other exotic animals along with some of the nearly 200 bird species observed here. A visitor center and exhibit are supported by the World Wildlife Fund and the Zoological Society of Milwaukee County.

Baboon Sanctuary and Belize City: 4 hours; US$65. As they are neither shy nor quiet, you are likely to see and definitely hear these primates that live in the riverine forests by the Belize River. The sanctuary visit is usually followed by a short tour of Belize City.

Crooked Tree Wildlife Sanctuary: A 3,000-acre preserve of lagoons and marshes 33 miles northwest of Belize City, this is a bird-watcher's mecca. There are dozens of species to be seen, but the sanctuary is best known for the thousands of jabiru storks, the largest flying bird in the hemisphere, that reside here during the dry season, from Oct to early May. Local tour companies can arrange a visit, but it is unlikely that your cruise ship will offer a shore excursion here, unless it is a nature or bird-watching type of cruise.

Hummingbird Highway and Mountain Pine Ridge: For hiking, the most accessible area is the 300-square-mile Mountain Pine Ridge, west of Belize City and south of Belize's capital, Belmopan, along the Hummingbird Highway, an area known for its scenic pine forests, streams, caves, and the 1,000-foot Hidden Valley Falls.

Caves Branch River: The Hummingbird Highway gives access to the Caves Branch River, which winds through the mountains into a tunnel that leads to an underground cave system through which the Caves Branch River flows. From artifacts found here, it is thought that the caves were used by ancient inhabitants for ceremonial purposes. Today visitors can enjoy an unusual "cave tubing" excursion.

The full-day excursion departs from Belize City by bus for a one-hour ride into the lush tropical countryside to where the cave excursion begins. Participants are given a flashlight to wear during their two-hour ride in an inflated inner tube, carried along by the slow-moving currents, and can view the stalactites and stalagmites that line the cave system. At the end of the journey, they are greeted with a picnic lunch. Changing facilities are available.

Cave Tubing and Rain Forest Exploration: 7 hours. Carrying your equipment and walking about forty-five minutes on a rain forest path, you reach the Sibun River site where your tubing adventure begins. Waterproof camera, sturdy closed shoes, sunscreen, hat, and change of clothes are recommended. The operation of the tour depends on weather conditions.

Other Mayan Sites: Among other important Mayan ruins in western Belize are the ceremonial center of Caracol, the most impressive Mayan site in Belize. and Xunantunich, a major center during the Classic period, 2 miles from the Guatemala border.

Xunantunich: 7 hours. The site, two hours by bus from the port, is situated on a limestone ridge with views of the hilly Cayo district, and it's composed of six large plazas surrounded by more than twenty-five temples and palaces

Tikal Expedition by Air: 9 hours. West of the town of San Ignacio, just across the Belize–Guatemala border, is one of the largest, most important Mayan sites in Central America. People often visit Tikal, from Belize. (See the Guatemala section that follows for information.) From the airport (10 miles from the port), a fifty-minute flight to Peten in Guatemala provides great views of Belize. In Peten your bus travels along Lago Peten Itza to Tikal for a three-hour tour of the famous Mayan site. Lunch is served at the site. Wildlife, such as howler and spider monkeys, coatimundi, parrots, keel-billed toucans, and other birds, is abundant.

The Cays

A short distance offshore is a string of tiny islands along the 185-mile-long barrier reef, the longest in the Western Hemisphere. Development is concentrated on Ambergris Caye, 35 miles to the north of Belize City, and Caye Caulker, 14 miles south of Ambergris Caye; another dozen have one or two hotels. San Pedro, the main town on Ambergris Caye, is usually a stop for small cruise ships where passengers can enjoy fabulous white-sand beaches, excellent deep-sea fishing, and snorkeling on the shallow-water reefs of the Hol Chan Marine Preserve, a 5-mile-square area of shallow-water coral gardens at the southern tip of Ambergris. Trips to Mayan sites and jungle retreats on the mainland depart daily from San Pedro.

Other locations along the reef that are often stops for small cruise ships are the Turneffe Islands, 18 miles east of Belize City, a large atoll with abundant fish and large rays; Lighthouse Reef, about 30 miles farther east, where Half Moon Cay is a sanctuary for nesting red-footed boobies and magnificent frigate birds; and Glovers Reef, 30 miles east of the southern coastal town of Dangriga. The coastal villages of Placencia and Punta Gorda in Belize are occasional ports of call by small ships.

Guatemala

www.visitguatemala.com

Guatemala is a land of superlatives. It has Central America's highest, most active volcano; the most prodigious Mayan ruins; the largest population; and the largest, most authentic population of indigenous people, who have clung the most tenaciously to their ancient culture and customs.

To many, Guatemala is the most beautiful and most interesting of the Central American seven. Certainly, the magnificent scenery, the Mayan antiquities, the colonial treasures, and the native Indians, with their exotic faces, dazzling dress, and colorful markets, make the country a photographer's dream.

About the size of Ohio, Guatemala offers an amazing variety of landscapes, from volcanic highlands clad with forests and dotted with lakes to lowlands covered with coffee, banana, and sugar plantations. From its lofty and rugged mountain peaks at more than 12,500 feet, the land is carved by dozens of rivers and falls west/southwest to the Pacific and east to a short coast on the Caribbean and a long border with Belize. To the west and north/northeast is a very long, irregular border with Mexico; to the south and southeast, El Salvador and Honduras.

Guatemala City, the capital, is the gateway to the country's western highlands, where the majority of the native Indians live. The town is a convenient base for touring the main attractions of the region, and its two superb museums alone would make it worth a visit.

Antigua: The former capital and oldest Spanish colonial city in Guatemala is one of the loveliest in Central America, with churches, houses, and flower-filled plazas dating from the 16th and 17th centuries. It has been declared a National Monument of the Americas.

Lake Atitlan: Northwest from Antigua, the Pan-American Highway leads to the breathtakingly

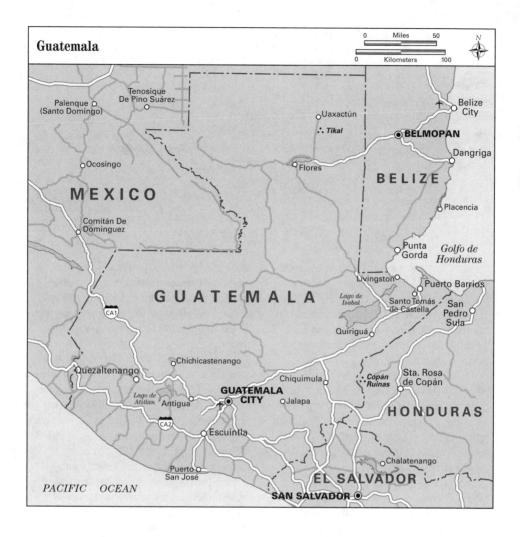

Guatemala

beautiful landscape of a mile-high lake surrounded by towering volcanoes. Around the shores of the lake are Indian villages whose people are directly descended from the Mayan tribes—Cakchiquel, Tzutuhil, and Quiche—who peopled the region when the Spaniards arrived in 1524. A road west continues to Quezaltenango, the country's second city and another good base for exploring more remote villages and hiking.

Chichicastenango (north of Lake Atitlan; 90 miles from Guatemala City). Perhaps the most popular market town in all Central America, Chichi, as it is known, is certainly the most photographed for the colorful Quiche Indians who

inhabit the area, their crafts, and the town's colonial churches.

The Caribbean Coast

Guatemala has only a small strip of land fronting the Caribbean where the Rio Dulce empties into the sea. Livingston, an old port that can only be reached by sea, is on the north side of the river; Puerto Barrios and Santo Tomás de Castilla, the newer port and the usual dock for cruise ships, are on the south.

Puerto Barrios: This was built as a company town by the United Fruit Company when it put in

Guatemala

Population: Eight million

Climate: Hot and humid on the coast; springlike weather in the highlands

Clothing: Comfortable, casual, light clothing for coastal areas

Currency: The Guatemalan quetzal (Q) is divided into 100 centavos. The quetzal fluctuates but is about Q8 to US$1.

Departure Tax: US$30

Electricity: 110 volts AC

Entry Formalities: Valid U.S. passport

Language: Spanish; some English in coastal areas

Time Zone: Central Standard Time

Telephone Area Code: 502

Vaccination Requirement: None

Information: Guatemala Consulate, 57 Park Ave., New York, NY 10016; (212) 686-3837

---

the railway used to ship its bananas to the coast, where they were loaded onto ships destined for the United States. Laid out in a grid, Puerto Barrios has wide streets and typical Caribbean wood frame houses, many on stilts. In the 1960s Santo Tomás de Castilla, a short distance to the southwest, was built to serve as the main port.

Livingston: Located just across the border from Belize, Livingston, with its lush tropical landscape and brightly painted wooden buildings, is a village caught in time. It has no airport and no road to the outside; the only way in is by sea. The gateway to Guatemala at the turn of the 20th century, when it was the principal port for goods transported down the Rio Dulce, it lost its raison d'être when the railroad and Puerto Barrios were built.

For some cruise ships, it is still a port of call and starting point for the journey up the Rio Dulce to Lake Izabal. The excursion up river can be made by cayucos, motorized dugout canoes, that take tourists on river trips.

Livingston's population of 2,000 or so is made up mostly of the Black Caribs, known in Central America as Garinagus or by their language, Garifuna. They are descendants of African slaves who escaped or were shipwrecked off the coast of St. Vincent and commingled with the Carib Indians there. In the late 18th century, after a major revolt against the British who had colonized St. Vincent, most of the Black Caribs were shipped off to Roatan, an island off the coast of Honduras. Over time they migrated to southern Belize, Guatemala, and Nicaragua, intermarrying with shipwrecked

sailors of other races and with the indigenous Mayas and developing a distinctive culture and language made up of African, Carib Indian, Mayan, and European elements. They also speak Spanish and English with a lilt similar to others in the Caribbean.

An interesting side note to history: At the time of the Columbus Quincentennial, the Caribs of Dominica, the last of the Carib tribes populating the Caribbean when Columbus arrived, established contacts with the Garinagus in Central America to try to learn more about their heritage by sharing their cultural traditions. If you compare the traditional crafts of the Caribs of Dominica and those of the Garinagus in Belize, the connection between the two peoples becomes obvious, particularly in the art of straw weaving, where the type of weaving, straw, and patterns used are so distinctive.

Rio Dulce Cruises: A boat trip up the Rio Dulce is, as one writer described it, an adventure straight out of *The African Queen*. From Livingston, the river passes through a steep-walled gorge thick with jungle greenery and streaming waterfalls and alive with egrets and other tropical birds. At the base of the gorge, the sulfurous water from a hot spring provides a delightful place for a swim.

Upon emerging from the gorge, the river widens into an area known as El Golfete, whose north side borders a 7,200-hectare nature reserve, **Biotopo Chocon–Machacas.** In addition to the beautiful river landscape, the reserve protects mangroves, tropical flora, and exotic wildlife, particularly the manatees that inhabit the waters.

The reserve runs for about 7 miles along the river and has a network of boat routes around the jungle lagoons, enabling passengers to get a close-up look at the wildlife. A nature trail begins at the visitor center.

At the western end of El Golfete is a restored 17th-century fortress, **Castillo de San Felipe de Lara,** built at the entrance to Lake Izabal (Lago de Izabel) to keep out marauding pirates, who ruled the seas of the Caribbean at the time and preyed on local villages and the commerce traveling on the river. Apparently the fortress was only minimally effective, as pirates were able to capture and burn it in 1686. Once the pirate threat was removed from the Caribbean, the fortress was used as a prison.

Lake Izabal, a large body whose fresh waters shelter the manatee, has not been developed for tourism, but some small cruise ships sail around the lake, stopping to visit the fort and take passengers from the village of Rio Dulce (also known as El Relleno) by bus to the region's main antiquity sites.

Carretera al Atlantico, the highway from the capital to the sea, is on the south side of the lake. At the Morales–La Ruidosa junction (Carretera al Atlantico, km 245), the highway west leads to Los Amates, less than a mile from the Maya archaeological site of Quirigua, in a lovely park setting. It is famous for the huge, intricately carved stelae that can be seen there. The site is open 7 a.m. to 5 p.m. daily; there is a small admission fee.

The Morales–La Ruidosa junction north crosses to the village of Rio Dulce, where a road leads to Flores, the gateway to El Peten, a vast lowland forest of which 50 square miles are a national park, with some of the most important antiquities in the Western Hemisphere.

Tikal National Park: In the dense jungle of El Peten, in the northeast region, is Tikal, the crown jewel of Guatemala's Mayan antiquities and the largest, most impressive ruins from the Classic period in the Mayan world. The vast area holds the ruins of approximately 3,000 structures. In the Great Plaza two awesome temples have been excavated, while the tops of three pyramids tower above the jungle's canopy to heights of more than 145 feet. In addition to the prodigious antiquities, the forest is alive with exotic flora and wildlife, including brightly colored parrots that squawk from the treetops and howler monkeys that swing noisily through the branches.

Flores is about a forty-five-minute drive away. Several lodges are situated near the site, enabling visitors to remain overnight. Some cruise ships offer excursions that travel by motor coach in one direction and by plane in the other. Tikal is located near the Belize border and is often visited from there.

Honduras

www.letsgohonduras.com

Stretching east–west between Guatemala and Nicaragua, with El Salvador on the south, Honduras is the second largest of the Central American seven and boasts a long, beautiful Caribbean coastline backed by tropical-jungle-clad mountains that climb to more than 9,000 feet. Much of the coast, with its beaches, wetlands, and lagoons full of manatees, howler monkeys, and other wildlife, is protected in coastal and marine parks.

A short distance off the Caribbean coast lie Honduras's best-known attractions—Roatan one of the Bay Islands, idyllic hideaways surrounded by fabulous coral reefs, an extension of the barrier reef off Mexico and Belize. The country's other well-known star is the spectacular Mayan ruin site at Copán, near the Guatemalan border.

Honduras's interior comprises mostly mountains and highland valleys—80 percent of its total 59,160 square miles is made up of terrain ranging from 1,800 feet to almost 9,500 feet above sea level.

Tegucigalpa, the capital, is situated in the central highlands at 3,217 feet in a bowl-shaped valley surrounded by pine-covered mountains and enjoying a springlike climate year-round. The hilly town, with its tile-roofed, pastel houses along cobblestone streets, has retained its colonial atmosphere. The main highway of the region connects Tegucigalpa with San Pedro Sula, the country's principal commercial center, and the coast.

In 1502, on his fourth and final voyage, Christopher Columbus sailed from Jamaica to explore the Central American landmass. He came ashore near Trujillo on the north coast and named it Honduras, meaning "depths" in Spanish, for the deep waters there.

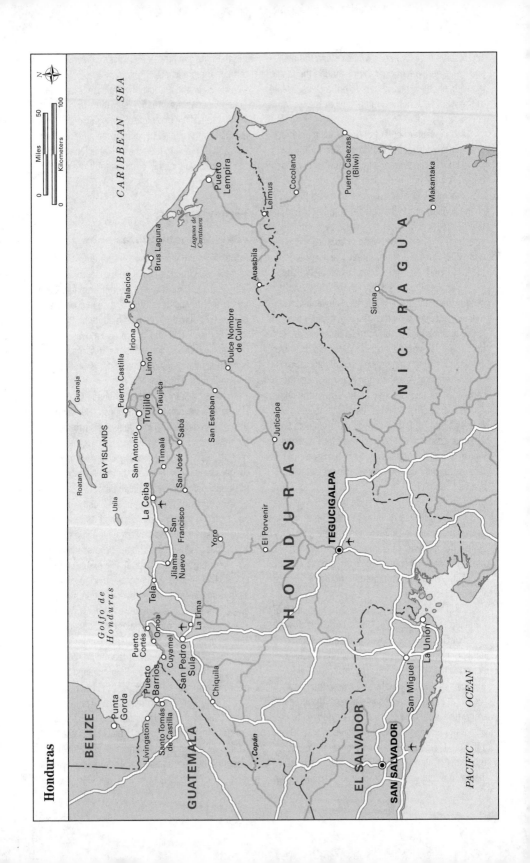

Honduras

Honduras

Population: 6.2 million

Government: A democratically elected government

Climate: Hot, tropical year-round in the lowlands; perpetual spring in the highlands.

Clothing: Comfortable, casual, light clothing for the coastal areas; hiking clothes and shoes for jungle excursions.

Currency: Lempira. There are 100 centavos in a lempira. US$1 is L19.

Departure Tax: US$33

Electricity: 110 volts AC

Entry Formalities: Valid US passport; on arrival, tourists get tourist cards valid for up to ninety days.

Languages: Spanish and English on the Caribbean coast and Bay Islands

Time Zone: Central Standard Time

Telephone Area Code: 505

Vaccination Requirement: None

Airlines: AeroHonduras, American, Continental, Delta, Northwest, TACA, United

Information: www.letsgohonduras.com; www.travel-to-honduras.com

Honduras Tourist Board, 2828 Coral Way, Suite 305, Miami, FL 33145; (305) 461-0600; (800) 410-9608

The town of **Trujillo**, founded in 1525 near the site of Columbus's landing, was the first capital of the Spanish colony, but soon the Spanish became more interested in the cooler highlands of the interior. Meanwhile the British grabbed the coast for its timber and the Bay Islands for their hidden bays and inlets, from which British pirates could prey on Spanish ships. It is said that by the early 1600s, Roatan had an estimated 5,000 British pirates. The notorious 18th-century pirate Henry Morgan, who later was rewarded by the British Crown—which named him governor of Jamaica—was among those who used the islands as a base.

To harvest the mahogany and other hardwoods from the forests, the British brought Jamaicans and other West Indians to Honduras. Today their descendants are largely people from the Caribbean coast, along with the mestizos of indigenous Indian and Spanish blood, and the Garinagus, who are a mixture of African and Carib Indians and known in the Eastern Caribbean as the Black Caribs.

In the late 18th century, after a revolt of the Black Caribs in St. Vincent, the British rounded up the survivors and shipped them to Roatan. From there the Garifuna, as they are sometimes called after their language, migrated to the mainland, creating fishing and farming communities along the coast from Belize to Nicaragua and developing their own religion, music, dance, and Garifuna language, a mix of West African, Arawak, and European speech.

The Bay Islands

Islas de la Bahía, an archipelago of three main islands—Roatan, Guanaja, and Utila—and many tiny cays, is located about 30 miles off the north coast. These islands are Honduras's prime tourist attractions, offering great diving and snorkeling on their extensive coral reefs. The marine gardens are a continuation of the barrier reef that starts off the coast of Mexico and extends for 185 miles to Honduras, making it the largest reef in the Western Hemisphere and second in the world only to Australia's Great Barrier Reef.

Culturally as well as scenically, the Bay Islands are a world apart from the mainland, having been occupied by the British from the 17th to the 19th centuries. Christopher Columbus landed on Guanaja in 1502, where he found a fairly large indigenous population. In less than twenty-five years, though, the population was decimated by the Spaniards who followed him, enslaving the islanders and sending them to work on the plantations of Cuba and in the silver mines of Mexico.

Before long English, French, and Dutch pirates took over the islands, and from these convenient bases they raided the Spanish galleons laden with gold and other treasures from the New World en route to Spain. Then, in 1782, after many attempts, the Spanish successfully wiped out the pirates' stronghold, and once again the islands were left uninhabited. A decade later, after the Black Carib

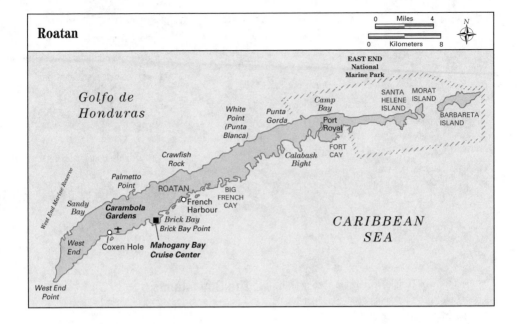

Roatan

0 Miles 4
0 Kilometers 8
N

Golfo de
Honduras

EAST END
National
Marine Park

White
Point
(Punta
Blanca)

Punta
Gorda

Camp
Bay

SANTA
HELENE
ISLAND

MORAT
ISLAND

Port
Royal

BARBARETA
ISLAND

Crawfish
Rock

Calabash
Bight

FORT
CAY

Palmetto
Point

ROATAN

BIG
FRENCH
CAY

Sandy
Bay

Carambola
Gardens

French
Harbour

CARIBBEAN
SEA

West End Marine Reserve

Brick Bay
Brick Bay Point

West
End

Coxen Hole

**Mahogany Bay
Cruise Center**

West End
Point

uprising in St. Vincent, the British shipped the survivors to Roatan. Although most made their way eventually to the mainland, Roatan still has one settlement of Garinagus at Punta Gorda.

The Bay Islands, along with the large Mosquitia territory in northeastern Honduras, remained British until 1859, when Great Britain ceded the territory to Honduras. Yet only in recent times, after Honduras required that Spanish be spoken in all schools, did the islanders begin to speak Spanish. English, spoken with a typical Caribbean lilt, remains their preferred language as well as their cultural orientation.

Roatan: Situated off the coast from La Ceiba, Roatan is the largest and most developed of the Bay Islands, with a population of about 10,000. The island, 30 miles long and only 1 to 3 miles wide, is surrounded by more than 60 miles of reef, making it a mecca for divers. Carnival Corporation and the government of Honduras have built a new $50 million port on the southwest coast of Roatan in an area known as Dixon Cove. Situated on 20 acres of waterfront, Mahogany Bay, as it is called, opened in 2009. The concept is similar to Carnival's port at Grand Turk, with a state-of-the-art pier for megaships and passenger facilities. Next to the pier is a welcome center with retail shops, restaurants,

and bars, along with a 60-foot lighthouse, a lagoon, and a nature trail. A transportation hub for taxis, car rentals, tour buses, and shore excursions is also available. Mahogany Bay is located next door to Coral Cay, a marine and nature park, and connected to it by a foot bridge.

The most beautiful part of the island is at West End, a small village with an idyllic, palm-shaded, white-sand beach washed by turquoise waters filled with colorful fish. Coxen Hole, the main town, is about a ten-minute drive from the airport. Here, in Coxen Hole, two miles away from Mahogany Bay, Royal Caribbean International is also building its own pier and terminal.

Among the island's resorts is the deluxe **Anthony's Key** (800-227-3483; www.anthonyskey .com), with good dive facilities. It also has dolphins that can be seen daily in waist deep water and a talk by a specialist on dolphin behavior: US$62. Also available is a swim, for US$84 for non-hotel-guests. Swims are scheduled at 9 a.m., noon, and 2:30 p.m. Also on the premises is a well-organized, well-displayed museum exhibit on the region's history and anthropology, which is funded by the resort, and a gift shop.

You can easily hire a taxi at the cruise ship dock in Coxen Hole for about US$50 for a two-hour tour, or rent a bicycle in the tiny town for about $5. An information kiosk and outdoor market with local crafts are at the pier.

The most popular excursion that cruise ships offer is a day at the beach and snorkeling at Tabyana Beach or at West End. They also have deep sea fishing and kayaking.

Guanaja: The most easterly of the three islands, Guanaja has rugged, mountainous terrain covered with forests and appears to be a mainland breakaway. Only about 11 miles long and 4 miles wide at its widest point, the island is surrounded by miles of coral reefs and a dozen or more cays. About 90 percent of the island has been declared a national forest reserve and marine park. The island caters mostly to affluent travelers.

Guanaja Town, known as the Venice of Honduras and called "Bonacca" by its inhabitants, is on a small cay just off the main island's east coast. Its wooden houses with sloping roofs are packed tight and rest on stilts. There are no roads and no cars on the cay; a labyrinth of walkways winding around the houses and narrow canals enable residents to bring their boats right up to their houses.

Utila: The smallest, least developed of the group has modest tourist facilities, appealing to budget travelers, and is, as yet, probably the cheapest place in the Caribbean to learn to dive. The islands are linked by daily air service from La Ceiba and San Pedro Sula to Roatan.

The North Coast

Honduras's entire north coast of 384 miles fronts the Caribbean Sea, with mountains of tropical jungle rising to more than 7,000 feet behind it. The towns of the north coast are Puerto Cortés, the main port where cruise ships usually dock; La Ceiba, the largest coastal town and jumping-off point for travel by air or boat to the Bay Islands; and Tela and Trujillo, known for their lovely, palm-fringed beaches and good fresh seafood. Rain, heaviest on the coast from Sept to Jan, can sometimes make the roads impassable.

Puerto Cortés: Located on the sea near the Guatemala border and 34 miles from San Pedro Sula, Puerto Cortés handles more than half of the country's exports. The docks are in the heart of town and are normally busy with cargo ships loading bananas, pineapples, and other produce for the two-day sail to Miami. There are some good beaches within a short drive, and the Spanish fortress at Omoa is a half-hour bus ride west from town.

Tela: In addition to its beaches, Tela has the **Lancetilla Botanical Gardens and Research Center,** begun in 1926 by United Fruit Company as an experimental station for tropical plants. The huge estate is a park with a visitor center and specimens of about every fruit tree and flower that grows in Central America. It's also a birder's haven: The gardens attract more than 200 species.

La Ceiba: Situated on the narrow coastal plain between the towering Cordillera Nombre de Dios mountains and the Caribbean, La Ceiba is a rich fishing and farming community surrounded by banana and pineapple plantations, mostly owned by Standard Fruit. **Pico Bonito National Park,** a few miles behind the town and covering about 300 square miles, is Honduras's largest national park and has magnificent forests and wildlife. On the coast 12 miles west of La Ceiba is the **Cuero-Salado Nature Reserve,** a large estuary formed by the Cuero and Salado Rivers that protects a multitude of animals, including manatees, howler monkeys, and many bird species.

Inland from the North Coast

San Pedro Sula: Honduras's second largest city is 34 miles south of Puerto Cortés in the Ulua River Valley, a large plain that is one of Honduras's most fertile, productive areas and the heart of banana country. Here Standard Fruit and United Fruit, which own a large part of northern Honduras, grow bananas and pineapples for export to the United States. Several of the vicinity's towns, ports, roads, and railways were built by the banana companies.

San Pedro Sula is a lively town with a population of about 325,900. It has an archaeological museum and a good central market where the National Association of Honduras Artisans has a wide selection of crafts from throughout the country.

Founded by the Spaniards in 1536, the town is today Honduras's major industrial and commercial center as well as the main center for the region's agricultural products. It is also the transportation hub for western Honduras and the gateway to Copán.

La Lima, 8 miles east of San Pedro, is a company town built by United Brands of Chiquita bananas fame, where you can visit the banana plantation and watch the packing operations. **Cusuco National Park,** 12 miles west of San Pedro, is a mountainous cloud forest with its highest peak at 7,398 feet; there is a visitor center. The 300-foot **Pulhapanzak Waterfall** and **Lago de Yojoa,** about 30 miles to the south, are popular recreation areas.

The Mayan Antiquities of Copán

Southwest of San Pedro Sula, via a 125-mile road that climbs the hills and upland valleys through coffee, tobacco, cornfields, and terraced hillsides are the ruins of Copán, among the most magnificent antiquities in the Americas, rivaling Tikal in Guatemala for top honors as Central America's most important archaeological site. Called the Athens of the Mayan World, Copán was a flourishing city for hundreds of years and reached its peak between A.D. 465 and 800 in the Mayan Classic period, when it was the artistic and scientific center. The region was inhabited by the Maya for about 2,800 years.

The main ceremonial center covers about 75 acres. The principal group of ruins includes the Great Plaza, with dozens of intricately carved stelae portraying the rulers of Copán, and the Hieroglyphic Stairway, the most dramatic monument. The stairway, 30 feet wide and 60 feet high, is covered with more than 2,200 glyphs that record the history of the Copán rulers. It is the longest pre-Columbian text ever found. Indeed, the temples and monuments of Copán have more reliefs and artistic embellishment than any other in the Mayan world—one reason they are so significant. The entire site is thought to have been built over earlier temples and other buildings.

The park has three other basic areas: The Ball Court was the social center of the city, and its unique features are the markers on the side walls, resembling macaw heads. Work here dates from the thirteenth ruler, known as "18 Rabbit," A.D. 711 to 736.

The Acropolis is divided into two large courts. The west court houses the elaborate Temple 11, built during the reign of Yax-Pac and meant to be his portal to the other world; and Temple 16, set between the east and west courts, which has the unique Altar "Q" at its base. Altar Q has been "read" completely and depicts each of the sixteen members of the Copán Dynasty, seated on their own glyph. In that of Yax-Pac, dynasty founder Yax-Kuk-Mo is passing the scepter of power to Yax-Pac.

The Tunnels: Archaeological excavations in Copán have led to the digging of more than 2½ miles of tunnels under the Acropolis, which have allowed scholars to view earlier stages of Copán's urban structure, as well as finding important tombs. Two tunnels are open to the public on a limited basis; only ten persons are allowed in at one time, and they must be accompanied by a guide. Rosalila Tunnel, under Temple 16, is said to be the best-preserved stucco building in the Mayan world. A full-size replica can be seen in the Mayan sculpture museum. Los Jaguares Tunnel is more than 2,100 feet long, with Galindo's Tomb (discovered more than a century ago), among other highlights.

Las Sepulturas Archaeological Site: Located 1 mile from the main Acropolis, this small site has been important in understanding how the Mayan elite lived in Copán's heyday. No guides are on the site, but one can be hired at the visitor center. New discoveries are made continuously; these findings are housed in the Mayan sculpture museum adjacent to the visitor center and in the town museum. Entrance fees: main park, US$15, including Las Sepulturas Archaeological Site; Museum of Mayan Sculpture, US$7; Museum of Archaeology (in town), US$3; Rosalila and Los Jaguares Tunnels, US$15. Normally cruise ship shore excursions include the cost of the park and museum entrance fees.

Casa K'inich: An interactive museum for children is located in the town of Copan Ruinas's main square. Here children learn about the Mayan culture by trying on ball game equipment and watching a game reenactment, practicing Maya math and writing, and counting in Ch'orti', a Mayan language. Casa K'inich—"house of sun"—is open Tues through Sat from 8 a.m. to noon and 1 to 5 p.m.; Sun 8 a.m. to noon only. Entrance is free, contact (505) 651-4105.

The pretty little town of **Copán Ruinas** is a mile or more from the ancient ruins. Its cobblestoned streets are lined with typical whitewashed adobe houses with red-tiled roofs, good restaurants and small inns; a colonial church anchors the plaza. There are hotels within walking distance of the Mayan site. Copán is a three-hour drive from San Pedro Sula and four hours from Puerto Cortés.

The Mosquito Coast

Located in the northeastern part of the country, La Mosquitia, or the Mosquito Coast, is one of Central America's largest wilderness areas, rich in wildlife. This swampy, heavily forested region is sparsely inhabited by the Miskito and Sumo Indians. Travel is mostly by boat, as there is only one road. Adventure and nature tours reach their destinations in the region by bush plane, four-wheel-drive vehicle, cayuco (dugout canoe) and mule pack, or on foot.

The **Rio Platano Reserve,** established by Honduras with the United Nations in 1980, is often described as the most beautiful nature reserve in Honduras. It protects a pristine river system that flows through a tropical rain forest and has abundant wildlife. Travel is by boat on the river, with camping in the forest. Air service to Palacios, a lilliputian hamlet and the most accessible locale to visit the reserve, operates from La Ceiba. There is also air service to Puerto Lempira, a small village and the largest coastal settlement in the Mosquito region, near the Nicaraguan border.

Nicaragua

www.intur.gob.ni

Although it has been almost two decades since a democratically elected government was voted into power and peace fell over the land, neither U.S. tourists nor cruise lines seem ready, as yet, to embrace Nicaragua as a major travel destination. When they do, they will find a beautiful country of tall mountains with pine-forested slopes, volcanoes, and lakes (including the largest lake in Central America), rain forests, lowlands drained by twenty-three rivers often traversing thick tropical jungles, and long shorelines on both its Caribbean and Pacific coasts. They will also see some of the Western Hemisphere's most historic towns, such as Granada and León, with lovely Spanish colonial architecture, and enjoy music, folklore, festivals, and markets brimming with handicrafts.

The largest country in Central America, Nicaragua is sandwiched between the Caribbean Sea on the east and the Pacific Ocean on the west. It is separated from Honduras, its neighbor on the north, by the 411-mile Rio Coco, Nicaragua's longest river; on the south, much of its border with Costa Rica is formed by the 120-mile Rio San Juan. Geographically, Nicaragua has three distinct regions: (1) the north-central mountains that fall east to the Caribbean in (2) a vast area of rivers and lowlands known as the Caribbean or Mosquito Coast, and (3) the Pacific lowland, which has the majority of the towns—including Managua, the capital—and people. The Pacific region also has about forty volcanoes, some reaching upward of 6,000 feet. The Momotombo volcano, on the southern shore of Lake Managua and clearly visible from the capital, is the national emblem. Just outside Managua is the **Masaya National Park,** with the Masaya volcano. It is one of the few summits of an active volcano that can be reached by car. A road leads directly to the lip of the cone, where you can look down into the smoking crater. The town of Masaya, 15 miles from Managua, is well known for its artisans, whose wares are on display in the town's colorful market.

The rich volcanic soil has made the Pacific corridor Nicaragua's most productive farming region. The region also has many lakes, including 5,067-square-mile Lake Nicaragua, Central America's largest and the tenth largest freshwater lake in the world. Granada, 28 miles from the capital at the foot of the Mombacho volcano on the northwestern shore of Lake Nicaragua, is Nicaragua's oldest city, founded by Hernandez de Córdoba in 1524. León Viejo, or Old León, at the foot of Momotombo, was also established by Córdoba in 1524, but it was destroyed by an earthquake in 1610 and covered with layers of ash from subsequent eruptions of the volcano. The present city of León is 19 miles away; it served as Nicaragua's capital until 1857, when the capital was moved to Managua. Among León's many attractions, the massive Metropolitan

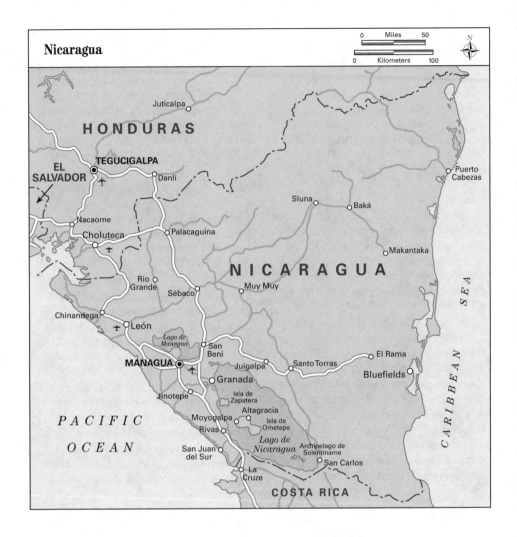

Nicaragua

Cathedral, begun in 1746 and completed a century later, is the largest in Central America and is famous for its huge paintings of the Stations of the Cross, considered masterpieces of Spanish colonial art.

Tourism has grown and ranks second as a source of national revenue. Hotel and resort development is moving along on the Pacific coast; the Caribbean shores, however, remain undeveloped and almost inaccessible, except at Puerto Cabezas in the north and Bluefields in the south.

Nicaragua is recapturing some of its past appeal to visitors through travel programs focusing on nature and light adventure. These might include visits to ranches and coffee plantations or a cruise on the Rio San Juan through the Indio Maiz National Reserve. The trip follows the course of the river from Lake Nicaragua to the Caribbean Sea along Nicaragua's border with Costa Rica. Now, for the first time, a few cruise ships are calling at San Juan del Sur, a small village on the Pacific coast that provides access to some of Nicaragua's main attractions. Given the town's limited facilities, you are probably better off taking one of your ship's shore excursions. One combines a visit to the heart of the coffee country with an equestrian show; another is a half-day trip to Granada and another is a full-day tour combining Granada, Masaya market, and Masaya Volcano National Park, with lunch at a local restaurant: eight hours.

Nicaragua

Population: 5.2 million

Government: A democratically elected government

Climate: Hot and humid on the coasts; springlike in the highlands

Currency: Cordoba, divided into 100 centavos. US$1 equals 21 cordobas.

Departure Tax: US$36

Electricity: 110 volts AC

Entry Formalities: A U.S. passport valid at least six months after entry date and a tourist card, issued for US$5 on arrival.

Languages: Spanish; English on the Caribbean coast and Corn Islands

Time Zone: Central Standard Time

Telephone Area Code: 505

Information: Nicaraguan Institute of Tourism, (505) 222-3333; (505) 254-5191; fax (505) 222-6610

Consulate of Nicaragua, 1627 New Hampshire Ave., NW, Washington, DC 20009; (202) 939-6570; fax: (202) 939-6542; www.intur.gob.ni

The Mosquito Coast

Hot, humid, and sparsely populated, the Caribbean or Mosquito Coast covers about half of Nicaragua and, with an average width of 60 miles, forms the widest skirt of lowlands in Central America. Much of it is covered with tropical rain forests that in some places are impenetrable jungle. The 325 miles of Caribbean shores are broken up by many river deltas and large lagoons created by the coursing of twenty-three rivers from the central mountains to the Caribbean Sea.

Nicaragua's Caribbean ports can be reached from Managua by air, but a preferred tourist route is via the town of El Rama and downriver by boat to Bluefields, a colorful old port on the Caribbean. The Mosquito region was never colonized by Spain, and indeed, tribal leaders asked for—and got—protection from the British against the Spaniards. Britain relinquished the territory to an independent Nicaragua in 1860, but English is still spoken on the coast and nearby islands, and, like so many pockets along the Central American coast with their mixed populations, there's a West Indian flavor here, too.

About 40 miles or so offshore from Bluefields are the tiny, idyllic **Corn Islands** (Islas del Maiz)—Grande and Pequeña—currently the only Nicaraguan Caribbean destinations occasionally visited by small cruise ships. The larger of the Corn Islands is only 4 miles square; the smaller is about 1 mile square. Both are fringed by sandy beaches,

crystal-clear waters, and coral reefs and are ideal for swimming, fishing, snorkeling, and diving, including exploring the wreck of a Spanish galleon a short distance offshore. The islanders are English-speaking Creoles and Garinagus.

Costa Rica

www.visitcostarica.com

Costa Rica is often called the Switzerland of Central America. A mountainous land with a long democratic tradition, no army, and one of the highest literacy rates in the Western Hemisphere, the country has managed miraculously, in recent years, to stay out of trouble.

A small, friendly country about the size of West Virginia, Costa Rica is bordered on the north by Nicaragua and on the south by Panama—countries plagued by political turmoil and armed conflicts throughout the 1980s. Yet peaceful Costa Rica succeeded in staying out of the conflicts that were tearing apart its neighbors while remaining their friend and, at the same time, maintaining a good relationship with the United States and often serving as mediator for all.

Most visitors come to Costa Rica to see its natural wonders, and cruise passengers are no exception. Costa Rica has become the very definition of ecotourism through its pioneering environmental efforts. Approximately 26 percent of the

Costa Rica

nation's land is under protection in more than thirty national parks, forestry reserves, wildlife refuges, and biological and private reserves (compared with 3 percent in the United States).

The designated areas protect a diverse landscape ranging from volcanic peaks and rain and cloud forests on mountain slopes, to dry and swamp forests in the lowlands, to dense mangrove and coral reefs along the coasts. The country has twelve distinct ecological systems containing 8,000 species of plants, including 1,200 varieties of orchids; 750 species of birds—more than in all of North America—and 10 percent of the world's

butterflies. In the national park system, which is made up of forty-five areas, at least one example of each ecosystem is represented.

Three chains of volcanic mountains form the Central Highlands, where the capital of Costa Rica, **San José,** with its year-round springlike weather, is located at an altitude of 3,805 feet. Depending on their ship's itinerary, cruise passengers often spend either the first or last night of their cruise in San José; visit the 19th-century National Cathedral and the wonderful National Museum, with a wealth of pre-Columbian artifacts; and shop at the Central Market.

Costa Rica

Population: 4.13 million

Government: A democratically elected government

Climate: Springlike climate in San José and the highlands; hot and tropical year-round on the coast; the dry season from Oct to May is the most comfortable period.

Clothing: Comfortable, casual, light clothing for the coastal areas; hiking clothes and shoes for jungle excursions.

Currency: Colón. US$1 equals about 505 colónes

Departure Tax: US$26

Electricity: 110 volts AC

Entry Formalities: No visa required for U.S. or Canadian citizens, but you must have a valid U.S. passport

Languages: Spanish and English

Time Zone: Central Standard Time

Telephone Area Code: 506

Vaccination Requirement: None

Airlines: LACSA, Aero Costa Rica, American, Continental, Delta, Northwest, Spirit, United, US Airways

Information: Costa Rica Tourist Bureau, P.O. Box 777-1000, San Jose, Costa Rica; www.visitcosta rica.com. The Tourist Board has a toll-free line to its San José offices, where English-speaking operators answer questions: (800) 343-6332.

Sarchi, a short trip from the capital, is a handicraft center known for its workshops that create the traditional, brightly painted oxcarts and interpret the colorful art onto many practical souvenirs. Shops sell other hardwood products as well as hammocks, straw, and leather.

San José is the gateway to many of the country's parks, with drive-to volcanoes, rain-forested mountains, and a lush countryside fresh with rushing rivers and rich with fertile valleys.

Poas Volcano National Park, an easy one-and-a-half-hour drive north of San José (22 miles north of Alajuela), is one of the most accessible and hence most popular parks. It provides the rare opportunity to drive almost to the crater rim of an active volcano at 8,000 feet, to peer down into it (when clouds don't obscure the view), and to hike in the surrounding forest. The crater is almost a mile across and 1,000 feet deep. There are small eruptions from time to time, but normally not enough to close the park (as in 1989, when eruption sent volcanic ash almost a mile into the air). A trail through a dwarf cloud forest heavy with mosses, lichens, and bromeliads and abundant with hummingbirds and other species leads to an extinct crater with a pretty lake.

Farther to the northwest, **Arenal National Park** protects the majestic Arenal volcano, the largest and most active in Central America. From its perfect cone, the 5,389-foot-high volcano puts on a spectacular display, sending smoke, ash, and exploding rocks into the air and lava tumbling down the slopes. At night, when the streams of orange-red lava glow, the sight is awesome. East of San José, **Irazu Volcano National Park** has Costa Rica's highest volcano, at 11,325 feet altitude.

The Caribbean Coast

Like so much of Central America, Costa Rica's Caribbean coast is sparsely settled and is the least accessible, less developed area of the country. Puerto Limón, the eastern gateway, almost at the center of the country's Caribbean coast, is a three-hour bus ride from San José. A hot, humid port city of about 60,000 people, Puerto Limón owes its creation in 1880 to the railway and banana industry, both of which have seen better days. In 1871 the government, eager to get the country's principal crop, coffee, more expeditiously to foreign markets, contracted Minor Keith, an American engineer, to build a railway from San José to the coast. The track took some twenty years to lay and cost thousands of lives because of malaria and yellow fever. It also changed Costa Rica forever by introducing Jamaicans into the population and bananas into the economy.

At first Keith brought workers from China and Italy, but in time he found that Jamaicans were

---

better able to withstand the weather and disease. To help defray some of the cost of building the railway, he planted bananas alongside the track, and in Limón, he built a pier and collected a share of the fee for its usage.

The banana business was so successful that by 1884, Keith was able to help Costa Rica pay its national debt and in exchange received a ninety-nine-year lease on the railway and thousands of acres of land along its route, where, of course, he planted more bananas. Five years later Keith and a rival company joined hands to form the United Fruit Company. It extended its base of operation from Guatemala to Panama and to a great extent controlled the power and politics of Central America's "banana republics" for almost a century.

After the railway had been completed, most of the Jamaicans stayed to work the banana plantations and railroad. Today the descendants of these English-speaking Jamaicans make up the majority of the population, which has largely retained a Jamaican or West Indian culture. However, that they kept their separate identity is not surprising considering the fact that the rest of Costa Rica did not accept them. Not until 1952 were they allowed Costa Rican citizenship. Even half a century later, there is little evidence of assimilation.

A cruise ship terminal at Puerto Limón, where two large cruise ships can dock at one time, has greatly improved the arrival experience for cruise passengers. Immediately outside the exit gate is a thriving market crammed full of inexpensive Costa Rican goods and crafts. For example, a beautifully carved, wooden salad bowl that could cost US$200 in New York can be had for $20. A kilo (2.2 pounds) of fine Costa Rican coffee is US$2.

Tortuguero National Park

North of Puerto Limón is a huge area of jungle-thick forests, swamps, and marshland crisscrossed by rivers and canals, a large part of which is protected by the Tortuguero National Park and, to the north, the Barra del Colorado National Refuge. Both are rich with birds and other wildlife.

Tortuguero takes its name from the large numbers of turtles that nest here from Aug to Nov. The national park, created in 1975 after a two-decade effort by conservationists, protects the nesting sites of four species—hawksbill, green, leatherback, and loggerhead turtles—on the beaches in the 50-mile stretch between the Matina River, which empties at Moin, and the Colorado River near the Nicaragua border.

The protected areas also include the low-lying hills, swamps, and forests that are home to monkeys, jaguars, raccoons, tapirs, and hundreds of species of birds. In addition, inland waterways support a wide variety of fish and other wildlife, including storks, herons, crocodiles, otters, manatees, and the gar, an unusual prehistoric fish said to be little changed for 90 million years.

Boat trips start at Moin, about 2 miles from Puerto Limón, and make their way through the swamps and marshes via a network of jungle-bordered canals, with signs like a highway, used by the people of the region as transportation. The area offers good sportfishing, while divers head to the reefs south of Limón.

Cahuita National Park

Cahuita, a small village about 25 miles southeast of Limón, is expanding as a tourist destination, attracting visitors for its laid-back lifestyle and the pretty beaches and reefs protected by the Cahuita National Park. Here the Caribbean Sea rolls in sometimes with force and breaks against the reefs. Behind the palm-edged beaches is a coastal rain forest full of birds and other wildlife.

Shore Excursions

With the growth of cruise traffic into Puerto Limón has come an increase in the number and diversity of excursions that cruise ships offer. The following are typical.

Tortuguero Canals: 4.5 hours; US$64. An hour's bus ride from the pier takes you to the Matina Embarcadero, where you are treated to a buffet of tropical fruits, soft drinks, and beers along with native music, before boarding a small boat to cruise through the jungle river system of natural and human-made canals used as waterways for transportation and exploration. The canals, paralleling Costa Rica's Caribbean coast, are surrounded by rain forest rich in flora and fauna, where you might see birds, monkeys, crocodiles, sloths, and toucans. Excursions often available by kayak.

Rio Reventazon White Water Rafting: 8 hours; US$99. The Reventazon River has some of Costa Rica's best 10 miles of Class II and III rapids. You travel southeast from Limón through fertile valleys and mountains with endless stretches of banana plantations. The river run starts near an abandoned railroad town in an area called Florida and passes through the beautiful valley where you might see toucans, herons, kingfishers, tanagers, and iguanas. En route, you'll stop for a buffet lunch prepared by the guides. *Participants must be able to swim.*

Costa Flores: 5 hours; US$64. Located on the border of the Braulio Carrillo National Park, Costa Flores is a 300-acre farm with more than 600 varieties of tropical flowers, said to be the largest tropical flower farm in the world. **Cahuita & Puerto Vargas National Park:** 5 hours; US$79. Puerto Vargas Reserve forms part of Cahuita National Park and has a variety of wildlife. Among the bird species in the swamp forest are the green ibis, green and rufous kingfishers, yellow-crowned night heron, and northern boat-billed heron; there are also four species of frogs. **Rain Forest Aerial Tram:** 8 hours; US$129. The Aerial Tram, a two-hour drive from Puerto Limón, is a decade-old ecotourism and research facility. The tram takes visitors through the rain forest canopy. The tram, located on a 1,000-acre private nature reserve adjacent to the Braulio Carrillo National Park. Some tram tours are combined with a zipline adventure.

Rain Forest Canopy Adventure: 4 hours; US$99. Ten platforms up to 197 feet high and 1,700 feet across give visitors an eye-level look at rain forest trees and spectacular views of the countryside. Cables are progressively more challenging, and guests have the option of experiencing only the first two platforms.

Sloth Sanctuary and Canoe Adventure: 5.5 hours; US$89. Seventy minutes of canoeing on the Estrella River. Expect to see rain forest denizens including monkeys, otters, caiman, butterflies, and amphibians. Guests will be introduced to sloths close-up at the Avioaros Center Sloth Sanctuary, followed by a guided walk through a humid tropical lowland forest.

Veragua Rainforest Research & Adventure Park, a world-class facility on a 4,000 acre private reserve surrounded by rainforest and adjacent to La Amistad International Park which Costa Rica shares with Panamá. The park, committed to conservation and scientific research with a biological research station, is less than one hour from Puerto Limón. With a naturalist guide, you visit the largest indoor nocturnal frog exhibit in the world, a butterfly garden, reptile vivarium, hummingbird garden, a gondola tram ride through the rainforest canopy, walking trails through the rainforest and a magnificent waterfall. Tour US$55 adult, $45 child; with the Canopy Tour $89.

The Pacific Coast

On Panama Canal cruises, Puerto Caldera, a modern container port about 6 miles from Puntarenas, the traditional port, is frequently used by cruise ships for passengers beginning or ending their cruise in San José, where they arrive or fly back to the United States. Depending on your ship's itinerary, you are likely to visit some of the national parks of the Pacific coast, some of which are remote from the capital and more readily accessible by ship.

Manuel Antonio National Park, near the Pacific coastal town of Quepos, is the smallest of the country's parks and one of the most popular. It protects beaches, rocky headlands, and a tropical forest that hosts a great variety of wildlife, including ocelots, three-toed sloths, squirrels, and howler and white-face monkeys—all often seen during hikes on the park's maintained trails. The park is three and a half hours by bus trip from San José.

Santa Rosa National Park, the first park to be established, covers 260 acres in the Pacific northwest and is the nesting ground for three turtle species: huge leatherbacks, the olive ridley, and the Pacific green. The park protects ten different habitats ranging from beaches and mangroves to dry forests and wooded savannas. The wildlife includes monkeys, anteaters, coatimundi, peccaries, and deer. **Palo Verde National Park,** a huge swampy refuge for migratory waterfowl, is also in the northwest.

Corcovado National Park, in the south on the Osa Peninsula near the Panama border, is remote from the capital. A popular stop for cruise ships, Corcovado's tropical rain forest and diverse habitat counts more than 500 species of trees, 285 species of birds, and 139 species of animals. Cruise ships often visit the **Marenco Biological Reserve,** which cannot be reached by road. There they hike a trail to the Rio Claro for swimming in freshwater pools and along beaches shaded by almond trees. This region is one of the last refuges for the rare scarlet macaw, often spotted in the trees by hikers.

Panama
www.visitpanama.com

The Panama Canal

Building the Panama Canal

History is replete with great endeavors, but few were as bold, difficult, dangerous, and controversial—yet successful and beneficial—as the Panama Canal. An engineering triumph by any measure, the Big Ditch, as it is often called, is a 50-mile-long channel traversing Panama at the narrowest point between the Atlantic and Pacific Oceans. A vital link in international trade for nearly a century, it has had a profound effect on world economic and commercial development. Annually, as many as 20,000 ships pass through it, carrying more than 200 million tons of cargo bound for destinations in the four corners of the world.

From the time the Spanish explorer Vasco Nuñez de Balboa crossed from the Atlantic to glimpse the Pacific in 1513, the dream of a waterway through the Isthmus of Panama was born. Under Charles I of Spain, the first survey for a proposed canal was made in 1534. What helped the search for a shortcut across Panama find new motivation was the California gold rush of 1849, when the lack of a safe way across the country by land hampered those in the eastern United States from participating in the bonanza. With the permission of Colombia, which controlled the isthmus area, a group of New York businessmen financed the building of a railroad, completed in 1855. It provided travel from the eastern United States to Panama by sea, crossing the Isthmus of Panama by rail, and sailing up the Pacific coast to California.

Yet the idea of a waterway persisted. In 1876 Colombia gave a French financial syndicate, headed by Lt. Lucien Napoleon Bonaparte Wyse, a French army officer, permission to construct a canal. The syndicate engaged Ferdinand de Lesseps, who had built the Suez Canal, for the project. De Lesseps, with little evidence to support it, said that a canal at sea level was feasible.

Despite tremendous support, enthusiasm, and feverish activity, the project was doomed from the start. For reasons of geography and topography, engineers say, digging a canal at sea level would not have worked regardless how much money, labor, and machinery de Lesseps had used. And if technical miscalculations had not been enough to defeat the French, tropical diseases were. Approximately 20,000 men died from yellow fever, malaria, and other illnesses in the two decades the French toiled. To these trials were added mismanagement and financial chicanery by no less than de Lesseps's son Charles and Gustave Eiffel, builder of the Paris tower. After $300 million in payout, the syndicate went bankrupt in 1889.

Meanwhile Theodore Roosevelt, a visionary who personified the American spirit of the times, wanted the United States to build a canal, which he saw as strategic for an expanding America and the link between the eastern United States and its new Pacific possessions—Hawaii and the Philippines, gained from the Spanish-American War in 1898.

After engineers studied sites in Nicaragua and Panama and a long, public debate was held, Congress approved Panama in 1902. But the battle was not over. Colombia said no and demanded more money for granting permission to the United States. The Panamanians, wanting the canal and eager for independence from Colombia, had their own ideas. With French aid and U.S. encouragement, they revolted; U.S. troops prevented Colombia from moving forces to stop them.

In 1903 the United States and Panama signed a treaty allowing America to build the canal. The following year, the United States bought the rights, property, and equipment of the French Canal Company for $40 million. Ironically, the equipment had deteriorated so much by then that most of it was worthless.

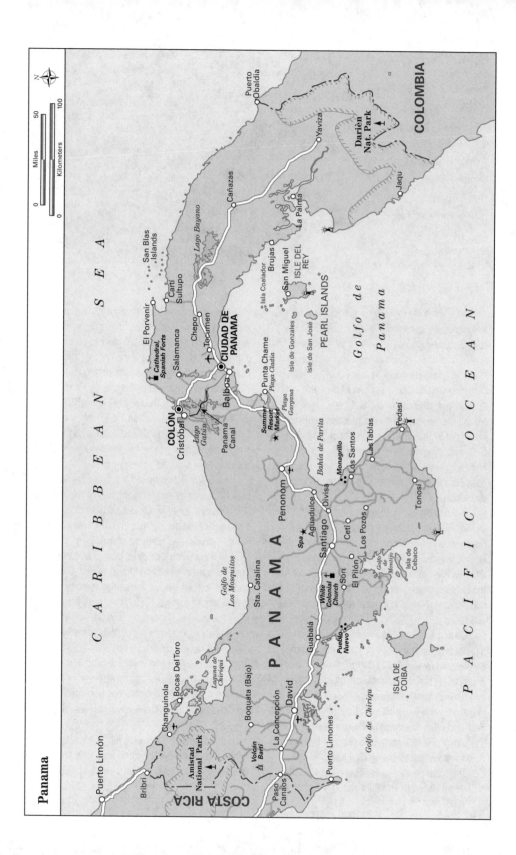

Panama

Faced with the difficulties of removing the rock necessary to create a sea-level canal, U.S. engineers, headed by Col. George W. Goethals, an Army Corps of Engineers career officer, concluded that a lock system would be less costly and provide better control. But the first order of business was to improve health conditions and particularly to control the mosquitoes that carried yellow fever and malaria. The job was given to Col. William C. Gorgas, who set about draining swamps and installing sewer systems. By 1906 yellow fever had been brought under control and malaria reduced dramatically.

Building the canal entailed three major projects on a grand scale: cutting a channel through the Continental Divide; digging an earthen dam—the largest ever built up to that time—across the Chagres River to create Gatun Lake, which became the largest artificial lake of its time; and designing and building three sets of enormous parallel locks and gates.

Cutting the 9-mile channel through Panama's mountain spine at the Culebra Cut—later named Gaillard Cut for Col. David DuBose Gaillard, the engineer in charge—was the most difficult part and took ten years. Enormous amounts of rock and shale were removed and hauled by rail to the Pacific to fill in marshes and build a causeway. Like the French, the U.S. team was plagued by rock and mudslides caused by the area's heavy rains.

The canal opened to traffic on Aug 15, 1914, six months ahead of schedule and at a cost of $387 million—$23 million below estimates. In the years since then, the United States has invested more than $3 billion in the canal, 70 percent of which was recovered, but basically the original structure is intact. Even though ships have gotten larger, the canal can still handle 90 percent of the world's oceangoing liners. By the time the canal had marked its 75h anniversary in 1989, more than five billion tons of goods and 700,000 ships had transited it. Now, over one million vessels have used the waterway since its opening.

In his *The Path Between the Seas,* the leading book on the history and construction of the Panama Canal, author David McCullough says that of its many achievements, perhaps the most remarkable is that "so vast and costly an undertaking . . . [was] done without graft, kickbacks, payroll padding [or] any of the hundred and one forms of corruption endemic to such works. . . . nor has there been even a hint of scandal . . . [or] charge of corruption in all the years that it has been in operation."

The canal's value is impossible to calculate. Just one example provides a dramatic illustration: From San Francisco, the voyage around South America is 13,000 miles and takes three weeks; to reach one side of the continent from the other via the canal, it's 4,600 miles and can be made in a week.

For Panama, it has meant jobs—more than 9,000 employees—and income from tolls and other revenue of about $800 million a year.

A New Day

At the stroke of midnight on Dec 31, 1999, while the world ushered in the new millennium, Panama celebrated its own once-in-a-lifetime event: the transfer of the Panama Canal, along with about $4 billion worth of property, from the United States to Panama. It included 569 square miles of real estate, transforming the barracks, hospitals, schools, airstrips, churches, houses, offices, and manicured lawns into private housing, hotels and other tourist facilities, a university, sports centers, and industrial parks.

Long before the big day, Panamanians had already laid plans and committed resources—an estimated $1 billion from Panamanian and foreign investors—to develop the Canal Zone for tourism, primarily in two directions: Colón 2000, an umbrella project to develop the city of Colón at the western mouth of the canal into a major Caribbean deep-water port for cruise tourism and trade and as a convention center with the makeover of the city's historical waterfront; and a similar, smaller development at the Pacific entry point. In between Panamanians are creating a tourism infrastructure with an eye to ecotourism particularly, with preservation of the Panama Canal watershed a top priority.

Panama claims to be giving more than lip service to ecotourism and expects the Panama Canal region to play a major role. Almost one-third of Panama is under protection through its national park system, which shelters more than 10,000 species of plants, including 1,200 orchid species, and 940 types of birds. Because the canal is surrounded by pristine rain forest, alive with wildlife, such projects as the **Gamboa Rainforest Resort at the Panama Canal** (507-314-9000; 877-800-1690; www.gamboaresort.com) seem to be ideal.

Located about midway across the Isthmus of Panama, about 25 miles from the Atlantic and Pacific Oceans, the resort sits at the fork of the Chagres River and Gatun Lake, in Soberania National Park, which is part of the watershed. In addition to its facilities—145 deluxe rooms, three restaurants, a pool, a spa, a marina, and meeting facilities—the resort has an education and research program, partly in cooperation with the Smithsonian Tropical Research Institute, which has trained the resort's guides. It has hiking trails; an observation deck over the canopy allows bird-watching, fishing, and other nature-oriented activities. River excursions and visits to nearby Indian villages are offered.

Among Panama's other ambitious projects, the $60 million restoration of the Panama Railroad has enabled passengers to travel by rail from ocean to ocean. The 82-acre site of the former School of the Americas, 5 miles from the Canal Free Zone, has been transformed into the **Meliá Panamá Canal** (507-470-1100; www.solmelia.com), managed by the Spanish hotel chain Sol Meliá. The 285-room hotel has a large pool, three restaurants, and a marina.

To expand the benefits of the cruise traffic, Panamanian authorities have encouraged cruise lines to design new itineraries that begin and end in Panama as well as having some ships turn around in the Gatun Lake at midpoint. The effort has paid off as many cruise ships have Panama as a destination in its own right with an increasing number of interesting shore excursions in the Canal Zone and elsewhere in the country.

The $5.25 billion expansion project to build a new lane of traffic along the Panama Canal is underway. Controversial for its environmental impact, the third set of locks will accommodate supertankers and larger cargo ships, each carrying 12,000 containers—as compared to the 5,000 containers now carried by Panamax ships. Thus, it will double the capacity, allowing more traffic and longer, wider ships, including the mega-cruiseships that now are too large to transit the present canal. In 2007, Constructora Urbana SA (CUSA), a Panamanian company, won the first bid to widen the canal. Its $41 million bid called for digging 4.1 miles of new channel, moving an estimated 46 million cubic feet of sediment and earth on the Pacific side of the canal. Work has begun , and the project is suppose to be completed in 2014, with the new locks open for transit in 2015. Stay tuned.

Shore Excursions

Samples of the excursions available to cruise passengers in the canal area follow. Your ship is also likely to have the more traditional city tours of

Colón at the canal's eastern end and Panama City on the west.

Rainforest Aerial Tram: 4.5 hours; US$99 adult; $79 child. The Gamboa Rainforest Resort at the Panama Canal is located on the Chagres River amid the 55,000-acre Soberania National Park. Here in this spectacular setting, the Aerial Tram enables you to see the forest canopy and get a bird's-eye view of the countryside. The tram rises from the forest floor and understory into the sunlit canopy to an observation tower. The Serpentarium, a butterfly house, botanical and orchid gardens, a reptile exhibit, and a model Emberá Indian village are also on the tour.

Ecological Adventure on Gatun Lake: 5.5 hours; US$49 adult; $39 child. At Gamboa Pier you board a 25-foot boat and travel to cargo ships waiting to cross the canal to Cerro Balboa on Gatun Lake, where the ecological tour begins. Your guide explains the flora and fauna here and its surprising importance to the canal operation. The visit continues to Monkey Island, where it's common to see monkeys and hopefully other wildlife. The last stop is the Miraflores Locks to watch the operation of the Panama Canal and see a model of the canal with a narrated video on its building and operation. Here, too, is the visitor center, with excellent exhibits.

Discover the Emberá Indian Culture: 5.5 hours; US$99 adult; $73 child. Panama's rich and diverse indigenous population accounts for about 8 percent of the total populace and comprises seven tribes. Although threatened by environmental degradation of their lands and incursions by outsiders, these tribal people have managed to preserve much of their culture. Upstream along the Chagres River, you will come into contact with the Emberá Indians. Also called Choco Indians, the Emberá live in houses built on stilts with cone-shaped roofs made of palm leaves. They sit on the floor, sleep on straw mats, and use a stepladder to climb up to their houses. Both men and women create crafts: basket weaving and ceramics for the women; woodcraft—cooking utensils, walking sticks, ritual sculptures, and altars—for the men. Perhaps their best skill is making piraguas or dugout canoes from cedar or yellow pine.

El Valle Ecological Paradise: 8 hours; US$69 adult; $54 child. The one-and-a-half-hour drive from Panama City to El Valle on the Pan-American Highway crosses the Bridge of the Americas and passes through beautiful, lush countryside. El Valle, at the edge of an extinct volcano, is famous for its ecological environment resplendent with flora and fauna; the town is a popular weekend escape for Panamanians. Visits are made to El Chorro Waterfall and Nispero Zoo.

Portobelo: The Pirate's Trail: 4.5 hours; US$43 adult; $31 child. Portobelo, one of the most important Spanish settlements in the New World, is an hour's scenic ride east from Colón on a road bordering the Caribbean coast much of the way. An excellent harbor (visited by Christopher Columbus), Portobelo was connected by a stone highway to Panama City—both transshipment ports for riches destined for Spain—and the end of two trails that crossed the jungles of the isthmus. When enough treasure had been accumulated here, caravans of sailing ships began their voyage back to Spain, trying to avoid pirates lying in wait.

Sir Francis Drake died of fever before he could capture the port and was buried in the bay, but other English buccaneers sacked it several times, including Sir Henry Morgan in 1688. In those days Portobelo was said to be the most heavily fortified Spanish coastal control point in the Americas. After viewing the early Spanish fortifications and customs house, you visit the Church of the Black Christ and hear its legend.

Atlantic to Pacific Railway Journey: 4.5 hours; US$149 adult; $119 child. The dome railway car, a refurbished 1938 Vintage Deluxe Observation Car, has full-length observation windows and booth-style seating. There are no preassigned seats, and capacity is limited. The air-conditioned car has restrooms and a bar. It shares an outside observation area with an executive train car.

Transiting the Panama Canal

More than two dozen cruise ships offer transcanal cruises regularly in the winter season, and another three dozen offer them seasonally in spring and fall, when they make their way between the Caribbean and Alaska; or the West Coast and the East Coast; or en route to and from South America in winter and Europe for the summer.

The Isthmus of Panama lies northeast–southwest across mountainous, tropical jungle terrain. Because of the lay of the land, ships sail mostly on a north–south course, rather than east–west as might be assumed.

Ships approaching from the Caribbean enter the waterway at Port Cristobál in Limón Bay; Colón, Panama's second largest town, is to the east. Port Cristobál is also the northern terminus of the railroad that runs alongside the canal. There may be as many as fifty ships waiting to transit, but cruise ships are given priority over cargo vessels. Normally, cruise ships complete the crossing in about eight hours, but it can take longer, depending on the number and speed of the ships ahead. Pilots from the Panama Canal Commission board all ships to guide them through the canal. The commission also provides every cruise ship with a commentator who gives a running account over the ship's public address system during the vessel's passage through the canal and of the history and operation of the canal.

From Port Cristobál, your ship follows a 6½-mile course at sea level along a 500-foot-wide channel south to the Gatun Locks, the first of three locks, where the vessel is lifted 85 feet in three stages to the level of Gatun Lake. As your ship inches forward on its own steam into the first and lowest of the three chambers, a towline is tossed to a Panamanian seaman, who connects it to a messenger line from an electric fifty-five-ton towing locomotive known as a mule, which runs on rails at the top of the lock on each side, pulling the ship into place in the chamber. Each mule can pull 70,000 pounds; the number attached to a ship is determined by the ship's size.

Above the first chamber is the control tower where the operator controls the flow of water through huge 18-foot culverts, or tunnels, located in the center and side walls of the locks. When the pilot gives the signal, the mules begin to roll forward to position your ship into the first chamber; slowly the great doors at the stern close.

With your ship inside the huge chamber, the tower operator opens the valves, and water spills out through the culverts at the rate of three million gallons a minute. It is like being on the bottom of a gigantic swimming pool, watching your ship rise as

water fills the enclosure. No pumps are used to fill or empty the chambers; the system works by gravity, with water flowing from one level to another through the large culverts to smaller culverts that open to the floor of the chambers.

The huge chambers—1,000 feet long by 110 feet wide—have concrete walls from 8 to 50 feet thick and floors from 13 to 20 feet deep. Each set of locks has parallel chambers of the same size to allow passage in both directions at the same time. Each lock holds 65.8 million gallons of water; every time a ship makes a complete transit, 52 million gallons of water flow into the sea. The colossal steel doors or gates—still the originals—at the end of each chamber are 65 feet wide and 7 feet thick, and vary from 47 to 82 feet in height; the largest weighs more than 700 tons. Yet they can be opened and closed with only a forty-horsepower motor.

When the water in the first chamber reaches the level of the water in the next lock, the gates between the two open, the mules pull your ship forward, and the doors behind your ship close. Again, water fills the chamber, and your ship rises to the water level of the third and final stage. When that step is completed, your ship sails onto Gatun Lake.

Covering an area of 163.38 square miles, Gatun Lake was created by carving out an enormous earthen dam across the Chagres Valley at the north end of the canal. The Chagres River flows into Gatun and Madden Lakes on the north side of the Continental Divide and, together with Miraflores Lake on the south side, supplies the water to operate the locks. The lakes' water levels are controlled by dams, ensuring a constant supply.

Your ship sails under its own power for 24 miles across Gatun Lake to the Gaillard Cut through a pretty landscape of forested hills and islets (the tops of submerged hills), where you can observe some of the region's wildlife. The most frequent visitors around your ship are brown pelicans; the treetops are often heavy with vultures; and high in the sky, magnificent frigate birds glide overhead. If you are good at spotting birds, off in the forest you might see toucans and macaws, and as the ship moves closer to the Pacific, you might begin to see boobies.

You will also be able to watch ships transiting the canal from the other direction; most will be cargo vessels, but occasionally a small private yacht or another cruise ship will pass, too. Expect a shower or two; depending on the time of year, the air can be balmy and pleasant or steamy. This is, after all, the middle of the jungle, even if it appears mechanized and manicured.

Some cruise ships on one-week Caribbean cruises go only as far as Gatun Lake, where they turn around and depart through the Gatun Locks back to the Atlantic side.

At about the midpoint of the canal, your ship leaves Gatun Lake and sails into the Gaillard Cut. This V-shaped channel, cut from granite and volcanic rock, is the narrowest stretch of the canal and was the most difficult to build. More than 230 million cubic yards of earth and rock were excavated from the 9-mile stretch to make it navigable. Originally the channel was 300 feet wide; later it was widened to 500 feet, and there is discussion about widening it further. It has a depth of 42 feet. While the sides have been stabilized, they are monitored constantly, and dredging never stops. About halfway along the cut on the west side, a bronze plaque honors the builders of the canal and the workers who died.

The cut ends at the entrance to the first of two sets of locks: Pedro Miguel Locks, with only one step of 31 feet, followed by the Miraflores Lake and the Miraflores Locks, which drop 54 feet in two steps. Here the process is reversed. Your ship will enter a chamber full of water, and as the water is drained out, your ship is lowered to the next level, and finally to the level of the Pacific. At the exit of the final lock is the Port of Balboa and, off in the distance to the south, Panama City. Directly in front is the lofty Bridge of the Americas, the bridge connecting the two sides of the waterway and part of the Interamerican Highway between North and South America.

Trivia buffs may like to know that for years the largest cruise ship to pass through the canal was Cunard's *QE2,* which was 963 feet long with a beam of 105—just 5 feet short of the locks' 110-foot width. However, most of the new large ships built to the specifications that allow them to transit the canal, referred to as Panamax ships, are a fraction longer and/or wider than the *QE2.* For example, NCL's *Norwegian Star* is 971 feet in length and has

a 105.6-foot beam. The amount these large ships pay has increased as well, normally up to $300,000 or more, but the least is still the 36 cents paid by Richard Halliburton to swim the canal in 1928.

The Panama Canal Operation

The Panama Canal operation is a model of efficiency. The canal operates 24 hours a day and 365 days a year, with as many as forty ships passing through daily. For most ships, the average Canal Waters Time—the total time spent at the Panama Canal, including waiting time and in-transit time—is just under 24 hours. A reservation system is available to provide a guaranteed priority transit upon request. The canal's ability to work at peak efficiency is attributed to its skilled technicians and year-round maintenance.

Miraflores Visitor Center

Located on the east side of the **Miraflores Locks,** the center enables visitors to watch vessels transiting the canal from a very short distance and learn about the canal's operation and watershed, the history of its construction, and its vital role in world trade. The center has a fully equipped theater, three observation terraces, snack bars, a panoramic-view restaurant, a gift shop, and four exhibition halls.

The History Hall provides background, explains the technical innovations that were integral to the canal's construction, and honors the hundreds of men and women who made it possible. The Hall of Water emphasizes the importance of water; the protection of the Canal Watershed, environment, and biodiversity; and the Canal Authority's commitment to managing this resource and the surrounding region. The Canal in Action is an amusing depiction of the canal operation and enables viewers to be inside a navigation simulator and one of the lock culverts and to view a virtual ocean-to-ocean transit. It also features the canal's ongoing improvements, modernization, and maintenance projects. The Canal in the World focuses on the importance of the canal to world trade, the trade routes it serves, its users, the types of vessels that transit, and the commodities they carry. It also gives an overview of studies conducted to guarantee the canal's future competitiveness and benefits to Panama.

Center admission for nonresidents: $8 adult; $5 ages five to seventeen; under five free. Hours: 9 a.m. to 5 p.m. daily; restaurant noon to 11 p.m. Information: (507) 276-8325; fax: (507) 276-8469; www.pancanal.com; cvm@pancanal.com.

The San Blas Islands

Of all the exotic destinations cruise ships visit in the Western Caribbean, none is more unusual than the San Blas Islands, an archipelago of low-lying islands off the northeast Caribbean coast of Panama. Upon approach, their thatched-roof dwellings shaded by crowds of palm trees look more like the islands of the South Seas than the Caribbean.

These islands are the home of the Kuna Indians, the only tribe of island dwellers in the Caribbean who have both survived and been able to maintain their ancient folkways more or less intact despite 500 years of contact with Europeans and other foreign cultures.

The San Blas Islands comprise about 400 islets plus a strip of land on the Panamanian coast, over which the Kuna claim sovereignty and maintain self-rule. There are forty-eight Kuna villages, with a total population of about 40,000, represented in a tribal council. The people move between the islands in dugout canoes, little changed from those of their ancestors. Their main crop is coconut, and in olden days, they were use as currency. Despite their isolation on these islands, they are unusually worldly and have accepted certain innovations, such as communications and education, while retaining their traditional way of life.

Normally, your first glimpse of the Kuna will be from your cruise ship, where as many as ten boats, full of Kuna women, will be doing a brisk business selling their colorful, unique molas, for which they are famous. Do not think these are the last of their stock. When you go ashore to visit a Kuna village, you will see the molas displayed on clotheslines strung the entire length of the village. Some are squares that can be made into pillow covers or framed; others appear on shirts and dresses. All are remarkably inexpensive, ranging from US$10 to $40 depending on the intricacy of the design. There is no need to try bargaining; these women may not be able to speak your language, but they understand money.

Molas represent a Kuna woman's wealth, like a dowry. They are elaborate reverse appliqué in bold, bright colors, incorporating stylized flowers, animals, birds, and supernatural motifs, and are made originally for the front and back panels of the blouse that the petite Kuna women wear. Occasionally you will see a mola that incorporates current events, such as the U.S. landing of troops in Panama, which crept into designs in 1990. To a newcomer molas may all seem alike, but upon closer examination the fineness of the stitches and sophistication of the motifs are the telling signs of a master craftswoman.

Kuna women also wear beaded bracelets drawn tightly on their arms and legs, gold nose rings, and layers of gold around their necks. They are a colorful bunch, irresistible to photographers. Most are happy for you to take their picture, often posing with a bright green parakeet, monkey, or iguana, but you must pay them $1 per click. The villagers are friendly, although rather stone-faced unless you take the time to admire someone's beautiful child—a gesture that usually draws a broad smile from the young mother. Their straight hair is jet black, and their facial features are similar to those of other Indian tribes of South America's Caribbean coast, whose common ancestors were the Arawaks, once populating all the islands of the Caribbean.

Index

About the Author

Kay Showker is a veteran writer, photographer, and lecturer on travel. Her assignments have taken her to more than one hundred countries in the Caribbean and around the world. She has appeared as a travel expert on CNN, ABC, CBS, and NBC, and radio stations across the country, as well as guest host on America Online and the Travel Channel.

Showker has written fourteen travel guides, six on the Caribbean. Her other books include *100 Best Resorts of the Caribbean* (Globe Pequot); *The Outdoor Traveler's Guide to the Caribbean* (Stewart, Tabori, & Chang), which won the Lowell Thomas Travel Awards when it was first published in 1992; *The Unofficial Guide to Cruises* (Wiley), named "The Best Guidebook of the Year" by the Lowell Thomas Travel Awards when it was first published in 1996; and two Fodor guides—*Egypt* and *Jordan and the Holy Land*.

She has written for *National Geographic Traveler, Travel + Leisure, Caribbean Travel and Life, Town & Country, Luxury Travel Advisor, Travel Etc., Travelife,* and other magazines and newspapers across the country. She served as senior editor of *Travel Weekly,* the industry's major trade publication, with which she was associated for eleven years.

A native of Kingsport, Tennessee, Ms. Showker received her B.A. in history from the University of Mary Washington and a master's degree in international affairs from the School of Advanced International Studies of Johns Hopkins University in Washington, D.C. Among her awards, she was the first journalist to receive Martinique's Sucrier d'Or, a professional achievement award and the first recipient of the Marcia Vickery Wallace Award, given annually by the Caribbean Tourism Organization and the Government of Jamaica to the leading travel journalist on the Caribbean. She was named the Travel Writer of the Year by the Bahamas Hotel Association.

Showker has served as a consultant to government and private organizations on travel and tourism. Ms. Showker is past president of the Society of American Travel Writers Northeast Chapter, and a member of the American Society of Journalists and Authors and the New York Travel Writers Association.